Ivor Horton's Beginning Java™ 2, JDK™ 5 Edition

Ivor Horton

Wiley Publishing, Inc.

Ivor Horton's Beginning Java™ 2, JDK™ 5 Edition

Published by
Wiley Publishing, Inc.
10475 Crosspoint Boulevard
Indianapolis, IN 46256
www.wiley.com

Copyright © 2005 by Ivor Horton

Published by Wiley Publishing, Inc., Indianapolis, Indiana

Published simultaneously in Canada

ISBN: 0-7645-6874-4

Manufactured in the United States of America

10 9 8 7 6 5 4 3 2

5B/RU/RS/QU/IN

For general information on our other products and services or to obtain technical support, please contact our Customer Care Department within the U.S. at (800) 762-2974, outside the U.S. at (317) 572-3993 or fax (317) 572-4002.

For technical support, please visit www.wiley.com/techsupport.

Wiley also publishes its books in a variety of electronic formats. Some content that appears in print may not be available in electronic books.

Library of Congress Cataloging-in-Publication Data

Horton, Ivor.
 Ivor Horton's Beginning Java 2, JDK 5 Edition / Ivor Horton.
   p. cm.
 Includes index.
 ISBN 0-7645-6874-4 (paper/website)
 1. Java (Computer program language) I. Title: *Ivor Horton's Beginning Java 2, JDK 5 Edition.* II. Title.
QA76.73.J38H6758 2004
005.13'3—dc22
                                         2004017036

About the Author

Ivor Horton started out as a mathematician, but shortly after graduating, he was lured into messing about with computers by a well-known manufacturer. He has spent many happy years programming occasionally useful applications in a variety of languages as well as teaching mainly scientists and engineers to do likewise. He has extensive experience in applying computers to problems in engineering design and to manufacturing operations in a wide range of industries. He is the author of a number of tutorial books on programming in C, C++, and Java. When not writing programming books or providing advice to others, he leads a life of leisure.

Credits

Executive Editor
Robert Elliott

Senior Development Editor
Kevin Kent

Technical Editors
Calvin Austin, J2SE 5.0 Specification Lead, Sun Microsystems
Wiley-Dreamtech India Pvt Ltd

Production Editor
William A. Barton

Copy Editor
Luann Rouff

Editorial Manager
Mary Beth Wakefield

Vice President & Executive Group Publisher
Richard Swadley

Vice President and Publisher
Joseph B. Wikert

Project Coordinator
Erin Smith

Graphics and Production Specialists
Karl Brandt
Jonelle Burns
Kelly Emkow
Carrie Foster
Lauren Goddard
Denny Hager
Joyce Haughey
Jennifer Heleine
Ron Terry

Quality Control Technicians
Joe Niesen
Susan Moritz
Brian H. Walls

Media Development Specialist
Travis Silvers

Proofreading and Indexing
TECHBOOKS Production Services

Cover Photograph
© Ian Capener

Foreword

You are probably reading this foreword with one of several things in mind. First, is this the right book for me, is the material current, and does the text reflect the final API? Second, what should I expect to learn and where should I start reading a book of this length?

Many of the forewords I have seen will lead you through an amusing anecdote or story and then mention a little about the author, but then fail to leave you any wiser about the answer to those questions. So, to get straight to the point and to answer the second question first, this is a book that you can start from page one and read right through to the end. If you haven't read any of Ivor Horton's books before, you are in for a pleasant surprise. Ivor's style is very accessible, which makes the content easy to follow and understand. I know, because I have read this book from cover to cover.

This edition of *Ivor Horton's Beginning Java 2, JDK 5 Edition* is based on the J2SE 5.0 platform. The J2SE 5.0 release is one of the most significant updates to the Java platform in many years and has been three years in the making. The release involved 160 experts worldwide, all working through the Java Community Process and focused on making the platform better for all developers. I have been involved with the project since day one as the Specification Lead for JSR 176, which defines the contents of J2SE 5.0. As such, I had a great interest in making sure that this book is accurate and matches the final API set. I've even compiled and run every code example twice, and there are a lot of great examples, as you will find out.

So what can you expect to learn from this new edition? First, Ivor covers the basic programming blocks and gets you started with your first Java program. Ivor then introduces the Java language changes step by step, including the new generic types, the enhanced `for` loop, enumerated types, and many others. You will also get to use the new language changes in later chapters and learn some of the other non-language features, such as XML DOM3 updates. So whether you are a new developer or already have some Java programming experience, you will gain the skills needed to work with the latest Java release.

In closing, I encourage you to read and enjoy what JDK 5.0 has to offer and find out how easy using J2SE 5.0 really is.

Calvin Austin
J2SE 5.0 Specification Lead
Sun Microsystems

Acknowledgments

While a book is usually attributed to the author, a book — particularly a large book such as this — is always the result of the efforts of a sizeable team of people. I'd therefore like to thank all the editorial and production staff at Wiley who worked so hard to produce this fifth edition of my Java tutorial from my initial draft.

I'd especially like to thank Calvin Austin of Sun Microsystems for his extensive technical input. He somehow found the time to go through the complete text and try out all the examples — twice — in spite of the considerable demands of his day job. Calvin's suggestions for improvements were invaluable, as was his ability to spot my mistakes, and I'm particularly grateful for his indications of where I'd missed some of the inevitable changes arising from the evolution of the J2SE 5.0 API during the beta phases. Any errors that remain are, of course, my own, but there are surely fewer of them as a consequence of Calvin's efforts.

I'd also like to thank readers of past editions of *Ivor Horton's Beginning Java* for their numerous suggestions for corrections and improvements. In addition to the many changes that I made in response to these, I also updated and reintroduced the chapters on using JDBC that were omitted from the previous edition, in response to requests from a number of readers. The greatly increased page count of this edition over the previous edition is only in part a consequence of restoring the JDBC tutorial. The bulk of the additional page count is attributable to new material relating to the features introduced by J2SE 5.0 that deliver exciting new capabilities for every Java programmer. The J2SE 5.0 release is truly a major step forward that encompasses important extensions to the Java language as well as major additions to the class libraries.

Finally I'd like to thank my wife, Eve, who provides unstinting support for whatever I happen to be doing and cheerfully accepts my complaints about the workload that I freely elected to undertake. She always manages to be on hand whenever I need sustenance or sympathy, or both, and undoubtedly I would never have finished this book without her.

Ivor Horton

Contents

Contents

Contents

Contents

Contents

Contents

Contents

Contents

Contents

Contents

Contents

Contents

Contents

Contents

Introduction

Welcome

Welcome to this edition of *Ivor Horton's Beginning Java 2, JDK 5 Edition*, a comprehensive and easy-to-use tutorial guide to learning the Java language and the Java 2 platform application program interface (API). This book provides you with the essential know-how for developing programs using the Java 2 Standard Edition 5.0 (J2SE 5.0) or later.

In this book, as well as teaching you Java, I'll introduce you to the wide variety of topics that will be relevant to you as a Java programmer. I have structured the book so that you learn Java programming in a carefully designed and logical way, and at each stage you'll be building on what you have learned at the previous stage.

Who Is This Book For?

Java programming is now a vast, well-established area that is still expanding as the capabilities of the language and associated libraries increase. Since its release, the growth of Java as the object-oriented language of choice for Internet programming, cross-platform applications, and teaching has been phenomenal. In my view this is due to three things: the system independent nature of Java, the simplicity and power of the language, and the extraordinary range of programming tasks for which Java is an effective and easy-to-use tool. Java is the language of choice of many programmers for major application development, offering advantages in ease of development and maintenance compared to other languages, as well as built-in capability to run on a variety of computers and operating systems without code changes. With Java you can do a lot more, more quickly, and more easily.

In this book I aim to provide you with a comprehensive understanding of the language, plus experience of programming in a range of Java application contexts to give you a solid base in each of these core areas. Every aspect of Java that is covered in the book is illustrated by fully working program examples that you can and should create and run for yourself. There are also exercises at the end of each chapter to give you the opportunity to try out what you've learned. With an understanding of the topics in this book, you can start to write fully featured and effective Java programs.

The word *Beginning* in the title refers more to the style of the book's teaching than to your skill level. It could equally well be called *Straight into Java*, because I designed the tutorial structure so that, whether you're a seasoned programmer from another language or a newcomer to programming in general, the book takes you straight to your floor.

I have assumed as a minimum that you know something about programming, in that you understand at least the fundamental concepts of how programs work. However, you don't need to have significant prior programming experience to use the book successfully. The pace of the book is fairly rapid, but without stinting on any of the necessary explanations of how Java works.

What's Covered in This Book

The book aims to teach you Java programming following a logical format:

❑   First, it covers some of the main terms and concepts that underpin programming in Java. This will give you a perspective and reference frame for the detail that follows.

❑   Second, it provides you with a clear explanation of all the features of the Java language — the basic data types, the control structures that manipulate data, the object-oriented features of the language, the way run-time errors are handled, and how threads are used. It also provides a solid introduction to generic types in Java and how you can apply them in your own programs. The book doesn't just explain what the language elements do, but also how you can apply them in practice.

❑   Third, it gives you an extensive introduction to the key packages in the Java class library — among others, the `java.math`, `java.io`, `java.nio`, `java.util`, `java.awt`, `java.awt.event`, `java.applet`, `javax.swing`, `javax.xml`, and `javax.sql` packages are all covered and illustrated with full working examples. These packages cover file handling, printing, collection classes, helper objects, graphical user interfaces, applets, XML, and relational database access and update.

❑   Fourth, it guides you through the process of building a substantial application, Sketcher, in which you apply the Java language capabilities and the Java class library in a realistic context. The sketching application will have menus, toolbars, and a status panel to give you a grounding in putting together a basic application user interface. You'll also implement the capability to draw and manipulate a number of elements, handle text, print sketches on your local printer, and save sketches to disk — including exporting and importing sketches in XML. Assembling an application with this range of functions will give you a much better understanding of how you apply Java in practical projects of your own, something that's hard to appreciate from any number of more trivial examples.

❑   Lastly, it introduces the fundamentals of SQL and then shows how you can use the JDBC capability that comes with the JDK to work with relational databases.

As you progress through these topics, I'll introduce you to the theory, and then illustrate it with an appropriate example and a clear explanation. You can learn quickly on a first read and look back over things to brush up on all the essential elements when you need to. The short examples in each chapter are designed mainly to illustrate a class and its methods or some new piece of theory in action. They focus specifically on showing you how the particular language feature or method works.

To get the most from the chapters, I strongly recommend that you try out the examples as you read. Type them in yourself, even if you have downloaded the example source code. It really does make a difference. The examples also provide a good base for experimentation and will hopefully inspire you to create programs of your own. It's important to try things out — you will learn as much (if not more) from your mistakes as you will from the things that work first time.

The source code for all of the example programs in the book is available at `http://www.wrox.com`.

What You Need to Use This Book

This book has been tested against the J2SE 5.0 release code, so you should be using JDK 5.0 or later. Other requirements for most of the chapters are fairly minimal: a copy of a text editor and a command-line window from which to run the Java tools. Details of the requirements for the book and how to acquire and install them are provided in Chapter 1.

Conventions

To help you get the most from the text and keep track of what's happening, I've used a number of conventions throughout the book.

For example, when discussing code, I have two conventions:

Italics are used to hold asides on programming code.

while:

> **These boxes hold important, not-to-be-forgotten information that is directly relevant to the surrounding text.**

When I introduce important words, I **highlight** them. I show keyboard strokes as Ctrl+A.

Command-line output is shown as:

```
C:\> java ShowStyle
When the command line and terminal output are shown, it's in this style.
```

Code that appears in the text, text that appears as part of an application GUI, and filenames are all identified as aVariable and MyFile.java.

Code fragments that show a particular mechanism or technique are shown with a shaded background:

```
if(life==aimless) {
    DoSomethingElse;
}
```

Where a previous code fragment has been changed in some way, the changes are shown highlighted:

```
if(life==aimless) {
    DoSomethingNew;
}
```

I presage code for complete working examples with a Try It Out section, which is used to split the code up where that's helpful, to highlight the component parts, and to show the progression of the application. When it's important, which is most of the time, I follow the code with a How It Works section to explain any salient points of the code in relation to previous theory. Complete new code examples in a Try It Out section are shown shaded:

```
public class Motto {
  public static void main(String[] args) {
    System.out.println("He who fights and runs away");
    System.out.println("Lives to runs away another day.");
  }
}
```

Complete code examples that are modifications of an earlier example show the new code as shaded:

```
public class Saying {
  public static void main(String[] args) {
    System.out.println("I used to think I was indecisive");
    System.out.println("but now I'm not so sure.");
  }
}
```

Finally, code fragments in a How It Works section that appeared in the complete example are shown unshaded like this:

```
System.out.println("I used to think I was indecisive");
System.out.println("but now I'm not so sure.");
```

Source Code

As you work through the examples in this book, you may choose either to type in all the code manually or to use the source code files that accompany the book. All of the source code used in this book is available for download at http://www.wrox.com. Once at the site, simply locate the book's title (either by using the Search box or by using one of the title lists) and click the Download Code link on the book's detail page to obtain all the source code for the book.

Because many books have similar titles, you may find it easiest to search by ISBN; for this book the ISBN is 0-7645-6874-4.

Once you download the code, just decompress it with your favorite compression tool. Alternately, you can go to the main Wrox code download page at http://www.wrox.com/dynamic/books/download .aspx to see the code available for this book and all other Wrox books.

Errata

We make every effort to ensure that there are no errors in the text or in the code. However, no one is perfect, and mistakes do occur. If you find an error in one of our books, such as a spelling mistake or a faulty piece of code, we would be very grateful for your feedback. By sending in errata you may save another reader hours of frustration, and at the same time you will be helping us provide even higher quality information.

To find the errata page for this book, go to `http://www.wrox.com` and locate the title using the Search box or one of the title lists. Then, on the book details page, click the Book Errata link. On this page you can view all errata that has been submitted for this book and posted by Wrox editors. A complete book list including links to each book's errata is also available at `www.wrox.com/misc-pages/booklist.shtml`.

If you don't spot "your" error on the Book Errata page, go to `www.wrox.com/contact/techsupport.shtml` and complete the form there to send us the error you have found. We'll check the information and, if appropriate, post a message to the book's errata page and fix the problem in subsequent editions of the book.

p2p.wrox.com

For author and peer discussion, join the P2P forums at `p2p.wrox.com`. The forums are a web-based system for you to post messages relating to Wrox books and related technologies and interact with other readers and technology users. The forums offer a subscription feature to e-mail you topics of interest of your choosing when new posts are made to the forums. Wrox authors, editors, other industry experts, and your fellow readers are present on these forums.

At `http://p2p.wrox.com` you will find a number of different forums that will help you not only as you read this book, but also as you develop your own applications. To join the forums, just follow these steps:

1. Go to `p2p.wrox.com` and click the Register link.
2. Read the terms of use and click Agree.
3. Complete the required information to join as well as any optional information you wish to provide and click Submit.
4. You will receive an e-mail with information describing how to verify your account and complete the joining process.

You can read messages in the forums without joining P2P but in order to post your own messages, you must join.

Once you join, you can post new messages and respond to messages other users post. You can read messages at any time on the web. If you would like to have new messages from a particular forum e-mailed to you, click the Subscribe to this Forum icon by the forum name in the forum listing.

For more information about how to use the Wrox P2P, be sure to read the P2P FAQs for answers to questions about how the forum software works as well as many common questions specific to P2P and Wrox books. To read the FAQs, click the FAQ link on any P2P page.

Introducing Java

This chapter will give you an appreciation of what the Java language is all about. Understanding the details of what I'll discuss in this chapter is not important at this stage; you will see all of the topics again in greater depth in later chapters of the book. The intent of this chapter is to introduce you to the general ideas that underpin what I'll be covering through the rest of the book, as well as the major contexts in which Java programs can be used and the kind of program that is applicable in each context.

In this chapter you will learn:

- ❑ The basic characteristics of the Java language
- ❑ How Java programs work on your computer
- ❑ Why Java programs are portable between different computers
- ❑ The basic ideas behind object-oriented programming
- ❑ How a simple Java program looks and how you can run it using the Java Development Kit
- ❑ What HTML is and how it is used to include a Java program in a web page

What Is Java All About?

Java is an innovative programming language that has become the language of choice for programs that need to run on a variety of different computer systems. First of all, Java enables you to write small programs called **applets**. These are programs that you can embed in web pages to provide some intelligence. Being able to embed executable code in a web page introduces a vast range of exciting possibilities. Instead of being a passive presentation of text and graphics, a web page can be interactive in any way that you want. You can include animations, games, interactive transaction processing — the possibilities are almost unlimited.

Of course, embedding program code in a web page creates special security requirements. As an Internet user accessing a page with embedded Java code, you need to be confident that it won't do anything that might interfere with the operation of your computer, or damage the data you have on your system. This implies that execution of the embedded code must be controlled in such a way that it will prevent accidental damage to your computer environment, as well as ensure that any Java code that was created with malicious intent is effectively inhibited. Java implicitly incorporates measures to minimize the possibility of such occurrences arising with a Java applet.

Java's support for the Internet and network-based applications generally doesn't end with applets. For example, Java Server Pages (JSP) provides a powerful means of building a server application that can dynamically create and download HTML pages to a client that are precisely customized for the specific request that is received. Of course, the pages that are generated by JSP can themselves contain Java applets.

Java also allows you to write large-scale application programs that you can run unchanged on any computer with an operating system environment in which Java is supported. This applies to the majority of computers in use today. You can even write programs that will work both as ordinary applications and as applets.

Java has matured immensely in recent years, particularly since the introduction of Java 2. The breadth of function provided by the standard core Java has grown incredibly. Java provides you with comprehensive facilities for building applications with an interactive graphical user interface (GUI), extensive image processing and graphics programming facilities, as well as support for accessing relational databases and communicating with remote computers over a network. Just about any kind of application can now be programmed effectively in Java, with the implicit plus of complete portability.

Of course, Java is still developing and growing. Amongst a myriad of other enhancements, release 1.4 of Java added a major additional capability, the ability to read and write XML. Java 5.0, which followed release 1.4, adds further new facilities, including important new language features as well as significant additions to the class libraries. You'll be learning about all of these in this book.

Features of The Java Language

The most important characteristic of Java is that it was designed from the outset to be machine independent. You can run Java programs unchanged on any machine and operating system combination that supports Java. Of course, there is still the slim possibility of the odd glitch, as you are ultimately dependent on the implementation of Java on any particular machine, but Java programs are intrinsically more portable than programs written in other languages. An application written in Java will only require a single set of source code statements, regardless of the number of different computer platforms on which it is run. In any other programming language, the application will frequently require the source code to be tailored to accommodate different computer environments, particularly if an extensive graphical user interface is involved. Java offers substantial savings in time and resources in developing, supporting, and maintaining major applications on several different hardware platforms and operating systems.

Possibly the next most important characteristic of Java is that it is **object-oriented**. The object-oriented approach to programming is also an implicit feature of all Java programs, so we will be looking at what this implies later in this chapter. Object-oriented programs are easier to understand and less time-consuming to maintain and extend than programs that have been written without the benefit of using objects.

Not only is Java object-oriented, but it also manages to avoid many of the difficulties and complications that are inherent in some other object-oriented languages, making it easy to learn and very straight-forward to use. By and large, it lacks the traps and "gotchas" that arise in some other programming languages. This makes the learning cycle shorter, and you need less real-world coding experience to gain competence and confidence. It also makes Java code easier to test.

Java has a built-in ability to support national character sets. You can write Java programs as easily for use in Greece or Japan as you can for English-speaking countries, always assuming you are familiar with the national languages involved, of course. You can even build programs from the outset to support several different national languages with automatic adaptation to the environment in which the code executes.

Learning Java

Java is not difficult to learn, but there is a great deal to it. Although the Java language is very powerful, it is fairly compact, so acquiring an understanding of it will take less time than you think. However, there's more to Java than just the language. To be able to program effectively in Java, you also need to understand the libraries that go with the language, and these are very extensive. In this book, the sequence in which you learn how the language works and how you apply it has been carefully structured so that you'll gain expertise and confidence with programming in Java through a relatively easy and painless process. As far as possible, each chapter avoids the use of things you haven't learned about already. A consequence, though, is that you won't be writing Java applications with a GUI right away. While it may be an appealing idea, this would be a bit like learning to swim by jumping in the pool at the deep end. Generally speaking, there is good evidence that by starting in the shallow end of the pool and learning how to float before you try to swim, you'll minimize the chance of drowning, and there is a high expectation that you'll end up being a competent swimmer.

Java Programs

As I have already noted, there are two basic kinds of programs you can write in Java. Programs that are to be embedded in a web page are called Java applets, and normal standalone programs are called Java applications. You can further subdivide Java applications into console applications, which only support character output to your computer screen (to the command line on a PC under Windows, for example), and windowed applications, which can create and manage multiple windows. The latter use the typical GUI mechanisms of window-based programs — menus, toolbars, dialogs, and so on.

While you are learning the Java language basics, you will be using console applications as examples to illustrate how things work. These are applications that use simple command-line input and output. With this approach you can concentrate on understanding the specifics of the language, without worrying about any of the complexity involved in creating and managing windows. Once you are comfortable with using all the features of the Java language, you'll move on to windowed applications and applet examples.

Learning Java — The Road Ahead

Before starting out on any journey, it is always helpful to have an idea of where you're heading and what route you should take, so let's take a look at a brief road map of where you'll be going with Java. There are five broad stages you'll progress through in learning Java using this book:

1. The first stage is this chapter. It sets out some fundamental ideas about the structure of Java programs and how they work. This includes such things as what object-oriented programming is all about and how an executable program is created from a Java source file. Getting these concepts straight at the outset will make learning to write Java programs that much easier for you.

2. Next, you'll learn how statements are put together, what facilities you have for storing basic data in a program, how you perform calculations, and how you make decisions based on the results of them. These are the nuts and bolts you need for the next stages.

3. In the third stage, you'll learn about **classes** — how you define them and how you can use them. Classes are blueprints for objects, so this is where you'll learn the object-oriented characteristics of Java. By the time you are through this stage, you will have learned all the basics of how the Java language works, so you'll be ready to progress further into how you can use it.

4. In the fourth stage, you'll learn how you can segment the activities that your programs carry out into separate tasks that can execute concurrently. This is particularly important for when you want to include several applets in a web page, and you don't want one applet to have to wait for another to finish executing before it can start. You may want a fancy animation to continue running while you play a game, for example, with both programs sitting in the same web page.

5. In the fifth stage, you'll learn in detail how you implement an application or an applet with a graphical user interface, and how you handle interactions with the user in this context. This amounts to applying the capabilities provided by the Java class libraries. When you finish this stage, you will be equipped to write your own fully fledged applications and applets in Java.

At the end of the book, you should be a knowledgeable Java programmer. The rest is down to experience.

Throughout this book I'll be using complete examples to explore how Java works. You should create and run all of the examples, even the simplest, preferably by typing them in yourself. Don't be afraid to experiment with them. If there is anything you are not quite clear on, try changing an example around to see what happens, or better still — write an example of your own. If you're uncertain how some aspect of Java that you have already covered works, don't look it up right away — try it out. Making mistakes is a very effective way to learn.

The Java Environment

You can run Java programs on a wide variety of computers using a range of operating systems. Your Java programs will run just as well on a PC running any supported version of Microsoft Windows as it will on Linux or a Sun Solaris workstation. This is possible because a Java program does not execute directly on your computer. It runs on a standardized environment called the **Java 2 Platform** that has been implemented as software on a wide variety of computers and operating systems. The Java Platform consists of two elements — a software implementation of a hypothetical computer called the **Java Virtual Machine** (**JVM**) and the Java Application Programming Interface (**Java API**), which is a set of software components that provides the facilities you need to write a fully fledged interactive application in Java.

A **Java compiler** converts the Java source code that you write into a binary program consisting of **byte-codes**. Bytecodes are machine instructions for the Java Virtual Machine. When you execute a Java program, a program called the **Java interpreter** inspects and deciphers the bytecodes for it, checks it out to ensure that it has not been tampered with and is safe to execute, and then executes the actions that the bytecodes specify within the Java Virtual Machine. A Java interpreter can run standalone, or it can be part of a web browser such as Netscape Navigator, Mozilla, or Microsoft Internet Explorer where it can be invoked automatically to run applets in a web page.

Because your Java program consists of bytecodes rather than native machine instructions, it is completely insulated from the particular hardware on which it is run. Any computer that has the Java environment implemented will handle your program as well as any other, and because the Java interpreter sits between your program and the physical machine, it can prevent unauthorized actions in the program from being executed.

In the past, there has been a penalty for all this flexibility and protection in the speed of execution of your Java programs. An interpreted Java program would typically run at only one-tenth of the speed of an equivalent program using native machine instructions. With present Java machine implementations, much of the performance penalty has been eliminated, and in programs that are not computation intensive — which is usually the case with the sort of program you would want to include in a web page, for example — you really wouldn't notice this anyway. With the JVM that is supplied with the current Java 2 Development Kit (JDK) available from the Sun web site, there are very few circumstances where you will notice any appreciable degradation in performance compared to a program compiled to native machine code.

Java Program Development

For this book you need the Java 2 Platform, Standard Edition (J2SE) version 5.0 or later. You can download the JDK from Sun for a variety of hardware platforms and operating systems, either directly from the Sun Java web site at `http://java.sun.com` (for Windows, Solaris, and Linux operating systems) or from sites that you can link to from there. The JDK you'll be using is available from `http://java.sun.com/j2se`. Versions of the Java Development Kit for Mac OS X are available from `http://devworld.apple.com/java/`.

Note that J2SE 5.0 succeeded J2SE 1.4. Normally, release 1.5 would have followed release 1.4, but it was decided to identify it as release 5.0 in recognition of the significance of the new features that are introduced by release 5.0 and the maturity of the product. Code module names in release 5.0 still use the denotation 1.5.0 so expect to see folder names incorporating 1.5.0 rather than 5.0, and you'll see 1.5.0 popping up in a few other places too, so don't let this confuse you.

One aspect of terminology also causes confusion sometimes — the Java Development Kit has been referred to at various times as the JDK — the Java Development Kit — and as the SDK — the Software Development Kit. The current usage with release 5.0 is JDK but with release 1.4 it was SDK, so if you see SDK this generally means the same as JDK. Just for consistency, I'll use JDK to refer to any Java Development Kit in the book.

To create the Java program source files that you will use with the JDK, you'll need a plaintext editor. Any editor will do as long as it does not introduce formatting codes into the contents of a file. Quite a number of shareware and freeware editors around are suitable, some of which are specific to Java, and you should have no trouble locating one. I find the JCreator editor is particularly good. There's a free version and a fee version with more functionality, but the free version is perfectly adequate for learning. You can download a free copy from `http://www.jcreator.com`. A good place to start looking if you want to investigate what other program text editors are available is the `http://www.download.com` web site.

A number of excellent professional Java program development environments are available, including products from Sun, Borland, Metrowerks, and Symantec. These all provide very friendly environments for creating and editing your Java source code and compiling and debugging your programs. These are powerful tools for the experienced programmer, but for learning Java using this book, I recommend that you resist the temptation to use any of these, especially if you are relatively new to programming. Instead, stick to using the JDK from Sun together with a suitable simple program text editor for creating your source code. So why am I suggesting that you will be better off *not* using a tool that makes programming easier and faster? There are several reasons. Firstly, the professional development systems tend to hide a lot of things you need to get to grips with so that you have a full understanding of how Java works. Secondly, the pro development environments are geared to managing complex applications with a large amount of code, which introduces complexity that you really are better off without while you are learning. Virtually all commercial Java development systems provide prebuilt facilities of their own to speed development. While this is very helpful for production program development, it really does get in the way when you are trying to learn Java. A further consideration is that productivity features supported by a commercial Java development are sometimes tied to a specific version of the Java 2 Platform. This means that some features of the latest version of Java may not work. The professional Java development tools are intended primarily for knowledgeable and experienced programmers, so start with one when you get to the end of the book.

Having said that, if you really do prefer to work with a commercial Java development system for whatever reason, and you have problems with running a particular example from the book, try it out with the JDK from the command line. The chances are good it will work okay.

Installing the JDK

You can obtain detailed instructions on how to install the JDK for your particular operating system from the Sun web site, so I won't go into all the variations for different systems here. However, you should watch out for a few things that may not leap out from the pages of the installation documentation.

First of all, the JDK and the documentation are separate, and you install them separately. The JDK for Windows is available in two versions — as a web install where components are downloaded incrementally, and as a full download of an .exe file that you just execute to start installation. The documentation for the JDK consists of a large number of HTML files structured in a hierarchy that are distributed in a ZIP archive. You will find it easier to install the JDK first, followed by the documentation. If you install the JDK to drive C: under Windows, the directory structure shown in Figure 1-1 will be created.

The jdk1.5.0 directory in Figure 1-1 is sometimes referred to as the root directory for Java. In some contexts it is also referred to as the Java home directory. The actual root directory name may have the release version number appended, in which case the actual directory name will be of the form jdk1.5.0_n where n is a release number, so in the first maintenance release, it will be jdk1.5.0_01, for example.

The sample directory contains sample applications that use JNLP, which is the Java Network Launching Protocol that is used for executing applications or applets from a network server without the need for a browser or the need to download and install the code.

You don't need to worry about the contents of most of these directories, at least not when you get started, but you should add the path for the jdk1.5.0\bin directory to the paths defined in your PATH environment variable. That way you will be able to run the compiler and the interpreter from anywhere without having to specify the path to it. If you installed the JDK to C:, then you need to add the path C:\jdk1.5.0\bin.

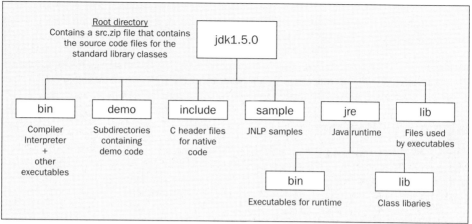

Figure 1-1

A word of warning — if you have previously installed a commercial Java development product, check that it has not modified your PATH environment variable to include the path to its own Java executables. If it has, when you try to run the Java compiler or interpreter, you are likely to get the versions supplied with the commercial product rather that those that came with the JDK. One way to fix this is to remove the path or paths that cause the problem. If you don't want to remove the paths that were inserted for the commercial product, you will have to use the full path specification when you want to run the compiler or interpreter from the JDK. The jre directory contains the Java Runtime facilities that are used when you execute a Java program. The classes in the Java libraries are stored in the jre\lib directory. They don't appear individually though. They are all packaged up in the archive, rt.jar. Leave this alone. The Java Runtime takes care of retrieving what it needs from the archive when your program executes.

The CLASSPATH environment variable is a frequent source of problems and confusion to newcomers to Java. The current JDK does *NOT* require CLASSPATH to be defined, and if it has been defined by some other Java version or system, it is likely to cause problems. Commercial Java development systems and versions of the Java Development Kit prior to 1.2 may well define the CLASSPATH environment variable, so check to see whether CLASSPATH has been defined on your system. If it has and you no longer have whatever defined it installed, you should delete it. If you have to keep the CLASSPATH environment variable — maybe because you want to keep the system that defined it or you share the machine with someone who needs it — you will have to use a command-line option to define CLASSPATH temporarily whenever you compile or execute your Java code. We will see how to do this a little later in this chapter.

If you want the JDK documentation installed in the hierarchy shown in Figure 1-1, then you should now extract the documentation from the archive to the root directory. This corresponds to C:\jdk1.5.0 if you installed the JDK to your C: drive. This will create a new subdirectory, docs, to the root directory, and install the documentation files in that. To look at the documentation, you just open the index.html file that is in the docs subdirectory.

Extracting the Source Code for the Class Libraries

The source code for the class libraries is included in the archive src.zip that you'll find in the jdk1.5.0 root directory. Once you have learned the basics of the Java language, browsing this source is very educational, and it can also be helpful when you are more experienced with Java in giving a better understanding of how things work—or when they don't, why they don't. You can extract the source files from the archive using the Winzip utility, the JAR utility that comes with the JDK, or any other utility that will unpack .zip archives—but be warned—there's a lot of it, and it takes a while!

Extracting the contents of src.zip to the root directory \jdk1.5.0 creates a new subdirectory, src, and installs the source code in subdirectories to this. To look at the source code for a particular class, just open the .java file that you are interested in using any plaintext editor.

Compiling a Java Program

Java source code is always stored in files with the extension .java. Once you have created the source code for a program and saved it in a .java file, you need to process the source using a Java compiler. Using the compiler that comes with the JDK, you would make the directory that contains your Java source file the current directory, and then enter the following command:

```
javac MyProgram.java
```

Here, javac is the name of the Java compiler, and MyProgram.java is the name of the program source file. This command assumes that the current directory contains your source file. If it doesn't, the compiler won't be able to find your source file. It also assumes that the source file corresponds to the Java language as defined in the current version of the JDK. There is a command-line option, -source, that you can use to specify the Java language version, so for JDK 5.0, the command above to execute the compiler is equivalent to:

```
javac -source 5 MyProgram.java
```

Note that you can also use 1.5 as the value with the source command-line option, in which case you could write the command like this:

```
javac -source 1.5 MyProgram.java
```

In practice you can ignore the -source command-line option unless you are compiling a Java program that was written using an older version of the JDK. For example, to compile code written for JDK 1.4 you would write:

```
javac -source 1.4 oldSourceCode.java
```

Here's a simple program you can try out the compiler on:

```java
public class MyProgram {
  public static void main(String[] args) {
    System.out.println("Rome wasn't burned in a day!");
  }
}
```

This just outputs a line of text to the command line. As this is just to try out the compiler, I won't explain how the program works at this point. Of course, you must type the code in exactly as shown and save the source file as MyProgram.java. If you have made any mistakes the compiler will issue error messages.

If you need to override an existing definition of the CLASSPATH environment variable — perhaps because it has been set by a Java development system you have installed — the command would be:

```
javac -classpath . MyProgram.java
```

The value of CLASSPATH follows the -classpath specification and here it is just a period. This defines just the path to the current directory, whatever that happens to be. This means that the compiler looks for your source file or files in the current directory. If you forget to include the period, the compiler will not be able to find your source files in the current directory. If you include the -classpath . command-line option in any event, it will do no harm.

Note that you should avoid storing your source files within the directory structure that was created for the JDK, as this can cause problems. Set up a separate directory of your own to hold the source code for a program and keep the code for each program in its own directory.

Assuming your program contains no errors, the compiler generates a bytecode program that is the equivalent of your source code. The compiler stores the bytecode program in a file with the same name as the source file, but with the extension .class. Java executable modules are always stored in a file with the extension .class. By default, the .class file will be stored in the same directory as the source file.

The command-line options we have introduced here are by no means all the options you have available for the compiler. You will be able to compile all of the examples in the book just knowing about the options we have discussed. There is a comprehensive description of all the options within the documentation for the JDK. You can also specify the -help command-line option to get a summary of the standard options you can use.

If you are using some other product to develop your Java programs, you will probably be using a much more user-friendly, graphical interface for compiling your programs that won't involve entering commands such as that shown above. However, the file name extensions for your source file and the object file that results from it will be just the same.

Executing a Java Application

To execute the bytecode program in the .class file with the Java interpreter in the JDK, you make the directory containing the .class file current and enter the command:

```
java -enableassertions MyProgram
```

Note that we use just the name MyProgram to identify the program, not the name of the file generated by the compiler, MyProgram.class. It is a common beginner's mistake to use the latter by analogy with the compile operation. If you put a .class file extension on MyProgram, your program won't execute, and you will get an error message:

```
Exception in thread "main" java.lang.NoClassDefFoundError: MyProgram/class
```

While the compiler expects to find the name of your source file, the java interpreter expects the name of a class, which is MyProgram in this case, not the name of a file. The MyProgram.class file contains the MyProgram class. We will explain what a class is shortly.

The -enableassertions option is necessary for JDK 5.0 programs that use assertions, and since you will be using assertions once you have learned about them it's a good idea to get into the habit of always using this option. You can abbreviate the -enableassertions option to -ea if you wish.

If you want to override an existing CLASSPATH definition, the option is the same as with the compiler. You can also abbreviate -classpath to -cp with the compiler or the Java interpreter. Here's how the command would look:

```
java -ea -cp . MyProgram
```

To execute your program, the Java interpreter analyzes and then executes the bytecode instructions. The Java Virtual Machine is identical in all computer environments supporting Java, so you can be sure your program is completely portable. As we already said, your program will run just as well on a Unix Java implementation as it will on that for Microsoft Windows, Solaris, Linux, OS/2, or any other operating system that supports Java. (Beware of variations in the level of Java supported though. Some environments, such as the Macintosh, tend to lag a little, so implementations for Java 2 will typically be available later than under Windows or Solaris.)

Executing an Applet

The Java compiler in the JDK will compile both applications and applets. However, an applet is not executed in the same way as an application. You must embed an applet in a web page before it can be run. You can then execute it either within a Java 2-enabled web browser, or by using the appletviewer, a bare-bones browser provided as part of the JDK. It is a good idea to use the appletviewer to run applets while you are learning. This ensures that if your applet doesn't work, it is almost certainly your code that is the problem, rather than some problem in integration with the browser.

If you have compiled an applet and included it in a web page stored as MyApplet.html in the current directory on your computer, you can execute it by entering the command:

```
appletviewer MyApplet.html
```

So how do you put an applet in a web page?

The Hypertext Markup Language

The Hypertext Markup Language, or **HTML** as it is commonly known, is used to define a web page. When you define a web page as an HTML document, it is stored in a file with the extension .html. An HTML document consists of a number of elements, and each element is identified by **tags**. The document will begin with <html> and end with </html>. These delimiters, <html> and </html>, are tags, and each element in an HTML document will be enclosed between a similar pair of tags between angle brackets. All element tags are case-insensitive, so you can use uppercase or lowercase, or even a mixture of the two, but by convention they are capitalized so they stand out from the text. Here is an example of an HTML document consisting of a title and some other text:

```
<html>
  <head>
    <title>This is the title of the document</title>
  </head>
  <body>
```

```
    You can put whatever text you like here. The body of a document can contain
    all kinds of other HTML elements, including <B>Java applets</B>. Note how each
    element always begins with a start tag identifying the element, and ends with
    an end tag that is the same as the start tag but with a slash added. The pair
    of tags around 'Java applets' in the previous sentence will display the text
    as bold.
  </body>
</html>
```

There are two elements that can appear directly within the <html> element, a <head> element and a <body> element, as in the example above. The <head> element provides information about the document, and is not strictly part of it. The text enclosed by the <title> element tags that appears here within the <head> element will be displayed as the window title when the page is viewed.

Other element tags can appear within the <body> element, and they include tags for headings, lists, tables, links to other pages, and Java applets. There are some elements that do not require an end tag because they are considered to be empty. An example of this kind of element tag is <hr/>, which specifies a horizontal rule, a line across the full width of the page. You can use the <hr/> tag to divide up a page and separate one type of element from another.

Adding an Applet to an HTML Document

For many element tag pairs, you can specify an **element attribute** in the starting tag that defines additional or qualifying data about the element. This is how a Java applet is identified in an <applet> tag. Here is an example of how you might include a Java applet in an HTML document:

```
<html>
  <head>
    <title> A Simple Program </title>
  </head>
  <body>
    <hr/>
    <applet code = "MyFirstApplet.class"  width = 300  height = 200 >
    </applet>
    <hr/>
  </body>
</html>
```

The two shaded lines between tags for horizontal lines specify that the bytecodes for the applet are contained in the file MyFirstApplet.class. The name of the file containing the bytecodes for the applet is specified as the value for the code attribute in the <applet> tag. The other two attributes, width and height, define the width and height of the region on the screen that will be used by the applet when it executes. These always have to be specified to run an applet. Here is the Java source code for a simple applet:

```
import javax.swing.JApplet;
import java.awt.Graphics;

public class MyFirstApplet extends JApplet {

  public void paint(Graphics g) {
    g.drawString("To climb a ladder, start at the bottom rung", 20, 90);
  }
}
```

Note that Java is case-sensitive. You can't enter `public` with a capital `P`—if you do, the program won't compile. This applet just displays a message when you run it. The mechanics of how the message gets displayed are irrelevant here—the example is just to illustrate how an applet goes into an HTML page. If you compile this code and save the previous HTML page specification in the file `MyFirstApplet.html` in the same directory as the Java applet code, you can run the applet using `appletviewer` from the JDK with the command:

```
appletviewer MyFirstApplet.html
```

This will display a window something like that shown in Figure 1-2:

Figure 1-2

In this particular case, the window is produced by Internet Explorer under Windows XP. Under other operating systems and browsers it is likely to look a little different. Since the height and width of the window for the applet are specified in pixels, the physical dimensions of the window will depend on the resolution and size of your monitor.

This example should work by default with Internet Explorer since the installation process for the JDK will install the Java plug-in for you. If it doesn't work, check the Internet Options . . . on the Tools menu for Internet Explorer. On the Advanced tab you should find an option titled "Use JRE v1.5.0 for <applet> (requires restart)"; make sure this option is checked. If you use Mozilla 1.x or Netscape 7.x, follow the instruction given in the installation documentation for the JDK to enable the plug-in.

Object-Oriented Programming in Java

As I said at the beginning of this chapter, Java is an object-oriented language. When you use a programming language that is not object-oriented, you must express the solution to every problem essentially in terms of numbers and characters—the basic kinds of data that you can manipulate in the language. In an object-oriented language like Java, things are different. Of course, you still have numbers and characters to work with—these are referred to as the **primitive data types**—but you can define other kinds of entities that are relevant to your particular problem. You solve your problem in terms of the entities or objects that occur in the context of the problem. This not only affects how a program is structured, but also the terms in which the solution to your problem is expressed. If your problem concerns baseball players, your Java program is likely to have `BaseballPlayer` objects in it; if you are producing a program dealing with fruit production in California, it may well have objects that are `Oranges` in it. Apart from seeming to be an inherently sensible approach to constructing programs, object-oriented programs are usually easier to understand.

In Java almost everything is an object. If you haven't delved into object-oriented programming before, or maybe because you have, you may feel this is a bit daunting. But fear not. Objects in Java are particularly easy. So easy, in fact, that you are going to start out by understanding some of the ideas behind Java objects right now. In that way you'll be on the right track from the outset.

This doesn't mean you are going to jump in with all the precise nitty-gritty of Java that you need for describing and using objects. You are just going to get the concepts straight at this point. You'll do this by taking a stroll through the basics using the odd bit of Java code where it helps the ideas along. All the code that you use here will be fully explained in later chapters. Concentrate on understanding the notion of objects first. Then you can ease into the specific practical details as you go along.

So What Are Objects?

Anything can be thought of as an object. Objects are all around you. You can consider `Tree` to be a particular class of objects: trees in general. The notion of a `Tree` in general is a rather abstract concept — although any tree fits the description, it is more useful to think of more specific types of tree. Hence, the Oak tree in my yard which I call `myOak`, the Ash tree in your yard which you call `thatDarnedTree`, and a `generalSherman`, the well-known redwood, are actual instances of specific types of tree, subclasses of `Tree` that in this case happen to be `Oak`, `Ash,` and `Redwood`. Note how we drop into the jargon here — **class** is a term that describes a specification for a collection of objects with common properties. Figure 1-3 shows some classes of trees and how you might relate them.

A class is a specification, or blueprint — expressed as a piece of program code — that defines what goes to make up a particular sort of object. A subclass is a class that inherits all the properties of the parent class, but that also includes extra specialization. Particular classes of `Tree`, such as `Oak` or `Ash`, have all the characteristics of the most general type, `Tree`; otherwise, they could not be considered to be such. However, each subclass of `Tree`, such as `Oak`, has its own characteristics that differentiate `Oak` objects from other types of `Tree`.

Of course, you define a class specification to fit what you want to do in your application context. There are no absolutes here. For my trivial problem, the specification of a `Tree` class might just consist of its species name and its height. If you are an arboriculturalist, then your problem with trees may require a much more complex class, or more likely a set of classes, that involves a mass of arboreal characteristics.

Every object that your program will use will have a corresponding class definition somewhere for objects of that type. This is true in Java as well as in other object-oriented languages. The basic idea of a class in programming parallels that of classifying things in the real world. It is a convenient and well-defined way to group things together.

An **instance** of a class is a technical term for an existing object of that class. `Ash` is a specification for a type of object, and `yourAsh` is an object constructed to that specification. So, `yourAsh` would be an instance of the class `Ash`. Once you have a class defined, then you can come up with objects, or instances, of that class. This raises the question of what differentiates an object of a given class from an object of another class, an `Ash` class object, say, from a `Redwood` object. In other words, what sort of information defines a class?

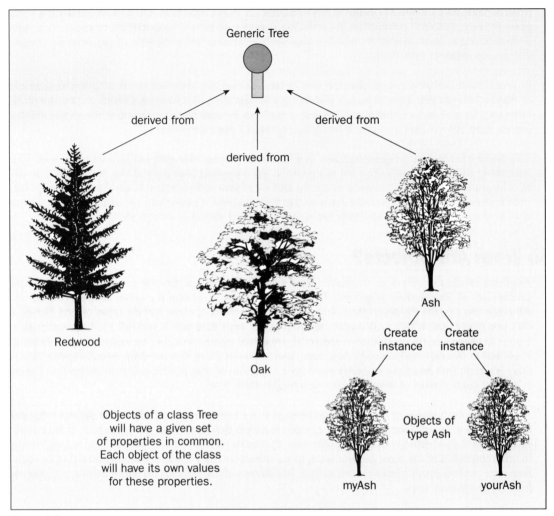

Figure 1-3

What Defines a Class of Objects?

You may have already guessed the answer. A class definition identifies all the parameters that define an object of that particular class, at least, so far as your needs go. Someone else might define the class differently, with a larger or smaller set of parameters to define the same sort of object — it all depends on what you want to do with the class. You decide what aspects of the objects you include to define that particular class of object, and you choose them depending on the kinds of problems that you want to address using the objects of the class. Let's think about a specific class of objects.

If you were defining a class Hat, for example, you might use just two parameters in the definition. You could include the type of hat as a string of characters such as "Fedora" or "Baseball cap" and its size as a numeric value. The parameters that define an object of a class are referred to as **instance variables** or **attributes** of a class, or class **fields**. The instance variables can be basic types of data such as numbers, but they can also be other class objects. For example, the name of a `Hat` object could be of type `String` — the class `String` defines objects that are strings of characters.

Of course there are lots of other things you could include to define a `Hat` if you wanted to, `color`, for example, which might be another string of characters such as `"Blue"`. To specify a class you just decide what set of attributes meet your requirements, and those are what you use. This is called **data abstraction** in the parlance of the object-oriented aficionado because you just abstract the attributes you want to use from the myriad possibilities for a typical object.

In Java the definition of the class `Hat` would look something like this:

```
class Hat {
   // Stuff defining the class in detail goes here.
   // This could specify the name of the hat, the size,
   // maybe the color, and whatever else you felt was necessary.
}
```

The name of the class follows the word `class`, and the details of the definition appear between the curly braces.

> Because the word *class* has this special role in Java it is called a *keyword*, and it is reserved for use only in this context. There are lots of other keywords in Java that you will pick up as we go along. You just need to remember that you must not use any of them for any other purposes.

I won't go into the detail of how the class `Hat` is defined, since you don't need it at this point. The lines appearing between the braces above are not code; they are actually **program comments**, because they begin with two successive forward slashes. The compiler will ignore anything on a line that follows two successive forward slashes in your Java programs, so you'll use this to add explanations to your programs. Generally, the more useful comments you can add to your programs, the better. You will see in Chapter 2 that there are other ways you can write comments in Java.

Each object of your class will have a particular set of values defined that characterize that particular object. You could have an object of type `CowboyHat`, which might be defined by values such as `"Stetson"` for the type of the hat, `"White"` for the color, and the size as 7. This is illustrated in Figure 1-4.

Although Figure 1-4 shows `CowboyHat` objects defined by a set of three values that you would not normally expect to change for a given instance, in general the parameter values that define an object are not necessarily fixed. You would expect the `type` and `size` attributes for a particular `CowboyHat` object to stay fixed since hats don't usually change their size — at least, not unless it's raining — but you could have other attributes, as illustrated in Figure 1-5.

You might have a parameter `owner`, which would record the owner's name, so the value stored as the attribute `owner` could be changed when the hat was sold or otherwise transferred to someone else. You might also have a parameter `hatOn`, for example, which would indicate whether the hat was on or off the owner's head; the value `true` would indicate that the owner was indeed wearing the hat, whereas the value `false` would mean that the hat had been removed and was just lying about somewhere.

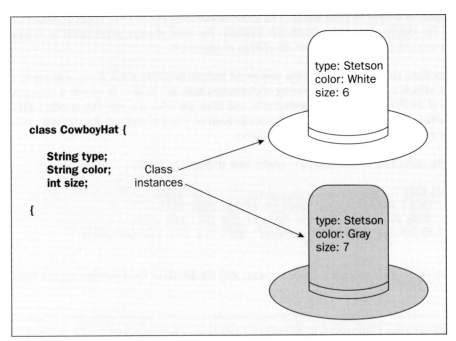

Figure 1-4

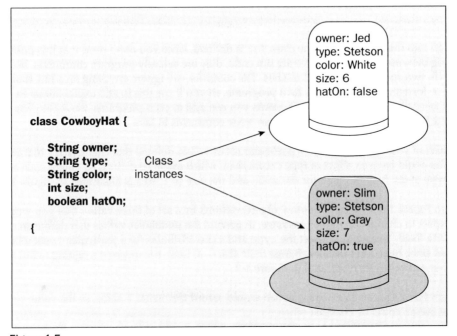

Figure 1-5

Operating on Objects

In spite of what you might think looking at Figure 1-5, a class object is not just a collection of various items of data. In addition to the parameters that characterize an object, a class specifies what you can do with an object of the class — that is, it defines the operations that are possible on objects of the class. Clearly, for objects to be of any use in a program, you need to decide what you can do with them. The operations that you specify for objects of a given type will depend on what sort of objects you are talking about, the attributes they contain, and how you intend to use them.

For the CowboyHat class in Figure 1-5, you may want to have operations that you could refer to as putHatOn and takeHatOff, which would have meanings that are fairly obvious from their names, and do make sense for CowboyHat objects. These operations on a particular CowboyHat object would set the value of hatOn for the object. To determine whether your CowboyHat was on or off, you would just need to look at this value. Conceivably, you might also have an operation changeOwner by which you could set the instance variable recording the current owner's name to a new value. Figure 1-6 shows two operations applied in succession to a CowboyHat object.

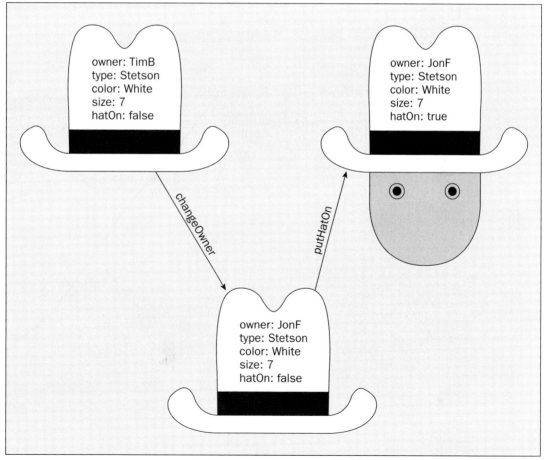

Figure 1-6

Of course, for each type of object you can have any operation that makes sense for you. If you want to have a shootHoleIn operation for Hat objects, that's no problem. You just have to define what that operation does to an object.

You are probably wondering at this point how an operation for a class is defined. As you'll see in detail a bit later, it boils down to a self-contained block of program code called a **method** that is identified by the name you give to it. You can pass data items — which can be integers, floating-point numbers, character strings, or class objects — to a method, and these will be processed by the code in the method. A method may also return a data item as a result. Performing an operation on an object amounts to *executing* the method that defines that operation for the object.

> Of course, the only operations you can perform on an instance of a particular class are those defined within the class, so the usefulness and flexibility of a class is going to depend on the thought that you give to its definition. We will be looking into these considerations more in Chapter 5.

Just so you'll recognize one when you see it, let's take a look at an example of a complete class definition. The code for the class CowboyHat we have been talking about might be as illustrated in Figure 1-7.

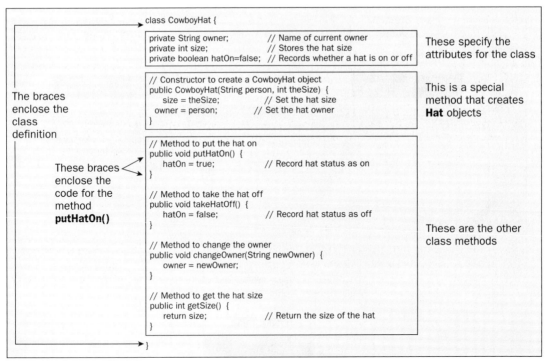

Figure 1-7

This code would be saved in a file with the name CowboyHat.java. The name of a file that contains the definition of a class is always the same as the class name, and the extension will be .java to identify that the file contains Java source code.

The code for the class definition appears between the braces that follow the identification for the class, as shown in Figure 1-7. The code for each of the methods in the class also appears between braces. The class has three instance variables, owner, size, and hatOn, and this last variable is always initialized as false. Each object that is created according to this class specification will have its own independent copy of each of these variables, so each object will have its own unique values for the owner, the hat size, and whether the hat is on or off. I omitted the type parameter in this version of the class to make the code a little bit shorter.

The keyword private, which has been applied to each instance variable, ensures that only code within the methods of the class can access or change the values of these directly. Methods of a class can also be specified as private. Being able to prevent access to some members of a class from outside is an important facility. It protects the internals of the class from being changed or used incorrectly. Someone using your class in another program can get access only to the bits to which you want them to have access. This means that you can change how the class works internally without affecting other programs that may use it. You can change any of the things inside the class that you have designated as private, and you can even change the code inside any of the public methods, as long as the method name and the number and types of values passed to it or returned from it remain the same.

Our CowboyHat class also has five methods, so you can do five different things with a CowboyHat object. One of these is a special method called a **constructor**, which creates a CowboyHat object — this is the method with the name, CowboyHat, that is the same as the class name. The items between the parentheses that follow the name of the constructor specify data that is to be passed to the method when it is executed — that is, when a CowboyHat object is created.

> In practice you might need to define a few other methods for the class to be useful; you might want to compare CowboyHat objects for example, to see if one was larger than another. However, at the moment you just need to get an idea of how the code looks. The details are of no importance here, as you'll return to all this in Chapter 5.

Java Program Statements

As you saw in the CowboyHat class example, the code for each method in the class appears between braces, and it consists of **program statements**. A semicolon terminates each program statement. A statement in Java can spread over several lines if necessary, since the end of each statement is determined by the semicolon, not by the end of a line. Here is a Java program statement:

```
hatOn = false;
```

If you wanted to, you could also write this as:

```
hatOn =
        false;
```

You can generally include spaces and tabs, and spread your statements over multiple lines to enhance readability if it is a particularly long statement, but sensible constraints apply. You can't put a space in the middle of a name for instance. If you write `hat On`, for example, the compiler will read this as two words.

Encapsulation

At this point we can introduce another bit of jargon you can use to impress or bore your friends — **encapsulation**. Encapsulation refers to the hiding of items of data and methods within an object. This is achieved by specifying them as `private` in the definition of the class. In the `CowboyHat` class, the instance variables `owner`, `type`, `size`, and `hatOn` were encapsulated. They were accessible only through the methods defined for the class. Therefore, the only way to alter the values they contain is to call a method that does that. Being able to encapsulate members of a class in this way is important for the security and integrity of class objects. You may have a class with data members that can take on only particular values. By hiding the data members and forcing the use of a method to set or change the values, you can ensure that only legal values are set.

I mentioned earlier another major advantage of encapsulation — the ability to hide the implementation of a class. By allowing only limited access to the members of a class, you have the freedom to change the internals of the class without necessitating changes to programs that use the class. As long as the external characteristics of the methods that can be called from outside the class remain unchanged, the internal code can be changed in any way that you, the programmer, want.

A particular object, an instance of `CowboyHat`, incorporates, or encapsulates, the `owner`, the `size` of the object, and the status of the hat in the instance variable `hatOn`. Only the constructor, and the `putHatOn()`, `takeHatOff()`, `changeOwner()`, and `getSize()` methods can be accessed externally.

> **Whenever I am referring to a method in the text, I will add a pair of parentheses after the method name to distinguish it from other things that have names. Some examples of this appear in the preceding paragraph. A method always has parentheses in its definition and in its use in a program, as you'll see, so it makes sense to represent it in this way in the text.**

Classes and Data Types

Programming is concerned with specifying how data of various kinds is to be processed, massaged, manipulated, or transformed. Since classes define the types of objects that a program will work with, you can consider defining a class to be the same as defining a data type. Thus, `Hat` is a type of data, as is `Tree`, and any other class you care to define. Java also contains a library of standard classes that provide you with a whole range of programming tools and facilities. For the most part then, your Java program will process, massage, manipulate, or transform class objects.

There are some basic types of data in Java that are not classes, and these are called **primitive types**. I will go into these in detail in the next chapter, but they are essentially data types for numeric values such as 99 or 3.75, for single characters such as *A* or *?*, and for logical values that can be `true` or `false`. Java also has classes that correspond to each of the primitive data types for reasons that you will see later on, so there is an `Integer` class that defines objects that encapsulate integers, for example. Every entity in your Java program that is not of a primitive data type will be an object of a class—either a class that you define yourself, a class supplied as part of the Java environment, or a class that you obtain from somewhere else, such as from a specialized support package.

Classes and Subclasses

Many sets of objects that you might define in a class can be subdivided into more specialized subsets that can also be represented by classes, and Java provides you with the capability to define one class as a more specialized version of another. This reflects the nature of reality. There are always lots of ways of dividing a cake—or a forest. `Conifer`, for example, could be a subclass of the class `Tree`. The `Conifer` class would have all the instance variables and methods of the `Tree` class, plus some additional instance variables and/or methods that make it a `Conifer` in particular. You refer to the `Conifer` class as a **subclass** of the class `Tree`, and the class `Tree` as a **superclass** of the class `Conifer`.

When you define a class such as `Conifer` using another class such as `Tree` as a starting point, the class `Conifer` is said to be **derived** from the class `Tree`, and the class `Conifer` **inherits** all the attributes of the class `Tree`.

Advantages of Using Objects

As I said at the outset, object-oriented programs are written using objects that are specific to the problem being solved. Your pinball machine simulator may well define and use objects of type `Table`, `Ball`, `Flipper`, and `Bumper`. This has tremendous advantages, not only in terms of easing the development process and making the program code easier to understand, but also in any future expansion of such a program. Java provides a whole range of standard classes to help you in the development of your program, and you can develop your own generic classes to provide a basis for developing programs that are of particular interest to you.

Because an object includes the methods that can operate on it as well as the data that defines it, programming using objects is much less prone to error. Your object-oriented Java programs should be more robust than the equivalent in a procedural programming language. Object-oriented programs take a little longer to design than programs that do not use objects since you must take care in the design of the classes that you will need, but the time required to write and test the code is sometimes substantially less than that for procedural programs. Object-oriented programs are also much easier to maintain and extend.

Java Program Structure

Let's summarize how a Java program is structured:

- ❑ A Java program always consists of one or more classes.

- ❑ You typically put the program code for each class in a separate file, and you must give each file the same name as that of the class that is defined within it.

- ❑ A Java source file name must have the extension `.java`.

Thus your file containing the class Hat will be called Hat.java and your file containing the class BaseballPlayer must have the file name BaseballPlayer.java.

A typical program consists of several files as illustrated in Figure 1-8.

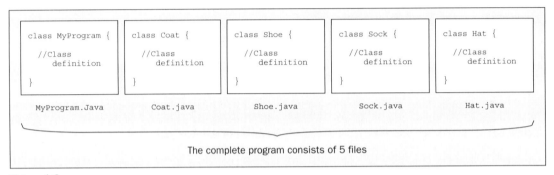

Figure 1-8

This program clearly majors on apparel, with four of the five classes representing clothing. Each source file contains a class definition, and all of the files that go to make up the program are stored in the same directory. The source files for your program contain all the code that you wrote, but this is not everything that is ultimately included in the program. There is also code from the **Java standard class library**, so let's take a peek at what that can do.

Java's Class Library

A library in Java is a collection of classes — usually providing related facilities — that you can use in your programs. The Java class library provides you with a whole range of goodies, some of which are essential for your programs to work at all, and some of which make writing your Java programs easier. To say that the standard class library covers a lot of ground would be something of an understatement, so I won't be going into it in detail here; however, you will be looking into how to apply many of the facilities it provides throughout the book.

Since the class library is a set of classes, it is stored in sets of files where each file contains a class definition. The classes are grouped together into related sets that are called **packages**, and each package is stored in a separate directory. A class in a package can access any of the other classes in the package. A class in another package may or may not be accessible. We will learn more about this in Chapter 5.

The package name is based on the path to the directory in which the classes belonging to the package are stored. Classes in the package java.lang for example are stored in the directory path java\lang (or java/lang under Unix). This path is relative to a particular directory that is automatically known by the Java run-time environment that executes your code. You can also create your own packages that will contain classes of your own that you want to reuse in different contexts, and that are related in some way.

The JDK includes a growing number of standard packages — well over 100 the last time I counted. Some of the packages you will meet most frequently are:

Package Name	Description
java.lang	These classes support the basic language features and the handling of arrays and strings. Classes in this package are always available directly in your programs by default because this package is always automatically loaded with your program.
java.io	Classes for data input and output operations.
java.util	This package contains utility classes of various kinds, including classes for managing data within collections or groups of data items.
javax.swing	These classes provide easy-to-use and flexible components for building graphical user interfaces (GUIs). The components in this package are referred to as Swing components.
java.awt	Classes in this package provide the original GUI components (JDK 1.1) as well as some basic support necessary for Swing components.
java.awt.geom	These classes define two-dimensional geometric shapes.
java.awt.event	The classes in this package are used in the implementation of windowed applications to handle events in your program. Events are things like moving the mouse, pressing the left mouse button, or clicking on a menu item.

As noted previously, you can use any of the classes from the java.lang package in your programs by default. To use classes from the other packages, you typically use import statements to identify the names of the classes that you need from each package. This allows you to reference the classes by the simple class name. Without an import statement you would need to specify the fully qualified name of each class from a package each time you refer to it. As we will see in a moment, the fully qualified name for a class includes the package name as well as the basic class name. Using fully qualified class names would make your program code rather cumbersome, and certainly less readable. It would also make them a lot more tedious to type in.

You can use an import statement to import the name of a single class from a package into your program, or all the class names. The two import statements at the beginning of the code for the applet you saw earlier in this chapter are examples of importing a single class name. The first was:

```
import javax.swing.JApplet;
```

This statement imports the JApplet class name that is defined in the javax.swing package. Formally, the name of the JApplet class is not really JApplet — it is the fully qualified name javax.swing.JApplet. You can use the unqualified name only when you import the class or the complete package containing it into your program. You can still reference a class from a package even if you don't import it though — you just need to use the full class name, javax.swing.JApplet. You could try this out with the applet you saw earlier if you like. Just delete the two import statements from the file and use the full class names in the program. Then recompile it. It should work the same as before. Thus, the fully qualified name for a class is the name of the package in which it is defined, followed by a period, followed by the name given to the class in its definition.

You could import the names of all the classes in the `javax.swing` package with the statement:

```
import javax.swing.*;
```

The asterisk specifies that all the class names are to be imported. Importing just the class names that your source code uses makes compilation more efficient, but when you are using a lot of classes from a package you may find it more convenient to import all the names. This saves typing reams of import statements for one thing. We will do this with examples of Java code in the book to keep the number of lines to a minimum. However, there are risks associated with importing all the names in a package. There may be classes with names that are identical to names you have given to your own classes, which would obviously create some confusion when you compile your code.

> **You will see more on how to use import statements in Chapter 5, as well as more about how packages are created and used, and you will be exploring the use of classes from the standard packages in considerable depth throughout the book.**

As I indicated earlier, the standard classes do not appear as files or directories on your hard disk. They are packaged up in a single compressed file, `rt.jar`, that is stored in the `jre/lib` directory. This directory is created when you install the JDK on your computer. A .jar file is a Java **ar**chive — a compressed archive of Java classes. The standard classes that your executable program requires are loaded automatically from `rt.jar`, so you don't have to be concerned with it directly at all.

Java Applications

Every Java application contains a class that defines a method called `main()`. The name of this class is the name that you use as the argument to the Java interpreter when you run the application. You can call the class whatever you want, but the method which is executed first in an application is always called `main()`. When you run your Java application, the method `main()` will typically cause methods belonging to other classes to be executed, but the simplest possible Java application program consists of one class containing just the method `main()`. As you will see below, the `main()` method has a particular fixed form, and if it is not of the required form, it will not be recognized by the Java interpreter as the method where execution starts.

You can see how this works by taking a look at just such a Java program. You need to enter the program code using your favorite plaintext editor, or if you have a Java development system with an editor, you can enter the code for the example using that. When you have entered the code, save the file with the same name as that used for the class and with the extension `.java`. For this example the file name will be `OurFirstProgram.java`. The code for the program is shown in Figure 1-9

The program consists of a definition for a class I have called `OurFirstProgram`. The class definition contains only one method, the method `main()`. The first line of the definition for the method `main()` is always of the form:

```
public static void main(String[] args)
```

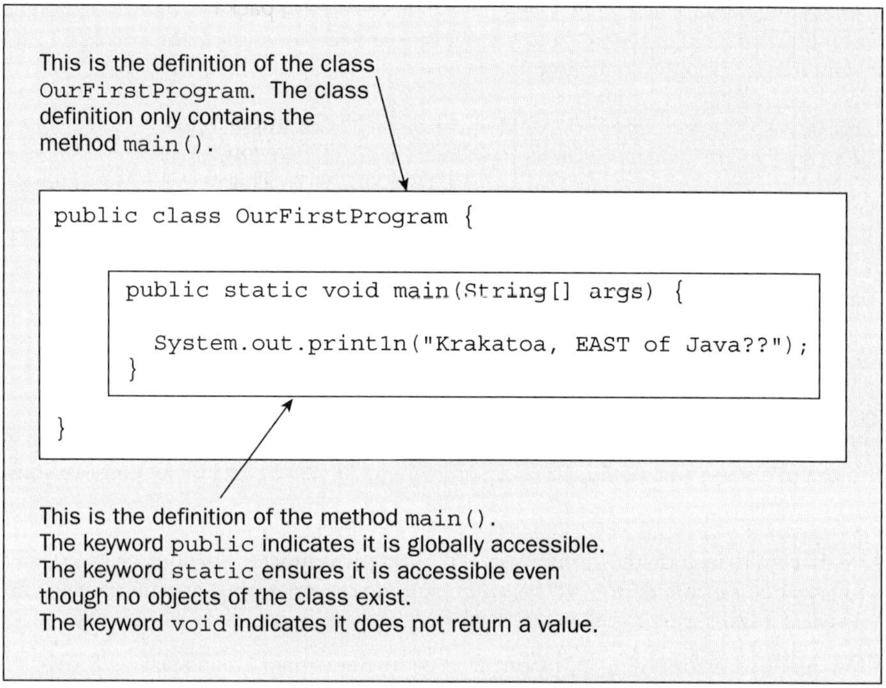

This is the definition of the class
OurFirstProgram. The class
definition only contains the
method main().

```
public class OurFirstProgram {

    public static void main(String[] args) {

        System.out.println("Krakatoa, EAST of Java??");
    }

}
```

This is the definition of the method main().
The keyword public indicates it is globally accessible.
The keyword static ensures it is accessible even
though no objects of the class exist.
The keyword void indicates it does not return a value.

Figure 1-9

The code for the method appears between the pair of curly braces. This version of the method has only one executable statement:

```
System.out.println("Krakatoa, EAST of Java??");
```

So what does this statement do? Let's work through it from left to right:

❑ System is the name of a standard class that contains objects that encapsulate the standard I/O devices for your system — the keyboard for command-line input and command-line output to the display. It is contained in the package java.lang, so it is always accessible just by using the simple class name System.

❑ The object out represents the standard output stream — the command line on your display screen — and is a data member of the class System. The member, out, is a special kind of member of the System class. Like the method main() in our OurFirstProgram class, it is static. This means that out exists even though there are no objects of type System (more on this in forthcoming chapters). Using the class name, System, separated from the member name out by a period — System.out — references the out member.

❑ The bit at the rightmost end of the statement, println("Krakatoa, EAST of Java??"), calls the println() method that belongs to the object out, and that outputs the text string that appears between the parentheses to your display. This demonstrates one way in which you can call a class method — by using the object name followed by the method name, with a period

separating them. The stuff between the parentheses following the name of a method is information that is passed to the method when it is executed. As we said, for `println()` it is the text we
want to output to the command line.

For completeness, the keywords `public`*,* `static`*, and* `void` *that appear in the method definition are
explained briefly in the annotations to the program code, but you need not be concerned if these still
seem a bit obscure at this point. I will be coming back to them in much more detail in Chapter 5.*

You can compile this program using the JDK compiler with the command

```
javac OurFirstProgram.java
```

or with the `-classpath` option specified:

```
javac -classpath . OurFirstProgram.java
```

If it didn't compile, there's something wrong somewhere. Here's a checklist of possible sources of the
problem:

❏ You forgot to include the path to the `jdk1.5.0\bin` directory in your `PATH`, or maybe you did
not specify the path correctly. This will result in your operating system not being able to find the
`javac` compiler that is in that directory.

❏ You made an error typing in the program code. Remember Java is case-sensitive, so
`OurfirstProgram` is not the same as `OurFirstProgram`, and of course, there must be no spaces
in the class name. If the compiler discovers an error, it will usually identify the line number in the
code where the error was found. In general, watch out for confusing zero, `0`, with a small letter `o`,
or the digit one, `1`, with the small letter `l`. All characters such as periods, commas, and semicolons
in the code are essential and must be in the right place. Parentheses, (), curly braces, {}, and square
brackets, [], always come in matching pairs and are not interchangeable.

❏ The source file name must match the class name exactly. The slightest difference will result in an
error. It must have the extension `.java`.

Once you have compiled the program successfully, you can execute it with the command:

```
java -ea OurFirstProgram
```

The `-ea` option is not strictly necessary since this program does not use assertions, but if you get used to
putting it in, you won't forget it when it is necessary. If you need the `-classpath` option specified:

```
java -ea -classpath . OurFirstProgram
```

Assuming the source file compiled correctly, and the `jdk1.5.0\bin` directory is defined in your path,
the most common reason for the program failing to execute is a typographical error in the class name,
`OurFirstProgram`. The second most common reason is writing the file name, `OurFirstProgram.class`,
in the command, whereas it should be just the class name, `OurFirstProgram`.

When you run the program, it will display the text:

```
Krakatoa, EAST of Java??
```

Java and Unicode

Programming to support languages that use anything other than the Latin character set has always been a major problem. There are a variety of 8-bit character sets defined for many national languages, but if you want to combine the Latin character set and Cyrillic in the same context, for example, things can get difficult. If you want to handle Japanese as well, it becomes impossible with an 8-bit character set because with 8 bits you have only 256 different codes so there just aren't enough character codes to go round. Unicode is a standard character set that was developed to allow the characters necessary for almost all languages to be encoded. It uses a 16-bit code to represent a character (so each character occupies 2 bytes), and with 16 bits up to 65,535 non-zero character codes can be distinguished. With so many character codes available, there is enough to allocate each major national character set its own set of codes, including character sets such as Kanji, which is used for Japanese and which requires thousands of character codes. It doesn't end there though. Unicode supports three encoding forms that allow up to a million additional characters to be represented.

As you'll see in Chapter 2, Java source code is in Unicode characters. Comments, identifiers (names in other words — see Chapter 2), and character and string literals can all use any characters in the Unicode set that represent letters. Java also supports Unicode internally to represent characters and strings, so the framework is there for a comprehensive international language capability in a program. The normal ASCII set that you are probably familiar with corresponds to the first 128 characters of the Unicode set. Apart from being aware that each character usually occupies 2 bytes, you can ignore the fact that you are handling Unicode characters in the main, unless of course you are building an application that supports multiple languages from the outset.

I say each Unicode character usually occupies 2 bytes because Java supports Unicode 4.0, which allows 32-bit characters called **surrogates**. You might think that the set of 64K characters that you can represent with 16 bits would be sufficient, but it isn't. Far-eastern languages such as Japanese, Korean, and Chinese alone involve more than 70,000 ideographs, and surrogates are used to represent characters that are not contained within the basic multilingual set that is defined by 16-bit characters.

Summary

In this chapter you've looked at the basic characteristics of Java, and how portability between different computers is achieved. I have also introduced you to the elements of object-oriented programming. There are bound to be some aspects of what I've discussed that you don't feel are completely clear to you. Don't worry about it. Everything I have discussed here I will be revisiting again in more detail later on in the book.

The essential points I have covered in this chapter are:

❏ Java applets are programs that are designed to be embedded in an HTML document. Java applications are standalone programs. Java applications can be console programs that only support text output to the screen, or they can be windowed applications with a GUI.

❏ Java programs are intrinsically object-oriented.

❏ Java source code is stored in files with the extension `.java`.

❏ Java programs are compiled to bytecodes, which are instructions for the Java Virtual Machine. The Java Virtual Machine is the same on all the computers on which it is implemented, thus ensuring the portability of Java programs.

❏ Java object code is stored in files with the extension `.class`.

❏ Java programs are executed by the Java interpreter, which analyses the bytecodes and carries out the operations they specify.

❏ The Java Development Kit (JDK) supports the compilation and execution of Java applications and applets.

Resources

You can download the source code for the examples in this book from `http://www.wrox.com`.

The source code download includes ancillary files, such as `.gif` files containing icons, for example, where they are used in the examples. I also include the solutions to the exercises that appear at the end of most chapters.

2

Programs, Data, Variables, and Calculation

In this chapter you'll look at the entities in Java that are not objects—numbers and characters. This will give you all the elements of the language you need to perform numerical calculations, and you'll apply these in a few working examples.

In this chapter you'll learn:

- ❑ How to declare and define variables of the basic integer and floating-point types
- ❑ How to write an assignment statement
- ❑ How integer and floating-point expressions are evaluated
- ❑ How to output data from a console program
- ❑ How mixed integer and floating-point expressions are evaluated
- ❑ What casting is and when you must use it
- ❑ What `boolean` variables are
- ❑ What determines the sequence in which operators in an expression are executed
- ❑ How to include comments in your programs

Data and Variables

A variable is a named piece of memory that you use to store information in your Java program—a piece of data of some description. Each named piece of memory that you define in your program is able to store data only of one particular type. If you define a variable to store integers, for example, you can't use it to store a value that is a decimal fraction, such as 0.75. If you've defined a variable that you use to refer to a `Hat` object, you can only use it to reference an object of type `Hat` (or any of its subclasses, as you'll see in Chapter 6). Since the type of data that each variable can store is fixed, the compiler can verify that each variable you define in your program is not used in a manner or a context that is inappropriate to its type. If a method in your program is supposed to process integers, the compiler will be able to detect when you inadvertently try to use the method with some other kind of data — for example, a string or a numerical value that is not integral.

Explicit data values that appear in your program are called **literals**. Each literal will also be of a particular type: 25, for example, is an integer literal of type `int`. I will go into the characteristics of the various types of literals that you can use as I discuss each variable type.

Before you can use a variable you must specify its name and type in a declaration statement. Before I describe how you write a declaration for a variable, let's consider what flexibility you have in choosing a name.

Naming Your Variables

The name that you choose for a variable, or indeed the name that you choose for anything in Java, is called an **identifier**. An identifier can be any length, but it must start with a letter, an underscore (_), or a dollar sign ($). The rest of an identifier can include any characters except those used as operators in Java (such as +, –, or *), but you will be generally better off if you stick to letters, digits, and the underscore character.

Java is case-sensitive, so the names `republican` and `Republican` are not the same. You must not include blanks or tabs in the middle of a name, so `Betty May` is out but you could have `BettyMay` or even `Betty_May`. Note that you can't have `6Pack` as a name since you cannot start a name with a numeric digit. Of course, you could use `sixPack` as an alternative.

Subject to the restrictions I have mentioned, you can name a variable almost anything you like, except for two additional restraints — you can't use keywords in Java as a name for something, and a name can't be anything that could be interpreted as a constant value — as a literal, in other words. Keywords are words that are an essential part of the Java language. You saw some keywords in the previous chapter, and you will learn a few more in this chapter. If you'd like to know what they all are now, see the complete list in Appendix A. The restriction on constant values is there because, although it is obvious why a name can't be 1234 or 37.5, constants can also be alphabetic, such as `true` and `false`, for example, which are literals of type `boolean`. Of course, the basic reason for these rules is that the compiler has to be able to distinguish between your variables and other things that can appear in a program. If you try to use a name for a variable that makes this impossible, then it's not a legal name.

Clearly, it makes sense to choose names for your variables that give a good indication of the sort of data they hold. If you want to record the size of a hat, for example, `hatSize` is not a bad choice for a variable name, whereas `qqq` would be a bad choice. It is a common convention in Java to start variable names with a lowercase letter and, where you have a name that combines several words, to capitalize the first letter of each word, as in `hatSize` or `moneyWellSpent`. You are in no way obliged to follow this convention but since almost all the Java world does, it helps to do so.

> *If you feel you need more guidance in naming conventions (and coding conventions in general) take a look at* `http://www.javasoft.com/docs/codeconv/`.

Variable Names and Unicode

Even though you may be entering your Java programs in an environment that stores ASCII characters, all Java source code is in Unicode. Although the original source code that you create may be ASCII, it is converted to Unicode characters internally, before it is compiled. While you can write any Java language statement using ASCII, the fact that Java supports Unicode provides you with immense flexibility. It means that the identifiers that you use in your source program can use any national language character set that is defined within the Unicode character set, so your programs can use French, Greek, or Russian variable names, for example, or even names in several different languages, as long as you have the means to enter them in the first place. The same applies to character data that your program defines.

Variables and Types

As I mentioned earlier, each variable that you declare can store values only of a type consistent with the data type of that variable. You specify the type of a particular variable by using a type name in the variable declaration. For instance, here's a statement that declares a variable that can store integers:

```
int numberOfCats;
```

The data type in this case is `int` and the variable name is `numberOfCats`. The semicolon marks the end of the statement. The variable, `numberOfCats`, can only store values of type `int`. Of course, `int` is a keyword.

Many of your variables will be used to reference objects, but let's leave those on one side for the moment, as they have some special properties. The only things in Java that are not objects are variables that correspond to one of eight basic data types, defined within the language. These fundamental types are referred to as **primitive types**, and they allow you to define variables for storing data that fall into one of three categories:

❑   Numeric values, which can be either integer or floating point

❑   Variables that store the code for a single Unicode character

❑   Logical variables that can assume the values `true` or `false`

All of the type names for the basic variable types are keywords in Java so you must not use them for other purposes. Let's take a closer look at each of the primitive data types and get a feel for how you can use them.

Integer Data Types

There are four types of variables that you can use to store integer data. All of these are signed; that is, they can store both negative and positive values. The four integer types differ in the range of values they can store, so the choice of type for a variable depends on the range of data values you are likely to need.

The four integer types in Java are:

Data Type	Description
byte	Variables of this type can have values from -128 to +127 and occupy 1 byte (8 bits) in memory
short	Variables of this type can have values from -32768 to 32767 and occupy 2 bytes (16 bits) in memory
int	Variables of this type can have values from -2147483648 to 2147483647 and occupy 4 bytes (32 bits) in memory
long	Variables of this type can have values from -9223372036854775808 to 9223372036854775807 and occupy 8 bytes (64 bits) in memory

Although I said the choice of type depends on the range of values that you want to be able to store, in practice you'll be using variables of type int or type long to store integers most of the time, for reasons that I'll explain a little later. Let's take a look at declarations of variables of each of these types:

```
byte smallerValue;
short pageCount;
int wordCount;
long bigValue;
```

Each of these statements declares a variable of the type specified.

The range of values that can be stored by each integer type in Java, as shown in the preceding table, is always the same, regardless of what kind of computer you are using. This is also true of the other primitive types that you will see later in this chapter and has the rather useful effect that your program will execute in the same way on computers that may be quite different. This is not necessarily the case with other programming languages.

Of course, although I have expressed the range of possible values for each type as decimal values, integers are stored internally as binary numbers, and it is the number of bits available to store each type that determines the maximum and minimum values, as shown in Figure 2-1.

For each of the binary numbers shown here, the leftmost bit is the sign bit, marked with an s. When the sign bit is 0 the number is positive, and when it is 1 the number is negative. Binary negative numbers are represented in what is called **2's complement form.** If you are not familiar with this, you will find an explanation of how it works in Appendix B.

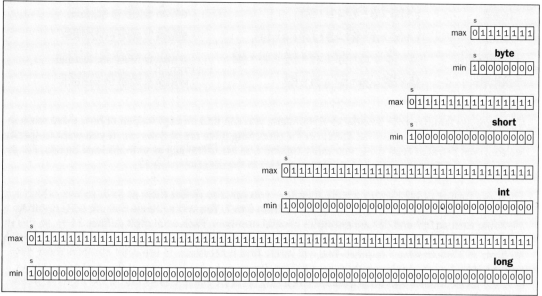

Figure 2-1

Integer Literals

An integer variable stores an integer value, so before you get to use integer variables you need to understand how you write integer values of various types. As I said earlier, a value of any kind in Java is referred to as a literal. So 1, 10.5, and "This is text" are all examples of literals.

Any integer literal that you specify as a sequence of decimal digits is of type `int` by default. Thus 1, -9999, and 123456789 are all literals of type `int`. If you want to define an integer literal of type `long`, you need to append an *L* to the value. The values 1L, -9999L, and 123456789L are all of type `long`. You can also use a lowercase letter *l*, but don't—it is too easily confused with the digit *1*.

You are perhaps wondering how you specify literals of type `byte` or `short`. Because of the way integer arithmetic works in Java, they just aren't necessary in the main. You'll see a couple of instances where an integer literal may be interpreted by the compiler as type `byte` or `short` later in this chapter, but these situations are the exception.

You can also specify integer literals to base 16—in other words, as **hexadecimal** numbers. Hexadecimal literals in Java have *0x* or *0X* in front of them and follow the usual convention of using the letters *A* to *F* (or *a* to *f*) to represent digits with values 10 to 15, respectively. In case you are a little rusty on hexadecimal values, here are some examples:

0x100	$1 * 16^2 + 0 * 16^1 + 0 * 16^0$	which is 256 in decimal
0x1234	$1 * 16^3 + 2 * 16^2 + 3 * 16^1 + 4 * 16^0$	which is 4660 in decimal
0xDEAF	$13 * 16^3 + 14 * 16^2 + 10 * 16^1 + 15 * 16^0$	which is 57007 in decimal
0xCAB	$12 * 16^2 + 10 * 16^1 + 11 * 16^0$	which is 3243 in decimal

If you are not familiar with hexadecimal numbers, you can find an explanation of how these work in Appendix B. All the hexadecimal literals in the preceding table are of type int. If you want to specify a hexadecimal literal of type long, you must append L to the literal just as with decimal literals. For example, 0x0FL is a hexadecimal literal that is equivalent to the decimal value 15.

There is a further possibility for integer literals — you can also define them as octal values, which is to base 8, and legal digits in an octal literal can be from 0 to 7. You write literals that are octal numbers with a leading zero, so 035 and 067 are examples of octal numbers. Each octal digit defines 3 bits, so this number base was used a lot more frequently in the days when machines used words of lengths that were a multiple of 3 bits to store a number. You will rarely find it necessary to use octal numbers these days, but you should take care not to use them by accident. If you put a leading zero at the start of an integer literal, the Java compiler will think you are specifying an octal value. Unless one of the digits is greater than 7, which results in the compiler flagging it as an error, you won't know that you have done this.

Declaring Integer Variables

As you saw earlier, you can declare a variable of type long with the statement:

```
long bigOne;
```

This statement is a declaration for the variable bigOne. This specifies that the variable bigOne will store a value of type long. When this statement is compiled, 8 bytes of memory will be allocated for the variable bigOne. Java does not automatically initialize a variable such as this. If you want your variables to have an initial value rather than a junk value left over from when the memory was last used, you must specify your own value in the declaration. To declare and initialize the variable bigOne to 2999999999, you just write:

```
long bigOne = 2999999999L;
```

The variable will be set to the value following the equal sign. It is good practice to always initialize your variables when you declare them. Note that if you try to use a variable in a calculation that has not had a value assigned to it, your program will not compile. There are also circumstances where the compiler cannot determine whether or not a variable has been initialized before it is used if you don't initialize it when you declare it, even though it may be obvious to you that it has been. This will also be flagged as an error, but if you get into the habit of always initializing variables when you declare them, you'll avoid all of these problems.

You can declare a variable just about anywhere in your program, but you must declare each variable before you use it in a calculation. The placement of the declaration has an effect on whether a particular variable is accessible at a given point in a program, and we will look deeper into the significance of this in the next chapter. Broadly, you should group related variable declarations together, immediately before the block of code that uses them.

You can declare and define multiple variables in a single statement. For example:

```
long bigOne = 999999999L, largeOne = 100000000L;
```

Here I have declared two variables of type `long`. A comma separates each variable from the next. You can declare as many variables as you like in a single statement, although it is usually better to stick to declaring one variable in each statement, as it helps to make your programs easier to read. A possible exception occurs with variables that are closely related — an (x,y) coordinate pair representing a point, for example, which you might reasonably declare as:

```
int xCoord = 0, yCoord = 0;          // Point coordinates
```

On the same line as the declaration of these two variables, we have a comment following the double slash, explaining what they are about. The compiler ignores everything from the double slash (`//`) until the end of the line. Explaining in comments what your variables are for is a good habit to get into, as it can be quite surprising how something that was as clear as crystal when you wrote it transmogrifies into something as clear as mud a few weeks later. You can add comments to your programs in other ways that we will see a little later in this chapter.

You can also spread a single declaration over several lines if you want. This also can help to make your program more readable. For example:

```
int miles    = 0,       // One mile is 8 furlongs
    furlongs = 0,       // One furlong is 220 yards
    yards    = 0,       // One yard is 3 feet
    feet     = 0;
```

This defines four variables of type `int` in a single statement with the names `miles`, `furlongs`, `yards`, and `feet`. Each variable has 0 as its initial value. Naturally, you must be sure that an initializing value for a variable is within the range of the type concerned; otherwise, the compiler will complain. Your compiler is intelligent enough to recognize that you can't get a quart into a pint pot, or, alternatively, a `long` constant into a variable of type `int`, `short`, or `byte`. Because the statement is spread over four lines, I am able to add a comment on each of the first three lines to explain something about the variable that appears on it.

To complete the set of variables that store integers you can declare and initialize a variable of type `byte` and one of type `short` with the following two statements:

```
byte luckyNumber = 7;
short smallNumber = 1234;
```

Here the compiler can deduce that the integer literals are to be of type `byte` and `short`, respectively, and convert the literals to the appropriate type. It is your responsibility to make sure the initial value will fit within the range of the variable that you are initializing. If it doesn't, the compiler will reject the statement and output an error message.

Most of the time you will find that variables of type `int` will cover your needs for dealing with integers, with type `long` being necessary now and again when you have some really big integer values to deal with. Variables of type `byte` and `short` do save a little memory, but unless you have a lot of values of these types to store, that is, values with a very limited range, they won't save enough to be worth worrying about. They also introduce complications when you use them in calculations, as you'll see shortly, so generally you should not use them unless it is absolutely necessary. Of course, when you are reading data from some external source, a disk file for instance, you'll need to make the type of variable for each data value correspond to what you expect to read.

Floating-Point Data Types

Numeric values that are not integral are stored as **floating-point** numbers. A floating-point number has a fixed number of digits of accuracy but with a very wide range of values. You get a wide range of values, even though the number of digits is fixed, because the decimal point can "float." For example, the values 0.000005, 500.0, and 5000000000000.0 can be written as $5×10^{-6}$, $5×10^2$, and $5×10^{12}$ respectively — you have just one digit 5 but you get three different numbers by moving the decimal point around.

There are two primitive floating-point types in Java, type `float` and type `double`. These give you a choice in the number of digits precision available to represent your data values, and in the range of values that can be accommodated:

Data Type	Description
float	Variables of this type can have values from -3.4E38 (-3.4 * 10^{38}) to +3.4E38 (+3.4 * 10^{38}) and occupy 4 bytes in memory. Values are represented with approximately 7 decimal digits accuracy.
double	Variables of this type can have values from -1.7E308 (-1.7 * 10^{308}) to +1.7E308 (+1.7 * 10^{308}) and occupy 8 bytes in memory. Values are represented with approximately 17 decimal digits accuracy. The smallest non-zero value that you can have is roughly ±4.9 * 10^{-324}.

> **All floating-point operations and the definitions for values of type `float` and type `double` conform to the IEEE 754 standard.**

As with integer calculations, floating-point calculations in Java will produce the same results on any computer.

Floating-Point Literals

Floating-point literals are of type `double` by default, so 1.0 and 345.678 are both of type `double`. When you want to specify a value of type `float`, you just append an *f*, or an *F*, to the value, so 1.0f and 345.678F are both literals of type `float`. If you are new to programming it is important to note that you must not include commas as separators when specifying numerical values in your program code. Where you might normally write a value as 99,786.5, in your code you must write it without the comma, as 99786.5.

When you need to write very large or very small floating-point values, you will usually want to write them with an exponent — that is, as a decimal value multiplied by a power of 10. You can do this in Java by writing the number as a decimal value followed by an *E*, or an *e*, preceding the power of 10 that you require. For example, the distance from the Earth to the Sun is approximately 149,600,000 kilometers, more conveniently written as 1.496E8. Since the *E* (or *e*) indicates that what follows is the exponent, this is equivalent to $1.496 * 10^8$. At the opposite end of the scale, the mass of an electron is around 0.0000000000000000000000000009 grams. This is much more convenient, not to say more readable, when it is written as 9.0E-28 grams.

Declaring Floating-Point Variables

You declare floating-point variables in a similar way to what you've already used for integers. You can declare and initialize a variable of type `double` with the following statement:

```
double sunDistance = 1.496E8;
```

This declares the variable with the name `sunDistance` and initializes it with the appropriate value.

Declaring a variable of type `float` is much the same. For example:

```
float electronMass = 9E-28F;
```

This defines and initializes the variable `electronMass`.

You can, of course, declare more than one variable of a given type in a single statement:

```
float hisWeight = 185.2F, herWeight = 108.5F;
```

Remember that you must put the *F* or *f* at the end of literals of type `float`. If you leave it out, the literal will be of type `double`, and the compiler won't convert it automatically to type `float`.

Fixing the Value of a Variable

Sometimes you will declare and initialize a variable with a value that should never change. For example:

```
int feet_per_yard = 3;
double mm_per_inch = 25.4;
```

Both these values should be fixed. There are always 3 feet to a yard, and an inch will always be 25.4 millimeters. Although they are fixed values for which you could use a literal in calculations, it is very convenient to store them in a variable because using suitable names makes it clear in your program what they mean. If you use the value 3 in your program code it could mean anything—but the name `feet_per_yard` leaves no doubt as to what it is.

However, ideally you'd like to prevent these variables from varying if possible. Accidental changes to the number of feet in a yard could make the results of your program suspect to say the least. Java provides you with a way to fix the value of any variable by using the `final` keyword when you declare it. For example:

```
final int FEET_PER_YARD = 3;      // Constant values
final double MM_PER_INCH = 25.4;  // that cannot be changed
```

The `final` keyword specifies that the value of a variable is final and must not be changed. The compiler will check your code for any violations of this and flag them as errors. I've used uppercase letters for the names of the variables here because it is a convention in Java to write constants in this way. This makes it easy to see which variables are defined as constant values. Obviously, any variable you declare as final must have an initial value assigned, as you can't specify it later.

Now that you know how to declare and initialize variables of the basic types, you are nearly ready to write a program. You just need to look at how you express the calculations you want carried out, and you store the results.

Arithmetic Calculations

You store the result of a calculation in a variable by using an **assignment statement**. An assignment statement consists of three elements: the name of the variable where you want the result stored; the assignment operator, =, which indicates that this is indeed an assignment operation; and an arithmetic expression that defines the calculation you want to perform. The whole thing is terminated by a semi-colon that marks the end of the assignment statement. Here's a simple example of an assignment statement:

```
numFruit = numApples + numOranges;      // Calculate the total fruit
```

When this statement executes, the value of the expression to the right of the assignment operator, =, is calculated, and the result is stored in the variable that appears to the left of the = sign. In this case, the values stored in the variables `numApples` and `numOranges` are added together, and the result is stored in the variable `numFruit`. Of course, you would have to declare all three variables before this statement.

Incrementing a variable by a given amount is a common requirement in programming. Look at the following assignment statement:

```
numApples = numApples + 1;
```

The result of evaluating the expression on the right of the = is one more than the value of `numApples`. This result is stored back in the variable `numApples`, so the overall effect of executing the statement is to increment the value in `numApples` by 1. You will see an alternative, more concise, way of producing the same effect shortly.

You can write multiple assignments in a single statement. Suppose you have three variables a, b, and c that you have defined to be of type `int`, and you want to set all three to 777. You can do this with the statement:

```
a = b = c = 777;
```

Note that an assignment is different from initialization in a declaration. Initialization causes a variable to have the value of the constant that you specify when it is created. An assignment involves copying data from one place in memory to another. For the preceding assignment statement, the compiler will have allocated some memory (4 bytes) to store the constant 777 as type `int`. This value will then be copied to the variable c. The value in c will be extracted and copied to b. Finally, the value in b will be copied to a. (However, strictly speaking, the compiler may optimize these assignments when it compiles the code to reduce the inefficiency of performing successive assignments of the same value in the way I have described.)

With simple assignments of a constant value to a variable of type `short` or `byte`, the constant will be stored as the type of the variable on the left of the =, rather than type `int`. For example:

```
short value = 0;
value = 10;
```

Here you have a declaration statement for the variable `value`, followed by an assignment statement. When the declaration executes, it will allocate space for the variable `value`, and arrange for its initial value to be 0. The assignment statement that follows the declaration statement needs to have 10 available as an integer literal of type `short`, occupying 2 bytes, because `value` is of type `short`. The value 10 will then be copied to the variable `value`.

Now let's look in more detail at how you perform calculations with integers.

Integer Calculations

The basic operators you use in calculations involving integers are +, -, *, and /, and these have the usual meanings — add, subtract, multiply, and divide, respectively. Each of these is a **binary** operator; that is, they combine two operands to produce a result — 2 + 3 for example will result in 5. An **operand** is just the term for a value to which an operator is applied. The priority or precedence that applies when an expression using these operators is evaluated is the same as you learned at school, so multiplication and division operations are executed before any addition or subtraction. Evaluating the expression:

```
20 - 3 * 3 - 9 / 3
```

will produce the value 8, since it is equivalent to 20 – 9 – 3.

As you will also have learned in school, you can use parentheses in arithmetic calculations to change the sequence of operations. Expressions within parentheses are always evaluated first, starting with the innermost when they are nested, so you use parentheses to override the default sequence of operations. Therefore, the expression

```
(20 - 3) * (3 - 9) / 3
```

is equivalent to 17 * (-6) / 3, which results in -34.

Of course, you use these operators with variables that store integer values as well as integer literals. You could calculate a value to be stored in a variable, `area`, of type `int` from values stored in the variables `length` and `width`, also of type `int`, by writing:

```
area = length*width;
```

As I said earlier, these arithmetic operators are binary operators, so called because they require two operands. There are also **unary** versions of the + and – operators that apply to a single operand to the right of the operator. Note that the unary – operator is not just a sign, as in a literal such as –345; it is an operator that has an effect. When applied to a variable, it results in a value that has the opposite sign to that of the value stored in the variable. For example, if the variable count has the value -10, the expression -count has the value +10. Of course, applying the unary + operator to the value of a variable results in the same value.

Let's try out some simple arithmetic in a working console application.

Try It Out   Apples and Oranges (or Console Yourself)

Key in the code for this example and save it in a file with the name Fruit.java. You will remember from the previous chapter that each source file will contain a class definition, and that the name of the file will be the same as that of the class with the extension .java. Store the file in a directory that is separate from the hierarchy containing the JDK. You can give the directory any name that you want, even the name Fruit if that helps to identify the program that it contains.

```
public class Fruit {
  public static void main(String[] args) {
    // Declare and initialize three variables
    int numOranges = 5;                     // Count of oranges
    int numApples = 10;                     // Count of apples
    int numFruit = 0;                       // Count of fruit

    numFruit = numOranges + numApples;      // Calculate the total fruit count
    // Display the result
    System.out.println("A totally fruity program");
    System.out.println("Total fruit is " + numFruit);
  }
}
```

Just to remind you, to compile this program using the JDK, first make sure that the current directory is the one containing your source file and then execute the following command:

```
javac Fruit.java
```

As I noted in the previous chapter, you may need to use the -classpath option if the CLASSPATH environment variable has been defined. If there are no errors, this will generate a file, Fruit.class, in the same directory, and this file contains the bytecodes for the program. To execute the program you invoke the Java interpreter with the class name for your application program:

```
java -ea Fruit
```

In some Java development environments, the output may not be displayed long enough for you to see it. If this is the case, you can add a few lines of code to get the program to wait until you press Enter before it ends. The additional lines to do this are shown shaded in the following listing:

```
import java.io.IOException;  // For code that delays ending the program
public class FruitWait {
  public static void main(String[] args) {
    // Declare and initialize three variables
    int numOranges = 5;                 // Count of oranges
    int numApples = 10;                 // Count of apples
    int numFruit = 0;                   // Count of fruit

    numFruit = numOranges + numApples;  // Calculate the total fruit count
    // Display the result
    System.out.println("A totally fruity program");
    System.out.println("Total fruit is " + numFruit);
    // Code to delay ending the program
    System.out.println("(press Enter to exit)");

    try {
      System.in.read();                 // Read some input from the keyboard

    } catch (IOException e) {           // Catch the input exception
      return;                           // and just return
    }
  }
}
```

I have changed the class name to `FruitWait` to distinguish it from the previous version of the program, so I can put it in a separate file in the code download for the book. I won't go into this extra code here. If you need to, just put it in for the moment. You will understand exactly how it works later in the book.

The stuff between the parentheses following `main`—that is, `String[] args`—provides a means of accessing data that is passed to the program from the command line when you run it. I will be going into this in detail later on in the book so you can just ignore it for now, though you must always include it in the first line of `main()`. If you don't, the program will compile but won't execute.

All that additional code in the body of the `main()` method just waits until you press Enter before ending the program. If necessary, you can include this in all of your console programs to make sure they don't disappear before you can read the output. It won't make any difference to how the rest of the program works. I will defer discussing in detail what is happening in the bit of code that I have added until I get to explaining exceptions in Chapter 7.

If you run this program with the additional code, the output will be similar to the window in Figure 2-2.

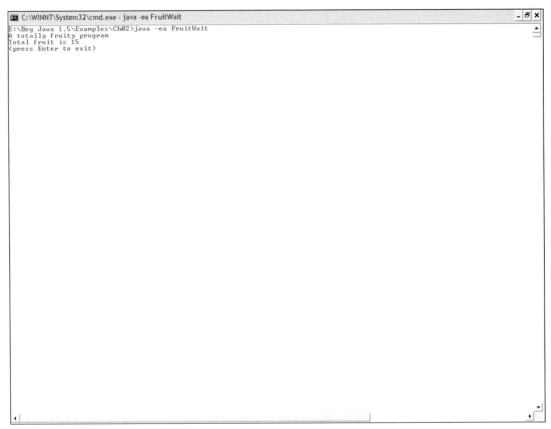

Figure 2-2

The basic elements of the code in the original version of the program are shown in Figure 2-3.

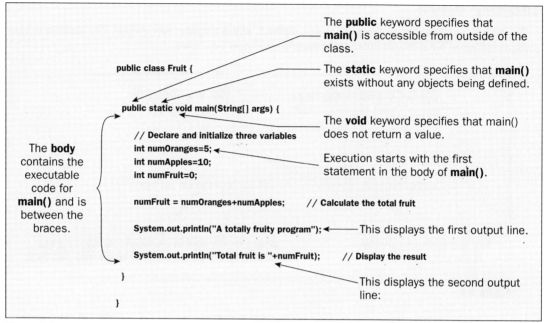

The **public** keyword specifies that **main()** is accessible from outside of the class.

The **static** keyword specifies that **main()** exists without any objects being defined.

public class Fruit {

public static void main(String[] args) {

The **void** keyword specifies that main() does not return a value.

// Declare and initialize three variables
int numOranges=5;
int numApples=10;
int numFruit=0;

Execution starts with the first statement in the body of **main()**.

The **body** contains the executable code for **main()** and is between the braces.

numFruit = numOranges+numApples;   // Calculate the total fruit

System.out.println("A totally fruity program"); ──── This displays the first output line.

System.out.println("Total fruit is "+numFruit);   // Display the result

This displays the second output line:

}

}

Figure 2-3

The program consists of just one class, Fruit, and just one method, main(). Execution of an application always starts at the first executable statement in the method main(). There are no objects of the class Fruit defined, but the method main() can still be executed because I have specified it as static. The method main() is always specified as public and static and with the return type void. The effects of these three keywords on the method are as follows:

public   Specifies that the method is accessible from outside the Fruit class

static   Specifies that the method is a class method that is to be executable, even though no class objects have been created. (Methods that are not static can be executed only for a particular object of the class, as you'll see in Chapter 5.)

void   Specifies that the method does not return a value

Don't worry if these are not completely clear to you at this point — you will meet them all again later.

The first three statements in main() declare the variables numOranges, numApples, and numFruit to be of type int and initialize them to the values 5, 10, and 0, respectively. The next statement adds the values stored in numOranges and numApples, and stores the result, 15, in the variable numFruit. We then generate some output from the program.

43

Producing Output

The next two statements use the `println()` method, which displays text output. The statement looks a bit complicated but it breaks down quite simply, as Figure 2-4 shows.

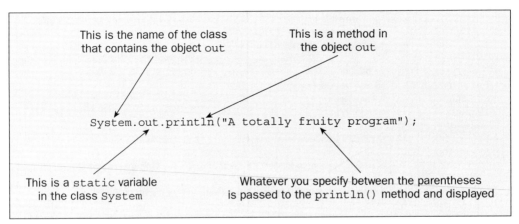

Figure 2-4

The text between double quotes, `"A totally fruity program"`, is a character string. Whenever you need a string constant, you just put the sequence of characters you want in the string between double quotes.

You can see from the annotations above how you execute methods that belong to an object. Here we execute the method `println()`, which belongs to the object `out`, which, in turn, is a variable that is a static member of the class `System`. Because the object `out` is static, it exists even if there are no objects of type `System` in existence. This is analogous to the use of the keyword `static` for the method `main()`.

Most objects in a program are not static members of a class though, so calling a method for an object typically just involves the object name and the method name. For instance, if you guessed, based on the last example, that to call the `putHatOn()` method for an object `cowboyHat` of the type `Hat` that I introduced in Chapter 1, you would write

    cowboyHat.putHatOn();

you would be right. Don't worry if you didn't though. We will be going into this again when we look at classes in detail. For the moment, any time you want to output something as text to the console, you will just write

    System.out.println(whateverWeWantToDisplay);

with whatever character string you want to display plugged in between the parentheses.

Thus, the second statement in the example:

    System.out.println("Total fruit is " + numFruit);

outputs the character string "Total fruit is " followed by the value of numFruit converted to characters, which is 15. So what's the + doing here—it's obviously not arithmetic we are doing, is it? The addition operator has a special effect when used with operands that are character strings—it joins them together to produce a single string. But numFruit is not a string, is it? No, but the left operand, "Total fruit is ", is, and this causes the compiler to decide that the whole thing is an expression working on character strings. Therefore, the compiler inserts code that converts the value of the right operand, numFruit, to a character string to be compatible with the left operand. The effect of the + operation is to tack the string representation of the value of numFruit onto the end of the string "Total fruit is ". The composite string is then passed to the println() method to display it on your screen. Dashed clever, these compilers.

If you wanted to output the value of numOranges as well, you could write:

```
System.out.println("Total fruit is " + numFruit + " and oranges = " + numOranges);
```

Try it out by adding it to the program if you like. You should get the following output:

```
Total fruit is 15 and oranges = 5
```

Integer Division and Remainders

When you divide one integer by another and the result is not exact, any remainder is discarded, so the final result is always an integer. The division 3/2, for example, produces the result 1, and 11/3 produces the result 3. This makes it easy to divide a given quantity equally amongst a given number of recipients. To divide numFruit equally between four children, you could write:

```
int numFruitEach = 0;          // Number of fruit for each child
numFruitEach = numFruit/4;
```

The result of division when the operands are positive is fairly obvious. It's the amount left over after dividing the right operand, called the **divisor**, into the left operand, referred to as the **dividend**, a whole number of times. The situation when either or both operands are negative deserves a little more exploration.

If you divide 7 by -3, the result will be -2. Similarly, if you divide -10 by 4 the result is -2. If you divide -5 by -3 the result is +1. The magnitude of the result of dividing a value a, by a value b, is the same, regardless of the sign of the operands, but the sign of the result depends on the sign of the operands. The sign of the result will be positive when the operands both have the same sign and negative when the operands are of different signs and the divisor is not greater than the dividend (in which case the result is zero). There is one peculiar exception to this. When the dividend is a negative integer of the largest possible magnitude and the divisor is -1, the result is the same as the dividend, which is negative and therefore violates the rule. You can see why this is so by considering specifics.

The value -2147483648 is the negative value of type int that has the largest magnitude. Dividing this by -1 should result in the value +2147483648, but the largest positive integer you can have as type int is 2147483647, so this result cannot be represented as type int. Therefore, the result is arbitrarily the original dividend, -2147483648.

Dividing by zero is something to be avoided. If you accidentally cause this to be attempted then your program will be terminated because an exception of type `ArithmeticException` will be thrown. You'll learn what exceptions are and what you can do about them in Chapter 7.

Of course, there are circumstances where you may want to obtain the remainder after a division, and on these occasions you can calculate the remainder using the modulus operator, `%`. If you wanted to know how many fruit were left after dividing the total by 4, you could write:

```
int remainder = 0;
remainder = numFruit%4;        // Calculate the remainder after division by 4
```

When either or both operands to the remainder operator are negative, the result may not seem to be obvious but keep in mind that it is related to the divide operation, so if you can work out what the result of a division will be, you can deduce the result of the remainder operation. You can get a clear idea of what happens by considering a few examples.

The result of the operation 8 % (-3) is +2. This will be evident if you recall that from the earlier discussion of division you know that the result of 8 / (-3) is -2. If you multiply the result of the division by the divisor, (-2) * (-3), the result is +6, so a remainder of +2 makes sense. The expression (-8) % 3 produces -2, which again you can deduce from the result of (-8) / 3 being -2. You have to add -2 to the result of (-2) * 3 to get the original value, -8. Lastly, (-8) % (-3) results in -2, which is also consistent with the divide operation applied to the same operands.

The modulus operator has the same precedence as multiplication and division and therefore executes before any add or subtract operations in the same expression. You could add these statements to the program, too, if you want to see the modulus operator in action. The following statement will output the results:

```
System.out.println("The number of fruit each is " + numFruitEach
                    + " and there are " + remainder + " left over.");
```

The Increment and Decrement Operators

If you want to increment an integer variable by one, you can use the increment operator instead of using an assignment. You write the increment operator as two successive plus signs, `++`. For example, if you have an integer variable `count` that you've declared as:

```
int count = 10;
```

you can then write the statement:

```
++count;        // Add 1 to count
```

This statement will increase the value of `count` to 11. If you want to decrease the value of `count` by 1 you can use the decrement operator, `--`:

```
--count;        // Subtract 1 from count
```

At first sight, apart from reducing the typing a little, this doesn't seem to have much of an advantage over writing:

```
count = count - 1;      // Subtract 1 from count
```

However, a big advantage of the increment and decrement operators is that you can use them in an expression. Try changing the arithmetic statement calculating the sum of numApples and numOranges in the previous example:

```
public class Fruit {
  public static void main(String[] args)   {
    // Declare and initialize three variables
    int numOranges = 5;
    int numApples = 10;
    int numFruit = 0;

    // Increment oranges and calculate the total fruit
    numFruit = ++numOranges + numApples;
    System.out.println("A totally fruity program");
    // Display the result
    System.out.println("Value of oranges is " + numOranges);
    System.out.println("Total fruit is " + numFruit);
  }
}
```

The lines that have been altered or added have been highlighted. In addition to the change to the numFruit calculation, an extra statement has been added to output the final value of numOranges. The value of numOranges will be increased to 6 before the value of numApples is added, so the value of numFruit will be 16. Thus, the statement changes the value stored in numOranges as well as the value stored in numFruit. You could try the decrement operation in the example as well.

A further property of the increment and decrement operators is that they work differently in an expression depending on whether you put the operator in front of the variable to which it applies, or following it. When you put the operator in front of a variable, as in the example you have just seen, it's called the **prefix form**. The converse case, with the operator following the variable, is called the **postfix form**. If you change the statement in the example to:

```
numFruit = numOranges++ + numApples;
```

and run it again, you'll find that numOranges still ends up with the value 6, but the total stored in numFruit has remained 15. This is because the effect of the postfix increment operator is to change the value of numOranges to 6 after the original value, 5, has been used in the expression to supply the value of numFruit. The postfix decrement operator works similarly, and both operators can be applied to any type of integer variable.

As you see, no parentheses are necessary in the expression numOranges++ + numApples. You could even write it as numOranges+++numApples and it will still mean the same thing but it is certainly a lot less obvious that this is the case. Someone who doesn't have all the rules for evaluating Java expressions at their fingertips might guess, wrongly, that the expression will execute as numOranges+(++numApples). Such potential confusion is really the programmer's fault. You can write it as (numOranges++) + numApples to make it absolutely clear where the ++ operator belongs. It is a good idea to always add parentheses to clarify things when there is some possibility of misinterpretation.

Computation with Shorter Integer Types

I have deliberately used variables of type `int` in all the previous examples. Computations with variables of the shorter integer types introduce some complications. This is because all binary integer operations in Java work only with both operands of type `int` or both operands of type `long`. The result is that with arithmetic expressions using variables of type `byte` or `short`, the values of the variables are first converted to type `int`, and the calculation is carried out using 32-bit arithmetic. The result will therefore be type `int` — a 32-bit integer. This has an interesting effect that you can see in the context of the previous example. Try changing the types of the variables `numOranges`, `numApples`, and `numFruit` in the original version of the program to type `short`, for example:

```
short numOranges = 5;
short numApples = 10;
short numFruit = 0;
```

You will find that the program will no longer compile. The problem is with the statement:

```
numFruit = numOranges + numApples;
```

Since the expression `numOranges + numApples` produces a 32-bit result, the compiler cannot store this value in `numFruit`, as the variable `numFruit` is only 16 bits long. To make the code acceptable to the compiler, you must modify the assignment statement so that the 32-bit result of the addition is converted back to a 16-bit number. You do this by changing the statement to:

```
numFruit = (short)(numOranges + numApples);
```

The statement now calculates the sum of `numOranges` and `numApples` and then converts, or **casts**, the 32-bit result to type `short` before storing it in `numFruit`. This is called an **explicit cast**, and the conversion process is referred to as **casting**. The cast to type `short` is the expression `(short)`, and the cast applies to whatever is immediately to the right of `(short)`, so the parentheses around the expression `numOranges + numApples` are necessary. Without them the cast would apply only to the variable `numOranges`, which is type `short` anyway, and the code would still not compile.

If the variables here were of type `byte`, you would need to cast the result of the addition to type `byte`. You would write such a cast as `(byte)`. This is a strong clue to how you write casts to other types. In general, you write a cast to any given type, `typename`, as the `typename` between parentheses — thus `(typename)`.

The effect of the cast to type `short` in the example is just to take the least significant 16 bits of the result, discarding the most significant 16 bits. The least significant bits are those at the right-hand end of the number because the bits in a binary number in Java increase in value from right to left. Thus, the most significant bits are those at the left-hand end. For the cast to type `byte` only the least significant 8 bits are kept. This means that if the magnitude of the result of the addition is such that more than 16 bits are necessary to represent it (or 8 bits in the case of a cast to `byte`), your answer will be wrong. You will get no indication from the compiler that this has occurred because it was you, after all, that expressly specified the cast, and the compiler assumes that you know what you are doing. To minimize the possibility for such hidden and mystifying errors, you should avoid explicit casts in your programs unless they are absolutely essential.

An integer arithmetic operation involving a value of type `long` will always be carried out using 64-bit values. If the other number in such an operation is not of type `long`, the compiler will arrange for it to be cast to type `long` before the operation is executed. For example:

```
long result = 0;
long factor = 10L;
int number = 5;
result = factor*number;
```

To execute the last statement, because the variable `factor` is of type `long`, the multiplication will be carried out using `long` values. The value stored in the variable `number` will be converted to type `long`, and that will be multiplied by the value of `factor`.

All other integer arithmetic operations involving types other than `long` are carried out with 32-bit values. Thus, you really need to consider only two kinds of integer literals:

❏   Type `long` for operations with 64-bit values where the value has an *L* appended.

❏   Type `int` for operations with 32-bit values for all other cases where there is no *L* at the end of the number.

Errors in Integer Arithmetic

If you divide an integer value by zero, no sensible result can be produced so an exception will be thrown, as I mentioned earlier in the chapter. An exception is the way of signaling errors in Java, which I will discuss in detail in Chapter 7. Using the `%` operator with a variable or expression for the right-hand operand that has a zero value will also cause an exception to be thrown.

Note that if an integer expression results in a value that is outside the range of the type of the result, the result will be truncated to the number of bits for the type you are using and therefore will be incorrect, but this will not be indicated in any way. It is up to you to make sure that the integer types that you are using in your program are always able to accommodate any value that might be produced by your calculations.

Problems can arise with intermediate results in some situations. Even when the ultimate result of an expression is within the legal range, the result of any intermediate calculation that is outside the range will be truncated, thus causing an incorrect result to be produced. To take a trivial example—if you multiply 1000000 by 2000000 and divide by 500000 using type `int`, you will not obtain the correct result if the multiplication is executed first This is because the result of the multiplication exceeds the maximum that can be stored as type `int`. Obviously where you know this sort of problem can occur, you may be able to circumvent it by using parentheses to make sure the division takes place first—but you need to remember that integer division produces an integer result, so a different sequence of execution can produce a different answer.

Floating-Point Calculations

The four basic arithmetic operators, `+`, `-`, `*`, `/`, are also available for use in floating-point expressions. You can try some of these out in another version of the `Fruit` program, which I'll call `AverageFruit`.

Try It Out   Average Fruit

Make the following changes to the `Fruit.java` file, and save this as `AverageFruit.java`. If necessary, you can add in the code we used earlier to make the program wait for the Enter key to be pressed before finishing.

```
public class AverageFruit {
  public static void main(String[] args) {
    // Declare and initialize three variables
    double numOranges = 50.0E-1;        // Initial value is 5.0
    double numApples = 1.0E1;           // Initial value is 10.0
    double averageFruit = 0.0;
    averageFruit = (numOranges + numApples)/2.0;
    System.out.println("A totally fruity program");
    System.out.println("Average fruit is " + averageFruit);
  }
}
```

This will produce the output:

```
A totally fruity program
Average fruit is 7.5
```

The program just computes the average number of fruits of different kinds by dividing the total by 2.0.

> As you can see, I have used various representations for the initializing values for the variables in the program, which are now of type `double`. It's not the ideal way to write 5.0, but at least it demonstrates that you can write a negative exponent value.

Other Floating-Point Arithmetic Operators

You can use `++` and `--` with floating-point variables, and they have the same effect as with integer variables, incrementing or decrementing the floating-point variable to which they are applied by 1.0. You can use them in prefix or postfix form, and their operation in each case is the same as with integer variables.

You can apply the modulus operator, `%`, to floating-point values, too. For an operation of the form:

```
floatOperand1 % floatOperand2
```

the result will be the floating-point remainder after dividing `floatOperand2` into `floatOperand1` an integral number of times. For example, the expression `12.6 % 5.1` will give the result 2.4. In general, the sign of the result of applying the modulus operator to floating-point values is the sign of the divi-dend. The magnitude of the result of a floating-point remainder operation is the largest integral value such that the magnitude of the result of multiplying the divisor by the result of the remainder operation does not exceed the dividend. For the more mathematically minded the result, r, of the expression `a % b`, where a and b are non-zero floating-point values, is defined by the expression `a-(n.b)`. The value n has the same sign as `a/b` and is the largest possible integer such that `a/n` is less than or equal to the true quotient `a/b`.

Error Conditions in Floating-Point Arithmetic

There are two error conditions that can occur with floating-point operations that are signaled by a special result value being generated. One occurs when a calculation produces a value that is outside the range that can be represented by the floating-point type you are using, and the other arises when the result is mathematically indeterminate, such as when your calculation is effectively dividing zero by zero.

To illustrate the first kind of error you could use a variable to specify the number of types of fruit. You could define the variable:

```
double fruitTypes = 2.0;
```

and then rewrite the calculation as:

```
averageFruit = (numOranges + numApples)/fruitTypes;
```

This in itself is not particularly interesting, but if we happened to set `fruitTypes` to 0.0, the output from the program would be:

```
A totally fruity program
Average fruit is Infinity
```

The value `Infinity` indicates a positive but effectively infinite result, in that it represents a value that is greater than the largest number that can be stored as type `double`. An effectively infinite result that was negative would be output as `-Infinity`. You don't actually need to divide by zero to produce this effect; any calculation that generates a value that exceeds the maximum value that can be represented as type `double` will have the same effect. For example, repeatedly dividing by a very small number, such as 1.0E-300, will yield an out-of-range result.

If you want to see what an indeterminate result looks like, you can replace the statement to calculate `averageFruit` with the following:

```
averageFruit = (numOranges - 5.0)/(numApples - 10.0);
```

This statement doesn't make much sense, but it produces an indeterminate result. The value of `averageFruit` is output as `NaN`. This value is referred to as *Not-a-Number*, indicating an indeterminate value. A variable with an indeterminate value will contaminate any subsequent expression in which it is used, so any operation involving an operand value of `NaN` will produce the same result of `NaN`.

A value that is `Infinity` or `-Infinity` will be unchanged when you add, subtract, or multiply by finite values, but if you divide any finite value by `Infinity` or `-Infinity` the result will be zero.

Mixed Arithmetic Expressions

You have probably guessed from earlier discussions that you can mix values of the basic types together in a single expression. The way mixed expressions are treated is governed by some simple rules that apply to each operator in such an expression. The rules, in the sequence in which they are checked, are:

❑ If either operand is of type `double`, the other is converted to `double` before the operation is carried out.

❑ If either operand is of type `float`, the other is converted to `float` before the operation is carried out.

❑ If either operand is of type `long`, the other is converted to `long` before the operation is carried out.

The first rule in the sequence that applies to a given operation is the one that is carried out. If neither operand is `double`, `float`, or `long`, they must be `int`, `short`, or `byte`, so they will be converted to type `int` where necessary and use 32-bit arithmetic to produce the result, as we saw earlier in the chapter.

Explicit Casting

It may well be that the default treatment of mixed expressions listed in the preceding section is not what you want. For example, suppose you have defined a `double` variable `result`; and two variables, `three` and `two`, of type `int` with the values 3 and 2, respectively. If you compute the value of `result` with the statement

```
result = 1.5 + three/two;
```

the value stored will be 2.5, since `three/two` will be executed as an integer operation and will produce the result 1. You may have wanted the term `three/two` to produce the value 1.5 so the overall result would be 3.0. You could do this using an explicit cast:

```
result = 1.5 + (double)three/two;
```

This causes the value stored in `three` to be converted to type `double` before the divide operation takes place. Then rule 1 applies for the divide operation, and the operand `two` is also converted to type `double` before the divide operation is executed. Hence, the value of `result` in this case will be 3.0.

> You can cast a value from any primitive type to any other, but you need to take care that you don't unintentionally lose information when you do so. Obviously casting from one integer type to another with a more limited range has the potential for losing information, as does casting any floating-point value to an integer. Casting from type `double` to type `float` can also produce an effective infinity when the original value is greater than the maximum value for a value of type `float`.

Automatic Type Conversions in Assignments

When the type of the result of an arithmetic expression on the right of an assignment operator differs from the type of the variable on the left, an automatic cast will be applied to the result as long as there is no possibility of losing information. If you think of the basic types that we have seen so far as being in the sequence

```
byte → short → int → long → float → double
```

then an automatic conversion will be made as long as it is upwards through the sequence of types, that is, from left to right. If you want to go in the opposite direction, from type double to type float or long, for example, then you must insert an explicit cast into your code for the result of the expression on the right of the assignment operator.

The op= Operators

The op= operators are used in statements of the form

```
lhs op= rhs;
```

where op can be any of the arithmetic operators +, -, *, /, %. It also works with some other operators you haven't seen yet. The preceding statement is basically a shorthand representation of the statement

```
lhs = lhs op (rhs);
```

The right-hand side (rhs) is in brackets because it is worked out first — then the result is combined with the left-hand side (lhs) using the operation op. Let's look at a few examples of this to make sure it's clear. To increment an int variable count by 5 you can write:

```
count += 5;
```

This has the same effect as the statement:

```
count = count + 5;
```

Of course, the expression to the right of the op= operator can be anything that is legal in the context, so the statement:

```
result /= a % b/(a + b);
```

is equivalent to:

```
result = result/(a % b/(a + b));
```

What I have said so far about op= operations is not quite the whole story. If the type of the result of the rhs expression is different from the type of lhs, the compiler will automatically insert a cast to convert the rhs value to the same type as lhs. This would happen with the last example if result was of type int and a and b were of type double, for example. This is quite different from the way the normal assignment operation is treated. A statement using the op= operator is really equivalent to:

```
lhs = (type_of_lhs)(lhs op (rhs));
```

The automatic conversion will be inserted by the compiler regardless of what the types of lhs and rhs are. Of course, this can result in information being lost due to the cast, and you will get no indication that it has occurred. This is different from ordinary assignment statements where an automatic cast will be allowed only when the range of values for the type of lhs is greater that the range for the type of rhs.

The complete set of `op=` operators are:

`+=`	`-=`	`*=`	`/=`	`%=`
`<<=`	`>>=`	`>>>=`	`&=`	`|=`	`^=`

You will meet the operators on the second row later in the book.

Mathematical Functions and Constants

Sooner or later you are likely to need mathematical functions in your programs, even if it's only to obtain an absolute value or calculate a square root. Java provides a range of methods that support such functions as part of the standard library that is stored in the package `java.lang`, and all these are available in your program automatically.

The methods that support various additional mathematical functions are implemented in the `Math` class as static methods, so to reference a particular function you can just write `Math` and the name of the method you wish to use separated by a period. For example, the `sqrt()` method calculates the square root of whatever you place between the parentheses. To use the `sqrt()` method to produce the square root of the floating-point value that you've stored in a variable, aNumber, you would write `Math.sqrt(aNumber)`.

The class `Math` includes a range of methods for standard trigonometric functions:

Method	Function	Argument Type	Result Type
`sin(arg)`	sine of the argument	`double` in radians	`double`
`cos(arg)`	cosine of the argument	`double` in radians	`double`
`tan(arg)`	tangent of the argument	`double` in radians	`double`
`asin(arg)`	$\sin^{-1}$ (arc sine) of the argument	`double`	`double` in radians, with values from $-\pi/2$ to $\pi/2$.
`acos(arg)`	$\cos^{-1}$ (arc cosine) of the argument	`double`	`double` in radians, with values from 0.0 to π.
`atan(arg)`	$\tan^{-1}$ (arc tangent) of the argument	`double`	`double` in radians, with values from $-\pi/2$ to $\pi/2$.
`atan2 (arg1,arg2)`	$\tan^{-1}$ (arc tangent) of arg1/arg2	Both `double`	`double` in radians, with values from $-\pi$ to π.

As with all methods, the arguments that you put between the parentheses following the method name can be any expression that produces a value of the required type. The toRadians() method in the Math class will convert a double argument that is an angular measurement in degrees to radians. There is a complementary method, toDegrees(), to convert in the opposite direction. The Math class also defines double values for e and π, which you can access as Math.E and Math.PI, respectively. If you are not familiar with these trigonometric operations you can safely ignore them.

You also have methods for evaluating hyperbolic functions, and you can ignore these too if they're not your bag:

Method	Function	Argument Type	Result Type
sinh(arg)	Hyperbolic sine of the argument, which is: $(e^{arg}-e^{-arg})/2$	double	double
cosh(arg)	Hyperbolic cosine of the argument, which is: $(e^{arg}+e^{-arg})/2$	double	double
tanh(arg)	Hyperbolic tangent of the argument, which is: $(e^{arg}-e^{-arg})/(e^{arg}+e^{-arg})$	double	double

You also have a range of numerical functions implemented as static methods in the Math class, and at least some of these will be useful to you:

Method	Function	Argument Type	Result Type
abs(arg)	Calculates the absolute value of the argument	int, long, float, or double	The same type as the argument
max (arg1,arg2)	Returns the larger of the two arguments, both of the same type	int, long, float, or double	The same type as the argument
min (arg1,arg2)	Returns the smaller of the two arguments, both of the same type	int, long, float, or double	The same type as the argument
ceil(arg)	Returns the smallest integer that is greater than or equal to the argument	double	double
floor(arg)	Returns the largest integer that is less than or equal to the argument	double	double

Table continued on following page

Method	Function	Argument Type	Result Type
round(arg)	Calculates the nearest integer to the argument value	float or double	Of type int for a float argument, of type long for a double argument
rint(arg)	Calculates the nearest integer to the argument value	double	double
IEEEremainder (arg1,arg2)	Calculates the remainder when arg1 is divided by arg2	Both of type double	Of type double

The `IEEEremainder()` method produces the remainder from `arg1` after dividing `arg2` into `arg1` the integral number of times that is closest to the exact value of `arg1/arg2`. This is somewhat different from the remainder operator. The operation `arg1 % arg2` produces the remainder after dividing `arg2` into `arg1` the integral number of times that does not exceed the absolute value of `arg1`. In some situations this can result in markedly different results. For example, executing the expression `9.0 % 5.0` results in 4.0, whereas the expression `Math.IEEEremainder(9.0,5.0)` results in –1.0. You can pick one approach to calculating the remainder or the other, to suit your requirements.

Where more than one type of argument is noted in the table, there are actually several methods, one for each type of argument, but all have the same name. We will see how this is possible in Java when we look at implementing class methods in Chapter 5.

There are methods defined in the `Math` class related to floating-point operations. The `signum()` method returns the **signum** of the floating-point argument, which may by of type `double` or of type `float`. The signum is returned as the same type as the argument, and the value is zero if the argument is zero, 1.0 if the argument is greater than zero, and -1.0 if the argument is less than zero. The `ulp()` method returns the size of the ULP (**U**nit in the **L**ast **P**lace) of the argument, which may be of type `double` or type `float`. The ULP is the smallest possible change in a floating-point value to produce the next higher or lower value. Another way of expressing this is that the ULP is the distance from one floating-point value to the next. Of course, the real values in between one floating-point value and the next cannot be represented exactly.

Several methods implement mathematical functions in the `Math` class. You'll probably be surprised at how often you find uses for some of these. The mathematical methods you have available are:

Method	Function	Argument Type	Result Type
sqrt(arg)	Calculates the square root of the argument	double	double
cbrt(arg)	Calculates the cube root of the argument	double	double

Method	Function	Argument Type	Result Type
pow (arg1,arg2)	Calculates the first argument raised to the power of the second argument, $arg1^{arg2}$	Both double	double
hypot(arg1,arg2)	Calculates the square root of $(arg1^2+arg2^2)$	Both double	double
exp(arg)	Calculates e raised to the power of the argument, e^{arg}	double	double
expm1(arg)	Calculates e raised to the power of the argument minus 1, e^{arg} -1	double	double
log(arg)	Calculates the natural logarithm (base e) of the argument	double	double
log1p(arg)	Calculates the natural logarithm (base e) of arg+1	double	double
log10(arg)	Calculates the base 10 logarithm of the argument.	double	double
random()	Returns a pseudo-random number greater than or equal to 0.0 and less than 1.0	None	double

You can try out a sample of the contents of the Math class in an example to make sure you know how they are used.

Try It Out   The Math Class

You are planning a new circular pond in which you want to keep fish. Your local aquatics supplier tells you that you can stock the pond with fish at the rate of 2 inches of fish length per square foot of pond surface area. Your problem is to calculate the radius of the pond that will accommodate 20 fish averaging 10 inches in length. The solution, of course, is to write a Java program — what else? The following program will calculate the radius of a pond, in feet and inches, that will provide a home for the number of fish you would like to keep:

```
public class PondRadius {
  public static void main(String[] args) {
    // Calculate the radius of a pond
    // which can hold 20 fish averaging 10 inches long
    int fishCount = 20;            // Number of fish in pond
    int fishLength = 10;           // Average fish length
    int lengthPerSqFt = 2;         // Fish length per square foot of surface
    double radius = 0.0;           // Pond radius in feet

    int feet = 0;                  // Pond radius - whole feet
```

```
        int inches = 0;                    //                    - and whole inches

        double pondArea = (double)(fishCount*fishLength)/lengthPerSqFt;
        radius = Math.sqrt(pondArea/Math.PI);
        feet = (int)Math.floor(radius); // Get the whole feet and nothing but the feet
        inches = (int)Math.round(12.0*(radius - feet));   // Get the inches

        System.out.println("To hold " + fishCount + " fish averaging " + fishLength +
                    " inches long you need a pond with an area of \n" +
                    pondArea + " square feet.");
        System.out.println("The radius of a pond with area " + pondArea +
                    " square feet is " +
                    feet + " feet " + inches + " inches");
    }
}
```

Save the program source file as `PondRadius.java`. When you compile and run it, you should get:

```
To hold 20 fish averaging 10 inches long you need a pond with an area of
100.0 square feet.
The radius of a pond with area 100.0 square feet is 5 feet 8 inches
```

How It Works

You first define the variables that specify initial data, followed by the variables `feet` and `inches` that you will use to store the result. You then calculate the pond surface area in feet with this statement:

```
double pondArea = (double)(fishCount*fishLength)/lengthPerSqFt;
```

You cast the total length of fish to be in the pond, `fishCount*fishLength`, to type `double` to force the division by the number of inches per square foot of pond surface to be done using floating-point values rather than integers.

The next calculation uses the `sqrt()` method to calculate the radius. Since the area of a circle with radius r is given by the formula πr^2, the radius must be $\sqrt{(\text{area}/\pi)}$, so you specify the argument to the `sqrt()` method as the expression `pondArea/Math.PI`, where `Math.PI` references the value of π that is defined in the `Math` class:

```
radius = Math.sqrt(pondArea/Math.PI);
```

The result is in feet as a value of type `double`.

To get the number of whole feet you use the `floor()` method:

```
feet = (int)Math.floor(radius);   // Get the whole feet and nothing but the feet
```

Note that the cast to type `int` of the value produced by the `floor()` method is essential in this statement; otherwise, you will get an error message from the compiler. The value returned from the `floor()` method is type `double`, and the compiler will not cast this to type `int` automatically because the process potentially loses information.

Finally, you get the number of inches by subtracting the value for whole feet from the original radius, multiplying the fraction of a foot by 12 to get the equivalent inches, and then rounding the result to the nearest integer using the `round()` method:

```
inches = (int)Math.round(12.0*(radius - feet));   // Get the inches
```

The constant for the number of inches per foot is written as a floating-point literal, 12.0, to be consistent with the rest of the expression for the value you pass to the `round()` method. If you were to write it as simply 12, it would be an integer literal of type `int`.

To output the result, you specify a combination (or concatenation) of strings and variables as arguments to the two `println()` method calls:

```
System.out.println("To hold " + fishCount + " fish averaging " + fishLength +
                   " inches long you need a pond with an area of \n" +
                   pondArea + " square feet.");
System.out.println("The radius of a pond with area " + pondArea +
                   " square feet is " +
                   feet + " feet " + inches + " inches");
```

Each statement is spread over three lines for convenience here. The \n that appears in the first output statement specifies a newline character, so the output will be on two lines. Anytime you want the next bit of output to begin a new line, just add \n to the output string. You can't enter a newline character just by typing it because when you do that the cursor just moves to the next line. That's why it's specified as \n. There are other characters like this that you cannot enter directly that we'll look into a little later in this chapter.

Importing the Math Class Methods

It would be a lot more convenient if you were able to avoid having to qualify the name of every method in the `Math` class that you use with the class name. The code would be a lot less cluttered if you could write `floor(radius)` instead of `Math.floor(radius)` for example. Well, you can. All you need to do is put the following statement at the beginning of the source file:

```
import static java.lang.Math.*;       // Import static class members
```

This statement makes the names of all the static members of the `Math` class available for use in your program code without having to qualify them with the class name. This includes constants such as `PI` as well as static methods. You can try this statement in the `PondRadius` example. With this statement at the beginning of the source file, you will be able to remove the qualification by the class name `Math` from all the members of this class that the program uses.

The * in the statement indicates that all static names are to be imported. If you wanted to import just the names from the `Math` class that the `PondRadius` program uses, you would write:

```
import static java.lang.Math.floor;   // Import floor
import static java.lang.Math.sqrt;    // Import sqrt
import static java.lang.Math.round;   // Import round
import static java.lang.Math.PI;      // Import PI
```

These statements import individually the four names from the `Math` class that the program references. You could use these four statements at the beginning of the program in place of the previous import statement that imports all the static names. I'll discuss this form of the import statement further in Chapter 5.

Storing Characters

Variables of type `char` store a single character code. They each occupy 16 bits, or 2 bytes, in memory because all characters in Java are stored as Unicode. To declare and initialize a character variable `myCharacter` you could use the statement:

```
char myCharacter = 'X';
```

This initializes the variable with the Unicode character representation of the letter `'X'`. You must always put single quotes as delimiters for a character literal in a statement as in this example, `'X'`. This is necessary to enable the compiler to distinguish between the character `'X'` and a variable with the name `X`. Note that you can't use double quotes as delimiters here because they are used to delimit a character string. A character string such as `"X"` is quite different from the literal of type `char`, `'X'`.

Character Escape Sequences

In general, the characters that you will be able to enter directly from your keyboard will be a function of the keys you have available and the set of character codes they map to according to your operating system. Whatever that is, it will be a small subset of the characters defined by the Unicode encoding. To enable you to enter any Unicode character as part of your program source code you can define Unicode characters by specifying the hexadecimal representation of the character codes in an **escape sequence**. An escape sequence is simply an alternative means of specifying a character that is often, but not exclusively, defined by its code. A backslash indicates the start of an escape sequence, so you have already met the escape sequence for a newline character, `\n`.

You create an escape sequence for a Unicode character by preceding the four hexadecimal digits of the character code by `\u`. Since the Unicode coding for the letter X is the hexadecimal value 0x0058 (the low-order byte is the same as the ASCII code), you could also declare and define `myCharacter` with the statement:

```
char myCharacter = '\u0058';
```

You place the escape sequence between single quotes to define the character literal. The result is the same as the previous statement where you used `'X'` as the initial value for `myCharacter`. You can enter any Unicode character in this way, as long as you know its code of course.

> **You can get more information on the full Unicode character set on the Internet by visiting** `http://www.unicode.org/`.

Because the backslash indicates the beginning of an escape sequence, you must always use the escape sequence, \\, to specify a backslash character as a character literal or in a text string.

As you have seen, you write a character string (a `String` literal, as we will see in Chapter 4) enclosed between double quotes, and a character literal between single quotes. For this reason you also need the escape sequences \' and \" to specify these characters. For example, to produce the output

```
"It's freezing in here", he said coldly.
```

you could write

```
System.out.println("\"It\'s freezing in here\", he said coldly.");
```

In fact, it's not strictly necessary to use an escape sequence to specify a single quote within a string, but obviously it will be when you want to specify a single quote as a character literal. Of course, it is always necessary to specify a double quote within a string using an escape sequence; otherwise, it would be interpreted as the end of the string.

There are other escape sequences that you use to define control characters:

\b	Backspace
\f	Form feed
\n	New line
\r	Carriage return
\t	Tab

Character Arithmetic

You can perform arithmetic on `char` variables. With `myCharacter` containing the character `'X'`, the statement:

```
myCharacter += 1;     // Increment to next character
```

will result in the value of `myCharacter` being changed to `'Y'`. This is because the Unicode code for `'Y'` is one more than the code for `'X'`. You could use the increment operator `++` to increase the code stored in `myCharacter` by just writing:

```
++myCharacter;        // Increment to next character
```

When you use variables of type `char` in an arithmetic expression, their values will be converted to type `int` to carry out the calculation. It doesn't necessarily make a whole lot of sense, but you could write the following statements that calculate with values of type `char`:

```
char aChar = 0;
char bChar = '\u0028';
aChar = (char)(2*bChar + 8);
```

These statements will leave the aChar variable holding the code for the letter X—which is 0x0058.

Try It Out   Arithmetic with Character Codes

This example will demonstrate arithmetic operations with values of type char:

```
public class CharCodeCalcs {
  public static void main(String[] args){
    char letter1 = 'A';               // letter1 is 'A'
    char letter2 = (char)(letter1+1); // letter2 is 'B'
    char letter3 = letter2;           // letter3 is also 'B'
    System.out.println("Here\'s a sequence of letters: "+ letter1 + letter2 +
                                                      (++letter3));

    // letter3 is now 'C'
    System.out.println("Here are the decimal codes for the letters:\n"+
                        letter1 + ": " + (int)letter1 +
                  "  " + letter2 + ": " + (int)letter2 +
                  "  " + letter3 + ": " + (int)letter3);
  }
}
```

This example will produce the following output:

```
Here's a sequence of letters: ABC
Here are the decimal codes for the letters:
A: 65   B: 66   C: 67
```

How It Works

The first three statements in main() define three variables of type char:

```
char letter1 = 'A';               // letter1 is 'A'
char letter2 = (char)(letter1+1); // letter2 is 'B'
char letter3 = letter2;           // letter3 is also 'B'
```

The cast to type char of the initial value for letter2 is essential. Without it, the code will not compile. The expression letter1+1 produces a result of type int, and the compiler will not insert an automatic cast to allow the value to be used as the initial value for letter2.

The next statement outputs three characters:

```
System.out.println("Here\'s a sequence of letters: "+ letter1 + letter2 +
                                                  (++letter3));
```

The first two characters displayed are those stored in letter1 and letter2. The third character is the value stored in letter3 after the variable has been incremented by 1.

By default, the println() method treats a variable of type char as a character for output. You can still output the value stored in a char variable as a numerical value simply by casting it to type int. The next statement demonstrates this:

```
System.out.println("Here are the decimal codes for the letters:\n"+
                   letter1 + ": " + (int)letter1 +
        "   " + letter2 + ": " + (int)letter2 +
        "   " + letter3 + ": " + (int)letter3);
```

This statement outputs the value of each of the three variables as a character followed by its decimal value.

Of course, you may prefer to see the character codes as hexadecimal values. You can display any value of type int as a hexadecimal string by enlisting the help of a static method that is defined in the Integer class in the standard library. Add an extra output statement to the example as the last statement in main():

```
System.out.println("Here are the hexadecimal codes for the letters:\n"+
                   letter1 + ": " + Integer.toHexString(letter1) +
        "   " + letter2 + ": " + Integer.toHexString(letter2) +
        "   " + letter3 + ": " + Integer.toHexString(letter3));
```

This statement will output the character codes as hexadecimal values, so you'll see this additional output:

```
Here are the hexadecimal codes for the letters:
A: 41  B: 42  C: 43
```

The toHexString() method generates a string representation of the argument you supply. Here you just have the name of a variable of type char as the argument in each of the three uses of the method but you could put any expression that results in a value of type int. Because the method requires an argument of type int, the compiler will insert a cast to type int for each of the arguments letter1, letter2, and letter3.

The Integer class is related to the primitive type int in that an object of type Integer "wraps" a value of type int. You will understand the significance of this better when you investigate classes in Chapter 5. There are also classes of type — Byte, Short, Long — that relate to values of the corresponding primitive types. The Long class also defines a static method toHexString() that you use to obtain a string that is a hexadecimal representation of a value of type long. These classes also contain other useful utility methods that I will introduce when a suitable context arises.

Of course, you can use the static import statement that I introduced in the context of the Math class to import the names of static members of other classes such as Integer and Long. For example, the following statement at the beginning of a source file would enable you to use the toHexString() method without having to qualify it with the Integer class name:

```
import static java.lang.Integer.toHexString;
```

Bitwise Operations

As you already know, all these integer variables we have been talking about are represented internally as binary numbers. A value of type int consists of 32 binary digits, known to us computer fans as bits. You can operate on the bits that make up integer values using the bitwise operators, of which there are four available:

&	AND
|	OR
^	Exclusive OR
~	Complement

Each of these operators operates on the individual bits in its operands as follows:

- ❏ The bitwise AND operator, &, combines corresponding bits in its two operands such that if the first bit AND the second bit are 1, the result is 1 — otherwise, the result is 0.

- ❏ The bitwise OR operator, |, combines corresponding bits such that if either or both bits are 1, then the result is 1. Only if both bits are 0 is the result 0.

- ❏ The bitwise exclusive OR (XOR) operator, ^, combines corresponding bits such that if both bits are the same the result is 0; otherwise, the result is 1.

- ❏ The complement operator, ~, takes a single operand in which it inverts all the bits, so that each 1 bit becomes 0, and each 0 bit becomes 1.

You can see the effect of these operators in the examples shown in Figure 2-5.

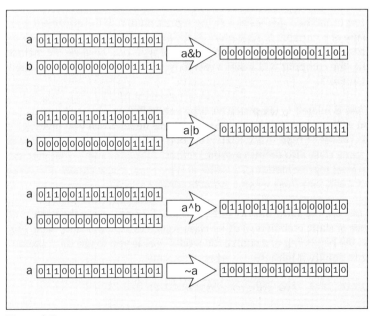

Figure 2-5

Figure 2-5 shows the binary digits that make up the operands and the results. Each of the three binary operations applies to each corresponding pair of bits from its operands in turn. The complement operator just flips the state of each bit in its operand so that 0 changes to 1 and 1 changes to 0 in the value that results.

Since you are concerned with individual bits when using bitwise operations, writing a constant as a normal decimal value is not going to be particularly convenient. For example, the bit pattern that is specified by the decimal value 24576 is not exactly self-evident. A much better way of writing binary values when you want to work with the bits is to express them as hexadecimal numbers, because you can convert from binary to hexadecimal, and vice versa, very quickly. There's more on this in Appendix B.

Converting from binary to hexadecimal is easy. Each group of four binary digits from the right corresponds to one hexadecimal digit. You just work out what the value of each four bits is and write the appropriate hexadecimal digit. For example, the value of a from the previous illustration is:

Binary	0110	0110	1100	1101
Decimal value	6	6	12	13
Hexadecimal	6	6	C	D

So the value of the variable a in hexadecimal is 0x66CD, where the 0x prefix indicates that this is a hexadecimal value. The variable b in the illustration has the hexadecimal value 0x000F. If you think of the variable b as a mask applied to a, you can view the & operator as keeping bits unchanged where the mask is 1 and setting the rest to 0. Mask is a term used to refer to a particular configuration of bits designed to select out specific bits when it is combined with a variable using a bitwise operator. So, if you want to select a particular bit out of an integer variable, just AND it with a mask that has that bit set to 1 and all the others as 0.

Using the AND and OR Operators

You can also envisage what the & operator does from another perspective — it forces a bit to 0 if the corresponding mask bit is 0, and leaves a bit unchanged if the mask bit is 1. Thus, the & operator provides you with a way to switch off specific bits in a word, leaving the rest as they were. Just create a mask with 0 bits in the positions that you want to make 0 and with 1 bits everywhere else. Similarly, the | operator forces a bit to be 1 when the mask bit is 1, and a mask bit of 0 leaves a bit unchanged so you can use the | operator to set particular bits in a word on.

The & and | operators are the most frequently used of the bitwise operators, mainly for dealing with variables where the individual bits are used as state indicators of some kind — for things that can be either true or false, or on or off. You could use a single bit as a state indicator determining whether something should be displayed, with the bit as 1, or not displayed, with the bit as 0. To take a simple example, to select the third bit from the right in the int variable indicators, you can write:

```
thirdBit = indicators & 0x4;      // Select the 3rd bit
```

The third bit of the variable thirdBit will be the same as the third bit in indicators and all the other bits will be zero. We can illustrate how this works if we assume the variable indicators contains the hexadecimal value 0xFF07:

	Hexadecimal	Binary			
indicators	0xFF07	1111	1111	0000	0111
mask value	0x4	0000	0000	0000	0100
indicators & 0x4	0x4	0000	0000	0000	0100

All these values should have 32 bits, and we are only showing 16 bits here, but you see all you need to know how it works. The mask value sets all the bits in the result to zero except for the third bit, which will be set to that of the indicators variable. Here, the result of the expression is non-zero because the third bit in indicators is 1.

On the other hand, if the variable indicators contained the value 0xFF09 the result would be different:

	Hexadecimal	Binary			
indicators	0xFF09	1111	1111	0000	1001
mask value	0x4	0000	0000	0000	0100
indicators & 0x4	0x0004	0000	0000	0000	0000

The result of the expression is now zero because the third bit of indicators is zero.

As I said, you can use the | operator to set a particular bit on. For example, to set the third bit in indicators on, you can write:

```
indicators = indicators | 0x4;    // Set the 3rd bit on
```

You can see how this applies to the last value you had for indicators:

	Hexadecimal	Binary			
indicators	0xFF09	1111	1111	0000	1001
mask value	0x4	0000	0000	0000	0100
indicators | 0x4	0xFF0D	1111	1111	0000	1101

As you can see, the effect is just to switch the third bit of indicators on. All the other bits are unchanged. Of course, if the third bit was already on, it would stay on.

You can also use the bitwise operators in the op= form. Setting the third bit in the variable indicators is usually written as:

```
indicators |= 0x4;
```

Although there is nothing wrong with the original statement, the one above is just a bit more concise.

To set a bit off you need to use the & operator again, with a mask that has 0 for the bit you want as 0, and 1 for all the others. To set the third bit of `indicators` off you could write:

```
indicators &= ~0x4;                      // Set the 3rd bit off
```

The ~ operator provides a useful way of specifying a value with all bits 1 apart from one. The literal 0x4 is a value with the third bit as zero and the other bits as 1. Applying the ~ operator to this flips each bit, so that the 0 bits are 1 and the 1 bit is zero. With `indicators` having the value 0xFF07, this would work as follows:

	Hexadecimal	Binary			
indicators	0xFF07	1111	1111	0000	0111
mask value	0x4	0000	0000	0000	0100
~0x4	0xFFFB	1111	1111	1111	1011
indicators & ~0x4	0xFF03	1111	1111	0000	0011

Let's see some of these bitwise operations in action.

Try It Out   Bitwise AND and OR Operations

This example just exercises some of the operations that you saw in the previous section:

```java
import static java.lang.Integer.toBinaryString;

public class BitwiseOps {
  public static void main(String[] args) {
    int indicators = 0xFF07;
    int selectBit3 = 0x4;          // Mask to select the 3rd bit

    // Try the bitwise AND to select the third bit in indicators
    System.out.println("indicators          = " +
                                    toBinaryString(indicators));
    System.out.println("selectBit3          = " +
                                    toBinaryString(selectBit3));
    indicators &= selectBit3;
    System.out.println("indicators & selectBit3  = " +
                                    toBinaryString(indicators));

    // Try the bitwise OR to switch the third bit on
    indicators = 0xFF09;
    System.out.println("\nindicators          = "+
                                    toBinaryString(indicators));
    System.out.println("selectBit3          = "+
                                    toBinaryString(selectBit3));
    indicators |= selectBit3;
    System.out.println("indicators | selectBit3  = " +
                                    toBinaryString(indicators));

    // Now switch the third bit off again
```

```
      indicators &= ~selectBit3;
      System.out.println("\nThe third bit in the previous value of indicators" +
                                              " has been switched off");
      System.out.println("indicators & ~selectBit3 = " +
                                           toBinaryString(indicators));

    }
  }
```

This example produces the following output:

```
indicators               = 1111111100000111
selectBit3               = 100
indicators & selectBit3  = 100

indicators               = 1111111100001001
selectBit3               = 100
indicators | selectBit3  = 1111111100001101

The third bit in the previous value of indicators has been switched off
indicators & ~selectBit3 = 1111111100001001
```

How It Works

The example uses the code fragments that I discussed in the previous section so you can see they work as described. One new capability introduced here is the use of the static `toBinaryString()` method that is defined in the `Integer` class. There's a static import statement for the name of this method so its use is not qualified by the class name in the example. The `toBinaryString()` method produces a string containing a binary representation of the value of type `int` that is passed as the argument to the method. You can see from the output for the value of `selectBit3` that the string does not include leading zeros. Obviously, the output would be better with leading zeros displayed but you need to know more about handling strings to be able to fix this. By the end of Chapter 4, you will be in a position to do so.

Using the Exclusive OR Operator

The ^ operator has the slightly surprising ability to interchange two values without moving either value somewhere else. The need for this turns up most frequently in tricky examination questions. Suppose you execute the following three statements:

```
a ^= b;
b ^= a;
a ^= b;
```

The effect of these statements is to interchange the values of a and b, but remember this works only for integers. We can try this out with a couple of arbitrary values for a and b, 0xD00F and 0xABAD, respectively — again, we will just look at 16 bits for each variable. The first statement changes a to a new value:

a ^= b	Hexadecimal	Binary			
a	0xD00F	1101	0000	0000	1111
b	0xABAD	1010	1011	1010	1101
a from a^b	0x7BA2	0111	1011	1010	0010

Now the next statement, which calculates a new value of b using the new value of a:

b ^= a	Hexadecimal	Binary			
a	0x7BA2	0111	1011	1010	0010
b	0xABAD	1010	1011	1010	1101
b from b^a	0xD00F	1101	0000	0000	1111

So b now has a value that looks remarkably like the value that a started out with. Let's look at the last step, which calculates a new value for a using the new value of b:

a ^= b	Hexadecimal	Binary			
a	0x7BA2	0111	1011	1010	0010
b	0xD00F	1101	0000	0000	1111
a from a^b	0xABAD	1010	1011	1010	1101

Lo and behold, the value of a is now the original value of b. In the old days, when all programmers wore lab coats, when computers were driven by steam, and when memory was measured in bytes rather than megabytes, this mechanism could be quite useful since you could interchange two values in memory without having to have extra memory locations available. So if antique computers are your thing, this may turn out to be a valuable technique. In fact, it's really much more useful than that. When you get to do some graphics programming later in the book, you'll see that this application of the exclusive OR operator is very relevant.

Don't forget—all of these bitwise operators can be applied only to integers. They don't work with any other type of value. As with the arithmetic expressions, the bitwise operations are carried out with 32 bits for integers of type short and of type byte, so a cast to the appropriate type is necessary for the result of the expression on the right of the assignment operator.

One note of caution: Special care is needed when initializing variables of type `byte` and type `short` with hexadecimal values to avoid being caught out. For example, you might be tempted to initialize a variable of type `byte` to binary 1111 1111 with the following statement:

```
byte allBitsOne = 0xFF;    // Wrong!!
```

In fact, this results in a compiler error message. The literal `0xFF` is 1111 1111, so what's the beef here? The beef is that `0xFF` is not 1111 1111 at all. The literal `0xFF` is type `int`, so it is the binary value 0000 0000 0000 0000 0000 0000 1111 1111. This happens to be equivalent to the decimal value 128, which is outside the range of type `byte`. The byte value you are looking for, 1111 1111, is equivalent to the decimal value -1, so the correct way to initialize `allBitsOne` to 1s is to write:

```
byte allBitsOne = 0xFFFFFFFF;    // Correct - well done!!
```

Now the compiler will happily chop off the high-order bits to produce the result you are looking for.

Shift Operations

Another mechanism that you have for working with integer variables at the bit level is *shifting*. You can shift the bits in an integer to the right or the left. You can also envisage the process of shifting binary digits right or left as dividing or multiplying by powers of two, respectively. Shifting the binary value of 3, which is 0011, to the left one bit multiplies it by two. It becomes binary 0110, which is decimal 6. Shifting it to the right by one bit divides it by 2. It becomes binary 0001, which is 1.

Java has three shift operators:

`<<`	Shift left, filling with zeros from the right.
`>>`	Shift right, propagating the sign bit from the left.
`>>>`	Shift right, filling with zeros from the left.

The effect of each of the shift operators is shown in Figure 2-6.

Of course, if the high-order bit in the `>>` operation in Figure 2-6 were zero, there would be three zeros at the leftmost end of the result.

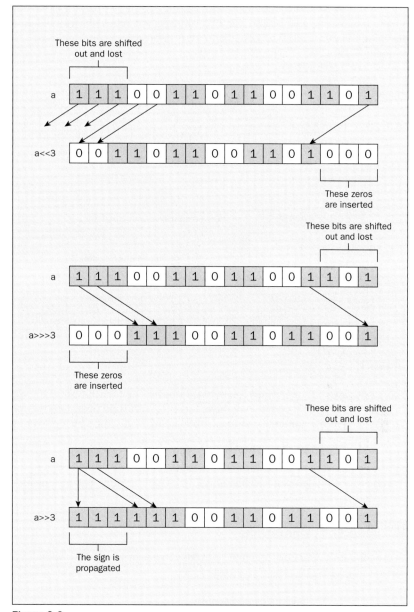

Figure 2-6

Shift operations are often used in combination with the other bitwise operators I have discussed to extract parts of an integer value. In many operating systems, a single 32-bit value is sometimes used to store multiple values. For example, you could store two 16-bit screen coordinates in a single 32-bit word. This is illustrated in Figure 2-7.

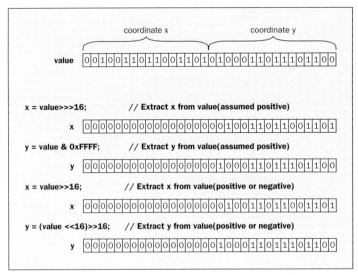

Figure 2-7

Figure 2-7 shows how the shift operations can be used to extract either the left or the right 16 bits from the variable `value`. You can see here why you have an extra shift right operation that propagates the leftmost bit. It is related to the notion of a shift as multiplying or dividing by a power of 2, and the implications of that in the context of negative integers represented in 2's complement form (see Appendix B). When the sign bit is not propagated, the shift right operation does not have a numerical interpretation for negative values because the sign bit is treated the same as any other bit, and zeros are inserted from the right. When the sign bit is propagated, the effect for negative values is the same as for positive values —namely, that each bit position shifted is a division by 2.

Try It Out   Using Shift Operations

This example uses the shift operators together with the bitwise operators to pack four values of type `char` into a variable of type `long`. Here's the code:

```java
import static java.lang.Long.toHexString;

public class PackingCharacters {
  public static void main(String[] args) {
    char letterA = 'A';
    char letterB = 'B';
    char letterC = 'C';
    char letterD = 'D';
    long packed = 0L;
    packed = letterD;                         // Store D
```

```
packed = (packed << 16) | letterC;    // Shift and add the next letter - C
packed = (packed << 16) | letterB;    // Shift and add the next letter - B
packed = (packed << 16) | letterA;    // Shift and add the next letter - A
System.out.println("packed now contains 0x" + toHexString(packed));

    // Now unpack the letters and output them
    long mask = 0xFFFF;                    // Rightmost 16 bits as 1
    char letter = (char)(packed & mask);   // Extract the rightmost letter
    System.out.println("From right to left the letters in packed are:");
    System.out.println("  " + letter + "  0x" + toHexString(letter));
    packed >>= 16;                         // Shift out the rightmost letter
    letter = (char)(packed & mask);        // Extract the new rightmost letter
    System.out.println("  " + letter + "  0x" + toHexString(letter));
    packed >>= 16;                         // Shift out the rightmost letter
    letter = (char)(packed & mask);        // Extract the new rightmost letter
    System.out.println("  " + letter + "  0x" + toHexString(letter));
    packed >>= 16;                         // Shift out the rightmost letter
    letter = (char)(packed & mask);        // Extract the new rightmost letter
    System.out.println("  " + letter + "  0x" + toHexString(letter));
  }
}
```

The output from this example will be:

```
packed now contains 0x44004300420041
From right to left the letters in packed are:
  A  0x41
  B  0x42
  C  0x43
  D  0x44
```

How It Works

The first four statements in `main()` define variables initialized with the letters to be packed into the variable, `packed`, of type `long` defined in the fifth statement in `main()`. The packing process begins by storing the first character in `packed`:

```
packed = letterD;                      // Store D
```

The rightmost 16 bits in `packed` now contain the character code D. This will eventually end up in the leftmost 16 bits of `packed`. The next statement inserts the next letter, C, into `packed`:

```
packed = (packed << 16) | letterC;     // Shift and add the next letter - C
```

The letter is inserted by first shifting the contents of `packed` left by 16 bits, and then ORing the value of `letterC` with the result. At this point, the leftmost 32 bits of `packed` are zero and the rightmost 32 bits contain D followed by C.

The next two statements repeat the same process to insert B and then A:

```
packed = (packed << 16) | letterB;     // Shift and add the next letter - B
packed = (packed << 16) | letterA;     // Shift and add the next letter - A
```

Now the variable `packed` holds the codes for all four characters in the sequence D, C, B, and A.

The output produced by the next statement confirms this:

```
System.out.println("packed now contains 0x" + toHexString(packed));
```

This statement uses the `toHexString()` method defined in the `Long` class to generate a string containing a hexadecimal representation of the value of `packed`. Because you have a static import statement for the name of this method, you don't need to qualify it with the class name. You can see from the output that this consists of the character code values 0x44, 0x43, 0x42, and 0x41, which are the codes for the letters D through A.

The program then demonstrates how you can use the shift operators combined with the bitwise AND to extract the four `char` values from `packed`. The first step is to define a `mask` to select the rightmost 16 bits in a value of type `long`:

```
long mask = 0xFFFF;                      // Rightmost 16 bits as 1
```

The next statement uses `mask` to pick out the rightmost character code in `packed`:

```
char letter = (char)(packed & mask);     // Extract the rightmost letter
```

The cast to type `char` of the value that results from ANDing `mask` with `packed` is necessary because the compiler will not insert an automatic cast from type `long` to type `char`.

The next two statements output a heading followed by the first letter as a letter and its code:

```
System.out.println("From right to left the letters in packed are:");
System.out.println("   " + letter + "   0x" + toHexString(letter));
```

To get at the next character along, you can shift out the character just extracted and AND the result with `mask` once again:

```
packed >>= 16;                           // Shift out the rightmost letter
letter = (char)(packed & mask);          // Extract the new rightmost letter
```

The result of the shift right operation is stored back in `packed`, so ANDing `mask` with `packed` extracts the next letter. Extraction of the next two letters is achieved by repeating exactly the same process of shifting and then ANDing with `mask`. From the output you can see that it all works as it should.

Methods for Bitwise Operations

In addition to the basic Java language facilities for operations on integers at the bit level, you also have some methods available in library classes that provide you with a few extra facilities. I won't go into great detail on these as they're rather specialized, but I'll outline the methods and explain what they do so you are aware of them.

The methods that implement bitwise operations are defined in the `Integer` and `Long` classes in the `java.lang` package. The methods in the `Integer` class apply to values of type `int`, and the methods in the `Long` class apply to values of type `long`. Both classes define the following methods for bitwise operations:

Method	Description
bitCount(arg)	Returns the number of 1 bits in the binary integer that you supply as arg. The count is returned as a value of type int.
highestOneBit(arg)	Returns an integer with a single 1 bit in the position corresponding to the leftmost 1 bit in arg. The value is returned as the same type as arg.
lowestOneBit(arg)	Returns an integer with a single 1 bit in the position corresponding to the rightmost 1 bit in arg. The value is returned as the same type as arg.
numberOfLeadingZeros(arg)	Returns the number of 0 bits preceding the leftmost 1 bit in arg. The value is returned as type int. If arg is zero, then the method returns the total number of bits in arg, which will be 32 for type int and 64 for type long.
numberOfTrailingZeros(arg)	Returns the number of 0 bits following the rightmost 1 bit in arg. The value is returned as type int. If arg is zero, then the method returns the total number of bits in arg, which will be 32 for type int and 64 for type long.
reverse(arg)	Returns the value that is obtained by reversing the order of bits in arg. The value is returned as the same type as arg.
rotateLeft(arg, distance)	Returns the value obtained by rotating the bits in arg left by distance bits positions, where distance is a value of type int. Rotation left means that bits shifted out on the left are shifted into vacated bit positions on the right. The value is returned as the same type as arg.
rotateRight(arg, distance)	Returns the value obtained by rotating the bits in arg right by distance bits positions, where distance is a value of type int. Rotation right means that bits shifted out on the right are shifted into vacated bit positions on the left. The value is returned as the same type as arg.

When you want to operate on a value of type int, you call the method for the Integer class, and for a value of type long you call the method in the Long class. The return value is of the same type as the argument in each case where the result is a transformed version of the argument. Where it is simply a count, the value returned is of type int.

If you think about what you would need to do yourself to implement what these methods do, you'll realize they can save a lot of effort. To count how many 1 bits there are in an integer, you would need to work through each of the bits in a loop checking for a 1 bit in each case. With the bitCount() method, you get the result with a single statement. It may well be faster than you could implement it for yourself, too. Let's consider some examples of how you use these methods.

First, suppose you define an integer variable as follows:

```
int data = 0x0F00;            // data is:   0000 0000 0000 0000 0000 1111 0000 0000
```

You can now apply the `bitCount()` method to this. You must use the method in the `Integer` class because `data` is of type `int`:

```
int bits = Integer.bitCount(data);     // Result is 4
```

The variable `bits` will be set to 4 because `data` contains four 1 bits. You use the method in the `Integer` class here because `data` is of type `int`. If you were working with an argument of type `long`, you would use the method in the `Long` class.

Here's a definition of another integer variable, this time of type `long`:

```
long number = 0xF00000000000000FL;
```

The bit pattern in `number` has the first byte as 1111 0000 and the last byte as 0000 1111; all the other bytes are zero. Note that the `L` on the end of the literal is essential here. Without it you are specifying a literal of type `int`, and type `int` only has 32 bits so you'll get an error message from the compiler.

You could rotate the bits in `number` left by two with the following statement:

```
long result = Long.rotateLeft(number, 2);
```

The variable `result` will be set to a value where the first byte is 0xC0, the last byte is 0x3F, and all the other bits are zero. The bits in `number` are shifted left by two bit positions, and the two 1 bits that are shifted out on the left will be shifted in on the right as this is a rotation operation on the bits.

Let's see some of these methods working for real.

Try It Out   Methods for Operations on Bits

You'll be able to see the effects of some of the methods I have discussed by just outputting the results of some of the operations. The example also makes use of another method that is defined in both the `Integer` and `Long` classes that you've seen in an earlier example — the `toBinaryString()` method, which creates a string representation of a binary integer. Here's the code:

```
import static java.lang.Long.*;

public class TryBitMethods {
  public static void main(String[] args) {
    long number = 0xF00000000000000FL;
    System.out.println("number:\n" + toBinaryString(number));
    long result = rotateLeft(number,2);
    System.out.println("number rotated left 2 bits:\n" + toBinaryString(result));
    result = rotateRight(number, 3);
    System.out.println("number rotated right 3 bits:\n" + toBinaryString(result));
    result = reverse(result);
    System.out.println("Previous result reversed:\n" + toBinaryString(result));
    System.out.println("Bit count in number:\n" + bitCount(number));
  }
}
```

This program will produce the following output:

```
number:
1111000000000000000000000000000000000000000000000000000000001111
number rotated left 2 bits:
1100000000000000000000000000000000000000000000000000000000111111
number rotated right 3 bits:
1111111000000000000000000000000000000000000000000000000000000001
Previous result reversed:
1000000000000000000000000000000000000000000000000000000001111111
Bit count in number: 8
```

I inserted \n characters in the output to put the binary value on the line following its description because it would not fit within the page width otherwise. You might find it more convenient to remove the newlines but insert spaces to make the binary values align vertically. They'll be easier to compare that way.

How It Works

The program applies a variety of the methods for bit operations in the Long class to the value in number. The toBinaryString() method in the Long class creates a string representation of the binary value that is passed to the method, and you output that using the println() method. By comparing the bit patterns produced by each method with the original, you can clearly see what the methods do. You might like to try the same thing with the methods in the Integer class. Because there is an import statement for all the static members of the Long class, none of the methods from the Long class that the program uses need to be qualified with the class name.

Variables with a Fixed Set of Integer Values

You will often need variables that can have values only from a predefined fixed set. For example, suppose you want to define an integer variable with the name weekday, which will store an integer value representing a day of the week. The variable ideally needs to be limited to seven possible values, one for each of Monday through Sunday. This is a situation where a facility called an **enumeration** is a natural choice. You could define an enumeration for this situation with the following declaration statement:

```
enum Day {Monday, Tuesday, Wednesday, Thursday, Friday, Saturday, Sunday }
```

This defines a new type, Day, for variables that can store only one or other of the values specified between the braces. The names Monday, Tuesday, and so on through to Sunday are called **enumeration constants**, and they identify the only values that are allowed for variables of type Day. In fact, these names will correspond to integer values, starting from 0 in this case, but they are not the same as integer variables because they exist only within the context of the enumeration, Day. Note the absence of a semi-colon at the end of the definition of the Day enumeration. Because you are defining a type here, no semi-colon is required after the closing brace. I used a capital D at the beginning of the type name, Day, because by convention, types that you define begin with a capital letter. The names for the enumeration constants would usually be written beginning with a lowercase letter, but in this case I used a capital letter at the beginning because that's how the days of the week are usually written. You could just as well write the enumeration constants with a lowercase letter.

With this new type, you can now define the variable weekday like this:

```
Day weekday = Day.Tuesday;
```

This declares the variable weekday to be of type Day, and initializes it with the value, Tuesday. Note that the enumeration constant must be qualified with the name of the enumeration type here. If you leave the qualifier out, the compiler will not recognize the constant. There is a way to get around this, but you'll have to wait until Chapter 5 to find out about it. You can set a variable of a given enumeration type only to one or other of the enumeration constants that you defined for the type.

An enumeration can contain as many or as few enumeration constants as you need. Here's an enumeration type for the months in the year:

```
enum Month { January, February, March    , April  , May     , June,
             July    , August  , September, October, November, December }
```

You could define a variable of this type like this:

```
Month current = Month.September;          // Initialize to September
```

If you later want to change the value stored in the variable, you can set it to a different enumeration constant:

```
current = Month.October;
```

The current variable will now contain the enumeration constant, October.

Let's see an enumeration in action in an example.

Try It Out   Using an Enumeration

Here's a program that defines the Day enumeration and some variables of that type:

```
public class TryEnumeration {
   // Define an enumeration type for days of the week
   enum Day {Monday, Tuesday,   Wednesday, Thursday,
                      Friday, Saturday, Sunday  }

   public static void main(String[] args) {

      // Define three variables of type Day
      Day yesterday = Day.Thursday;
      Day today = Day.Friday;
      Day tomorrow = Day.Saturday;

      // Output the values of the Day variables
      System.out.println("Today is " + today);
      System.out.println("Tomorrow will be " + tomorrow);
      System.out.println("Yesterday was " + yesterday);
   }
}
```

This will produce the following output:

```
Today is Friday
Tomorrow will be Saturday
Yesterday was Thursday
```

How It Works

The code itself is essentially what you saw in the previous section. There is the declaration of the enumeration type, Day, followed by the main() method that contains definitions of three variables of that type. You then have output statements for the values of the three variables.

The output is very interesting. It doesn't display the numerical values of the variables of type Day, but their names. This is the default way in which a value of an enumeration type is represented as a string because the names are more important than the values in most enumeration types. After all, the values that they have are arbitrarily assigned here and serve only to differentiate one enumeration constant from another.

Note that because the statement that defines Day is defining a new type, you cannot position it within the body of the main() method, or indeed any other method that you might define. The definition for Day could appear in a separate source file with the name Day.java, and the example would work just as well.

This is just a small fraction of the capabilities of enumerations. I introduced them at this point because enumeration constants — the values that a variable of an enumeration type may have — are always integers. You will find out more about how you can use them as you progress through subsequent chapters, but you will have to wait until Chapter 6 for the full story.

Boolean Variables

Variables of type boolean can have only one of two values, true or false. The values true and false are boolean literals. The boolean type is named after the mathematician George Boole, who invented Boolean algebra, and variables of this type are described as boolean variables. You can define a variable of type boolean called state with the following statement:

```
boolean state = true;
```

This statement also initializes the variable state with the value true.

You can also set the value of a boolean variable in an assignment statement. For example, the statement

```
state = false;
```

sets the value of the variable state to false.

At this point you can't do much with a boolean variable, other than to set its value to true or false, but as you will see in the next chapter, boolean variables become much more useful in the context of decision-making in a program, particularly when we can use expressions that produce a result of type boolean.

Several operators combine `boolean` values, including operators for `boolean` AND, `boolean` OR, and `boolean` negation (these are `&&`, `||`, and `!`, respectively), as well as comparison operators that produce a `boolean` result. Rather than go into these here in the abstract, I will defer discussion until the next chapter, where I will also explain how you can apply them in practice to alter the sequence of execution in a program.

> Note that variables of type `boolean` differ from the other primitive data types in that they cannot be cast to any other basic type, and the other primitive types cannot be cast to type `boolean`.

Operator Precedence

I have already introduced the idea of a pecking order for operators that determines the sequence in which they are executed in a statement. A simple arithmetic expression such as 3 + 4*5 results in the value 23 because the multiply operation is executed first—it takes precedence over the addition operation. I can now formalize the position by classifying all the operators present in Java according to their precedence. Each operator in Java has a set priority or precedence in relation to the others, as shown in the following table. Operators with a higher precedence are executed before those of a lower precedence. Precedence is highest for operators in the top line in the table, down through to the operators in the bottom line, which have the lowest precedence. Operators that appear on the same line of the table have the same precedence:

Operator Precedence Group	Associativity
(), [], postfix ++, postfix --	left
unary +, unary -, prefix ++, prefix --, ~, !	right
(type), new	left
*, /, %	left
+, -	left
<<, >>, >>>	left
< ,<= , >, >=, instanceof	left
==, !=	left
&	left
^	left
|	left
&&	left
||	left
?:	left
=, +=, -=, *=, /=, %=, <<=, >>=, >>>=, &=, |=, ^=	right

Most of the operators that appear in the table you have not seen yet, but you will meet them all in this book eventually, and it is handy to have them all gathered together in a single precedence table that you can refer to when necessary.

By definition, the postfix ++ operator changes the value of its operand after the other operators in the expression in which it appears have been executed, despite its high precedence. In this case, precedence determines what it applies to; in other words, the postfix ++ acts only on the variable that appears immediately before it. For this reason the expression `numOranges+++numApples` that we saw earlier in the chapter is evaluated as `(oranges++) + apples` rather than `oranges + (++apples)`.

The sequence of execution of operators with equal precedence in a statement is determined by a property called associativity. The operators that appear on the same line in the table above form a group of operators that are either left-associative or right-associative. A left-associative operator attaches to its immediate left operand. This results in an expression involving several left-associative operators with the same precedence in the same expression being executed in sequence, starting with the leftmost and ending with the rightmost. Right-associative operators of equal precedence in an expression bind to their right operand and consequently are executed from right to left. For example, if you write the statement:

```
a = b + c + 10;
```

the left associativity of the group to which the + operator belongs implies that this is effectively:

```
a = (b + c) + 10;
```

On the other hand, = and op= are right-associative, so if you have int variables a, b, c, and d each initialized to 1, the statement:

```
a += b = c += d = 10;
```

sets a to 12, b and c to 11, and d to 10. The statement is equivalent to:

```
a += (b = (c += (d = 10)));
```

Note that these statements are intended to illustrate how associativity works and are not a recommended approach to coding.

You will probably find that you will learn the precedence and associativity of the operators in Java by just using them in your programs, so don't spend time trying to memorize them. You may need to refer back to the table from time to time, but as you gain experience you will gain a feel for where the operators sit and eventually you will automatically know when you need parentheses and when not.

Program Comments

I have been adding comments in all the examples so far, so you already know that everything following // in a line is ignored by the compiler (except when the // appears in a character string between double quotes of course). Another use for // is to change lines of code into comments so that they don't get executed — to "comment them out" in other words. If you want to remove some code from a program temporarily, you just add // at the beginning of each line that you want to eliminate. Removing the // later restores the line of code.

It is often convenient to include multiple lines of comment in a program — for example, at the beginning of a method to explain what it does. An alternative to using // at the beginning of each line in a block of comments is to put /* at the beginning of the first comment line and */ at the end of the last comment line. Everything between the /* and the next */ will be ignored. By this means you can annotate your programs, as shown here for example:

```
/******************************************
 * This is a long explanation of        *
 * some particularly important          *
 * aspect of program operation.         *
 ****************************************/
```

Here I have used asterisks to highlight the comment. Of course, you can frame blocks like this in any way that you like, or even not at all, just so long as there is /* at the beginning and */ at the end.

Documentation Comments

You can also include comments in a program that are intended to produce separate documentation for the program. These are called **documentation comments**. A program called javadoc processes the documentation comments in the source code for a program to generate separate documentation for the code. All the documentation that you get with the JDK is produced in this way.

The documentation that is generated by javadoc is in the form of HTML web pages that can be viewed using a browser such as Netscape Navigator or Internet Explorer. A full discussion of documentation comments is outside the scope of this book — not because they are difficult, they aren't. However, it would require a lot of pages to cover them properly, and there are already a lot of pages in the book. I will just describe them sufficiently so that you will recognize documentation comments when you see them.

A documentation comment begins with /** and ends with */. An example of a simple documentation comment is:

```
/**
 This is a documentation comment.
 */
```

Any asterisks at the beginning of each line in a documentation comment are ignored, as are any spaces preceding the first asterisk.

A documentation comment can also include HTML tags, as well as special tags beginning with @ that are used to document methods and classes in a standard form. The @ character is followed by a keyword that defines the purpose of the tag. Here are some of the keywords that you can use:

@author   Used to define the author of the code. For example, I could specify that I am the author by adding the tag:

```
/**

 @author Ivor Horton

 */
```

@deprecated	Used in the documentation of library classes and methods to indicate that they have been superseded and generally should not be used in new applications. This is primarily used within the class libraries to identify obsolete methods.
@exception	Used to document exceptions that the code can throw and the circumstance which can cause this to occur. For example, you might add the following documentation comment preceding your definition of a method to indicate the type of exception that the method may throw: `/**` `@exception IOException   When an I/O error occurs.` `*/`
{@link}	Generates a link to another part of the documentation within the documentation that is produced. You can use this tag to embed a link to another class or method within descriptive text for your code. The curly brackets are used to separate the link from the rest of the in-line text.
@param	Used to describe the parameters for a method.
@return	Used to document the value returned from a method.
@see	Used to specify cross-references to some other part of the code, such as another class or a method. It can also reference a URL.
@throws	A synonym for @exception.
@version	Used to describe the current version of the code.

You can use any HTML tags within a documentation comment except for header tags. The HTML tags you insert are used to structure and format the documentation appropriately when it is viewed, and javadoc will add HTML tags to format the comments that include the special @ tags mentioned in the preceding table.

The outline here really only gives you a hint as to what documentation comments are and doesn't do justice to the power and scope of javadoc. For that you need to look into it in detail. If you want to see real examples of javadoc comments, take a look at one or other of the source code files for the library classes. The JDK comes with the javadoc program and its documentation. javadoc also has its own home page on the Javasoft web site at http://java.sun.com/j2se/javadoc/.

Summary

In this chapter you have seen all of the basic types of variables that are available in Java. The discussion of boolean variables will be more meaningful in the context of the next chapter since their primary use is in decision-making and modifying the execution sequence in a program.

The important points you have learned in this chapter are:

❏ The integer types are byte, short, int, and long, occupying 1, 2, 4, and 8 bytes, respectively.

❏ Variables of type char occupy 2 bytes and can store a single Unicode character code.

❏ Integer expressions are evaluated using 64-bit operations for variables of type long, and using 32-bit operations for all other integer types. You must, therefore, add a cast for all assignment operations storing a result of type byte, type short, or type char.

❏ A cast will be automatically supplied where necessary for op= assignment operations.

❏ The floating-point types are float and double, occupying 4 and 8 bytes, respectively.

❏ Values that are outside the range of a floating-point type are represented by a special value that is displayed as either Infinity or -Infinity.

❏ Where the result of a floating-point calculation is indeterminate, the value is displayed as NaN. Such values are referred to as Not-a-Number.

❏ You use an enumeration type to define variables that can be assigned values only from a fixed set that you specified as part of the enumeration.

❏ Variables of type boolean can have only either the value true or the value false.

❏ The order of execution of operators in an expression is determined by their precedence. Where operators are of equal precedence, the order of execution is determined by their associativity.

Exercises

You can download the source code for the examples in the book and the solutions to the following exercises from http://www.wrox.com.

1. Write a console program to define and initialize a variable of type byte to 1, and then successively multiply it by 2 and display its value 8 times. Explain the reason for the last result.

2. Write a console program to declare and initialize a double variable with some value such as 1234.5678. Then retrieve the integral part of the value and store it in a variable of type long, and the first four digits of the fractional part and store them in an integer of type short. Display the value of the double variable by outputting the two values stored as integers.

3. Write a program that defines a floating-point variable initialized with a dollar value for your income and a second floating-point variable initialized with a value corresponding to a tax rate of 35 percent. Calculate and output the amount of tax you must pay with the dollars and cents stored as separate integer values (use two variables of type int to hold the tax, perhaps taxDollars and taxCents).

4. The diameter of the Sun is approximately 865,000 miles. The diameter of the Earth is approximately 7,600 miles. Use the methods in the class Math to calculate:

❏ The volume of the Earth in cubic miles

❏ The volume of the Sun in cubic miles

❏ The ratio of the volume of the Sun to the volume of the Earth

Loops and Logic

In this chapter you'll look at how you make decisions and choices in your Java programs. You will also learn how to make your programs repeat a set of actions until a specific condition is met. In this chapter you'll learn:

- ❏ How you compare data values
- ❏ How you can define logical expressions
- ❏ How you can use logical expressions to alter the sequence in which program statements are executed
- ❏ How you can select different expressions depending on the value of a logical expression
- ❏ How to choose between options in a fixed set of alternatives
- ❏ How long your variables last
- ❏ How you can repeat a block of code a given number of times
- ❏ How you can repeat a block of code as long as a given logical expression is true
- ❏ How you can break out of loops and statement blocks
- ❏ What assertions are and how you use them

All your programs of any consequence will use at least some, and often most, of the language capabilities and programming techniques I will cover in this chapter, so make sure you have a good grasp of them.

But first, how do you make decisions in code, and so affect the way the program runs?

Making Decisions

Making choices will be a fundamental element in all your programs. You need to be able to make decisions like, "If the user wants to enter more data, then read another value from the keyboard" or "If the bank balance is large, buy the car with the go-faster stripes, else renew the monthly bus ticket." Whatever decision you want to make, in programming terms it requires the ability to make comparisons between variables, constants, and the values of expressions and then execute one group of statements or another, depending on the result of a given comparison. Thus, the first step to understanding how you make decisions in a program is to look at how you make comparisons.

Making Comparisons

Java provides you with six relational operators for comparing two data values. The data values you are comparing can be variables, constants, or expressions with values drawn from Java's primitive data types—byte, short, int, long, char, float or double.

Relational Operators	Description
>	Produces the value true if the left operand is greater than the right operand, and false otherwise.
>=	Produces the value true if the left operand is greater than or equal to the right operand, and false otherwise.
==	Produces the value true if the left operand is equal to the right operand, and false otherwise.
!=	Produces the value true if the left operand is not equal to the right operand, and false otherwise.
<=	Produces the value true if the left operand is less than or equal to the right operand, and false otherwise.
<	Produces the value true if the left operand is less than the right operand, and false otherwise.

As you see, each operator produces either the value true or the value false, and so is eminently suited to the business of making decisions. This also implies that you can use a boolean variable to store the result of a comparison. You saw how to declare variables of type boolean in the previous chapter. For example, you could define a boolean variable state and set its value to be the result of an expression using a comparison as follows:

```
boolean state = false;    // Define and initialize the variable
state = x - y < a + b;    // Store the result of comparing x-y with a+b
```

The value of the variable state will be set to true in the assignment statement if x - y is less than a + b, and to false otherwise.

To understand how the preceding expression is evaluated, take a look back at the precedence table for operators that I introduced in the last chapter. You'll see that the comparison operators are all of lower precedence than the arithmetic operators, so arithmetic operations will always be completed before any comparisons are made, unless of course there are parentheses dictating otherwise. The expression

```
x - y == a + b
```

will produce the result true if x - y is equal to a + b, since these arithmetic sub-expressions will be evaluated first, and the values that result will be the operands for the == operator. Of course, it is helpful to put the parentheses in, even though they are not strictly necessary. It leaves no doubt as to what is happening if you write:

```
(x - y) == (a + b)
```

Note that if the left and right operands of a relational operator are of differing types, values will be promoted in the same way as you saw in the previous chapter for mixed arithmetic expressions. So if aDouble is of type double and number is of type int in the following expression:

```
aDouble < number + 1
```

the result of the expression number + 1 will be calculated as type int, and this value will be promoted to type double before comparing it with the value of aDouble.

The if Statement

The first statement you'll look at that can make use of the result of a comparison is the if statement. The if statement, in its simplest configuration, is of the form

```
if(expression)
    statement;
```

where expression can be any expression that produces a value true or false. You can see a graphical representation of this logic in Figure 3-1.

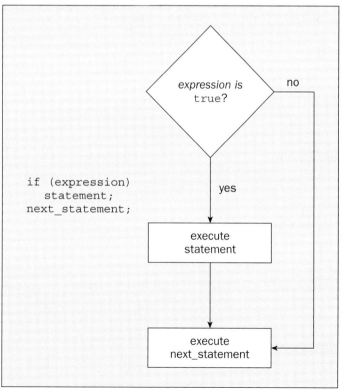

Figure 3-1

If the value of `expression` is `true`, the statement that follows the `if` is executed; otherwise, it isn't. A practical example of this is as follows:

```
if(number%2 != 0)              // Test if number is odd
    ++number;                  // If so make it even
```

The `if` condition between the parentheses tests whether the value of `number` is odd by comparing the remainder that results from dividing it by 2 with 0. If the remainder isn't equal to 0, the value of `number` is odd, so you add 1 to make it even. If the value of number is even, the statement incrementing `number` will not be executed.

> **Note how the statement on the second line is indented. This is to show that it is subject to the `if` condition. You should always indent statements in your Java programs as cues to the program structure. You will gather more guidelines on the use of statement indenting as you work with more complicated examples.**

You may sometimes see a simple `if` written on a single line. The previous example could have been written:

```
if(number%2 != 0) ++number;   // If number is odd, make it even
```

This is perfectly legal. The compiler ignores excess spaces and newline characters — the semicolon acts as the delimiter for a statement. Writing an `if` in this way saves a little space, and occasionally it can be an aid to clarity, when you have a succession of such comparisons, for example, but generally it is better to write the action statement on a separate line from the condition being tested.

Statement Blocks

In general, wherever you can have one executable statement in Java, you can also have a block of statements enclosed between braces. This applies to the statements within a statement block, so you can always nest a statement block between braces inside another statement block, and you can do this to any depth. The ability to use a block wherever you can have a statement means that you can use a statement block within the basic `if` statement that you just saw. Therefore, the `if` statement can equally well be of the form:

```
if(expression) {
    statement 1;
    statement 2;
    ...
    statement n;
}
```

Now if the value of `expression` is `true`, all the statements enclosed in the following block will be executed. Of course, without the braces to enclose the block, the code no longer has a statement block:

```
if(expression)
   statement 1;
   statement 2;
   ...
   statement n;
```

Here, only the first statement, `statement 1`, will be omitted when the `if` expression is `false`; the remaining statements will always be executed regardless of the value of `expression`. You can see from this that indenting is just a visual cue to the logic. It has no effect on how the program code executes. This looks as though the sequence of statements belongs to the `if`, but only the first statement does because there are no braces. The indenting is incorrect and misleading here and the code should be written as:

```
if(expression)
   statement 1;
statement 2;
   ...
statement n;
```

> In this book, I have adopted the convention of having the opening brace on the same line as the `if` condition. The closing brace will then be aligned with the first character, `i`, in the keyword `if`. I will indent all the statements within the block from the braces so that they are easily identified as belonging to the block. This is consistent with the pattern I have been using with a block defining a class and a block belonging to a method. There are other conventions that you can use if you prefer. In another common convention, the braces bounding a block appear on their own line and are aligned. The most important consideration is that you are consistent in whatever convention you adopt.

As a practical example of an `if` statement that includes a statement block, you could write:

```
if(number%2 != 0) {                           // Test if number is odd
   // If so make it even and output a message
   ++number;
   System.out.println("Number was forced to be even and is now " + number);
}
```

Now both statements between the braces are executed if the `if` expression is `true`, and neither of them is executed if the `if` expression is `false`.

It is good practice to always put opening and closing braces around the code dependent on an `if` condition, even when there is only a single action statement. This helps to make the code easier to follow and will minimize the possibility of the program logic being confused.

Statement blocks are more than just a convenient way of grouping statements together — they affect the life and accessibility of variables. You'll learn more about statement blocks when I discuss variable scope later in this chapter. In the meantime, let's look a little deeper into what you can do with the `if` statement.

The else Clause

You can extend the basic `if` statement by adding an `else` clause. This provides an alternative choice of statement, or statement block, that is executed when the `expression` in the `if` statement is `false`. You can see the syntax of this statement, and how the program's control flow works, in Figure 3-2.

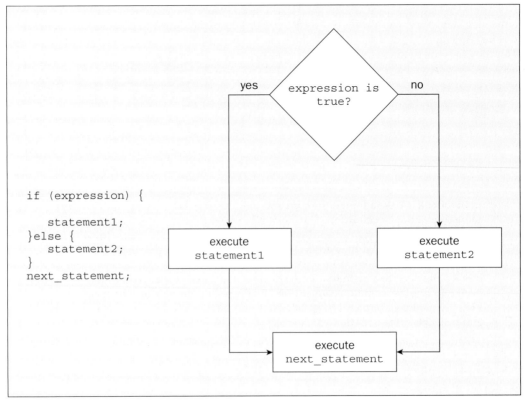

```
if (expression) {

    statement1;
}else {
    statement2;
}
next_statement;
```

Figure 3-2

This provides an explicit choice between two courses of action — one for when the `if` expression is `true` and another for when it is `false`.

You can apply this in a console program and try out the `random()` method from the `Math` class at the same time.

if-else

When you have entered the program text, save it in a file called `NumberCheck.java`. Compile it and then run it a few times to see what results you get.

```java
public class NumberCheck {
    public static void main(String[] args) {
        int number = 0;
```

```
number = 1+(int)(100*Math.random());   // Get a random integer between 1 & 100
if(number%2 == 0) {                     // Test if it is even
  System.out.println("You have got an even number, " + number); // It is even

} else {
  System.out.println("You have got an odd number, " + number);  // It is odd
}
  }
}
```

How It Works

You saw the `random()` method that is defined in the standard class `Math` in the previous chapter. It returns a random value of type `double` between 0.0 and 1.0, but the result is always less than 1.0, so the largest number you will get is 0.9999... (with the number of recurring digits being limited to the maximum number that the type `double` will allow, of course). Consequently, when you multiply the value returned by 100.0 and convert this value to type `int` with the explicit cast, you discard any fractional part of the number and produce a random integer between 0 and 99. Adding 1 to this will result in a random integer between 1 and 100, which you store in the variable `number`. You then generate the program output in the `if` statement. If the value of `number` is even, the first `println()` call is executed; otherwise, the second `println()` call in the `else` clause is executed.

Note the use of indentation here. It is evident that `main()` is within the class definition because of the indentation relative to the first line of the class definition. The code for `main()` is clearly distinguished because it is indented relative to the first line of the method. You can also see immediately which statement is executed when the `if` expression is `true`, and which applies when it is `false`.

Nested if Statements

The statement that is executed when an `if` expression is `true` can be another `if`, as can the statement in an `else` clause. This enables you to express such convoluted logic as "if my bank balance is healthy, then I will buy the car if I have my check book with me, else I will buy the car if I can get a loan from the bank." An `if` statement that is nested inside another can also itself contain a nested `if`. You can continue nesting `if`s one inside the other like this for as long as you still know what you are doing — or even beyond if you enjoy confusion.

To illustrate the nested `if` statement, I can modify the `if` from the previous example:

```
if(number%2 == 0) {                     // Test if it is even
  if(number < 50) {                     // Output a message if number is < 50
    System.out.println("You have got an even number < 50, " + number);
  }

} else {
  System.out.println("You have got an odd number, " + number); // It is odd
}
```

Now the message for an even value is displayed only if the value of `number` is also less than 50. There are three possible outcomes from this code fragment — if `number` is even and less than 50, you will see a message to that effect; if `number` is even and is not less than 50, there will be no output; and finally, if `number` is odd, a message will be displayed.

The braces around the nested `if` are necessary here because of the `else` clause. The braces constrain the nested `if` in the sense that if it had an `else` clause, it would have to appear between the braces enclosing the nested `if`. If the braces were not there, the program would still compile and run but the logic would be different. Let's see how.

With nested `if`s, the question of to which `if` statement a particular `else` clause belongs often arises. If you remove the braces from the code above, you have:

```
if(number%2 == 0)                      // Test if it is even
   if(number < 50 )                    // Output a message if number is < 50
      System.out.println("You have got an even number < 50, " + number);
else
   System.out.println("You have got an odd number, " + number); // It is odd
```

This has substantially changed the logic from the previous version, in spite of the fact that the indentation implies otherwise. The `else` clause now belongs to the nested `if` that tests whether number is less than 50, so the second `println()` call is executed only for *even* numbers that are greater than or equal to 50. This is clearly not what was intended since it makes nonsense of the output in this case, but it does illustrate the rule for connecting `else`s to `if`s, which is:

> An `else` **always belongs to the nearest preceding** `if` **in the same block that is not already spoken for by another** `else`.

You need to take care that the indenting of statements with nested `if`s is correct. It is easy to convince yourself that the logic is as indicated by the indentation, even when this is completely wrong.

Let's try the `if-else` combination in another program:

Try It Out   Deciphering Characters the Hard Way

Create the class `LetterCheck`, and code its `main()` method as follows:

```
public class LetterCheck {
   public static void main(String[] args) {
      char symbol = 'A';
      symbol = (char)(128.0*Math.random());     // Generate a random character

      if(symbol >= 'A') {                        // Is it A or greater?
         if(symbol <= 'Z') {                     // yes, and is it Z or less?
            // Then it is a capital letter
            System.out.println("You have the capital letter " + symbol);

         } else {                                // It is not Z or less
            if(symbol >= 'a') {                  // So is it a or greater?
               if(symbol <= 'z') {               // Yes, so is it z or less?
                  // Then it is a small letter
                  System.out.println("You have the small letter " + symbol);

               } else {                          // It is not less than z
                  System.out.println(
```

```
                    "The code is greater than a but it's not a letter");
            }

        } else {
            System.out.println(
                        "The code is less than a and it's not a letter");
            }
        }

        } else {
        System.out.println("The code is less than A so it's not a letter");
        }
    }
}
```

How It Works

This program figures out whether the character stored in the variable `symbol` is an uppercase letter, a lowercase letter, or some other character. The program first generates a random character with a numeric code between 0 and 127, which corresponds to the characters in the basic 7-bit ASCII (ISO 646) character set. The Unicode coding for the ASCII characters is numerically the same as the ASCII code values. Within this character set, the letters `'A'` to `'Z'` are represented by a contiguous group of ASCII codes with decimal values from 65 to 90. The lowercase letters are represented by another contiguous group with ASCII code values that have decimal values from 97 to 122. So to convert any capital letter to a lowercase letter, you just need to add 32 to the character code.

The `if` statements are a bit convoluted so let's look at the diagram of the logic in Figure 3-3.

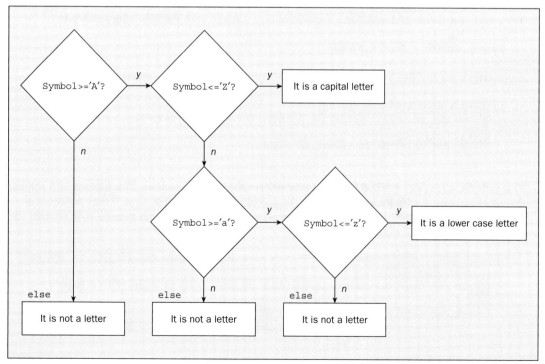

Figure 3-3

You have four `if` statements altogether. The first `if` tests whether `symbol` is `'A'` or greater. If it is, it could be a capital letter, a small letter, or possibly something else. But if it isn't, it is not a letter at all, so the `else` for this `if` statement (toward the end of the program) produces a message to that effect.

The nested `if` statement, which is executed if `symbol` is `'A'` or greater, tests whether it is `'Z'` or less. If it is, then `symbol` definitely contains a capital letter, and the appropriate message is displayed. If it isn't then it may be a small letter, so another `if` statement is nested within the `else` clause of the first nested `if` to test for this possibility.

The `if` statement in the `else` clause tests for `symbol` being greater than `'a'`. If it isn't, you know that `symbol` is not a letter, and a message is displayed. If it is, another `if` checks whether `symbol` is `'z'` or less. If it is you have a small letter, and if not you don't have a letter at all.

You will have to run the example a few times to get all the possible messages to come up. They all will— eventually.

After having carefully crafted our convoluted and cumbersome condition checking, I can now reveal that there is a much easier way to achieve the same result. You'll see that in the section "Logical Operators" that follows immediately after a brief word on working with enumeration values.

Comparing Enumeration Values

You can't compare variables of an enumeration type using the comparison operators but you can using a method that every enumeration object provides. Suppose you define an enumeration type as:

```
enum Season { spring, summer, fall, winter }
```

You could now define and initialize a variable of type `Season` with the following statement:

```
Season season = Season.summer;
```

If you later want to check what the `season` variable currently holds, you could write

```
if(season.equals(Season.spring)) {
  System.out.println("Spring has sprung, the grass is riz.");
} else {
  System.out.println("It isn\'t Spring!");
}
```

This calls the `equals()` method for the enumeration referred to by `season`. This method will compare the value in `season` with the value between the parentheses and result in `true` if they are equal or `false` if they are unequal. You could use the `equals()` method to compare `season` with another variable of type `Season`, for example:

```
Season best = Season.winter;            // A new variable initialized to winter
if(season.equals(best)) {
  System.out.println("season is the same as best, and is equal to "+ best);
} else {
  System.out.println(" season has the value "+season +
                          " and best has the value " + best);
}
```

After defining the variable, best, you test whether the value of season is the same value as best. If it is, the first output statement will be executed. If best and season are not equal, the output statement in the else block will be executed.

Logical Operators

The tests you have put in the if expressions have been relatively simple so far. Real life is typically more complicated. You will often want to combine a number of conditions so that you execute a particular course — for example, if they are all true simultaneously. You can ride the roller coaster if you are over 12 years old, over 4 feet tall, and less than 6 feet 6. Failure on any count and it's no-go. Sometimes, though, you may need to test for any one of a number of conditions being true — for example, you get a lower price entry ticket if you are under 16, or over 65.

You can deal with both of these cases, and more, using **logical operators** to combine several expressions that have a value true or false. Because they operate on boolean values, they are also referred to as **boolean operators**. There are five logical operators that operate on boolean values:

Symbol	Long Name
&	logical AND
&&	conditional AND
|	logical OR
||	conditional OR
!	logical negation (NOT)

These are very simple; the only point of potential confusion is the fact that you have the choice of two operators for each of AND and OR. The extra operators are the bitwise & and | from the previous chapter that you can also apply to boolean values where they have an effect that is subtly different from && and ||. I'll first consider what each of these is used for in general terms; then I'll look at how you can use them in an example.

Logical AND Operations

You can use either AND operator, && or &, where you have two logical expressions that must both be true for the result to be true — that is, you only want to be rich and healthy. Either AND operator will produce the same result from the logical expression. I will come back to how they differ in a moment. First, let's explore how they are used. All of the following discussion applies equally well to & as well as &&.

Let's see how logical operators can simplify the last example. You could use the && operator if you were testing a variable of type char to determine whether it contained an uppercase letter or not. The value being tested must be both greater than or equal to 'A' AND less than or equal to 'Z'. Both conditions must be true for the value to be a capital letter. Taking the example from our previous program, with a value stored in a char variable symbol, you could implement the test for an uppercase letter in a single if by using the && operator:

```
if(symbol >= 'A' && symbol <= 'Z')
    System.out.println("You have the capital letter " + symbol);
```

If you look at the precedence table in Chapter 2, you'll see that the relational operators will be executed before the && operator, so no parentheses are necessary. Here, the output statement will be executed only if both of the conditions combined by the operator && are true. However, as I have said before, it is a good idea to add parentheses if they make the code easier to read. It also helps to avoid mistakes.

In fact, the result of an && operation is very simple. It is true only if both operands are true; otherwise, the result is false.

You can now rewrite the set of ifs from the last example.

Try It Out   **Deciphering Characters the Easy Way**

You can replace the outer if-else loop and its contents in LetterCheck.java as shown in the following code:

```
public class LetterCheck2 {
  public static void main(String[] args) {
    char symbol = 'A';
    symbol = (char)(128.0*Math.random());          // Generate a random character
    if(symbol >= 'A' && symbol <= 'Z') {           // Is it a capital letter
      System.out.println("You have the capital letter " + symbol);
    } else {
      if(symbol >= 'a' && symbol <= 'z') {     // or is it a small letter?
        System.out.println("You have the small letter " + symbol);
      } else {                                 // It is not less than z
        System.out.println("The code is not a letter");
      }
    }
  }
}
```

The output should be the same as the previous version of the code.

How It Works

Using the && operator has condensed the example down quite a bit. You now can do the job with two ifs, and it's certainly easier to follow what's happening.

You might want to note that when the statement in an else clause is another if, the if is sometimes written on the same line as the else, as in:

```
if(symbol >= 'A' && symbol <= 'Z') {            // Is it a capital letter
  System.out.println("You have the capital letter " + symbol);
} else if(symbol >= 'a' && symbol <= 'z') {     // or is it a small letter?
  System.out.println("You have the small letter " + symbol);

} else {                                        // It is not less than z
  System.out.println("The code is not a letter");
}
```

I think the original is clearer in this particular case, but writing else if can sometimes make the code easier to follow.

&& versus &

So what distinguishes && from & ? The difference between them is that the conditional && will not bother to evaluate the right-hand operand if the left-hand operand is `false`, since the result is already determined in this case to be `false`. This can make the code a bit faster when the left-hand operand is `false`.

For example, consider the following statements:

```
int number = 50;
if(number<40 && (3*number - 27)>100) {
   System.out.println("number = " + number);
}
```

Here the expression `(3*number - 27)>100` will never be executed since the expression `number<40` is always `false`. On the other hand, if you write the statements as

```
int number = 50;
if(number<40 & (3*number - 27)>100) {
   System.out.println("number = " + number);
}
```

the effect is different. The whole logical expression is always evaluated, so even though the left-hand operand of the & operator is `false` and the result is a forgone conclusion once that is known, the right-hand operand `((3*number - 27)>100)` will still be evaluated.

So, you can just use && all the time to make your programs a bit faster and forget about &, right? Wrong — it all depends on what you are doing. Most of the time you can use &&, but there are occasions when you will want to be sure that the right-hand operand is evaluated. Equally, in some instances, you want to be certain the right-hand operand won't be evaluated if the left operand is `false`.

For example, the first situation can arise when the right-hand expression involves modifying a variable — and you want the variable to be modified in any event. An example of a statement like this is:

```
if(++value%2 == 0 & ++count < limit) {
   // Do something
}
```

Here, the variable `count` will be incremented in any event. If you use && instead of &, `count` will be incremented only if the left operand of the AND operator is `true`. You get a different result depending on which operator is used.

I can illustrate the second situation with the following statement:

```
if(count > 0 && total/count > 5) {
   // Do something...
}
```

In this case, the right operand for the && operation will be executed only if the left operand is `true` — that is, when `count` is positive. Clearly, if you were to use & here, and `count` happened to be zero, you would be attempting to divide the value of `total` by 0, which in the absence of code to prevent it would terminate the program.

Logical OR Operations

The OR operators, | and ||, apply when you want a true result if either or both of the operands are true. The logical OR, ||, has a similar effect to the logical AND, in that it omits the evaluation of the right-hand operand when the left-hand operand is true. Obviously if the left operand is true, the result will be true regardless of whether the right operand is true or false.

Let's take an example. A reduced entry ticket price is issued to under 16-year-olds and to those aged 65 or over; this could be tested using the following if:

```
if(age < 16 || age>= 65) {
   ticketPrice *= 0.9;          // Reduce ticket price by 10%
}
```

The effect here is to reduce ticketPrice by 10 percent if either condition is true. Clearly in this case, both conditions cannot be true.

With an | or an || operation, you get a false result only if both operands are false. If either or both operands are true, the result is true.

Boolean NOT Operations

The third type of logical operator, !, applies to one boolean operand, and the result is the inverse of the operand value. So if the value of a boolean variable, state, is true, then the expression !state has the value false, and if it is false, then !state evaluates to true. To see how the operator is used with an expression, you could rewrite the code fragment you used to provide discounted ticket price as:

```
if(!(age >= 16 && age < 65)) {
   ticketPrice *= 0.9;          // Reduce ticket price by 10%
}
```

The expression (age >= 16 && age < 65) is true if age is from 16 to 64. People of this age do not qualify for the discount, so the discount should be applied only when this expression is false. Applying the ! operator to the result of the expression does what you want.

You could also apply the ! operator in an expression that was a favorite of Charles Dickens:

```
!(Income>Expenditure)
```

If this expression is true, the result is misery, at least as soon as the bank starts bouncing your checks.

Of course, you can use any of the logical operators in combination if necessary. If the theme park decides to give a discount on the price of entry to anyone who is under 12 years old and under 48 inches tall, or to someone who is over 65 and over 72 inches tall, you could apply the discount with this test:

```
if((age < 12 && height < 48) || (age > 65 && height > 72)) {
   ticketPrice *= 0.8;              // 20% discount on the ticket price
}
```

The parentheses are not strictly necessary here, as && has a higher precedence than ||, but adding the parentheses makes it clearer how the comparisons combine and makes it a little more readable.

Don't confuse the bitwise operators &, |, and ! with the logical operators that look the same. Which type of operator you are using in any particular instance is determined by the type of operand with which you use it. The bitwise operators apply to integer types and produce an integer result. The logical operators apply to operands that have boolean values and produce a result of type boolean—true or false. You can use both bitwise and logical operators in an expression if it is convenient to do so.

Character Testing Using Standard Library Methods

While testing characters using logical operators is a useful way of demonstrating how these operators work, in practice there is an easier way. The standard Java packages provide a range of standard methods to do the sort of testing for particular sets of characters such as letters or digits that you have been doing with if statements. They are all available within the Character class, which is automatically available in your programs. For example, you could have written the if statement in the LetterCheck2 program as shown in the following example.

Try It Out   Deciphering Characters Trivially

In the following example, the if expressions in main() that were in the LetterCheck2 class have been replaced by expressions that call methods in the Character class to do the testing:

```java
import static java.lang.Character.isLowerCase;
import static java.lang.Character.isUpperCase;

public class LetterCheck3 {
  public static void main(String[] args) {
    char symbol = 'A';
    symbol = (char)(128.0*Math.random());        // Generate a random character

    if(isUpperCase(symbol)) {
      System.out.println("You have the capital letter " + symbol);

    } else {
      if(isLowerCase(symbol)) {
        System.out.println("You have the small letter " + symbol);

      } else {
        System.out.println("The code is not a letter");
      }
    }
  }
}
```

How It Works

Because you have the import statements for the isUpperCase and isLowerCase method names at the beginning of the source file, you can call these methods without using the Character class name as qualifier. The isUpperCase() method returns true if the char value that you pass to it is uppercase, and false if it is not. Similarly, the isLowerCase() method returns true if the char value you pass to it is lowercase.

The following table shows some of the other methods included in the `Character` class that you may find useful for testing characters. In each case, you put the argument of type `char` that is to be tested between the parentheses following the method name.

Method	Description
isDigit()	Returns the value `true` if the argument is a digit (0 to 9), and `false` otherwise.
isLetter()	Returns the value `true` if the argument is a letter, and `false` otherwise.
isLetterOrDigit()	Returns the value `true` if the argument is a letter or a digit, and `false` otherwise.
isWhitespace()	Returns the value `true` if the argument is whitespace, which is any one of the following characters: space (' ') tab ('\t') newline ('\n') carriage return ('\r') form feed ('\f') The method returns `false` otherwise.

You will find information on other methods in the class `Character` in the JDK documentation for the class.

The Conditional Operator

The **conditional operator** is sometimes called a **ternary operator** because it involves three operands. It is best understood by looking at an example. Suppose you have two variables of type int with the names `yourAge` and `myAge`, and you want to assign the greater of the values stored in `yourAge` and `myAge` to a third variable, `older`, which is also of type int. You can do this with the following statement:

```
older = yourAge>myAge ? yourAge : myAge;
```

The conditional operator has a logical expression as the first of its three operands — in this case, it is the expression `yourAge>myAge`. If this expression is `true`, the operand that follows the ? symbol — in this case, `yourAge` — is evaluated to produce the value resulting from the operation. If the expression `yourAge>myAge` is `false`, the third operand which comes after the colon — in this case, `myAge` — is evaluated to produce the value from the operation. Thus, the result of this conditional expression is `yourAge`, if `yourAge` is greater than `myAge`, and `myAge` otherwise. This value is then stored in the variable `older`. The use of the conditional operator in this assignment statement is equivalent to the if statement:

```
if(yourAge > myAge) {
    older = yourAge;
```

```
    } else {
      older = myAge;
    }
```

Remember, though, the conditional operator is an operator and not a statement, so you can use it in a more complex expression involving other operators.

The conditional operator can be written generally as:

```
    logical_expression ? expression1 : expression2
```

If the `logical_expression` evaluates as `true`, the result of the operation is the value of `expression1`, and if `logical_expression` evaluates to `false`, the result is the value of `expression2`. Note that if `expression1` is evaluated because `logical_expression` is `true`, then `expression2` will not be, and vice versa.

You can use the conditional operator in lots of circumstances, and one common application of it is to control output, depending on the result of an expression or the value of a variable. You can vary a message by selecting one text string or another depending on the condition specified.

Try It Out   Conditional Plurals

Type in the following code, which will add the correct ending to `'hat'` depending on how many hats you have:

```
    public class ConditionalOp {
      public static void main(String[] args) {
        int nHats = 1;                          // Number of hats
        System.out.println("I have " + nHats + " hat" + (nHats == 1 ? "." : "s."));

        nHats++;                                // Increment number of hats
        System.out.println("I have " + nHats + " hat" + (nHats == 1 ? "." : "s."));
      }
    }
```

The output from this program will be:

```
    I have 1 hat.
    I have 2 hats.
```

How It Works

The result of executing the conditional operator in the program is a string containing just a period when the value of `nHats` is 1, and a string containing an `s` followed by a period in all other cases. The effect of this is to cause the output statement to automatically adjust the output between singular and plural. You can use the same technique in other situations, such as where you need to choose "he" or "she" for example, as long as you are able to specify a logical expression to differentiate the situation in which you should use one rather than the other. A more challenging application you could try is to append "st", "nd", "rd", or "th" to a date value, such as in "3rd November" or "4th July".

The switch Statement

You use the switch statement to select from multiple choices based on a set of fixed values for a given expression. The expression must produce a result of an integer type other than long, or a value of an enumeration type. Thus, the expression that controls a switch statement can result in a value of type char, byte, short, or int, or an enumeration constant.

In normal use the switch statement operates rather like a rotary switch in that you can select one of a fixed number of choices. For example, on some makes of washing machine you choose between the various possible machine settings in this way, with positions for cotton, wool, synthetic fiber, and so on, which you select by turning the knob to point to the option that you want.

Here's a switch statement reflecting this logic for a washing machine:

```
switch(wash) {
  case 1:                          // wash is 1 for Cotton
    System.out.println("Cotton selected");
    break;
  case 2:                          // wash is 2 for Linen
    System.out.println("Linen selected");
    break;
  case 3:                          // wash is 3 for Wool
    System.out.println("Wool selected");
    break;
  default:                         // Not a valid value for wash
    System.out.println("Selection error");
    break;
}
```

The selection in the switch statement is determined by the value of the expression that you place between the parentheses after the keyword switch. In this case it's simply the variable wash that would need to be previously declared as of type char, byte, short, or int. You define the possible switch options by one or more **case values**, also called **case labels**, which you define using the keyword case. In general, a case label consists of the case keyword followed by a constant value that is the value that will select the case, followed by a colon. The statements to be executed when the case is selected follow the case label. You place all the case labels and their associated statements between the braces for the switch statement. You have three case values in the preceding example, plus a special case with the label default, which is another keyword. A particular case value is selected if the value of the switch expression is the same as that of the particular case value. The default case is selected when the value of the switch expression does not correspond to any of the values for the other cases. Although I've written the cases in the preceding switch sequenced by their case values, they can be in any order.

When a particular case is selected, the statements that follow that case label are executed. So if wash has the value 2, the statements that follow:

```
case 2:                          // wash is 2 for Linen
```

are executed. In this case, these are:

```
System.out.println("Linen selected");
break;
```

When a `break` statement is executed here, it causes execution to continue with the statement following the closing brace for the `switch`. The `break` is not mandatory as the last statement for each case, but if you don't put a `break` statement at the end of the statements for a case, the statements for the next case in sequence will be executed as well, through to whenever another `break` is found or the end of the `switch` block is reached. This is not usually what you want. The `break` after the `default` statements in our example is not strictly necessary, but it does protect against the situation when you might add another case label at the end of the `switch` statement block, and overlook the need for the `break` at the end of the last case.

You need a case label for each choice to be handled in the `switch`, and the case values must all be different. The `default` case you have in the preceding example is, in general, optional. As I said, it is selected when the value of the expression for the `switch` does not correspond with any of the case values that you have defined. If you don't specify a `default` case and the value of the `switch` expression does not match any of the case labels, none of the statements in the `switch` will be executed, and execution continues at the statement following the closing brace of the `switch` statement.

You could rewrite the previous `switch` statement to use a variable of an enumeration type as the expression controlling the `switch`. Suppose you have defined the `WashChoice` enumeration type like this:

```
enum WashChoice { cotton, linen, wool }          // Define enumeration type
```

You can now code the switch statement like this:

```
WashChoice wash = WashChoice.linen;              // Initial definition of variable
// Some more code that might change the value of wash...

switch(wash) {
  case cotton:
    System.out.println("Cotton selected");
    break;
  case linen:
    System.out.println("Linen selected");
    break;
  case wool:
    System.out.println("Wool selected");
    break;
}
```

The `switch` is controlled by the value of the `wash` variable. Note how you use the enumeration constants as case values. You must write them *without* the enumeration type name as a qualifier in this context; otherwise, the code will not compile. Using enumeration constants as the case values makes the `switch` much more self-explanatory. It is perfectly clear what each case applies to. Because you cannot assign a value to a variable of an enumeration type that is not a defined enumeration constant, it is not necessary to include a default case here.

The General Case of the switch Statement

I have illustrated the logic of the general `switch` statement in the flowchart shown in Figure 3-4.

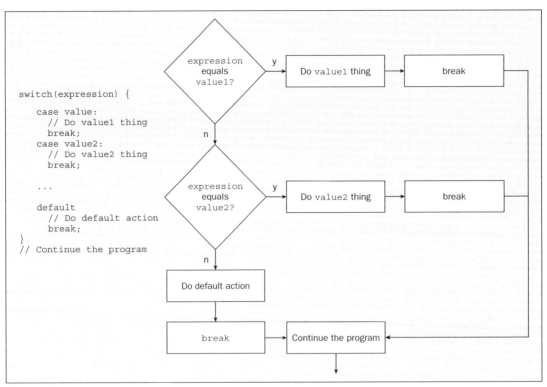

Figure 3-4

Each `case` value is notionally compared with the value of an expression. If one matches, then the code for that case is executed, and the `break` branches to the first statement after the `switch`. As I said earlier, if you don't include the `break` statements, the logic is quite different, as shown in Figure 3-5.

Now when a case label value is equal to the `switch` expression, the code for that case is executed, and followed by the statements for all the other cases that succeed the case that was selected, including that for the default case if that follows. This is not usually what you want, so make sure you don't forget the `break` statements.

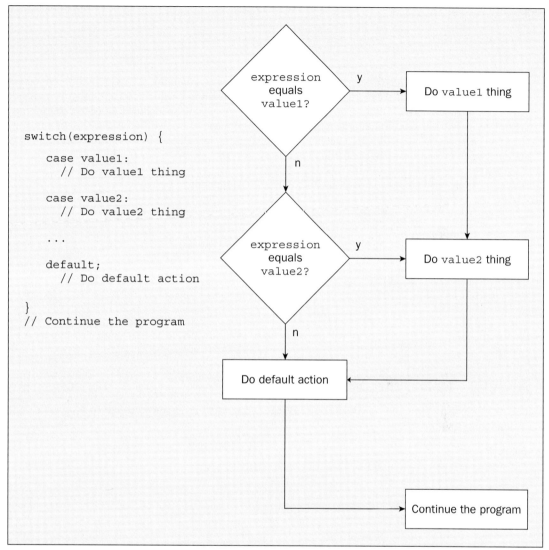

```
switch(expression) {

    case value1:
      // Do value1 thing

    case value2:
      // Do value2 thing

    ...

    default;
      // Do default action

}
// Continue the program
```

Figure 3-5

You can arrange to execute the same statements for several different case labels, as in the following switch statement:

```
char yesNo = 'N';
// more program logic...

switch(yesNo) {
  case 'n': case 'N':
      System.out.println("No selected");
      break;
```

```
    case 'y': case 'Y':
        System.out.println("Yes selected");
        break;
}
```

Here the variable yesNo receives a character from the keyboard somehow. You want a different action depending on whether the user enters 'Y' or 'N', but you want to be able to accept either uppercase or lowercase entries. This switch does just this by putting the case labels together. Note that there is no default case here. If yesNo contains a character other than those identified in the case statements, the switch statement has no effect. In practice, you might add a default case in this kind of situation to output a message indicating when the value in yesNo is not valid.

Of course, you could also implement this logic using if statements:

```
if(yesNo=='n' || yesNo=='N') {
  System.out.println("No selected");

} else {
  if(yesNo=='y' || yesNo=='Y') {
    System.out.println("Yes selected");
  }
}
```

I prefer the switch statement as I think it's easier to follow, but you decide for yourself. Let's try an example.

Try It Out   **Making the switch**

This example uses a switch controlled by an integer type and a switch controlled by a variable of an enumeration type:

```
public class TrySwitch {
    enum WashChoice {cotton, linen, wool, synthetic}      // Define enumeration type

    public static void main(String[] args) {
        WashChoice wash = WashChoice.cotton;    // Variable to define the choice of wash

        // The clothes variable specifies the clothes to be washed by an integer value
        // 1:shirts    2:sweaters   3:socks    4:sheets 5:pants
        int clothes = 3;

        switch(clothes) {
          case 1:
            System.out.println("Washing shirts.");
            wash = WashChoice.cotton;
            break;
          case 2:
            System.out.println("Washing sweaters.");
            wash = WashChoice.wool;
            break;
          case 3:
            System.out.println("Washing socks.");
            wash = WashChoice.wool;
```

```
      break;
    case 4:
      System.out.println("Washing sheets.");
      wash = WashChoice.linen;
      break;
    case 5:
      System.out.println("Washing pants.");
      wash = WashChoice.synthetic;
      break;
    default:
      System.out.println("Unknown washing - default synthetic.");
      wash = WashChoice.synthetic;
      break;
  }
  // Now select the wash temperature
  System.out.println("Wash is "+ wash);
  switch(wash) {
    case wool:
      System.out.println("Temperature is 120.");
      break;
    case cotton:
      System.out.println("Temperature is 170.");
      break;
    case synthetic:
      System.out.println("Temperature is 130.");
      break;
    case linen:
      System.out.println("Temperature is 180.");
      break;
  }
  }
}
```

You should get the following output from this example:

```
Washing socks.
Wash is wool
Temperature is 120.
```

How It Works

This looks like a lot of code, but it's because of the number of cases in the two `switch` statements. You first define an enumeration type, `WashChoice`. You then define a variable of this type in the `main()` method with the following statement:

```
WashChoice wash = WashChoice.cotton;   // Variable to define the choice of wash
```

The initial value for `wash` here is arbitrary. You could have chosen any of the possible enumeration constants for the `WashChoice` type.

Next, you define and initialize a variable identifying the type of clothes to be washed:

```
int clothes = 3;
```

The initial value for `clothes` corresponds to socks and in a more practical example would be arrived at by means other than just assigning the value. You use the `clothes` variable to control the next `switch` statement. For each case in the `switch`, you output what is to be washed and set the value for the `wash` variable to the appropriate enumeration constant. You would usually put a default case in this sort of `switch` statement because its control expression is numeric, and if the value was derived by some computation or other, there is always the possibility of an invalid value being produced. If there is no default case and the `switch` expression results in a value that does not correspond to any of the cases, execution will just continue with the statement following the `switch` block.

After the first `switch`, you output the wash type:

```
System.out.println("Wash is "+ wash);
```

You saw in the previous chapter that the string representation of a value that is an enumeration constant is the name of the value as it appears in the type definition.

Lastly, you use the `wash` variable as the expression selecting a case in the next `switch`. Because a variable of an enumeration type must have an enumeration constant as a value, and all possible values are represented by cases in the `switch`, you don't need a default case here.

Note that you could have defined the values for the various types of clothes as constant values:

```
final int SHIRTS = 1;
final int SWEATERS = 2;
final int SOCKS = 3;
final int SHEETS = 4;
final int PANTS = 5;
```

The value set for the `clothes` variable would then have been much more obvious:

```
int clothes = SOCKS;
```

Of course, you could also have used an enumeration for the `clothes` type, too, but I'll leave you to work out what that would look like.

Variable Scope

The **scope** of a variable is the part of the program over which the variable name can be referenced — in other words, where you can use the variable in the program. Every variable that I have declared so far in program examples has been defined within the context of a method, the method `main()`. Variables that are declared within a method are called **local variables**, as they are only accessible within the confines of the method in which they are declared. However, they are not necessarily accessible everywhere in the code for the method in which they are declared. Look at the next code fragment, which shows variables defined within nested blocks:

```
{
    int n = 1;                          // Declare and define n

    // Reference to n is OK here
```

```
// Reference to m here is an error because m does not exist yet

{
  // Reference to n here is OK too
  // Reference to m here is still an error

  int m = 2;                                 // Declare and define m

  // Reference to m and n are OK here - they both exist
}       // m dies at this point

// Reference to m here is now an error
// Reference to n is still OK though
}         // n dies at this point so you can't refer to it in following statements
```

A variable does not exist before its declaration; you can refer to it only after it has been declared. It continues to exist until the end of the block in which it is defined, and that includes any blocks nested within the block containing its declaration. The variable n is created as the first statement in the outer block. It continues to exist within the inner block too. The variable m exists only within the inner block because that's where its declaration appears. After the brace at the end of the inner block, m no longer exists so you can't refer to it. The variable n is still around though and it survives until the closing brace of the outer block.

So, the rule that determines the accessibility of local variables is simple. Local variables are accessible only from the point in the program where they are declared to the end of the block that contains the declaration. At the end of the block in which they are declared, they cease to exist. I can demonstrate this with an example:

Try It Out   Scoping

Here's a version of the main() method that demonstrates how variable scope works:

```
public class Scope {
  public static void main(String[] args) {
    int outer = 1;                                 // Exists throughout the method

    {
      // You cannot refer to a variable before its declaration
      // System.out.println("inner = " + inner);   // Uncomment this for an error

      int inner = 2;
      System.out.println("inner = " + inner);       // Now it is OK
      System.out.println("outer = " + outer);       // and outer is still here

      // All variables defined in the enclosing outer block still exist,
      // so you cannot redefine them here
      // int outer = 5;                              // Uncomment this for an error
    }

    // Any variables declared in the previous inner block no longer exist
    // so you cannot refer to them
    // System.out.println("inner = " + inner);       // Uncomment this for an error
```

```
            // The previous variable, inner, does not exist so you can define a new one
            int inner = 3;
            System.out.println("inner = " + inner);     // ... and output its value
            System.out.println("outer = " + outer);     // outer is still around
      }
   }
```

As it stands, this program will produce the following output:

```
inner = 2
outer = 1
inner = 3
outer = 1
```

If you uncomment any or all of the three statements as suggested, it won't compile:

```
javac Scope.java
Scope.java:11: Undefined variable: inner
        System.out.println("inner = " + inner);   // Uncomment this for an error
                                          ^

1 error
javac Scope.java
Scope.java:19: Variable 'outer' is already defined in this method.
            int outer = 5;                         // Uncomment this for an error
                ^

1 error

javac Scope.java
Scope.java:23: Undefined variable: inner
          System.out.println("inner = " + inner);   // Uncomment this for an error
                                            ^

1 error
```

How It Works

The main() method in this program has one block nested inside the block that contains the code for the method. The variable outer is defined right at the start, so you can refer to this anywhere within the method main(), including inside the nested block. You are not allowed to re-declare a variable, so the commented statement that re-declares outer within the inner block will cause a compiler error if you remove the double slash at the beginning of the line.

The variable inner is defined inside the nested block with the initial value 2, and you can refer to it anywhere from its declaration to the end of the inner block. After the closing brace of the inner block, the variable inner no longer exists, so the commented output statement that refers to inner is illegal. However, since the variable inner has expired, you can declare another one with the same name and with the initial value 3.

Note that all this is just to demonstrate the lifetime of local variables. It is not good practice to redefine variables that have expired, because of the obvious potential for confusion. Also, although I have only used variables of type int in the preceding example, scoping rules apply to variables of any type.

> There are other variables called *class variables* that have much longer lifetimes when they are declared in a particular way. The variables PI and E in the standard library class Math are examples of these. They hang around as long as your program is executing. There are also variables that form part of a class object called *instance variables*. You'll learn more about these in Chapter 5.

Loops

A **loop** allows you to execute a statement or block of statements repeatedly. The need to repeat a block of code arises in almost every program. If you did the first exercise at the end of the last chapter, based on what you had learned up to that point, you would have come up with a program along the lines of the following:

```java
public class TryExample1_1 {
  public static void main(String[] args) {
    byte value = 1;
    value *= 2;
    System.out.println("Value is now "+value);
    value *= 2;
    System.out.println("Value is now "+value);
    value *= 2;
    System.out.println("Value is now "+value);
    value *= 2;
    System.out.println("Value is now "+value);
    value *= 2;
    System.out.println("Value is now "+value);
    value *= 2;
    System.out.println("Value is now "+value);
    value *= 2;
    System.out.println("Value is now "+value);
    value *= 2;
    System.out.println("Value is now "+value);
  }
}
```

The same pair of statements has been entered eight times. This is a rather tedious way of doing things. If the program for the company payroll had to include separate statements to do the calculation for each employee, it would never get written. A loop removes this sort of difficulty. You could write the method main() to do the same as the code above as follows:

```java
public static void main(String[] args) {
  byte value = 1;
  for (int i=0; i<8 ; i++) {
    value *= 2;
    System.out.println("Value is now " + value);
  }
}
```

This uses one particular kind of loop—called a `for` loop. The `for` loop statement on the third line causes the statements in the following block to be repeated eight times. The number of times it is to be repeated is determined by the stuff between parentheses following the keyword `for`—you'll see how in a moment. The point is you could, in theory, repeat the same block of statements as many times as you want—a thousand or a million or a billion—it is just as easy and it doesn't require any more lines of code. The primary purpose of the `for` loop is to execute a block of statements a given number of times.

In general, a loop has two parts to it; it has a **loop body**, which is a single statement or block of statements defining the code that is to be repeated, and it has a **loop control mechanism** that determines how many times the loop body will execute.

Varieties of Loop

There are four kinds of loop statements you can use. I'll introduce these in outline first to give an overview of all the possibilities:

1. The numerical `for` loop:

```
for (initialization_expression ; loop_condition ; increment_expression) {
    // statements
}
```

I have described this loop as the *numerical* `for` loop as a rough indication of how it is used, and to distinguish it from another variety of `for` loop that I'll come to in a moment. The numerical `for` loop is usually just referred to as a `for` loop. The loop body for this loop is the block of statements between the braces. This can be just a single statement, in which case the braces are optional. The code to control the `for` loop appears in parentheses following the keyword `for`.

As you can see, the loop control mechanism has three parts separated by semicolons. The first part, the `initialization_expression`, executes once before the loop starts. You typically use this expression to initialize a counter for the number of loop iterations—for example, `i = 0`. With a loop controlled by a counter, which can be an integer or a floating-point variable, you can count up or down by whatever increment or decrement you choose until the variable reaches some defined limit.

Execution of this loop continues as long as the condition you specify in the second part of the control mechanism, the `loop_condition`, is `true`. This expression is checked at the beginning of each loop iteration, and as long as it is true, the loop body executes. When `loop_condition` is `false`, the loop ends and execution continues with the statement following the loop block. For example, if you used `i<10` as the `loop_condition` expression, the loop would continue as long as the variable `i` has a value less than 10. The third part of the control information between the parentheses, the `increment_expression`, is usually used to increment the loop counter. This is executed at the end of each loop iteration. This could be `i++`, which would increment the loop counter, i, by one. Of course, you might want to increment the loop counter in steps other than 1. For example, you might write i += 2 as the increment_expression to go in steps of 2, or even something more complicated such as i = 2*i+1.

2. The collection-based for loop:

```
for (type identifier : iterable_expression) {
   // statements
}
```

You won't be able to fully appreciate the capabilities of this loop until you have learned about Collection classes in Chapter 14, so I'll just give you a brief indication here of what you can do with it so you know about all the loop statements you have available. This for loop has two control elements separated by a colon that appear between the parentheses following the for keyword. The first element is an identifier of the type that you specify, and the second is an expression specifying a collection of objects or values of the specified type. The loop will execute once for each item of the specified type that appears in the collection, and you can refer to the current item in the loop body using the identifier that you specified as the first control element. You can apply this form of for loop to arrays as well as collections. You will learn about arrays — and how you can use this loop with an array — in Chapter 4.

3. The while loop:

```
while (expression) {
   // statements
}
```

This loop executes as long as the logical expression between the parentheses is true. When expression is false, the loop ends and execution continues with the statement following the loop block. The expression is tested at the beginning of the loop, so if it is initially false, the loop body will not be executed at all. An example of a while loop condition might be yesNo=='Y' || yesNo=='y'. This expression would be true if the variable yesNo contained 'y' or 'Y', so yesNo might hold a character entered from the keyboard in this instance.

4. The do while loop:

```
do {
   // statements
} while (expression);
```

This loop is similar to the while loop, except that the expression controlling the loop is tested at the end of the loop block. This means that the loop body always executes at least once, even if the expression is always false.

The basic logic of each of the four kinds of loop is shown in Figure 3-6.

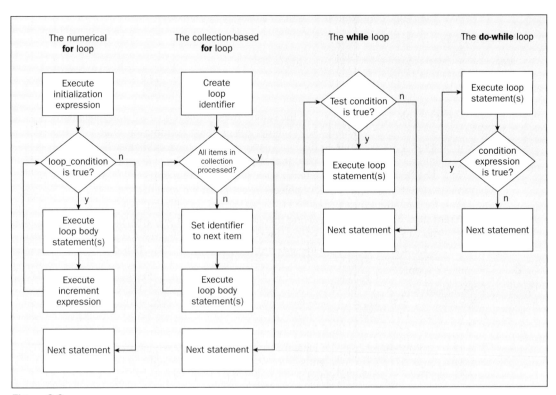

Figure 3-6

The two versions of the `for` loop have quite different mechanisms controlling the number of iterations. You can also see quite clearly that the primary difference between the `while` loop and the `do while` loop is where the test is carried out.

Let's explore each of these loops in turn and see how they work in a practical context.

Try It Out   The Numerical for Loop

Let's start with a very simple example. Suppose you want to calculate the sum of the integers from 1 to a given value. You can do this using the `for` loop as shown in the following example:

```
public class ForLoop {
  public static void main(String[] args) {
    int limit = 20;                      // Sum from 1 to this value
    int sum = 0;                         // Accumulate sum in this variable

    // Loop from 1 to the value of limit, adding 1 each cycle
    for(int i = 1; i <= limit; i++) {
      sum += i;                          // Add the current value of i to sum
```

```
        }
        System.out.println("sum = " + sum);
      }
    }
```

This program will produce the output

```
sum = 210
```

but you can try it out with different values for `limit`.

How It Works

All the work is done in the `for` loop. The loop counter is `i`, and this is declared and initialized within the `for` loop statement. The syntax of this `for` loop is shown in Figure 3-7.

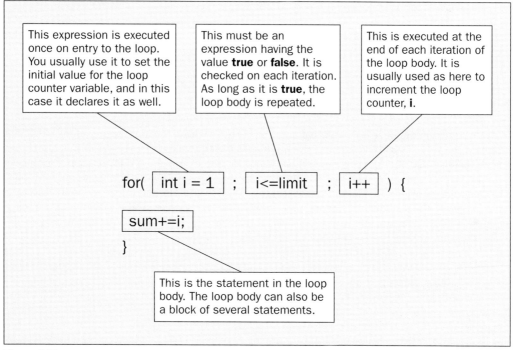

Figure 3-7

As you see, there are three elements that control the operation of the `for` loop, and they appear between the parentheses that follow the keyword `for`. In sequence, their purpose is to:

❑   Set the initial conditions for the loop, particularly the loop counter

❑   Specify the condition for the loop to continue

❑   Increment the loop counter

They are always separated by semicolons, but as you will see later, any or all of them can be omitted.

The first control element is executed when the loop is first entered. Here you declare and initialize the loop counter i. Because it is declared within the loop, it will not exist outside it. If you try to output the value of i after the loop with a statement such as

```
System.out.println("Final value of i = " + i);   // Will not work outside the loop
```

you'll find that the program will no longer compile.

Where the loop body consists of just a single statement, you can omit the braces and write the loop like this:

```
for (int i = 1; i <= limit; i++)
    sum += i;                           // Add the current value of i to sum
```

In general, it's better practice to keep the braces in as it makes it clearer where the loop body ends.

If you need to initialize and/or declare other variables for the loop, you can do it here by separating the declarations by commas. For example, you could write:

```
for (int i = 1, j = 0; i <= limit; i++) {
    sum += i * j++;                     // Add the current value of i*j to sum
}
```

In this fragment, I initialize an additional variable j, and, to make the loop vaguely sensible, I have modified the value to add the sum to i*j++, which is the equivalent of i*(i-1) in this case. Note that j will be incremented after the product i*j has been calculated. You could declare other variables here, but note that it would not make sense to declare sum at this point. If you can't figure out why, delete or comment out the original declaration of sum in the example and put it in the for loop instead to see what happens. The program won't compile—right? After the loop ends, the variable sum no longer exists, so you can't reference it. This is because all variables that you declare within the loop control expressions are logically within the block that is the body of the loop.

The second control element in a for loop is a logical expression that is checked at the beginning of each iteration through the loop. If the expression is true, the loop continues, the loop body executes, and as soon as it is false, the loop is finished. In our program, the loop ends when i is greater than the value of limit.

The third control element in a for loop typically increments the loop variable, as you have seen in the example. You can put multiple expressions here, too, so you could rewrite the previous code fragment that added j to the loop as:

```
for (int i = 1, j = 0; i <= limit; i++, j++) {
    sum+=i*j;                           // Add the current value of i*j to sum
}
```

Again, there can be several expressions here, and they do not need to relate directly to the control of the loop. You could even rewrite the original loop for summing integers so that the summation occurs in the loop control element:

```
for (int i = 1; i <= limit; sum += i, i++) {
    ;
}
```

Now the loop statement is empty — you just have the semicolon to terminate it. This version of the code doesn't really improve things though as it's certainly not so easy to see what is happening and there are hazards in writing the loop this way. If you were to reverse the sequence of adding to sum and incrementing i as follows:

```
for (int i = 1; i <= limit; i++, sum += i) {   // Wrong!!!
    ;
}
```

you would generate the wrong answer. This is because the expression i++ will be executed before sum += i, so the wrong value of i is used.

You can omit any or all of the elements that control the for loop, but you must include the semicolons. It is up to you to make sure that the loop does what you want. I could rewrite the loop in the program as:

```
for(int i = 1; i <= limit; ) {
    sum += i++;                              // Add the current value of i to sum
}
```

I have simply transferred the operation of incrementing i from the for loop control expression to the loop body. The for loop works just as before. However, this is not a good way to write the loop, as it makes it much less obvious how the loop counter is incremented.

Counting Using Floating-Point Values

You can use a floating-point variable as the loop counter if you need to. This may be needed when you are calculating the value of a function for a range of fractional values. Suppose you wanted to calculate the area of a circle with values for the radius from 1 to 2 in steps of 0.2. You could write this as:

```
for(double radius = 1.0; radius <= 2.0; radius += 0.2) {
    System.out.println("radius = " + radius + " area = " + Math.PI*radius*radius);
}
```

This will produce the following output:

```
radius = 1.0 area = 3.141592653589793
radius = 1.2 area = 4.523893421169302
radius = 1.4 area = 6.157521601035994
radius = 1.5999999999999999 area = 8.04247719318987
radius = 1.7999999999999998 area = 10.178760197630927
radius = 1.9999999999999998 area = 12.566370614359169
```

The area has been calculated using the formula (r^2 with the standard value PI defined in the Math class, which is 3.14159265358979323846. Although you may have intended the values of radius to increment from 1.0 to 2.0 in steps of 0.2, they don't quite make it. The value of radius is never exactly 2.0 or any of the other intermediate values because 0.2 cannot be represented exactly as a binary floating-point value. If you doubt this, and you are prepared to deal with an infinite loop, change the loop to:

```
// BE WARNED - THIS LOOP DOES NOT END
for(double radius = 1.0; radius != 2.0; radius += 0.2) {
  System.out.println("radius = " + radius + " area = " + Math.PI*radius*radius);
}
```

If the value of radius reaches 2.0, the condition radius ! =2.0 will be false and the loop will end, but unfortunately, it doesn't. Its last value before 2 will be approximately 1.999 . . . and the next value will be something like 2.1999 . . . and so it will never be 2.0. From this you can deduce a golden rule:

> **Never use tests that depend on an exact value for a floating-point variable to control a loop.**

Try It Out   The Collection-Based for Loop

You can't do a whole lot with the collection-based for loop yet. This will come into its own later in the book, especially after Chapter 14, and you'll be learning more about what you can do with it in the next chapter. One thing that it does apply to and that you have learned something about is an enumeration. Here's how you could apply the collection-based for loop to iterate through all the possible values in an enumeration:

```
public class CollectionForLoop {
  enum Season { spring, summer, fall, winter }   // Enumeration type definition

  public static void main(String[] args) {
    for(Season season : Season.values()) {       // Vary over all values
      System.out.println(" The season is now " + season);
    }
  }
}
```

This will generate the following output:

```
The season is now spring
The season is now summer
The season is now fall
The season is now winter
```

How It Works

Figure 3-8 shows the way the collection-based for loop works.

The season variable of type Season that appears in the first control expression between the parentheses for the for loop will be assigned a different enumeration constant value of each iteration of the loop. The second control expression, following the colon, identifies the collection that is the source of values for the variable declared in the first control expression. In this case it is an enumeration, but in general, there are other collections you can use, as you'll see in Chapter 14. In the next chapter you'll be learning about arrays where both forms of for loop can be used.

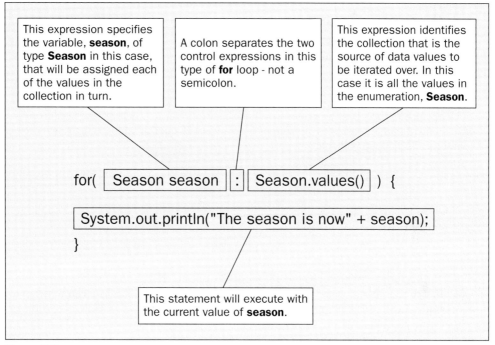

This expression specifies the variable, **season**, of type **Season** in this case, that will be assigned each of the values in the collection in turn.

A colon separates the two control expressions in this type of **for** loop - not a semicolon.

This expression identifies the collection that is the source of data values to be iterated over. In this case it is all the values in the enumeration, **Season**.

```
for( Season season : Season.values() ) {

    System.out.println("The season is now" + season);

}
```

This statement will execute with the current value of **season**.

Figure 3-8

In this example, the enumeration defines four values, spring, summer, fall, and winter, so the variable season will be assigned each of these values in turn, as the output shows.

Try It Out   The while Loop

You can write the program for summing integers again using the while loop, which will show you how the loop mechanism differs from the for loop:

```
public class WhileLoop {
  public static void main(String[] args) {
    int limit = 20;                      // Sum from 1 to this value
    int sum = 0;                         // Accumulate sum in this variable
    int i = 1;                           // Loop counter

    // Loop from 1 to the value of limit, adding 1 each cycle
    while(i <= limit) {
      sum += i++;                        // Add the current value of i to sum
    }
    System.out.println("sum = " + sum);
  }
}
```

You should get the following result:

```
sum = 210
```

How It Works

The `while` loop is controlled wholly by the logical expression that appears between the parentheses that follow the keyword `while`. The loop continues as long as this expression has the value `true`, and how it ever manages to arrive at the value `false` to end the loop is up to you. You need to be sure that the statements within the loop will eventually result in this expression being `false`. Otherwise, you have a loop that continues indefinitely.

How the loop ends in the example is clear. You have a simple count as before, and you increment i in the loop statement that accumulates the sum of the integers. Sooner or later i will exceed the value of `limit`, and the `while` loop will end.

You don't always need to use the testing of a count limit as the loop condition. You can use any logical condition you want.

Try It Out   The do while Loop

And last, but not least, you have the do `while` loop.

As I said at the beginning of this topic, the do `while` loop is much the same as the `while` loop, except for the fact that the continuation condition is checked at the end of the loop. You can write an integer-summing program with this kind of loop too:

```
public class DoWhileLoop {
  public static void main(String[] args) {
    int limit = 20;                     // Sum from 1 to this value
    int sum = 0;                        // Accumulate sum in this variable
    int i = 1;                          // Loop counter

    // Loop from 1 to the value of limit, adding 1 each cycle
    do {
      sum += i;                         // Add the current value of i to sum
      i++;
    } while(i <= limit);

    System.out.println("sum = " + sum);
  }
}
```

The output will be the same as the previous example.

How It Works

The statements within the loop are always executed at least once because the condition that determines whether the loop should continue is tested at the end of each iteration. Within the loop you add the value of i to sum, and then increment it. When i exceeds the value of `limit`, the loop ends, at which point sum will contain the sum of all the integers from 1 to `limit`.

The loop statement here has braces around the block of code that is within the loop. You could rewrite the loop so that only one statement was within the loop body, in which case the braces are not required. For example:

```
do
  sum += i;                          // Add the current value of i to sum
while(++i <= limit);
```

Of course, you can and should still put the braces in. I advise that you always use braces around the body of a loop, even when it is only a single statement.

There are often several ways of writing the code to produce a given result, and this is true here — you could also move the incrementing of the variable i back inside the loop and write it as follows:

```
do {
  sum += i++;                        // Add the current value of i to sum
} while (i <= limit);
```

The value of i is now incremented using the postfix increment operator. If you were to use the prefix form, you would get the wrong result. Note that the semicolon after the while condition is present in each version of the loop. This is part of the loop statement so you must not forget to put it in. The primary reason for using this loop over the while loop would be if you want to be sure that the loop code always executes at least once.

Nested Loops

You can nest loops of any kind one inside another to any depth. Let's look at an example where you can use nested loops.

A **factorial** of an integer, n, is the product of all the integers from 1 to n. It is written as $n!$. It may seem a little strange if you haven't come across it before, but the factorial of an integer is very useful for calculating combinations and permutations of things. For example, $n!$ is the number of ways you can arrange n different things in sequence, so a deck of cards can be arranged in 52! different sequences. Let's try calculating some factorial values.

Try It Out   Calculating Factorials

This example will calculate the factorial of every integer from 1 up to a given limit. Enter the following code:

```
public class Factorial {
  public static void main(String[] args) {
    long limit = 20L;         // Calculate factorials of integers up to this value
    long factorial = 1L;      // A factorial will be stored in this variable

    // Loop from 1 to the value of limit
    for (long i = 1L; i <= limit; i++) {
      factorial = 1L;         // Initialize factorial

      for (long factor = 2; factor <= i; factor++) {
        factorial *= factor;
      }
      System.out.println(i + "! is " + factorial);
    }
  }
}
```

This program will produce the following output:

```
1! is 1
2! is 2
3! is 6
4! is 24
5! is 120
6! is 720
7! is 5040
8! is 40320
9! is 362880
10! is 3628800
11! is 39916800
12! is 479001600
13! is 6227020800
14! is 87178291200
15! is 1307674368000
16! is 20922789888000
17! is 355687428096000
18! is 6402373705728000
19! is 121645100408832000
20! is 2432902008176640000
```

How It Works

All the variables used in this example are of type `long`. Factorial values grow very rapidly so by using type `long` you allow much larger factorials to be calculated than if you used type `int`. You still could have declared `factor` and `i` as type `int` without limiting the size of the factorial value that the program can produce, but the compiler would then need to insert casts to make the `int` values type `long` whenever they were involved in an operation with a value of type `long`.

The outer loop, controlled by `i`, walks through all the integers from 1 to the value of `limit`. In each iteration of the outer loop, the variable `factorial` is initialized to 1, and the nested loop calculates the factorial of the current value of `i` using `factor` as the control counter that runs from 2 to the current value of `i`. The resulting value of `factorial` is then displayed before going to the next iteration of the outer loop.

Although you have nested a `for` loop inside another `for` loop here, as I said at the outset, you can nest any kind of loop inside any other. You could have written the nested loop as:

```java
for (long i = 1L; i <= limit; i++) {
  factorial = 1L;            // Initialize factorial
  long factor = 2L;
  while (factor <= i) {
    factorial *= factor++;
  }
  System.out.println(i + "! is " + factorial);
}
```

Now you have a `while` loop nested in a `for` loop. It works just as well, but it is rather more naturally coded as two nested `for` loops because they are both controlled by a counter.

If you have been concentrating, you may well have noticed that you don't really need nested loops to display the factorial of successive integers. You can do it with a single loop that multiplies the current factorial value by the loop counter. However, this would be a very poor demonstration of a nested loop.

The continue Statement

There are situations where you may want to skip all or part of a loop iteration. Suppose you want to sum the values of the integers from 1 to some limit, except that you don't want to include integers that are multiples of three. You can do this using an `if` and a `continue` statement:

```
for(int i = 1; i <= limit; i++) {
  if(i % 3 == 0) {
    continue;                         // Skip the rest of this iteration
  }
  sum += i;                           // Add the current value of i to sum
}
```

The `continue` statement is executed in this example when i is an exact multiple of 3, causing the rest of the current loop iteration to be skipped. Program execution continues with the next iteration if there is one, and if not, with the statement following the end of the loop block. The `continue` statement can appear anywhere within a block of loop statements. You may even have more than one `continue` in a loop.

The Labeled continue Statement

Where you have nested loops, there is a special form of the `continue` statement that enables you to stop executing the inner loop — not just the current iteration of the inner loop — and continue at the beginning of the next iteration of the outer loop that immediately encloses the current loop. This is called the **labeled continue statement**.

To use the labeled `continue` statement, you need to identify the loop statement for the enclosing outer loop with a **statement label**. A statement label is simply an identifier that is used to reference a particular statement. When you need to reference a particular statement, you write the statement label at the beginning of the statement in question, separated from the statement by a colon. Let's look at an example:

Try It Out   **Labeled continue**

You could add a labeled `continue` statement to omit the calculation of factorials of odd numbers greater than 10. This is not the best way to do this, but it does demonstrate how the labeled `continue` statement works:

```
public class Factorial2 {
  public static void main(String[] args) {
    long limit = 20L;           // to calculate factorial of integers up to this value
    long factorial = 1L;        // factorial will be calculated in this variable

    // Loop from 1 to the value of limit
```

```
        OuterLoop:
        for(long i = 1L; i <= limit; i++) {
          factorial = 1;                    // Initialize factorial
          for(long j = 2L; j <= i; j++) {
            if(i > 10L && i % 2L == 1L) {
              continue OuterLoop;           // Transfer to the outer loop
            }
            factorial *= j;
          }
          System.out.println(i + "! is " + factorial);
        }
      }
    }
```

If you run this it will produce the following output:

```
1! is 1
2! is 2
3! is 6
4! is 24
5! is 120
6! is 720
7! is 5040
8! is 40320
9! is 362880
10! is 3628800
12! is 479001600
14! is 87178291200
16! is 20922789888000
18! is 6402373705728000
20! is 2432902008176640000
```

How It Works

The outer loop has the label OuterLoop. In the inner loop, when the condition in the if statement is true, the labeled continue is executed causing an immediate transfer to the beginning of the next iteration of the outer loop. The condition in the if statements causes the calculation of the factorial to be skipped for odd values greater than 10.

In general, you can use the labeled continue to exit from an inner loop to any enclosing outer loop, not just the one immediately enclosing the loop containing the labeled continue statement.

Using the break Statement in a Loop

You have seen how to use the break statement in a switch block. Its effect is to exit the switch block and continue execution with the first statement after the switch. You can also use the break statement to break out from a loop. When break is executed within a loop, the loop ends immediately, and execution continues with the first statement following the loop. To demonstrate this, you will write a program to find prime numbers. In case you have forgotten, a prime number is an integer that is only exactly divisible by itself and 1.

Try It Out   **Calculating Primes I**

There's a little more code to this than the previous example. This program will find all the primes from 2 to 50:

```
public class Primes {
   public static void main(String[] args) {
      int nValues = 50;                  // The maximum value to be checked
      boolean isPrime = true;            // Is true if we find a prime

      // Check all values from 2 to nValues
      for(int i = 2; i <= nValues; i++) {
         isPrime=true;                   // Assume the current i is prime

         // Try dividing by all integers from 2 to i-1
         for(int j = 2; j < i; j++) {
            if(i % j == 0) {             // This is true if j divides exactly
               isPrime = false;          // If we got here, it was an exact division
               break;                    // so exit the loop
            }
         }
         // We can get here through the break, or through completing the loop
         if(isPrime)                     // So is it prime?
            System.out.println(i);       // Yes, so output the value
      }
   }
}
```

You should get the following output:

```
2
3
5
7
11
13
17
19
23
29
31
37
41
43
47
```

How It Works

There are much more efficient ways to calculate primes, but this program does demonstrate the break statement in action. The first step in main() is to declare two variables:

```
int nValues = 50;                  // The maximum value to be checked
boolean isPrime = true;            // Is true if we find a prime
```

The first variable is the upper limit for integers to be checked to see if they are prime. The isPrime variable will be used to record whether a particular value is prime or not.

The basic idea of the program is to go through the integers from 2 to the value of nValues and check each one to see if it has an integer divisor less than itself. The nested loops do this:

```
for(int i = 2; i <= nValues; i++) {
  isPrime=true;                 // Assume the current i is prime

  // Try dividing by all integers from 2 to i-1
  for(int j = 2; j < i; j++) {
    if(i % j == 0) {            // This is true if j divides exactly
      isPrime = false;          // If we got here, it was an exact division
      break;                    // so exit the loop
    }
  }
  // We can get here through the break, or through completing the loop
  if(isPrime)                   // So is it prime?
    System.out.println(i);      // Yes, so output the value
}
```

The outer loop is indexed by i and steps through the possible values that need to be checked for primeness. The inner loop is indexed by j, the value of j being a trial divisor. This determines whether any integer less than the value being tested for primality is an exact divisor.

The checking is done in the if statement in the inner loop. If j divides i exactly, i%j will be 0, so isPrime will be set to false. In this case the break will execute to exit the inner loop — there is no point in continuing as you now know that the value being tested is not prime. The next statement to be executed will be the if statement after the closing brace of the inner loop block. You can also reach this point by a normal exit from the loop that occurs when the value is prime so you need a way to determine whether the current value of i was found to be prime or not. The isPrime variable solves this problem. You just check the value of isPrime and if it has the value true, you have a prime to display so you execute the println() call.

You could simplify this example if you used the labeled continue statement instead of the break statement:

Try It Out   Calculating Primes II

Try the following changes to the code in the Primes class:

```
public class Primes2 {
  public static void main(String[] args) {
    int nValues = 50;                      // The maximum value to be checked

    // Check all values from 2 to nValues
    OuterLoop:
    for(int i = 2; i <= nValues; i++) {
      // Try dividing by all integers from 2 to i-1
      for(int j = 2; j < i; j++) {
        if(i%j == 0) {                     // This is true if j divides exactly
```

```
        continue OuterLoop;        // so exit the loop
      }
    }
    // We only get here if we have a prime
    System.out.println(i);         // so output the value
  }
}
}
```

If you've keyed it in correctly, you'll get the same output as the previous example.

How It Works

You no longer need the `isPrime` variable to indicate whether you have a prime or not, as the output statement can be reached only through a normal exit from the inner loop. When this occurs it means you have found a prime. If you get an exact divisor in the inner loop, it implies that the current value of `i` is not prime, so the labeled `continue` statement transfers immediately to the next iteration of the outer loop.

Breaking Indefinite Loops

You will find that sometimes you need to use a loop where you don't know in advance how many iterations will be required. This can arise when you are processing external data items that you might be reading in from the keyboard, for example, and you cannot know in advance how many there will be. You can often use a `while` loop in these circumstances, with the loop condition determining when the loop should end, but sometimes it can be convenient to use an indefinite loop instead and use a `break` statement in the loop body to end the loop. An indefinite loop is a loop where the control condition is such that the loop apparently continues to execute indefinitely. In this case, the mechanism to end the loop must be in the body of the loop.

Try It Out   Calculating Primes III

Suppose you want the `Primes` program to generate a given number of primes, rather than check up to a given integer value. In this case, you don't know how many numbers you need to check to generate the required number of primes. This is a case where an indefinite loop is useful. You can code this as follows:

```
public class FindPrimes {
  public static void main(String[] args) {
    int nPrimes = 50;                   // The maximum number of primes required

    OuterLoop:
    for(int i = 2; ; i++) {             // This loop runs forever

      // Try dividing by all integers from 2 to i-1
      for(int j = 2; j < i; j++) {
        if(i % j == 0) {                // This is true if j divides exactly
          continue OuterLoop;           // so exit the loop
        }
      }
      // We only get here if we have a prime
      System.out.println(i);            // so output the value
```

```
         if(--nPrimes == 0) {              // Decrement the prime count
            break;                         // It is zero so we have them all
         }
      }
   }
}
```

This program will output the first 50 primes.

How It Works

This program is very similar to the previous version. The principal differences are that nPrimes contains the number of primes required, so the program will produce the first 50 primes, instead of finding the primes between 2 and 50, and the for outer loop, controlled by i, has the loop condition omitted, so the loop has no direct mechanism for ending it. The loop must be terminated by the code within the loop; otherwise, it will continue to execute indefinitely.

Here the termination of the outer loop is controlled by the if statement following the output statement. As you find each prime, the value is displayed, after which the value of nPrimes is decremented in the if statement:

```
   if(--nPrimes == 0) {        // Decrement the prime count
      break;                   // It is zero so we have them all
   }
```

The break statement will be executed when nPrimes has been decremented to zero, and this will exit the outer loop.

The Labeled break Statement

Java also makes a labeled break statement available to you. This enables you to jump immediately to the statement following the end of any enclosing statement block or loop that is identified by the label in the labeled break statement. The label precedes the opening brace of the block that it identifies. Figure 3-9 illustrates how the labeled break statement works.

The labeled break enables you to break out to the statement following an enclosing block or loop that has an identifying label, regardless of how many levels of nested blocks there are. You might have several loops nested one within the other, for example, where you could use the labeled break to exit from the innermost loop (or indeed any of them) to the statement following the outermost loop. You just need to add a label to the beginning of the relevant block or loop that you want to break out of, and use that label in the break statement.

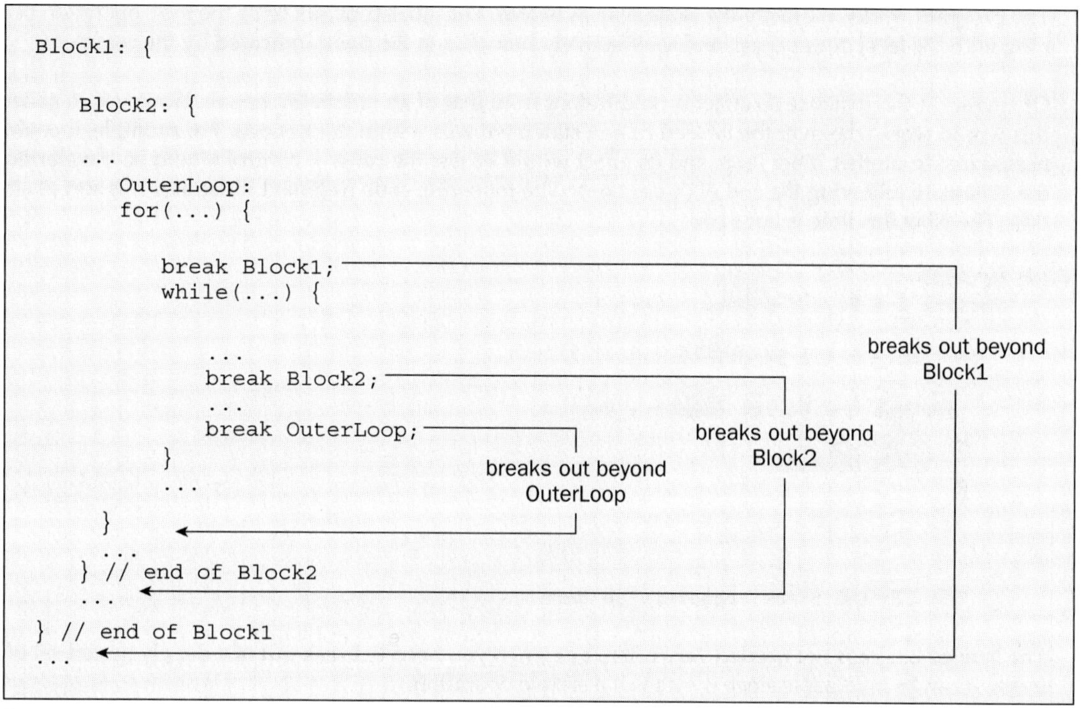

```
Block1: {

    Block2: {

    ...
        OuterLoop:
        for(...) {

            break Block1;
            while(...) {

                ...
                break Block2;
                ...
                break OuterLoop;
            }
            ...
        }
        ...
    } // end of Block2
    ...
} // end of Block1
...
```

breaks out beyond
OuterLoop

breaks out beyond
Block2

breaks out beyond
Block1

Figure 3-9

Just to see it working you can alter the previous example to use a labeled break statement:

```java
public class FindPrimes2 {
  public static void main(String[] args) {
    int nPrimes = 50;                      // The maximum number of primes required

    // Check all values from 2 to nValues
    OuterLoop:
    for(int i = 2; ; i++) {                         // This loop runs forever

      // Try dividing by all integers from 2 to i-1
      for(int j = 2; j < i; j++) {
        if(i % j == 0) {                   // This is true if j divides exactly
          continue OuterLoop;              // so exit the loop
        }
      }
      // We only get here if we have a prime
      System.out.println(i);               // so output the value
      if(--nPrimes == 0) {                 // Decrement the prime count
        break OuterLoop;                   // It is zero so we have them all
      }
    }
    // break OuterLoop goes to here
  }
}
```

The program works in exactly the same way as before. The labeled `break` ends the loop operation beginning with the label `OuterLoop`, and so effectively branches to the point indicated by the comment.

Of course, in this instance its effect is no different from that of an unlabeled `break`. However, in general this would work wherever the labeled `break` statement was within `OuterLoop`. For example, it could be nested inside another inner loop, and its effect would be just the same — control would be transferred to the statement following the end of `OuterLoop`. The following code fragment illustrates this sort of situation. The label this time is `Outside`:

```
Outside:
for(int i = 0 ; i< count1 ; i++) {
  ...
  for(int j = 0 ; j< count2 ; j++) {
    ...
    for(int k = 0 ; k< count3 ; k++) {
      ...
      break Outside;
      ...
    }
  }
}
// The labeled break transfers to here...
```

The labeled `break` is not needed very often, but when you need to break out of a deeply nested set of loops, it can be invaluable since it makes it a simple operation.

Assertions

Every so often you will find that the logic in your code leads to some logical condition that should always be `true`. If you test an integer and establish that it is odd, it is certainly true that it cannot be even, for example. You may also find yourself writing a statement or statements that, although they could be executed in theory, in practice they never really should be. I don't mean by this the usual sorts of errors that occur, such as some incorrect data being entered somehow, which should be handled ordinarily by the normal code. I mean circumstances where if the statements were to be executed, it would imply that something was very seriously wrong with the program or its environment. These are precisely the circumstances to which **assertions** apply.

A simple assertion is a statement of the form

```
assert logical_expression;
```

Here, `assert` is a keyword, and `logical_expression` is any expression that results in a value of `true` or `false`. When this statement executes, if `logical_expression` evaluates to `true`, then the program continues normally. If `logical_expression` evaluates to `false`, the program will be terminated with an error message starting with:

```
java.lang.AssertionError
```

This will be followed by more information about where the error occurred in the code. When this occurs, the program is said to *assert*.

Let's consider an example. Suppose you have a variable of type int that stores the number of days in the current month. You might use it like this:

```
if(daysInMonth == 30) {
   System.out.println("Month is April, June, September, or November");

} else if(daysInMonth == 31) {
   System.out.println(
             "Month is January, March, May, July, August, October, or December.");
} else {
   assert daysInMonth == 28 || daysInMonth == 29;
   System.out.println("Month is February.");
}
```

You are presuming that daysInMonth is valid — that is, it has one of the values 28, 29, 30, or 31. Maybe it came from a file that is supposed to be accurate so you should not need to check it, but if it turns out not to be valid, the assertion will detect it and end the program.

You could have written this slightly differently:

```
if(daysInMonth == 30) {
   System.out.println("Month is April, June, September, or November");

} else if(daysInMonth == 31) {
   System.out.println(
             "Month is January, March, May, July, August, October, or December.");

} else if(daysInMonth == 28 || daysInMonth == 29) {
   System.out.println("Month is February.");

} else {
   assert false;
}
```

Here, if daysInMonth is valid, the program should never execute the last else clause. An assertion with the logical expression as false will always assert, and terminate the program.

For assertions to have an effect when you run your program, you must specify the -enableassertions option. For example:

```
java -enableassertions MyProg
```

You can also use its abbreviated form -ea:

```
java -ea MyProg
```

If you don't specify this option when you run the program, assertions will be ignored.

More Complex Assertions

There is a slightly more complex form of assertions that have this form:

```
assert logical_expression : string_expression;
```

Here, `logical_expression` must evaluate to a `boolean` value, either `true` or `false`. If `logical_expression` is `false` then the program will terminate with an error message including the string that results from `string_expression`.

For example, you could have written the assertion in the last code fragment as:

```
assert false : "daysInMonth has the value " + daysInMonth;
```

Now if the program asserts, the output will include information about the value of `daysInMonth`.

Let's see how it works in practice.

Try It Out   A Working Assertion

Here's some code that is guaranteed to assert—if you compile and execute it right:

```
public class TryAssertions {
  public static void main(String args[]) {
    int daysInMonth = 32;
    if(daysInMonth == 30) {
      System.out.println("Month is April, June, September, or November");

    } else if(daysInMonth == 31) {
      System.out.println(
            "Month is January, March, May, July, August, October, or December.");

    } else if(daysInMonth == 28 || daysInMonth == 29) {
      System.out.println("Month is February.");

    } else {
      assert false;
    }
  }
}
```

Don't forget that, once you have compiled the program, you must execute it with assertions enabled, like this:

```
java -enableassertions TryAssertions
```

You should then get the following output:

```
java.lang.AssertionError
 at TryAssertions.main(TryAssertions.java:15)
Exception in thread "main"
```

How It Works

Since you have set `daysInMonth` to an invalid value, the assertion statement is executed, and that results in the error message. You could try out the other form of the assertion in the example:

```
assert false : "daysInMonth has the value " + daysInMonth;
```

Now you should see that the output includes the string resulting from the second expression in the assertion statement:

```
java.lang.AssertionError: daysInMonth has the value 32
  at TryAssertions.main(TryAssertions.java:15)
Exception in thread "main"
```

I will use assertions from time to time in the examples in subsequent chapters.

Summary

In this chapter you have learned about all of the essential mechanisms for making decisions in Java. You have also learned all of the looping facilities that you have available when programming in Java. The essential points I have covered are:

- ❑ You can use **relational operators** to compare values, and such comparisons result in values of either `true` or `false`.

- ❑ You can combine basic comparisons and logical variables in more complex logical expressions by using **logical operators**.

- ❑ The `if` statement is a basic decision-making tool in Java. It enables you to choose to execute a block of statements if a given logical expression has the value `true`. You can optionally execute another block of statements if the logical expression is `false` by using the `else` keyword.

- ❑ You can use the **conditional operator** to choose between two expressions depending on the value of a logical expression.

- ❑ You can use the `switch` statement to choose from a fixed number of alternatives.

- ❑ The variables in a method come into existence at the point at which you declare them and cease to exist after the end of the block that immediately encloses their declaration. The program extent where the variable is accessible is the **scope** of the variable.

- ❑ You have four ways of repeating a block of statements: a numerical `for` loop, a collection-based `for` loop, a `while` loop, or a `do while` loop.

- ❑ The `continue` statement enables you to skip to the next iteration in the loop containing the `continue` statement.

- ❑ The labeled `continue` statement enables you to skip to the next iteration in a loop enclosing the labeled `continue` that is identified by the label. The labeled loop need not be that immediately enclosing the labeled `continue`.

- ❑ The `break` statement enables you to break out of a loop or block of statements in which it appears.

❑   The labeled `break` statement enables you to break out of a loop or block of statements that encloses it that is identified by the label. This is not necessarily the block that encloses it directly.

❑   You use an assertion statement to verify logical conditions that should always be `true`, or as code in parts of a program that should not be reached, but theoretically can be.

Exercises

You can download the source code for the examples in the book and the solutions to the following exercises from `http://www.wrox.com`.

1.   Write a program to display a random choice from a set of six choices for breakfast (you could use any set; for example, scrambled eggs, waffles, fruit, cereal, toast, or yogurt).

2.   When testing whether an integer is a prime, it is sufficient to try to divide by integers up to the square root of the number being tested. Rewrite the program example from this chapter to use this approach.

3.   A lottery requires that you select six different numbers from the integers 1 to 49. Write a program to do this for you and generate five sets of entries.

4.   Write a program to generate a random sequence of capital letters that does not include vowels.

Arrays and Strings

In this chapter you'll start to use Java objects. You'll first be introduced to arrays, which enable you to deal with a number of variables of the same type through a single variable name, and then you'll look at how to handle character strings. By the end of this chapter you'll have learned:

- ❑ What arrays are and how you declare and initialize them
- ❑ How you access individual elements of an array
- ❑ How you can use individual elements of an array
- ❑ How to declare arrays of arrays
- ❑ How you can create arrays of arrays with different lengths
- ❑ How to create `String` objects
- ❑ How to create and use arrays of `String` objects
- ❑ What operations are available for `String` objects
- ❑ What `StringBuffer` objects are and how they relate to operations on `String` objects
- ❑ What operations are available for `StringBuffer` objects

Some of what I discuss in this chapter relates to objects, and as I have not yet covered in detail how you define a class (which is an object type definition), I will have to skate over some aspects of how objects work, but all will be revealed in Chapter 5.

Arrays

With the basic built-in Java data types that you've seen in the previous chapters, each identifier corresponds to a single variable. But when you want to handle sets of values of the same type — the first 1,000 primes, for example — you really don't want to have to name them individually. What you need is an **array**.

Let's first get a rough idea of what an array is and how it works. An array is an object that is a named set of variables of the same type. Each variable in the array is called an **array element**. To reference a particular element in an array, you use the array name combined with an integer value of type int, called an **index**. You put the index between square brackets following the array name; for example, data[99] refers to the element in the data array corresponding to the index value 99. The index for an array element is the offset of that particular element from the beginning of the array. The first element will have an index of 0, the second will have an index of 1, the third an index of 2, and so on. Thus, data[99] refers to the hundredth element in the data array. The index value does not need to be an integer literal. It can be any expression that results in a value of type int that is equal to or greater than zero. Obviously a for loop is going to be very useful for processing array elements — which is one reason why you had to wait until now to hear about arrays.

Array Variables

An array variable and the array it refers to are separate entities. The memory that is allocated for an array variable stores a **reference** to an array object, not the array itself. The array object itself is a distinct entity that will be elsewhere in memory. All variables that refer to objects store references that record the memory locations of the objects they refer to.

You are not obliged to create an array when you declare an array variable. You can first create the array variable and later use it to store a reference to a particular array.

You could declare the integer array variable primes with the following statement:

```
int[] primes;            // Declare an integer array variable
```

The variable primes is now a placeholder for an integer array that you have yet to define. No memory has been allocated to hold an array itself at this point. The primes variable is simply a location in memory that can store a reference to an array. You will see in a moment that to create the array itself you must specify its type and how many elements it is to contain. The square brackets following the type in the previous statement indicates that the variable is for referencing an array of int values, and not for storing a single value of type int. The type of the array variable is int[].

You may come across an alternative notation for declaring an array variable:

```
int primes[];            // Declare an integer array variable
```

Here the square brackets appear after the variable name, rather than after the type name. This is exactly equivalent to the previous statement so you can use either notation. Many programmers prefer the original notation, as int[] tends to indicate more clearly that the type is an array of values of type int.

Defining an Array

Once you have declared an array variable, you can define an array that it will reference:

```
primes = new int[10];        // Define an array of 10 integers
```

This statement creates an array that will store 10 values of type int, and stores a **reference** to the array in the variable primes. The reference is simply where the array is in memory. You could also declare the array variable and define the array of type int to hold 10 prime numbers with a single statement, as shown in Figure 4-1.

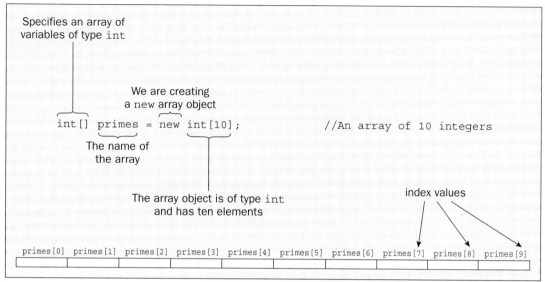

Figure 4-1

The first part of the definition specifies the type of the array. The element type name, int in this case, is followed by an empty pair of square brackets to indicate you are declaring an array rather than a single variable of type int. The part the statement that follows the equals sign defines the array. The keyword new indicates that you are allocating new memory for the array, and int[10] specifies you want capacity for 10 variables of type int in the array. Since each element in the primes array is a variable of type int that requires 4 bytes, the whole array will occupy 40 bytes, plus 4 bytes for the primes variable to store the reference to the array. When an array is created like this, all the array elements are initialized to a default value automatically. The initial value is zero in the case of an array of numerical values, is false for boolean arrays, is '\u0000' for arrays storing type char, and is null for an array of a class type.

Consider the statement:

```
double[] myArray = new double[100];
```

This statement is a declaration of the array variable myArray. The statement also defines the array, since the array size is specified. The variable myArray will refer to an array of 100 values of type double, and each element will have the value 0.0 assigned by default. Because there are 100 elements in this array, the legal index values range from 0 to 99.

The Length of an Array

You can refer to the length of the array — the number of elements it contains — using length, a data member of the array object. For example, for the array myArray that you defined in the previous section, you can refer to its length as myArray.length, which will have the value 100. You can use the length member of an array to control a numerical for loop that iterates over the elements of an array.

Accessing Array Elements

As I mentioned earlier, you refer to an element of an array by using the array name followed by the element's index value enclosed between square brackets. You can specify an index value by any expression that produces a zero or positive result of type int. If you use a value of type long as an index, you will get an error message from the compiler; if your calculation of an index uses long variables and the result is of type long, you will need to cast it to type int. You will no doubt recall from Chapter 2 that arithmetic expressions involving values of type short and type byte produce a result of type int, so you can use those in an index expression.

You refer to the first element of the primes array that was declared previously as primes[0], and you reference the fifth element in the array as primes[4]. The maximum index value for an array is one less than the number of elements in the array. Java checks that the index values you use are valid. If you use an index value that is less than 0, or greater than the index value for the last element in the array, an **exception** will be thrown — throwing an exception is just the way errors at execution time are signaled, and there are different types of exceptions for signaling various kinds of errors. The exception type in this case is an IndexOutOfBoundsException. When such an exception is thrown, your program will normally be terminated. You'll be looking at exceptions in detail in Chapter 7, including how you can deal with exceptions and prevent termination of your program.

The primes array is an example of what is sometimes referred to as a **one-dimensional array**, because each of its elements is referenced using one index — running from 0 to 9 in this case. You'll see later that arrays can also have two or more dimensions, the number of dimensions being the same as the number of indexes required to access an element of the array.

Reusing Array Variables

As I explained at the beginning of this chapter, an array variable is separate from the array that it references. Rather like the way an ordinary variable can store different values at different times, you can use an array variable to store a reference to different arrays at different points in your program. Suppose you have declared and defined the variable primes as before, like this:

```
int[] primes = new int[10];    // Allocate an array of 10 integer elements
```

This produces an array of 10 elements of type int. Perhaps a bit later in your program you want to use the array variable primes to refer to a larger array, with 50 elements, say. You could simply write:

```
primes = new int[50];          // Allocate an array of 50 integer elements
```

Now the primes variable refers to a new array of values of type int that is entirely separate from the original. When this statement is executed, the previous array of 10 elements is discarded, along with all the data values you may have stored in it. The variable primes can now be used to reference only elements of the new array. This is illustrated in Figure 4-2.

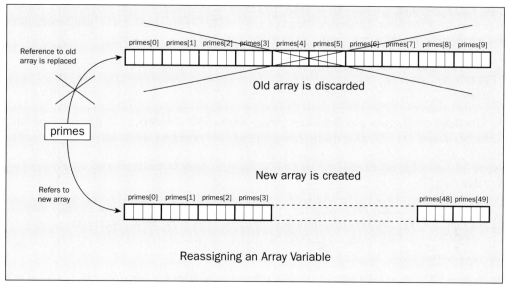

Figure 4-2

After executing the statement shown in Figure 4-2, the array variable `primes` now points to a new integer array of 50 elements with index values running from 0 to 49. Although you can change the array that an array variable references, you can't alter the type of value that an element stores. All the arrays referenced by a given variable must correspond to the original type that you specified when you declared the array variable. The variable `primes`, for example, can only reference arrays of type `int[]`. You have used an array of elements of type `int` in the illustration, but the same thing applies equally well when you are working with arrays of elements of type `long` or `double` or of any other type. Of course, you are not restricted to working with arrays of elements of primitive types. You can create arrays of elements to store references to any type of object, including objects of the classes that you will be defining yourself in Chapter 5.

Initializing Arrays

You can initialize the elements in an array with your own values when you declare it, and at the same time determine how many elements it will have. To do this, you simply add an equals sign followed by the list of element values enclosed between braces following the specification of the array variable. For example, you could define and initialize an array with the following statement:

```
int[] primes = {2, 3, 5, 7, 11, 13, 17};    // An array of 7 elements
```

This creates the `primes` array with sufficient elements to store all of the initializing values that appear between the braces — seven in this case. The array size is determined by the number of initial values so no other information is necessary to define the array. The values are assigned to the array elements in sequence so in this example `primes[0]` will have the initial value 2, `primes[1]` will have the initial value 3, `primes[2]` will have the initial value 5, and so on through the rest of the elements in the array.

If you specify initializing values for an array, you must include values for *all* the elements. If you want to set only some of the array elements to specific values explicitly, you must use an assignment statement for each element for which you supply a value. For example:

```
int[] primes = new int[100];
primes[0] = 2;
primes[1] = 3;
```

The first statement declares and defines an integer array of 100 elements, all of which will be initialized to zero by default. The two assignment statements then set values for the first two array elements.

You can also initialize the elements in an array using a `for` loop to iterate over all the elements and set the value for each:

```
double[] data = new double[50];         // An array of 50 values of type double
for(int i = 0 ; i<data.length ; i++) { // i from 0 to data.length-1
   data[i] = 1.0;
}
```

For an array with `length` elements, the index values for the elements run from 0 to `length-1`. The `for` loop control statement is written so that the loop variable `i` starts at 0 and will be incremented by 1 on each iteration up to `data.length-1`. When `i` is incremented to `data.length`, the loop will end. Thus, this loop sets each element of the array to 1. Using a `for` loop in this way is one standard idiom for iterating over the elements in an array. You'll see later that you can use the collection-based `for` loop for iterating over and *accessing* the values of the array elements. Here you are *setting* the values so the collection-based `for` loop cannot be applied.

Using a Utility Method to Initialize an Array

You can also use a method that is defined in the `Arrays` class in the `java.util` package to initialize an array. For example, to initialize the data array defined as in the previous fragment, you could use the following statement:

```
Arrays.fill(data, 1.0);                    // Fill all elements of data with 1.0
```

The first argument to the `fill()` method is the name of the array to be filled. The second argument is the value to be used to set the elements. This method will work for arrays of any primitive type. Of course, for this statement to compile correctly you would need an `import` statement at the beginning of the source file:

```
import java.util.Arrays;
```

This statement imports the `Arrays` class name into the source file so you can use it as you have in the preceding code line. Without the `import` statement, you can still access the `Arrays` class using the fully qualified name. In this case the statement to initialize the array would be:

```
java.util.Arrays.fill(data, 1.0);          // Fill all elements of data with 1.0
```

This is just as good as the previous version of the statement.

Of course, because `fill()` is a static method in the `Arrays` class, you could import the method name into your source file:

```
import static java.util.Arrays.fill;
```

Now you can call the method with the name unadorned with the class name:

```
fill(data, 1.0);                        // Fill all elements of data with 1.0
```

Initializing an Array Variable

You can initialize an array variable with a reference to an existing array. For example, you could declare the following array variables:

```
long[] even = {2L, 4L, 6L, 8L, 10L};
long[] value = even;
```

Here the array reference stored in `even` is used to initialize the array `value` in its declaration. This has the effect shown in Figure 4-3.

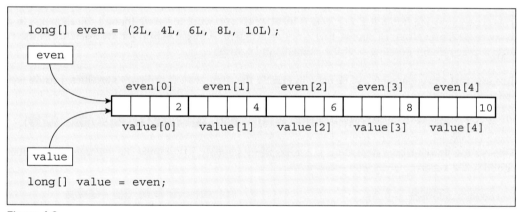

Figure 4-3

You have created two array variables, but you have only one array. Both arrays refer to the same set of elements, and you can access the elements of the array through either variable name — for example, `even[2]` refers to the same variable as `value[2]`. One use for this is when you want to switch the arrays referenced by two variables. If you were sorting an array by repeatedly transferring elements from one array to another, by flipping the array you were copying from with the array you were copying to, you could use the same code. For example, if you declared array variables as:

```
double[] inputArray = new double[100];    // Array to be sorted
double[] outputArray = new double[100];   // Reordered array
double[] temp;                            // Temporary array reference
```

when you want to switch the array referenced by `outputArray` to be the new input array, you could write:

```
temp = inputArray;          // Save reference to inputArray in temp
inputArray = outputArray;   // Set inputArray to refer to outputArray
outputArray = temp;         // Set outputArray to refer to what was inputArray
```

None of the array elements are moved here. Just the addresses of where the arrays are located in memory are swapped, so this is a very fast process. Of course, if you want to replicate an array, you have to define a new array of the same size and type, and then copy the value of each element of the old array individually to your new array.

Using Arrays

You can use array elements in expressions in exactly the same way as you might use a single variable of the same data type. For example, if you declare an array samples, you can fill it with random values between 0.0 and 100.0 with the following code:

```
double[] samples = new double[50];      // An array of 50 double values
for(int i = 0; i < samples.length; i++) {
  samples[i] = 100.0*Math.random();     // Generate random values
}
```

This shows how the numerical for loop is ideal when you want to iterate though the elements in an array to set their values. Of course, this is not an accident. A major reason for the existence of the for loop is precisely for iterating over the elements in an array.

To show that array elements can be used in exactly the same way as ordinary variables, I could write the following statement:

```
double result = (samples[10]*samples[0] - Math.sqrt(samples[49]))/samples[29];
```

This is a totally arbitrary calculation, of course. More sensibly, to compute the average of the values stored in the samples array, you could write:

```
double average = 0.0;                    // Variable to hold the average

for(int i = 0; i < samples.length; i++) {
  average += samples[i];                 // Sum all the elements
}
average /= samples.length;               // Divide by the total number of elements
```

Within the loop, you accumulate the sum of all the elements of the array samples in the variable average. You then divide this sum by the number of elements.

Notice how you use the length of the array, samples.length, all over the place. It appears in the for loop, and in floating-point form as a divisor to calculate the average. When you use arrays, you will often find that references to the length of the array are strewn all through your code. As long as you use the length member of the array, the code is independent of the number of array elements. If you change the number of elements in the array, the code will automatically deal with that. You should always use the length member when you need to refer to the length of an array—never use explicit values.

Using the Collection-Based for Loop with an Array

You can use a collection-based `for` loop as an alternative to the numerical `for` loop when you want to process the values of all the elements in an array. For example, you could rewrite the code fragment from the previous section that calculated the average of the values in the `samples` array like this:

```
double average = 0.0;           // Variable to hold the average
for(double value : samples) {
  average += value;             // Sum all the elements
}
average /= samples.length;      // Divide by the total number of elements
```

The `for` loop will iterate through the values of all elements of type `double` in the `samples` array in sequence. The `value` variable will be assigned the value of each element of the `samples` array in turn. Thus, the loop achieves the same result as the numerical `for` loop that you used earlier — the sum of all the elements will be accumulated in `average`. Of course, when you want to process only data from part of the array, you still must use the numerical `for` loop with the loop counter ranging over the indexes for the elements you want to access.

It's important to remember that the collection-based `for` loop iterates over the *values* stored in an array. It does not provide access to the elements for the purpose of setting their values. Therefore, you use it only when you are accessing all the values stored in an array to use them in some way. If you want to recalculate the values in the array, use the numerical `for` loop.

Let's try out an array in an improved program to calculate prime numbers:

Try It Out   Even More Primes

Try out the following code, derived, in part, from the code you used in Chapter 3:

```
import static java.lang.Math.ceil;
import static java.lang.Math.sqrt;

public class MorePrimes {
  public static void main(String[] args) {
    long[] primes = new long[20];       // Array to store primes
    primes[0] = 2L;                     // Seed the first prime
    primes[1] = 3L;                     // and the second
    int count = 2;                      // Count of primes found - up to now,
                                        // which is also the array index

    long number = 5L;                   // Next integer to be tested

    outer:
    for( ; count < primes.length; number += 2L) {
      // The maximum divisor we need to try is square root of number
      long limit = (long)ceil(sqrt((double)number));

      // Divide by all the primes we have up to limit
      for(int i = 1; i < count && primes[i] <= limit; i++) {
        if(number%primes[i] == 0L) {    // Is it an exact divisor?
          continue outer;               // Yes, so try the next number
        }
```

```
      }
      primes[count++] = number;            // We got one!
    }

    for(long n : primes) {
      System.out.println(n);               // Output all the primes
    }
  }
}
```

This program computes as many prime numbers as the capacity of the primes array will allow.

How It Works

Any number that is not a prime must be a product of prime factors, so you only need to divide a prime number candidate by prime numbers that are less than or equal to the square root of the candidate to test for whether it is prime. This is fairly obvious if you think about it. For every factor a number has that is greater than the square root of the number, the result of division by this factor is another factor that is less than the square root. You perhaps can see this more easily with a specific example. The number 24 has a square root that is a bit less than 5. You can factorize it as 2 * 12, 3 * 8, 4 * 6; then you come to cases where the first factor is greater than the square root so the second is less, 6 * 4, 8 * 3, etc., and so you are repeating the pairs of factors you already have.

You first declare the array primes to be of type long, and define it as having 20 elements. You set the first two elements of the primes array to 2 and 3, respectively, to start the process off, as you will use the primes you have in the array as divisors when testing a new candidate.

The variable count is the total number of primes you have found, so this starts out as 2 because you have already stored 2 and 3 in the first two elements of the primes array. Note that because you use count as the for loop control variable, you omit the first expression between parentheses in the loop statement, as the initial value of count has already been set.

You store the candidate to be tested in number, with the first value set as 5. The for loop statement labeled outer is slightly unusual. First of all, the variable count that determines when the loop ends is not incremented in the for loop statement, but in the body of the loop. You use the third control expression between the for loop parentheses to increment number in steps of two, since you don't want to check even numbers. The for loop ends when count is equal to the length of the array. You test the value in number in the inner for loop by dividing number by all of the prime numbers you have in the primes array that are less than, or equal to, the square root of the candidate. If you get an exact division, the value in number is not prime, so you go immediately to the next iteration of the outer loop via the continue statement.

You calculate the limit for divisors you need to try with the following statement:

```
long limit = (long)ceil(sqrt((double)number));
```

The sqrt() method from the Math class produces the square root of number as a double value, so if number has the value 7, for example, a value of about 2.64575 will be returned. This is passed to the ceil() method, which is also a member of the Math class. The ceil() method returns a value of type double that is the minimum whole number that is not less than the value passed to it. With number as 7, this will return 3.0, the smallest integral value not less than the square root of 7. You want to use this number as the limit for your integer divisors, so you cast it to type `long` and store the result in `limit`. You are able to call the `sqrt()` and `ceil()` methods without qualifying their names with the class to which they belong because you have imported their names into the source file.

If you don't get an exact division, you exit normally from the inner loop and execute the statement

```
primes[count++] = number;              // We got one!
```

Because `count` is the number of values you have stored, it also corresponds to the index for the next free element in the `primes` array. Thus, you use `count` as the index to the array element in which you want to store the value of `number`, and then increment `count`.

When you have filled the `primes` array, the `outer` loop will end and you output all the values in the array in the loop:

```
for(long n : primes) {
    System.out.println(n);             // Output all the primes
}
```

This loop will iterate through all the elements of type `long` in the `primes` array in sequence. On each iteration n will contain the value of the current element, so that will be written out by the `println()` method.

You can express the logical process of this program as the following sequence of steps:

1. Take the **number** in question and determine its square root.

2. Set the **limit** for divisors to be the smallest integer that is greater than this square root value.

3. Test to see if the **number** can be divided exactly (without remainder) by any of the **primes** already in the `primes` **array** that are less than the **limit** for divisors.

4. If any of the existing primes divide into the current **number**, discard the current **number** and start a new iteration of the loop with the next candidate **number**.

5. If none of the divisors divide into **number** without a remainder, it is a prime, so enter the existing **number** in the first available empty slot in the array and then move to the next iteration for a new candidate **number**.

6. When the **array** of primes is full, stop looking for new primes and output all the prime number values from the array.

Arrays of Arrays

You have worked only with one-dimensional arrays up to now, that is, arrays that use a single index. Why would you ever need the complications of using more indexes to access the elements of an array?

Consider a specific example. Suppose that you have a fanatical interest in the weather, and you are intent on recording the temperature each day at 10 separate geographical locations throughout the year. Once you have sorted out the logistics of actually collecting this information, you can use an array of 10 elements corresponding to the number of locations, where each of these elements is an array of 365 elements to store the temperature values. You would declare this array with the statement

```
float[][] temperature = new float[10][365];
```

This is called a **two-dimensional array**, since it has two dimensions — one with index values running from 0 to 9, and the other with index values from 0 to 364. The first index relates to a geographical location, and the second index corresponds to the day of the year. That's much handier than a one-dimensional array with 3650 elements, isn't it?

Figure 4-4 shows the organization of the two-dimensional array.

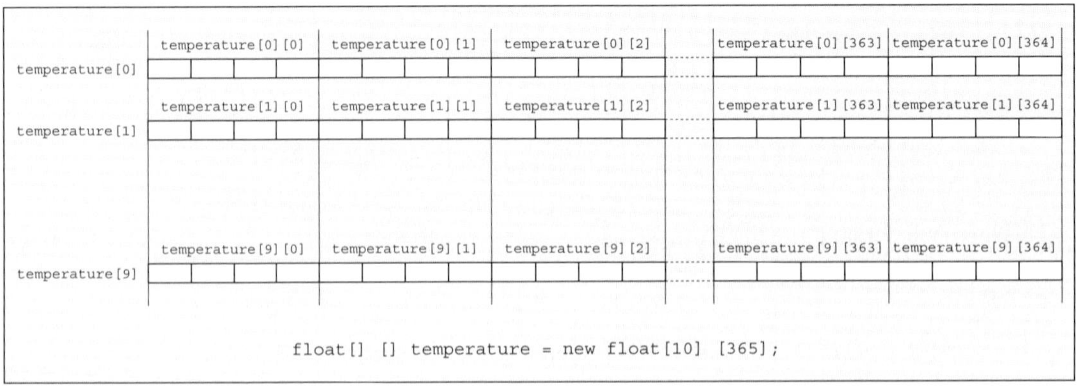

Figure 4-4

There are 10 one-dimensional arrays that make up the two-dimensional array, and they each have 365 elements. In referring to an element, the first pair of square brackets encloses the index for a particular array and the second pair of square brackets encloses the index value for an element within that array. So to refer to the temperature for day 100 for the sixth location, you would use `temperature[5][99]`. Since each `float` variable occupies 4 bytes, the total space required to store the elements in this two-dimensional array is 10x365x4 bytes, which is a total of 14,600 bytes.

For a fixed value for the second index in a two-dimensional array, varying the first index value is often referred to as accessing a **column** of the array. Similarly, fixing the first index value and varying the second, you access a **row** of the array. The reason for this terminology should be apparent from Figure 4-4.

You could equally well have used two statements to create the last array, one to declare the array variable and the other to define the array:

```
float [][] temperature;              // Declare the array variable
temperature = new float[10][365];    // Create the array
```

The first statement declares the array variable `temperature` for two-dimensional arrays of type `float`. The second statement creates the array with ten elements, each of which is an array of 365 elements of type `float`.

Let's exercise this two-dimensional array in a program to calculate the average annual temperature for each location.

Try It Out   The Weather Fanatic

To save you having to wander around 10 different locations armed with a thermometer, you'll generate the temperatures as random values between -10 degrees and 35 degrees. This assumes you are recording temperatures in degrees Celsius. If you prefer Fahrenheit, you could generate values from 14 degrees to 95 degrees to cover the same range.

```
public class WeatherFan {
   public static void main(String[] args) {
      float[][] temperature = new float[10][365];      // Temperature array

      // Generate random temperatures
      for(int i = 0; i<temperature.length; i++) {
         for(int j = 0; j < temperature[i].length; j++) {
            temperature[i][j] = (float)(45.0*Math.random() - 10.0);
          }
       }

      // Calculate the average per location
      for(int i = 0; i<temperature.length; i++) {
         float average = 0.0f;       // Place to store the average

         for(int j = 0; j < temperature[i].length; j++) {
            average += temperature[i][j];
         }

         // Output the average temperature for the current location
         System.out.println("Average temperature at location "
               + (i+1) + " = " + average/(float)temperature[i].length);
       }
    }
 }
```

When I ran the program, I got the following output:

```
Average temperature at location 1 = 12.2733345
Average temperature at location 2 = 12.012519
Average temperature at location 3 = 11.54522
Average temperature at location 4 = 12.490543
Average temperature at location 5 = 12.574791
Average temperature at location 6 = 11.950315
Average temperature at location 7 = 11.492908
Average temperature at location 8 = 13.176439
Average temperature at location 9 = 12.565457
Average temperature at location 10 = 12.981103
```

You should get different results.

How It Works

After declaring the array `temperature` you fill it with random values using nested `for` loops. Note how `temperature.length` used in the outer loop refers to the length of the first dimension, 10 in this case. In the inner loop you use `temperature[i].length` to refer to the length of the second dimension, 365. You could use any index value here; `temperature[0].length` would have been just as good for all the elements, since the lengths of the rows of the array are all the same in this case.

The `Math.random()` method generates a value of type `double` from 0.0 up to, but excluding, 1.0. This value is multiplied by 45.0 in the expression for the temperature, which results in values between 0.0 and 45.0. Subtracting 10.0 from this value gives you the range you require, -10.0 to 35.0.

You then use another pair of nested `for` loops, controlled in the same way as the first, to calculate the averages of the stored temperatures. The outer loop iterates over the locations and the inner loop sums all the temperature values for a given location. Before the execution of the inner loop, the variable `average` is declared and initialized, and this is used to accumulate the sum of the temperatures for a location in the inner loop. After the inner loop has been executed, you output the average temperature for each location, identifying the locations by numbers 1 to 10, one more than the index value for each location. Note that the parentheses around `(i+1)` here are essential. To get the average, you divide the variable `average` by the number of samples, which is `temperature[i].length`, the length of the array holding temperatures for the current location. Again, you could use any index value here since, as you have seen, they all return the same value, 365.

You could write the nested loop to calculate the average temperatures as nested collection-based `for` loops, like this:

```
int location = 0;                           // Location number
for(float[] temperatures : temperature) {
    float average = 0.0f;      // Place to store the average

    for(float t : temperatures) {
        average += t;
    }

    // Output the average temperature for the current location
    System.out.println("Average temperature at location "
            + (++location) + " = " + average/(float)temperatures.length);
}
```

The outer loop iterates over the elements in the array of arrays, so the loop variable `temperatures` will reference each of the one-dimensional arrays in `temperature` in turn. The type of the `temperatures` variable is `float[]` because it stores a reference to a one-dimensional array from the array of one-dimensional arrays, `temperature`.

The inner `for` loop iterates over the elements in the array that is currently referenced by `temperatures`, and the loop variable `t` will be assigned the value of each element from the `temperatures` in turn. You have to define an extra variable, `location`, to record the location number as this was previously provided by the loop variable `i`, which is not present in this version. You increment the value of `location` in the output statement using the prefix form of the increment operator so the location values will be 1, 2, 3, and so on.

Arrays of Arrays of Varying Length

When you create an array of arrays, the arrays in the array do not need to be all the same length. You could declare an array variable, `samples`, with the statement:

```
float[][] samples;                          // Declare an array of arrays
```

This declares the array object `samples` to be of type `float[][]`. You can then define the number of elements in the first dimension with the statement:

```
samples = new float[6][];                   // Define 6 elements, each is an array
```

The `samples` variable now references an array with six elements, each of which can hold a reference to a one-dimensional array. You can define these arrays individually if you want:

```
samples[2] = new float[6];                  // The 3rd array has 6 elements
samples[5] = new float[101];                // The 6th array has 101 elements
```

This defines two of the six possible one-dimensional arrays that can be referenced through elements of the `samples` array. The third element in the `samples` array now references an array of 6 elements of type `float`, and the sixth element of the `samples` array references an array of 101 elements of type `float`. Obviously, you cannot use an array until it has been defined, but you could conceivably use these two and define the others later—not a likely approach though!

If you wanted the array `samples` to have a triangular shape, with one element in the first row, two elements in the second row, three in the third row, and so on, you could define the arrays in a loop:

```
for(int i = 0; i<samples.length; i++) {
    samples[i] = new float[i+1];            // Allocate each array
}
```

The effect of this is to produce the array layout that is shown in Figure 4-5.

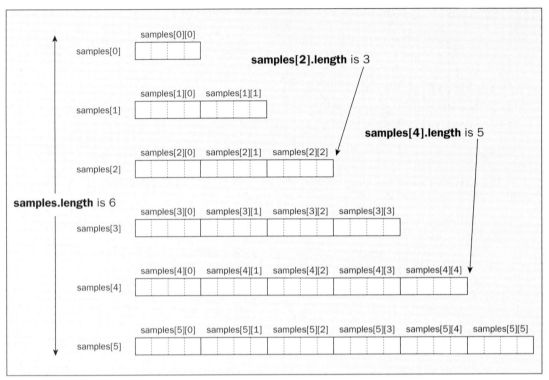

Figure 4-5

The 21 elements in the array will occupy 84 bytes. When you need a two-dimensional array with rows of varying length, allocating them to fit the requirement can save a considerable amount of memory compared to just using rectangular arrays where the row lengths are all the same.

To check out that the array is as shown in Figure 4-5, you could define it in a program using the code fragments you have just seen and include statements to display the `length` member for each of the one-dimensional arrays.

You could use a numerical `for` loop to initialize the elements in the `samples` array, even though the rows may differ in length:

```
for(int i = 0; i < samples.length; i++) {
  for(int j = 0 ; j<samples[i].length ; j++) {
    samples[i][j] = 99.0f;              // Initialize each element to 99
  }
}
```

The upper limit for the control variable in the inner loop is `samples[i].length`. The expression `samples[i]` references the current row in the two-dimensional array so `samples[i].length` is the number of elements in the current row. The outer loop iterates over the rows in the `samples` array, and the inner loop iterates over all the elements in a row.

You can also achieve the same result with slightly less code using the `fill()` method from the `Arrays` class that you saw earlier:

```
for(int i = 0; i < samples.length; i++) {
    java.util.Arrays.fill(samples[i], 99.0f); // Initialize elements in a row to 99
}
```

Because the `fill()` method fills all the elements in a row, you need only one loop that iterates over the rows of the array.

Multidimensional Arrays

You are not limited to two-dimensional arrays either. If you are an international java bean grower with multiple farms across several countries, you could arrange to store the results of your bean counting in the array declared and defined in the following statement:

```
long[][][] beans = new long[5][10][30];
```

The array, `beans`, has three dimensions. It provides for holding bean counts for each of up to 30 fields per farm, with 10 farms per country in each of 5 countries.

You can envisage this as just a three-dimensional array, but remember that `beans` is really an array of five elements, each of which holds a reference to a two-dimensional array, and each of these two-dimensional arrays can be different. For example, if you really want to go to town, you can declare the array `beans` with the statement:

```
long[][][] beans = new long[3][][];                    // Three two-dimensional arrays
```

Each of the three elements in the first dimension of `beans` can hold a different two-dimensional array, so you could specify the first dimension of each explicitly with the following statements:

```
beans[0] = new long[4][];
beans[1] = new long[2][];
beans[2] = new long[5][];
```

These three arrays have elements that each hold a one-dimensional array, and you can also specify the sizes of these independently. Note how the empty square brackets indicate there is still a dimension undefined. You could give the arrays in each of these elements random dimensions between 1 and 7 with the following code:

```
for(int i = 0; i<beans.length; i++)            // Vary over 1st dimension
    for(int j = 0; j<beans[i].length; j++)     // Vary over 2nd dimension
        beans[i][j] = new long[(int)(1.0 + 6.0*Math.random())];
```

If you can find a sensible reason for doing so, or if you are just a glutton for punishment, you can extend this to four or more dimensions.

Arrays of Characters

All the arrays you have defined have contained elements storing numerical values so far. You can also have arrays of characters. For example, you can declare an array variable of type `char[]` to hold 50 characters with the following statement:

```
char[] message = new char[50];
```

Keep in mind that characters are stored as Unicode in Java so each element occupies 2 bytes.

If you wanted to initialize every element of this array to a space character, you could either use a `for` loop to iterate over the elements of the array, or just use the `fill()` method in the `Arrays` class, like this:

```
java.util.Arrays.fill(message, ' ');              // Store a space in every element
```

Of course, you could use the `fill()` method to initialize the elements with any character you wish. If you put `'\n'` as the second argument to the `fill()` method, the array elements would all contain a newline character.

You can also define the size of an array of type `char[]` by the characters it holds initially:

```
char[] vowels = { 'a', 'e', 'i', 'o', 'u'};
```

This defines an array of five elements, initialized with the characters appearing between the braces. This is fine for things like vowels, but what about proper messages?

Using an array of type `char`, you can write statements such as:

```
char[] sign = {'F', 'l', 'u', 'e', 'n', 't', ' ',
               'G', 'i', 'b', 'b', 'e', 'r', 'i', 's', 'h', ' ',
               's', 'p', 'o', 'k', 'e', 'n', ' ',
               'h', 'e', 'r', 'e'};
```

Well, you get the message — just — but it's not a very friendly way to deal with it. It looks like a collection of characters, which is what it is. What you really need is something a bit more integrated — something that looks like a message, but still gives you the ability to get at the individual characters if you want. What you need is a `String`.

Strings

You will need to use character strings in most of your programs — headings, names, addresses, product descriptions, messages — the list is endless. In Java, ordinary strings are objects of the class `String`. The `String` class is a standard class that comes with Java, and it is specifically designed for creating and processing strings. The definition of the `String` class is in the `java.lang` package so it will be accessible in all your programs by default.

String Literals

You have already made extensive use of string literals for output. Just about every time the `println()` method was used in an example, you used a string literal as the argument. A **string literal** is a sequence of characters between double quotes:

```
"This is a string literal!"
```

This is actually a `String` literal with a capital `S` — in other words, a constant object of the class `String` that the compiler creates for use in your program.

As I mentioned in Chapter 2, some characters can't be entered explicitly from the keyboard so you can't include them directly in a string literal. You can't include a newline character by pressing the Enter key since this will move the cursor to a new line. You also can't include a double quote character as it is in a string literal because this is used to indicate where a string literal begins and ends. You can specify all of these characters in a string in the same way as you did for `char` constants in Chapter 2 — you use an escape sequence. All the escape sequences you saw when you looked at `char` constants apply to strings. The statement

```
System.out.println("This is \na string constant!");
```

will produce the output

```
This is
a string constant!
```

since \n is interpreted as a newline character. Like values of type `char`, strings are stored internally as Unicode characters. You can also include Unicode character codes in a string as escape sequences of the form \unnnn where nnnn are the four hexadecimal digits of the Unicode coding for a particular character. The Greek letter π, for example, is \u03C0.

You will recall from my preliminary discussion of classes and objects in Chapter 1 that a class usually contains data members and methods, and naturally, this is true of the `String` class. The sequence of characters in the string is stored in a data member of the `String` object and the methods for the `String` object enable you to process the data in a variety of ways. I'll go into the detail of how a class is defined in Chapter 5, so in this chapter I'll concentrate on how you can create and use objects of the class `String` without explaining the mechanics of why things work the way that they do. You already know how to define a `String` literal. The next step is to learn how you declare a `String` variable and how you create `String` objects.

Creating String Objects

Just to make sure there is no confusion in your mind, a `String` variable is simply a variable that stores a reference to an object of the class `String`. You declare a `String` variable in much the same way as you define a variable of one of the basic types. You can also initialize it in the declaration, which is generally a good idea:

```
String myString = "My inaugural string";
```

This declares the variable myString as type String and initializes it with a reference to a String object encapsulating the string "My inaugural string". You can store a reference to another string in a String variable, once you have declared it, by using an assignment. For example, you can change the value of the String variable myString to the statement:

```
myString = "Strings can be knotty";
```

The effect of this is illustrated in Figure 4-6:

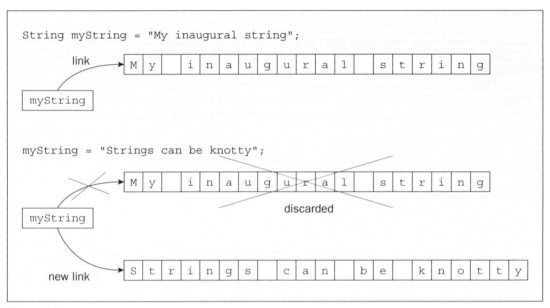

Figure 4-6

The String object itself is distinct from the variable you use to refer to it. In the same way as you saw with array objects, the variable myString stores a reference to a String object, not the object itself, so in other words, a String variable records where the String object is in memory. When you declare and initialize myString, it references the object corresponding to the initializing string literal. When you execute the assignment statement, the original reference is overwritten by the reference to the new string and the old string is discarded. The variable myString then contains a reference to the new string.

String objects are said to be **immutable**—which just means that they cannot be changed. This means that you cannot extend or otherwise modify the string that an object of type String represents. When you execute a statement that combines existing String objects, you are *always* creating a new String object as a result. When you change the string referenced by a String variable, you throw away the reference to the old string and replace it with a reference to a new one. The distinction between a String variable and the string it references is not apparent most of the time, but you will see situations later in this chapter where it is important to understand this, so keep it in mind.

You should also keep in mind that characters in a string are Unicode characters, so each one typically occupies 2 bytes, with the possibility that they can be 4 bytes if you are using characters represented as surrogates. This is also not something you need worry about most of the time, but there are occasions where you need to be conscious of that, too.

Of course, you can declare a variable of type `String` in a method without initializing it:

```
String anyString;            // Uninitialized String variable
```

The `anyString` variable that you have declared here does not refer to anything. However, if you try to compile a program that attempts to use `anyString` before it has been initialized by some means, you will get an error. If you don't want a `String` variable to refer to anything at the outset — for example, if you may or may not assign a `String` object to it before you use the variable — then you must initialize it to a special `null` value:

```
String anyString = null;     // String variable that doesn't reference a string
```

The literal `null` is an object reference value that does not refer to anything. Because an array is essentially an object, you can also use `null` as the value for an array variable that does not reference anything.

You can test whether a `String` variable refers to anything or not by a statement such as:

```
if(anyString == null) {
   System.out.println("anyString does not refer to anything!");
}
```

The variable `anyString` will continue to be `null` until you use an assignment to make it reference a particular string. Attempting to use a variable that has not been initialized is an error. When you declare a `String` variable, or any other variable that is not an array, in a block of code without initializing it, the compiler can detect any attempts to use the variable before it has a value assigned and will flag it as an error. As a rule, you should always initialize variables as you declare them.

You can use the literal `null` when you want to discard a `String` object that is currently referenced by a variable. Suppose you define a `String` variable like this:

```
String message = "Only the mediocre are always at their best";
```

A little later in the program, you want to discard the string that `message` references. You can just write this statement:

```
message = null;
```

The value `null` replaces the original reference stored so `message` now does not refer to anything.

Arrays of Strings

You can create arrays of strings. You declare an array of `String` objects with the same mechanism that you used to declare arrays of elements for the basic types. You just use the type `String` in the declaration. For example, to declare an array of five `String` objects, you could use the statement:

```
String[] names = new String[5];
```

It should now be apparent that the argument to the method `main()` is an array of `String` objects because the definition of the method always looks like this:

```
public static void main(String[] args) {
  // Code for method...
}
```

You could also declare an array of `String` objects where the initial values determine the size of the array:

```
String[] colors = {"red", "orange", "yellow", "green", "blue", "indigo", "violet"};
```

This array will have 7 elements because there are 7 initializing string literals between the braces.

Of course, as with arrays storing elements of primitive types, you can create arrays of strings with any number of dimensions.

You can try out arrays of strings with a small example.

Try It Out   Twinkle, Twinkle, Lucky Star

Let's create a console program to generate your lucky star for the day:

```
public class LuckyStars {
  public static void main(String[] args) {
    String[] stars = {
                       "Robert Redford"  , "Marilyn Monroe",
                       "Boris Karloff"   , "Lassie",
                       "Hopalong Cassidy", "Trigger"
                     };
    System.out.println("Your lucky star for today is "
                       + stars[(int)(stars.length*Math.random())]);
  }
}
```

When you compile and run this program, it will output your lucky star. For example, I was fortunate enough to get the following result:

```
Your lucky star for today is Marilyn Monroe
```

How It Works

This program creates the array `stars` of type `String[]`. The array length will be set to however many initializing values appear between the braces in the declaration statement, which is 6 in this case.

You select a random element from the array by creating a random index value within the output statement with the expression `(int)(stars.length*Math.random())`. Multiplying the random number produced by the method `Math.random()` by the length of the array, you will get a value between 0.0

and 6.0 because the value returned by `random()` will be between 0.0 and 1.0. The result won't ever be exactly 6.0 because the value returned by the `random()` method is strictly less than 1.0, which is just as well as this would be an illegal index value. The result is then cast to type `int` and will result in a value from 0 to 5, making it a valid index value for the `stars` array.

Thus the program selects a random string from the array and displays it, so you should see different output if you execute the program repeatedly.

Operations on Strings

There are many kinds of operations that can be performed on strings, but let's start with one you have used already, joining two or more strings together to form a new, combined string. This is often called **string concatenation**.

Joining Strings

To join two `String` objects to form a new, single string you use the + operator, just as you have been doing with the argument to the `println()` method in the program examples thus far. The simplest use of this is to join two strings together:

```
myString = "The quick brown fox" + " jumps over the lazy dog";
```

This will join the two strings on the right of the assignment and store the result in the `String` variable `myString`. The + operation generates a completely new `String` object that is separate from the two original `String` objects that are the operands, and this new object is stored in `myString`. Of course, you also use the + operator for arithmetic addition, but if either of the operands for the + operator is a `String` object or literal, then the compiler will interpret the operation as string concatenation and will convert the operand that is not a `String` object to a string.

Here's an example of concatenation strings referenced by `String` variables:

```
String date = "31st ";
String month = "December";
String lastDay = date + month;          // Result is "31st December"
```

If a `String` variable that you use as one of the operands to + contains `null`, then this will automatically be converted to the string `"null"`. So if the `month` variable contained `null` instead of a reference to the string "December", the result of the concatenation with `date` would be the string `"31st null"`.

Note that you can also use the += operator to concatenate strings. For example:

```
String phrase = "Too many";
phrase += " cooks spoil the broth";
```

After executing these statements, the variable phrase will refer to the string "Too many cooks spoil the broth". Of course, this does not modify the string "Too many". The string that is referenced by phrase after this statement has been executed is a completely new String object. This is illustrated in Figure 4-7.

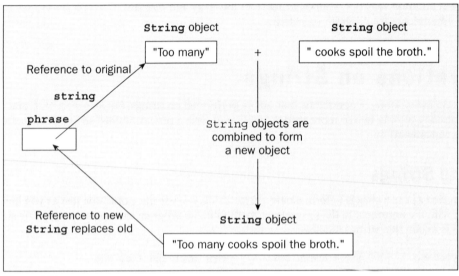

Figure 4-7

Let's see how some variations on the use of the + operator with String objects work in an example.

Try It Out   String Concatenation

Enter the following code for the class JoinStrings:

```java
public class JoinStrings {
    public static void main(String[] args) {

        String firstString = "Many ";
        String secondString = "hands ";
        String thirdString = "make light work";

        String myString;                    // Variable to store results

        // Join three strings and store the result
        myString = firstString + secondString + thirdString;
        System.out.println(myString);

        // Convert an integer to String and join with two other strings
        int numHands = 99;
        myString = numHands + " " + secondString + thirdString;
        System.out.println(myString);

        // Combining a string and integers
```

```
    myString = "fifty five is " + 5 + 5;
    System.out.println(myString);

    // Combining integers and a string
    myString = 5 + 5 + " is ten";
    System.out.println(myString);
  }
}
```

If you run this example, it will produce some interesting results:

```
Many hands make light work
99 hands make light work
fifty five is 55
10 is ten
```

How It Works

The first line of output is quite straightforward. It simply joins the three string values stored in the String variables, firstString, secondString, and thirdString, into a single string and stores this in the variable myString.

The second line of output is a use of the + operator you have used regularly with the println() method, but clearly something a little more complicated is happening here. This is illustrated in Figure 4-8.

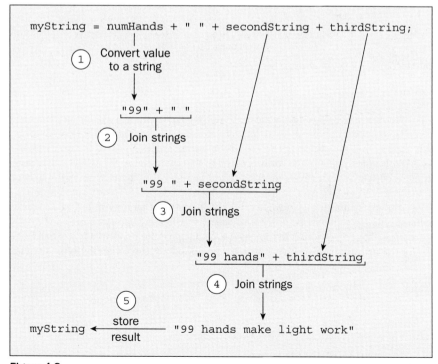

Figure 4-8

159

Behind the scenes, the value of the variable numHands is being converted to a string that represents this value as a decimal number. This is prompted by the fact that it is combined with the string literal, " ". Dissimilar types in a binary operation cannot be operated on, so one operand must be converted to the type of the other if the operation is to be possible. Here the compiler arranges that the numerical value stored in numHands is converted to type String to match the type of the right operand of the + operator. If you look back at the table of operator precedences, you'll see that the associativity of the + operator is from left to right, so the strings are combined in pairs starting from the left, as shown in Figure 4-8.

The left-to-right associativity of the + operator is important in understanding the next two lines of output. The two statements involved in creating these strings look very similar. Why does 5 + 5 result in 55 in one statement, and 10 in the other? The reason is illustrated in Figure 4-9.

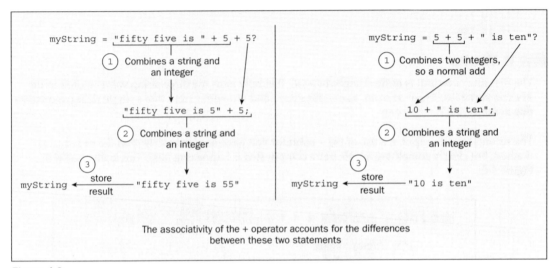

Figure 4-9

The essential difference between the two is that the first statement always has at least one operand of type String, so the operation is one of string concatenation, whereas in the second statement the first operation is an arithmetic addition because both operands are integers. In the first statement, each of the integers is converted to type String individually. In the second, the numerical values are added, and the result, 10, is converted to a string representation to allow the literal " is ten" to be concatenated.

You don't need to know about this at this point, but in case you were wondering, the conversion of values of the basic types to type String is actually accomplished by using a static method, toString(), of a standard class that corresponds to the basic type. Each of the primitive types has an equivalent class defined, so for the primitive types I have already discussed are the following **wrapper classes**:

Basic Type	Wrapper Class
byte	Byte
short	Short

Basic Type	Wrapper Class
int	Integer
long	Long
float	Float
double	Double
boolean	Boolean
char	Character

The classes in the table are called wrapper classes because objects of each of these class types "wrap" a value of the corresponding primitive type. Whenever a value of one of the basic types appears as an operand to + and the other operand is a `String` object, the compiler arranges to pass the value of the basic type as the argument to the `toString()` method that is defined in the corresponding wrapper class. The `toString()` method returns the `String` equivalent of the value. All of this happens automatically when you are concatenating strings using the + operator. As you will see, not only these classes have a `toString()` method — all classes do. I won't go into the further significance of these classes now, as I'll be covering these in more detail in Chapter 5.

The `String` class also defines a method, `valueOf()`, that will create a `String` object from a value of any of the basic types. You just pass the value you want converted to a string as the argument to the method. For example:

```
String doubleString = String.valueOf(3.14159);
```

You call the `valueOf()` method using the name of the class `String`, as shown in the preceding line. This is because the method is a `static` member of the `String` class. You'll learn what `static` means in this context in Chapter 5. A literal or variable of any of the basic types can be passed to the `valueOf()` method, and it will return a `String` representation of the value.

Comparing Strings

Here's where the difference between the `String` variable and the string it references will become apparent. To compare values stored in variables of the primitive types for equality, you use the == operator. This does *not* apply to `String` objects (or any other objects). The expression

```
string1 == string2
```

will check whether the two `String` variables refer to the same string. If they reference separate strings, this expression will have the value `false`, regardless of whether or not the strings happen to be identical. In other words, the expression above does not compare the strings themselves; it compares the references to the strings, so the result will be `true` only if `string1` and `string2` both refer to one and the same string. You can demonstrate this with a little example.

Two Strings, Identical but Not the Same

In the following code, you test to see whether `string1` and `string3` refer to the same string:

```
public class MatchStrings {
  public static void main(String[] args) {

    String string1 = "Too many ";
    String string2 = "cooks";
    String string3 = "Too many cooks";

  // Make string1 and string3 refer to separate strings that are identical
    string1 += string2;

    // Display the contents of the strings
    System.out.println("Test 1");
    System.out.println("string3 is now: " + string3);
    System.out.println("string1 is now: " + string1);

    if(string1 == string3)                  // Now test for identity
      System.out.println("string1 == string3 is true." +
                         " string1 and string3 point to the same string");
    else
      System.out.println("string1 == string3 is false." +
                    " string1 and string3 do not point to the same string");

    // Now make string1 and string3 refer to the same string
    string3 = string1;
    // Display the contents of the strings
    System.out.println("\n\nTest 2");
    System.out.println("string3 is now: " + string3);
    System.out.println("string1 is now: " + string1);

    if(string1 == string3)                  // Now test for identity
      System.out.println("string1 == string3 is true." +
                         " string1 and string3 point to the same string");
    else
      System.out.println("string1 == string3 is false." +
                    " string1 and string3 do not point to the same string");
  }
}
```

You have created two scenarios in this example. In the first, the variables `string1` and `string3` refer to separate `String` objects that happen to encapsulate identical strings. In the second, they both reference the same `String` object. The program will produce the following output:

```
Test 1
string3 is now: Too many cooks
string1 is now: Too many cooks
string1==string3 is false. string1 and string3 do not point to the same string

Test 2
string3 is now: Too many cooks
string1 is now: Too many cooks
string1==string3 is true. string1 and string3 point to the same string
```

How It Works

The three variables `string1`, `string2`, and `string3` are initialized with the string literals you see. After executing the assignment statement, the string referenced by `string1` will be identical to that referenced by `string3`, but as you see from the output, the comparison for equality in the `if` statement returns `false` because the variables refer to two separate strings. Note that if you were to just initialize `string1` and `string2` with the same string literal, `"Too many cooks"`, only one `String` object would be created, which both variables would reference. This would result in both comparisons being `true`.

Next you change the value of `string3` so that it refers to the same string as `string1`. The output demonstrates that the `if` expression has the value `true`, and that the `string1` and `string3` objects do indeed refer to the same string. This clearly shows that the comparison is not between the strings themselves, but between the references to the strings. So how do you compare the strings?

Comparing Strings for Equality

To compare two `String` variables, that is, to decide whether the strings they reference are equal or not, you must use the `equals()` method, which is defined for objects of type `String` . For example, to compare the `String` objects referenced by the variables `string1` and `string3` you could write the statement:

```
if(string1.equals(string3)) {
    System.out.println("string1.equals(string3) is true." +
                       " so strings are equal.");
}
```

This calls the `equals()` method for the `String` object referenced by `string1` and passes `string3` as the argument. The `equals()` method does a case-sensitive comparison of corresponding characters in the strings and returns `true` if the strings are equal and `false` otherwise. Two strings are equal if they are the same length, that is, have the same number of characters, and each character in one string is identical to the corresponding character in the other.

Of course, you could also use the `equals()` method for the string referenced by `string3` to do the comparison:

```
if(string3.equals(string1)) {
    System.out.println("string3.equals(string1) is true." +
                       " so strings are equal.");
}
```

This is just as effective as the previous version.

To check for equality between two strings ignoring the case of the string characters, you use the method `equalsIgnoreCase()`. Let's put these methods in the context of an example to see them working.

Try It Out   String Identity

Make the following changes to the `MatchStrings.java` file of the previous example:

```
public class MatchStrings2 {
  public static void main(String[] args) {

    String string1 = "Too many ";
```

```
   String string2 = "cooks";
   String string3 = "Too many cooks";

   // Make string1 and string3 refer to separate strings that are identical
   string1 += string2;

   // Display the contents of the strings
   System.out.println("Test 1");
   System.out.println("string3 is now: " + string3);
   System.out.println("string1 is now: " + string1);

   if(string1.equals(string3)) {                  // Now test for equality
     System.out.println("string1.equals(string3) is true." +
                            " so strings are equal.");
   } else {
     System.out.println("string1.equals(string3) is false." +
                        " so strings are not equal.");
   }

   // Now make string1 and string3 refer to strings differing in case
   string3 = "TOO many cooks";
   // Display the contents of the strings
   System.out.println("\n\nTest 2");
   System.out.println("string3 is now: " + string3);
   System.out.println("string1 is now: " + string1);

   if(string1.equals(string3)) {                  // Compare for equality
     System.out.println("string1.equals(string3) is true " +
                        " so strings are equal.");
   } else {
     System.out.println("string1.equals(string3) is false" +
                        " so strings are not equal.");
   }

   if(string1.equalsIgnoreCase(string3)) {        // Compare, ignoring case
     System.out.println("string1.equalsIgnoreCase(string3) is true" +
                            " so strings are equal ignoring case.");
   } else {
     System.out.println("string1.equalsIgnoreCase(string3) is false" +
                            " so strings are different.");
   }
  }
 }
}
```

Of course, if you don't want to have to create another source file, leave the class name as it was before, as MatchStrings. If you run this example, you should get the following output:

```
Test 1
string3 is now: Too many cooks
string1 is now: Too many cooks
string1.equals(string3) is true. so strings are equal.


Test 2
string3 is now: TOO many cooks
```

```
string1 is now: Too many cooks
string1.equals(string3) is false so strings are not equal.
string1.equalsIgnoreCase(string3) is true so strings are equal ignoring case.
```

How It Works

In the if expression, you've called the equals() method for the object string1 to test for equality with string3. This is the syntax you've been using to call the method println() in the object out. In general, to call a method belonging to an object, you write the object name, then a period, and then the name of the method. The parentheses following the method name enclose the information to be passed to the method, which is string3 in this case. The general form for calling a method for an object is shown in Figure 4-10.

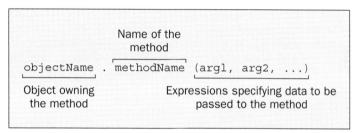

Figure 4-10

> You'll learn more about this in Chapter 5, when you look at how to define your own classes. For the moment, just note that you don't necessarily need to pass any arguments to a method because some methods don't require any. On the other hand, several arguments can be required. It all depends on how the method was defined in the class.

The equals() method requires one argument that you put between the parentheses. This must be the String object that is to be compared with the original object. As you saw earlier, the method returns true if the string passed to it (string3 in the example) is identical to the string pointed to by the String object that owns the method; in this case, string1. As you also saw in the previous section, you could just as well call the equals() method for the object string3, and pass string1 as the argument to compare the two strings. In this case, the expression to call the method would be:

```
string3.equals(string1)
```

and you would get exactly the same result.

The next line in the program code after outputting the values of string3 and string1 is:

```
if(string1.equals(string3)) {                    // Now test for equality
  System.out.println("string1.equals(string3) is true." +
                     " so strings are equal.");
} else {
  System.out.println("string1.equals(string3) is false." +
                     " so strings are not equal.");
}
```

The output from this shows that calling the `equals()` method for `string1` with `string3` as the argument returns `true`. After the `if` statement you make `string3` reference a new string. You then compare the values of `string1` and `string3` once more, and, of course, the result of the comparison is now `false`.

Finally, you compare `string1` with `string3` using the `equalsIgnoreCase()` method. Here the result is `true` since the strings differ only in the case of the first three characters.

String Interning

Having convinced you of the necessity for using the `equals` method for comparing strings, I can now reveal that there is a way to make comparing strings with the `==` operator effective. The mechanism to make this possible is called **string interning**. String interning ensures that no two `String` objects encapsulate the same string, so all `String` objects encapsulate unique strings. This means that if two `String` variables reference strings that are identical, the references must be identical, too. To put it another way, if two `String` variables contain references that are not equal, they must refer to strings that are different. So how do you arrange that all `String` objects encapsulate unique strings? You just call the `intern()` method for every new `String` object that you create. To show how this works, I can amend a bit of an earlier example:

```
String string1 = "Too many ";
String string2 = "cooks";
String string3 = "Too many cooks";

// Make string1 and string3 refer to separate strings that are identical
string1 += string2;
string1 = string1.intern();              // Intern string1
```

The `intern()` method will check the string referenced by `string1` against all the `String` objects currently in existence. If it already exists, the current object will be discarded, and `string1` will contain a reference to the existing object encapsulating the same string. As a result, the expression `string1 == string3` will evaluate to `true`, whereas without the call to `intern()` it evaluated to `false`.

All string constants and constant `String` expressions are automatically interned. That's why `string1` and `string3` would reference the same object if you were to use the same initializing string literal. Suppose you add another variable to the previous code fragment:

```
String string4 = "Too " +"many ";
```

The reference stored in `string4` will be automatically the same as the reference stored in `string1`. Only `String` expressions involving variables need to be interned explicitly by calling `intern()`. You could have written the statement that created the combined string to be stored in `string1` with this statement:

```
string1 = (string1 + string2).intern();
```

This now interns the result of the expression `(string1 + string2)`, ensuring that the reference stored in `string1` will be unique.

String interning has two benefits. First, it reduces the amount of memory required for storing `String` objects in your program. If your program generates a lot of duplicate strings then this will be significant.

Second, it allows the use of `==` instead of the `equals()` method when you want to compare strings for equality. Since the `==` operator just compares two references, it will be much faster than the `equals()` method, which involves a sequence of character-by-character comparisons. This implies that you may make your program run much faster, but only in certain cases. Keep in mind that the `intern()` method has to use the `equals()` method to determine whether a string already exists. More than that, it will compare the current string against a succession of, and possibly all, existing strings in order to determine whether the current string is unique. Realistically, you should stick to using the `equals()` method in the majority of situations and use interning only when you are sure that the benefits outweigh the cost.

Checking the Start and End of a String

It can be useful to be able to check just part of a string. You can test whether a string starts with a particular character sequence by using the `startsWith()` method for the `String` object. The argument to the method is the string that you want to look for at the beginning of the string. The argument string can be of any length, from one character up to the length of the original string you are testing. If `string1` has been defined as `"Too many cooks"`, the expression `string1.startsWith("Too")` will have the value `true`. So would the expression `string1.startsWith("Too man")`. Here's an example of using the method:

```
String string1 = "Too many cooks";
if(string1.startsWith("Too")) {
   System.out.println("The string does start with \"Too\" too!");
}
```

The comparison is case-sensitive so the expression `string1.startsWith("tOO")` would result in the value `false`.

A complementary method `endsWith()` checks for what appears at the end of a string, so the expression `string1.endsWith("cooks")` will have the value `true`. The test is case-sensitive here, too.

Sequencing Strings

You'll often want to place strings in order — for example, when you have a collection of names. Testing for equality doesn't help because to sort strings you need to be able to determine whether one string is greater than or less than another. What you need is the `compareTo()` method in the `String` class. This method compares the `String` object for which it is called with the `String` argument you pass to it and returns an integer that is negative if the `String` object is less than the argument that you passed, zero if the `String` object is equal to the argument, and positive if the `String` object is greater than the argument. Of course, sorting strings requires a clear definition of what the terms *less than*, *equal to*, and *greater than* mean when applied to strings, so I'll explain that first.

The `compareTo()` method compares two strings by comparing successive corresponding characters, starting with the first character in each string. The process continues until either corresponding characters are found to be different, or the last character in one or both strings is reached. Characters are compared by comparing their Unicode representations — so two characters are equal if the numeric values of their Unicode representations are equal. One character is greater than another if the numerical value of its Unicode representation is greater than that of the other. A character is less than another if its Unicode code is less than that of the other.

One string is greater than another if the first character that differs from the corresponding character in the other string is greater than the corresponding character in the other string. So if `string1` has the value `"mad dog"`, and `string2` has the value `"mad cat"`, then the expression

```
string1.compareTo(string2)
```

will return a positive value as a result of comparing the fifth characters in the strings: the `'d'` in `string1` with the `'c'` in `string2`.

What if the corresponding characters in both strings are equal up to the end of the shorter string, but the other string has more characters? In this case the longer string is greater than the shorter string, so `"catamaran"` is greater than `"cat"`.

One string is less than another string if it has a character less than the corresponding character in the other string, and all the preceding characters are equal. Thus, the following expression will return a negative value:

```
string2.compareTo(string1)
```

Two strings are equal if they contain the same number of characters and corresponding characters are identical. In this case the `compareTo()` method returns 0.

You can exercise the `compareTo()` method in a simple example.

Try It Out   Ordering Strings

In this example you'll create three strings that you can compare using the `compareTo()` method. Enter the following code:

```java
public class SequenceStrings {
  public static void main(String[] args) {

    // Strings to be compared
    String string1 = "A";
    String string2 = "To";
    String string3 = "Z";

    // Strings for use in output
    String string1Out = "\"" + string1 + "\"";      // string1 with quotes
    String string2Out = "\"" + string2 + "\"";      // string2 with quotes
    String string3Out = "\"" + string3 + "\"";      // string3 with quotes

    // Compare string1 with string3
    if(string1.compareTo(string3) < 0) {
      System.out.println(string1Out + " is less than " + string3Out);

    } else {
      if(string1.compareTo(string3) > 0) {
        System.out.println(string1Out + " is greater than " + string3Out);
      } else {
        System.out.println(string1Out + " is equal to " + string3Out);
      }
```

```
      }

    // Compare string2 with string1
    if(string2.compareTo(string1) < 0) {
      System.out.println(string2Out + " is less than " + string1Out);

    } else {
      if(string2.compareTo(string1) > 0) {
        System.out.println(string2Out + " is greater than " + string1Out);
      } else {
        System.out.println(string2Out + " is equal to " + string1Out);
      }
    }
  }
}
```

The example will produce the following output:

```
"A" is less than "Z"
"To" is greater than "A"
```

How It Works

You should have no trouble with this example. It declares and initializes three `String` variables, `string1`, `string2`, and `string3`. You then create three further `String` variables that correspond to the first three strings with double quote characters at the beginning and the end. This is just to simplify the output statements. You then have an `if` with a nested `if` to compare `string1` with `string3`:

```
    if(string1.compareTo(string3) < 0) {
      System.out.println(string1Out + " is less than " + string3Out);

    } else {
      if(string1.compareTo(string3) > 0) {
        System.out.println(string1Out + " is greater than " + string3Out);
      } else {
        System.out.println(string1Out + " is equal to " + string3Out);
      }
    }
```

The outer `if` statement determines whether `string1` is less than `string3`. If it is, then a message is displayed. If `string1` is not less than `string3`, then either they are equal or `string1` is greater than `string3`. The inner `if` statement determines which is the case and outputs a message accordingly.

You compare `string2` with `string1` in the same way.

As with the `equals()` method, the argument to the method `compareTo()` can be any expression that results in a `String` object.

Accessing String Characters

When you are processing strings, sooner or later you will need to access individual characters in a `String` object. To refer to a character at a particular position in a string you use an index of type `int` that is the offset of the character position from the beginning of the string.

This is exactly the same principle you used for referencing an array element. The first character in a string is at position 0, the second is at position 1, the third is at position 2, and so on. However, although the principle is the same, the practice is not. You can't use square brackets to access characters in a string — you must use a method.

Extracting String Characters

You can extract a character from a `String` object by using the `charAt()` method. This accepts an integer argument that is the offset of the character position from the beginning of the string — in other words, an index. If you attempt to use an index that is less than 0 or greater than the index for the last position in the string, you will cause an **exception** to be thrown, which will cause your program to be terminated. I will discuss exactly what exceptions are, and how you should deal with them, in Chapter 7. For the moment, just note that the specific type of exception thrown in this case is called `StringIndexOutOfBoundsException`. Its name is rather a mouthful, but quite explanatory.

To avoid unnecessary errors of this kind, you obviously need to be able to determine the length of a `String` object. To obtain the length of a string, you just need to call its `length()` method. Note the difference between this and the way you got the length of an array. Here you are calling a method, `length()`, for a `String` object, whereas with an array you were accessing a data member, `length`. You can explore the use of the `charAt()` and `length()` methods in the `String` class with another example.

Try It Out   **Getting at Characters in a String**

In the following code, the soliloquy is analyzed character-by-character to determine the vowels, spaces, and letters that appear in it:

```java
public class StringCharacters {
  public static void main(String[] args) {
    // Text string to be analyzed
    String text = "To be or not to be, that is the question;"
                 +"Whether 'tis nobler in the mind to suffer"
                 +" the slings and arrows of outrageous fortune,"
                 +" or to take arms against a sea of troubles,"
                 +" and by opposing end them?";
    int spaces  = 0,                              // Count of spaces
        vowels  = 0,                              // Count of vowels
        letters = 0;                              // Count of letters

    // Analyze all the characters in the string
    int textLength = text.length();               // Get string length

    for(int i = 0; i < textLength; i++) {
      // Check for vowels
      char ch = Character.toLowerCase(text.charAt(i));
      if(ch == 'a' || ch == 'e' || ch == 'i' || ch == 'o' || ch == 'u') {
        vowels++;
      }

      //Check for letters
      if(Character.isLetter(ch)) {
        letters++;
      }
```

```
        // Check for spaces
        if(Character.isWhitespace(ch)) {
          spaces++;
        }
      }
    }

    System.out.println("The text contained vowels:      " + vowels + "\n" +
                       "                       consonants: " + (letters-vowels) + "\n"+
                       "                       spaces:     " + spaces);
  }
}
```

Running the example, you'll see:

```
The text contained vowels:     60
                   consonants: 93
                   spaces:     37
```

How It Works

The `String` variable `text` is initialized with the quotation you see. All the counting of letter characters is done in the `for` loop, which is controlled by the index `i`. The loop continues as long as `i` is less than the length of the string, which is returned by the method `text.length()` and which you saved in the variable `textLength`.

Starting with the first character, which has the index value 0, you retrieve each character from the string by calling its `charAt()` method. You use the loop index `i` as the index to the character position string. The method returns the character at index position `i` as a value of type `char`, and you convert this to lowercase, where necessary, by calling the `static` method `toLowerCase()` in the class `Character`. The character to be converted is passed as an argument, and the method returns either the original character or, if it is uppercase, the lowercase equivalent. This enables you to deal with all the characters in the string as if they were lowercase.

There is an alternative to using the `toLowerCase()` method in the `Character` class. The `String` class also contains a `toLowerCase()` method that will convert a whole string to lowercase and return a reference to the converted string. You could convert the string `text` to lowercase with the statement:

```
text = text.toLowerCase();                    // Convert string to lower case
```

This statement replaces the original string with the lowercase equivalent. If you wanted to retain the original, you could store the reference to the lowercase string in another variable of type `String`. The `String` class also defines the `toUpperCase()` method for converting a string to uppercase, which you use in the same way as the `toLowerCase()` method.

The `if` expression checks for any of the vowels by ORing the comparisons with the five vowels together. If the expression is `true`, you increment the `vowels` count. To check for a letter of any kind you use the `isLetter()` method in the `Character` class, and accumulate the total letter count in the variable `letters`. This enables you to calculate the number of consonants by subtracting the number of vowels from the total number of letters. Finally, the loop code checks for a space by using the `isWhitespace()` method in the class `Character`. This method returns `true` if the character passed as an argument is a

Unicode whitespace character. As well as spaces, whitespace in Unicode also includes horizontal and vertical tab, newline, carriage return, and form-feed characters. If you just wanted to count the spaces in the text, you could explicitly compare for a space character. After the `for` loop ends, you just output the results.

Searching Strings for Characters

There are two methods available to you in the `String` class that will search a string: `indexOf()` and `lastIndexOf()`. Each of these comes in four different flavors to provide a range of search possibilities. The basic choice is whether you want to search for a single character or for a substring, so let's look first at the options for searching a string for a given character.

To search a string `text` for a single character, `'a'` for example, you could write:

```
int index = 0;                    // Position of character in the string
index = text.indexOf('a');        // Find first index position containing 'a'
```

The method `indexOf()` will search the contents of the string `text` forwards from the beginning and return the index position of the first occurrence of `'a'`. If `'a'` is not found, the method will return the value -1.

> **This is characteristic of both search methods in the class String. They always return either the index position of what is sought or -1 if the search objective is not found. It is important that you check the index value returned for -1 before you use it to index a string; otherwise, you will get an error when you don't find what you are looking for.**

If you wanted to find the last occurrence of `'a'` in the `String` variable `text`, you just use the method `lastIndexOf()`:

```
index = text.lastIndexOf('a');         // Find last index position containing 'a'
```

The method searches the string backwards, starting with the last character in the string. The variable `index` therefore contains the index position of the last occurrence of `'a'`, or -1 if it is not found.

You can now find the first and last occurrences of a character in a string, but what about the ones in the middle? Well, there's a variation of each of the preceding methods that has a second argument to specify a "from position" from which to start the search. To search forwards from a given position, `startIndex`, you would write:

```
index = text.indexOf('a', startIndex);
```

This version of the method `indexOf()` searches the string for the character specified by the first argument starting with the position specified by the second argument. You could use this to find the first `'b'` that comes after the first `'a'` in a string with the following statements:

```
int aIndex = -1;                        // Position of 1st 'a'
int bIndex = -1;                        // Position of 1st 'b' after 'a'
aIndex = text.indexOf('a');             // Find first 'a'
if(aIndex >= 0) {                       // Make sure you found 'a'
    bIndex = text.indexOf('b', ++aIndex);  // Find 1st 'b' after 1st 'a'
}
```

Once you have the index value from the initial search for `'a'`, you need to check that `'a'` was really found by verifying that `aIndex` is not negative. You can then search for `'b'` from the position following `'a'`. As you can see, the second argument of this version of the method `indexOf()` is separated from the first argument by a comma. Since the second argument is the index position from which the search is to start, and `aIndex` is the position at which `'a'` was found, you should increment `aIndex` to the position following `'a'` before using it in the search for `'b'` to avoid checking for `'b'` in the position you already know contains `'a'`.

If `'a'` happened to be the last character in the string, it wouldn't matter, since the `indexOf()` method just returns –1 if the index value is beyond the last character in the string. If you somehow supplied a negative index value to the method, it would simply search the whole string from the beginning.

Of course, you could use the `indexOf()` method to count how many times a particular character occurred in a string:

```
int aIndex = -1;                        // Search start position
int count = 0;                          // Count of 'a' occurrences
while((aIndex = text.indexOf('a', ++aIndex)) > -1) {
    ++count;
}
```

The `while` loop condition expression calls the `indexOf()` method for the `String` object referenced by `text` and stores the result in the variable `aIndex`. If the value stored is greater than –1, it means that `'a'` was found, so the loop body executes and `count` is incremented. Because `aIndex` has –1 as its initial value, the search starts from index position 0 in the string, which is precisely what you want. When a search reaches the end of the string without finding `'a'`, –1 will be returned by the `indexOf()` method and the loop will end.

Searching for Substrings

The `indexOf()` and `lastIndexOf()` methods also come in versions that accept a string as the first argument, which will search for this string rather than a single character. In all other respects they work in the same way as the character searching methods you have just seen. I can summarize the complete set of `indexOf()` methods in the following table:

Method	Description
indexOf(int ch)	Returns the index position of the first occurrence of the character ch in the String for which the method is called. If the character ch does not occur, -1 is returned.
indexOf(int ch, int index)	Same as the preceding method, but with the search starting at position index in the string. If the value of index is outside the legal limits for the String object, -1 is returned.
indexOf(String str)	Returns the index position of the first occurrence of the substring str in the String object for which the method is called. If the substring str does not occur, -1 is returned.
indexOf(String str, int index)	Same as the preceding method, but with the search starting at position index in the string. If the value of index is outside the legal limits for the String object, -1 is returned.

The four flavors of the lastIndexOf() method have the same parameters as the four versions of the indexOf() method. The difference is that the last occurrence of the character or substring that is sought is returned by the lastIndexOf() method.

The startsWith() method that I mentioned earlier in the chapter also comes in a version that accepts an additional argument that is an offset from the beginning of the string being checked. The check for the matching character sequence then begins at that offset position. If you have defined a string as

```
String string1 = "The Ides of March";
```

then the expression String1.startsWith("Ides", 4) will have the value true.

I can show the indexOf() and lastIndexOf() methods at work with substrings in an example.

Try It Out   Exciting Concordance Entries

You'll use the indexOf() method to search the quotation you used in the last "Try It Out" example for "and" and the lastIndexOf() method to search for "the".

```
public class FindCharacters {
  public static void main(String[] args) {
    // Text string to be analyzed
    String text = "To be or not to be, that is the question;"
              + " Whether 'tis nobler in the mind to suffer"
              + " the slings and arrows of outrageous fortune,"
              + " or to take arms against a sea of troubles,"
              + " and by opposing end them?";
```

```
int andCount = 0;                  // Number of and's
int theCount = 0;                  // Number of the's

int index = -1;                    // Current index position

String andStr = "and";             // Search substring
String theStr = "the";             // Search substring

// Search forwards for "and"
index = text.indexOf(andStr);      // Find first 'and'
while(index >= 0) {
   ++andCount;
   index += andStr.length();       // Step to position after last 'and'
   index = text.indexOf(andStr, index);
}

// Search backwards for "the"
index = text.lastIndexOf(theStr);  // Find last 'the'
while(index >= 0) {
   ++theCount;
   index -= theStr.length();       // Step to position before last 'the'
   index = text.lastIndexOf(theStr, index);
}
System.out.println("The text contains " + andCount + " ands\n"
                 + "The text contains " + theCount + " thes");
   }
}
```

The program will produce the following output:

```
The text contains 2 ands
The text contains 5 thes
```

> If you were expecting the `"the"` count to be 3, note that there is one instance in
> `"whether"` and another in `"them"`. If you want to find three, you need to refine your
> program to eliminate such pseudo-occurrences by checking the characters on either
> side of the `"the"` substring.

How It Works

You define the `String` variable, `text`, as before, and set up two counters, `andCount` and `theCount`, for the two words. The variable `index` keeps track of the current position in the string. You then have `String` variables `andStr` and `theStr` holding the substrings you will be searching for.

To find the instances of `"and"`, you first find the index position of the first occurrence of `"and"` in the string `text`. If this index is negative, `text` does not contain `"and"`, and the `while` loop will not execute, as the condition is `false` on the first iteration. Assuming there is at least one `"and"`, the `while` loop block executes and `andCount` is incremented for the instance of `"and"` you have just found. The `indexOf()` method returns the index position of the first character of the substring, so you have to move the index forward to the character following the last character of the substring you have just found. This is done by adding the length of the substring, as shown in Figure 4-11.

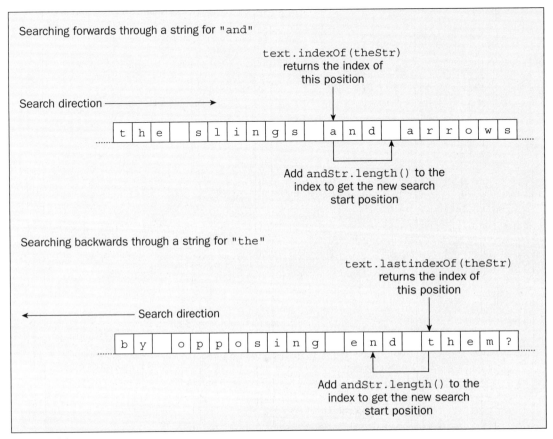

Figure 4-11

You are then able to search for the next occurrence of the substring by passing the new value of index to the indexOf() method. The loop continues as long as the index value returned is not -1.

To count the occurrences of the substring "the" the program searches the string text backwards, by using the method lastIndexOf() instead of indexOf(). This works in much the same way, the only significant difference being that you decrement the value of index, instead of incrementing it. This is because the next occurrence of the substring has to be at least that many characters back from the first character of the substring you have just found. If the string "the" happened to occur at the beginning of the string you are searching, the lastIndexOf() method would be called with a negative value for index. This would not cause any problem — it would just result in -1 being returned in any event.

Extracting Substrings

The `String` class includes the `substring()` method, which will extract a substring from a string. There are two versions of this method. The first version will extract a substring consisting of all the characters from a given index position up to the end of the string. This works as illustrated in the following code fragment:

```
String place = "Palm Springs";
String lastWord = place.substring(5);
```

After executing these statements, `lastWord` will contain the string `"Springs"`, which corresponds to the substring starting at index position 5 in `place` through to the end of the string. The method copies the substring from the original to form a new `String` object. This version of the method is useful when a string has basically two constituent substrings, but a more common requirement is to be able to extract several substrings from a string in which each substring is separated from the next by a particular delimiter character such as a comma, a slash, or even just a space. The second version of `substring()` will help with this.

The second version of the `substring()` method enables you to extract a substring from a string by specifying the index positions of the first character in the substring and one beyond the last character of the substring as arguments to the method. With the variable `place` being defined as before, the following statement will result in the variable `segment` being set to the string `"ring"`:

```
String segment = place.substring(7, 11);
```

> The `substring()` method is not like the `indexOf()` method when it comes to illegal index values. The `indexOf()` method returns -1 when you supply an invalid index value to it. With either version of the `substring()` method, an exception will be thrown if you specify an index that is outside the bounds of the string. As with the `charAt()` method, the `substring()` method will throw a `StringIndexOutOfBoundsException` **exception.**

You can see how `substring()` works with a more substantial example.

Try It Out   Word for Word

You can use the `indexOf()` method in combination with the `substring()` method to extract a sequence of substrings that are separated by spaces in a single string:

```
public class ExtractSubstrings {
    public static void main(String[] args) {
        String text = "To be or not to be";      // String to be segmented
        int count = 0;                            // Number of substrings
        char separator = ' ';                     // Substring separator

        // Determine the number of substrings
        int index = 0;
        do {
            ++count;                              // Increment count of substrings
```

```
      ++index;                                    // Move past last position
      index = text.indexOf(separator, index);
    } while (index != -1);

    // Extract the substring into an array
    String[] subStr = new String[count];          // Allocate for substrings
    index = 0;                                     // Substring start index
    int endIndex = 0;                              // Substring end index
    for(int i = 0; i < count; i++) {
      endIndex = text.indexOf(separator,index);   // Find next separator

      if(endIndex == -1) {                         // If it is not found
        subStr[i] = text.substring(index);         // extract to the end
      } else {                                           // otherwise
        subStr[i] = text.substring(index, endIndex);    // to end index
      }

      index = endIndex + 1;                        // Set start for next cycle
    }

    // Display the substrings
    for(String s : subStr) {                       // For each string in subStr
      System.out.println(s);                       // display it
    }
  }
}
```

When you run this example, you should get the following output:

```
To
be
or
not
to
be
```

How It Works

After setting up the string `text` to be segmented into substrings, a `count` variable to hold the number of substrings, and the separator character, `separator`, the program has three distinct phases:

1. The first phase counts the number of substrings by using the `indexOf()` method to find separators. The number of separators is always one less than the number of substrings. By using the `do-while` loop, you ensure that the value of `count` will be one more than the number of separators because there will always be one loop iteration for when the separator is not found.

2. The second phase extracts the substrings in sequence from the beginning of the string and stores them in an array of `String` variables that has `count` elements. A separator follows each substring from the first to the penultimate so you use the version of the `substring()` method that accepts two index arguments for these. The last substring is signaled by a failure to find the separator character when `index` will be -1. In this case you use the `substring()` method with a single argument to extract the substring through to the end of the string `text`.

3. The third phase simply outputs the contents of the array by displaying each element in turn, using a collection-based `for` loop. The `String` variable, s, defined in the loop will reference each string in the array in turn. You display each string by passing s as the argument to the `println()` method.

What you have been doing here is breaking a string up into **tokens** — substrings in other words — that are separated by **delimiters** — characters that separate one token from the next. This is such a sufficiently frequent requirement that Java provides you with an easier way to do this — using the `split()` method in the `String` class.

Tokenizing a String

The `split()` method in the `String` class is specifically for splitting a string into tokens. It does this in a single step, returning all the tokens from a string as an array of `String` objects. To do this it makes use of a facility called **regular expressions** that I'll discuss in detail in Chapter 15. However, you can still make use of the `split()` method without knowing about how regular expressions work so I'll largely ignore this aspect here. Just keep the `split()` method in mind when you get to Chapter 15.

The `split()` method expects two arguments. The first argument is a `String` object that specifies a **pattern** for a delimiter. Any delimiter that matches the pattern is assumed to be a separator for a token. Here I will talk only about patterns that are simply a set of possible delimiter characters in the string. But as you'll see in Chapter 15, the pattern for delimiters can be much more sophisticated than this. The second argument to the `split()` method is an integer value that is a count of the maximum number of times the pattern can be applied to find tokens and, therefore, affects the maximum number of tokens that can be found. If you specify the second argument as zero, the pattern will be applied as many times as possible, and any trailing empty tokens will be discarded. This can arise if several delimiters at the end of the string are being analyzed. If you specify the limit as a negative integer, the pattern will also be applied as many times as possible, but trailing empty tokens will be retained and returned. As I said earlier, the tokens found by the method are returned in an array of type `String[]`.

The key to tokenizing a string is providing the appropriate pattern defining the set of possible delimiters. At its simplest, a pattern can be a string containing a sequence of characters, each of which is a delimiter. You must specify the set of delimiters in the string between square brackets. This is necessary to distinguish a simple set of delimiter characters from more complex patterns. Examples are the string `"[abc]"` defining `'a'`, `'b'`, and `'c'` as delimiters, or `"[, .:;]"` specifying a comma, a period, a space, a colon, or a semicolon as delimiters. There are many more powerful ways of defining a pattern, but I will defer discussing that until Chapter 15.

To see how the `split()` method works, consider the following code fragment:

```
String text = "to be or not to be, that is the question.";
String[] words = text.split("[, .]", 0);   // Delimiters are comma, space, or period
```

The first statement defines the string to be analyzed and split into tokens. The second statement calls the `split()` method for the text object to tokenize the string. The first argument to the method specifies a comma, a space, or a period as possible delimiters. The second argument specifies the limit on the number of applications of the delimiter pattern as zero, so it will be applied as many times as necessary to tokenize the entire string. The `split()` method returns a reference to an array of strings that will be stored in the `words` variable. In case you hadn't noticed, these two lines of code do the same thing as most of the code in `main()` in the previous working example!

Another version of the split() method requires a single argument of type String specifying the pattern. This is equivalent to using the version with two arguments, where the second argument is zero, so you could write the second statement in the previous code fragment as:

```
String[] words = text.split("[, .]");   // Delimiters are comma, space, or period
```

This will produce exactly the same result as when you specify the second argument as 0. Now, it's time to explore the behavior of the split() method in an example.

Try It Out   Using a Tokenizer

Here you'll split a string completely into tokens with alternative explicit values for the second argument to the split() method to show the effect:

```java
public class StringTokenizing {
  public static void main(String[] args) {
    String text = "To be or not to be, that is the question.";  // String to segment
    String delimiters = "[, .]";              // Delimiters are comma, space, and period
    int[] limits = {0, -1};                   // Limit values to try

    // Analyze the string
    for(int limit : limits) {
      System.out.println("\nAnalysis with limit = " + limit);
      String[] tokens = text.split(delimiters, limit);
      System.out.println("Number of tokens: " + tokens.length);
      for(String token : tokens) {
        System.out.println(token);
      }
    }
  }
}
```

The program will generate two blocks of output. The first block of output corresponding to a limit value of 0 is:

```
Analysis with limit = 0
Number of tokens: 11
To
be
or
not
to
be

that
is
the
question
```

The second block of output corresponding to a limit value of -1 is:

```
Analysis with limit = -1
Number of tokens: 12
```

```
To
be
or
not
to
be

that
is
the
question
```

In this second case, you have an extra empty line at the end.

How It Works

The string identifying the possible delimiters for tokens in the text is defined by the statement

```
String delimiters = "[, .]";          // Delimiters are comma, space, and period
```

The characters between the square brackets are the delimiters, so here you have specified that comma, space, and period are delimiters. If you want to include other characters as delimiters, just add them between the square brackets. For example, the string `"[, .:;!?]"` adds a colon, a semicolon, an exclamation point, and a question mark to the original set of three delimiters.

You also have an array of values for the second argument to the `split()` method call:

```
int[] limits = {0, -1};               // Limit values to try
```

I included only two initial values for array elements to keep the amount of output in the book at a minimum, but you should try a few extra values.

The outer collection-based `for` loop iterates over the limit values in the `limits` array. The `limit` variable will be assigned the value of each element in the `limits` array in turn. The same string is split into tokens on each iteration, with the current limit value as the second argument to the `split()` method. You display the number of tokens produced by the `split()` method by outputting the length of the array that it returns. You then output the contents of the array that the `split()` method returns in the nested collection-based `for` loop. The loop variable, `token`, will reference each string in the `tokens` array in turn.

If you look at the first block of output, you will see that an array of 11 tokens was returned by the `split()` method. The text being analyzed contains 10 words, and the extra token arises because there are two successive delimiters, a comma followed by a space, in the middle of the string, which causes an empty token to be produced. It is possible to make the `split()` method recognize a comma followed (or preceded) by one or more spaces as a single delimiter but you'll have to wait until Chapter 15 to find out how it's done.

The second block of output has 12 tokens. This is because there is an extra empty token at the end of the list of tokens that is eliminated when the second argument to the `split()` method is 0. The extra token is there because the end of the string is always a delimiter, so the period followed by the end of the string identifies an empty token.

Modified Versions of String Objects

You can use a couple of methods to create a new String object that is a modified version of an existing String object. These methods don't change the original string, of course — as I said, String objects are immutable.

To replace one specific character with another throughout a string, you can use the replace() method. For example, to replace each space in the string text with a slash, you could write:

```
String newText = text.replace(' ', '/');      // Modify the string text
```

The first argument of the replace() method specifies the character to be replaced, and the second argument specifies the character that is to be substituted in its place. I have stored the result in a new variable newText here, but you could save it back in the original String variable, text, if you wanted to effectively replace the original string with the new modified version.

To remove whitespace from the beginning and end of a string (but not the interior) you can use the trim() method. You could apply this to a string as follows:

```
String sample = "   This is a string   ";
String result = sample.trim();
```

After these statements execute, the String variable result will contain the string "This is a string". This can be useful when you are segmenting a string into substrings and the substrings may contain leading or trailing blanks. For example, this might arise if you were analyzing an input string that contained values separated by one or more spaces.

Creating Character Arrays from String Objects

You can create an array of variables of type char from a String object by using the toCharArray() method that is defined in the String class. Because this method creates an array of type char and returns a reference to it, you only need to declare the array variable of type char[] to hold the array reference—you don't need to allocate the array. For example:

```
String text = "To be or not to be";
char[] textArray = text.toCharArray();      // Create the array from the string
```

The toCharArray() method returns an array containing the characters of the String variable text, one per element, so textArray[0] will contain 'T', textArray[1] will contain 'o', textArray[2] will contain ' ', and so on.

You can also extract a substring as an array of characters using the method getChars(), but in this case you do need to create an array that is large enough to hold the characters and pass it as an argument to the method. Of course, you can reuse a single array to store characters when you want to extract and process a succession of substrings one at a time and thus avoid having to repeatedly create new arrays. Of necessity, the array you are using must be large enough to accommodate the longest substring. The method getChars() expects four arguments. In sequence, these are:

❑   The index position of the first character to be extracted from the string (type int)

❑   The index position following the last character to be extracted from the string (type int)

❑ The name of the array to hold the characters extracted (type char[])

❑ The index of the array element to hold the first character (type int)

You could copy a substring from text into an array with the following statements:

```
String text = "To be or not to be";
char[] textArray = new char[3];
text.getChars(9, 12, textArray, 0);
```

This will copy characters from text at index positions 9 to 11 inclusive, so textArray[0] will be 'n', textArray[1] will be 'o', and textArray[2] will be 't'.

Using the Collection-Based for Loop with a String

You can't use a String object directly as the source of values for a collection-based for loop, but you have seen already that you can use an array. The toCharArray() method therefore provides you with a way to iterate over the characters in a string using a collection-based for loop. Here's an example:

```
String phrase = "The quick brown fox jumped over the lazy dog.";
int vowels = 0;
for(char ch : phrase.toCharArray()) {
  ch = Character.toLowerCase(ch);
  if(ch == 'a' || ch == 'e' || ch == 'i' || ch == 'o' || ch == 'u') {
    ++vowels;
  }
}
System.out.println("The phrase contains " + vowels + " vowels.");
```

This fragment calculates the number of vowels in the String phrase by iterating over the array of type char[] that the toCharArray() method for the string returns. The result of passing the value of the loop variable ch to the static toLowerCase() method in the Character class is stored back in ch. Of course, you could also use a numerical for loop to iterate over the element's characters in the string directly using the charAt() method.

Obtaining the Characters in a String as an Array of Bytes

You can extract characters from a string into a byte[] array using the getBytes() method in the class String. This converts the original string characters into the character encoding used by the underlying operating system — which is usually ASCII. For example:

```
String text = "To be or not to be";       // Define a string
byte[] textArray = text.getBytes();        // Get equivalent byte array
```

The byte array textArray will contain the same characters as in the String object, but stored as 8-bit characters. The conversion of characters from Unicode to 8-bit bytes will be in accordance with the default encoding for your system. This will typically mean that the upper byte of the Unicode character is discarded, resulting in the ASCII equivalent. Of course, it is quite possible that a string may contain Unicode characters that cannot be represented in the character encoding in effect on the local machine. In this case, the effect of the getBytes() method is unspecified.

Creating String Objects from Character Arrays

The `String` class also has a static method, `copyValueOf()`, to create a `String` object from an array of type `char[]`. You will recall that a static method of a class can be used even if no objects of the class exist.

Suppose you have an array defined as follows:

```
char[] textArray = {'T', 'o', ' ', 'b', 'e', ' ', 'o', 'r', ' ',
                    'n', 'o', 't', ' ', 't', 'o', ' ', 'b', 'e' };
```

You can then create a `String` object encapsulating these characters as a string with the following statement:

```
String text = String.copyValueOf(textArray);
```

This will result in the object `text` referencing the string `"To be or not to be"`.

You could achieve the same result like this:

```
String text = new String(textArray);
```

This calls a constructor for the `String` class, which creates a new object of type `String` that encapsulates a string containing the characters from the array. The `String` class defines several constructors for defining `String` objects from various types of arrays. You'll learn more about constructors in Chapter 5.

Another version of the `copyValueOf()` method can create a string from a subset of the array elements. It requires two additional arguments to specify the index of the first character in the array to be extracted and the count of the number of characters to be extracted. With the array defined as previously, the statement

```
String text = String.copyValueOf(textArray, 9, 3);
```

extracts three characters starting with `textArray[9]`, so `text` will contain the string `"not"` after this operation.

There's a class constructor that will do the same thing:

```
String text = new String(textArray, 9, 3);
```

The arguments are the same here as for the `copyValueOf()` method, and the result is the same.

Mutable Strings

`String` objects cannot be changed, but you have been creating strings that are combinations and modifications of existing `String` objects, so how is this done? Java has two other standard classes that encapsulate strings, the `StringBuffer` class and the `StringBuilder` class, and both `StringBuffer` and `StringBuilder` objects can be altered directly. Strings that can be changed are referred to as **mutable**

strings, in contrast to `String` objects that are **immutable strings**. Java uses objects of the `StringBuffer` class type internally to perform many of the operations that involve combining `String` objects. Once the required string has been formed as a `StringBuffer` object, it is then converted to an object of type `String`.

You have the choice of using either a `StringBuffer` object or a `StringBuilder` object whenever you need a string that you can change directly, so what's the difference? In terms of the operations these two classes provide, there is no difference, but `StringBuffer` objects are safe for use by multiple threads, whereas `StringBuilder` objects are not. You'll be learning about threads in Chapter 16, but in case you're not familiar with the term, **threads** are just independent execution processes within a program that can execute concurrently. For example, an application that involves acquiring data from several remote sites could implement the data transfer from each remote site as a separate thread. This would allow these relatively slow operations to execute in parallel, sharing processor time in a manner determined by the operating system. This usually means that the elapsed time for acquiring all the data from the remote sites would be much less than if the operations were executed sequentially in a single thread of execution.

Of course, if concurrent threads of execution access the same object, there is potential for problems. Complications can arise when one thread might be accessing an object while another is in the process of modifying it. When this sort of thing is possible in your application, you must use the `StringBuffer` class to define mutable strings if you want to avoid trouble. The `StringBuffer` class operations have been coded to prevent errors arising from concurrent access by two or more threads. If you are sure that your mutable strings will be accessed only by a single thread of execution, then you should use `StringBuilder` objects because operations on these will be faster than with `StringBuffer` objects.

So when should you use mutable `String` objects rather than immutable `String` objects? `StringBuffer` and `StringBuilder` objects come into their own when you are transforming strings frequently — adding, deleting, or replacing substrings in a string. Operations will be faster and easier using mutable objects. If you have mainly static strings that you occasionally need to concatenate in your application, then `String` objects will be the best choice. Of course, if you want to, you can mix the use of both mutable and immutable in the same program.

As I said, the `StringBuilder` class provides the same set of operations as the `StringBuffer` class. I'll describe mutable string operations in terms of the `StringBuffer` class for the rest of this chapter because this is always a safe choice, but don't forget that all the operations that I discuss in the context of `StringBuffer` are available with the `StringBuilder` class, which will be faster but not thread-safe.

Creating StringBuffer Objects

You can create a `StringBuffer` object that contains a given string with the following statement:

```
StringBuffer aString = new StringBuffer("A stitch in time");
```

This declares a `StringBuffer` object, `aString`, and initializes it with the string `"A stitch in time"`. When you are initializing a `StringBuffer` object, you must use this syntax, with the keyword `new`, the `StringBuffer` class name, and the initializing value between parentheses. You cannot just use the string as the initializing value as you did with `String` objects. This is because there is rather more to a `StringBuffer` object than just the string that it contains initially, and, of course, a string literal is a `String` object by definition.

You can also create a `StringBuffer` object using a reference stored in a variable of type `String`:

```
String phrase = "Experience is what you get when you're expecting something else.";
StringBuffer buffer = new StringBuffer(phrase);
```

The `StringBuffer` object, `buffer`, will contain a string that is the same as that encapsulated by the `String` object, `phrase`.

You can just create the `StringBuffer` variable, in much the same way as you created a `String` variable:

```
StringBuffer myString = null;
```

This variable does not refer to anything until you initialize it with a defined `StringBuffer` object. For example, you could write:

```
myString = new StringBuffer("Many a mickle makes a muckle");
```

This statement creates a new `StringBuffer` object encapsulating the string `"Many a mickle makes a muckle"` and stores the reference to this object in `myString`. You can also initialize a `StringBuffer` variable with an existing `StringBuffer` object:

```
StringBuffer aString = myString;
```

Both `myString` and `aString` will now refer to a single `StringBuffer` object.

The Capacity of a StringBuffer Object

The `String` objects that you have been using each contain a fixed string, and when you create a `String` object, memory is allocated to accommodate however many Unicode characters are in the string it encapsulates. Everything is fixed so memory usage is not a problem. A `StringBuffer` object is a little different. It contains a block of memory called a **buffer**, which may or may not contain a string, and if it does, the string need not occupy the entire buffer. Thus, the length of a string in a `StringBuffer` object can be different from the length of the buffer that the object contains. The length of the buffer is referred to as the **capacity** of the `StringBuffer` object.

Once you have created a `StringBuffer` object, you can find the length of the string it contains, by using the `length()` method for the object:

```
StringBuffer aString = new StringBuffer("A stitch in time");
int theLength = aString.length();
```

If the object `aString` were defined as in the preceding declaration, the variable `theLength` would have the value 16. However, the capacity of the object is larger, as illustrated in Figure 4-12.

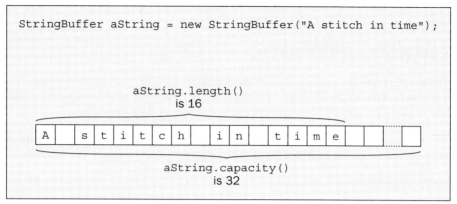

Figure 4-12

When you create a StringBuffer object from an existing string, the capacity will be the length of the string plus 16. Both the capacity and the length are in units of Unicode characters, so twice as many bytes will be occupied in memory.

The capacity of a StringBuffer object is not fixed though. It grows automatically as you add to the string to accommodate a string of any length. You can also specify the initial capacity when you create a StringBuffer object. For example, the following statement creates a StringBuffer object with a specific value for the capacity:

```
StringBuffer newString = new StringBuffer(50);
```

This will create an object, newString, with the capacity to store 50 characters. If you omitted the capacity value in this declaration, the object would have a default capacity of 16 characters. Thus, the StringBuffer object that you create here has a buffer with a capacity of 50 characters that is initially empty — no string is stored in it.

A String object is always a fixed string, so capacity is irrelevant — it is always just enough to hold the characters in the string. A StringBuffer object on the other hand is a container in which you can store a string of any length, and it has a capacity at any given instant for storing a string up to a given size. Although you can set the capacity, it is unimportant in the sense that it is just a measure of how much memory is available to store Unicode characters at this particular point in time. You can get by without worrying about the capacity of a StringBuffer object at all since the capacity required to cope with what your program is doing will always be provided automatically. It just gets increased as necessary.

So why have I mentioned the capacity of a StringBuffer object at all? While it's true you can use StringBuffer objects ignoring their capacity, the capacity of a StringBuffer object is important in the sense that it affects the amount of overhead involved in storing and modifying a string. If the initial capacity is small, and you store a string that is long, or you add to an existing string significantly, extra memory will need to be allocated. Allocating additional memory will take time, and if it occurs frequently, it can add a substantial overhead to the processor time your program needs to complete the task. It is more efficient to make the capacity of a StringBuffer sufficient for the needs of your program.

To find out what the capacity of a `StringBuffer` object is at any given time, you use the `capacity()` method for the object:

```
int theCapacity = aString.capacity();
```

This method will return the number of Unicode characters the object can currently hold. For `aString` defined as shown, this will be 32. When you create a `StringBuffer` object containing a string, its capacity will be 16 characters greater than the minimum necessary to hold the string.

The `ensureCapacity()` method enables you to change the default capacity of a `StringBuffer` object. You specify the minimum capacity you need as the argument to the method. For example:

```
aString.ensureCapacity(40);
```

If the current capacity of the `aString` object is less than 40, this will increase the capacity of `aString` by allocating a new larger buffer, but not necessarily with a capacity of 40. The capacity will be the larger of either the value that you specify, 40 in this case, or twice the current capacity plus 2, which is 66, given that `aString` is defined as before. You might want to do this sort of thing when you are reusing an existing `StringBuffer` object in a new context where the strings are longer.

Changing the String Length for a StringBuffer Object

You can change the length of the string contained in a `StringBuffer` object with the method `setLength()`. Note that the length is a property of the string the object holds, as opposed to the capacity, which is a property of the string buffer. When you increase the length for a `StringBuffer` object, you are adding characters to the existing string and the extra characters will contain `'\u0000'`. A more common use of this method would be to decrease the length, in which case the string will be truncated. If `aString` contains `"A stitch in time"`, the statement

```
aString.setLength(8);
```

will result in `aString` containing the string `"A stitch"`, and the value returned by the `length()` method will be 8. The characters that were cut from the end of the string by this operation are lost.

To increase the length to what it was before, you could write:

```
aString.setLength(16);
```

Now `aString` will contain the string

```
"A stitch\u0000\u0000\u0000\u0000\u0000\u0000\u0000\u0000"
```

The `setLength()` method does not affect the capacity of the object unless you set the length to be greater than the capacity. In this case the capacity will be increased to accommodate the new string length to a value that is twice the original capacity plus two if the length you set is less than this value. If you specify a length that is greater than twice the original capacity plus two, the new capacity will be the same as the length you set. If the capacity of `aString` is 66, executing the statement

```
aString.setLength(100);
```

will set the capacity of the object, aString, to 134. If you supplied a value for the length of 150, then the new capacity would be 150. You must not specify a negative length here. If you do, a StringIndexOutOfBoundsException exception will be thrown.

Adding to a StringBuffer Object

The append() method enables you to add a string to the end of the existing string stored in a StringBuffer object. This method comes in quite a few flavors, but perhaps the simplest adds a String constant to a StringBuffer object.

Suppose you define a StringBuffer object with the following statement:

```
StringBuffer aString = new StringBuffer("A stitch in time");
```

You can add to it with the statement:

```
aString.append(" saves nine");
```

after which aString will contain "A stitch in time saves nine". The length of the string contained in the StringBuffer object is increased by the length of the string that you add. You don't need to worry about running out of space though. The capacity will always be increased automatically whenever necessary to accommodate the longer string.

The append() method returns a reference to the extended StringBuffer object, so you could also assign it to another StringBuffer object. Instead of the previous statement, you could have written:

```
StringBuffer bString = aString.append(" saves nine");
```

Now both aString and bString point to the same StringBuffer object.

If you take a look at the operator precedence table back in Chapter 2, you will see that the ' . ' operator (sometimes called the member selection operator) that you use to execute a particular method for an object has left-to-right associativity. You can therefore write multiple append operations in a single statement:

```
StringBuffer proverb = new StringBuffer();              // Capacity is 16
proverb.append("Many").append(" hands").append(" make").
            append(" light").append(" work.");
```

The second statement is executed from left to right, so that the string contained in the object proverb is progressively extended until it contains the complete string. The reference that each call to append() returns is used to call append() again for the same object, proverb.

Appending a Substring

Another version of the append() method adds part of a String object to a StringBuffer object. This version of append() requires you to specify two additional arguments: the index position of the first character in the String object that is to be appended and the total number of characters to be appended.

To illustrate the workings of this, suppose you create a `StringBuffer` object and a `String` object with the following statements:

```
StringBuffer buf = new StringBuffer("Hard ");
String aString = "Waxworks";
```

You can then append part of the `aString` object to the `buf` object with this statement:

```
buf.append(aString, 3, 4);
```

This operation is shown in Figure 4-13.

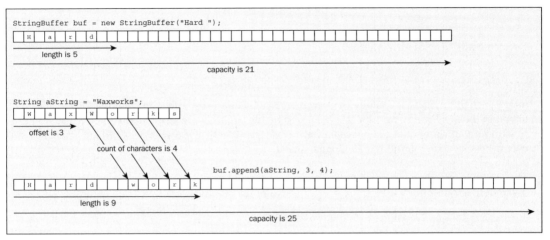

Figure 4-13

This operation appends a substring of `aString` consisting of four characters starting at index position 3 to the `StringBuffer` object `buf`. The object `buf` will then contain the string `"Hard work"`. The capacity of the `StringBuffer` object is automatically increased by the length of the appended substring, if necessary.

Appending Basic Types

You have a set of versions of the `append()` method that will enable you to `append()` the string equivalent of values of any of the primitive types to a `StringBuffer` object. These versions of `append()` will accept arguments of any of the following types: `boolean`, `char`, `byte`, `short`, `int`, `long`, `float`, or `double`. In each case, the value is converted to a string equivalent of the value, which is appended to the object, so a `boolean` variable will be appended as either "true" or "false", and for numeric types the string will be a decimal representation of the value. For example:

```
StringBuffer buf = new StringBuffer("The number is ");
long number = 999;
buf.append(number);
```

will result in `buf` containing the string `"The number is 999"`.

There is nothing to prevent you from appending constants to a `StringBuffer` object. For example, if you now execute the statement

```
buf.append(12.34);
```

the object `buf` will contain `"The number is 99912.34"`.

There is also a version of the `append()` method that accepts an array of type `char` as an argument. The contents of the array are appended to the `StringBuffer` object as a string. A further variation on this enables you to append a subset of the elements from an array of type `char` by using two additional arguments: one to specify the index of the first element to be appended, and another to specify the total number of elements to be appended. An example of how you might use this is as follows:

```
char[] text = { 'i', 's', ' ', 'e', 'x', 'a', 'c', 't', 'l', 'y'};
buf.append(text, 2, 8);
```

This appends the string `"exactly"` to buf, so after executing this statement `buf` contains `"The number is 99912.34 exactly"`.

You may be somewhat bemused by the plethora of `append()` method options, so let's collect all the possibilities together. You can append any of the following types to a `StringBuffer` object:

boolean	char	String	Object
int	long	float	double
byte	short		

You can also append an array of type `char[]` and a subset of the elements of an array of type `char[]`. In each case the `String` equivalent of the argument is appended to the string in the `StringBuffer` object.

I haven't discussed type `Object` yet—I included it in the table here for the sake of completeness. You will learn about this type of object in Chapter 6.

Finding the Position of a Substring

You can search the buffer of a `StringBuffer` object for a given substring by calling the `lastIndexOf()` method. The simpler of the two versions of this method requires just one argument, which is the string you are looking for, and the method returns the index position of the last occurrence of the string you are searching for as a value of type `int`. The method returns -1 if the substring is not found. For example:

```
StringBuffer phrase = new StringBuffer("one two three four");
int position = phrase.lastIndexOf("three");
```

The value returned is the index position of the first character of `"three"` in `phrase`, which will be 8. Remember, the first character is at index position 0. Of course, if the argument to the `lastIndexOf()` method were `"t"`, the result would be the same because the method finds the last occurrence of the substring in the buffer.

The second version of the `lastIndexOf()` method requires an additional argument that specifies the index position in the buffer where the search is to start. For example:

```
position = phrase.lastIndexOf("three", 6);
```

This statement starts the search at index position 6 so the first six characters (index values 0 to 5) in the buffer will not be examined. Obviously, because the `lastIndexOf()` method finds the last occurrence of the substring, this version of the method does not help you find multiple occurrences. It just provides a way for you to avoid searching some initial part of the buffer when you know in advance where you expect the substring to be found.

Replacing a Substring in the Buffer

You use the `replace()` method for a `StringBuffer` object to replace a contiguous sequence of characters with a given string. The string that you specify as the replacement can contain more characters than the substring being replaced, in which case the string will be extended as necessary. The `replace()` method requires three arguments. The first two are of type `int` and specify the start index in the buffer and one beyond the end index of the substring to be replaced. The third argument is of type `String` and is the string to be inserted. Here's an example of how you might use the `replace()` method:

```
StringBuffer phrase = new StringBuffer("one two three four");
String substring = "two";
String replacement = "twenty";
int position = phrase.lastIndexOf(substring);              // Find start of "two"
phrase.replace(position, position+substring.length(), replacement);
```

The first three statements define the original `StringBuffer` object, the `substring` to be replaced, and the string to replace the `substring`. The next statement uses the `lastIndexOf()` method to find the position of the first character of the last occurrence of `substring` in phrase. The last statement uses the `replace()` method to substitute `replacement` in place of `substring`. To get the index value for one beyond the last character of `substring`, you just add the length of `substring` to its position index. Because `replacement` is a string containing more characters than `substring`, the length of the string in phrase will be increased, and the new contents will be `"one twenty three four"`.

I have not bothered to insert code to check for the possibility of -1 being returned in the preceding code fragment, but naturally in a real-world context it is essential to do this to avoid the program being terminated when the `substring` is not present.

Inserting Strings

To insert a string into a `StringBuffer` object, you use the `insert()` method of the object. The first argument specifies the index of the position in the object where the first character is to be inserted. For example, if `buf` contains the string `"Many hands make light work"`, the statement

```
buf.insert(4, " old");
```

will insert the string `" old"` starting at index position 4, so `buf` will contain the string `"Many old hands make light work"` after executing this statement.

Many versions of the `insert()` method accept a second argument of any of the same range of types that apply to the `append()` method, so you can use any of the following with the `insert()` method:

boolean	char	String	Object
int	long	float	double
byte	short		

In each case the string equivalent of the second argument is inserted starting at the index position specified by the first argument. You can also insert an array of type `char[]`, and if you need to insert a subset of an array of type `char[]` into a `StringBuffer` object, you can call the version of `insert()` that accepts four arguments:

Method	Description

insert(int index,
        char[] str,
        int offset,
        int length)
	Inserts a substring into the `StringBuffer` object starting at position `index`. The substring is the `String` representation of `length` characters from the `str[]` array, starting at position `offset`.

If the value of `index` is outside the range of the string in the `StringBuffer` object, or the `offset` or `length` values result in illegal indexes for the array `str`, then an exception of type `StringIndexOutOfBoundsException` will be thrown.

Extracting Characters from a Mutable String

The `StringBuffer` class includes the `charAt()` and `getChars()` methods, both of which work in the same way as the methods of the same name in the `String` class which you've already seen. The `charAt()` method extracts the character at a given index position, and the `getChars()` method extracts a range of characters and stores them in an array of type `char` starting at a specified index position. You should note that there is no equivalent to the `getBytes()` method for `StringBuffer` objects.

Other Mutable String Operations

You can change a single character in a `StringBuffer` object by using the `setCharAt()` method. The first argument indicates the index position of the character to be changed, and the second argument specifies the replacement character. For example, the statement

```
buf.setCharAt(3, 'Z');
```

will set the fourth character in the string to `'Z'`.

You use the `deleteCharAt()` method to remove a single character from a `StringBuffer` object at the index position specified by the argument. For example:

```
StringBuffer phrase = new StringBuffer("When the boats come in");
phrase.deleteCharAt(10);
```

After these statements have executed, `phrase` will contain the string `"When the bats come in"`.

If you want to remove several characters from a `StringBuffer` object you use the `delete()` method. This method requires two arguments: The first is the index of the first character to be deleted and the second is the index position following the last character to be deleted. For example:

```
phrase.delete(5, 9);
```

This statement will delete the substring `"the "` from `phrase`, so it will then contain the string `"When bats come in"`.

You can completely reverse the sequence of characters in a `StringBuffer` object with the `reverse()` method. For example, if you define the object with the declaration

```
StringBuffer palindrome = new StringBuffer("so many dynamos");
```

you can then transform it with the statement

```
palindrome.reverse();
```

which results in `palindrome` containing the useful phrase "somanyd ynam os".

Creating a String Object from a StringBuffer Object

You can produce a `String` object from a `StringBuffer` object by using the `toString()` method of the `StringBuffer` class. This method creates a new `String` object and initializes it with the string contained in the `StringBuffer` object. For example, to produce a `String` object containing the proverb that you created in the previous section, you could write:

```
String saying = proverb.toString();
```

The object `saying` will contain `"Many hands make light work"`.

The `toString()` method is used extensively by the compiler together with the `append()` method to implement the concatenation of `String` objects. When you write a statement such as:

```
String saying = "Many" + " hands" + " make" + " light" + " work";
```

the compiler will implement this as:

```
String saying = new StringBuffer().append("Many").append(" hands").
                        append(" make").append(" light").
                        append(" work").toString();
```

The expression to the right of the = sign is executed from left to right, so the segments of the string are appended to the `StringBuffer` object that is created until finally the `toString()` method is invoked to convert it to a `String` object. `String` objects can't be modified, so any alteration or extension of a `String` object will involve the use of a `StringBuffer` object, which can be changed.

It's time to see a `StringBuffer` object in action.

Using a StringBuffer Object to Assemble a String

This example just exercises some of the `StringBuffer` operations you have seen by assembling a string from an array of words and then inserting some additional characters into the string:

```
public class UseStringBuffer {
  public static void main(String[] args) {
    StringBuffer sentence = new StringBuffer(20);
    System.out.println("\nStringBuffer object capacity is "+ sentence.capacity()+
                    " and string length is "+sentence.length());

    // Append all the words to the StringBuffer object
    String[] words = {"Too"   , "many", "cooks", "spoil", "the" , "broth"};
    sentence.append(words[0]);
    for(int i = 1 ; i<words.length ; i++) {
      sentence.append(' ').append(words[i]);
    }

    // Show the result
    System.out.println("\nString in StringBuffer object is:\n" +
                                                sentence.toString());
    System.out.println("StringBuffer object capacity is now "+ sentence.capacity()+
                    " and string length is "+sentence.length());

    // Now modify the string by inserting characters
    sentence.insert(sentence.lastIndexOf("cooks")+4,"ie");
    sentence.insert(sentence.lastIndexOf("broth")+5, "er");
    System.out.println("\nString in StringBuffer object is:\n" + sentence);
    System.out.println("StringBuffer object capacity is now "+ sentence.capacity()+
                    " and string length is "+sentence.length());

  }
}
```

The output from this example will be:

```
StringBuffer object capacity is 20 and string length is 0

String in StringBuffer object is:
Too many cooks spoil the broth
StringBuffer object capacity is now 42 and string length is 30

String in StringBuffer object is:
Too many cookies spoil the brother
StringBuffer object capacity is now 42 and string length is 34
```

How It Works

You first create a `StringBuffer` object with a buffer capacity of 20 characters with the following statement:

```
StringBuffer sentence = new StringBuffer(20);
```

The output statement that follows just displays the buffer capacity and the initial string length. You obtain these by calling the `capacity()` and `length()` methods, respectively, for the `sentence` object. The string length is zero because you have not specified any buffer contents.

The next four statements create an array of words and append those words to `sentence`:

```
String[] words = {"Too"  , "many", "cooks", "spoil", "the" , "broth"};
sentence.append(words[0]);
for(int i = 1 ; i<words.length ; i++) {
  sentence.append(' ').append(words[i]);
```

To start the process of building the string, you append the first word from the `words` array to `sentence`. You then append all the subsequent words in the `for` loop, preceding each word with a space character.

The next output statement displays the buffer contents as a string by calling the `toString()` method for `sentence` to create a `String` object. You then output the buffer capacity and string length for `sentence` once more. The output shows that the capacity has been automatically increased to 42 and the length of the string is 30.

In the last phase of the program you insert the string `"ie"` after the substring `"cook"` with the statement

```
sentence.insert(sentence.lastIndexOf("cooks")+4,"ie");
```

The `lastIndexOf()` method returns the index position of the last occurrence of `"cooks"` in `sentence` so you add 4 to this to specify the insertion position after the last letter of `"cook"`. You use the same mechanism to insert the string `"er"` following `"broth"` in the buffer.

Finally, you output the string and the capacity and string length with the last two statements in `main()`:

```
System.out.println("\nString in StringBuffer object is:\n" + sentence);
System.out.println("StringBuffer object capacity is now "+ sentence.capacity()+
                   " and string length is "+sentence.length());
```

Note that the first output statement does not call the `toString()` method explicitly. The compiler will insert the call for you to convert the `StringBuffer` object to a `String` object. This is necessary to make it compatible with the + operator for `String` objects.

Summary

You should now be thoroughly familiar with how to create and use arrays. Most people have little trouble dealing with one-dimensional arrays, but arrays of arrays are a bit trickier so try to practice using these.

You have also acquired a good knowledge of what you can do with `String` objects, as well as `StringBuffer` and `StringBuilder` objects. Most operations with these objects are very straightforward and easy to understand. Being able to decide which methods you should apply to the solution of specific problems is a skill that will come with a bit of practice.

The essential points that I have discussed in this chapter are:

❑   You use an array to hold multiple values of the same type, identified through a single variable name.

❑   You reference an individual element of an array by using an index value of type int. The index value for an array element is the offset of that element from the first element in the array.

❑   An array element can be used in the same way as a single variable of the same type.

❑   You can obtain the number of elements in an array by using the length member of the array object.

❑   An array element can also contain an array, so you can define arrays of arrays, or arrays of arrays of arrays, and so on.

❑   A String object stores a fixed character string that cannot be changed. However, you can assign a given String variable to a different String object.

❑   You can obtain the number of characters stored in a String object by using the length() method for the object.

❑   The String class provides methods for joining, searching, and modifying strings — the modifications being achieved by creating a new String object.

❑   StringBuffer and StringBuilder objects can store a string of characters that you can modify.

❑   StringBuffer and StringBuilder objects support the same set of operations. StringBuffer objects are safe when accessed by multiple threads of execution whereas StringBuilder object are not.

❑   You can get the number of characters stored in a StringBuffer object by calling its length() method, and you can find out the current maximum number of characters it can store by using its capacity() method.

❑   You can change both the length and the capacity for a StringBuffer object.

❑   You can create a String object from a StringBuffer object by using the toString() method of the StringBuffer object.

Exercises

You can download the source code for the examples in the book and the solutions to the following exercises from http://www.wrox.com.

1.   Create an array of String variables and initialize the array with the names of the months from January to December. Create an array containing 12 random decimal values between 0.0 and 100.0. Display the names of each month along with the corresponding decimal value. Calculate and display the average of the 12 decimal values.

2.   Write a program to create a rectangular array containing a multiplication table from 1 * 1 up to 12 * 12. Output the table as 13 columns with the numeric values right-aligned in columns. (The first line of output will be the column headings, the first column with no heading, then the numbers 1 to 12 for the remaining columns. The first item in each of the succeeding lines is the row heading, which ranges from 1 to 12.)

3. Write a program that sets up a `String` variable containing a paragraph of text of your choice. Extract the words from the text and sort them into alphabetical order. Display the sorted list of words. You could use a simple sorting method called the bubble sort. To sort an array into ascending order the process is as follows:

   a. Starting with the first element in the array, compare successive elements (0 and 1, 1 and 2, 2 and 3, and so on).

   b. If the first element of any pair is greater than the second, interchange the two elements.

   c. Repeat the process for the whole array until no interchanges are necessary. The array elements will now be in ascending order.

4. Define an array of ten `String` elements each containing an arbitrary string of the form `"month/day/year"`; for example, `"10/29/99"` or `"12/5/01"`. Analyze each element in the array and output the date represented in the form 29th October 1999.

5. Write a program that will reverse the sequence of letters in each word of your chosen paragraph from Exercise 3. For instance, `"To be or not to be."` would become `"oT eb ro ton ot eb."`

Defining Classes

In this chapter you'll explore the heart of the Java language—classes. Classes specify the objects you use in object-oriented programming. These form the basic building blocks of any Java program, as you saw in Chapter 1. Every program in Java involves classes, since the code for a program can appear only within a class definition.

You'll be exploring the details of how a class definition is put together, how to create your own classes, and how to use classes to solve your own computing problems. And in the next chapter, you'll build on this to look at how object-oriented programming helps you work with sets of related classes.

By the end of this chapter you will have learned:

- ❏ What a class is, and how you define a class
- ❏ How to implement class constructors
- ❏ How to define class methods
- ❏ What method overloading is
- ❏ What a recursive method is and how it works
- ❏ How to create objects of a class type
- ❏ What packages are and how you can create and use them
- ❏ What access attributes are and how you should use them in your class definitions
- ❏ What nested classes are and how you use them
- ❏ When you should add the `finalize()` method to a class
- ❏ What native methods are

What Is a Class?

As you saw in Chapter 1, a class is a prescription for a particular kind of object — it defines a new **type**. You use the definition of a class to create objects of that class type — that is, to create objects that incorporate all the components specified as belonging to that class.

> *In case that's too abstract, look back to the previous chapter where you used the* String *class. The* String *class is a comprehensive definition for a* String *object, with all the operations you are likely to need specified. Whenever you create a new* String *object, you are creating an object with all the characteristics and operations specified by the class definition. Every* String *object has all the methods that the* String *class defines built in. This makes* String *objects indispensable, and string handling within a program easy.*

The String class lies toward one end of a spectrum in terms of complexity in a class. The String class is intended to be usable in any program. It includes facilities and capabilities for operating on String objects to cover virtually all circumstances in which you are likely to use strings. In most cases your own classes won't need to be this elaborate. You will typically be defining a class to suit your particular application, and you will make it as simple or complex as necessary. Some classes, such as a Plane or a Person, for example, may well represent objects that can potentially be very complicated, but the application requirements may be very limited. A Person object might just contain a name, address, and phone number, for example, if you are just implementing an address book. In another context, in a payroll program perhaps, you might need to represent a Person with a whole host of properties, such as age, marital status, length of service, job code, pay rate, and so on. How you define a class depends on what you intend to do with objects of your class.

In essence, a class definition is very simple. There are just two kinds of things that you can include in a class definition:

- ❏ **Fields** — These are variables that store data items that typically differentiate one object of the class from another. They are also referred to as **data members** of a class.

- ❏ **Methods** — These define the operations you can perform for the class — so they determine what you can do to, or with, objects of the class. Methods typically operate on the fields — the variables of the class.

The fields in a class definition can be of any of the primitive types, or they can be references to objects of any class type, including the one that you are defining.

The methods in a class definition are named, self-contained blocks of code that typically operate on the fields that appear in the class definition. Note, though, that this doesn't necessarily have to be the case, as you might have guessed from the main() methods you have written in all the examples up to now.

Fields in a Class Definition

An object of a class is also referred to as an **instance** of that class. When you create an object, the object will contain all the fields that were included in the class definition. However, the fields in a class definition are not all the same — there are two kinds.

One kind of field is associated with the class, and is shared by all objects of the class. There is only one copy of each of these kinds of fields no matter how many class objects are created, and they exist even if no objects of the class have been created. This kind of variable is referred to as a **class variable** because the field belongs to the class and not to any particular object, although as I've said, all objects of the class will share it. These fields are also referred to as **static fields** because you use the `static` keyword when you declare them.

The other kind of field in a class is associated with each object uniquely — each instance of the class will have its own copy of each of these fields, each with its own value assigned. These fields differentiate one object from another, giving an object its individuality — the particular name, address, and telephone number in a given `Person` object, for example. These are referred to as **non-static fields** or **instance variables** because you specify them without using the `static` keyword, and each instance of a class type will have its own independent set.

Because this is extremely important to understand, let's summarize the two kinds of fields that you can include in your classes:

❑ **Non-static fields, also called instance variables** — Each object of the class will have its own copy of each of the non-static fields or instance variables that appear in the class definition. Each object will have its own values for each instance variable. The name *instance variable* originates from the fact that an object is an *instance* or an occurrence of a class, and the values stored in the instance variables for the object differentiate the object from others of the same class type. An instance variable is declared within the class definition in the usual way, with a type name and a variable name, and can have an initial value specified.

❑ **Static fields, also called class variables** — A given class will have only one copy of each of its static fields or class variables, and these will be shared between and among all the objects of the class. Each class variable exists even if no objects of the class have been created. Class variables belong to the class, and they can be referenced by any object or class method, not just methods belonging to instances of that class. If the value of a static field is changed, the new value is available equally in all the objects of the class. This is quite different from non-static fields, where changing a value for one object does not affect the values in other objects. A static field must be declared using the keyword `static` preceding the type name.

Look at Figure 5-1, which illustrates the difference between class variables and instance variables.

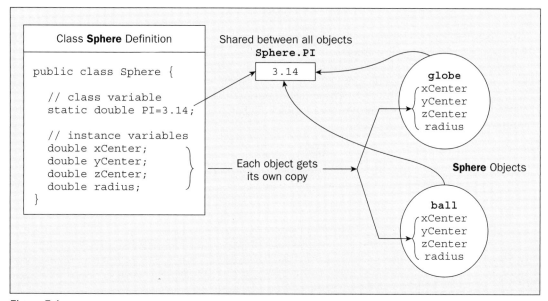

Figure 5-1

Figure 5-1 shows a schematic of a class, Sphere, that has one class variable, PI, and four instance variables, radius, xCenter, yCenter, and zCenter. Each of the objects, globe and ball, will have its own set of variables with the names radius, xCenter, yCenter, and zCenter, but both will share a single copy of the class variable PI.

Why would you need two kinds of variables in a class definition? The instance variables are clearly necessary since they store the values that distinguish one particular object from another. The radius and the coordinates of the center of the sphere are fundamental to determining how big a particular Sphere object is, and where it is in space. However, although the variable PI is a fundamental parameter for every sphere — to calculate the volume, for example — it would be wasteful to store a value for PI in every Sphere object, since it is always the same. As you know, it is also available from the standard class Math so it is somewhat superfluous in this case, but you get the general idea. So one use for class variables is to hold constant values such as (that are common to all objects of the class.

Another use for class variables is to track data values that are common to all objects of a class and that need to be available even when no objects have been defined. For example, if you wanted to keep a count of how many objects of a class have been created in your program, you could define a variable to store the count of the number of objects as a class variable. It would be essential to use a class variable, because you would still want to be able to use your count variable even when no objects have been declared.

Methods in a Class Definition

The methods that you define for a class provide the actions that can be carried out using the variables specified in the class definition. Analogous to the variables in a class definition are two varieties of methods — **instance methods** and **class methods.** You can execute class methods even when no objects of a class exist, whereas instance methods can be executed only in relation to a particular object, so if no objects exist, you have no way to execute any of the instance methods defined in the class. Again, like class variables, class methods are declared using the keyword static, so they are sometimes referred to as **static methods.** You saw in the previous chapter that the valueOf() method is a static member of the String class.

Since static methods can be executed when there are no objects in existence, they cannot refer to instance variables. This is quite sensible if you think about it — trying to operate with variables that might not exist would be bound to cause trouble. In fact the Java compiler won't let you try. If you reference an instance variable in the code for a static method, it won't compile — you'll just get an error message. The main() method, where execution of a Java application starts, must always be declared as static, as you have seen. The reason for this should be apparent by now. Before an application starts execution, no objects exist, so to start execution, you need a method that is executable even though there are no objects around — a static method therefore.

The Sphere class might well have an instance method volume() to calculate the volume of a particular object. It might also have a class method objectCount() to return the current count of how many objects of type Sphere have been created. If no objects exist, you could still call this method and get the count 0.

Note that although instance methods are specific to objects of a class, there is only ever one copy of each instance method in memory that is shared by all objects of the class, as it would be extremely expensive to replicate all the instance methods for each object. A special mechanism ensures that each time you call a method the code executes in a manner that is specific to an object, but I'll defer explaining how this is possible until a little later in this chapter.

Apart from the `main()` method, perhaps the most common use for static methods is when you use a class just as a container for a bunch of utility methods, rather than as a specification for a set of objects. All executable code in Java has to be within a class, but lots of general-purpose functions you need don't necessarily have an object association — calculating a square root, for example, or generating a random number. The mathematical functions that are implemented as class methods in the standard `Math` class are good examples. These methods don't relate to class objects at all — they operate on values of the primitive types. You don't need objects of type `Math`; you just want to use the methods from time to time, and you can do this as you saw in Chapter 2. The `Math` class also contains some class variables containing useful mathematical constants such as e and π.

Accessing Variables and Methods

You'll normally want to access variables and methods that are defined within a class from outside it. You will see later that it is possible to declare class members with restrictions on accessing them from outside, but let's cover the principles that apply where the members are accessible. I'll consider accessing static members — that is, static fields and methods — and instance members separately.

You can access a static member of a class using the class name, followed by a period, followed by the member name. With a class method you also need to supply the parentheses enclosing any arguments to the method after the method name. The period here is called the dot operator. So, if you wanted to calculate the square root of π, you could access the class method `sqrt()` and the class variable `PI` that are defined in the `Math` class as follows:

```
double rootPi = Math.sqrt(Math.PI);
```

This shows how you call a static method — you just prefix it with the class name and put the dot operator between them. You also reference the static data member, `PI`, in the same way — as `Math.PI`. If you have a reference to an object of a class type available, then you can also use that to access a static member of the class because every object always has access to the static members of its class. You just use the variable name, followed by the dot operator, followed by the member name.

Of course, as you've seen in previous chapters, you can import the names of the static members of the class by using an `import` statement. You can then refer to the names of the static members you have imported into your source file without qualifying their names at all.

Instance variables and methods can be called only using an object reference, because by definition they relate to a particular object. The syntax is exactly the same as I have outlined for static members. You put the name of the variable referencing the object followed by a period, followed by the member name. To use a method `volume()` that has been declared as an instance method in the `Sphere` class, you might write:

```
double ballVolume = ball.volume();
```

Here the variable `ball` is of type `Sphere` and it contains a reference to an object of this type. You call its `volume()` method, which calculates the volume of the `ball` object, and the result that is returned is stored in the variable `ballVolume`.

Defining Classes

To define a class you use the keyword class followed by the name of the class, followed by a pair of braces enclosing the details of the definition. Let's consider a concrete example to see how this works in practice. The definition of the Sphere class that I mentioned earlier could be:

```
class Sphere {
    static final double PI = 3.14;        // Class variable that has a fixed value
    static int count = 0;                 // Class variable to count objects

    // Instance variables
    double radius;                        // Radius of a sphere

    double xCenter;                       // 3D coordinates
    double yCenter;                       // of the center
    double zCenter;                       // of a sphere

    // Plus the rest of the class definition...
}
```

You name a class using an identifier of the same sort you've been using for variables. By convention, though, class names in Java begin with a capital letter, so the class name is Sphere with a capital S. If you adopt this approach, you will be consistent with most of the code you come across. You could enter this source code and save it as the file Sphere.java. You'll be adding to this class definition and using it in a working example a little later in this chapter.

You may have noticed that in the examples in previous chapters the keyword public in this context preceded the keyword class in the first line of the class definition. The effect of the keyword public is bound up with the notion of a **package** containing classes, but I'll defer discussing this until a little later in this chapter when you have a better idea of what makes up a class definition.

The keyword static in the first line of the Sphere class definition specifies the variable PI as a class variable rather than an instance variable. The variable PI is also initialized with the value 3.14. The keyword final tells the compiler that you do not want the value of this variable to be changed, so the compiler will check that this variable is not modified anywhere in your program. Obviously, this is a very poor value for (. You would normally use Math.PI — which is defined to 20 decimal places, close enough for most purposes.

> Whenever you want to fix the initial value that you specify for a variable — that is, make it a constant — you just need to declare the variable with the keyword final. By convention, constants have names in capital letters.

You have also declared the next variable, count, using the keyword static. All objects of the Sphere class will have access to and share the one copy of count and the one copy of PI that exist. You have initialized the variable count to 0, but since you have not declared it using the keyword final, you can change its value.

The next four variables in the class definition are instance variables, as they don't have the keyword static applied to them. Each object of the class will have its own separate set of these variables, storing the radius and the coordinates of the center of the sphere. Although you haven't put initial values for these variables here, you could do so if you wanted. If you don't specify an initial value, a default value will be assigned automatically when the object is created. Fields of numeric types will be initialized with zero, fields of type char will be initialized with '\u000', and fields that store class references or references to arrays will be initialized with null.

There has to be something missing from the definition of the Sphere class — there is no way to set the value of radius and the other instance variables once a particular Sphere object is created. There is nothing to update the value of count either. Adding these things to the class definition involves using methods, so the next step is to understand how a method is put together.

Defining Methods

You have been producing versions of the main() method since Chapter 1, so you already have an idea of how a method is constructed. Nonetheless, I'll go through how you define methods from the beginning to make sure everything is clear.

I'll start with the fundamental concepts. A method is a self-contained block of code that has a name, and has the property that it is reusable — the same method can be executed from as many different points in a program as you require. Methods also serve to break up large and complex calculations that might involve many lines of code into more manageable chunks. You execute a method by **calling** it using its name, and the method may or may not return a value when its execution finishes. Methods that do not return a value are always called in a statement that just specifies the call. Methods that do return a value are usually called from within an expression, and the value that is returned by such a method is used in the evaluation of the expression. If a method that returns a value is called by itself in a statement, not in an expression in other words, then the value it returns is discarded.

The basic structure of a method is shown in Figure 5-2.

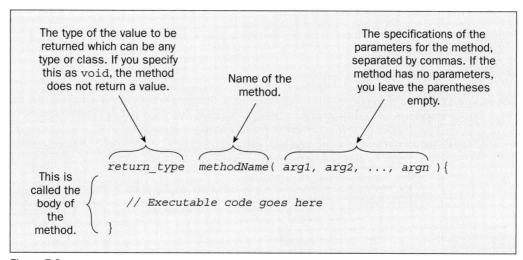

Figure 5-2

When you specify the return type for a method, you are defining the type for the value that will be returned by the method when you execute it. The method must always return a value of this type. To define a method that does not return a value, you specify the return type as void. Something called an **access attribute** can optionally precede the return type in a method definition, but I'll defer looking into this until later in this chapter.

The **parameters** to a method appear in its definition between the parentheses following the method name. These specify what information is to be passed to the method when you execute it, and the values that you supply for the parameters when you call a method are described as **arguments**. The parameter names are used in the body of the method to refer to the corresponding argument values that you supply when you call the method. Your methods do not have to have parameters specified. A method that does not require any information to be passed to it when it is executed has an empty pair of parentheses after the name.

Returning from a Method

To return a value from a method when its execution is complete you use a return statement. For example:

```
    return return_value;                    // Return a value from a method
```

After executing the return statement in a method, the program continues from the point where the method was called. The value return_value that is returned by the method can be any expression that produces a value of the type specified for the return value in the declaration of the method. Methods that return a value — that is, methods declared with a return type other than void — must always finish by executing a return statement that returns a value of the appropriate type. Note, though, that you can put several return statements within a method if the logic requires this. If a method does not return a value, you can just use the keyword return by itself to end execution of the method:

```
    return;                                 // Return from a method
```

For methods that do not return a value, falling through the closing brace enclosing the body of the method is equivalent to executing a return statement.

The Parameter List

The **parameter list** appears between the parentheses following the method name. This specifies the type of each value that can be passed as an argument to the method, and the variable name that is used in the body of the method to refer to each argument value passed to the method when it is called. The difference between a **parameter** and an **argument** is sometimes confusing because people often, incorrectly, use them interchangeably. I will try to differentiate them consistently, as follows:

❑   A *parameter* has a name and a type and appears in the parameter list in the definition of a method. A parameter defines the type of value that can be passed to the method when it is called.

❑   An *argument* is a value that is passed to a method when it is executed, and the value of the argument is referenced by the parameter name during execution of the method. Of course, the type of the argument value must be consistent with the type specified for the corresponding parameter in the definition of the method.

This is illustrated in Figure 5-3.

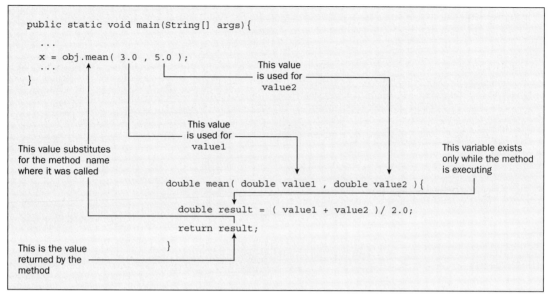

Figure 5-3

In Figure 5-3 you have the definition of a method `mean()`. The definition of this method can appear only within the definition of a class, but the rest of the class definition has been omitted so as not to clutter up the diagram. You can see that the method has two parameters, `value1` and `value2`, both of which are of type `double`. The parameter names are used to refer to the arguments `3.0` and `5.0`, respectively, within the body of the method when it is called by the statement shown. Since this method has not been defined as `static`, you can call it only for an object of the class. In the example, the `mean()` method for the object `obj` is called.

When you call the `mean()` method from another method (from `main()` in this case, but it could be from some other method), the values of the arguments you pass are the initial values assigned to the corresponding parameters before execution of the body of the method begins. You can use any expression you like for an argument when you call a method, as long as the value it produces is of the same type as the corresponding parameter in the definition of the method. With the method `mean()`, both parameters are of type `double`, so both argument values must always be of type `double`.

The method `mean()` declares the variable `result`, which exists only within the body of the method. This variable will be newly created each time you execute the method and will be destroyed when execution of the method ends. All the variables that you declare within the body of a method are local to the method, and are only around while the method is being executed. Variables declared within a method are called **local variables** because they are local to the method. The scope of a local variable is as I discussed in Chapter 2, from the point at which you declare it to the closing brace of the immediately enclosing block, and local variables are not initialized automatically. If you want your local variables to have initial values, you must supply the initial value when you declare them.

How Argument Values Are Passed to a Method

You need to be clear about how the argument values are passed to a method; otherwise, you may run into problems. In Java, all argument values are transferred to a method using what is called the **pass-by-value** mechanism. Figure 5-4 illustrates how this works.

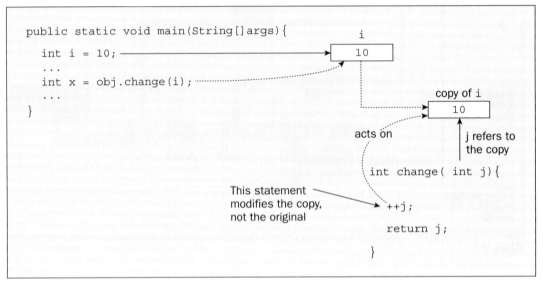

```
public static void main(String[]args){                          i

    int i = 10;                                               10

    ...
    int x = obj.change(i);
    ...                                                          copy of i

}                                                              10


                                                    acts on        j refers to
                                                                   the copy

                                                     int change( int j){

                                  This statement
                                  modifies the copy,
                                  not the original        ++j;

                                                        return j;

                                                     }
```

Figure 5-4

Pass-by-value just means that for each argument value that you pass to a method, a copy of the value is made, and it is the copy that is passed to the method and referenced through the parameter name, not the original value. This implies that if you use a variable of any of the primitive types as an argument, the method cannot modify the value of this variable in the calling program. In the example shown in Figure 5-4, the change() method will modify the copy of i that is created automatically and referenced using the parameter name j. Thus, the value of j that is returned will be 11, and this will be stored in the variable x when the return from the method executes. However, the original value of i will remain at 10.

> While the pass-by-value mechanism applies to all types of arguments, the effect for objects is different from that for variables of the primitive types. You can change an object, as you will see a little later in this chapter, because a variable of a class type contains a reference to an object, not the object itself. Thus, when you use a variable of a class type as an argument to a method, a copy of a *reference* to the object is passed to the method, not a copy of the object itself. Because a copy of a reference still refers to the same object, the parameter name used in the body of a method will refer to the original object that was passed as the argument.

Final Parameters

You can specify any of the parameters for a method as `final`. This has the effect of preventing modification of any argument value that is substituted for the parameter when you call the method. The compiler will check that your code in the body of the method does not attempt to change any final parameters. Since the pass-by-value mechanism makes copies of values of the basic types, `final` really makes sense only when it is applied to parameters that are references to class objects, as you'll see later on.

Specifying a parameter of a class as `final` is of limited value. It does prevent accidental modification of the object reference that is passed to the method, but it does not prevent modification of the object itself.

A much more important use for the `final` keyword is for declaring classes or method as final, and you'll learn more about this in Chapter 6.

Defining Class Methods

You define a class method by adding the keyword `static` to its definition. For example, the class `Sphere` could have a class method to return the value stored in the static variable `count`:

```
class Sphere {
  // Class definition as before...
  // Static method to report the number of objects created
  static int getCount() {
    return count;                            // Return current object count
  }
}
```

This method needs to be a class method because you want to be able to get at the count of the number of objects that exist even when it is zero. You can amend the `Sphere.java` file to include the definition of `getCount()`.

> Remember that you cannot directly refer to any of the instance variables in the class within a static method. This is because a static method can be executed when no objects of the class have been created, and therefore no instance variables exist.

Accessing Class Data Members in a Method

An instance method can access any of the data members of the class, just by using the appropriate name. Let's extend the class `Sphere` a little further by adding a method to calculate the volume of a `Sphere` object:

```
class Sphere {
  static final double PI = 3.14;       // Class variable that has a fixed value
  static int count = 0;                // Class variable to count objects

  // Instance variables
  double radius;                       // Radius of a sphere
```

```
double xCenter;                          // 3D coordinates
double yCenter;                          // of the center
double zCenter;                          // of a sphere

// Static method to report the number of objects created
static int getCount(){
  return count;                          // Return current object count
}

// Instance method to calculate volume
double volume() {
  return 4.0/3.0*PI*radius*radius*radius;
}

// Plus the rest of the class definition...
}
```

You can see that the `volume()` method is an instance method because it is not declared as static. It has no parameters, but it does return a value of type `double` — the required volume. The method uses the class variable `PI` and the instance variable `radius` in the volume calculation — this is the expression `4.0/3.0*PI*radius*radius*radius` (corresponding to $(4/3)\pi r^3$) in the `return` statement. The value that results from this expression will be returned to the point where the method is called for a `Sphere` object.

You know that each object of the class will have its own separate set of instance variables, so how is an instance variable for a particular object selected in a method? How does the `volume()` method pick up the value of a `radius` variable for a particular `Sphere` object?

The Variable this

Every instance method has a variable with the name `this` that refers to the current object for which the method is being called. The compiler uses `this` implicitly when your method refers to an instance variable of the class. For example, when the method `volume()` refers to the instance variable `radius`, the compiler will insert the `this` object reference so that the reference will be equivalent to `this.radius`. The return statement in the definition of the `volume()` method is actually:

```
return 4.0/3.0*PI*this.radius*this.radius*this.radius;
```

The statement actually refers to the `radius` field for the object referenced by the variable `this`. In general, every reference to an instance variable is in reality prefixed with `this`. You could put it in yourself, but there's no need, the compiler does it for you. In fact, it is not good practice to clutter up your code with `this` unnecessarily. However, there are occasions where you have to include it, as you will see.

When you execute a statement such as

```
double ballVolume = ball.volume();
```

where `ball` is an object of the class `Sphere`, the variable `this` in the method `volume()` will refer to the object `ball`, so the instance variable `radius` for the `ball` object will be used in the calculation.

> I mentioned earlier that only one copy of each instance method for a class exists in memory, even though there may be many different objects. You can see that the variable `this` allows the same instance method to work for different class objects. Each time an instance method is called, the `this` variable is set to reference the particular class object to which it is being applied. The code in the method will then relate to the specific members of the object referred to by `this`.

You have seen that there are four different potential sources of data available to you when you write the code for a method:

❑ Arguments passed to the method, which you refer to by using the parameter names

❑ Data members, both instance variables and class variables, which you refer to by their names

❑ Local variables that you declare in the body of the method

❑ Values that are returned by other methods that are called from within the method

The names of variables that are declared within a method are local to the method. You can use a name for a local variable or a parameter in a method that is the same as that of a instance variable. If you find it necessary or convenient to do this, then you must use the name `this` when you refer to the data member of the class from within the method. The variable name by itself will always refer to the variable that is local to the method, not the instance variable.

For example, suppose you wanted to add a method to change the radius of a `Sphere` object to a new radius value that is passed as an argument. You could code this as:

```
void changeRadius(double radius) {
  // Change the instance variable to the argument value
  this.radius = radius;
}
```

In the body of the `changeRadius()` method, `this.radius` refers to the instance variable, and `radius` by itself refers to the parameter. No confusion in the duplication of names exists here. It is clear that you are receiving a radius value as a parameter with the name `radius` and storing it in the `radius` variable for the class object.

Initializing Data Members

You have seen how you were able to supply an initial value for the static members `PI` and `count` in the `Sphere` class with the following declaration:

```
class Sphere {
  static final double PI = 3.14;      // Class variable that has a fixed value
  static int count = 0;               // Class variable to count objects

  // Rest of the class...
}
```

You can also initialize ordinary non-static data members in the same way. For example:

```
class Sphere {
    static final double PI = 3.14;        // Class variable that has a fixed value
    static int count = 0;                 // Class variable to count objects

    // Instance variables
    double radius = 5.0;                  // Radius of a sphere

    double xCenter = 10.0;                // 3D coordinates
    double yCenter = 10.0;                // of the center
    double zCenter = 10.0;                // of a sphere

    // Rest of the class...
}
```

Now every object of type Sphere will start out with a radius of 5.0 and have the center at the point 10.0, 10.0, 10.0.

Some things can't be initialized with a single expression. For example, if you had a large array as a data member that you wanted to initialize, with a range of values that required some kind of calculation, this could be a job for an **initialization block**.

Using Initialization Blocks

An initialization block is a block of code between braces that is executed before an object of the class is created. There are two kinds of initialization blocks:

❑ A **static initialization block** is a block defined using the keyword static and is executed once when the class is loaded. A static initialization block can initialize only static data members of the class.

❑ A **non-static initialization block** is executed for each object that is created and thus can initialize instance variables in a class.

This is easiest to understand by considering a working example.

Try It Out   **Using an Initialization Block**

Let's define a simple class with a static initialization block first of all:

```
class TryInitialization {
    static int[] values = new int[10];           // Static array member

    // Initialization block
    static {
        System.out.println("Running initialization block.");
        for(int i=0; i<values.length; i++) {
            values[i] = (int)(100.0*Math.random());
        }
    }
```

```
    // List values in the array for an object
    void listValues() {
      System.out.println();                        // Start a new line
      for(int value : values) {
        System.out.print(" " + value);             // Display values
      }
      System.out.println();                        // Start a new line
    }

    public static void main(String[] args) {
      TryInitialization example = new TryInitialization();
      System.out.println("\nFirst object:");
      example.listValues();

      example = new TryInitialization();
      System.out.println("\nSecond object:");
      example.listValues();
    }
  }
```

When you compile and run this, you will get identical sets of values for the two objects — as might be expected since the `values` array is static:

```
Running initialization block.

First object:

 40 97 88 63 58 48 84 5 32 67

Second object:

 40 97 88 63 58 48 84 5 32 67
```

How It Works

The `TryInitialization` class has a static member, `values`, that is an array of 10 integers. The static initialization block is the code

```
    static {
      System.out.println("Running initialization block.");
      for(int i=0; i<values.length; i++) {
        values[i] = (int)(100.0*Math.random());
      }
    }
```

This initializes the `values` array with pseudo-random integer values generated in the `for` loop. The output statement in the block is there just to record when the initialization block executes. Because this initialization block is static, it is only ever executed once during program execution, when the class is loaded.

The `listValues()` method provides you with a means of outputting the values in the array. The `print()` method you are using in the `listValues()` method works just like `println()`, but without starting a new line before displaying the output, so you get all the values on the same line.

In `main()`, you generate an object of type `TryInitialization` and then call its `listValues()` method. You then create a second object and call the `listValues()` method for that. The output demonstrates that the initialization block only executes once, and that the values reported for both objects are the same.

Because the `values` array is a static member of the class, you could list the element's values through a static method that would not require any objects to have been created. Try temporarily adding the keyword `static` to the declaration of the `listValues()` method in the class:

```
static void listValues() {
  System.out.println();                    // Start a new line
  for(int value : values) {
    System.out.print(" " + value);         // Display values
  }
  System.out.println();                    // Start a new line
}
```

You can now call the method using the class name, so add two extra statements at the beginning of `main()`:

```
System.out.println("\nNo object:");
TryInitialization.listValues();
```

If you compile and execute the program with these changes, you will get an additional record of the values in the `values` array. You still get the output from calling `listValues()` using the two object references. Every object has access to the static members of its class. Of course, the values in the output will be different from the previous execution because they are pseudo-random values.

If you restore the program to its original state, and then delete the `static` modifier before the initialization block and recompile and run the program again, you will get the output along the lines of:

```
Running initialization block.

First object:

 66 17 98 59 99 18 40 96 40 21

Running initialization block.

Second object:

 57 86 79 31 75 99 51 5 31 44
```

Now you have a non-static initialization block. You can see from the output that the values are different for the second object because the non-static initialization block is executed each time an object is created. In fact, the `values` array is static, so the array is shared between all objects of the class. You could demonstrate this by amending `main()` to store each object separately and calling `listValues()` for the first object after the second object has been created. Amend the `main()` method in the program to read as follows:

```
    public static void main(String[] args) {
      TryInitialization example = new TryInitialization();
      System.out.println("\nFirst object:");
      example.listValues();
      TryInitialization nextexample = new TryInitialization();
      System.out.println("\nSecond object:");
      nextexample.listValues();

      example.listValues();
    }
```

While you have demonstrated that this is possible, you will not normally want to initialize static variables with a non-static initialization block.

As I said at the outset, a non-static initialization block can initialize instance variables, too. If you want to demonstrate this, you just need to remove the `static` modifier from the declaration of `values` and compile and run the program once more.

You can have multiple initialization blocks in a class, in which case they execute in the sequence in which they appear. The static blocks execute when the class is loaded, and the non-static blocks execute when each object is created. Initialization blocks are useful, but you need more than that to create objects properly.

Constructors

When you create an object of a class, a special kind of method called a **constructor** is always invoked. If you don't define any constructors for your class, the compiler will supply a **default constructor** in the class, which does nothing. The default constructor is also described as the **no-arg constructor** because it requires no arguments to be specified when it is called. The primary purpose of a constructor is to provide you with the means of initializing the instance variables uniquely for the object that is being created. If you are creating a `Person` object with the name John Doe, then you want to be able to initialize the member holding the person's name to `"John Doe"`. This is precisely what a constructor can do. Any initialization blocks that you have defined in a class are always executed before a constructor.

A constructor has two special characteristics that differentiate it from other class methods:

❑   A constructor never returns a value, and you must not specify a return type — not even of type `void`.

❑   A constructor always has the same name as the class.

To see a practical example you could add a constructor to the `Sphere` class definition:

```
class Sphere {
  static final double PI = 3.14;      // Class variable that has a fixed value
  static int count = 0;               // Class variable to count objects

  // Instance variables
  double radius;                      // Radius of a sphere
```

```
      double xCenter;                      // 3D coordinates
      double yCenter;                      // of the center
      double zCenter;                      // of a sphere

      // Class constructor
      Sphere(double theRadius, double x, double y, double z) {
        radius = theRadius;                // Set the radius

        // Set the coordinates of the center
        xCenter = x;
        yCenter = y;
        zCenter = z;
        ++count;                           // Update object count
      }

      // Static method to report the number of objects created
      static int getCount() {
        return count;                      // Return current object count
      }

      // Instance method to calculate volume
      double volume() {
        return 4.0/3.0*PI*radius*radius*radius;
      }
    }
```

The definition of the constructor is shaded above. You are accumulating quite a lot of code to define the Sphere class, but as it's just an assembly of the pieces you have been adding, you should find it all quite straightforward.

As you can see, the constructor has the same name as the class and has no return type specified. A constructor can have any number of parameters, including none. The default constructor has no parameters, as is indicated by its alternative description — the no-arg constructor. In this case the Sphere class constructor has four parameters, and each of the instance variables is initialized with the value of the appropriate parameter. Here's a situation where you might have used the name radius for the parameter, in which case you would need to use the keyword this to refer to the instance variable of the same name. The last action of the constructor is to increment the class variable count by 1, so that count accumulates the total number of objects created.

The Default Constructor

As I said, if you don't define any constructors for a class, the compiler will supply a default constructor that has no parameters and does nothing. Before you defined a constructor for the Sphere class, the compiler would have supplied one, defined like this:

```
  Sphere() {
  }
```

It has no parameters and no statements in its body so it does nothing — except enable you to create an object of type Sphere, of course. The object created by the default constructor will have fields with their default values set. If you have defined any non-static initialization blocks within a class, they will be executed each time any constructor executes, immediately before the execution of the code in the body of the constructor. Whenever you create an object, a constructor will be called. When you have not defined any constructors for a class, the default constructor will be called each time you create an object of that class type.

Note that if you define a constructor of any kind for a class, the compiler will not supply a default constructor. If you still need a default constructor — and you will find many occasions when you do — you must define it explicitly in addition to the other constructors in the class.

Creating Objects of a Class

When you declare a variable of type Sphere with the following statement:

```
Sphere ball;                                    // Declare a variable
```

no constructor is called because no object is created. All you have created at this point is the variable ball, which can store a reference to an object of type Sphere, if and when you create one. Figure 5-5 shows this.

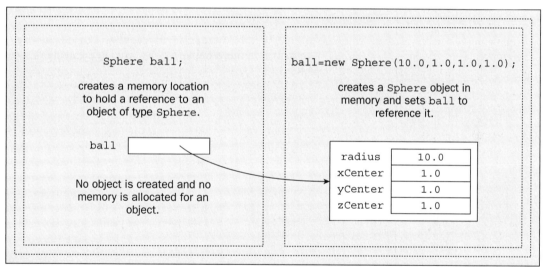

Figure 5-5

You will recall from the discussion of string objects and arrays that the variable and the object it references are distinct entities. To create an object of a class you must use the keyword new followed by a call to a constructor. To initialize ball with a reference to an object, you could write:

```
ball = new Sphere(10.0, 1.0, 1.0, 1.0);         // Create a sphere
```

Now you have a Sphere object with a radius of 10.0 located at the coordinates (1.0, 1.0, 1.0). The object is created in memory and will occupy a sufficient number of bytes to accommodate all the data necessary to define the object. The variable `ball` records where in memory the object is — it acts as a reference to the object. This is illustrated in Figure 5-5.

Of course, you can do the whole thing in one step, with the following statement:

```
Sphere ball = new Sphere(10.0, 1.0, 1.0, 1.0);    // Create a sphere
```

This declares the variable `ball` and defines the `Sphere` object to which it refers.

You can create another variable that refers to the same object as `ball`:

```
Sphere myBall = ball;
```

Now the variable `myBall` refers to the same object as `ball`. You still have only one object, but you have two different variables that reference it. You could have as many variables as you like referring to the same object.

As I mentioned earlier, the separation of the variable and the object has an important effect on how objects are passed to a method, so let's look at that in more detail.

Passing Objects to a Method

When you pass an object as an argument to a method, the mechanism that applies is called **pass-by-reference,** because a copy of the reference contained in the variable is transferred to the method, not a copy of the object itself. The effect of this is shown in Figure 5-6.

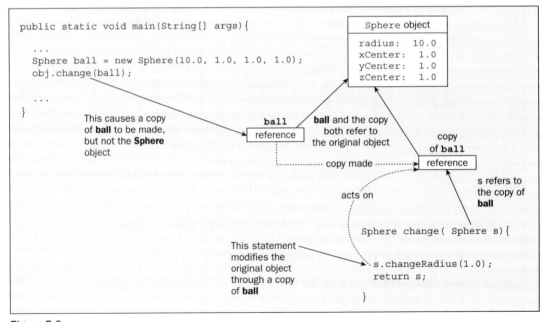

Figure 5-6

Figure 5-6 presumes you have defined a method, changeRadius(), in the class Sphere, that will alter the radius value for an object, and that you have a method change() in some other class that calls changeRadius(). When the variable ball is used as an argument to the method change(), the pass-by-reference mechanism causes a copy of the contents of ball to be made and stored in s. The variable ball just stores a reference to the Sphere object, and the copy contains that same reference and therefore refers to the same object. No copying of the actual object occurs. This is a major plus in terms of efficiency when passing arguments to a method. Objects can be very complex, involving a lot of instance variables. If objects themselves were always copied when passed as arguments, it could be very time-consuming and make the code very slow.

Since the copy of the reference from ball refers to the same object as the original, when the changeRadius() method is called, the original object will be changed. You need to keep this in mind when writing methods that have objects as parameters because this is not always what you want.

In the example shown, the method change() returns the modified object. In practice, you would probably want this to be a distinct object, in which case you would need to create a new object from s. You will see how you can write a constructor to do this a little later in this chapter.

> Remember that this only applies to objects. If you pass a variable of type int or double to a method, for example, a copy of the value is passed. You can modify the value passed as much as you want in the method, but it won't affect the original value.

The Lifetime of an Object

The lifetime of an object is determined by the variable that holds the reference to it—assuming there is only one. If you have the declaration

```
Sphere ball = new Sphere(10.0, 1.0, 1.0, 1.0);   // Create a sphere
```

then the Sphere object that the variable ball refers to will die when the variable ball goes out of scope. This will be at the end of the block containing this declaration. Where an instance variable is the only one referencing an object, the object survives as long as the instance variable owning the object survives.

> A slight complication can arise with objects, though. As you have seen, several variables can reference a single object. In this case, the object survives as long as a variable still exists somewhere that references the object.

As you have seen before, you can reset a variable to refer to nothing by setting its value to null. If you write the statement

```
ball = null;
```

the variable ball no longer refers to an object, and assuming there is no other object referencing it, the Sphere object it originally referenced will be destroyed. Note that while the object has been discarded, the variable ball still continues to exist and you can use it to store a reference to another Sphere object. The lifetime of an object is determined by whether any variable anywhere in the program still references it.

The process of disposing of dead objects is called **garbage collection**. Garbage collection is automatic in Java, but this doesn't necessarily mean that objects disappear from memory straight away. It can be some time after the object becomes inaccessible to your program. This won't affect your program directly in any way. It just means you can't rely on memory occupied by an object that is done with being available immediately. For the most part it doesn't matter; the only circumstances where it might would be if your objects were very large, millions of bytes, say, or you were creating and getting rid of very large numbers of objects. In this case, if you are experiencing problems you can try to call the static gc() method that is defined in the System class to encourage the Java Virtual Machine (JVM) to do some garbage collecting and recover the memory that the objects occupy:

```
System.gc();
```

This is a best efforts deal on the part of the JVM. When the gc() method returns, the JVM will have tried to reclaim the space occupied by discarded objects, but there's no guarantee that it will all be recovered. There's also the possibility that calling the gc() method may make things worse. If the garbage collector is executing some preparations for recovering memory, your call will undo that and in this way slow things up.

Defining and Using a Class

To put what you know about classes to use, you can use the Sphere class in an example.

You will be creating two source files. In a moment you'll create the file CreateSpheres.java, which will contain the definition of the CreateSpheres class that will have the method main() defined as a static method. As usual, this is where execution of the program starts. The other file will be the Sphere.java file, which contains the definition of the Sphere class that you have been assembling. The Sphere class definition should look like this:

```
class Sphere {
    static final double PI = 3.14;        // Class variable that has a fixed value
    static int count = 0;                 // Class variable to count objects

    // Instance variables
    double radius;                        // Radius of a sphere

    double xCenter;                       // 3D coordinates
    double yCenter;                       // of the center
    double zCenter;                       // of a sphere
    // Class constructor
    Sphere(double theRadius, double x, double y, double z) {
        radius = theRadius;               // Set the radius

        // Set the coordinates of the center
        xCenter = x;
        yCenter = y;
        zCenter = z;
        ++count;                          // Update object count
    }

    // Static method to report the number of objects created
```

```
    static int getCount() {
      return count;                              // Return current object count
    }

    // Instance method to calculate volume
    double volume() {
      return 4.0/3.0*PI*radius*radius*radius;
    }
  }
```

Both files need to be in the same directory or folder—I suggest you name the directory CreateSpheres. Then copy or move the latest version of Sphere.java to this directory.

Try It Out   Using the Sphere Class

Enter the following code for the file CreateSpheres.java:

```
class CreateSpheres {
  public static void main(String[] args) {
    System.out.println("Number of objects = " + Sphere.getCount());

    Sphere ball = new Sphere(4.0, 0.0, 0.0, 0.0);        // Create a sphere
    System.out.println("Number of objects = " + ball.getCount());

    Sphere globe = new Sphere(12.0, 1.0, 1.0, 1.0);      // Create a sphere
    System.out.println("Number of objects = " + Sphere.getCount());

    // Output the volume of each sphere
    System.out.println("ball volume = " + ball.volume());
    System.out.println("globe volume = " + globe.volume());
  }
}
```

Compile the source files and then run CreateSpheres, and you should get the following output:

```
Number of objects = 0
Number of objects = 1
Number of objects = 2
ball volume = 267.94666666666666
globe volume = 7234.559999999999
```

This is the first time you have run a program involving two source files. If you are using the JDK compiler, then compile CreateSpheres.java with the current directory as CreateSpheres using the command:

```
javac CreateSpheres.java
```

The compiler will find and compile the Sphere.java source file automatically. If all the source files for a program are in the current directory, then compiling the file containing a definition of main() will compile all the source files for the program.

Note that by default the `.class` files generated by the compiler are stored in the current directory — that is, the directory containing your source code. If you want the `.class` files stored in a different directory, then you can use the `-d` option with the Java compiler to specify where they should go. For example, to store the class files in a directory called `C:\classes`, you would type:

```
javac -d C:/classes CreateSpheres.java
```

How It Works

The `Sphere` class definition includes a constructor that will create objects, and the method `volume()` to calculate the volume of a particular sphere. It also contains the `static` method `getCount()` you saw earlier, which returns the current value of the class variable `count`. You need to define this method as `static` because you want to able to call it regardless of how many objects have been created, including the situation when there are none.

The method `main()` in the `CreateSpheres` class puts the `Sphere` class through its paces. When the program is compiled, the compiler will look for a file with the name `Sphere.class`. If it does not find the `.class` file, it will look for `Sphere.java` to provide the definition of the class `Sphere`. As long as this file is in the current directory, the compiler will be able to find it and compile it.

The first thing the program does is call the `static` method `getCount()`. Because no objects exist, you must use the class name to call it at this point. You then create the object `ball`, which is a `Sphere` object, with a radius of 4.0 and its center at the origin point (0.0, 0.0, 0.0). You call the `getCount()` method again, this time using the object name. This demonstrates that you can call a `static` method through an object. You create another `Sphere` object, `globe`, with a radius of 12.0. You call the `getCount()` method again, this time using the class name. Static methods like this are usually called using the class name. After all, the reason for calling this particular method would be to find out how many objects exist, so presumably you cannot be sure that any objects exist at that point. A further reason to use the class name rather than a reference to an object when calling a static method is that it makes it quite clear in the source code that it *is* a static method that is being called. You can't call a non-static method using the class name.

The program finally outputs the volume of both objects by calling the `volume()` method for each, from within the expressions, specifying the arguments to the `println()` method calls.

Method Overloading

Java allows you to define several methods in a class with the same name, as long as each method has a unique set of parameters. Defining two or more methods with the same name in a class is called **method overloading**.

The name of a method together with the types and sequence of the parameters form the **signature** of the method; the signature of each method in a class must be distinct to allow the compiler to determine exactly which method you are calling at any particular point. The return type has no effect on the signature of a method. You cannot differentiate between two methods just by the return type. This is because the return type is not necessarily apparent when you call a method. For example, suppose you write a statement such as:

```
Math.round(value);
```

Although the preceding statement is pointless since it discards the value that the `round()` method produces, it does illustrate why the return type cannot be part of the signature for a method. The compiler has no way to know from this statement what the return type of the method `round()` is supposed to be. Thus, if there were several different versions of the method `round()`, and the return type were the only distinguishing aspect of the method signature, the compiler would be unable to determine which version of `round()` you wanted to use.

You will find many circumstances where it is convenient to use method overloading. You have already seen that the `Math` class contains two versions of the method `round()`, one that accepts an argument of type `float` and the other that accepts an argument of type `double`. You can see now that method overloading makes this possible. It would be rather tedious to have to use a different name for each version of `round()` when they both do essentially the same thing. The `valueOf()` method in the `String` class is another example. There is a version of this method for each of the basic types. One context in which you will regularly need to use overloading is when you write constructors for your classes, which you'll look at now.

Multiple Constructors

Constructors are methods that can be overloaded, just like any other method in a class. In most situations, you will want to generate objects of a class from different sets of initial defining data. If you just consider the `Sphere` class, you could conceive of a need to define a `Sphere` object in a variety of ways. You might well want a constructor that accepted just the (x, y, z) coordinates of a point, and have a `Sphere` object created with a default radius of 1.0. Another possibility is that you may want to create a default `Sphere` with a radius of 1.0 positioned at the origin, so no arguments would be specified at all. This requires two constructors in addition to the one you have already written. Let's try it then.

Try It Out   **Multiple Constructors for the Sphere Class**

The code for the extra constructors is as follows:

```
class Sphere {
  // First Constructor and variable declarations
  ...
  // Construct a unit sphere at a point
  Sphere(double x, double y, double z) {
    xCenter = x;
    yCenter = y;
    zCenter = z;
    radius = 1.0;
    ++count;                        // Update object count
  }


  // Construct a unit sphere at the origin
  Sphere() {
    xCenter = 0.0;
    yCenter = 0.0;
    zCenter = 0.0;
    radius = 1.0;
    ++count;                        // Update object count
  }

  // The rest of the class as before...
}
```

The statements in the default constructor that set three fields to zero are not really necessary, as the fields would be set to zero by default. They are there just to emphasize that the primary purpose of a constructor is to enable you to set initial values for the fields.

If you add the following statements to the CreateSpheres class, you can test out the new constructors:

```
public class CreateSpheres {
  public static void main(String[] args) {
    System.out.println("Number of objects = " + Sphere.getCount());

    Sphere ball = new Sphere(4.0, 0.0, 0.0, 0.0);          // Create a sphere
    System.out.println("Number of objects = " + ball.getCount());

    Sphere globe = new Sphere(12.0, 1.0, 1.0, 1.0);          // Create a sphere
    System.out.println("Number of objects = " + Sphere.getCount());

    Sphere eightBall = new Sphere(10.0, 10.0, 0.0);
    Sphere oddBall = new Sphere();
    System.out.println("Number of objects = " + Sphere.getCount());

    // Output the volume of each sphere
    System.out.println("ball volume = " + ball.volume());
    System.out.println("globe volume = " + globe.volume());
    System.out.println("eightBall volume = " + eightBall.volume());
    System.out.println("oddBall volume = " + oddBall.volume());
  }
}
```

Now the program should produce the following output:

```
Number of objects = 0
Number of objects = 1
Number of objects = 2
Number of objects = 4
ball volume = 267.94666666666666
globe volume = 7234.559999999999
eightBall volume = 4.1866666666666665
oddBall volume = 4.1866666666666665
```

How It Works

When you create a Sphere object, the compiler selects the constructor to use based on the types of the arguments you have specified. So, the first of the new constructors is applied in the first statement that you added to main(), as its signature fits with the argument types used. The second statement that you added clearly selects the last constructor, as no arguments are specified. The other additional statements are there just to generate some output corresponding to the new objects. You can see from the volumes of eightBall and oddBall that they both are of radius 1 — in both instances the result is the value of $4\pi/3$.

It is the number and types of the parameters that affect the signature of a method, not the parameter names. If you wanted a constructor that defined a Sphere object at a point, by specifying the diameter rather than the radius, you have a problem. You might try to write it as:

```
// Illegal constructor!!!
// This WON'T WORK because it has the same signature as the original!!!
Sphere(double diameter, double x, double y, double z) {
   xCenter = x;
   yCenter = y;
   zCenter = z;
   radius = diameter/2.0;
   ++count;
}
```

If you add this method to the `Sphere` class and recompile, you'll get a compile-time error. This constructor has four arguments of type `double`, so its signature is identical to the first constructor that you wrote for the class. This is not permitted — hence the compile-time error. When the number of parameters is the same in two overloaded methods, at least one pair of corresponding parameters must be of different types.

Calling a Constructor from a Constructor

One class constructor can call another constructor in the same class in its first executable statement. This can often save duplicating a lot of code. To refer to another constructor in the same class, you use `this` as the method name, followed by the appropriate arguments between parentheses. In the `Sphere` class, you could have defined the constructors as:

```
class Sphere {
   // Construct a unit sphere at the origin
   Sphere() {
      radius = 1.0;
      // Other data members will be zero by default
      ++count;                    // Update object count
   }

   // Construct a unit sphere at a point
   Sphere(double x, double y, double z)
   {
      this();                     // Call the constructor with no arguments
      xCenter = x;
      yCenter = y;
      zCenter = z;
   }

   Sphere(double theRadius, double x, double y, double z) {
      this(x, y, z);              // Call the 3 argument constructor
      radius = theRadius;         // Set the radius
   }
   // The rest of the class as before...
}
```

In the constructor that accepts the point coordinates as arguments, you call the default constructor to set the radius and increment the count of the number of objects. In the constructor that sets the radius, as well as the coordinates, you call the constructor with three arguments to set the coordinates, which in turn will call the constructor that requires no arguments.

Duplicating Objects Using a Constructor

When you were looking at how objects were passed to a method, you came across a requirement for duplicating an object. The need to produce an identical copy of an object occurs surprisingly often.

> Java provides a `clone()` method, but the details of using it must wait for the next chapter.

Suppose you declare a `Sphere` object with the following statement:

```
Sphere eightBall = new Sphere(10.0, 10.0, 0.0);
```

Later in your program you want to create a new object `newBall`, which is identical to the object `eightBall`. If you write

```
Sphere newBall = eightBall;
```

this will compile okay but it won't do what you want. You might remember from my earlier discussion that the variable `newBall` references the same object as `eightBall`. You don't have a distinct object. The variable `newBall`, of type `Sphere`, is created but no constructor is called, so no new object is created.

Of course, you could create `newBall` by specifying the same arguments to the constructor as you used to create `eightBall`. In general, however, it may be that `eightBall` has been modified in some way during execution of the program, so you don't know that its instance variables have the same values — for example, the position might have changed. This presumes that you have some other class methods that alter the instance variables. You could provide the capability for duplicating an existing object by adding a constructor to the class that will accept an existing `Sphere` object as an argument:

```
// Create a sphere from an existing object
Sphere(final Sphere oldSphere) {
   radius = oldSphere.radius;
   xCenter = oldSphere.xCenter;
   yCenter = oldSphere.yCenter;
   zCenter = oldSphere.yCenter;
   ++count;                                  // Increment the object count
}
```

This works by copying the values of the instance variables of the `Sphere` object that is passed as the argument to the corresponding instance variables of the new object. Thus the new object that this constructor creates will be identical to the `Sphere` object that is passed as the argument.

Now you can create `newBall` as a distinct object by writing:

```
Sphere newBall = new Sphere(eightBall);        // Create a copy of eightBall
```

The next section recaps what you have learned about methods and constructors with another example.

Using Objects

You'll create a program to do some simple 2D geometry. This will give you an opportunity to use more than one class. You'll define two classes, a class that represents point objects and a class that represents line objects; you'll then use these to find the point at which two lines intersect. Call the example `TryGeometry`, so this will be the name of the directory or folder in which you should save the program files. Quite a few lines of code are involved, so you'll put it together piecemeal and get an understanding of how each piece works as you go.

Try It Out   The Point Class

You first define a basic class for point objects:

```java
import static java.lang.Math.sqrt;

class Point {
  // Coordinates of the point
  double x;
  double y;

  // Create a point from coordinates
  Point(double xVal, double yVal) {
    x = xVal;
    y = yVal;
  }

  // Create a point from another Point object
  Point(final Point oldPoint) {
    x = oldPoint.x;                        // Copy x coordinate
    y = oldPoint.y;                        // Copy y coordinate
  }

  // Move a point
  void move(double xDelta, double yDelta) {
    // Parameter values are increments to the current coordinates
    x += xDelta;
    y += yDelta;
  }

  // Calculate the distance to another point
  double distance(final Point aPoint) {
    return sqrt((x - aPoint.x)*(x - aPoint.x) + (y - aPoint.y)*(y - aPoint.y));
  }

  // Convert a point to a string
  public String toString() {
    return Double.toString(x) + ", " + y;      // As "x, y"
  }
}
```

You should save this as `Point.java` in the directory `TryGeometry`.

How It Works

This is a simple class that has just two instance variables, x and y, which are the coordinates of the Point object. At the moment you have two constructors. One will create a Point object from a coordinate pair passed as arguments of type double, and the other will create a new Point object from an existing one.

Three methods are included in the class. First you have the move() method, which moves a Point to another position by adding an increment to each of the coordinates. You also have the distance() method, which calculates the distance from the current Point object to the Point object passed as the argument. This uses the Pythagorean theorem to compute the distance, as shown in Figure 5-7.

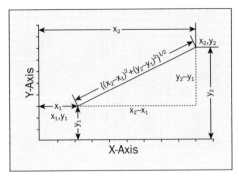

Figure 5-7

Finally, you have a method toString(), which returns a string representation of the coordinates of the current point. If a class defines the toString() method, an object of that class can be used as an operand of the string concatenation operator +, so you can implement this in any of your classes to allow objects to be used in this way. The compiler will automatically insert a call to toString() when necessary. For example, suppose thePoint is an object of type Point, and you write the statement:

```
System.out.println("The point is at " + thePoint);
```

The toString() method will be automatically invoked to convert the object referenced by the variable thePoint to a String, and the resultant string will be appended to the String literal. You have specified the toString() method as public, as this is essential here for the class to compile. I will defer explanations as to why this is necessary until a little later in this chapter.

Note how you use the static toString() method defined in the Double class to convert the x value to a String. The compiler will insert a call to the same method automatically for the y value, as the left operand of the + operation is a String object. Note that you could equally well have used the valueOf() method in the String class. In this case the statement would be written like this:

```
        return String.valueOf(x) + ", " + y;      // As "x, y"
```

Try It Out   The Line Class

You can use `Point` objects in the definition of the class `Line`:

```
class Line {
  Point start;                               // Start point of line
  Point end;                                 // End point of line

  // Create a line from two points
  Line(final Point start, final Point end) {
    this.start = new Point(start);
    this.end = new Point(end);
  }

  // Create a line from two coordinate pairs
  Line(double xStart, double yStart, double xEnd, double yEnd) {
    start = new Point(xStart, yStart);       // Create the start point
    end = new Point(xEnd, yEnd);             // Create the end point
  }

  // Calculate the length of a line
  double length() {
    return start.distance(end);              // Use the method from the Point class
  }

  // Convert a line to a string
  public String toString() {
    return "(" + start+ "):(" + end + ")";   // As "(start):(end)"
  }                                          // that is, "(x1, y1):(x2, y2)"
}
```

You should save this as the file `Line.java` in the `TryGeometry` directory.

How It Works

You shouldn't have any difficulty with this class definition, as it is very straightforward. The `Line` class stores two `Point` objects as instance variables. There are two constructors for `Line` objects — one accepting two `Point` objects as arguments and the other accepting the (x, y) coordinates of the start and end points. You can see how you use the variable `this` to differentiate the class instance variables, `start` and `end`, from the parameter names in the constructor.

Note how the constructor that accepts `Point` objects works:

```
// Create a line from two points
Line(final Point start, final Point end) {
  this.start = new Point(start);
  this.end = new Point(end);
}
```

With this implementation of the constructor, two new `Point` objects are created that will be identical to, but independent of, the objects passed to the constructor. If you don't think about what happens, you might be tempted to write it as:

```
// Create a line from two points - a poor implementation!
Line(final Point start, final Point end) {
   this.start = start;            // Dependent on external object!!!
   this.end = end;                // Dependent on external object!!!
}
```

The important thing you should notice here is that the way the constructor is implemented could cause problems that might be hard to track down. In this version of the constructor no new points are created. The `start` and `end` members of the object refer to the `Point` objects that passed as arguments. The `Line` object will be implicitly dependent on the `Point` objects that are used to define it. If these were changed outside the `Line` class, by using the `move()` method, for example, this would "silently" modify the `Line` object. You might consciously decide that this is what you want, so the `Line` object continues to be dependent on its associated `Point` objects. The rationale for this in a drawing package, for example, might be that this would allow a point to be moved, and all lines based on the point would also be moved accordingly. However, this is different from allowing such interdependencies by accident. In general, you should take care to avoid creating implicit dependencies between objects unless they are what you intended.

In the `toString()` method for the `Line` class, you are able to use the `Point` objects directly in the formation of the `String` representation of a `Line` object. This works because the `Point` class also defines a `toString()` method.

You've now defined two classes. In these class definitions, you've included the basic data that defines an object of each class type. You've also defined some useful methods for operating on objects, and added constructors for a variety of input parameters. Note how the `Point` class is used in the definition of the `Line` class. It is quite natural to define a line in terms of two `Point` objects, and the `Line` class is much simpler and more understandable than if it were defined entirely in terms of the individual x and y coordinates. To further demonstrate how classes can interact, and how you can solve problems directly, in terms of the objects involved, let's devise a method to calculate the intersection of two `Line` objects.

Creating a Point from Two Lines

You can add the method to determine the point of intersection between two lines to the `Line` class. Figure 5-8 illustrates how the mathematics works out.

You can ignore the mathematics if you want to, as it is not the most important aspect of the example. If you are willing to take the code in the new constructor on trust, then skip to the next "Try It Out" section. On the other hand, you shouldn't find it too difficult if you can still remember what you did in high school.

One way to get the intersection of two lines is to use equations like those shown. These are called parametric equations because they use a parameter value (s or t) as the variable for determining points on each line. The parameters s and t vary between 0 and 1 to give points on the lines between the defined start and end points. When a parameter s or t is 0 the equations give the coordinates of the start point of a line, and when the parameter value is 1 you get the end point of the line.

Where two lines intersect, the equations for the lines must produce the same (x, y) values, so, at this point, the right-hand sides of the equations for x for the two lines must be equal, and the same goes for the equations for y. This will give you two equations in s and t, and with a bit of algebraic juggling you can eliminate s to get the equation shown for t. You can then replace t in the equations, defining line 1 to get x and y for the intersection point.

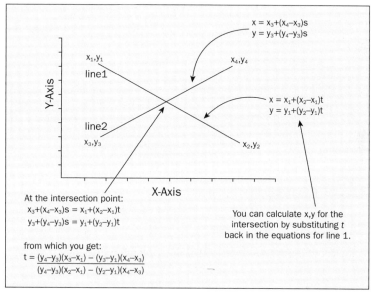

Figure 5-8

Try It Out — Calculating the Intersection of Two Lines

You can use these results to write the additional method you need in the `Line` class. Add the following code to the class definition in `Line.java`:

```java
// Return a point as the intersection of two lines
Point intersects(final Line line1) {
  Point localPoint = new Point(0, 0);

  double num = (this.end.y - this.start.y)*(this.start.x - line1.start.x) -
               (this.end.x - this.start.x)*(this.start.y - line1.start.y);

  double denom = (this.end.y - this.start.y)*(line1.end.x - line1.start.x) -
                 (this.end.x - this.start.x)*(line1.end.y - line1.start.y);

  localPoint.x = line1.start.x + (line1.end.x - line1.start.x)*num/denom;
  localPoint.y = line1.start.y + (line1.end.y - line1.start.y)*num/denom;

  return localPoint;
}
```

Since the `Line` class definition refers to the `Point` class, the `Line` class can't be compiled without the other being available. When you compile the `Line` class, the compiler will compile the other class, too.

How It Works

The `intersects()` method is called for one `Line` object and takes another `Line` object as the argument. In the code, the local variables `num` and `denom` are the numerator and denominator in the expression for `t` in Figure 5-8. You then use these values to calculate the x and y coordinates for the intersection point.

> If the lines are parallel, the denominator in the equation for `t` will be zero, something you should really check for in the code. For the moment you'll ignore it and end up with coordinates that are `Infinity` if it occurs.

Note how you get at the values of the coordinates for the `Point` objects defining the lines. The dot notation for referring to a member of an object is just repeated when you want to reference a member of a member. For example, for the object `line1`, the expression `line1.start` refers to the `Point` object at the beginning of the line. Therefore, `line1.start.x` refers to its x coordinate, and `line1.start.y` accesses its y coordinate.

Now you have a `Line` class defined that you can use to calculate the intersection point of two `Line` objects. You need a program to test the code out.

Try It Out   The TryGeometry Class

You can exercise the two classes you have defined with the following code in the method `main()`:

```
public class TryGeometry {
  public static void main(String[] args) {
    // Create two points and display them
    Point start = new Point(0.0, 1.0);
    Point end = new Point(5.0, 6.0);
    System.out.println("Points created are " + start + " and " + end);


    // Create two lines and display them
    Line line1 = new Line(start, end);
    Line line2 = new Line(0.0, 3.0, 3.0, 0.0);
    System.out.println("Lines created are " + line1 + " and " + line2);

    // Display the intersection
    System.out.println("Intersection is " + line2.intersects(line1));

    // Now move the end point of line1 and show the new intersection
    end.move(1.0, -5.0);
    System.out.println("Intersection is " + line1.intersects(line2));
  }
}
```

Save the `TryGeometry.java` file in the `TryGeometry` directory along with the other two class files, `Point.java` and `Line.java`. The program will produce the following output:

```
Points created are 0.0, 1.0 and 5.0, 6.0
Lines created are (0.0, 1.0):(5.0, 6.0) and (0.0, 3.0):(3.0, 0.0)
Intersection is 1.0, 2.0
Intersection is 1.0, 2.0
```

How It Works

You first create two `Point` objects, which you will use later in the program to create the object `line1`. You then display the points using the `println()` method. The `toString()` method that you defined in the `Point` class is used automatically to generate the `String` representation for each `Point` object.

After creating `line1` from the two points, you use the other constructor in the `Line` class to create `line2` from two pairs of coordinates. You then display the two lines. The `toString()` member of the `Line` class is invoked here to create the `String` representation of each `Line` object, and this in turn calls the `toString()` method in the `Point` class.

The next statement calls the `intersects()` method from the `line2` object and returns the `Point` object at the intersection of the two lines, `line1` and `line2`, as part of the argument to the `println()` method that outputs the point. As you see, you are not obliged to save an object when you create it. Here you just use it to create the string to be displayed. Once the output statement has executed, the intersection point object is discarded.

You use the `move()` method in the class `Point` to modify the coordinates of the object `end` that you used to create `line1`. You then get the intersection of the two lines again, this time calling the `intersects()` method from `line1`. The output demonstrates that `line1` is independent of the object `end`, as moving the point has made no difference to the intersection.

If you change the constructor in the `Line` class to the version you saw earlier that does not create new `Point` objects to define the line, you can run the example again to see the effect. The output will be:

```
Points created are 0.0, 1.0 and 5.0, 6.0
Lines created are (0.0, 1.0):(5.0, 6.0) and (0.0, 3.0):(3.0, 0.0)
Intersection is 1.0, 2.0
Intersection is 2.0, 1.0
```

Changing the `end` object now alters the line, so you get a different intersection point for the two lines after you move the `end` point. This is because the `Line` object, `line1`, contains references to the `Point` objects defined in `main()`, not references to independent `Point` objects.

Recursion

The methods you have seen so far have been called from within other methods, but a method can also call itself. A method that calls itself is described as a **recursive method,** and the process is referred to as **recursion.** You can also have indirect recursion where a method A calls another method B, which in turn calls the method A. Clearly you must include some logic in a recursive method so that it will eventually stop calling itself if the process is not to continue indefinitely. You can see how this might be done with a simple example.

You can write a method that will calculate integer powers of a variable — in other words, evaluate x^n, or $x*x...*x$ where x is multiplied by itself n times. You can use the fact that you can obtain x^n by multiplying x^{n-1} by x. To put this in terms of a specific example, you can calculate 2^4 as 2^3 multiplied by 2, and you can get 2^3 by multiplying 2^2 by 2, and 2^2 is produced by multiplying 2^1, which is 2, of course, by 2.

Try It Out   **Calculating Powers**

Here is the complete program, including the recursive method `power()`:

```
public class PowerCalc {
  public static void main(String[] args) {
    double x = 5.0;
    System.out.println(x + " to the power 4 is " + power(x,4));
    System.out.println("7.5 to the power 5 is " + power(7.5,5));
    System.out.println("7.5 to the power 0 is " + power(7.5,0));
    System.out.println("10 to the power -2 is " + power(10,-2));
  }

  // Raise x to the power n
  static double power(double x, int n) {
    if(n > 1)
      return x*power(x, n-1);           // Recursive call
    else if(n < 0)
      return 1.0/power(x, -n);          // Negative power of x
    else
      return n == 0 ? 1.0 : x;          // When n is 0 return 1, otherwise x
  }
}
```

This program will produce the following output:

```
5.0 to the power 4 is 625.0
7.5 to the power 5 is 23730.46875
7.5 to the power 0 is 1.0
10 to the power -2 is 0.01
```

How It Works

The `power()` method has two parameters, the value x and the power n. The method performs four different actions, depending on the value of n:

$n > 1$	A recursive call to `power()` is made with n reduced by 1, and the value that is returned is multiplied by x. This is effectively calculating xn as x times xn-1.
$n < 0$	x-n is equivalent to $1/xn$ so this is the expression for the return value. This involves a recursive call to `power()` with the sign of n reversed.
$n = 0$	x0 is defined as 1, so this is the value returned.
$n = 1$	x1 is x, so x is returned.

Just to make sure the process is clear you can work through the sequence of events as they occur in the calculation of 5^4.

Level	Description	Relevant Code
1	The first call of the power() method passes 5.0 and 4 as arguments. Since the second argument, n, is greater than 1, the power() method is called again in the return statement, with the second argument reduced by 1.	```power(5.0, 4) {
if(n > 1)
return 5.0*power(5.0, 4-1);
...
}```
2	The second call of the power() method passes 5.0 and 3 as arguments. Since the second argument, n, is still greater than 1, the power() method is called again in the return statement, with the second argument reduced by 1.	```power(5.0, 3) {
if(n > 1)
return 5.0*power(5.0, 3-1);
...
}```
3	The third call of the power() method passes 5.0 and 2 as arguments. Since the second argument, n, is still greater than 1, the power() method is called again, with the second argument again reduced by 1.	```power(5.0, 2) {
if(n > 1)
return 5.0*power(5.0, 2-1);
...
}```
4	The fourth call of the power() method passes 5.0 and 1 as arguments. Since the second argument, n, is not greater than 1, the value of the first argument, 5.0, is returned to level 3.	```power(5.0, 1) {
if(n > 1)
...
else
return 5.0;
}```
3	Back at level 3, the value returned, 5.0, is multiplied by the first argument, 5.0, and returned to level 2.	```power(5.0, 2) {
if(n>1)
...
else
return 5.0*5.0;
}```
2	Back at level 2, the value returned, 25.0, is multiplied by the first argument, 5.0, and returned to level 1.	```power(5.0, 3) {
if(n > 1)
...
else
return 5.0*25.0;
}```
1	Back at level 1, the value returned, 125.0, is multiplied by the first argument, 5.0, and 625.0 is returned as the result of calling the method in the first instance.	```power(5.0, 4) {
if(n > 1)
...
else
return 5.0*125.0;
}```

You can see from this that the `power()` method is called four times in all. The calls cascade down through four levels until the value of n is such that it allows a value to be returned. The return values ripple up through the levels until you are eventually back at the top, and 625.0 is returned to the original calling point.

As a rule, you should use recursion only where there are evident advantages in the approach, as recursive method calls have quite of lot of overhead. This particular example could be more easily programmed as a loop, and it would execute much more efficiently. You could also use the `Math.pow()` method to produce the result. One example of where recursion can be applied very effectively is in the handling of data structures such as trees. Unfortunately these don't make convenient illustrations of how recursion works at this stage of the learning curve because of their complexity.

Before you can dig deeper into classes, you need to take an apparent detour to understand what a package is in Java.

Understanding Packages

> Packages are fundamental to Java programs so make sure you understand this section.

Packages are implicit in the organization of the standard classes as well as your own programs, and they influence the names you can use for classes and the variables and methods they contain. Essentially, a **package** is a uniquely named collection of classes. The primary reason for grouping classes in packages is to avoid possible name clashes with your own classes when you are using prewritten classes in an application. The names used for classes in one package will not interfere with the names of classes in another package or your program because the class names in a package are all qualified by the package name. Thus, the `String` class you have been using is in the `java.lang` package, so the full name of the class is `java.lang.String`. You have been able to use the unqualified name because all the classes in the `java.lang` package are always available in your program code; there's an implicit `import` statement in effect for all the names in the `java.lang` package. If you happened to have defined a class of your own with the name `String`, using the name `String` would refer to your class, but you could still use the library class that has the same name by using its full name in your code, `java.lang.String`.

Every class in Java is contained in a package, including all those you have defined in the examples. You haven't seen many references to package names so far because you have been implicitly using the **default package** to hold your classes, and this doesn't have a name.

All of the standard classes in Java are contained within a set of packages, and each package contains classes that are related in some way. The package that contains most of the standard classes that you have used so far is called `java.lang`, so called because the classes in this package provide Java language–related support. You haven't seen any explicit reference to `java.lang` in your code either, because this package is automatically available to your programs. Things are arranged this way because some of the classes in `java.lang`, such as `String`, are used in every program. If you use a class from the other packages containing standard classes, you will need either to use the fully qualified name of the class or to explicitly import the full class name into your program in a way that I'll come to shortly.

Packaging Up Your Classes

Putting one of your classes in a named package is very simple. You just add a package statement as the first statement in the source file containing the class definition. Note that it must always be the *first* statement. Only comments or blank lines are allowed to precede the package statement. A **package statement** consists of the keyword `package` followed by the package name and is terminated by a semicolon. If you want the classes in a package to be accessible outside the package, you must declare the class using the keyword `public` in the first line of your class definition. Class definitions that aren't preceded by the keyword `public` are accessible only from methods in classes that belong to the same package.

For example, to include the `Sphere` class in a package called `Geometry`, the contents of the file `Sphere.java` would need to be:

```
package Geometry;

public class Sphere {
   // Details of the class definition
}
```

Each class that you want to include in the package `Geometry` must contain the same package statement at the beginning, and you must save all the files for the classes in the package in a directory with the same name as the package, that is, `Geometry`. Note the use of the `public` keyword in the definition of the `Sphere` class. This makes the class accessible generally. If you omit the `public` keyword from the class definition, the class would be accessible only from methods in classes that are in the `Geometry` package.

Note that you would also need to declare the constructors and methods in the class as `public` if you want them to be accessible from outside of the package. I will return to this in more detail a little later in this chapter.

Packages and the Directory Structure

Packages are actually a little more complicated than they appear at first sight, because a package is intimately related to the directory structure in which it is stored. You already know that the definition of a class with the name `ClassName` must be stored in a file with the name `ClassName.java`, and that all the files for classes within a package `PackageName` must be included in a directory with the name `PackageName`. You can compile the source for a class within a package and have the `.class` file that is generated stored in a different directory, but the directory name must still be the same as the package name.

As you are aware from the existence of the `java.lang` package that contains the `String` class, a package can have a composite name that is a combination of two or more simple names. You can specify a package name as any sequence of names separated by periods. For example, you might have developed several collections of classes dealing with geometry, perhaps one that works with 2D shapes and another with 3D shapes. In this case you might include the class `Sphere` in a package with the statement:

```
package Geometry.Shapes3D;
```

and the class for circles in a package using the statement:

```
package Geometry.Shapes2D;
```

237

In this situation, the files containing the classes in the `Geometry.Shapes3D` packages are expected to be in the directory `Shapes3D` and the files containing the classes in the `Geometry.Shapes2D` packages are expected to be in the directory `Shapes2D`. Both of these directories must be subdirectories of a directory with the name `Geometry`. In general, you can have as many names as you like separated by periods to identify a package, but the package name must reflect the directory structure in which the package is stored. This is illustrated in Figure 5-9.

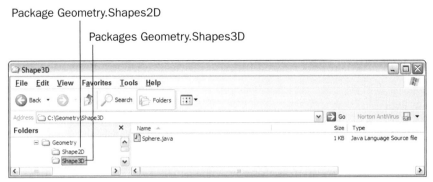

Figure 5-9

Compiling a Package

Compiling the classes in a package can be a bit tricky unless you are clear on how you go about it. I'll describe what you need to do assuming you are using the JDK under Microsoft Windows. The path to the package directory must be explicitly made known to the compiler in the value that is set for `CLASSPATH`, even when the current directory is the one containing the package. The easiest way to specify `CLASSPATH` is by using the `-classpath` option when you invoke the compiler.

The path to the package directory is the path to the directory that *contains* the package directory, and therefore does not include the package directory itself. For example, if you have stored the source files for classes that are in the `Geometry` package in the directory with the path `C:\Beg Java Stuff\ Geometry`, then the path to the `Geometry` directory is `C:\Beg Java Stuff`. Many beginners mistakenly specify the path as `C:\Beg Java Stuff\Geometry`, in which case the package will not be found.

As I said, you can tell the compiler about the path to your package by using the `-classpath` option on the command line. Assuming that the `Geometry` directory is a subdirectory of `C:\Beg Java Stuff`, you could compile the `Line.java` source file with the command:

```
javac -classpath "C:\Beg Java Stuff" Line.java
```

This will result in both the `Line.java` and `Point.java` files being compiled, since `Line.java` refers to the other class. Because the directory in the path contains spaces, you have to enclose the path string between double quotes.

If the `Point` and `Line` classes were not interrelated, you could still compile the two source files or, indeed, any number of source files, in the `Geometry` package with the following command:

```
javac -classpath "C:\Beg Java Stuff" *.java
```

Accessing a Package

How you access a package when you are compiling a program that uses the package depends on where you have put it. There are a couple of options here. The first, but not the best, is to leave the .class files for the classes in the package in the directory with the package name.

Let's look at that before going on to the second possibility.

With the .class files in the original package directory, either the path to your package must appear in the string that has been set for the CLASSPATH environment variable, or you must use the -classpath option on the command line when you invoke the compiler or the interpreter. This overrides the CLASSPATH environment variable if it happens to be set. Note that it is up to you to make sure that the classes in your package are in the right directory. Java will not prevent you from saving a file in a directory that is quite different from that appearing in the package statement. Of the two options here, using the -classpath option on the command line is preferable, because it sets the classpath transiently each time and can't interfere with anything you do subsequently. In any event, you can explore both possibilities.

If you elect to use the CLASSPATH environment variable, it needs to contain only the paths to your packages. The standard packages that are supplied with Java do not need to be considered, as the compiler and the interpreter can always find them. For example, you might set it under Windows 98 by adding the following command to your autoexec.bat file:

```
set CLASSPATH=.;C:\MySource;C:\MyPackages
```

Now the compiler and the interpreter will look for program files and the directories containing your packages in the current directory, which is specified by the period in the classpath string, and the directories C:\MySource and C:\MyPackages. Of course, you can have as many paths as you want defined in CLASSPATH. They just need to be separated by semicolons under Windows. If you are using Windows XP, then you can create and set environment variables through the Advanced tab in the System Properties dialog that you can access through Control Panel.

Under Unix, the equivalent mechanism to set CLASSPATH might be:

```
CLASSPATH=.:/usr/local/mysource:/usr/local/mypackages
```

If you are using the JDK, you can always specify where your packages can be found by using the -classpath option when you execute the Java compiler or the interpreter. This has the advantage that it applies only for the current compilation or execution, so you can easily set it to suit each run. The command to compile MyProgram.java defining the classpath as in the preceding environment variable would be:

```
javac -classpath ".;C:\MySource;C:\MyPackages" MyProgram.java
```

If you don't set the classpath in one of these ways, or you set it incorrectly, Java will not be able to find the classes in any new packages you might create. Remember that the period identifies the current directory as one of the directories in which files can be found. If you forget to specify the period in the -classpath string when compiling your program, the compiler will not be able to find your program source file. If you omit the period from the -classpath string when executing your program, you will get a message to the effect that main() cannot be found and your program will not run.

Another way to make your packages available once you have compiled them is by making them **extensions** to the set of standard packages.

Using Extensions

Extensions are `.jar` files stored within the `ext` directory that is created when you install the JDK. The default directory structure that is created is shown in Figure 5-10.

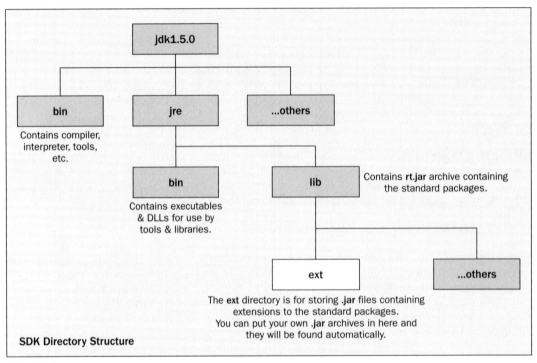

Figure 5-10

The classes and packages in the `.jar` archives that you place in the `ext` directory will automatically be accessible when you compile or run your Java programs, without the need to set the `CLASSPATH` environment variable or use the `-classpath` command-line option. When you create a `.jar` file for a package, you need to make sure that you add the `.class` files with the directory structure corresponding to the package name — you can't just add the `.class` files to the archive. For example, suppose you want to store the `Geometry` package in an archive. Assuming you have already compiled the package and the current directory contains the package directory, the following command can be used to create the archive:

```
C:\Beg Java Stuff>jar cvf Geometry.jar Geometry\*.class
```

This will create the archive `Geometry.jar`, and add all the `.class` files that are in the `Geometry` directory to it. All you now need to do to make the package available to any program that needs it is to copy it to the `ext` directory in the JDK directory hierarchy shown in Figure 5-10.

The `jar` utility does a lot more than I have described here. If you want to know more about what it can do, look into the "Tools and Utilities" section of the JDK documentation.

Adding Classes from a Package to Your Program

You used the `import` statement frequently in examples but nonetheless I'll describe it here from the ground up. Assuming they have been defined with the `public` keyword, you can add all or any of the classes in a named package to the code in your program by using an **import statement.** You can then reference the classes that you make available to your program through the `import` statement just by using the class names. For example, to make available all the classes in the package `Geometry.Shapes3D` to a source file, you just need to add the following `import` statement to the beginning of the file:

```
import Geometry.Shapes3D.*;   // Include all classes from this package
```

The keyword `import` is followed by the specification of what you want to import. The wildcard *, following the period after the package name, selects all the classes in the package, rather like selecting all the files in a directory. Now you can refer to any public class in the package just by using the class name. Again, the names of other classes in your program must be different from the names of the classes in the package. Importing all the names in a package is not an approach you should adopt generally as it defeats the primary objective of putting classes in packages. It's usually better to import just the names from a package that your code references.

If you want to add a particular class rather than an entire package, you specify its name explicitly in the `import` statement:

```
import Geometry.Shapes3D.Sphere;   // Include the class Sphere
```

This includes only the `Sphere` class in the source file. By using a separate `import` statement for each individual class from the package, you ensure that your source file includes only the classes that you need. This reduces the likelihood of name conflicts with your own classes, particularly if you are not fully familiar with the contents of the package and it contains a large number of classes.

> Note that the * can be used only to select all the classes in a package. You can't use `Geometry.*` to select all the packages in the `Geometry` directory.

Packages and Names in Your Programs

A package creates a self-contained environment for naming your classes. As I've said, this is the primary reason for having packages in Java. You can specify the names for classes in one package without worrying about whether the same names have been used elsewhere. Java makes this possible by treating the package name as part of the class name—actually as a prefix. This means that the class `Sphere` in the package `Geometry.Shapes3D` has the full name `Geometry.Shapes3D.Sphere`. If you don't use an `import` statement to incorporate the class in your program, you can still make use of the class by referring to it using its full class name. If you needed to do this with the class `Sphere`, you might declare a variable with the statement:

```
Geometry.Shapes3D.Sphere ball = new Geometry.Shapes3D.Sphere(10.0, 1.0, 1.0, 1.0);
```

While this is rather verbose and certainly doesn't help the readability of the program, it does ensure you will have no conflict between this class and any other `Sphere` class that might be part of your program. You can usually contrive that your class names do not conflict with those in the commonly used standard Java packages, but in cases where you can't manage this, you can always fall back on using fully qualified class names. Indeed, on some occasions, you have to do this. This is necessary when you are using two different classes from different packages that share the same basic class name.

Importing Static Class Members

As you have seen in some of the examples, you can import the names of static members of a class from a named package into your program. This allows you to reference such static members by their simple unqualified names. In the `Sphere` class that you developed earlier in this chapter, you could have used the constant `PI` that is defined in the `Math` class by using its fully qualified name, `Math.PI`, in the definition of the volume method:

```
double volume() {
    return 4.0/3.0*Math.PI*radius*radius*radius;
}
```

This obviates the need for the static member of the `Sphere` class with the name `PI` and would provide a much more accurate definition of the value of π.

However, the `Math` prefix to the name `PI` doesn't really add to the clarity of the code, and it would be better without it. You can remove the need for prefixing `PI` with the `Math` class name by importing the `PI` member name from the `Math` class:

```
import static java.lang.Math.PI;

class Sphere {
    // Class details as before...
    double volume() {
        return 4.0/3.0*PI*radius*radius*radius;
    }
}
```

It is clear what `PI` means here and the code is not cluttered up with the class name prefix.

You can also import all the static members of a class using `*` notation. For example:

```
import static java.lang.Math.*;      // Import all static members of the Math class
```

With this statement at the beginning of a source file, you can refer to any of the static members of the `Math` class without qualifying them with the class name. Thus you can use methods such as `sqrt()`, `abs()`, `random()`, and so on, without the need for the `Math` prefix to the method names. Of course, using the `*` notation to import all the static names in a class does increase the risk of clashes between the names you are importing and the names you define in your code.

Note that the `import` statement, and that includes its use for importing static members of a class, applies only to classes that are defined in a named package. This is particularly relevant in the context of static import. If you want to import the names of a static member of a class that you define, then you *must* put the definition of a class in a named package. You cannot import the names of static members of a class that is defined in the default package that has no name. The class name in a static `import` statement must always be qualified with its package name.

Standard Packages

All of the standard classes that are provided with Java are stored in standard packages. There is a substantial and growing list of standard packages (more than 150 in JDK 5) but some of the ones you may hear about most frequently are:

`java.lang`	Contains classes that are fundamental to Java (e.g., the Math class) and all of these are available in your programs automatically. You do not need an import statement to include them.
`java.io`	Contains classes supporting stream input/output operations.
`java.nio`	Contains classes supporting the new input/output operations that were introduced in JDK1.4—especially with files.
`java.nio.channels`	Contains more classes supporting new input/output operations—the ones that actually read and write files.
`java.awt`	Contains classes that support Java's graphical user interface (GUI). While you can use these classes for GUI programming, it is almost always easier and better to use the alternative Swing classes.
`javax.swing`	Provides classes supporting the "Swing" GUI components. These are not only more flexible and easier to use than the `java.awt` equivalents, but they are also implemented largely in Java with minimal dependency on native code.
`javax.swing.border`	Classes to support generating borders around Swing components.
`javax.swing.event`	Classes supporting event handling for Swing components.
`java.awt.event`	Contains classes that support event handling.
`java.awt.geom`	Contains classes for drawing and operating with 2D geometric entities.
`java.applet`	Contains classes that enable you to write applets—programs that are embedded in a web page.
`java.util`	Contains classes that support a range of standard operations for managing collections of data, accessing date and time information, and analyzing strings.

The standard packages and the classes they contain cover an enormous amount of ground, so even in a book of this size it is impossible to cover them all exhaustively. There are now many more classes in the standard packages included with JDK 5 than there are pages in this book. However, you will be applying some classes from all of the packages in the preceding table, plus one or two others besides, in later chapters of the book.

Standard Classes Encapsulating the Primitive Data Types

You saw in the previous chapter that you have classes available that allow you to define objects that encapsulate values of each of the primitive data types in Java. These classes are:

```
Boolean        Character       Byte

Short          Integer         Long

Float          Double
```

These are all contained in the package `java.lang` along with quite a few other classes, such as the `String` and `StringBuffer` classes that you saw in Chapter 4. Each of these classes encapsulates a value of the corresponding primitive type and includes methods for manipulating and interrogating objects of the class, as well as a number of very useful static methods that provide utility functions for the underlying primitive types.

You have methods in these classes for converting from values of primitive types to strings. Each class provides a static `toString()` method to convert a value of the corresponding primitive type to a `String` object, as you saw in the last chapter. There is also a non-static `toString()` method in each class that returns a `String` representation of a class object.

Conversely, there are methods to convert from a `String` object to a primitive type. For example, the static `parseInt()` member in the `Integer` class accepts a `String` representation of an integer as an argument and returns the equivalent value as type `int`. An alternative version of this method accepts a second argument of type `int` that specifies the radix to be used when interpreting the string. This enables you to parse strings that are hexadecimal or octal values, for example. If the `String` object cannot be parsed for any reason, if it contains invalid characters, for example, the method will throw an exception of type `NumberFormatException`. All the standard classes encapsulating numerical primitive types define static methods to parse strings. You have the methods `parseShort()`, `parseByte()`, `parseInt()`, and `parseLong()` in the classes for integer types, and `parseFloat()` and `parseDouble()` for floating-point classes. The `Boolean` class defines a static method `valueOf()` that converts a string to the `Boolean` value `true` if the string is equal to `"true"` ignoring case. Any other string will result in `false` being returned.

Each class also defines a `value()` method that returns the value that is encapsulated by an object as a value of the corresponding primitive type. For example, if you have created an object `number` of type `Double` that encapsulates the value 1.14159, then the expression `number.value()` will result in the value 1.14159 as type `double`.

The classes that wrap numerical primitive types each contain the `static final` constants `MAX_VALUE` and `MIN_VALUE` that define the maximum and minimum values that can be represented. The floating-point classes also define the constants `POSITIVE_INFINITY`, `NEGATIVE_INFINITY`, and `NaN` (it stands for **Not a Number**, as it is the result of $0/0$), so you can use these in comparisons to test whether such values have arisen during calculations. Alternatively, you can test floating-point values with the static methods `isInfinite()` and `isNaN()` — you pass your variable as an argument, and the methods return `true` for an infinite value or the `NaN` value, respectively. Remember that an infinite value can arise without necessarily dividing by zero. Any computation that results in an exponent that is too large to be represented will produce either `POSITIVE_INFINITY` or `NEGATIVE_INFINITY`.

Many other operations are supported by these classes, so it is well worth browsing the JDK documentation for them. In particular, the `Character` class defines a large number of static methods for testing and classifying characters.

Autoboxing Values of Primitive Types

Circumstances can arise surprisingly often where you want to pass values of a primitive type to a method that requires the argument to be a reference to an object. The compiler will supply automatic conversions of primitive values to the corresponding class type when circumstances permit this. This can arise when you pass a value of type `int` to a method where the parameter type is type `Integer`, for example. Conversions from a primitive type to the corresponding class type are called **boxing conversions**, and automatic conversions of this kind are described as **autoboxing**.

The compiler will also insert unboxing conversions when necessary to convert a reference to an object of a wrapper class for a primitive type such as `double` to the value that it encapsulates. The compiler does this by inserting a call to the `value()` method for the object. You can see this in action in the following little example.

Try It Out   Autoboxing in Action

This program is contrived to force boxing and unboxing conversions to occur:

```java
public class AutoboxingInAction {
  public static void main(String[] args) {
    int[] values = { 3, 97, 55, 22, 12345 };
    Integer[] objs = new Integer[values.length];  // Array to store Integer objects

    // Call method to cause boxing conversions
    for(int i = 0 ; i<values.length ; i++) {
      objs[i] = boxInteger(values[i]);
    }

    // Use method to cause unboxing conversions
    for(Integer intObject : objs) {
      unboxInteger(intObject);
    }
  }

  // Method to cause boxing conversion
  public static Integer boxInteger(Integer obj) {
    return obj;
  }

  // Method to cause unboxing conversion
  public static void unboxInteger(int n) {
    System.out.println("value = " + n);
  }
}
```

This example will produce the following output:

```
value = 3
value = 97
value = 55
value = 22
value = 12345
```

How It Works

You have defined the `boxInteger()` method with a parameter type of type `Integer`. When you call this method in the first `for` loop in `main()`, you pass values of type `int` to it from the `values` array. Because the `boxInteger()` method requires the argument to be a reference to an object of type `Integer`, the compiler arranges for autoboxing to occur by inserting a boxing conversion to convert the integer value to an object of type `Integer`. The method returns a reference to the object that results, and you store this in the `Integer[]` array `objs`.

The second `for` loop in `main()` passes each reference to an `Integer` object from the `objs` array to the `unboxInteger()` method. Because you have specified the method parameter type as type `int`, the method cannot accept a reference to an object of type `Integer` as the argument directly. The compiler inserts an unboxing convert to obtain the value of type `int` that the object encapsulates. This value is then passed to the method, and you output it.

Autoboxing is particular useful when you need to insert values of primitive types into a collection — you will meet the collection classes that are available in the class libraries in Chapter 14, but you'll see more on boxing and unboxing conversions in Chapter 13.

Controlling Access to Class Members

I have not yet discussed in any detail how you control the accessibility of class members from outside the class — from a method in another class in other words. You know that you can refer to any of the static members of the same class in the code for a static class method, and a non-static method can refer to any member of the same class. The degree to which variables and methods within one class are accessible from other classes is a bit more complicated. It depends on what **access attributes** you have specified for the members of a class, whether the classes are in the same package, and whether you have declared the class as public. This is why you had to understand packages first.

Using Access Attributes

Let's start by considering classes that are in the same package. Within a given package, any class has direct access to any other class name in the same package — for declaring variables or specifying method parameter types, for example — but the variables and methods that are members of that other class are not necessarily accessible. The accessibility of these is controlled by **access attributes**. The name of a class in one package can be accessed from a class in another package only if the class to be accessed is declared as `public`. Classes not declared as `public` can be accessed only by classes within the same package.

You have four possibilities when specifying an access attribute for a class member, and each possibility has a different effect overall. The options you have for specifying the accessibility of a variable or a method in a class are:

Attribute	Permitted Access
No access attribute	From methods in any class in the same package
public	From methods in any class anywhere as long as the class has been declared as public
private	Accessible only from methods inside the class. No access from outside the class at all.
protected	From methods in any class in the same package and from any subclass anywhere

The table shows you how the access attributes you set for a class member determine the parts of the Java environment from which you can access it. I will discuss subclasses in the next chapter, so don't worry about these for the moment. I will describe how and when you use the protected attribute then. Note that public, private, and protected are all keywords. Specifying a member as public makes it completely accessible, and at the other extreme, making it private restricts access to members of the same class.

This may sound more complicated than it actually is. Look at Figure 5-11, which shows the access allowed between classes within the same package.

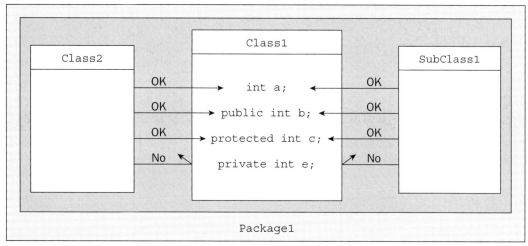

Figure 5-11

Within a package such as package1 in Figure 5-11, only the private members of the class Class1 can't be directly accessed by methods in other classes in the same package. If you declare a class member to be private, it can be accessed only by methods in the same class.

As I said earlier, a class definition must have an access attribute of `public` if it is to be accessible from outside the package that contains it. Figure 5-12 shows the situation where the classes seeking access to the members of a public class are in different packages.

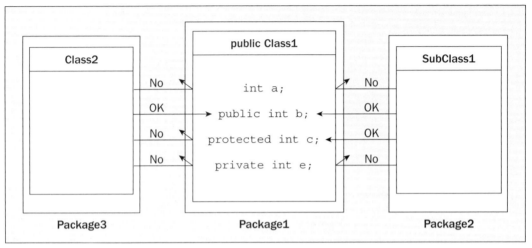

Figure 5-12

Here access is more restricted. The only members of `Class1` that can be accessed from an ordinary class, `Class2`, in another package, are those specified as `public`. Keep in mind that the class `Class1` must also have been defined with the attribute `public` for this to be the case. A class that is not defined as `public` cannot be accessed at all from a class in another package.

From a subclass of `Class1` that is in another package, the members of `Class1` without an access attribute cannot be reached, and neither can the `private` members — these can never be accessed externally under any circumstances.

Specifying Access Attributes

As you probably gathered from the diagrams in the previous section, to specify an access attribute for a class member, you just add the appropriate keyword to the beginning of the declaration. Here is the `Point` class you saw earlier, but now with access attributes defined for its members:

Try It Out   Accessing the Point Class

Make the following changes to your `Point` class. If you save it in a new directory, do make sure `Line.java` is copied there as well. It will be useful later if they are in a directory with the name `Geometry`.

```
import static java.lang.Math.sqrt;

public class Point {
  // Create a point from its coordinates
```

```
public Point(double xVal, double yVal) {
   x = xVal;
   y = yVal;
}

// Create a Point from an existing Point object
public Point(final Point aPoint) {
   x = aPoint.x;
   y = aPoint.y;
}
   // Move a point
public void move(double xDelta, double yDelta) {
   // Parameter values are increments to the current coordinates
   x += xDelta;
   y += yDelta;
}

// Calculate the distance to another point
public double distance(final Point aPoint) {
   return sqrt((x - aPoint.x)*(x - aPoint.x)+(y - aPoint.y)*(y - aPoint.y));
}

// Convert a point to a string
public String toString() {
   return Double.toString(x) + ", " + y;      // As "x, y"
}

// Coordinates of the point
private double x;
private double y;
}
```

The members have been resequenced within the class, with the `private` members appearing last. You should maintain a consistent ordering of class members according to their access attributes, as it makes the code easier to follow. The ordering adopted most frequently is for the most accessible members to appear first and the least accessible last, but a consistent order is more important than the particular order you choose.

How It Works

Now the instance variables x and y cannot be accessed or modified from outside the class, as they are private. The only way these can be set or modified is through methods within the class, either with constructors or the `move()` method. If it is necessary to obtain the values of x and y from outside the class, as it might well be in this case, a simple function would do the trick. For example:

```
public double getX() {
   return x;
}
```

Couldn't be easier really, could it? This makes x freely available, but prevents modification of its value from outside the class. In general, such methods are referred to as **accessor** methods and usually have the form getXXX(). Methods that allow a private data member to be changed are called **mutator** methods and are typically of the form setXXX(), where a new value is passed as an argument. For example:

```
public void setX(double inputX) {
   x = inputX;
}
```

It may seem odd to use a method to alter the value of a private data member when you could just make it public. The main advantage of using a method in this way is that you can apply validity checks on the new value that is to be set and prevent inappropriate values from being assigned. Of course, if you really don't want to allow the value of a private member to be changed, you don't include a mutator method for the class.

Choosing Access Attributes

As you can see from the table of access attributes, all the classes you have defined so far have had members that are freely accessible within the same package. This applies both to the methods and the variables that were defined in the classes. This is not good object-oriented programming practice. As I said in Chapter 1, one of the ideas behind objects is to keep the data members encapsulated so they cannot be modified by all and sundry, even from other classes within the same package. On the other hand, the methods in your classes that provide the operations you want to allow with objects of the class type generally need to be accessible. They provide the outside interface to the class and define the set of operations that are possible with objects of the class. Therefore, in the majority of situations with simple classes (i.e., no subclasses), you should be explicitly specifying your class members as either public or private, rather than omitting the access attributes.

Broadly, unless you have good reasons for declaring them otherwise, the variables in a public class should be private and the methods that will be called from outside the class should be public. Even where access to the values of the variables from outside a class is necessary, you don't need to make them public or leave them without an access attribute. As you've just seen, you can provide access quite easily by adding a simple public method to return the value of a data member.

Of course, there are always exceptions:

❑ For classes in a package that are not public, and therefore not accessible outside the package, it may sometimes be convenient to allow other classes in the package direct access to the data members.

❑ If you have data members that have been specified as final so that their values are fixed and they are likely to be useful outside the class, you might as well declare them to be public.

❑ You may well have methods in a class that are intended to be used only internally by other methods in the same class. In this case you should specify these as private.

❑ In a class like the standard class Math, which is just a convenient container for utility functions and standard data values, you'll want to make everything public.

All of this applies to simple classes. You'll see in the next chapter, when you will be looking at subclasses, that there are some further aspects of class structure that you must take into account.

Using Package and Access Attributes

Let's put together an example that uses a package that you will create. You could put the `Point` and `Line` classes that you defined earlier in a package you could call `Geometry`. You can then write a program that will import these classes and test them. You should already have the `Geometry` directory set up if you followed my suggestion with the previous example.

Try It Out   Packaging Up the Line and Point Classes

The source and `.class` files for each class in the package must be in a directory with the name `Geometry`. Remember that you need to ensure the path to the directory (or directories if you are storing `.class` files separately) `Geometry` appears in the `CLASSPATH` environment variable setting before you try to compile or use either of these two classes. You can best do this by specifying the `-classpath` option when you run the compiler or the interpreter.

To include the class `Point` in the package, the code in `Point.java` will be:

```java
package Geometry;

import static java.lang.Math.sqrt;
public class Point {

  // Create a point from its coordinates
  public Point(double xVal, double yVal) {
    x = xVal;
    y = yVal;
  }

  // Create a Point from an existing Point object
  public Point(final Point aPoint) {
    x = aPoint.x;
    y = aPoint.y;
  }

    // Move a point
  public void move(double xDelta, double yDelta) {
    // Parameter values are increments to the current coordinates
    x += xDelta;
    y += yDelta;
  }

  // Calculate the distance to another point
  public double distance(final Point aPoint) {
    return sqrt((x - aPoint.x)*(x - aPoint.x)+(y - aPoint.y)*(y - aPoint.y));
  }

  // Convert a point to a string
  public String toString() {
    return Double.toString(x) + ", " + y;     // As "x, y"
  }
```

```
    // Retrieve the x coordinate
    public double getX() {
      return x;
    }

    // Retrieve the y coordinate
    public double getY() {
      return y;
    }

    // Set the x coordinate
    public void setX(double inputX) {
      x = inputX;
    }

    // Set the y coordinate
    public void setY(double inputY) {
      y = inputY;
    }

    // Coordinates of the point
    private double x;
    private double y;
  }
```

Note that you have added the getX(), getY(), setX(), and setY() methods to the class to make the private data members accessible.

The Line class also needs to be amended to make the methods public and to declare the class as public. You'll have to change its intersects() method so that it can access the private data members of Point objects using the set...() and get...() methods in the Point class. The code in Line.java, with changes highlighted, will be:

```
  package Geometry;

  public class Line {

    // Create a line from two points
    public Line(final Point start, final Point end) {
      this.start = new Point(start);
      this.end = new Point(end);
    }

    // Create a line from two coordinate pairs
    public Line(double xStart, double yStart, double xEnd, double yEnd) {
      start = new Point(xStart, yStart);      // Create the start point
      end = new Point(xEnd, yEnd);            // Create the end point
    }

    // Calculate the length of a line
    public double length() {
      return start.distance(end);             // Use the method from the Point class
```

```
    }

    // Return a point as the intersection of two lines -- called from a Line object
    public Point intersects(final Line line1) {

      Point localPoint = new Point(0, 0);

      double num =(this.end.getY() - this.start.getY())
               * (this.start.getX()-line1.start.getX())
               - (this.end.getX() - this.start.getX())
               * (this.start.getY() - line1.start.getY());

      double denom = (this.end.getY() - this.start.getY())
                   * (line1.end.getX() - line1.start.getX())
                   - (this.end.getX() - this.start.getX())
                   * (line1.end.getY() - line1.start.getY());

      localPoint.setX(line1.start.getX() + (line1.end.getX() -
                                    line1.start.getX())*num/denom);
      localPoint.setY(line1.start.getY() + (line1.end.getY() -
                                    line1.start.getY())*num/denom);

      return localPoint;
    }

    // Convert a line to a string
    public String toString() {
      return "(" + start+ "):(" + end + ")";   // As "(start):(end)"
    }                                           // that is, "(x1, y1):(x2, y2)"

    // Data members
    Point start;                                // Start point of line
    Point end;                                  // End point of line
  }
```

Here you have left the data members of the class without an access attribute so they are accessible from the Point class, but not from classes outside the Geometry package.

How It Works

The package statement at the beginning of each source file defines the package to which the class belongs. Remember, you still have to save it in the correct directory, Geometry. Without the public attribute, the classes would not be available to classes outside the Geometry package.

Since you have declared the data members in the class Point as private, they will not be accessible directly. You have added the methods getX(), getY(), setX(), and setY() to the Point class to make the values accessible to any class that needs them.

The static import statement that you added earlier for the sqrt() method in the Math class allows the distance() method to access the sqrt() method without using the Math qualifier.

The Line class hasn't been updated since the earlier example, so you first have to sort out the access attributes. The two instance variables are declared as before, without any access attribute, so they can be accessed from within the package but not from classes outside the package. This is an occasion where exposing the data members within the package is very convenient, and you can do it without exposing the data members to any classes using the package. And you have updated the intersects() method to reflect the changes in accessibility made to the members of the Point class.

You can now write the program that is going to import and use the package that you have just created.

Try It Out   Testing the Geometry Package

You can create a succession of points, and create a line joining each pair of successive points in the sequence. You can then calculate the total line length.

```
import Geometry.*;     // Import the Point and Line classes

public class TryPackage {
  public static void main(String[] args) {
    double[][] coords = { {1.0, 0.0}, {6.0, 0.0}, {6.0, 10.0},
                          {10.0,10.0}, {10.0, -14.0}, {8.0, -14.0}};
    // Create an array of points and fill it with Point objects
    Point[] points = new Point[coords.length];
    for(int i = 0; i < coords.length; i++)
      points[i] = new Point(coords[i][0],coords[i][1]);

    // Create an array of lines and fill it using Point pairs
    Line[] lines = new Line[points.length - 1];
    double totalLength = 0.0;                      // Store total line length here
    for(int i = 0; i < points.length - 1; i++) {
      lines[i] = new Line(points[i], points[i+1]); // Create a Line
      totalLength += lines[i].length();            // Add its length
      System.out.println("Line "+(i+1)+' ' +lines[i] +
                    " Length is " + lines[i].length());

    }
    // Output the total length
    System.out.println("\nTotal line length = " + totalLength);
  }
}
```

You should save this as TryPackage.java in the directory TryPackage. If the path to your Geometry directory on a PC running Windows is C:\Packages\Geometry, you can compile this with the following command:

```
javac -classpath ".;C:\Packages" TryPackage.java
```

This assumes the current directory is the one containing the TryPackage.java file, which will be the TryPackage directory if you followed my suggestion. The **-classpath** option specifies two paths separated by a semicolon. The first path, specified by a period, is the current directory. This is necessary to enable the TryPackage.java source file to be found. The second path is C:\Packages, which is the directory containing your Geometry package. Without this the compiler will not be able to find the classes in the Geometry package, and the compilation will fail.

Once you have a successful compilation, you can execute the program with the command:

```
java -classpath ".;C:\Packages" TryPackage
```

When the program executes, you should see the following output:

```
Line 1 (1.0, 0.0):(6.0, 0.0)    Length is 5.0
Line 2 (6.0, 0.0):(6.0, 10.0)    Length is 10.0
Line 3 (6.0, 10.0):(10.0, 10.0)    Length is 4.0
Line 4 (10.0, 10.0):(10.0, -14.0)    Length is 24.0
Line 5 (10.0, -14.0):(8.0, -14.0)    Length is 2.0

Total line length = 45.0
```

How It Works

This example is a handy review of how you can define arrays and also shows that you can declare an array of objects in the same way as you declare an array of one of the basic types. The dimensions of the array of arrays, `coords`, are determined by the initial values that you specified between the braces. The number of values within the outer braces determines the first dimension. Each of the elements in the array is itself an array of length two, with each pair of element values enclosed within their own braces.

Since there are six sets of these, you have an array of six elements, each of which is itself an array of two elements. Each of these elements corresponds to the (x, y) coordinates of a point.

> You can see from this that you could create an array of arrays with each row having a different number of elements. The number of initializing values that appear between each inner pair of braces determines the length of each row, so the rows could all be of different lengths in the most general case.

You declare an array of `Point` objects with the same length as the number of (x, y) pairs in the `coords` array. This array is filled with `Point` objects in the `for` loop, which you create using the pairs of coordinate values from the `coords` array.

Since each pair of `Point` objects will define a `Line` object, you need one less element in the `lines` array than you have in the `points` array. You create the elements of the lines array in the second `for` loop using successive `Point` objects and accumulate the total length of all the line segments by adding the length of each `Line` object to `totalLength` as it is created. On each iteration of the `for` loop, you output the details of the current line. Finally, you output the value of `totalLength`, which in this case is 45.

Note that the `import` statement in `TryPackage.java` adds the classes from the `Geometry` package to your program. These classes can be added to any application using the same `import` statement. You might like to try putting the classes in the `Geometry` package in a `.jar` file and try it out as an extension. Let's look at one other aspect of generating your own packages — compiling just the classes in the package without any program that makes use of them. You can try this out on the `Geometry` package if you delete the `Line.class` and `Point.class` files from the package directory.

First, make the directory, `C:\Packages`, that contains the package directory current. Now you can compile just the classes in the `Geometry` package with the following command:

```
javac -classpath "C:\Packages" Geometry/*.java
```

This will compile both the `Line` and `Point` classes so you should see the `.class` files restored in the `Geometry` directory. The files to be compiled are specified relative to the current directory as `Geometry/*.java`. Under Microsoft Windows this could equally well be `Geometry\*.java`. This specifies all files in the `Geometry` subdirectory to the current directory. The classpath must contain the path to the package directory; otherwise, the compiler will not be able to find the package. You have defined it here using the `-classpath` option. You haven't specified the current directory in the classpath string because you do not have any files there that need to be compiled. If you had included it in the classpath string, it would not have made any difference — the classes in the `Geometry` package would compile just the same.

Nested Classes

All the classes you have defined so far have been separate from each other — each stored away in its own source file. Not all classes have to be defined like this. You can put the definition of one class inside the definition of another class. The inside class is called a **nested class**. A nested class can itself have another class nested inside it, if need be.

When you define a nested class, it is a member of the enclosing class in much the same way as the other class members. A nested class can have an access attribute just like other class members, and the accessibility from outside the enclosing class is determined by the attributes in the same way:

```
public class Outside {

  // Nested class
  public class Inside {
    // Details of Inside class...
  }

  // More members of Outside class...
}
```

Here the class `Inside` is nested inside the class `Outside`. The `Inside` class is declared as a public member of `Outside`, so it is accessible from outside `Outside`. Obviously, a nested class should have some specific association with the enclosing class. Arbitrarily nesting one class inside another would not be sensible. The enclosing class here is referred to as a **top-level class**. A top-level class is a class that contains a nested class but is not itself a nested class.

The nested class here has meaning only in the context of an object of type `Outside`. This is because the `Inside` class is not declared as a static member of the class `Outside`. Until an object of type `Outside` has been created, you can't create any `Inside` objects. However, when you declare an object of a class containing a nested class, no objects of the nested class are necessarily created — unless of course the enclosing class's constructor creates them. For example, suppose you create an object with the following statement:

```
Outside outer = new Outside();
```

No objects of the nested class, `Inside`, are created. If you now wish to create an object of the type of the nested class, you must refer to the nested class type using the name of the enclosing class as a qualifier.

For instance, having declared an object of type `Outside`, you can create an object of type `Inside` as follows:

```
Outside.Inside inner = outer.new Inside();          // Define a nested class object
```

Here you have created an object of the nested class type that is associated with the object `outer` that you created earlier. You are creating an object of type `Inside` in the context of the object `outer`. Within non-static methods that are members of `Outside`, you can use the class name `Inside` without any qualification, as it will be automatically qualified by the compiler with the `this` variable. So you could create a new `Inside` object from within the method of the object `Outside`:

```
Inside inner = new Inside();                         // Define a nested class object
```

This statement is equivalent to:

```
this.Inside inner = this.new Inside();               // Define a nested class object
```

All this implies that a static method cannot create objects of a non-static nested class type. Because the `Inside` class is not a static member of the `Outside` class, such a member could refer to an object which does not exist — which would be an error if there are no `Inside` objects extant in the context of an `Outside` object. Because `Inside` is not a static member of the `Outside` class, if a static method in the `Outside` class tried to create an object of type `Inside` directly, without first invoking an object of type `Outside`, it would be trying to create an object outside of that object's legitimate scope — an illegal maneuver.

Further, because the `Inside` class is not a static member of the `Outside` class, it cannot in turn contain any static data members itself. Since `Inside` is not static, it cannot act as a freestanding class with static members — this would be a logical contradiction.

You typically use nested classes to define objects that at least have a strong association with objects of the enclosing class type, and often there is a tight coupling between the two. A further use for nested classes is for grouping a set of related classes under the umbrella of an enclosing class. You will be using this approach in examples later on in the book.

Static Nested Classes

To make objects of a nested class type independent of objects of the enclosing class type, you can declare the nested class as `static`:

```
public class Outside {
  public static class Skinside {
    // Details of Skinside
  }

  // Nested class
  public class Inside {
    // Details of Inside class...
  }
  // More members of Outside class...
}
```

Now with `Skinside` inside `Outside` declared as `static`, you can declare objects of this nested class type independent from any objects of type `Outside`, and regardless of whether you have created any `Outside` objects or not. For example:

```
Outside.Skinside example = new Outside.Skinside();
```

This is significantly different from what you needed to do for a non-static nested class. Now you must use the nested class name qualified by the enclosing class name as the type for creating the object. Thus, the name of a static nested class exists within the context of the outer class and therefore the nested class name is qualified by the enclosing class name. Note that a static nested class can have static members, whereas a non-static nested class cannot. A class containing both a static and a non-static nested class is illustrated in Figure 5-13.

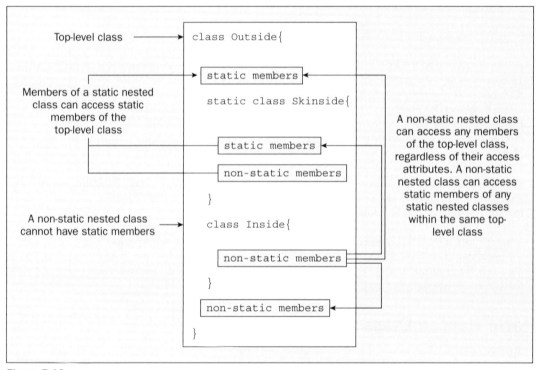

Figure 5-13

If the preceding discussion seems a bit confusing in the abstract, you will get a better idea of how a nested class works in practice with a simple example. You will create a class `MagicHat` that will define an object containing a variable number of `Rabbit` objects. You will put the definition for the class `Rabbit` inside the definition of the class `MagicHat`, so `Rabbit` will be an example of a nested class. The basic structure of `MagicHat.java` will be:

```
public class MagicHat {
    // Definition of the MagicHat class...
```

```
    // Nested class to define a rabbit
    static class Rabbit {
      // Definition of the Rabbit class...
    }
  }
```

Here the nested class is defined as `static` because you want to be able to have static members of this class. You will see a little later in the chapter how it might work with a non-static nested class.

Try It Out   Rabbits out of Hats

Let's add the detail of the `MagicHat` class definition:

```
import java.util.Random;                           // Import Random class

public class MagicHat {
  static int maxRabbits = 5;                        // Maximum rabbits in a hat
  static Random select = new Random();              // Random number generator

  // Constructor for a hat
  public MagicHat(String hatName) {
    this.hatName = hatName;                          // Store the hat name
    rabbits = new Rabbit[1+select.nextInt(maxRabbits)]; // Random rabbits

    for(int i = 0; i < rabbits.length; i++) {
      rabbits[i] = new Rabbit();                     // Create the rabbits
    }
  }

  // String representation of a hat
  public String toString() {
    // Hat name first...
    String hatString = "\n" + hatName + " contains:\n";

    for(Rabbit rabbit : rabbits) {
      hatString += "     " + rabbit;                 // Add the rabbits strings
    }
    return hatString;
  }

  private String hatName;                            // Name of the hat
  private Rabbit rabbits[];                          // Rabbits in the hat

  // Nested class to define a rabbit
  static class Rabbit {
    // Definition of the Rabbit class...
  }
}
```

You can save the source file in a new directory, `TryNestedClass`. Instead of the old `Math.random()` method that you have been using up to now to generate pseudo-random values, you are using an object of the class `Random` that is defined in the `java.util` package. An object of type `Random` has a variety of methods to generate pseudo-random values of different types, and with different ranges. The method `nextInt()` that you are using here returns an integer that is zero or greater, but less than the integer value you pass as an argument. Thus, if you pass the length of an array to it, it will generate a random index value that will always be legal for the array size.

You can now add the definition of the `Rabbit` class. When you create a `Rabbit` object, you want it to have a unique name so you can distinguish one `Rabbit` from another. You can generate unique names by selecting one of a limited set of fixed names and then appending an integer that is different each time the base name is used. Here's what you need to add for the `Rabbit` class definition:

```
public class MagicHat {

  // Definition of the MagicHat class - as before...

  // Nested class to define a rabbit
  static class Rabbit {
    // A name is a rabbit name from rabbitNames followed by an integer
    static private String[] rabbitNames = {"Floppsy", "Moppsy",
                                           "Gnasher", "Thumper"};
    static private int[] rabbitNamesCount = new int[rabbitNames.length];
    private String name;                         // Name of the rabbit

    // Constructor for a rabbit
    public Rabbit() {
      int index = select.nextInt(rabbitNames.length);   // Get random name index
      name = rabbitNames[index] + (++rabbitNamesCount[index]);
    }

    // String representation of a rabbit
    public String toString() {
      return name;
    }
  }
}
```

Note that the constructor in the `Rabbit` class can access the `select` member of the enclosing class, `MagicHat`, without qualification. This is possible only with static members of the enclosing class — you can't refer to non-static members of the enclosing class here because there is no object of type `MagicHat` associated with it.

You can use the following application class to try out the nested class:

```
public class TryNestedClass {
  static public void main(String[] args) {
    // Create three magic hats and output them
    System.out.println(new MagicHat("Gray Topper"));
    System.out.println(new MagicHat("Black Topper"));
    System.out.println(new MagicHat("Baseball Cap"));
  }
}
```

You should save this source file in the same directory as `MagicHat.java`. When I ran the program, I got the following output:

```
Gray Topper contains:
    Floppsy1    Moppsy1    Gnasher1    Floppsy2    Thumper1

Black Topper contains:
    Moppsy2    Gnasher2    Floppsy3    Floppsy4

Baseball Cap contains:
    Moppsy3
```

You are likely to get something different.

How It Works

Each `MagicHat` object will contain a random number of `Rabbit` objects. The constructor for a `MagicHat` object stores the name of the hat in its private member `hatName` and generates a `Rabbit` array with at least one, and up to `maxRabbits`, elements. This is done with the expression `1+select.nextInt(maxRabbits)`. Calling `nextInt()` with the argument `maxRabbits` will return a value that is from 0 to `maxRabbits-1`, inclusive. Adding 1 to this will result in a value from 1 to `maxRabbits`, inclusive. The array so created is then filled with `Rabbit` objects.

The `MagicHat` class also has a `toString()` method that returns a `String` object containing the name of the hat and the names of all the rabbits in the hat. This assumes that the `Rabbit` class also has a `toString()` method defined. You will be able to use the `toString()` implicitly in an output statement when you create and display `MagicHat` class objects.

The base names that you use to generate rabbit names are defined in the `static` array `rabbitNames[]` in the `Rabbit` class. The count for each base name, which you will append to the base name to produce a unique name for a rabbit, is stored in the `static` array `rabbitNamesCount[]`. This has the same number of elements as the `rabbitNames` array, and each element stores a value to be appended to the corresponding name in the `rabbitNames` array. The `Rabbit` class has the data member `name` to store a name that is initialized in the constructor. A random base name is selected from the `rabbitNames[]` array using an index value from 0 up to one less than the length of this array. You then append the current count for the name incremented by 1, so successive uses of any base name, such as `Gnasher`, for example, will produce names `Gnasher1`, `Gnasher2`, and so on. The `toString()` method for the class returns the name for the `Rabbit` object.

The `main()` method in `TryNestedClass` creates three `MagicHat` objects and outputs the string representation of each of them. Putting the object as an argument to the `println()` method will call the `toString()` method for the object automatically, and the `String` object that is returned will be output to the screen.

If you look at the `.class` files that are produced by the compiler, the `Rabbit` class has its own file with the name `MagicHat$Rabbit.class`. Thus the name of the nested `Rabbit` class is qualified by the name of the class that contains it, `MagicHat`.

Using a Non-Static Nested Class

In the previous example, you could make the `Rabbit` class non-static by deleting the keyword `static` from its definition. However, if you try that, the program will no longer compile and run. The problem is the static data members `rabbitNames` and `rabbitNamesCount` in the `Rabbit` class. You saw earlier that a non-static nested class cannot have static members, so you must find an alternative way of dealing with names if you want to make `Rabbit` a non-static nested class.

You could consider making these arrays non-static. This has several disadvantages. First, each `Rabbit` object would have its own copy of these arrays — an unnecessary duplication of data. A more serious problem is that the naming process would not work. Because each object has its own copy of the `rabbitNamesCount` array, the names that are generated are not going to be unique.

The answer is to keep `rabbitNames` and `rabbitNamesCount` as static, but put them in the `MagicHat` class instead. Let's see that working.

Try It Out   Accessing the Top-Level Class Members

You need to modify the class definition to the following:

```
public class MagicHat {
  static int maxRabbits = 5;                        // Maximuum rabbits in a hat
  static Random select = new Random();              // Random number generator
  static private String[] rabbitNames = {"Floppsy", "Moppsy",
                                          "Gnasher", "Thumper"};
  static private int[] rabbitNamesCount = new int[rabbitNames.length];

  // Constructor for a hat
  public MagicHat(final String hatName) {
    this.hatName = hatName;                          // Store the hat name
    rabbits = new Rabbit[1+select.nextInt(maxRabbits)]; // Random rabbits

    for(int i = 0; i < rabbits.length; i++) {
      rabbits[i] = new Rabbit();                      // Create the rabbits
    }
  }

  // String representation of a hat
  public String toString() {
    // Hat name first...
    String hatString = "\n" + hatName + " contains:\n";

    for(Rabbit rabbit : rabbits) {
      hatString += "    " + rabbit;                   // Add the rabbits strings
    }
    return hatString;
  }
  private String hatName;                             // Name of the hat
  private Rabbit rabbits[];                           // Rabbits in the hat

  // Nested class to define a rabbit
  class Rabbit {
    private String name;                             // Name of the rabbit
```

```
    // Constructor for a rabbit
    public Rabbit() {
      int index = select.nextInt(rabbitNames.length);  // Get random name index
      name = rabbitNames[index] + (++rabbitNamesCount[index]);
    }

    // String representation of a rabbit
    public String toString() {
      return name;
    }
  }
}
```

The only changes are the deletion of the `static` keyword in the definition of the `Rabbit` class and the movement of data members relating to rabbit names to the `MagicHat` class. You can run this with the same version of `TryNestedClass`, and it should produce output much the same as before.

How It Works

Although the output is much the same, what is happening is distinctly different. The `Rabbit` objects that are created in the `MagicHat` constructor are now associated with the current `MagicHat` object that is being constructed. The `Rabbit()` constructor call is actually `this.Rabbit()`.

Using a Nested Class Outside the Top-Level Class

You can create objects of an inner class outside the top-level class containing the inner class. As I discussed, how you do this depends on whether the nested class is a static member of the enclosing class. With the first version of the `MagicHat` class, with a static `Rabbit` class, you could create an independent rabbit by adding the following statement to the end of `main()`:

```
System.out.println("An independent rabbit: " + new MagicHat.Rabbit());
```

This `Rabbit` object is completely free — there is no `MagicHat` object to contain and restrain it. In the case of a non-static `Rabbit` class, things are different. Let's try this using a modified version of the previous program.

Try It Out   Free-Range Rabbits (Almost)

You can see how this works by modifying the `main()` method in `TryNestedClass` to create another `MagicHat` object, and then create a `Rabbit` object for it:

```
static public void main(String[] args) {
  // Create three magic hats and output them
  System.out.println(new MagicHat("Gray Topper"));
  System.out.println(new MagicHat("Black Topper"));
  System.out.println(new MagicHat("Baseball Cap"));

  MagicHat oldHat = new MagicHat("Old hat");          // New hat object
  MagicHat.Rabbit rabbit = oldHat.new Rabbit();       // Create rabbit object
  System.out.println(oldHat);                         // Show the hat
  System.out.println("\nNew rabbit is: " + rabbit);   // Display the rabbit
}
```

The output produced is as follows:

```
Gray Topper contains:
 Thumper1

Black Topper contains:
 Moppsy1 Thumper2 Thumper3

Baseball Cap contains:
 Floppsy1 Floppsy2 Thumper4

Old hat contains:
 Floppsy3 Thumper5 Thumper6 Thumper7 Thumper8

New rabbit is: Thumper9
```

How It Works

The new code first creates a `MagicHat` object, `oldHat`. This will have its own rabbits. You then use this object to create an object of the class `MagicHat.Rabbit`. This is how a nested class type is referenced — with the top-level class name as a qualifier. You can only call the constructor for the nested class in this case by qualifying it with a `MagicHat` object name. This is because a non-static nested class can refer to members of the top-level class — including instance members. Therefore, an instance of the top-level class must exist for this to be possible.

Note how the top-level object is used in the constructor call. The object name qualifier goes before the keyword `new`, which precedes the constructor call for the inner class. This creates an object, `rabbit`, in the context of the object `oldHat`. This doesn't mean `oldHat` has `rabbit` as a member. It means that if top-level members are used in the inner class, they will be the members for `oldHat`. You can see from the example that the name of the new rabbit is not part of the `oldHat` object, although it is associated with `oldHat`. You could demonstrate this by modifying the `toString()` method in the `Rabbit` class to:

```
public String toString() {
   return name + " parent: "+hatName;
}
```

If you run the program again, you will see that when each `Rabbit` object is displayed, it will also show its parent hat.

Local Nested Classes

You can define a class inside a method — where it is called a **local nested class**. It is also referred to as a **local inner class**, since a non-static nested class is often referred to as an **inner class**. You can create objects of a local inner class only locally — that is, within the method in which the class definition appears. This is useful when the computation in a method requires the use of a specialized class that is not required or used elsewhere. A good example is listeners for events that arise as a result of user interaction with an application. You'll learn about listeners in Chapter 18.

A local inner class can refer to variables declared in the method in which the definition appears, but only if they are `final`.

The finalize() Method

You have the option of including a method `finalize()` in a class definition. This method is called automatically by Java before an object is finally destroyed and the space it occupies in memory is released. In practice this may be some time after the object is inaccessible in your program. When an object goes out of scope, it is dead as far as your program is concerned, but the Java Virtual Machine may not get around to disposing of the remains until later. When it does, it calls the `finalize()` method for the object. The form of the `finalize()` method is:

```
protected void finalize() {
   // Your clean-up code...
}
```

This method is useful if your class objects use resources that require some special action when they are destroyed. Typically these are resources that are not within the Java environment and not guaranteed to be released by the object itself. These could be such things as graphics resources, fonts or other drawing-related resources that are supplied by the host operating system, or external files on the hard disk. Leaving these around after an object is destroyed wastes system resources and, in some circumstances (with graphics resources under some older versions of Windows, for example) if you waste enough of them, your program, and possibly other programs the system is supporting, may stop working. For most classes this is not necessary, but if an object opened a disk file for example, but did not guarantee its closure, you would want to make sure that the file was closed when the object was destroyed. You can implement the `finalize()` method to take care of this.

Another use for the `finalize()` method is to record the fact that the object has been destroyed. You could implement the `finalize()` method for the `Sphere` class to decrement the value of the static member `count`, for example. This would make `count` a measure of how many `Sphere` objects were around, rather than how many had been created. It would, however, not be an accurate measure for reasons that I will come to in a moment.

You cannot rely on an object being destroyed when it is no longer available to your program code. Unless your program calls the `System.gc()` method, the Java Virtual Machine will get rid of unwanted objects and free the memory they occupy only if it runs out of memory, or if there is no activity within your program — for example, when waiting for input. As a result, objects may not get destroyed until execution of your program ends. You also have no guarantee as to when a `finalize()` method will be called. All you are assured is that it will be called before the memory that the object occupied is freed. Nothing time-sensitive should be left to the `finalize()` method.

If you don't allow for the possibility of your objects hanging around, this can cause problems. For example, suppose you create an object in a method that opens a file, and rely on the `finalize()` method to close it. If you then call this method in a loop, you may end up with a large number of files open at one time, since the object that is created in each call of the method will not necessarily be destroyed immediately on return from the method. This introduces the possibility of your program attempting to have more files open simultaneously than the host operating system allows. In this situation, you should make sure a file is closed when you have finished with it, by including an object method to close it explicitly — for example, `close()`.

The `System` class also provides another possible approach. You can suggest to the JVM that the `finalize()` methods for all discarded objects should be run, if they haven't been already. You just call the `runFinalization()` method:

```
System.runFinalization();
```

This is another of those "best efforts" deals on the part of the JVM. It will do its very best to run `finalize()` for any dead objects that are lying around before returning from the `runFinalization()` method, but like with a lot of things in this life, there are no guarantees.

Native Methods

It is possible to include in a class a method that is implemented in some other programming language, such as C or C++, external to the Java Virtual Machine. To specify such a method within a class definition, you use the keyword `native` in the declaration of the method. For example:

```
public native long getData();      // Declare a method that is not in Java
```

Of course, the method will have no body in Java since it is defined elsewhere, where all the work is done, so the declaration ends with a semicolon. The implementation of a native method will need to use an interface to the Java environment. The standard API for implementing native methods in C, for example, is called JNI — the Java Native Interface.

The major drawback to using native methods in Java is that your program will no longer be portable. Security requirements for applets embedded in web pages require that the code must all be written in Java — using native methods in an applet is simply not possible. Since the primary reasons for using Java are the portability of the code and the ability to produce applets, the need for you to add native methods to your Java programs will be minimal. I will therefore not delve any deeper into this topic.

Summary

In this chapter you've learned all the essentials of defining your own classes. You can now create your own class types to fit the context of the problems you are dealing with. You will build on this in the next chapter to enable you to add more flexibility to the operations on your class objects by learning how to realize polymorphism.

The important points covered in this chapter are:

❑ A class definition specifies the variables and methods that are members of the class.

❑ Each class must be saved in a file with the same name as the class, and with the extension `.java`.

❑ Class variables are declared using the keyword `static`, and one instance of each class variable is shared among all objects of a class.

❑ Each object of a class will have its own instance variables — these are variables declared without using the keyword `static`.

❑ Methods that are specified as `static` can be called even if no class objects exist, but a `static` method cannot refer to instance variables.

❑ Methods that are not specified as `static` can access any of the variables in the class directly.

❑ Recursive methods are methods that call themselves.

❑ Access to members of a class is determined by the access attributes that are specified for each of them. These can be `public`, `private`, `protected`, package `private`, or nothing at all.

❑ Classes can be grouped into a package. If a class in a package is to be accessible from outside the package, the class must be declared using the keyword `public`.

❑ To designate that a class is a member of a package, you use a `package` statement at the beginning of the file containing the class definition.

❑ To add classes from a package to a file, you use an `import` statement immediately following any package statement in the file.

❑ A nested class is a class that is defined within the definition of another class. Objects of a nested class type can be created only in the context of an object of the outer class type.

❑ Objects of a static nested class type can be created independently, but the static nested class name must be qualified by the outer class name.

❑ A native method is a method implemented in a language other than Java. Java programs containing native methods cannot be applets and are no longer portable.

Exercises

You can download the source code for the examples in the book and the solutions to the following exercises from `http://www.wrox.com`.

1. Define a class for rectangle objects defined by two points, the top-left and bottom-right corners of the rectangle. Include a constructor to copy a rectangle, a method to return a rectangle object that encloses the current object and the rectangle passed as an argument, and a method to display the defining points of a rectangle. Test the class by creating four rectangles and combining these cumulatively to end up with a rectangle enclosing them all. Output the defining points of all the rectangles you create.

2. Define a class, `mcmLength`, to represent a length measured in meters, centimeters, and millimeters, each stored as integers. Include methods to add and subtract objects, to multiply and divide an object by an integer value, to calculate an area resulting from the product of two objects, and to compare objects. Include constructors that accept three arguments — meters, centimeters, and millimeters; one integer argument in millimeters; one `double` argument in centimeters; and no arguments, which creates an object with the length set to zero. Check the class by creating some objects and testing the class operations.

3. Define a class, `tkgWeight`, to represent a weight in tons, kilograms, and grams, and include a similar range of methods and constructors as the previous example. Demonstrate this class by creating and combining some class objects.

4. Put both the previous classes in a package called `Measures`. Import this package into a program that will calculate and display the total weight of the following: 200 carpets — size: 4 meters by 2 meters 9 centimeters, that weigh 1.25 kilograms per square meter; and 60 carpets — size: 3 meters 57 centimeters by 5 meters, that weigh 1.05 kilograms per square meter.

Extending Classes and Inheritance

A very important part of object-oriented programming allows you to create a new class based on a class that has already been defined. The class that you use as the base for your new class can be one that you have defined, a standard class in Java, or a class defined by someone else — perhaps from a package supporting a specialized application area.

This chapter focuses on how you can reuse existing classes by creating new classes based on the ones you have and explores the ramifications of using this facility, and the additional capabilities it provides. You will also delve into an important related topic — **interfaces** — and how you can use them.

In this chapter you will learn:

- ❑ How to reuse classes by defining a new class based on an existing class
- ❑ What polymorphism is and how to define your classes to take advantage of it
- ❑ What an abstract method is
- ❑ What an abstract class is
- ❑ What an interface is and how you can define your own interfaces
- ❑ How to use interfaces in your classes
- ❑ How interfaces can help you implement polymorphic classes

Using Existing Classes

Let's start by understanding the jargon. Defining a new class based on an existing class is called **derivation**. The new class, or **derived class**, is referred to as a **direct subclass** of the class from which it is derived. The original class is called a **base class** because it forms the base for the definition of the derived class. The original class is also referred to as a **superclass** of the derived class.

You can also derive a new class from a derived class, which in turn was derived from some other derived class, and so on. This is illustrated in Figure 6-1.

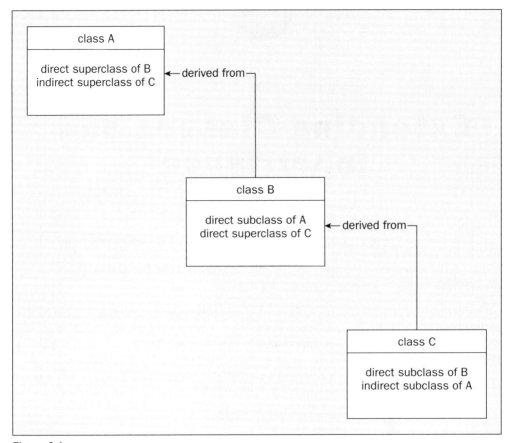

Figure 6-1

This shows just three classes in a hierarchy, but there can be as many as you like.

Let's consider a more concrete example. You could define a class `Dog` that could represent a dog of any kind:

```
class Dog {
    // Members of the Dog class...
}
```

This might contain a data member identifying the name of a particular dog, such as *Lassie* or *Poochy*, and another data member to identify the breed, such as *Border Collie* or *Pyrenean Mountain Dog*. From the `Dog` class, you could derive a `Spaniel` class that represented dogs that were spaniels:

```
class Spaniel extends Dog {
    // Members of the Spaniel class...
}
```

The extends keyword that you use here identifies that Dog is a base class for Spaniel, so an object of type Spaniel will have members that are inherited from the Dog class, in addition to the members of the Spaniel class that appear in its definition. The breed would be *Spaniel* for all instances of the class Spaniel although in general the name for each spaniel would be different. The Spaniel class might have some additional data members that characterize the specifics of what it means to be a spaniel. You will see in a moment how you can arrange for the base class data members to be set appropriately.

A Spaniel object is a specialized instance of a Dog object. This reflects real life. A spaniel is obviously a dog and will have all the properties of a basic dog, but it has some unique characteristics of its own that distinguish it from all the dogs that are not spaniels. The inheritance mechanism that adds all the properties of the base class — Dog in this instance — to those in the derived class is a good model for the real world. The members of the derived class define the properties that differentiate it from the base type, so when you derive one class from another, you can think of your derived class as a specification for objects that are specializations of the base class object. Another way of thinking about this is that the base class defines a set of objects and a derived class defines a specific subset of those that have particular defining characteristics.

Class Inheritance

In summary, when you derive a new class from a base class, the process is additive in terms of what makes up a class definition. The additional members that you define in the new class establish what makes a derived class object different from a base class object. Any members that you define in the new class are in addition to those that are already members of the base class. For your Spaniel class that you derived from Dog, the data members to hold the name and the breed that are defined for the class Dog would automatically be in the class Spaniel. A Spaniel object will always have a complete Dog object inside it — with all its data members and methods. This does not mean that all the members defined in the Dog class are available to methods that are specific to the Spaniel class. Some are and some aren't. The inclusion of members of a base class in a derived class so that they are accessible in that derived class is called **class inheritance**. An **inherited member** of a base class is one that is *accessible* within the derived class. If a base class member is not accessible in a derived class, then it is not an inherited member of the derived class, but base class members that are not inherited still form part of a derived class object.

An inherited member of a derived class is a full member of that class and is freely accessible to any method in the class. Objects of the derived class type will contain all the inherited members of the base class — both fields and methods, as well as the members that are specific to the derived class. Remember that a derived class object always contains a complete base class object within it, including all the fields and methods that are not inherited. The next step is to take a closer look at how inheritance works and how the access attribute of a base class member affects its visibility in a derived class.

You need to consider several aspects of defining and using a derived class. First of all, you need to know which members of the base class are inherited in the derived class. I will explain what this implies for data members and methods separately — there are some subtleties here you should be quite clear on. I will also look at what happens when you create an object of the derived class. There are some wrinkles in this context that require closer consideration. Let's start by looking at the data members that are inherited from a base class.

Inheriting Data Members

Figure 6-2 shows which access attributes permit a class member to be inherited in a subclass. It shows what happens when the subclass is defined in either the same package or a different package from that containing the base class. Remember that inheritance implies accessibility of the member in a derived class, not just presence.

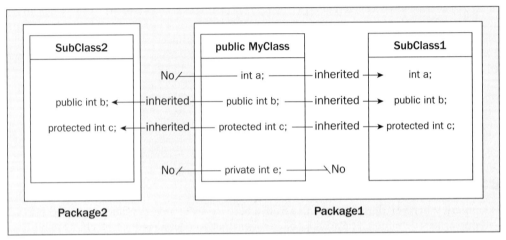

Figure 6-2

> Remember that a class itself can be specified as public. This makes the class accessible from any package anywhere. A class that is not declared as public can be accessed only from classes within the same package. This means, for example, that you cannot define objects of a non-public class type within classes in other packages. It also means that to derive a new class from a class in a different package, the base class must be declared as public. If the base class is not declared as public, it cannot be reached directly from outside the package.

As you can see from Figure 6-2, a subclass that you define in the same package as its base class inherits everything except for private data members of the base. If you define a subclass outside the package containing the base class, the private data members are not inherited, and neither are any data members in the base class that you have declared without access attributes. Members defined as private in the base class are never inherited under any circumstances. The base class, MyClass, must be declared as public in Package1, otherwise it would not be accessible from Package2 as the base class for SubClass2.

You should also be able to see where the explicit access specifiers now sit in relation to one another. The public specifier is the least restrictive on class members since a public member is available everywhere, protected comes next, and prevents access from classes outside of a package, but does not limit inheritance — provided the class itself is `public`. Putting no access specifier on a class member limits access to classes within the same package and prevents inheritance in subclasses that are defined in a different package. The most restrictive is `private` since access is constrained to the same class.

The inheritance rules apply to members of a class that you have declared as `static` — as well as non-static members. You will recall that only one occurrence of each `static` variable in a class exists and is shared by all objects of the class, whereas each object has its own set of instance variables. So, for example, a variable that you declare as `private` and `static` in the base class is not inherited in a derived class, whereas a variable that you declare as `protected` and `static` will be inherited and will be shared between all objects of a derived class type, as well as objects of the base class type.

Hidden Data Members

You can define a data member in a derived class with the same name as a data member in the base class. This is not a recommended approach to class design generally, but it's possible that it can arise unintentionally. When it occurs, the base class data member may still be inherited, but will be hidden by the derived class member with the same name. The hiding mechanism applies regardless of whether the respective types or access attributes are the same or not — the base class member will be hidden in the derived class if the names are the same.

Any use of the derived class member name will always refer to the member defined as part of the derived class. To refer to the inherited base class member, you must qualify it with the keyword `super` to indicate it is the member of the superclass that you want. Suppose you have a data member `value` as a member of the base class, and a data member with the same name in the derived class. In the derived class, the name `value` references the derived class member, and the name `super.value` refers to the member inherited from the base class. Note that you cannot use `super.super.something` to refer to a member name hidden in the base class of a base class.

In most situations you won't need to refer to inherited data members in this way, as you would not deliberately set out to use duplicate names. The situation can commonly arise if you are using a class as a base that is subsequently modified by adding data members — it could be a Java library class, for example, or some other class in a package designed and maintained by someone else. Since your code did not presume the existence of the base class member with the same name as your derived class data member, hiding the inherited member is precisely what you want. It allows the base class to be altered without breaking your code.

Inherited Methods

Ordinary methods in a base class, by which I mean methods that are not constructors, are inherited in a derived class in the same way as the data members of the base class. Those methods declared as `private` in a base class are not inherited, and those that you declare without an access attribute are inherited only if you define the derived class in the same package as the base class. The rest are all inherited.

Constructors are different from ordinary methods. Constructors in the base class are never inherited, regardless of their attributes. You can look into the intricacies of constructors in a class hierarchy by considering how derived class objects are created.

Objects of a Derived Class

I said at the beginning of this chapter that a derived class extends a base class. This is not just jargon — it really does do this. As I have said several times, inheritance is about what members of the base class are *accessible* in a derived class, not what members of the base class *exist* in a derived class object. An object of a subclass will contain *all* the members of the original base class, plus any new members that you have defined in the derived class. This is illustrated in Figure 6-3.

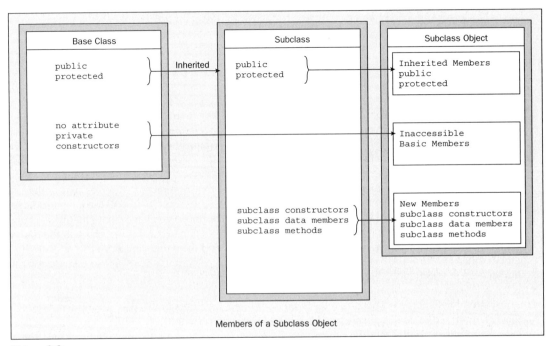

Figure 6-3

The base members are all there in a derived class object — you just can't access some of them in the methods that you have defined for the derived class. The fact that you can't access some of the base class members does not mean that they are just excess baggage — they are essential members of your derived class objects. A Spaniel object needs all the Dog attributes that make it a Dog object, even though some of these may not be accessible to the Spaniel methods. Of course, the base class methods that are inherited in a derived class can access all the base class members, including those that are not inherited.

Though the base class constructors are not inherited in your derived class, you can still call them to initialize the base class members. More than that, if you don't call a base class constructor from your derived class constructor, the compiler will try to arrange to do it for you. The reasoning behind this is that since a derived class object has a base class object inside it, a good way to initialize the base part of a derived class object is using a base class constructor.

To understand this better, let's take a look at how it works in practice.

Deriving a Class

Let's take a simple example. Suppose you have defined a class to represent an animal as follows:

```
public class Animal {
  public Animal(String aType) {
    type = new String(aType);
  }

  public String toString() {
    return "This is a " + type;
  }

  private String type;
}
```

This has a member, `type`, to identify the type of animal, and its value is set by the constructor. You also have a `toString()` method for the class to generate a string representation of an object of the class.

You can now define another class, based on the class `Animal`, to define dogs. You can do this immediately, without affecting the definition of the class `Animal`. You could write the basic definition of the class `Dog` as:

```
public class Dog extends Animal {
  // constructors for a Dog object

  private String name;          // Name of a Dog
  private String breed;         // Dog breed
}
```

You use the keyword `extends` in the definition of a subclass to identify the name of the direct superclass. The class `Dog` will inherit only the method `toString()` from the class `Animal`, since the `private` data member and the constructor cannot be inherited. Of course, a `Dog` object will have a `type` data member that needs to be set to `"Dog"`, it just can't be accessed by methods that you define in the `Dog` class. You have added two new instance variables in the derived class. The `name` member holds the name of the particular dog, and the `breed` member records the kind of dog it is. All you need to add is the means of creating `Dog` class objects.

Derived Class Constructors

You can define two constructors for the subclass `Dog`, one that just accepts an argument for the name of a dog and another that accepts both a name and the breed of the `Dog` object. For any derived class object, you need to make sure that the `private` base class member, `type`, is properly initialized. You do this by calling a base class constructor from the derived class constructor:

```
public class Dog extends Animal {
  public Dog(String aName) {
    super("Dog");              // Call the base constructor
    name = aName;              // Supplied name
    breed = "Unknown";         // Default breed value
  }
```

```
   public Dog(String aName, String aBreed) {
      super("Dog");                              // Call the base constructor
      name = aName;                              // Supplied name
      breed = aBreed;                            // Supplied breed
   }

   private String name;                          // Name of a Dog
   private String breed;                         // Dog breed
}
```

The statement in the derived class constructors that calls the base class constructor is:

```
   super("Dog");                                 // Call the base constructor
```

The use of the super keyword here as the method name calls the constructor in the superclass — the direct base class of the class Dog, which is the class Animal. This will initialize the private member type to "Dog" since this is the argument passed to the base constructor. The superclass constructor is always called in this way in the subclass, using the name super rather than the base class constructor name Animal. The super keyword has other uses in a derived class. You have already seen that you can access a hidden member of the base class by qualifying the member name with super.

Calling the Base Class Constructor

You should always call an appropriate base class constructor from the constructors in your derived class. The base class constructor call must be the first statement in the body of the derived class constructor. If the first statement in a derived class constructor is not a call to a base class constructor, the compiler will insert a call to the default base class constructor for you:

```
   super();                           // Call the default base constructor
```

Unfortunately, this can result in a compiler error, even though the offending statement was inserted automatically. How does this come about?

When you define your own constructor in a class, as is the case for the Animal class, no default constructor is created by the compiler. It assumes you are taking care of all the details of object construction, including any requirement for a default constructor. If you have not defined your own default constructor in a base class — that is, a constructor that has no parameters — when the compiler inserts a call to the default constructor from your derived class constructor, you will get a message saying that the constructor is not there.

Try It Out   **Testing a Derived Class**

You can try out the Dog class with the following code:

```
   public class TestDerived {
     public static void main(String[] args) {
       Dog aDog = new Dog("Fido", "Chihuahua");    // Create a dog
       Dog starDog = new Dog("Lassie");            // Create a Hollywood dog
```

```
        System.out.println(aDog);          // Let's hear about it
        System.out.println(starDog);       // and the star
    }
}
```

Of course, the files containing the `Dog` and `Animal` class definition must be in the same directory as `TestDerived.java`. The example produces the following rather uninformative output:

```
This is a Dog
This is a Dog
```

How It Works

Here you create two `Dog` objects and then output information about them using the `println()` method. This will implicitly call the `toString()` method for each. You could try commenting out the call to `super()` in the constructors of the derived class to see the effect of the compiler's efforts to call the default base class constructor.

You have called the inherited method `toString()` successfully, but this knows only about the base class data members. At least you know that the `private` member, `type`, is being set up properly. What you really need though is a version of `toString()` for the derived class.

Overriding a Base Class Method

You can define a method in a derived class that has the same signature as a method in the base class. The access attribute for the method in the derived class can be the same as that in the base class or less restrictive, but it cannot be more restrictive. This means that if you declare a method as `public` in the base class, for example, any derived class definition of the method must also be declared as `public`. You cannot omit the access attribute in the derived class in this case, or specify it as `private` or `protected`.

When you define a new version of a base class method in this way, the derived class method will be called for a derived class object, not the method inherited from the base class. The method in the derived class **overrides** the method in the base class. The base class method is still there though, and it is still possible to call it in a derived class. Let's see an overriding method in a derived class in action.

Try It Out   Overriding a Base Class Method

You can add the definition of a new version of `toString()` to the definition of the derived class, `Dog`:

```
// Present a dog's details as a string
public String toString() {
    return "It's " + name + " the " + breed;
}
```

With this change to the example, the output will now be:

```
It's Fido the Chihuahua
It's Lassie the Unknown
```

How It Works

The `toString()` method in the `Dog` class **overrides** the base class method because it has the same signature. You will recall from the last chapter that the signature of a method is determined by its name and the parameter list. So, now whenever you use the `toString()` method for a `Dog` object either explicitly or implicitly, this method will be called — not the base class method.

> Note that you are obliged to declare the `toString()` method as `public`. **When you override a base class method, you cannot change the access attributes of the new version of the method to be more stringent than that of the base class method that it overrides. Since** `public` **is the least stringent access attribute, you have no other choice.**

Of course, ideally you would like to output the member, `type`, of the base class, but you can't reference this in the derived class because it is not inherited. However, you can still call the base class version of `toString()`. It's another job for the `super` keyword.

Try It Out   Calling a Base Class Method from a Derived Class

You can rewrite the derived class version of `toString()` to call the base method:

```
// Present a dog's details as a string
public String toString() {
   return super.toString() + "\nIt's " + name + " the " + breed;
}
```

Running the example again will produce the following output:

```
This is a Dog
It's Fido the Chihuahua
This is a Dog
It's Lassie the Unknown
```

How It Works

You use the `super` keyword to identify the base class version of `toString()` that is hidden by the derived class version. You used the same notation to refer to superclass data members that were hidden by derived class data members with the same name. Calling the base class version of `toString()` returns the `String` object for the base part of the object. You then append extra information to this about the derived part of the object to produce a `String` object specific to the derived class.

Choosing Base Class Access Attributes

You now know the options available to you in defining the access attributes for classes you expect to use to define subclasses. You know what effect the attributes have on class inheritance, but how do you decide which you should use?

There are no hard and fast rules — what you choose will depend on what you want to do with your classes in the future, but there are some guidelines you should consider. They follow from basic object-oriented principles:

❑ You should declare the methods that make up the external interface to a class as `public`. As long as there are no overriding methods defined in a derived class, public base class methods will be inherited and fully available as part of the external interface to the derived class. You should not normally make data members public unless they are constants intended for general use.

❑ If you expect other people will use your classes as base classes, your classes will be more secure if you keep data members `private`, and provide `public` methods for accessing and manipulating them when necessary. In this way you control how a derived class object can affect the base class data members.

❑ Making base class members `protected` allows them to be accessed from other classes in the same package, but prevents direct access from a class in another package. Base class members that are `protected` are inherited in a subclass and can, therefore, be used in the implementation of a derived class. You can use the `protected` option when you have a package of classes in which you want uninhibited access to the data members of any class within the same package — because they operate in a closely coupled way, for instance — but you want free access to be limited to subclasses in other packages.

❑ Omitting the access attribute for a class member makes it directly available to other classes in the same package, while preventing it from being inherited in a subclass that is not in the same package — it is effectively `private` when viewed from another package.

Polymorphism

Class inheritance is not just about reusing classes that you have already defined as a basis for defining a new class. It also adds enormous flexibility to the way in which you can program your applications, with a mechanism called **polymorphism**. So what is polymorphism?

The word *polymorphism* generally means the ability to assume several different forms or shapes. In programming terms it means the ability of a single variable of a given type to be used to reference objects of different types and to automatically call the method that is specific to the type of object the variable references. This enables a single method call to behave differently, depending on the type of the object to which the call applies. This is illustrated in Figure 6-4.

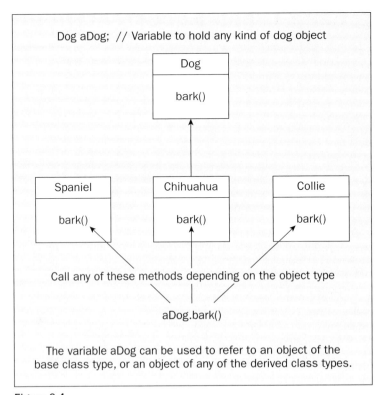

Figure 6-4

A few requirements must be fulfilled to get polymorphic behavior, so let's step through them.

First of all, polymorphism works with derived class objects. It also depends on a new capability that is possible within a class hierarchy that you haven't met before. Up to now you have always been using a variable of a given type to reference objects of the same type. Derived classes introduce some new flexibility in this. Of course, you can store a reference to a derived class object in a variable of the derived class type, but you can also store it in a variable of any direct or indirect base class type. More than that, a reference to a derived class object *must* be stored in a variable of a direct or indirect class type for polymorphism to work. For example, Figure 6-4 illustrates how a variable of type Dog can be used to store a reference to an object of any type derived from Dog. If the Dog class were derived from the Animal class here, a variable of type Animal could also be used to reference Spaniel, Chihuahua, or Collie objects.

Polymorphism means that the actual type of the object involved in a method call determines which method is called, rather than the type of the variable being used to store the reference to the object. In Figure 6-4, if aDog contains a reference to a Spaniel object, the bark() method for that object will be called. If it contains a reference to a `Collie` object, the `bark()` method in the `Collie` class will be called. To get polymorphic operation when calling a method, the method must be declared as a member of the base class — the class type of the variable you are using — as well as being declared as a member of the class type of the object involved. So in the example, the `Dog` class must contain a `bark()` method, as must each of the derived classes. You cannot call a method for a derived class object using a variable of a base class type if the method is not a member of the base class. Any definition of the method in a derived class must have the same signature as in the base class and must have an access specifier that is no more restrictive.

Methods that have the same signature have the same name, and have parameter lists with the same number of parameters where corresponding parameters are of the same type. You have a bit more flexibility with the return type when you are defining a polymorphic method. For polymorphic behavior, the return type of the method in the derived class must either be the same as that of the base class method, or must be of a type that is a subclass of the base class type. Where the return types are different but the return type of the method in the derived class is a subclass of the return type in the base class, the return types are said to be **covariant**. Thus the type of object returned by the derived class method is just a specialization of the type returned by the base class method. For example, suppose that you have a method defined in a base class `Animal` that has a return type of type `Animal`:

```
public class Animal {
   Animal createCreature() {
      // Code to create an Animal object and return a reference to it...
   }

   // Rest of the class definition...
}
```

You can redefine the `createCreature()` method in a derived class `Dog` like this:

```
public class Dog extends Animal {
   Dog createCreature() {
      // Code to create a Dog object and return a reference to it...
   }

   // Rest of the class definition...
}
```

As long as the return type for the method in the derived class is a subclass of the base class type, as you have here, even though the return types are different you can still get polymorphic behavior. I can summarize the conditions that need to be met if you want to use polymorphism as follows:

- ❏ The method call for a derived class object must be through a variable of a base class type.

- ❏ The method called must be defined in the derived class.

- ❏ The method called must also be declared as a member of the base class.

- ❏ The method signatures for the method in the base and derived classes must be the same.

- ❏ Either the method return type must be the same in the base and derived classes or the return type must be covariant.

- ❏ The method access specifier must be no more restrictive in the derived class than in the base.

281

When you call a method using a variable of a base class type, polymorphism results in the method that is called being selected based on the type of the object stored, not the type of the variable. Because a variable of a base type can store a reference to an object of any derived type, the kind of object stored will not be known until the program executes. Thus the choice of which method to execute has to be made dynamically when the program is running — it cannot be determined when the program is compiled. The bark() method that is called through the variable of type Dog in the earlier illustration may do different things depending on what kind of object the variable references. As you will see, this introduces a whole new level of capability in programming using objects. It implies that your programs can adapt at run time to accommodate and process different kinds of data quite automatically.

Note that polymorphism applies only to methods. It does not apply to data members. When you access a data member of a class object, the variable type always determines the class to which the data member belongs. This implies that a variable of type Dog can only be used to access data members of the Dog class. Even when it references an object of type Spaniel, for example, you can only use it to access data members of the Dog part of a Spaniel object.

Using Polymorphism

As you have seen, polymorphism relies on the fact that you can assign an object of a subclass type to a variable that you have declared as being of a superclass type. Suppose you declare the variable:

```
Animal theAnimal = null;                  // Declare a variable of type Animal
```

You can quite happily make theAnimal refer to an object of any of the subclasses of the class Animal. For example, you could use it to reference an object of type Dog:

```
theAnimal = new Dog("Rover");
```

As you might expect, you could also initialize the variable theAnimal to reference an object when you declare it:

```
Animal theAnimal = new Dog("Rover");
```

This principle applies quite generally. You can use a variable of a base class type to store a reference to an object of any class type that you have derived, directly or indirectly, from the base. You can see what magic can be wrought with this in practice by extending the previous example. You can add a new method to the class Dog that will display the sound a Dog makes. You can add a couple of new subclasses that represent some other kinds of animals.

Try It Out   Enhancing the Dog Class

First of all you will enhance the class Dog by adding a method to display the sound that a dog makes:

```
public class Dog extends Animal {
  // A barking method
  public void sound() {
    System.out.println("Woof     Woof");
  }

  // Rest of the class as before...
}
```

You can also derive a class `Cat` from the class `Animal`:

```java
public class Cat extends Animal {
  public Cat(String aName) {
    super("Cat");                   // Call the base constructor
    name = aName;                   // Supplied name
    breed = "Unknown";              // Default breed value
  }

  public Cat(String aName, String aBreed) {
    super("Cat");                   // Call the base constructor
    name = aName;                   // Supplied name
    breed = aBreed;                 // Supplied breed
  }

  // Return a String full of a cat's details
  public String toString() {
    return super.toString() + "\nIt's " + name + " the " + breed;
  }

  // A miaowing method
  public void sound() {
    System.out.println("Miiaooww");
  }

  private String name;              // Name of a cat
  private String breed;             // Cat breed
}
```

Just to make it a crowd, you can derive another class — of ducks:

```java
public class Duck extends Animal {
  public Duck(String aName) {
    super("Duck");                  // Call the base constructor
    name = aName;                   // Supplied name
    breed = "Unknown";              // Default breed value
  }

  public Duck(String aName, String aBreed) {
    super("Duck");                  // Call the base constructor
    name = aName;                   // Supplied name
    breed = aBreed;                 // Supplied breed
  }

  // Return a String full of a duck's details
  public String toString() {
    return super.toString() + "\nIt's " + name + " the " + breed;
  }

  // A quacking method
  public void sound() {
    System.out.println("Quack quackquack");
  }
}
```

```
        private String name;                    // Duck name
        private String breed;                   // Duck breed
    }
```

You can fill the whole farmyard, if you need the practice, but three kinds of animal are sufficient to show you how polymorphism works.

You need to make one change to the class `Animal`. To select the method `sound()` dynamically for derived class objects, it needs to be a member of the base class. You can add a content-free version of `sound()` to the class `Animal`:

```
class Animal {
    // Rest of the class as before...

    // Dummy method to be implemented in the derived classes
    public void sound(){}
}
```

Only a particular `Animal` object will make a specific sound, so the `sound()` method in the class does nothing. You need a program that will use these classes. To give the classes a workout, you can create an array of type `Animal` and populate its elements with different subclass objects. You can then select an object random from the array, so that there is no possibility that the type of the object selected is known ahead of time. Here's the code to do that:

```
import java.util.Random;

public class TryPolymorphism {
  public static void main(String[] args) {
    // Create an array of three different animals
    Animal[] theAnimals = {
                           new Dog("Rover", "Poodle"),
                           new Cat("Max", "Abyssinian"),
                           new Duck("Daffy","Aylesbury")
                          };

    Animal petChoice;                       // Choice of pet

    Random select = new Random();           // Random number generator
    // Make five random choices of pet
    for(int i = 0; i < 5; i++) {
      // Choose a random animal as a pet
      petChoice = theAnimals[select.nextInt(theAnimals.length)];

      System.out.println("\nYour choice:\n" + petChoice);
      petChoice.sound();                    // Get the pet's reaction
    }
  }
}
```

When I ran this I got the following output:

```
Your choice:
This is a Duck
It's Daffy the Aylesbury
Quack quackquack
Your choice:
This is a Cat
It's Max the Abyssinian
Miiaooww

Your choice:
This is a Duck
It's Daffy the Aylesbury
Quack quackquack
Your choice:
This is a Duck
It's Daffy the Aylesbury
Quack quackquack

Your choice:
This is a Cat
It's Max the Abyssinian
Miiaooww
```

The chances are good that you will get a different set from this, and a different set again when you rerun the example. The output from the example clearly shows that the methods are being selected at run time, depending on which object happens to get stored in the variable petChoice.

How It Works

The definition of the sound() method in the Animal class has no statements in the body, so it will do nothing if it is executed. You will see a little later in this chapter how you can avoid including the empty definition for the method but still get polymorphic behavior in the derived classes.

You need the import statement because you use a Random class object in the example to produce pseudo-random index values in the way you have seen before. The array theAnimals of type Animal contains a Dog object, a Cat object, and a Duck object. You select objects randomly from this array in the for loop using the Random object select, and store the selection in petChoice. You then call the toString() and sound() methods using the object reference stored. The effect is that the appropriate method is selected automatically to suit the object stored, so the program operates differently depending on what type of object is referenced by petChoice.

Of course, you call the toString() method implicitly in the argument to println(). The compiler will insert a call to this method to produce a String representation of the object referenced by petChoice. The particular toString() method will automatically be selected to correspond with the type of object referenced by petChoice. This would still work even if you had not included the toString() method in the base class. You'll see a little later in this chapter that there is a toString() method in every class that you define, regardless of whether you define one or not.

Polymorphism is a fundamental part of object-oriented programming. You'll be making extensive use of polymorphism in many of the examples you will develop later in the book, and you will find that you use it often in your own applications and applets. But this is not all there is to polymorphism in Java, and I will come back to it again later in this chapter.

Multiple Levels of Inheritance

As I indicated at the beginning of the chapter, there is nothing to prevent a derived class from being used as a base class. For example, you could derive a class Spaniel from the class Dog without any problem:

Try It Out   A Spaniel Class

Start the Spaniel class off with this minimal code:

```
class Spaniel extends Dog {
  public Spaniel(String aName) {
    super(aName, "Spaniel");
  }
}
```

To try this out you can add a Spaniel object to the array theAnimals in the previous example, by changing the statement to:

```
Animal[] theAnimals = {
                    new Dog("Rover", "Poodle"),
                    new Cat("Max", "Abyssinian"),
                    new Duck("Daffy","Aylesbury"),
                    new Spaniel("Fido")
                  };
```

Don't forget to add in the comma after the Duck object. Try running the example again a few times.

How It Works

The class Spaniel will inherit members from the class Dog, including the members of Dog that are inherited from the class Animal. The class Dog is a direct superclass, and the class Animal is an indirect superclass of the class Spaniel. The only additional member of Spaniel is the constructor. This calls the Dog class constructor using the keyword super and passes the value of aName and the String object "Spaniel" to it.

If you run the TryPolymorphism class a few times, you should get a choice of the Spaniel object from time to time. Thus, the class Spaniel is also participating in the polymorphic selection of the methods toString() and sound(), which in this case are inherited from the parent class, Dog. The inherited toString() method works perfectly well with the Spaniel object, but if you wanted to provide a unique version, you could add it to the Spaniel class definition. This would then be automatically selected for a Spaniel object rather than the method inherited from the Dog class.

Abstract Classes

In the `Animal` class, you introduced a version of the `sound()` method that did nothing because you wanted to call the `sound()` method in the subclass objects dynamically. The method `sound()` has no meaning in the context of the generic class `Animal`, so implementing it does not make much sense. This situation often arises in object-oriented programming. You will often find yourself creating a superclass from which you will derive a number of subclasses, just to take advantage of polymorphism.

To cater for this, Java has **abstract classes**. An abstract class is a class in which one or more methods are declared, but not defined. The bodies of these methods are omitted, because, as in the case of the method `sound()` in the `Animal` class, implementing the methods does not make sense. Since they have no definition and cannot be executed, they are called **abstract methods**. The declaration for an abstract method ends with a semicolon and you specify the method with the keyword `abstract` to identify it as such. To declare that a class is abstract you just use the keyword `abstract` in front of the `class` keyword in the first line of the class definition.

You could have defined the class `Animal` as an abstract class by amending it as follows:

```
public abstract class Animal {
  public abstract void sound();    // Abstract method

  public Animal(String aType) {
    type = new String(aType);
  }

  public String toString() {
    return "This is a " + type;
  }

  private String type;
}
```

The previous program will work just as well with these changes. It doesn't matter whether you prefix the class name with `public abstract` or `abstract public`, they are equivalent, but you should be consistent in your usage. The sequence `public abstract` is typically preferred. The same goes for the declaration of an abstract method, but both `public` and `abstract` must precede the return type specification, which is `void` in this case.

An `abstract` method cannot be `private` since a `private` method cannot be inherited and therefore cannot be redefined in a subclass.

You cannot instantiate an object of an abstract class, but you can declare a variable of an abstract class type. With the new abstract version of the class `Animal`, you can still write:

```
Animal thePet = null;                    // Declare a variable of type Animal
```

just as you did in the `TryPolymorphism` class. You can then use this variable to store objects of the subclasses, `Dog`, `Spaniel`, `Duck`, and `Cat`.

When you derive a class from an abstract base class, you don't have to define all the abstract methods in the subclass. In this case the subclass will also be abstract and you won't be able to instantiate any objects of the subclass either. If a class is abstract, you must use the `abstract` keyword when you define it, even if it only inherits an abstract method from its superclass. Sooner or later you must have a sub-class that contains no abstract methods. You can then create objects of this class type.

The Universal Superclass

I must now reveal something I have been keeping from you. *All* the classes that you define are sub-classes by default — whether you like it or not. All your classes have a standard class, Object, as a base, so Object is a superclass of every class. You never need to specify the class Object as a base in the definition of your classes — it happens automatically.

There are some interesting consequences of having Object as a universal superclass. For one thing, a variable of type Object can store a reference to an object of any class type. This is useful when you want to write a method that needs to handle objects of unknown type. You can define a parameter to the method of type Object, in which case a reference to any type of object can be passed to the method. When necessary you can include code in the method to figure out what kind of object it actually is (you'll see some of the tools that will enable you to do this a little later in this chapter).

Of course, your classes will inherit members from the class Object. These all happen to be methods, of which seven are public, and two are protected. The seven public methods are:

Method	Purpose
toString()	This method returns a String object that describes the current object. In the inherited version of the method, this will be the name of the class, followed by '@' and the hexadecimal representation for the object. This method is called automatically when you concatenate objects with String variables using +. You can override this method in your classes to return your own String object for your class.
equals()	This compares the reference to the object passed as an argument with the reference to the current object and returns true if they are equal. Thus true is returned if the current object and the argument are the same object (not just equal — they must be one and the same object). It returns false if they are different objects, even if the objects have identical values for their data members.
getClass()	This method returns an object of type Class that identifies the class of the current object. You'll see a little more about this later in this chapter.
hashCode()	This method calculates a hashcode value for an object and returns it as type int. Hashcode values are used in classes defined in the package java.util for storing objects in hash tables. You'll see more about this in Chapter 14.
notify()	This is used to wake up a thread associated with the current object. I'll discuss how threads work in Chapter 16.
notifyAll()	This is used to wake up all threads associated with the current object. I'll also discuss this in Chapter 16.
wait()	This method causes a thread to wait for a change in the current object. I'll discuss this method in Chapter 16, too.

Note that `getClass()`, `notify()`, `notifyAll()`, and `wait()` cannot be overridden in your own class definitions — they are *fixed* with the keyword `final` in the class definition for `Object` (see the section on the `final` modifier later in this chapter).

It should be clear now why you could get polymorphic behavior with `toString()` in your derived classes when your base class did not define the method. There is always a `toString()` method in all your classes that is inherited from `Object`.

The two `protected` methods that your classes inherit from `Object` are:

Method	Purpose
`clone()`	This will create an object that is a copy of the current object regardless of type. This can be of any type, as an `Object` variable can refer to an object of any class. Note that this does not work with all class objects and does not always do precisely what you want, as you will see later in this section.
`finalize()`	This is the method that is called to clean up when an object is destroyed. As you saw in the previous chapter, you can override this to add your own clean-up code.

Since all your classes will inherit the methods defined in the `Object` class you should look at them in a little more detail.

The toString() Method

You have already made extensive use of the `toString()` method, and you know that it is used by the compiler to obtain a `String` representation of an object when necessary. It is obvious now why you must always declare the `toString()` method as `public` in a class. It is declared as such in the `Object` class and you can't declare it as anything else.

You can see what the `toString()` method that is inherited from the `Object` class will output for an object of one of your classes by commenting out the `toString()` method in `Animal` class in the previous example. A typical sample of the output for an object is:

```
Your choice:
Spaniel@b75778b2
It's Fido the Spaniel
Woof    Woof
```

The second line here is generated by the `toString()` method implemented in the `Object` class. This will be inherited in the `Animal` class, and it is called because you no longer override it. The hexadecimal digits following the @ in the output are the hashcode of the object.

Determining the Type of an Object

The `getClass()` method that all your classes inherit from `Object` returns an object of type `Class` that identifies the class of an object. Suppose you have a variable `pet` of type `Animal` that might contain a reference to an object of type Dog, Cat, Duck, or even Spaniel. To figure out what sort of thing it really refers to, you could write the following statements:

```
Class objectType = pet.getClass();          // Get the class type
System.out.println(objectType.getName());    // Output the class name
```

The method getName() is a member of the Class class, and it returns the fully qualified name of the actual class of the object for which it is called as a String object. Thus, the second statement will output the name of the class for the pet object. If pet referred to a Duck object, this would output:

```
Duck
```

This is the fully qualified name in this case, as the class is in the default package, which has no name. For a class defined in a named package, the class name would be prefixed with the package name. If you just wanted to output the class identity, you need not explicitly store the Class object. You can combine both statements into one:

```
System.out.println(pet.getClass().getName());   // Output the class name
```

This will produce the same output as before.

Remember that the Class object returns the actual class of an object. Suppose you define a String object like this:

```
String saying = "A stitch in time saves nine.";
```

You could store a reference to this String object as type Object:

```
Object str = saying;
```

The following statement will display the type of str:

```
System.out.println(str.getClass().getName());
```

This statement will output the type name as java.lang.String. The fact that the reference is stored in a variable of type Object does not affect the underlying type of the object itself.

When your program is executing, there are instances of the Class class in existence that represent each of the classes and interfaces in your program (I'll explain what an interface type is a little later in this chapter). There is also a Class object for each array type in your program as well as every primitive type. The Java Virtual Machine generates these when your program is loaded. Since Class is primarily intended for use by the Java Virtual Machine, it has no public constructors, so you can't create objects of type Class yourself.

Although you can use the forName() method to get the Class object corresponding to a particular "class or interface type, there is a more direct way. If you append .class to the name of any class, interface, or primitive type, you have a reference to the Class object for that class. For example, java.lang.String.class references the Class object for the String class and Duck.class references the Class object for the Duck class. Similarly, int.class is the class object for the primitive type, int, and double.class is the one corresponding to type `double`. This may not seem particularly relevant at this point, but keep it in mind. Because there is only one `Class` object for each class or interface type, you can test for the class of an object programmatically. Given a variable `pet` of type `Animal`, you could check whether the object referenced was of type `Duck` with the following statement:

```
if(pet.getClass()== Duck.class) {
   System.out.println("By George - it is a duck!");
}
```

This tests whether the object referenced by `pet` is of type `Duck`. Because each `Class` object is unique, this is a precise test. If `pet` contained a reference to an object that was a subclass of `Duck`, the result of the comparison in the `if` would be `false`. You'll see a little later in this chapter that you have an operator in Java, `instanceof`, that does almost the same thing — but not quite.

Note that the `Class` class is not an ordinary class. It is an example of a **generic type**. I'll discuss generic types in detail in Chapter 13, but for now be aware that `Class` really defines a set of classes. Each class, interface, array type, and primitive type that you use in your program will be represented by an object of a unique class from the set defined by the `Class` generic type.

Copying Objects

As you saw in the summary at the beginning of this section, the `protected` method `clone()` that is inherited from the `Object` class will create a new object that is a copy of the current object. It will do this only if the class of the object to be cloned indicates that cloning is acceptable. This is the case if the class implements the `Cloneable` interface. Don't worry about what an interface is at this point — you'll learn about this a little later in this chapter.

The `clone()` method that is inherited from `Object` clones an object by creating a new object of the same type as the current object and setting each of the fields in the new object to the same value as the corresponding fields in the current object. When the data members of the original object refer to class objects, the objects referred to are not duplicated when the clone is created — only the references are copied from the fields in the old object to the fields in the cloned object. This isn't typically what you want to happen — both the old and the new class objects can now be modifying a single shared object that is referenced through their corresponding data members, not recognizing that this is occurring.

If objects are to be cloned, the class must implement the `Cloneable` interface. I will discuss interfaces later in this chapter where you will see that implementing an interface typically involves implementing a specific set of methods. All that is required to make a class implement this interface is to declare it in the first line of the class definition. This is done using the `implements` keyword. For example:

```
class Dog implements Cloneable {
  // Details of the definition of the class...
}
```

This makes `Dog` objects cloneable because you have declared that the class implements the interface.

You will understand the implications of the inherited `clone()` method more clearly if you consider a simple specific instance. Let's suppose you define a class `Flea` that has a method that allows the name to be changed:

```
public class Flea extends Animal implements Cloneable {
  // Constructor
  public Flea(String aName, String aSpecies) {
    super("Flea");                       // Pass the type to the base
    name = aName;                        // Supplied name
    species = aSpecies;                  // Supplied species
  }

  // Change the flea's name
  public void setName(String aName) {
    name = aName;                        // Change to the new name
  }

  // Return the flea's name
  public String getName() {
    return name;
  }

  // Return the species
  public String getSpecies() {
    return species;
  }

  public void sound() {
    System.out.println("Psst");
  }

  // Present a flea's details as a String
  public String toString() {
    return super.toString() + "\nIt's " + name + " the " + species;
  }

  // Override inherited clone() to make it public
  public Object clone() throws CloneNotSupportedException {
    return super.clone();
  }

  private String name;                   // Name of flea!
  private String species;                // Flea species
}
```

You have defined accessor methods for the name and the species. You don't need them now but they will be useful later. By implementing the Cloneable interface you are indicating that you are happy to clone objects of this class. Since you have said that Flea is cloneable, you must implement the Cloneable interface in the base class too, so the Animal class needs to be changed to:

```
public class Animal implements Cloneable {
  // Details of the class as before...
}
```

No other changes are necessary to the Animal class here. You can now define a class PetDog that contains a Flea object as a member that is also cloneable:

```
public class PetDog extends Animal implements Cloneable {
  // Constructor
  public PetDog(String name, String breed) {
    super("Dog");
    petFlea = new Flea("Max","circus flea");        // Initialize petFlea
    this.name = name;
    this.breed = breed;
  }

  // Rename the dog
  public void setName(String name) {
    this.name = name;
  }

  // Return the dog's name
  public String getName() {
    return name;
  }

  // Return the breed
  public String getBreed() {
    return breed;
  }

  // Return the flea
  public Flea getFlea() {
    return petFlea;
  }

  public void sound() {
    System.out.println("Woof");
  }

  // Return a String for the pet dog
  public String toString() {
    return super.toString() + "\nIt's " + name + " the "
         + breed + " & \n" + petFlea;
  }

  // Override inherited clone() to make it public
  public Object clone() throws CloneNotSupportedException {
    return super.clone();
  }

  private Flea petFlea;            // The pet flea
  private String name;            // Dog's name
  private String breed;           // Dog's breed
}
```

To make it possible to clone a `PetDog` object, you override the inherited `clone()` method with a `public` version that calls the base class version. Note that the inherited method throws the `CloneNotSupportedException` so you must declare the method as shown — otherwise, it won't compile. You will be looking into what exceptions are in the next chapter.

You can now create a `PetDog` object with the statement:

```
PetDog myPet = new PetDog("Fang", "Chihuahua");
```

After seeing my pet, you want one just like it, so you can clone him:

```
PetDog yourPet = (PetDog)myPet.clone();
```

Now you have individual `PetDog` objects that regrettably contain references to the same `Flea` object. The `clone()` method will create the new `PetDog` object, `yourPet`, and copy the reference to the `Flea` object from the `petFlea` data member in `myPet` to the member with the same name in `yourPet`. If you decide that you prefer the name "Gnasher" for `yourPet`, you can change the name of your pet with the statement:

```
yourPet.setName("Gnasher");
```

Your dog will probably like a personalized flea, too, so you can change the name of its flea with the statement:

```
yourPet.getFlea().setName("Atlas");
```

Unfortunately, `Fang`'s flea will also be given the name `Atlas` because, under the covers, `Fang` and `Gnasher` both share a common `Flea`. If you want to demonstrate this, you can put all the classes together in an example, with the following class:

```
// Test cloning
public class TestCloning {
  public static void main(String[] args) {
    try {
      PetDog myPet = new PetDog("Fang", "Chihuahua");
      PetDog yourPet = (PetDog)myPet.clone();
      yourPet.setName("Gnasher");                // Change your dog's name
      yourPet.getFlea().setName("Atlas");        // Change your dog's flea's name
      System.out.println("\nYour pet details:\n"+yourPet);
      System.out.println("\nMy pet details:\n"+ myPet);

    } catch(CloneNotSupportedException e) {
      e.printStackTrace(System.err);
    }
  }
}
```

Don't worry about the `try` and `catch` blocks — these are necessary to deal with the exception that I mentioned earlier. You'll learn all about exceptions in Chapter 7. Just concentrate on the code between the braces following `try`. If you run the example, it will output the details on `myPet` and `yourPet` after the name for `yourPet` has been changed. Both names will be the same, so the output will be:

```
C:\Java\3668\Ch06\TestFlea>java TestFlea
Your pet details:
This is a Dog
It's Gnasher the Chihuahua &
This is a Flea
It's Atlas the circus flea
```

```
My pet details:
This is a Dog
It's Fang the Chihuahua &
This is a Flea
It's Atlas the circus flea
```

Choosing a name for your pet's flea has changed the name for my pet's flea, too. Unless you really want to share objects between the variables in two separate objects, you should implement the `clone()` method in your class to do the cloning the way you want. As an alternative to cloning (or in addition to), you could add a constructor to your class to create a new class object from an existing object. This creates a duplicate of the original object properly. You saw how you can do this in the previous chapter. If you implement your own `public` version of `clone()` to override the inherited version, you would typically code this method in the same way as you would the constructor to create a copy of an object. You could implement the `clone()` method in the `PetDog` class like this:

```
public Object clone() throws CloneNotSupportedException {
   PetDog pet = new PetDog(name, breed);
   pet.setName("Gnasher");
   pet.getFlea().setName("Atlas");

   return pet;
}
```

Here the method creates a new `PetDog` object using the name and breed of the current object. You then call the two objects' `setName()` methods to set the clones' names. If you compile and run the program, again with this change, altering the name of `myPet` will not affect `yourPet`. Of course, you could use the inherited `clone()` method to duplicate the current object and then explicitly clone the `Flea` member to refer to an independent object:

```
// Override inherited clone() to make it public
public Object clone() throws CloneNotSupportedException {
   PetDog pet = (PetDog)super.clone();
   pet.petFlea = (Flea)petFlea.clone();

   return pet;
}
```

The new object created by the inherited `clone()` method is of type `PetDog`, but it is returned as a reference of type `Object`. To access the `thePet` member, you need a reference of type `PetDog`, so the cast is essential. The same is true of the cloned `Flea` object. The effect of this version of the `clone()` method is the same as the previous version.

Methods Accepting a Variable Number of Arguments

You can write a method so that it will accept an arbitrary number of arguments when it is called, and the arguments that are passed do not need to be of the same type. The reason I have waited until now to mention this is that understanding how this works depends on having an understanding of the role of the Object class. You indicate that a method will accept a variable number of arguments by specifying the last parameter as follows:

```
Object ... args
```

The method can have zero or more parameters preceding this, but this must be last for obvious reasons. The ellipsis (three periods) between the type name Object and the parameter name args enables the compiler to determine that the argument list is variable. The parameter name args represents an array of type Object[], and the argument values are available in the elements of the array as type Object. Within the body of the method, the length of the args array tells you how many arguments were supplied.

Let's consider a very simple example to demonstrate the mechanism. Suppose you want to implement a static method that will accept any number of arguments and output the arguments to the command line — whatever they are. You could code it like this:

```
public static void printAll(Object ... args) {
  for(Object arg : args) {
    System.out.print("   "+arg);
  }
  System.out.println();
}
```

The arguments can be anything at all. Values of primitive types will be autoboxed because the method expects reference arguments. The loop will output the string representation of each of the arguments on a single line, the string being produced by invoking the toString() method for whatever the argument is.

Let's see it working.

Try It Out   Displaying Any Old Arguments

Here's a program that will exercise the printAll() method:

```
public class TryVariableArgumentList {
  public static void main(String[] args) {
    printAll( 2, "two", 4, "four", 4.5, "four point five");   // Six arguments
    printAll();                                                // No arguments
    printAll(25, "Anything goes", true, 4E4, false);          // Five arguments
  }

  public static void printAll(Object ... args) {
    for(Object arg : args) {
      System.out.print("   "+arg);
    }
    System.out.println();
  }
}
```

This program will produce the following output:

```
2   two   4   four   4.5   four point five

25   Anything goes   true   40000.0   false
```

How It Works

You can see from the output that the `printAll()` works as advertised and will accept an arbitrary number of arguments. The first call of the `printAll()` method mixes arguments of type `int`, type `String`, and type `double`. The numerical values are converted to objects the corresponding wrapper class types by boxing conversions that the compiler inserts. The output strings are then produced by calls to the `toString()` method for the objects, also expedited by the compiler. The second call to the method results in an empty line. The last line of output shows that autoboxing works with `boolean` values as well as values of the other primitive types.

One use for the variable argument list capability in the class libraries is to define the `printf()` method in the `PrintStream` class. This method will produce formatted output for an arbitrary sequence of values of various types, where the formatting is specified by the first argument to the method. `System.out` happens to be of type `PrintStream` so you can use `printf()` to produce formatted output to the command line. I'll discuss how you use the `printf()` method to produce output with more precise control over the format in which it is displayed in Chapter 8 in the context of streams.

Limiting the Types in a Variable Argument List

You don't have to specify the type of the variable argument list as type `Object`; you can specify it as any class or interface type. The arguments must be of the type that you specify, or any subtype of that type. Specifying the type of the variable argument list as `Object` maximizes flexibility because any types of argument can be supplied, but there may be occasions where you want to restrict the types of the arguments that can be supplied. For example, if you want to define a method that computes the average of an arbitrary number of values that are to be supplied as individual arguments, then you really want to be sure that the arguments can only be numerical values. Here's how you could do this:

```
public static double average(Double ... args) {
   if(args.length == 0) {
     return 0.0;
   }
   double ave = 0.0;
   for(double value : args) {
     ave += value;
   }
   return ave/args.length;
}
```

In this case the arguments must be of type `Double` or of a type derived from `Double`, or — because of autoboxing conversion supplied by the compiler — of type `double`. You could try this out in an example.

Try It Out   **Limiting the Types Allowed in a Variable Argument List**

You need to add only a simple version of `main()` to call the `average()` method a few times to show it in action:

```
public class TryLimitedVariableArgumentList {
   public static void main(String[] args) {
      System.out.println(average(1.0,2.0,3.0,4.0,5.0));
      System.out.println(average(3.14, 1.414, 1.732));
```

```
        System.out.println(average(new Double(7),new Double(8),new Double(9),
                                               new Double(10)));
    }

    // Average of a variable number of values
    public static double average(Double ... args) {
      if(args.length == 0) {
        return 0.0;
      }
      double ave = 0.0;
      for(double value : args) {
        ave += value;
      }
      return ave/args.length;
    }
  }
```

This example produces the following output:

```
3.0
2.0953333333333335
8.5
```

How It Works

The `average()` method allows an arbitrary number of arguments to be supplied when it is called. The arguments can be references of type `Double` or a type derived from `Double`, or of type `double`. When the arguments are of type `double`, the compiler inserts autoboxing conversions to type `Double` for them so the values are received in the method as that type. If you were to attempt to pass values of type `int` as arguments to the `average()` method, the compiler would flag this as an error because there is no automatic conversion from type `int` to type `Double`.

Casting Objects

You can cast an object to another class type, but only if the current object type and the new class type are in the same hierarchy of derived classes, and one is a superclass of the other. For example, earlier in this chapter you defined the classes `Animal`, `Dog`, `Spaniel`, `Cat`, and `Duck`, and these classes are related in the hierarchy shown in Figure 6-5.

You can cast a reference to an object of a class upwards through its direct and indirect superclasses. For example, you could cast a reference to an object of type `Spaniel` directly to type `Dog`, type `Animal`, or type `Object`. You could write:

```
Spaniel aPet = new Spaniel("Fang");
Animal theAnimal = (Animal)aPet;         // Cast the Spaniel to Animal
```

When you are assigning an object reference to a variable of a superclass type, you do not have to include the cast. You could write the assignment as:

```
Animal theAnimal = aPet;                 // Cast the Spaniel to Animal
```

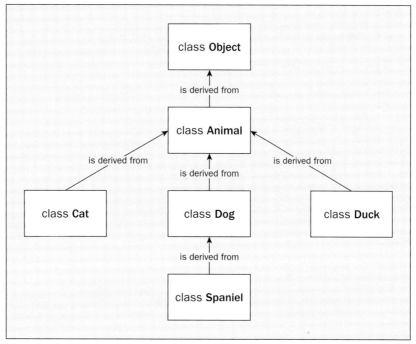

Figure 6-5

This would work just as well. The compiler is always prepared to insert a cast to a superclass type when necessary.

When you cast an object reference to a superclass type, Java retains full knowledge of the actual class to which the object belongs. If this were not the case, polymorphism would not be possible. Since information about the original type of an object is retained, you can cast down a hierarchy as well. However, you must always write the cast explicitly since the compiler is not prepared to insert it. For the cast to work, the object must be a legitimate instance of the class you are casting to — that is, the class you are casting to must be the original class of the object, or must be a superclass of the object. For example, you could cast a reference stored in the variable theAnimal shown in the preceding example to type Dog or type Spaniel, since the object was originally a Spaniel, but you could not cast it to Cat or Duck, since an object of type Spaniel does not have Cat or Duck as a superclass. To cast theAnimal to type Dog, you would write:

```
Dog aDog = (Dog)theAnimal;               // Cast from Animal to Dog
```

Now the variable aDog refers to an object of type Spaniel that also happens to be a Dog. Remember, you can only use the variable aDog to call the polymorphic methods from the class Spaniel that override methods that exist in Dog. You can't call methods that are not defined in the Dog class. If you want to call a method that is in the class Spaniel and not in the class Dog, you must first cast aDog to type Spaniel.

Although you cannot cast between unrelated objects, from `Spaniel` to `Duck` for example, you can achieve a conversion by writing a suitable constructor, but obviously only where it makes sense to do so. You just write a constructor in the class to which you want to convert and make it accept an object of the class you are converting from as an argument. If you really thought `Spaniel` to `Duck` was a reasonable conversion, you could add the constructor to the `Duck` class:

```
public Duck(Spaniel aSpaniel) {
    // Back legs off, and staple on a beak of your choice...
    super("Duck");              // Call the base constructor
    name = aSpaniel.getName();
    breed = "Barking Coot";  // Set the duck breed for a converted Spaniel
}
```

This assumes you have added a method, `getName()`, in the class `Dog`, which will be inherited in the class `Spaniel`, and which returns the value of `name` for an object. This constructor accepts a `Spaniel` and turns out a `Duck`. This is quite different from a cast though. This creates a completely new object that is separate from the original, whereas a cast presents the same object as a different type.

When to Cast Objects

You will have cause to cast objects in both directions through a class hierarchy. For example, whenever you execute methods polymorphically, you will be storing objects in a variable of a base class type and calling methods in a derived class. This will generally involve casting the derived class objects to the base class. Another reason you might want to cast up through a hierarchy is to pass an object of several possible subclasses to a method. By specifying a parameter as base class type, you have the flexibility to pass an object of any derived class to it. You could pass a `Dog`, `Duck`, or `Cat` object to a method as an argument for a parameter of type `Animal`, for example.

The reason you might want to cast down through a class hierarchy is to execute a method unique to a particular class. If the `Duck` class has a method `layEgg()`, for example, you can't call this using a variable of type `Animal`, even though it references a `Duck` object. As I said, casting downwards through a class hierarchy always requires an explicit cast.

Try It Out   Casting Down to Lay an Egg

Let's amend the `Duck` class and use it along with the `Animal` class in an example. Add `layEgg()` to the `Duck` class as:

```
public class Duck extends Animal {
  public void layEgg() {
    System.out.println("Egg laid");
  }
    // Rest of the class as before...
}
```

If you now try to use this with the code:

```
public class LayEggs {
  public static void main(String[] args) {
    Duck aDuck = new Duck("Donald", "Eider");
```

```
        Animal aPet = aDuck;          // Cast the Duck to Animal
        aPet.layEgg();                // This won't compile!
      }
    }
```

you will get a compiler message to the effect that layEgg() is not found in the class Animal.

Since you know this object is really a Duck, you can make it work by writing the call to layEgg() in the preceding code as:

```
    ((Duck)aPet).layEgg();            // This works fine
```

The object pointed to by aPet is first cast to type Duck. The result of the cast is then used to call the method layEgg(). If the object were not of type Duck, the cast would cause an exception to be thrown.

> **In general, you should avoid explicitly casting objects as much as possible because it increases the potential for an invalid cast and can therefore make your programs unreliable. Most of the time, you should find that if you design your classes carefully, you won't need explicit casts very often.**

Identifying Objects

There are circumstances when you may not know exactly what sort of object you are dealing with. This can arise if a derived class object is passed to a method as an argument for a parameter of a base class type for example, in the way I discussed in the previous section. In some situations you may need to cast the object to its actual class type, perhaps to call a class-specific method. If you try to make the cast and it turns out to be illegal, an exception will be thrown, and your program will end unless you have made provision for catching the exception. One way to obviate this situation is to verify that the object is of the type you expect before you make the cast.

You saw earlier in this chapter how you could use the getClass() method to obtain the Class object corresponding to the class type, and how you could compare it to a Class instance for the class you are looking for. You can also do this using the instanceof operator. For example, suppose you have a variable pet of type Animal, and you want to cast it to type Duck. You could code this as:

```
    Duck aDuck;                       // Declare a duck

    if(pet instanceof Duck) {
      aDuck = (Duck)pet;              // It is a duck so the cast is OK
      aDuck.layEgg();                 // and You can have an egg for tea
    }
```

If pet does not refer to a Duck object, an attempt to cast the object referenced by pet to Duck would cause an exception to be thrown. This code fragment will execute the cast and lay an egg only if pet does point to a Duck object. The preceding code fragment could have been written much more concisely as:

```
    if(pet instanceof Duck) {
      ((Duck)pet).layEgg();           // It is a duck so You can have an egg for tea
    }
```

So what is the difference between this and using `getClass()`? Well, it's quite subtle. The `instanceof` operator checks whether a cast of the object referenced by the left operand to the type specified by the right operand is legal. The result will be `true` if the object is the same type as the right operand, *or of any subclass type*. You can illustrate the difference by choosing a slightly different example.

Suppose `pet` stores a reference to an object of type `Spaniel`. You want to call a method defined in the `Dog` class, so you need to check that `pet` does really reference a `Dog` object. You can check whether you have a `Dog` object or not with the following statements:

```
if(pet instanceof Dog) {
   System.out.println("You have a dog!");
} else {
   System.out.println("It's definitely not a dog!");
}
```

You will get confirmation that you have a `Dog` object here even though it is actually a `Spaniel` object. This is fine though for casting purposes. As long as the `Dog` class is in the class hierarchy for the object, the cast will work okay, so the operator is telling you what you need to know. However, suppose you write:

```
if(pet.getClass() == Dog.class)
   System.out.println("You have a dog!");
else
   System.out.println("It's definitely not a dog!");
```

Here the `if` expression will be `false` because the class type of the object is `Spaniel`, so its `Class` object is different from that of `Dog.class` — you would have to write `Spaniel.class` instead of `Dog.class` to get the value `true` from the `if` expression.

You can conclude from this that for casting purposes you should always use the `instanceof` operator to check the type of a reference. You only need to resort to checking the `Class` object corresponding to a reference when you need to confirm the exact type of the reference.

More on Enumerations

When I introduced enumerations in Chapter 2, I said that there was more to enumerations than simply a type with a limited range of integer values. In fact, an enumeration type is a special form of class. When you define an enumeration type in your code, the enumeration constants that you specify are created as instances of a class that has the `Enum` class, which is defined in the `java.lang` package, as a superclass. The object that corresponds to each enumeration constant stores the name of the constant in a field, and the enumeration class type inherits the `toString` method from the `Enum` class. The `toString()` method in the `Enum` class returns the original name of the enumeration constant, so that's why you get the name you gave to an enumeration constant displayed when you output it using the `println()` method.

You have seen that you can put the definition of an enumeration type within the definition of a class. You can also put the definition is a separate source file. In this case you specify the name of the file containing the enumeration type definition in the same way as for any other class type. An enumeration that you define in its own source file can be accessed by any other source file in exactly the same way as any other class definition.

An object representing an enumeration constant also stores an integer field. By default, each constant in an enumeration will be assigned an integer value that is different from all the other constants in the enumeration. The values are assigned to the enumeration constants in the sequence in which you specify them, starting with zero for the first constant, 1 for the second, and so on. You can retrieve the value for a constant by calling its `ordinal()` method, but you should not need to do this in general.

You have already seen back in Chapter 3 that you can compare values of an enumeration type for equality using the `equals()` method. For example, assuming that you have defined an enumeration type, `Season`, with enumeration constants `spring`, `summer`, `fall`, and `winter`, you could write the following:

```
Season now = Season.winter;
if(now.equals(Season.winter))
   System.out.println("It is definitely winter!");
```

The `equals()` method is inherited from the `Enum` class in your enumeration class type. Your enumeration class type will also inherit the `compareTo()` method that compares instances of the enumeration based on their ordinal values. It returns a negative integer if the value for the instance for which the method is called is less than the instance that you pass as the argument, 0 if they are equal, and a positive integer if the value of the current instance is greater than the value for the argument. Thus, the sequence in which you specify the enumeration constants when you define them determines the order that the `compareTo()` method implements. You might use it like this:

```
if(now.compareTo(Season.summer) > 0)
   System.out.println("It is definitely getting colder!");
```

The `values()` method for an enumeration that I introduced in Chapter 3 is a static member of your enumeration class type. This method returns a collection object containing all the enumeration constants that you can use in a collection-based `for` loop. You'll learn about collection classes in Chapter 14.

Adding Members to an Enumeration Class

Because an enumeration is a class, you have the possibility to add your own methods and fields when you define the enumeration type. You can also add your own constructors to initialize any additional fields you introduce. Let's take an example. Suppose you want to define an enumeration for clothing sizes — jackets, say. Your initial definition might be like this:

```
public enum JacketSize { small, medium, large, extra_large, extra_extra_large }
```

You then realize that you would really like to record the average chest size applicable to each jacket size. You could amend the definition of the enumeration like this:

```
public enum JacketSize { small(36), medium(40), large(42),
                extra_large(46), extra_extra_large(48);

  // Constructor
  JacketSize(int chestSize) {
    this.chestSize = chestSize;
  }
  // Method to return the chest size for the current jacket size
```

```
    public int chestSize() {
      return chestSize;
    }

    private int chestSize;                    // Field to record chest size
  }
```

Note how the list of enumeration constants now ends with a semicolon. Each constant in the list has the corresponding chest size between parentheses, and this value will be passed to the constructor that you have added to the class. In the previous definition of JacketSize, the appearance of each enumeration constant results in a call to the default constructor for the class. In fact, you could put an empty pair of parentheses after the name of each constant, and it would still compile. However, this would not improve the clarity of the code. Because you have defined a constructor, no default destructor will be defined for the enumeration class, so you cannot write enumeration constants just as names. You must put the parentheses enclosing a value for the chest size following each enumeration constant. Of course, if you wanted to have the option of omitting the chest size for some of the constants in the enumeration, you could define your own default constructor and assign a default value for the chestSize field.

Even though you have added your own constructor, the fields inherited from the base class, Enum, that store the name of the constant and its ordinal value, will still be set appropriately. The ordering of the constants that compareTo() implements will still be determined by the sequence in which the constants appear in the definition. Note that you must not declare a constructor in an enumeration class as public. If you do, the enum class definition will not compile. The only modifier that you are allowed to apply to a constructor in class defining an enumeration is private, which will result in the constructor being callable only from inside the class.

The chest size is recorded in a private data member so there is also a chestSize() method to allow the value of chestSize to be retrieved.

Let's see it working.

Try It Out   Embroidering an Enumeration

First, create a new directory for the example and save the JacketSize.java file containing the definition of the enumeration from the previous section in it. Now create another file containing the following definition:

```
public enum JacketColor { red, orange, yellow, blue, green }
```

This should be in a file with the name JacketColor.java.

Now you can define a class that represents a jacket:

```
public class Jacket {
  public Jacket(JacketSize size, JacketColor color) {
    this.size = size;
    this.color = color;
  }

  public String toString() {
    StringBuffer str = new StringBuffer("Jacket ");
```

```
        return str.append(size).append(" in ").append(color).toString();
    }

    private JacketSize size;
    private JacketColor color;
}
```

Finally, you need a file containing code to try out some jackets:

```
public class TryEnumeration {
    public static void main(String[] args) {

        // Define some jackets
        Jacket[] jackets = { new Jacket(JacketSize.medium, JacketColor.red),
                             new Jacket(JacketSize.extra_large, JacketColor.yellow),
                             new Jacket(JacketSize.small, JacketColor.green),
                             new Jacket(JacketSize.extra_extra_large, JacketColor.blue)
                           };

        // Output colors available
        System.out.println("Jackets colors available are:\n");
        for(JacketColor color: JacketColor.values()) {
            System.out.print("   " + color);
        }

        // Output sizes available
        System.out.println("\n\nJackets sizes available are:\n");
        for(JacketSize size: JacketSize.values()) {
            System.out.print("   " + size);
        }

        System.out.println("\n\nJackets in stock are:");
        for(Jacket jacket: jackets) {
            System.out.println(jacket);
        }
    }
}
```

When you compile and execute this program you will get the following output:

```
Jackets colors available are:

   red   orange   yellow   blue   green

Jackets sizes available are:

   small   medium   large   extra_large   extra_extra_large

Jackets in stock are:
Jacket medium in red
Jacket extra_large in yellow
Jacket small in green
Jacket extra_extra_large in blue
```

How It Works

The `main()` method in the `TryEnumeration` class defines an array of `Jacket` objects. It then lists the sizes and colors available for a jacket simply by using the collection-based `for` loop to list the constants in each enumeration. Because the enumeration constants are objects, the compiler inserts a call to the `toString()` method for the objects to produce the output. You use the same kind of `for` loop to list the contents of the array of `Jacket` objects. This also involves an implicit call to the `toString()` method for each `Jacket` object.

Because you have defined the `JacketSize` and `JacketColor` enumerations in separate classes, they are accessible from any source file in the same directory. To make them even more widely available, you could put them in a package.

The `Jacket` class uses the enumeration types to define private fields recording the size and color of a jacket. Note how the `toString()` method in the `Jacket` class is able to use the size and color members as though they were strings. The compiler will insert a call to the `toString()` method for the enumeration type that applies. You can override the `toString()` method for an enumeration type. For example, you might decide you prefer to define the `toString()` method in the `JacketSize` enumeration like this:

```
public String toString() {
   switch(this)  {
      case small:
         return "S";
      case medium:
         return "M";
      case large:
         return "L";
      case extra_large:
         return "XL";
      default:
         return "XXL";
   }
}
```

Note how you can use `this` as the control expression for the `switch` statement. This is because `this` references the current instance, which is an enumeration constant. Because the expression is an enumeration constant, the case labels are the constant names. They do not need to be qualified by the name of the enumeration. With this implementation of `toString()` in the `JacketSize` enumeration, the output will be:

```
Jackets colors available are:

 red   orange   yellow   blue   green

Jackets sizes available are:

 S   M   L   XL   XXL

Jackets in stock are:
Jacket M in red
Jacket XL in yellow
Jacket S in green
Jacket XXL in blue
```

Thus, you can see from this example that you can treat an enumeration type just like any other class type.

Designing Classes

A basic problem in object-oriented programming is deciding how the classes in your program should relate to one another. One possibility is to create a hierarchy of classes by deriving classes from a base class that you have defined and adding methods and data members to specialize the subclasses. The `Animal` class and the subclasses derived from it are an example of this. Another possibility is to define a set of classes that are not hierarchical, but that have data members that are themselves class objects. A `Zoo` class might well have objects of types derived from `Animal` as members, for example. You can have class hierarchies that contain data members that are class objects — you already have this with the classes derived from `Animal` since they have members of type `String`. The examples so far have been relatively clear-cut as to which approach to choose, but it is not always so evident. Quite often you will have a choice between defining your classes as a hierarchy and defining classes that have members that are class objects. Which is the best approach to take?

Like almost all questions of this kind, there are no clear-cut answers. If object-oriented programming were a process that you could specify by a fixed set of rules that you could just follow blindly, you could get the computer to do it. There are some guidelines though, and some contexts in which the answer may be more obvious.

Aside from the desirability of reflecting real-world relationships between types of objects, the need to use polymorphism is a primary reason for using subclasses (or interfaces, as you'll see shortly). This is the essence of object-oriented programming. Having a range of related objects that can be treated equivalently can greatly simplify your programs. You have seen how having various kinds of animals specified by classes derived from a common base class, `Animal`, allows us to act on different types of animals as though they are the same, producing different results depending on what kind of animal is being dealt with, and all this automatically.

A Classy Example

Many situations involve making judgments about the design of your classes. The way to go may well boil down to a question of personal preference. Let's try to see how the options look in practice by considering a simple example. Suppose you want to define a class `PolyLine` to represent geometric entities that consist of a number of connected line segments, as illustrated in the Figure 6-6.

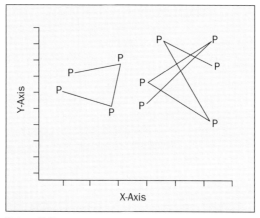

Figure 6-6

Figure 6-6 shows two polylines, one defined by four points, the other defined by six points.

It seems reasonable to represent points as objects of a class `Point`. Points are well-defined objects that will occur in the context of all kinds of geometric entities. You have seen a class for points earlier, which you put in the `Geometry` package. Rather than repeat the whole class, let's just define the bare bones of what you need in this context:

```
public class Point {
    // Create a point from its coordinates
    public Point(double xVal, double yVal) {
        x = xVal;
        y = yVal;
    }

    // Create a point from another point
    public Point(Point point) {
        x = point.x;
        y = point.y;
    }

    // Convert a point to a string
    public String toString() {
        return x+","+y;
    }

    // Coordinates of the point
    protected double x;
    protected double y;
}
```

Save the source file containing this code in a new directory, `TryPolyLine`. You'll add all the files for the example to this directory. Both data members of `Point` will be inherited in any subclass because they are specified as `protected`. They are also insulated from interference from outside the package containing the class. The `toString()` method will allow `Point` objects to be concatenated to a `String` object for automatic conversion—in an argument passed to the `println()` method, for example.

The next question you might ask is, "Should I derive the class `PolyLine` from the class `Point`?" This has a fairly obvious answer. A polyline is clearly not a kind of point, so it is not logical to derive the class `PolyLine` from the `Point` class. This is an elementary demonstration of what is often referred to as the "*is a*" test. If you can say that one kind of object "*is a*" specialized form of another kind of object, you may have a good case for a derived class (but not always—there may be other reasons not to!). If not, you don't.

The complement to the "*is a*" test is the "*has a*" test. If one object "*has a*" component that is an object of another class, you have a case for a class member. A `House` object "*has a*" door, so a variable of type `Door` is likely to be a member of the class `House`. The `PolyLine` class will contain several points, which looks promising, but you should look a little more closely at how you might store them, as there are some options.

Designing the PolyLine Class

With the knowledge you have of Java, an array of `Point` objects looks like a good candidate to be a member of the class. There are disadvantages, though. A common requirement with polylines is to be able to add a segment or two to an existing object. With an array storing the points you will need to create a new array each time you add a segment, then copy all the points from the old array to the new one. This could be time-consuming if you have a `PolyLine` object with a lot of segments.

You have another option. You could create a **linked list** of points. In its simplest form, a linked list of objects is an arrangement where each object in the list has a reference to the next object as a data member. As long as you have a variable containing a reference to the first `Point` object, you can access all the points in the list, as shown in Figure 6-7.

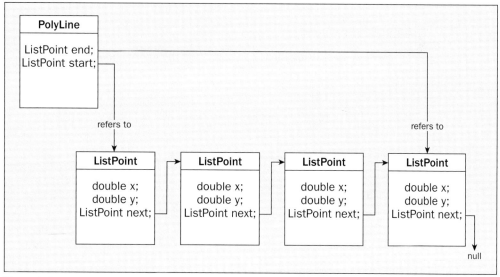

Figure 6-7

Figure 6-7 illustrates the basic structure you might have for a linked list of points stored as a `PolyLine`. The points are stored as members of `ListPoint` objects. In addition to constructors, the `PolyLine` class will need a method to add points, but before you look into that, let's consider the `ListPoint` class in more detail.

You could take one of at least three approaches to define the `ListPoint` class, and you could make arguments in favor of all three.

❑   You could define the `ListPoint` class with the *x* and *y* coordinates stored explicitly. The main argument against this would be that you have already encapsulated the properties of a point in the `Point` class, so why not use it?

❑   You could regard a `ListPoint` object as something that contains a reference to a `Point` object, plus members that refer to previous and following `ListPoint` objects in the list. This is not an unreasonable approach. It is easy to implement and not inconsistent with an intuitive idea of a `ListPoint`.

❑   You could view a `ListPoint` object as a specialized kind of `Point`, so you would derive the `ListPoint` class from `Point`. Whether or not this is reasonable depends on whether you see this as valid. To my mind, this is stretching the usual notion of a point somewhat—I would not use this.

The best option looks to me to be the second approach. You could implement the `ListPoint` class with a data member of type `Point`, which defines a basic point with its coordinates. A `ListPoint` object would have an extra data member, `next`, of type `ListPoint` that is intended to contain a reference to the next object in the list. With this arrangement, you can find all the points in a `Polyline` object by starting with its `start` member, which stores a reference to its first `ListPoint` object. This contains a reference to the next `ListPoint` object in its `next` member, which in turn contains a reference to the next, and so on through to the last `ListPoint` object. You'll know it is the last one because its `next` member, which usually points to the next `ListPoint` object, will be `null`. Let's try it.

Try It Out   The ListPoint Class

You can define the `ListPoint` class using the `Point` class with the following code:

```
public class ListPoint {
  // Constructor
  public ListPoint(Point point) {
    this.point = point;                  // Store point reference
    next = null;                         // Set next ListPoint as null
  }

  // Set the pointer to the next ListPoint
  public void setNext(ListPoint next) {
    this.next = next;                    // Store the next ListPoint
  }

  // Get the next point in the list
  public ListPoint getNext() {
    return next;                         // Return the next ListPoint
  }

  // Return String representation
  public String toString() {
    return "(" + point + ")";
  }

  private ListPoint next;                // Refers to next ListPoint in the list
  private Point point;                   // The point for this list point
}
```

Save this file in the same directory as the `Point` class, `TryPolyLine`.

How It Works

A `ListPoint` object is a means of creating a list of `Point` objects that originate elsewhere so you don't need to worry about duplicating `Point` objects stored in the list. You can just store the reference to the `Point` object passed to the constructor in the data member, `point`. The data member, `next`, should contain a reference to the next `ListPoint` in the list, and since that is not defined here, you set `next` to `null`.

The `setNext()` method will enable the `next` data member to be set for the existing last point in the list when a new point is added to the list. A reference to the new `ListPoint` object will be passed as an argument to the method. The `getNext()` method enables the next point in the list to be determined, so this method is the means by which you can iterate through the entire list.

By implementing the `toString()` method for the class, you enable the automatic creation of a `String` representation for a `ListPoint` object when required. Here you differentiate the `String` representation of the `ListPoint` object by enclosing the `String` representation of `point` between parentheses.

You could now have a first stab at implementing the `PolyLine` class.

Try It Out   The PolyLine Class

You can define the `PolyLine` class to use the `ListPoint` class as follows:

```
public class PolyLine {
  // Construct a polyline from an array of points
  public PolyLine(Point[] points) {
    if(points != null) {                    // Make sure there is an array
      for(Point p : points) {
        addPoint(p);
      }
    }
  }

  // Add a Point object to the list
  public void addPoint(Point point) {
    ListPoint newEnd = new ListPoint(point);     // Create a new ListPoint
    if(start == null) {
      start = newEnd;                            // Start is same as end
    } else {
      end.setNext(newEnd);                 // Set next variable for old end as new end
    }
    end = newEnd;                               // Store new point as end
  }

  // String representation of a polyline
  public String toString() {
    StringBuffer str = new StringBuffer("Polyline:");
    ListPoint nextPoint = start;               // Set the 1st point as start
    while(nextPoint != null) {
      str.append(" "+ nextPoint);              // Output the current point
      nextPoint = nextPoint.getNext();         // Make the next point current
    }
    return str.toString();
  }

  private ListPoint start;               // First ListPoint in the list
  private ListPoint end;                 // Last ListPoint in the list
}
```

This source file also goes in the `TryPolyLine` directory.

You might want to be able to add a point to the list by specifying a coordinate pair. You could overload the addPoint() method to do this:

```
// Add a point defined by a coordinate pair to the list
public void addPoint(double x, double y) {
  addPoint(new Point(x, y));
}
```

You just created a new Point object in the expression that is the argument to the other version of addPoint().

You might also want to create a PolyLine object from an array of coordinates. The constructor to do this would be:

```
// Construct a polyline from an array of coordinates
public PolyLine(double[][] coords) {
  if(coords != null) {
    for(int i = 0; i < coords.length ; i++) {
      addPoint(coords[i][0], coords[i][1]);
    }
  }
}
```

How It Works

The PolyLine class has the data members start and end that you saw in Figure 6-7. These will reference the first and last points of the list, or null if the list is empty. Storing the end point in the list is not essential since you can always find it by going through the list starting with start. However, having a reference to the last point saves a lot of time when you want to add a point to the list. The constructor accepts an array of Point objects and starts the process of assembling the object, by creating a list containing one ListPoint object produced from the first element in the array. It then uses the addPoint() method to add all the remaining points in the array to the list.

Adding a point to the list is deceptively simple. All the addPoint() method does is create a ListPoint object from the Point object passed as an argument, sets the next member of the old end point in the list to refer to the new point, and finally stores a reference to the new end point in the member end.

The toString() method will return a string representing the PolyLine object as a list of point coordinates. Note how the next member of the ListPoint objects controls the loop that runs through the list. When the last ListPoint object is reached, the next member will be returned as null, and the while loop will end. You can now give the PolyLine class a whirl.

Try It Out   Using PolyLine Objects

You can create a simple example to illustrate use of the PolyLine class:

```
public class TryPolyLine {
  public static void main(String[] args) {
    // Create an array of coordinate pairs
    double[][] coords = { {1., 1.}, {1., 2.}, { 2., 3.},
                          {-3., 5.}, {-5., 1.}, {0., 0.} };
```

```
// Create a polyline from the coordinates and display it
PolyLine polygon = new PolyLine(coords);
System.out.println(polygon);
// Add a point and display the polyline again
polygon.addPoint(10., 10.);
System.out.println(polygon);

// Create Point objects from the coordinate array
Point[] points = new Point[coords.length];
for(int i = 0; i < points.length; i++)
points[i] = new Point(coords[i][0],coords[i][1]);

// Use the points to create a new polyline and display it
PolyLine newPoly = new PolyLine(points);
System.out.println(newPoly);
  }
}
```

Remember that all three classes, Point, ListPoint, and PolyLine, need to be together in the same directory as this class, which will be the TryPolyLine directory if you followed my initial suggestion. If you have keyed everything in correctly, the program will output three PolyLine objects:

```
Polyline: (1.0,1.0) (1.0,2.0) (2.0,3.0) (-3.0,5.0) (-5.0,1.0) (0.0,0.0)
Polyline: (1.0,1.0) (1.0,2.0) (2.0,3.0) (-3.0,5.0) (-5.0,1.0) (0.0,0.0)
                                                               (10.0,10.0)
Polyline: (1.0,1.0) (1.0,2.0) (2.0,3.0) (-3.0,5.0) (-5.0,1.0) (0.0,0.0)
```

The first and the third lines of output are the same, with the coordinates from the coords array. The second has the extra point (10, 10) at the end.

The PolyLine class works well enough but it doesn't seem very satisfactory. Adding all the code to create and manage a list for what is essentially a geometric entity is not very object-oriented is it? Come to think of it, why are you making a list of points? Apart from the type of the data members of the ListPoint class, there's very little to do with Point objects in its definition; it's all to do with the linking mechanism. You might also have lots of other requirements for lists. If you were implementing an address book for instance, you would want a list of names. A cookery program would need a list of recipes. You might need lists for all kinds of things — maybe even a list of lists! Let's see if there's a better approach.

Let's put together a more general-purpose linked list and then use it to store polylines as before. You should save the source files for this in a new directory, as you will implement it as a whole new example. I'll put the source files in a directory with the name TryLinkedList in the code download for the book.

A General-Purpose Linked List

The key to implementing a simple, general-purpose linked list is the Object class discussed earlier in this chapter. Because the Object class is a superclass of every class, a variable of type Object can be used to store any kind of object. You could re-implement the ListPoint class in the form of a ListItem class. This will represent an element in a linked list that can reference any type of object:

```
class ListItem {
  // Constructor
  public ListItem(Object item) {
    this.item = item;              // Store the item
    next = null;                   // Set next as end point
  }

  // Return class name & object
  public String toString() {
    return "ListItem " + item ;
  }

  ListItem next;                   // Refers to next item in the list
  Object item;                     // The item for this ListItem
}
```

It's basically similar to the `ListPoint` class except that you have omitted the methods to set and retrieve the next member reference. You'll see why these are not necessary in a moment. The `toString()` method assumes that the object referenced by `item` implements a `toString()` method. You won't use the `toString()` method here when you come to exercise the general linked list class you're implementing, but it is a good idea to implement the `toString()` method for your classes anyway. If you do, class objects can always be output using the `println()` method, which is very handy for debugging.

You can now use objects of this class in a definition of a class that will represent a linked list.

Defining a Linked List Class

The mechanics of creating and handling the linked list will be similar to what you had in the `PolyLine` class, but externally you need to deal in the objects that are stored in the list, not in terms of `ListItem` objects. In fact, you don't need to have the `ListItem` class separate from the `LinkedList` class. You can make it an inner class:

```
public class LinkedList {
  // Default constructor - creates an empty list
  public LinkedList() {}

  // Constructor to create a list containing one object
  public LinkedList(Object item) {
    if(item != null) {
      current=end=start=new ListItem(item); // item is the start and end
    }
  }

  // Construct a linked list from an array of objects
  public LinkedList(Object[] items) {
    if(items != null) {
      // Add the items to the list
      for(int i = 0; i < items.length; i++) {
        addItem(items[i]);
      }
      current = start;
    }
  }
```

```
// Add an item object to the list
public void addItem(Object item) {
  ListItem newEnd = new ListItem(item);    // Create a new ListItem
  if(start == null) {                       // Is the list empty?
    start = end = newEnd;                   // Yes, so new element is start and end
  } else {                                  // No, so append new element
    end.next = newEnd;                      // Set next variable for old end
    end = newEnd;                           // Store new item as end
  }
}

// Get the first object in the list
public Object getFirst() {
  current = start;
  return start == null ? null : start.item;
}

// Get the next object in the list
public Object getNext() {
  if(current != null) {
    current = current.next;                 // Get the reference to the next item
  }
  return current == null ? null : current.item;
}

private ListItem start = null;              // First ListItem in the list
private ListItem end = null;                // Last ListItem in the list
private ListItem current = null;            // The current item for iterating
private class ListItem {
  // ListItem class definition as before...
}
}
```

Save this source file in the new directory for the example. You can use this class to create a linked list containing any types of objects. The class has data members to track the first and last items in the list, plus the member current, which will be used to iterate through the list. You have three class constructors. The default constructor creates an empty list. You have a constructor to create a list with a single object, and another to create a list from an array of objects. Any list can also be extended by means of the addItem() method. Each of the constructors, apart from the default, sets the current member to the first item in the list, so if the list is not empty, this will refer to a valid first item.

You can see that because the ListItem class is a member of the LinkedList class, you can refer to its data members directly within methods in the LinkedList class. This obviates the need for any methods in the ListItem class to get or set its fields. Since it is private it will not be accessible outside the LinkedList class so there is no risk associated with this — as long as you code the LinkedList class correctly, of course.

The addItem() method works in much the same way as the addPoint() method did in the PolyLine class. It creates a new ListItem object and updates the next member of the previous last item to refer to the new one. The complication is the possibility that the list might be empty. The check in the if takes care of this. You take special steps if start holds a null reference.

The getFirst() and getNext() methods are intended to be used together to access all the objects stored in the list. The getFirst() method returns the object stored in the first ListItem object in the list and sets the current data member to refer to the first ListItem object. After calling the getFirst() method, successive calls to the getNext() method will return subsequent objects stored in the list. The method updates current to refer to the next ListItem object, each time it is called. When the end of the list is reached, getNext() returns null.

Try It Out   Using the General Linked List

You can now define the PolyLine class so that it uses a LinkedList object. All you need to do is put a LinkedList variable as a class member that you initialize in the class constructors, and implement all the other methods you had in the previous version of the class to use the LinkedList object:

```
public class PolyLine {
  // Construct a polyline from an array of coordinate pairs
  public PolyLine(double[][] coords) {
    Point[] points = new Point[coords.length];    // Array to hold points

    // Create points from the coordinates
    for(int i = 0; i < coords.length ; i++) {
      points[i] = new Point(coords[i][0], coords[i][1]);
    }

    // Create the polyline from the array of points
    polyline = new LinkedList(points);
  }

  // Construct a polyline from an array of points
  public PolyLine(Point[] points) {
    polyline = new LinkedList(points);            // Create the polyline
  }

  // Add a Point object to the list
  public void addPoint(Point point) {
    polyline.addItem(point);                      // Add the point to the list
  }

  // Add a point from a coordinate pair to the list
  public void addPoint(double x, double y) {
    polyline.addItem(new Point(x, y));            // Add the point to the list
  }

  // String representation of a polyline
  public String toString() {
    StringBuffer str = new StringBuffer("Polyline:");
    Point point = (Point) polyline.getFirst();
                                                  // Set the 1st point as start
    while(point != null) {
      str.append(" ("+ point+ ")");               // Append the current point
      point = (Point)polyline.getNext();          // Make the next point current
    }
    return str.toString();
```

```
    }

    private LinkedList polyline;                    // The linked list of points
}
```

You can exercise this using the same code as last time — in the `TryPolyLine.java` file. Copy this file to the directory for this example.

How It Works

The `PolyLine` class implements all the methods that you had in the class before, so the `main()` method in the `TryPolyLine` class works just the same. Under the covers, the methods in the `PolyLine` class work a little differently. The work of creating the linked list is now in the constructor for the `LinkedList` class. The `PolyLine` class constructors just assemble a point array if necessary, and call the `LinkedList` constructor. Similarly, the `addPoint()` method creates a `Point` object from the coordinate pair it receives and passes it to the `addItem()` method for the `LinkedList` object, `polyline`.

Note that the cast from `Point` to `Object` when the `addItem()` method is called is automatic. A cast from any class type to type `Object` is always automatic because the cast is up the class hierarchy — remember that all classes have `Object` as a base. In the `toString()` method, you must insert an explicit cast to store the object returned by the `getFirst()` or the `getNext()` method. This cast is down the hierarchy so you must specify the cast explicitly.

You could use a variable of type `Object` to store the objects returned from `getFirst()` and `getNext()`, but this would not be a good idea. You would not need to insert the explicit cast, but you would lose a valuable check on the integrity of the program. You put objects of type `Point` into the list, so you would expect objects of type `Point` to be returned. An error in the program somewhere could result in an object of another type being inserted. If the object is not of type `Point` — due to the said program error, for example — the cast to type `Point` will fail and you will get an exception. A variable of type `Object` can store anything. If you use this, and something other than a `Point` object is returned, it would not register at all.

Now that you have gone to the trouble of writing your own general linked list class, you may be wondering why someone hasn't done it already. Well, they have! The `java.util` package defines a `LinkedList` class that is much better than this one. Still, putting your own together was good experience, and I hope you found it educational, if not interesting. The way you have implemented the `LinkedList` class here is not the best approach. In Chapter 13 you will learn about **generic types**, which enable you to define a linked list class that is type-safe. You'll look at the standard class in the `java.util` package that implements a linked list using the generic types capability described in Chapter 14.

Using the final Modifier

You have already used the `final` keyword to fix the value of a static data member of a class. You can also apply this keyword to the definition of a method, and to the definition of a class.

It may be that you want to prevent a subclass from overriding a method in your class. When this is the case, simply declare that method as `final`. Any attempt to override a `final` method in a subclass will result in the compiler flagging the new method as an error. For example, you could declare the method `addPoint()` as `final` within the class `PolyLine` by writing its definition in the class as:

```
    public final void addPoint(Point point) {
        ListPoint newEnd = new ListPoint(point);   // Create a new ListPoint
        end.setNext(newEnd);                       // Set next variable for old end as new end
        end = newEnd;                              // Store new point as end
    }
```

Any class derived from `PolyLine` would not be able to redefine this method. Obviously, an `abstract` method cannot be declared as `final`—because it must be defined in a subclass somewhere.

If you declare a class as `final`, you prevent any subclasses from being derived from it. To declare the class `PolyLine` as `final`, you would define it as:

```
    public final class PolyLine {
        // Definition as before...
    }
```

If you now attempt to define a class based on `PolyLine`, you will get an error message from the compiler. An abstract class cannot be declared as `final` since this would prevent the abstract methods in the class from ever being defined. Declaring a class as `final` is a drastic step that prevents the functionality of the class being extended by derivation, so you should be very sure that you want to do this.

Interfaces

In the classes that you derived from the class `Animal`, you had a common method, `sound()`, that was implemented individually in each of the subclasses. The method signature was the same in each class, and the method could be called polymorphically. The main point to defining the class `Animal` first and then subsequently defining the classes `Dog`, `Cat`, and so on, from it was to be able to get polymorphic behavior. When all you want is a set of one or more methods to be implemented in a number of different classes so that you can call them polymorphically, you can dispense with the base class altogether.

You can achieve the same result much more simply by using a Java facility called an **interface**. The name indicates its primary use—specifying a set of methods that represent a particular class interface, which can then be implemented appropriately in a number of different classes. All of the classes will then share this common interface, and the methods in it can be called polymorphically through a variable of the interface type. This is just one aspect of what you can do using an interface. I will start by examining what an interface is from the ground up and then look at what you can do with it.

An **interface** is essentially a collection of related constants and/or abstract methods, and in most cases it will contain just methods. An interface doesn't define what a method does. It just defines its form—its name, its parameters, and its return type, so by definition the methods in an interface are abstract.

To make use of an interface, you **implement** the interface in a class—that is, you declare that the class implements the interface and you write the code for each of the methods that the interface declares as part of the class definition. When a class implements an interface, any constants that were defined in the interface definition are available directly in the class, just though they were inherited from a base class. An interface can contain either constants, or abstract methods, or both.

As Figure 6-8 illustrates, the methods in an interface are always `public` and `abstract`, so you do not need to specify them as such; it is considered bad programming practice to specify any attributes for them, and you definitely cannot add any attributes other than the defaults, `public` and `abstract`. This implies that methods declared in an interface can never be `static`, so an interface always declares instance methods. The constants in an interface are always `public`, `static`, and `final`, so you do not need to specify the attributes for these either.

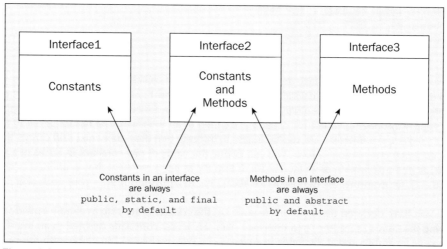

Figure 6-8

An interface is defined just like a class, but using the keyword `interface` rather than the keyword `class`. You store an interface definition in a `.java` file with the same name as the interface. The name that you give to an interface must be different from that of any other interface or class in the same package. Just as for classes, the members of the interface — the constants and/or method declarations — appear between a pair of braces that delimit the body of the interface definition.

Encapsulating Constants in a Program

You will often find that a program makes use of a set of constant values that you really want to define only once. You might have values representing standard colors that your program uses or perhaps constants that are used in calculations such as conversion factors from one set of units to another. In Java versions prior to 5.0, a common approach was to define a set of related constants in an interface and then implement the interface in any class that used any of the constants. This approach has largely been made obsolete by the static import capability.

The capability to import static members of a class that was introduced in Java 5 provides an excellent way of dealing with constants in a program. However, the use of an interface for such purposes has been very widespread in the past, so I'll first explain briefly how that works to equip you for when you run into it. I'll then explain how you use static import to access constants that you have defined in a class, which is a much cleaner and better way of making a set of constants available wherever they are needed.

Constants in an Interface

Suppose you are writing a program that converts measurements between metric and imperial units. Here's how the constants that such a program might use could be defined in an interface:

```
public interface ConversionFactors {
    double INCH_TO_MM = 25.4;
    double OUNCE_TO_GRAM = 28.349523125;
    double POUND_TO_GRAM = 453.5924;
    double HP_TO_WATT = 745.7;
    double WATT_TO_HP = 1.0/HP_TO_WATT;
}
```

The `ConversionFactors` interface defines five constants for conversions of various kinds. Constants defined in an interface are automatically `public`, `static`, and `final`. You have no choice about this — constants defined in an interface always have these attributes. Since they are static and final, you must always supply initializing values for constants defined in an interface. The names given to these in the `ConversionFactors` interface use capital letters to indicate that they are `final` and cannot be altered — this is a common convention in Java. You can define the value of one constant in terms of a preceding constant, as in the definition of `WATT_TO_HP`. If you try to use a constant that is defined later in the interface — if, for example, the definition for `WATT_TO_HP` appeared first — your code will not compile.

Because you have declared the interface as `public`, the constants are also available outside the package containing the `ConversionFactors` interface. You can access constants defined in an interface in the same way as for public and static fields in a class — by just qualifying the name with the name of the interface. For example, you could write:

```
public class MyClass {
    // This class can access any of the constants defined in ConversionFactors
    // by qualifying their names...
    public static double poundsToGrams(double pounds) {
        return pounds*ConversionFactors.POUND_TO_GRAM;
    }

    // Plus the rest of the class definition...
}
```

Since the `ConversionFactors` interface includes only constants, a class can gain access to them using their unqualified names by declaring that it implements the interface. This has been the technique employed in the past. For example, here's a class that implements the `ConversionFactors` interface:

```
public class MyOtherClass implements ConversionFactors {
    // This class can access any of the constants defined in ConversionFactors
    // using their unqualified names, and so can any subclasses of this class...
    public static double poundsToGrams(double pounds) {
        return pounds*POUND_TO_GRAM;
    }

    // Plus the rest of the class definition...
}
```

The constants defined in the `ConversionFactors` interface are now members of `MyOtherClass` and therefore will be inherited in any derived classes.

While this technique of using an interface as a container for constants works and has been widely used in the past, using a class to contain the constants as static fields and then importing the names of the fields as required provides a simpler more effective approach. This is now the recommended technique for handling sets of constants in a program. Let's see how it works.

Constants Defined in a Class

You could define a class to hold the same set of constants that you saw defined in an interface in the previous section, like this:

```
package conversions;                                    // Package for conversions

public class ConversionFactors {
   public static final double INCH_TO_MM = 25.4;
   public static final double OUNCE_TO_GRAM = 28.349523125;
   public static final double POUND_TO_GRAM = 453.5924;
   public static final double HP_TO_WATT = 745.7;
   public static final double WATT_TO_HP = 1.0/HP_TO_WATT;
}
```

Of course, you can access the members of the ConversionsFactors class from outside by using the qualified names of the data members—ConversionFactors.HP_TO_WATT, for example. An alternative and possibly more convenient approach is to import the static members of the class into any class that needs to use any of the constants. This will allow the constants to be referred to by their unqualified names. In this case, the class must be in a named package, because the import statement cannot be applied to the unnamed package.

Here's how you might use it:

```
import static conversions.ConversionFactors.*;    // Import static members

public class MyOtherClass {
   // This class can access any of the constants defined in ConversionFactors

   public static double poundsToGrams(double pounds) {
      return pounds*POUND_TO_GRAM;
   }

   // Plus the rest of the class definition...
}
```

Now you can access any of the static members of the ConversionFactors class using their unqualified names from any source file. All that is necessary is the import statement for the static members of the class. Alternatively, you could just import the static members you want to use. For example, you could use the following import statement if you just wanted to use the constant with the name POUND_TO_GRAM:

```
import static conversions.ConversionFactors.POUND_TO_GRAM;
```

Let's see it working in an example.

Try It Out   Importing Constants into a Program

Save the `ConversionFactors` class definition `ConversionFactors.java` in a directory with the name `conversions`. Here's a simple class that uses the constants defined in the utility class `ConversionFactors`:

```
import static conversions.ConversionFactors.*;    // Import static members

public class TryConversions {
  public static double poundsToGrams(double pounds) {
    return pounds*POUND_TO_GRAM;
  }

  public static double inchesToMillimeters(double inches) {
    return inches*INCH_TO_MM;
  }

  public static void main(String args[]) {
    int myWeightInPounds = 180;
    int myHeightInInches = 75;
    System.out.println("My weight in pounds: " +myWeightInPounds +
                    " \t-in grams: "+ (int)poundsToGrams(myWeightInPounds));
    System.out.println("My height in inches: " +myHeightInInches +
            " \t-in millimeters: "+ (int)inchesToMillimeters(myHeightInInches));
  }
}
```

Save the `TryConversions.java` file in the `TryConversions` directory. Don't forget that you must include the path to your conversions package when you compile this program. If the `conversions` directory is a subdirectory of `C:\MyPackages`, the command to compile the program with `TryConversions` as the current directory would be:

```
javac -classpath .:C:\MyPackages TryConversions.java
```

When you compile and execute this example, you should see the following output:

```
My weight in pounds: 180      -in grams: 81646
My height in inches: 75       -in millimeters: 1905
```

How It Works

The fact that you have used only static methods to access the constants from the utility class is unimportant — it's just to keep the example simple. They are equally accessible from instance methods in a class.

The two conversion methods use the conversion factors defined in the `ConversionFactors` class. Because you have imported the static fields from the `ConversionFactors` class in the `conversions` package into the `TryConversion.java` source file, you can use the unqualified names to refer to the constants.

Interfaces Declaring Methods

The primary use for an interface is to define the external form of a set of methods that represent a particular functionality. Let's consider an example. Suppose that you want to define an interface declaring a set of methods to be used for conversions between metric and imperial measurements. You could define such an interface like this:

```
public interface Conversions {
   double inchesToMillimeters (double inches);
   double ouncesToGrams(double ounces);
   double poundsToGrams(double pounds);
   double hpToWatts(double hp);
   double wattsToHP(double watts);
}
```

This interface declares five methods to perform conversions. Every method declared in the interface must have a definition within the class that implements the interface if you are going to create objects of the class. A class that implements this interface would look like this:

```
public class MyClass implements Conversions {
   // Implementations for the methods in the Conversions interface
   // Definitions for the other class members...
}
```

Since the methods in an interface are, by definition, public, you must use the public keyword when you define them in your class—otherwise, your code will not compile. The implementation of an interface method in a class must not have an access specifier that is more restrictive than that implicit in the abstract method declaration, and you can't get less restrictive than `public`.

A class can implement more than one interface. In this case, you write the names of all the interfaces that the class implements separated by commas following the `implements` keyword. Here's an example:

```
public class MyClass implements Conversions, Definitions, Detections {
   // Definition of the class including implementation of interface methods
}
```

This class implements three interfaces with the names `Conversions`, `Definitions`, and `Detections`. The class body will contain definitions for the methods declared in all three interfaces.

Try It Out   Implementing an Interface

You can use the `Conversions` interface in a modified version of the previous example. Redefine the `TryConversions` class in the `TryConversions.java` source file as follows:

```
import static conversions.ConversionFactors.*;   // Import static members

public class TryConversions implements Conversions {
  public double wattsToHP (double watts) {
    return watts*WATT_TO_HP;
  }
  public double hpToWatts (double hp) {
    return hp*HP_TO_WATT;
  }
```

```
    public double ouncesToGrams(double ounces) {
      return ounces*OUNCE_TO_GRAM;
    }

    public double poundsToGrams(double pounds) {
      return pounds*POUND_TO_GRAM;
    }

    public double inchesToMillimeters(double inches) {
      return inches*INCH_TO_MM;
    }

    public static void main(String args[]) {
      int myWeightInPounds = 180;
      int myHeightInInches = 75;

      TryConversions converter = new TryConversions();
      System.out.println("My weight in pounds: " +myWeightInPounds +
        " \t-in grams: "+ (int)converter.poundsToGrams(myWeightInPounds));
      System.out.println("My height in inches: " + myHeightInInches
                    + " \t-in millimeters: "
                    + (int)converter.inchesToMillimeters(myHeightInInches));
    }
  }
```

Save the file in a new directory, `TryConversion2`, and add a source file containing the definition for the `Conversions` interface to the same directory. You name a file containing an interface definition in a similar way to that of a class — the file name should be the same as the interface name, with the extension `.java`. Thus, the source file containing the `Conversions` interface definition will be `Conversions.java`.

How It Works

The methods you were using in the original definition of the class are now not declared as `static`. Since interface methods are by definition instance methods, you cannot declare them as static in the class that implements the interface. As the methods are now instance methods, you have to create a `TryConversions` object, `converter`, to call them.

Of course, in this particular instance, statically importing the constants that are used by the interface method implementations is a clumsy way of doing things. Since the constants are clearly related to the methods, it would probably be better to define all the constants in the `Conversions` interface in addition to the method declarations.

Of course, you don't *have to* implement every method in the interface, but there are some consequences if you don't.

A Partial Interface Implementation

You can omit the implementation of one or more of the methods from an interface in a class that implements the interface, but in this case the class inherits some abstract methods from the interface so you would need to declare the class itself as `abstract`:

```
import static conversions.ConversionFactors.INCH_TO_MM;
import static conversions.ConversionFactors.OUNCE_TO_GRAM;

public abstract class MyClass implements Conversions {
  // Implementation of two of the methods in the interface
  public double inchesToMillimeters(double inches) {
    return inches*INCH_TO_MM;
  }

  public double ouncesToGrams(double ounces) {
    return ounces*OUNCE_TO_GRAM;
  }

  // Definition of the rest of the class...
}
```

You cannot create objects of type `MyClass`. To arrive at a useful class, you must define a subclass of `MyClass` that implements the remaining methods in the interface. The declaration of the class as `abstract` is mandatory when you don't implement all of the methods that are declared in an interface. The compiler will complain if you forget to do this.

Now that you know how to write the code to implement an interface, you can tie up a loose end that was left earlier in this chapter. I mentioned that you need to implement the interface `Cloneable` to use the inherited method `clone()`. In fact this interface is empty with no methods or constants, so all you need to do to implement it in a class is to specify that the class in question implements it. This means that you just need to write something like:

```
public MyClass implements Cloneable {
  // Detail of the class...
}
```

The sole purpose of the `Cloneable` interface is to act as a flag signaling that you are prepared to allow objects of your class to be cloned. Even though you have defined a public `clone()` method in your class, the compiler will not permit the `clone()` method to be called for objects of your class type unless you also specify that your class implements `Cloneable`.

Extending Interfaces

You can define one interface based on another by using the keyword `extends` to identify the base interface name. This is essentially the same form as you use to derive one class from another. The interface doing the extending acquires all the methods and constants from the interface it extends. For example, the interface `Conversions` would perhaps be more useful if it contained the constants that the original interface `ConversionFactors` contained. This would obviate the need for a separate class containing the constants, so there would be no need for the static import statement.

You could do this by defining the interface `Conversions` as follows:

```
public interface Conversions extends ConversionFactors {
  double inchesToMillimeters (double inches);
  double ouncesToGrams(double ounces);
```

```
    double poundsToGrams(double pounds);
    double hpToWatts(double hp);
    double wattsToHP(double watts);
}
```

Now the interface `Conversions` also contains the members of the interface `ConversionFactors`. Any class implementing the `Conversions` interface will have the constants from `ConversionFactors` available to implement the methods. Analogous to the idea of a superclass, the interface `ConversionFactors` is referred to as a **super-interface** of the interface `Conversions`.

Of course, since the constants and the methods involved in conversion operations are closely related, it would have been much better to put them all in a single interface definition. But then it wouldn't demonstrate one interface extending another.

Interfaces and Multiple Inheritance

Unlike a class, which can extend only one other class, an interface can extend any number of other interfaces. To define an interface that inherits the members of several other interfaces, you specify the names of the interfaces separated by commas following the keyword `extends`. For example:

```
public interface MyInterface extends HisInterface, HerInterface {
    // Interface members - constants and abstract methods...
}
```

Now `MyInterface` will inherit all the methods and constants that are members of `HisInterface` and `HerInterface`. This is described as **multiple inheritance**. In Java, classes do not support multiple inheritance, only interfaces do.

Some care is necessary when you use this capability. If two or more super-interfaces declare a method with the same signature — that is, with identical names and parameters — the method must have the same return type in all the interfaces that declare it. If they don't, the compiler will report an error. This is because it would be impossible for a class to implement both methods, as they have the same signature. If the method is declared identically in all the interfaces that declare it, then a single definition in the class will satisfy all the interfaces. As I said in the previous chapter, every method in a class must have a unique signature, and the return type is not part of it.

Using Interfaces

What you have seen up to now has primarily illustrated the mechanics of creating an interface and incorporating it into a class. The really interesting question is — what should you use interfaces for?

An interface that declares methods defines a standard set of operations. Different classes can add such a standard interface by implementing it. Thus, objects of a number of different class types can share a common set of operations. Of course, a given operation in one class may be implemented quite differently from how it is implemented in another class. But the way in which you invoke the operation is the same for objects of all class types that implement the interface. For this reason it is often said that an interface defines a **contract** for a set of operations.

I hinted at the third and perhaps most important use of interfaces at the beginning of this discussion. An interface defines a type, so you can expedite polymorphism across a set of classes that implement the same interface. This is an extremely useful and powerful facility. Let's have a look at how this works.

Interfaces and Polymorphism

You can't create objects of an interface type, but you can create a variable of an interface type. For example:

```
Conversions converter = null;        // Variable of the Conversions interface type
```

If you can't create objects of type `Conversions`, what good is it? Well, you use it to store a reference to an object of any class type that implements `Conversions`. This means that you can use this variable to call the methods declared in the `Conversions` interface polymorphically. The `Conversions` interface is not a good example to show how this works. Let's consider a real-world parallel that I can use to better demonstrate this idea, that of home audio/visual equipment and a remote control. I'm grateful to John Ganter who suggested this idea to me after reading a previous edition of this book.

You almost certainly have a TV, a hi-fi, a VCR, and maybe a DVD player around your home, and each of them will have its own remote control. All the remote controls will probably have some common subset of buttons — power on/off, volume up, volume down, mute, and so on. Once you have more than four or so remotes cluttering the place up, you might consider one of those fancy universal remote control devices to replace them — sort of a single definition of a remote control, to suit all equipment.

A universal remote has a lot of similarities to an interface. By itself a universal remote does nothing. It defines a set of buttons for standard operations, but the operation of each button must be programmed specifically to suit each kind of device that you want to control. You can represent the TV, VCR, DVD, and so on by classes, each of which will make use of the same remote control interface — the set of buttons if you like — but each in a different way. Even though it uses the same button on the remote, Power On for the TV, for example, is quite different from Power On for the VCR. Let's see how that might look in a concrete example.

Try It Out   Defining Interfaces

Here's how you might define an interface to model a simple universal remote:

```
public interface RemoteControl {
   boolean powerOnOff();                  // Returns new state, on = true
   int volumeUp(int increment);           // Returns new volume level
   int volumeDown(int decrement);         // Returns new volume level
   void mute();                           // Mutes sound output
   int setChannel(int channel);           // Set the channel number and return it
   int channelUp();                       // Returns new channel number
   int channelDown();                     // Returns new channel number
}
```

The methods declared here in the `RemoteControl` interface should be self-explanatory. I have included just a few of the many possible remote operations here to conserve space in the book. You could add more if you want. You could have separate power on and power off methods, for example, tone controls, and so on. There is no definition for any of these methods here. Methods declared in an interface are always `abstract` — by definition. Nor is there an access attribute for any of them. Methods declared in an interface are always `public` by default.

Now any class that requires the use of the functionality provided by a `RemoteControl` just has to declare that it implements the interface and include the definitions for each of the methods in the interface. For example, here's the TV:

```java
import static java.lang.Math.max;
import static java.lang.Math.min;

public class TV implements RemoteControl {
  public TV(String make, int screensize) {
    this.make = make;
    this.screensize = screensize;
    // In practice you would probably have more
    // arguments to set the max and min channel
    // and volume here plus other characteristics for a particular TV.
  }

  public boolean powerOnOff() {
    power = !power;
    System.out.println(make + " "+ screensize + " inch TV power "
                    + (power ? "on.":"off."));
    return power;
  }

  public int volumeUp(int increment) {
    if(!power) {                        // If the power is off
      return 0;                         // Nothing works
    }

    // Set volume - must not be greater than the maximum
    volume += increment;
    volume = min(volume, MAX_VOLUME);
    System.out.println(make + " "+ screensize + " inch TV volume level: "
                    + volume);
    return volume;
  }

  public int volumeDown(int decrement) {
    if(!power) {                        // If the power is off
      return 0;                         // Nothing works
    }

    // Set volume - must not be less than the minimum
    volume -= decrement;
    volume = max(volume, MIN_VOLUME);
    System.out.println(make + " "+ screensize + " inch TV volume level: "
                    + volume);
    return volume;
  }

  public void mute() {
    if(!power) {                        // If the power is off
      return;                           // Nothing works
    }

    volume = MIN_VOLUME;
    System.out.println(make + " "+ screensize + " inch TV volume level: "
                    + volume);
  }
```

```java
    public int setChannel(int newChannel) {
        if(!power) {                        // If the power is off
          return 0;                         // Nothing works
        }

        // Channel must be from MIN_CHANNEL to MAX_CHANNEL
        if(newChannel>=MIN_CHANNEL && newChannel<=MAX_CHANNEL)
          channel = newChannel;
        System.out.println(make + " "+ screensize + " inch TV tuned to channel: "
                        + channel);
        return channel;
    }

    public int channelUp() {
        if(!power) {                        // If the power is off
          return 0;                         // Nothing works
        }

        // Wrap channel up to MIN_CHANNEL when MAX_CHANNEL is reached
        channel = channel<MAX_CHANNEL ? ++channel : MIN_CHANNEL;
        System.out.println(make + " "+ screensize + " inch TV tuned to channel: "
                        + channel);
        return channel;
    }

    public int channelDown() {
        if(!power)   {                      // If the power is off
          return 0;                         // Nothing works
        }

        // Wrap channel down to MAX_CHANNEL when MIN_CHANNEL is reached
        channel = channel>MIN_CHANNEL ? --channel : MAX_CHANNEL;
        System.out.println(make + " "+ screensize + " inch TV tuned to channel: "
                        + channel);
        return channel;
    }

    private String make = null;
    private int screensize = 0;
    private boolean power = false;

    private int MIN_VOLUME = 0;
    private int MAX_VOLUME = 100;
    private int volume = MIN_VOLUME;

    private int MIN_CHANNEL = 0;
    private int MAX_CHANNEL = 999;
    private int channel = 0;
}
```

This class implements all the methods declared in the RemoteControl interface, and each method outputs a message to the command line so you'll know when it is called. Of course, if you omitted any of the interface method definitions in the class, the class would be abstract and you would have to declare it as such.

A VCR class might also implement RemoteControl:

```java
import static java.lang.Math.max;
import static java.lang.Math.min;

public class VCR implements RemoteControl {
  public VCR(String make) {
    this.make = make;
  }

  public boolean powerOnOff() {
    power = !power;
    System.out.println(make + " VCR power "+ (power ? "on.":"off."));
    return power;
  }

  public int volumeUp(int increment) {
     if(!power) {                        // If the power is off
       return 0;                         // Nothing works
  }

     // Set volume - must not be greater than the maximum
     volume += increment;
     volume = min(volume, MAX_VOLUME);
     System.out.println(make + " VCR volume level: "+ volume);
     return volume;
  }

  public int volumeDown(int decrement) {
    if(!power) {                         // If the power is off
      return 0;                          // Nothing works
    }

     // Set volume - must not be less than the minimum
     volume -= decrement;
     volume = max(volume, MIN_VOLUME);
     System.out.println(make + " VCR volume level: "+ volume);
     return volume;
  }

  public void mute() {
    if(!power) {                         // If the power is off
      return;                            // Nothing works
    }

     volume = MIN_VOLUME;
     System.out.println(make + " VCR volume level: "+ volume);
  }

  public int setChannel(int newChannel) {
    if(!power) {                         // If the power is off
      return 0;                          // Nothing works
    }
```

```
        // Channel must be from MIN_CHANNEL to MAX_CHANNEL
        if(newChannel>=MIN_CHANNEL && newChannel<=MAX_CHANNEL) {
          channel = newChannel;
        }
        System.out.println(make + " VCR tuned to channel: "+ channel);
        return channel;
      }

      public int channelUp() {
        if(!power) {                          // If the power is off
          return 0;                           // Nothing works
        }

        // Wrap channel round to MIN_CHANNEL when MAX_CHANNEL is reached
        channel = channel<MAX_CHANNEL ? ++channel : MIN_CHANNEL;
        System.out.println(make + " VCR tuned to channel: "+ channel);
        return channel;
      }

      public int channelDown() {
        if(!power) {                          // If the power is off
          return 0;                           // Nothing works
        }

        // Wrap channel round to MAX_CHANNEL when MIN_CHANNEL is reached
        channel = channel>MIN_CHANNEL ? --channel : MAX_CHANNEL;
        System.out.println(make + " VCR tuned to channel: "+ channel);
        return channel;
      }

      private String make = null;
      private boolean power = false;

      private int MIN_VOLUME = 0;
      private int MAX_VOLUME = 100;
      private int volume = MIN_VOLUME;

      private int MIN_CHANNEL = 0;
      private int MAX_CHANNEL = 99;
      private int channel = 0;
    }
```

Of course, you could continue and define classes for other kinds of devices that used the remote, but these two are sufficient to demonstrate the principle.

Let's see how you can use the RemoteControl interface and these two classes in a working example.

Try It Out   Polymorphism Using an Interface Type

You want to demonstrate polymorphic behavior with these classes. By introducing a bit of "randomness" into the example, you can avoid having any prior knowledge of the objects involved. Here's the class to operate both TV and VCR objects via a variable of type RemoteControl:

```
import static java.lang.Math.random;

public class TryRemoteControl {
  public static void main(String args[]) {
    RemoteControl remote = null;

    // You will create five objects to operate using our remote
    for(int i = 0 ; i<5 ; i++) {
      // Now create either a TV or a VCR at random
      if(random()<0.5)
        // Random choice of TV make and screen size
        remote = new TV(random()<0.5 ? "Sony" : "Hitachi",
                        random()<0.5 ? 32 : 28);
      else // Random choice of VCR
        remote = new VCR(random()<0.5 ? "Panasonic": "JVC");

      // Now operate it, whatever it is
      remote.powerOnOff();             // Switch it on
      remote.channelUp();              // Set the next channel up
      remote.volumeUp(10);             // Turn up the sound
    }
  }
}
```

This should be in the same directory as the source files for the other two classes and the interface. When you compile and run this, you should see output recording a random selection of five TV and VCR objects operated by the RemoteControl variable. I got:

```
Sony 28 inch TV power on.
Sony 28 inch TV tuned to channel: 1
Sony 28 inch TV volume level: 10
Panasonic VCR power on.
Panasonic VCR tuned to channel: 1
Panasonic VCR volume level: 10
Sony 32 inch TV power on.
Sony 32 inch TV tuned to channel: 1
Sony 32 inch TV volume level: 10
JVC VCR power on.
JVC VCR tuned to channel: 1
JVC VCR volume level: 10
Sony 28 inch TV power on.
Sony 28 inch TV tuned to channel: 1
Sony 28 inch TV volume level: 10
```

How It Works

The variable remote is of type RemoteControl so you can use it to store a reference to any class object that implements the RemoteControl interface. Within the for loop, you create either a TV or a VCR object at random. The TV or VCR object will be of a randomly chosen make, and any TV object will be either 28 inches or 32 inches — again chosen at random. The object that is created is then operated through remote by calling its powerOnOff(), channelUp(), and volumeUp() methods. Since the type of the object is determined at run time, and at random, the output demonstrates you are clearly seeing polymorphism in action here through a variable of an interface type.

Using Multiple Interfaces

Of course, a `RemoteControl` object in the previous example can be used to call only the methods that are declared in the interface. If a class implements some other interface besides `RemoteControl`, then to call the methods declared in the second interface you would need either to use a variable of that interface type to store the object reference or to cast the object reference to its actual class type. Suppose you have a class defined as:

```
public MyClass implements RemoteControl, AbsoluteControl {
    // Class definition including methods from both interfaces...
}
```

Since this class implements `RemoteControl` and `AbsoluteControl`, you can store an object of type `MyClass` in a variable of either interface type. For example:

```
AbsoluteControl ac = new MyClass();
```

Now you can use the variable `ac` to call methods declared in the `AbsoluteControl` interface. However, you cannot call the methods declared in the `RemoteControl` interface using `ac`, even though the object reference that it holds has these methods. One possibility is to cast the reference to the original class type, like this:

```
((MyClass)ac).powerOnOff();
```

Since you cast the reference to type `MyClass`, you can call any of the methods defined in that class. You can't get polymorphic behavior like this though. The compiler will determine the method that is called when the code is compiled. To call the methods in the `RemoteControl` interface polymorphically, you would have to have the reference stored as that type. Provided you know that the object is of a class type that implements the `RemoteControl` interface, you can get from the reference store in the variable `ac` to a reference of type `RemoteControl`. Like this, for example:

```
if(ac instanceof RemoteControl)
    ((RemoteControl)ac).mute();
```

Even though the interfaces `RemoteControl` and `AbsoluteControl` are unrelated, you can cast the reference in `ac` to type `RemoteControl`. This is possible because the object that is referenced by `ac` is actually of type `MyClass`, which happens to implement both interfaces and therefore incorporates both interface types.

If you got a bit lost in this last section don't worry about it. You won't need this level of knowledge about interfaces very often.

Method Parameters of Interface Types

Of course, you can specify that a parameter to a method is of an interface type. This has a special significance in that a reference to an object of any type can be passed as an argument as long as the object type implements the interface. By specifying a parameter as an interface type you are implying that the method is interested only in the interface methods. As long as an object is of a type that implements those methods, it is acceptable as an argument.

This technique of making a parameter an interface type is used extensively within the class libraries. The `String`, `StringBuilder`, and `StringBuffer` classes (plus the `CharBuffer` class that you'll meet later in the book) all implement the `CharSequence` interface. You'll see lots of class methods that have a parameter of type `CharSequence`, in which case such methods will accept references to any of the class types I've mentioned as arguments. For example, the `StringBuilder` and `StringBuffer` classes both have constructors with a parameter of type `CharSequence`. You can therefore create new objects of these two class types from any of the four classes that implement the interface.

Nesting Classes in an Interface Definition

You can put the definition of a class inside the definition of an interface. The class will be an inner class to the interface. An inner class to an interface will be `static` and `public` by default. The code structure would be like this:

```
interface Port {
   // Methods & Constants declared in the interface...

   class Info {
      // Definition of the class...
   }
}
```

This declares the interface `Port` with an inner class `Info`. Objects of the inner class would be of type `Port.Info`. You might create one with a statement like this:

```
Port.Info info = new Port.Info();
```

The standard class library includes a number of interfaces with inner classes, including one with the name `Port` (in the `javax.sound.sampled` package) that has an inner class with the name `Info`, although the `Info` class does not have the default constructor that I have used in the illustration here. The circumstances where you might define a class as an inner class to an interface would be when objects of the inner class type have a strong logical association with the interface.

A class that implements the interface would have no direct connection with the inner class to the interface — it would just need to implement the methods declared by the interface, but it is highly likely it would make use of objects of the inner class type.

Interfaces and the Real World

An interface type is sometimes used to reference an object that encapsulates something that exists outside of Java, such as a particular physical device. This is done when the external device does not require methods implemented in Java code because all the function is provided externally. The interface method declarations just identify the mechanism for operating on the external object.

The example of the `Port` interface in the library is exactly that. A reference of type `Port` refers to an object that is a physical port on a sound card, such as that for the speaker or the microphone. The inner class, `Port.Info`, defines objects that encapsulate data to define a particular port. You can't create a `Port` object directly since there is no class of type `Port`. Indeed, it doesn't necessarily make sense to do so since your system may not have any ports. Assuming your PC has sound ports, you obtain a reference of type `Port` to an object that encapsulates a real port, such as the microphone, by calling a static method defined in another class. The argument to the method would be a reference to an object of type `Port.Info` specifying the kind of port that you want. All of the methods defined in the `Port` interface would correspond to methods written in native machine code that would operate on the port. To call them you just use the `Port` reference that you have obtained.

Anonymous Classes

There are occasions where you need to define a class for which you will only ever want to define one object in your program, and the only use for the object is to pass it directly as an argument to a method. In this case, as long as your class extends an existing class, or implements an interface, you have the option of defining the class as an **anonymous class.** The definition for an anonymous class appears in the new expression, in the statement where you create and use the object of the class, so that there is no necessity to provide a name for the class.

I will illustrate how this is done using an example. Suppose you want to define an object of a class that implements the interface `ActionListener` for one-time use. You could do this as follows:

```
pickButton.addActionListener(new ActionListener() {
                    // Code to define the class
                    // that implements the ActionListener interface
                }
            );
```

The class definition appears in the new expression that creates the argument to the `addActionListener()` method. This method requires a reference of type `ActionListener` — in other words, a reference to a class that implements the `ActionListener` interface. The parentheses following the name of the interface indicate you are creating an object reference of this type, and the details of the class definition appear between the parentheses. The anonymous class can include data members as well as methods, but obviously not constructors because the class has no name. Here, all the methods declared in the `ActionListener` interface would need to be defined. You'll be using this approach in practice when you are implementing window-based applications later in the book.

If the anonymous class extends an existing class, the syntax is much the same. In this case, you are calling a constructor for the base class and, if this is not a default constructor, you can pass arguments to it by specifying them between the parentheses following the base class name. The definition of the anonymous class must appear between braces, just as in the previous example.

An anonymous class can be convenient where the class definition is short and simple. You shouldn't use the approach to define classes of any complexity as it will make the code very difficult to understand.

Summary

You should now understand polymorphism and how to apply it. You will find that this technique can be utilized to considerable advantage in the majority of your Java programs. It will certainly appear in many of the examples in the remaining chapters.

The important points I have covered in this chapter are:

❏ An abstract method is a method that has no body defined for it and is declared using the key-word `abstract`.

❏ An abstract class is a class that contains one or more abstract methods. It must be defined with the attribute `abstract`.

❏ You can define one class based on another. This is called class derivation or inheritance. The base class is called a superclass, and the derived class is called a subclass. A superclass can also be a subclass of another superclass.

❏ A subclass inherits certain members of its superclass. An inherited member of a class can be referenced and used as though it were declared as a normal member of the class.

❏ A subclass does not inherit the superclass constructors.

❏ The `private` members of a superclass are not inherited in a subclass. If the subclass is not in the same package as the superclass, then members of the superclass that do not have an access attribute are not inherited.

❏ The first statement in the body of a constructor for a subclass should call a constructor for the superclass. If it does not, the compiler will insert a call for the default constructor for the superclass.

❏ A subclass can re-implement, or overload, the methods inherited from its superclass. If two or more subclasses, with a common base class, re-implement a common set of methods, these methods can be selected for execution at run time.

❏ A variable of a superclass can point to an object of any of its subclasses. Such a variable can then be used to execute the subclass methods inherited from the superclass.

❏ A subclass of an abstract class must also be declared as `abstract` if it does not provide definitions for all of the abstract methods inherited from its superclass.

❏ You can import the static members of a class that is defined in a named package to allow the static members to be referenced by their unqualified names.

❏ An enumeration type is a specialized form of class, and the enumeration constants that you define are instances of the enumeration class type.

❏ A class defined inside another class is called a nested class or inner class. An inner class may itself contain inner classes.

❏ An interface can contain constants, abstract methods, and inner classes.

❏ A class can implement one or more interfaces by declaring them in the class definition and including the code to implement each of the interface methods.

❏ A class that does not define all the methods for an interface it implements must be declared as `abstract`.

❏ If several classes implement a common interface, the methods declared as members of the interface can be executed polymorphically.

Exercises

You can download the source code for the examples in the book and the solutions to the following exercises from `http://www.wrox.com`.

1. Define an abstract base class `Shape` that includes `protected` data members for the (x, y) position of a shape, a `public` method to move a shape, and a `public abstract` method `show()` to output a shape. Derive subclasses for lines, circles, and rectangles. Also, define the class `PolyLine` that you saw in this chapter with `Shape` as its base class. You can represent a line as two points, a circle as a center and a radius, and a rectangle as two points on diagonally opposite corners. Implement the `toString()` method for each class. Test the classes by selecting ten random objects of the derived classes, and then invoking the `show()` method for each. Use the `toString()` methods in the derived classes.

2. Define a class, `ShapeList`, that can store an arbitrary collection of any objects of subclasses of the `Shape` class.

3. Implement the classes for shapes using an interface for the common methods, rather than inheritance from the superclass, while still keeping `Shape` as a base class.

4. Extend the `LinkedList` class that you defined in this chapter so that it supports traversing the list backwards as well as forwards.

5. Add methods to the class `LinkedList` to insert and delete elements at the current position.

6. Implement a method in the `LinkedList` class to insert an object following an object passed as an argument. (Assume the objects stored in the list implement an `equals()` method that compares the `This` object with an object passed as an argument and returns `true` if they are equal.)

Exceptions

Java uses exceptions as a way of signaling serious problems when you execute a program. The standard classes use them extensively. Since they arise in your Java programs when things go wrong, and if something can go wrong in your code, sooner or later it will, they are a very basic consideration when you are designing and writing your programs.

The reason I've been sidestepping the question of exceptions for the past six chapters is that you first needed to understand classes and inheritance before you could understand what an exception is and appreciate what happens when an exception occurs. Now that you have a good grasp of these topics I can delve into how to use and deal with exceptions in a program.

In this chapter you'll learn:

❑ What an exception is

❑ How you handle exceptions in your programs

❑ The standard exceptions in Java

❑ How to guarantee that a particular block of code in a method will always be executed

❑ How to define and use your own types of exceptions

❑ How to throw exceptions in your programs

The Idea Behind Exceptions

An exception usually signals an error and is so called because errors in your Java programs are bound to be the exception rather than the rule — by definition! An exception doesn't always indicate an error though — it can also signal some particularly unusual event in your program that deserves special attention.

If you try to deal with the myriad and often highly unusual error conditions that might arise in the midst of the code that deals with the normal operation of the program, your program structure will soon become very complicated and difficult to understand. One major benefit of having an error signaled by an exception is that it separates the code that deals with errors from the code that is executed when things are moving along smoothly. Another positive aspect of exceptions is that they provide a way of enforcing a response to particular errors. With many kinds of exceptions, you must include code in your program to deal with them; otherwise, your code will not compile.

One important idea to grasp is that not all errors in your programs need to be signaled by exceptions. Exceptions should be reserved for the unusual or catastrophic situations that can arise. A user entering incorrect input to your program for instance is a normal event and should be handled without recourse to exceptions. The reason for this is that dealing with exceptions involves quite a lot of processing over-head, so if your program is handling exceptions a lot of the time it will be a lot slower than it needs to be.

An exception in Java is an object that's created when an abnormal situation arises in your program. This exception object has fields that store information about the nature of the problem. The exception is said to be *thrown* — that is, the object identifying the exceptional circumstance is tossed as an argument to a specific piece of program code that has been written specifically to deal with that kind of problem. The code receiving the exception object as a parameter is said to *catch* it.

The situations that cause exceptions are quite diverse, but they fall into four broad categories:

Code or data errors	For example, you attempt an invalid cast of an object, you try to use an array index that's outside the limits for the array, or an integer arithmetic expression has a zero divisor.
Standard method exceptions	For example, if you use the `substring()` method in the `String` class, it can throw a `StringIndexOutOfBoundsException` exception.
Throwing your own exceptions	You'll see later in this chapter how you can throw a few of your own when you need to.
Java errors	These can be due to errors in executing the Java Virtual Machine, which runs your compiled program, but usually arise as a consequence of an error in your program.

Before you look at how you make provision in your programs for dealing with exceptions, you should understand what specific classes of exceptions could arise.

Types of Exceptions

An exception is always an object of some subclass of the standard class `Throwable`. This is true for exceptions that you define and throw yourself, as well as the standard exceptions that arise due to errors in your code. It's also true for exceptions that are thrown by methods in one or another of the standard packages.

Two direct subclasses of the class `Throwable` — the class `Error` and the class `Exception` — cover all the standard exceptions. Both these classes themselves have subclasses that identify specific exception conditions. Figure 7-1 shows the hierarchy to which these classes belong.

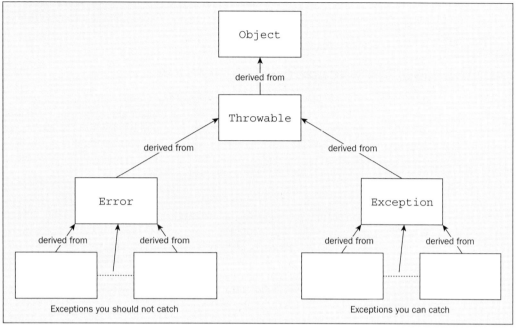

Figure 7-1

Error Exceptions

The exceptions that are defined by the Error class and its subclasses are characterized by the fact that they all represent conditions that you aren't expected to do anything about, so you aren't expected to catch them. Error has three direct subclasses — ThreadDeath, LinkageError, and VirtualMachineError:

❑ The first of these sounds the most serious, but in fact it isn't. A ThreadDeath exception is thrown whenever an executing thread is deliberately stopped, and for the thread to be destroyed properly, you should not catch this exception. In some circumstances you might want to catch it — for clean-up operations, for example — in which case you must be sure to rethrow the exception to allow the thread to die peacefully. When a ThreadDeath exception is thrown and not caught, it's the thread that ends, not the program. I will deal with threads in detail in Chapter 16.

❑ The LinkageError exception class has subclasses that record serious errors with the classes in your program. Incompatibilities between classes or attempting to create an object of a non-existent class type are the sorts of things that cause these exceptions to be thrown.

❑ The VirtualMachineError class has four subclasses that specify exceptions that will be thrown when a catastrophic failure of the Java Virtual Machine occurs. You aren't prohibited from trying to deal with these exceptions, but in general, there's little point in attempting to catch them.

The exceptions that correspond to objects of classes derived from LinkageError and VirtualMachineError are all the result of catastrophic events or conditions. You can do little or nothing to recover from them during the execution of the program. In these sorts of situations, all you

341

can usually do is read the error message that is generated by the exception being thrown and then, particularly in the case of a `LinkageError` exception, try to figure out what might be wrong with your code to cause the problem.

RuntimeException Exceptions

For almost all the exceptions that are represented by subclasses of the `Exception` class, you must include code in your programs to deal with them if your code may cause them to be thrown. If a method in your program has the potential to generate an exception of a type that has `Exception` as a superclass, you must either handle the exception within the method or register that your method may throw such an exception. If you don't, your program will not compile. You'll see in a moment how to handle exceptions and how to specify that a method can throw an exception.

One group of subclasses of `Exception` that is exempted from this is comprised of those derived from `RuntimeException`. The reason that `RuntimeException` exceptions are treated differently, and that the compiler allows you to ignore them, is that they generally arise because of serious errors in your code. In most cases you can do little to recover the situation. However, in some contexts for some of these exceptions, this is not always the case, and you may well want to include code to recognize them. Quite a lot of subclasses of `RuntimeException` are used to signal problems in various packages in the Java class library. Let's look at the exception classes that have `RuntimeException` as a base that are defined in the `java.lang` package.

The subclasses of `RuntimeException` defined in the standard package `java.lang` are:

Class Name	Exception Condition Represented
ArithmeticException	An invalid arithmetic condition has arisen, such as an attempt to divide an integer value by zero.
IndexOutOfBoundsException	You've attempted to use an index that is outside the bounds of the object it is applied to. This may be an array, a `String` object, or a `Vector` object. The `Vector` class is defined in the standard package `java.util`. You will be looking into the `Vector` class in Chapter 14.
NegativeArraySizeException	You tried to define an array with a negative dimension.
NullPointerException	You used an object variable containing `null`, when it should refer to an object for proper operation — for example, calling a method or accessing a data member.
ArrayStoreException	You've attempted to store an object in an array that isn't permitted for the array type.
ClassCastException	You've tried to cast an object to an invalid type — the object isn't of the class specified, nor is it a subclass or a superclass of the class specified.
IllegalArgumentException	You've passed an argument to a method that doesn't correspond with the parameter type.

Class Name	Exception Condition Represented
SecurityException	Your program has performed an illegal operation that is a security violation. This might be trying to read a file on the local machine from an applet.
IllegalMonitorStateException	A thread has tried to wait on the monitor for an object that the thread doesn't own. (You'll look into threads in Chapter 16.)
IllegalStateException	You tried to call a method at a time when it was not legal to do so.
UnsupportedOperationException	This is thrown if you request an operation to be carried out that is not supported.

In the normal course of events you shouldn't meet up with the last three of these. The ArithmeticException turns up quite easily in your programs, as does the IndexOutOfBoundsException. A mistake in a for loop limit will produce the latter. In fact there are two subclasses of IndexOutOfBoundsException that specify the type of exception thrown more precisely — ArrayIndexOutOfBoundsException and StringIndexOutOfBoundsException. A NullPointerException can also turn up relatively easily, as can ArrayStoreException, ClassCastException, and IllegalArgumentException, surprisingly enough. The last three here arise when you are using a base class variable to call methods for derived class objects. Explicit attempts to perform an incorrect cast, or store a reference of an incorrect type, or pass an argument of the wrong type to a method will all be picked up by the compiler. These exceptions can, therefore, arise only from using a variable of a base type to hold references to a derived class object.

The IllegalArgumentException class is a base class for two further exception classes, IllegalThreadStateException and NumberFormatException. The former arises when you attempt an operation that is illegal in the current thread state. The NumberFormatException exception is thrown by the valueOf() or decode() methods in the classes representing integers — that is, the classes Byte, Short, Integer, and Long. The parseXXX() methods in these classes can also throw this exception. The exception is thrown if the String object you pass as an argument to the conversion method is not a valid representation of an integer — if it contains invalid characters, for example. In this case a special return value cannot be used, so throwing an exception is a very convenient way to signal that the argument is invalid.

You'll be trying out some of the RuntimeException exceptions later in the chapter, as some of them are very easy to generate, but let's see what other sorts of exception classes have Exception as a base.

Other Subclasses of Exception

For all the other classes derived from the class Exception, the compiler will check that you've either handled the exception in a method where the exception may be thrown or that you've indicated that the method can throw such an exception. If you do neither, your code won't compile. You'll look more at how you ensure that the code does compile in the next two sections.

Apart from a few that have `RuntimeException` as a base, all exceptions thrown by methods in the Java class library are of a type that you must deal with. In Chapter 8 you will be looking at input and output where the code will be liberally sprinkled with provisions for exceptions being thrown.

> **You'll see later in this chapter that when you want to define your own exceptions, you do this by subclassing the** `Exception` **class. Wherever your exception can be thrown by a method, the compiler will verify either that it is caught in the method or that the method definition indicates that it can be thrown by the method, just as it does for the built-in exceptions.**

Dealing with Exceptions

As I discussed in the previous sections, if your code can throw exceptions other than those of type `Error` or type `RuntimeException` (you can assume that I generally include the subclasses when I talk about `Error` and `RuntimeException` exceptions), you must do something about it. Whenever you write code that can throw an exception, you have a choice. You can supply code within the method to deal with any exception that is thrown, or you can essentially ignore it by enabling the method containing the exception-throwing code to pass it on to the code that called the method.

Let's first see how you can pass an exception on.

Specifying the Exceptions a Method Can Throw

Suppose you have a method that can throw an exception that is neither a subclass of `RuntimeException` nor of `Error`. This could be an exception of type `IOException`, for example, which can be thrown if your method involves some file input or output operations. If the exception isn't caught and disposed of in the method, you must at least declare that the exception can be thrown. But how do you do that?

You do it simply by adding a `throws` clause in the definition of the method. Suppose you write a method that uses the methods from classes that support input/output that are defined in the package `java.io`. You'll see in the chapters devoted to I/O operations that some of these can throw exceptions represented by objects of classes `IOException` and `FileNotFoundException`. Neither of these is a subclass of `RuntimeException` or `Error`, so the possibility of an exception being thrown needs to be declared. Since the method can't handle any exceptions it might throw, for the simple reason that you don't know how to do it yet, it must be defined as:

```
double myMethod() throws IOException, FileNotFoundException {
  // Detail of the method code...
}
```

As the preceding fragment illustrates, to declare that your method can throw exceptions you just put the `throws` keyword after the parameter list for the method. Then add the list of classes for the exceptions that might be thrown, separated by commas. This has a knock-on effect — if another method calls this method, it too must take account of the exceptions this method can throw. After all, calling a method that can throw an exception is clearly code where an exception may be thrown. The calling method definition must either deal with the exceptions or declare that it can throw these exceptions as well. It's a simple choice. You either pass the buck or decide that the buck stops here. The compiler checks for this and your code will not compile if you don't do one or the other. The reasons for this will become obvious when you look at the way a Java program behaves when it encounters an exception.

Handling Exceptions

If you want to deal with the exceptions where they occur, you can include three kinds of code blocks in a method to handle them — try, catch, and finally blocks:

❑ A try block encloses code that may give rise to one or more exceptions. Code that can throw an exception that you want to catch must be in a try block.

❑ A catch block encloses code that is intended to handle exceptions of a particular type that may be thrown in the associated try block. I'll get to how a catch block is associated with a try block in a moment.

❑ The code in a finally block is always executed before the method ends, regardless of whether any exceptions are thrown in the try block.

Let's dig into the detail of try and catch blocks first and then come back to the application of a finally block a little later.

The try Block

When you want to catch an exception, the code in the method that might cause the exception to be thrown must be enclosed in a try block. Code that can cause exceptions need not be in a try block, but in this case, the method containing the code won't be able to catch any exceptions that are thrown and the method must declare that it can throw the types of exceptions that are not caught.

A try block is simply the keyword try, followed by braces enclosing the code that can throw the exception:

```
try {
   // Code that can throw one or more exceptions
}
```

Although I am discussing primarily exceptions that you must deal with here, a try block is also necessary if you want to catch exceptions of type Error or RuntimeException. When you come to a working example in a moment, you will use an exception type that you don't have to catch, simply because exceptions of this type are easy to generate.

The catch Block

You enclose the code to handle an exception of a given type in a catch block. The catch block must immediately follow the try block that contains the code that may throw that particular exception. A catch block consists of the keyword catch followed by a single parameter between parentheses that identifies the type of exception that the block is to deal with. This is followed by the code to handle the exception enclosed between braces:

```
try {
   // Code that can throw one or more exceptions

} catch(ArithmeticException e) {
   // Code to handle the exception
}
```

This `catch` block handles only `ArithmeticException` exceptions. This implies that this is the only kind of exception that can be thrown in the `try` block. If others can be thrown, this won't compile. I will come back to handling multiple exception types in a moment.

In general, the parameter for a `catch` block must be of type `Throwable` or one of the subclasses of the class `Throwable`. If the class that you specify as the parameter type has subclasses, the `catch` block will be expected to process exceptions of that class type, plus all subclasses of the class. If you specified the parameter to a `catch` block as type `RuntimeException`, for example, the code in the `catch` block would be invoked for exceptions defined by the class `RuntimeException`, or any of its subclasses.

You can see how this works with a simple example. It doesn't matter what the code does — the important thing is that it throws an exception you can catch.

Try It Out   Using a try and a catch Block

The following code is really just an exhaustive log of the program's execution:

```
public class TestTryCatch {
  public static void main(String[] args) {
     int i = 1;
     int j = 0;

     try {
       System.out.println("Try block entered " + "i = "+ i + " j = "+j);
       System.out.println(i/j);                   // Divide by 0 - exception thrown
       System.out.println("Ending try block");

     } catch(ArithmeticException e) {             // Catch the exception
       System.out.println("Arithmetic exception caught");
     }

     System.out.println("After try block");
     return;
   }
}
```

If you run the example, you should get the following output:

```
Try block entered i = 1 j = 0
Arithmetic exception caught
After try block
```

How It Works

The variable j is initialized to 0, so that the divide operation in the try block will throw an ArithmeticException exception. You must use the variable j with the value 0 here because the Java compiler will not allow you to explicitly divide by zero — that is, the expression i/0 will not compile. The first line in the try block will enable you to track when the try block is entered, and the second line will throw an exception. The third line can be executed only if the exception isn't thrown — which can't occur in this example.

This shows that when the exception is thrown, control transfers immediately to the first statement in the catch block. It's the evaluation of the expression that is the argument to the println() method that throws the exception, so the println() method never gets called. After the catch block has been executed, execution then continues with the statement following the catch block. The statements in the try block following the point where the exception occurred aren't executed. You could try running the example again after changing the value of j to 1 so that no exception is thrown. The output in this case will be:

```
Try block entered i = 1 j = 1
1
Ending try block
After try block
```

From this you can see that the entire try block is executed. Execution then continues with the statement after the catch block. Because no arithmetic exception was thrown, the code in the catch block isn't executed.

> You need to take care when adding try blocks to existing code. A try block is no different to any other block between braces when it comes to variable scope. Variables declared in a try block are available only until the closing brace for the block. It's easy to enclose the declaration of a variable in a try block, and, in doing so, inadvertently limit the scope of the variable and cause compiler errors.

The catch block itself is a separate scope from the try block. If you want the catch block to output information about objects or values that are set in the try block, make sure the variables are declared in an outer scope.

try catch Bonding

The try and catch blocks are bonded together. You must not separate them by putting statements between the two blocks, or even by putting braces around the try keyword and the try block itself. If you have a loop block that is also a try block, the catch block that follows is also part of the loop. You can see this with a variation of the previous example.

Try It Out   A Loop Block That Is a try Block

You can make j a loop control variable and count down so that eventually you get a zero divisor in the loop:

```
public class TestLoopTryCatch {
  public static void main(String[] args) {
```

```
         int i = 12;

     for(int j=3 ;j>=-1 ; j--)
       try {
          System.out.println("Try block entered " + "i = "+ i + " j = "+j);
          System.out.println(i/j);                // Divide by 0 - exception thrown
         System.out.println("Ending try block");

        } catch(ArithmeticException e) {          // Catch the exception
          System.out.println("Arithmetic exception caught");
        }

     System.out.println("After try block");
     return;
   }
 }
```

This will produce the following output:

```
Try block entered i = 12 j = 3
4
Ending try block
Try block entered i = 12 j = 2
6
Ending try block
Try block entered i = 12 j = 1
12
Ending try block
Try block entered i = 12 j = 0
Arithmetic exception caught
Try block entered i = 12 j = -1
-12
Ending try block
After try block
```

How It Works

The `try` and `catch` blocks are all part of the loop because the `catch` is inextricably bound to the `try`. You can see this from the output. On the fourth iteration, you get an exception thrown because `j` is 0. However, after the `catch` block is executed, you still get one more iteration with `j` having the value –1. Of course, it would be better programming style to include braces for the loop block that enclosed the `try`/`catch` combination, but then it would have been obvious that they were both in the loop and would not demonstrate the point of the example.

Even though the `try` and `catch` blocks are both within the `for` loop, they have separate scopes. Variables declared within the `try` block cease to exist when an exception is thrown. You can demonstrate that this is so by declaring an arbitrary variable—`k`, say—in the `try` block, and then adding a statement to output `k` in the `catch` block. Your code will not compile in this case.

Suppose you wanted the loop to end when an exception was thrown. You can easily arrange for this. Just put the whole loop in a `try` block, thus:

```
public static void main(String[] args) {
    int i = 12;
    try {
      System.out.println("Try block entered.");
      for(int j=3 ;j>=-1 ; j--) {
        System.out.println("Loop entered " + "i = "+ i + " j = "+j);
        System.out.println(i/j);          // Divide by 0 - exception thrown
      }
      System.out.println("Ending try block");

    } catch(ArithmeticException e) {     // Catch the exception
      System.out.println("Arithmetic exception caught");
    }

    System.out.println("After try block");
    return;
}
```

With this version of `main()`, the previous program will produce the following output:

```
Try block entered.
Loop entered i = 12 j = 3
4
Loop entered i = 12 j = 2
6
Loop entered i = 12 j = 1
12
Loop entered i = 12 j = 0
Arithmetic exception caught
After try block
```

Now, you no longer get the output for the last iteration because control passes to the `catch` block when the exception is thrown, and that is now outside the loop.

Multiple catch Blocks

If a `try` block can throw several different kinds of exception, you can put several `catch` blocks after the `try` block to handle them:

```
try {
  // Code that may throw exceptions

} catch(ArithmeticException e) {
  // Code for handling ArithmeticException exceptions
} catch(IndexOutOfBoundsException e) {
  // Code for handling IndexOutOfBoundsException exceptions
}
// Execution continues here...
```

Exceptions of type `ArithmeticException` will be caught by the first `catch` block, and exceptions of type `IndexOutOfBoundsException` will be caught by the second. Of course, if an `ArithmeticException` exception is thrown, only the code in that `catch` block will be executed. When it is complete, execution continues with the statement following the last `catch` block.

When you need to catch exceptions of several different types that may be thrown in a try block, the order of the catch blocks can be important. When an exception is thrown, it will be caught by the first catch block that has a parameter type that is the same as that of the exception, or a type that is a super-class of the type of the exception. An extreme case would be if you specified the catch block parameter as type Exception. This will catch any exception that is of type Exception, or of a class type that is derived from Exception. This includes virtually all the exceptions you are likely to meet in the normal course of events.

This has implications for multiple catch blocks relating to exception class types in a hierarchy. The catch blocks must be in sequence with the most derived type first, and the most basic type last. Otherwise, your code will not compile. The simple reason for this is that if a catch block for a given class type precedes a catch block for a type that is derived from the first, the second catch block can never be executed, and the compiler will detect that this is the case.

Suppose you have a catch block for exceptions of type ArithmeticException and another for excep-tions of type Exception as a catch-all. If you write them in the following sequence, exceptions of type ArithmeticException could never reach the second catch block because they will always be caught by the first:

```
// Invalid catch block sequence - won't compile!
try {
  // try block code

} catch(Exception e) {
  // Generic handling of exceptions
} catch(ArithmeticException e) {
  // Specialized handling for these exceptions
}
```

Of course, this won't get past the compiler — it would be flagged as an error.

To summarize — if you have catch blocks for several exception types in the same class hierarchy, you must put the catch blocks in order, starting with the lowest subclass first and then progressing to the highest superclass.

In principle, if you're only interested in generic exceptions, all the error handling code can be localized in one catch block for exceptions of the superclass type. However, in general it is more useful and better practice to have a catch block for each of the specific types of exceptions that a try block can throw.

The finally Block

The immediate nature of an exception being thrown means that execution of the try block code breaks off, regardless of the importance of the code that follows the point at which the exception was thrown. This introduces the possibility that the exception leaves things in an unsatisfactory state. You might have opened a file, for example, and because an exception was thrown, the code to close the file is not executed.

The finally block provides the means for you to clean up at the end of executing a try block. You use a finally block when you need to be sure that some particular code is run before a method returns, no matter what exceptions are thrown within the associated `try` block. A `finally` block is always executed, regardless of whether or not exceptions are thrown during the execution of the associated `try` block. If a file needs to be closed, or a critical resource released, you can guarantee that it will be done if the code to do it is put in a `finally` block.

The `finally` block has a very simple structure:

```
finally {
   // Clean-up code to be executed last
}
```

Just like a `catch` block, a `finally` block is associated with a particular `try` block, and it must be located immediately following any `catch` blocks for the `try` block. If there are no `catch` blocks, then you position the `finally` block immediately after the `try` block. If you don't do this, your program will not compile.

> **The primary purpose for the `try` block is to identify code that may result in an exception being thrown. However, you can use it to contain code that doesn't throw exceptions for the convenience of using a `finally` block. This can be useful when the code in the `try` block has several possible exit points — break or return statements, for example — but you always want to have a specific set of statements executed after the `try` block has been executed to make sure things are tidied up, such as closing any open files. You can put these in a `finally` block. Note: If a value is returned within a `finally` block, this return overrides any return statement executed in the `try` block.**

Structuring a Method

You've looked at the blocks you can include in the body of a method, but it may not always be obvious how they are combined. The first thing to get straight is that a `try` block plus any corresponding `catch` blocks and the `finally` block all bunch together in that order:

```
try {
   // Code that may throw exceptions...

} catch(ExceptionType1 e) {
   // Code to handle exceptions of type ExceptionType1 or subclass
} catch(ExceptionType2 e) {
   // Code to handle exceptions of type ExceptionType2 or subclass
... // more catch blocks if necessary
} finally {
   // Code always to be executed after try block code
}
```

You can't have just a `try` block by itself. Each `try` block must always be followed by at least one block that is either a `catch` block or a `finally` block.

You must not include other code between a `try` block and its `catch` blocks, or between the `catch` blocks and the `finally` block. You can have other code that doesn't throw exceptions after the `finally` block, and you can have multiple `try` blocks in a method. In this case, your method might be structured as shown in Figure 7-2.

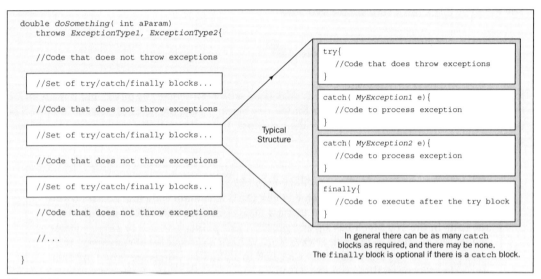

Figure 7-2

In many cases, a method will need only a single `try` block followed by all the `catch` blocks for the exceptions that need to be processed in the method, perhaps followed by a `finally` block. Java, however, gives you the flexibility to have as many `try` blocks as you want. This makes it possible for you to separate various operations in a method by putting each of them in their own `try` block—an exception thrown as a result of a problem with one operation does not prevent subsequent operations from being executed.

The `throws` clause that follows the parameter list for the method identifies exceptions that can be thrown in this method, but which aren't caught by any of the `catch` blocks within the method. You saw this earlier in this chapter. Exceptions that aren't caught can be thrown by code anywhere in the body of the method—in code not enclosed by a `try` block.

Execution Sequence

You saw how the sequence of execution proceeds with the simple case of a `try` block and a single `catch` block. You also need to understand the sequence in which code executes when you have the `try-catch-finally` combinations of blocks, when different exceptions are thrown. This is easiest to comprehend by considering an example. You can use the following code to create a range of exceptions and conditions.

Try It Out   Execution Sequence of a try Block

It will be convenient, in this example, to use an input statement to pause the program. The method you will use can throw an exception of a type defined in the `java.io` package. You'll start by importing the `java.io.IOException` class name into the source file. Give the class that contains `main()` the name

TryBlockTest. You'll define another method, `divide()`, in this class that will be called in `main()`. The overall structure of the `TryBlockTest` class source file will be:

```
import java.io.IOException;

public class TryBlockTest {
  public static void main(String[] args) {
    // Code for main()..
  }

  // Divide method
  public static int divide(int[] array, int index) {
    // Code for divide()...
  }
}
```

The idea behind the `divide()` method is to pass it an array and an index as arguments. By choosing the values in the array and the index value judiciously, you'll be able to cause exceptions of type `ArithmeticException` and `ArrayIndexOutOfBoundsException` to be thrown. You'll need a `try` block plus two `catch` blocks for the exceptions, and you'll throw in a `finally` block for good measure. Here's the code for `divide()`:

```
public static int divide(int[] array, int index) {
  try {
    System.out.println("\nFirst try block in divide() entered");
    array[index + 2] = array[index]/array[index + 1];
    System.out.println("Code at end of first try block in divide()");
    return array[index + 2];

  } catch(ArithmeticException e) {
    System.out.println("Arithmetic exception caught in divide()");
  } catch(ArrayIndexOutOfBoundsException e) {
    System.out.println("Index-out-of-bounds exception caught in divide()");
  } finally {
    System.out.println("finally block in divide()");
  }

  System.out.println("Executing code after try block in divide()");
  return array[index + 2];
}
```

You can define the `main()` method with the following code:

```
public static void main(String[] args) {
  int[] x = {10, 5, 0};                    // Array of three integers

  // This block only throws an exception if the divide() method does
  try {
    System.out.println("First try block in main() entered");
    System.out.println("result = " + divide(x,0));  // No error
    x[1] = 0;                                // Will cause a divide by zero
    System.out.println("result = " + divide(x,0));  // Arithmetic error
    x[1] = 1;                                // Reset to prevent divide by zero
    System.out.println("result = " + divide(x,1));  // Index error
```

```
    } catch(ArithmeticException e) {
      System.out.println("Arithmetic exception caught in main()");
    } catch(ArrayIndexOutOfBoundsException e) {
      System.out.println("Index-out-of-bounds exception caught in main()");
    }

    System.out.println("Outside first try block in main()");
    System.out.println("\nPress Enter to exit");

    // This try block is just to pause the program before returning
    try {
      System.out.println("In second try block in main()");
      System.in.read();                          // Pauses waiting for input...
      return;

    } catch(IOException e) {             // The read() method can throw exceptions
      System.out.println("I/O exception caught in main()");
    } finally {                                  // This will always be executed
      System.out.println("finally block for second try block in main()");
    }

    System.out.println("Code after second try block in main()");
  }
```

Because the read() method for the object in (this object represents the standard input stream and complements the out object, which is the standard output stream) can throw an I/O exception, it must be called in a try block and have an associated catch block, unless you choose to add a throws clause to the header line of main().

If you run the example, it will produce the following output:

```
First try block in main()entered

First try block in divide() entered
Code at end of first try block in divide()
finally block in divide()
result = 2

First try block in divide() entered
Arithmetic exception caught in divide()
finally block in divide()
Executing code after try block in divide()
result = 2

First try block in divide() entered
Index-out-of-bounds exception caught in divide
finally block in divide()
Executing code after try block in divide()
Index-out-of-bounds exception caught in main()
Outside first try block in main()

Press Enter to exit
In second try block in main()

finally block for second try block in main()
```

How It Works

All the try, catch, and finally blocks in the example have output statements so you can trace the sequence of execution.

Within the divide() method, the code in the try block can throw an exception of type ArithmeticException if the element array[index + 1] of the array passed to it is 0. It can also throw an ArrayIndexOutOfBoundsException exception in the try block if the index value passed to it is negative, or it results in index + 2 being beyond the array limits. Both these exceptions are caught by one or other of the catch blocks, so they will not be apparent in the calling method main().

Note, however, that the last statement in divide() can also throw an exception of type ArrayIndexOutOfBoundsException:

```
return array[index+2];
```

This statement is outside the try block, so the exception will not be caught. The exception will therefore be thrown by the method when it is called in main(). However, you aren't obliged to declare that the divide() method throws this exception because the ArrayIndexOutOfBoundsException class is a subclass of RuntimeException and is therefore exempted from the obligation to deal with it.

The main() method has two try blocks. The first try block encloses three calls to the divide() method. The first call will execute without error; the second call will cause an arithmetic exception in the method; and the third call will cause an index-out-of-bounds exception. There are two catch blocks for the first try block in main() to deal with these two potential exceptions.

The read() method in the second try block in main() can cause an I/O exception to be thrown. Since this is one of the exceptions that the compiler will check for, you must either put the statement that calls the read() method in a try block and have a catch block to deal with the exception or declare that main() throws the IOException exception. If you don't do one or the other, the program will not compile.

Using the read() method in this way has the effect of pausing the program until the Enter key is pressed. You'll be looking at read(), and other methods for I/O operations, in the next four chapters. The IOException class is in the package java.io, so you need the import statement for this class because you refer to it in the catch block using its unqualified name. Of course, if you referred to it as java.io.IOException, you would not need to import the class name. Remember that only classes defined in java.lang are included in your program automatically.

Normal Execution of a Method

The first line of output from the TryBlockTest example indicates that execution of the try block in main() has begun. The next block of four lines of output from the example is the result of a straight-forward execution of the divide() method. No exceptions occur in divide(), so no catch blocks are executed.

The code at the end of the divide() method, following the catch blocks, isn't executed because the return statement in the try block ends the execution of the method. However, the finally block in divide() is executed before the return to the calling method occurs. If you comment out the return statement at the end of the divide() method's try block and run the example again, the code that follows the finally block will be executed.

The sequence of execution when no exceptions occur is shown in Figure 7-3.

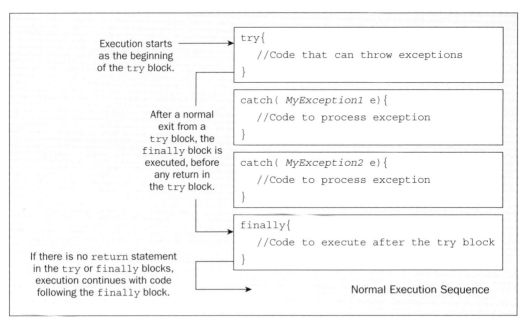

Figure 7-3

Figure 7-3 illustrates the normal sequence of execution in an arbitrary `try-catch-finally` set of blocks. If there's a return statement in the `try` block, this will be executed immediately after the `finally` block completes execution — so this prevents the execution of any code following the `finally` block. A return statement in a `finally` block will cause an immediate return to the calling point, and the code following the `finally` block wouldn't be executed in this case.

Execution When an Exception Is Thrown

The next block of five lines in the output correspond to an `ArithmeticException` being thrown and caught in the `divide()` method. The exception is thrown because the value of the second element in the array x is zero. When the exception occurs, execution of the code in the `try` block is stopped, and you can see that the code that follows the `catch` block for the exception in the `divide()` method is then executed. The `finally` block executes next, followed by the code after the `finally` block. The value in the last element of the array isn't changed from its previous value, because the exception occurs during the computation of the new value, before the result is stored.

The general sequence of execution in an arbitrary `try-catch-finally` set of blocks when an exception occurs is shown in Figure 7-4.

Execution of the `try` block stops at the point where the exception occurs, and the code in the `catch` block for the exception is executed immediately. If there is a `return` statement in the `catch` block, this isn't executed until after the `finally` block has been executed. As I discussed earlier, if a `return` statement that returns a value is executed within a `finally` block, that value will be returned, not the value from any previous `return` statement.

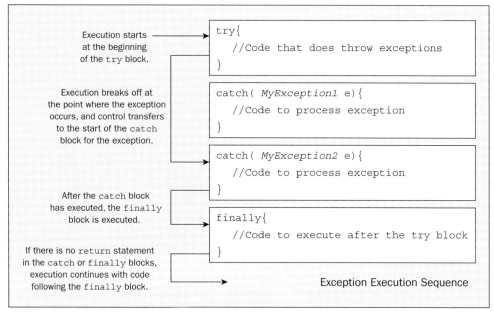

Figure 7-4

Execution When an Exception Is Not Caught

The next block of six lines in the output is a consequence of the third call to the divide() method. This causes an ArrayIndexOutOfBoundsException to be thrown in the try block, which is then caught. However, the code at the end of the method, which is executed after the finally block, throws another exception of this type. This can't be caught in the divide() method because the statement causing it isn't in a try block. Since this exception isn't caught in the divide() method, the method terminates immediately and the same exception is thrown in main() at the point where the divide() method was called. This causes the code in the relevant catch block in main() to be executed in consequence.

An exception that isn't caught in a method is always propagated upwards to the calling method. It will continue to propagate up through each level of calling method until either it is caught or the main() method is reached. If it isn't caught in main(), the program will terminate and a suitable message will be displayed. This situation is illustrated in Figure 7-5.

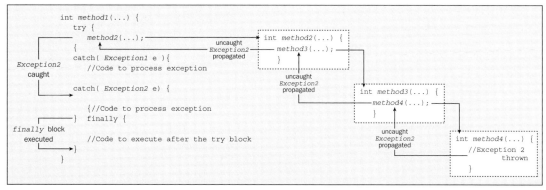

Figure 7-5

Figure 7-5 shows `method1()` calling `method2()`,which calls `method3()`, which calls `method4()`, in which an exception of type `Exception2` is thrown. This exception isn't caught in `method4()`, so execution of `method4()` ceases, and the exception is thrown in `method3()`. It isn't caught and continues to be rethrown until it reaches `method1()` where there's a `catch` block to handle it.

In our `TryBlockTest` example, execution continues in `main()` with the output statements outside the first `try` block. The `read()` method pauses the program until you press the Enter key. No exception is thrown, and execution ends after the code in the `finally` block is executed. The `finally` block is tied to the `try` block that immediately precedes it and is executed even though there's a return statement in the `try` block.

Nested *try* Blocks

I won't be going into these in detail, but you should note that you can have nested `try` blocks, as Figure 7-6 illustrates.

The `catch` blocks for the outer `try` block can catch any exceptions that are thrown, but not caught, by any code within the block, including code within inner `try-catch` blocks. In the example shown in Figure 7-6, the `catch` block for the outer `try` block will catch any exception of type `Exception2`. Such exceptions could originate anywhere within the outer `try` block. The illustration shows two levels of nesting, but you can specify more if you know what you're doing.

```
try {
    try {
        //1st inner try block code...
    } catch( Exception1 ) {
        //...
    }
    //Outer try block code...
    try {
        //2nd inner try block code...
    }catch( Exception1 e ) {
        //try block code...
    }

}catch( Exception2 e ){
    //Outer catch block code...
}
```

Exceptions of type `Exception2` thrown anywhere in here that are not caught will be caught by the `catch` block for the outer `try` block.

Figure 7-6

Rethrowing Exceptions

Even though you may need to recognize that an exception has occurred in a method by implementing a `catch` clause for it, this is not necessarily the end of the matter. In many situations, the calling program may need to know about it — perhaps because it will affect the continued operation of the program or because the calling program may be able to compensate for the problem.

If you need to pass an exception that you have caught on to the calling program, you can rethrow it from within the `catch` block using a `throw` statement. For example:

```
try {
  // Code that originates an arithmetic exception

} catch(ArithmeticException e) {
  // Deal with the exception here
  throw e;                       // Rethrow the exception to the calling program
}
```

The `throw` statement is the keyword `throw` followed by the exception object to be thrown. When you look at how to define our own exceptions later in this chapter, you'll be using exactly the same mechanism to throw them.

Exception Objects

Well, you now understand how to put `try` blocks together with `catch` blocks and `finally` blocks in your methods. You may be thinking at this point that it seems a lot of trouble to go to just to display a message when an exception is thrown. You may be right, but whether you can do very much more depends on the nature and context of the problem. In many situations a message may be the best you can do, although you can produce messages that are a bit more informative than those you've used so far in our examples. For one thing, I have totally ignored the exception object that is passed to the `catch` block.

The exception object that is passed to a `catch` block can provide additional information about the nature of the problem that originated it. To understand more about this, let's first look at the members of the base class for exceptions `Throwable` because these will be inherited by all exception classes and are therefore contained in every exception object that is thrown.

The Throwable Class

The `Throwable` class is the class from which all Java exception classes are derived — that is, every exception object will contain the methods defined in this class. The `Throwable` class has two constructors: a default constructor and a constructor that accepts an argument of type `String`. The `String` object that is passed to the constructor is used to provide a description of the nature of the problem causing the exception. Both constructors are public.

Objects of type `Throwable` contain two items of information about an exception:

❑   A message, which I have just referred to as being initialized by a constructor

❑   A record of the execution stack at the time the object was created

The **execution stack** keeps track of all the methods that are in execution at any given instant. It provides the means whereby executing a return gets back to the calling point for a method. The record of the execution stack that is stored in the exception object consists of the line number in the source code where the exception originated followed by a trace of the method calls that immediately preceded the point at which the exception occurred. This is made up of the fully qualified name for each of the methods called, plus the line number in the source file where each method call occurred. The method calls are in sequence with the most recent method call appearing first. This will help you to understand how this point in the program was reached.

The `Throwable` class has the following public methods that enable you to access the message and the stack trace:

Method	Description
`getMessage()`	This returns the contents of the message, describing the current exception. This will typically be the fully qualified name of the exception class (it will be a subclass of `Throwable`) and a brief description of the exception.
`printStackTrace()`	This will output the message and the stack trace to the standard error output stream — which is the screen in the case of a console program.
`printStackTrace(PrintStream s)`	This is the same as the previous method except that you specify the output stream as an argument. Calling the previous method for an exception object e is equivalent to: `e.printStackTrace(System.err);`

Another method, `fillInStackTrace()`, will update the stack trace to the point at which this method is called. For example, if you put a call to this method in the `catch` block:

```
e.fillInStackTrace();
```

the line number recorded in the stack record for the method in which the exception occurred will be the line where `fillInStackTrace()` is called. The main use of this is when you want to rethrow an exception (so it will be caught by the calling method) and record the point at which it is rethrown. For example:

```
e.fillInStackTrace();                    // Record the throw point
throw e;                                 // Rethrow the exception
```

In practice, it's often more useful to throw an exception of your own. You'll see how to define your own exceptions in the next section, but first, let's exercise some of the methods defined in the `Throwable` class and see the results.

Try It Out   Dishing the Dirt on Exceptions

The easiest way to try out some of the methods I've just discussed is to make some judicious additions to the catch blocks in the divide() method you have in the TryBlockTest class example:

```java
public static int divide(int[] array, int index) {
  try {
    System.out.println("\nFirst try block in divide() entered");
    array[index + 2] = array[index]/array[index + 1];
    System.out.println("Code at end of first try block in divide()");
    return array[index + 2];

  } catch(ArithmeticException e) {
    System.err.println("Arithmetic exception caught in divide()\n" +
                       "\nMessage in exception object:\n\t" +
                       e.getMessage());
    System.err.println("\nStack trace output:\n");
    e.printStackTrace();
    System.err.println("\nEnd of stack trace output\n");
  } catch(ArrayIndexOutOfBoundsException e) {
    System.err.println("Index-out-of-bounds exception caught in divide()\n" +
                       "\nMessage in exception object:\n\t" + e.getMessage());
    System.err.println("\nStack trace output:\n");
    e.printStackTrace();
    System.out.println("\nEnd of stack trace output\n");
  } finally {
    System.err.println("finally clause in divide()");
  }
  System.out.println("Executing code after try block in divide()");
  return array[index + 2];
}
```

If you recompile the program and run it again, it will produce all the output as before, but with extra information when exceptions are thrown in the divide() method. The new output generated for the ArithmeticException will be:

```
Message in exception object:
      / by zero

Stack trace output:

java.lang.ArithmeticException: / by zero
      at TryBlockTest.divide(TryBlockTest.java:54)
      at TryBlockTest.main(TryBlockTest.java:15)
End of stack trace output
```

The additional output generated for the ArrayIndexOutOfBoundsException will be:

```
Message in exception object:
      3

Stack trace output:
```

```
java.lang.ArrayIndexOutOfBoundsException:   3
        at TryBlockTest.divide(TryBlockTest.java:54)
        at TryBlockTest.main(TryBlockTest.java:17)

End of stack trace output
```

How It Works

The extra lines of code in each of the `catch` blocks in the `divide()` method output the message associated with the exception object e by calling its `getMessage()` method. You could have just put e here, which would invoke the `toString()` method for e, and, in this case, the class name for e would precede the message. There are a couple of extra `println()` calls around the call to `printStackTrace()` to make it easier to find the stack trace in the output. These are called for the standard error stream object, `System.err`, for consistency with the stack trace output.

The first stack trace, for the arithmetic exception, indicates that the error originated at line 54 in the source file `TryBlockText.java` and the last method call was at line 15 in the same source file. The second stack trace provides similar information about the index-out-of-bounds exception, including the offending index value. As you can see, with the stack trace output, it's very easy to see where the error occurred and how this point in the program was reached.

Standard Exceptions

The majority of predefined exception classes in Java don't add further information about the conditions that created the exception. The type alone serves to differentiate one exception from another in most cases. This general lack of additional information is because it can be gleaned in the majority of cases only by prior knowledge of the computation that is being carried out when the exception occurs, and the only person who is privy to that is you, since you're writing the program.

This should spark the glimmer of an idea. If you need more information about the circumstances surrounding an exception, you're going to have to obtain it and, equally important, communicate it to the appropriate point in your program. This leads to the notion of defining your own exceptions.

Defining Your Own Exceptions

There are two basic reasons for defining your own exception classes:

❏   You want to add information when a standard exception occurs, and you can do this by rethrowing an object of your own exception class.

❏   You may have error conditions that arise in your code that warrant the distinction of a special exception class.

However, you should bear in mind that there's a lot of overhead in throwing exceptions, so it is not a valid substitute for "normal" recovery code that you would expect to be executed frequently. If you have recovery code that will be executed often, then it doesn't belong in a `catch` block, but rather in something like an `if-else` statement.

Let's see how you create your own exceptions.

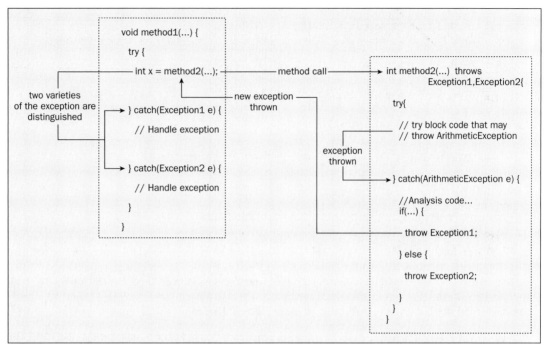

Figure 7-7

Figure 7-7 shows how two different circumstances causing an `ArithmeticException` in `method2()` are differentiated in the calling method, `method1()`. The `method2()` method can throw an exception either of type `Exception1` or of type `Exception2`, depending on the analysis that is made in the `catch` block for the `ArithmeticException` type. The calling method has a separate `catch` block for each of the exceptions that may be thrown.

You could also define a new exception class that had instance variables to identify the problem more precisely. Let's suppose that in the last example you wanted to provide more information to the calling program about the error that caused each exception in the `divide()` method. The primary exception can be either an `ArithmeticException` or an `ArrayIndexOutOfBoundsException`, but since you're dealing with a specific context for these errors, you could give the calling program more information by throwing your own exceptions.

Let's take the `ArithmeticException` case as a model and define an exception class to use in the program to help identify the reason for the error more precisely.

Try It Out   Defining Your Own Exception Class

You can define the class that will correspond to an `ArithmeticException` in the `divide()` method as:

```
public class ZeroDivideException extends Exception {
   private int index = -1;        // Index of array element causing error

   // Default Constructor
   public ZeroDivideException(){ }
```

```
      // Standard constructor
      public ZeroDivideException(String s) {
         super(s);                                  // Call the base constructor
      }

      public ZeroDivideException(int index) {
         super("/ by zero");                        // Call the base constructor
         this.index = index;                        // Set the index value
      }

      // Get the array index value for the error
      public int getIndex() {
         return index;                              // Return the index value
      }
   }
```

How It Works

As you've derived the `ZeroDivideException` class from the `Exception` class, the compiler will check that the exceptions thrown are either caught or identified as thrown in a method. Your class will inherit all the members of the class `Throwable` via the `Exception` class, so you'll get the stack trace record and the message for the exception maintained for free. It will also inherit the `toString()` method, which is satisfactory in this context, but this could be overridden if desired.

You've added a data member, `index`, to store the index value of the zero divisor in the array passed to `divide()`. This will give the calling program a chance to fix this value if appropriate in the `catch` block for the exception. In this case, the `catch` block would also need to include code that would enable the `divide()` method to be called again with the corrected array.

Let's now put it to work in another variation on the `TryBlockTest` example.

Try It Out   Using the Exception Class

You need to use the exception class in two contexts — in the `divide()` method when you catch a standard `ArithmeticException` and in the calling method `main()` to catch the new exception. Let's modify `divide()` first:

```
   public static int divide(int[] array, int index) throws ZeroDivideException {
      try {
         System.out.println("First try block in divide() entered");
         array[index + 2] = array[index]/array[index + 1];
         System.out.println("Code at end of first try block in divide()");
         return array[index + 2];

      } catch(ArithmeticException e) {
         System.out.println("Arithmetic exception caught in divide()");
         throw new ZeroDivideException(index + 1);     // Throw new exception
      } catch(ArrayIndexOutOfBoundsException e) {
         System.out.println(
                  "Index-out-of-bounds index exception caught in divide()");
      }
      System.out.println("Executing code after try block in divide()");
      return array[index + 2];
   }
```

The first change is to add the `throws` clause to the method definition. Without this you'll get an error message from the compiler. The second change adds a statement to the `catch` block for `ArithmeticException` exceptions that throws a new exception.

This new exception needs to be caught in the calling method `main()`:

```
public static void main(String[] args) {
  int[] x = {10, 5, 0};                  // Array of three integers

  // This block only throws an exception if method divide() does
  try {
    System.out.println("First try block in main()entered");
    System.out.println("result = " + divide(x,0));  // No error
    x[1] = 0;                            // Will cause a divide by zero
    System.out.println("result = " + divide(x,0));  // Arithmetic error
    x[1] = 1;                            // Reset to prevent divide by zero
    System.out.println("result = " + divide(x,1));  // Index error
  } catch(ZeroDivideException e) {
    int index = e.getIndex();            // Get the index for the error
    if(index > 0) {                      // Verify it is valid and now fix the array
      x[index] = 1;                      // ...set the divisor to 1...
      x[index + 1] = x[index - 1];       // ...and set the result
      System.out.println("Zero divisor corrected to " + x[index]);
    }
  } catch(ArithmeticException e) {
    System.out.println("Arithmetic exception caught in main()");
  } catch(ArrayIndexOutOfBoundsException e) {
    System.out.println("Index-out-of-bounds exception caught in main()");
  }
  System.out.println("Outside first try block in main()");
}
```

You should put the revised `TryBlockTest` class file and the file for the `ZeroDivideException` class together in the same directory. In the download, they'll be in the `TryBlockTest3` directory for Chapter 7.

How It Works

All you need to add in `main()` is the `catch` block for the new exception. You need to make sure that the index value for the divisor stored in the exception object is positive so that another exception is not thrown when you fix up the array. As you arbitrarily set the array element that contained the zero divisor to 1, it makes sense to set the array element holding the result to the same as the dividend. You can then let the method `main()` stagger on.

> A point to bear in mind is that the last two statements in the `try` block will not have been executed. After the `catch` block has been executed, the method continues with the code following the `try-catch` block set. In practice you would need to consider whether to ignore this. One possibility is to put the whole of the `try-catch` block code in `main()` in a loop that would normally only run one iteration, but where this could be altered to run additional iterations by setting a flag in the `catch` block.

This is a rather artificial example—so what sort of circumstances could justify this kind of fixing up of the data in a program? If the data originated through some kind of instrumentation measuring physical parameters such as temperatures or pressures—in a chemical manufacturing plant or an oil refinery, for example—the data may contain spurious zero values from time to time. Rather than abandon the whole calculation you might well want to amend these as they occur and press on to process the rest of the data.

Summary

In this chapter you have learned what exceptions are and how to deal with them in your programs. You should make sure that you consider exception handling as an integral part of developing your Java programs. The robustness of your program code depends on how effectively you deal with the exceptions that can be thrown within it.

The important concepts you have explored in this chapter are:

❏ Exceptions identify errors that arise in your program.

❏ Exceptions are objects of subclasses of the Throwable class.

❏ Java includes a set of standard exceptions that may be thrown automatically, as a result of errors in your code, or may be thrown by methods in the standard classes in Java.

❏ If a method throws exceptions that aren't caught, and aren't represented by subclasses of the Error class or by subclasses of the RuntimeException class, then you must identify the exception classes in a throws clause in the method definition.

❏ If you want to handle an exception in a method, you must place the code that may generate the exception in a try block. A method may have several try blocks.

❏ Exception handling code is placed in a catch block that immediately follows the try block that contains the code that can throw the exception. A try block can have multiple catch blocks that each deals with a different type of exception.

❏ A finally block is used to contain code that must be executed after the execution of a try block, regardless of how the try block execution ends. A finally block will always be executed before execution of the method ends.

❏ You can throw an exception by using a throw statement. You can throw an exception anywhere in a method. You can also rethrow an existing exception in a catch block to pass it to the calling method.

❏ You can define your own exception classes that, in general, should be derived from the class Exception.

Exercises

You can download the source code for the examples in the book and the solutions to the following exercises from http://www.wrox.com.

1. Write a program that will generate exceptions of type `NullPointerException`, `NegativeArraySizeException`, and `IndexOutOfBoundsException`. Record the catching of each exception by displaying the message stored in the exception object and the stack trace record.

2. Add an exception class to the last example that will differentiate between the index-out-of-bounds error possibilities, rethrow an appropriate object of this exception class in `divide()`, and handle the exception in `main()`.

3. Write a program that calls a method that throws an exception of type `ArithmeticException` at a random iteration in a `for` loop. Catch the exception in the method and pass the iteration count when the exception occurred to the calling method by using an object of an exception class you define.

4. Add a `finally` block to the method in the previous example to output the iteration count when the method exits.

Understanding Streams

This is the first of four chapters devoted to streams and file input and output. This chapter introduces **streams**, and deals with keyboard input, and output to the command line.

By the end of this chapter, you will have learned:

❑ What a stream is and what the main classes that Java provides to support stream operations are

❑ What stream readers and writers are and what they are used for

❑ How to read data from the keyboard

❑ How to format data that you write to the command line

Streams and the New I/O Capability

The package that supports stream input/output is java.io, and it is vast. It defines over seventy classes and interfaces, many of which have a large number of methods. It is therefore quite impractical to go into them all in detail in a book of this kind. Refer to the Java documentation for more information. My strategy in this and the following three chapters will be to take a practical approach. The idea is to provide an overall grounding of the concepts involved and to equip you with enough detailed knowledge to be able to do a number of specific, useful, and practical things in your programs. These are:

❑ To be able to read data of various kinds from the keyboard

❑ To be able to create formatted output to the command line

❑ To be able to read and write files containing basic data

❑ To be able to read and write files containing objects

To achieve this, I'll give you an overview of what the important stream classes do and how they interrelate, together with an outline of the classes that operate on streams. I'll go into the detail selectively, just exploring the classes and methods that you need to accomplish specific things. I'll also be sticking to the latest and greatest I/O capability that was first introduced in the JDK 1.4 and continues in JDK 5.0, which makes it unnecessary to delve into a lot of the original stream classes.

Up to and including Java 1.3, the only way to read and write disk files was to use a **stream**. The new I/O capability in the `java.nio` and `java.nio.channels` packages enables you to read and write files that contain data of the primitive Java types, as well as strings, and completely supersedes the stream I/O capability in this context. While all the old I/O facilities are still there, the new I/O capability is much more efficient and in many ways easier to use, so I'll limit the discussions of streams for handling files to the extent necessary for you to understand the new I/O capability. I'll go into the new I/O capability in detail in the next two chapters.

Two areas where you must still use the facilities provided by the stream classes are reading from the keyboard and writing to the command line. I cover both of these in this chapter along with some general aspects of the stream classes and the relationships between them. The new file I/O capability does not provide for objects to be written and read, so you still need to use streams for this. You will be looking into how you read and write objects to a file in Chapter 12.

Understanding Streams

A **stream** is an abstract representation of an input or output device that is a source of, or destination for, data. You can write data to a stream and read data from a stream. You can visualize a stream as a sequence of bytes that flows into or out of your program. Figure 8-1 illustrates how physical devices map to streams.

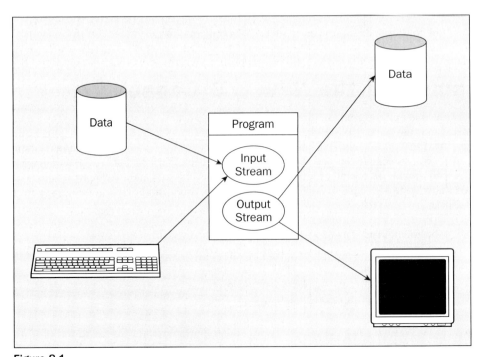

Figure 8-1

Input and Output Streams

When you write data to a stream, the stream is called an **output stream**. The output stream can go to any device to which a sequence of bytes can be transferred, such as a file on a hard disk, or a phone line connecting your system to a remote system. An output stream can also go to your display screen, but only at the expense of limiting it to a fraction of its true capability. Stream output to your display is output to the command line. When you write to your display screen using a stream, it can display characters only, not graphical output. Graphical output requires more specialized support that I'll discuss from Chapter 17 onwards.

> *Note that while a printer can be considered notionally as a stream, printing in Java does not work this way. A printer in Java is treated as a graphical device, so sending output to the printer is very similar to displaying graphical output on your display screen. You'll learn how printing works in Java in Chapter 21.*

You read data from an **input stream**. In principle, this can be any source of serial data, but is typically a disk file, the keyboard, or a remote computer.

Under normal circumstances, file input and output for the machine on which your program is executing is available only to Java *applications*. It's not available to Java applets except to a strictly limited extent. If this were not so, a malicious Java applet embedded in a web page could trash your hard disk. An IOException will normally be thrown by any attempted operation on disk files on the local machine in a Java applet. The directory containing the .class file for the applet and its subdirectories are freely accessible to the applet. Also, the security features in Java can be used to control what an applet (and an application running under a Security Manager) can access so that an applet can access only files or other resources *for which it has explicit permission.*

The main reason for using a stream as the basis for input and output operations is to make your program code for these operations independent of the device involved. This has two advantages. First, you don't have to worry about the detailed mechanics of each device, which are taken care of behind the scenes. Second, your program will work for a variety of input/output devices without any changes to the code.

Stream input and output methods generally permit very small amounts of data, such as a single character or byte, to be written or read in a single operation. Transferring data to or from a stream like this may be extremely inefficient, so a stream is often equipped with a **buffer** in memory, in which case it is called a **buffered stream**. A buffer is simply a block of memory that is used to batch up the data that is transferred to or from an external device. Reading or writing a stream in reasonably large chunks will reduce the number of input/output operations necessary and thus make the process more efficient.

When you write to a buffered output stream, the data is sent to the buffer and not to the external device. The amount of data in the buffer is tracked automatically, and the data is usually sent to the device when the buffer is full. However, you will sometimes want the data in the buffer to be sent to the device before the buffer is full, and methods are provided to do this. This operation is usually termed **flushing** the buffer.

Buffered input streams work in a similar way. Any read operation on a buffered input stream will read data from the buffer. A read operation for the device that is the source of data for the stream will be read only when the buffer is empty and the program has requested data. When this occurs, a complete buffer-full of data will be read automatically from the device, if sufficient data is available.

Binary and Character Streams

The java.io package supports two types of streams—**binary streams,** which contain binary data, and **character streams,** which contain character data. Binary streams are sometimes referred to as **byte streams.** These two kinds of streams behave in different ways when you read and write data.

When you write data to a binary stream, the data is written to the stream as a series of bytes, exactly as it appears in memory. No transformation of the data takes place. Binary numerical values are just written as a series of bytes, 4 bytes for each value of type int, 8 bytes for each value of type long, 8 bytes for each value of type double, and so on. As you saw in Chapter 2, Java stores its characters internally as Unicode characters, which are 16-bit characters, so each Unicode character is written to a binary stream as 2 bytes, the high byte being written first. Supplementary Unicode characters that are surrogates consist of two successive 16-bit characters, in which case the two sets of 2 bytes are written in sequence to the binary stream with the high byte written first in each case.

Character streams are used for storing and retrieving text. You may also use character streams to read text files not written by a Java program. All binary numeric data has to be converted to a textual representation before being written to a character stream. This involves generating a character representation of the original binary data value. Reading numeric data from a stream that contains text involves much more work than reading binary data. When you read a value of type int from a binary stream, you know that it consists of 4 bytes. When you read an integer from a character stream, you have to determine how many characters from the stream make up the value. For each numerical value you read from a character stream, you have to be able to recognize where the value begins and ends and then convert the **token**—the sequence of characters that represents the value—to its binary form. Figure 8-2 illustrates this.

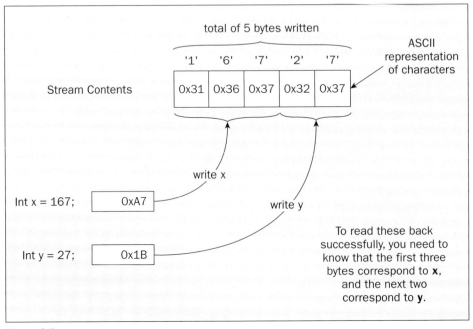

Figure 8-2

When you write strings to a stream as character data, by default the Unicode characters are automatically converted to the local representation of the characters in the host machine, and these are then written to the stream. When you read a string, the default mechanism converts the data from the stream back to Unicode characters from the local machine representation. With character streams, your program reads and writes Unicode characters, but the stream will contain characters in the equivalent character encoding used by the local computer.

You don't have to accept the default conversion process for character streams. Java allows named mappings between Unicode characters and sets of bytes to be defined, called **charsets**, and you can select an available charset that should apply when data is transferred to, or from, a particular character stream. I won't be going into this in detail, but you can find more information on defining and using charsets in the JDK documentation for the `Charset` class.

The Classes for Input and Output

There are quite a number of stream classes, but as you will see, they form a reasonably logical structure. Once you see how they are related, you shouldn't have much trouble using them. I will work through the class hierarchy from the top down, so you will be able to see how the classes hang together and how you can combine them in different ways to suit different situations.

The package `java.io` contains the classes that provide the foundation for Java's support for stream I/O:

Class	Description
InputStream	The base class for byte stream input operations.
OutputStream	The base class for byte stream output operations.

`InputStream` and `OutputStream` are both **abstract** classes. As you are well aware by now, you cannot create instances of an abstract class — these classes serve only as a base from which to derive classes with more concrete input or output capabilities. However, both of the classes declare methods that define a basic set of operations for the streams they represent, so the fundamental characteristics of how a stream is accessed are set by these classes. Both classes implement the `Closeable` interface. This interface declares just one method, `close()`, which should close the stream and release any resources that the stream object is holding. Generally, the `InputStream` and `OutputStream` classes, and their subclasses, represent byte streams and provide the means of reading and writing binary data as a series of bytes.

Basic Input Stream Operations

As you saw in the previous section, the `InputStream` class is abstract, so you cannot create objects of this class type. Nonetheless, input stream objects are often accessible via a reference of this type, so the methods identified in this class are what you get. The `InputStream` class includes three methods for reading data from a stream:

Method	Description
read()	This method is abstract in the InputStream class, so it has to be defined in a subclass. The method returns the next byte available from the stream as type int. If the end of the stream is reached, the method will return the value -1. An exception of type IOException will be thrown if an I/O error occurs.
read(byte[] array)	This method reads bytes from the stream into successive elements of array. The maximum of array.length bytes will be read. The method will not return until the input data is read or the end of the stream is detected. The method returns the number of bytes read or -1 if no bytes were read because the end of the stream was reached. If an I/O error occurs, an exception of type IOException will be thrown. If the argument to the method is null then a NullPointerException will be thrown. An input/output method that does not return until the operation is completed is referred to as a **blocking** method, and you say that the methods **blocks** until the operation is complete.
read(byte[] array, int offset, int length)	This works in essentially the same way as the previous method, except that up to length bytes are read into array starting with the element array[offset].

The data is read from the stream by these methods simply as bytes. No conversion is applied to the bytes read. If any conversion is required — for a stream containing bytes in the local character encoding, for example — you must provide a way to handle this. You will see how this might be done in a moment.

You can skip over bytes in an InputStream by calling its skip() method. You specify the number of bytes to be skipped as an argument of type long, and the actual number of bytes skipped is returned, also a value of type long. This method can throw an IOException if an error occurs.

You can close an InputStream by calling its close() method. Once you have closed an input stream, subsequent attempts to access or read from the stream will cause an IOException to be thrown because the close() operation will have released the resources held by the stream object, including the source of the data, such as a file.

The InputStream class has the seven direct subclasses shown in Figure 8-3.

You will be using the FileInputStream class in Chapter 11 for reading disk files and the ObjectInputStream class in Chapter 12 for reading objects from a file.

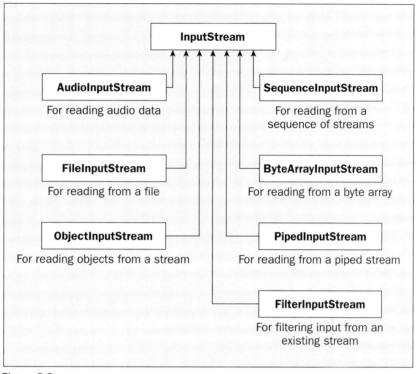

Figure 8-3

The `FilterInputStream` class has a further nine direct subclasses that provide more specialized ways of filtering or transforming data from an input stream. You'll be using only the `BufferedInputStream` class, but here's the complete set, with an indication of what each of them does:

BufferedInputStream	Buffers input from another stream in memory to make the read operations more efficient.
DataInputStream	Reads data of primitive types from a binary stream.
CheckedInputStream	Reads an input stream and maintains a checksum for the data that is read to verify its integrity.
CipherInputStream	Reads data from an encrypted input stream.
DigestInputStream	Reads data from an input stream and updates an associated message digest. A message digest is a mechanism for combining an arbitrary amount of data from a stream into a fixed-length value that can be used to verify the integrity of the data.
InflaterInputStream	Reads data from a stream that has been compressed, such as a ZIP file, for example.

Table continued on following page

`LineNumberInputStream`	Reads data from a stream and keeps track of the current line number. The line number starts at 0 and is incremented each time a newline character is read.
`ProgressMonitorInputStream`	Reads data from an input stream and uses a progress-monitor to monitor reading the stream. If reading the stream takes a significant amount of time, a progress dialog will be displayed offering the option to cancel the operation. This is used in window-based applications for operations that are expected to be time-consuming.
`PushbackInputStream`	Adds the capability to return the last byte that was read back to the input stream so you can read it again.

You can create a `BufferedInputStream` object from any other input stream, since the constructor accepts a reference of type `InputStream` as an argument. The `BufferedInputStream` class overrides the methods inherited from `InputStream`. For example, in the following code:

```
BufferedInputStream keyboard = new BufferedInputStream(System.in);
```

the argument `System.in` is the static member of the `System` class that encapsulates input from the keyboard and is of type `InputStream`. You'll be looking into how you can best read input from the keyboard a little later in this chapter.

The effect of wrapping a stream in a `BufferedInputStream` object is to buffer the underlying stream in memory so that data can be read from the stream in large chunks — up to the size of the buffer that is provided. The data is then made available to the `read()` methods directly from memory, and a real read operation from the underlying stream is executed only when the buffer is empty. With a suitable choice of buffer size, the number of input operations that are needed will be substantially reduced, and the process will be a whole lot more efficient. This is because for most input streams, each read operation carries quite a bit of overhead, beyond the time required to actually transfer the data. In the case of a disk file, for example, the transfer of data from the disk to memory can start only once the read/write head has been positioned over the track that contains the data and the disk has rotated to the point where the read/write head is over the point in the track where the data starts. This delay before the transfer of data begins will typically be several milliseconds and will often be much longer than the time required to transfer the data. Thus, by minimizing the number of separate read operations that are necessary, you can substantially reduce the total time needed to read a significant amount of data.

The buffer size that you get by default when you call the `BufferedInputStream` constructor as in the previous code fragment is 8192 bytes. This will be adequate for most situations where modest amounts of data are involved. The `BufferedInputStream` class also defines a constructor that accepts a second argument of type `int` that enables you to specify the size in bytes of the buffer to be used.

Deciding on a suitable size for a buffer is a matter of judgment. You need to think about how the buffer size will affect operations in your program. The total amount of data involved, as well as the amount that you need to process at one time, also comes into it. For example, you will usually want to choose a buffer size that is a multiple of the amount of data that your program will request in each read operation. Suppose you expect your program to read and process 600 bytes at a time, for instance. In this case, you should choose a buffer size that is a multiple of 600 bytes. The multiple, and therefore the total buffer size, is a balance between the amount of memory required for the buffer and its effect on the efficiency of your program. If you expect to be processing 100 sets of data, each of 600 bytes, you might settle on a buffer size of 6000 bytes as a reasonable choice. Each buffer-full would then consist of 10 sets of data, and there would need to be only 10 physical read operations to refill the buffer.

Basic Output Stream Operations

The OutputStream class contains three write() methods for writing binary data to the stream. As can be expected, these mirror the read() methods of the InputStream class. This class is also abstract, so only subclasses can be instantiated. The principal direct subclasses of OutputStream are shown in Figure 8-4.

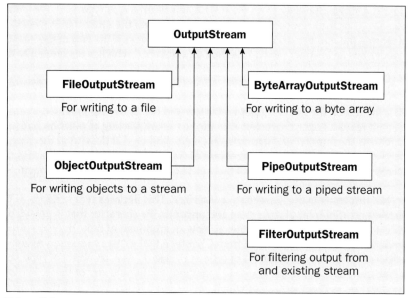

Figure 8-4

You'll be using the FileOutputStream class that is derived from OutputStream when you write files in the next chapter, and you'll investigate the methods belonging to the ObjectOutputStream class in Chapter 12, when you learn how to write objects to a file.

Note that this is not the complete set of output stream classes. The FilterOutputStream class has a further seven subclasses, including the BufferedOutputStream class, which does for output streams what the BufferedInputStream class does for input streams. There is also the PrintStream class, which you will be looking at a little later in this chapter, since output to the command line is via a stream object of this type.

Stream Readers and Writers

Stream readers and **writers** are objects that can read and write byte streams as character streams. So a character stream is essentially a byte stream fronted by a reader or a writer. The base classes for stream readers and writers are:

Class	Description
Reader	The base class for reading a character stream
Writer	The base class for writing a character stream

Reader and Writer are both abstract classes. Both classes implement the Closeable interface, which declares the close() method. The Reader class also implements the Readable interface, which declares the read() method for reading characters into a CharBuffer object that is passed as the argument to the method. I'll discuss CharBuffer objects in Chapters 10 and 11 in the context of reading and writing files. The Reader class defines two further read() methods. One of these requires no arguments and reads and returns a single character from the stream and returns it as type int. The other expects an array of type char[] as the argument and reads characters into the array that is passed to the method. The method returns the number of characters that were read or -1 if the end of the stream is reached. Finally, the reader has an abstract read() method as a member, which is declared like this:

```
public abstract int read(char[] buf, int offset, int length) throws IOException;
```

This method is the reason the Reader class is abstract and has to be implemented in any concrete subclass. The method reads length characters into the buf array starting at position buf[offset]. The method also returns the number of characters that were read or -1 if the end of the stream was reached. All three read() methods can throw an exception of type IOException, and the read method declared in Readable can also throw an exception of NullPointerException if the argument is null.

The Writer class implements the Appendable interface. This declares two versions of the append() method; one takes an argument of type char and appends the character that is passed to it to whatever stream the Writer encapsulates, and the other accepts an argument of type CharSequence and appends that to the underlying stream. You'll recall from Chapter 6 that a CharSequence reference can be a reference to an object of type String, an object of type StringBuilder, an object of type StringBuffer, or an object of type CharBuffer, so the append() method will handle any of these. The Writer class has five write() methods as members, all of which have a void return type and throw an IOException if an I/O error occurs:

write(int ch)	Writes the character corresponding to the low-order 2 bytes of the integer argument, ch
write(char[] buf)	Writes the array of characters buf
write(char[] buf, int offset, int length)	This is an abstract method that writes length characters from buf starting at buf[offset]
write(String str)	Writes the string str
write(String str, int offset, int length)	Writes length characters from str starting with the character at index position offset in the string

The `Reader` and `Writer` classes and their subclasses are not really streams themselves, but provide the methods you can use for reading and writing an underlying stream as a character stream. Thus, a `Reader` or `Writer` object is typically created using an underlying `InputStream` or `OutputStream` object that encapsulates the connection to the external device, which is the ultimate source or destination of the data.

Using Readers

The `Reader` class has the direct subclasses shown in Figure 8-5.

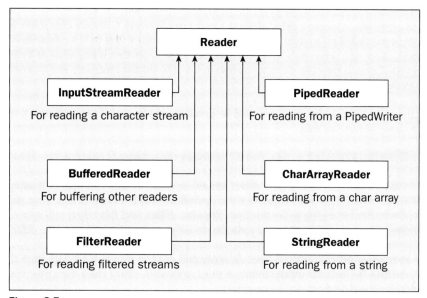

Figure 8-5

The concrete class that you would use to read an input stream as a character stream is `InputStreamReader`. You could create an `InputStreamReader` object like this, for example:

```
InputStreamReader keyboard = new InputStreamReader(System.in);
```

The parameter to the `InputStreamReader` constructor is of type `InputStream`, so you can pass an object of any class derived from `InputStream` to it. The sample above creates an `InputStreamReader` object, `keyboard`, from the object `System.in`, the keyboard input stream.

The `InputStreamReader` class defines the abstract `read()` method that it inherits from `Reader` and redefines the `read()` method without parameters. These methods read bytes from the underlying stream and return them as Unicode characters using the default conversion from the local character encoding. In addition to the preceding example, there are also three further constructors for `InputStreamReader` objects:

`InputStreamReader(InputStream in, Charset s)`	Constructs an object with `in` as the underlying stream. The object will use `s` to convert bytes to Unicode characters.

Table continued on following page

`InputStreamReader(InputStream in,` `            CharsetDecoder dec)`	Constructs an object that will use the charset decoder `dec` to transform bytes that are read from the stream `in` to a sequence of Unicode characters
`InputStreamReader(InputStream in,` `            String charsetName)`	Constructs an object that will use the charset identified in the name `charsetName` to convert bytes that are read from the stream `in` to a sequence of Unicode characters

A `java.nio.charset.Charset` object defines a mapping between Unicode characters and bytes. A `Charset` can be identified by a name that is a string that conforms to the IANA conventions for `Charset` registration. A `java.nio.charset.CharsetDecoder` object converts a sequence of bytes in a given charset to bytes. Consult the class documentation in the JDK for the `Charset` and `CharsetDecoder` classes for more information.

Of course, the operations with a reader would be much more efficient if you buffered it using a `BufferedReader` object like this:

```
BufferedReader keyboard = new BufferedReader(new InputStreamReader(System.in));
```

Here, you wrap an `InputStreamReader` object around `System.in` and then buffer it using a `BufferedReader` object. This will make the input operations much more efficient. Your read operations will be from the buffer belonging to the `BufferedReader` object, and this object will take care of filling the buffer from `System.in` when necessary via the underlying `InputStreamReader` object.

A `CharArrayReader` object is created from an array and enables you to read data from the array as though it were from a character input stream. A `StringReader` object class does essentially the same thing, but obtains the data from a `String` object.

Using Writers

The main subclasses of the `Writer` class are as shown in Figure 8-6.

I'll just discuss a few details of the most commonly used of these classes.

The `OutputStreamWriter` class writes characters to an underlying binary stream. It also has a subclass, `FileWriter`, that writes characters to a stream encapsulating a file. Both of these are largely superseded by the I/O facilities introduced in Java 1.4 that you'll explore starting in the next chapter.

Note that the `PrintWriter` class has no particular relevance to printing, in spite of its name. The `PrintWriter` class defines methods for formatting binary data as characters and writing it to a character stream. It defines overloaded `print()` and `println()` methods that accept an argument of each of the basic data types, of type `char[]`, of type `String`, and of type `Object`. The data that is written is a character representation of the argument. Numerical values and objects are converted to a string representation using the static `valueOf()` method in the `String` class. Overloaded versions of this method exist for all of the primitive types plus type `Object`. In the case of an argument that is an `Object` reference, the `valueOf()` method just calls the `toString()` method for the object to produce the string to be written to the stream. The `print()` methods just write the string representation of the argument, whereas the `println()` method appends \n to the output. You can create a `PrintWriter` object from a stream or from another `Writer` object.

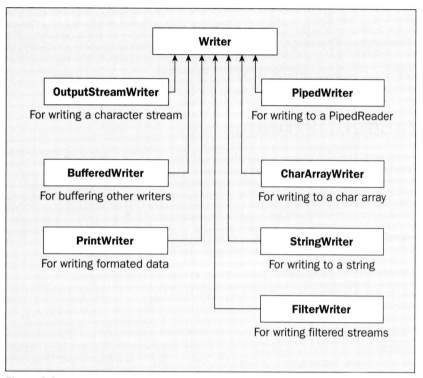

Figure 8-6

An important point to note when using a `PrintWriter` object is that its methods do not throw I/O exceptions. To determine whether any I/O errors have occurred, you have to call the `checkError()` method for the `PrintWriter` object. This method will return `true` if an error occurred and `false` otherwise.

The `StringWriter` and `CharArrayWriter` classes are for writing character data to a `StringBuffer` object, or an array of type `char[]`. You would typically use these to perform data conversions so that the results are available to you from the underlying array, or string. For example, you could combine the capabilities of a `PrintWriter` with a `StringWriter` to obtain a `String` object containing binary data converted to characters:

```
StringWriter strWriter = new StringWriter();
PrintWriter writer = new PrintWriter(strWriter);
```

Now you can use the methods for the `writer` object to write to the `StringBuffer` object underlying the `StringWriter` object:

```
double value = 2.71828;
writer.println(value);
```

You can get the result back as a `StringBuffer` object from the original `StringWriter` object:

```
StringBuffer str = strWriter.getBuffer();
```

Of course, the formatting done by a `PrintWriter` object does not help make the output line up in neat columns. If you want that to happen, you have to do it yourself. You'll see how you might do this for command-line output a little later in this chapter.

Let's now turn to keyboard input and command-line output.

The Standard Streams

Your operating system will typically define three standard streams that are accessible through members of the `System` class in Java:

❑   A **standard input stream** that usually corresponds to the keyboard by default. This is encapsulated by the `in` member of the `System` class and is of type `InputStream`.

❑   A **standard output stream** that corresponds to output on the command line. This is encapsulated by the `out` member of the `System` class and is of type `PrintStream`.

❑   A **standard error output stream** for error messages that usually maps to the command-line output by default. This is encapsulated by the `err` member of the `System` class and is also of type `PrintStream`.

You can reassign any of these to another stream within a Java application. The `System` class provides the static methods `setIn()`, `setOut()`, and `setErr()` for this purpose. The `setIn()` method requires an argument of type `InputStream` that specifies the new source of standard input. The other two methods expect an argument of type `PrintStream`.

Since the standard input stream is of type `InputStream`, you are not exactly overwhelmed by the capabilities for reading data from the keyboard in Java. Basically, you can read a byte or an array of bytes using a `read()` method as standard, and that's it. If you want more than that, reading integers, or decimal values, or strings as keyboard input, you're on your own. Let's see what you can do to remedy that.

Getting Data from the Keyboard

To get sensible input from the keyboard, you have to be able to scan the stream of characters and recognize what they are. When you read a numerical value from the stream, you have to look for the digits and possibly the sign and decimal point, figure out where the number starts and ends in the stream, and finally convert it to the appropriate value. To write the code to do this from scratch would take quite a lot of work. Fortunately, you can get a lot of help from the class libraries. One possibility is to use the `java.util.Scanner` class, but I'll defer discussion of that until Chapter 15 because you need to understand another topic before you can use `Scanner` objects effectively. The `StreamTokenizer` class in the `java.io` package is another possibility, so let's look further into that.

The term **token** refers to a data item such as a number or a string that will, in general, consist of several consecutive characters of a particular kind from the stream. For example, a number is usually a sequence of characters that consists of digits, maybe a decimal point, and sometimes a sign in front. The class has the name `StreamTokenizer` because it can read characters from a stream and parse it into a series of tokens that it recognizes.

You create a `StreamTokenizer` object from a stream reader object that reads data from the underlying input stream. To read the standard input stream `System.in` you can use an `InputStreamReader` object that converts the raw bytes that are read from the stream from the local character encoding to Unicode characters before the `StreamTokenizer` object sees them. In the interests of efficiency it would be a good idea to buffer the data from the `InputStreamReader` through a `BufferedReader` object that will buffer the data in memory. With this in mind, you could create a `StreamTokenizer` object like this:

```
StreamTokenizer tokenizer = new StreamTokenizer(
                    new BufferedReader(
                      new InputStreamReader(System.in)));
```

The argument to the `StreamTokenizer` object is the original standard input stream `System.in` inside an `InputStreamReader` object that converts the bytes to Unicode inside a `BufferedReader` object that supplies the stream of Unicode characters via a buffer in memory.

Before you can make use of the `StreamTokenizer` object for keyboard input, you need to understand a bit more about how it works.

Tokenizing a Stream

The `StreamTokenizer` class defines objects that can read an input stream and parse it into tokens. The input stream is read and treated as a series of separate bytes, and each byte is regarded as a Unicode character in the range `'u\0000'` to `'u\00FF'`. A `StreamTokenizer` object in its default state can recognize the following kinds of tokens:

Token	Description
Numbers	A sequence consisting of the digits 0 to 9, plus possibly a decimal point, and a + or – sign.
Strings	Any sequence of characters between a pair of single quotes or a pair of double quotes.
Words	Any sequence of letters or digits 0 to 9 beginning with a letter. A letter is defined as any of A to Z and a to z or \u00A0 to \u00FF. A word follows a whitespace character and is terminated by another whitespace character, or any character other than a letter or a digit.
Comments	Any sequence of characters beginning with a forward slash, /, and ending with the end-of-line character. Comments are ignored and not returned by the tokenizer.
Whitespace	All byte values from \u0000 to \u0020, which includes space, backspace, horizontal tab, vertical tab, line feed, form feed, and carriage return. Whitespace acts as a delimiter between tokens and is ignored (except within a quoted string).

To retrieve a token from the stream, you call the `nextToken()` method for the `StreamTokenizer` object:

```
int tokenType = 0;
try {
  while((tokenType = tokenizer.nextToken()) != tokenizer.TT_EOF) {
     // Do something with the token...
  }
```

```
    } catch (IOException e) {
      e.printStackTrace(System.err);
      System.exit(1);
    }
```

The nextToken() method can throw an exception of type IOException, so the call is in a try block. The value returned depends on the token recognized, and indicates its type, and from this value you can determine where to find the token itself. In the preceding fragment, you store the value returned in tokenType and compare its value with the constant TT_EOF. This constant is a static field of type int in the StreamTokenizer class that is returned by the nextToken() method when the end of the stream has been read. Thus the while loop continues until the end of the stream is reached. The token that was read from the stream is itself stored in one of two instance variables of the StreamTokenizer object. If the data item is a number, it is stored in a public data member nval, which is of type double. If the data item is a quoted string or a word, a reference to a String object that encapsulates the data item is stored in the public data member sval, which is of type String, of course. The analysis that segments the stream into tokens is fairly simple, and the way in which an arbitrary stream is broken into tokens is illustrated in Figure 8-7.

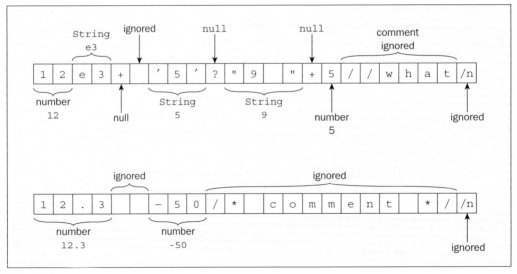

Figure 8-7

As I've said, the int value returned by the nextToken() method indicates what kind of data item was read. It can be any of the following constant values defined in the StreamTokenizer class:

Token Value	Description
TT_NUMBER	The token is a number that has been stored in the public field nval of type double in the tokenizer object.
TT_WORD	The token is a word that has been stored in the public field sval of type String in the tokenizer object.

Token Value	Description
TT_EOF	The end of the stream has been reached.
TT_EOL	An end-of-line character has been read. This is set only if the `eolIsSignificant()` method has been called with the argument, `true`. Otherwise, end-of-line characters are treated as whitespace and ignored.

If a quoted string is read from the stream, the value that is returned by `nextToken()` will be the quote character used for the string as type `int` — either a single quote or a double quote. In this case, you retrieve the reference to the string that was read from the `sval` member of the tokenizer object. The value indicating what kind of token was read last is also available from a public data member `ttype`, of the `StreamTokenizer` object, which is of type `int`.

Customizing a Stream Tokenizer

The default tokenizing mode can be modified by calling one or other of the following methods:

Method	Description
`resetSyntax()`	Resets the state of the tokenizer object so no characters have any special significance. This has the effect that all characters are regarded as ordinary and are read from the stream as single characters. The value of each character will be stored in the `ttype` field.
`ordinaryChar(int ch)`	Sets the character `ch` as an ordinary character. An ordinary character is a character that has no special significance. It will be read as a single character whose value will be stored in the `ttype` field. Calling this method will not alter the state of characters other than the argument value.
`ordinaryChars(int low, int hi)`	Causes all characters from `low` to `hi` inclusive to be treated as ordinary characters. Calling this method will not alter the state of characters other than those specified by the argument values.
`whitespaceChars(int low, int hi)`	Causes all characters from `low` to `hi` inclusive to be treated as whitespace characters. Unless they appear in a string, whitespace characters are treated as delimiters between tokens. Calling this method will not alter the state of characters other than those specified by the argument values.
`wordChars(int low, int hi)`	Specifies that the characters from `low` to `hi` inclusive are word characters. A word is at least one of these characters. Calling this method will not alter the state of characters other than those specified by the argument values.
`commentChar(int ch)`	Specifies that `ch` is a character that indicates the start of a comment. All characters to the end of the line following the character `ch` will be ignored. Calling this method will not alter the state of characters other than the argument value.

Table continued on following page

Method	Description
quoteChar(int ch)	Specifies that matching pairs of the character ch enclose a string. Calling this method will not alter the state of characters other than the argument value.
slashStarComments(boolean flag)	If the argument is false, this switches off recognizing comments between /* and */. A true argument switches it on again.
slashSlashComments(boolean flag)	If the argument is false, this switches off recognizing comments starting will a double slash. A true argument switches it on again.
lowerCaseMode(boolean flag)	An argument of true causes strings to be converted to lowercase before being stored in sval. An argument of false switches off lowercase mode.
pushback()	Calling this method causes the next call of the nextToken() method to return the ttype value that was set by the previous nextToken() call and to leave sval and nval unchanged.

If you want to alter a tokenizer, it is usually better to reset it by calling the resetSyntax() method and then calling the other methods to set the tokenizer up the way that you want. If you adopt this approach, any special significance attached to particular characters will be apparent from your code. The resetSyntax() method makes all characters, including whitespace and ordinary characters, so that no character has any special significance. In some situations you may need to set a tokenizer up dynamically to suit retrieving each specific kind of data that you want to extract from the stream. When you want to read the next character as a character, whatever it is, you just need to call resetSyntax() before calling nextToken(). The character will be returned by nextToken() and stored in the ttype field. To read anything else subsequently, you have to set the tokenizer up appropriately.

Let's see how you can use this class to read data items from the keyboard.

Try It Out   Creating a Formatted Input Class

One way of reading formatted input is to define your own class that uses a StreamTokenizer object to read from standard input. You can define a class, FormattedInput, that will define methods to return various types of data items entered via the keyboard:

```
import java.io.StreamTokenizer;
import java.io.BufferedReader;
import java.io.InputStreamReader;
import java.io.IOException;

public class FormattedInput {

    // Method to read an int value...

    // Method to read a double value...
```

```
      // Plus methods to read various other data types...

      // Helper method to read the next token
      private int readToken() {
        try {
          ttype = tokenizer.nextToken();
          return ttype;

        } catch (IOException e) {   // Error reading in nextToken()
          e.printStackTrace(System.err);
          System.exit(1);           // End the program
        }
        return 0;
      }


      // Object to tokenize input from the standard input stream
      private StreamTokenizer tokenizer = new StreamTokenizer(
                                    new BufferedReader(
                                      new InputStreamReader(System.in)));
      private int ttype;              // Stores the token type code
    }
```

The default constructor will be quite satisfactory for this class, because the instance variable `tokenizer` is already initialized. The `readToken()` method is there for use in the methods that will read values of various types. It makes the `ttype` value returned by `nextToken()` available directly, and saves having to repeat the `try` and `catch` blocks in all the other methods.

All you need to add are the methods to read the data values that you want. Here is one way to read a value of type `int`:

```
      // Method to read an int value
      public int readInt() {
        for (int i = 0; i < 5; i++) {

          if (readToken() == tokenizer.TT_NUMBER) {
            return (int) tokenizer.nval;    // Value is numeric, so return as int
          } else {
            System.out.println("Incorrect input: " + tokenizer.sval
                            + " Re-enter an integer");
            continue;                       // Retry the read operation
          }


        }
        System.out.println("Five failures reading an int value"
                      + " - program terminated");
        System.exit(1);                     // End the program
        return 0;
      }
```

This method gives the user five chances to enter a valid input value before terminating the program. Terminating the program is likely to be inconvenient to say the least in many circumstances. If you instead make the method throw an exception in the case of failure here, and let the calling method decide what to do, this would be a much better way of signaling that the right kind of data could not be found.

You can define your own exception class for this. Let's define it as the type `InvalidUserInputException`:

```
public class InvalidUserInputException extends Exception {
  public InvalidUserInputException() {}

  public InvalidUserInputException(String message) {
    super(message);
  }
}
```

You haven't had to add anything to the base class capability. You just need the ability to pass your own message to the class. The significant thing you have added is your own exception type name.

Now you can change the code for the `readInt()` method so it works like this:

```
public int readInt() throws InvalidUserInputException {
  if (readToken() != tokenizer.TT_NUMBER) {
    throw new InvalidUserInputException(" readInt() failed. "
                                + "Input data not numeric");
  }
  return (int) tokenizer.nval;
}
```

If you need a method to read an integer value and return it as one of the other integer types, `byte`, `short`, or `long`, you could implement it in the same way, but just cast the value in `nval` to the appropriate type. You might want to add checks that the original value was an integer, and maybe that it was not out of range for the shorter integer types. For example, to do this for type `int`, you could code it as:

```
public int readInt() throws InvalidUserInputException {
  if (readToken() != tokenizer.TT_NUMBER) {
    throw new InvalidUserInputException(" readInt() failed. "
                                + "Input data not numeric");
  }

  if (tokenizer.nval > (double) Integer.MAX_VALUE
          || tokenizer.nval < (double) Integer.MIN_VALUE) {
    throw new InvalidUserInputException(" readInt() failed. "
                                + "Input outside range of type int ");
  }

  if (tokenizer.nval != (double) (int) tokenizer.nval) {
    throw new InvalidUserInputException(" readInt() failed. "
                                + "Input not an integer");
  }
  return (int) tokenizer.nval;
}
```

The `Integer` class makes the maximum and minimum values of type `int` available in the public members `MAX_VALUE` and `MIN_VALUE`. Other classes corresponding to the basic numeric types provide similar fields. To determine whether the value in `nval` is really a whole number, you cast it to an integer, then cast it back to `double` and see whether it is the same value.

To implement `readDouble()`, the code is very simple. You don't need the cast for the value in `nval` since it is type `double` anyway:

```
public double readDouble() throws InvalidUserInputException {
  if (readToken() != tokenizer.TT_NUMBER) {
    throw new InvalidUserInputException(" readDouble() failed. "
                                      + "Input data not numeric");
  }
  return tokenizer.nval;
}
```

A `readFloat()` method would just need to cast `nval` to type `float`.

Reading a string is slightly more involved. You could allow input strings to be quoted or unquoted as long as they were alphanumeric and did not contain whitespace characters. Here's how the method might be coded to allow that:

```
public String readString() throws InvalidUserInputException {
  if (readToken() == tokenizer.TT_WORD || ttype == '\"'
        || ttype == '\'') {
    return tokenizer.sval;
  } else {
    throw new InvalidUserInputException(" readString() failed. "
                                      + "Input data is not a string");
  }
}
```

If either a word or a string is recognized, the token is stored as type `String` in the `sval` field of the `StreamTokenizer` object.

Let's see if it works.

Try It Out   Formatted Keyboard Input

You can try out the `FormattedInput` class in a simple program that iterates round a loop a few times to give you the opportunity to try out correct and incorrect input:

```
public class TestFormattedInput {
  public static void main(String[] args) {
    FormattedInput kb = new FormattedInput();
    for (int i = 0; i < 5; i++) {
      try {
        System.out.print("Enter an integer: ");
        System.out.println("Integer read: " + kb.readInt());
        System.out.print("Enter a double value: ");
        System.out.println("Double value read: " + kb.readDouble());
        System.out.print("Enter a string: ");
        System.out.println("String read: " + kb.readString());
      } catch (InvalidUserInputException e) {
        System.out.println("InvalidUserInputException thrown.\n"
```

```
                                       + e.getMessage());
              }
          }
       }
    }
```

It is best to run this example from the command line. Some Java development environments are not terrific when it comes to keyboard input. If you try a few wrong values, you should see your exception being thrown.

How It Works

This just repeats requests for input of each of the three types of value you have provided methods for, over five iterations. Of course, after an exception of type InvalidUserInputException is thrown, the loop will go straight to the start of the next iteration — if there is one.

This code isn't foolproof. Bits of an incorrect entry can be left in the stream to confuse subsequent input and you can't enter floating-point values with exponents. However, it does work after a fashion and it's best not to look a gift horse in the mouth.

Writing to the Command Line

Up to now, you have made extensive use of the println() method from the PrintStream class in your examples to output formatted information to the screen. The out object in the expression System.out.println() is of type PrintStream. This class outputs data of any of the basic types as a string. For example, an int value of 12345 becomes the string "12345" as generated by the valueOf() method from the String class. However, you also have the PrintWriter class that I discussed earlier in the chapter to do the same thing since this class has all the methods that PrintStream provides.

The principle difference between the two classes is that with the PrintWriter class you can control whether or not the stream buffer is flushed when the println() method is called, whereas with the PrintStream class you cannot. The PrintWriter class will flush the stream buffer only when one of the println() methods is called, if automatic flushing is enabled. A PrintStream object will flush the stream buffer whenever a newline character is written to the stream, regardless of whether it was written by a print() or a println() method.

Both the PrintWriter and PrintStream classes format basic data as characters. In addition to the print() and println() methods that do this, they also define the printf() method mentioned in Chapter 6. This method gives you a great deal more control over the format of the output and will also accept an arbitrary number of arguments to be formatted and displayed.

The printf() Method

The printf() method that is defined in the PrintStream and PrintWriter classes will produce formatted output for an arbitrary sequence of values of various types, where the formatting is specified by the first argument to the method. System.out happens to be of type PrintStream, so you can use printf() to produce formatted output to the command line. The PrintStream and PrintWriter classes define two versions of the printf() method:

`printf(String format, Object ... args)`	Outputs the values of the elements in `args` according to format specifications in `format`. An exception of type `NullPointerException` will be thrown if `format` is `null`.
`printf(Locale loc, String format, Object ... args)`	This version works as the preceding version does except that the output is tailored to the locale specified by the first argument. I'll explain how you define objects of the `java.util.Locale` class type a little later in this chapter.

The format parameter is a string that should contain at least one format specification for each of the argument values that follow the format argument. The format specification for an argument value just defines how the data is to be presented and is of the following general form:

```
%[argument_index$][flags][width][.precision]conversion
```

The square brackets around components of the format specification indicate that they are optional, so the minimum format specification if you omit all of the optional parts is `%conversion`.

The options that you have for the various components of the format specification for a value are:

`conversion`	This is a single character specifying how the argument is to be presented. The commonly used values are: `'d'`, `'o'`, and `'x'` apply to integer values and specify that the output representation of the value should be decimal, octal, or hexadecimal, respectively. `'f'`, `'g'`, and `'a'` apply to floating-point values and specify that the output representation should be decimal notation, scientific notation (with an exponent), or hexadecimal with an exponent, respectively. `'c'` specifies that the argument value is a character and should be displayed as such. `'s'` specifies that the argument is a string. `'b'` specifies that the argument is a boolean value, so it will be output as `"true"` or `"false"`. `'h'` specifies that the hashcode of the argument is to be output in hexadecimal form. `'n'` specifies the platform line separator so `"%n"` will have the same effect as `"\n"`.

Table continued on following page

`argument_index`	This is a decimal integer that identifies one of the arguments that follow the format string by its sequence number, where `"1$"` refers to the first argument, `"2$"` refers to the second argument, and so on. You can also use `'<'` in place of a sequence number followed by `$` to indicate that the argument should be the same as that of the previous format specification in the format string. Thus `"<"` specifies that the format specification applies to the argument specified by the preceding format specification in the format string.
`flags`	This is a set of flag characters that modify the output format. The flag characters that are valid depend on the conversion that is specified. The most-used ones are:
	`'-'` and `'^'` apply to anything and specify that the output should be left-justified and uppercase, respectively.
	`'+'` forces a sign to be output for numerical values.
	`'0'` forces numerical values to be zero-padded.
`width`	Specifies the field width for outputting the argument and represents the minimum number of characters to be written to the output.
`precision`	This is used to restrict the output in some way depending on the conversion. Its primary use is to specify the number of digits of precision when outputting floating-point values.

The best way to explain how you use this is through examples. I'll start with the simplest and work up from there.

Formatting Numerical Data

I suggest that you set up a program source file with an empty version of `main()` into which you can plug a succession of code fragments to try them out.

The minimal format specification is a percent sign followed by a conversion specifier for the type of value you want displayed. For example:

```
int a = 5, b = 15, c = 255;
double x = 27.5, y = 33.75;
System.out.printf("x = %f y = %g", x, y);
System.out.printf(" a = %d b = %x c = %o", a, b, c);
```

Executing this fragment produces the following output:

```
x = 27.500000 y = 33.750000 a = 5 b = f c = 377
```

There is no specification of the argument to which each format specifier applies, so the default action is to match the format specifiers to the arguments in the sequence in which they appear. You can see from the output that you get six decimal places after the decimal point for floating-point values, and the field width is set to be sufficient to accommodate the number of characters in each output value. Although there are two output statements, all the output appears on a single line, so you can deduce that `printf()`

works like the `print()` method in that it just transfers output to the command line starting at the current cursor position.

The integer values also have a default output field width that is sufficient for the number of characters in the output. Here you have output values in normal decimal form, in hexadecimal form, and in octal representation. Note that there must be at least as many arguments as there are format specifiers. If you remove c from the argument list in the last `printf()` call, you will get an exception of type `MissingFormatArgumentException` thrown. If you have more arguments than there are format specifiers in the format string, on the other hand, the excess arguments are simply ignored.

By introducing the argument index into the specification in the previous code fragment, you can demonstrate how that works:

```
int a = 5, b = 15, c = 255;
double x = 27.5, y = 33.75;
System.out.printf("x = %2$f y = %1$g", x, y);
System.out.printf(" a = %3$d b = %1$x c = %2$o", a, b, c);
```

This produces the following output:

```
x = 33.750000 y = 27.500000 a = 255 b = 5 c = 17
```

Here you have reversed the sequence of the floating-point arguments in the output by using the argument index specification to select the argument for the format specifier explicitly. The integer values are also output in a different sequence from the sequence in which the arguments appear.

To try out the use of `"<"` as the argument index specification, you could add the following statement to the preceding fragment:

```
System.out.printf("%n a = %3$d b = %<x c = %<o", a, b, c);
```

This will produce the following output on a new line:

```
a = 255 b = ff c = 377
```

You could equally well use `"\n"` in place of `"%n"` in the format string. The second and third format specifiers use `"<"` as the argument index, so all three apply only to the value of the first argument. The arguments b and c are ignored.

Note that if the format conversion is not consistent with the type of the argument to which you apply it, an exception of type `IllegalFormatConversion` will be thrown. This would occur if you attempted to output any of the variables a, b, and c, which are of type int, with a specifier such as `"%f"`, which applies only to floating-point values.

Specifying the Width and Precision

You can specify the field width for any output value. Here's an example of that:

```
int a = 5, b = 15, c = 255;
double x = 27.5, y = 33.75;
System.out.printf("x = %15f y = %8g", x, y);
System.out.printf(" a = %1$5d b = %2$5x c = %3$2o", a, b, c);
```

Executing this will result in the following output:

```
x =       27.500000 y = 33.750000 a =    5 b =    f c = 377
```

You can see from the output that you get the width that you specify only if it is sufficient to accommodate all the characters in the output value. The second floating-point value, y, occupies a field width of 9, not the 8 that is specified. When you want your output to line up in columns, you must be sure to specify a field width that is sufficient to accommodate every output value.

Where the specified width exceeds the number of characters for the value, the field is padded on the left with spaces so the value appears right-justified in the field. If you want the output left-justified in the field, you just use the '-' flag character. For example:

```
System.out.printf("%na = %1$-5d b = %2$-5x c = %3$-5o", a, b, c);
```

This statement produces output left-justified in the fields, thus:

```
a = 5      b = f      c = 377
```

You can add a precision specification for floating-point output:

```
double x = 27.5, y = 33.75;
System.out.printf("x = %15.2f y = %14.3g", x, y);
```

Here the precision for the first value is two decimal places, and the precision for the second value is 3 decimal places. Therefore, you will get the following output:

```
x =           27.50 y =        33.750
```

Formatting Characters and Strings

The following code fragment outputs characters and their code values:

```
int count = 0;
for(int ch = 'a' ; ch<= 'z' ; ch++) {
  System.out.printf("     %1$4c%1$4x", ch);
  if(++count%6 == 0) {
    System.out.printf("%n");
  }
}
```

Executing this produces the following output:

```
a   61     b   62     c   63     d   64     e   65     f   66
g   67     h   68     i   69     j   6a     k   6b     l   6c
m   6d     n   6e     o   6f     p   70     q   71     r   72
s   73     t   74     u   75     v   76     w   77     x   78
y   79     z   7a
```

First the format specification %1$4c is applied to the first and only argument following the format string. This outputs the value of ch as a character because of the 'c' conversion specification, and in a field width of 4. The second specification is %1$4x, which outputs the same argument—because of the 1$— as hexadecimal because the conversion is 'x' and in a field width of 4.

You could write the output statement in the loop as:

```
System.out.printf("     %1$4c%<4x", ch);
```

The second format specifier is %<x, which will output the same argument as the preceding format specifier because of the '<' following the % sign.

Because a % sign always indicates the start of a format specifier, you must use "%%" in the format string when you want to output a % character. For example:

```
int percentage = 75;
System.out.printf("\n%1$d%%", percentage);
```

The format specifier %1$d outputs the value of percentage as a decimal value. The %% that follows in the format string will display a percent sign, so the output will be:

```
75%
```

You use the %s specifier to output a string. Here's an example that will output the same string twice:

```
String str = "The quick brown fox.";
System.out.printf("%nThe string is:%n%s%n%1$25s", str);
```

This produces the following output:

```
The string is:
The quick brown fox.
        The quick brown fox.
```

The first instance of str in the output is produced by the "%s" specification that follows the first "%n", and the second instance is produced by the "%1$25s" specification. The "%1$25s" specification has a field width that is greater than the length of the string so the string appears right-justified in the output field. You could apply the '-' flag to obtain the string left-justified in the field.

You have many more options and possibilities for formatted output. Try experimenting with them yourself, and if you want details of more specifier options, read the JDK documentation for the printf() method in the PrintStream class.

The Locale Class

You can pass an object of type java.util.Locale as the first argument to the printf() method, preceding the format string and the variable number of arguments that you want displayed. The Locale object specifies a language or a country + language context that affects the way various kinds of data, such as dates or monetary amounts, is presented.

You have three constructors available for creating Locale objects that accept one, two, or three arguments of type String. The first argument specifies a language as a string of two lowercase letters representing a Language Code defined by the standard ISO-639. Examples of language codes are "fr" for French, "en" for English, and "be" for Belarusian. The second argument specifies a country as a string of two uppercase letters representing a Country Code defined by the ISO-3166 standard. Examples of country codes are "US" for the USA, "GB" for the United Kingdom, and "CA" for Canada. The third argument is a vendor or browser-specific code such as "WIN" for Windows or "MAC" for Macintosh.

However, rather than using a class constructor, more often than not you'll use one of the Locale class static constants that provide predefined Locale objects for common national contexts. For example, you have constants JAPAN, ITALY, and GERMANY for countries and JAPANESE, ITALIAN, and GERMAN for the corresponding languages. Consult the JDK documentation for the Locale class for a complete list of these.

Formatting Data into a String

The printf() method produces the string that is output by using an object of type java.util
.Formatter, and it is the Formatter object that is producing the output string from the format string and the argument values. A Formatter object is also used by a static method format() that is defined in the String class, and you can use this method to format data into a string that you can use wherever you like — for displaying data in a component in a windowed application, for example. The static format() method in the String class comes in two versions, and the parameter lists for these are the same as for the two versions of the printf() method in the PrintStream class just discussed, one with the first parameter as a Locale object followed by the format string parameter and the variable parameter list and the other without the Locale parameter. Thus, all the discussion of the format specification and the way it interacts with the arguments you supply applies equally well to the String.format() method, and the result is returned as type String.

For example, you could write the following to output floating-point values:

```
double x = 27.5, y = 33.75;
String outString = String.format("x = %15.2f y = %14.3g", x, y);
```

outString will contain the data formatted according to the first argument to the format() method. You could pass outString to the print() method to output it to the command line:

```
System.out.print(outString);
```

You will get the following output:

```
x =           27.50 y =          33.750
```

This is exactly the same output as you got earlier using the printf() method, but obviously outString is available for use anywhere.

You can use a java.util.Formatter object directly to format data. You first create the Formatter object like this:

```
StringBuffer buf = new StringBuffer();
java.util.Formatter formatter = new java.util.Formatter(buf);
```

The Formatter object will generate the formatted string in the StringBuffer object buf — you could also use a StringBuilder object for this purpose, of course. You now use the format() method for the formatter object to format your data into buf like this:

```
double x = 27.5, y = 33.75;
formatter.format("x = %15.2f y = %14.3g", x, y);
```

If you want to write the result to the command line, the following statement will do it:

```
System.out.print(buf);
```

The result of executing this sequence of statements will be exactly the same as from the previous fragment.

A `Formatter` object can format data and transfer it to destinations other than `StringBuilder` and `StringBuffer` objects, but I'll defer discussion of this until I introduce file output in Chapter 10.

Summary

In this chapter, I have introduced the facilities for inputting and outputting basic types of data to a stream. The important points I have discussed include the following:

❑ A stream is an abstract representation of a source of serial input or a destination for serial output.

❑ The classes supporting stream operations are contained in the package `java.io`.

❑ Two kinds of stream operations are supported: binary stream operations will result in streams that contain bytes, and character stream operations are for streams that contain characters in the local machine character encoding.

❑ No conversion occurs when characters are written to, or read from, a byte stream. Characters are converted from Unicode to the local machine representation of characters when a character stream is written.

❑ Byte streams are represented by subclasses of the classes `InputStream` and `OutputStream`.

❑ Character stream operations are provided by subclasses of the `Reader` and `Writer` classes.

❑ The `printf()` method that is defined in the `PrintStream` and `PrintWriter` classes formats an arbitrary number of argument values according to a format string that you supply. You can use this method for the `System.out` object to produce formatted output to the command line.

❑ The static `format()` method that is defined in the `String` class will format an arbitrary number of argument values according to a format string that you supply and return the result as a `String` object. This method works in essentially the same way as the `printf()` method in the `PrintStream` class.

❑ An object of the `Formatter` class that is defined in the `java.util` package can format data into a `StringBuilder` or `StringBuffer` object, as well as other destinations.

Exercises

You can download the source code for the examples in the book and the solutions to the following exercises from `http://www.wrox.com`.

1. Use a `StreamTokenizer` object to parse a string entered from the keyboard containing a series of data items separated by commas and output each of the items on a separate line.

2.   Create a class defining an object that will parse each line of input from the keyboard that contains items separated by an arbitrary delimiter (for example, a colon, or a comma, or a forward slash, and so on) and return the items as an array of type `String[]`. For example, the input might be:

```
1/one/2/two
```

The output would be returned as an array of type `String[]` containing `"1"`, `"one"`, `"2"`, `"two"`.

3.   Write a program to generate 20 random values of type `double` between -50 and +50 and use the `printf()` method for `System.out` to display them with two decimal places in the following form:

```
 1) +35.93    2) -46.94    3) +42.27    4) +32.09    5) +29.21
 6) +13.87    7) -47.87    8) +30.67    9) -25.20   10) +29.67
11) +48.62   12)  +6.70   13) +28.97   14) -41.64   15) +16.67
16) +17.01   17)  +9.62   18) -15.21   19)  +7.46   20)  +4.09
```

4.   Use a `Formatter` object to format 20 random values of type `double` between -50 and +50 and output the entire set of 20 in a single call of `System.out.print()` or `System.out.println()`.

Accessing Files and Directories

In this chapter, you'll explore how you identify, access, and manipulate files and directories on your hard drive. This will include the ability to create new files and directories, but not to read or write files. You'll get to that starting in the next chapter.

In this chapter you will learn:

- ❑ How you create `File` objects and use them to examine files and directories
- ❑ How you can use `File` class methods to examine the contents of the hard drives on your system
- ❑ How to create new files and directories on your hard drive
- ❑ How to create temporary files
- ❑ How you create `FileOutputStream` objects

Working with File Objects

It is easy to forget that a `File` object doesn't actually represent a file. You need to keep reminding yourself that a `File` object encapsulates a **pathname** or **reference** to what may or may not be a physical file or directory on your hard disk, *not* the physical file or directory itself. The fact that you create a `File` object does not determine that a file or directory actually exists. This is not as strange as it might seem at first sight. After all, you will often be defining a `File` object that encapsulates a path to a new file or directory that you intend to create later in your program.

As you'll see, a `File` object serves two purposes:

- ❑ It enables you to check the pathname that it encapsulates against the physical file system and see whether it corresponds to a real file or directory.
- ❑ You can use it to create file stream objects.

The `File` class provides several methods for you to test the path that a `File` object encapsulates in various ways, as well as the physical file or directory it may represent. You can determine whether or not an object does represent a path to an existing file or directory, for example. If a `File` object does correspond to a real file, you have methods available that you can use to modify the file in a number of ways.

Creating File Objects

You have a choice of four constructors for creating `File` objects. The simplest accepts a `String` object as an argument that specifies a path for a file or a directory. For example, you could write the statement:

```
File myDir = new File("C:/jdk1.5.0/src/java/io");
```

This creates a `File` object encapsulating the path `C:/j2sdk1.4.0/src/java/io`. On my system, this happens to be the path to the directory `io`, which contains the classes in the `java.io` package. On the various flavors of the Microsoft Windows operating system, you can also use an escaped backslash separator, `\\`, when you define a path, instead of `/`, if you wish, but paths do tend to look rather busy if you do. For example:

```
File myDir = new File("C:\\jdk1.5.0\\src\\java\\io");
```

It also requires more typing.

Note that the `File` class constructor here does not check the string that you pass as the argument in any way, so there is no guarantee that a `File` object encapsulates a valid representation of a path on your system at all. For example, this will compile and execute perfectly well:

```
File junk = new File("dwe\n:;?cc/.*\naaf%)(");        // Not a valid path!
```

The argument to the constructor here does not define a valid file or directory path — at least not under any operating system that I am familiar with — but that statement compiles and executes. You can therefore deduce that you can pass *any* string as an argument to the `File` class constructor. It is up to you to ensure that it is valid for your system.

To specify a pathname to a file, you just need to make sure that the string that you pass as an argument to the constructor does refer to a file and not a directory. For example:

```
File myFile = new File("C:/jdk1.5.0/src/java/io/File.java");
```

This statement sets the object `myFile` to correspond to the source file for the definition of the class, `File`.

An important and easily overlooked characteristic of `File` objects is that they are **immutable**. Once you have created a `File` object you cannot change the path it encapsulates. You will see later that you can change the name of the physical file that a `File` object references by using the `rename()` method belonging to the `File` object, but this will not change the `File` object itself. The `File` object will still encapsulate the original path so that once the file name has been changed, the path encapsulated by the `File` object will no longer refer to an existing file. This can be confusing if you don't realize this is the case. Using this `File` object to test subsequently whether the file exists, for example, will return `false`.

You can also create a `File` object that represents a pathname for a file by using a constructor that allows you to specify the directory that contains the file and the file name separately. The directory that contains the file is usually referred to as the **parent** directory. Two constructors allow you to do this, and they offer you a choice as to how you specify the parent directory. In one, the first argument is a reference to a `File` object that encapsulates the path for the directory containing the file. In the other, the first argument specifies the parent directory path as a `String` object. The second argument in both cases is a `String` object identifying the file name.

For example, on my system, I can identify the Java source file for the `File` class with the statements:

```
File myDir = new File("C:/jdk1.5.0/src/java/io");     // Parent directory
File myFile = new File(myDir, "File.java");           // The path to the file
```

The first statement creates a `File` object that refers to the directory for the package `io`, and the second statement creates a `File` object that corresponds to the file `File.java` in that directory.

You could use the second of the two constructors to achieve the same result as the previous two statements:

```
File myFile = new File("C:/jdk1.5.0/src/java/io", "File.java");
```

Using a `File` object to specify the directory is much more useful than using a string directly. For one thing, using a `File` object enables you to verify that the directory does really exist before attempting to access the file or files that you are interested in. You can also create the directory if necessary, as you will see.

The fourth constructor allows you to define a `File` object from an object of type `URI` that encapsulates a **u**niform **r**esource **i**dentifier, commonly known as a **URI**. As you are undoubtedly aware, a URI is used to reference a resource on the World Wide Web and the most common form of URI is a **URL** — a **u**niform **r**esource **l**ocator. A URL usually consists of a protocol specification such as `HTTP`, a host machine identification such as `www.wrox.com`, plus a name that refers to a particular resource on that machine, such as `misc-pages/booklist.shtml`; so, for example, `http://www.wrox.com/misc-pages/booklist.shtml` is a URL that references a page on a Wrox Press server that contains a list of Java books published by Wrox Press and the file downloads that are available for each of them.

The `URI` class provides several constructors for creating URI objects, but getting into the detail of these is too much of a diversion from our present topic — dealing with local files. However, the simplest constructor just accepts a reference to a `String` object and you could use this to create a `File` object like this:

```
File remoteFile = new File(
                new URI(http://www.wrox.com/misc-pages/booklist.shtml));
```

References to physical files inevitably tend to be system-dependent since each operating system will have its own conventions for specifying a path to a file. If you refer to a particular file in the directory `C:\My Java Stuff` under Windows, this path will not be recognized under Unix. However, Java provides capabilities that enable you to avoid system dependencies when you specify file paths, at least to some extent, so let's look at those in more detail.

Portable Path Considerations

The `File` class contains a static member, `separator`, of type `String`, that defines the separator used between names in a path by your operating system. Under Unix, this will be defined as `"/"`, and under MS Windows it will be `"\\"`. As you have seen, when you are specifying a path by a string under Windows, you can use either of these characters as a pathname separator. Another static field, `separatorChar`, defines the same separator character as type `char` for convenience, so you can use whichever suits you. The `File` class also defines the system default character for separating one path from another as the static member `pathSeparator`, which is of type `String`, or as the static member `pathSeparatorChar`, which is of type `char`. The path separator is a semicolon under MS Windows and a colon under Unix.

Of course, the specific makeup of a path is system-dependent, but you could have used the `separator` field in the `File` class to specify the path for `myFile` in a slightly more system-independent way, like this:

```
File myFile = new File("C:" + File.separator + "jdk1.5.0" + File.separator +
                       "src" + File.separator + "java" + File.separator +
                       "io", "File.java");
```

This defines the same path as the earlier statement but without using an explicit separator character between the names in the path. While you have specified the pathname separator character in a portable fashion, the argument to the `File` class constructor is still specific to Windows because you have specified the drive letter as part of the path. To remove the Windows-specific element in the file path you would have to omit the drive letter from the path specification. In this case you would have a **relative path** specification.

Absolute and Relative Paths

In general, the pathname that you use to create a `File` object has two parts: an optional prefix followed by a series of names separated by the system default separator character for pathnames. Under MS Windows the prefix for a path on a local drive will be a string defining the drive, such as `"C:\\"` or `"C:/"`. Under Unix the prefix will be a forward slash, `"/"`. A path that includes a prefix is an **absolute path,** and since it includes a prefix, it is not system-independent. A path without a prefix is a **relative path**, and as long as it consists of one or more names separated by characters specified as `File.separator` or `File.separatorChar`, it should be portable across different systems. The last name in a path can be a directory name or a file name. All other names must be directory names. If you use anything other than this — if you use any system-specific conventions to specify the path, for example — naturally you no longer have a system-independent path specification.

The pathnames you have used in the preceding code fragments have all been absolute paths, since you included the drive letter in the path for Windows or a forward slash to identify the Unix root directory. If you omit this, you have a relative path, and the pathname string will be interpreted as a path *relative* to the current directory. This implies that you can reference a file that is in the same directory as your program by just the file name.

For example:

```
File myFile = new File("output.txt");
```

This statement creates a `File` object encapsulating a pathname string that is just the name "output.txt". This will be interpreted as being the name of a file in the current directory when the `File` object is used. Unless it has been changed programmatically, the current directory will be the directory that was current when program execution was initiated. You will see in a moment how you can obtain the absolute path from a `File` object, regardless of how the `File` object was created.

You could also refer to a file in a subdirectory of the current directory using a relative path:

```
File myFile = new File("dir" + File.separator + "output.txt");
```

Thus, you can use a relative path specification to reference files in the current directory, or in any subdirectory of the current directory, and since a relative path does not involve the system-dependent prefix, this will work across different operating systems.

As you have seen, an absolute path in a Windows environment can have a prefix that is an explicit drive specification, but you can also use the **UNC** (**U**niversal **N**aming **C**onvention) representation of a path, which provides a machine-independent way of identifying paths to shared resources on a network. The name is slightly misleading in that UNC paths are found predominantly in the MS Windows family of operating systems. The UNC representation of a path always begins with two backslashes, followed by the machine name, followed by the share name. In the MS Windows environment, a UNC path will be of the form:

```
\\servername\directory_path\filename
```

In environments other than MS Windows that support the UNC path specification, it may be written in the form:

```
//servername/directory_path/filename
```

On a computer with the name `myPC`, with a shared directory `shared`, you could create a `File` object as follows:

```
File myFile = new File("//myPC/shared/jdk1.5.0/src/java/io", "File.java");
```

If you are keen to practice your typing skills, you could also write this as:

```
File myFile = new File(File.separator + File.separator + "myPC" +
                       File.separator + "shared" + File.separator +
                       "jdk1.4" + File.separator + "src" + File.separator +
                       "java" + File.separator + "io", "File.java");
```

If you want to create a `File` object that refers to the root directory under Unix, you just use "/" as the path.

Accessing System Properties

While you can specify a relative path to a file that is not system-dependent, in some circumstances you might want to specify a path that is independent of the current environment, but where the current directory, or even a subdirectory of the current directory, is not a convenient place to store a data file. In this case, accessing one of the **system properties** can help. A system property specifies values for parameters related to the system environment in which your program is executing. Each system property is identified by a unique name and has a value associated with the name that is defined as a string. A set of standard system properties is always available, and you can access the values of any of these by passing the name of the property that you are interested in to the static getProperty() method that is defined in the System class.

For example, the directory that is the default base for relative paths is defined by the property that has the name "user.dir", so you can access the path to this directory with the statement:

```
String currentDir = System.getProperty("user.dir");
```

You could then use this to specify explicitly where the file with the name "output.txt" is located:

```
File dataFile = new File(currentDir, "output.txt");
```

Of course, this is equivalent to just specifying the file name as the relative path, so you have not achieved anything new. However, another system property with the name "user.home" has a value that defines a path to the user's home directory. You could therefore specify that the "output.txt" file is to be in this directory as follows:

```
File dataFile = new File(System.getProperty("user.home"), "output.txt");
```

The location of the user's home directory is system-dependent, but wherever it is you can access it in this way without building system dependencies into your code.

Naturally, you could specify the second argument to the constructor here to include directories that are to be subdirectories of the home directory. For instance:

```
File dataFile = new File(System.getProperty("user.home"),
                         "dir" + File.separator + "output.txt");
```

On my system this defines the path:

```
C:\Documents and Settings\Ivor Horton\dir\output.txt
```

If you want to plug this code fragment into a main() method and see what path the resultant File object encapsulates, the following statement will output the absolute path for you:

```
System.out.println(dataFile.getAbsolutePath());
```

This uses the getAbsolutePath() method for the File object to obtain the absolute path as a reference to a String object. I will come back to this method in a moment.

If you would like to see what the full set of standard system properties are, you will find the complete list in the JDK documentation for the static getProperties() method in the System class. You can also retrieve the current set of properties on your system and their values by calling the getProperties() method, so let's put a little program together to do that.

Getting the Default System Properties

Here's the program to list the keys and values for the current set of system properties on your computer:

```
public class TryProperties {
    public static void main(String[] args) {
        java.util.Properties properties = System.getProperties();
        properties.list(System.out);
    }
}
```

This will output all the system properties.

How It Works

The `getProperties()` method returns the set of system properties encapsulated in an object of type `Properties`. The `Properties` class is defined in the `java.util` package, and the program uses the fully qualified class name rather than an import statement for it. You call the `list()` method for the `Properties` object to output the properties to the stream that is passed as the argument, in this case `System.out`, which corresponds to your display screen.

Setting System Properties

As I discussed in the previous section, once you know the key for a system property you can obtain its value, which is a `String` object, by calling the static `getProperty()` method in the `System` class and passing the key for the property you are interested in as the argument. You can also change the value for a system property by calling the static `setProperty()` method in the `System` class. The `setProperty()` method expects two arguments; the first is a `String` object identifying the property to be changed, and the second is a `String` object that is the new property value.

You also have the possibility to remove the current value that is set for a property by using the static `clearProperty()` method in the `System` class. You just pass a string specifying the property key as the argument. For example:

```
String oldValue = System.clearProperty("java.class.path");
```

This statement will remove the Java classpath specification, so you won't want to do this unless you have good reason to do so. The `clearProperty()` method returns the value that was set for the property before it was cleared as a reference of type `String`. It is possible that the Java security manager may not permit this operation to be carried out, in which case an exception of type `SecurityException` will be thrown. The method will throw an exception of type `NullPointerException` if the argument is `null`, or an exception of type `IllegalArgumentException` if you pass an empty string as the argument.

For a specific example of where you might want to set a system property, suppose that you wanted to change the specification for the system property that specifies the current working directory. That property has the key `"user.dir"`, so you could use the following statement:

```
System.setProperty("user.dir", "C:/MyProg");
```

Executing this statement changes the current working directory to `"C:/MyProg"`. Now when you are using a relative path, it will be relative to this directory. You can change the system property that defines the current directory as often as you like in your program, so you can always adjust the current directory to be the one containing the file you are working with if that is convenient. Of course, when you do this, you need to be sure that the directory does exist, so it would be wise to verify that the directory is there before executing the call to the `setProperty()` method. That sort of verification is the next topic of this chapter.

Testing and Checking File Objects

The `File` class provides more than 30 methods that you can apply to `File` objects, so I will just introduce the ones that will be most useful to you, grouped by the sorts of things that they do.

First of all, you can get information about a `File` object itself by using the following methods:

Method	Description
getName()	Returns a `String` object containing the name of the file without the path — in other words, the last name in the path stored in the object. For a `File` object representing a directory, just the directory name is returned.
getPath()	Returns a `String` object containing the path for the `File` object — including the file or directory name.
isAbsolute()	Returns `true` if the `File` object refers to an absolute pathname, and `false` otherwise. Under MS Windows, an absolute pathname begins with either a drive letter followed by a colon and then a backslash or a double backslash. Under Unix, an absolute path is specified from the root directory down.
getParent()	Returns a `String` object containing the name of the parent directory of the file or directory represented by the current `File` object. This will be the original path without the last name. The method returns `null` if there is no parent specified. This will be the case if the `File` object was created for a file in the current directory by just using a file name.
getParentFile()	Returns the parent directory as a `File` object, or `null` if this File object does not have a parent.
toString()	Returns a `String` representation of the current `File` object and is called automatically when a `File` object is concatenated with a `String` object. You have used this method implicitly in output statements. The string that is returned is the same as that returned by the `getPath()` method.
hashCode()	Returns a hashcode value for the current `File` object. You will see more about what hashcodes are used for in Chapter 14.
equals()	You use this method for comparing two `File` objects for equality. If the `File` object passed as an argument to the method has the same path as the current object, the method returns `true`. Otherwise, it returns `false`.

```
        System.out.println(myFile + (myFile.isHidden() ? " is" : " is not")
                           + " hidden");
        System.out.println("You can" + (myFile.canRead() ? " " : "not ")
                           + "read " + myFile);
        System.out.println("You can" + (myFile.canWrite() ? " " : "not ")
                           + "write " + myFile);
        return;
    }
}
```

On my machine, the above example produces the following output:

```
C:\jdk1.5.0\src\java\io is a directory.
C:\jdk1.5.0\src\java\io\File.java does exist
C:\jdk1.5.0\src\java\io\File.java is a file.
C:\jdk1.5.0\src\java\io\File.java is not hidden
You can read C:\jdk1.5.0\src\java\io\File.java
You can write C:\jdk1.5.0\src\java\io\File.java
```

How It Works

This program first creates an object corresponding to the directory containing the java.io package. You will need to check the path to this directory on your own system and insert that as the argument to the constructor of the File object. The output statement then uses the conditional operator ?: in conjunction with the isDirectory() method to display a message. If isDirectory() returns true, then " is" is selected. Otherwise, " is not" is selected. The program then creates another File object corresponding to the file File.java and displays further information about the file using the same sort of mechanism. Finally, the program uses the canRead() and canWrite() methods to determine whether read and write access to the file is permitted.

If you are using MS Windows, you might like to try out the separator \\ with this example and see if it makes a difference.

You can use the following methods for a File object to obtain further information about the file or directory, if it exists:

Method	Description
list()	If the current File object represents a directory, a String array is returned containing the names of the members of the directory. If the directory is empty, the array will be empty. If the current File object is a file, null is returned. The method will throw an exception of type SecurityException if access to the directory is not authorized.
listFiles()	If the object for which this method is called is a directory, it returns an array of File objects corresponding to the files and directories in that directory. If the directory is empty, then the array that is returned will be empty. The method will return null if the object is not a directory, or if an I/O error occurs. The method will throw an exception of type SecurityException if access to the directory is not authorized.

Table continued on following page

Method	Description
length()	Returns a value of type long that is the length, in bytes, of the file represented by the current File object. If the pathname for the current object references a file that does not exist, then the method will return zero. If the pathname refers to a directory, then the value returned is undefined.
lastModified()	Returns a value of type long that represents the time that the directory or file represented by the current File object was last modified. This time is the number of milliseconds since midnight on 1st January 1970 GMT. It returns zero if the file does not exist.

A static method defined in the File class, listRoots(), returns an array of File objects. Each element in the array that is returned corresponds to a root directory in the current file system. The path to every file in the system will begin with one or another of these roots. In the case of a Unix system, for example, the array returned will contain just one element corresponding to the single root on a Unix system, /. Under MS Windows, the array will contain an element for each logical drive that you have, including floppy drives, CD drives, and DVD drives. The following statements will list all the root directories on your system:

```
File[] roots = File.listRoots();
    for(File root : roots) {
       System.out.println(root);
}
```

The for loop lists the elements of the array returned by the listRoots() method.

With a variation on the last example, you can try out some of these methods.

Try It Out   Getting More Information

You can arrange to list all the files in a directory and record when they were last modified with the following program:

```
import java.io.File;
import java.util.Date;                  // For the Date class

public class TryFile2 {
  public static void main(String[] args) {

    // Create an object that is a directory
    File myDir = new File("C:/jdk1.5.0/src/java/io");
    System.out.println(myDir.getAbsolutePath()
                 + (myDir.isDirectory() ? " is " : " is not ")
                 + "a directory");
    System.out.println("The parent of " + myDir.getName() + " is "
                 + myDir.getParent());

    // Get the contents of the directory
    File[] contents = myDir.listFiles();
```

```
    // List the contents of the directory
    if (contents != null) {
      System.out.println("\nThe " + contents.length
                           + " items in the directory " + myDir.getName()
                           + " are:");
      for (File file : contents) {
        System.out.println(file + " is a "
                   + (file.isDirectory() ? "directory" : "file")
                   + " last modified on:\n"
                   + new Date(file.lastModified()));
      }
    } else {
      System.out.println(myDir.getName() + " is not a directory");
    }

    System.exit(0);
  }
}
```

Again, you need to use a path that is appropriate for your system. You should not have any difficulty seeing how this works. The first part of the program creates a `File` object representing the same directory as in the previous example. The second part itemizes all the files and subdirectories in the directory. The output will look something like this:

```
C:\jdk1.5.0\src\java\io is a directory
The parent of io is C:\jdk1.5.0\src\java

The 80 items in the directory io are:
C:\jdk1.5.0\src\java\io\Bits.java is a file last modified on
Thu Dec 11 00:20:12 GMT 2003
C:\jdk1.5.0\src\java\io\BufferedInputStream.java is a file last modified on
Thu Dec 11 00:20:12 GMT 2003
C:\jdk1.5.0\src\java\io\BufferedOutputStream.java is a file last modified on
Thu Dec 11 00:20:12 GMT 2003
C:\jdk1.5.0\src\java\io\BufferedReader.java is a file last modified on
Thu Dec 11 00:20:12 GMT 2003
C:\jdk1.5.0\src\java\io\BufferedWriter.java is a file last modified on
Thu Dec 11 00:20:12 GMT 2003
                 .
                 .
                 .
```

and so on.

How It Works

You can see from the output that the `getName()` method just returns the file name or the directory name, depending on what the `File` object represents.

The `listFiles()` method returns a `File` array, with each element of the array representing a member of the directory, which could be a subdirectory or a file. You store the reference to the array returned by the method in the array variable `contents`. After outputting a heading, you check that the array is not `null`. You then list the contents of the directory in the collection-based `for` loop. You use the `isDirectory()`

method to determine whether each item is a file or a directory and create the output accordingly. You could just as easily have used the `isFile()` method here. The `lastModified()` method returns a `long` value that represents the time, in milliseconds, when the file was last modified since midnight on 1st January 1970. To get this to a more readable form, you use the value to create a `Date` object, and the `toString()` method for the class returns what you see in the output. The `Date` class is defined in the `java.util` package (see Chapter 15). You have imported this into the program file, but you could just as well use the fully qualified class name `java.util.Date` instead. If the `contents` array is `null`, you just output a message. You could easily add code to output the length of each file here, if you want.

There is a standard system property with the key `"java.home"` that identifies the directory that is the root directory of the Java run-time environment. If you have installed the JDK (rather than just a JRE), this will be the `jre` subdirectory to the JDK subdirectory, which on my system is `C:/jdk1.5.0`. In this case, the value of `java.home` will be `"C:/jdk1.5.0/jre"`. You could therefore use this to refer to the file in the previous example in a system-independent way. If you create a `File` object from the value of the `java.home` property, calling its `getParent()` method will return the parent directory as a `String` object. This will be the JDK home directory, so you could use this as the base directory to access the source files for the class libraries, like this:

```
File myDir = new File(new File(System.getProperty("java.home")).getParent(),
                      "src" + File.separator+"java" + File.separator+"io");
```

As long as the JRE that is in effect is the one installed as part of the JDK, you have a system-independent way of accessing the source files for the library classes.

Filtering a File List

The `list()` and `listFiles()` methods in the `File` class are overloaded with versions that accept an argument used to filter a file list. This enables you to get a list of those files with a given extension, or with names that start with a particular sequence of characters. For example, you could ask for all files starting with the letter *T*, which might return the two files you created above: "TryFile.java" and "TryFile2.java". The argument that you pass to the `list()` method must be a variable of type `FilenameFilter`, whereas the `listFiles()` method is overloaded with versions to accept arguments of type `FilenameFilter` or `FileFilter`. Both `FilenameFilter` and `FileFilter` are interfaces that contain the abstract method `accept()`. The `FilenameFilter` interface is defined in the `java.io` package as:

```
public interface FilenameFilter {
  public abstract boolean accept(File directory, String filename);
}
```

The `FileFilter` interface, which is also defined in `java.io`, is very similar:

```
public interface FileFilter {
  public abstract boolean accept(File pathname);
}
```

The only distinction between these two interfaces is the parameter list for the method that they both declare. The `accept()` method in the `FilenameFilter` class has two parameters for you to specify: the directory plus the file name to identify a particular file, so this is clearly aimed at testing whether a given file should be included in a list of files. The `accept()` method for the `FileFilter` interface has just a single parameter of type `File`, and this is used to filter files and directories.

The object that you pass as an argument to the `list()` or `listFiles()` method must implement either the `FilenameFilter` or the `FileFilter` interface, respectively. The filtering of the list is achieved by the `list()` or `listFiles()` method by calling the method `accept()` that is defined for your object for every item in the raw list. If the method returns `true`, the item stays in the list, and if it returns `false`, the item is not included. Obviously, these interfaces act as a vehicle to allow the mechanism to work, so you need to define your own class that implements the appropriate interface. If you are using the `list()` method, your class must implement the `FilenameFilter` interface. If you are using the `listFiles()` method, you can implement either interface. How you actually filter the filenames is entirely up to you. You can arrange to do whatever you like within the class that you define. You can see how this works by extending the previous example a little further.

Try It Out   Using the FilenameFilter Interface

You can define a class to specify a file filter as:

```java
import java.io.File;
import java.io.FilenameFilter;

public class FileListFilter implements FilenameFilter {
  private String name;        // File name filter
  private String extension;   // File extension filter

  // Constructor
  public FileListFilter(String name, String extension) {
    this.name = name;
    this.extension = extension;
  }

  public boolean accept(File directory, String filename) {
    boolean fileOK = true;

    // If there is a name filter specified, check the file name
    if (name != null) {
      fileOK &= filename.startsWith(name);
    }

    // If there is an extension filter, check the file extension
    if (extension != null) {
      fileOK &= filename.endsWith('.' + extension);
    }

    return fileOK;
  }
}
```

This uses the methods `startsWith()` and `endsWith()`, which are defined in the `String` class that I discussed in Chapter 4. Save this source in the same directory as the previous example, as `FileListFilter.java`.

Now you need a modified version of your `TryFile2.java` code as follows:

```java
import java.io.File;
import java.io.FilenameFilter;
import java.util.Date;                        // For the Date class

public class TryFile3 {
  public static void main(String[] args) {

    // Create an object that is a directory
    File myDir = new File("C:/jdk1.5.0/src/java/io");
    System.out.println(myDir.getAbsolutePath()
                       + (myDir.isDirectory() ? " is " : " is not ")
                       + "a directory");
    System.out.println("The parent of " + myDir.getName() + " is "
                       + myDir.getParent());

    // Define a filter for java source files beginning with F
    FilenameFilter select = new FileListFilter("F", "java");

    // Get the contents of the directory
    File[] contents = myDir.listFiles(select);

    // List the contents
    if (contents != null) {
      System.out.println("\nThe " + contents.length
                         + " matching items in the directory, "
                         + myDir.getName() + ", are:");
      for (File file : contents) {
        System.out.println(file + " is a "
                         + (file.isDirectory() ? "directory" : "file")
                         + " last modified on\n"
                         + new Date(file.lastModified()));
      }
    } else {
      System.out.println(myDir.getName() + " is not a directory");
    }

    return;
  }
}
```

It is best to continue with our numbering convention and call the above script `TryFile3.java`. I put both source files for this example in a new directory, `TryFile3`. When you run this code, you should get something like the following:

```
C:\jdk1.5.0\src\java\io is a directory
The parent of io is C:\jdk1.5.0\src\java

The 15 matching items in the directory, io, are:
D:\jdk1.5.0\src\java\io\File.java is a file last modified on
Fri Jan 23 00:23:26 GMT 2004
D:\jdk1.5.0\src\java\io\FileDescriptor.java is a file last modified on
Fri Jan 23 00:31:14 GMT 2004
```

```
D:\jdk1.5.0\src\java\io\FileFilter.java is a file last modified Fri Jan 23 00:23:26
GMT 2004
D:\jdk1.5.0\src\java\io\FileInputStream.java is a file last modified on
Fri Jan 23 00:23:26 GMT 2004
      .
      .
      .
```

and so on.

How It Works

Our `FileListFilter` class has two instance variables — name and `extension`. The name variable stores the file name prefix, and `extension` selects file types to be included in a list. The constructor sets these variables, and the value of either can be omitted when the constructor is called by specifying the appropriate argument as `null`. If you want a really fancy filter, you can have just one argument to the constructor and specify the filter as `*.java`, or `A*.java`, or even `A*.j*`. You would just need a bit more code in the constructor or possibly the `accept()` method to analyze the argument. Our implementation of the `accept()` method here returns `true` only if the file name that is passed to it by the `list()` method has initial characters that are identical to `name`, and the file extension is the same as that stored in `extension`.

In the modified example, you construct an object of our filter class using the string "F" as the file name prefix and the string ".java" as the extension. This version of the example will now list only files with names beginning with F and with the extension .java.

Creating and Modifying Files and Directories

There are methods defined in the `File` class that you can use to change the physical file by making it read-only or renaming it. There are also methods that enable you to create files and directories, and to delete them. The methods that provide you with these capabilities are the following:

Method	Description
renameTo(File path)	The file represented by the current object will be renamed to the path represented by the `File` object passed as an argument to the method. Note that this does *not* change the current `File` object in your program — it alters the physical file. Thus, the file that the `File` object represents will no longer exist after executing this method, because the file will have a new name and possibly will be located in a different directory. If the file's directory in the new path is different from the original, the file will be moved. The method will fail if the directory in the new path for the file does not exist, or if you don't have write access to it. If the operation is successful, the method will return `true`. Otherwise, it will return `false`.
setReadOnly()	Sets the file represented by the current object as read-only and returns `true` if the operation is successful.

Table continued on following page

417

Method	Description
mkdir()	Creates a directory with the path specified by the current File object. The method will fail if the parent directory of the directory to be created does not already exist. The method returns true if it is successful and false otherwise.
mkdirs()	Creates the directory represented by the current File object, including any parent directories that are required. It returns true if the new directory is created successfully and false otherwise. Note that even if the method fails, some of the directories in the path may have been created.
createNewFile()	Creates a new empty file with the pathname defined by the current File object as long as the file does not already exist. The method returns true if the file was created successfully. Note that this method will create a file only in an existing directory — it will not create any directories specified by the path.

createTempFile(
  String prefix,
  String suffix,
  File directory)
	This is a static method that creates a temporary file in the directory directory, with a name created using the first two arguments, and returns a File object corresponding to the file created. The string prefix represents the start of the file name and must be at least three characters long. The string suffix specifies the file extension. The file name will be formed from prefix followed by five or more generated characters, followed by suffix. If suffix is null, .tmp will be used. If prefix or suffix are too long for file names on the current system, they will be truncated, but neither will be truncated to less than three characters. If the directory argument is null, the system temporary directory will be used. If the file cannot be created, an IOException will be thrown. If prefix has less than three characters, an IllegalArgumentException will be thrown.

createTempFile(
  String prefix,
  String suffix)
	Calling this method is equivalent to calling the preceding version with the last argument as null:
	createTempFile(String prefix, String suffix, null)

delete()	This will delete the file or directory represented by the current File object and return true if the delete was successful. It won't delete directories that are not empty. To delete a directory, you must first delete the files it contains.
deleteOnExit()	Causes the file or directory represented by the current File object to be deleted when the program ends. This method does not return a value. The deletion will be attempted only if the JVM terminates normally. Once you call the method for a File object, the delete operation is irrevocable, so you will need to be cautious with this method.

Note that, in spite of the name, the files that you create by using the createTempFile() method are not necessarily temporary, as they will not be deleted automatically. You must use delete() or deleteOnExit() to ensure that files you no longer require are removed.

You can arrange for a temporary file to be deleted automatically at the end of the program by calling the `deleteOnExit()` method for the `File` object. For example, you might write:

```
File tempFile = File.createTempFile("list", null);
tempFile.deleteOnExit();
```

The first statement will create a temporary file with a name of the form `listxxxxx.tmp` in the default temporary directory. The xxxxx part of the name is generated automatically. Since you did not supply a `suffix`, the file extension will be `.tmp` by default. The second statement calls the `deleteOnExit()` method for `tempFile`, so you are assured that this file won't be left lying around after the program finishes. You can apply the `deleteOnExit()` method to any `File` object, not just those corresponding to temporary files, but do so with caution. As has been noted, the delete is irrevocable once you have called the method!

You will be trying out some of these methods in examples later in this chapter. Now that you understand how to define objects encapsulating a path in a Java program, you can move on to creating file stream objects. I'll introduce file output streams first.

Creating File Output Streams

You use a `FileOutputStream` object when you want to write to a physical file on a disk. The `FileOutputStream` class is derived from the `OutputStream` class and therefore inherits the methods of that class for writing to a file. However, I won't bother going into detail on these or the versions in the `FileOutputStream` class that override them, as you will be using the new file channel capability to write to a file.

There are five constructors for `FileOutputStream` objects:

Constructor	Description
`FileOutputStream(` `String filename)`	Creates an output stream for the file `filename`. The existing contents of the file will be overwritten. If the file cannot be opened for any reason, an exception of type `FileNotFoundException` will be thrown.

`FileOutputStream(`
    `String filename,`
    `boolean append)`
	Creates an output stream for the file `filename`. Data written to the file will be appended following the existing contents if append is `true`. If append is `false`, any existing file contents will be overwritten. If the file cannot be opened for any reason, an exception of type `FileNotFoundException` will be thrown.

`FileOutputStream(` `File file)`	Creates a file output stream for the file represented by the object `file`. Any existing file contents will be overwritten. If the file cannot be opened, an exception of type `FileNotFoundException` will be thrown.

Table continued on following page

Constructor	Description

FileOutputStream(
    File file,
    boolean append)
	Creates a file output stream for the file represented by the object file. Data written to the file will be appended following the existing contents if append is true. If append is false, any existing file contents will be overwritten. If the file cannot be opened for writing for any reason, an exception of type FileNotFoundException will the thrown.

FileOutputStream(FileDescriptor desc)	Creates an output stream corresponding to the argument desc. A FileDescriptor object represents an existing connection to a file, so since the file must exist, this constructor does not throw an exception of type FileNotFoundException.

The first four constructors will create the file if it does not already exist, but only if the parent directory exists, so it's a good idea to check this before calling the constructor. All of these constructors can throw a SecurityException if writing to the file is not authorized on your system, although by default there is no security manager for an application, in which case there are no restrictions on writing files. Once you have created a FileOutputStream object, the physical file is automatically opened, ready to be written. Once you have written the file, using a **channel** (as you'll see in Chapter 10), you can close the file by calling the close() method for the FileOutputStream object. This also closes the file channel and releases all system resources associated with the stream.

To create a stream object of type FileOutputStream, you will typically create a File object first and then pass that to a FileOutputStream constructor. This approach enables you to check the properties of the file using the File object before you try to create the stream and in this way avoid potential problems. Of course, you can create a FileOutputStream object directly from a String object that defines the path and file name, but it is generally much less convenient to do this. I will come back to the third possibility — creating a file stream object from a FileDescriptor object — in a moment.

In passing, here's how you would create a file output stream directly from the file name:

```
FileOutputStream outputFile = null;     // Place to store the stream reference
try {
  outputFile = new FileOutputStream("myFile.txt");
} catch(FileNotFoundException e) {
  e.printStackTrace(System.err);
}
```

If the file cannot be opened, the constructor will throw a FileNotFoundException, which won't be very convenient in most circumstances. You must put the call to the constructor in a try block and catch the exception if you want the code to compile, unless of course you arrange for the method containing the constructor call to pass on the exception with a throws clause. The exception will be thrown if the path refers to a directory rather than a file, or if the parent directory in the path does not exist. If the file does not exist, but the directory that is supposed to contain it does exist, the constructor will create a new file for you. Of course, you must declare the outputFile variable prior to the try block. If you declare it within the try block, the variable will not exist outside it. Creating a File object first enables you to check the file out and deal with any potential problems. Let's look at ways in which you can apply this.

Ensuring a File Exists

Let's suppose that you want to append data to a file if it exists and create a new file if it doesn't. Either way, you want to end up with a file output stream to work with. You will need to go through several checks to achieve this:

❑   Use the `File` object to verify that it actually represents a file rather than a directory. If it doesn't, you can't go any further, so output an error message.

❑   Use the `File` object to decide whether the file exists. If it doesn't, ensure that you have a `File` object with an absolute path. You need this to obtain and check out the parent directory.

❑   Get the path for the parent directory and create another `File` object using this path. Use the new `File` object to check whether the parent directory exists. If it doesn't, create it using the `mkDirs()` method for the new `File` object.

Let's look at how that might be done in practice.

Try It Out   Ensuring That a File Exists

You could guarantee a file is available with the following code:

```java
import java.io.File;
import java.io.FileOutputStream;
import java.io.FileNotFoundException;

public class GuaranteeAFile {
  public static void main(String[] args) {
    String filename = "C:/Beg Java Stuff/Bonzo/Beanbag/myFile.txt";
    File aFile = new File(filename);    // Create the File object

    // Verify the path is a file
    if (aFile.isDirectory()) {

      // Abort after a message
      // You could get input from the keyboard here and try again...
      System.out.println("The path " + aFile.getPath()
                      + " does not specify a file. Program aborted.");
      System.exit(1);
    }

    // If the file doesn't exist
    if (!aFile.isFile()) {
      // Check the parent directory...
      aFile = aFile.getAbsoluteFile();
      File parentDir = new File(aFile.getParent());
      if (!parentDir.exists()) {         // ... and create it if necessary
        parentDir.mkdirs();
      }
    }

    FileOutputStream outputFile = null;// Place to store the stream reference
    try {
```

```
          // Create the stream opened to append data
          outputFile = new FileOutputStream(aFile, true);
      } catch (FileNotFoundException e) {
        e.printStackTrace(System.err);
      }
      System.exit(0);
    }
  }
```

Don't forget to change the file name and path if the `filename` string isn't convenient in your environment. After executing this code, you should find that all the necessary directories and the file have been created if they don't already exist. You can try this out with paths with a variety of directory levels. Delete them all when you are done, though.

How It Works

You call `isDirectory()` in the `if` statement to see whether the path is just a directory. Instead of aborting at this point, you could invite input of a new path from the keyboard, but I'll leave that for you to try. Next, you check whether the file exists. If it doesn't, you call `getAbsoluteFile()` to ensure that our `File` object has a parent path. If you don't do this and you have a file specified with a parent, in the current directory, for example, then `getParent()` will return `null`. Having established the `File` object with an absolute path, you create a `File` object for the directory containing the file. If this directory does not exist, calling `mkdirs()` will create all the directories required for the path so that you can then safely create the file stream. The `FileOutputStream` constructor can in theory throw a `FileNotFoundException`, although not in our situation here. In any event, you must put the `try` and `catch` block in for the exception.

A further possibility is that you might start with two strings defining the directory path and the file name separately. You might then want to be sure that you had a valid directory before you created the file. You could do that like this:

```
String dirname = "C:/Beg Java Stuff";   // Directory name
String filename = "charData.txt";        // File name

File dir = new File(dirname);            // File object for directory
if (!dir.exists()) {                     // If directory does not exist...
  if (!dir.mkdirs()) {                   // ...create it
    System.out.println("Cannot create directory: " + dirname);
    System.exit(1);
  }
} else if (!dir.isDirectory()) {
  System.err.println(dirname + " is not a directory");
  System.exit(1);
}

// Now create the file...
```

If the directory doesn't exist, you call `mkdirs()` inside the nested `if` to create it. Since the method returns `false` if the directory was not created, this will determine whether or not you have indeed managed to create the directory.

Avoiding Overwriting a File

In some situations when the file does exist, you may not want it to be overwritten. Here is one way you could avoid overwriting a file if it already exists:

```
String filename = "C:/Beg Java Stuff/myFile.txt";
File aFile = new File(filename);
FileOutputStream outputFile = null;     // Place to store the stream reference
if (aFile.isFile()) {
  System.out.println("myFile.txt already exists.");
} else {
  // Create the file stream
  try {
    // Create the stream opened to append data
    outputFile = new FileOutputStream(aFile);
    System.out.println("myFile.txt output stream created");
  } catch (FileNotFoundException e) {
    e.printStackTrace(System.err);
  }
}
```

Of course, if you want to be sure that the path will in fact result in a new file being created when it doesn't already exist, you would need to put in the code from the previous example that checks out the parent directory. The preceding fragment avoids overwriting the file, but it is not terribly helpful. If the file exists, you create the same `FileOutputStream` object as before, but if it doesn't, you just toss out an error message. In practice, you are more likely to want the program to take some action so that the existing file is protected but the new file still gets written. One solution would be to rename the original file in some way if it exists, and then create the new one with the same name as the original. This takes a little work though.

Try It Out   Avoiding Overwriting a File

Without worrying about plugging in the code that ensures that the file directory exists, here is how you could prevent an existing file from being overwritten. As always, you should change the file name and path to suit your environment if necessary.

```
import java.io.File;
import java.io.FileOutputStream;
import java.io.FileNotFoundException;

public class AvoidOverwritingFile {
  public static void main(String[] args) {
    String filepath = "C:/Beg Java Stuff/myFile.txt";
    File aFile = new File(filepath);
    FileOutputStream outputFile = null;     // Stores the stream reference
    if (aFile.isFile()) {
      File newFile = aFile;                 // Start with the original file
```

```
            // Append "_old" to the file name repeatedly until it is unique
            do {
              String name = newFile.getName();      // Get the name of the file
              int period =
                name.indexOf('.');                   // Find the separator for the extension
              newFile = new File(newFile.getParent(),
                                 name.substring(0, period) + "_old"
                                 + name.substring(period));
            } while(newFile.exists());              // Stop when no such file exists
            aFile.renameTo(newFile);                // Rename the file
          }

          // Now we can create the new file
          try {

            // Create the stream opened to append data
            outputFile = new FileOutputStream(aFile);
            System.out.println("myFile.txt output stream created");
          } catch (FileNotFoundException e) {
            e.printStackTrace(System.err);
          }
          System.exit(0);
      }
    }
```

If you run this a few times, you should see some _old_old... files created.

How It Works

If the file exists, the code in the if block executes. This stores the reference to the original File object in newFile as a starting point for the do-while loop that follows. Each iteration of the loop appends the string "_old" to the name of the file and creates a new File object using this name in the original directory. The expression in the loop condition tests whether the new File object referenced by newFile corresponds to an existing file. If it does, the original file cannot be renamed to this name so the loop continues and adds a further occurrence of _old to the file name. Eventually, this process should arrive at a name that does not correspond to an existing file as long as the permitted file name length of the system in not exceeded. At this point the loop ends and the original file is renamed to the name corresponding to newFile.

I use the getParent() method in the loop to obtain the parent directory for the file, and the getName() method returns the file name. I have to split the file name into the name part and the extension to append the "_old" string, and the charAt() method for the String object gives the index position of the period separating the name from the file extension. Of course, this code presumes the existence of a file extension since I define my original file name with one. It is quite possible to deal with files that don't have an extension, but I'll leave that as a little digression for you.

FileDescriptor Objects

A FileOutputStream object has a method getFD() that returns an object of type FileDescriptor that represents the current connection to the physical file. You cannot create a FileDescriptor object yourself. You can only obtain a FileDescriptor object by calling the getFD() method for an object that represents a file stream. Once you have closed the stream, you can no longer obtain the `FileDescriptor` object for it since the connection to the file will have been terminated.

You can use a `FileDescriptor` object to create other stream objects when you want to have several connected to the same file concurrently. Since a `FileDescriptor` object represents an existing connection, you can only use it to create streams with read and/or write permissions that are consistent with the original stream. You can't use the `FileDescriptor` object from a `FileOutputStream` to create a `FileInputStream`, for example.

If you look at the documentation for the `FileDescriptor` class, you'll see that it also defines three public static data members: `in`, `out`, and `err`, which are themselves of type `FileDescriptor`. These correspond to the standard system input, the standard system output, and the standard error stream, respectively, and they are there as a convenience for when you want to create byte or character stream objects corresponding to the standard streams.

> Don't confuse the data members of the `FileDescriptor` class with the data members of the same name defined by the `System` class in the `java.lang` package. The `in`, `out`, and `err` data members of the `System` class are of type `PrintStream`, so they have the `print()`, `println()`, and `printf()` methods. The `FileDescriptor` data members do not. A `PrintStream` object is a stream, whereas a `FileDescriptor` object is not.

Summary

In this chapter, I've discussed the facilities for inspecting physical files and directories and for writing basic types of data to a file. The important points I have discussed include the following:

- ❑ An object of the class `File` can encapsulate a file or directory path. The path encapsulated by a `File` object does not necessarily correspond to a physical file or directory.

- ❑ You can use a `File` object to test whether the path it encapsulates refers to a physical file or directory. If it does not, there are methods available to create it together with any directories that are part of the path that may also be required.

- ❑ The `File` class defines static methods for creating temporary files.

- ❑ An object of type `FileDescriptor` can also identify a physical file.

- ❑ A `FileOutputStream` object can be created from a `File` object, and the file will be opened for writing. If the file does not exist, it will be created where possible.

Exercises

You can download the source code for the examples in the book and the solutions to the following exercises from `http://www.wrox.com`.

1. Modify the example that avoids overwriting a file to permit the file path to be entered as a command-line argument and to allow for file names that do not have extensions.

2. File names on many systems are not of unlimited length, so appending _old to file names may break down at some point. Modify the example that avoids overwriting a file to append a three-digit numerical value to the file name to differentiate it from the existing file instead of just adding _old. The program should check for the presence of three digits at the end of the name for the existing file and replace this with a value incremented by an amount to make it unique. (That is, increment the last three digits by 1 until a unique file name is created.)

3. Write a program that will list all the directories in a directory defined by a path supplied as a command-line argument, or all the directories on a system if no command-line argument is present. (Hint: The listRoots() method will give you the roots on a system and the listFiles() method will give you an array of File objects for the files and directories in any given directory — including a root.)

Writing Files

In this chapter, you'll be looking at ways in which basic data can be written to a file using the new file input/output capability that was introduced in the 1.4 release of the JDK and that continues in JDK 5.0. This mechanism for file I/O largely superseded the read/write capability provided by readers and writers from the `java.io` package when applied to file streams. Since the new file I/O does everything that the old capability does, and does it better, I'll focus just on that.

In this chapter you'll learn:

- ❏ The principles of reading and writing files using the new I/O capability
- ❏ How you obtain a file channel for a file
- ❏ How you create a buffer and load it with data
- ❏ What view buffers are and how you use them
- ❏ How you use a channel object to write the contents of a buffer to a file

File I/O Basics

If you are new to programming file operations, there are a couple of things about how they work that may not be apparent to you and can be a source of confusion so I'll clarify these before I go any further. If you already know how input and output for disk files work, you can skip this section.

First, let's consider the nature of a file. Once you have written data to a file, what you have is just a linear sequence of bytes. The bytes in a file are referenced by their offset from the beginning, so the first byte is byte 0, the next byte is byte 1, the third byte is byte 2, and so on through to the end of the file. If there are n bytes in a file, the last byte will be at offset n-1. There is no specific information in the file about how the data originated or what it represents unless you explicitly put it there. Even if there is, you need to know that it's there and read and interpret the data accordingly.

For example, if you write a series of 25 binary values of type int to a file, it will contain 100 bytes. Nothing in the file will indicate that the data consists of 4-byte integers so there is nothing to prevent you from reading the data back as 50 Unicode characters or 10 long values followed by a string, or any other arbitrary collection of data items that corresponds to 100 bytes. Of course, the result is unlikely to be very meaningful unless you interpret the data in the form in which it was originally written. This implies that to read data from a file correctly, you need to have prior knowledge of the structure and format of the data that is in the file.

The form of the data in the file may be recorded or implied in many ways. For example, one way that the format of the data in a file can be communicated is to use an agreed file name extension for data of a particular kind, such as .java for a Java source file or .jpg for a graphical image file or .wav for a sound file. Each type of file has a predefined structure, so from the file extension you know how to interpret the data in the file. Of course, another way of transferring data so that it can be interpreted correctly is to use a generalized mechanism for communicating data and its structure, such as XML. You will be looking into how you can work with XML in your Java applications in Chapters 22 and 23.

You can access an existing file to read it or write it in two different ways, described as **sequential access** or **random access**. The latter is sometimes referred to as **direct access**. Sequential access to a file is quite straightforward and works pretty much as you would expect. Sequential read access involves reading bytes from the file starting from the beginning with byte 0. Of course, if you are interested only in the file contents starting at byte 100, you can just read and ignore the first 100 bytes. Sequential write access involves writing bytes to the file starting at the beginning if you are replacing the existing data or writing a new file, and writing bytes starting at the end if you are appending new data to an existing file.

The term random access is sometimes misunderstood initially. Just like sequential access, random access is just a way of accessing data in a file and has nothing to do with how the data in the file is structured or how the physical file was originally written. You can access any file randomly for reading and/or writing. When you access a file randomly, you can read one or more bytes from the file starting at any point. For example, you could read 20 bytes starting at the 13th byte in the file (which will be the byte at offset 12, of course) and then read 50 bytes starting at the 101st byte or any other point that you choose. Similarly, you can update an existing file in random access mode by writing data starting at any point in the file. In random access mode, the choice of where to start reading or writing and how many bytes you read or write is entirely up to you. You just need to know the offset for the byte where a read or write operation should start. Of course, for these to be sensible and successful operations, you have to have a clear idea of how the data in the file is structured.

First a note of caution: Before running any of the examples in this chapter, be sure to set up a separate directory for storing the files that you are using when you are testing programs. It's also not a bad idea to back up any files and directories on your system that you don't want to risk losing. But of course, you do back up your files regularly anyway — right?

The old adage "If anything can go wrong, it will," applies particularly in this context, as does the complementary principle "If anything can't go wrong, it will." Remember also that the probability of something going wrong increases in proportion to the inconvenience it is likely to cause.

File Input and Output

The new file I/O capabilities that were introduced in Java 1.4 provided the potential for substantially improved performance over the I/O facilities of previous releases, the only cost being some slight increase in complexity. Three kinds of objects are involved in reading and writing files using the new I/O capability:

❑ A file stream object that encapsulates the physical file that you are working with. You saw how to create `FileOutputStream` objects at the end of the previous chapter, and you use these for files to which you want to write. In the next chapter, you will be using `FileInputStream` objects for files that you want to read.

❑ One or more **buffer** objects in which you put the data to be written to a file, or from which you get the data that has been read. You'll learn about buffer objects in the next section.

❑ A **channel** object that provides the connection to the file and does the reading or writing of the data using one or more buffer objects. You'll see how to obtain a channel from a file stream object later in this chapter.

The way in which these types of objects work together is illustrated in Figure 10-1.

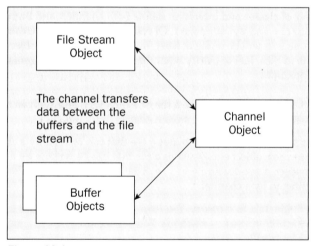

Figure 10-1

The process for writing and reading files is basically quite simple. To write to a file, you load data into one or more buffers that you have created and then call a method for the channel object to write the data to the file that is encapsulated by the file stream. To read from a file, you call a method for the channel object to read data from the file into one or more buffers, and then retrieve the data from the buffers.

You will be using four classes defined in the `java.io` package when you are working with files. As I've said, the `FileInputStream` and `FileOutputStream` classes define objects that provide access to a file for reading or writing, respectively. You use an object of type `RandomAccessFile` when you want to access a file randomly, or when you want to use a single channel to both read from and write to a file. You'll be exploring this, along with the `FileInputStream` class, in the next chapter. You will see from the JDK documentation for the `FileInputStream`, `FileOutputStream`, and `RandomAccessFile` classes that they each provide methods for I/O operations. However, I'll ignore these, as you'll be using the services of a file channel to perform operations with objects of these stream classes. The only method from these classes that you will be using is the `close()` method, which closes the file and any associated channel.

Channels

Channels were introduced in the 1.4 release of Java to provide a faster capability for input and output operations with files, network sockets, and piped I/O operations between programs than the methods provided by the stream classes. I will be discussing channels only in the context of files, not because the other uses for channels are difficult, but just to keep the book focused on the essentials so that the potential for a hernia is minimized. The channel mechanism can take advantage of buffering and other capabilities of the underlying operating system and therefore is considerably more efficient than using the operations provided directly within the file stream classes. As I said earlier, a channel transfers data between a file and one or more buffers. I'll first introduce the overall relationships between the various classes that define channels and buffers, and then look into the details of how you use channels with file streams.

A considerable number of classes and interfaces define both channels and buffers. They also have similar names such as `ByteBuffer` and `ByteChannel`. Of course, `File` and file stream objects are also involved in file I/O operations, so you will be using at least four different types of objects working together when you read from or write to files. Just to clarify what they all do, here's a summary of the essential role of each of them in file operations:

❑ A `File` object encapsulates a path to a file or a directory, and such an object encapsulating a file path can be used to construct a file stream object.

❑ A `FileInputStream` object encapsulates a file that can be read by a channel. A `FileOutputstream` object encapsulates a file that can be written by a channel. As you will see in the next chapter, a `RandomAccessFile` object can encapsulate a file that can be both read from and written to by a channel.

❑ A buffer just holds data in memory. You load the data that you want to write to a file into a buffer using the buffer's `put()` methods. You use a buffer's `get()` methods to retrieve data that has been read from a file.

❑ You obtain a `FileChannel` object from a file stream object or a `RandomAccessFile` object. You use a `FileChannel` object to read and/or write a file using the `read()` and `write()` methods for the `FileChannel` object, with a buffer or buffers as the source or destination of the data.

The channel interfaces and classes that you will be using are in the `java.nio.channels` package. The classes that define buffers are defined in the `java.nio` package. In a program that reads or writes files, you will therefore need import statements for class names from at least three packages, the two packages I have just introduced plus the `java.io` package.

Channel Operations

A series of channel interfaces exists, each of which declares a set of one or more related operations that a channel may perform. They all extend a common interface, Channel, which declares two methods:

❑   The close() method, which closes a channel

❑   The isOpen() method, which tests the state of the channel, returning true if it is open and false otherwise

Note that closing a channel does not necessarily close the file to which the channel is attached, but closing a file also closes its channel. The channel interfaces are related as illustrated in the hierarchy shown in Figure 10-2.

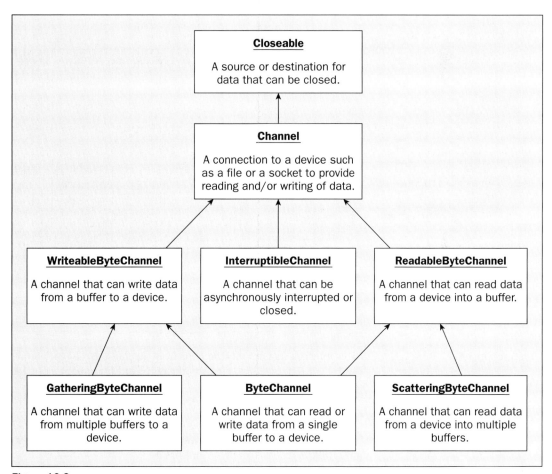

Figure 10-2

Each arrow points from a given interface to an interface that it extends. The ByteChannel interface simply combines the operations specified by the ReadableByteChannel and WritableByteChannel interfaces without declaring any additional methods. The ScatteringByteChannel interface extends the ReadableByteChannel interface by adding methods that allow data to be read and distributed amongst several separate buffers in a single operation. The GatheringByteChannel interface adds methods to those of the WritableByteChannel interface to permit writing from a number of separate buffers in a single operation. The InterruptibleChannel interface is implemented by classes encapsulating channels for network sockets and other interruptible devices; I will be concentrating on file operations so I won't discuss this interface further.

The methods that each interface in the hierarchy declares are as follows:

Interface	Method and Description
Closeable	void close() Closes the source or destination and releases any resources associated with it.
Channel	void close() Closes the channel boolean isOpen() Returns true if the channel is open and false otherwise.
ReadableByteChannel	int read(ByteBuffer input) Reads bytes from a channel into the buffer specified by the argument and returns the number of bytes read, or -1 if the end of the stream is reached.
WritableByteChannel	int write(ByteBuffer output) Writes bytes from the buffer specified by the argument to the channel and returns the number of bytes written.
ByteChannel	This interface just inherits methods from the ReadableByteChannel and WritableByteChannel interfaces. No additional methods are declared.
ScatteringByteChannel	int read(ByteBuffer[] inputs) Reads bytes from the channel into the array of buffers specified by the argument and returns the number of bytes read or -1 if the end of the stream is reached. int read(ByteBuffer[] inputs, int offset, int length) Reads bytes from the channel into length buffers from the array specified by the first argument starting with the buffer inputs[offset].

Interface	Method and Description
`GatheringByteChannel`	`int write(ByteBuffer[] outputs)`
	Writes bytes from the array of buffers specified by the argument to the channel, and returns the number of bytes written.
	`int write(ByteBuffer[] outputs, int offset,` `int length)`
	Writes bytes to the channel from `length` buffers from the array specified by the first argument, starting with the buffer `outputs[offset]`.

All of these methods can throw exceptions of one kind or another, and I'll go into details on these when you come to apply them. Note that a channel works only with buffers of type `ByteBuffer`. Other kinds of buffers do exist as you'll see, but you can't use them directly with the `read()` and `write()` methods for a channel. You'll see what determines the number of bytes read or written in an operation when I discuss buffers in detail shortly.

File Channels

A `FileChannel` object defines a channel for a physical file and provides an efficient mechanism for reading, writing, and manipulating the file. You can't create a `FileChannel` directly. You first have to create a file stream object for the file, then obtain a reference to the `FileChannel` object for the file by calling the `getChannel()` method for the file stream object. Here's how you would obtain the channel for a `FileOutputStream` object:

```
File aFile = new File("C:/Beg Java Stuff/myFile.text");
FileOutputStream outputFile = null;    // Place to store an output stream reference
try {
  // Create the stream opened to write
  outputFile = new FileOutputStream(aFile);
} catch (FileNotFoundException e) {
  e.printStackTrace(System.err);
  System.exit(1);
}
// Get the channel for the file
FileChannel outputChannel = outputFile.getChannel();
```

The `FileChannel` class implements all of the channel interfaces that I discussed in the previous section, so any `FileChannel` object incorporates the methods you have seen for both reading and writing a file. However, a `FileChannel` object obtained from a `FileOutputStream` object will not be able to read from the file since the stream permits only output. Similarly, a `FileChannel` obtained from a `FileInputStream` object can only read from the file. If you try to perform a read operation on a file opened just for output, a `NonReadableChannelException` will be thrown. Attempting to write to a file opened for input will result in a `NonWritableChannelException` being thrown.

Once you have obtained a reference to a file channel, you are ready to read from or write to the file, but you need to learn a bit more about buffers before you can try that out.

Buffers

All the classes that define buffers have the abstract `Buffer` class as a base. The `Buffer` class therefore defines the fundamental characteristics common to all buffers. A particular buffer can store a sequence of elements of a given type, and an element can be of any primitive data type other than `boolean`. Thus, you can create buffers to store `byte` values, `char` values, `short` values, `int` values, `long` values, `float` values, or `double` values. The following classes in the `java.nio` package define these buffers:

Class	Description
ByteBuffer	A buffer that stores values of type `byte`. You can also store the binary values of any of the other primitive types in this buffer, except for type `boolean`. Each binary value that you store will occupy a number of bytes in the buffer determined by the type — values of type `char` or `short` will occupy 2 bytes, `int` values will occupy 4 bytes, and so on. Only buffers of this type can be used in a file I/O operation.
CharBuffer	A buffer that stores only values of type `char`
ShortBuffer	A buffer that stores only values of type `short`
IntBuffer	A buffer that stores only values of type `int`
LongBuffer	A buffer that stores only values of type `long`
FloatBuffer	A buffer that stores only values of type `float`
DoubleBuffer	A buffer that stores only values of type `double`

I keep repeating "except for type `boolean`" every so often, so I had better address that. The various types of buffers provide only for the numerical data types, and type `boolean` does not fit into this category. Of course, you may actually want to record some `boolean` values in a file. In this case, you have to devise a suitable alternative representation. You could use integer values 0 and 1, or perhaps strings `"true"` and `"false"`, or even characters `'t'` and `'f'`. You could even represent a `boolean` value as a single bit and pack eight of them at a time into a single byte, but this is likely to be worthwhile only if you have a lot of them. Which approach you choose will depend on what is most convenient in the context in which you are using the `boolean` values.

While you have seven different classes defining buffers, a channel uses only buffers of type `ByteBuffer` to read or write data. The other types of buffers in the table above are called **view buffers**, because they are usually created as views of an existing buffer of type `ByteBuffer`. You'll see how and why a little later in this chapter.

Buffer Capacity

Each type of buffer stores elements of a specific kind — a `ByteBuffer` object holds bytes, a `LongBuffer` object holds integers of type `long`, and so on for the other buffer types. The capacity of a buffer is the maximum number of values it can contain, not the number of bytes — unless, of course, it stores elements of type `byte`. The capacity of a buffer is fixed when you create it and cannot be changed subsequently. You can obtain the capacity for a buffer object as a value of type `int` by calling the `capacity()`

method that it inherits from the `Buffer` class. Figure 10-3 shows the capacities of different buffers when each occupies the same amount of memory.

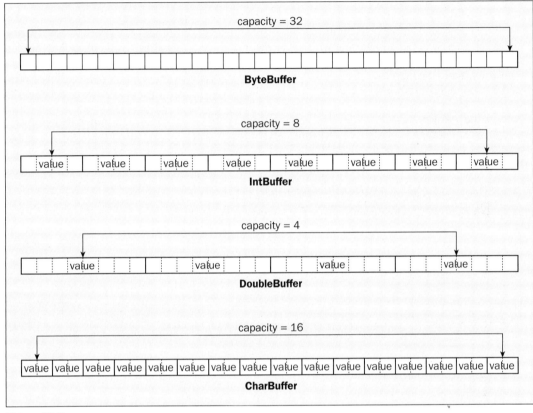

Figure 10-3

Of course, for a buffer that stores bytes, the capacity is the maximum number of bytes it can hold, but for a buffer of type `DoubleBuffer`, for example, which stores `double` values, the capacity is the maximum number of values of type `double` you can put in it. Values in a buffer are indexed from zero, so the index position for referencing values in a buffer runs from 0 to `capacity-1`.

Buffer Position and Limit

A buffer also has a **limit** and a **position**, both of which affect data transfer operations to or from the buffer. In the case of a `ByteBuffer`, the position and limit control read and write operations executed by a channel using the buffer.

The position is the index position of the next buffer element to be read or written. This may sound a little strange, but keep in mind that a `ByteBuffer` can be for file input or output and you can transfer values into and out of other types of buffer. Consider a couple of examples. With a `ByteBuffer` that you are using for file output, the position identifies the location in the buffer of the next byte to be written to the file. For a `ByteBuffer` used for file input, the position identifies where the next byte that is read from the file will be stored in the buffer. When you transfer one or more values into a `DoubleBuffer` or an `IntBuffer` for example, the position indicates where the first value will be stored in the buffer. When you are extracting values, the position indicates the location of the first value to be extracted.

The limit is the index position in a buffer of the first value that should not be read or written. Thus, elements can be read or written starting with the element at `position` and up to and including the element at `limit-1`. Thus if you want to fill a buffer, the position must be at zero since this is where the first data item will go, and the limit must be equal to the capacity since the last data item has to be stored at the last element in the buffer, which is `capacity-1`.

You use the position and limit for a `ByteBuffer` to determine what bytes in the buffer are involved in a read or write operation executed by a channel. How the position and limit affect I/O operations is easier to understand if you take a specific example. First consider an operation that writes data from the buffer to a file. This is illustrated in Figure 10-4.

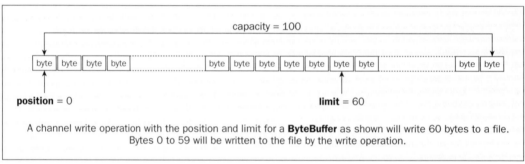

A channel write operation with the position and limit for a **ByteBuffer** as shown will write 60 bytes to a file. Bytes 0 to 59 will be written to the file by the write operation.

Figure 10-4

When a file write operation is executed by a channel using a given `ByteBuffer`, elements from the buffer will be written to the file starting at the index specified by the position. Successive bytes will be written to the file up to, and including, the byte at index position `limit-1`. Thus with the buffer shown in Figure 10-4, 60 bytes will be written to the file. When you want to write all the data from a buffer, you should set the buffer position to 0 and the limit to the buffer capacity. In this case the limit will be an index value that is one beyond the index value for the last byte in the buffer, so `limit-1` will refer to the last byte.

For a read operation, data that is read from the file is stored in a `ByteBuffer` starting at the byte at the index given by the buffer's position. Assuming that the end of the file is not reached before all the bytes are read, bytes will continue to be read up to and including the byte at the index `limit-1`. Thus, the number of bytes read will be `limit-position`, and the bytes will be stored in the buffer from the byte at `position` up to and including the byte at `limit-1`.

As I said at the beginning of this section, the position and limit are involved when you load data into a buffer or retrieve data from it. This applies for any type of buffer. The position specifies where the next value will be inserted in a buffer or retrieved from it. As you'll see, the position will usually be automatically incremented to point to the next available position when you insert or extract values in a buffer.

The limit acts as a constraint to indicate where the data in a buffer ends, a bit like an end-of-file marker. You cannot insert or extract elements beyond the position specified by the limit.

Since a buffer's position is an index, it must be greater than or equal to zero. You can also deduce that it must also be less than or equal to the limit. Clearly, the limit cannot be greater than the capacity of a buffer. Otherwise, you could be trying to write elements to positions beyond the end of the buffer. However, as you have seen, it can be equal to it. These relationships can be expressed as:

```
0 ≤ position ≤ limit ≤ capacity
```

As a general rule, if your code attempts to do things directly or indirectly that result in these relationships being violated, an exception will be thrown.

When you create a new independent buffer, its capacity will be fixed at a value that you specify. It will also have a position of zero and its limit will be set to its capacity. When you create a view buffer from an existing `ByteBuffer`, the contents of the view buffer start at the current position for the `ByteBuffer`. The capacity and limit for the view buffer will be set to the limit for the original buffer, divided by the number of bytes in an element in the view buffer. The limit and position for the view buffer will subsequently be independent of the limit and position for the original buffer.

Setting the Position and Limit

You can set the position and limit for a buffer explicitly by using the following methods that are defined in the `Buffer` class:

Method	Description
`position(int newPosition)`	Sets the position to the index value specified by the argument. The new position value must be greater than or equal to zero, and not greater than the current limit; otherwise, an exception of type `IllegalArgumentException` will be thrown. If the buffer's mark is defined (I will explain the mark in the next section) and greater than the new position, it will be discarded.
`limit(int newLimit)`	Sets the limit to the index value specified by the argument. If the buffer's position is greater than the new limit it will be set to the new limit. If the buffer's mark is defined and exceeds the new limit, it will be discarded. If the new limit value is negative or greater than the buffer's capacity, an exception of type `IllegalArgumentException` will be thrown.

Both of these methods return a reference of type `Buffer` for the object for which they were called. This enables you to chain calls to these methods together in a single statement. For example, given a buffer reference `buf`, you could set both the position and the limit with the statement:

```
buf.limit(512).position(256);
```

This assumes the capacity of the buffer is at least 512 elements. If you are explicitly setting both the limit and the position, you should always choose the sequence in which you set them to avoid setting a position that is greater than the limit. If the buffer's limit starts out less than the new position you want to set, attempting to set the position first results in an `IllegalArgumentException` being thrown. Setting the limit first to a value less than the current position will have a similar effect. If you want to avoid checking the current limit and position when you want to reset both, you can always do it safely like this:

```
buf.position(0).limit(newLimit).position(newPosition);
```

Of course, the new position and limit values must be legal; otherwise, an exception will still be thrown. In other words, `newPosition` must be non-negative and less than `newLimit`. To be 100 percent certain that setting a new position and limit is going to work, you could code it something like this:

```
if(newPosition >= 0 && newLimit > newPosition) {
  buf.position(0).limit(newLimit).position(newPosition);
} else {
  System.out.println("Illegal position:limit settings."
               + "Position: " + newPosition + " Limit: "+ newLimit);
}
```

You can determine whether there are any elements between the position and the limit in a buffer by calling the `hasRemaining()` method for the buffer:

```
if (buf.hasRemaining()) {            // If limit-position is >0
  System.out.println("We have space in the buffer!");
}
```

You can also find out how many values can currently be accommodated by using the `remaining()` method. For example:

```
System.out.println("The buffer can accommodate " + buf.remaining() +
                                " more elements.");
```

Of course, the value returned by the `remaining()` method will be the same as the expression `buf.limit()-buf.position()`.

Creating Buffers

None of the classes that define buffers have public constructors available. Instead, you use a static factory method to create a buffer. You will typically create a buffer object of type `ByteBuffer` by calling the static `allocate()` method for the class. You pass a value of type `int` as an argument to the method that defines the capacity of the buffer — the maximum number of bytes that the buffer must accommodate. For example:

```
ByteBuffer buf = ByteBuffer.allocate(1024);      // Buffer of 1024 bytes capacity
```

When you create a new buffer using the `allocate()` method for the buffer class, it will have a position of zero, and its limit will be set to its capacity. The buffer that the preceding statement creates will therefore have a position of 0, and a limit and capacity of 1024.

You can also create other types of buffers in the same way. For example:

```
// Buffer stores 100 float values
FloatBuffer floatBuf = FloatBuffer.allocate(100);
```

This creates a buffer with a capacity to store 100 values of type `float`. Since each element occupies 4 bytes, the data in this buffer will occupy 400 bytes. The buffer's initial position will be 0, and its limit and capacity will be 100.

In practice, you are unlikely to want to create buffers other than `ByteBuffer` objects in this way, since you cannot use them directly for channel I/O operations. You will usually create a `ByteBuffer` object first and then create any view buffers that you need from this buffer.

View Buffers

You can use a `ByteBuffer` object to create a buffer of any of the other types I have introduced that shares all or part of the memory that the original `ByteBuffer` uses to store data. Such a buffer is referred to as a **view buffer** because it provides a view of the contents of the byte buffer as elements of another data type. Data is always transferred to or from a file as a series of bytes, but it will typically consist of data values of a mix of types other than type `byte`. A view buffer therefore has two primary uses: for loading data items that are not of type `byte` into a `ByteBuffer` prior to writing it to a file, and accessing data that has been read from a file as values that are other than type `byte`.

You could create a view buffer of type `IntBuffer` from a `ByteBuffer` object like this:

```
ByteBuffer buf = ByteBuffer.allocate(1024);    // Buffer of 1024 bytes capacity
IntBuffer intBuf = buf.asIntBuffer();          // Now create a view buffer
```

The content of the view buffer, `intBuf`, that you create here will start at the byte buffer's current position, which in this case is zero since it is newly created. The remaining bytes in `buf` will effectively be shared with the view buffer. At least, the maximum number of them that is a multiple of 4 will be, since `intBuf` stores elements of type `int` that require 4 bytes each. The view buffer will have an initial position of 0, and a capacity and limit of 256. This is because 256 elements of type `int` completely fill the 1024 bytes remaining in `buf`. If you had allocated `buf` with 1023 bytes, then `intBuf` would have mapped to 1020 bytes of `buf` and would have a capacity and limit of 255.

You could now use this view buffer to load the original buffer with values of type `int`. You could then use the original byte buffer to write the `int` values to a file. As I said at the outset, view buffers have a similar role when you are reading a file. You would have a primary buffer of type `ByteBuffer` into which you read bytes from a file, and then you might access the contents of the `ByteBuffer` through a view buffer of type `DoubleBuffer` to enable you to retrieve the data that is read from the file as values of type `double`.

The `ByteBuffer` class defines the following methods for creating view buffers for a byte buffer object:

Method	Description
asCharBuffer()	Returns a reference to a view buffer of type CharBuffer
asShortBuffer()	Returns a reference to a view buffer of type ShortBuffer
asIntBuffer()	Returns a reference to a view buffer of type IntBuffer
asLongBuffer()	Returns a reference to a view buffer of type LongBuffer
asFloatBuffer()	Returns a reference to a view buffer of type FloatBuffer
asDoubleBuffer()	Returns a reference to a view buffer of type DoubleBuffer
asReadOnlyBuffer()	Returns a reference to a read-only view buffer of type ByteBuffer

In each case, the view buffer's contents start at the current position of the original byte buffer. The position of the view buffer itself is initially set to zero, and its capacity and limit are set to the number of bytes remaining in the original byte buffer divided by the number of bytes in the type of element that the view buffer holds. Figure 10-5 illustrates a view buffer of type IntBuffer that is created after the initial position of the byte buffer has been incremented by 2, possibly after inserting a value of type char into the byte buffer:

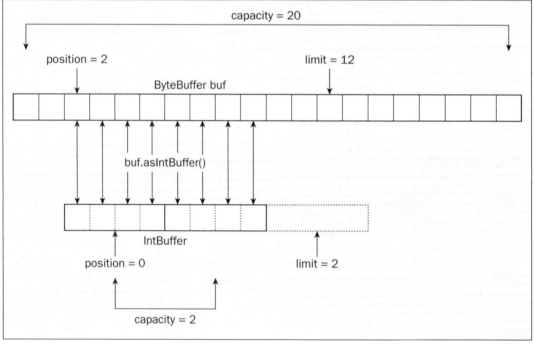

Figure 10-5

You can create as many view buffers from a buffer of type `ByteBuffer` as you want, and they can overlap or not as you require. A view buffer always maps to bytes in the byte buffer starting at the current position. You will frequently want to map several different view buffers to a single byte buffer so that each provides a view of a different segment of the byte buffer in terms of a particular type of value. Figure 10-6 illustrates this situation.

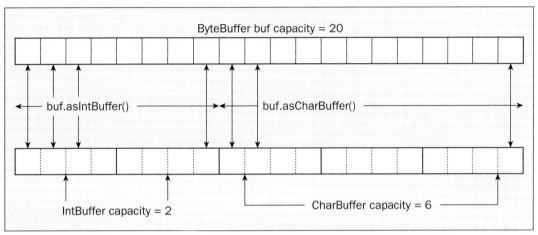

Figure 10-6

The diagram illustrates a byte buffer with a view buffer of type `IntBuffer` mapped to the first 8 bytes, and a view buffer of type `CharBuffer` mapped to the last 12 bytes. All you need to do to achieve this is to ensure that the position of the byte buffer is set appropriately before you create each view buffer.

Duplicating and Slicing Buffers

You can duplicate any of the buffers I have discussed by calling the `duplicate()` method for a buffer. The method returns a reference to a buffer with the same type as the original, and which shares the contents and memory of the original buffer. The duplicate buffer initially has the same capacity, position, and limit as the original. However, although changes to the contents of the duplicate will be reflected in the original, and vice versa, the position and limit for the original buffer and the duplicate are independent of one other. One use for a duplicate buffer is when you want to access different parts of a buffer's contents concurrently. You can retrieve data from a duplicate buffer without affecting the original buffer in any way. A buffer and its duplicate are illustrated in Figure 10-7.

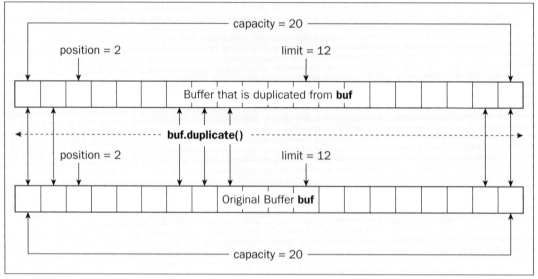

Figure 10-7

Thus a duplicate buffer is not really a new buffer in memory. It is just a new object that provides an alternative route to accessing the same block of memory that is being used to buffer the data. The `duplicate()` method returns a reference of a new object of the same type as the original, but has no independent data storage. It merely shares the memory that belongs to the original buffer object but with independent position and limit values.

You can also **slice** any of the buffers you have seen. Calling the `slice()` method for a buffer will return a reference to a new buffer object of the same type as the original that shares the elements that remain in the original buffer. Slicing a buffer is illustrated in Figure 10-8.

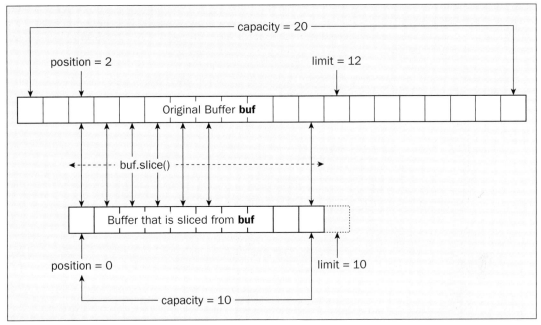

Figure 10-8

A buffer produced by the `slice()` method maps to a part of the original buffer starting at the element at its current position, up to and including the element at `limit-1`. Of course, if the position of the original buffer object is zero and the limit is equal to the capacity, the `slice()` method effectively produces the same result as the `duplicate()` method — that is, the entire buffer will be shared. Slicing a buffer gives you access to the data in a given part of a buffer through two or more separate routes, each with its own independent position and limit.

Creating Buffers by Wrapping Arrays

You can also create a buffer by wrapping an existing array of the same type as the buffer elements by calling one of the static `wrap()` methods that are inherited from the `Buffer` class. This method creates a buffer that already contains the data in the array. For example, you could create a `ByteBuffer` object by wrapping an array of type `byte[]`, like this:

```
String saying = "Handsome is as handsome does.";
byte[] array = saying.getBytes();                    // Get string as byte array
ByteBuffer buf = ByteBuffer.wrap(array);
```

These statements convert the `saying` string to a byte array using the default platform charset and create a byte buffer containing the array. Of course, you could convert the string to a byte array and create the buffer in a single statement:

```
ByteBuffer buf = ByteBuffer.wrap(saying.getBytes());
```

443

In any event, the buffer object will not have memory of its own to store the data. The buffer will be backed by the byte array that you have used to define it so modifications to the values in the buffer will alter the array, and vice versa. The capacity and limit for the buffer will be set to the length of the array, and its position will be zero.

You can also wrap an array to create a buffer so that the position and limit correspond to a particular sequence of elements in the array. For example:

```
String saying = "Handsome is as handsome does.";
byte[] array = saying.getBytes();            // Get string as byte array
ByteBuffer buf = ByteBuffer.wrap(array, 9, 14);
```

This creates a buffer by wrapping the whole array as before, but the position and limit are set using the second and third argument. Thus in effect, the second and third arguments to the `wrap()` method specify the subsection of the array that is to be read or written next. This is illustrated in Figure 10-9.

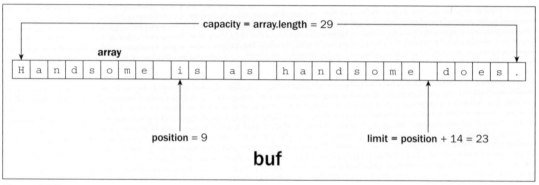

Figure 10-9

The buffer's capacity will be `array.length` and the position is set to the value of the second argument, 9. The third argument specifies the number of buffer elements that can be read or written so this value will be added to the position to define the limit. If either the second argument value or the sums of the second and third argument values do not represent legal index values for the array, then an exception of type `IndexOutOfBoundsException` will be thrown.

You can also wrap arrays of other primitive types to create a buffer of the corresponding type. For example:

```
long[] numbers = { 1, 1, 2, 3, 5, 8, 13, 21, 34, 55, 89};
LongBuffer numBuf = LongBuffer.wrap(numbers);
```

The buffer of type `LongBuffer` that you create here will have a capacity of `array.length`, which will be 11. The buffer position will be set to 0 and the limit will be set to the capacity. In a similar manner you can create buffers from arrays of any of the other basic types with the exception of type `boolean`.

If a buffer object has been created from an array, you can obtain a reference to the backing array that is storing the data in the buffer by calling the `array()` method for the buffer. For example, for the buffer created by the previous code fragment, you could obtain a reference to the original array like this:

```
long[] data = numBuf.array();
```

The variable `data` will now contain a reference to the original array, `numbers`, which you used to create `numBuf`. If the buffer had not been created from an array, the `array()` method will throw an exception of type `UnsupportedOperationException`.

If a buffer object is passed to a method as an argument, you might need to determine whether or not it has a backing array — before you can call its `array()` method for example, if you plan to alter the buffer's contents by changing the elements in the array. The `hasArray()` method for a buffer object will return `true` if the buffer was created from an array, and `false` otherwise. Typical usage of this method is something like this:

```
if(numBuf.hasArray()) {
   long[] data = numBuf.array();
   // Modify the data array directly to alter the buffer...

} else {
   // Modify the buffer using put() methods for the buffer object...
}
```

Obviously, you would take the trouble to do this only if modifying the backing array was a whole lot more convenient or faster than using `put()` methods for the buffer. You will see how you use `put()` methods to modify the contents of a buffer very soon in this chapter.

Wrapping Strings

You can create buffers of type `CharBuffer` by wrapping an object of any type that implements the `CharSequence` interface, so this enables you to wrap objects of type `String`, type `StringBuilder`, and type `StringBuffer`. You can also wrap an array of type `char[]` to create a `CharBuffer` object containing the contents of the array. For example:

```
String wisdom = "Many a mickle makes a muckle.";
CharBuffer charBuf = CharBuffer.wrap(wisdom);
```

The `CharBuffer` object and the `String` object share the same memory. Since a `String` object is immutable, the buffer that results from this is read-only. Attempting to transfer data into the buffer will result in an exception of type `ReadOnlyBufferException` being thrown. If you expect to be modifying the buffer, one approach is to obtain the contents of the `String` as an array of type `char[]` and wrap that to create the buffer. Here's how you can do that:

```
String wisdom = "Many a mickle makes a muckle.";
CharBuffer charBuf = CharBuffer.wrap(wisdom.toCharArray());
```

The buffer now wraps an array of type `char[]` that contains the same sequence of characters as the original string. You can now modify the buffer, but of course this won't affect the original `String` object, only the underlying array that you created.

You could also create a `StringBuilder` or `StringBuffer` object from the `String` object and wrap that. For example:

```
String wisdom = "Many a mickle makes a muckle.";
CharBuffer charBuf = CharBuffer.wrap(new StringBuffer(wisdom));
```

Now you have a `CharBuffer` object wrapping a backing `StringBuffer` object.

Of course, wrapping a string as I've illustrated here is quite different from wrapping a byte array that is produced from a string, as described earlier. Here you are creating a buffer containing Unicode characters, whereas before you were creating a buffer containing characters represented by an 8-bit encoding.

Marking a Buffer

You use the **mark** property for a buffer to record a particular index position in the buffer that you want to be able to return to later. You can set the mark to the current position by calling the `mark()` method for a buffer object that is inherited from the `Buffer` class. For example:

```
buf.mark();                                    // Mark the current position
```

This method also returns a reference of type `Buffer` so you could chain it with the methods for setting the limit and position:

```
buf.limit(512).position(256).mark();
```

This will set the mark to 256, the same as the position, which is set after the limit has been set to 512.

After a series of operations that alter the position, you can reset the buffer's position to the mark that you have set previously by calling the `reset()` method that is inherited from the `Buffer` class:

```
buf.reset();                                   // Reset position to last marked
```

If you have not set the mark, or if it has been discarded by an operation to set the limit or the position, the `reset()` method will throw an exception of type `InvalidMarkException`. The mark for a view buffer operates independently of the mark for the buffer from which it was created.

You probably won't need to mark a buffer most of the time. The sort of situation where you could use it is where you are scanning some part of a buffer to determine what kind of data it contains — after reading a file, for example. You could mark the point where you started the analysis, and then return to that point by calling `reset()` for the buffer when you have figured out how to handle the data.

Buffer Data Transfers

Of course, before you can use a channel to write the contents of a buffer to a file, you must load the buffer with the data. Methods for loading data into a buffer are referred to as **put** methods. Similarly, when a channel has read data from a file into a buffer, you are likely to want to retrieve the data from the buffer. In this case you use the buffer's **get** methods.

Two kinds of operations transfer data values to or from a buffer.

❑ A **relative** put or get operation transfers one or more values starting at the buffer's current position. In this case the position is automatically incremented by the number of values transferred.

❑ In an **absolute** put or get operation, you explicitly specify an index for the position in the buffer where the data transfer is to begin. In this case the buffer's position will not be updated, so it will remain at the index value it was before the operation was executed.

Transferring Data into a Buffer

The `ByteBuffer` class and all the view buffer classes have two `put()` methods for transferring a single value of the buffer's type to the buffer. One is a relative put method that transfers an element to a given index position in the buffer, and the other is an absolute put method that places the element at an index position that you specify as an argument. All the buffer classes also have three relative put methods for bulk transfer of elements of the given type. Let's consider the `put()` methods for a `ByteBuffer` object as an example.

Method	Description
`put(byte b)`	Transfers the byte specified by the argument to the buffer at the current position and increments the position by 1. An exception of type `BufferOverflowException` will be thrown if the buffer's position is not less than its limit.
`put(int index, byte b)`	Transfers the byte specified by the second argument to the buffer at the index position specified by the first argument. The buffer position is unchanged. An exception of type `IndexOut OfBoundsException` will be thrown if the index value is negative or greater than or equal to the buffer's limit.
`put(byte[] array)`	Transfers all the elements of `array` to this buffer starting at the current position. The position will be incremented by the length of the array. An exception of type `BufferOverflow Exception` will be thrown if there is insufficient space in the buffer to accommodate the contents of the array.
`put(byte[] array, int offset, int length)`	Transfers bytes from `array[offset]` to `array[offset+length-1]` inclusive to the buffer. If there is insufficient space for them in the buffer, an exception of type `BufferOverflowException` will be thrown.
`put(ByteBuffer src)`	Transfers the bytes remaining in `src` to the buffer. This will be `src.remaining()` elements from the buffer `src` from its `position` index to `limit-1`. If there is insufficient space to accommodate these, then an exception of type `Buffer OverflowException` will be thrown. If `src` is identical to the current buffer — you are trying to transfer a buffer to itself, in other words — an exception of type `IllegalArgument Exception` will be thrown.

Each of these methods returns a reference to the buffer for which it was called. If the buffer is read-only, any of these methods will throw an exception of type `ReadOnlyBufferException`. You'll see how a buffer can be read-only when I discuss using view buffers in more detail. Each buffer object that stores elements of a given primitive type — `CharBuffer`, `DoubleBuffer`, or whatever — will have `put()` methods analogous to those for `ByteBuffer`, but with arguments of a type appropriate to the type of element in the buffer.

The `ByteBuffer` class has some extra methods that enable you to transfer binary data of other primitive types to the buffer. For example, you can transfer a value of type `double` to a buffer of type `ByteBuffer` with either of the following methods:

Method	Description
`putDouble(double value)`	Transfers the double value specified by the argument to the buffer at the current position and increments the position by 8. If there are less than 8 bytes remaining in the buffer, an exception of type `BufferOverflowException` will be thrown.
`putDouble(int index, double value)`	Transfers the `double` value specified by the second argument to the buffer starting at the index position specified by the first argument. The buffer's position will be unchanged. If there are less than 8 bytes remaining in the buffer, an exception of type `BufferOverflowException` will be thrown. If index is negative or the buffer's limit is less than or equal to index+7, the method will throw an exception of type `IndexOutOfBoundsException`.

Note that these provide for transferring only single values. If you want to transfer an array of values you must use a loop. Similar pairs of methods to the preceding are defined in the `ByteBuffer` class to transfer values of other primitive types. These are the methods `putChar()`, `putShort()`, `putInt()`, `putLong()`, and `putFloat()`, each of which transfers a value of the corresponding type. Like the other `put()` methods you have seen, these all return a reference to the buffer for which they are called. This is to allow you to chain the calls for these methods together in a single statement if you wish. For example:

```
String text = "Value of e";
ByteBuffer buf = ByteBuffer.allocate(text.length()+ sizeof(Math.E));
buf.put(text.getBytes()).putDouble(Math.E);
```

Here, you write the string to the buffer by converting it to bytes by calling its `getBytes()` method, and passing the result to the `put()` method for the buffer. The `put()` method returns a reference to the buffer, `buf`, so you use that to call the `putDouble()` method to write the 8 bytes for the `double` value, `Math.E`, to the buffer. Of course, `putDouble()` also returns a reference to `buf`, so you could chain further calls together in the same statement if you so wished. Here the buffer capacity has been allocated so that it exactly accommodates the data to be loaded, so the capacity will be 18 bytes.

Note that you are transferring the string characters to the buffer as bytes in the local character encoding in the previous code fragment, not as Unicode characters. To transfer them as the original Unicode characters, you could code the operations like this:

```
char[] array = text.toCharArray();          // Create char[] array from the string
ByteBuffer buf = ByteBuffer.allocate(50);   // Buffer of 50 bytes capacity
// Now use a loop to transfer array elements one at a time
for (char ch; array) {
  buf.putChar(ch);
}
buf.putDouble(Math.E);                       // Transfer the binary double value
```

Here you use a collection-based `for` loop to write the elements of the array that you create from `text` to the buffer.

Using View Buffers

View buffers are intended to make it easier to transfer data elements of various basic types to or from a `ByteBuffer`. The only slightly tricky part is that you have to keep track of the position for the original `ByteBuffer` object yourself when you use a view buffer, since operations with the view buffer will not update the position for the backing byte buffer. You could do what the previous code fragment does using view buffers:

```
String text = "Value of e";
ByteBuffer buf = ByteBuffer.allocate(50);    // The original byte buffer
CharBuffer charBuf = buf.asCharBuffer();     // Create view buffer
charBuf.put(text);                           // Transfer string via view buffer

// Update byte buffer position by the number of bytes we have transferred
buf.position(buf.position() + 2*charBuf.position());

buf.putDouble(Math.E);                       // Transfer binary double value
```

Putting data into a view buffer with a relative put operation updates only the position of the view buffer. The position for the backing `ByteBuffer` is unchanged, so you must increment it to account for the number of bytes occupied by the Unicode characters that you have written. Since you transfer the eight bytes for the constant `Math.E` directly using `buf`, the position in `buf` will be incremented by 8 automatically. Of course, it's essential that you update the buffer's position to account for the characters you have transferred before you transfer the floating-point value. If you don't, you'll overwrite the first 8 bytes of the character data.

Preparing a Buffer for Output to a File

You have seen that a buffer starts out with its position set to 0 — the first element position — and with its limit set to the capacity. The state of a view buffer reflects the state of the byte buffer from which it is created. Suppose you create a byte buffer with the following statement:

```
ByteBuffer buf = ByteBuffer.allocate(80);
```

449

You can now create a view buffer from this byte buffer that you can use to store values of type `double` with the statement:

```
DoubleBuffer doubleBuf = buf.asDoubleBuffer();
```

The view buffer's initial state will be as shown in Figure 10-10.

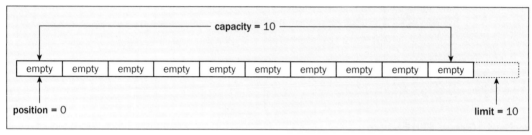

Figure 10-10

The limit is automatically set to the capacity, 10, so it points to the position that is one beyond the last value. You could load six values of type `double` into this buffer with the following statements:

```
double[] data = { 1.0, 1.414, 1.732, 2.0, 2.236, 2.449 };
doubleBuf.put(data);             // Transfer the array elements to the buffer
```

The `put()` operation automatically increments the position for the view buffer. Now the buffer will be as shown in Figure 10-11.

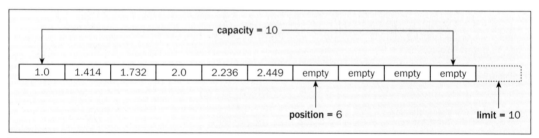

Figure 10-11

The position and limit values are now set to values ready for more data to be added to the buffer. The value of `position` points to the first empty element, and `limit` points to one beyond the last empty element. Of course, the position for the backing `ByteBuffer` is still in its original state, but you can update that to correspond with the data you have loaded into the view buffer with the statement:

```
buf.Position(8*doubleBuf.Position());
```

If you now want to write the data you have in the byte buffer to a file, you must change the values for `position` and `limit` in the byte buffer to identify the elements that are to be written. A file write operation will write data elements starting from the element in the buffer at the index specified by `position`, and up to and including the element at the index `limit-1`. To write the data to the file, the limit for the byte buffer needs to be set to the current position, and the position needs to be set back to zero. You could do this explicitly using the methods you have seen. For example:

```
// Limit to current position and position to 0
buf.limit(buf.position()).position(0);
```

This will first set the limit to the byte referenced by the current position, and then reset the position back to the first byte, byte 0. However, you don't need to specify the operation in such detail. The `Buffer` class conveniently defines the `flip()` method that does exactly this, so you would normally set up the buffer to be written to a file like this:

```
// Limit to current position and position to 0
buf.flip();
```

The `flip()` method returns the buffer reference as type `Buffer`, so you can chain this operation on the buffer with others in a single statement. So, after you have loaded your byte buffer with data, don't forget to flip it before you write it to a file. If you don't, your data will not be written to the file, but garbage may well be. If you loaded the data using a view buffer, you also have to remember to update the byte buffer's position before performing the flip.

Let's cover two other methods that modify the limit and/or the position for a buffer. The `clear()` method sets the limit to the capacity and the position to zero, so it restores these values to the state they had when the buffer was created. This doesn't reset the data in the buffer though. The contents are left unchanged. You'll typically call the `clear()` method when you want to reuse a buffer, either to load new data into it ready to be written, or to read data into it from a channel. The `rewind()` method simply resets the position to zero, leaving the limit unchanged. This enables you to reread the data that is in the buffer. Both of these methods are defined in the base class `Buffer` and both return a reference to the buffer of type `Buffer`, so you can chain these operations with others that are defined in the `Buffer` class.

Writing to a File

To start with, you will be using the simplest `write()` method for a file channel that writes the data contained in a single `ByteBuffer` object to a file. The number of bytes written to the file is determined by the buffer's position and limit when the `write()` method executes. Bytes will be written starting with the byte at the buffer's current position. The number of bytes written is `limit-position`, which is the number returned by the `remaining()` method for the buffer object. The `write()` method returns the number of bytes that were actually written as a value of type `int`.

A channel `write()` operation can throw any of five different exceptions:

Exception	Description
NonWritableChannelException	Thrown if the channel was not opened for writing.
ClosedChannelException	Thrown if the channel is closed. Calling the `close()` method for the file channel will close the channel, as will calling the `close()` method for the file stream.

Table continued on following page

Exception	Description
AsynchronousCloseException	Thrown if another thread closes the channel while the write operation is in progress.
ClosedByInterruptException	Thrown if another thread interrupts the current thread while the write operation is in progress.
IOException	Thrown if some other I/O error occurs.

The first of these is a subclass of RuntimeException, so you do not have to catch this exception. The other four are subclasses of IOException, which must be caught, so you will normally put the write() method call in a try block. If you want to react specifically to one or other of these last four exceptions, you will need to add a catch block for that specific type. Otherwise, you can just include a single catch block for type IOException to catch all four types of exception. For example, if you have set up a ByteBuffer buf, ready to be written, you might code the write operation like this:

```
File aFile = new File("C:/Beg Java Stuff/myFile.text");
FileOutputStream outputFile = null;     // Place to store an output stream reference

try {
  // Create the stream opened to write
  outputFile = new FileOutputStream(aFile);
} catch (FileNotFoundException e) {
  e.printStackTrace(System.err);
}
// Get the channel for the file
FileChannel outputChannel = outputFile.getChannel();
try {
  outputChannel.write(buf);                // Write the buffer contents to the file
} catch (IOException e) {
  e.printStackTrace(System.err);
}
```

A write() method for a channel will return only when the write operation is complete, but this does not guarantee that the data has actually been written to the file. Some of the data may still reside in the native I/O buffers. If the data you are writing is critical and you want to minimize the risk of losing it in the event of a system crash, you can force all outstanding output operations to a file that were previously executed by the channel to be completed by calling the force() method for the FileChannel object like this:

```
try {
  outputChannel.force();                 // Force data transfer to the file
} catch (IOException e) {
  e.printStackTrace(System.err);
}
```

The force() method will throw a ClosedChannelException if the channel is closed, or an IOException if some other I/O error occurs. Note that the force() method guarantees only that all data will be written for a local storage device. If the ultimate destination for the data is a storage device elsewhere on a network, you have no direct way to guarantee that the data gets written to the device.

Only one write operation can be in progress for a given file channel at any time. If you call `write()` while a `write()` operation that was initiated by another thread is in progress, your call to the `write()` method will block until the write that's in progress has been completed.

File Position

The position of a file is the index position of where the next byte is to be read or written. The first byte in a file is at position zero so the value for a file's position is the offset of the next byte from the beginning. Don't confuse the file position with the position in a buffer that I discussed earlier — the two are quite independent, but of course they are connected. When you write a buffer to a file using the `write()` method discussed in the previous section, the byte in the buffer at the buffer's current position will be written to the file at its current position. This is illustrated in Figure 10-12.

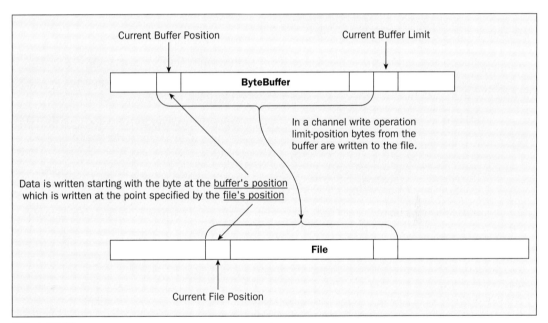

Figure 10-12

The file channel object keeps track of the current position in the file. If you created the file stream to append to the file by using a `FileOutputStream` constructor with the append mode argument as `true`, then the file position recorded by the channel for the file will start out at the byte following the last byte. Otherwise, the initial file position will be the first byte of the file. The file position will generally be incremented by the number of bytes written each time you write to the file. There is one exception to this. The `FileChannel` class defines a special `write()` method that does the following:

Method	Description
`write(ByteBuffer buf, long position)`	This writes the contents of the buffer, `buf`, to the file at the position specified by the second argument, and not the file position recorded by the channel. Bytes from the buffer are written starting at the buffer's current position, and `buf.remaining()` bytes will be written. This does not update the channel's file position.

This method can throw any of the following exceptions:

Exception	Description
`IllegalArgumentException`	Thrown if you specify a negative value for the file position
`NonWritableChannelException`	Thrown if the file was not opened for writing
`ClosedChannelException`	Thrown if the channel is closed
`AsynchronousCloseException`	Thrown if another thread closes the channel while the write operation is in progress
`ClosedByInterruptException`	Thrown if another thread interrupts the current thread while the write operation is in progress
`IOException`	Thrown if any other I/O error occurs

You might use this version of the `write()` method in a sequence of writes to update a particular part of the file without disrupting the primary sequence of write operations. For example, you might record a count of the number of records in a file at the beginning. As you add new records to the file, you could update the count at the beginning of the file without changing the file position recorded by the channel, which would be pointing to the end of the file where new data is to be written.

You can find out what the current file position is by calling the `position()` method for the `FileChannel` object. This returns the position as type `long` rather than type `int` since it could conceivably be a large file with a lot more than two billion bytes in it. You can also set the file position by calling a position method for the `FileChannel` object, with an argument of type `long` that specifies a new position. For example, if you have a reference to a file channel stored in a variable `outputChannel`, you could alter the file position with the following statements:

```
try {
  outputChannel.position(fileChannel.position() - 100);
} catch (IOException e) {
  e.printStackTrace(System.err);
}
```

This moves the current file position back by 100 bytes. This could be because you have written 100 bytes to the file and want to reset the position so you can rewrite it. The call to the `position()` method should normally be in a `try` block because it can throw an exception of type `IOException` if an I/O error occurs.

You can set the file position beyond the end of the file. If you then write to the file, the bytes between the previous end of the file and the new position will contain junk values. If you try to read from a position beyond the end of the file, an end-of-file condition will be returned immediately.

When you are finished with writing a file you should close it by calling the `close()` method for the file stream object. This will close the file and the file channel. A `FileChannel` object defines its own `close()` method that will close the channel but not the file.

Now, after that marathon drive through the basic tools you need to write a file, it's time to start exercising your disk drive. Let's try an example.

Try It Out   Using a Channel to Write a String to a File

You will write the string `"Garbage in, garbage out\n"` to a file with the name `charData.txt` that you will create in the directory `Beg Java Stuff` on your C: drive. If you want to write to a different drive and/or directory, just change the program accordingly. Here is the code:

```java
import java.io.File;
import java.io.FileOutputStream;
import java.io.IOException;
import java.io.FileNotFoundException;
import java.nio.ByteBuffer;
import java.nio.channels.FileChannel;

public class WriteAString {
  public static void main(String[] args) {
    String phrase = new String("Garbage in, garbage out\n");
    String dirname = "C:/Beg Java Stuff";     // Directory name
    String filename = "charData.txt";         // File name

    File dir = new File(dirname);             // File object for directory

    // Now check out the directory
    if (!dir.exists()){                       // If directory does not exist
      if (!dir.mkdir()){                      // ...create it
        System.out.println("Cannot create directory: " + dirname);
        System.exit(1);
      }
    } else if (!dir.isDirectory()) {
      System.err.println(dirname + " is not a directory");
      System.exit(1);
    }

    // Create the filestream
    File aFile = new File(dir, filename);     // File object for the file path
    FileOutputStream outputFile = null;       // Place to store the stream reference
    try {
```

```
      outputFile = new FileOutputStream(aFile, true);
      System.out.println("File stream created successfully.");
    } catch (FileNotFoundException e) {
      e.printStackTrace(System.err);
    }

    // Create the file output stream channel and the buffer
    FileChannel outChannel = outputFile.getChannel();
    ByteBuffer buf = ByteBuffer.allocate(1024);
    System.out.println("New buffer:            position = " + buf.position()
                    + "\tLimit = " + buf.limit() + "\tcapacity = "
                    + buf.capacity());

    // Load the data into the buffer
    for (char ch : phrase.toCharArray()) {
      buf.putChar(ch);
    }

    System.out.println("Buffer after loading: position = " + buf.position()
                    + "\tLimit = " + buf.limit() + "\tcapacity = "
                    + buf.capacity());
    buf.flip();                            // Flip the buffer ready for file write
    System.out.println("Buffer after flip:    position = " + buf.position()
                    + "\tLimit = " + buf.limit() + "\tcapacity = "
                    + buf.capacity());

    // Write the file
    try {
      outChannel.write(buf);               // Write the buffer to the file channel
      outputFile.close();                  // Close the O/P stream & the channel
      System.out.println("Buffer contents written to file.");
    } catch (IOException e) {
      e.printStackTrace(System.err);
    }
    System.exit(0);
  }
}
```

The program produces some command-line output to trace what is going on. After you have compiled and run this program, you should see the following output:

```
File stream created successfully.
New buffer:            position = 0      Limit = 1024    capacity = 1024
Buffer after loading: position = 48      Limit = 1024    capacity = 1024
Buffer after flip:    position = 0       Limit = 48      capacity = 1024
Buffer contents written to file.
```

You can inspect the contents of the file charData.txt using a plaintext editor. They will look something like the following.

```
G a r b a g e   i n ,   g a r b a g e   o u t (
```

There are spaces between the characters as displayed because the output is 8-bit characters and you are writing Unicode characters to the file where 2 bytes are written for each character in the original string. Your text editor may represent the first of each byte pair as something other than spaces, or possibly not at all, as they are bytes that contain zero. You might even find that your plaintext editor will display only the first 'G'. If so, try to find another editor. If you run the example several times, the phrase will be appended to the file for each execution of the program.

> **Don't be too hasty deleting this or other files that you'll write later in this chapter, as you'll reuse some of them in the next chapter when you start exploring how to read files.**

How It Works

You first define three `String` objects:

- ❏ `phrase` — The string that you will write to the file
- ❏ `dirname` — The name of the directory you will create
- ❏ `filename` — The name of the file

In the `try` block, you create a `File` object to encapsulate the directory path. If this directory does not exist, the `exists()` method will return `false`, and the `mkdir()` method for `dir` will be called to create it. If the `exists()` method returns `true`, you make sure that the `File` object represents a directory and not a file by calling the `isDirectory()` method for the `File` object.

Having established the directory one way or another, you create a `File` object, `aFile`, to encapsulate the path to the file. You use this object to create a `FileOutputStream` object that will append data to the file. Omitting the second argument to the `FileOutputStream` constructor or specifying it as `false` would make the file stream overwrite any existing file contents. The file stream has to be created in a `try` block because the constructor can throw a `FileNotFoundException`. Once you have a `FileOutputStream` object, you call its `getChannel()` method to obtain a reference to the channel that you'll use to write the file.

The next step is to create a `ByteBuffer` object and load it up with the characters from the string. You create a buffer with a capacity of 1024 bytes. This is so you can see clearly the difference between the capacity and the limit after flipping. You could have created a buffer exactly the size required with the following statement:

```
ByteBuffer buf = ByteBuffer.allocate(2*phrase.length());
```

You can see how the position, limit, and capacity values change from the output. You use the `putChar()` method for the buffer object to transfer the characters one at a time in a collection-based `for` loop that iterates over the elements in an array of type `char[]` that you create from the original string. You then output the information about the buffer status again. The limit is still as it was, but the position has increased by the number of bytes written.

Finally, you write the contents of the buffer to the file. You can see here how flipping the buffer before the operation sets up the limit and position ready for writing the data to the file.

The `FileChannel` object has a `size()` method that will return the length of the file, in bytes, as a value of type `long`. You could try this out by adding the following statement immediately after the statement that writes the buffer to the channel:

```
System.out.println("The file contains " + outChannel.size() + " bytes.");
```

You should see that 48 bytes are written to the file each time, since `phrase` contains 24 characters. The `size()` method returns the total number of bytes in the file, so the number will grow by 48 each time you run the program.

Using a View Buffer to Load Data into a Byte Buffer

The code in the previous example is not the only way of writing the string to the buffer. You could have used a view buffer, like this:

```
ByteBuffer buf = ByteBuffer.allocate(1024);
CharBuffer charBuf = buf.asCharBuffer();
charBuf.put(phrase);                          // Transfer string to buffer
buf.limit(2*charBuf.position());              // Update byte buffer limit

// Create the file output stream channel
FileChannel outChannel = outputFile.getChannel();

// Write the file
try {
  outChannel.write(buf);            // Write the buffer to the file channel
  outputFile.close();               // Close the output stream & the channel
} catch(IOException e) {
  e.printStackTrace(System.err);
}
```

Transferring the string via a view buffer of type `CharBuffer` is much simpler. The only fly in the ointment is that the backing `ByteBuffer` has no knowledge of this. The position for `buf` is still sitting firmly at zero with the limit set as the capacity, so flipping it won't set it up ready to write to the channel. However, all you have to do is set the limit corresponding to the number of bytes you transferred to the view buffer.

Of course, if you were writing the file for use by some other program, writing Unicode characters could be very inconvenient if the other program environment did not understand it. Let's see how you would write the data as bytes in the local character encoding.

Try It Out   **Writing a String as Bytes**

I will leave out the directory validation to keep the code shorter but remember that you should normally put this check in your programs. Here's the code:

```
import java.io.File;
import java.io.FileOutputStream;
import java.io.IOException;
import java.io.FileNotFoundException;
import java.nio.ByteBuffer;
import java.nio.channels.FileChannel;
```

```
public class WriteAStringAsBytes {
  public static void main(String[] args) {

    String phrase = new String("Garbage in, garbage out\n");
    String dirname = "C:/Beg Java Stuff";        // Directory name
    String filename = "byteData.txt";

    File aFile = new File(dirname, filename);

    // Create the file output stream
    FileOutputStream file = null;
    try {
      file = new FileOutputStream(aFile, true);
    } catch (FileNotFoundException e) {
      e.printStackTrace(System.err);
    }
    FileChannel outChannel = file.getChannel();
    ByteBuffer buf = ByteBuffer.allocate(phrase.length());
    byte[] bytes = phrase.getBytes();

    buf.put(bytes);
    buf.flip();

    try {
      outChannel.write(buf);
      file.close();                              // Close the output stream & the channel
    } catch (IOException e) {
      e.printStackTrace(System.err);
    }
  }
}
```

If you run this a couple of times and look into the `byteData.txt` file with your plaintext editor, you should find:

```
Garbage in, garbage out
Garbage in, garbage out
```

You have no gaps between the letters this time because the Unicode characters were converted to bytes in the default character encoding on your system by the `getBytes()` method for the string.

How It Works

You create the file stream and the channel essentially as in the previous example. This time the buffer is created with the precise amount of space you need. Since you'll be writing each character as a single byte, the buffer capacity needs to be only the length of the string `phrase`.

You convert the string to a byte array in the local character encoding using the `getBytes()` method defined in the `String` class. You transfer the contents of the array to the buffer using the relative `put()` method for the channel. After a quick flip of the buffer, you use the channel's `write()` method to write the buffer's contents to the file.

You could have written the conversion of the string to an array plus the sequence of operations with the buffer and the channel write operation much more economically, if less clearly, like this:

```
outChannel.write((ByteBuffer)(buf.put(phrase.getBytes()).flip()));
```

This makes use of the fact that the buffer methods you are using here return a reference to the buffer so you can chain them together. You would put this statement in the `try` block in place of the existing statement that writes to the channel. Of course, you would also need to delete the three statements that precede the `try` block.

Writing Varying Length Strings to a File

So far, the strings you have written to the file have all been of the same length. It is very often the case that you will want to write a series of strings of different lengths to a file. In this case, if you want to recover the strings from the file, you need to provide some information in the file that allows the beginning and/or end of each string to be determined. One possibility is to write the length of each string to the file immediately preceding the string itself.

To do this, you can use a view buffer. Let's see how that might work in an example that writes strings of various lengths to a file.

Try It Out   Writing Multiple Strings to a File

This example just writes a series of useful proverbs to a file:

```java
import java.io.File;
import java.io.FileOutputStream;
import java.io.IOException;
import java.io.FileNotFoundException;
import java.nio.ByteBuffer;
import java.nio.channels.FileChannel;

public class WriteProverbs {
  public static void main(String[] args) {
    String dirName = "c:/Beg Java Stuff";        // Directory for the output file
    String fileName = "Proverbs.txt";            // Name of the output file
    String[] sayings = {
      "Indecision maximizes flexibility.",
      "Only the mediocre are always at their best.",
      "A little knowledge is a dangerous thing.",
      "Many a mickle makes a muckle.",
      "Who begins too much achieves little.",
      "Who knows most says least.",
      "A wise man sits on the hole in his carpet."
    };
    File aFile = new File(dirName, fileName);

    FileOutputStream outputFile = null;
    try {
      outputFile = new FileOutputStream(aFile, true);
    } catch (FileNotFoundException e) {
```

```
      e.printStackTrace(System.err);
      System.exit(1);
    }
    FileChannel outChannel = outputFile.getChannel();

    // Create a buffer to accommodate the longest string + its length value
    int maxLength = 0;
    for (String saying : sayings) {
      if(maxLength < saying.length())
        maxLength = saying.length();
    }

    ByteBuffer buf = ByteBuffer.allocate(2*maxLength + 4);

    // Write the file
    try {
      for (String saying : sayings) {
        buf.putInt(saying.length()).asCharBuffer().put(saying);
        buf.position(buf.position() + 2*saying.length()).flip();
        outChannel.write(buf);         // Write the buffer to the file channel
        buf.clear();
      }
      outputFile.close();              // Close the output stream & the channel
      System.out.println("Proverbs written to file.");
    } catch (IOException e) {
      e.printStackTrace(System.err);
      System.exit(1);
    }
    System.exit(0);
  }
}
```

When you execute this, it should produce the following rather terse output:

```
Proverbs written to file.
```

You can check the veracity of this assertion by inspecting the contents of the file with a plaintext editor.

How It Works

The program writes the strings from the array `sayings` to the file.

You create a `String` array, `sayings[]`, that contains seven proverbs that are written to the stream in the `for` loop. You put the length of each proverb in the buffer using the `putInt()` method for the `ByteBuffer` object. You then use a view buffer of type `CharBuffer` to transfer the string to the buffer. The contents of the view buffer will start at the current position for the byte buffer. This corresponds to the byte immediately following the string length value.

Transferring the string into the view buffer causes only the view buffer's position to be updated. The byte buffer's position is still pointing back at the byte following the string length where the first character of the string was written. You therefore have to increment the position for the byte buffer by twice the number of characters in the string before flipping it to make it ready to be written to the file.

461

The first time you run the program, the file doesn't exist, so it will be created. You can then look at the contents. If you run the program again, the same proverbs will be appended to the file, so there will be a second set. Alternatively, you could modify the `sayings[]` array to contain different proverbs the second time around. Each time the program runs, the data will be added at the end of the existing file.

After writing the contents of the byte buffer to the file, you call its `clear()` method to reset the position to zero and the limit back to the capacity. This makes it ready for transferring the data for the next proverb on the next iteration. Remember that it doesn't change the contents of the buffer though.

Using a Formatter Object to Load a Buffer

You saw the `java.util.Formatter` class when I introduced the `printf()` method that you can use with the `System.out` stream object back in Chapter 8. The `Formatter` class defines a constructor that accepts a reference of type `java.lang.Appendable` as an argument, and because the `Printstream` and `PrintWriter` classes implement the `Appendable` interface, you can construct a `Formatter` object that will format data into these objects. The `CharBuffer` class also implements the `Appendable` interface so you can create a `Formatter` object that will format data into a view buffer of type `CharBuffer`. Here's how you might create a `Formatter` object ready for use with a view buffer:

```
ByteBuffer buf = ByteBuffer.allocate(1024);    // Byte buffer
CharBuffer charBuf = buf.asCharBuffer();       // View buffer
Formatter formatter = new Formatter(charBuf); // Formatter to write view buffer
```

You can now use the `format()` method for the `Formatter` object to format data values into the view buffer `charBuf`. You'll recall that the `format()` method works just like `printf()` — with the first argument being a format string and the arguments that follow specifying the data values to be formatted. Of course, writing data into the view buffer leaves the backing byte buffer's limit unchanged, so you must update this to reflect the data that is now in the buffer before attempting to write the buffer's contents to the channel. You can see how this works with a simple example:

Try It Out   Using a Formatter Object to Load a Buffer

Here's the code to use a `Formatter` object to prepare the data to be written to a file:

```java
import java.io.File;
import java.io.FileOutputStream;
import java.io.IOException;
import java.io.FileNotFoundException;
import java.nio.ByteBuffer;
import java.nio.CharBuffer;
import java.nio.channels.FileChannel;
import java.util.Formatter;

public class UsingAFormatter {
  public static void main(String[] args) {
    String[] phrases = {"Rome wasn't burned in a day.",
                        "It's a bold mouse that sits in the cat's ear.",
                        "An ounce of practice is worth a pound of instruction."
                       };
    String dirname = "C:/Beg Java Stuff";    // Directory name
    String filename = "Phrases.txt";         // File name
```

```java
File dir = new File(dirname);                 // File object for directory

// Now check out the directory
if (!dir.exists()){                           // If directory does not exist
  if (!dir.mkdir()){                          // ...create it
    System.out.println("Cannot create directory: " + dirname);
    System.exit(1);
  }
} else if (!dir.isDirectory()) {
  System.err.println(dirname + " is not a directory");
  System.exit(1);
}

// Create the filestream
File aFile = new File(dir, filename);   // File object for the file path
FileOutputStream outputFile = null;     // Place to store the stream reference
try {
  outputFile = new FileOutputStream(aFile, true);
  System.out.println("File stream created successfully.");
} catch (FileNotFoundException e) {
  e.printStackTrace(System.err);
}

// Create the file output stream channel
FileChannel outChannel = outputFile.getChannel();

// Create byte buffer to hold data to be written
ByteBuffer buf = ByteBuffer.allocate(1024);
System.out.println("\nByte buffer:");
System.out.printf("position = %2d  Limit = %4d  capacity = %4d%n",
                  buf.position(), buf.limit(), buf.capacity());

// Create a view buffer
CharBuffer charBuf = buf.asCharBuffer();
System.out.println("Char view buffer:");
System.out.printf("position = %2d  Limit = %4d  capacity = %4d%n",
                  charBuf.position(),charBuf.limit(),charBuf.capacity());
Formatter formatter = new Formatter(charBuf);

// Write to the view buffer using a formatter
int number = 0;                               // Proverb number
for(String phrase : phrases) {
  formatter.format("%nProverb%3d: %s", ++number, phrase);
  System.out.println("\nView buffer after loading:");
  System.out.printf("position = %2d  Limit = %4d  capacity = %4d%n",
                    charBuf.position(), charBuf.limit(),charBuf.capacity());
  charBuf.flip();                             // Flip the view buffer
  System.out.println("View buffer after flip:");
  System.out.printf("position = %2d  Limit = %4d  length = %4d%n",
                    charBuf.position(),charBuf.limit(),charBuf.length());
  buf.limit(2*charBuf.length());              // Set byte buffer limit

  System.out.println("Byte buffer after limit update:");
  System.out.printf("position = %2d  Limit = %4d  length = %4d%n",
```

```
                                 buf.position(),buf.limit(), buf.remaining());

        // Write the file
        try {
          outChannel.write(buf);                    // Write the buffer to the file channel
          System.out.println("Buffer contents written to file.");
          buf.clear();
          charBuf.clear();
        } catch (IOException e) {
         e.printStackTrace(System.err);
         System.exit(1);
        }
      }
      try {
        outputFile.close();                         // Close the O/P stream & the channel
      } catch (IOException e) {
        e.printStackTrace(System.err);
      }
    }
  }
}
```

With this example I got the following output:

```
File stream created successfully.

Byte buffer:
position =  0  Limit = 1024  capacity = 1024
Char view buffer:
position =  0  Limit =  512  capacity =  512

View buffer after loading:
position = 42  Limit =  512  capacity =  512
View buffer after flip:
position =  0  Limit =   42  length =   42
Byte buffer after limit update:
position =  0  Limit =   84  length =   84
Buffer contents written to file.

View buffer after loading:
position = 59  Limit =  512  capacity =  512
View buffer after flip:
position =  0  Limit =   59  length =   59
Byte buffer after limit update:
position =  0  Limit =  118  length =  118
Buffer contents written to file.

View buffer after loading:
position = 67  Limit =  512  capacity =  512
View buffer after flip:
position =  0  Limit =   67  length =   67
Byte buffer after limit update:
position =  0  Limit =  134  length =  134
Buffer contents written to file.
```

You can inspect the contents of the file with a plaintext editor. Remember that the data is written as Unicode characters.

How It Works

You first create an array of three strings that will be written to the file. You can add more to the array if you like. I kept it at three to keep the volume of output down. You've seen the first part of the code that sets up the `File`, `FileOutputStream`, and `FileChannel` objects before, so I'll go straight to where the buffer is loaded.

You set up the buffers with the statements:

```
ByteBuffer buf = ByteBuffer.allocate(1024);
CharBuffer charBuf = buf.asCharBuffer();
```

Some output statements between these record the initial state of the byte buffer. After outputting the state of the view buffer `charBuf`, you create the `Formatter` object you'll use to load the buffer:

```
Formatter formatter = new Formatter(charBuf);
```

The `format()` method for the `Formatter` object will write data to `charBuf`.

After defining the variable `number` that will store the proverb sequence number, you load the buffer and write to the file in a `for` loop:

```
for(String phrase : phrases) {
  // Load the buffer...
  // Write the buffer to the file...
}
```

This loop iterates over each of the strings in the `phrases` array. You load a proverb from `phrases` into the view buffer with the statement:

```
formatter.format("%nProverb%3d: %s", ++number, phrase);
```

This will transfer the incremented value of `number` followed by the string `phrase`, formatted according to the first argument to the `format()` method. This will update the position for the view buffer, but not the byte buffer.

You flip the view buffer with the statement:

```
charBuf.flip();                              // Flip the view buffer
```

Flipping the view buffer sets its limit as the current position and resets its position to 0. The `length()` method for the view buffer returns the number of characters in the buffer, which is `limit-position`. You could obtain the same result by calling the remaining method that the `CharBuffer` class inherits from the `Buffer` class. You update the limit for the byte buffer with the statement:

```
buf.limit(2*charBuf.length());               // Set byte buffer limit
```

Since each Unicode character occupies 2 bytes, the statement sets the byte buffer limit to twice the number of characters in `charBuf`.

With the byte buffer set up ready to be written to the channel, you write the data to the file with the statement:

```
outChannel.write(buf);              // Write the buffer to the file channel
```

You now need to reset the limit and position for both the byte buffer and the view buffer to be ready for the next proverb to be written. The following two statements do this:

```
buf.clear();
charBuf.clear();
```

Calling the `clear()` method for a buffer sets the buffer's position back to 0 and its limit to the capacity.

This example looks a little more complicated than it really is because of all the statements tracing the states of the buffer. If you delete these, you'll find the code is quite short.

The output shown for this example was produced on a Microsoft Windows system where a newline is written as two characters, CR and LF. If you are using Linux or other operating systems that represent a newline as a single NL character, the values for `position` after the buffer has been loaded by the `Formatter` object will be less if a newline character is in the data that was loaded.

Direct and Indirect Buffers

When you allocate a byte buffer by calling the static `allocate()` method for the `ByteBuffer` class, you get an **indirect buffer**. An indirect buffer is not used by the native I/O operations, which have their own buffers. Data to be written to a file has to be copied from your indirect buffer to the buffer that the native output routine uses before the write operation can take place. Similarly, after a read operation the data is copied from the input buffer used by your operating system to the indirect buffer that you allocate.

Of course, with small buffers and limited amounts of data being read, using an indirect buffer doesn't add much overhead. With large buffers and lots of data, it can make a significant difference though. In this case, you can use the `allocateDirect()` method in the `ByteBuffer` class to allocate a **direct buffer**. The JVM will try to make sure that the native I/O operation makes use of the direct buffer, thus avoiding the overhead of the data copying process. The allocation and de-allocation of a direct buffer carries its own overhead, which may outweigh any advantages gained if the buffer size and data volumes are small.

You can test whether a buffer object encapsulates a direct buffer by calling its `isDirect()` method. This will return `true` if it is a direct buffer and `false` otherwise.

You could try this out by making a small change to the `WriteProverbs` example. Just replace the statement

```
ByteBuffer buf = ByteBuffer.allocate(2*maxLength + 4);
```

with the following two statements:

```
ByteBuffer buf = ByteBuffer.allocateDirect(2*maxLength + 4);
System.out.println("Buffer is "+ (buf.isDirect()?"":"not")+"direct.");
```

This will output a line telling you whether the program is working with a direct buffer or not. If it is, it will produce the following output:

```
Buffer is direct.
Proverbs written to file.
```

Writing Numerical Data to a File

Let's see how you could set up the primes-generating program from Chapter 4 to write primes to a file instead of outputting them. You will base the new code on the MorePrimes version of the program. Ideally, you could add a command-line argument to specify how many primes you want. This is not too difficult. Here's how the code will start off:

```
import static java.lang.Math.ceil;
import static java.lang.Math.sqrt;
import static java.lang.Math.min;

public class PrimesToFile {
  public static void main(String[] args) {
    int primesRequired = 100;                    // Default prime count
    if (args.length > 0) {
      try {
        primesRequired = Integer.valueOf(args[0]).intValue();
      } catch (NumberFormatException e) {
        System.out.println("Prime count value invalid. Using default of "
                           + primesRequired);
      }
      // Code to generate the primes...

      // Code to write the file...
    }
  }
}
```

Here, if you don't find a command-line argument that you can convert to an integer, you just use a default count of 100. The static import statements allow you to use the static methods in the Math class that you'll need for the calculation without qualifying their names.

You can now generate the primes with code similar to that in Chapter 4 as follows:

```
long[] primes = new long[primesRequired];  // Array to store primes
primes[0] = 2;                             // Seed the first prime
primes[1] = 3;                             // and the second

int count = 2;                             // Count of primes found up to now
long number = 5;                           // Next integer to be tested

outer:
for (; count < primesRequired; number += 2) {

    // The maximum divisor we need to try is square root of number
```

```
          long limit = (long)ceil(sqrt((double)number));

          // Divide by all the primes we have up to limit
          for (int i = 1; i < count && primes[i] <= limit; i++)
            if (number % primes[i] == 0)          // Is it an exact divisor?
              continue outer;                     // yes, try the next number

          primes[count++] = number;               // We got one!
      }
```

Now all you need to do is add the code to write the primes to the file. Let's put this into a working
example.

Try It Out   **Writing Primes to a File**

Here's the complete example, with the additional code to write the file shown shaded:

```
import static java.lang.Math.ceil;
import static java.lang.Math.sqrt;
import static java.lang.Math.min;
import java.io.File;
import java.io.FileOutputStream;
import java.io.IOException;
import java.io.FileNotFoundException;
import java.nio.ByteBuffer;
import java.nio.LongBuffer;
import java.nio.channels.FileChannel;

public class PrimesToFile {
  public static void main(String[] args) {
    int primesRequired = 100;                     // Default count
    if (args.length > 0) {
      try {
        primesRequired = Integer.valueOf(args[0]).intValue();
      } catch (NumberFormatException e) {
        System.out.println("Prime count value invalid. Using default of "
                        + primesRequired);
      }
    }

    long[] primes = new long[primesRequired];  // Array to store primes
    primes[0] = 2;                             // Seed the first prime
    primes[1] = 3;                             // and the second
    // Count of primes found - up to now, which is also the array index
    int count = 2;
    // Next integer to be tested
    long number = 5;

    outer:
    for (; count < primesRequired; number += 2) {

      // The maximum divisor we need to try is square root of number
```

```
        long limit = (long)ceil(sqrt((double)number));

        // Divide by all the primes we have up to limit
        for (int i = 1; i < count && primes[i] <= limit; i++)
          if (number % primes[i] == 0)                  // Is it an exact divisor?
            continue outer;                             // yes, try the next number

        primes[count++] = number;                       // We got one!
      }

    File aFile = new File("C:/Beg Java Stuff/primes.bin");
    FileOutputStream outputFile = null;
    try {
      outputFile = new FileOutputStream(aFile);  // Create the file stream
    } catch (FileNotFoundException e) {
      e.printStackTrace(System.err);
      System.exit(1);
    }
    FileChannel file = outputFile.getChannel();  // Get the channel from the stream
    final int BUFFERSIZE = 100;                  // Byte buffer size
    ByteBuffer buf = ByteBuffer.allocate(BUFFERSIZE);
    LongBuffer longBuf = buf.asLongBuffer();     // View buffer for type long

    // Count of primes written to file
    int primesWritten = 0;

    while (primesWritten < primes.length) {
      longBuf.put(primes,                        // Array to be written
                  primesWritten,                 // Index of 1st element to write
                  min(longBuf.capacity(), primes.length - primesWritten));
      buf.limit(8*longBuf.position());           // Update byte buffer position
      try {
        file.write(buf);
        primesWritten += longBuf.position();
      } catch (IOException e) {
        e.printStackTrace(System.err);
        System.exit(1);
      }
      longBuf.clear();
      buf.clear();
    }

    try {
      System.out.println("File written is " + file.size() + " bytes.");
      outputFile.close();                        // Close the file and its channel
    } catch (IOException e) {
      e.printStackTrace(System.err);
      System.exit(1);
    }
    System.exit(0);
  }
}
```

If you don't supply the number of primes you want as a command-line argument, this program produces the following output:

```
File written is 800 bytes.
```

This looks reasonable since you wrote 100 values of type `long` as binary data and they are 8 bytes each.

How It Works

You create a `FileOutputStream` object and obtain the channel in the way that you have previously. Since you did not specify that you want to append to the file when you create the stream object, the file will be overwritten each time you run the program.

You create the `ByteBuffer` object with a capacity of 100 bytes. This is a poor choice for the buffer size as it is not an exact multiple of 8 — so it doesn't correspond to a whole number of prime values. However, I chose this value to make the problem of managing the buffer more interesting. You can change the buffer size by change the value specified for `BUFFERSIZE`.

The primes will be transferred to the buffer through a view buffer of type `LongBuffer` that you obtain from the original byte buffer. Since the buffer is too small to hold all the primes, you have to load it and write the primes to the file in a loop.

The `primesWritten` variable counts how many primes have been written to the file, so you use this to control the `while` loop that writes the primes to the file. The loop continues as long as `primesWritten` is less than the number of elements in the primes array. The number of primes that the `LongBuffer` object can hold corresponds to `longBuf.capacity()`. You can transfer this number of primes to the buffer as long as there is that many left in the array still to be written to the file, so you transfer a block of primes to the buffer like this:

```
longBuf.put(primes,                          // Array to be written
            primesWritten,                   // Index of 1st element to write
          min(longBuf.capacity(), primes.length - primesWritten));
```

The first argument to the `put()` method is the array that is the source of the data, and the second argument is the index position of the first element to be transferred. The third argument will be the capacity of the buffer as long as there is more than that number of primes still in the array. If there is less than this number on the last iteration, you transfer `primes.length-primesWritten` values to the buffer.

Since you are using a relative put operation, loading the view buffer will change the position for that buffer to reflect the number of values transferred to it. However, the backing byte buffer that you use in the channel write operation will still have its limit and position unchanged. You therefore set the limit for the byte buffer with the statement:

```
buf.limit(8*longBuf.position());
```

Since each prime occupies 8 bytes, multiplying the position value for the view buffer by 8 gives you the number of bytes occupied in the primary buffer. You then go ahead and write that buffer to the file and increment `primesWritten` by the position value for the view buffer, since this will be the number of primes that were written. Before the next iteration you call `clear()` for both buffers to reset their positions and limits to their original states — to 0 and the capacity, respectively. When you have written all the primes, the loop ends and you output the length of the file before closing it.

Since this file contains binary data, you will not want to view it except perhaps for debugging purposes.

Writing Mixed Data to a File

Sometimes, you may want to write more than one kind of binary data to a file. You may want to mix integers with floating-point values with text perhaps. One way to do this is to use multiple view buffers. You can get an idea of how this works by outputting some text along with each binary prime value in the previous example. Rather than taking the easy route by just writing the same text for each prime value, let's add a character representation of the prime value preceding each binary value. You'll add something like "prime = nnn" ahead of each binary value.

The first point to keep in mind is that if you ever want to read the file successfully, you can't just dump strings of varying lengths in it. You would have no way to tell where the text ended and where the binary data began. You either have to fix the length of the string so you know how many bytes correspond to text when you read the file, or you must provide data in the file that specifies the length of the string. Let's therefore choose to write the data corresponding to each prime as three successive data items:

1. A count of the length of the string as binary value (it would sensibly be an integer type but you'll make it type double since you need the practice)

2. The string representation of the prime value "prime = nnn", where obviously the number of digits will vary

3. The prime as a binary value of type long

The basic prime calculation will not change at all, so you need only update the shaded code at the end in the previous example that writes the file.

The basic strategy you will adopt is to create a byte buffer and then create a series of view buffers that map the three different kinds of data into it. A simple approach would be to write the data for one prime at a time, so let's try that first. Setting up the file stream and the channel will be more or less the same:

```
File aFile = new File("C:/Beg Java Stuff/primes.txt");
FileOutputStream outputFile = null;
try {
  outputFile = new FileOutputStream(aFile);
} catch (FileNotFoundException e) {
  e.printStackTrace(System.err);
  System.exit(1);
}
FileChannel file = outputFile.getChannel();
```

The file extension has been changed to .txt to differentiate it from the original binary file that you wrote with the previous version. You will want to make use of both the binary file and this file when you are looking into file read operations in the next chapter, so don't delete them.

The byte buffer has to be large enough to hold the double value that counts the characters in the string, the string itself, plus the long value for the prime. The original byte buffer with 100 bytes capacity will be plenty big enough so let's go with that:

```
final int BUFFERSIZE = 100;                    // Buffer size in bytes
ByteBuffer buf = ByteBuffer.allocate(BUFFERSIZE);
```

You need to create three view buffers from the byte buffer, one that will hold the double value for the count, one for the string, and one for the binary prime value, but you have a problem, which is illustrated in Figure 10-13.

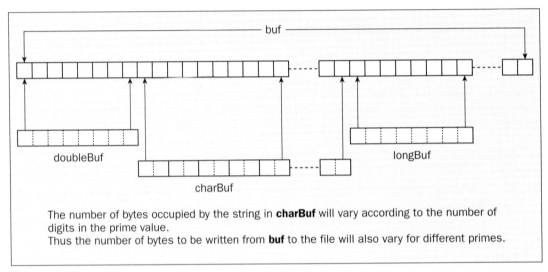

The number of bytes occupied by the string in **charBuf** will vary according to the number of digits in the prime value.
Thus the number of bytes to be written from **buf** to the file will also vary for different primes.

Figure 10-13

Because the length of the string depends on the number of decimal digits in the prime value, you don't know where it ends. This implies you can't map the last buffer, longBuf, to a fixed position in the byte buffer, buf. You are going to have to set this buffer up dynamically inside the file-writing loop after you figure out how long the string for the prime is. You can set up the first two view buffers outside the loop though:

```
DoubleBuffer doubleBuf = buf.asDoubleBuffer();
buf.position(8);
CharBuffer charBuf = buf.asCharBuffer();
```

The first buffer that will hold the string length as type double will map to the beginning of the byte buffer, buf. The view buffer into which you will place the string needs to map to the position in buf immediately after the space required for the double value — 8 bytes from the beginning of buf in other words. Remember that the first element in a view buffer maps to the current position in the byte buffer. Thus, you can just set the position for buf to 8 before creating the view buffer, charBuf. All that's now needed is the loop that will load up the first two view buffers, create the third view buffer and load it, and then write the file. Let's put the whole thing together as a working example.

Try It Out   Using Multiple View Buffers

The code for the loop is shaded in the following complete program:

```java
import static java.lang.Math.ceil;
import static java.lang.Math.sqrt;
import java.io.File;
import java.io.FileOutputStream;
import java.io.IOException;
import java.io.FileNotFoundException;
import java.nio.ByteBuffer;
import java.nio.LongBuffer;
import java.nio.DoubleBuffer;
import java.nio.CharBuffer;
import java.nio.channels.FileChannel;

public class PrimesToFile2 {
  public static void main(String[] args) {
    int primesRequired = 100;                   // Default count
    if (args.length > 0) {
      try {
        primesRequired = Integer.valueOf(args[0]).intValue();
      } catch (NumberFormatException e) {
        System.out.println("Prime count value invalid. Using default of "
                        + primesRequired);
      }
    }

    long[] primes = new long[primesRequired];   // Array to store primes
    primes[0] = 2;                              // Seed the first prime
    primes[1] = 3;                              // and the second

    // Count of primes found - up to now, which is also the array index
    int count = 2;
    long number = 5;                            // Next integer to be tested

    outer:
    for (; count < primesRequired; number += 2) {

      // The maximum divisor we need to try is square root of number
      long limit = (long)ceil(sqrt((double)number));

      // Divide by all the primes we have up to limit
      for (int i = 1; i < count && primes[i] <= limit; i++)
        if (number % primes[i] == 0)            // Is it an exact divisor?
          continue outer;                       // yes, try the next number

      primes[count++] = number;                 // We got one!
    }

    File aFile = new File("C:/Beg Java Stuff/primes.txt");
    FileOutputStream outputFile = null;
    try {
```

```
      outputFile = new FileOutputStream(aFile);
    } catch (FileNotFoundException e) {
      e.printStackTrace(System.err);
      System.exit(1);
    }
    FileChannel file = outputFile.getChannel();
    final int BUFFERSIZE = 100;    // Buffer size in bytes
    ByteBuffer buf = ByteBuffer.allocate(BUFFERSIZE);

    DoubleBuffer doubleBuf = buf.asDoubleBuffer();
    buf.position(8);
    CharBuffer charBuf = buf.asCharBuffer();
    LongBuffer longBuf = null;
    String primeStr = null;

    for (long prime : primes) {
      primeStr = "prime = " + prime;                   // Create the string
      doubleBuf.put(0,(double)primeStr.length());  // Store the string length
      charBuf.put(primeStr);                          // Store the string
      buf.position(2*charBuf.position() + 8);         // Position for 3rd buffer
      longBuf = buf.asLongBuffer();                   // Create the buffer
      longBuf.put(prime);                             // Store the binary long value
      buf.position(buf.position() + 8);               // Set position after last value
      buf.flip();                                     // and flip
      try {
        file.write(buf);                              // Write the buffer as before.
      } catch (IOException e) {
        e.printStackTrace(System.err);
        System.exit(1);
      }
      buf.clear();
      doubleBuf.clear();
      charBuf.clear();
    }
    try {
      System.out.println("File written is " + file.size() + " bytes.");
      outputFile.close();                             // Close the file and its channel
    } catch (IOException e) {
      e.printStackTrace(System.err);
      System.exit(1);
    }
    System.exit(0);
  }
}
```

With the default number of primes to be produced, this example should produce the following output:

```
File written is 3742 bytes.
```

How It Works

I'll discuss only the body of the collection-based `for` loop that iterates over the elements in the `primes` array because that's the new function in the example.

You create the string first because you need to know its length so you can put that in the buffer first. You insert the length as type `double` in the view buffer, `doubleBuf`. You then put the string into `charBuf` as this buffer already maps to the position starting 8 bytes along from the start of `buf`. Next, you update the position in `buf` to the element following the string. This allows you to map `longBuf` to the byte buffer correctly. After creating the third view buffer, `longBuf`, you load the prime value. You then update the position for `buf` to the byte following this value. This will be the position as previously set plus 8. Finally, you flip `buf` to set the position and limit for writing, and then the channel writes to the file.

If you inspect the file with a plaintext editor you should get an idea of what is in the file. You should be able to see the Unicode strings separated by the binary values you have written to the file. Of course, the binary value won't look particularly meaningful when viewed as characters.

This example writes the file one prime at a time, so it's not going to be very efficient. It would be better to use a larger buffer and load it with multiple primes. Let's see how you can do that with another version of the program.

Try It Out   Multiple Records in a Buffer

You will be loading the byte buffer using three different view buffers repeatedly to put data for as many primes into the buffer as you can. The basic idea is illustrated in Figure 10-14.

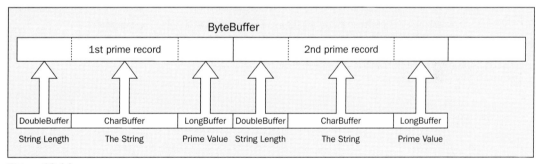

Figure 10-14

I'll just show the new code that replaces the code in the previous example here. This is the code that allocates the buffers and writes the file:

```
import static java.lang.Math.ceil;
import static java.lang.Math.sqrt;
import java.io.File;
// Remaining import statements as before...

public class PrimesToFile3 {
  public static void main(String[] args) {
```

```
// Code as in the previous example...

final int BUFFERSIZE = 1024;                          // Buffer size in bytes - bigger!
ByteBuffer buf = ByteBuffer.allocate(BUFFERSIZE);
String primeStr = null;
int primesWritten = 0;
while (primesWritten < primes.length) {
  while (primesWritten < primes.length) {
    primeStr = "prime = " + primes[primesWritten];
    if ((buf.position() + 2*primeStr.length() + 16) > buf.limit()) {
      break;
    }
    buf.asDoubleBuffer().put(0, (double)primeStr.length());
    buf.position(buf.position() + 8);
    buf.position(buf.position()
                      + 2*buf.asCharBuffer().put(primeStr).position());
    buf.asLongBuffer().put(primes[primesWritten++]);
    buf.position(buf.position() + 8);
  }
  buf.flip();
  try {
    file.write(buf);
  } catch (IOException e) {
    e.printStackTrace(System.err);
    System.exit(1);
  }
  buf.clear();
}
try {
  System.out.println("File written is " + file.size() + " bytes.");
  outputFile.close();                                 // Close the file and its channel
} catch (IOException e) {
  e.printStackTrace(System.err);
  System.exit(1);
}
System.exit(0);
  }
}
```

You should get the same output as for the previous example here.

How It Works

To start with, you just create a byte buffer with a capacity of 1024 bytes. All the view buffers are created inside the inner `while` loop. Both loops end when `primesWritten`, which counts the number of primes written to the file, reaches a value that equals the length of the `primes` array. The inner loop loads up the buffer and the outer loop writes the contents of the buffer to the file.

The first step in the inner loop is to create the prime string. This makes it possible to check whether there is enough free space in the byte buffer to accommodate the string plus the two binary values — the string length as type `double` and the prime itself of type `long`. If there isn't enough space, the `break` statement will be executed so the inner loop will end, and the channel will write the buffer contents to the file after flipping it. After the buffer has been written, the buffer's `clear()` method is called to reset the position to 0 and the limit to the capacity.

When there is space in the byte buffer, the inner loop loads the buffer starting with the statement:

```
buf.asDoubleBuffer().put(0, (double)primeStr.length());
```

This creates a view buffer of type `DoubleBuffer` and calls its `put()` method to transfer the length of the string to the buffer. You don't save the view buffer reference because you will need a different view buffer on the next iteration — one that maps to the position in the byte buffer following the data you are transferring for the current prime.

The next statement increments the position of the byte buffer by the number of bytes in the string length value. You then execute the statement:

```
buf.position(buf.position()
                   + 2*buf.asCharBuffer().put(primeStr).position());
```

This statement is a little complicated so let's dissect it. The expression for the argument to the `position()` method within the parentheses executes first. This calculates the new position for `buf` as the current position, given by `buf.position()`, plus the value resulting from the expression

```
2*buf.asCharBuffer().put(primeStr).position()
```

The subexpression, `buf.asCharBuffer()`, creates a view buffer of type `CharBuffer`. You call the `put()` method for this buffer to transfer `primeStr` to it, and this returns a reference to the `CharBuffer` object. You use this reference to call the `put()` method for the `CharBuffer` object to transfer the string. You use the reference that `put()` returns to call the `position()` method for the `CharBuffer` object, which will return the position after the string has been transferred, so multiplying this value by 2 gives the number of bytes occupied by the string in `buf`. Thus, you update the position for `buf` to the point following the string that you transfer to the buffer.

The last step in the loop is to execute the following statements:

```
buf.asLongBuffer().put(primes[primesWritten++]);
buf.position(buf.position() + 8);
```

The first statement here transfers the binary prime value to the buffer via a view buffer of type `LongBuffer` and increments the count of the number of primes written to the file. The second statement updates the position for `buf` to the next available byte. The inner `while` loop then continues with the next iteration to load the data for the next prime into the buffer. This will continue until there is insufficient space for data for another prime, whereupon the inner loop will end, and the buffer will be written to the file.

Gathering-Write Operations

I'll introduce one further file channel output capability before you try reading a file — the ability to transfer data to a file from several buffers in sequence in a single write operation. This is called a **gathering-write** operation. The advantage of this capability is that it avoids the necessity to copy information into a single buffer before writing it to a file. A gathering-write operation is one side of what are called **scatter-gather I/O operations**. You will look into the other side — the **scattering-read** operation — in the next chapter.

Just to remind you of what I said earlier, a file channel has two methods that can perform a gathering-write operation:

Method	Description
`write(ByteBuffers[] buffers)`	Writes bytes from each of the buffers in the `buffers` array to the file in sequence, starting at the channel's current file position

`write(ByteBuffers[] buffers,`
`        int offset,`
`        int length)`
	Writes data to the file starting at the channel's current file position from `buffers[offset]` to `buffers[offset+length-1]` inclusive and in sequence

Both these methods can throw the same five exceptions as the write method for a single `ByteBuffer` object. The second of these methods can also throw an `IndexOutOfBoundsException` if `offset` or `offset+length-1` is not a legal index value for the `buffers` array.

The data that is written from each buffer to the file is determined from that buffer's position and limit, in the way you have seen. One obvious application of the gathering-write operation is when you are reading data from several different files into a number of buffers, and you want to merge the data into a single file. You can see how it works by using a variation on the primes-writing program.

Try It Out   The Gathering Write

To simulate conditions where a gathering-write could apply, you will set up the string length, the string itself, and the binary prime value in separate byte buffers. You will also write the prime string as bytes in the local encoding.

Here's the code:

```
import static java.lang.Math.ceil;
import static java.lang.Math.sqrt;
import java.io.File;
import java.io.FileOutputStream;
import java.io.IOException;
import java.io.FileNotFoundException;
import java.nio.ByteBuffer;
import java.nio.LongBuffer;
import java.nio.DoubleBuffer;
import java.nio.CharBuffer;
import java.nio.channels.FileChannel;

public class GatheringWrite {
  public static void main(String[] args) {
    int primesRequired = 100;    // Default count
```

```java
if (args.length > 0) {
  try {
    primesRequired = Integer.valueOf(args[0]).intValue();
  } catch (NumberFormatException e) {
    System.out.println("Prime count value invalid. Using default of "
                         + primesRequired);
  }
}

long[] primes = new long[primesRequired];    // Array to store primes
primes[0] = 2;                                // Seed the first prime
primes[1] = 3;                                // and the second
// Count of primes found - up to now, which is also the array index
int count = 2;
long number = 5;                             // Next integer to be tested

outer:
for (; count < primesRequired; number += 2) {

  // The maximum divisor we need to try is square root of number
  long limit = (long)ceil(sqrt((double) number));

  // Divide by all the primes we have up to limit
  for (int i = 1; i < count && primes[i] <= limit; i++) {
    if (number % primes[i] == 0) {           // Is it an exact divisor?
      continue outer;                        // yes, try the next number

    }
  }
  primes[count++] = number;                  // We got one!
}

File aFile = new File("C:/Beg Java Stuff/primes2.txt");  // Different file!
FileOutputStream outputFile = null;
try {
  outputFile = new FileOutputStream(aFile);
} catch (FileNotFoundException e) {
  e.printStackTrace(System.err);
  System.exit(1);
}
FileChannel file = outputFile.getChannel();

ByteBuffer[] buffers = new ByteBuffer[3];    // Array of buffer references
buffers[0] = ByteBuffer.allocate(8);         // To hold a double value
buffers[2] = ByteBuffer.allocate(8);         // To hold a long value

String primeStr = null;
for (long prime : primes) {
  primeStr = "prime = " + prime;
  buffers[0].putDouble((double) primeStr.length()).flip();
  buffers[1] = ByteBuffer.allocate(primeStr.length());
  buffers[1].put(primeStr.getBytes()).flip();
  buffers[2].putLong(prime).flip();
  try {
```

```
          file.write(buffers);
        } catch (IOException e) {
          e.printStackTrace(System.err);
          System.exit(1);
        }
        buffers[0].clear();
        buffers[2].clear();
      }

      try {
        System.out.println("File written is " + file.size() + " bytes.");
        outputFile.close();                        // Close the file and its channel
      } catch (IOException e) {
        e.printStackTrace(System.err);
        System.exit(1);
      }

      System.out.println("File closed");
      System.exit(0);
    }
  }
```

When you execute this, it should produce the following output:

```
File written is 2671 bytes.
File closed
```

The length of the file is considerably less than before, because you are writing the string as bytes rather than Unicode characters. The part of the code that is different is shaded, and I'll concentrate on that.

How It Works

You use three byte buffers—one for the string length, one for the string itself, and one for the binary prime value:

```
ByteBuffer[] buffers = new ByteBuffer[3];     // Array of buffer references
```

You create a `ByteBuffer[]` array with three elements to hold references to the buffers that you need. The buffers holding the string length and the prime value are fixed in length so you are able to create those straight away to hold 8 bytes each:

```
buffers[0] = ByteBuffer.allocate(8);          // To hold a double value
buffers[2] = ByteBuffer.allocate(8);          // To hold a long value
```

You have to create the buffer to hold the string dynamically, inside the `for` loop that iterates over all the prime values you have in the `primes` array.

After assembling the prime string, you transfer the length to the first buffer:

```
buffers[0].putDouble((double) primeStr.length()).flip();
```

Note that you flip the buffer in the same statement after the data value has been transferred, so it is set up ready to be written to the file.

Next, you create the buffer to accommodate the string, load the byte array equivalent of the string, and flip the buffer:

```
buffers[1] = ByteBuffer.allocate(primeStr.length());
buffers[1].put(primeStr.getBytes()).flip();
```

All of the `put()` methods for the byte buffers you are using in this example automatically update the buffer position, so you can flip each buffer as soon as the data is loaded. As an alternative to allocating this byte buffer directly to accommodate the byte array from the string, you could call the static `wrap()` method in the `ByteBuffer` class that wraps a byte array. You could achieve the same as the previous two statements with the following single statement:

```
buffers[1] = ByteBuffer.wrap(primeStr.getBytes());
```

Since the `wrap()` method creates a buffer with a capacity that is the same as the length of the array, with the position set to zero, and the limit to the capacity, you don't need to flip the buffer — it is already in a state to be written.

The three buffers are ready, so you write the array of buffers to the file like this:

```
try {
  file.write(buffers);
} catch (IOException e) {
  e.printStackTrace(System.err);
  System.exit(1);
}
```

This applies the gathering-write operation to write the contents of the three buffers in the array to the file.

Finally, you ready the first and third buffers for the next iteration by calling the `clear()` method for each of them:

```
buffers[0].clear();
buffers[2].clear();
```

Of course, the second buffer is re-created on each iteration, so there's no need to clear it. Surprisingly easy, wasn't it?

Summary

In this chapter, I have discussed the facilities for checking out physical files and directories and writing basic types of data to a file. The important points that I've discussed include:

- ❑ An object of the class `File` can represent the path to a physical file.

- ❑ An object of type `FileDescriptor` can also represent a physical file.

- ❑ A `FileOutputStream` object can be created from a `File` object, and the file will be opened for writing. If the file does not exist, it will be created where possible.

❏ A `FileChannel` object for a file is returned by the `getChannel()` method for a file stream object.

❏ A buffer contains data to be written to a file or data that has been read from a file. Only `ByteBuffer` objects can be used directly in file I/O operations.

❏ A buffer's position is the index position of the first element in the buffer to be written or read. A buffer's limit specifies the index position of the first element that is not to be written or read.

❏ A view buffer is a buffer that allows the data in a backing byte buffer to be viewed as being of a particular basic type.

❏ You insert data into a buffer using its `put()` methods and retrieve data from it using its `get()` methods. Relative `get()` and `put()` methods increment the buffer's position, whereas absolute `get()` and `put()` methods do not.

❏ You write the contents of a `ByteBuffer` object to a file using a `write()` method belonging to the `FileChannel` object for the file.

❏ The amount of data transferred between a buffer and a file in an I/O operation is determined by the buffer's position and limit. Data is read or written starting at the file's current position.

Exercises

You can download the source code for the examples in the book and the solutions to the following exercises from `http://www.wrox.com`.

1. Modify the example that writes proverbs to a file to separate the proverbs using a delimiter character. You will need to choose a delimiter character that will not appear in normal text.

2. Write a program that, using an integer array of date values containing month, day, and year as integers for some number of dates (10, say, so the integer array will be two-dimensional with 10 rows and 3 columns), will write a file with a string representation of each date written as Unicode characters. For example, the date values 3,2,1990 would be written to the file as 2nd March 1990. Make sure that the date strings can be read back, either by using a separator character of some kind to mark the end of each string or by writing the length of each string before you write the string itself.

3. Extend the previous example to write a second file at the same time as the first, but containing the month, day, and year values as binary data. You should have both files open and be writing to both at the same time.

4. Write a program that, for a given `String` object defined in the code, will write strings to a file in the local character encoding (as bytes) corresponding to all possible permutations of the words in the string. For example, for the string the fat cat, you would write the strings the fat cat, the cat fat, cat the fat, cat fat the, fat the cat, and fat cat the, to the file, although not necessarily in that sequence. (Don't use very long strings; with n words in the string, the number of permutations is $n!$).

Reading Files

In this chapter you'll investigate how you read files containing basic types of data. You'll be exploring how to read files sequentially or at random and how you can open a file for both read and write operations.

In this chapter you'll learn:

❏ How to obtain a file channel for reading a file

❏ How to use buffers in file channel read operations

❏ How to read different types of data from a file

❏ How to retrieve data from random positions in a file

❏ How you can read from and write to the same file

❏ How you can do direct data transfer between channels

❏ What a memory-mapped file is and how you can access a memory-mapped file

❏ What a file lock is and how you can lock all or part of a file

File Read Operations

The process for reading a file parallels that of writing a file. You obtain a `FileChannel` object from a file stream, and use the channel to read data from the file into one or more buffers. Initially you will be using a channel object that you obtain from a `FileInputStream` object to read a file. Later you will be using a `FileChannel` object obtained from a `RandomAccessFile` object to read and write the same file. Like the `FileOutputStream` class, the `FileInputStream` class defines its own methods for file input, as does the `RandomAccessFile` class. However, I'll completely ignore these because the file channel methods for reading the file are much more efficient and will eventually supersede the stream methods. In any event, if you are curious to see how the old stream input mechanism works you can find details about the methods that read from a file stream in the descriptions for the `FileInputStream` and `RandomAccessFile` classes in the documentation that accompanies the JDK.

The starting point for reading a file is to create a `FileInputStream` object. Creating `FileInputStream` objects is not very different from creating `FileOutputStream` objects, so I'll explain how you do that first.

> **In the examples in this chapter you'll be reading some of the files that you created in the last chapter, so I hope that you kept them.**

Creating File Input Streams

A `FileInputStream` object encapsulates a file that is essentially intended to be read so the file must already exist and contain some data. It follows that a constructor for this class type can create an object only for a file that already exists. You have three constructors for `FileInputStream` objects, each of which takes a single argument.

First of all, you can create a `FileInputStream` object from a `String` object that specifies the file name. For example:

```
FileInputStream inputFile = null;        // Place to store the input stream reference
try {
   inputFile = new FileInputStream("C:/Beg Java Stuff/myFile.txt");

} catch(FileNotFoundException e) {
   e.printStackTrace(System.err);
   System.exit(1);
}
```

The `try` block is necessary here because this constructor will throw a `FileNotFoundException` if the file does not exist or the argument to the constructor specifies a directory rather than a file.

You can also use a `File` object to identify the file, like this:

```
File aFile = new File("C:/Beg Java Stuff/myFile.txt");
FileInputStream inputFile = null;        //Place to store the input stream reference
try {
   inputFile = new FileInputStream(aFile);

} catch(FileNotFoundException e) {
   e.printStackTrace(System.err);
   System.exit(1);
}
```

This constructor can also throw a `FileNotFoundException`, so again, you must create the `FileInputStream` object within a `try` block. Using a `File` object to create a `FileInputStream` object is the preferred approach because you can check that the file exists before creating the stream and thus avoid the possibility of throwing a `FileNotFoundException`.

The third possibility is to use a `FileDescriptor` object that you have obtained by calling the `getFD()` method for an existing `FileInputStream` object, or possibly a `RandomAccessFile` object. For example:

```
File aFile = new File("C:/Beg Java Stuff/myFile.text");
FileInputStream inputFile1 = null;     // Place to store an input stream reference
FileDescriptor fd = null;              // Place to store the file descriptor

try {
  // Create the stream opened to write
  inputFile1 = new FileInputStream(aFile);
  fd = inputFile1.getFD();             // Get the file descriptor for the file

} catch(IOException e) {               // For IOException or FileNotFoundException
  e.printStackTrace(System.err);
  System.exit(1);
}

// You can now create another input stream for the file from the file descriptor...
FileInputStream inputFile2 = new FileInputStream(fd);
```

The `getFD()` method can throw an exception of type `IOException` if an I/O error occurs. Because `IOException` is a superclass of `FileNotFoundException`, the `catch` block will catch either type of exception.

I'm sure that you noticed that the constructor call that creates `inputFile2` is not in a `try` block. This is not an oversight. When you create the `FileInputStream` object from a `FileDescriptor` object, the `FileNotFoundException` cannot be thrown since a `FileDescriptor` object always refers to an existing file. This is because a `FileDescriptor` object can be obtained only from a file stream object that already encapsulates a connection to a physical file, so there can be no doubt that the file is real.

As with the `FileOutputStream` constructors, any of the `FileInputStream` constructors will throw a `SecurityException` if a security manager exists on the system and read access to the file is not permitted. Since this is a type of `RuntimeException`, you don't have to catch it.

File Channel Read Operations

You obtain a reference to a `FileChannel` object that you can use to read a file by calling the `getChannel()` method of a `FileInputStream` object. Because a `FileInputStream` object opens a file as read-only, only channel read operations are legal. The channel returned by a `FileInputStream` object has three basic read operations available, each of which reads bytes starting at the byte indicated by the current position in the file. The file position will be incremented by the number of bytes read. The three `read()` methods for a `FileChannel` object are:

`read(ByteBuffer buf)`	Tries to read `buf.remaining()` bytes (equivalent to `limit-position` bytes) from the file into the buffer, `buf`, starting at the buffer's current position. The number of bytes read is returned as type `int`. The value is -1 if the channel reaches the end-of-file during the operation. The buffer position will be incremented by the number of bytes read and the buffer's limit will be left unchanged.
`read(ByteBuffer[] buffers)`	Tries to read bytes into each of the buffers in the `buffers` array in sequence. Bytes will be read into each buffer starting at the point defined by that buffer's position. The number of bytes read into each buffer is defined by the `remaining()` method for that buffer. The `read()` method returns the total number of bytes read as type `int`, or -1 if the channel reaches the end-of-file during the operation. Each buffer's position will be incremented by the number of bytes read into it. Each buffer's limit will be unchanged.

`read(ByteBuffer[] buffers,`
`    int offset,`
`    int length)`
	This operates in the same way as the previous method except that bytes are read starting with the buffer `buffers[offset]`, and up to and including the buffer `buffers[offset+length-1]`. This method will throw an exception of type `IndexOutOfBoundsException` if `offset` or `offset+length-1` are not valid index values for the `buffers` array.

As you can see, all three `read()` methods read data into one or more buffers of type `ByteBuffer`. Since you can use only `ByteBuffer` objects to receive the data read from the file, you can read data from a file only via a channel as a series of bytes. How you interpret these bytes afterwards though is up to you.

All three methods can throw exceptions of any of the following types:

`NonReadableChannelException`	Thrown if the file was not opened for reading
`ClosedChannelException`	Thrown if the channel is closed
`AsynchronousCloseException`	Thrown if the channel is closed by another thread while the read operation is in progress
`ClosedByInterruptException`	Thrown if another thread interrupts the current thread while the read operation is in progress
`IOException`	Thrown if some other I/O error occurs

The first of these is a subclass of `RuntimeException` so you are not obliged to catch this exception. If you don't need to identify the other exceptions individually, you can use a single `catch` block for exceptions of type `IOException` to catch any of them.

The `FileChannel` object keeps track of the file's current position, and this is initially set to zero, corresponding to the first byte available from the file. Each read operation increments the channel's file position by the number of bytes read, so the next read operation will start at that point, assuming you don't modify the file position by some other means. When you need to change the file position in the channel — to reread the file, for example — you just call the position() method for the FileChannel object, with the index position of the byte where you want the next read to start as the argument to the method. For example, with a reference to a FileChannel object stored in a variable inChannel, you could reset the file position back to the beginning of the file with the following statements:

```
try {
  inChannel.position(0);    // Set file position to first byte

} catch(IOException e) {
  e.printStackTrace();
}
```

This method will throw a ClosedChannelException if the channel is closed, or an IOException if some other error occurs, so you need to put the call in a try block. It can also throw an IllegalArgumentException if the argument you supply to the method is negative. IllegalArgumentException is a subclass of RuntimeException. You can legally specify a position beyond the end of the file, but a subsequent read operation will just return -1 indicating that the end-of-file has been reached.

Calling the position() method with no argument specified returns the current file position. This version of the method can also throw exceptions of type ClosedChannelException and IOException so you must put the call in a try block or make the calling method declare the exceptions in a throws clause.

The amount of data read from a file into a byte buffer is determined by the position and limit for the buffer when the read operation executes, as Figure 11-1 illustrates. Bytes are read into the buffer starting at the byte in the buffer given by its position; and assuming sufficient bytes are available from the file, a total of limit-position bytes from the file will be stored in the buffer.

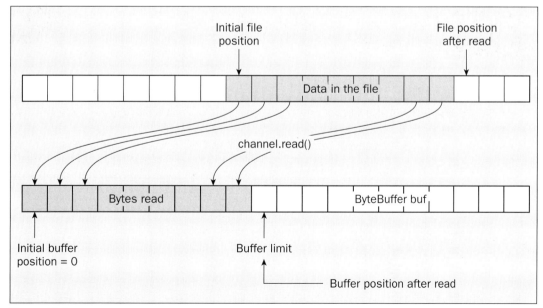

Figure 11-1

You'll see some other channel `read()` methods later that you can use to read data from a particular point in a file.

Reading a Text File

You can now attempt to read the very first file that you wrote in the previous chapter — `charData.txt`. You wrote this file as Unicode characters, so you must take this into account when interpreting the contents of the file.

Your first step will be to define a `File` object encapsulating the file path and create a `FileInputStream` object from that. You can then obtain a reference to the channel from the `FileInputStream` object that you'll use to read the file. I won't include all the checking here that you should apply to validate the file path, as you know how to do that:

```
File aFile = new File("C:/Beg Java Stuff/charData.txt");
FileInputStream inFile = null;

try {
  inFile = new FileInputStream(aFile);

} catch(FileNotFoundException e) {
  e.printStackTrace(System.err);
  System.exit(1);
}
FileChannel inChannel = inFile.getChannel();
```

Of course, you can only read the data from the file as bytes into a byte buffer. You create a `ByteBuffer` object exactly as you saw previously when you were writing the file. You know that you wrote 48 bytes at a time to the file — you wrote the string `"Garbage in, garbage out\n"` that consists of 24 Unicode characters. However, you tried appending to the file an arbitrary number of times, so you should provide for reading as many Unicode characters as there are in the file. You can set up the `ByteBuffer` with exactly the right size for the data from a single write operation with the following statement:

```
ByteBuffer buf = ByteBuffer.allocate(48);
```

The code that you use to read from the file needs to allow for an arbitrary number of 24-character strings in the file. Of course, it will also allow for the end-of-file being reached while you are reading the file. You can read from the file into the buffer like this:

```
try {
  while(inChannel.read(buf) != -1) {
    // Code to extract the data that was read into the buffer...
    buf.clear();                        // Clear the buffer for the next read
  }
  System.out.println("EOF reached.");

} catch(IOException e) {
  e.printStackTrace(System.err);
  System.exit(1);
}
```

The file is read in the expression you use for the `while` loop condition. The `read()` method will return -1 when the end-of-file is reached, so that will end the loop. Within the loop you have to extract the data from the buffer, do what you want with it, and then clear the buffer to be ready for the next read operation.

Getting Data from the Buffer

After each read operation, the buffer's position will point to the byte following the last byte that was read. Before you attempt to extract any data from the buffer, you therefore need to flip the buffer to reset the position back to the beginning of the data, and the limit to the byte following the last byte of data that was read. One way to extract bytes from the buffer is to use the `getChar()` method for the `ByteBuffer` object. This will retrieve a Unicode character from the buffer at the current position and increment the position by 2. This could work like this:

```
buf.flip();
StringBuffer str = new StringBuffer(buf.remaining()/2);
while(buf.hasRemaining())
  str.append(buf.getChar());

System.out.println("String read: "+ str.toString());
```

This code should replace the comment in the previous fragment that appears at the beginning of the `while` loop. You first create a `StringBuffer` object in which you will assemble the string. This is the most efficient way to do this — using a `String` object would result in the creation of a new `String` object each time you add a character to the string. Of course, because there's no possibility of multiple threads accessing the string, you could use a `StringBuilder` object here instead of the `StringBuffer` object and gain a little more efficiency. The `remaining()` method for the buffer returns the number of bytes read after the buffer has been flipped, so you can just divide this by 2 to get the number of characters read. You extract characters one at a time from the buffer in the `while` loop and append them to the `StringBuffer` object. The `getChar()` method increments the buffer's position by 2 each time, so eventually `hasRemaining()` will return `false` when all the characters have been extracted, and the loop will end. You then just convert the `StringBuffer` to a `String` object and output the string on the command line.

This approach works okay, but a better way is to use a view buffer of type `CharBuffer`. The `toString()` method for the `CharBuffer` object will give you the string that it contains directly. Indeed, you can boil the whole thing down to a single statement:

```
System.out.println("String read: " +
            ((ByteBuffer)(buf.flip())).asCharBuffer().toString());
```

The `flip()` method returns a reference of type `Buffer`, so you have to cast it to type `ByteBuffer` to make it possible to call the `asCharBuffer()` method for the buffer object. This is necessary because the `asCharBuffer()` method is defined in the `CharBuffer` class, not in the `Buffer` class.

You can assemble these code fragments into a working example.

Try It Out   Reading Text from a File

Here's the code for the complete program to read the `charData.txt` file that you wrote in the previous chapter:

```java
import java.io.File;
import java.io.FileInputStream;
import java.io.IOException;
import java.io.FileNotFoundException;
import java.nio.ByteBuffer;
import java.nio.channels.FileChannel;
public class ReadAString {
  public static void main(String[] args) {
    File aFile = new File("C:/Beg Java Stuff/charData.txt");
    FileInputStream inFile = null;

    try {
      inFile = new FileInputStream(aFile);

    } catch(FileNotFoundException e) {
      e.printStackTrace(System.err);
      System.exit(1);
    }

    FileChannel inChannel = inFile.getChannel();
    ByteBuffer buf = ByteBuffer.allocate(48);
    try {
      while(inChannel.read(buf) != -1) {
        System.out.println("String read: " +
                        ((ByteBuffer)(buf.flip())).asCharBuffer().toString());
        buf.clear();                       // Clear the buffer for the next read
      }
      System.out.println("EOF reached.");
      inFile.close();                      // Close the file and the channel

    } catch(IOException e) {
      e.printStackTrace(System.err);
      System.exit(1);
    }
    System.exit(0);
  }
}
```

When you compile and run this, you should get output something like the following:

```
String read: "Garbage in, garbage out

String read: "Garbage in, garbage out

String read: "Garbage in, garbage out

EOF reached.
```

The number of lines of output depends on how many times you ran the example that wrote the file. The gap between the lines of output occurs because each string ends with a ' \n ' character.

How It Works

Nothing is new here beyond what I have already discussed. If you want to output the length of the file, you could add a statement to call the `size()` method for the `inChannel` object:

```
System.out.println("File contains "+ inChannel.size() + " bytes.");
```

Immediately before the `while` loop would be a good place to put it, as the `size()` method can throw an `IOException`. You might also like to modify the code to output the buffer's position and limit before and after the read. This will show quite clearly how these change when the file is read.

Reading Binary Data

When you read binary data, you still read bytes from the file, so the process is essentially the same as you used in the previous example. To read a binary file, you create a `FileInputStream` object and get the `FileChannel` object from it, and then you read the data into a byte buffer. You could set up a file channel to read the `primes.bin` file that you created in the previous chapter, like this:

```
File aFile = new File("C:/Beg Java Stuff/primes.bin");
FileInputStream inFile = null;

try {
  inFile = new FileInputStream(aFile);

} catch(FileNotFoundException e) {
  e.printStackTrace(System.err);
  System.exit(1);
}
FileChannel inChannel = inFile.getChannel();
```

You have some options for the size of the byte buffer. The number of bytes in the buffer should be a multiple of 8 because a prime value is of type `long`, but other than that you can make it whatever size you like. You could allocate a buffer to accommodate the number of primes that you want to output to the command line — six values, say. This would make accessing the data very easy since you need to set up a view buffer of type `LongBuffer` only each time you read from the file. One thing against this is that reading such a small amount of data from the file in each read operation would not be a very efficient way to read the file. Before data transfer can start for a read operation, you have significant delay, usually of the order of several milliseconds, waiting for the disk to rotate until the data that you want to read is under the read heads. Therefore, the more read operations you use to retrieve a given amount of data from the file, the longer it takes. However, in the interests of understanding the mechanics of this, let's see how it would work anyway. The buffer would be created like this:

```
final int PRIMECOUNT = 6;                    // Number of primes to read at a time
ByteBuffer buf = ByteBuffer.allocate(8*PRIMECOUNT);
```

You can then read the primes in a `while` loop inside a `try` block:

```
long[] primes = new long[PRIMECOUNT];
try {
  while(inChannel.read(buf) != -1) {
```

```
    // Access the primes via a view buffer of type LongBuffer...
    // Output the primes read...
    buf.clear();                        // Clear the buffer for the next read
  }
  System.out.println("EOF reached.");
  inFile.close();                       // Close the file and the channel

} catch(IOException e) {
  e.printStackTrace(System.err);
  System.exit(1);
}
```

You can create a view buffer of type `LongBuffer` that will help you get at the primes once a block of data has been read from the file. You obtain the view buffer by calling the `asLongBuffer()` method for the byte buffer, `buf`. The `LongBuffer` class offers you a choice of four `get()` methods for accessing values of type `long` in the buffer:

`get()`	Extracts a single value of type `long` from the buffer at the current position and returns it. The buffer position is then incremented by 1.
`get(int index)`	Extracts a single value of type `long` from the buffer position specified by the argument and returns it. The current buffer position is not altered. Remember: The buffer position is in terms of values.
`get(long[] values)`	Extracts `values.length` values of type `long` from the buffer starting at the current position and stores them in the array `values`. The current position is incremented by the number of values retrieved from the buffer. The method returns a reference to the buffer as type `LongBuffer`. If insufficient values are available from the buffer to fill the array that you pass as the argument — in other words, `limit-position` is less than `values.length` — the method will throw an exception of type `BufferUnderflowException`, no values will be transferred to the array, and the buffer's position will be unchanged.
`get(long[] values, int offset, int length)`	Extracts `length` values of type `long` from the buffer starting at the current position and stores them in the `values` array, starting at `values[offset]`. The current position is incremented by the number of values retrieved from the buffer. The method returns a reference to the buffer as type `LongBuffer`. If there are insufficient values available from the buffer — in other words, `limit-position` is less than `length` — the method will throw an exception of type `BufferUnderflowException`. In this case no values will be transferred to the array, and the buffer's position will be unchanged.

The `BufferUnderflowException` class is a subclass of `RuntimeException`, so you are not obliged to catch this exception, although it may be useful to do so if you want to avoid references to array elements that have not been loaded with data from the buffer.

With the buffer size you have specified in the previous code fragment, perhaps the simplest way to access the primes in the buffer is like this:

```
    LongBuffer longBuf = ((ByteBuffer)(buf.flip())).asLongBuffer();
    System.out.println();                              // Newline for the buffer contents
    while(longBuf.hasRemaining()) {                    // While there are values
      System.out.print("   " + longBuf.get());         // output them on the same line
    }
```

If you wanted to collect the primes into an array, using the form of get() method that transfers values to an array will be more efficient than writing a loop to transfer them one at a time, but you have to be careful. Let's try it out in an example to see why.

Try It Out   Reading a Binary File

You will read the primes six at a time into an array. Here's the program:

```
import java.io.File;
import java.io.FileInputStream;
import java.io.IOException;
import java.io.FileNotFoundException;
import java.nio.ByteBuffer;
import java.nio.channels.FileChannel;

public class ReadPrimes {
  public static void main(String[] args) {
    File aFile = new File("C:/Beg Java Stuff/primes.bin");
    FileInputStream inFile = null;

    try {
      inFile = new FileInputStream(aFile);

    } catch(FileNotFoundException e) {
      e.printStackTrace(System.err);
      System.exit(1);
    }

    FileChannel inChannel = inFile.getChannel();
    final int PRIMECOUNT = 6;
    ByteBuffer buf = ByteBuffer.allocate(8*PRIMECOUNT);
    long[] primes = new long[PRIMECOUNT];
    try {
      while(inChannel.read(buf) != -1) {
        ((ByteBuffer)(buf.flip())).asLongBuffer().get(primes);

        // List the primes read on the same line
        System.out.println();
        for(long prime : primes) {
          System.out.printf("%10d", prime);
        }

        buf.clear();                      // Clear the buffer for the next read
      }
      System.out.println("\nEOF reached.");
      inFile.close();                     // Close the file and the channel

    } catch(IOException e) {
```

```
        e.printStackTrace(System.err);
        System.exit(1);
    }
    System.exit(0);
  }
}
```

You get a whole lot of prime values, six to a line, and then, when you almost have them all displayed, you suddenly get the latter part of the following output:

```
        2           3           5           7          11          13
       17          19          23          29          31          37
. . .
      467         479         487         491         499         503
Exception in thread "main" java.nio.BufferUnderflowException
at java.nio.LongBuffer.get(LongBuffer.java:650)
at java.nio.LongBuffer.get(LongBuffer.java:674)
at ReadPrimes.main(ReadPrimes.java:27)
Exception in thread "main"
```

How It Works

The reason is doesn't work very well is that the number of primes in the file is not divisible by the number of primes that you read into the view buffer. This is determined by the number of elements in the primes array. On the last iteration of the while loop that reads the file, you have insufficient values to fill the array so the get() method throws an exception of type BufferUnderflowException.

One way to deal with this is to catch the exception that is thrown. It's not a particularly good way because of the overhead in throwing and catching exceptions, but let's see how you could do it anyway. You could rewrite the while loop like this:

```
        int primesRead = 0;
        while(inChannel.read(buf) != -1) {
          try {
            ((ByteBuffer)(buf.flip())).asLongBuffer().get(primes);
            primesRead = primes.length;

          } catch(BufferUnderflowException e) {
            LongBuffer longBuf = buf.asLongBuffer();
            primesRead = longBuf.remaining();
            longBuf.get(primes,0, primesRead);
          }

          // List the primes read on the same line
          System.out.println();
          for(int i = 0 ; i<primesRead ; i++) {
            System.out.printf("%10d", primes[i]);
          }

          buf.clear();                          // Clear the buffer for the next read
        }
```

When the exception is thrown on the last iteration, you catch it and read the remaining values in the view buffer using the alternate form of the get() method, where the second argument specifies the first array element in which to store a value, and the third argument specifies the number to be stored. To take account of the possibility that less than the whole array will contain primes when you output it, you set the number of primes that are read in the loop. Note that you must set the value of primesRead inside the catch block before you execute the get() method. Afterwards, the number remaining will be zero. Of course, you now have to use a different for loop to output the primes, as the last block of output won't fill the array.

Of course, although this works, it is a very poor way to deal with the problem. A better way is to avoid it altogether, like this:

```
int primesRead = 0;
while(inChannel.read(buf) != -1) {
  LongBuffer longBuf = ((ByteBuffer)(buf.flip())).asLongBuffer();
  primesRead = longBuf.remaining();
  longBuf.get(primes,0, longBuf.remaining());

  // List the primes read on the same line
  System.out.println();
  for(int i = 0 ; i< primesRead ; i++) {
    System.out.printf("%10d", primes[i]);
  }

  buf.clear();                        // Clear the buffer for the next read
}
```

The shaded lines reflect changes to the code in the original example. Now you always read the number of values available in longBuf, so you can't cause the BufferUnderflowException to be thrown.

A further possibility is to use a buffer large enough to hold all the primes in the file. You can work this out from the value returned by the size() method for the channel — which is the length of the file in bytes. You could do that like this:

```
final int PRIMECOUNT = (int)inChannel.size()/8;
```

Of course, you also must alter the for loop that outputs the primes so it doesn't attempt to put them all on the same line. There is a hazard with this though if you don't know how large the file is. Unless your computer is unusually replete with RAM, it could be inconvenient if the file contains the first billion primes. It might be as well to add an assertion to protect against an excess of primes:

```
assert inChannel.size()<=100000;
final int PRIMECOUNT = (int)inChannel.size()/8;
```

Now the program will not proceed if you have more than 100,000 primes in the file. Don't forget that to execute a program with assertions, you must specify the -enableassertions option.

Reading Mixed Data

The `primes.txt` file that you created in the previous chapter contains data of three different types. You have the string length as a binary value of type `double` of all things, followed by the string itself describing the prime value, followed by the binary prime value as type `long`. Reading this file is a little trickier than it looks at first sight.

To start with you'll set up the file input stream and obtain the channel for the file. Since, apart from the name of the file, this is exactly the same as in the previous example, I won't repeat it here. Of course, the big problem is that you don't know ahead of time exactly how long the strings are. You have two strategies to deal with this:

❑   You can read the string length in the first read operation, then read the string and the binary prime value in the next. The only downside to this approach is that it's not a particularly efficient way to read the file, as you will have read operations that each read a very small amount of data.

❑   You can set up a sizable byte buffer of an arbitrary capacity and just fill it with bytes from the file. You can then sort out what you have in the buffer. The problem with this approach is that the buffer's contents may well end part way through one of the data items from the file. You will have to do some work to detect this and figure out what to do next, but this will be much more efficient than the first approach since you will vastly reduce the number of read operations that are necessary to read the entire file.

Let's try the first approach first, as it's easier.

To read the string length you need a byte buffer with a capacity to hold a single value of type `double`:

```
ByteBuffer lengthBuf = ByteBuffer.allocate(8);
```

You can create a byte buffer to hold both the string and the binary prime value, but only after you know the length of the string. Remember, you wrote the string as Unicode characters so you must allow 2 bytes for each character in the original string. Some variables will come in handy:

```
int strLength = 0;         // Stores the string length
ByteBuffer buf = null;     // Stores a reference to the second byte buffer
byte[] strChars = null;    // Stores a reference to an array to hold the string
```

Since you need two read operations to get at all the data for a single prime, your strategy for reading the entire file will have to provide for this. A good approach would be to put both read operations in an indefinite loop and use a `break` statement to exit the loop when you hit the end-of-file (EOF). Here's how you can read the file using this technique:

```
while(true) {
   if(inChannel.read(lengthBuf) == -1)       // Read the string length, if it's EOF
     break;                                   // exit the loop

   lengthBuf.flip();
   strLength = (int)lengthBuf.getDouble();   // Extract length & convert to int
   buf = ByteBuffer.allocate(2*strLength+8); // Buffer for string & prime
```

```
if(inChannel.read(buf) == -1) {          // Read string & binary prime value
  assert false;                          // Should not get here!
  break;                                 // Exit loop on EOF
}

buf.flip();
strChars = new byte[2*strLength];        // Create the array for the string
buf.get(strChars);                       // Extract string & binary prime value

System.out.printf("String length: %3s  String: %-12s  Binary Value: %3d%n",
            strLength, ByteBuffer.wrap(strChars).asCharBuffer(),buf.getLong());

lengthBuf.clear();                       // Clear the buffer for the next read
}
```

After reading the string length into `lengthBuf` you can create the second buffer and allocate an array of type `byte[]` to store the bytes corresponding to the string characters. With this approach you don't need any view buffers at all to get at the data from the file. The `getDouble()` method for `lengthBuf` provides you with the length of the string. You get the bytes that form the string using the `get()` method for `buf`. You obtain the binary prime value using the `getLong()` method for `buf` in the argument to the `printf()` method. To access the bytes in the `strChars` array as a string, you wrap the array in a byte buffer and then create a view buffer of type `CharBuffer` from that. Of course, if you find a string length value, there ought to be a string and a binary prime, so you have an assertion to signal something has gone wrong if this turns out not to be the case.

Let's see how it works out in practice.

Try It Out   Reading Mixed Data from a File

Here's the complete program code:

```
import java.io.FileInputStream;
import java.io.IOException;
import java.io.File;
import java.io.FileNotFoundException;

import java.nio.ByteBuffer;
import java.nio.channels.FileChannel;

public class ReadPrimesMixedData {
  public static void main(String[] args) {
    File aFile = new File("C:/Beg Java Stuff/primes.txt");
    FileInputStream inFile = null;

    try {
      inFile = new FileInputStream(aFile);

    } catch(FileNotFoundException e) {
      e.printStackTrace(System.err);
      System.exit(1);
    }

    FileChannel inChannel = inFile.getChannel();
    try {
```

```
        ByteBuffer lengthBuf = ByteBuffer.allocate(8);
        int strLength = 0;              // Stores the string length
        ByteBuffer buf = null;          // Stores a reference to the second byte buffer
        byte[] strChars = null;         // A reference to an array to hold the string

        while(true) {
          if(inChannel.read(lengthBuf) == -1)  // Read the string length,
            break;                             // if its EOF exit the loop

          lengthBuf.flip();

          // Extract the length and convert to int
          strLength = (int)lengthBuf.getDouble();

          // Buffer for the string & the prime
          buf = ByteBuffer.allocate(2*strLength+8);

          if(inChannel.read(buf) == -1) {   // Read the string & binary prime value
            assert false;                   // Should not get here!
            break;                          // Exit loop on EOF
          }
          buf.flip();
          strChars = new byte[2*strLength]; // Create the array for the string
          buf.get(strChars);                // Extract the string

          System.out.printf("String length: %3s  String: %-12s  Binary Value: %3d%n",
                  strLength, ByteBuffer.wrap(strChars).asCharBuffer(),buf.getLong());
          lengthBuf.clear();                // Clear the buffer for the next read
        }

        System.out.println("\nEOF reached.");
        inFile.close();                     // Close the file and the channel

      } catch(IOException e) {
        e.printStackTrace(System.err);
        System.exit(1);
      }
      System.exit(0);
    }
  }
```

Don't forget that you need to specify the -enableassertions option when you execute it. You should get the following output:

```
String length:   9 String: prime = 2      Binary Value:   2
String length:   9 String: prime = 3      Binary Value:   3
String length:   9 String: prime = 5      Binary Value:   5
```

and so on down to the end:

```
String length:  11 String: prime = 523    Binary Value: 523
String length:  11 String: prime = 541    Binary Value: 541

EOF reached.
```

How It Works

You read the file with a relatively straightforward process. On each iteration of the loop that reads the file, you first read 8 bytes into `lengthBuf` since this will be the length of the following string as a value of type `double`. Knowing the length of the string, you are able to create a second buffer, `buf`, to accommodate the string plus the 8-byte `long` value that is the prime in binary. The string is extracted as an array of bytes using the `get()` method for the buffer, and you view this as a Unicode string by wrapping the array in a `ByteBuffer` and viewing that as a `CharBuffer`. You read the binary prime value from the byte buffer, `buf`, by calling its `getLong()` method. The loop continues until the read operation using `lengthBuf` reaches the end-of-file. If you reach EOF while reading data into `buf`, this means that the file structure is not as it should be and the program will assert. The `'-'` flag in the string format specification `"%-12s"` in the format string for the `printf()` method left-justifies the string in the output field; without this the string would align on the right rather than the left and the output wouldn't look so pretty.

You can choose other ways of extracting the string from `buf`. Here's how you might use a view buffer to do it:

```
char[] str = new char[strLength]; // Array to hold the string
buf.asCharBuffer().get(str);
System.out.printf("String length: %3s  String: %-12s  Binary Value: %3d%n",
                  strLength, new String(str),
                  ((ByteBuffer)(buf.position(2*strLength))).getLong());
```

You use the `get()` method for the view buffer to extract the string as an array of characters. You then create a `String` object from this array in the argument to the `printf()` method. Extracting data from the view buffer leaves the position value for the byte buffer unchanged, so you have to modify the position before calling `getLong()` to extract the binary value.

You could also use the `getChar()` method for the byte buffer to retrieve the string characters one at a time:

```
char[] str = new char[strLength]; // Array to hold the string
for(int i = 0 ; i<str.length ; i++) {
  str[i] = buf.getChar();
}
System.out.printf("String length: %3s  String: %-12s  Binary Value: %3d%n",
                  strLength, new String(str), buf.getLong());
```

You retrieve the string characters in a `for` loop. Because the `getChar()` method does update the position for `buf`, you can just call `getLong()` to access the binary prime value.

Compacting a Buffer

The alternative approach to reading the file is to read bytes from the file into a large buffer for efficiency and then figure out what is in it. Processing the data will need to take account of the possibility that the last data item in the buffer may be incomplete — part of a `double` or `long` value or part of a string. The essence of this approach is therefore as follows:

1. Read from the file into the buffer.

2. Extract the string length, the string, and the binary prime value from the buffer repeatedly until no more complete values are available.

3. Shift any bytes that are left over in the buffer back to the beginning of the buffer. These will be some part of a complete set of the string length, the string, and the binary prime value. Go back to point 1 to read more from the file.

The buffer classes provide the `compact()` method for performing the operation you need in the third step here to shift bytes that are left over back to the beginning. An illustration of the action of the `compact()` method on a buffer is shown in Figure 11-2.

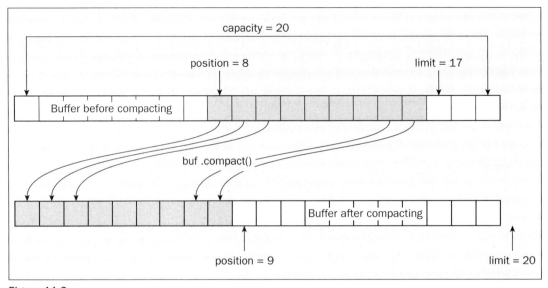

Figure 11-2

As you can see, the compacting operation copies everything in the buffer, which will be the data elements from the buffer's current position up to but not including the buffer's limit, to the beginning of the buffer. The position is then set to the element following the last element that was copied, and the limit is set to the capacity. This is precisely what you want when you have worked partway through the data in an input buffer and you want to add some more data from the file. Compacting the buffer sets the position and limit such that the buffer is ready to receive more data. The next read operation using the buffer will add data at the end of what was left in the buffer.

Try It Out   Reading into a Large Buffer

Here are the changes to the original program code to read data into a large buffer:

```
import java.io.FileInputStream;
import java.io.IOException;
import java.io.File;
import java.io.FileNotFoundException;
import java.nio.ByteBuffer;
import java.nio.channels.FileChannel;

public class ReadPrimesMixedData2 {
```

```java
public static void main(String[] args) {
  File aFile = new File("C:/Beg Java Stuff/primes.txt");
  FileInputStream inFile = null;
  try {
    inFile = new FileInputStream(aFile);
  } catch(FileNotFoundException e) {
    e.printStackTrace(System.err);
    System.exit(1);
  }
  FileChannel inChannel = inFile.getChannel();
  try {
    ByteBuffer buf = ByteBuffer.allocateDirect(1024);
    buf.position(buf.limit());             // Set the position for the loop operation
    int strLength = 0;                     // Stores the string length
    byte[] strChars = null;                // Array for string

    while(true) {
      if(buf.remaining() < 8) {            // Verify enough bytes for string length
        if(inChannel.read(buf.compact()) == -1)
          break;
        buf.flip();
      }
      strLength = (int)buf.getDouble();

      // Verify enough bytes for complete string
      if(buf.remaining()<2*strLength) {
        if(inChannel.read(buf.compact()) == -1)
          break;
        buf.flip();
      }
      strChars = new byte[2*strLength];
      buf.get(strChars);

      if(buf.remaining()<8) {              // Verify enough bytes for prime value
        if(inChannel.read(buf.compact()) == -1)
          break;
        buf.flip();
      }

      System.out.printf("String length: %3s  String: %-12s  Binary Value: %3d%n",
              strLength, ByteBuffer.wrap(strChars).asCharBuffer(),buf.getLong());
    }
    System.out.println("\nEOF reached.");
    inFile.close();                        // Close the file and the channel

  } catch(IOException e) {
    e.printStackTrace(System.err);
    System.exit(1);
  }
  System.exit(0);
  }
}
```

This should result in the same output as the previous example.

How It Works

All the work is done in the indefinite `while` loop. Before the loop executes you create a direct buffer with a capacity of 1024 bytes by calling the `allocateDirect()` method. A direct buffer will be faster if you are reading a lot of data from a file, as the data is transferred directly from the file to our buffer. The code within the loop determines whether there are data values in the buffer by calling the `remaining()` method for the buffer object. The default settings for the buffer, with the position at zero and the limit at the capacity, would suggest falsely that there is data in the buffer, so you set the position to the limit initially so that the `remaining()` method will return zero.

Within the loop you first check whether there are sufficient bytes for the `double` value that specifies the string length. On the first iteration, this will definitely not be the case, so the `compact()` method will be called to compact the buffer, and the reference to `buf` that is returned will be passed to the `read()` method for `inChannel` to read data from the file. You then flip the buffer and get the length of the string. Of course, data in the file should be in groups of three items — the string length, the string, the binary prime value — so the end-of-file should be detected trying to obtain the first of these by the `read()` method for the channel returning -1. In this case you exit the loop by executing a `break` statement.

Next you get the string itself, after checking that you have sufficient bytes left in the buffer. You should never find EOF, so you put an assertion rather than a break if EOF is detected. Finally, you obtain the binary prime value in a similar way and output the group of three data items. The loop continues until all data has been read and processed and EOF is recognized when you are looking for a string length value.

Copying Files

You probably don't need a file copy program, as your operating system is bound to provide a facility for this. However, it is a useful way of demonstrating how a file channel for any input file can transfer data directly to a file channel for an output file without involving explicit buffers.

A file channel defines two methods for direct data transfer:

``transferTo(long position,
         long count,
         WritableByteChannel dst)```
	Attempts to transfer `count` bytes from this channel to the channel `dst`. Bytes are read from this channel starting at the file position specified by `position`. The position of this channel is not altered by this operation, but the position of `dst` will be incremented by the number of bytes written. Fewer than `count` bytes will be transferred if this channel's file has fewer than `count` bytes remaining, or if `dst` is non-blocking and has fewer than `count` bytes free in its system output buffer. The number of bytes transferred is returned as a value of type `int`.

`transferFrom(ReadableByteChannel src,`
`            long position,`
`            long count)`
	Attempts to transfer `count` bytes to this channel from the channel `src`. Bytes are written to this channel starting at the file position specified by `position`. The position of this channel is not altered by the operation, but the position of `src` will be incremented by the number of bytes read from it. If `position` is greater than the size of the file, then no bytes will be transferred. Fewer than `count` bytes will be transferred if the file corresponding to `src` has fewer than `count` bytes remaining in the file or if it is non-blocking and has fewer than `count` bytes free in its system input buffer. The number of bytes transferred is returned as a value of type `int`.

A channel that was obtained from a `FileInputStream` object will support only the `transferTo()` method. Similarly, a channel that was obtained from a `FileOutputStream` object will support only the `transferFrom()` method. Both of these methods can throw any of the following flurry of exceptions:

`IllegalArgumentException`	Thrown if either `count` or `position` is negative
`NonReadableChannelException`	Thrown if the operation attempts to read from a channel that was not opened for reading
`NonWritableChannelException`	Thrown if the operation attempts to write to a channel that was not opened for writing
`ClosedChannelException`	Thrown if either channel involved in the operation is closed
`AsynchronousCloseException`	Thrown if either channel is closed by another thread while the operation is in progress
`ClosedByInterruptException`	Thrown if another thread interrupts the current thread while the operation is in progress
`IOException`	Thrown if some other I/O error occurs

The value of these methods lies in the potential for using the I/O capabilities of the underlying operating system directly. Where this is possible, the operation is likely to be much faster than copying from one file to another in a loop using the `read()` and `write()` methods you have seen.

A file copy program is an obvious candidate for trying out these methods.

Try It Out   **Direct Data Transfer between Channels**

This example is a program that will copy the file that is specified by a command-line argument. You'll copy the file to a backup file that you'll create in the same directory as the original. You'll create the name of the new file by appending `"_backup"` to the original file name as many times as necessary to form a unique file name. That operation is a good candidate for writing a helper method:

```
// Method to create a unique backup File object
public static File createBackupFile(File aFile) {
    aFile = aFile.getAbsoluteFile();             // Ensure you have an absolute path
    File parentDir = new File(aFile.getParent());    // Get the parent directory
    String name = aFile.getName();                   // Get the file name
    int period = name.indexOf('.');              // Find the extension separator
    if(period == -1) {                           // If there isn't one
      period = name.length();                    // set it to the end of the string
    }
    String nameAdd = "_backup";                  // String to be appended

    // Create a File object that is unique
    File backup = aFile;
    while(backup.exists()) {                      // If the name already exists...
        name = backup.getName();                 // Get the current name of the file
      backup = new File(parentDir, name.substring(0,period) // add _backup again
                    + nameAdd + name.substring(period));
        period += nameAdd.length();              // Increment separator index
    }      return backup;
}
```

This method assumes the argument has already been validated as a real file. After making sure that `aFile` is not a relative path, you extract the basic information you need to create the new file — the parent directory, the file name, and where the period separator is, if there is one. You then create a `File` variable, `backup`, that you initialize using the original file name and path. The `while` loop will execute as long as the name already exists as a file, and will repeatedly append instances of `"_backup"` until a unique file name is arrived at.

You can now write the `main()` method to use the `createBackupFile()` method to create the destination file for the file copy operation:

```
import java.io.File;
import java.io.FileInputStream;
import java.io.FileOutputStream;
import java.io.FileNotFoundException;
import java.io.IOException;
import java.nio.channels.FileChannel;

public class FileCopy {
  public static void main(String[] args) {
    if(args.length==0) {
      System.out.println("No file to copy. Application usage is:\n"+
                    "java -classpath . FileCopy \"filepath\"" );
      System.exit(1);
    }
    File fromFile = new File(args[0]);
```

```
      if(!fromFile.exists()) {
        System.out.printf("File to copy, %s, does not exist.",
                                          fromFile.getAbsolutePath());
        System.exit(1);
      }

      File toFile = createBackupFile(fromFile);
      FileInputStream inFile = null;
      FileOutputStream outFile = null;
      try {
        inFile = new FileInputStream(fromFile);
        outFile = new FileOutputStream(toFile);

      } catch(FileNotFoundException e) {
        e.printStackTrace(System.err);
        assert false;
      }

      FileChannel inChannel = inFile.getChannel();
      FileChannel outChannel = outFile.getChannel();

      try {
        int bytesWritten = 0;
        long byteCount = inChannel.size();
        while(bytesWritten<byteCount) {
          bytesWritten += inChannel.transferTo(bytesWritten,
                                        byteCount-bytesWritten,
                                        outChannel);
        }

        System.out.printf("File copy complete. %d bytes copied to %s%n",
                                  byteCount, toFile.getAbsolutePath());
        inFile.close();
        outFile.close();

      } catch(IOException e) {
        e.printStackTrace(System.err);
        System.exit(1);
      }
      System.exit(0);
  }

  // Code for createBackupFile() goes here...
}
```

You could try this out by copying the file containing the primes as binary values using the command:

```
java -enableassertions FileCopy "C:/Beg Java Stuff/primes.bin"
```

You should get output something like the following:

```
File copy complete. 4000 bytes copied to C:\Beg Java Stuff\primes_backup.bin
```

Of course, the file path will be your path, not mine. In any event, you should be able to check that the new file's contents are identical to the original.

How It Works

You first obtain the command-line argument and create a `File` object from it with the following code:

```
if(args.length==0) {
  System.out.println("No file to copy. Application usage is:\n"+
                     "java -classpath . FileCopy \"filepath\"" );
  System.exit(1);
}
File fromFile = new File(args[0]);
```

If there's no command-line argument, you supply a message explaining how to use the program before exiting.

Next, you verify that this is a real file:

```
if(!fromFile.exists()) {
    System.out.printf("File to copy, %s, does not exist.",
                              fromFile.getAbsolutePath());
    System.exit(1);
}
```

If it isn't, there's nothing you can do, so you bail out of the program.

Creating a `File` object for the backup file is a piece of cake:

```
File toFile = createBackupFile(fromFile);
```

You saw how this helper method works earlier in this chapter.

You now create a pair of file stream objects to work with:

```
FileInputStream inFile = null;
FileOutputStream outFile = null;
try {
  inFile = new FileInputStream(fromFile);
  outFile = new FileOutputStream(toFile);

} catch(FileNotFoundException e) {
  e.printStackTrace(System.err);
  assert false;
}
```

Since you checked the `File` objects, you know you won't see a `FileNotFoundException` being thrown, but you still must provide for the possibility. Of course, the `FileInputStream` object corresponds to the file name entered on the command line. Creating the `FileOutputStream` object will result in a new empty file being created, ready for loading with the data from the input file.

Next, you get the channel for each file from the file streams:

```
FileChannel inChannel = inFile.getChannel();
FileChannel outChannel = outFile.getChannel();
```

Once you have the channel objects, you transfer the contents of the input file to the output file like this:

```
try {
  int bytesWritten = 0;
  long byteCount = inChannel.size();
  while(bytesWritten<byteCount) {
    bytesWritten += inChannel.transferTo(bytesWritten,
                                          byteCount-bytesWritten,
                                          outChannel);
  }
  System.out.printf("File copy complete. %d bytes copied to %s%n",
                               byteCount, toFile.getAbsolutePath());
  inFile.close();
  outFile.close();

} catch(IOException e) {
  e.printStackTrace(System.err);
  System.exit(1);
}
```

You copy the data using the `transferTo()` method for `inChannel`. You could equally well use the `transferFrom()` method for `outChannel`. The chances are good that the `transferTo()` method will transfer all the data in one go. The `while` loop is there just in case it doesn't. The loop condition checks whether the number of bytes written is less than the number of bytes in the file. If it is, the loop executes another transfer operation for the number of bytes left in the file, with the file position specified as the number of bytes written so far.

Random Access to a File

You can already read from or write to a file at random. The `FileChannel` class defines both a `read()` and a `write()` method that operate at a specified position in the file:

`read(ByteBuffer buf, long position)`	Reads bytes from the file into `buf` in the same way as you have seen previously except that bytes are read starting at the file position specified by the second argument. The channel's position is not altered by this operation. If `position` is greater than the number of bytes in the file, then no bytes are read.
`write(ByteBuffer buf, long position)`	Writes bytes from `buf` to the file in the same way as you have seen previously except that bytes are written starting at the file position specified by the second argument. The channel's position is not altered by this operation. If `position` is less than the number of bytes in the file, then bytes from that point will be overwritten. If `position` is greater than the number of bytes in the file then the file size will be increased to this point before bytes are written. In this case the bytes between the original end-of-file and where the new bytes are written will contain junk values.

These methods can throw the same exceptions as the corresponding method accepting a single argument; plus, they may throw an exception of type `IllegalArgumentException` if a negative file position is specified.

Let's see how you can access a file randomly using the preceding `read()` method.

Try It Out   Reading a File Randomly

To show how easy it is to read from random positions in a file, you will write an example to extract a random selection of values from our `primes.bin` file. Here's the code:

```
import java.io.File;
import java.io.FileInputStream;
import java.io.FileOutputStream;
import java.io.FileNotFoundException;
import java.io.IOException;
import java.nio.ByteBuffer;
import java.nio.channels.FileChannel;

public class RandomFileRead {
  public static void main(String[] args) {
    File aFile = new File("C:/Beg Java Stuff/primes.bin");
    FileInputStream inFile = null;
    FileOutputStream outFile = null;

    try {
      inFile = new FileInputStream(aFile);

    } catch(FileNotFoundException e) {
      e.printStackTrace(System.err);
      System.exit(1);
    }
    FileChannel inChannel = inFile.getChannel();

    final int PRIMESREQUIRED = 10;
    ByteBuffer buf = ByteBuffer.allocate(8*PRIMESREQUIRED);

    long[] primes = new long[PRIMESREQUIRED];
    int index = 0;                           // Position for a prime in the file

    try {
      // Count of primes in the file
      final int PRIMECOUNT = (int)inChannel.size()/8;

      // Read the number of random primes required
      for(int i = 0 ; i<PRIMESREQUIRED ; i++) {
        index = 8*(int)(PRIMECOUNT*Math.random());
        inChannel.read(buf, index);              // Read the value
        buf.flip();
        primes[i] = buf.getLong();               // Save it in the array
        buf.clear();
      }

      // Output the selection of random primes 5 to a line in field width of 12
```

```
      int count = 0;                                 // Count of primes written
      for(long prime : primes) {
        System.out.printf("%12d", prime);
        if(++count%5 == 0) {
          System.out.println();
        }
      }
      inFile.close();                                // Close the file and the channel

   } catch(IOException e) {
      e.printStackTrace(System.err);
      System.exit(1);
   }
      System.exit(0);
  }
}
```

When I ran this, I got the following output:

```
      359         107         383         109           7
      173         443         337          17         113
```

You should get something similar but not the same because the random number generator is seeded using the current clock time. The number of random selections is fixed, but you could easily add code for a value to be entered on the command line.

How It Works

You access a random prime in the file by generating a random position in the file with the expression `8*(int)(PRIMECOUNT*Math.random())`. The value of `index` is a pseudo-random integer that can be from 0 to the number of primes in the file minus one, multiplied by 8 since each prime occupies 8 bytes. Since `buf` has a capacity of 8 bytes, only one prime will be read each time. You store each randomly selected prime in an element of the `primes` array. Finally, you output the primes five to a line in a field width of 12 characters.

The need to be able to access and update a file randomly arises quite often. Even with a simple personnel file, for example, you are likely to need the capability to update the address or the phone number for an individual. Assuming you have arranged for the address and phone number entries to be of a fixed length, you could update the data for any entry simply by overwriting it. If you want to read from and write to the same file you can just create two file streams and get two file channels for the file, one for input and one for output. Let's try that, too.

Try It Out   Reading and Writing a File Randomly

You can modify the previous example so that you overwrite each random prime that you retrieve with the value `99999L` to make it stand out from the rest. This will mess up the `primes_backup.bin` file that you will use here, but you can always run the program that will copy files to copy `primes.bin` if you want to restore it. Here's the code:

```
import java.io.File;
import java.io.FileInputStream;
import java.io.FileOutputStream;
import java.io.FileNotFoundException;
import java.io.IOException;
import java.nio.ByteBuffer;
import java.nio.channels.FileChannel;

public class RandomReadWrite {
  public static void main(String[] args)
  {
    File aFile = new File("C:/Beg Java Stuff/primes_backup.bin");
    FileInputStream inFile = null;
    FileOutputStream outFile = null;

    try {
      inFile = new FileInputStream(aFile);
      outFile = new FileOutputStream(aFile, true);

    } catch(FileNotFoundException e) {
      e.printStackTrace(System.err);
      System.exit(1);
    }
    FileChannel inChannel = inFile.getChannel();
    FileChannel outChannel = outFile.getChannel();

    final int PRIMESREQUIRED = 10;
    ByteBuffer buf = ByteBuffer.allocate(8);

    long[] primes = new long[PRIMESREQUIRED];
    int index = 0;                              // Position for a prime in the file
    final long REPLACEMENT = 99999L;            // Replacement for a selected prime

    try {
      final int PRIMECOUNT = (int)inChannel.size()/8;
      System.out.println("Prime count = "+PRIMECOUNT);
      for(int i = 0 ; i<PRIMESREQUIRED ; i++) {
        index = 8*(int)(PRIMECOUNT*Math.random());
        inChannel.read(buf, index);             // Read at a random position
        buf.flip();                             // Flip the buffer
        primes[i] = buf.getLong();              // Extract the prime
        buf.flip();                             // Flip to ready for insertion
        buf.putLong(REPLACEMENT);               // Replacement into buffer
        buf.flip();                             // Flip ready to write
        outChannel.write(buf, index);           // Write the replacement to file
        buf.clear();                            // Reset ready for next read
      }

      int count = 0;                            // Count of primes written
      for(long prime : primes) {
        System.out.printf("%12d", prime);
        if(++count%5 == 0) {
          System.out.println();
        }
      }
    }
```

```
            inFile.close();                     // Close the file and the channel
            outFile.close();

        } catch(IOException e) {
            e.printStackTrace(System.err);
            System.exit(1);
        }
            System.exit(0);
    }
}
```

This will output from the file a set of ten random prime selections that have been overwritten. If you want to verify that you have indeed overwritten these values in the file, you can run the ReadPrimes example that you wrote earlier in this chapter with the file name as "primes_backup.bin".

How It Works

All you had to do to write the file as well as read it was to create a FileOutputStream object for the file in addition to the FileInputStream object and access its file channel. You are then able to use one channel for writing to the file and the other for reading it. The output file stream was opened in append mode so that any additional values written to the file would be added to the end of the file.

You can read and write sequentially or at random. The channel read() and write() methods you are using here explicitly specify the position where the data is to be read or written as an argument. In this case the file position recorded by the channel does not change. You could equally well change the file position for the channel before performing the read or write, like this:

```
            for(int i = 0 ; i<PRIMESREQUIRED ; i++) {
              index = 8*(int)(PRIMECOUNT*Math.random());
              inChannel.read(buf, index);          // Read at a random position
              buf.flip();                          // Flip the buffer
              primes[i] = buf.getLong();           // Extract the prime
              buf.flip();                          // Flip to ready for insertion
              buf.putLong(REPLACEMENT);            // Replacement into buffer
              buf.flip();                          // Flip ready to write
              outChannel.write(buf, index);        // Write the replacement to file
              buf.clear();                         // Reset ready for next read
            }
```

Now the file positions recorded by the channels are set explicitly and each channel's position is updated when it executes an I/O operation. Note that the position() method for a channel does not return a reference to the channel object so you cannot chain the position() and read() method calls together. You can do this only with buffer objects.

One problem with the example as it stands is that some of the selections could be 99999L, which is patently not prime. You could fix this by checking each value you store in the primes array:

```
    for(int i = 0 ; i<PRIMESREQUIRED ; i++)
    {
      while(true)
      {
        index = 8*(int)(PRIMECOUNT*Math.random());
        inChannel.read(buf, index);              // Read at a random position
```

```
      buf.flip();                        // Flip the buffer
      primes[i] = buf.getLong();         // Extract the prime
      if(primes[i] != REPLACEMENT) {
        break;                           // It's good so exit the inner loop
      } else {
        buf.clear();                     // Clear ready to read another
      }
    }
  }
  buf.flip();                            // Flip to ready for insertion
  buf.putLong(REPLACEMENT);              // Replacement into buffer
  buf.flip();                            // Flip ready to write
  outChannel.write(buf, index);          // Write the replacement to file
  buf.clear();                           // Reset ready for next read
}
```

The while loop now continues if the value read from the file is the same as REPLACEMENT, so another random file position will be selected. This continues until something other than the value of REPLACE-MENT is found. Of course, if you run the example often enough, you won't have enough primes in the file to fill the array, so the program will loop indefinitely looking for something other than REPLACEMENT. You could deal with this in several ways . For example, you could count how many iterations have occurred in the while loop and bail out if it reaches the number of primes in the file. You could also inspect the file first to see whether there are sufficient primes in the file to fill the array. If there are exactly 10, you can fill the array immediately. I'll leave it to you to fill in these details.

Read/Write Operations with a Single File Channel

If you want to be able to read from and write to a file using a single channel, you must use the channel provided by a RandomAccessFile object. A RandomAccessFile object is not related to the other file stream classes since its only base class is Object. Its original purpose was to provide random access to a file, which the other file stream classes could not, but as you have seen, this capability has been usurped by a channel anyway.

Two constructors are available for creating RandomAccessFile objects, and both require two argu-ments. For one constructor, the first argument is a File object that identifies the file path, and the sec-ond is a String object that specifies the access mode. The other constructor offers the alternative of using a String object as the first argument specifying the file path, with the second argument defining the access mode as before.

The access mode can be any of the following four values:

"r"	Indicates that you just want to read the file. In this mode the file cannot be written.
"rw"	Indicates that you want to open the file to allow both read and write operations.
"rwd"	Indicates that you want to allow both read and write operations but you want all write operations to force immediate writing of data to the device.
"rws"	Indicates that you want to allow both read and write operations but you want all write operations to force immediate writing of data and metadata (such as the file length) to the device.

If you specify the mode as anything other than the four shown in the preceding table, the constructor will throw an `IllegalArgumentException`. You use the `"rwd"` and `"rws"` mode when you are writing to a local device and you want the data to be written immediately to minimize the possibility of data loss in the event of a system crash. The `"rwd"` mode requires fewer operations than `"rws"` mode for write operations because writing the data and the metadata typically involves a separate low-level write operation.

To create a `RandomAccessFile` object, you could write:

```
File myPrimes = new File("c:/Beg Java Stuff/primes.bin");
RandomAccessFile primesFile = null;
try {
  primesFile = new RandomAccessFile(myPrimes, "rw");

} catch(FileNotFoundException e) {
  e.printStackTrace(System.err);
  assert false;
}
```

This will create the random access file object `primesFile`, corresponding to the physical file `primes.bin`, and will open it for both reading and writing.

If the file does not exist when you specify `"rw"`, `"rwd"`, or `"rws"` as the mode, the file will be created automatically as long as the parent directory exists. Of course, the implicit assumption is that you intend to write to the file before you try to read it. If you specify the mode as `"r"`, the file must already exist. If it doesn't, the constructor will throw a `FileNotFoundException`. The same exception will be thrown if the file exists but cannot be opened for some reason. Like the file stream class constructors, a `RandomAccessFile` constructor can throw a `SecurityException` if a security manager exists and access to the file is denied.

You obtain the `FileChannel` object from a `RandomAccessFile` object in the same way as for the file stream objects you have been working with:

```
FileChannel ioChannel = primesFile.getChannel();
```

You can now use this channel to read from and write to the file sequentially or at random. It should be a trivial exercise for you to modify the previous example to use a channel from a `RandomAccessFile` object instead of the channels for the two file stream objects.

If you check the documentation for the `RandomAccessFile` class, you will find that it, too, records the file position and it describes it as a file-pointer. It also defines the `getFilePointer()` method for obtaining the current value of the file-pointer and the `seek()` method that alters it. The file-pointer for a `RandomAccessFile` object is identical to the file position recorded by its channel, and changes to one are immediately reflected in the other.

Memory-Mapped Files

A memory-mapped file is a file that has its contents mapped into an area of virtual memory in your computer. This enables you to reference or update the data in the file directly without performing any explicit file read or write operations on the physical file yourself. When you reference a part of the file that is not actually in real memory, it will be automatically paged in by your operating system. The memory that a file maps to may be paged in or out by the operating system, just like any other memory in your computer, so its immediate availability in real memory is not guaranteed. Because of the potentially immediate availability of the data it contains, a memory-mapped file is particularly useful when you need to access the file randomly. Your program code can reference the data in the file just as though it were all resident in memory.

Mapping a file into memory is implemented by a `FileChannel` object. The `map()` method for a `FileChannel` object will return a reference to a buffer of type `MappedByteBuffer` that will map to a specified part of the channel's file:

`map(int mode, long position, long size)`	Maps a region of the channel's file to a buffer of type `MappedByteBuffer`. The file region that is mapped starts at `position` in the file and is of length `size` bytes. The first argument, `mode`, specifies how the buffer's memory may be accessed and can be any of the following three constant values, which are defined in the `MapMode` class, which is a static inner class of the `FileChannel` class:
	`MapMode.READ_ONLY` — This is valid if the channel was opened for reading the file — in other words, if the channel was obtained from a `FileInputStream` object or a `RandomAccessFile` object. In this mode the buffer is read-only. If you try to modify the buffer's contents, an exception of type `ReadOnlyBufferException` will be thrown.
	`MapMode.READ_WRITE` — This is valid if the channel was obtained from a `RandomAccessFile` object with `"rw"`, `"rwd"`, or `"rws"` as its access mode. You can access and change the contents of the buffer and any changes to the contents will be propagated to the file, possibly later if the access mode is `"rw"`.
	`MapMode.PRIVATE` — This mode is for a "copy-on-write" mapping. This option for `mode` is also valid only if the channel was obtained from a `RandomAccessFile` object with `"rw"` as its access mode. You can access or change the buffer, but changes will not be propagated to the file. Private copies of modified portions of the buffer will be created and used for subsequent buffer accesses.

When you access or change data in the `MappedByteBuffer` object that is returned when you call the `map()` method for a `FileChannel` object, you are effectively accessing the file that is mapped to the buffer. Once you have called the `map()` method, the file mapping and the buffer that you have established are independent of the `FileChannel` object. You can close the channel, and the mapping of the file into the `MappedByteBuffer` object will still be valid and operational.

Because the `MappedByteBuffer` class is a subclass of the `ByteBuffer` class, you have all the `ByteBuffer` methods available for a `MappedByteBuffer` object. This implies that you can create view buffers for a `MappedByteBuffer` object, for instance.

The `MappedByteBuffer` class defines three methods of its own to add to those inherited from the `ByteBuffer` class:

`force()`	If the buffer was mapped in `MapMode.READ_WRITE` mode, this method forces any changes made to the buffer's contents to be written to the file and returns a reference to the buffer. For buffers created with other access modes, this method has no effect.
`load()`	Tries on a "best efforts" basis to load the contents of the buffer into memory and returns a reference to the buffer.
`isLoaded()`	Returns `true` if it is likely that this buffer's contents are available in physical memory and `false` otherwise.

The `load()` method is dependent on external operating system functions executing to achieve the desired result, so the result cannot in general be guaranteed. Similarly, when you get a `true` return from the `isLoaded()` method, this is an indication of a probable state of affairs rather than a guarantee. This doesn't imply any kind of problem. It just means that accessing the data in the mapped byte buffer may take longer that you might expect in some instances. Using a memory-mapped file through a `MappedByteBuffer` is simplicity itself, so let's try it.

Try It Out   Using a Memory-Mapped File

You will access and modify the `primes_backup.bin` file using a `MappedByteBuffer`, so you may wish to rerun the file copy program to restore it to its original condition. Here's the code:

```
import java.io.File;
import java.io.RandomAccessFile;
import java.io.FileNotFoundException;
import java.io.IOException;
import java.nio.MappedByteBuffer;
import java.nio.channels.FileChannel;
import static java.nio.channels.FileChannel.MapMode.READ_WRITE;

public class MemoryMappedFile {
  public static void main(String[] args) {
    File aFile = new File("C:/Beg Java Stuff/primes_backup.bin");
    RandomAccessFile ioFile = null;
    try {
      ioFile = new RandomAccessFile(aFile,"rw");
    } catch(FileNotFoundException e) {
      e.printStackTrace(System.err);
      System.exit(1);
    }
    FileChannel ioChannel = ioFile.getChannel();
    final int PRIMESREQUIRED = 10;
    long[] primes = new long[PRIMESREQUIRED];

    int index = 0;                              // Position for a prime in the file
    final long REPLACEMENT = 999999L;           // Replacement for a selected prime

    try {
```

```
        final int PRIMECOUNT = (int)ioChannel.size()/8;
        MappedByteBuffer buf = ioChannel.map(READ_WRITE, 0L,ioChannel.size()).load();
        ioChannel.close();                           // Close the channel

        for(int i = 0 ; i<PRIMESREQUIRED ; i++) {
          index = 8*(int)(PRIMECOUNT*Math.random());
          primes[i] = buf.getLong(index);
          buf.putLong(index, REPLACEMENT);
        }
        int count = 0;                               // Count of primes written
        for(long prime : primes) {
          System.out.printf("%12d", prime);
          if(++count%5 == 0) {
            System.out.println();
          }
        }
        ioFile.close();                              // Close the file and the channel
      } catch(IOException e) {
        e.printStackTrace(System.err);
        System.exit(1);
      }
      System.exit(0);
    }
  }
```

This should output ten randomly selected primes, but some or all of the selections may turn out to be 999999L, the value of REPLACEMENT if you have not refreshed the contents of primes_backup.bin. The highlighted lines of code are those that are new or different compared to the previous example.

How It Works

The only statements of interest are those that are shaded because the others you have seen before. You can see import statements for RandomAccessFile and MappedByteBuffer class names, and you import the static member of the MapMode inner class to the FileChannel class that you will use in the code.

You create a RandomAccessFile object with "rw" access to the file:

```
        ioFile = new RandomAccessFile(aFile,"rw");
```

This statement executes in a try block since it can throw a FileNotFoundException. You could also use the "rwd" or "rws" access modes if you want any changes written to the physical file immediately.

You get the file channel for the ioFile object with the statement:

```
        FileChannel ioChannel = ioFile.getChannel();
```

You then create and load a MappedByteBuffer object with the statement:

```
        MappedByteBuffer buf = ioChannel.map(READ_WRITE, 0L,ioChannel.size()).load();
```

The buffer is created with the READ_WRITE mode, which permits the buffer to be accessed or modified. The buffer maps to the entire file because you specify the start file position as zero, and the length that is mapped as the length of the file. The map() method returns a reference to the MappedByteBuffer object that is created and you use this to call its `load()` method to request that the contents of the file be loaded into memory immediately. The `load()` method also returns the same buffer reference, and you store that in `buf`.

Note that it is not essential to call the `load()` method before you access the data in the buffer. If the data is not available when you try to access it through the `MappedByteBuffer` object, it will be loaded for you. Try running the example with the call to `load()` removed. It should work the same as before.

The next statement closes the file channel because it is no longer required:

```
ioChannel.close();                          // Close the channel
```

It is not essential to close the channel but doing so demonstrates that memory-mapped file operations are independent of the channel once the mapping has been established.

Inside the `for` loop, you retrieve a value from the buffer at a random position, `index`:

```
primes[i] = buf.getLong(index);
```

Note that you have not needed to execute any explicit `read()` operations. The file contents are available directly through the buffer and any read operations that need to be executed to make the data you are accessing available are initiated automatically.

Next, you change the value at the position from which you retrieved the value to store in `primes[i]`:

```
buf.putLong(index, REPLACEMENT );
```

This will change the contents of the buffer, and this change will subsequently be written to the file at some point. When this occurs depends on the underlying operating system.

Finally, you output the contents of the `primes` array. You have been able to access and modify the contents of the file without having to execute any explicit I/O operations on the file. This is potentially much faster than using explicit read and write operations. How much faster depends on how efficiently your operating system handles memory-mapped files and whether the way in which you access the data results in a large number of page faults.

Memory-mapped files have one risky aspect that you need to consider, and we'll look at that in the next section.

Locking a File

You need to take care that an external program does not modify a memory-mapped file that you are working with, especially if the file could be truncated externally while you are accessing it. If you try to access a part of the file through a `MappedByteBuffer` that has become inaccessible because a segment has been chopped off the end of the file by another program, then the results are somewhat unpredictable. You may get a junk value back that your program may not recognize as such, or an exception of some kind may be thrown. You can acquire a lock on the file to prevent this sort of problem. A file lock simply ensures your right of access to the file and may also inhibit the ability of others to change or possibly access the file as long as your lock is in effect. This facility is available only if the underlying operating system supports file locking.

A lock on a file is encapsulated by an object of the `FileLock` class, which is defined in the `java.nio.channels` package. The `lock()` method for a `FileChannel` object tries to obtain an exclusive lock on the channel's file. Acquiring an exclusive lock on a file ensures that another program cannot access the file at all, and is typically used when you want to write to a file, or when any modification of the file by another process will cause you problems. Here's one way to obtain an exclusive lock on a file:

```
FileLock ioFileLock = null;
try {
   ioFileLock = ioChannel.lock();

} catch (IOException e) {
   e.printStackTrace(System.err);
   System.exit(1);
}
```

This method attempts to acquire an exclusive lock on the channel's file so that no other program or thread can access the file while this channel holds the lock. A prerequisite for obtaining an exclusive lock is that the file has been opened for both reading and writing so the code fragment assumes that this applies to `ioChannel`. If another program or thread already has a lock on the file, the `lock()` method will block until the lock on the file is released and can be acquired by this channel. The lock that is acquired is owned by the channel, `ioChannel`, and will be automatically released when the channel is closed. By saving the reference to the `FileLock` object, you can release the lock on the file when you are done by calling the `release()` method for the `FileLock` object. This invalidates the lock so file access is no longer restricted. You can call the `isValid()` method for a `FileLock` object to determine whether it is valid. A return value of `true` indicates a valid lock; otherwise, `false` will be returned indicating that the lock is not valid. Note that once created, a `FileLock` object is immutable. It also has no further effect on file access once it has been invalidated. If you want to lock the file a second time, you must acquire a new lock.

Having your program hang until a lock is acquired is not an ideal situation. It is quite possible a file could be locked permanently — at least until the computer is rebooted — because of a programming error in another program, in which case your program will hang indefinitely. The `tryLock()` method for a channel offers an alternative way of requesting a lock that does not block. It either returns a reference to a valid `FileLock` object or returns `null` if the lock could not be acquired. This gives your program a chance to do something else or retire gracefully:

```
FileLock ioFileLock = null;
try {
   ioFileLock = ioChannel.tryLock();
   if(ioFileLock == null) {
      System.out.println("The file's locked - again!! Oh, I give up...");
      System.exit(1);
   }
} catch (IOException e) {
   e.printStackTrace(System.err);
   System.exit(1);
}
```

You'll see a better response to a lock than this in an example, but you get the idea.

Locking Part of a File

Overloaded versions of the `lock()` and `tryLock()` methods allow you to specify just the part of the file you want to obtain a lock on so you don't lock the whole file:

`lock(long position,`
`    long size,`
`    boolean shared)`
	Requests a lock on the region of this channel's file starting at `position` and of length `size`. If the last argument is `true`, the lock requested is a shared lock. If it is `false`, the lock requested is an exclusive lock. If the lock cannot be obtained for any reason, the method will block until the lock can be obtained or the channel is closed by another thread.

`tryLock(long position,`
`    long size,`
`    boolean shared)`
	This works in the same way as the previous method, except that `null` will be returned if the requested lock cannot be acquired. This avoids the potential for hanging your program indefinitely.

A shared lock allows concurrent read access to the file by several processes. The effect of a shared lock is to prevent an exclusive lock being acquired by another program that overlaps the region that is locked. However, a shared lock does permit another program to acquire a shared lock on a region of the file that may overlap the region to which the original shared lock applies. This implies that more than one program may be accessing the same region of the file, so the effect of a shared lock is simply to ensure that your code is not prevented from doing whatever it is doing by some other program with a shared lock on the file. Some operating systems do not support shared locks, in which case the request will always be treated as an exclusive lock regardless of what you requested.

Note that a single Java Virtual Machine (JVM) does not allow overlapping locks, so different threads running on the same JVM cannot have overlapping locks on a file. However, the locks within two or more JVMs on the same computer can overlap. If another program changing the data in a file would cause a problem for you, then the safe thing to do is to obtain an exclusive lock on the file you are working with. If you want to test for the presence of an overlapping lock, you can call the `overlaps()` method for your lock object.

Practical File Locking Considerations

You can apply file locks in any context, not just with memory-mapped files. The fact that all or part of a file can be locked by a program means that you cannot ignore file locking when you are writing a real-world Java application that may execute in a context where file locking is supported. You need to include at least shared file locks for regions of a file that your program uses. In some instances, though, you'll want to use exclusive locks since external changes to a file's contents can still be a problem even when the parts you are accessing cannot be changed. As I've said, you can obtain an exclusive lock only on a channel that is open for both reading and writing; and an exception of type `NonReadableChannelException` or `NonWritableChannelException` will be thrown, as appropriate, if you have opened the file just for input or just for output. This means that if you really must have an exclusive lock on a file, you have to have opened it for reading and writing, and this means that you will have obtained the `FileChannel` object from a `RandomAccessFile` object that you created with the mode as `"rw"`, `"rws"`, or `"rwd"`.

You don't need to obtain a lock on an entire file. Generally, if it is likely that other programs will be using the same file concurrently, it is not reasonable practice to lock everyone else out, unless it is absolutely necessary, such as a situation in which you may be performing a transacted operation that must either succeed or fail entirely. Circumstances where it would be necessary are when the correctness of your program result is dependent on the entire file's contents not changing. If you were computing a checksum for a file, for example, you would need to lock the entire file. Any changes made while your checksum calculation is in progress are likely to make it incorrect.

Most of the time it is quite sufficient to lock the portion of the file you are working with, and then release it once you are done with it. You can get an idea of how you might do this in the context of the program that lists the primes from the `primes.bin` file.

Try It Out   Using a File Lock

You will lock the region of the `primes.bin` file that you intend to read, and then release it after the read operation is complete. You will use the `tryLock()` method since it does not block, and try to acquire the lock again if it fails to return a reference to a `FileLock` object. To do this sensibly you need to be able to pause the current thread rather than roaring round a tight loop frantically calling the `tryLock()` method. I'll bring forward a capability from Chapter 16 to do this for you. You can pause the current thread by 200 milliseconds with the following code:

```
try {
  Thread.sleep(200);     // Wait for 200 milliseconds

} catch(InterruptedException e) {
  e.printStackTrace(System.err);
}
```

The static `sleep()` method in the `Thread` class causes the current thread to sleep for the number of milliseconds specified by the argument. While the current thread is sleeping, other threads can execute, so whoever has a lock on our file has a chance to release it.

Here's the code for the complete example:

```
import java.io.File;
import java.io.FileInputStream;
import java.io.IOException;
import java.io.FileNotFoundException;
import java.nio.ByteBuffer;
import java.nio.LongBuffer;
import java.nio.channels.FileChannel;
import java.nio.channels.FileLock;

public class LockingPrimesRead {
  public static void main(String[] args) {
    File aFile = new File("C:/Beg Java Stuff/primes.bin");
    FileInputStream inFile = null;

    try {
      inFile = new FileInputStream(aFile);
    } catch(FileNotFoundException e) {
      e.printStackTrace(System.err);
      System.exit(1);
```

```
      }

      FileChannel inChannel = inFile.getChannel();
      final int PRIMECOUNT = 6;
      ByteBuffer buf = ByteBuffer.allocate(8*PRIMECOUNT);
      long[] primes = new long[PRIMECOUNT];

      try {
        int primesRead = 0;
        FileLock inLock = null;

        // File reading loop
        while(true) {
          int tryLockCount = 0;

          // Loop to get a lock on the file region you want to read
          while(true) {
            inLock = inChannel.tryLock(inChannel.position(), buf.remaining(), true);
            if(inLock != null) {                    // If you have a lock
              System.out.println("\nAcquired file lock.");
              break;                                // exit the loop
            }

            if(++tryLockCount>=100) {               // If you've tried too often
              System.out.printf("Failed to acquire lock after %d tries."+
                                              "Terminating...%n", tryLockCount);
              System.exit(1);                       // end the program
            }

            // Wait 200 msec before the next try for a file lock
            try {
                Thread.sleep(200);                  // Wait for 200 milliseconds
            } catch(InterruptedException e) {
                e.printStackTrace(System.err);
            }
          }

          // You have a lock so now read the file
          if(inChannel.read(buf) == -1) {
            break;
          }
          inLock.release();                         // Release lock as read is finished
          System.out.println("Released file lock.");

          LongBuffer longBuf = ((ByteBuffer)(buf.flip())).asLongBuffer();
          primesRead = longBuf.remaining();
          longBuf.get(primes,0, longBuf.remaining());
          for(int i = 0 ; i< primesRead ; i++) {
            if(i%6 == 0) {
              System.out.println();
            }
            System.out.printf("%12d", primes[i]);
          }
          buf.clear();                              // Clear the buffer for the next read
        }
```

```
        System.out.println("\nEOF reached.");
        inFile.close();                        // Close the file and the channel

    } catch(IOException e) {
        e.printStackTrace(System.err);
        System.exit(1);
    }
        System.exit(0);
    }
}
```

This will output primes from the file just as the ReadPrimes example does, but interspersed with comments showing where you acquire and release the file lock.

How It Works

The overall while loop for reading the file is now indefinite since you need to obtain a file lock before reading the file. You attempt to acquire the file lock in the inner while loop with the statement:

```
inLock = inChannel.tryLock(inChannel.position(), buf.remaining(), true);
```

This requests a shared lock on buf.remaining() bytes in the file starting with the byte at the current file position. You can't get an exclusive lock on a file unless it has been opened for both reading and writing, and this doesn't apply here. Acquiring a shared lock on just the part of the file that you want to read ensures that other programs are not prevented from accessing the file, but the bit you are working with cannot be changed externally. Another program cannot acquire an exclusive overlapping lock, but it can acquire a shared overlapping lock.

You have to test the value returned by the tryLock() method for null to determine whether you have obtained a lock or not. The if statement that does this is quite simple:

```
            if(inLock != null) {                 // If you have a lock
             System.out.println("\nAcquired file lock.");
             break;                              // exit the loop
            }
```

If inLock is not null, you have a lock on the file, so you exit the loop to acquire the lock. If inLock is null, you then check how often you have tried to acquire a lock and failed:

```
            if(++tryLockCount>=100) {            // If you've tried too often
              System.out.printf("Failed to acquire lock after %d tries."+
                                         "Terminating...%n", tryLockCount);
              System.exit(1);                    // end the program
            }
```

The only reason for the string concatenation here is that the string won't fit in the width of the page. If you have already tried 100 times to obtain a lock, you give up and exit the program. If it's fewer tries than this, you're prepared to give it another try, but first you pause the current thread:

```
            try {
                Thread.sleep(200);                   // Wait for 200 milliseconds
```

```
        } catch(InterruptedException e) {
            e.printStackTrace(System.err);
        }
```

This will pause the current thread for 200 milliseconds, which will provide an opportunity for the program that has an exclusive lock on the file to release it. After returning from the `sleep()` method, the `while` loop continues for another try at acquiring a lock.

Once you have acquired a lock, you read the file in the usual way and release the lock:

```
if(inChannel.read(buf) == -1) {
  break;
}
inLock.release();                           // Release lock as read is finished
System.out.println("Released file lock.");
```

By releasing the lock immediately after reading the file, you ensure that the amount of time the file is blocked is a minimum. Of course, if the `read()` method returns -1 because EOF has been reached, you won't call the `release()` method for the `FileLock` object here because you exit the outer loop. However, after exiting the outer `while` loop you close the file stream and the channel, and closing the channel will release the lock.

Summary

In this chapter, I have discussed the various ways in which you can read basic types of data from a file. The important points I have discussed include:

❑ You can read a file using a `FileChannel` object obtained from a `FileInputStream` object or from a `RandomAccessFile` object.

❑ You can use a channel obtained from a `RandomAccessFile` object that was created with mode `"rw"`, `"rwd"`, or `"rws"` to both read and write the file.

❑ Data that is read from a file using a channel is stored in one or more buffers of type `ByteBuffer`.

❑ You can use view buffers to interpret the data read from a file as any basic type other than `boolean`.

❑ A memory-mapped file enables you to access data in the file as though it were resident in memory. You access a memory-mapped file through a `MappedByteBuffer` object.

❑ Acquiring an exclusive lock on a file ensures that no other program can access the file while you hold the lock. You can obtain an exclusive lock only on a file you have opened for both reading and writing.

❑ Acquiring a shared lock on a file ensures that your program has access to the file in circumstances where other programs may be accessing the same file, and protects the region of the file you have locked from being altered.

Exercises

You can download the source code for the examples in the book and the solutions to the following exercises from http://www.wrox.com.

1. Write a program to read back and list the contents of the file written by the first exercise in the previous chapter.

2. Extend the ReadPrimes example that you produced in this chapter to optionally display the *n*th prime, when *n* is entered from the keyboard.

3. Extend the ReadPrimes program further to output a given number of primes, starting at a given number. For example, output 15 primes starting at the 30th. The existing capabilities should be retained.

4. Write a program that will output the contents of a file to the command line as groups of eight hexadecimal digits with five groups to a line, each group separated from the next by a space.

5. Write a program that will allow either one or more names and addresses to be entered from the keyboard and appended to a file, or the contents of the file to be read back and output to the command line.

6. Modify the previous example to store an index to the name and address file in a separate file. The index file should contain each person's second name, plus the position where the corresponding name and address can be found in the name and address file. Provide support for an optional command argument allowing a person's second name to be entered. When the command-line argument is present, the program should then find the name and address and output it to the command line.

Serializing Objects

In this chapter, you'll see how you can transfer objects to and from a stream. By the end of this chapter you will have learned:

- ❑ What serialization is and how you make a class serializable
- ❑ How to write objects to a file
- ❑ What transient fields in a class are
- ❑ How to write basic types of data to an object file
- ❑ How to implement the `Serializable` interface
- ❑ How to read objects from a file
- ❑ How to implement serialization for classes containing objects that are not serializable by default

Storing Objects in a File

The process of storing and retrieving objects in an external file is called **serialization**. Writing an object to a file is referred to as serializing the object, and reading an object from a file is called deserializing an object. Serialization is concerned with writing objects and the fields they contain to a stream, so this excludes `static` members of a class. Static fields will have whatever values are assigned by default in the class definition. Note that an array of any type is an object and can be serialized, even an array of values of a primitive type, such as type `int` or type `double`.

I think you will be surprised at how easy this is. Perhaps the most impressive aspect of the way serialization is implemented in Java is that you can generally read and write objects of almost any class type, including objects of classes that you have defined yourself, without adding any code to the classes involved to support this mechanism. For the most part, everything is taken care of automatically.

Two classes from the `java.io` package are used for serialization. An `ObjectOutputStream` object manages the writing of objects to a file, and reading the objects back is handled by an object of the class `ObjectInputStream`. As you saw in Chapter 8 and as Figure 12-1 illustrates, these are derived from `OutputStream` and `InputStream`, respectively.

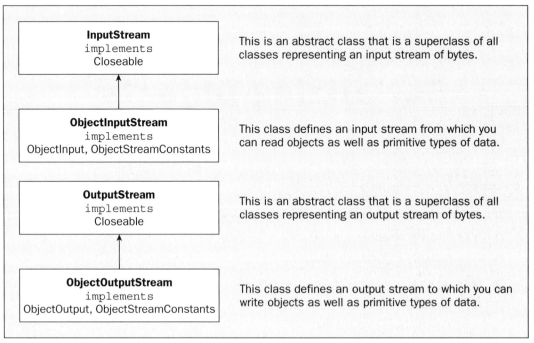

InputStream
`implements`
Closeable

This is an abstract class that is a superclass of all classes representing an input stream of bytes.

ObjectInputStream
`implements`
ObjectInput, ObjectStreamConstants

This class defines an input stream from which you can read objects as well as primitive types of data.

OutputStream
`implements`
Closeable

This is an abstract class that is a superclass of all classes representing an output stream of bytes.

ObjectOutputStream
`implements`
ObjectOutput, ObjectStreamConstants

This class defines an output stream to which you can write objects as well as primitive types of data.

Figure 12-1

The `ObjectInput` and `ObjectOutput` interfaces extend the `DataInput` and `DataOutput` interfaces that declare methods for reading and writing data of the primitive types and add the methods for reading and writing objects. Both object stream classes implement the `ObjectStreamConstants` interface, which defines constants that are used to identify elements of an object in the stream.

Writing an Object to a File

To write objects to a file, the constructor for the `ObjectOutputStream` class requires a reference to a `FileOutputStream` object as an argument, and this object defines the stream that encapsulates the file in which you intend to store your objects. You could create an `ObjectOutputStream` object with the following statements:

```
File theFile = new File("MyFile");
// Check out the file...

// Create the object output stream for the file
ObjectOutputStream objectOut = null;
try {
  objectOut = new ObjectOutputStream(new FileOutputStream(theFile));
```

```
  } catch(IOException e) {
    e.printStackTrace(System.err);
    System.exit(1);
  }
```

You know from your earlier investigations into file output that the `FileOutputStream` constructor can throw a `FileNotFoundException` if the `File` object that you pass to the constructor represents a directory rather than a file, or if the file does not exist and cannot be created for some reason. In addition, the `ObjectOutputStream` constructor will throw an `IOException` if an error occurs while the stream header is being written to the file. The `catch` block here will handle either of these exceptions because the `IOException` class is a superclass of the `FileNotFoundException` class.

While the previous code fragment will work perfectly well, it does not result in a stream that is particularly efficient because each output operation will write directly to the file. In practice you will probably want to buffer write operations to the file in memory, in which case you would create the `ObjectOutputStream` object like this:

```
objectOut = new ObjectOutputStream(
            new BufferedOutputStream(
            new FileOutputStream(theFile)));
```

The `BufferedOutputStream` constructor creates an object that buffers the `OutputStream` object that is passed to it, so here you get a buffered `FileOutputStream` object that you pass to the `ObjectOutputStream` constructor. With this arranged, each write operation to the `ObjectOutputStream` will write to the `BufferedOutputStream` object. The `BufferedOutputStream` object will write the data to an internal buffer. Data from the buffer will be written to the file whenever the buffer is full, or when you close the stream by calling its `close()` method or flush the stream by calling its `flush()` method. By default, the buffer has a capacity of 2048 bytes. If you want to use a buffer of a different size, you can use the `BufferedOutputStream` constructor, which accepts a second argument of type `int` that defines the size of the buffer in bytes.

To write an object to the file `MyFile`, you call the `writeObject()` method for `objectOut` with a reference to the object to be written as the argument. Since this method accepts a reference of type `Object` as an argument, you can pass a reference of any class type to the method and this includes `enum` types and arrays. Three basic conditions have to be met for an object to be written to a stream:

❏   The class must be declared as `public`.

❏   The class must implement the `Serializable` interface.

❏   If the class has a direct or indirect base class that is not serializable, then that base class must have a default constructor — that is, a constructor that requires no arguments. The derived class must take care of transferring the base class data members to the stream.

Implementing the `Serializable` interface is a lot less difficult than it sounds, and you will see how in a moment. Later I will come back to the question of how to deal with a non-serializable base class.

If `myObject` is an instance of a public class that implements `Serializable`, then to write `myObject` to the stream that you defined previously, you would use the following statement:

```
try {
  objectOut.writeObject(myObject);

} catch(IOException e) {
  e.printStackTrace(System.err);
  System.exit(1);
}
```

The `writeObject()` method can throw any of the following three exceptions:

`InvalidClassException`	Thrown when there is something wrong with the class definition for the object being written. This might be because the class is not `public`, for instance.
`NotSerializableException`	Thrown if the object's class, or the class of a data member of the class, does not implement the `Serializable` interface.
`IOException`	Thrown when a file output error occurs.

The first two exception classes here are subclasses of `ObjectStreamException`, which is itself a subclass of `IOException`. Thus, you can catch any of them with a `catch` block for `IOException`. Of course, if you want to take some specific action for any of these then you can catch them individually. Just be sure to put the `catch` blocks for the first two types of exception before the one for `IOException`.

The call to `writeObject()` takes care of writing everything to the stream that is necessary to reconstitute the object later in a read operation. This includes information about the class and all its superclasses, as well as the contents and types of the data members of the class. Remarkably, this works even when the data members are themselves class objects, as long as they are objects of `Serializable` classes. Our `writeObject()` call will cause the `writeObject()` method for each object that is a data member to be called, and this mechanism continues recursively until everything that makes up our object has been written to the stream. Each independent object that you write to the stream requires a separate call to the `writeObject()` method, but the objects that are members of an object are taken care of automatically. This is not completely foolproof in that the relationships between the class objects can affect this process, but for the most part this is all you need to do. You will be using serialization to write fairly complex objects to files in Chapter 21.

Writing Basic Data Types to an Object Stream

You can write data of any of the primitive types using the methods declared in the `DataInput` interface and defined in the `ObjectOutputStream` class for this purpose. For writing individual items of data of various types, you have the following methods:

`writeByte(int b)`	`writeByte(byte b)`	`writeChar(int ch)`
`writeShort(int n)`	`writeInt(int n)`	`writeLong(long n)`
`writeFloat(float x)`	`writeDouble(double x)`	

None of these methods returns a value, and they can all throw an IOException since they are output operations.

When you want to write a String object to the file as an object, you would normally use the writeObject() method. You can also write a string to the file as a sequence of bytes using the writeBytes() method, passing a reference to a String as the argument to the method. In this case, each character in the string is converted to a byte using the default charset. You can write a string simply as a sequence of Unicode characters by using the writeChars() method, again with a reference of type String as the argument. This writes each Unicode character in the string as 2 bytes. Note that the writeBytes() and writeChars() methods write just a sequence of bytes or characters. No information about the original String object is written so the fact that these characters belonged to a string is lost.

You have two methods defined in the ObjectOutputStream class that apply to arrays of bytes:

write(byte[] array)	Writes the contents of array to the file as bytes.

write(byte[] array,
    int offset,
    int length)
	Writes length elements from array to the file starting with array[offset].

In both cases just bytes are written to the stream as binary data, not the array object itself. An array of type byte[] will be written to the stream as an object by default, so you will need to use these methods only if you do not want an array of type byte[] written as an object.

You can mix writing data of the basic types and class objects to the stream. If you have a mixture of objects and data items of basic types that you want to store in a file, you can write them all to the same ObjectOutputStream. You just have to make sure that you read everything back in the sequence and form that it was written.

Implementing the Serializable Interface

A necessary condition for objects of a class to be serializable is that the class implements the Serializable interface, but this may not be sufficient, as you'll see. In most instances, you need only declare that the class implements the Serializable interface to make the objects of that class type serializable. No other code is necessary. For example, the following declares a class that implements the interface:

```
public MyClass implements Serializable {
  // Definition of the class...
}
```

As long as all the fields in MyClass are serializable, then simply declaring that the class implements the Serializable interface is sufficient to make objects of type MyClass serializable. If your class is derived from another class that implements the Serializable interface, then your class also implements Serializable so you don't have to declare that this is the case. Let's try this out on a simple class to verify that it really works.

Try It Out   Writing Objects to a File

You will first define a serializable class that has some arbitrary fields with different data types:

```java
import java.io.Serializable;

public class Junk implements Serializable {
  private static java.util.Random generator = new java.util.Random();
  private int answer;                                // The answer
  private double[] numbers;                          // Valuable data
  private String thought;                            // A unique thought

  public Junk(String thought) {
    this.thought = thought;
    answer = 42;                                     // Answer always 42

    numbers = new double[3+generator.nextInt(4)]; // Array size 3 to 6
    for(int i = 0 ; i<numbers.length ; i++) {        // Populate with
      numbers[i] = generator.nextDouble();           // random values
    }
  }

  public String toString() {
    StringBuffer strBuf = new StringBuffer(thought);
    strBuf.append('\n').append(String.valueOf(answer));
    for(int i = 0 ; i<numbers.length ; i++) {
      strBuf.append("\nnumbers[")
            .append(String.valueOf(i))
            .append("] = ")
            .append(numbers[i]);
    }
    return strBuf.toString();
  }
}
```

An object of type `Junk` has three instance fields: a simple integer that is always 42, a `String` object, and an array of `double` values. The `toString()` method provides a `String` representation of a `Junk` object that you can output to the command line. The static field `generator` will not be written to the stream when an object of type `Junk` is serialized. The only provision you have made for serializing objects of type `Junk` is to declare that the class implements the `Serializable` interface.

You can write objects of this class type to a file with the following program:

```java
import java.io.ObjectOutputStream;
import java.io.BufferedOutputStream;
import java.io.FileOutputStream;
import java.io.IOException;

public class SerializeObjects {
  public static void main(String[] args) {
    Junk obj1 = new Junk("A green twig is easily bent.");
```

```
    Junk obj2 = new Junk("A little knowledge is a dangerous thing.");
    Junk obj3 = new Junk("Flies light on lean horses.");
    ObjectOutputStream objectOut = null;
    try {
       // Create the object output stream
       objectOut = new ObjectOutputStream(
                     new BufferedOutputStream(
                       new FileOutputStream("C:/Beg Java Stuff/JunkObjects.bin")));

       // Write three objects to the file
       objectOut.writeObject(obj1);              // Write object
       objectOut.writeObject(obj2);              // Write object
       objectOut.writeObject(obj3);              // Write object
       System.out.println("\n\nobj1:\n" + obj1
                        +"\n\nobj2:\n" + obj2
                        +"\n\nobj3:\n" + obj3);

    } catch(IOException e) {
      e.printStackTrace(System.err);
      System.exit(1);
    }

    // Close the stream
    try {
       objectOut.close();                          // Close the output stream

    } catch(IOException e) {
      e.printStackTrace(System.err);
      System.exit(1);
    }
  }
}
```

When I ran this, I got the following output:

```
obj1:
A green twig is easily bent.
42
numbers[0] = 0.20157825618636616
numbers[1] = 0.7123542196242817
numbers[2] = 0.8027761971323069

obj2:
A little knowledge is a dangerous thing.
42
numbers[0] = 0.929629487353265
numbers[1] = 0.5402881072148746
numbers[2] = 0.03259660544653753
numbers[3] = 0.94945294401263
numbers[4] = 0.17383591141346522

obj3:
Flies light on lean horses.
42
```

```
numbers[0] = 0.6765377168813207
numbers[1] = 0.3933764846876555
numbers[2] = 0.7633265658906377
numbers[3] = 0.31411955819992887
```

You should get something vaguely similar.

How It Works

You first create three objects of type `Junk` in the `main()` method. You then define a variable that will hold the object output stream reference. If you were to define this variable within the first `try` block, then it would not exist beyond the end of the `try` block so you could not refer to it after that point. Within the `try` block you create the `ObjectOutputStream` object that you will use to write objects to the file `C:/Beg Java Stuff/JunkObjects.bin` via a buffered output stream. Each `Junk` object is written to the file by passing it to the `writeObject()` method for the `ObjectOutputStream` object. Each object will be written to the file, including the values of its three instance fields, `answer`, `thought`, and `numbers`. The `String` object and the array are written to the file as objects. This is taken care of automatically and requires no special provision within the code. The static field `generator` is not written to the file.

Before you exit the program, you close the stream by calling its `close()` method. You could put the call to `close()` within the first `try` block, but if an exception were thrown due to an I/O error, the method would not get called. By putting it in a separate `try` block you ensure that you do call the `close()` method. The stream would be closed automatically when the program terminates but it is good practice to close any streams as soon as you are done with them. You'll read the objects back from the file a little later in this chapter.

Conditions for Serialization

In general, you could encounter a small fly in the ointment. For implementing the `Serializable` interface to be sufficient to make objects of the class serializable, all the fields in the class must be serializable (or `transient` — which I'll come to), and all superclasses of the class must also be serializable. This implies that the fields must be either of primitive types or of class types that are themselves serializable.

If a superclass of your class is not serializable, it still may be possible to make your class serializable. The conditions that must be met for this to be feasible are:

❏   Each superclass that is not serializable must have a public default constructor — a constructor with no parameters.

❏   Your class must be declared as implementing the `Serializable` interface.

❏   Your class must take responsibility for serializing and deserializing the fields for the superclasses that are not serializable.

This will usually be the case for your own classes, but one or two classes that come along with Java do not implement the `Serializable` interface, and what's more, you can't make them serializable because they do not have a public default constructor. The `Graphics` class in the package `java.awt` is an example of such a class — you will see more of this class when you get into programming using windows. All is not lost, however. You have an escape route. As long as you know how to reconstruct any fields that were not serializable when you read an object back from a stream, you can still serialize your objects by declaring the non-serializable fields as `transient`.

Transient Data Members of a Class

If your class has fields that are not serializable, or that you just don't want to have written to the stream, you can declare them as `transient`. For example:

```
public class MyClass implements Serializable {
   transient protected Graphics g;      // Transient class member

   // Rest of the class definition
}
```

Declaring a data member as `transient` prevents the `writeObject()` method from attempting to write the data member to the stream. When the class object is read back, it will be created properly, including any members that you declared as `transient`. They just won't have their values set, because they were not written to the stream. Unless you arrange for something to be done about it, the transient fields will be `null`.

You may well want to declare some data members of a class as `transient`. You would do this when they have a value that is not meaningful long term or out of context — objects that represent the current time, or today's date, for example. You must either provide code to explicitly reconstruct the members that you declare as `transient` when the object that contains them is read from the stream or accept the defaults for these that apply when the objects are recreated.

Reading an Object from a File

Reading objects back from a file is just as easy as writing them. First, you need to create an `ObjectInputStream` object for the file. To do this you just pass a reference to a `FileInputStream` object that encapsulates the file to the `ObjectInputStream` class constructor:

```
File theFile = new File("MyFile");
// Perhaps check out the file...

// Create the object output stream for the file
ObjectInputStream objectIn = null;
try {
   objectIn = new ObjectInputStream(new FileInputStream(theFile));

} catch(IOException e) {
   e.printStackTrace(System.err);
   System.exit(1);
}
```

The `ObjectInputStream` constructor will throw an exception of type `StreamCorruptedException` — a subclass of `IOException` — if the stream header is not correct, or of type `IOException` if an error occurs while reading the stream header. Of course, as you saw in the previous chapter, the `FileInputStream` constructor can throw an exception of type `FileNotFoundException`.

Once you have created the `ObjectInputStream` object, you call its `readObject()` method to read an object from the file:

```
Object myObject = null;
try {
  myObject = objectIn.readObject();

} catch(ClassNotFoundException e){
  e.printStackTrace(System.err);
  System.exit(1);

} catch(IOException e){
  e.printStackTrace(System.err);
  System.exit(1);
}
```

The readObject() method can throw the following exceptions:

ClassNotFoundException	Thrown if the class for an object read from the stream cannot be found.
InvalidClassException	Thrown if something is wrong with the class for an object. This is commonly caused by using a definition for a class when you read an object from a stream that is different from the definition in effect when you wrote it.
StreamCorruptedException	When objects are written to the stream, additional control data is written so that the object data can be validated when it is read back. This exception is thrown when the control information in the stream violates consistency checks.
OptionalDataException	Thrown when basic types of data are read rather than an object. For example, if you wrote a String object using the writeChars() method and then attempted to read it back using the readObject() method, this exception would be thrown.
IOException	Thrown if an error occurred reading the stream.

Clearly, if you do not have a full and accurate class definition for each type of object that you want to read from the stream, the stream object will not know how to create the object and the read will fail. The last four of the five possible exceptions are flavors of IOException, so you can use that as a catchall as you have in the preceding code fragment. However, ClassNotFoundException is derived from Exception, so you must put a separate catch block for this exception in your program. Otherwise, the code will not compile.

As the code fragment implies, the readObject() method will return a reference to the object as type Object, so you need to cast it to the appropriate class type to use it. Note that arrays are considered to be objects and are treated as such during serialization, so if you explicitly read an array from a file, you will have to cast it to the appropriate array type.

For example, if the object in the previous code fragment was of type MyClass, you could read it back from the file with the statements:

```
MyClass theObject = null;              // Store the object here

try {
  theObject = (MyClass)(objectIn.readObject());

} catch(ClassNotFoundException e) {
  e.printStackTrace(System.err);
  System.exit(1);

} catch(IOException e) {
  e.printStackTrace(System.err);
  System.exit(1);
}
```

To deserialize the object, you call the readObject() method and cast the reference that is returned to type MyClass.

Armed with the knowledge of how the readObject() method works, you can now read the file that you wrote in the previous example.

Try It Out   **Deserializing Objects**

You can read the file containing Junk objects with the following code:

```
import java.io.FileInputStream;
import java.io.BufferedInputStream;
import java.io.ObjectInputStream;
import java.io.IOException;
import java.io.EOFException;

class DeserializeObjects {
  public static void main(String args[]) {
    ObjectInputStream objectIn = null;  // Stores the stream reference
    int objectCount = 0;                // Number of objects read
    Junk object = null;                 // Stores an object reference
    try {
      objectIn = new ObjectInputStream(
                   new BufferedInputStream(
                     new FileInputStream("C:/Beg Java Stuff/JunkObjects.bin")));

      // Read from the stream until we hit the end
      while(true) {
        object = (Junk)objectIn.readObject();// Read an object
        objectCount++;                        // Increment the count
        System.out.println(object);           // Output the object
      }

    } catch(ClassNotFoundException e) {
      e.printStackTrace(System.err);
      System.exit(1);
```

```
        } catch(EOFException e) {                    // This will execute when we reach EOF
          System.out.println("EOF reached. "+ objectCount + " objects read.");

        } catch(IOException e) {                      // This is for other I/O errors
          e.printStackTrace(System.err);
          System.exit(1);
        }

        // Close the stream
        try {
          objectIn.close();                           // Close the input stream

        } catch(IOException e) {
          e.printStackTrace(System.err);
          System.exit(1);
        }
      }
    }
```

Don't forget that you need to put the `Junk.java` source file in the same directory as this source file. I got the following output from this example:

```
A green twig is easily bent.
42
numbers[0]  =  0.20157825618636616
numbers[1]  =  0.7123542196242817
numbers[2]  =  0.8027761971323069
A little knowledge is a dangerous thing.
42
numbers[0]  =  0.929629487353265
numbers[1]  =  0.5402881072148746
numbers[2]  =  0.03259660544653753
numbers[3]  =  0.94945294401263
numbers[4]  =  0.17383591141346522
Flies light on lean horses.
42
numbers[0]  =  0.6765377168813207
numbers[1]  =  0.3933764846876555
numbers[2]  =  0.7633265658906377
numbers[3]  =  0.31411955819992887
EOF reached. 3 objects read.
```

You should get output corresponding to the objects that were written to your file.

How It Works

You first define the `objectIn` variable that will store the reference to the stream. You will use the `objectCount` variable to accumulate a count of the total number of objects read from the stream. The `object` variable stores the reference to each object that you read. To make the program a little more general, the read operation is in a loop to show how you might read the file when you don't know how many objects there are in it. To read each object, you just call the `readObject()` method for the input stream and cast the reference returned to type `Junk` before storing it in `object`.

So you can see what you have read from the file, the string representation of each object is displayed on the command line. The `while` loop will continue to read objects from the stream indefinitely. When the end of the file is reached, an exception of type `EOFExcepion` will be thrown. This will effectively terminate the loop, and the code in the `catch` block for this exception will execute. This outputs a message to the command line showing the number of objects that were read. As you can see, you get back all the objects that you wrote to the file originally. This is obviously very encouraging — getting fewer objects than you wrote would be inconvenient to say the least, and getting more would be worrying.

Determining the Class of a Deserialized Object

Clearly, since the `readObject()` method returns the object that it reads from the stream as type `Object`, you need to know what the original type of the object was to be able to cast it to its actual type. For the most part, you will know what the class of the object is when you read it back. It is possible that in some circumstances you won't know exactly, but you have a rough idea, in which case you can test it. To bring the problem into sharper focus, consider a hypothetical situation.

Suppose you have a file containing objects that represent employees. The basic characteristics of all employees are defined in a base class, `Person`, but various different types of employee are represented by subclasses of `Person`. You might have subclasses `Manager`, `Secretary`, `Admin`, and `ShopFloor`, for example. The file can contain any of the subclass types in any sequence. Of course, you can cast any object read from the file to type `Person` because that is the base class, but you want to know precisely what each object is so you can call some type-specific methods. Since you know what the possible types are, you can check the type of the object against each of these types and cast accordingly:

```
Person person = null;
try {
  person = (Person)objectIn.readObject();
  if(person instanceof Manager)
    processManager((Manager)person);
  else if(person instanceof Secretary)
    processSecretary((Secretary)person);
    // and so on...

} catch (IOException e){
}
```

Here you determine the specific class type of the object read from the file before calling a method that deals with that particular type of object. Don't forget though that the `instanceof` operator does not guarantee that the object being tested is actually of the type tested for — `Manager`, say. The object could also be of any type that is a subclass of `Manager`. In any event, the cast to type `Manager` will be perfectly legal.

Where you need to be absolutely certain of the type, you can use a different approach:

```
if(person.getClass().getName().equals(Manager))
    processManager((Manager)person);
  else if(person.getClass().getName().equals(Secretary))
    processSecretary((Secretary)person);
  // and so on...
```

This calls the `getClass()` method (inherited from `Object`) for the object read from the file and that returns a reference to the `Class` object representing the class of the object. Calling the `getName()` method for the `Class` object returns the fully qualified name of the class. This approach guarantees that the object is of the type for which you are testing, and is not a subclass of that type.

Another approach would be to just execute a cast to a particular type, and catch the `ClassCastException` that is thrown when the cast is invalid. This is fine if you do not expect the exception to be thrown under normal conditions, but if on a regular basis the object read from the stream might be other than the type to which you are casting, you will be better off with code that avoids the need to throw and catch the exception because this adds quite a lot of overhead.

Reading Basic Data from an Object Stream

The `ObjectInputStream` class defines the methods declared in the `DataInput` interface for reading basic types of data back from an object stream and binary values. They are:

`readBoolean()`	`readByte()`	`readChar()`	`readShort()`
`readInt()`	`readLong()`	`readFloat()`	`readDouble()`

They each return a value of the corresponding type, and they can all throw an `IOException` if an error occurs, or an `EOFException` if the end-of-file is reached.

Just to make sure that the process of serializing and deserializing objects is clear, let's try it again in another simple example.

Using Object Serialization

Back in Chapter 6, you produced an example that created `PolyLine` objects containing `Point` objects in a generalized linked list. This is a good basis for demonstrating how effectively serialization takes care of handling objects that are members of objects. You can just modify the class `TryPolyLine` to use serialization.

Try It Out   Serializing a Linked List

The classes `PolyLine`, `Point`, and `LinkedList` and the inner class `ListItem` are exactly the same as in Chapter 6 except that you need to implement the `Serializable` interface in each of them.

The `PolyLine` definition needs to be amended to:

```
import java.io.Serializable;

public final class PolyLine implements Serializable  {
  // Class definition as before...
}
```

The `Point` definition needs a similar change:

```
import java.io.Serializable;

public class Point implements Serializable {
  // Class definition as before...
}
```

The `LinkedList` class and its inner class likewise:

```
import java.io.Serializable;

public class LinkedList implements Serializable {
  // Class definition as before...
  private class ListItem implements Serializable {
    // Inner class definition as before...
  }
}
```

Of course, each file must also have an `import` statement for the `java.io.Serializable` class as in the preceding code.

The modified version of the `TryPolyLine` class to write the `PolyLine` objects to a stream looks like this:

```
import java.io.ObjectOutputStream;
import java.io.BufferedOutputStream;
import java.io.FileOutputStream;
import java.io.ObjectInputStream;
import java.io.BufferedInputStream;
import java.io.FileInputStream;
import java.io.IOException;

public class TryPolyLine {
  public static void main(String[] args) {
    // Create an array of coordinate pairs
    double[][] coords = { {1., 1.}, {1., 2.}, { 2., 3.},
                          {-3., 5.}, {-5., 1.}, {0., 0.} };

    // Create a polyline from the coordinates and display it
    PolyLine polygon = new PolyLine(coords);
    System.out.println(polygon);

    // Add a point and display the polyline again
    polygon.addPoint(10., 10.);
    System.out.println(polygon);

    // Create Point objects from the coordinate array
    Point[] points = new Point[coords.length];
    for(int i = 0; i < points.length; i++)
      points[i] = new Point(coords[i][0],coords[i][1]);

    // Use the points to create a new polyline and display it
    PolyLine newPoly = new PolyLine(points);
    System.out.println(newPoly);

    // Write both polyline objects to the file
    try {
      // Create the object output stream
      ObjectOutputStream objectOut =
                  new ObjectOutputStream(
                    new BufferedOutputStream(
                      new FileOutputStream("C:/Beg Java Stuff/Polygons.bin")));
```

539

```
      objectOut.writeObject(polygon);              // Write first object
      objectOut.writeObject(newPoly);              // Write second object
      objectOut.close();                           // Close the output stream

  } catch(IOException e) {
      e.printStackTrace(System.err);
      System.exit(1);
  }
  // Read the objects back from the file
  System.out.println("\nReading objects from the file: ");
  try {
    ObjectInputStream objectIn =
                new ObjectInputStream(
                  new BufferedInputStream (
                    new FileInputStream("C:/Beg Java Stuff/Polygons.bin")));

    PolyLine theLine = (PolyLine)objectIn.readObject();
    System.out.println(theLine);                 // Display the first object
    theLine = (PolyLine)objectIn.readObject();
    System.out.println(theLine);                 // Display the second object
    objectIn.close();                            // Close the input stream

  } catch(ClassNotFoundException  e) {
      e.printStackTrace(System.err);
      System.exit(1);

  } catch(IOException e){
      e.printStackTrace(System.err);
      System.exit(1);
  }
 }
}
```

This produces the following output:

```
Polyline: (1.0,1.0) (1.0,2.0) (2.0,3.0) (-3.0,5.0) (-5.0,1.0) (0.0,0.0)
Polyline: (1.0,1.0) (1.0,2.0) (2.0,3.0) (-3.0,5.0) (-5.0,1.0) (0.0,0.0) (10.0,10.0)
Polyline: (1.0,1.0) (1.0,2.0) (2.0,3.0) (-3.0,5.0) (-5.0,1.0) (0.0,0.0)

Reading objects from the file:
Polyline: (1.0,1.0) (1.0,2.0) (2.0,3.0) (-3.0,5.0) (-5.0,1.0) (0.0,0.0) (10.0,10.0)
Polyline: (1.0,1.0) (1.0,2.0) (2.0,3.0) (-3.0,5.0) (-5.0,1.0) (0.0,0.0)
```

How It Works

You create two different `PolyLine` objects in the same manner as in the original example, and you display them on standard output as before. You then create an `ObjectOutputStream` for the file, `Polygons.bin`, in the `C:\Beg Java Stuff` directory and write each of the `PolyLine` objects to the file using the `writeObject()` method. You should adjust the file name and directory to suit your environment if necessary. You then call the `close()` method to close the output stream. You don't need to explicitly write the `LinkedList` and `Point` objects to the stream. These are part of the `PolyLine` object, so they are taken care of automatically. The same goes for when you read the `PolyLine` objects back. All the subsidiary objects are reconstructed automatically.

To read the file, you create an `ObjectInputStream` object for `Polygons.bin`. You read the first object using the `readObject()` method and store the reference to it in the variable `theObject`. You then output the object, `read`, to the standard output stream. You repeat the same process for the second `PolyLine` object. It couldn't be simpler really, could it?

Serializing Classes Yourself

Earlier I identified situations where the default serialization that you used in the example won't work. One such situation occurs if your class has a superclass that is not serializable. As I said earlier, to make it possible to overcome this, the superclass must have a default constructor, and you must take care of serializing the fields that are inherited from the superclass yourself. If the superclass does not have a default constructor and you do not have access to the original definition of the superclass, you have a problem with no obvious solution.

Another situation where the default serialization mechanism won't be satisfactory is where your class has fields that don't travel well. If you use the `hashCode()` method that your classes will inherit from `Object`, then the `hashcode()` value for an object will be derived from its internal address. When you read the object back from a file its address will be different and therefore so will its hashcode. You may have a class with vast numbers of fields with zero values, for example, that you may not want to have written to the file. These are all cases where do-it-yourself serialization is needed.

To implement and control the serialization of a class yourself, you must implement two `private` methods in the class: one for input from an `ObjectInputStream` object and the other for output to an `ObjectOutputStream` object. The `readObject()` and `writeObject()` methods for the stream will call these methods to perform I/O on the stream if you implement them.

Even though it isn't necessary in this class, let's take the `PolyLine` class as a demonstration vehicle for how this works. To do your own serialization, the class would be:

```
class PolyLine implements Serializable {
  // Class definition as before...

    // Serialized input method
    private void readObject(ObjectInputStream in) throws IOException {
      // Code to do the serialized input...
    }

    // Serialized output method
    private void writeObject(ObjectOutputStream out)
       throws IOException, ClassNotFoundException {
      // Code to do the serialized output...
    }
  }
```

These two methods must have exactly the same signature in any class where they are required, and they must be declared as `private`.

In a typical situation, you will want to use the default serialization operations provided by the object stream and just add your own code to fix up the data members that you want to take care of — or have to in the case of a non-serialized base class. To get the default serialization done on input, you just call the `defaultReadObject()` method for the stream in your serialization method:

```
    private void readObject(ObjectInputStream in) throws IOException {
      in.defaultReadObject();                    // Default serialized input
      // Your code to do serialized input...
    }
```

You can get the default serialized output operation in a similar fashion by calling the
defaultWriteObject() method for the stream object that is passed to your output method.
Obviously, you must read back the data in exactly the same sequence as it was written, so the two
methods will have essentially mirror operations on the same sequence of data items.

Serialization Problems and Complications

For most classes and applications, serialization will work in a straightforward fashion. You will have situations that can cause confusion though. One such situation is when you want to write several versions of
the same object to a file. You need to take care to ensure that the result is what you want. Suppose you
write an object to a file — a PolyLine object, say. A little later in your code, you modify the PolyLine
object in some way, by moving a point perhaps, and you now write the same object to the file again in its
modified state. What happens? Does the file contain the two versions of the object? The answer — perhaps
surprisingly — is no. Let's explore this in a little more detail.

Try It Out   Serializing Variations on an Object

Let's start by defining a very simple serializable class that you can use in our example:

```
import java.io.Serializable;

public class Data implements Serializable {
  private int value;

  public Data(int init) {
    value = init;
  }

  // Method to compare two Data objects
  public boolean equals(Object obj) {
    if(obj instanceof Data && ((Data)obj).value == value) {
      return true;
    }
    return false;
  }

  public void setValue(int val) {
    value = val;
  }

  public int getValue() {
    return value;
  }
}
```

Objects of type `Data` have a single field of type `int`. Two `Data` objects are equal if their `value` fields contain the same value. You can alter the `value` field for an object by calling its `setValue()` method so you can easily create variations on the same object. Now you can write an example that will write variations on a single instance of type `Data` to a file and then read them back:

```java
import java.io.ObjectOutputStream;
import java.io.BufferedOutputStream;
import java.io.FileOutputStream;
import java.io.ObjectInputStream;
import java.io.BufferedInputStream;
import java.io.FileInputStream;
import java.io.IOException;

public class TestData {
  public static void main(String[] args) {
    Data data = new Data(1);
    try {
      // Create the object output stream
      ObjectOutputStream objectOut =
                  new ObjectOutputStream(
                    new BufferedOutputStream(
                      new FileOutputStream("C:/Beg Java Stuff/dataObjects.bin")));

      // Write three variants of the object to the file
      objectOut.writeObject(data);                // Write object
      System.out.println("1st Object written has value: "+data.getValue());
      data.setValue(2);                           // Modify the object
      objectOut.writeObject(data);                // and write it again
      System.out.println("2nd Object written has value: "+data.getValue());
      data.setValue(3);                           // Modify the object again...
      objectOut.writeObject(data);                // and write it once more
      System.out.println("3rd Object written has value: "+data.getValue());
      objectOut.close();                          // Close the output stream

    } catch(IOException e) {
      e.printStackTrace(System.err);
      System.exit(1);
    }

    // Read the three objects back from the file
    System.out.println("\nReading objects from the file: ");
    try {
      ObjectInputStream objectIn =
                  new ObjectInputStream(
                    new BufferedInputStream(
                      new FileInputStream("C:/Beg Java Stuff/dataObjects.bin")));

      Data data1 = (Data)objectIn.readObject();
      Data data2 = (Data)objectIn.readObject();
      Data data3 = (Data)objectIn.readObject();
      System.out.println("1st object is " + (data1.equals(data2)? "" : "not ")
                    + "Equal to 2nd object.");
      System.out.println("2nd object is " + (data2.equals(data3)? "" : "not ")
                    + "Equal to 3rd object.");
```

```
        System.out.println("data1 = "+data1.getValue()   // Display object values
                    + "   data2 = " + data2.getValue()
                    + "   data3 = "+data3.getValue());
        objectIn.close();                                 // Close the input stream

    } catch(ClassNotFoundException e) {
        e.printStackTrace(System.err);
        System.exit(1);
    } catch(IOException e) {
        e.printStackTrace(System.err);
        System.exit(1);
    }
  }
}
```

This is a simple program that writes three objects to the file and records on the command line what objects were written. It then reads the objects back from the file and writes details of the objects that were read to the command line. When you run it you should see the following output:

```
1st Object written has value: 1
2nd Object written has value: 2
3rd Object written has value: 3

Reading objects from the file:
1st object is Equal to 2nd object.
2nd object is Equal to 3rd object.
data1 = 1   data2 = 1   data3 = 1
```

All three objects that you read from the file are equal and identical to the first object that was written. This seems rather strange and unexpected so let's try to understand what is happening here.

How It Works

As you know, all variables of a class type store references, not objects, and you may have several different variables referring to the same object in your program. For this reason, the serialization output process keeps track of the objects that are written to the stream. Any attempt to write the same object to the stream will not result in duplicates of the object being written. Only a **handle**, which is a sort of reference, will be written to the stream, and this will point to the first occurrence of the object in the stream.

Thus, in the example, the modified versions of the Data object will not be written to the file. The first write operation writes the original object referenced by Data to the stream. For the second and third write operations, the serialization process detects that you are writing an object that has previously been written to the file, and so only a handle that refers to the original unmodified version of the object will be written, and so the changes will be lost. This explains why, when you read the three objects back from the file, they all turn out to be identical. This is not what you intended in this case, so how can you avoid this?

Resetting an Object Output Stream

The appropriate course of action in such situations is obviously going to be application-dependent, but in the previous example it is clear — you want each version of Data explicitly written to the file. You can make the `ObjectOutputStream` object forget the objects it has previously written to a stream by calling its `reset()` method:

```
objectOut.reset();                                      // Reset the stream
```

This clears the record that is kept within the stream object of what has been written and writes a "reset marker" to the stream. When an `ObjectInputStream` object reads a "reset marker" it too clears its record of what has been read, so that subsequent object read operations will be as if the stream started at that point. To make effective use of this, your code will clearly need to accommodate the possibility of multiple versions of the same object existing in the stream. It's your code, so you will know what you want to do. To make the example work as you want, you can reset the stream before each output operation after the first call to `writeObject()`, like this:

```
objectOut.writeObject(data);                    // Write object
System.out.println("1st Object written has value: "+data.getValue());
data.setValue(2);                               // Modify the object
objectOut.reset();
objectOut.writeObject(data);                    // and write it again
System.out.println("2nd Object written has value: "+data.getValue());
data.setValue(3);                               // Modify the object again...
objectOut.reset();
objectOut.writeObject(data);                    // and write it once more
System.out.println("3rd Object written has value: "+data.getValue());
```

If you insert the calls to `reset()` in the original code and run the example again, you should get the output you were expecting.

A further complication arises with serialized objects when you change the definition of a class in some way. When an object is written to a file, part of the information identifying the class is a sort of hashcode, called a **version ID**, that is intended to ensure that the definition of the class used when you are reading an object from a file is the same as the class definition that was used when the object was written. Even cosmetic changes between writing and reading a stream, such as changing the name of a field, can alter the version ID, so in this case a read operation will fail with an `InvalidClassException` being thrown. In general, you need to make sure that the class definitions in a program reading a file are the same as those used when the file was written, although you can explicitly set the version number and deal with any changes yourself.

For more complex situations, it is possible to take complete control of the serialization process within your classes by implementing the `Externalizable` interface. This is important when the class definition for the object involves change over time. With careful programming you can accommodate modifications to classes without invalidating existing serialized objects. A detailed discussion of what is involved in this is outside the scope of this book.

Summary

In this chapter you have explored how you can write objects to a file and read them back. Making your class serializable makes it very easy to save your application data in a file. While what I have discussed is by no means exhaustive, you now know enough to deal with straightforward object serialization. The important points in this chapter are:

❏ To make objects of a class serializable the class must implement the `Serializable` interface.

❏ If a class has a superclass that does not implement the `Serializable` interface, then the superclass must have a public default constructor if it is to be possible to serialize the class.

❏ Objects are written to a file using an `ObjectOutputStream` object and read from a file using and `ObjectInputStream` object.

❏ Objects are written to a file by calling the `writeObject()` method for the `ObjectOutputStream` object corresponding to the file.

❏ Objects are read from a file by calling the `readObject()` method for the `ObjectInputStream` object `corresponding` to the file.

❏ When necessary — for example, if a superclass is not serializable — you can implement the `readObject()` and `writeObject()` methods for your classes.

Exercises

You can download the source code for the examples in the book and the solutions to the following exercises from `http://www.wrox.com`.

1. Define a `Person` class to encapsulate a person's name and address with the name and address being fields of type `Name` and `Address`. Write a program to allow names and addresses to be entered from the keyboard and stored as `Person` objects in a file. Once the file exists new entries should be appended to the file.

2. Extend the previous example to optionally list all the names and addresses contained within the file on the command line.

3. Extend the previous example to add an index based on the person's name for each person entered at the keyboard to locate the corresponding `Person` object in the object file. The index file will contain entries of type `IndexEntry`, each of which encapsulates a name and a file position in the object file. The index file should be a separate file from the original file containing `Person` objects.

Note: You will probably find it easiest to delete the previous file before you run this example so that the object file can be reconstructed along with the index file. You can't get the file position in an object stream in the same way as you can with a channel. However, you can use the sequence number for an object as the index — the first object being 1, the second being 2, and so on.

4. Use the index file to provide random direct access to the object file for querying random names entered from the keyboard. Entering a name from the keyboard should result in the address for the individual, or a message indicating the entry is not present in the file. The process will be to first search the index file for an object with a name field matching the keyboard entry. When an `IndexEntry` is found, you use the sequence number it contains to retrieve the appropriate `Person` object.

Generic Class Types

Generic class types are not a separate capability from the class and interface types that you have seen in earlier chapters. The facility for defining generic class and interface types is an extension of the ordinary definition of classes and interfaces that you are already familiar with that enables you to define families of classes and interfaces. In this chapter you will learn:

- ❑   What a generic type is

- ❑   How you define a generic type

- ❑   How you specify type parameters for a generic type

- ❑   What parameter type bounds are and how you use them

- ❑   What wildcard type specifications are and how you use them

- ❑   How you define bounds for a wildcard

- ❑   How you define and use parameterized methods

What Are Generic Types?

A **generic type**, which is also referred to as a **parameterized type**, is a class or interface type definition that has one or more type parameters. You define an actual class or interface type from a generic type by supplying a type argument for each of the type parameters that the generic type has. It'll be easier to understand what this means with a concrete example of where and how you could apply the concept.

I'm sure you recall the LinkedList class that you first saw in Chapter 6 and used in an example in the previous chapter. You used the LinkedList class to encapsulate a linked list of Point objects, but the idea of a linked list applies to any set of objects that you want to organize in this way. A linked list is just one example of classes that define objects for organizing other objects of a given type into a collection in some way. Such classes are described as **collection classes** for obvious reasons, and in Chapter 14 you'll meet a variety of these that are defined in the java.util package.

The `LinkedList` class that you implemented in Chapter 6 can organize objects of any given type into a linked list. This clearly has the advantage that the code for a single class defines a linked list class that you can use for objects of any kind, but it has significant disadvantages, too. When you were adding `Point` objects to a `LinkedList` object, nothing in the code prevented you from adding a `Line` object, or indeed any type of object, to the same linked list. Of course, if you were to do this inadvertently, the result would be a disaster, because when you retrieved objects from the list, you would not know that some of the objects were not of type `Point`. If you attempted to use an object as a `Point` object that was actually type `Line` or type `String`, your program would fail.

To avoid such problems, ideally what you need is a `LinkedList` class that is typesafe. By typesafe I mean that when you are using a `LinkedList` object to store `Point` objects, no possibility of any other type of object being added exists. In other words, you want a class that will always prevent you from accidentally adding objects of the wrong type. Of course, you can define a `LinkedList` class that works only with objects of type `Point`. You just use parameters of type `Point` in the methods that you use to add objects to the list and to retrieve them. The problem with this solution is that you must write a new `LinkedList` class for every type of object that you want to organize in this way, so you end up with a `LinkedLineList` class, a `LinkedPointList` class, a `LinkedElephantList` class—well, you can see the problem.

That's *exactly* where generic types come in. Generic types provide a way for you to define a generic `LinkedList` class that can transform itself into a class that defines a typesafe `LinkedList` class for objects of any type that you want to organize in a linked list. Broadly, a **generic type** can assume the guise of any particular class from the set or family of classes that it represents. You just supply the appropriate type arguments for the parameters in the generic type and it will behave as that particular class. Let's see how that works in practice.

Defining a Generic Class Type

I'll use the `LinkedList` class as a model for showing how you define a generic type because you already know how a linked list works. A definition of a generic class type looks very much like the definition of an ordinary class, but with a parameter specification added following the class name. Here's how the `LinkedList` class from Chapter 6 looks as an outline of a generic type:

```
public class LinkedList<T> {                      // T is the type parameter
  // Generic type definition...
}
```

The parameter that appears between the angled brackets, `<>`, that follows the generic type name, `LinkedList`, is called a **type parameter**. The name, `T`, identifies the type parameter, and you use the parameter name in the definition of the methods and fields in the generic type where there is a dependency on the argument value for this parameter in the implementation detail. Occurrences of the type parameter name in the definition of a generic type are called **type variables** because they will be replaced by a value that is a type, in a similar way to how method parameters are replaced by the arguments that you supply.

Although I've used a single letter, `T`, as the type parameter name to indicate that the argument should be a **T**ype, you can use any legal identifier. For example, you could use `InsertYourTypeHere` as the parameter name, but this would make the code in the body of the generic type definition rather cumbersome.

It's generally best to keep the parameter names as short as possible—ideally as a single letter. Within the text I'll append angled brackets to a generic type name to differentiate when I'm referring to a generic type such as `LinkedList<>` from when I'm referring to an ordinary class or interface type. While the `LinkedList<>` example is a generic *class* type, you can equally well define generic *interface* types, and you'll find quite a number of these in the standard packages. You'll be working with the `Iterable<>` and `Comparable<>` generic interface types from the `java.lang` package later in this chapter.

To create a class from the generic type, `LinkedList<>`, you just supply an appropriate argument for the parameter between the angled brackets. All occurrences of the type variable, `T`, that appear in the definition will be replaced by the type argument that you supply. This will result in a class type that you can use to create an object that implements a linked list that will store objects of the type that you specified, as illustrated in Figure 13-1.

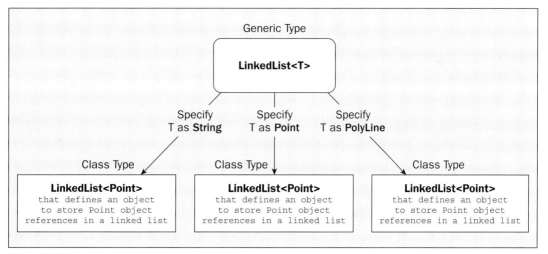

Figure 13-1

Thus, a generic type essentially defines a set of types, the set being produced by different arguments for the parameters or parameters for the generic type. Note that although Figure 13-1 show three *types* being defined, there aren't three classes. There's just the generic class type to which you supply a type argument to produce a particular type. The three types in Figure 13-1 are produced by plugging the three type arguments shown into the generic type.

You can supply only a class or interface type such as type `String` or type `Point` as an argument for a type parameter in a generic type. In other words, you cannot use a primitive type such as `int` or type `double` as an argument, although, of course, you can use type `Integer` or type `Double`. When you create a particular type from the generic type definition by supplying an argument value for `T`, the argument will be substituted for every occurrence of `T` in the generic type specification. This applies to fields as well as the definitions of methods in the generic type.

You put a generic type definition in a source file with the extension `.java`, just like an ordinary class, so you could save the code for the preceding outline generic type as `LinkedList.java`. It will even compile as it is, although it's not very useful at the moment.

Implementing a Generic Type

You can easily convert the definition of the LinkedList class you were working with earlier into a generic type. Here's how an initial stab at a LinkedList<> generic type definition would look:

```
public class LinkedList<T> {
  // Default constructor - creates an empty list
  public LinkedList() {}

  // Constructor to create a list containing one object
  public LinkedList(T item) {
    if(item != null) {
      current=end=start=new ListItem(item);        // item is the start and end
    }
  }

  // Construct a linked list from an array of objects
  public LinkedList(T[] items) {
    if(items != null) {
      // Add the items to the list
      for(int i = 0; i < items.length; i++) {
        addItem(items[i]);
      }
      current = start;
    }
  }

  // Add an item object to the list
  public void addItem(T item) {
    ListItem newEnd = new ListItem(item);    // Create a new ListItem
    if(start == null) {                      // Is the list empty?
      start = end = newEnd;                  // Yes, so new element is start and end
    } else {                                 // No, so append new element
      end.next = newEnd;                     // Set next variable for old end
      end = newEnd;                          // Store new item as end
    }
  }
  // Get the first object in the list
  public T getFirst() {
    current = start;
    return start == null ? null : start.item;
  }

  // Get the next object in the list
  public T getNext() {
    if(current != null) {
      current = current.next;                // Get the reference to the next item
    }
    return current == null ? null : current.item;
  }

  private ListItem start = null;         // First ListItem in the list
  private ListItem end = null;           // Last ListItem in the list
  private ListItem current = null;       // The current item for iterating
```

```
        private class ListItem {

          // Constructor
          public ListItem(T item) {
            this.item = item;              // Store the item
            next = null;                   // Set next as end point
          }

          // Return class name & object
          public String toString() {
            return "ListItem " + item ;
          }

          ListItem next;                   // Refers to next item in the list
          T item;                          // The item for this ListItem
        }
    }
```

The shaded lines reflect changes to the original LinkedList class definition that you created in Chapter 6. Each of the lines that have been modified in the body of the generic type definition have just had the type variable, T, substituted wherever the type Object appeared in the original. The item field in the ListItem inner class is now of type T, for example, and the return type for the getNext() method is now type T. All the methods that make use of the parameter T in their definitions will be customized by the argument type that is supplied for T when you define a type from the generic type. A generic type definition can include ordinary methods that do not involve any parameters in their definitions as well as methods that do. This just means that the ordinary methods are not customized for particular instances of the generic type.

You now have a generic LinkedList<T> type that you can use to create a new LinkedList class for storing objects of any type that you want. Let's look at how you use it.

Instantiating a Generic Type

You use the generic type name followed by a class or interface type name between angled brackets to define a new type. For example:

```
    LinkedList<String> strings;            // A variable of type LinkedList<String>
```

This just defines a variable with the name strings. The type for this variable is LinkedList<String>, which is from the generic type that you defined in the previous section. As a result of this statement, the compiler will use the type argument String that you supplied to replace every instance of the type variable, T, in the generic type definition to arrive at the notional class type definition for LinkedList<String>.

Of course, you can define an object when you define the variable, like this:

```
    LinkedList<String> strings = new LinkedList<String>();
```

This calls the default constructor for the LinkedList<String> class type to define an object that implements a linked list of String objects.

The argument that you supply to a generic type could also be a type that you define using a generic type. Look at this example:

```
LinkedList<LinkedList<String>> texts = new LinkedList<LinkedList<String>>();
```

Here you have created an object that implements a linked list in which you can store objects that are linked lists of type LinkedList<String>. Thus, you have defined a linked list of linked lists!

To apply the new generic LinkedList<> type that you have defined in a working context, let's repeat the TryPolyLine example from Chapter 6 but using a type that is generated from the LinkedList<> generic type.

Try It Out   Using a Generic Linked List Type

First you need a modified version of the PolyLine class that uses the LinkedList<T> generic type:

```
public class PolyLine {
  // Construct a polyline from an array of coordinate pairs
  public PolyLine(double[][] coords) {
    Point[] points = new Point[coords.length];    // Array to hold points

    // Create points from the coordinates
    for(int i = 0; i < coords.length ; i++) {
      points[i] = new Point(coords[i][0], coords[i][1]);
    }

    // Create the polyline from the array of points
    polyline = new LinkedList<Point>(points);      // Create list of Point objects
  }

  // Construct a polyline from an array of points
  public PolyLine(Point[] points) {
    polyline = new LinkedList<Point>(points);      // Create list of Point objects
  }

  // Add a Point object to the list
  public void addPoint(Point point) {
    polyline.addItem(point);                       // Add the point to the list
  }

  // Add a point from a coordinate pair to the list
  public void addPoint(double x, double y) {
    polyline.addItem(new Point(x, y));             // Add the point to the list
  }

  // String representation of a polyline
  public String toString() {
    StringBuffer str = new StringBuffer("Polyline:");
    Point point = (Point) polyline.getFirst();
                                                   // Set the 1st point as start
    while(point != null) {
      str.append(" ("+ point+ ")");                // Append the current point
      point = (Point)polyline.getNext();           // Make the next point current
```

```
        }
        return str.toString();
    }

    private LinkedList<Point> polyline;              // The linked list of points
}
```

I have shaded all the lines that have been changed from the original version—yes, all three of them! The constructor calls that create objects implementing a linked list now use the LinkedList<T> generic type with Point as the type argument. The polyline field is now of type LinkedList<Point>.

Put this source file in a directory along with the Point class source file that you created in Chapter 6, and the source file containing the LinkedList<> generic type. You can then add the following source file that will try out the new version of the PolyLine class:

```
public class TryGenericLinkedList {
    public static void main(String[] args) {
        // Create an array of coordinate pairs
        double[][] coords = { {1., 1.}, {1., 2.}, { 2., 3.},
                              {-3., 5.}, {-5., 1.}, {0., 0.} };

        // Create a polyline from the coordinates and display it
        PolyLine polygon = new PolyLine(coords);
        System.out.println(polygon);
        // Add a point and display the polyline again
        polygon.addPoint(10., 10.);
        System.out.println(polygon);

        // Create Point objects from the coordinate array
        Point[] points = new Point[coords.length];
        for(int i = 0; i < points.length; i++) {
          points[i] = new Point(coords[i][0],coords[i][1]);
        }
        // Use the points to create a new polyline and display it
        PolyLine newPoly = new PolyLine(points);
        System.out.println(newPoly);
    }
}
```

Apart from the class name, this is the same as the TryPolyLine source file that you created in Chapter 6. Compiling this program results in five .class files. Two of these are the result of compiling LinkedList.java. The source for generic type compiles into LinkedList.class plus the LinkedList$ListItem.class corresponding to the inner class. When you execute this example, it produces the same output as the example in Chapter 6.

How It Works

The PolyLine class creates the LinkedList<Point> type from the LinkedList<T> generic type that will implement a linked list of Point objects because of this statement:

```
    private LinkedList<Point> polyline;              // The linked list of points
```

The class type that results from this is produced by passing `Point` as the argument for the type variable `T` in the `LinkedList<T>` generic type definition. This process is described as **type erasure** because all occurrences of the type variable `T` are eliminated, so you end up with a notional class with the following definition:

```
public class LinkedList {
  // Default constructor - creates an empty list
  public LinkedList() {}

  // Constructor to create a list containing one object
  public LinkedList(Object item) {
    if(item != null) {
      current=end=start=new ListItem(item); // item is the start and end
    }
  }

  // Construct a linked list from an array of objects
  public LinkedList(Object[] items) {
    if(items != null) {
      // Add the items to the list
      for(int i = 0; i < items.length; i++) {
        addItem(items[i]);
      }
      current = start;
    }
  }

  // Add an item object to the list
  public void addItem(Object item) {
    ListItem newEnd = new ListItem(item);   // Create a new ListItem
    if(start == null) {                     // Is the list empty?
      start = end = newEnd;                 // Yes, so new element is start and end
    } else {                                // No, so append new element
      end.next = newEnd;                    // Set next variable for old end
      end = newEnd;                         // Store new item as end
    }
  }
  // Get the first object in the list
  public Object getFirst() {
    current = start;
    return start == null ? null : start.item;
  }

  // Get the next object in the list
  public Object getNext() {
    if(current != null) {
      current = current.next;               // Get the reference to the next item
    }
    return current == null ? null : current.item;
  }

  private ListItem start = null;            // First ListItem in the list
  private ListItem end = null;              // Last ListItem in the list
  private ListItem current = null;          // The current item for iterating
```

```
    private class ListItem {

      // Constructor
      public ListItem(Point item) {
        this.item = item;                    // Store the item
        next = null;                         // Set next as end point
      }

      // Return class name & object
      public String toString() {
        return "ListItem " + item ;
      }

      ListItem next;                         // Refers to next item in the list
      Object item;                           // The item for this ListItem
    }
  }
```

The type parameter following the class name in the original generic type definition has been removed, and all occurrences of the type variable Point within the class definition have been replaced by type Object. Type Object is chosen by the compiler to replace the type variable because type Object is the ultimate superclass class from which type Point is derived. The type that the compiler selects to replace a type variable is the **leftmost bound** of the type variable. Type Object is the default leftmost bound that applies to any class type because all classes have type Object as their ultimate superclass, but you'll see later in the chapter how you can specify a different leftmost bound for a type parameter and what the reasons are for doing this.

Of course, this class doesn't exist as a separate entity. The preceding code represents a description of how the generic type behaves when you supply a type argument as type Point. Looking at the class that now works with references of type Object, you may wonder what the advantage of being able to specify the type parameter is; after all, you can supply a reference to an object of any type for a parameter of type Object. The answer is that the type variable you supply is used by the compiler to ensure compile-time type safety. When you use an object of type LinkedList<Point> in your code, the compiler checks that you use it only to store objects of type Point and flags any attempt to store objects of other types as an error. When you call methods for an object of type LinkedList<Point>, the compiler will ensure that you supply references only of type Point where the original method parameter was specified as the type parameter.

You use the methods in the parameterized type in the same way as those in the original LinkedList class definition. Everything is very straightforward, and you now have a PolyLine implementation that uses a typesafe linked list. I think you'll agree that the essentials of defining and using a generic type could be described as a piece of cake.

Using Primitive Type Wrapper Class Types as Arguments

On occasion you will want to store values of a primitive type in a collection such as a linked list. In this situation you use the generic type with one of the wrapper classes for values of primitive types as the type argument — these are the classes Integer, Short, Double, and so on that are defined in the java.lang package. Here's how you could use the LinkedList<T> generic type to hold values of type double:

```
LinkedList<Double> temperatures = new LinkedList<Double>();
```

Here you have created a linked list that will store objects of type `Double`, and the autoboxing facility that you met in Chapter 5 makes it very easy to use the `LinkedList<Double>` object directly with values of type `double`. For example, to effectively add a value of type `double` to the linked list you have just created, you could write:

```
temperatures.addItem(10.5);
```

Because the parameter type for this method for the `LinkedList<Double>` object is of type `Double`, the compiler will automatically insert a boxing conversion to convert the `double` value 10.5 to an object of type `Double` that encapsulates it. Thus, the creation of the appropriate wrapper class object is taken care of automatically, so you can use the linked list object as though it stored values of the primitive type.

Let's see if the linked list type can really take the heat.

Try It Out   Autoboxing with Generic Types

In this example you'll create an instance of the `LinkedList<T>` generic type and use that to store random temperature values of type `double`. Here's the code:

```
public class TryAutoboxing {
  public static void main(String[] args) {
    LinkedList<Double> temperatures = new LinkedList<Double>();

    // Insert 6 temperature values 0 to 25 degress Centigrade
    for(int i = 0 ; i<6 ; i++) {
      temperatures.addItem(25.0*Math.random());
    }

    System.out.printf("%.2f degrees Fahrenheit%n",
                            toFahrenheit(temperatures.getFirst()));
    Double value = null;
    while((value=temperatures.getNext()) != null) {
      System.out.printf("%.2f degrees Fahrenheit%n", toFahrenheit(value));
    }
  }

    // Convert Centigrade to Fahrenheit
    public static double toFahrenheit(double temperature) {
      return 1.8*temperature+32.0;
    }
}
```

This will output something similar to the following:

```
72.88 degrees Fahrenheit
32.80 degrees Fahrenheit
38.36 degrees Fahrenheit
65.76 degrees Fahrenheit
65.92 degrees Fahrenheit
67.56 degrees Fahrenheit
```

How It Works

Here you create an object of type `LinkedList<Double>` from the parameterized type to store elements of type `Double` in the linked list. When you pass a value of type `double` to the `addItem()` method of the linked list class that you have created, the compiler inserts a boxing conversion to type `Double` because that's the argument type that the method requires.

When you extract `Double` objects from the linked list and pass them to the `toFahrenheit()` method, the compiler automatically inserts an unboxing conversion to extract the original `double` values and those will be passed to the method. You could equally well use the reference returned by `getFirst()` or `getNext()` in an arithmetic expression; you would get the same unboxing conversion provided automatically.

You can see how the `printf()` method is helpful in making the output more readable by limiting the display of temperature values to two decimal places after the decimal point.

The Runtime Type of Generic Type Instances

Suppose you create two different types from the `LinkedList<T>` generic type:

```
LinkedList<Double> numbers = new LinkedList<Double>();    // List to store numbers
LinkedList<String> proverbs = new LinkedList<String>();   // List to store strings
```

Clearly the variables `numbers` and `proverbs` are instances of different class types. One type represents a linked list that stores values of type `Double`, and the other represents a linked list that stores values of type `String`. However, things are not quite as straightforward as that. Because you have only one generic type, both classes share the same `Class` object at runtime, which is the `Class` object that corresponds to the generic type, so their class type names will be identical. Indeed, *all* types that you generate from a given generic type share the same class name at run time. You can demonstrate this with the following simple example.

Try It Out   The Run-Time Types of Generic Type Instances

In this example you'll create two different instances of the `LinkedList<T>` generic type and see what their type names are:

```
public class TestClassTypes {
  public static void main(String[] args) {

  LinkedList<String> proverbs = new LinkedList<String>();
  LinkedList<Double> numbers = new LinkedList<Double>();
   System.out.println("numbers class name " + numbers.getClass().getName());
   System.out.println("proverbs class name " + proverbs.getClass().getName());
   System.out.println("Compare Class objects: "
                     + numbers.getClass().equals(proverbs.getClass()));

  }
 }
```

This will produce the following output:

```
numbers class name LinkedList
proverbs class name LinkedList
Compare Class objects: true
```

How It Works

You call the `getClass()` method that is inherited from the `Object` class to obtain the `Class` objects for the objects referenced by proverbs and numbers. You then call the `getName()` method for the `Class` object to get the run-time type name. In both instances the type name is `LinkedList`. The fact that the run-time types are identical is further confirmed by the comparison of the `Class` objects for the `LinkedList<String>` and `LinkedList<Double>` objects, and the output shows they are identical.

Thus, you have the unavoidable conclusion that all instances of a given type share the same `Class` object at run-time, and therefore the same run-time type. Of course, this does not mean that the objects are the same type. For example, the following statement will not compile:

```
proverbs = (LinkedList<String>)numbers;   // Illegal cast - will not compile
```

The compiler knows that these objects are really of different types and will not allow you to do this.

However, not a lot prevents you from doing the following:

```
Object obj = (Object)numbers;
proverbs = (LinkedList<String>)obj;       // Will result in a compiler warning
```

Here the cast of `numbers` to type `Object` is legal—every class has `Object` as a base so the compiler will allow this. With the second statement, though, the compiler knows only that you are casting a reference of type `Object` and therefore cannot identify this as an illegal operation. Even at run time this will not be checked because the run-time type of the reference stored in `obj` will be `LinkedList`, the same as that of `proverbs`. This means that you will end up with a reference to an object that is really of type `LinkedList<Double>` in a variable of type `LinkedList<String>`. You will discover that this is a problem only when you attempt to call methods for the object. If you want to verify that this is the case, you can add the following code to the end of the example:

```
Object obj = (Object)numbers;
System.out.println("obj class name " + obj.getClass().getName());
proverbs = (LinkedList<String>)obj;
System.out.println("obj in proverbs class name " + proverbs.getClass().getName());
```

The example will then produce the following output:

```
numbers class name LinkedList
proverbs class name LinkedList
compare: true
obj class name LinkedList
obj in proverbs class name LinkedList
```

You can deduce from this that the type checking related to the use of types produced by a generic type happens at compile time, not at run time. At run time the class types of all the types that you generate from a given parameterized type are the same, so you have no programmatic way to differentiate them. You can further conclude that casts to types that you produce from a generic type are unchecked and inherently risky. Where such casts in your code are recognized by the compiler, you will get a warning message to indicate that you have a potential problem. You should use such casts only when they are absolutely necessary, and always double-check that the cast is valid. Of course, you do encounter instances where such casts are unavoidable. One example is when you are deserializing objects that are instances of a class produced from a generic type. You'll be trying this a little later in this chapter.

One further point to keep in mind about types that you create from a generic type: Because all types that you produce from a generic type have the same run-time type, you cannot use the instanceof *operator to test for such types.*

Relationships between Generic Type Instances

It's easy to be misled about whether types you create from a generic type are related. Suppose you create an object as follows:

```
LinkedList<String> strings = new LinkedList<String>();      // A list of strings
```

You have created a linked list that will store objects of type String. Suppose you now create another object with the following statement:

```
LinkedList<Object> things = new LinkedList<Object>();      // A list of objects
```

This object stores objects of type Object organized as a linked list. Of course, it also stores objects of any class type that is a subclass of Object, so any class type is acceptable. Is there any relationship between the type of things, LinkedList<Object>, and the type of strings, LinkedList<String>? Superficially, you might jump to the conclusion that there is; after all, Object is a superclass of every class type, including type String. However, if you think about it, the relationship between the type arguments is an irrelevancy, and the conclusion would be wrong. The types just happen to be produced by a single generic type, LinkedList<>, but there's no reason why the type argument that you use should establish any relationship between these types, no more than there would be between two ordinary collection classes that you might define to store String objects and Object objects.

Multiple Type Parameters

The LinkedList<T> generic type has a single type parameter, but in general you can define a generic type with as many type parameters as you wish. Suppose that you want to define a generic type that defines a set of classes that encapsulate a pair of objects of arbitrary types. This would typically arise where one object is used as a key to access the other in a collection. For example, you might store Person objects in a collection that encapsulates personal details such as the name, the address, and the phone number. You could associate each Person object with a Name object that you use as a key to retrieve the Person object. One way of establishing the association between an object and its key would be to encapsulate both in another object — of type Pair, say.

Here's how you might define a generic type, Pair<K, V>, that is to be used for defining classes that encapsulate a key/value pair of any type:

```
public class Pair <KeyType, ValueType> {
  // Constructor
  public Pair(KeyType key, ValueType aValue) {
    key = aKey;
    value = aValue;
  }

  // Get the key for this pair
  public getKey() {
    return key;
  }
```

```
// Get the value for this pair
public getValue() {
  return value;
}

// Set the value for this pair
public setValue(ValueType aValue) {
  value = aValue;
}

private KeyType key;
private ValueType value;
}
```

Obviously, a practical definition would be more complicated than this — you'd need a means of comparing key objects, for example — but it suffices to demonstrate how you can use two parameters in the definition of a generic type.

Here's an example of how you could use this generic type:

```
Pair<String, String> entry = new Pair<String, String>("Fred Thrump",
                                                      "212 222 3333");
```

This creates an object of type `Pair<String, String>` and stores a reference to it in the variable with the name `entry`.

Type Parameter Scope

The scope of a type parameter is the entire generic class definition, but excluding any static members or initializers in the class. This implies that you cannot specify the type of a static field within a generic type definition by the type variable for the generic type. Similarly, static methods cannot have parameters or return types that are type variables corresponding to the type parameter, and you must not use the type variables in the bodies of static method definitions.

This does not mean that static methods cannot be parameterized — I am talking only about type variables corresponding to parameters that apply to a generic type definition. You'll see later in this chapter that you can define **generic methods** that have their own independent parameterized definitions involving their own set of parameters, and such parameterized methods may be static or non-static.

Static Fields in a Generic Type

Even though all types produced from a given generic type share the same run-time type, they still have their own independent static fields. For example, suppose you were to add a static field — count, say — of type int to the LinkedList<> type definition to record the number of objects created. You'd then add a statement to the constructor to increment count each time it was called. Each type instance, such as LinkedList<String> or LinkedList<Point>, would have its own copy of count, so the static count member of the LinkedList<String> type would correctly reflect the number of times the LinkedList<String> constructor had been called.

Type Parameter Bounds

In some situations you will be defining a generic type where you want to constrain the type arguments that are supplied to define a class instance so that they extend a particular class, or implement specific interfaces, or even both. The reason for this would be that your generic type has to make some assumptions about the capabilities of the objects an instance of the type will be dealing with. Such constraints are called **type parameter bounds**. The first bound that you specify for a type parameter can be a class type or an interface type. Any additional bounds after the first for a type parameter can be interface types only. If you don't specify any bounds for a type parameter, it will have type `Object` as its implicit bound because all classes have this type as their ultimate base class.

To understand how you specify a type parameter bound, consider a simple example of where this applies. Suppose that you wanted to modify the `LinkedList<T>` generic type that you saw earlier so that objects of classes produced by this type would be serializable. Not only would `LinkedList<T>` need to implement the `Serializable` interface, but objects of type `T` that were stored in the list would, too. The definition for the generic type would therefore look like this:

```
class LinkedList<T extends Serializable> implements Serializable {
  // Default constructor - creates an empty list
  public LinkedList() {}

  // Constructor to create a list containing one object
  public LinkedList(T item) {
    if(item != null) {
      current=end=start=new ListItem(item);       // item is the start and end
    }
  }

  // Construct a linked list from an array of objects
  public LinkedList(T[] items) {
    if(items != null) {
      // Add the items to the list
      for(int i = 0; i < items.length; i++) {
        addItem(items[i]);
      }
      current = start;
    }
  }

  // Add an item object to the list
  public void addItem(T item) {
    ListItem newEnd = new ListItem(item);     // Create a new ListItem
    if(start == null) {                       // Is the list empty?
      start = end = newEnd;                   // Yes, so new element is start and end
    } else {                                  // No, so append new element
      end.next = newEnd;                      // Set next variable for old end
      end = newEnd;                           // Store new item as end
    }
  }
  // Get the first object in the list
  public T getFirst() {
    current = start;
    return start == null ? null : start.item;
  }
```

```
    // Get the next object in the list
    public T getNext() {
      if(current != null) {
        current = current.next;              // Get the reference to the next item
      }
      return current == null ? null : current.item;
    }

    private ListItem start = null;           // First ListItem in the list
    private ListItem end = null;             // Last ListItem in the list
    private ListItem current = null;         // The current item for iterating

    private class ListItem implements Serializable {

      // Constructor
      public ListItem(T item) {
        this.item = item;                    // Store the item
        next = null;                         // Set next as end point
      }

      // Return class name & object
      public String toString() {
        return "ListItem " + item ;
      }

      ListItem next;                         // Refers to next item in the list
      T item;                                // The item for this ListItem
    }
  }
```

The only changes to the previous version of the generic type definition are the two shaded lines. Notice how you use the extends keyword regardless of whether the type parameter bound is a class or an interface. Of course, this applies only to bounds for type parameters in a generic type. Where the generic type itself implements an interface, you use the implements keyword, and where it extends a class, you use the extends keyword, just as you would for an ordinary class type. Of course, the ListItem inner class must also implement the Serializable interface because you need ListItem objects to be serializable.

Where you need to specify a type parameter that has several bounds, you use a special notation. You put & between the type names that are bounds following the extends keyword. Here's how that looks:

```
class MyType<T extends FancyClass & Serializable & MyInterface> {
  // Code defining the generic type...
}
```

The parameter for the MyType<> generic type has three bounds: the FancyClass class and the interfaces Serializable and MyInterface. All type arguments for T to the MyType<T> parameterized type must extend the FancyClass class and implement both the Serializable and the MyInterface interfaces.

Let's see if the serializable LinkedList<> generic type works.

Try It Out   Using Parameter Bounds in a Generic Type

This example exercises the last version of the `LinkedList<>` generic type by serializing a list of integers and then deserializing it. Here's the code:

```java
import java.io.FileOutputStream;
import java.io.FileInputStream;
import java.io.ObjectOutputStream;
import java.io.ObjectInputStream;
import java.io.IOException;
import static java.lang.Math.random;

public class TrySerializableLinkedList {
  public static void main(String[] args) {
    LinkedList<Integer> numbers = new LinkedList<Integer>();
    for(int i = 0 ; i<10 ; i++) {
      numbers.addItem(1+(int)(100.0*random())); // Add ten random integers 1 to 100
    }

    System.out.println("\nnumbers list contains:");
    listAll(numbers);                               // List contents of numbers

    // Now serialize the list to a file
    String filename = "C:/Beg Java Stuff/Numbers.bin";
    try {
      ObjectOutputStream objOut = new ObjectOutputStream(
                                      new FileOutputStream(filename));
      objOut.writeObject(numbers);
      objOut.close();
    } catch(IOException e) {
      e.printStackTrace();
      System.exit(1);
    }

    LinkedList<Integer> values = null;       // Variable to store list from the file

    // Deserialize the list from the file
    try {
      ObjectInputStream objIn = new ObjectInputStream(
                                      new FileInputStream(filename));
      values = (LinkedList<Integer>)(objIn.readObject());
      objIn.close();
    } catch(IOException e) {
      e.printStackTrace();
      System.exit(1);
    } catch(ClassNotFoundException e) {
      e.printStackTrace();
      System.exit(1);
    }

    System.out.println("\nvalues list contains:");
    listAll(values);                               // List contents of values
  }
```

```
// Helper method to list the contents of a linked list
static void listAll(LinkedList<Integer> list) {
  Integer number = list.getFirst();
  int count = 0;
  do {
    System.out.printf("%5d",number);
    if(++count%5 == 0 ) {
      System.out.println();
    }
  } while((number = list.getNext()) != null);
}
}
```

Include the source file for `LinkedList<>` in the same directory as this source file. When you compile this program, you will get the following message from the compiler:

```
TrySerializableLinkedList.java:36: warning: [unchecked] unchecked cast
found    : java.lang.Object
required: LinkedList<java.lang.Integer>
        values = (LinkedList<Integer>)(objIn.readObject());
                                       ^
```

```
1 warning
```

This example will produce output along the following lines:

```
numbers list contains:
    56   79   36   64   43
    78   81    3   36   56

values list contains:
    56   79   36   64   43
    78   81    3   36   56
```

How It Works

You first create a linked list of type `LinkedList<Integer>` that stores objects of type `integer`:

```
LinkedList<Integer> numbers = new LinkedList<Integer>();
```

You populate this list with ten `Integer` objects that encapsulate random integer values from 1 to 100 in the `for` loop:

```
for(int i = 0 ; i<10 ; i++) {
  numbers.addItem(1+(int)(100.0*random())); // Add ten random integers 1 to 100
}
```

This relies on autoboxing to create the `Integer` objects to be passed as arguments to the `addItem()` method.

The static `listAll()` method is a helper method that lists the contents of a linked list of integers, and you call that to output what is stored in the `numbers` linked list.

Since the linked list is now supposed to be serializable, you demonstrate that this in the case by writing the `numbers` object to the file in the way you saw in the previous chapter. You then read it back and store a reference to the list read from the file in a new variable, `values`. The statement in the `try` block that reads the object from the file is:

```
values = (LinkedList<Integer>)(objIn.readObject());
```

The `readObject()` method returns a reference of type `Object`, so you must cast it to type `LinkedList<Integer>` before storing it in `values`. The compiler recognizes that this cast is unchecked at run time, so you get the warning message shown earlier as a result of this statement. However, you have no alternative to casting in this instance.

Having read the `LinkedList<Integer>` from the file, you demonstrate that it is indeed the same as the original by listing its contents via a call to the `listAll()` method. The output shows that the serialization and deserialization operations were successful.

Generic Types and Generic Interfaces

A generic type can implement one or more interface types, including generic interface types. The syntax that you use for this is the same as for ordinary class and interface types, the only difference being that each generic type name will be followed by its type parameter list between angled brackets. For example:

```
public class MyClass<T> implements MyInterface<T> {
   // Details of the generic type definitions
}
```

You can see how this works by taking a practical example.

Enabling the Collection-Based for Loop

The `for` loop you have been using to extract the elements stored in a linked list, such as in the `TryAutoboxing` example at the beginning of this chapter, for example, was rather cumbersome. Wouldn't it be nice if you could use the collection-based `for` loop with the classes produced from the `LinkedList<>` generic type? It's not that difficult, so let's see how to do it.

For an object of a container class type to be usable with the collection-based `for` loop, the class must fulfill just one requirement—it must implement the generic `Iterable<>` interface that is defined in the `java.lang` package. The `Iterable<>` interface is a generic type that declares a single method, `iterator()`, that returns a reference of type `Iterator<>`, which is another generic interface type. All your class has to do then is declare that it implements the `Iterable<>` interface and provide an implementation for the `iterator()` method.

Here's the outline of what you need to add to the `LinkedList<>` generic type that you developed at the beginning of this chapter to make it usable with the collection-based `for` loop:

```
import java.util.Iterator;

public class LinkedList<T> implements Iterable<T> {
```

```
    // Returns an iterator for this list
    public Iterator<T> iterator() {
        // Code to return a reference to an iterator for this list...
    }

    // Rest of the LinkedList<T> generic type definition as before...
}
```

The generic `LinkedList<>` class type now implements the generic `Iterable<>` interface type, and they share a common type parameter. The type argument that you supply for `LinkedList<>` also applies to `Iterable<>`. You can see why the `Iterable<>` and `Iterator<>` interfaces need to be generic types. The type parameter allows them to be automatically adapted to any type. Because these interfaces are defined as generic types, you can define classes that contain sets of objects of any type and enable them to be iterated over using the collection-based `for` loop by implementing the `Iterable<>` interface. The interface will automatically be customized to work with whatever type of object a particular container contains.

The `Iterator<T>` type that is the return type for the `iterator()` method is a generic interface type that is defined in the `java.util` package. Thus your implementation of the `iterator()` method must return an object of a class type that implements the `Iterator<>` interface. This implies that for your class to define an iterator, it must implement the methods that are declared in the `Iterator<>` interface. These methods provide a mechanism for iterating once over each of the elements in a collection in turn and may also provide the ability to remove elements. The methods that the `Iterator<>` interface declares are the following:

`T next()`	Returns a reference of type `T` to the next object that is available from the iterator and throws an exception of type `java.util.NoSuchElementException` if no further elements are available. `T` is the type parameter for the generic interface and corresponds to the type of objects stored in the container. Note that you'll also see `E` used as the type parameter that represents `Element` instead of `T` for `Type`.
`boolean hasNext()`	Returns `true` if at least one more element is available from the iterator, so calling the `next()` method for the iterator returns a reference to the object in the container. The method returns `false` if no more elements are available from the iterator. Thus this method provides a way to check whether calling the `next()` method for the iterator will return a reference or throw an exception.
`void remove()`	If the remove operation is supported, this method removes the last element that was retrieved by the preceding `next()` method call from the collection. If the remove operation is supported, this method throws an exception of type `java.lang.UnsupportedOperationException`. It will also throw an exception of type `java.lang.IllegalStateException` if the `next()` method has not been called for the iterator object prior to calling the `remove()` method.

The basic idea of the first two methods is to provide a mechanism for iterating over all the elements in a collection such as the linked lists produced by the LinkedList<> generic type. Suppose that you have a LinkedList<String> reference stored in a variable, strings, where LinkedList<> is the version that implements Iterable<>. The mechanism for retrieving elements from the linked list works like this:

```
Iterator<String> iter = strings.iterator();    // Get an iterator
String str = null;                             // Stores an element from the list
while(iter.hasNext()) {                        // If there are more elements
  str = iter.next();                           // Get the next one...
  // Do something with str...
}
```

The while loop continues to retrieve elements from iter as long as the hasNext() method returns true. Within the loop, successive elements are retrieved by calling the next() method. You don't need to put this loop in a try block because the exception that the next() method can throw is of a type derived from RuntimeException. Removing an element would just involve calling the remove() method for strings after a call of the next() method, typically after you have analyzed the object retrieved to determine that you really do want to remove it. The exceptions that the remove() method can throw are also derived from RuntimeException so you are not obliged to catch them.

Implementing an Iterator Capability

As I said in the previous section, the iterator() method in the LinkedList<> type must return an object reference as type Iterator<>, so the class type for the object must implement the Iterator<> interface. You could define a class representing an iterator as an inner class to the LinkedList<> generic class type:

```
import java.util.Iterator;

public class LinkedList<T> implements Iterable<T> {

  // Returns an iterator for this list
  public Iterator<T> iterator() {
    return new ListIterator();         // Create iterator of the inner class type
  }

  // Inner class defining iterator objects for this linked list
  private class ListIterator implements Iterator<T> {
    // Constructor
    public ListIterator() {
      // Code to initialize the iterator...
    }

    // Method to test whether more elements are available
    public boolean hasNext() {
      // Code to determine if there are more elements...
    }

    // Method to return the next available object from the linked list
    public T next() {
      // Code to return the next element...
    }
```

```
      // Method to remove the last element retrieved from the linked list
      public void remove() {
        // Code to remove the element last accessed by next()...
      }

      // Any other members needed for ListIterator<T>...
    }
    // Rest of the LinkedList<T> generic type definition as before...
  }
```

You have added an inner class to define an iterator object for a linked list. The ListIterator class defines the methods declared in the Iterator<> interface plus a constructor. Note that you do not need to specify a type parameter for the ListIterator class. Only the interface that is implemented by the ListIterator class is parameterized, and that uses the type variable name for the outer class. The type argument you supply for the container type will also apply to the methods declared by the Iterator<> interface that are implemented by the ListIterator inner class.

A ListIterator object is able to access the members of its parent LinkedList<> object directly, but because it must provide a one-pass iteration through the elements in the linked list, it will need to track what is happening during successive calls of the next() method. You can provide this by adding a field of type T to the ListIterator class to record the element from the linked list that will be available when the next() method is called next. You can easily initialize such a field in the constructor and then implement the other methods to make use of it. The inner class definition would then look like this:

```
    private class ListIterator implements Iterator<T> {
      // Constructor
      public ListIterator() {
        nextElement = getFirst();
      }

      // Method to test whether more elements are available
      public boolean hasNext() {
        return nextElement != null;
      }

      // Method to return the next available object from the linked list
      public T next() {
        T element = nextElement;
        if(element == null) {
          throw new java.util.NoSuchElementException();
        }
        nextElement = getNext();
        return element;
      }

      // Method to remove the last element retrieved from the linked list
      // You don't want to support this operation for the linked list
      // so just throw the exception
      public void remove() {
        throw new IllegalStateException();
      }

      private T nextElement;
    }
```

If you add this inner class to the definition of `LinkedList<>`, you can use a new version of the `TryAutoboxing` example to try it out.

Here's a version of the original `TryAutoboxing` example that has been modified to use the collection-based `for` loop:

```
public class TryAutoboxing {
  public static void main(String[] args) {
    LinkedList<Double> temperatures = new LinkedList<Double>();

    // Insert 6 temperature values 0 to 25 degrees Centigrade
    for(int i = 0 ; i<6 ; i++) {
      temperatures.addItem(25.0*Math.random());
    }

    // Collection-based for loop used with LinkedList<Double>
    for(Double value : temperatures) {
      System.out.printf("%.2f degrees Fahrenheit%n", toFahrenheit(value));
    }
  }

  // Convert Centigrade to Fahrenheit
  public static double toFahrenheit(double temperature) {
    return 1.8*temperature+32.0;
  }
}
```

Put the source file for this class in the same directory as the new version of `LinkedList<>` that implements the `Iterable<>` interface. If you use the old version, the program will not compile.

The output will be the same as the previous version of `TryAutoboxing`.

How It Works

The collection-based `for` loop requires an iterator of type `Iterator<T>` that it uses to iterate over the members of a collection or an array. Clearly, all arrays implement the `Iterator<>` interface; otherwise, you couldn't use them with this form of `for` loop. Because the `LinkedList<>` type now implements `Iterable<>`, you can use the collection-based `for` loop with any `LinkedList<>` collection, as the example demonstrates.

A Parameterized Type for Binary Trees

Let's consider another kind of container as a candidate for being a generic type. A binary tree is a structure for organizing data in the form of a tree, where each node in the tree has at most two child nodes. One interesting application of a binary tree is for sorting. Figure 13-2 shows an example of integers organized in a binary tree structure.

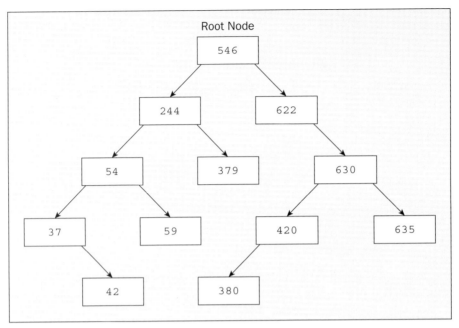

Figure 13-2

The first node in a binary tree is called the **root node**, because this node is the root of the tree and is the starting point for accessing nodes in the tree. Each node in a binary tree, including the root node, can have two child nodes, usually referred to as the **left child node** and the **right child node**. Thus, each node in a binary tree may have zero, one, or two child nodes, and Figure 13-2 contains examples of all three possibilities.

By constructing the tree so that for each node the object stored as the left node is always less than the object represented by the node and the object in the right node is always greater, you'll be able to extract the objects that are stored in the tree so that they are in sequence. The tree in Figure 13-2 has been constructed like this. For every node that has child nodes, the left child node is always less than the current node, and the right child node is always greater. Adding a node to a tree involves starting with the root node and seeing whether the new node is less than or greater than the current node. This establishes whether it is a potential left node or right node for the root node. If the root node already has a child node in the position where the new node belongs, you repeat the comparison process with the child node. Eventually you'll find a child node position that is `null` where the new node fits, so that's where you put it. Clearly, a recursive method will help make this process easy. Given that you have constructed a tree in this manner and that you know the root node, you can work your way through all the nodes in a tree by following the left and right child nodes in an orderly fashion to obtain all the objects in the tree in sequence. Since all the nodes are similar, the use of recursion will help to simplify this process, too.

Because a binary tree is a structure you can apply to organizing objects of any type, it is an obvious candidate for being a generic type. It also provides another example of where being able to constrain the type parameter is important. The way the tree is constructed implies that you must be able to compare objects that are added to a tree. This means that every object in the tree must have a method available for comparing objects. Making the object type implement an interface that declares a method that compares objects is the way to do this. A binary tree implementation also provides an example of a situation where you can apply the power of recursion to very good effect.

Defining the Generic Type

You can come to some general conclusions about what the characteristics of your BinaryTree<> class are going to be by considering how it will work. Objects of type Node are going to be a fundamental part of a binary tree. The Node objects in the tree are really part of the inner workings of the container so they don't need to be known about or accessible externally. It is therefore appropriate if you define Node objects by a private inner class to the BinaryTree<> class. All nodes in a binary tree must be different, but you can allow duplicate data items to be added to a tree by providing for a count of the number of identical objects to be recorded in a Node object. Obviously, as a minimum, a BinaryTree<> object will have to store the Node object that is the root node for the tree and provide a method for adding new nodes. It'll also need a method for returning all the data that was stored in the tree in sequence, so you need some facility for packaging this. The generic LinkedList<> type from the previous example provides a convenient facility for this.

The type for objects that can be added to the tree must have a method for comparing them. The Comparable<> interface that is defined in the java.lang package declares a single method, the compareTo() method, that will fit the bill. The compareTo() method returns a negative integer if the object for which it is called is less than the argument to the method, 0 if it equals the argument, and a positive integer if it is greater, so it does precisely what you need for placing new values in a BinaryTree<> class object. If you specify the Comparable<> interface as a constraint on the type parameter for the BinaryTree<> class, it ensures that all objects added to a BinaryTree<> object implement the compareTo() method. Because the Comparable<> interface is defined as a parameterized type, it fits exactly with what you want here.

Here's a first stab at outlining the BinaryTree<> generic type:

```
public class BinaryTree<T extends Comparable<T>> {

  // Add a value to the tree
  public void add(T value) {
    // Add a value to the tree...
  }


  // Create a list containing the values from the tree in sequence
  public LinkedList<T> sort() {
    // Code to extract object from the tree in sequence
    // and insert then in a LinkedList object and return that...
  }

  LinkedList<T> values;                        // Stores sorted values
  private Node root;                           // The root node

  // Private inner class defining nodes
  private class Node {
    Node(T value) {
      obj = value;
      count = 1;
    }
```

```
      T obj;                        // Object stored in the node
      int count;                    // Count of identical nodes
      Node left;                    // The left child node
      Node right;                   // The right child node
    }
  }
```

No `BinaryTree<>` constructor is defined because the default constructor suffices. The default no-arg constructor creates an object with the root node as `null`. Thus, all objects are added to the tree by calling the `add()` method. The `sort()` method returns a `LinkedList<>` object that it creates, containing the objects that were stored in the tree in ascending sequence.

The inner `Node` class has four fields that store the value, the count of the number of values identical to this, and references to its left and right child nodes. The constructor just initializes the `obj` and `count` fields in the `Node` object that is created, leaving `left` and `right` with their default values of `null`. Of course, when a `Node` object is first created, it won't have any child nodes, and the count of identical objects in the tree will be 1. Let's look at how objects will be inserted into a tree.

Inserting Objects in a Binary Tree

It's easy to see how adding an object to the tree can be a recursive operation in general. The process is illustrated in Figure 13-3.

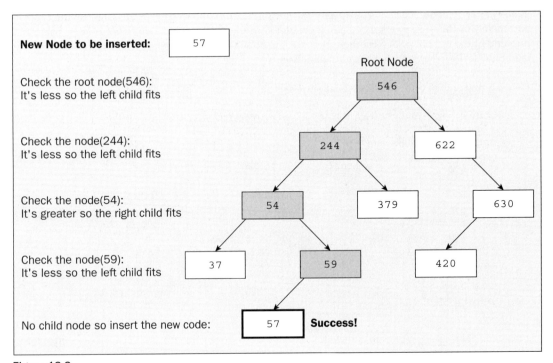

Figure 13-3

The shaded nodes in Figure 13-3 are the ones that have to be considered in the process of inserting the value 57 in the tree. To find where the new node for an object should be placed in relation to the existing nodes, you'll start with the root node to see which of its child nodes represents a potential position for the new node. If the candidate child node that you choose already exists, then you must repeat the process you've just gone through with the root node with the chosen child node. Of course, this child node may itself have child nodes so the process may need to be repeated again. You should be able to visualize how this can continue until either you find a child node that contains an object that is identical to the one contained in the new node or you find a vacant child node position where the new node fits.

You can implement the `add()` method in the `BinaryTree<>` generic type definition like this:

```
public void add(T value) {
  if(root == null) {              // If there's no root node
    root = new Node(value);       // store it in the root
  } else {                        // Otherwise...
    add(value, root);             // add it recursively
  }
}
```

If the root node is `null`, the `add()` method creates a new root node containing the value to be inserted. If root is not `null`, then the node where it fits in the tree must be found, and this is the function performed by another version of the `add()` method that accepts two arguments specifying the value to be inserted into the tree and the node where it might be inserted. The second argument allows the method to be called recursively. This method can be private as it does not need to be accessed externally. You could implement it like this:

```
private void add(T value, Node node) {
  int comparison = node.obj.compareTo(value);
  if(comparison == 0) {             // If it is equal to the current node
    ++node.count;                   // just increment the count
    return;
  }
  if(comparison > 0) {              // If it's less than the current node
    if(node.left == null) {         // and the left child node is not null
      node.left = new Node(value);  // Store it as the left child node
    } else {                        // Otherwise...
      add(value, node.left);        // ...add it to the left node
    }
  } else {                          // It must be greater than the current node
    if(node.right == null) {        // so it must go to the right...
      node.right = new Node(value);
    } else {
      add(value, node.right);
    }
  }
}
```

This method is called only with a non-`null` second argument. The first step is to compare the object to be inserted, which is given by the first argument, `value`, with the object stored in the current node, specified by the second argument. If the new object equals the one stored in the current node, you need to update the count only for the current node and you are done.

If the new object is not equal to that stored in the current node, you first check whether it's less. Remember: The compareTo() method returns a positive integer when the object for which it is called is greater than the argument, so the value of comparison being positive means that the new object is less than that in the current node. That makes it a candidate for the left child node of the current node, but only if the left child node is null. If the left child node is not null, you call the add() method recursively to add the object relative to the left node. You've tested for zero and positive values of comparison, so the only other possibility is that the comparison value is negative. In this case you repeat the same procedure, but with the right child node. This process finds the place for the new node containing the inserted object so that each node has only a left child that is less than the current node and a right child that is greater. In fact, for any node, the values stored in the whole left subtree will be less than the current node, and the values in the whole right subtree will be greater. Now that you've got them in, you have to figure out how you're going to get them out again.

Extracting Objects from the Binary Tree

Calling the sort() method for a BinaryTree<> object will return a LinkedList<> object containing the objects from the tree in ascending sequence. The process for selecting the objects to be inserted into the linked list is also recursive. You can define the sort() method like this:

```
public LinkedList<T> sort() {
    values = new LinkedList<T>();      // Create a linked list
    treeSort(root);                    // Sort the objects into the list
    return values;
}
```

The LinkedList<> object is a field in the BinaryTree<> object and the sort() method eventually returns a reference to it. You create a new LinkedList<> object each time to hold the sorted values of type T from the tree. The sort() method could be called several times for a BinaryTree<> object, with the contents of the binary tree being changed in the intervening period, so you must be sure you create the linked list from scratch each time. The real work of inserting the objects from the tree into the linked list values is going to be done by the recursive treeSort() method. You can get an inkling of how this will work if you recall that the left child node object of every node will be less than the current node, which will be less than the right child node. Therefore, you want to access the objects in the sequence:

```
left child node - node - right child node
```

Of course, the child nodes may themselves have child nodes, *but the same applies to them.* Take the left child node, for example. The objects here should be accessed in the sequence:

```
left child of left child node - left child node - right child of left child node
```

The same goes for the right child node and its children. All you have to do is express this as code, and you can do that like this:

```
private void treeSort(Node node) {
    if(node != null) {                 // If the node isn't null
        treeSort(node.left);           // process its left child

        // List the duplicate objects for the current node
        for(int i = 0 ; i<node.count ; i++) {
            values.addItem(node.obj);
        }
```

```
    treeSort(node.right);                // Now process the right child
  }
}
```

If the node that is passed to the `treeSort()` method is `null`, nothing further is left to do so the method returns. If the argument is not `null`, you process the left child node, then the node that was passed as the argument, then the right child node — just as you saw earlier. That does it all. The actual insertion of an object into the linked list always occurs in the `for` loop. This loop typically executes one iteration because most of the time, no duplicate objects are in the tree. The value of the left child node, if it exists, is always added to the linked list before the value of the current node because you don't add the value from the current node until the `treeSort()` method call for the left child returns. Similarly, the value from the right child node will always be added to the linked list after that of the current node.

You're ready to give the `BinaryTree<>` generic type a whirl.

Try It Out   Sorting Using a Binary Tree

You'll need to create a directory to hold the three source files for this program. When you've set that up, copy the `LinkedList.java` source file from the previous example to the new directory. You can then add the `BinaryTree.java` source file containing the following code to the directory:

```java
public class BinaryTree<T extends Comparable<T>> {

  // Add a value to the tree
  public void add(T value) {
    if(root == null) {                   // If there's no root node
      root = new Node(value);            // store it in the root
    } else {                             // Otherwise...
      add(value, root);                  // add it recursively
    }
  }

  // Recursive insertion of an object
  private void add(T value, Node node) {
    int comparison = node.obj.compareTo(value);
    if(comparison == 0) {                // If it is equal to the current node
      ++node.count;                      // just increment the count
      return;
    }
    if(comparison > 0) {                 // If it's less than the current node
      if(node.left == null) {            // and the left child node is not null
        node.left = new Node(value);     // Store it as the left child node
      } else {                           // Otherwise...
        add(value, node.left);           // ...add it to the left node
      }
    } else {                             // It must be greater than the current node
      if(node.right == null) {           // so it must go to the right...
        node.right = new Node(value);
      } else {
        add(value, node.right);
      }
    }
  }
}
```

```
// Create a list containing the values from the tree in sequence
public LinkedList<T> sort() {
  values = new LinkedList<T>();       // Create a linked list
  treeSort(root);                     // Sort the objects into the list
  return values;
}

// Extract the tree nodes in sequence
private void treeSort(Node node) {
  if(node != null) {                  // If the node isn't null
    treeSort(node.left);              // process its left child

    // List the duplicate objects for the current node
    for(int i = 0 ; i<node.count ; i++) {
      values.addItem(node.obj);
    }
    treeSort(node.right);             // Now process the right child
  }
}

LinkedList<T> values;                 // Stores sorted values
private Node root;                    // The root node

// Private inner class defining nodes
private class Node {
  Node(T value) {
    obj = value;
    count = 1;
  }

  T obj;                              // Object stored in the node
  int count;                          // Count of identical nodes
  Node left;                          // The left child node
  Node right;                         // The right child node
  }
}
```

You can try out sorting integers and strings using `BinaryTree<>` objects with the following code:

```
public class TryBinaryTree {
  public static void main(String[] args) {
    int[] numbers = new int[30];
    for(int i = 0 ; i<numbers.length ; i++) {
      numbers[i] = (int)(1000.0*Math.random());    // Random integers 0 to 999
    }

    // List starting integer values
    int count = 0;
    System.out.println("Original values are:");
    for(int number : numbers) {
      System.out.printf("%6d", number);
      if(++count%6 == 0) {
        System.out.println();
```

```
      }
    }

    // Create the tree and add the integers to it
    BinaryTree<Integer> tree = new BinaryTree<Integer>();
    for(int number:numbers) {
      tree.add(number);
    }

    // Get sorted values
    LinkedList<Integer> values = tree.sort();
    count = 0;
    System.out.println("\nSorted values are:");
    for(Integer value : values) {
      System.out.printf("%6d", value);
      if(++count%6 == 0) {
        System.out.println();
      }
    }

    // Create an array of words to be sorted
    String[] words = {"vacillate", "procrastinate", "arboreal", "syzygy",
                      "xenocracy", "zygote"       , "mephitic", "soporific",
                      "grisly"   , "gristly" };

    // List the words
    System.out.println("\nOriginal word sequence:");
    for(String word : words) {
      System.out.printf("%-15s", word);
        if(++count%5 == 0) {
          System.out.println();
        }
    }

    // Create the tree and insert the words
    BinaryTree<String> cache = new BinaryTree<String>();
    for(String word : words) {
      cache.add(word);
    }

    // Sort the words
    LinkedList<String> sortedWords = cache.sort();

    // List the sorted words
    System.out.println("\nSorted word sequence:");
    count = 0;
    for(String word : sortedWords) {
      System.out.printf("%-15s", word);
      if(++count%5 == 0) {
        System.out.println();
      }
    }
  }
}
```

The output should be along the lines of the following:

```
Original values are:
    110    136    572    589    605    832
    565    765    514    616    347    724
    152    527    124    324     42    508
    621    653    480    236      1    793
    324     31    127    170    724    546

Sorted values are:
      1     31     42    110    124    127
    136    152    170    236    324    324
    347    480    508    514    527    546
    565    572    589    605    616    621
    653    724    724    765    793    832

Original word sequence:
vacillate        procrastinate   arboreal        syzygy          xenocracy
zygote           mephitic        soporific       grisly          gristly

Sorted word sequence:
arboreal         grisly          gristly         mephitic        procrastinate
soporific        syzygy          vacillate       xenocracy       zygote
```

How It Works

You have defined `BinaryTree<>` as a parameterized type with a type parameter that is constrained to implement the parameterized interface type `Comparable<>`. Thus, a type argument that you use with the `BinaryTree<>` generic type must implement the `Comparable<>` interface. If it doesn't, the code won't compile. This ensures that all objects added to a `BinaryTree<>` object will have the `compareTo()` function available. The definition for `BinaryTree<>` also demonstrates that a generic type definition can include a field of another generic type—`LinkedList<>` in this instance. The `LinkedList<>` field type is determined by the type argument supplied to the `BinaryTree<>` generic type.

After creating and displaying an array of 30 random integer values, you define a `BinaryTree<Integer>` object that will store objects of type `Integer`. The following statement does this:

```
BinaryTree<Integer> tree = new BinaryTree<Integer>();
```

You then insert the integers into the binary tree in a loop:

```
for(int number:numbers) {
  tree.add(number);
}
```

The parameter type for the `add()` method will be type `Integer`, but autoboxing automatically takes care of converting your arguments of type `int` to objects of type `Integer`.

Calling the `sort()` method for the `BinaryTree` object, `values`, returns the objects from the tree contained in a `LinkedList` object:

```
LinkedList<Integer> values = tree.sort();
```

This creates a variable with the name `list` that is of type `LinkedList` from the `LinkedList<T>` generic type. This type that results from eliminating the parameters from the generic type is referred to as a **raw type**.

The class that corresponds to the raw type is produced by removing the type parameters from the generic type definition and replacing each instance of a type variable in the definition by the leftmost bound of its correspond type parameter. This process of mapping from a generic type to a non-generic type is called **type erasure** because all occurrences of the type variable are effectively erased from the generic class definition. A raw type exists as a consequence of implementing generic types using type erasure.

Since in the absence of any explicit type parameter bounds every type parameter `T` is implicitly bounded by type `Object`, all occurrences of `T` in a generic type definition will be replaced by `Object` to produce the raw type. This is important for interface types such as `Iterable<>` and `Comparable<>` in the standard packages. Interfaces in the standard packages that define methods are generally defined as generic types for maximum flexibility. When you implement such an interface in an ordinary class without specifying a type argument, your class is implementing the raw type, so the methods in the interface will be declared with parameters and/or return types of type `Object`.

Suppose you have specified that the type parameter `T` for a parameterized type is bounded by the type `Comparable<>`. This is the case for the `BinaryTree<>` type that you implemented earlier. In the raw type for the parameterized type, all occurrences of the type variable `T` will be replaced by `Comparable`. The raw type corresponding to `Comparable<>` will be produced by using type `Object` as the replacement for the type parameter because no parameter constraints are specified for the `Comparable<>` generic type. Thus for the `BinaryTree<>` type that you defined earlier, the raw type definition will be produced by replacing the type variable, `T`, in the definition of `BinaryTree<>` by `Comparable`. This may be what you want for a valid raw type in this case. The parameter type to the `add()` method will be `Comparable`, so you can pass an object of any class type that implements the `Comparable` interface to it. However, in other instances where methods with a return type are specified by a type parameter, you may want the raw type to be produced using `Object` as the upper bound for the type parameter. This applies to the serializable version of the `LinkedList<>` generic type where the bound on the type parameter is `Serializable`. It might be better to have the `getFirst()` and `getNext()` methods return a reference of type `Object` instead of type `Serializable`. You can accomplish this quite easily by simply defining the first bound for the type parameter as type `Object`, like this:

```
class LinkedList<T extends Object & Serializable> implements Serializable {
    // Class definition as before...
}
```

Now the leftmost bound for the type parameter is type `Object`, so the raw type will be produced by replacing the type variable `T` by `Object` in the generic type definition.

You can store a reference of any of the types produced from a generic type in a variable of the corresponding raw type. For example, you could write:

```
list = new LinkedList<String>();
```

However, this is legal for compatibility with code written before generic types were available in Java. Therefore, you should not regard it as part of your normal programming repertoire as it's an inherently risky practice.

Using Wildcards as Type Parameter Arguments

You express a particular type from the set defined by a generic type by supplying a type argument for each of its type parameters. For example, to specify the `BinaryTree<>` type that stores objects of type `String`, you specify the type argument as `String` — so the type is `BinaryTree<String>`. Instead of supplying a specific type as the type argument for a generic type, you can specify the argument as `?`, in which case you have specified the type argument as a **wildcard**. A wildcard type represents any class or interface type.

You can declare variables of a generic type using a wildcard type argument. For example:

```
BinaryTree<?> tree = new BinaryTree<Double>();
```

The `tree` variable is of type `BinaryTree<?>` so you can store a reference to any type of `BinaryTree<>` object in it. In this instance you have stored a reference to an object of type `BinaryTree<Double>`, but `BinaryTree<String>` or `BinaryTree<AnyType>` would be equally acceptable — as long as the type argument is not a primitive type. You can think of the use of a variable of a wildcard type as loosely paralleling the use of a variable of type `Object`. Because the `tree` variable type is the result of a wildcard type argument, the actual type of the reference stored is not known, so you cannot use this variable to call methods specific to the object that it references.

You can use a wildcard type argument to specify a method parameter type where there is no dependency in the code on the actual type argument. If you specify the type of a parameter to a method as `BinaryTree<?>`, then the method will accept an argument of type `BinaryTree<String>`, `BinaryTree<Double>`, or indeed any `BinaryTree<>` type. To make this clearer, let's consider a specific situation where you might use a wildcard as an argument for a method parameter of a generic type.

In the previous example, the `main()` method listed the objects in the `LinkedList<>` object that the `sort()` method returns by executing a specific loop for each of the two cases — `Integer` objects and `String` objects. You could write a static method that would list the items stored in a linked list, whatever they are. Here's how you could define such a method as a static member of the `TryBinaryTree` class:

```
public static void listAll(LinkedList<?> list) {
  for(Object obj : list) {
    System.out.println(obj);
  }
}
```

The parameter type for the `listAll()` method uses a wildcard specification instead of an explicit type argument. Thus, the method accepts an argument of any `LinkedList<>` type. Because every object will have a `toString()` method regardless of the actual type, the argument passed to `println()` in the body of the method will always be valid. Now you could list the integers in the `values` object of type `LinkedList<Integer>` with the statement:

```
listAll(values);
```

You could also list the contents of the `sortedWords` object of type `LinkedList<String>` with the statement:

```
      listAll(sortedWords);
```

You can plug these code fragments, including the definition of the method, of course, into the
TryBinaryTree class and recompile to see it working.

Try It Out   Using a Wildcard Type Argument

Here's a modified version of the previous example:

```
public class TryWildCard {
  public static void main(String[] args) {
    int[] numbers = new int[30];
    for(int i = 0 ; i<numbers.length ; i++) {
      numbers[i] = (int)(1000.0*Math.random());    // Random integers 0 to 999
    }
    // List starting integer values
    int count = 0;
    System.out.println("Original values are:");
    for(int number : numbers) {
      System.out.printf("%6d", number);
      if(++count%6 == 0) {
        System.out.println();
      }
    }

    // Create the tree and add the integers to it
    BinaryTree<Integer> tree = new BinaryTree<Integer>();
    for(int number:numbers) {
      tree.add(number);
    }

    // Get sorted values
    LinkedList<Integer> values = tree.sort();
    System.out.println("\nSorted values are:");
    listAll(values);

    // Create an array of words to be sorted
    String[] words = {"vacillate", "procrastinate", "arboreal",
                      "syzygy", "xenocracy", "zygote",
                      "mephitic", "soporific", "grisly", "gristly" };

    // List the words
    System.out.println("\nOriginal word sequence:");
    for(String word : words) {
      System.out.printf("%-15s", word);
        if(++count%5 == 0) {
          System.out.println();
        }
    }

    // Create the tree and insert the words
    BinaryTree<String> cache = new BinaryTree<String>();
    for(String word : words) {
      cache.add(word);
    }
```

```
      // Sort the words
      LinkedList<String> sortedWords = cache.sort();

      // List the sorted words
      System.out.println("\nSorted word sequence:");
      listAll(sortedWords);
    }

    // List the elements in any linked list
    public static void listAll(LinkedList<?> list) {
      for(Object obj : list) {
        System.out.println(obj);
      }
    }
  }
```

You should get essentially the same output as before except that the sorted data will be listed with each item on a separate line.

How It Works

You have a static method defined in the `TryWildcard` class that will list the elements in any `LinkedList<>` object. You use this to list the contents of objects of type `LinkedList<Integer>` and `LinkedList<String>`. The `listAll()` method relies on only the `toString()` method being implemented for the objects retrieved from the linked list, and this will be the case for any type of object because the `toString()` method will always be inherited from the `Object` class.

Constraints on a Wildcard

It may be the case that you'd like to limit a wildcard specification to some extent — after all, allowing any non-primitive type at all is an incredibly wide specification. You can explicitly constrain a wildcard specification. One possibility is to specify that it extends another type. This type of constraint is described as an **upper bound** of the wildcard type because it implies that any subclass of the type that the wildcard extends is acceptable, including the type itself, of course.

For example, suppose you wanted to implement a method that would write the objects stored in a `LinkedList<>` object to a file. A prerequisite would be that the objects in the list implement the `Serializable` interface, whatever type they are. You could define a static method to do this using a constraint on the wildcard type specification:

```
    public static void saveAll(LinkedList<? extends java.io.Serializable>  list) {
      // Serialize the objects from the list...
    }
```

The parameter to the `listAll()` method is of type:

```
    LinkedList<? extends java.io.Serializable>
```

This says that the argument to the `listAll()` method can be a linked list of objects of any type as long as they implement the `Serializable` interface. Knowing that the objects in the list implement the `Serializable` interface means that you can serialize them without knowing exactly what type they are.

You can just pass an object reference to the `writeObject()` method for the stream, and everything will be taken care of.

To make the upper bound for a wildcard type `Object` you just write it as `? extends Object`. You might think that specifying a wildcard with an upper bound that is type `Object` is stating the obvious and not a useful thing to do. However, it does have a very useful effect. It forces the specification to represent only class types, and not interface types, so you can use this when you want to specify any type, as long as it's a class type.

You can also constrain a wildcard type specification by specifying that it is a superclass of a given type. In this case you use the `super` keyword to define a **lower bound** for the wildcard. Here's an example:

```
public static void analyze(LinkedList<? super MyClass> list) {
   // Code to do whatever with the list...
}
```

In this case you are saying that the elements in the list that is passed as the argument to the `analyze()` method must be of type `MyClass`, or of a type that `MyClass` extends or implements. This should ring a bell in relation to the `BinaryTree<>` generic type from earlier in this chapter. A wildcard that is a superclass of a given type sounds like a good candidate for what you were looking for to make the `BinaryTree<>` type more flexible, and it would accept a type argument that possibly inherited an implementation of the `Comparable<>` interface. You could modify the definition to the following to allow this:

```
public class BinaryTree<T extends Comparable<? super T>> {
   // Details exactly as before...
}
```

The only change you have made to the `BinaryTree<>` type definition is that you've changed the type parameter for the `Comparable<>` interface to a wildcard that is a superclass of `T`, the type parameter for `BinaryTree<>`. The effect is to allow any type argument to be accepted that implements the `Comparable<>` interface or inherits an implementation of it. This should allow the `BinaryTree<>` type to be used with classes such as the `Manager` class, which could not be used as a type argument in the previous `BinaryTree<>` implementation. Let's prove it.

Try It Out   **A More Flexible Binary Tree**

You'll need the definition of the `Person` and `Manager` classes that you saw earlier. The `Person` class definition is:

```
public class Person implements Comparable<Person> {
  public Person(String name) {
    this.name = name;
  }

  public int compareTo(Person person) {
    if( person == this) {
      return 0;
    }
    return this.name.compareTo(person.name);
  }
```

```
   public String toString() {
      return name;
   }

   protected String name;
}
```

The `Manager` class definition is:

```
public class Manager extends Person {
   public Manager(String name, int level) {
      super(name);
      this.level = level;
   }

   public String toString() {
      return "Manager "+ super.toString() + " level: " + level;
   }

   protected int level;
}
```

You can put the `Person` and `Manager` class definitions in the same directory as the following source file, which stores `Manager` objects in a `BinaryTree<Manager>` object:

```
public class TryFlexibleBinaryTree {
   public static void main(String[] args) {

      BinaryTree<Manager> people = new BinaryTree<Manager>();
      Manager[] managers = { new Manager("Jane", 1), new Manager("Joe", 3),
                             new Manager("Freda", 3), new Manager("Albert", 2)};
      for(Manager manager: managers){
         people.add(manager);
         System.out.println("Added "+ manager);
      }
      System.out.println();
      listAll(people.sort());
   }

   // List the elements in any linked list
   public static void listAll(LinkedList<?> list) {
      for(Object obj : list) {
         System.out.println(obj);
      }
   }
}
```

You'll also need the modified version of `BinaryTree<>` and the source file for `LinkedList<>`. The output should be:

```
Added Manager Jane level: 1
Added Manager Joe level: 3
Added Manager Freda level: 3
Added Manager Albert level: 2
```

```
Manager Albert level: 2
Manager Freda level: 3
Manager Jane level: 1
Manager Joe level: 3
```

How It Works

The output demonstrates that the `BinaryTree<>` generic type works with a type argument that implements `Comparable<>` even when the implementation is inherited. The use of a wildcard with a lower bound as the parameter for the constraint adds the flexibility to allow inherited implementations of the constraint type. This is usually what you will want for any constraint on a type argument for a parameterized type, so you should always use this pattern with constraints for all your generic types unless you have a reason not to.

More on the Class Class

I mentioned back in Chapter 6 that the `Class` class is not an ordinary class type; rather, it's defined as a parameterized type. The `Class<>` object for a given type such as `Person` or `java.lang.String` in your application is produced by supplying the type as the argument for the generic type parameter, so of type `Class<Person>` and `Class<java.lang.String>` in these two instances. Because these class types are produced from a generic type, many of the methods have parameters or return types that are specifically the type argument — `Person` or `java.lang.String` in the two examples I've cited.

The `Class<>` type defines a lot of methods, but I'll mention only a few of them here as their application is beyond the scope of this book. You'll probably find that the primary use you have for `Class<>` is obtaining the class of an object by calling the `getClass()` method for the object. However, you also get a number of other useful methods with an object of a `Class<>` type:

Method	Purpose
`forName()`	This is a static method that you can use to get the `Class<>` object for a known class or interface type. You pass the fully qualified name of the type as a `String` object to this method, and it returns a `Class<>` object (e.g., `Class<String>`) for the type that has the name you have supplied. If no class or interface of the type you specify exists, a `ClassNotFoundException` exception is thrown.
`newInstance()`	This method calls the default constructor for the class represented by the current `Class<>` object and returns a new object of that type. When things don't work as they should, this method can throw exceptions of type `IllegalAccessException` if the class or its no-arg constructor is not accessible or of type `InstantiationsException` if the `Class<>` object represents an abstract class, an interface, an array type, a primitive type, or void, or if the class does not have a no-arg constructor. It can also throw an exception of type `ExceptionInitializerError` if the object initialization fails, or of `SecurityException` if no permission for creating the new object exists.

Table continued on following page

Method	Purpose
getSuperclass()	This method returns a Class<> object for the superclass of the class represented by the current Class<> object. Where the type represented is a class type that is not a derived class or is an array type, the method will return a Class<> object for the Object class. If the current Class<> object represents the Object class or a primitive type or void, then null is returned.
isInterface()	This method returns true if the current Class<> object represents an interface.
getInterfaces()	This method returns an array of type Class[] containing objects that represent the interfaces implemented by the class or interface type corresponding to the current Class<> object. If the class or interface does not implement any interfaces, the array that is returned will have a length of 0.
toString()	This method returns a String object representing the current Class object.

Because Class<> is a generic type, you can define a method in a generic type definition with a parameter of type Class<T>. This is helpful when you need to be able to create an object of type T. You can't call a T class constructor because you don't know what type T is, but you can create an object of type T by calling the newInstance() method for an object of type Class<T>. For example:

```
public class AGenericType<T> {

   public T makeObject(Class<T> cobj) {
     T obj = cobj.newInstance();
     // Set the values of fields in obj...
     return obj;
   }

   // Other code for the definition...
}
```

The type argument will result in a specific class<T> type for the cobj parameter to the makeObject() method, so given a Class<T> object, you can always create an object of type T at run time even though at compile time type T is unknown.

As I said, the preceding list of methods for the Class<> type is not exhaustive. A number of other methods defined in the class enable you to find out details of the contents of a class — the fields, the public methods defined in the class, or even classes that are defined within the class. If you need this kind of capability, you can find out more by browsing the API documentation relating to the Class<> generic type that comes with the JDK.

Arrays and Parameterized Types

Arrays of elements that are of a specific type produced from a generic type are not allowed. For example, although it looks quite reasonable, the following statement is not permitted and will result in a compiler error message:

```
LinkedList<String>[] lists = new LinkedList<String>[10];    // Will not compile!!!
```

Although you can declare a field in a generic type by specifying the type using a type variable, you are not allowed to create arrays of elements using a type variable. For example, you can define a data member like this:

```
public class MyType<T> {
   // The methods and data members of the type...
   private T[] data;                                        // This is OK
}
```

While defining the data field as being of type T[] is legal and will compile, the following is not legal and will not compile:

```
public class MyType<T> {
   // Constructor
   public MyType() {
      data = new T[10];                                     // Not allowed!!
   }

   // The methods and data members of the type...
   private T[] data;                                        // This is OK
}
```

In the constructor you are attempting to create an array of elements of the type given by the type variable T, and this is not permitted.

However, you can define arrays of elements of a generic type where the element type is the result of an unbounded wildcard type argument. For example, you can define the following array:

```
LinkedList<?>[] lists = new LinkedList<?>[10];              // OK
```

Each element in the array can store a reference to any specific LinkedList<> type, and they could all be different types. Just so that you can believe it, let's try it.

Try It Out   A Wildcard Array

You can modify the previous TryWildcard example to demonstrate using a wildcard type in an array:

```
public class TryWildCardArray {
  public static void main(String[] args) {
    BinaryTree<?>[] trees = {new BinaryTree<Integer>(), new BinaryTree<String>()};
    LinkedList<?>[] lists = new LinkedList<?>[trees.length];

    int[] numbers = new int[30];
    for(int i = 0 ; i<numbers.length ; i++) {
      numbers[i] = (int)(1000.0*Math.random());    // Random integers 0 to 999
    }
    // List starting integer values
    int count = 0;
    System.out.println("Original values are:");
    for(int number : numbers) {
```

```
      System.out.printf("%6d", number);
      if(++count%6 == 0) {
        System.out.println();
      }
    }

    // Add the integers to first tree
    for(int number:numbers) {
      ((BinaryTree<Integer>)trees[0]).add(number);
    }

    // Create an array of words to be sorted
    String[] words = {"vacillate", "procrastinate", "arboreal", "syzygy",
                      "xenocracy", "zygote", "mephitic", "soporific",
                      "grisly", "gristly" };

    // List the words
    System.out.println("\nOriginal word sequence:");
    for(String word : words) {
      System.out.printf("%-15s", word);
        if(++count%5 == 0) {
          System.out.println();
        }
    }

    // Insert the words into second tree
    for(String word : words) {
      ((BinaryTree<String>)trees[1]).add(word);
    }

    // Sort the values in both trees
    for(int i = 0 ; i<lists.length ; i++){
    lists[i] = trees[i].sort();
  }

    // List the sorted values from both trees
    for(LinkedList<?> list : lists){
      System.out.println("\nSorted results:");
      listAll(list);
    }
  }

  // List the elements in any linked list
  public static void listAll(LinkedList<?> list) {
    for(Object obj : list) {
      System.out.println(obj);
    }
  }
}
```

You should copy the `BinaryTree.java` and `LinkedList.java` source files to the directory containing `TryWildcardArray.java`. When you compile this program, you will get two warnings from the compiler from the statements that involve explicit casts. The output will be similar to that from the previous example. The sorted lists of values will be output one value per line because that's how the `listAll()` method displays them.

How It Works

You create two array using wildcard type specifications:

```
BinaryTree<?>[] trees = {new BinaryTree<Integer>(), new BinaryTree<String>()};
LinkedList<?>[] lists = new LinkedList<?>[trees.length];
```

The length of the `trees` array is determined by the number of values in the initializing list — two in this case. You can see that you can happily initialize the array with references to objects of different specific types as long as they are produced from the generic type `BinarayTree<>`. The `lists` array is of type `LinkedList<?>[]` and is defined as having the same number of elements as the `trees` array. You'll store the `LinkedList<>` references returned by the `sort()` method in these elements eventually.

After creating the array of random integer values, you add them to a binary tree in a loop:

```
for(int number:numbers) {
  ((BinaryTree<Integer>)trees[0]).add(number);
}
```

You can't call the `add()` method while the reference stored in `trees[0]` is of type `BinaryTree<?>` because the compiler cannot decide on the form of the `add()` method without having a specific type argument available. The type argument determines the parameter type for the method. Without that there's no way to decide how the argument to the method is to be passed. You must cast the reference to a specific type, `BinaryTree<Integer>` in this case, to allow the `add()` method for that type to be called. You get a warning from the compiler at this point because the compiler cannot verify that this cast is valid. If it isn't, calling the `add()` method will cause an exception to be thrown at run time so you have to accept responsibility for it. Actually, it works, and the integer values will be converted automatically to type `Integer`.

You then create an array of `String` objects as you did in the previous version and add these to the second binary tree:

```
for(String word : words) {
  ((BinaryTree<String>)trees[1]).add(word);
}
```

Again it is necessary to cast the reference in `trees[1]` to type `BinaryTree<String>`, and this results in the second warning from the compiler.

You sort the contents of the binary trees in another loop:

```
for(int i = 0 ; i<lists.length ; i++){
lists[i] = trees[i].sort();
```

Sorting a tree is not dependent on a specific type. You can call the `sort()` method without a cast because the operation does not depend on a type argument. The method returns a `LinkedList<>` reference of a specific type, `LinkedList<Integer>` in the first call and `LinkedList<String>` in the second, but the `lists` array is of type `LinkedList<?>` so you can store references of any `LinkedList<>` type in it.

You list the sorted values stored in the lists that result from calls to the `sort()` method for the `BinaryTree<>` objects in a loop:

```
for(LinkedList<?> list : lists){
  System.out.println("\nSorted results:");
  listAll(list);
}
```

The loop variable is of a wildcard type, `LinkedList<?>`, and it iterates over the elements in the `lists` array. This is fine here because the static `listAll()` method does not require a particular type of `LinkedList<>` reference as the argument; it works for `LinkedList` types created from the `LinkedList<>` generic type using any type argument.

Note that you can create arrays of a generic type only using a wildcard specification that is unbounded. If you specify an upper or lower bound for a wildcard type argument when defining an array type, it will be flagged by the compiler as an error.

Parameterized Methods

You can define a method with its own independent set of one or more type parameters, in which case you have a **parameterized method**, which is also referred to as a **generic method**. You can have parameterized methods in an ordinary class. Methods within a generic type definition can also have independent parameters.

You could modify the `listAll()` method that you defined in the `TryWildcardArray` class in the previous example so that it is a parameterized method. Here's how that would look:

```
public static <T> void listAll(LinkedList<T> list) {
  for(T obj : list) {
    System.out.println(obj);
  }
}
```

The `<T>` following the `public` and `static` keywords is the type parameter list for the generic method. Here you have only one type parameter, `T`, but you could have more. The type parameter list for a generic method always appears between angled brackets and should follow any modifiers such as `public` and `static`, as you have here, and should precede the return type.

Not that calling this version of the `listAll()` method does not require the type argument to be supplied explicitly. The type argument will be deduced from the parameter type supplied when the method is called. If you replace the `listAll()` code in the previous example by the version here, you should find that it works just as well. No other changes to the program are necessary to make use of it.

You could also gain some advantage by using parameterized methods in the `BinaryTree<>` type definition. With the present version of this generic type, the `add()` method accepts an argument of type `T`, which is the type argument. In general, you might want to allow subclasses of T to be added to a `BinaryTree<T>` object. Harking back to the `Person` and `Manager` classes you saw earlier, it might well be the case that you would want to add `Manager` objects and objects of any subclass of `Person` to a `BinaryTree<Person>` container. You could accommodate this by redefining the `add()` method in the class as an independently parameterized method:

```
public <E extends T> void add(E value) {
    if(root == null) {                  // If there's no root node
        root = new Node(value);         // store it in the root
    } else {                            // Otherwise...
        add(value, root);               // add it recursively
    }
}
```

Now the method has an independent parameter, E. This parameter has an upper bound, which in this case is the type variable for the `BinaryTree<>` type. Thus, you are saying here that the `add()` method accepts an argument of any type that is type T, or a subclass of T. This clearly adds flexibility to the use of `BinaryTree<>` objects. You have no need to change the body of the method in this case. All the flexibility is provided simply by the way you have defined the method parameter.

Of course, you must also alter the other version of the `add()` method that is defined in `BinaryTree<>` to have an independent parameter:

```
private <E extends T> void add(E value, Node node) {
    int comparison = node.obj.compareTo(value);
    if(comparison == 0) {                    // If it is equal to the current node
        ++node.count;                        // just increment the count
        return;
    }
    if(comparison > 0) {                     // If it's less than the current node
        if(node.left == null) {              // and the left child node is not null
            node.left = new Node(value);     // Store it as the left child node
        } else {                             // Otherwise...
            add(value, node.left);           // ...add it to the left node
        }
    } else {                                 // It must be greater than the current node
        if(node.right == null) {             // so it must go to the right...
            node.right = new Node(value);
        } else {
            add(value, node.right);
        }
    }
}
```

Although you've used the same identifier, E, as the type parameter for this method, it has nothing to do with the E you used as the type parameter for the previous version of `add()`. The scope of a parameter for a method is just the method itself, so the two Es are quite separate and independent of one another. You could use K or some other parameter name here if you want to make it absolutely obvious.

Let's give it a whirl.

Try It Out   Using Parameterized Methods

First, create a directory to hold the source files for this example and copy the files containing the Person and Manager class definitions to it. You'll also need the `BinaryTree.java` file containing the version with the parameterized `add()` methods and the source file for the `LinkedList<>` generic type. Here's the program to make use of these:

```
public class TryParameterizedMethods {
  public static void main(String[] args) {

    BinaryTree<Person> people = new BinaryTree<Person>();

    // Create and add some Manager objects
    Manager[] managers = { new Manager("Jane",1), new Manager("Joe",3),
                                         new Manager("Freda",3)};

    for(Manager manager : managers){
      people.add(manager);
    }

    // Create and add some Person objects objects
    Person[] persons = {new Person("Will"), new Person("Ann"), new Person("Mary"),
                        new Person("Tina"), new Person("Stan")};
    for(Person person : persons) {
      people.add(person);
    }

    listAll(people.sort());  // List the sorted contents of the tree
  }

  // Parameterized method to list the elements in any linked list
  public static <T> void listAll(LinkedList<T> list) {
    for(T obj : list) {
      System.out.println(obj);
    }
  }
}
```

The output should be as follows:

```
Ann
Manager Freda level: 3
Manager Jane level: 1
Manager Joe level: 3
Mary
Stan
Tina
Will
```

How It Works

You create an object of a `BinaryTree` type that will store `Person` objects:

```
BinaryTree<Person> people = new BinaryTree<Person>();
```

You then define an array of `Manager` objects and add those to the people binary tree:

```
Manager[] managers = { new Manager("Jane",1), new Manager("Joe",3),
                                     new Manager("Freda",3)};
for(Manager manager : managers){
  people.add(manager);
}
```

The `add()` method is defined as a parameterized method in the `BinaryTree<>` type definition, where the method's parameter, `E`, has an upper bound that is the type variable for the `BinaryTree<>` type. This enables the `add()` method to accept arguments that are of a type that can be type `Person` or any subclass of `Person`. You defined the `Manager` class with `Person` as the base class so the `add()` method happily accepts arguments of type `Manager`.

Just to demonstrate that you can, you create an array of `Person` objects and add those to the `people` binary tree:

```
Person[] persons = {new Person("Will"), new Person("Ann"), new Person("Mary"),
                    new Person("Tina"), new Person("Stan")};
for(Person person : persons) {
  people.add(person);
}
```

You now have a mix of `Person` and `Manager` objects in the binary tree. You list the contents of the binary tree in ascending alphabetical order by calling the parameterized `listAll()` method that you defined as a static member of the `TryParameterizedMethods` class:

```
listAll(people.sort());   // List the sorted contents of the tree
```

The argument to the `listAll()` method is of type `BinaryTree<Person>`, so the compiler supplies `Person` as the type argument to the method. This means that within the method, the loop iterates over an array of `Person` references using a loop variable of type `Person`. The output demonstrates that the mix of `Person` and `Manager` objects were added to the binary tree correctly and are displayed in the correct sequence.

Generic Constructors

A constructor is a specialized kind of method and you can define class constructors with their own independent parameters. You can define parameterized constructors for both ordinary classes and generic class types. Let's take an example.

Suppose you want to add a constructor to the `BinaryTree<>` type definition that will accept an argument that is an array of items to be added to the binary tree. In this case, defining the constructor as a parameterized method gives you the same flexibility you have with the `add()` method. Here's how the constructor definition looks:

```
public <E extends T> BinaryTree(E[] items) {
  for(E item : items) {
    add(item);
  }
}
```

The constructor parameter is `E`. You have defined this with an upper bound of `T`, so the argument to the constructor can be an array of elements of the type specified by the type variable `T` or any subclass of `T`. For example, if you define a binary tree of type `BinaryTree<Person>`, then you can pass an array to the constructor with elements of type `Person` or any type that is a subclass of `Person`.

Let's try it.

595

Try It Out   Using a Parameterized Constructor

The definition of `BinaryTree<>` will now be as follows:

```java
public class BinaryTree<T extends Comparable<T>> {

  // No-arg constructor
  public BinaryTree() {}

  // Parameterized constructor
  public <E extends T> BinaryTree(E[] items) {
    for(E item : items) {
      add(item);
    }
  }

  // Add a value to the tree
  public <E extends T> void add(E value) {
    if(root == null) {                    // If there's no root node
      root = new Node(value);             // store it in the root
    } else {                              // Otherwise...
      add(value, root);                   // add it recursively
    }
  }

  // Recursive insertion of an object
  private <E extends T> void add(E value, Node node) {
    int comparison = node.obj.compareTo(value);
    if(comparison == 0) {                 // If it is equal to the current node
      ++node.count;                       // just increment the count
      return;
    }
    if(comparison > 0) {                  // If it's less than the current node
      if(node.left == null) {             // and the left child node is not null
        node.left = new Node(value);      // Store it as the left child node
      } else {                            // Otherwise...
        add(value, node.left);            // ...add it to the left node
      }
    } else {                              // It must be greater than the current node
      if(node.right == null) {            // so it must go to the right...
        node.right = new Node(value);
      } else {
        add(value, node.right);
      }
    }
  }

  // Create a list containing the values from the tree in sequence
  public LinkedList<T> sort() {
    treeSort(root);                                  // Sort the objects into the list
    return values;
  }
```

```
      // Extract the tree nodes in sequence
      private void treeSort(Node node) {
        if(node != null) {                      // If the node isn't null
          treeSort(node.left);                  // process its left child

          // List the duplicate objects for the current node
          for(int i = 0 ; i<node.count ; i++) {
            values.addItem(node.obj);
          }
          treeSort(node.right);                 // Now process the right child
        }
      }

      LinkedList<T> values = new LinkedList<T>();    // Stores sorted values
      private Node root;                             // The root node

      // Private inner class defining nodes
      private class Node {
        Node(T value) {
          obj = value;
          count = 1;
        }

        T obj;                                  // Object stored in the node
        int count;                              // Count of identical nodes
        Node left;                              // The left child node
        Node right;                             // The right child node
      }
    }
```

The only changes from the previous version are the addition of the constructor that accepts an array as an argument and the definition of the no-arg constructor, which is not supplied by the compiler when you explicitly define a constructor of your own. Put this source file in a new directory and copy the LinkedList.java, Person.java, and Manager.java files from the previous example to this directory.

You can add the following source file to try out the parameterized constructor:

```
public class TryParameterizedConstructor {
  public static void main(String[] args) {
    Manager[] managers = {new Manager("Jane",1), new Manager("Joe",3),
                          new Manager("Freda",3), new Manager("Bert", 2),
                          new Manager("Ann", 2),new Manager("Dave", 2)};
    BinaryTree<Person> people = new BinaryTree<Person>(managers);
    listAll(people.sort());
  }

  // List the elements in any linked list
  public static <T> void listAll(LinkedList<T> list) {
    for(T obj : list) {
      System.out.println(obj);
    }
  }
}
```

The output will be:

```
Manager Ann level: 2
Manager Bert level: 2
Manager Dave level: 2
Manager Freda level: 3
Manager Jane level: 1
Manager Joe level: 3
```

How It Works

After you create an array of `Manager` objects you create a `BinaryTree<Person>` object with the contents of the `managers` array as the initial contents of the binary tree:

```
BinaryTree<Person> people = new BinaryTree<Person>(managers);
```

Because the constructor has an independent parameter and that parameter has the type variable for the `BinaryTree<>` type as its upper bound, the constructor accepts the `managers` array as the argument because it is a subclass of `Person`, the type argument that you use to specify the type of the binary tree object.

The output shows that the array elements were added to the binary tree and were successfully extracted and stored in sequence in a linked list by the `sort()` method.

Parameterized Types and Inheritance

You can define a class as a subclass of a class type that is an instance of a generic type. For example, you could derive a new class from type `LinkedList<Person>` or from type `BinaryTree<String>`. Methods and fields will be inherited from the base class in the usual way. However, you can encounter complications because of the way the compiler translates methods that involve type arguments into bytecodes, so let's first understand that process.

Each method that involves parameters and/or the return value type specified by a type argument is translated by the compiler to a method with the same name, but with the type of each parameter whose type is a type variable replaced by its leftmost bound. Where the type of the return value is a type variable, then that, too, is replaced by its leftmost bound. Casts are inserted in the body of the translated method where necessary to produce the actual types required. You'll find that an example will help clarify this.

Earlier you saw a version of the `LinkedList<>` type defined as:

```
public LinkedList<T extends Object & Serializable> {
  public void addItem(T item) {
    // Code for the method...
  }

  // More code for the type definition...
}
```

If you define an object of type `LinkedList<String>`, notionally the `addItem()` method for the object is like this:

```
         public void addItem(String item) {
            // Code for the method...
         }
```

However, the compiler will translate the `addItem()` method to the following:

```
         public void addItem(Object item) {
            // Code for the method...
            // References to fields originally of type T will be cast to type String
            // as will values returned by method calls originally of type T.
         }
```

Normally you don't need to be aware of this. However, suppose you derive a new class from type `LinkedList<String>`:

```
      public class SpecialList extends LinkedList<String> {

         // Override base class version of addItem() method
         public void addItem(String item) {
            // New code for the method...
         }

         // Rest of the code for SpecialList...
      }
```

Here you are quite correctly overriding the version of `addItem()` that your class inherits from `LinkedList<String>`. Because the compiler chooses to compile the method to bytecodes with a different signature, as it is your method doesn't override the base class at all. The base class method parameter will be of type `Object`, whereas the parameter for your version of the method is of type `String`. To fix the problem the compiler will create a **bridge method** in your derived `SpecialList` class that looks like this:

```
      public void addItem(Object item) {
         addItem((String)item);                 // Call derived class version
      }
```

The effect of the bridge method is to convert any calls to the inherited version of `addItem()` to a call to your version, thus making your override of the base class method effective.

However, the approach adopted by the compiler has implications for you. You must take care not to define methods in your derived class that have the same signature as an inherited method. Since the compiler changes the parameter types and return types involving type variables to their bounds, you must consider the inherited methods in these terms when you are defining your derived class methods. If a method in a class that you have derived from a generic type has the same signature as the erasure of an inherited method, your code will not compile.

Summary

In this chapter you have learned the essentials of how generic types are defined and used. In the next chapter you'll see how the `java.util` package provides you with an extensive range of standard generic types you can use in your programs. The important points you have seen in this chapter include:

❏ A generic type, which is also referred to as a parameterized type, defines a family of classes or interfaces using one or more type parameters. Container classes are typically defined as generic types.

❏ The argument you supply for a type parameter can be a class type or an interface type. It cannot be a primitive type.

❏ You can limit the scope of type arguments for a given type parameter by specifying one or more bounds for the parameter using the extends keyword. The first bound can be a class or interface type; the second and subsequent bounds must be interface types.

❏ You define a specific type from a generic type by supplying a type argument for each type parameter.

❏ All types produced from a given generic type share the same run-time type.

❏ A parameterized method defines a family of methods using one or more independent type parameters.

❏ A parameterized method can be a member of an ordinary class type or a generic type.

❏ You can use wildcards as type arguments in a parameterized type in situations where there is no dependency on a specific type.

❏ You can constrain a wildcard type argument with either an upper bound that you specify using the extends keyword or with a lower bound that you specify using the super keyword.

Exercises

You can download the source code for the examples in the book and the solutions to the following exercises from http://www.wrox.com.

1. A stack is a container that stores objects in a manner indicated by its name — in a vertical stack where only the object at the top of the stack is accessible. It works rather like a sprung stack of plates in a cafeteria. Only the top plate is at counter level and, therefore, is the only one you can access. When you add a plate to the stack, the existing plates are pushed down so the new plate is now the one that you can access. Define a generic Stack<> type with a method push() that adds the object that is passed as an argument to the top of the stack, and with a method pop() that removes and returns the object that is currently at the top of the stack. The pop() method should return null when the stack is empty. Demonstrate the operation of your Stack<> implementation by storing and retrieving 10 strings and 10 Double objects in stacks of a suitable type.

2. Implement and demonstrate a listAll() method in the Stack<> class definition that will list the objects in the stack.

3. Modify your Stack<> type to make it serializable. Demonstrate that this is the case by creating a Stack<String> object and adding 10 strings to it, then serializing and deserializing the Stack<String> object, and listing the contents of the deserialized stack.

The Collections Framework

In this chapter you'll look at the Java collections framework, which consists of generic types that represent sets of collection classes. These generic types are defined in the `java.util` package, and they provide you with a variety of ways for structuring and managing collections of objects in your programs. In particular, the collection types enable you to deal with situations where you don't know in advance how many objects you'll need to store, or where you need a bit more flexibility in the way in which you access an object from a collection than the indexing mechanism provided by an array.

In this chapter you will learn:

- ❑ What sets, sequences, and maps are, and how they work

- ❑ What a `Vector<T>` collection object is and how to use `Vector<T>` objects in your programs

- ❑ How to manage `Vector<T>` objects so that storing and retrieving elements is typesafe

- ❑ What a `Stack<T>` collection is and how you use it

- ❑ How you use the `LinkedList<T>` collections

- ❑ How you store and retrieve objects in a hash table represented by a `HashMap<K,V>` object

- ❑ How you can generate hashcodes for your own class objects

Understanding the Collections Framework

The Java collections framework is a set of generic types that you use to create **collection classes** that support various ways for you to store and manage objects of any kind in memory. As I'm sure you appreciate from the previous chapter, a collection class is simply a class that organizes a set of objects of a given type in a particular way, such as in a linked list or a pushdown stack. The majority of types that make up the collections framework are defined in the `java.util` package.

Using a generic type for your collections of objects means that you get static checking by the compiler for whatever types of objects you want to manage. This ensures that you do not inadvertently attempt to store objects of the wrong type in a collection. The collections framework includes a professional implementation of a generic type that implements a linked list, which is vastly superior to the linked list that you took so much trouble to develop for yourself first as an ordinary class back in Chapter 6, and later as a generic type in Chapter 13. However, the effort wasn't entirely wasted as you now have a good idea of how linked lists work and how generic types are defined.

You'll find that the collections framework is a major asset in most of your programs. When you want an array that automatically expands to accommodate however many objects you throw into it, or you need to be able to store and retrieve an object based on what it is rather than using an index or a sequence number, then look no further. You get all this and more in the generic types implemented within the collections framework.

The collections framework involves too much for me to discuss it in complete detail, but you'll be looking at how you can apply some representative examples of collections that you're likely to need most often. You'll be exploring the capabilities provided by the following generic types in detail:

Generic Class/Interface Type	Description
The `Iterator<T>` interface type	Declares methods for iterating through elements of a collection, one at a time. You met this interface in the previous chapter.
The `Vector<T>` type	Supports an array-like structure for storing any type of object. The number of objects that you can store in a `Vector<T>` object increases automatically as necessary.
The `Stack<T>` type	Supports the storage of any type of object in a pushdown stack.
The `LinkedList<T>` type	Supports the storage of any type of object in a doubly-linked list, which is a list that you can iterate though forwards or backwards.
The `HashMap<K,V>` type	Supports the storage of an object of type `V` in a hash table, sometimes called a map. The object is stored using an associated key object of type `K`. To retrieve an object you just supply its associated key.

I'll start by looking in general terms at various possible types of collections for objects.

Collections of Objects

In Chapter 13 you put together a generic type that defined a linked list. An object of type `LinkedList<T>` represented an example of a **collection** of objects of type `T`, where `T` could be any class or interface type. A **collection** is the term used to describe any object that represents a set of objects grouped together and organized in a particular way in memory. A class that defines collection objects is often referred to as a **container class**. A linked list is just one of a number of ways of organizing objects together in a collection.

There are three main types of collections that organize objects in different ways, called **sets**, **sequences**, and **maps**. Let's first get an understanding of how these three types of collections work in principle and then come back to look at the generic types that implement versions of these. One point I'd like to emphasize about the following discussion is that when I talk about a collection of objects, I mean a collection of *references* to objects. In Java, collections store references only — the objects themselves are external to the collection.

Sets

A **set** is probably the simplest kind of collection you can have. Here the objects are not ordered in any particular way at all, and objects are simply added to the set without any control over where they go. It's a bit like putting things in your pocket — you just put things in and they rattle around inside your pocket in no particular order. Figure 14-1 illustrates the idea of a set.

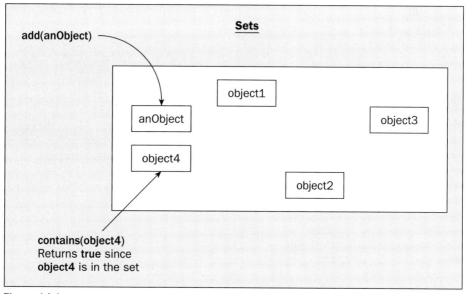

Figure 14-1

You can add objects to a set and iterate over all the objects in a set. You can also check whether a given object is a member of the set or not. For this reason you cannot have duplicate objects in a set — each object in the set must be unique. Of course, you can also remove a given object from a set, but only if you know what the object is in the first place — in other words, if you have a reference to the object in the set.

There are variations on the basic set that I have described here. For example, sets can be ordered, so objects added to a set will be inserted into a sequence of objects ordered according to some criterion of comparison. Such sets require that the objects to be stored are of a class type that defines methods suitable for comparing the objects.

Sequences

The linked list that you have already explored to some extent is an example of a more general type of collection called a **sequence**. A primary characteristic of a sequence is that the objects are stored in a linear fashion, not necessarily in any particular order, but organized in an arbitrary fixed sequence with a beginning and an end. This contrasts with the set discussed in the previous section, where there is no order at all. An ordinary array is basically another example of a sequence, but is much more limited than the equivalent collection because it holds a fixed number of elements.

Collections generally have the capability to expand to accommodate as many elements as necessary. The Vector<T> type, for example, is an example of a sequence that provides similar functionality to an array, but also has the capability to accommodate as many new elements as you wish to add to it. Figure 14-2 illustrates the organization of objects in the various types of sequence collections that you have available.

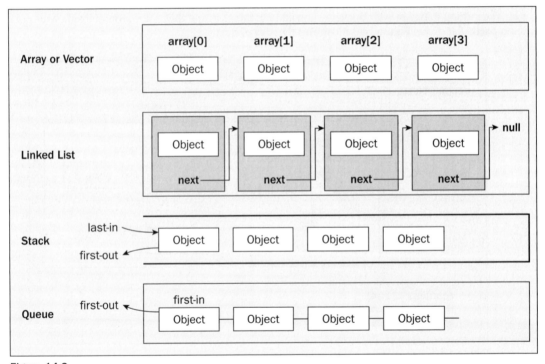

Figure 14-2

Because a sequence is linear, you will be able to add a new object only at the beginning or at the end, or insert a new object following a given object position in the sequence—after the fifth, say. Generally, you can retrieve an object from a sequence in several ways. You can select the first or the last; you can get the object at a given position—as in indexing an array; or you can search for an object identical to a given object by checking all the objects in the sequence either backwards or forwards. You can also iterate through the sequence backwards or forwards accessing each object in turn. You didn't implement all these capabilities in the linked list class in Chapter 6, but you could have.

You have essentially the same options for deleting objects from a sequence as you have for retrieving them; that is, you can remove the first or the last, you can delete the object at a particular position in the sequence, or you can remove an object that is equal to a given object. Sequences have the facility to store several copies of the same object at different places in the sequence. This is not true of all types of collections, as you already know from the outline of a set in the previous section.

A **stack**, which is a last-in, first-out (LIFO) storage mechanism, is also considered to be a sequence, as is a **queue**, which is usually a first-in, first-out (FIFO) mechanism. As you'll see, the Java collections framework implements a queue as a **priority queue** in which elements in the queue are ordered, which implies that FIFO won't apply in general. The elements are in ascending sequence from the head of the queue so it's more a case of "lowest in, first out." It's easy to see that a linked list can act as a stack, since using the methods to add and remove objects at the end of a list makes the list operate as a stack. Similarly, only adding objects by using the method to add an object to the end of a linked list, and only retrieving objects from the head of the list, makes it operate as a FIFO queue.

In the Java collections framework, types that define sequences are subdivided into two subgroups, **lists** and **queues**. Vectors, linked lists, and stacks are all lists.

Maps

A **map** is rather different from a set or a sequence collection because each entry involves a pair of objects. A map is also referred to sometimes as a **dictionary** because of the way it works. Each object that is stored in a map has an associated **key** object, and the object and its key are stored together as a pair. The key determines where the object is stored in the map, and when you want to retrieve an object, you must supply the appropriate key — so it acts as the equivalent of a word that you look up in a regular dictionary. Figure 14-3 shows how a map works.

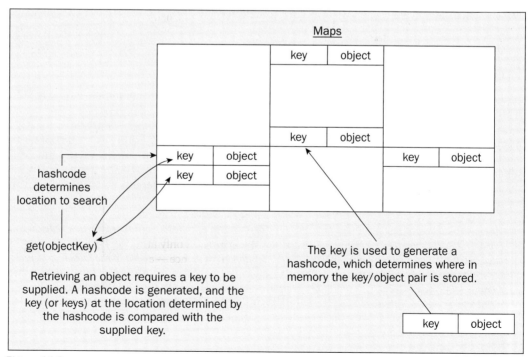

Figure 14-3

A key can be any kind of object that you want to use to reference the object stored. Because the key has to uniquely identify the object, all the keys in a map must be different. To put this in context, suppose you were creating a program to provide an address book. You might store all the details of each person — their name, address, phone number, or whatever — in a single object of type Entry perhaps, and store a reference to the object in a map. The key is the mechanism for retrieving objects, so assuming that all names are different, a person's name would be a natural choice for the key. Thus the entries in the map in this case would be Name/Entry pairs. You would supply a Name object as the key, and get back the Entry object corresponding to the key, which might encapsulate data such as the address and/or the phone number. You might well have another map in this application where entries were keyed on the phone number. Then you could retrieve an entry corresponding to a given number. Of course, in practice, names are not unique — hence, the invention of such delightful attachments to the person as social security numbers.

Hashing

Where a key/object pair is stored in a map is determined from the key by a process known as **hashing**. Hashing processes the key object to produce an integer value called a **hashcode**. The hashCode() method that is defined in the Object class produces a hashcode of type int for an object. The hashcode is typically used to calculate an offset from the start of the memory that has been allocated within the map for storing objects, and the offset determines the location where the key/object pair is to be stored. Ideally the hashing process should result in values that are uniformly distributed within a given range, and every key should produce a different hashcode. In general, this may not be the case. However, there are ways of dealing with hashcodes that don't turn out to be ideal, so it is not a problem. The implementations for map collections usually have provision for dealing with the situation where two or more different key objects produce the same hashcode. I will explain keys and hashcodes in a little more detail when I discuss using maps later in this chapter.

Now let's look at how you can move through a collection.

Iterators

In the LinkedList<T> class that you developed in Chapter 13 you implemented the Iterable<> interface for getting the objects from the list. This resulted in your LinkedList<> type being able to make an **iterator** available. As you know, an iterator is an object that you can use once to retrieve all the objects in a collection one by one. Someone dealing cards from a deck one by one is acting as an iterator for the card deck — without the shuffle, of course. Implementing the Iterable<> interface was a much better approach to accessing the members of a list than the technique that you originally implemented, and it made the collection usable with a collection-based for loop. Using an **iterator** is a standard mechanism for accessing each of the elements in a collection.

*It is worth noting at this point that Java also provides something called an **enumerator** that is defined by any class that implements the java.util.Enumeration<> generic interface type. An enumerator provides essentially the same capability as an iterator, but it is recommended in the Java documentation that you use an iterator in preference to an enumerator for collections. There's nothing particularly wrong with enumerators — it's just that the Iterator<> interface declares an optional remove() method that the Enumeration<> interface does not, and the methods in the Iterator<> interface have shorter names than those in the Enumeration<> interface, so code that uses them will be less cluttered.*

Any collection object that represents a set or a sequence can create an object of type `Iterator<>` that behaves as an iterator. Types representing maps do not have methods for creating iterators. However, as you'll see, a map class provides methods to enable the keys or objects, or indeed the key/object pairs, to be viewed as a set, so you can then obtain an iterator to iterate over the objects in the set view of the map. An `Iterator<>` object encapsulates references to all the objects in the original collection in some sequence, and they can be accessed one by one using the `Iterator<>` interface methods that you saw in the previous chapter. In other words, an iterator provides an easy way to get at all the objects in a collection one at a time. Just to remind you, the basic mechanism for using an iterator in Java is illustrated in Figure 14-4.

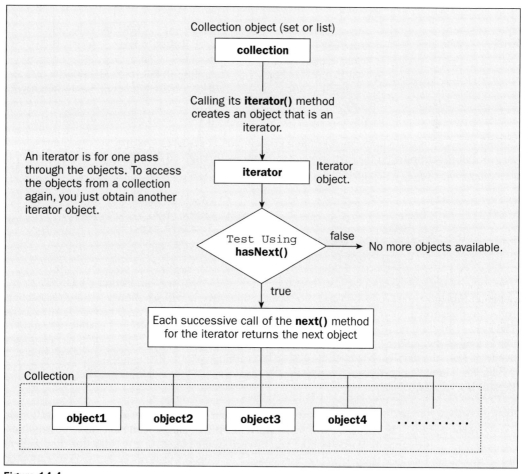

Figure 14-4

The `Iterator<>` interface in `java.util` declares the following three methods:

Method	Description
`T next()`	Returns an object as type `T` starting with the first and sets the `Iterator<T>` object to return the next object on the next call of this method. If there is no object to be returned, the method throws a `NoSuchElementException` exception.
`boolean hasNext()`	Returns `true` if there is a next object to be retrieved by a call to `next()`.
`void remove()`	Removes the last object returned by `next()` from the collection that supplied the `Iterator<T>` object. If `next()` has not been called or if you call `remove()` twice after calling `next()`, an `IllegalStateException` will be thrown. Not all iterators support this method, in which case an `UnsupportedOperationException` exception will be thrown if you call it.

Calling the `next()` method for an object that implements `Iterator<>` returns successive objects from the collection, starting with the first, so you can progress through all the objects in a collection very easily with a loop such as the following:

```
MyClass item;                      // Store an object from the collection
while(iter.hasNext()) {            // Check that there's another
   item = iter.next();             // Retrieve next object
   // Do something with item...
}
```

This code fragment assumes that `iter` is of type `Iterator<MyClass>` and stores a reference to an object obtained from whatever collection class you were using. As you will see shortly, most objects that are collections have an `iterator()` method that returns an iterator for the current contents of the collection. The `next()` method returns an object as the original type so there's no need for casting. The loop continues as long as the `hasNext()` method returns `true`, which indicates that there is at least one more object available from the iterator. When all the objects have been accessed, the `hasNext()` method will return `false`. Each time you need to go through the objects in a collection you obtain another iterator, as an iterator is a "use once" object.

The iterator you've seen here is a one-way street—you can go through the objects in a collection one at a time, once, and that's it. This is fine for many purposes but not all, so you have other possibilities for accessing the entire contents of a collection. You can access the objects in any collection that implements the `Iterable<>` interface using the collection-based `for` loop. If this is not enough, there's another kind of iterator that is more flexible than the one you've seen so far—called a **list iterator**.

List Iterators

The `ListIterator<>` interface that is defined in `java.util` declares methods that you can use to traverse a collection of objects backwards or forwards. You don't have to elect for a particular direction either. You can change from forwards to backwards and *vice versa* at any time so an object can be retrieved more than once.

The `ListIterator<>` interface extends the `Iterator<>` interface type so the iterator methods you have already seen and used still apply. The methods defined in the `ListIterator<>` interface that you use to traverse the list of objects are:

Method	Description
`T next()`	Retrieves the next object in sequence as the type of the objects in the collection — the same as for the `Iterator<>` interface.
`boolean hasNext()`	Returns `true` if there is an object that will be returned by `next()`.
`int nextIndex()`	Returns the index of the object that will be returned by the next call to `next()` as type `int`, or returns the number of elements in the list if the `ListIterator<>` object is at the end of the list.
`T previous()`	Returns the previous object in sequence in the list. You use this method to run backwards through the list.
`boolean hasPrevious()`	Returns `true` if the next call to `previous()` will return an object.
`int previousIndex()`	Returns the index of the object that will be returned by the next call to `previous()`, or returns -1 if the `ListIterator<>` object is at the beginning of the list.

You can alternate between calls to `next()` and `previous()` to go backwards and forwards through the list. Calling `previous()` immediately after calling `next()` will return the same element — and *vice versa*.

With a `ListIterator<>` object you can add and replace objects as well as remove them from the collection. `ListIterator` declares the following methods for this:

Method	Description
`void remove()`	Removes the last object that was retrieved by `next()` or `previous()`. The `UnsupportedOperation` exception is thrown if the remove operation is not supported for this collection, and an `IllegalStateException` will be thrown if `next()` or `previous()` have not yet been called for the iterator.
`void add(T obj)`	Adds the argument immediately before the object that would be returned by the next call to `next()`, and after the object that would be returned by the next call to `previous()`. The call to `next()` after the `add()` operation will return the object that was added. The next call to `previous()` will not be affected. This method throws an `UnsupportedOperationException` if objects cannot be added, a `ClassCastException` if the class of the argument prevents it from being added, and `IllegalOperationException` if there is some other reason why the add cannot be done.

Table continued on following page

609

Method	Description
`void set(T obj)`	Replaces the last object retrieved by a call to `next()` or `previous()`. If neither `next()` nor `previous()` have been called, or `add()` or `remove()` have been called most recently, an `IllegalStateException` will be thrown. If the `set()` operation is not supported for this collection an `UnsupportedOperationException` will be thrown. If the class of the reference passed as an argument prevents the object from being stored in the collection, a `ClassCastException` will be thrown. If some other characteristic of the argument prevents it from being stored in the collection, an `IllegalArgumentException` will be thrown.

Now that you know more about iterators, you need to find out a bit about the collection classes themselves to make use of them.

Collection Classes

You have a total of 15 classes in `java.util` that you can use to manage collections of objects, and they support collections that are sets, lists, queues, and maps, as follows:

	Class	Description
Sets:	`HashSet<T>`	An implementation of a set that uses `HashMap<>` under the covers. Although a set is by definition unordered, there has to be some way to find an object reasonably efficiently. The use of a `HashMap` object to implement the set enables store and retrieve operations to be done in a constant time. However, the order in which elements of the set are accessed is not necessarily constant over time.
	`LinkedHashSet<T>`	Implements a set using a hash table with all the entries linked in a doubly-linked list. This class can be used to make a copy of any set such that iteration ordering is preserved — something that does not apply to a `HashSet<>`.
	`TreeSet<T>`	An implementation of a set that orders the objects in the set in ascending sequence. This means that an iterator obtained from a `TreeSet<>` object will provide the objects in ascending sequence. The `TreeSet<>` classes use a `TreeMap<>` object under the covers.
	`EnumSet<T extends Enum<T>>`	Implements a specialized set that stores enum values from a single enum type, `T`

	Class	Description
Lists:	Vector<T>	Implements a list as an array that automatically increases in size to accommodate as many elements as you need. Objects are stored and retrieved using an index as in a normal array. You can also use an iterator to retrieve objects from a Vector<>. The Vector<> type is one of two container classes in the java.util package that are synchronized — that is, it is well behaved when concurrently accessed by two or more threads. I will discuss threads and synchronization in Chapter 16.
	Stack<T>	This class is derived from Vector<> and "adds methods to implement a stack — a last-in first-out storage mechanism.
	LinkedList<T>	Implements a linked list. The linked list defined by this class can also be used as a stack or a queue.
	ArrayList<T>	Implements an array that can vary in size and can also be accessed as a linked list. This provides a similar function to the Vector<> generic type but is unsynchronized so it is not safe for use by multiple threads.
Queues:	PriorityQueue<T>	Implements a priority queue in which objects are ordered in ascending sequence from the head of the queue. The order is determined either by a Comparator<> object supplied to the constructor for the collection class that can be used to compare objects, or through the compareTo() method declared in the Comparable<> interface that the object type implements.
Maps:	Hashtable<K,V>	Implements a map with keys of type K and values of type V where all keys must be non-null. The class defining a key must implement the hashcode() method and the equals() method to work effectively. This type, like Vector<>, is synchronized so it's safe to use by two or more threads.
	HashMap<K,V>	Implements a map where objects of type V are stored using keys of type K. This collection allows null objects to be stored and allows a key to be null (only one of course, since keys must be unique).

Table continued on following page

Class	Description
LinkedHashMap<K,V>	Implements a map storing values of type V using keys of type K with all of its entries in a doubly-linked list. This class can be used to create a copy of a map of any type such that the order of the entries in the copy is the same as the original.
WeakHashMap<K,V>	Implements a map storing values of type V using keys of type K such that if a key to an object is no longer referenced ordinarily, the key/object pair will be discarded. This contrasts with HashMap<> where the presence of the key in the map maintains the life of the key/object pair, even though the program using the map no longer has a reference to the key and therefore cannot retrieve the object.
IdentityHashMap<K,V>	Implements a map storing values of type V using keys of type K using a hash table where comparisons in searching the map for a key or a value compares references, not objects. This implies that two keys are equal only if they are the same key. The same applies to values.
TreeMap<K,V>	Implements a map storing values of type V using keys of type K such that the objects are arranged in ascending key order.

In addition to the generic types listed in the table, the java.util.concurrent package defines further collection class types that are specifically designed to support concurrent operations by multiple threads. I won't be discussing these in this chapter.

The generic types representing sets, lists, and queues are related in the manner shown in Figure 14-5.

The shaded boxes identify generic types that you would use to define collections. The others are abstract types that you cannot instantiate. All types that define sequences share a common base class, AbstractCollection<>. This class defines methods for the operations that are common to sets, lists, and queues. The operations provided by the AbstractCollection<> class include adding objects to a collection, removing objects, providing an iterator for a collection, and testing for the presence of one or more objects in a collection.

The parameterized types that define maps of various kinds are related as shown in Figure 14-6.

All the concrete types that define maps have the AbstractMap<> type as a common base class. This provides an outline implementation of operations that apply to maps, thus simplifying the definitions of the more specialized types of maps.

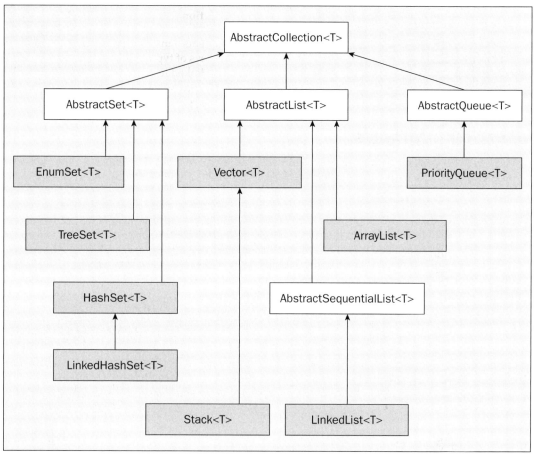

Figure 14-5

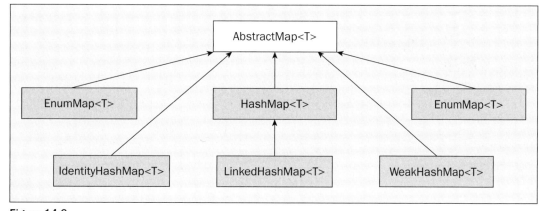

Figure 14-6

I don't have the space to go into all these classes in detail, but to show you some examples of how and where these can be applied, I'll describe the three generic types that you are likely to find most useful, `Vector<T>`, `LinkedList<T>`, and `HashMap<K,V>`. These are representative examples of the most frequently used collections, and once you have worked with these you'll have little difficulty with the others. Before I get into the specifics of using these classes, I'll introduce the interfaces that they implement, because these define the operations that the collection classes support and thus define the ways in which you can apply them.

Collection Interfaces

The `java.util` package defines eight generic collection interface types that determine the methods that you use to work with each type of collection class. These interfaces are related in the manner shown in Figure 14-7.

You can see that the interfaces for maps have no connection to the interfaces implemented by sets and lists. You can also see that the map interfaces do not implement the `Iterable<>` interface, so you cannot use the collection-based `for` loop to iterate over the objects in a map. However, the `Map<>` interface declares a `values()` method that returns a collection view of the objects in a map as type `Collection<>`. You can then use the `Collection<>` reference with a collection-based `for` loop to access the contents of the map because the `Collection<>` type extends `Iterable<>`.

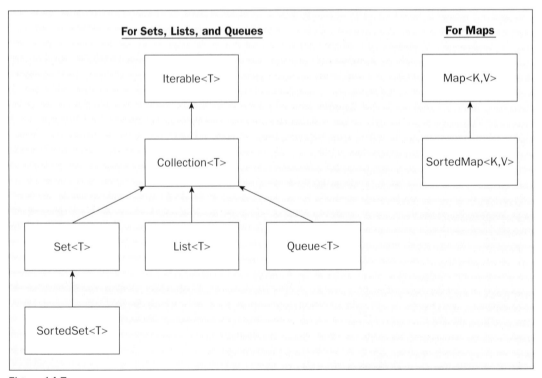

Figure 14-7

There are four basic collection interfaces, the `Set<>`, `List<>`, `Queue<>`, and `Map<>` interfaces, that relate to the fundamental organization of objects in a collection. The first three inherit the members of `Iterable<>` and `Collection<>`, so sets, lists, and queues share the characteristics specified by these two interfaces. `SortedSet<>` and `SortedMap<>` are specialized versions of their respective superinterfaces that add methods that provide for ordering objects within a collection. Don't confuse the `Collection<>` interface with the `Collections` class (with an *s*) that you will see later. The two other interfaces for collections are `SortedSet<>`, which extends the `Set<>` interface, and `SortedMap<>`, which extends the `Map<>` interface. These two interfaces are implemented by collection classes that maintain their contents in ascending order.

These interfaces are implemented amongst the classes in the `java.util` package as follows:

Interface Type	Implemented by
Set<T>	HashSet<T>, LinkedHashSet<T>, EnumSet<T>
SortedSet<T>	TreeSet<T>
List<T>	Vector<T>, Stack<T>, ArrayList<T>, LinkedList<T>
Queue<T>	PriorityQueue<T>, LinkedList<T>
Map<K,V>	Hashtable<K,V>, HashMap<K,V>, LinkedHashMap<K,V>, WeakHashMap<K,V>, IdentityHashMap<K,V>
SortedMap<T>	TreeMap<T>

The `LinkedList<>` type implements both the `List<>` interface and the `Queue<>` interface, so it really does have a dual personality in that you can regard a `LinkedList<>` object as a linked list or as a queue.

Keep in mind that any collection class object that implements the `Collection<>` interface can be referenced using a variable of type `Collection<>`. This means that any of the list or set collections can be referenced in this way; only the map class types are excluded (but not entirely, as you can obtain a set from a map, and the classes implementing a map can provide a view of the values stored as a `Collection<>` reference). You will see that using a parameter of type `Collection<>` is a standard way of passing a list or a set to a method.

These interfaces involve quite a large number of methods, so rather than go through them in the abstract, let's see them at work in the context of specific collection class types. I'll consider the `Vector<>` type first since it is close to the notion of an array and you are already familiar with that.

Using Vectors

The `Vector<T>` parameterized type defines a sequence collection of elements of any type `T`. A `Vector<>` object works rather like an array, but with the additional feature that it can grow itself automatically when you need more capacity. The `Vector<>` type implements the `List<>` interface, so you can also access the contents of containers of this type as a list.

> Like arrays, vectors hold object references only, not actual objects. To keep the text simple I'll refer to a `Vector<>` as holding objects, and I'll make the distinction only when it's important. However, you should keep in mind that all the collection classes you're about to encounter hold object references.

Creating a Vector

You have four constructors for a `Vector<>`. The default constructor creates an empty `Vector<>` object with the capacity to store up to a default number of objects of the type argument that you supply. The default capacity of a `Vector<>` object is ten objects, and the `Vector<>` object will double in size when you add an object when it is full. For example:

```
Vector<String> transactions = new Vector<String>();
```

This statement creates an empty vector with a capacity for ten `String` objects. If the default capacity isn't suitable for what you want to do, you can set the initial capacity of the `Vector<>` object explicitly when you create it by using a different constructor. You just specify the capacity you require as an argument of type `int`. For example:

```
Vector<String> transactions = new Vector<String>(100);
```

The `Vector<>` object you're defining here will store 100 strings initially. It will also double in capacity each time you exceed the current capacity. The process of doubling the capacity of a vector when more space is required can be quite inefficient. For example, if you end up storing 7000 `String` object references in the `Vector<>` you've just defined, it will actually have space for 12800 object references. The capacity doubling mechanism means that the capacity will always be a value of the form $100*2^n$, and the smallest n to accommodate 7000 references is 128. As each object reference requires 4 bytes, you'll be occupying more than 20 K of memory unnecessarily.

One way of avoiding this is to specify the amount by which the `Vector` should be incremented as well as the initial capacity when you create the `Vector` object. Both of these arguments to the constructor are of type `int`. For example:

```
Vector<String> transactions = new Vector<String>(100,10);
```

This `Vector<>` object has an initial capacity of 100, but the capacity will only be increased by 10 elements each time more space is required.

Why not increment the vector object by 1 each time then? The reason is that the process of incrementing the capacity takes time because it involves copying the contents to a new area of memory. The bigger the vector is, the longer the copy takes, and that will affect your program's performance if it happens very often.

The last constructor creates a `Vector<>` object containing object references from another collection. It is passed to the constructor as an argument of type `Collection<>`. Since all the set and list collection classes implement the `Collection<>` interface, the constructor argument can be of any set or list class type, including another `Vector<>`. The objects are stored in the `Vector<>` object that is created; they are stored in the sequence in which they are returned from the iterator for the `Collection<>` object that is passed as the argument.

Let's see a vector working.

Try It Out   Using a Vector

I'll take a very simple example here, just storing a few strings in a vector:

```java
import java.util.Vector;

public class TrySimpleVector {
  public static void main(String[] args) {
    Vector<String> names = new Vector<String>();
    String[] firstnames = { "Jack", "Jill", "John",
                            "Joan", "Jeremiah", "Josephine"};

    // Add the names to the vector
    for(String firstname : firstnames) {
      names.add(firstname);
    }

    // List the contents of the vector
    for(String name : names) {
      System.out.println(name);
    }
  }
}
```

If you compile and run this, it will list the names that are defined in the program.

How It Works

You first create a vector to store strings using the default constructor:

```java
Vector<String> names = new Vector<String>();
```

This vector will have the default capacity to store ten references to strings. You copy the references to the `Vector<String>` object, names, in the first `for` loop. The `add()` method adds the object to the vector at the next available position.

The second `for` loop iterates over the `String` references in the vector:

```java
for(String name : names) {
  System.out.println(name);
}
```

All collection classes that are sequences implement the `Iterable<>` interface so you can always use the collection-based `for` loop to access the contents of the collection. Of course, you could also use an iterator. The following code will produce the same result as the `for` loop:

```
java.util.Iterator<String> iter = names.iterator();
while(iter.hasNext()) {
    System.out.println(iter.next());
}
```

The `iter` object provides a one-time pass through the contents of the `names` collection. The `boolean` value returned by the `hasNext()` method determines whether or not the loop should continue. The `next()` method returns the object reference as the type argument you used to create the vector so no casting is necessary.

You are spoiled for choice when accessing elements stored in a vector because you have a third mechanism you can use. The `get()` method for a `Vector<>` object returns a reference to the object at an index position specified by the argument to the method. The argument to the `get()` method is a zero-based index, just like an array. To iterate over all the index values for elements in a vector you need to know how many elements are stored in it; the `size()` method supplies this as a value of type `int`. You can combine these facilities to provide the following alternative to the collection-based `for` loop:

```
for(int i = 0 ; i<names.size() ; i++) {
    System.out.println(names.get(i));
}
```

The collection-based `for` loop is the simplest and clearest mechanism for iterating over the contents of a vector. The `get()` method is useful for accessing an element stored at a particular index position.

The Capacity and Size of a Vector

Although I said earlier that a `Vector<>` works like an array, you can now appreciate that this isn't strictly true. One significant difference is in the information you can get about the storage space it provides. An array has a single measure, its length, which is the count of the total number of elements it can reference. A vector has two measures relating to the space it provides — the **capacity** and the **size**, as Figure 14-8 illustrates.

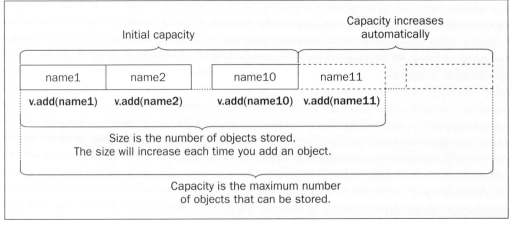

Figure 14-8

Obtaining and Ensuring Capacity

The **capacity** of a Vector<> is the maximum number of objects that it can hold at any given instant. Of course, the capacity can vary over time, because when you store an object in a Vector<> object that is full, its capacity will automatically increase. For example, the Vector<> object transactions that you defined in the last of the constructor examples earlier had an initial capacity of 100. You also specified the capacity increment as 10. After you've stored 101 objects in it, its capacity will be 110 objects. A vector typically contains fewer objects than its capacity.

You can obtain the capacity of a Vector<> by calling its capacity() method, which returns the current capacity as a value of type int. For example:

```
int namesMax = names.capacity();          // Get current capacity
```

If this statement follows the definition you have for names in the previous example, the variable namesMax will have the value 10.

You can also ensure that a Vector has a sufficient capacity for your needs by calling its ensureCapacity() method. For example:

```
names.ensureCapacity(150);                 // Set minimum capacity to 150
```

If the capacity of names is less than 150, the capacity will be increased to that value. If it's already 150 or greater, it will be unchanged by this statement. The argument you specify for ensureCapacity() is of type int. There's no return value.

Changing the Size

When you first create a Vector<> object of a given size, no element references are stored in it. The space allocated for an element reference will be occupied once you've stored a reference in it. The number of elements you have stored in a Vector<> is referred to as its **size**. The size of a Vector<> clearly can't be greater than the capacity. As you've seen, you can obtain the size of a Vector<> object as a value of type int by calling the size() method for the object. You could use the size() method in conjunction with the capacity() method to calculate the number of free entries in the Vector object transactions with the statement:

```
int freeCount = names.capacity() - names.size();
```

You will usually increase the size value for a Vector<> indirectly by storing an object in it, but you can also change the size directly by calling a method. Using the method setSize(), you can increase and decrease the size. For example:

```
names.setSize(50);                         // Set size to 50
```

The size of the names vector is set to the argument value (of type int). If the names vector has less than 50 elements occupied, the additional elements up to 50 will be filled with null references. If it already contains more than 50 objects, all object references in excess of 50 will be discarded. The objects themselves may still be available if other references to them exist.

Looking back to the situation I discussed earlier, you saw how the effects of incrementing the capacity by doubling each time the current capacity was exceeded could waste memory. A Vector<> object provides you with a direct way of dealing with this — the trimToSize() method. This just changes the capacity to match the current size. For example:

```
names.trimToSize();              // Set capacity to size
```

If the size of the names is 30 when this statement executes, then the capacity will be set to 30. Of course, you can still add more objects to the Vector<> object, as it will grow to accommodate them by whatever increment is in effect.

Storing Objects in a Vector

The simplest way to store an object in a vector is to use the add() method as you did in the last example. To store a name in the names vector, you could write:

```
transactions.add(aName);
```

This will add a reference to the object aName to the Vector<> object called names. The new entry will be added at the end of the existing objects in the vector, and the size of the vector will be increased by 1. All the objects that were already stored in the vector remain at their previous index position.

You can also store an object at a particular index position in a Vector<> object using another version of add() that has two parameters. The first argument is the index position and the second argument is the object to be stored. The index value must be less than or equal to the size of the vector, which implies that either there is already an object reference at this position or it is the position at the end of the Vector that is next in line to receive one. The index value is the same as for an array — an offset from the first element — so you reference the first element using an index value of zero. For example, to insert the object aName as the third entry of names, you would write:

```
names.add(2, aName);
```

The index value is of type int and represents the index value for the position of the new object. The new object, aName, is inserted in front of the object that previously corresponded to the index value 2, so objects stored in elements with index values equal to or greater than 2 will be shuffled along, and their index values will increase by 1. If you specify an index value argument that is negative, or greater than or equal to the size of the vector, the method will throw an ArrayIndexOutOfBoundsException.

To change an element in a vector you use the set() method. This accepts two arguments: The first argument is the index position where the object specified by the second argument is to be stored. To change the third element in the Vector object from names to newName, you would write:

```
names.set(2, newName);
```

The method returns a reference to the object that was previously stored at this position. This gives you a chance to hang on to the displaced object if you want to keep it. If the first argument is negative, or is greater than or equal to the current size of the Vector, the method will throw an ArrayIndexOutOfBoundsException.

You can add all the objects from another collection to a vector, either appended at the end or inserted following a given index position. For example, to append the contents of a `LinkedList<>` object, `myNamesList` — and here I'm referring to the `java.util.LinkedList<>` type, not the homemade version — to a `Vector<>` object, `names`, you would write:

```
names.addAll(myNamesList);
```

The parameter to the method is of type `Collection<T>`, so because the `names` vector is of type `Vector<String>`, the object reference passed as the argument must be of type `Collection<String>`. Here, this implies that `myNamesList` is of type `LinkedList<String>`.

To insert the collection objects at a particular position relative to the existing objects in the vector, you specify the index position as the first argument. So to insert the objects from `myNamesList` starting at index position `i`, you would write:

```
names.addAll(i, myNamesList);
```

The object originally at position `i`, and objects originally to the right of position `i`, will all be shuffled to the right to make room for the new objects. If the index value passed as the first argument is negative, or is not less than the size of `names`, an `ArrayIndexOutOfBoundsException` object will be thrown. Adding a collection will increase the size of the vector by the number of objects added.

Retrieving Objects from a Vector

As you saw in the simple example earlier, if you have the index for an element, you can obtain the element at a particular position by using the `get()` method for the `Vector<>`. For the `names` vector you could write:

```
String name = names.get(4);
```

This statement will retrieve the fifth element in the vector. The return type for the `get()` method is determined by the type argument you used to create the `Vector<>` object.

Note that the `get()` method will throw an exception of type `ArrayIndexOutOfBoundsException` if the argument is an illegal index value. The index must be non-negative and less than the size of the vector.

You can retrieve the first element in a `Vector<>` by using the `firstElement()` method. For example:

```
String name = names.firstElement();
```

You can also retrieve the last element in a `Vector<>` by using the method `lastElement()` in a similar manner. However, a vector has a flavor of a list about it, and if you want to process the objects in your vector like a list, you can obtain an iterator.

Accessing Elements in a Vector through a List Iterator

You've already seen how you can obtain all the elements in a `Vector<>` object by using an `Iterator<>` object that you obtain from the `Vector<>` object so I won't repeat it. You can also obtain a `ListIterator` reference from a vector by calling the `listIterator()` method:

```
ListIterator<String> listIter = names.listIterator();
```

Now you can go backwards or forwards though the objects using the `ListIterator` methods that you saw earlier.

It is also possible to obtain a `ListIterator<>` object that encapsulates just a part of the vector, using a version of the `listIterator()` method that accepts an argument specifying the index position of the first vector element in the iterator:

```
ListIterator<String> listIter = names.listIterator(2);
```

This statement results in a list iterator that encapsulates the elements from names from the element at index position 2 to the end. The argument must not be negative and must be less than the size of names; otherwise, an `IndexOutOfBoundsException` will be thrown. Take care not to confuse the interface name `ListIterator`, with a capital *L*, with the method of the same name, with a small *l*.

To cap that, you can retrieve an internal subset of the objects in a vector as a collection of type `List<>` using the `subList()` method:

```
List<String> list = names.subList(2, 5);    //Extract elements 2 to 4 as a sublist
```

The first argument is the index position of the first element from the vector to be included in the list, and the second index is the element at the upper limit — *not* included in the list. Thus this statement extracts elements 2 to 4, inclusive. Both arguments to `subList()` must be positive, the first argument must be less than the size of the vector, and the second argument must not be greater than the size; otherwise, an `IndexOutOfBoundsException` will be thrown.

You have lots of ways of using the `subList()` method in conjunction with other methods, for example:

```
ListIterator<String> listIter = names.subList(5, 15).listIterator(2);
```

The call to `subList()` returns a `List<String>` object that encapsulates the elements from names at index positions 5 to 14, inclusive. You then call the `listIterator()` method for this `List<String>` object, which will return a list iterator of type `ListIterator<String>` for elements in the list from index position 2 to the end in the `List<String>` collection. This corresponds to elements 7 to 14, inclusive, from the original names vector. You can use this iterator to roam backwards and forwards through elements 7 to 14 from the names vector to your heart's content.

Extracting All the Elements from a Vector

A `Vector<>` object provides you with tremendous flexibility in use, particularly with the capability to automatically adjust its capacity. Of course, the flexibility you get through using a `Vector<>` object comes at a price. There is always some overhead involved when you're retrieving elements. For this reason, there may be times when you want to retrieve the elements contained in a `Vector<>` object as a regular array. The method `toArray()` will do this for you. You would typically use the method `toArray()` to obtain the elements of a `Vector<>` object, names, as follows:

```
String[] data = names.toArray(new String[names.size()]);
```

The argument to the `toArray()` method must be an array of the same type or a supertype of the type of elements in the vector. If it isn't, an exception of type `ArrayStoreException` will be thrown. If the argument is `null`, then an exception of type `NullPointerException` will be thrown. If the array you pass as the argument is not large enough to accommodate all the elements in the vector, then a new array will be created, and a reference to that will be returned. The `toArray()` method here returns an array of type `String[]` containing all the elements from `names` in the correct sequence.

It's worth noting that the `java.util.Arrays` class that you first met back in Chapter 3 defines a static parameterized method, `asList()`, that will convert an array of a given type, `T`, into a `List<T>` collection. The argument is the array of type `T` that you want to convert, and the reference returned is of type `List<T>`. For example:

```
String[] people = { "Brian", "Beryl", "Belinda", "Barry", "Bill", "Barbara" };
List<String> nameList = java.util.Arrays.asList(people);
```

Note that the `List<>` reference that is returned does not have storage independent of the array. The `List<>` object is backed by the array you pass as the argument. From the interface hierarchy that you saw earlier you know that a `List<String>` reference is also a `Collection<String>` reference. You can therefore pass it as an argument to a `Vector<String>` constructor. For example:

```
Vector<String> names = new Vector<String>( java.util.Arrays.asList(people));
```

Here you are calling the constructor that accepts an argument of type `Collection<>`. You thus have a way to create a `Vector<>` object containing the elements from a predefined array. Of course, the type of elements in the array must be consistent with the type argument for the vector you are creating.

Removing Objects from a Vector

You can remove the reference at a particular index position by calling the `remove()` method with the index position of the object as the argument. For example:

```
names.remove(3);
```

will remove the fourth reference from `names`. The references following this will now be at index positions that are one less than they were before, so what was previously the fifth object reference will now be at index position 3. Of course, the index value that you specify must be legal for the `Vector<>` object on which you're operating, meaning greater than or equal to 0 and less than its `size()`; otherwise, an exception of type `IndexOutOfBoundsException` will be thrown. This version of the `remove()` method returns a reference to the object removed, so it provides a means for you to retain a reference to the object after you remove it from the vector:

```
String name = names.remove(3);
```

Here you save a reference to the object that was removed from the `names` vector in `name`.

Sometimes, you'll want to remove a particular reference, rather than the reference at a given index. If you know what the object is that you want to remove, you can use another version of the `remove()` method to delete it:

```
boolean deleted = names.remove(aName);
```

This will search the `names` vector from the beginning to find the first reference to the object `aName` and remove it. If the object is found and removed from the vector, the method returns `true`; otherwise, it returns `false`.

Another way to remove a single element is to use the `removeElementAt()` method, which requires an argument specifying the index position for the element to be removed. This is clearly similar to the version of `remove()` that accepts an index as an argument, the difference being that here the return type is `void`. This is because the element is always removed if the index you supply is valid, and an exception of type `ArrayIndexOutOfBoundsException` is thrown if it isn't.

There is also a `removeAll()` method that accepts an argument of type `Collection<>`, which removes elements from the collection passed to the method if they are present in the vector. The method returns `true` if the `Vector` object is changed by the operation — that is, at least one element was removed. You could use this in conjunction with the `subList()` method to remove a specific set of elements:

```
names.removeAll(names.subList(5,15));
```

This will remove elements 5 to 14, inclusive, from the `Vector<String>` object `names`, plus any duplicates of those objects that are in the vector.

The `retainAll()` method provides you with a backhanded removal mechanism. You pass a reference of type `Collection<>` as the argument to the method that contains the elements to be retained. Any elements not in the collection you pass to the method will be removed. For example, you could keep the elements at index positions 5 to 14, inclusive, and discard the rest with the statement:

```
names.retainAll(names.subList(5,15));
```

The method returns `true` if the vector has been changed — in other words, if at least one element has been removed as a result of the operation. The method will throw an exception of type `NullPointerException` if the argument is `null`.

If you want to discard all the elements in a `Vector`, you can use the `removeAllElements()` method to empty the `Vector` in one go:

```
transactions.removeAllElements();     // Dump the whole lot
```

This removes all the elements and sets the size to zero. The `clear()` method that is declared in the `List<>` interface is identical in function to the `removeAllElements()` method so you can use that to empty a vector if you prefer.

With all these ways of removing elements from a `Vector<>` object, there's a lot of potential for ending up with an empty vector. It's often handy to know whether a vector contains elements or not, particularly if there's been a lot of adding and deleting of elements. You can determine whether a vector contains elements by calling its `isEmpty()` method. This returns `true` if the `Vector<>` object has zero size, and `false` otherwise.

Note that a `Vector<>` object may contain only `null` references, but this doesn't mean the `size()` will be zero or that the `isEmpty()` method will return `true`. To empty a `Vector<>` object you must actually remove the elements, not just set the elements to `null`.

Searching a Vector

You can get the index position of an object stored in a vector by passing the object as an argument to the indexOf() method. For example, the statement

```
int position = names.indexOf(aName);
```

will search the names vector from the beginning for the object aName using the equals() method for the argument, so your aName class type needs to have a proper implementation of equals() for this to work. The variable position will contain either the index of the first reference to the object in transactions or -1 if the object isn't found.

Another available version of the method indexOf() accepts a second argument specifying the index position where the search for the object should begin. The main use for this arises when an object can be referenced more than once in a vector. You can use the method in this situation to recover all occurrences of any particular object, as follows:

```
String aName = "Fred";                                // Name to be found
int count = 0;                                         // Number of occurrences
int position = -1;                                     // Search starting index
while(++position<names.size()) {                       // Search with a valid index
  if((position = names.indexOf(aName, position))<0) {  // Find next
    break;
  }
  ++count;
}
```

This code fragment counts the number of occurrences of a given name in the names vector. The while loop will continue as long as the method indexOf() returns a valid index value and the index isn't incremented beyond the end of the vector names. Figure 14-9 shows how this works.

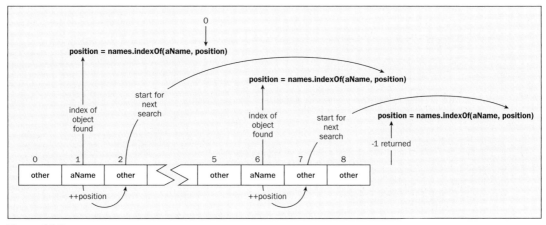

Figure 14-9

On each while loop iteration, the indexOf() method will search names from the element given by the index stored in the variable position. The initial value of -1 is incremented in the while loop condition, so on the first iteration it is 0. On subsequent iterations where `indexOf()` finds an occurrence of `aName`, the loop condition increments `position` to the next element ready for the next search. When no further references to the object can be found from the position specified by the second argument, the method `indexOf()` will return –1, and the loop will end by executing the break statement. If `aName` happens to be found in the last element in the vector at index position `size-1`, the value of `position` will be incremented to `size` by the loop condition expression, so the expression will be `false` and the loop will end.

Applying Vectors

Let's implement a simple example to see how using a `Vector<>` container works out in practice. You'll write a program to model a collection of people, where you can add the names of the persons that you want in the crowd from the keyboard. You'll first define a class to represent a person:

```
public class Person {
  // Constructor
  public Person(String firstName, String surname) {
    this.firstName = firstName;
    this.surname = surname;
  }

  public String toString() {
    return firstName + " " + surname;
  }

  private String firstName;          // First name of person
  private String surname;            // Second name of person
}
```

The only data members are the `String` members to store the first and second names for a person. By overriding the default implementation of the `toString()` method provided by the `Object` class, you allow objects of the `Person` class to be used as arguments to the `println()` method for output, since as you are well aware by now, `toString()` will be automatically invoked in this case.

Now you can define an example with which you can try your skills as a casting director.

Try It Out   Creating the Crowd

You can now add a class containing a `main()` method to try storing `Person` objects in a vector. You can call it `TryVector`:

```
import java.util.Vector;
import java.util.ListIterator;
import java.io.BufferedReader;
import java.io.InputStreamReader;
import java.io.IOException;

public class TryVector {
  public static void main(String[] args) {
    Person aPerson = null;                  // A person object
```

```
      Vector<Person> filmCast = new Vector<Person>();

      // Populate the film cast
      for( ; ; ) {                            // Indefinite loop
        aPerson = readPerson();               // Read in a film star
        if(aPerson == null) {                 // If null obtained...
          break;                              // We are done...
        }
        filmCast.add(aPerson);                // Otherwise, add to the cast
      }

      int count = filmCast.size();
      System.out.println("You added " + count +
        (count == 1 ? " person":  " people") + " to the cast.\n");
      System.out.println("The vector currently has room for "
                  + (filmCast.capacity() - count) + " more people.\n");

      // Show who is in the cast using an iterator
      ListIterator<Person> thisLot = filmCast.listIterator();

      while(thisLot.hasNext()) {         // Output all elements
        System.out.println( thisLot.next());
      }
    }

    // Read a person from the keyboard
    static Person readPerson() {
      // Read in the first name and remove blanks front and back
      String firstName = null;
      String surname = null;
      System.out.println("\nEnter first name or ! to end:");
      try {
        firstName = keyboard.readLine().trim();     // Read and trim a string

        if(firstName.charAt(0) == '!') {            // Check for ! entered
          return null;                              // If so, we are done...
        }

        // Read in the surname, also trimming blanks
        System.out.println("Enter surname:");
        surname = keyboard.readLine().trim();        // Read and trim a string
      } catch(IOException e) {
        System.err.println("Error reading a name.");
        e.printStackTrace();
        System.exit(1);
      }
      return new Person(firstName,surname);
    }


  static BufferedReader keyboard = new BufferedReader(
                                  new InputStreamReader(System.in));

}
```

With a modest film budget, I got the following output (my input is in bold):

```
Enter first name or ! to end:
Marilyn
Enter surname:
Monroe

Enter first name or ! to end:
Slim
Enter surname:
Pickens

Enter first name or ! to end:
Hopalong
Enter surname:
Cassidy

Enter first name or ! to end:
Mae
Enter surname:
West

Enter first name or ! to end:
!
You added 4 people to the cast.

The vector currently has room for 6 more people.

Marilyn Monroe
Slim Pickens
Hopalong Cassidy
Mae West
```

How It Works

Here you'll be assembling an all-star cast for a new blockbuster. The method `main()` creates a `Person` variable, which will be used as a temporary store for an actor or actress, and a `Vector<Person>` object, `filmCast`, to hold the entire cast.

The `for` loop uses the `readPerson()` method to obtain the necessary information from the keyboard and create a `Person` object. If `!` is entered from the keyboard, `readPerson()` will return `null`, and this will end the input process for cast members.

You output the number of stars entered with these statements:

```
int count = filmCast.size();
System.out.println("You added " + count +
  (count == 1 ? " person":  " people") + " to the cast.\n");
```

The `size()` method returns the number of objects in the vector, which is precisely what you want. The complication introduced by the conditional operator is just to make the grammar in the output sentence correct.

To output the space remaining in the vector you calculate the difference between the capacity and the size:

```
System.out.println("The vector currently has room for "
                + (filmCast.capacity() - count) + " more people.\n");
```

This is interesting but irrelevant because the vector will accommodate as many stars as you care to enter.

Finally, you output the members of the cast using a `ListIterator<Person>` object — just to try it out. You could do the job just as well with an `Iterator<Person>` object or even simply a collection-based `for` loop. Using an iterator for listing the members of the cast is still relatively simple:

```
ListIterator<Person> thisLot = filmCast.listIterator();

while(thisLot.hasNext()) {          // Output all elements
   System.out.println( thisLot.next());
}
```

Instead of an iterator, you could also have used the `get()` method for the `filmCast` object to retrieve the actors:

```
for(int i = 0 ; i<filmCast.size() ; i++)
   System.out.println(filmCast.get());
```

The collection-based `for` loop would be the simplest way of all for listing the contents of the vector:

```
for(Person person : filmCast) {
   System.out.println(person);
}
```

The static `getPerson()` method is a convenient way of managing the input. The input source is the static class member defined by the following statement:

```
static BufferedReader keyboard = new BufferedReader(
                                 new InputStreamReader(System.in));
```

The keyboard object is `System.in` wrapped in an `InputStreamReader` object that is wrapped in a `BufferedReader` object. The `InputStreamReader` object provides conversion of the input from the byte stream `System.in` to characters. The `BufferedReader` object buffers the data read from the `InputStreamReader`. Because the input consists of a series of strings, entered one to a line of input, the `readLine()` method does everything you need. The calls to `readLine()` must be in a `try` block because it can throw an exception of type `IOException`. The call to the `trim()` method for the `String` object returned by the `readLine()` method just removes any spurious leading or trailing blanks.

Sorting a Collection

The output from the last example appears in the sequence in which you enter it. If you want to be socially correct, say, in the creation of a cast list, you should arrange them in alphabetical order. You could write your own method to sort `Person` objects in the `filmCast` object, but it will be a lot less trouble to take advantage of another feature of the `java.util` package, the `Collections` class — not to be confused with the `Collection<>` interface. The `Collections` class defines a variety of handy static methods that you can apply to collections, and one of them happens to be a `sort()` method.

The `sort()` method will sort lists only — that is, collections that implement the `List<>` interface. Obviously, there also has to be some way for the `sort()` method to determine the order of objects from the list that it is sorting — in your case, `Person` objects. The most suitable way to do this for `Person` objects is to implement the `Comparable<>` interface for the class. As you know, the `Comparable<>` interface declares only one method, `compareTo()`. You saw this method in the previous chapter so you know it returns –1, 0, or +1 depending on whether the current object is less than, equal to, or greater than the argument passed to the method. If the `Comparable<>` interface is implemented for the type of object stored in a collection, you can just pass the collection object as an argument to the `sort()` method. The collection is sorted in place so there is no return value.

You can implement the `Comparable<>` interface very easily for your `Person` class, as follows:

```java
public class Person implements Comparable<Person> {
  // Constructor
  public Person(String firstName, String surname) {
    this.firstName = firstName;
    this.surname = surname;
  }

  public String toString() {
    return firstName + " " + surname;
  }

  // Compare Person objects
  public int compareTo(Person person) {
    int result = surname.compareTo(person.surname);
    return result == 0 ? firstName.compareTo(((Person)person).firstName):result;
  }

  private String firstName;    // First name of person
  private String surname;      // Second name of person
}
```

You use the `compareTo()` method for `String` objects to compare the surnames, and if the surnames are equal, the result is determined from the first names.

You can just pass your `Vector<Person>` object to the `sort()` method, and this will use the `compareTo()` method in the `Person` class to compare members of the list.

Let's see if it works for real.

Try It Out   Sorting the Stars

You can now add statements to the `main()` method in `TryVector` to sort the cast members:

```
public static void main(String[] args) {
   // Code as previously...

   // Now sort the vector contents and list it
   Collections.sort(filmCast);
   System.out.println("\nThe cast is ascending sequence is:\n");
   for(Person person : filmCast) {
      System.out.println(person);
   }
}
```

You'll need the following `import` statement to the `TryVector.java` file:

```
import java.util.Collections;
```

If you run the example with these changes, you'll get additional output with the cast in alphabetical order. Here's what I got when I entered the same data as last time:

```
Input record and output exactly as before...

The cast is ascending sequence is:

Hopalong Cassidy
Marilyn Monroe
Slim Pickens
Mae West
```

How It Works

Passing the `filmCast` object to the static `sort()` method in the `Collections` class sorts the objects in the vector in place. Like shelling peas!

The `sort()` method is actually a parameterized method so it works for any type that implements the `Comparable<>` interface. The way the method parameter is defined is interesting:

```
static <T extends Comparable<? super T>> void sort(List<T> list)
```

You'll recall from the discussion of parameterized types in the previous chapter that using a wildcard with the superclass constraint that you see here specifies that the type argument can be any type that implements the `Comparable<>` interface or inherits an implementation from a superclass. The method parameter is of type `List<T>` rather than `Collection<T>` because the `List<>` interface provides methods that allow the position where elements are inserted to be determined. It also provides the `listIterator()` method that returns a `ListIterator<T>` object that allows iteration forwards or backwards through the objects in the collection.

Stack Storage

A stack is a storage mechanism that works on a last-in, first-out basis, often abbreviated to LIFO. Don't confuse this with FIFO, which is first-in first-out, or FIFI, which is a name for a poodle. The operation of a stack is analogous to the plate stack you see in some self-service restaurants and is illustrated in Figure 14-10. The stack of plates is supported by a spring that allows the stack of plates to sink into a hole in the countertop so that only the top plate is accessible. The plates come out in the reverse order to the way they went in, so the cold plates are at the bottom, and the hot plates, fresh from the dishwasher, are at the top.

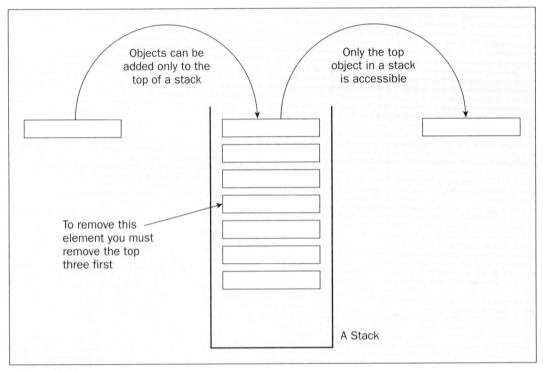

Figure 14-10

A stack in Java doesn't have a spring, but it does have all the facilities of a Vector<> object because the generic Stack<> type is derived from the Vector<> type. Of course, since you know the Vector<> class implements the List<> interface, a Stack<> object is also a List<>.

The Stack<> class adds five methods to those inherited from Vector<>, two of which provide you with the LIFO mechanism; the other three give you extra capabilities. These methods are:

Method	Description
T push(T obj)	Pushes the object of type T that you pass as the argument to the method onto the top of the stack. It also returns the reference you pass as the argument.

Method	Description
`T pop()`	Pops the object off the top of the stack and returns it. This removes the reference from the stack. If the stack contains no references when you call this method, an exception of type `EmptyStackException` will be thrown.
`T peek()`	This method allows you to take a look at the object reference at the top of the stack without popping it off the stack. It returns the reference from the top of the stack without removing it. Like the previous method, this method can throw an exception of type `EmptyStackException`.
`int search(Object obj)`	This will return an `int` value, which is the position on the stack of the reference to the object that you pass as the argument. The reference at the top of the stack is at position 1, the next reference is at position 2, and so on. Note that this is quite different from referencing elements in a `Vector<>` or an array, where indexes start at 0. If the object isn't found on the stack, –1 is returned.
`boolean empty()`	This method returns `true` if the stack is empty, and `false` otherwise.

The only constructor for a `Stack` object is the no-arg constructor. This calls the default constructor for the base class, `Vector<>`, so you'll always get an initial capacity for 10 objects, but since it's basically a `Vector<>`, it will grow automatically in the same way.

One possible point of confusion is the relationship between the top of a `Stack<>` object and the elements in the underlying `Vector<>` object. Intuitively, you might think that the top of the stack is going to correspond to the first element in the vector, with index 0. If so, you would be totally *wrong*! The `push()` method for a `Stack<>` object is analogous to `add()` for a `Vector<>`, which adds an object to the end of the vector. Thus, the top of the stack corresponds to the end of the vector.

Let's try a `Stack<>` object out in an example so you get a feel for how the methods are used.

Try It Out   Dealing Cards

You can use a `Stack<>` object along with another useful method from the `Collections` class to simulate dealing cards from a card deck. You'll need a way of representing a card suit and a card rank. An enum type will work well because `enum` types have a fixed set of constant values. Here's how you can define the suits:

```
public enum Suit {
   CLUBS, DIAMONDS, HEARTS, SPADES
}
```

The sequence in which the suits are defined here determines their sort order, so CLUBS is the lowest and SPADES is the highest. Save this source file as `Suit.java` in a new directory for the files for this example.

You can define the possible card face values just as easily:

```
public enum Rank {
  TWO,   THREE, FOUR, FIVE, SIX,   SEVEN,
  EIGHT, NINE,  TEN,  JACK, QUEEN, KING, ACE
}
```

TWO is the lowest card face value, and ACE is the highest. You can save this as Rank.java. You're now ready to develop the class that will represent cards. Here's an initial outline:

```
public class Card {
  public Card(Rank rank, Suit suit) {
    this.rank = rank;
    this.suit = suit;
  }

  private Suit suit;
  private Rank rank;
}
```

Your Card class has two data members that are both enumeration types. One defines the suit, and the other defines the face value of the card.

You will undoubtedly need to display a card, so you will need a String representation of a Card object. The toString() method will do this for us:

```
public class Card {
  public String toString() {
    return rank + " of " + suit;
  }

  // Other members as before...
}
```

The String representation of an enum constant is the name you assign to the constant, so the String representation of a Card object with the suit value as CLUBS and the rank value as FOUR will be "FOUR of CLUBS".

In general, you will probably need to be able to compare cards, so you could also make the Card class implement the Comparable<> interface:

```
public class Card implements Comparable<Card> {
  // Compare two cards
  public int compareTo(Card card) {
    if(suit.equals(card.suit)) {              // First compare suits
      if(rank.equals(card.rank)) {            // So check face values
        return 0;                             // They are equal
      }
      return rank.compareTo(card.rank)<0 ? -1 : 1;
    } else {                                  // Suits are the same
```

```
        return suit.compareTo(card.suit)<0 ? -1 : 1;  // Sequence is C<D<H<S
      }
    }

    // Other members as before...
  }
```

You can see the benefit of the `Comparable<>` interface being a generic type. The `Card` class implements the `Comparable<Card>` interface, so the `compareTo()` method works with `Card` objects and no cast is necessary in the operation. The suit first determines the card sequence. If the two cards are of the same suit, then you compare the face values. To compare enum values for equality you use the `equals()` method. The `Enum<>` class that is the base for all enum types implements the `Comparable<>` interface so you use the `compareTo()` method to determine the sequencing of enum values.

You could represent a hand of cards that is dealt from a deck as an object of type `Hand`. A `Hand` object will need to be able to accommodate an arbitrary number of cards, as this depends on what game the hand is intended for. You can define the `Hand` class using a `Vector<Card>` object to store the cards:

```
// Class defining a hand of cards
import java.util.Vector;

public class Hand {
  // Add a card to the hand
  public void add(Card card) {
    hand.add(card);
  }

  public String toString() {
    StringBuilder str = new StringBuilder();
    for(Card card : hand) {
      str.append(" "+ card);
    }
    return str.toString();
  }

  private Vector<Card> hand = new Vector<Card>();  // Stores a hand of cards
}
```

The default constructor generated by the compiler will create a `Hand` object containing an empty `Vector<Card>` member, hand. The `add()` member will add the `Card` object passed as an argument by adding it to the hand vector. You also have implemented a `toString()` method here that creates a string that combines the rank name with the suit name. You use the collection-based `for` loop to traverse the cards in the hand and construct a string representation of the complete hand. You might be tempted to use the `pop()` method in a loop to iterate over the cards in the hand but the `pop()` method removes an object from the stack, so using it here would remove all the cards from the hand.

It might be as well to provide a way to sort the cards in a hand. You could do this by adding a `sort()` method to the `Hand` class:

```
import java.util.Vector;
import java.util.Collections;
```

```
public class Hand {
  // Sort the hand
  public Hand sort() {
    Collections.sort(hand);
    return this;
  }

  // Rest of the class as before...
}
```

The `Card` class implements the `Comparable<>` interface, so you can use the static `sort()` method in the `Collections` class to sort the cards in the hand. `return this` returns the current `Hand` object after it has been sorted. This will make the use of the `sort()` method a little more convenient, as you'll see when you put the `main()` method together.

You might well want to compare hands in general, but this is completely dependent on the context. The best approach to accommodate this when required would be to derive a game-specific class from `Hand` — a `PokerHand` class, for example — and make it implement its own version of the `compareTo()` method in the `Comparable<>` interface.

The last class that you'll define will both represent a deck of cards and deal a hand:

```
import java.util.Stack;

public class CardDeck {
  // Create a deck of 52 cards
  public CardDeck() {
    for(Suit suit : Suit.values())
      for(Rank rank : Rank.values())
        deck.push(new Card(rank, suit));
  }

  // Deal a hand
  public Hand dealHand(int numCards) {
    Hand hand = new Hand();
    for(int i = 0; i<numCards; i++) {
      hand.add((Card)deck.pop());
    }
    return hand;
  }

  private Stack<Card> deck = new Stack<Card>();
}
```

The card deck is stored as a `Stack<Card>` object, `deck`. In the constructor, the nested `for` loops create the cards in the deck. For each suit in turn, you generate all the `Card` objects for each rank and push them onto the `Stack<>` object, `deck`. The `values()` method for an `enum` type returns a collection containing all the `enum` constants so that's how the loop iterates over all possible suits and ranks.

The `dealHand()` method creates a `Hand` object, and then pops `numCards` `Card` objects off the deck stack and adds each of them to `hand`. The `Hand` object is then returned. At the moment your deck is completely sequenced. You need a method to shuffle the deck before you deal:

```
import java.util.Stack;
import java.util.Collections;

public class CardDeck {
  // Shuffle the deck
  public void shuffle() {
    Collections.shuffle(deck);
  }

  // Rest of the class as before...
}
```

With the aid of another `static` parameterized method from the `Collections` class it couldn't be easier. The `shuffle()` method in `Collections` shuffles the contents of any collection that implements the `List<>` interface. The `Stack<>` class implements `List<>` so you can use the `shuffle()` method to produce a shuffled deck of `Card` objects. For those interested in the details of shuffling, this `shuffle()` method randomly permutes the list by running backwards through its elements swapping the current element with a randomly chosen element between the first and the current element. The time taken to complete the operation is proportional to the number of elements in the list.

An overloaded version of the `shuffle()` method allows you to supply an object of type `Random` as the second argument, which is used for selecting elements at random while shuffling.

The final piece is a class that defines `main()`:

```
class TryDeal {
  public static void main(String[] args) {
    CardDeck deck = new CardDeck();
    deck.shuffle();

    Hand myHand = deck.dealHand(5).sort();
    Hand yourHand = deck.dealHand(5).sort();
    System.out.println("\nMy hand is" + myHand);
    System.out.println("\nYour hand is" + yourHand);
  }
}
```

I got the following output:

```
My hand is:
 NINE of DIAMONDS SEVEN of HEARTS TWO of CLUBS FOUR of CLUBS NINE of SPADES

Your hand is
 FIVE of CLUBS KING of CLUBS TWO of DIAMONDS KING of HEARTS TEN of SPADES
```

You will almost certainly get something different.

How It Works

Your code for `main()` first creates a `CardDeck` object and calls its `shuffle()` method to randomize the sequence of `Card` objects. You then create two `Hand` objects of five cards with the following statements:

```
Hand myHand = deck.dealHand(5).sort();
Hand yourHand = deck.dealHand(5).sort();
```

The `dealHand()` method returns a `Hand` object that you use to call its `sort()` method. Because the `sort()` method returns a reference to the `Hand` object after sorting, you are able to call it in a single statement like this. The `Hand` object that the `sort()` method returns is stored in the local variable, either `myHand` or `yourHand` as the case may be. The output statements just display the hands that were dealt.

A `Stack` object is particularly well suited to dealing cards, as you want to remove each card from the deck as it is dealt, and this is done automatically by the `pop()` method, which retrieves an object. When you need to go through all the objects in a `Stack` collection without removing them, you can use a collection-based `for` loop, just as you did for the `Vector<Card>` object in the `toString()` method in the `Hand` class. Of course, since the `Stack<>` class is derived from `Vector<>`, all the `Vector<>` class methods are available for a stack when you need them.

I think you'll agree that using a stack is very simple. A stack is a powerful tool in many different contexts. A stack is often applied in applications that involve syntactical analysis, such as compilers and interpreters — including those for Java.

Linked Lists

The `LinkedList<>` generic collection type implements a generalized linked list. You have already seen quite a few of the methods that the class implements, as the members of the `List<>` interface are implemented in the `Vector<>` class. Nonetheless, let's quickly review the methods that the `LinkedList<>` class implements. There are two constructors: a default constructor that creates an empty list and a constructor that accepts a `Collection<>` argument that will create a `LinkedList<>` object containing the objects from the collection that is passed to it.

To add objects to a list you have the `add()` and `addAll()` methods, exactly as I discussed for a `Vector<>` object. You can also add an object at the beginning of a list using the `addFirst()` method, and you can add one at the end using `addLast()`. Both methods accept an argument of type corresponding to the type argument you supplied when you created the `LinkedList<>` object, and neither returns a value. Of course, the `addLast()` method provides the same function as the `add()` method.

To retrieve an object at a particular index position in the list, you can use the `get()` method, as in the `Vector<>` class. You can also obtain references to the first and last objects in the list by using the `getFirst()` and `getLast()` methods, respectively. To remove an object you can use the `remove()` method with an argument that is either an index value or a reference to the object that is to be removed. The `removeFirst()` and `removeLast()` methods do what you would expect.

Replacing an existing element in the list at a given index position is achieved by using the `set()` method. The first argument is the index value and the second argument is the new object at that position. The old object is returned, and the method throws an `IndexOutOfBoundsException` if the index value is not within the limits of the list. The `size()` method returns the number of elements in the list.

As with a `Vector<>` object, you can obtain an `Iterator<>` object by calling `iterator()`, and you can obtain a `ListIterator<>` object by calling `listIterator()`. You'll recall that an `Iterator<>` object allows you only to go forward through the elements, whereas a `ListIterator<>` object enables you to iterate backwards or forwards.

You could change the `TryPolyLine` example from Chapter 6 to use a `LinkedList<>` collection object rather than your homemade version.

Try It Out   **Using a Genuine Linked List**

Put this example in a new directory, `TryNewPolyLine`. You can use the `TryPolyLine` class that contains `main()` and the `Point` class exactly as they are, so if you still have them, copy the source files to the new directory. You just need to change the `PolyLine` class definition:

```java
import java.util.LinkedList;

public class PolyLine {
  // Construct a polyline from an array of points
  public PolyLine(Point[] points) {
    // Add the  points
    for(Point point : points) {
      polyline.add(point);
    }
  }
  // Construct a polyline from an array of coordinate
  public PolyLine(double[][] coords) {
    for(double[] xy : coords) {
      addPoint(xy[0], xy[1]);
    }
  }

  // Add a Point object to the list
  public void addPoint(Point point) {
    polyline.add(point);                  // Add the new point
  }

  // Add a point to the list
  public void addPoint(double x, double y) {
    polyline.add(new Point(x, y));
  }

  // String representation of a polyline
  public String toString() {
    StringBuffer str = new StringBuffer("Polyline:");

    for(Point point : polyline) {
      str.append(" "+ point);             // Append the current point
    }
    return str.toString();
  }

  private LinkedList<Point> polyline = new LinkedList<Point>();
}
```

The class is a lot simpler because the `LinkedList<>` class provides all the mechanics of operating a linked list. Since the interface to the `PolyLine` class is the same as the previous version, the original version of `main()` will run unchanged and produce exactly the same output.

How It Works

The only interesting bit is the change to the `PolyLine` class. `Point` objects are now stored in the linked list implemented by the `LinkedList<>` object, `polyline`. You use the `add()` method to add points in the constructors, and the `addPoint()` methods. Using a collection class makes the `PolyLine` class very straightforward.

I changed the implementation of the second constructor in the `PolyLine` class to illustrate how you can use the collection-based `for` loop with a two-dimensional array:

```
public PolyLine(double[][] coords) {
  for(double[] xy : coords) {
    addPoint(xy[0], xy[1]);
  }
}
```

The `coords` parameter to the constructor is a two-dimensional array of elements of type `double`. This is effectively a one-dimensional array of references to one-dimensional arrays that have two elements each, corresponding to the *x* and *y* coordinate values for a point. Thus, you can use the collection-based `for` loop to iterate over the array of arrays. The loop variable is `xy`, which is of type `double[]` and has two elements. Within the loop, you pass the elements of the array `xy` as arguments to the `addPoint()` method. This method then creates a `Point` object and adds it to the `LinkedList<Point>` collection, `polyline`.

Using Maps

As you saw at the beginning of this chapter, a **map** is a way of storing data that minimizes the need for searching when you want to retrieve an object. Each object is associated with a key that is used to determine where to store the reference to the object, and both the key and the object are stored in the map. Given a key, you can always go more or less directly to the object that has been stored in the map based on the key. It's important to understand a bit more about how the storage mechanism works for a map, and in particular what the implications of using the default hashing process are. You will explore the use of maps primarily in the context of the `HashMap<>` generic class type.

The Hashing Process

The implementation of a map in the Java collections framework provided by the `HashMap<>` class sets aside an array in which it will store key and object pairs. The index to this array is produced from the key object by using the hashcode for the object to compute an offset into the array for storing key/object pairs. By default, this uses the `hashCode()` method for the object that's used as a key. This is inherited in all classes from `Object` so this is the method that produces the basic hashcode unless the `hashcode()` method is redefined in the class for the key. The `HashMap<>` class doesn't assume that the basic hashcode is adequate. To try to ensure that the hashcode that is actually used has the characteristics required for an efficient map, the basic hashcode is further transformed within the `HashMap<>` object.

An entry in the table that is used to store key/value pairs is called a bucket. The hashcode produced from the key selects a particular bucket in which a key/value pair should be stored. This is illustrated in Figure 14-11.

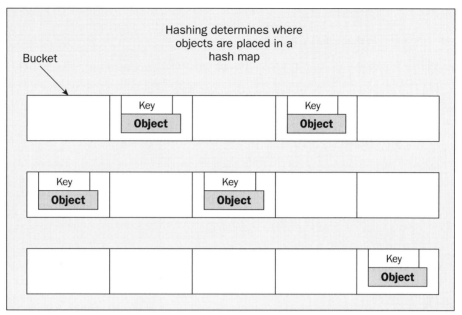

Figure 14-11

Note that, while every key must be unique, each key doesn't have to result in a unique hashcode. When two or more different keys produce the same hash value, it's called a **collision**. A HashMap<> object deals with collisions by storing all the key/object pairs that have the same hash value in a linked list. If this occurs very often, it is obviously going to slow up the process of storing and retrieving data. Retrieving an object that resulted in a collision when it was stored is a two-stage process. The key will be hashed to find the location where the key/object pair should be. The linked list then has to be searched to sort out the particular key you are searching on from all the others that have the same hash value. There is therefore a strong incentive to minimize collisions, and the price of reducing the possibility of collisions in a hash table is having plenty of empty space in the table.

The Object class defines the method hashCode(), so any object can be used as a key and it will hash by default. The method as it is implemented in Object in Java, however, isn't a panacea. Since it usually uses the memory address where an object is stored to produce the hash value, distinct objects always produce different hash values. In one sense this is a plus, because the more likely it is that a unique hash value will be produced for each key, the more efficient the operation of the hash map is going to be. The downside is that different object instances that have identical data will produce different hash values, so you can't compare them.

This becomes a nuisance if you use the default hashCode() method in objects that you're using as keys. In this case, an object stored in a hash map can never be retrieved using a different key object instance, even though that key object may be identical in all other respects. Yet this is precisely what you'll want to do in many cases.

Consider an application such as a simple address book. You might store map entries keyed on the names of the people to whom the entries relate, and you would want to search the map based on a name that was entered from the keyboard. However, the object representing the newly entered name is inevitably going to be distinct from that used as a key for the entry. Using the former, you won't be able to find the entry corresponding to the name.

The solution to this problem is to somehow make a hash of the instance variables of the object. Then, by comparing the values of the data members of the new name object with those for the name objects used as keys in the hash map, you'll be able to make a match.

Using Your Own Class Objects as Keys

For objects of one of your own classes to be usable as keys in a hash table, you must override the equals() method of the Object class. In its default form, equals() accepts an object of the same class as an argument and returns a boolean value. The equals() method is used by methods in the HashMap<> class to determine when two keys are equal, so in order to enable the changes discussed in the previous section, your version of this method should return true when two different objects contain identical data values.

You can also override the default hashCode() method, which returns the hash value for the object as type int. The hashCode() method is used to generate the int value that is the key. Your hashCode() method should produce hashcodes that are reasonably uniform over the possible range of keys, and generally unique for each key.

Generating Hashcodes

The various techniques for generating hashcodes form a big topic, and I can only scratch the surface here. How you write the hashCode() method for your class is up to you, but it needs to meet certain requirements if it is to be effective. A hashcode is returned by the hashcode() method as a value of type int. You should aim to return a hashcode that has a strong probability of being unique to the object, and the hashcodes that you produce for the range of different objects that you'll be working with should be as widely distributed across the range of int values as possible.

To achieve the uniqueness, you will typically want to combine the values of all the data members in an object to produce the hashcode, so the first step is to produce an integer corresponding to each data member. You must then combine these integers to generate the return value that will be the hashcode for the object. One technique you can use to do this is to multiply each of the integers corresponding to the data members by a different prime number and then sum the results. This should produce a reasonable distribution of values that have a good probability of being different for different objects. It doesn't matter which prime numbers you use as multipliers, as long as:

❏   They aren't so large as to cause the result to fall outside the range of type int

❏   You use a different one for each data member

So how do you get from a data member of a class to an integer? Generating an integer for data members of type String is easy: you just call the hashCode() method for the member. This has been implemented in the String class to produce good hashcode values that will be the same for identical strings (take a look at the source code if you want to see how). You can use integer data members as they are, but floating-point data members need a bit of judgment. If they have a small range in integer terms, you need to multiply them by a value that's going to result in a unique integer when they are cast to type int. If they have a very large range in integer terms you may need to scale them down.

Suppose you intended to use a `Person` object as a key in a hash table, and the class data members were `firstName` and `surname` of type `String` and `age` of type `int`. You could implement the `hashCode()` method for the class as:

```
public int hashCode() {
    return 13*firstName.hashCode() + 17*surname.hashCode() + 19*age;
}
```

Wherever a data member is an object of another class rather than a variable of one of the basic types, you need to implement the `hashCode()` method for that class. You can then use that in the computation of the hashcode for the key class.

Creating a HashMap Container

As you saw earlier in this chapter, all map classes implement the `Map<>` interface, so an object of any map class can be referenced using a variable of type `Map<>`. You will look in detail at the `HashMap<>` class since it is good for most purposes. There are four constructors you can use to create a `HashMap<K,V>` object:

Constructor	Description
`HashMap()`	Creates a map with the capacity to store a default number of objects. The default capacity is 16 objects, and the default load factor (more on the load factor below) is 0.75.
`HashMap(int capacity)`	Creates a map with the capacity to store the number of objects you specify in the argument and a default load factor of 0.75.
`HashMap(int capacity,float loadFactor)`	Creates a hash table with the capacity and load factor that you specify.
`HashMap(Map<? extends K, ? extends V> map)`	Creates a map with the capacity and load factor of the `Map` object passed as an argument.

To create a map using the default constructor, you can write something like this:

```
HashMap<String,Person> theMap = new HashMap<String,Person>();
```

This statement creates a `HashMap<>` object that can store `Person` objects with associated keys of type `String`.

The **capacity** for a map is simply the number of key/object pairs it can store. The capacity increases automatically as necessary, but this is a relatively time-consuming operation. The capacity value of the map is combined with the hashcode for the key that you specify to compute the index that determines where an object and its key are to be stored. To make this computation produce a good distribution of index values, you should ideally use prime numbers for the capacity of a hash table when you specify it yourself. For example:

```
HashMap myMap = new HashMap(151);
```

This map has a capacity for 151 objects and their keys, although the number of objects stored can never actually reach the capacity. You must always have spare capacity in a map for efficient operation. With too little spare capacity, you have an increased likelihood that keys will generate the same table index, so collisions become more likely.

The **load factor** is used to decide when to increase the size of the hash table. When the size of the table reaches a value that is the product of the load factor and the capacity, the capacity will be increased automatically to twice the old capacity plus 1 — the plus one ensuring it is at least odd, if not prime. The default load factor of 0.75 is a good compromise, but if you want to reduce it you could do so by using the third constructor:

```
// Create a map with a 60% load factor
HashMap<String,Person> aMap = new HashMap<String,Person>(151, 0.6f);
```

This map will work a bit more efficiently than the current default, but at the expense of having more unoccupied space. When 90 objects have been stored, the capacity will be increased to 303, (2*151+1).

Storing, Retrieving, and Removing Objects

Storing, retrieving, and removing objects in a HashMap<> is very simple. The four methods involved in these operations are:

Method	Description
V put(K key, V value)	Stores the object value in the map using the key specified by the first argument. value will displace any existing object associated with key, and a reference to the previous object for the key will be returned. If no object was previously stored for key or the key was used to store null as an object, null is returned.
void putAll(Map<? extends K,? extends V> map)	Transfers all the key/object pairs from map to the current map, replacing any objects that exist with the same keys.

Method	Description
`V get(Object key)`	Returns the object stored with the same key as the argument. If no object was stored with this key or `null` was stored as the object, `null` is returned. Note that the object remains in the table.
`V remove(Object key)`	Removes the entry associated with `key` if it exists and returns a reference to the object. A `null` is returned if the entry does not exist, or if `null` was stored using `key`.

If you attempt to retrieve an object using `get()` and a `null` is returned, it is still possible that a `null` was stored as the object associated with the key that you supplied to the `get()` method. You can determine if this is the case by passing your key object to the `containsKey()` method for the map. This will return `true` if the key is stored in the map.

You should ensure that the value returned from the `put()` method is `null`. If you don't, you may unwittingly displace an object that was stored in the table earlier using the same key. The following code fragment illustrates how you might do that:

```
HashMap<String,Integer> aMap = new HashMap<String,Integer>();
String myKey = "Goofy";
int value = 12345;
Integer oldValue = null;
for (int i = 0 ; i<4 ; i++) {
  if((oldValue = aMap.put(myKey, value++)) != null) {
    System.out.println("Uh-oh, we bounced an object: " + oldValue);
  }
}
```

Of course, you could throw your own exception here instead of displaying a message on the command line. The second parameter to the `put()` method for the `aMap` object will be of type `Integer`, so the compiler supplies an autoboxing conversion for the `int` value that is passed as the argument.

If you execute this fragment it will generate the following output:

```
Uh-oh, we bounced an object: 12345
Uh-oh, we bounced an object: 12346
Uh-oh, we bounced an object: 12347
```

When the first value is stored, there's nothing stored in the map for the key, so there's no message. For all subsequent attempts to store objects, the previous object is displaced, and a reference to it is returned.

Note that the `get()` operation will return a reference to the object associated with the key, but it does not remove it from the table. To retrieve an object and delete the entry containing it from the table, you must use the `remove()` method. This removes the object corresponding to the key and returns a reference to it:

```
int objectValue = aMap.remove(myKey);
```

As noted in the table, if there's no stored object corresponding to myKey, or null was stored as the object, null will be returned. If you were to append this statement to the previous fragment, a reference to an Integer object encapsulating the value 12348 would be returned. Since you store it in a variable of type int, the compiler will insert an unboxing conversion for the return value.

Processing all the Elements in a Map

The Map<> interface provides three ways of obtaining a collection view of the contents of a map. You can obtain all the keys from a Map<K, V> object as an object of type Set<K>. You can also get a Collection<V> object that references all the objects in the map. Key/object pairs are stored in a map as objects of type that implement the Map.Entry<K, V> interface. This is a generic interface type that is defined within the Map<K, V> interface. You can get all the key/object pairs from the map as an object of type Set<Map.Entry<K, V>>.

Note that the Set<> or Collection<> object that you get is essentially a view of the contents of a map, so changes to a HashMap<> object will be reflected in the associated Set<> or Collection<>, and vice versa. The three methods involved are:

Method	Description
keySet()	Returns a Set<K> object referencing the keys from the map
entrySet()	Returns a Set<Map.Entry<K, V>> object referencing the key/object pairs — each pair being an object of type Map.Entry<K, V>
values()	Returns a Collection<V> object referencing the objects stored in the map

Let's first see how you can use a set of keys. The keySet() method for a HashMap<K, V> object returns a Set<K> object referencing the set of keys that you can either use directly to access the keys, or use indirectly to get at the objects stored in the map. For a HashMap<String, Integer> object aMap, you could get the set of all the keys in the map with the statement:

```
Set<String> keys = aMap.keySet();
```

Now you can get an iterator for this set of keys with the statement:

```
Iterator<String> keyIter = keys.iterator();
```

You can use the iterator() method for the object keys to iterate over all the keys in the map. Of course, you can combine these two operations to get the iterator directly. For example:

```
Iterator<String> keyIter = aMap.keySet().iterator();   // Get the iterator

while(keyIter.hasNext()) {                              // Iterate over the keys
  System.out.println(keyIter.next());
}
```

This iterates over all the keys and outputs them. Of course, you could use the keys to extract the objects but the Collection<> object that is returned by the values() method provides you with a more direct way of doing this. Here's how you could list the objects stored in aMap, assuming it is of type HashMap<String,Integer>:

```
Collection<Integer> collection = aMap.values();
for(Integer i : collection) {
  System.out.println(i);
}
```

This uses a collection-based for loop to iterate over the elements in the collection of objects that the values() method returns.

Of course, the Set<> interface has Iterable<> as a superinterface, so you could use the collection-based for loop directly with the object that the keySet() method returns:

```
Set<String> keys = aMap.keySet();
for(String key : keys) {
  System.out.println(key);
}
```

That's much neater than messing about with an iterator, isn't it? In general, the collection-based for loop will provide you with code that is easier to understand than an iterator.

The method entrySet() returns a Set<Map.Entry<K,V>> object referencing the key/object pairs. In a similar way that you used for the set of keys, you use a for loop to access the Map.Entry<> objects. Each Map.Entry<K,V> object will contain the following methods to operate on it:

Method	Description
K getKey()	Returns the key for the Map.Entry<K,V> object.
V getValue()	Returns the object for the Map.Entry<K,V> object.
V setValue(V new)	Sets the object for this Map.Entry<K,V> object to the argument and returns the original object. Remember that this alters the original map. This method throws:
	UnsupportedOperationException if put() is not supported by the underlying map
	ClassCastException if the argument cannot be stored because of its type
	IllegalArgumentException if the argument is otherwise invalid
	NullPointerException if the map does not allow null objects to be stored. This last exception does not apply to HashMap<>.

A Map.Entry<> object will also need an equals() method for comparisons with another Map.Entry<> object passed as an argument, and a hashCode() method to compute a hashcode for the Map.Entry object. With a set of Map.Entry<> objects you can obviously access the keys and the corresponding objects using a collection-based for loop, and you can modify the object part of each key/object pair if you need to.

You have waded through a lot of the theory for HashMap<> objects; let's put together an example that applies it.

You can create a very simple phone book that uses a map. We won't worry too much about error recovery so as not to bulk up the code. You'll use a variation of the last version of the Person class that you saw earlier in this chapter in the example where you were sorting objects in a vector. Copy the source file to a new directory called TryHashMap or something similar. Besides the Person class, you'll need to create a PhoneNumber class and an Entry class that represents an entry in your phone book combining a name and a number. You could add other stuff such as the address, but this is not necessary to show the principles. You'll also define a PhoneBook class to represent the phone book.

Try It Out   Using a HashMap Map

You need to improve your old Person class to make Person objects usable as keys in the map that you will use — to store the phone book entries. You must add an equals() method to do this, and you'll override the default hashCode() method just to show how this can work. The extended version of the class will be as follows:

```
import java.io.Serializable;

public class Person implements Comparable<Person>, Serializable {
  public boolean equals(Object person) {
    return compareTo((Person)person) == 0;
  }

  public int hashCode() {
    return 7*firstName.hashCode()+13*surname.hashCode();
  }

  // The rest of the class as before...
}
```

You've added to the previous version of the class two methods that override the equals() and hash-code() methods inherited from Object. Because the String class defines a good hashCode() method, you can easily produce a hash code for a Person object from the data members. To implement the equals() method you just call the compareTo() method that you implemented for the Comparable<> interface. You have also made the class serializable just in case it comes in useful at some point.

There's another thing you can do that will definitely be useful. You can add to the Person class a static method that will read data for a Person object from the keyboard:

```
import java.io.BufferedReader;
import java.io.InputStreamReader;
import java.io.IOException;
import java.io.Serializable;
```

```
public class Person implements Comparable<Person>, Serializable {
  // Read a person from the keyboard
  public static readPerson() {
    String firstName = null;
    String surname = null;
    try {
      System.out.print("Enter first name: ");
      firstName = keyboard.readLine().trim();
      System.out.print("Enter surname: ");
      surname = keyboard.readLine().trim();
    } catch(IOException e) {
      System.err.println("Error reading a name.");
      e.printStackTrace();
      System.exit(1);
    }
    return new Person(firstName,surname);
  }

  private static BufferedReader keyboard = new BufferedReader(
                                      new InputStreamReader(System.in));
  // Rest of the class as before...
}
```

You should have no trouble seeing how this works as it's almost identical to the `readPerson()` method you used previously in this chapter.

You can make the PhoneNumber class very simple:

```
import java.io.Serializable;

class PhoneNumber implements Serializable {
  public PhoneNumber(String areacode, String number) {
    this.areacode = areacode;
    this.number = number;
  }

  public String toString() {
    return areacode + " " + number;
  }

  private String areacode;
  private String number;
}
```

You could do a whole lot of validity checking of the number here, but it's not important for the example.

However, you could use a `static` method to read a number from the keyboard, so let's add that, too:

```
import java.io.BufferedReader;
import java.io.InputStreamReader;
import java.io.IOException;
import java.io.Serializable;
```

```
class PhoneNumber implements Serializable {
  // Read a phone number from the keyboard
  public static PhoneNumber readNumber() {
    String area = null;                        // Stores the area code
    String localcode = null;                   // Stores the local code
    try {
      System.out.print("Enter area code: ");
      area = keyboard.readLine().trim();
      System.out.print("Enter local code: ");
      localcode = keyboard.readLine().trim();
      System.out.print("Enter the number: ");
      localcode += " " + keyboard.readLine().trim();
    } catch(IOException e) {
      System.err.println("Error reading a phone number.");
      e.printStackTrace();
      System.exit(1);
    }
    return new PhoneNumber(area,localcode);
  }

  private static BufferedReader keyboard = new BufferedReader(
                                  new InputStreamReader(System.in));
  // Rest of the class as before...
}
```

This is again very similar to the `readPerson()` method. You don't need a separate variable to store the number that is entered. You just append the string that is read to `localcode`, with a space character inserted to make the output look nice. In practice, you'd certainly want to verify that the input was valid, but you don't need this to show how a hash map works.

An entry in the phone book will combine the name and the number and would probably include other things such as the address. You can get by with the basics:

```
import java.io.Serializable;

class BookEntry implements Serializable {
  public BookEntry(Person person, PhoneNumber number) {
    this.person = person;
    this.number = number;
  }

  public Person getPerson() {
    return person;
  }

  public PhoneNumber getNumber() {
    return number;
  }

  public String toString() {
    return person.toString() + '\n' + number.toString();
  }
```

```
    // Read an entry from the keyboard
    public static BookEntry readEntry() {
      return new BookEntry(Person.readPerson(), PhoneNumber.readNumber());
    }

    private Person person;
    private PhoneNumber number;
  }
```

This is all pretty standard stuff. In the `static readEntry()` method, you just make use of the methods that create `Person` and `PhoneNumber` objects using input from the keyboard, so this becomes very simple.

The class that implements the phone book is next — called the `PhoneBook` class, of course:

```
import java.io.Serializable;
import java.util.HashMap;

class PhoneBook implements Serializable {
  public void addEntry(BookEntry entry) {
    phonebook.put(entry.getPerson(), entry);
  }

  public BookEntry getEntry(Person key) {
    return phonebook.get(key);
  }

  public PhoneNumber getNumber(Person key) {
    return getEntry(key).getNumber();
  }

  private HashMap<Person,BookEntry> phonebook = new HashMap<Person,BookEntry>();
}
```

To store `BookEntry` objects you use a `HashMap<Person, BookEntry>` member, `phonebook`. You'll use the `Person` object corresponding to an entry as the key, so the `addEntry()` method has to retrieve only the `Person` object from the `BookEntry` object that is passed to it and use that as the first argument to the `put()` method for `phonebook`.

All you need now is a class containing `main()` to test these classes:

```
public class TryPhoneBook {
  public static void main(String[] args) {
    PhoneBook book = new PhoneBook();                    // The phone book
    FormattedInput in = new FormattedInput();            // Keyboard input
    Person someone;
    for(;;) {
      System.out.println("Enter 1 to enter a new phone book entry\n"+
                         "Enter 2 to find the number for a name\n"+
                         "Enter 9 to quit.");
      int what = 0;                                      // Stores input selection
      try {
        what = in.readInt();
```

```
        } catch(InvalidUserInputException e) {
          System.out.println(e.getMessage()+"\nTry again.");
          continue;
        }

        switch(what) {
          case 1:
            book.addEntry(BookEntry.readEntry());
            break;
          case 2:
            someone = Person.readPerson();
            BookEntry entry = book.getEntry(someone);
            if(entry == null) {
              System.out.println("The number for " + someone +
                                 " was not found. ");
            } else {
              System.out.println("The number for " + someone +
                                 " is " + entry.getNumber());
            }
            break;
          case 9:
            System.out.println("Ending program.");
            return;
          default:
            System.out.println("Invalid selection, try again.");
            break;
        }
      }
    }
  }
}
```

You're using the FormattedInput class that you developed in Chapter 8 to read the input values, so copy the source file for this class along with the source file for the InvalidUserInputException class, which is also from Chapter 8, to the directory for this example.

This is what the example produces with my input:

```
Enter 1 to enter a new phone book entry
Enter 2 to find the number for a name
Enter 9 to quit.
1
Enter first name:
Algernon
Enter surname:
Lickspittle
Enter area code:
914
Enter local code:
321
Enter the number :
3333
Enter 1 to enter a new phone book entry
Enter 2 to find the number for a name
```

```
Enter 9 to quit.
2
Enter first name:
Algernon
Enter surname:
Lickspittle
The number for Algernon Lickspittle is 914 321 3333
Enter 1 to enter a new phone book entry
Enter 2 to find the number for a name
Enter 9 to quit.
9
```

Ending program.

Of course, you can try it with several entries if you have the stamina.

How It Works

The main() method runs an ongoing loop that will continue until a 9 is entered. When a 1 is entered, the addEntry() method for the PhoneBook object is called with the expression BookEntry.readEntry() as the argument. The static method readEntry() calls the static methods in the Person class and the PhoneNumber class to read from the keyboard and create objects of these classes. The readEntry() method then passes these objects to the constructor for the BookEntry class, and the object that is created is returned. This object will be added to the HashMap member of the PhoneBook object.

If a 2 is entered, the getEntry() method is called. The argument expression calls the readPerson() member of the Person class to obtain the Person object corresponding to the name entered from the keyboard. This object is then used to retrieve an entry from the map in the PhoneBook object. Of course, if there is no such entry null will be returned, so you have to check for it and display an appropriate message.

Try It Out	Storing a Map in a File

This phone book is not particularly useful. The process of echoing what you just keyed in doesn't hold one's interest for long. What you need is a phone book that is held in a file. That's not difficult. You just need to add a constructor and another method to the PhoneBook class:

```java
import java.io.File;
import java.io.FileInputStream;
import java.io.ObjectInputStream;
import java.io.FileOutputStream;
import java.io.ObjectOutputStream;
import java.io.IOException;
import java.io.Serializable;
import java.util.HashMap;

class PhoneBook implements Serializable {
  public PhoneBook() {
    if(filename.exists())                       // If there's a phone book in a file...
    try {
      ObjectInputStream in = new ObjectInputStream(
      new FileInputStream(filename));
      phonebook = (HashMap<Person, BookEntry>)in.readObject();  //...read it in.
      in.close();
```

```
        } catch(ClassNotFoundException e) {
          e.printStackTrace();
          System.exit(1);
        } catch(IOException e) {
          e.printStackTrace();
          System.exit(1);
        }
    }

    public void save() {
      try {
        System.out.println("Saving phone book");
        ObjectOutputStream out = new ObjectOutputStream(
                                      new FileOutputStream(filename));
        out.writeObject(phonebook);
        System.out.println("Done");
        out.close();

      } catch(IOException e) {
        e.printStackTrace();
        System.exit(1);
      }
    }

    private File filename = new File("Phonebook.bin");

    // Other members of the class as before...
  }
```

The new private data member `filename` defines the name of the file where the map holding the phone book entries is to be stored. Since you have specified only the file name and extension, the file will be assumed to be in the current directory. The `filename` object is used in the constructor that now reads the `HashMap<>` object from the file if it exists. If it doesn't exist, the constructor does nothing, and the `PhoneBook` object will use the default empty `HashMap` object. The cast of the reference returned by the `readObject()` method to type `HashMap<Person, BookEntry>` will cause the compiler to issue a warning message to the effect that you have an unchecked cast. There is no way around this since the compiler cannot know what the type of the object that is read from the file will be. Everything will be fine as long as you know what you are doing!

The `save()` method provides for storing the map away, so you will need to call this method before ending the program.

To make the program a little more interesting you could add a method to the `PhoneBook` class that will list all the entries in a phone book. Ideally, the entries should be displayed in alphabetical order by name. One way to do this would be to create a linked list containing the entries and use the static `sort()` method that the `Collections` class defines to sort them. The `sort()` method expects an argument that is of type `List<>`, where the type of elements in the list implements the `Comparable<>` interface. Thus, to be able to sort the entries in the phone book, the `BookEntry` class must implement the `Comparable<>` interface. This is quite easy to arrange:

```
import java.io.Serializable;

class BookEntry implements Comparable<BookEntry>, Serializable {
  public int compareTo(BookEntry entry) {
    return person.compareTo(entry.getPerson());
  }
  // Rest of the class as before...
}
```

For the purpose of sorting the entries, you'll want to use the sort order of the Person objects to determine the sort order of the BookEntry objects. Because the Person class already implements the Comparable<> interface, you can implement the compareTo() method in the BookEntry class by calling the method for the Person object in the entry.

Now you can implement the listEntries() method in the PhoneBook class to list the entries in alphabetical order:

```
import java.io.File;
import java.io.FileInputStream;
import java.io.ObjectInputStream;
import java.io.FileOutputStream;
import java.io.ObjectOutputStream;
import java.io.IOException;
import java.io.Serializable;
import java.util.HashMap;
import java.util.LinkedList;
import java.util.Collections;

class PhoneBook implements Serializable {
  // List all entries in the book
  public void listEntries() {
    // Get the entries as a linked list
    LinkedList<BookEntry> entries = new LinkedList<BookEntry>(phonebook.values());
    Collections.sort(entries);                  // Sort the entries

    for(BookEntry entry : entries) {
      System.out.println(entry);
    }
  }
  // Other members as before...
}
```

Listing the entries in name sequence is relatively simple. Calling the values() method for the phonebook object returns the objects in the map, which are BookEntry objects, as a Collection<>. You pass this to the constructor for the LinkedList<BookEntry> class to obtain an object of that type. The LinkedList<> class implements the List<> interface, so you can pass the entries object to the sort() method to sort the entries. It's then a simple matter of using the collection-based for loop to iterate through the sorted entries to output them.

You can update main() to take advantage of the new features of the PhoneBook class:

```
class TryPhoneBook {
  public static void main(String[] args) {
    PhoneBook book = new PhoneBook();            // The phone book
    FormattedInput in = new FormattedInput();    // Keyboard input
    Person someone;

    for(;;) {
      System.out.println("Enter 1 to enter a new phone book entry\n"+
                         "Enter 2 to find the number for a name\n"+
                         "Enter 3 to list all the entries\n" +
                         "Enter 9 to quit.");
      int what = 0;
      try {
        what = in.readInt();

      } catch(InvalidUserInputException e) {
        System.out.println(e.getMessage()+"\nTry again.");
        continue;
      }

      switch(what) {
        case 1:
          book.addEntry(BookEntry.readEntry());
          break;
        case 2:
          someone = Person.readPerson();
          BookEntry entry = book.getEntry(someone);
          if(entry == null) {
            System.out.println("The number for " + someone +
                               " was not found. ");
          } else {
            System.out.println("The number for " + someone +
                               " is " + entry.getNumber());
          }
          break;
        case 3:
          book.listEntries();
          break;
        case 9:
          book.save();
          System.out.println("Ending program.");
          return;
        default:
          System.out.println("Invalid selection, try again.");
          break;
      }
    }
  }
}
```

How It Works

The first changes here are an updated prompt for input and a new case in the switch to list the entries
in the phone book. The other change is to call the save() method to write the map that stores the phone
book to a file before ending the program.

> Be aware of the default hashCode() method in the Object class when storing maps. The hashcodes are generated from the address of the object, and getting a key object back from a file in exactly the same place in memory is about as likely as finding hairs on a frog. The result is that the hashcode generated from the key when it is read back will be different from what was originally produced, so you will never find the entry in the map to which it corresponds.
>
> If you override the default hashCode() method, then the hashcodes are produced from the data members of the key objects, so they are always the same regardless of where the key objects are stored in memory.

The first time you run this version of TryPhoneBook it will create a new file and store the entire phone book in it. On subsequent occasions the PhoneBook constructor will read from the file, so all the previous entries are available.

In the next chapter you'll move on to look at some of the other components from the java.util package.

Summary

All of the classes in this chapter will be useful sooner or later when you're writing your own Java programs. You'll be applying many of them in examples throughout the remainder of the book.

The important elements you've covered are:

❏ The Java collections framework provides you with a range of collection classes implemented as generic types. These enable you to organize your data in various ways.

❏ You can use a Vector<> object as a kind of flexible array that expands automatically to accommodate any number of objects stored.

❏ The Stack<> class is derived from the Vector class and implements a pushdown stack.

❏ The HashMap<> class defines a hash map in which objects are stored based on an associated key.

❏ An Iterator<> is an interface for retrieving objects from a collection sequentially. An Iterator<> object allows you to access all the objects it contains serially — but only once. There's no way to go back to the beginning.

❏ The ListIterator<> interface provides methods for traversing the objects in a collection backwards or forwards.

❏ Objects stored in any type of collection can be accessed using Iterator<> objects.

❏ Objects stored in a Vector<>, a Stack<>, or a LinkedList<> can be accessed using ListIterator<> objects.

Exercises

You can download the source code for the examples in the book and the solutions to the following exercises from `http://www.wrox.com`.

1. Implement a version of the program to calculate prime numbers that you saw in Chapter 4 to use a `Vector<>` object instead of an array to store the primes. (Hint: Remember the `Integer` class.)

2. Write a program to store a deck of 52 cards in a linked list in random sequence using a `Random` class object. You can represent a card as a two-character string — `"1C"` for the ace of clubs, `"JD"` for the jack of diamonds, and so on. Output the cards from the stack as four hands of 13 cards.

3. Extend the program from this chapter that used a map to store names and telephone numbers such that you can enter a number to retrieve the name.

4. Implement a phone book so that just a surname can be used to search, and have all the entries corresponding to the name display.

A Collection of Useful Classes

In this chapter you'll be looking at some more very useful classes in the `java.util` package, but this time they are not collection classes — just a collection of classes. You will also be looking at the facilities provided by classes in the `java.util.regex` package that implement regular expressions in Java. Support for regular expressions is a very powerful and important feature of Java.

In this chapter you'll learn:

- ❑ How to use the static methods in the `Arrays` class for filling, comparing, sorting, and searching arrays

- ❑ How to use the `Observable` class and the `Observer` interface to communicate between objects

- ❑ What facilities the `Random` class provides

- ❑ How to create and use `Date` and `Calendar` objects

- ❑ What regular expressions are and how you can create and use them

- ❑ What a `Scanner` class does and how you use it

Utility Methods for Arrays

The `Arrays` class in `java.util` provides you with a set of static methods for operating on arrays. You have methods for sorting and searching arrays, as well as methods for comparing two arrays of elements of a basic type. You also have methods for filling arrays of elements with a given value. Let's look at the simplest method first, the `fill()` method for filling an array.

Filling an Array

The need to fill an array with a specific value arises quite often, and you already met the static `fill()` method that is defined in the `Arrays` class back in Chapter 4. The `fill()` method comes in a number of overloaded versions of the form:

```
fill(type[] array, type value)
```

Here *type* is a placeholder for the types supported by various versions of the method. The method stores `value` in each element of `array`. The return type is `void` so there is no return value. There are versions supporting *type* as any of the following:

boolean		byte	char	float	double
short		int	long	Object	

Here's how you could fill an array of integers with a particular value:

```
long[] values = new long[1000];
java.util.Arrays.fill(values, 888L);   // Every element as 888
```

It's quite easy to initialize multidimensional arrays. To initialize a two-dimensional array, for example, you just treat it as an array of one-dimensional arrays. For example:

```
int[][] dataValues = new int[10][20];
for(int[] row : dataValues) {
  Arrays.fill(row, 99);
}
```

This will set every element on the `dataValues` array to 99. The loop iterates over the 10 arrays of 20 elements that make up the `dataValues` array. If you want to set the rows in the array to different values, you could do it like this:

```
int initial = 0;
int[][] dataValues = new int[10][20];
for(int[] row : dataValues) {
  Arrays.fill(row, ++initial);
}
```

This will result in the first row of 20 elements being set to 1, the second row of 20 elements to 2, and so on through to the last row of 20 elements that will be set to 10.

The version of `fill()` accepting an array argument of type `Object[]` will obviously process an array of any class type. You could fill an array of `Person` objects like this:

```
Person[] people = new Person[100];
java.util.Arrays(people, new Person("John", "Doe"));
```

This will insert a reference to the object passed as the second argument to the `fill()` method in every element of the `people` array. Note that there is only one `Person` object that all the array elements reference.

There is a further form of `fill()` method that accepts four arguments. This is of the form:

```
fill(type[] array, int fromIndex, int toIndex, type value)
```

This will fill part of `array` with `value`, starting at `array[fromIndex]` up to and including `array[toIndex-1]`. There are versions of this method for the same range of types at the previous set of `fill()` methods. This variety of `fill()` will throw an exception of type `IllegalArgumentException` if `fromIndex` is greater than `toIndex`. It will also throw an exception of type `ArrayIndexOutOfBoundsException` if `fromIndex` is negative or `toIndex` is greater than `array.length`. Here's an example of using this form of the `fill()` method:

```
Person[] people = new Person[100];
java.util.Arrays(people, 0, 50, new Person("Jane", "Doe");
java.util.Arrays(people, 50, 100, new Person("John", "Doe");
```

This will set the first 50 elements to reference one `Person` object and the second 50 elements to reference another.

Comparing Arrays

There are nine overloaded versions of the static `equals()` method for comparing arrays defined in the `Arrays` class, one for each of the types that apply to the `fill()` method. All versions of `equals()` are of the form:

```
boolean equals(type[] array1, type[] array2)
```

The method returns `true` if `array1` is equal to `array2` and `false` otherwise. The two arrays are equal if they contain the same number of elements and the values of all corresponding elements in the two arrays are equal. If `array1` and `array2` are both `null`, they are also considered to be equal.

When floating-point arrays are compared, `0.0` is considered to be equal to `-0.0`, and two elements that contain `NaN` are also considered to be equal. When arrays with elements of a class type are compared, the elements are compared by calling the `equals()` method for the class. If you have not implemented the `equals()` method in your own classes, then the version inherited from the `Object` class will be used. This compares references, not objects, and so returns `true` only if both object references refer to the same object.

Here's how you can compare two arrays:

```
String[] numbers = {"one", "two", "three", "four" };
String[] values = {"one", "two", "three", "four" };
if(java.util.Arrays.equals(numbers, values)) {
  System.out.println("The arrays are equal");
} else {
  System.out.println("The arrays are not equal");
}
```

In this fragment both arrays are equal so the `equals()` method will return `true`.

Sorting Arrays

The static `sort()` method in the `Arrays` class will sort the elements of an array that you pass as the argument into ascending sequence. The method is overloaded for eight of the nine types (`boolean` is excluded) we saw for the `fill()` method for each of two versions of `sort()`:

```
void sort(type[] array)

void sort(type[] array, int fromIndex, int toIndex)
```

The first variety sorts the entire array into ascending sequence. The second variety sorts the elements from `array[fromIndex]` to `array [toIndex-1]` into ascending sequence. This will throw an exception of type `IllegalArgumentException` if `fromIndex` is greater than `toIndex`. It will also throw an exception of type `ArrayIndexOutOfBoundsException` if `fromIndex` is negative or `toIndex` is greater than `array.length`.

Obviously, you can pass an array of elements of any class type to the versions of the `sort()` method that have the first parameter as type `Object[]`. If you are using either variety of the `sort()` method to sort objects, then the class type of the objects must support the `Comparable<>` interface since the `sort()` method uses the `compareTo()` method to compare objects.

Here's how we can sort an array of strings:

```
String[] numbers = {"one", "two", "three", "four", "five",
                    "six", "seven", "eight"};
java.util.Arrays.sort(numbers);
```

After executing these statements, the elements of the array `numbers` will contain:

```
"eight" "five" "four" "one" "seven" "six" "three" "two"
```

Two additional versions of the `sort()` method for sorting arrays of type `Object[]` are both parameterized methods. These are for sorting arrays in which the order of elements is determined by using an external comparator object. The class type of the comparator object must implement the `java.util.Comparator<>` interface. One advantage of using an external comparator for sorting a collection of objects is that you can have several comparators that can impose different orderings depending on the circumstances. For example, in some cases you might want to sort a name file ordering by first name within second name. On other occasions you might want to sort by second name within first name. You can't do this using the `Comparable<>` interface implemented by the class. The first version of the `sort()` method that makes use of a comparator is:

```
<T>void sort(T[] array, Comparator<? super T> comparator)
```

This will sort the elements of the entire array passed as the first argument using the comparator passed as the second argument.

The second version of the `sort()` method using a comparator is:

```
<T>void sort(T[] array,
             int fromIndex, int toIndex, Comparator<? super T>  comparator)
```

This sorts the elements of the array from index position `fromIndex` up to but excluding the element at index position `toIndex`.

The wildcard parameter to the `Comparator<>` type specifies that the type argument to the comparator can be `T` or any superclass of `T`. This implies that so far as the `sort()` method is concerned it can sort an array of elements of type `T` using a `Comparator<>` object that can compare objects of type `T` or that can compare objects of any superclass of `T`. To put this in a specific context, this means that you can use an object of type `Comparator<Person>` to sort an array of objects of type `Manager`, where `Manager` is a subclass of `Person`.

The `Comparator<>` interface declares two methods. First is the `compare()` method, which is used by the `sort()` method for comparing elements of the array of type `T[]`. The method compares two objects of type `T` that are passed as arguments, so it's of the form:

```
int compare(T obj1, T obj2)
```

The method returns a negative integer, zero, or a positive integer, depending on whether `obj1` is less than, equal to, or greater than `obj2`. The method will throw an exception of type `ClassCastException` if the types of the argument you pass are such that they cannot be compared by the comparator.

The second method declared by the `Comparator<>` interface is the `equals()` method, which is used for comparing `Comparator<>` objects for equality. The method is of the form:

```
boolean equals(Object comparator)
```

This compares the current `Comparator<>` object with another object of a type that also implements the `Comparator<>` interface that you pass as the argument. It returns a `boolean` value indicating whether the current comparator object and the argument impose the same ordering on a collection of objects. I think it would be a good idea to see how sorting using a `Comparator<>` object works in practice.

Try It Out   Sorting Using a Comparator

You can borrow the version of the `Person` class that implements the `Comparable<>` interface from the `TryVector` example in Chapter 14 for this example. Copy the `Person.java` file to the directory you set up for this example. The comparator will need access to the first name and the surname for a `Person` object to make comparisons, so you'll need to add methods to the `Person` class to allow that:

```
public class Person implements Comparable<Person> {
  public String getFirstName() {
    return firstName;
  }

  public String getSurname() {
    return surname;
  }
  // Rest of the class as before...
}
```

You can now define a class for a comparator that applies to `Person` objects:

```java
import java.util.Comparator;

public class ComparePersons implements Comparator<Person> {
  // Method to compare Person objects - order is descending
  public int compare(Person person1, Person person2) {
    int result = -person1.getSurname().compareTo(person2.getSurname());
    return result == 0 ?
          -person1.getFirstName().compareTo(person2.getFirstName()) : result;
  }

  // Method to compare with another comparator
  public boolean equals(Object collator) {
    if(this == collator) {              // If argument is the same object
      return true;                       // then it must be equal
    }
    if(collator == null) {              // If argument is null
      return false;                      // then it can't be equal
    }
    return getClass() == collator.getClass(); // Class must be the same for equal
  }
}
```

Just to make it more interesting and to demonstrate that it's this comparator and not the `compareTo()` method in the `Person` class that's being used by the `sort()` method, this comparator establishes a descending sequence of `Person` objects. By switching the sign that the `compareTo()` method returns, you invert the sort order here. Thus, sorting using this comparator will sort `Person` objects in descending alphabetical order by surname and then by first name within surname.

You can try this out with the following program:

```java
import java.util.Arrays;

public class TrySortingWithComparator {
  public static void main(String[] args) {
    Person[] authors = {
            new Person("Danielle", "Steel"), new Person("John", "Grisham"),
            new Person("Tom", "Clancy"),     new Person("Christina", "Schwartz"),
            new Person("Patricia", "Cornwell"), new Person("Bill", "Bryson")
                       };

    System.out.println("Original order:");
    for(Person author : authors) {
      System.out.println(author);
    }

    Arrays.sort(authors, new ComparePersons());  // Sort using comparator

    System.out.println("\nOrder after sorting using comparator:");
    for(Person author : authors) {
      System.out.println(author);
    }
```

```
      Arrays.sort(authors);                        // Sort using Comparable method

      System.out.println("\nOrder after sorting using Comparable method:");
      for(Person author : authors) {
        System.out.println(author);
      }
    }
  }
```

This example will produce the following output:

```
Original order:
Danielle Steel
John Grisham
Tom Clancy
Christina Schwartz
Patricia Cornwell
Bill Bryson

Order after sorting using comparator:
Danielle Steel
Christina Schwartz
John Grisham
Patricia Cornwell
Tom Clancy
Bill Bryson

Order after sorting using Comparable method:
Bill Bryson
Tom Clancy
Patricia Cornwell
John Grisham
Christina Schwartz
Danielle Steel
```

How It Works

After defining the authors array of Person objects, you sort them with the statement:

```
Arrays.sort(authors, new ComparePersons());  // Sort using comparator
```

The second argument is an instance of the ComparePersons class, which is a comparator for Person objects because it implements the Comparator<Person> interface. The sort() method calls the compare() method to establish the order between Person objects, and you defined this method like this:

```
public int compare(Person person1, Person person2) {
  int result = -person1.getSurname().compareTo(person2.getSurname());
  return result == 0 ? -person1.getFirstName().compareTo(person2.getFirstName())
                                                                : result;
}
```

The primary comparison is between surnames and returns a result that is the opposite of that produced by the `compareTo()` method for `String` objects. Since the order established by the `compareTo()` method is ascending, your `compare()` method establishes a descending sequence. If the surnames are equal, the order is determined by the first names, again inverting the sign of the value returned by the `compareTo()` method to maintain descending sequence. Of course, you could have coded this method by switching the arguments, `person1` and `person2`, instead of reversing the sign:

```
public int compare(Person person1, Person person2) {
    int result = person2.getSurname().compareTo(person1.getSurname());
    return result == 0 ? person2.getFirstName().compareTo(person1.getFirstName())
                                                                  : result;

}
```

This would establish a descending sequence for `Person` objects.

You call the `sort()` method a second time with the statement:

```
Arrays.sort(authors);                          // Sort using Comparable method
```

Because you have not supplied a comparator, the `sort()` method expects the class type of the elements to be sorted to have implemented the `Comparable<>` interface. Fortunately your `Person` class does, so the authors get sorted. This time the result is in ascending sequence because that's what the `compareTo()` method establishes.

Searching Arrays

The static `binarySearch()` method in the `Arrays` class will search the elements of a sorted array for a given value using the binary search algorithm. This works only if the elements of the array are in ascending sequence, so if they are not, you should call the `sort()` method to sort the array in ascending sequence before calling the `binarySearch()` method. The binary search algorithm works by repeatedly subdividing the sequence of elements to find the target element value, as illustrated in Figure 15-1.

The figure shows two searches of an array of integers. The first step is always to compare the target with the element at the approximate center of the array. The second step is to examine the element at the approximate center of the left or right half of the array, depending of whether the target is less than or greater than the element. This process of subdividing and examining the element at the middle of the interval continues until the target is found, or the interval consists of a single element that is different from the target. When the target is found, the result is the index position of the element that is equal to the target. You should be able to see from this process that the algorithm implicitly assumes that the elements are in ascending order.

You have eight overloaded versions of the `binarySearch()` method supporting the same range of types that you saw with the `fill()` method earlier. The `boolean` type is not supported by the `binarySearch()` method:

```
binarySearch(type[] array, type value)
```

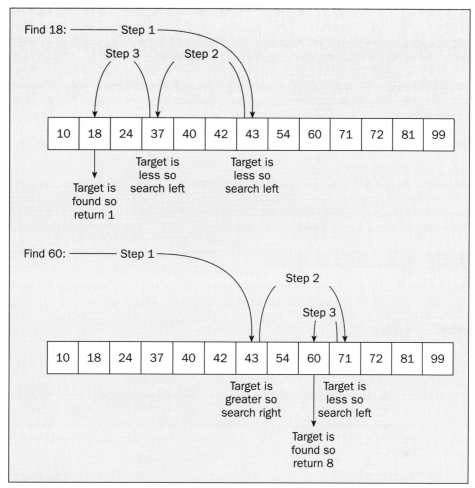

Figure 15-1

You have an additional version of the `binarySearch()` method for searching an array of type `Object[]` for which you can supply a reference to a `Comparator<>` object as the fourth argument.

All versions of the `binarySearch()` method return a value of type `int`, which is the index position in array where `value` was found. Of course, it is possible that the value is not in the array. In this case a negative integer is returned that is produced by taking the value of the index position of the first element that is greater than the value, reversing its sign, and subtracting 1. For example, suppose you have an array of integers containing the element values 2, 4, 6, 8, and 10:

```
int[] numbers = {2, 4, 6, 8, 10};
```

You could search for the value 7 with the statement:

```
int position = java.util.Arrays.binarySearch(numbers, 7);
```

The value of `position` will be `-4`, because the element at index position 3 is the first element that is greater than 7. The return value is calculated as `-3-1`, which is `-4`. This mechanism guarantees that if the value sought is not in the array, then the return value is always negative, so you'll always be able to tell whether a value is in the array by examining the sign of the result.

Unless you are using a method that uses a comparator for searching arrays of objects, the class type of the array elements must implement the `Comparable` interface. Here's how we could search for a string in an array of strings:

```
String[] numbers ={"one", "two", "three", "four", "five", "six", "seven"};

java.util.Arrays.sort(numbers);
int position = java.util.Arrays.binarySearch(numbers, "three");
```

We have to sort the `numbers` array; otherwise, the binary search won't work. After executing these statements the value of `position` will be 6.

Try It Out   In Search of an Author

You could search the `authors` array from the previous example. Copy the source file for the `Person` class to a new directory for this example. Here's the code to try a binary search:

```
import java.util.Arrays;

public class TryBinarySearch {
  public static void main(String[] args) {
    Person[] authors = {
            new Person("Danielle", "Steel"), new Person("John", "Grisham"),
            new Person("Tom", "Clancy"),     new Person("Christina", "Schwartz"),
            new Person("Patricia", "Cornwell"), new Person("Bill", "Bryson")
                        };

    Arrays.sort(authors);                           // Sort using Comparable method

    System.out.println("\nOrder after sorting into ascending sequence:");
    for(Person author : authors) {
      System.out.println(author);
    }

    // Search for authors
    Person[] people = {
            new Person("Christina", "Schwartz"),    new Person("Ned", "Kelly"),
            new Person("Tom", "Clancy"),            new Person("Charles", "Dickens")
                      };
      int index = 0;
    System.out.println("\nIn search of authors:");
    for(Person person : people) {
      index = Arrays.binarySearch(authors, person);
      if(index >= 0) {
        System.out.println(person + " was found at index position " + index);
      } else {
```

```
            System.out.println(person + " was not found. Return value is " + index);
          }
        }
      }
    }
```

This example will produce the following output:

```
Order after sorting into ascending sequence:
Bill Bryson
Tom Clancy
Patricia Cornwell
John Grisham
Christina Schwartz
Danielle Steel

In search of authors:
Christina Schwartz was found at index position 4
Ned Kelly was not found. Return value is -5
Tom Clancy was found at index position 1
Charles Dickens was not found. Return value is -4
```

How It Works

You create and sort the `authors` array in the same way as you did in the previous example. The elements in the `authors` array are sorted into ascending sequence because you use the `sort()` method without supplying a comparator, and the `Comparable<>` interface implementation in the `Person` class imposes ascending sequence on objects.

You create the `people` array containing `Person` objects that may or may not be authors. You use the `binarySearch()` method to check whether the elements from the `people` array appear in the `authors` array in a loop:

```
for(Person person : people) {
  index = Arrays.binarySearch(authors, person);
  if(index >= 0) {
    System.out.println(person + " was found at index position " + index);
  } else {
    System.out.println(person + " was not found. Return value is " + index);
  }
}
```

The `person` variable will reference each of the elements in turn. If the `person` object appears in the `authors` array, the index will be non-negative, and the first output statement in the `if` will execute; otherwise, the second output statement will execute. You can see from the output that everything works as expected.

Observable and Observer Objects

The `Observable` class provides you with an interesting mechanism for communicating a change in one class object to a number of other class objects. One use for this mechanism is in graphical user interface (GUI) programming where you often have one object representing all the data for the application — a text document, for example, or a geometric model of a physical object — and several other objects that represent views of the data that are displayed in separate windows, where each shows a different representation or perhaps a subset of the data. This is referred to as the **document/view architecture** for an application, or sometimes the **model/view architecture.** This is a contraction of something referred to as the model/view/controller architecture, and we will come back to this when we discuss creating **GUIs.** The document/view terminology is applied to any collection of application data — geometry, bitmaps, or whatever. It isn't restricted to what is normally understood by the term *document*. Figure 15-2 illustrates the document/view architecture.

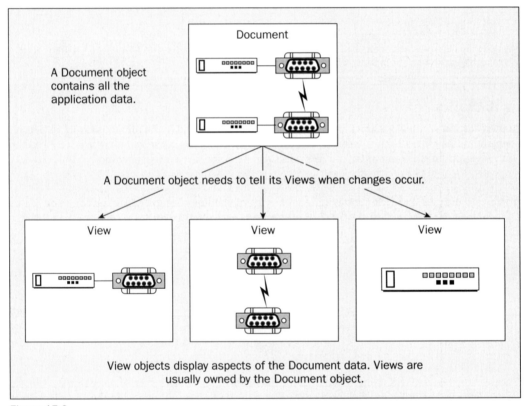

A Document object contains all the application data.

Document

A Document object needs to tell its Views when changes occur.

View

View

View

View objects display aspects of the Document data. Views are usually owned by the Document object.

Figure 15-2

When the `Document` object changes, all the views need to be notified that a change has occurred, since they may well need to update what they display. The document is **observable,** and all the views are **observers.** This is exactly what the `Observable` class is designed to achieve when used in combination with an interface, `Observer`. A document can be considered to be an `Observable` object, and a view can be thought of as an `Observer` object. This enables the view to respond to changes in the document.

The document/view architecture portrays a many-to-many relationship. A document may have many observers, and a view may observe many documents.

Defining Classes of Observable Objects

You use the `java.util.Observable` class in the definition of a class of objects that may be observed. You simply derive the class for objects to be monitored — Document, say — from the class `Observable`.

Any class that may need to be notified when a `Document` object has been changed must implement the interface `Observer`. This doesn't in itself cause the `Observer` objects to be notified when a change in an observed object occurs; it just establishes the potential for this to happen. You need to do something else to link the observers to the observable, which we'll come to in a moment.

The definition of the class for observed objects could be of the form:

```
public class Document extends Observable {
  // Details of the class definitions
}
```

The class `Document` here will inherit methods from the class `Observable` that operate the communications to the `Observer` objects.

A class for observers could be defined as:

```
public class View implements Observer {
  // Method for the interface
  public void update(Observable theObservableObject, Object arg) {
    // This method is called when the observed object changes
  }

  // Rest of the class definition...
}
```

To implement the `Observer` interface, you need to define just one method, `update()`. This method is called automatically when an associated `Observable` object changes. The first argument that is passed to the `update()` method is a reference to the `Observable` object that changed and caused the method to be called. This enables the `View` object to access public methods in the associated `Observable` object, which would be used to access the data to be displayed, for example. The second argument passed to `update()` is used to convey additional information to the `Observer` object.

Observable Class Methods

The `Observable` class maintains an internal record of all the `Observer` objects related to the object to be observed. Your class, derived from `Observable`, will inherit the data members that deal with this. Your class of observable objects will also inherit nine methods from the class `Observable`. These are the following:

Method	Description
addObserver(Observer o)	Adds the object passed as an argument to the internal record of observers. Only Observer objects in the internal record will be notified when a change in the Observable object occurs.
deleteObserver(Observer o)	Deletes the object passed as an argument from the internal record of observers.
deleteObservers()	Deletes all observers from the internal record of observers.
notifyObservers(Object arg)	Calls the update() method for all of the Observer objects in the internal record if the current object has been set as changed. The current object is set as changed by calling the setChanged() method below. The current object and the argument passed to the notifyObservers() method will be passed to the update() method for each Observer object.
notifyObservers()	Calling this method is equivalent to the previous method with a null argument. (See the setChanged() method below.)
countObservers()	The count of the number of Observer objects for the current object is returned as type int.
setChanged()	Sets the current object as changed. You must call this method before calling the notifyObservers() method. Note that this method is protected.
hasChanged()	Returns true if the object has been set as changed, and false otherwise.
clearChanged()	Resets the changed status of the current object to unchanged. Note that this method is also protected.

It's fairly easy to see how these methods are used to manage the relationship between an Observable object and its associated observers. To connect an observer to an Observable object, the Observer object must be registered with the Observable object by calling its addObserver() method. Once this is done the Observer will be notified automatically when changes to the Observable object occur. An observable object is responsible for adding Observer objects to its internal record through the addObserver() method. In practice, the Observer objects are typically created as objects that are dependent on the Observable object, and then they are added to the record, so there's an implied ownership relationship.

This makes sense if you think about how the mechanism is often used in an application using the document/view architecture. A document has permanence since it represents the data for an application. A view is a transient presentation of some or all of the data in the document, so a Document object should naturally create and own its View objects. A view will be responsible for managing the interface to the application's user, but the update of the underlying data in the Document object would be carried out by methods in the Document object, which would then notify other View objects that a change has occurred.

Of course, you're in no way limited to using the `Observable` class and the `Observer` interface in the way in which I've described here. You can use them in any context where you want changes that occur in one class object to be communicated to others. We can exercise the process in a silly example.

Try It Out   Observing the Observable

We'll first define a class for an object that can exhibit change:

```
import java.util.Observable;

public class JekyllAndHyde extends Observable {
  public void drinkPotion() {
    name = "Mr.Hyde";
    setChanged();
    notifyObservers();
  }

  public String getName() {
    return name;
  }

  private String name = "Dr. Jekyll";
}
```

Now we can define the class of person who's looking out for this kind of thing:

```
import java.util.Observer;
import java.util.Observable;

public class Person implements Observer {
  // Constructor
  public Person(String name, String says) {
    this.name = name;
    this.says = says;
  }

  // Called when observing an object that changes
  public void update(Observable thing, Object o) {
    System.out.println("It's " + ((JekyllAndHyde)thing).getName() +
                       "\n" + name + ": " + says);
  }

  private String name;              // Person's identity
  private String says;              // What they say when startled
}
```

We can gather a bunch of observers to watch Dr. Jekyll with the following class:

```
// Try out observers
import java.util.Observer;

public class Horrific {
  public static void main(String[] args) {
```

```
        JekyllAndHyde man = new JekyllAndHyde();        // Create Dr. Jekyll

      Observer[] crowd = {
        new Person("Officer","What's all this then?"),
        new Person("Eileen Backwards", "Oh, no, it's horrible - those teeth!"),
        new Person("Phil McCavity", "I'm your local dentist - here's my card."),
        new Person("Slim Sagebrush", "What in tarnation's goin' on here?"),
        new Person("Freaky Weirdo", "Real cool, man. Where can I get that stuff?")
                        };

      // Add the observers
      for(Observer observer : crowd) {
        man.addObserver(observer);
      }
      man.drinkPotion();                                // Dr. Jekyll drinks up
    }
  }
```

If you compile and run this, you should get the following output:

```
It's Mr.Hyde
Freaky Weirdo: Real cool, man. Where can I get that stuff?
It's Mr.Hyde
Slim Sagebrush: What in tarnation's goin' on here?
It's Mr.Hyde
Phil McCavity: I'm your local dentist - here's my card.
It's Mr.Hyde
Eileen Backwards: Oh, no, it's horrible - those teeth!
It's Mr.Hyde
Officer: What's all this then?
```

How It Works

`JekyllAndHyde` is a very simple class with just two methods. The `drinkPotion()` method encourages Dr. Jekyll to do his stuff, and the `getName()` method enables anyone who is interested to find out who he is. The class extends the `Observable` class, so we can add observers for an object of this class.

The revamped `Person` class implements the `Observer` interface, so an object of this class can observe an `Observable` object. When notified of a change in the object being observed, the `update()` method will be called. Here, it just outputs who the person is and what they say.

In the `Horrific` class, after defining Dr. Jekyll in the variable `man`, you create an array, `crowd`, of type `Observer` to hold the observers—which are of type `Person`, of course. You can use an array of type `Observer` because the class `Person` implements the `Observer` interface. We pass two arguments to the `Person` class constructor: a name and a string indicating what the person will say when they see a change in Dr. Jekyll. We add each of the observers for the `man` object in the `for` loop.

Calling the `drinkPotion()` method for the object `man` results in the internal name being changed, the `setChanged()` method being called for the `man` object, and the `notifyObservers()` method that is inherited from the `Observable` class being called. This causes the `update()` method for each of the registered observers to be called, which generates the output. If you comment out the `setChanged()` call in the `drinkPotion()` method, and compile and run the program again, you'll get no output. Unless `setChanged()` is called, the observers aren't notified.

Now let's move on to look at the `java.util.Random` class.

Generating Random Numbers

You have already used the `Random` class a little, but let's investigate this in more detail. The `Random` class enables you to create multiple random number generators that are independent of one another. Each object of the class is a separate random number generator. Any `Random` object can generate pseudo-random numbers of types `int`, `long`, `float`, or `double`. These numbers are created using an algorithm that takes a *seed* and *grows* a sequence of numbers from it. Initializing the algorithm twice with the same seed would produce the same sequence because the algorithm is deterministic.

The integer values generated will be uniformly distributed over the complete range for the type, and the floating-point values will be uniformly distributed over the range 0.0 to 1.0 for both types. You can also generate numbers of type `double` with a **Gaussian** (or normal) distribution that has a mean of 0.0 and a standard deviation of 1.0. This is the typical bell-shaped curve that represents the probability distribution for many random events. Figure 15-3 illustrates the various flavors of random number generator that you can define.

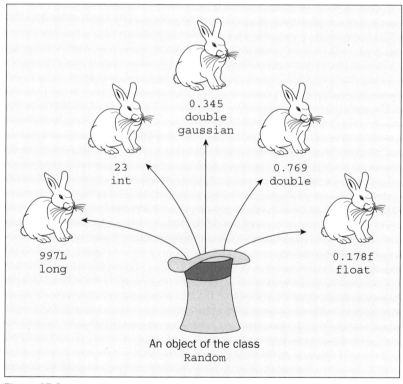

Figure 15-3

There are two constructors for a `Random` object. The default constructor will create an object that uses the current time from your computer clock as the seed value for generating pseudo-random numbers. The other constructor accepts an argument of type `long` that will be used as the seed.

```
Random lottery = new Random();          // Sequence not repeatable
Random repeatable = new Random(997L);   // Repeatable sequence
```

If you use the default constructor, the sequence of numbers that is generated will be different each time a program is run, although beware of creating two generators in the same program with the default constructor. The time resolution used is 1 millisecond, so if you create two objects in successive statements they will usually generate the same sequence, because the times used for the starting seed values will be identical.

`Random` objects that you create using the same seed will always produce the same sequence, which can be very important when you are testing a program. Testing a program where the output is not repeatable can be a challenge! A major feature of random number generators created using a given seed in Java is that not only will they always produce the same sequence of pseudo-random numbers from a given seed, but they will also do so even on totally different computers.

Random Operations

The public methods provided by a `Random` object are:

Method	Description
`nextInt()`	Returns a pseudo-random number of type `int`. Values generated will be uniformly distributed across the complete range of values for a number of type `int`.
`nextInt(int limit)`	Returns a pseudo-random number of type `int` that is greater than or equal to 0, and less than `limit` — very useful for creating random array index values.
`nextLong()`	Returns a pseudo-random number of type `long`. Values generated will be uniformly distributed across the complete range of values for a number of type `long`.
`nextFloat()`	Returns a pseudo-random number of type `float`. Values generated will be uniformly distributed across the range 0.0f to 1.0, including 0.0f but excluding 1.0f.
`nextDouble()`	Returns a pseudo-random number of type `double`. Values generated will be uniformly distributed across the range 0.0 to 1.0, including 0.0 but excluding 1.0.
`nextGaussian()`	Returns a pseudo-random number of type `double` selected from a Gaussian distribution. Values generated will have a mean of 0.0 and a standard deviation of 1.0.
`nextBoolean()`	Returns `true` or `false` as pseudo-random values.

Method	Description
nextBytes(byte[] bytes)	Fills the array, bytes, with pseudo-random values.
setSeed(long seed)	Resets the random number generator to generate values using the value passed as an argument as a starting seed for the algorithm.

To produce a pseudo-random number of a particular type, you just call the appropriate method for a Random object. You can repeat the sequence of numbers generated by a Random object that you created with a seed value, by calling the setSeed() method with the same seed value as an argument.

We can give the Random class an outing with a simple program that simulates throwing a pair of dice. We'll assume you get six throws to try to get a double six.

Try It Out   **Using Random Objects**

Here's the program:

```
import java.util.Random;
import java.io.IOException;

public class Dice {
  public static void main(String[] args) {
    System.out.println("You have six throws of a pair of dice.\n" +
             "The objective is to get a double six. Here goes...\n");

    Random diceValues = new Random();      // Random number generator
    String[] goes = {"First",  "Second", "Third",
                     "Fourth", "Fifth",  "Sixth"};
    int die1 = 0;                          // First die value
    int die2 = 0;                          // Second die value

    for(String go : goes)  {
      die1 = 1 + diceValues.nextInt(6);            // Number from 1 to 6
      die2 = 1 + diceValues.nextInt(6);            // Number from 1 to 6
      System.out.println(go + " throw: " + die1 + ", " + die2);

      if(die1 + die2 == 12) {                       // Is it double 6?
        System.out.println("    You win!!");        // Yes !!!
        return;
      }
    }
    System.out.println("Sorry, you lost...");
    return;
  }
}
```

If you compile this program you should get output that looks something like this:

```
You have six throws of a pair of dice.
The objective is to get a double six. Here goes...
```

677

```
First throw: 3, 2
Second throw: 1, 1
Third throw: 1, 2
Fourth throw: 5, 3
Fifth throw: 2, 2
Sixth throw: 6, 4
Sorry, you lost...
```

How It Works

You use one random number generator here that you create using the default constructor, so it will be seeded with the current time and will produce a different sequence of values each time the program is run. You simulate throwing the dice in the `for` loop. For each throw you need a random number between 1 and 6 to be generated for each die. The easiest way to produce this is to add 1 to the value returned by the `nextInt()` method when you pass 6 as the argument. If you wanted to make a meal of it, you could obtain the same result by using the statement:

```
die1 = 1 + abs(diceValues.nextInt())%6;                    // Number from 1 to 6
```

Remember that the pseudo-random integer values that you get from the version of the `nextInt()` method you are using here will be uniformly distributed across the whole range of possible values for type `int`, positive and negative. That's why you need to use the `abs()` method from the `Math` class here to make sure you end up with a positive die value. The remainder after dividing the value resulting from `abs(diceValues.nextInt())` by 6 will be between 0 and 5. Adding 1 to this produces the result you want.

> *Remember that the odds against a double six are 36:1, so you'll only succeed once on average out of every six times you run the example.*

Now let's move on to look at dates and times.

Dates and Times

Quite a few classes in the `java.util` package are involved with dates and times, including the `Date` class, the `Calendar` class, and the `GregorianCalendar` class. In spite of the class name, a `Date` class object actually defines a particular instant in time to the nearest millisecond, measured from January 1, 1970, 00:00:00 GMT. Since it is relative to a particular instant in time, it also corresponds to a date. The `Calendar` class is the base class for `GregorianCalendar`, which represents the sort of day/month/year calendar everybody is used to and also provides methods for obtaining day, month, and year information from a `Date` object. A `Calendar` object is always set to a particular date — a particular instant on a particular date to be precise — but you can change it by various means. From this standpoint a `GregorianCalendar` object is more like one of those desk calendars that just show one date, and you can flip over the days, months, or years to show another date.

You also have the `TimeZone` class that defines a time zone that can be used in conjunction with a calendar, and that you can use to specify the rules for clock changes due to daylight saving time. The ramifications of handling dates and times are immense so you'll only be able to dabble here, but at least you will get the basic ideas. Let's take a look at `Date` objects first.

The Date Class

With the `Date` class you can create an object that represents a given date and time. You have two ways to do this using the following constructors:

Method	Description
`Date()`	Creates an object based on the current time of your computer clock to the nearest millisecond
`Date(long time)`	Creates an object based on the time value in milliseconds since 00:00:00 GMT on January 1, 1970 that is passed as an argument

With either constructor, you create a `Date` object that represents a specific instant in time to the nearest millisecond. Carrying dates around as the number of milliseconds since the dawn of the year 1970 won't grab you as being incredibly user-friendly — but I'll come back to how we can interpret a `Date` object better in a moment. The `Date` class provides four methods for comparing `Date` objects:

Comparison Methods	Description
`after(Date earlier)`	Returns `true` if the current object represents a date that's later than the date represented by the argument `earlier`, and `false` otherwise.
`before(Date later)`	Returns `true` if the current object represents a date that's earlier than the date represented by the argument `later`, and `false` otherwise.
`equals(Object aDate)`	Returns `true` if the current object and the argument represent the same date and time, and `false` otherwise. This implies that they would both return the same value from `getTime()`.
`compareTo(Date date)`	This method is the result of the `Date` class implementing the `Comparable<Date>` interface. As you've seen in other contexts, this method returns a negative integer, zero, or a positive integer depending on whether the current object is less than, equal to, or greater than the argument. The presence of this method in the class means that you can use the `sort()` method in the `Arrays` class to sort an array of `Date` objects, or the `sort()` method in the `Collections` class to sort a collection of dates.

The `equals()` method returns `true` if two different `Date` objects represent the same date and time. Since the `hashCode()` method is also implemented for the class, you have all you need to use `Date` objects as keys in a hash table.

Interpreting Date Objects

The `DateFormat` class is an abstract class that you can use to create meaningful `String` representations of `Date` objects. It isn't in the `java.util` package though — it's defined in the package `java.text`. You have four standard representations for the date and the time, and these are identified by constants defined in the DateFormat class. The effects of these will vary in different countries, because the representation for the date and the time will reflect the conventions of those countries. The constants in the DateFormat class defining the four formats are:

Date Format	Description
SHORT	A completely numeric representation for a date or a time, such as 2/2/97 or 4:15 a.m.
MEDIUM	A longer representation than SHORT, such as 5-Dec-97
LONG	A longer representation than MEDIUM, such as December 5, 1997
FULL	A comprehensive representation of the date or the time such as Friday, December 5, 1997 AD or 4:45:52 PST (Pacific Standard Time)

A java.util.Locale object identifies information that is specific to a country, a region, or a language. You can define a Locale object for a specific country, for a specific language, for a country and a language, or for a country and a language and a variant, the latter being a vendor- or browser-specific code such as WIN or MAC. When you are creating a Locale object, you use ISO codes to specify the language and/or the country. The language codes are defined by ISO-639. Countries are specified by the country codes in the standard ISO-3166. You can find the country codes on the Internet at:

```
http://www.chemie.fu-berlin.de/diverse/doc/ISO_3166.html
```

or

```
http://www.iso.org/iso/en/prods-services/iso3166ma/index.html
```

You can also get a list of the country codes as an array of String objects by calling the static getISOCountries() method. For example:

```
String[] countryCodes = java.util.Locale.getISOCountries();
```

You can find the language codes at:

```
http://www.ics.uci.edu/pub/ietf/http/related/iso639.txt
```

or

```
http://www.loc.gov/standards/iso639-2/englangn.html
```

You can also get the language codes that are defined by the standard in a String object:

```
String[] languages = java.util.Locale.getISOLanguages();
```

For some countries, the easiest way to specify the locale, if you don't have the ISO codes on the tip of your tongue, is to use one of the Locale objects defined within the Locale class. In Java 2 these are:

US	CANADA	CANADA_FRENCH	PRC
UK	GERMANY	FRANCE	ITALY
JAPAN	KOREA	CHINA	TAIWAN

Because the `DateFormat` class is `abstract`, you can't create objects of the class directly, but you can obtain `DateFormat` objects by using any of the following `static` methods that are defined in the class, each of which returns a value of type `DateFormat`:

Static Method	Description
`getTimeInstance()`	Returns a time formatter for the default locale that uses the default style for the time
`getTimeInstance(` `    int timeStyle)`	Returns a time formatter for the default locale that uses the style for the time specified by the argument

`getTimeInstance(`
`    int style,`
`    Locale aLocale)`
	Returns a time formatter for the locale specified by the second argument that uses the style for the time that is specified by the first argument

`getDateInstance()`	Returns a date formatter for the default locale that uses the default style for the date
`getDateInstance(int dateStyle)`	Returns a date formatter for the default locale that uses the style for the date specified by the argument

`getDateInstance(`
`    int dateStyle,`
`    Locale aLocale)`
	Returns a date formatter for the locale specified by the second argument that uses the style for the date that is specified by the first argument

`getInstance()`	Returns a default date and time formatter that uses the SHORT style for both the date and the time
`getDateTimeInstance()`	Returns a date and time formatter for the default locale that uses the default style for both the date and the time

`getDateTimeInstance(`
`    int dateStyle,`
`    int timeStyle)`
	Returns a date and time formatter for the current locale that uses the styles for the date and the time specified by the arguments

`getDateTimeInstance(`
`    int dateStyle,`
`    int timeStyle,`
`    Locale aLocale)`
	Returns a date and time formatter for aLocale with the styles for the date and the time as specified by the first two arguments

When you've obtained a `DateFormat` object for the country and the style that you want, and the sort of data you want to format — the date or the time or both — you're ready to produce a `String` from the `Date` object.

All you need to do is to pass the `Date` object to the `format()` method for the `DateFormat` object. For example:

```
Date today = new Date();                    // Object for now - today's date
DateFormat fmt = DateFormat.getDateTimeInstance(DateFormat.FULL,
                                            DateFormat.FULL, Locale.US);
String formatted = fmt.format(today);
```

The first statement creates a `Date` object that represents the instant in time when the call to the `Date` constructor executes. The second statement creates a `DateFormat` object that can format the date and time encapsulated by a `Date` object. In this case the formatting style for the data and the time, specified by the first two arguments to the static `getDateTimeInstance()`, is defined by the `FULL` constant in the `DateFormat` class. This provides the most detailed specification of the date and time. The third argument to the `getDateTimeInstance()` method, `Locale.US`, determines that the formatting should correspond to that required for the United States. The `Locale` class defines constants for other major countries and languages. The third statement applies the `format()` method of the `fmt` object to the `Date` object that was created. After executing these statements, the `String` variable `formatted` will contain a full representation of the date and the time when the `Date` object `today` was created.

You can try out some dates and formats in a simple example.

Try It Out   Producing Dates and Times

This example will show the four different date formats for four countries:

```
// Trying date formatting
import java.util.Locale;
import java.text.DateFormat;
import java.util.Date;
import static java.util.Locale.*;       // Import names of constants
import static java.text.DateFormat.*;   // Import names of constants

public class TryDateFormats {
  public static void main(String[] args) {
    Date today = new Date();
    Locale[] locales = {US, UK, GERMANY, FRANCE};
    int[] styles = {FULL, LONG, MEDIUM, SHORT};
    String[] styleNames = {"FULL", "LONG", "MEDIUM", "SHORT"};

    // Output the date for each locale in four styles
    DateFormat fmt = null;
    for(Locale locale : locales) {
      System.out.println("\nThe Date for " +
                      locale.getDisplayCountry() + ":");
      for(int i = 0 ; i<styles.length ; i++) {
        fmt = DateFormat.getDateInstance(styles[i], locale);
        System.out.println( "\tIn " + styleNames[i] +
                      " is " + fmt.format(today));
      }
    }
  }
}
```

When I compiled and ran this it produced the following output:

```
The Date for United States:
  In FULL is Sunday, March 28, 2004
  In LONG is March 28, 2004
  In MEDIUM is Mar 28, 2004
  In SHORT is 3/28/04

The Date for United Kingdom:
  In FULL is 28 March 2004
  In LONG is 28 March 2004
  In MEDIUM is 28-Mar-2004
  In SHORT is 28/03/04

The Date for Germany:
  In FULL is Sonntag, 28. März 2004
  In LONG is 28. März 2004
  In MEDIUM is 28.03.2004
  In SHORT is 28.03.04

The Date for France:
  In FULL is dimanche 28 mars 2004
  In LONG is 28 mars 2004
  In MEDIUM is 28 mars 2004
  In SHORT is 28/03/04
```

How It Works

By statically importing the constants from the `Locale` and `DateFormat` classes, you obviate the need to qualify the constants in the program and thus make the code a little less cluttered. The program creates a `Date` object for the current date and time and an array of `Locale` objects for four countries using values defined in the `Locale` class. It then creates an array of the four possible styles, and another array containing a `String` representation for each style that will be used in the output.

The output is produced in the nested `for` loops. The outer collection-based `for` loop iterates over the countries, and the inner loop iterates over the four styles for each country. The inner loop uses a loop control variable so you can select from the `styleNames` array. A `DateFormat` object is created for each combination of style and country, and the `format()` method for the `DateFormat` object is called to produce the formatted date string in the inner call to `println()`.

You could change the program in a couple ways. You could initialize the `locales[]` array with the expression `DateFormat.getAvailableLocales()`. This will return an array of type `Locale` containing all of the supported locales, but be warned — there are a lot of them. You'll also find that the characters won't display for many countries because your machine doesn't support the country-specific character set. You could also use the method `getTimeInstance()` or `getDateTimeInstance()` instead of `getDateInstance()` to see what sort of output they generate.

Under the covers, a `DateFormat` object contains a `DateFormatSymbols` object that contains all the strings for the names of days of the week and other fixed information related to time and dates. This class is also in the `java.text` package. Normally you don't use the `DateFormatSymbols` class directly, but it can be useful when all you want are the days of the week.

Obtaining a Date Object from a String

The parse() method for a DateFormat object interprets a String object passed as an argument as a date and time, and returns a Date object corresponding to the date and the time. The parse() method will throw a ParseException if the String object can't be converted to a Date object, so you must call it within a try block.

The String argument to the parse() method must correspond to the country and style that you used when you obtained the DateFormat object. This makes it a bit tricky to use successfully. For example, the following code will parse the string properly:

```
Date aDate;
DateFormat fmt = DateFormat.getDateInstance(DateFormat.FULL, Locale.US);
try {
   aDate = fmt.parse("Saturday, July 4, 1998 ");
   System.out.println("The Date string is: " + fmt.format(aDate));

} catch(java.text.ParseException e) {
   System.out.println(e);
}
```

This works because the string is what would be produced by the locale and style. If you omit the day from the string, or you use the LONG style or a different locale, a ParseException will be thrown.

Gregorian Calendars

The Gregorian calendar is the calendar generally in use today in the western world and is represented by an object of the GregorianCalendar class. A GregorianCalendar object encapsulates time zone information, as well as date and time data. You have no less than seven constructors for GregorianCalendar objects, from the default that creates a calendar with the current date and time in the default locale for your machine through to a constructor specifying the year, month, day, hour, minute, and second. The default suits most situations.

You can create a calendar with a statement such as:

```
GregorianCalendar calendar = new GregorianCalendar();
```

This will be set to the current instant in time, and you can retrieve this as a Date object by calling the getTime() method for the calendar:

```
Date now = calendar.getTime();
```

You can create a GregorianCalendar object encapsulating a specific date and/or time with any of the following constructors:

```
GregorianCalendar(int year, int month, int day)
GregorianCalendar(int year, int month, int day, int hour, int minute)
GregorianCalendar(int year, int month, int day, int hour, int minute, int second)
```

The day argument is the day within the month, so the value can be from 1 to 28, 29, 30, or 31, depending on the month and whether it's a leap year or not. The month value is zero-based so January is 0 and December is 11.

The `GregorianCalendar` class is derived from the abstract `Calendar` class from which it inherits a large number of methods and static constants for use with these methods. The constants include month values with the names JANUARY to DECEMBER so you could create a calendar object with the statement:

```
GregorianCalendar calendar = new GregorianCalendar(1967, Calendar.MARCH, 10);
```

If you statically import the constant members of the `GregorianCalendar` class you'll be able to use constants such as MARCH and DECEMBER without the need to qualify them with the class name. The time zone and locale will be the default for the computer on which this statement executes. If you want to specify a time zone, there is a `GregorianCalendar` constructor that accepts an argument of type `java.util.TimeZone`. You can get the default `TimeZone` object by calling the static `getDefault()` method, but if you are going to the trouble of specifying a time zone, you probably want something other than the default. To create a particular time zone you need to know its ID. This is a string specifying a region or country plus a location. For example, here are some examples of time zone IDs:

"Europe/Stockholm"	"Asia/Novosibirsk"	"Pacific/Guam"
"Antarctica/Palmer"	"Atlantic/South_Georgia"	"Africa/Accra"
"America/Chicago"	"Indian/Comoro"	"Europe/London"

To obtain a reference to a `TimeZone` object corresponding to a given time zone ID, you pass the ID to the static `getTimeZone()` method. For example, we could create a `Calendar` object for the Chicago time zone like this:

```
GregorianCalendar calendar =
      new GregorianCalendar(TimeZone.getTimeZone("America/Chicago"));
```

If you want to know what all the time zones IDs are, you could list them like this:

```
String[] ids = TimeZone.getAvailableIDs();
for(String id : ids) {
  System.out.println(id);
}
```

Be prepared for a lot of output though, as there are well over 500 time zone IDs.

The calendar created from a `TimeZone` object will have the default locale. If you want to specify the locale explicitly, you have a constructor that accepts a `Locale` reference as the second argument. For example:

```
GregorianCalendar calendar =
      new GregorianCalendar(TimeZone.getTimeZone("America/Chicago"). Locale.US);
```

You can also create a `Calendar` object from a locale:

```
GregorianCalendar calendar =
      new GregorianCalendar(Locale.UK);
```

This will create a calendar set to the current time in the default time zone within the UK.

Setting the Date and Time

If you have a `Date` object available, you have a `setTime()` method that you can pass a `Date` object to set a `GregorianCalendar` object to the time specified by the `Date` object:

```
GregorianCalendar calendar = new GregorianCalendar();
calendar.setTime(date);
```

More typically you will want to set the date and/or time with explicit values such as day, month, and year, and you have several overloaded versions of the `set()` method for setting various components of the date and time. These are inherited in the `GregorianCalendar` class from its superclass, the `Calendar` class. You can set a `GregorianCalendar` object to a particular date like this:

```
GregorianCalendar calendar = new GregorianCalendar();
calendar.set(1995, 10, 29);  // Date set to 29th November 1999
```

The three arguments to the `set()` method here are the year, the month, and the day as type `int`. You need to take care with this method because it's easy to forget that the month is zero-based, with January specified by 0. Note that the fields reflecting the time setting within the day will not be changed. They will remain at whatever they were. You can reset all fields for a `GregorianCalendar` object to zero by calling its `clear()` method, so calling `clear()` before you call `set()` here would ensure that the time fields are all zero.

The other versions of the `set()` method are:

```
set(int year, int month, int day, int hour, int minute)
set(int year, int month, int day, int hour, int minute, int second)
set(int field, int value)
```

It's obvious what the first two of these do. In each case the fields not explicitly set will be left at their original values. The third version of `set()` sets a field specified by one of the integer constants defined in the `Calendar` class for this purpose:

Field	Value
AM_PM	Can have the values AM or PM, which correspond to values of 0 and 1
DAY_OF_WEEK	Can have the values SUNDAY, MONDAY, etc., through to SATURDAY, which correspond to values of 1 to 7
DAY_OF_YEAR	Can be set to a value from 1 to 366
MONTH	Can be set to a value of JANUARY, FEBRUARY, etc., through to DECEMBER, corresponding to values of 0 to 11
DAY_OF_MONTH or DATE	Can be set to a value from 1 to 31
WEEK_OF_MONTH	Can be set to a value from 1 to 6
WEEK_OF_YEAR	Can be set to a value from 1 to 54
HOUR_OF_DAY	A value from 0 to 23

Field	Value
HOUR	A value from 1 to 12 representing the current hour in the a.m. or p.m.
MINUTE	The current minute in the current hour — a value from 0 to 59
SECOND	The second in the current minute, 0 to 59
MILLISECOND	The millisecond in the current second, 0 to 999
YEAR	The current year — for example, 2004
ERA	Can be set to either `GregorianCalendar.BC` or `GregorianCalendar.AD` (both values being defined in the `GregorianCalendar` class)
ZONE_OFFSET	A millisecond value indicating the offset from GMT
DST_OFFSET	A millisecond value indicating the offset for daylight saving time in the current time zone

Qualifying the names of these constants with the class name `GregorianCalendar` can make the code look cumbersome but you can use static import for the constants to simplify things:

```
import static java.util.Calendar.*;
import static java.util.GregorianCalendar.*;
```

The static `import` statement imports only the names of static members that are defined in a class, not the names of inherited members. Therefore, you need two `import` statements if you want access to all the constants you can use with the `GregorianCalendar` class.

With these two `import` statements in effect, you can write statements like this

```
GregorianCalendar calendar = new GregorianCalendar();
calendar.set(DAY_OF_WEEK, TUESDAY);
```

Getting Date and Time Information

You can get information such as the day, the month, and the year from a `GregorianCalendar` object by using the `get()` method and specifying what you want as an argument. The possible arguments to the `get()` method are those defined in the table of constants above identifying calendar fields. All values returned are of type `int`. For example, you could get the day of the week with the statement:

```
int day = calendar.get(calendar.DAY_OF_WEEK);
```

You could now test this for a particular day using the constant defined in the class:

```
if(day == calendar.SATURDAY)
   // Go to game...
```

Since the values for `day` are integers, you could equally well use a `switch` statement:

```
switch(day) {
  case Calendar.MONDAY:
  // do the washing...
  break;
  case Calendar.MONDAY:
  // do something else...
  break;
  // etc...
}
```

Modifying Dates and Times

Of course, you might want to alter the current instant in the calendar, and for this you have the `add()` method. The first argument determines what units you are adding in, and you specify this argument using the same field designators as in the previous list. For example, you can add 14 to the year with the statement:

```
calendar.add(calendar.YEAR, 14);   // 14 years into the future
```

To go into the past, you just make the second argument negative:

```
calendar.add(calendar.MONTH, -6);   // Go back 6 months
```

You can increment or decrement a field of a calendar by 1 using the `roll()` method. This method modifies the field specified by the first argument by +1 or –1, depending on whether the second argument is `true` or `false`. For example, to decrement the current month in the object `calendar`, you would write:

```
calendar.roll(calendar.MONTH, false);   // Go back a month
```

The change can affect other fields. If the original month were January, rolling it back by one would make the date December of the previous year.

Of course, having modified a `GregorianCalendar` object, you can get the current instant back as a `Date` object using the `getTime()` method that we saw earlier. You can then use a `DateFormat` object to present this in a readable form.

Comparing Calendars

Checking the relationship between dates represented by `Calendar` objects is a fairly fundamental requirement and you have four methods available for comparing them:

Method	Description
`before()`	Returns `true` if the current object corresponds to a time before that of the `Calendar` object passed as an argument. Note that this implies a `true` return can occur if the date is the same but the time is different.
`after()`	Returns `true` if the current object corresponds to a time after that of the `Calendar` object passed as an argument.

Method	Description
equals()	Returns true if the current object corresponds to a time that is identical to that of the Calendar object passed as an argument.
compareTo(Calendar c)	Returns a value of type int that is negative, zero, or positive depending on whether the time value for the current object is less than, equal to, or greater than the time value for the argument.

These are very simple to use. To determine whether the object thisDate defines a time that precedes the time defined by the object today, you could write:

```
if(thisDate.before(today)) {
  // Do something...
}
```

Alternatively you could write the same thing as:

```
if(today.after(thisDate)) {
  // Do something...
}
```

It's time to look at how we can use calendars.

Try It Out   Using a Calendar

This example will deduce important information about when you were born. It uses the FormattedInput class from Chapter 8 to get input from the keyboard, so copy this class and the source file for the InvalidUserInputException class to a new directory for the source files for this example. Here's the code:

```
import java.util.GregorianCalendar;
import java.text.DateFormatSymbols;
import static java.util.Calendar.*;

class TryCalendar {
  public static void main(String[] args) {
    FormattedInput in = new FormattedInput();

    // Get the date of birth from the keyboard
    int day = 0, month = 0, year = 0;
    System.out.println("Enter your birth date as dd mm yyyy: ");
    try {
      day = in.readInt();
      month = in.readInt();
      year = in.readInt();
    } catch(InvalidUserInputException e) {
      System.out.println("Invalid input - terminating...");
      System.exit(1);
```

```
        }

        // Create birth date calendar - month is 0 to 11
        GregorianCalendar birthdate = new GregorianCalendar(year, month-1,day);
        GregorianCalendar today = new GregorianCalendar();      // Today's date

        // Create this year's birthday
        GregorianCalendar birthday = new GregorianCalendar(
                                        today.get(YEAR),
                                        birthdate.get(MONTH),
                                        birthdate.get(DATE));

        int age = today.get(today.YEAR) - birthdate.get(YEAR);

        String[] weekdays = new DateFormatSymbols().getWeekdays(); // Get day names

        System.out.println("You were born on a " +
                        weekdays[birthdate.get(DAY_OF_WEEK)]);
        System.out.println("This year you " +
                        (birthday.after(today)    ?"will be " : "are ") +
                        age + " years old.");
        System.out.println("In " + today.get(YEAR) + " your birthday " +
                        (today.before(birthday)? "will be": "was") +
                        " on a "+ weekdays[birthday.get(DAY_OF_WEEK)] +".");
    }
}
```

I got the following output:

```
Enter your birth date as dd mm yyyy:
5 12 1964
You were born on a Saturday
This year you will be 40 years old.
In 2004 your birthday will be on a Sunday.
```

How It Works

You start by prompting for the day, month, and year for a date of birth to be entered through the keyboard as integers. You then create a `GregorianCalendar` object corresponding to this date. Note the adjustment of the month — the constructor expects January to be specified as 0. You need a `GregorianCalendar` object for today's date so you use the default constructor for this. To compute the age this year, you just have to subtract the year of birth from this year, both of which you get from the `GregorianCalendar` objects.

To get at the strings for the days of the week, you create a `DateFormatSymbols` object and call its `getWeekdays()` method. This returns an array of eight `String` objects, the first of which is empty to make it easy to index using day numbers from 1 to 7. The second element in the array contains "Sunday". You can also get the month names using the `getMonths()` method.

To display the day of the week for the date of birth you call the `get()` method for the `GregorianCalendar` object `birthdate`, and use the result to index the `weekdays[]` array. To determine the appropriate text in the next two output statements, you use the `after()` and `before()` methods for `Calendar` objects to compare today with the birthday date this year.

Regular Expressions

You saw some elementary capability for searching strings when I discussed the `String` class back in Chapter 4. You have much more sophisticated facilities for analyzing strings by searching for patterns known as **regular expressions**. Regular expressions are not unique to Java. Perl is perhaps better known for its support of regular expressions. Many word processors, especially on Unix, support regular expressions, and there are specific utilities for regular expressions, too.

So what is a regular expression? A regular expression is simply a string that describes a pattern that is to be used to search for matches within some other string. It's not simply a passive sequence of characters to be matched, though. A regular expression is essentially a mini-program for a specialized kind of computer called a **state-machine**. This isn't a real machine but a piece of software specifically designed to interpret a regular expression and analyze a given string based on the operations implicit in a regular expression.

The regular expression capability in Java is implemented through two classes in the `java.util.regex` package: the `Pattern` class, which defines objects that encapsulate regular expressions, and the `Matcher` class, which defines an object that encapsulates a state-machine that can search a particular string using a given `Pattern` object. The `java.util.regex` package also defines the `PatternSyntaxException` class, which defines exception objects thrown when a syntax error is found when compiling a regular expression to create a `Pattern` object.

Using regular expressions in Java is basically very simple:

1. You create a `Pattern` object by passing a string containing a regular expression to the static `compile()` method in the `Pattern` class.

2. You then obtain a `Matcher` object, which can search a given string for the pattern, by calling the `matcher()` method for the `Pattern` object with the string that is to be searched as the argument.

3. You call the `find()` method (or some other methods, as you will see) for the `Matcher` object to search the string.

4. If the pattern is found, you query the `Matcher` object to discover the whereabouts of the pattern in the string and other information relating to the match.

While this is a straightforward process that is easy to code, the hard work is in defining the pattern to achieve the result that you want. This is an extensive topic since in their full glory regular expressions are immensely powerful and can be very complicated. There are books devoted entirely to this, so my aim is to give you enough of a bare-bones understanding of how regular expressions work that you will be in a good position to look into the subject in more depth if you need to. Although regular expressions can look quite fearsome, don't be put off. They are always built step-by-step, so although the result may look complicated and obscure, they are not necessarily difficult to put together. Regular expressions are a lot of fun and a sure way to impress your friends and maybe confound your enemies.

Defining Regular Expressions

You may not have heard of regular expressions before reading this book and, therefore, may think you have never used them. If so, you are almost certainly wrong. Whenever you search a directory for files of a particular type, `"*.java"`, for example, you are using a form of regular expression. However, to say that regular expressions can do much more than this is something of an understatement. To get an understanding of what you can do with regular expressions, you'll start at the bottom with the simplest kind of operation and work your way up to some of the more complex problems they can solve.

Creating a Pattern

In its most elementary form, a regular expression just does a simple search for a substring. For example, if you want to search a string for the word *had*, the regular expression is exactly that. So the string defining this particular regular expression is `"had"`. Let's use this as a vehicle for understanding the programming mechanism for using regular expressions. You can create a `Pattern` object for the expression `"had"` with the statement:

```
Pattern had = Pattern.compile("had");
```

The static `compile()` method in the `Pattern` class returns a reference to a `Pattern` object that contains the compiled regular expression. The method will throw an exception of type `java.util.regex.PatternSyntaxException` if the regular expression passed as the argument is invalid. However, you don't have to catch this exception as it is a subclass of `RuntimeException` and therefore is unchecked. The compilation process stores the regular expression in a `Pattern` object in a form that is ready to be processed by a `Matcher` state-machine.

A further version of the `compile()` method enables you to control more closely how the pattern will be applied when looking for a match. The second argument is a value of type `int` that specifies one or more of the following flags that are defined in the `Pattern` class:

`CASE_INSENSITIVE`	Matches ignoring case, but assumes only US-ASCII characters are being matched.
`MULTILINE`	Enables the beginning or end of lines to be matched anywhere. Without this flag only the beginning and end of the entire sequence will be matched.
`UNICODE_CASE`	When this is specified in addition to `CASE_INSENSITIVE`, case-insensitive matching will be consistent with the Unicode standard.
`DOTALL`	Makes the expression . (which we will see shortly) match any character, including line terminators.
`LITERAL`	Causes the string specifying a pattern to be treated as a sequence of literal characters, so escape sequences, for example, will not be recognized as such.
`CANON_EQ`	Matches taking account of canonical equivalence of combined characters. For example, some characters that have diacritics may be represented as a single character or as a single character with a diacritic followed by a diacritic character. This flag will treat these as a match.
`COMMENTS`	Allows whitespace and comments in a pattern. Comments in a pattern start with # so from the first # to the end of the line will be ignored.
`UNIX_LINES`	Enables Unix lines mode, where only `'\n'` is recognized as a line terminator.

All these flags are unique single-bit values within a value of type `int` so you can combine them by ORing them together or by simple addition. For example, you can specify the `CASE_INSENSITIVE` and the `UNICODE_CASE` flags with the expression:

```
Pattern.CASE_INSENSITIVE | Pattern.UNICODE_CASE
```

Or you can write this as:

```
Pattern.CASE_INSENSITIVE + Pattern.UNICODE_CASE
```

Beware of using addition when you want to add a flag to a variable representing an existing set of flags. If the flag already exists, addition will produce the wrong result because the addition of the two corresponding bits will result in a carry to the next bit. ORing will always produce the correct result.

If you wanted to match `"had"` ignoring case, you could create the pattern with the statement:

```
Pattern had = Pattern.compile("had", Pattern.CASE_INSENSITIVE);
```

In addition to the exception thrown by the first version of the `compile()` method, this version will throw an exception of type `IllegalArgumentException` if the second argument has bit values set that do not correspond to one of the flag constants defined in the `Pattern` class.

Creating a Matcher

Once you have a `Pattern` object, you can create a `Matcher` object that can search a particular string, like this:

```
String sentence = "Smith, where Jones had had 'had', had had 'had had'.";
Matcher matchHad = had.matcher(sentence);
```

The first statement defines the string `sentence` that you want to search. To create the `Matcher` object, you call the `matcher()` method for the `Pattern` object with the string to be analyzed as the argument. This will return a `Matcher` object that can analyze the string that was passed to it. The parameter for the `matcher()` method is actually of type `CharSequence`. This is an interface that is implemented by the `String`, `StringBuffer`, and `StringBuilder` classes so you can pass a reference of any of these types to the method. The `java.nio.CharBuffer` class also implements `CharSequence`, so you can pass the contents of a `CharBuffer` to the method, too. This means that if you use a `CharBuffer` to hold character data you have read from a file, you can pass the data directly to the `matcher()` method to be searched.

An advantage of Java's implementation of regular expressions is that you can reuse a `Pattern` object to create `Matcher` objects to search for the pattern in a variety of strings. To use the same pattern to search another string, you just call the `matcher()` method for the `Pattern` object with the new string as the argument. You then have a new `Matcher` object that you can use to search the new string.

You can also change the string that a `Matcher` object is to search by calling its `reset()` method with a new string as the argument. For example:

```
matchHad.reset("Had I known, I would not have eaten the haddock.");
```

This will replace the previous string, `sentence`, in the `Matcher` object, so it is now capable of searching the new string. Like the `matcher()` method in the `Pattern` class, the parameter type for the `reset()` method is `CharSequence`, so you can pass a reference of type `String`, `StringBuffer`, `StringBuilder`, or `java.nio.CharBuffer` to it.

Searching a String

Now that you have a `Matcher` object, you can use it to search the string. Calling the `find()` method for the `Matcher` object will search the string for the next occurrence of the pattern. If it finds the pattern, the method stores information about where it was found in the `Matcher` object and returns `true`. If it doesn't find the pattern, the `find()` method returns `false`. When the pattern has been found, calling the `start()` method for the `Matcher` object returns the index position in the string where the first character in the pattern was found. Calling the `end()` method returns the index position following the last character in the pattern. Both index values are returned as type `int`. Therefore, you could search for the first occurrence of the pattern like this:

```
if(m.find()) {
    System.out.println("Pattern found. Start: "+m.start()+" End: "+m.end());
} else {
    System.out.println("Pattern not found.");
}
```

Note that you must not call `start()` or `end()` for the `Matcher` object before you have succeeded in finding the pattern. Until a pattern has been matched, the `Matcher` object is in an undefined state and calling either of these methods will result in an exception of type `IllegalStateException` being thrown.

You will usually want to find all occurrences of a pattern in a string. When you call the `find()` method, searching starts at an index position in the string called the **append position** and stops either when the pattern is found and the value `true` is returned or when the end of the string is reached, in which case the return value is `false`. The append position is initially zero, corresponding to the beginning of the string, but it is updated if the pattern is found. Each time the pattern is found, the new append position will be the index position of the character immediately following the last character in the text that matched the pattern. The next call to `find()` will start searching at this new append position. Thus, you can easily find all occurrences of the pattern by searching in a loop like this:

```
while(m.find()) {
    System.out.println(" Start: "+m.start()+" End: "+m.end());
}
```

At the end of this loop the append position will be at the index position of the character following the last occurrence of the pattern in the string. If you want to reset the append position back to zero, you just call an overloaded version of `reset()` for the `Matcher` object that has no arguments:

```
m.reset();                              //Reset this matcher
```

This resets the `Matcher` object to its original state before any search operations were carried out.

To make sure you understand the searching process, let's put it all together in an example.

Try It Out   Searching for a Substring

Here's a complete example to search a string for a pattern:

```java
import java.util.regex.Matcher;
import java.util.regex.Pattern;
import java.util.Arrays;

class TryRegex {
  public static void main(String args[]) {
    // A regex and a string in which to search are specified
    String regEx = "had";
    String str = "Smith, where Jones had had 'had', had had 'had had'.";

    // The matches in the output will be marked (fixed-width font required)
    char[] marker = new char[str.length()];
    Arrays.fill(marker,' ');
    // So we can later replace spaces with marker characters

    // Obtain the required matcher
    Pattern pattern = Pattern.compile(regEx);
    Matcher m = pattern.matcher(str);

    // Find every match and mark it
    while( m.find() ){
      System.out.println("Pattern found at Start: "+m.start()+" End: "+m.end());
      Arrays.fill(marker,m.start(),m.end(),'^');
    }

    // Show the object string with matches marked under it
    System.out.println(str);
    System.out.println(new String(marker));
  }
}
```

This will produce the following output:

```
Pattern found at Start: 19 End: 22
Pattern found at Start: 23 End: 26
Pattern found at Start: 28 End: 31
Pattern found at Start: 34 End: 37
Pattern found at Start: 38 End: 41
Pattern found at Start: 43 End: 46
Pattern found at Start: 47 End: 50
Smith, where Jones had had 'had', had had 'had had'.
                   ^^^ ^^^  ^^^   ^^^ ^^^  ^^^ ^^^
```

How It Works

You first define a string, regEx, containing the regular expression, and a string, str, that you'll search:

```java
String regEx = "had";
String str = "Smith, where Jones had had 'had', had had 'had had'.";
```

You also create an array, marker, of type char[] with the same number of elements as str, that you'll use to indicate where the pattern is found in the string:

```
char[]  marker = new char[str.length()];
```

You fill the elements of the marker array with spaces initially using the static fill() method from the Arrays class discussed earlier:

```
Arrays.fill(marker,' ');
```

Later you'll replace some of the spaces in the array with '^' to indicate where the pattern has been found in the original string.

After compiling the regular expression regEx into a Pattern object, pattern, you create a Matcher object, m, from pattern, which applies to the string str:

```
Pattern pattern = Pattern.compile(regEx);
Matcher m = pattern.matcher(str);
```

You then call the find() method for m in the while loop condition:

```
while( m.find() ){
    System.out.println("Pattern found at Start: "+m.start()+" End: "+m.end());
    Arrays.fill(marker, m.start(), m.end(), '^');
}
```

This loop continues as long as the find() method returns true. On each iteration you output the index values returned by the start() and end() methods, which reflect the index position where the first character of the pattern was found, and the index position following the last character. You also insert the '^' character in the marker array at the index positions where the pattern was found — again using the fill() method. The loop ends when the find() method returns false, implying that there are no more occurrences of the pattern in the string.

When the loop ends you have found all occurrences of the pattern in the string, so you output the string str with the contents of the marker array immediately below it on the next line. As long as the command-line output uses a fixed-width font, the '^' characters will mark the positions where the pattern appears in the string.

You'll reuse this example as you delve into further options for regular expressions by plugging in different definitions for regEx and the string that is searched, str. The output will be more economical if you delete or comment out the statement in the while loop that outputs the start and end index positions.

Matching an Entire String

On some occasions you want to try to match a pattern against an entire string — in other words, you want to establish that the complete string you are searching is a match for the pattern. Suppose you read an input value into your program as a string. This might be from the keyboard or possibly through a dialog box managing the entry data in graphical user interface for an application. You might want to be sure that the input string is an integer, for example. If input should be of a particular form, you can use a regular expression to determine whether it is correct or not.

The `matches()` method for a `Matcher` object tries to match the entire input string with the pattern and returns `true` only if there is a match. The following code fragment demonstrates how this works:

```
String input = null;
// Read into input from some source...

Pattern yes = Pattern.compile("yes");
Matcher m = pattern.matcher(input);

if(m.matches()) {                         // Check if input matches "yes"
  System.out.println("Input is yes.");
} else {
  System.out.println("Input is not yes.");
}
```

Of course, this illustration is trivial, but later you'll see how you can define more sophisticated patterns that can check for a range of possible input forms.

Defining Sets of Characters

A regular expression can be made up of ordinary characters, which are upper- and lowercase letters and digits, plus sequences of **meta-characters**, which are characters that have a special meaning. The pattern in the previous example was just the word `"had"`, but what if you wanted to search a string for occurrences of `"hid"` or `"hod"` as well as `"had"`, or even any three-letter word beginning with `"h"` and ending with `"d"`?

You can deal with any of these possibilities with regular expressions. One option is to specify the middle character as a wildcard by using a period; a period is one example of a meta-character. This meta-character matches any character except end-of-line, so the regular expression `"h.d"`, represents any sequence of three characters that starts with `"h"` and end with `"d"`. Try changing the definitions of `regEx` and `str` in the previous example to:

```
String regEx = "h.d";
String str = "Ted and Ned Hodge hid their hod and huddled in the hedge.";
```

If you recompile and run the example again, the last two lines of output will be:

```
Ted and Ned Hodge hid their hod and huddled in the hedge.
                  ^^^       ^^^     ^^^            ^^^
```

You can see that you didn't find `"Hod"` in `Hodge` because of the capital `"H"`, but you found all the other sequences beginning with `"h"` and ending with `"d"`.

Of course, the regular expression `"h.d"` would also have found `"hzd"` or `"hNd"` if they had been present, which is not what you want. You can limit the possibilities by replacing the period with just the collection of characters you are looking for between square brackets, like this:

```
String regEx = "h[aio]d";
```

The `[aio]` sequence of meta-characters defines what is called a **simple class** of characters, consisting in this case of `"a"`, `"i"`, or `"o"`. Here the term *class* is used in the sense of a set of characters, not a class that defines a type. If you try this version of the regular expression in the previous example, the last two lines of output will be:

```
Ted and Ned Hodge hid their hod and huddled in the hedge.
             ^^^         ^^^
```

The regular expression now matches all sequences that begin with `"h"` and end with `"d"` and have a middle letter of `"a"` or `"i"` or `"o"`.

You can define character classes in a regular expression in a variety of ways. Here are some examples of the more useful forms:

`[aeiou]`	This is a simple class that any of the characters between the square brackets will match — in this example, any vowel. You used this form in the code fragment above to search for variations on `"had"`.
`[^aeiou]`	This represents any character except those appearing to the right of the `^` character between the square brackets. Thus, here you have specified any character that is not a vowel. Note this is any *character*, not any letter, so the expression `"h[^aeiou]d"` will look for `"h!d"` or `"h9d"` as well as `"hxd"` or `"hWd"`. Of course, it will reject `"had"` or `"hid"` or any other form with a vowel as the middle letter.
`[a-e]`	This defines an inclusive range — any of the letters `"a"` to `"e"` in this case. You can also specify multiple ranges. For example:
`[a-cs-zA-E]`	This corresponds to any of the characters from `"a"` to `"c"`, from `"s"` to `"z"`, or from `"A"` to `"E"`.
	If you want to specify that a position must contain a digit, you could use `[0-9]`. To specify that a position can be a letter or a digit you could express it as `[a-zA-Z0-9]`.

You can use any of these in combination with ordinary characters to form a regular expression. For example, suppose you want to search some text for any sequence beginning with `"b"`, `"c"`, or `"d"`, with `"a"` as the middle letter, and ending with `"d"` or `"t"`. You could define the regular expression to do this as:

```
String regEx = "[b-d]a[dt]";
```

This expression will match any occurrence of `"bad"`, `"cad"`, `"dad"`, `"bat"`, `"cat"`, or `"dat"`.

Logical Operators in Regular Expressions

You can use the `&&` operator to combine classes that define sets of characters. This is particularly useful when you use it combined with the negation operator, `^`, that appears in the second row of the table in the preceding section. For example, if you want to specify that any lowercase consonant is acceptable, you could write the expression that will match this as:

```
"[b-df-hj-np-tv-z]"
```

However, this can much more conveniently be expressed as the pattern:

```
"[a-z&&[^aeiou]]"
```

This produces the intersection (in other words, the characters common to both sets) of the set of characters "a" through "z" with the set that is not a lowercase vowel. To put it another way, the lowercase vowels are subtracted from the set "a" through "z" so you are left with just the consonants.

The | operator is a logical OR that you use to specify alternatives. A regular expression to find "hid", "had", or "hod" could be written as "hid|had|hod". You can try this in the previous example by changing the definition of regEx to:

```
String regEx = "hid|had|hod";
```

Note that the | operation means either the whole expression to the left of the operator or the whole expression to the right, not just the characters on either side as alternatives.

You could also use the | operator to define an expression to find sequences beginning with an uppercase or lowercase "h", followed by a vowel, and ending in "d", like this:

```
String regEx = "[h|H][aeiou]d";
```

The first pair of square brackets encloses the choice of "h" or "H". The second pair of square brackets determines that the next character is any vowel. The last character must always be "d". With this as the regular expression in the example, the "Hod" in *Hodge* will be found as well as the other variations.

Predefined Character Sets

You also have a number of predefined character classes that provide you with a shorthand notation for commonly used sets of characters. Here are some that are particularly useful:

.	This represents any character, as you have already seen.
\d	This represents any digit and is therefore shorthand for [0-9].
\D	This represents any character that is not a digit. It is therefore equivalent to [^0-9].
\s	This represents any whitespace character.
\S	This represents any non-whitespace character and is therefore equivalent to [^\s].
\w	This represents a word character, which corresponds to an upper- or lowercase letter or a digit or an underscore. It is therefore equivalent to [a-zA-Z_0-9].
\W	This represents any character that is not a word character, so it is equivalent to [^\w].

Note that when you are including any of the sequences that start with a backslash in a regular expression, you need to keep in mind that Java treats a backslash as the beginning of an escape sequence. Therefore, you must specify the backslash in the regular expression as \\. For example, to find a sequence of three digits, the regular expression would be "\\d\\d\\d". This is peculiar to Java because of the significance of the backslash in Java strings, so it doesn't necessarily apply to other environments that support regular expressions, such as Perl.

Obviously, you may well want to include a period, or any of the other meta-characters, as part of the character sequence you are looking for. To do this you can use an escape sequence starting with a backslash in the expression to define such characters. Since Java strings interpret a backslash as the start of a Java escape sequence, the backslash itself has to be represented as \\, the same as when using the predefined character sets that begin with a backslash. Thus, the regular expression to find the sequence "had." would be "had\\.".

The earlier search you tried with the expression "h.d" found embedded sequences such as "hud" in the word huddled. You could use the \s set that corresponds to any whitespace character to prevent this by defining regEx like this:

```
String regEx = "\\sh.d\\s";
```

This searches for a five-character sequence that starts and ends with any whitespace character. The output from the example will now be:

```
Ted and Ned Hodge hid their hod and huddled in the hedge.
                  ^^^^^          ^^^^^
```

You can see that the marker array shows the five-character sequences that were found. The embedded sequences are now no longer included, as they don't begin and end with a whitespace character.

To take another example, suppose you want to find hedge or Hodge as words in the sentence, bearing in mind that there's a period at the end. You could do this by defining the regular expression as:

```
String regEx = "\\s[h|H][e|o]dge[\\s|\\.]";
```

The first character is defined as any whitespace by \\s. The next character is defined as either "h" or "H" by [h|H]. This can be followed by either "e" or "o" specified by [e|o]. This is followed by plaintext dge with either a whitespace character or a period at the end, specified by [\\s|\\.]. This doesn't cater for all possibilities. Sequences at the beginning of the string will not be found, for example, nor will sequences followed by a comma. We'll see how to deal with these next.

Matching Boundaries

So far you have been trying to find the occurrence of a pattern anywhere in a string. In many situations you will want to be more specific. You may want to look for a pattern that appears at the beginning of a line in a string but not anywhere else, or maybe just at the end of any line. As you saw in the previous example, you may want to look for a word that is not embedded — you want to find the word "cat" but not the "cat" in "cattle" or in "Popacatapetl", for example. The previous example worked for the string you were searching but would not produce the right result if the word you were looking for was followed by a comma or appeared at the end of the text. However, you have other options for specifying the pattern. You can use a number of special sequences in a regular expression when you want to match a particular boundary. For example, these are especially useful:

^	Specifies the beginning of a line. For example, to find the word Java at the beginning of any line you could use the expression `"^Java"`.
$	Specifies the end of a line. For example, to find the word Java at the end of any line you could use the expression `"Java$"`. Of course, if you were expecting a period at the end of a line the expression would be `"Java\\.$"`.
\b	Specifies a word boundary. To find words beginning with `'h'` and ending with `'d'` you could use the expression `"\\bh.d\\b"`.
\B	A non-word boundary — the complement of \b above.
\A	Specifies the beginning of the string being searched. To find the word The at the very beginning of the string being searched you could use the expression `"\\AThe\\b"`. The `\\b` at the end of the regular expression is necessary to avoid finding Then or There at the beginning of the input.
\z	Specifies the end of the string being searched. To find the word hedge followed by a period at the end of a string, you could use the expression `"\\bhedge\\.\\z"`.
\Z	The end of input except for the final terminator. A final terminator will be a newline character (`"\n"`) if `Pattern.UNIX_LINES` is set. Otherwise, it can also be a carriage return (`"\r"`), a carriage return followed by a newline, a next-line character (`"\u0085"`), a line separator (`"\u2028"`), or a paragraph separator (`"\u2029"`).

While you have moved quite a way from the simple search for a fixed substring offered by the `String` class methods, you still can't search for sequences that may vary in length. If you wanted to find all the numerical values in a string, which might be sequences such as `1234` or `23.45` or `999.998`, for example, you don't yet have the ability to do that. You can fix that now by taking a look at **quantifiers** in a regular expression, and what they can do for you.

Using Quantifiers

A quantifier following a subsequence of a pattern determines the possibilities for how that subsequence of a pattern can repeat. Let's take an example. Suppose you want to find any numerical values in a string. If you take the simplest case, we can say an integer is an arbitrary sequence of one or more digits. The quantifier for one or more is the meta-character +. You have also seen that you can use \d as short-hand for any digit (remembering, of course, that it becomes \\d in a Java `String` literal), so you could express any sequence of digits as the regular expression:

```
"\\d+"
```

Of course, a number may also include a decimal point and may be optionally followed by further digits. To indicate something can occur just once or not at all, as is the case with a decimal point, you can use the quantifier ?. You can write the pattern for a sequence of digits followed by a decimal point as:

```
"\\d+\\.?"
```

To add the possibility of further digits, you can append `\\d+` to what you have so far to produce the expression:

```
"\\d+\\.?\\d+"
```

This is a bit untidy. You can rewrite this as an integral part followed by an optional fractional part by putting parentheses around the bit for the fractional part and adding the `?` operator:

```
"\\d+(\\.\\d+)?"
```

However, this isn't quite right. You can have `2.` as a valid numerical value, for example, so you want to specify zero or more appearances of digits in the fractional part. The `*` quantifier expresses that, so maybe you should use:

```
"\\d+(\\.\\d*)?"
```

You are still missing something, though. What about the value .25 or the value -3? The optional sign in front of a number is easy, so let's deal with that first. To express the possibility that – or + can appear, you can use `[-|+]`, and since this either appears or it doesn't, you can extend it to `[+|-]?`. So to add the possibility of a sign you can write the expression as:

```
"[+|-]?\\d+(\\.\\d*)?"
```

You have to be careful how you allow for numbers beginning with a decimal point. You can't allow a sign followed by a decimal point or just a decimal point by itself to be interpreted as a number, so you can't say a number starts with zero or more digits or that the leading digits are optional. You could define a separate expression for numbers without leading digits like this:

```
"[+|-]?\\.\\d+"
```

Here then is an optional sign followed by a decimal point and at least one digit. With the other expression there is also an optional sign so you can combine these into a single expression to recognize either form, like this:

```
"[+|-]?(\\d+(\\.\\d*)?)|(\\.\\d+)"
```

This regular expression identifies substrings with an optional plus or minus sign followed by either a substring defined by `"\\d+(\\.\\d*)?"` or a substring defined by `"\\.\\d+"`. You might be tempted to use square brackets instead of parentheses here, but this would be quite wrong as square brackets define a set of characters, so any single character from the set is a match.

That was probably a bit more work than you anticipated, but it's often the case that things that look simple at first sight can turn out to be a little tricky. Let's try that out in an example.

Try It Out   Finding Integers

This is similar to the code we have used in previous examples except that here we will just list each substring that is found to correspond to the pattern:

```
import java.util.regex.Pattern;
import java.util.regex.Matcher;

public class FindingIntegers {
  public static void main(String args[]) {
    String regEx = "[+|-]?(\\d+(\\.\\d*)?)|(\\.\\d+)";
    String str = "256 is the square of 16 and -2.5 squared is 6.25 " +
                                 "and -.243 is less than 0.1234.";
    Pattern pattern = Pattern.compile(regEx);
    Matcher m = pattern.matcher(str);
    int i = 0;
    String subStr = null;
    while(m.find()) {
      System.out.println(m.group());                    // Output the substring matched
    }
  }
}
```

This will produce the following output:

```
256
16
-2.5
6.25
.243
0.1234
```

How It Works

Well, you found all the numbers in the string, so our regular expression works well, doesn't it? You can't do that with the methods in the `String` class. The only new code item here is the method, `group()`, that you call in the `while` loop for the `Matcher` object, m. This method returns a reference to a `String` object containing the subsequence corresponding to the last match of the entire pattern. Calling the `group()` method for the `Matcher` object m is equivalent to the expression `str.substring(m.start(), m.end())`.

Tokenizing a String

You saw back in Chapter 4 that you could tokenize a string using the `split()` method for a `String` object. As I mentioned then, the `split()` method does this by applying a regular expression — in fact, the first argument to the method is interpreted as a regular expression. This is because the expression `text.split(str, limit)`, where text is a `String` variable, is equivalent to the expression:

```
Pattern.compile(str).split(text, limit)
```

This means that you can apply all of the power of regular expressions to the identification of delimiters in the string. To demonstrate that this is the case I'll repeat the example from Chapter 4, but modify the first argument to the `split()` method so only the words in the text are included in the set of tokens.

Try It Out   Extracting the Words from a String

Here's the code for the modified version of the example:

```
public class StringTokenizing {
  public static void main(String[] args) {
    String text = "To be or not to be, that is the question."; // String to segment
    String delimiters = "\\s+|,\\s*|\\.\\s*";

    // Analyze the string
    String[] tokens = text.split(delimiters);

    // Output the tokens
    System.out.println("Number of tokens: " + tokens.length);
    for(String token : tokens) {
      System.out.println(token);
    }
  }
}
```

Now you should get the following output:

```
Number of tokens: 10
To
be
or
not
to
be
that
is
the
question
```

How It Works

The program produces 10 tokens in the output, which is the number of words in the text. The original version in Chapter 4 treated a comma followed by a space as two separate tokens and produced an empty token as a result. The substring ",\\s*" in the regular expression for the delimiters specifies that a comma followed by zero or more whitespace characters should be treated as a single token. The delimiters string is still relatively simplistic in that it does not include other delimiters that are likely to be found in text in general, such as ? or !, and it does not allow for spaces preceding punctuation characters. I'll leave it to you to fix this.

Search and Replace Operations

You can implement a search and replace operation very easily using regular expressions. Whenever you call the `find()` method for a `Matcher` object, you can call the `appendReplacement()` method to replace the subsequence that was matched. You create a revised version of the original string in a new `StringBuffer` object that you supply to the method. You have two arguments to the `appendReplacement()` method. The first is a reference to the `StringBuffer` object that is to contain the new string, and the second is the replacement string for the matched text. You can see how this works by considering a specific example.

Suppose you define a string to be searched as:

```
String joke = "My dog hasn't got any nose.\n"
            +"How does your dog smell then?\n"
            +"My dog smells horrible.\n";
```

You now want to replace each occurrence of `"dog"` in the string by `"goat"`. You first need a regular expression to find `"dog"`:

```
String regEx = "dog";
```

You can compile this into a pattern and create a `Matcher` object for the string `joke`:

```
Pattern doggone = Pattern.compile(regEx);
Matcher m = doggone.matcher(joke);
```

You are going to assemble a new version of `joke` in a `StringBuffer` object that you can create like this:

```
StringBuffer newJoke = new StringBuffer();
```

This is an empty `StringBuffer` object ready to receive the revised text. We can now search for and replace instances of `"dog"` in `joke` by calling the `find()` method for m and calling `appendReplacement()` each time it returns `true`:

```
while(m.find()) {
    m.appendReplacement(newJoke, "goat");
}
```

Each call of `appendReplacement()` copies characters from `joke` to `newJoke` starting at the character where the previous `find()` operation started and ending at the character preceding the first character matched: at `m.start()-1`, in other words. The method will then append the string specified by the second argument to `newJoke`. This process is illustrated in Figure 15-4.

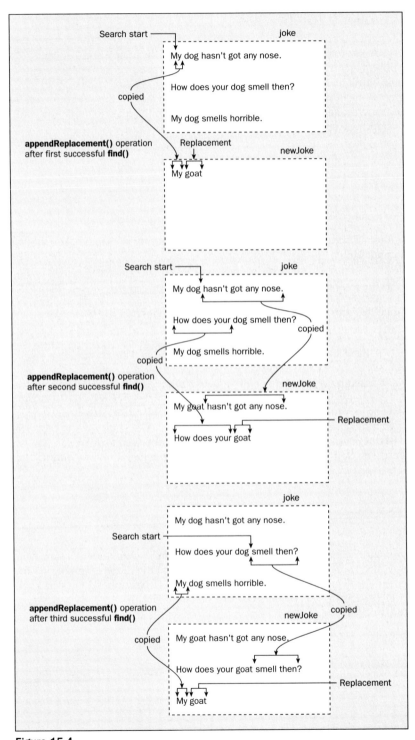

Figure 15-4

The `find()` method will return `true` three times, once for each occurrence of `"dog"` in `joke`. When the three steps shown in the diagram have been completed, the `find()` method returns `false` on the next loop iteration, terminating the loop. This leaves `newJoke` in the state shown in the last box in Figure 15-4. All we now need to complete `newJoke` is a way to copy the text from `joke` that comes after the last subsequence that was found. The `appendTail()` method for the `Matcher` object does that:

```
m.appendTail(newJoke);
```

This will copy the text starting with the `m.end()` index position from the last successful match through to the end of the string. Thus this statement copies the segment `" smells horrible."` from `joke` to `newJoke`. We can put all that together and run it.

Try It Out   Search and Replace

Here's the code I have just discussed assembled into a complete program:

```java
import java.util.regex.Pattern;
import java.util.regex.Matcher;

class SearchAndReplace {
  public static void main(String args[]) {
    String joke = "My dog hasn't got any nose.\n"
                  +"How does your dog smell then?\n"
                  +"My dog smells horrible.\n";
    String regEx = "dog";

    Pattern doggone = Pattern.compile(regEx);
    Matcher m = doggone.matcher(joke);

    StringBuffer newJoke = new StringBuffer();
    while(m.find()) {
      m.appendReplacement(newJoke, "goat");
    }
    m.appendTail(newJoke);
    System.out.println(newJoke.toString());
  }
}
```

When you compile and execute this you should get the following output:

```
My goat hasn't got any nose.
How does your goat smell then?
My goat smells horrible.
```

How It Works

Each time the `find()` method returns `true` in the `while` loop condition, you call the `appendReplacement()` method for the `Matcher` object `m`. This copies characters from `joke` to `newJoke`, starting with the index position where the `find()` method started searching, and ending at the character preceding the first character in the match, which will be at `m.start()-1`. The method then appends the replacement string, `"goat"`, to the contents of `newJoke`.

Once the loop finishes, the `appendTail()` method copies characters from `joke` to `newJoke`, starting with the character following the last match at `m.end()` through to the end of `joke`. Thus, you end up with a new string similar to the original, but which has each instance of `"dog"` replaced by `"goat"`.

You can use the search and replace capability to solve some string manipulation problems very easily. For example, if you want to make sure that any sequence of one or more whitespace characters is replaced by a single space, you can define the regular expression as `"\\s +"` and the replacement string as a single space `" "`. To eliminate all spaces at the beginning of each line, you can use the expression `"^\\s+"` and define the replacement string as empty, `""`.

Using Capturing Groups

Earlier you used the `group()` method for a `Matcher` object to retrieve the subsequence matched by the entire pattern defined by the regular expression. The entire pattern represents what is called a **capturing group** because the `Matcher` object captures the subsequence corresponding to the pattern match. Regular expressions can also define other capturing groups that correspond to parts of the pattern. Each pair of parentheses in a regular expression defines a separate capturing group in addition to the group that the whole expression defines. In the earlier example, you defined the regular expression by the statement:

```
String regEx = "[+|-]?(\\d+(\\.\\d*)?)|  (\\.\\d+)";
```

This defines three capturing groups other than the whole expression: one for the subexpression `(\\d+(\\.\\d*)?)`, one for the subexpression `(\\.\\d*)`, and one for the subexpression `(\\.\\d+)`. The `Matcher` object stores the subsequence that matches the pattern defined by each capturing group, and what's more, you can retrieve them.

To retrieve the text matching a particular capturing group, you need a way to identify the capturing group that you are interested in. To this end, capturing groups are numbered. The capturing group for the whole regular expression is always number 0. Counting their opening parentheses from the left in the regular expression numbers the other groups. Thus, the first opening parenthesis from the left corresponds to capturing group 1, the second opening parenthesis corresponds to capturing group 2, and so on for as many opening parentheses as there are in the whole expression. Figure 15-5 illustrates how the groups are numbered in an arbitrary regular expression.

As you see, it is easy to number the capturing groups as long as you can count left parentheses. Group 1 is the same as Group 0 because the whole regular expression is parenthesized. The other capturing groups in sequence are defined by `(B)`, `(C(D))`, `(D)`, and `(E)`.

To retrieve the text matching a particular capturing group after the `find()` method returns `true`, you call the `group()` method for the `Matcher` object with the group number as the argument. The `groupCount()` method for the `Matcher` object returns a value of type `int` that specifies the number of capturing groups within the pattern — that is, excluding group 0, which corresponds to the whole pattern. Therefore, you have all you need to access the text corresponding to any or all of the capturing groups in a regular expression.

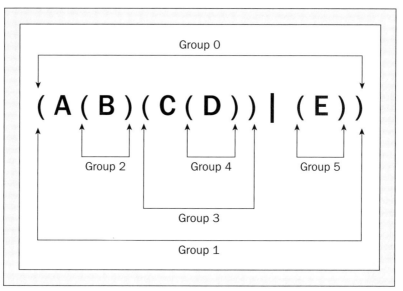

Figure 15-5

Try It Out   Capturing Groups

Let's modify our earlier example to output the text matching each group:

```java
import java.util.regex.Pattern;
import java.util.regex.Matcher;

public class TryCapturingGroups {
  public static void main(String args[]) {
    String regEx = "[+|-]?(\\d+(\\.\\d*)?)|(\\.\\d+)";
    String str = "256 is the square of 16 and -2.5 squared is 6.25 " +
                                "and -.243 is less than 0.1234.";
    Pattern pattern = Pattern.compile(regEx);
    Matcher m = pattern.matcher(str);
    while(m.find()) {
      for(int i = 0; i<=m.groupCount() ; i++) {
        System.out.println("Group " + i + ": " + m.group(i)); // Group i substring
      }
    }
  }
}
```

This produces the following output:

```
Group 0: 256
Group 1: 256
Group 2: null
Group 3: null
Group 0: 16
```

```
Group 1: 16
Group 2: null
Group 3: null
Group 0: -2.5
Group 1: 2.5
Group 2: .5
Group 3: null
Group 0: 6.25
Group 1: 6.25
Group 2: .25
Group 3: null
Group 0: .243
Group 1: null
Group 2: null
Group 3: .243
Group 0: 0.1234
Group 1: 0.1234
Group 2: .1234
Group 3: null
```

How It Works

The regular expression here defines four capturing groups:

❑ Group 0: The whole expression.

❑ Group 1: The subexpression `(\\d+(\\.\\d*)?)`

❑ Group 2: The subexpression `(\\.\\d*)`

❑ Group 3: The subexpression `(\\.\\d+)`

After each successful call of the `find()` method for the `Matcher` object m, you output the text captured by each group in turn by passing the index value for the group to the `group()` method. Note that because you want to output group 0 as well as the other groups, you start the loop index from 0 and allow it to equal the value returned by `groupCount()` so as to index over all the groups.

You can see from the output that group 1 corresponds to numbers beginning with a digit, and group 3 corresponds to numbers starting with a decimal point, so either one or the other of these is always `null`. Group 2 corresponds to the subpattern within group 1 that matches the fractional part of a number that begins with a digit, so the text for this can be non-`null` only when the text for group 1 is non-`null` and the number has a decimal point.

Juggling Captured Text

Since you can get access to the text corresponding to each capturing group in a regular expression, you can move such blocks of text around. The `appendReplacement()` method has special provision for recognizing references to capturing groups in the replacement text string. If $n, where n is an integer, appears in the replacement string, it will be interpreted as the text corresponding to group n. You can therefore replace the text matched to a complete pattern by any sequence of your choosing of the subsequences corresponding to the capturing groups in the pattern. That's hard to describe in words, so let's demonstrate it with an example.

Try It Out   Rearranging Captured Group Text

I'm sure you remember that the `Math.pow()` method requires two arguments; the second argument is the power to which the first argument must be raised. Thus, to calculate 16^3 you can write:

```
double result = Math.pow(16.0, 3.0);
```

Let's suppose a weak programmer on your team has written a Java program in which the two arguments have mistakenly been switched, so in trying to compute 16^3 the programmer has written:

```
double result = Math.pow(3.0, 16.0);
```

Of course, this computes 3^{16}, which is not quite the same thing. Let's suppose further that this sort of error is strewn throughout the source code and in every case the arguments are the wrong way round. You would need a month of Sundays to go through manually and switch the argument values, so let's see if regular expressions can rescue the situation.

What you need to do is find each occurrence of `Math.pow()` and switch the arguments around. The intention here is to understand how you can switch things around, so I'll keep it simple and assume that the argument values to `Math.pow()` are always a numerical value or a variable name.

The key to the whole problem is to devise a regular expression with capturing groups for the bits you want to switch — the two arguments. Be warned: This is going to get a little messy, not difficult, though — just messy.

You can define the first part of the regular expression that will find the sequence `"Math.pow("` at any point, and where you want to allow an arbitrary number of whitespace characters, you can use the sequence `\\s*`. You'll recall that `\\s` in a Java string specifies the predefined character class `\s`, which is whitespace. The `*` quantifier specifies zero or more of them. If you allow for whitespace between `Math.pow` and the opening parenthesis for the arguments, and some more whitespace after the opening parenthesis, the regular expression will be:

```
"(Math.pow)\\s*\\(\\s*"
```

You have to specify the opening parenthesis by `"\\("`. An opening parenthesis is a meta-character, so you have to write it as an escape sequence.

The opening parenthesis will be followed by the first argument, which I said could be a number or a variable name. You created a regular expression to identify a number earlier:

```
"[+|-]?(\\d+(\\.\\d*)?)|(\\.\\d+)"
```

To keep things simple, you'll assume that a variable name is just any sequence of letters, digits, or underscores that begins with a letter or an underscore. This will avoid getting involved with qualified names. You can match a variable name with the expression:

```
"[a-zA-Z_]\\w*"
```

You can therefore match either a variable name or a number with the pattern:

```
"((([a-zA-Z_]\\w*)|([+|-]?(\\d+(\\.\\d*)?)|(\\.\\d+)))"
```

This just ORs the two possibilities together and parenthesizes the whole thing so it will be a capturing group.

A comma that may be surrounded by zero or more whitespace characters on either side will follow the first argument. You can match that with the pattern:

```
\\s*,\\s*
```

The pattern to match the second argument will be exactly the same as the first:

```
"((([a-zA-Z_]\\w*)|([+|-]?(\\d+(\\.\\d*)?)|(\\.\\d+)))"
```

Finally, this must be followed by a closing parenthesis that may or may not be preceded by whitespace:

```
\\s*\\)
```

You can put all this together to define the entire regular expression as the value for a `String` variable:

```
String regEx = "(Math.pow)"                                          // Math.pow
    + "\\s*\\(\\s*"                                                   // Opening (
    + "((([a-zA-Z_]\\w*)|([+|-]?(\\d+(\\.\\d*)?)|(\\.\\d+)))"          // First argument
    + "\\s*,\\s*"                                                     // Comma
    + "((([a-zA-Z_]\\w*)|([+|-]?(\\d+(\\.\\d*)?)|(\\.\\d+)))"          // Second argument
    + "\\s*\\)";                                                      // Closing (
```

Here you assemble the string literal for the regular expression by concatenating six separate string literals. Each of these corresponds to an easily identified part of the method call. If you count the left parentheses, excluding the escaped parenthesis of course, you can also see that capturing group 1 corresponds with the method name, group 2 is the first method argument, and group 8 is the second method argument.

You can put this in the following example:

```
import java.util.regex.Pattern;
import java.util.regex.Matcher;

public class RearrangeText {
  public static void main(String args[]) {
    String regEx = "(Math.pow)"                                          // Math.pow
    + "\\s*\\(\\s*"                                                       // Opening (
    + "((([a-zA-Z_]\\w*)|([+|-]?(\\d+(\\.\\d*)?)|(\\.\\d+)))"              // First argument
    + "\\s*,\\s*"                                                         // Comma
    + "((([a-zA-Z_]\\w*)|([+|-]?(\\d+(\\.\\d*)?)|(\\.\\d+)))"              // Second argument
    + "\\s*\\)";                                                          // Closing (

    String oldCode =
        "double result = Math.pow( 3.0, 16.0);\n"
      + "double resultSquared = Math.pow(2 ,result );\n"
      + "double hypotenuse = Math.sqrt(Math.pow(2.0, 30.0)+Math.pow(2 , 40.0));\n";
```

```
        Pattern pattern = Pattern.compile(regEx);
        Matcher m = pattern.matcher(oldCode);

        StringBuffer newCode = new StringBuffer();
        while(m.find()) {
          m.appendReplacement(newCode, "$1\\($8,$2\\)");
        }
        m.appendTail(newCode);

        System.out.println("Original Code:\n"+oldCode.toString());
        System.out.println("New Code:\n"+newCode.toString());
      }
    }
```

You should get the following output:

```
Original Code:
double result = Math.pow( 3.0, 16.0);
double resultSquared = Math.pow(2 ,result );
double hypotenuse = Math.sqrt(Math.pow(2.0, 30.0)+Math.pow(2 , 40.0));

New Code:
double result = Math.pow(16.0,3.0);
double resultSquared = Math.pow(result,2);
double hypotenuse = Math.sqrt(Math.pow(30.0,2.0)+Math.pow(40.0,2));
```

How It Works

You have defined the regular expression so that separate capturing groups identify the method name and both arguments. As you saw earlier, the method name corresponds to group 1, the first argument to group 2, and the second argument to group 8. You therefore define the replacement string to the appendReplacement() method as "$1\\($8,$2\\)". The effect of this is to replace the text for each method call that is matched by the following, in sequence:

$1	The text matching capturing group 1, which will be the method name
\\(	A left parenthesis
$8	The text matching capturing group 8, which will be the second argument
,	A comma
$2	The text matching capturing group 2, which will be the first argument
\\)	A right parenthesis

The call to appendTail() is necessary to ensure that any text left at the end of oldCode following the last match for regEx gets copied to newCode.

In the process, you have eliminated any superfluous whitespace that was lying around in the original text.

Using a Scanner

The `java.util.Scanner` class defines objects that use regular expressions to scan character input from a variety of sources and present the input as a sequence of tokens of various primitive types or as strings. For example, you can use a `Scanner` object to read data values of various types from a file or a stream, including the standard stream `System.in`. Indeed, using a `Scanner` object would have saved you the trouble of developing the `FomattedInput` class back in Chapter 8 — still, it was good practice, wasn't it?

The facilities provided by the `Scanner` class are quite extensive, so I won't be able to go into all of it in detail because of space limitations. I'll just provide you with an idea of how the scanner mechanisms you are likely to find most useful can be applied. Once you have a grasp of the basics, I'm sure you'll find the other facilities quite easy to use.

Creating Scanner Objects

You can create a `Scanner` object by passing an object encapsulating the source of the data to be scanned to a `Scanner` constructor. You have five overloaded `Scanner` constructors that accept a single argument of any of the following types:

    InputStream   File   ReadableByteChannel   Readable   String

The `Scanner` object that is created will be able to read data from whichever source you supply as the argument to the constructor. `Readable` is an interface implemented by objects of type such as `BufferedReader`, `CharBuffer`, `FileReader`, `InputStreamReader`, and a number of other readers, so you can create a `Scanner` object that will scan any of these. For input from an external source, such as an `InputStream` or a `File` object, bytes will be converted into characters using the default charset in effect. Where you want to specify a charset that is to be used for the conversion from bytes to characters, you use constructors that accept a second argument of type `String` that specifies the charset name.

When you specify the argument to a constructor as type `File`, the constructor can throw an exception of type `FileNotFoundException`, so you must call the method in a `try` block in this instance or specify that your method making the call may throw an exception of type `FileNotFoundException`.

Of course, read operations for some sources may also result in an exception of type `IOException` being thrown. If this occurs, the `Scanner` object interprets this as signaling that the end of input has been reached. You can test whether an `IOException` has been thrown when reading from a source by calling the `ioException()` method for the `Scanner` object; the method returns `true` if the source has thrown an exception of type `IOException`..

Let's take the obvious example of a source from which you might want to interpret data. To obtain a `Scanner` object that will scan input from the keyboard, you could use the following statement:

    java.util.Scanner keyboard = new java.util.Scanner(System.in);

Creating a `Scanner` object to read from a file is a little more laborious because of the exception that may be thrown:

```
java.util.Scanner fileScan = null;
try {
  fileScan = new java.util.Scanner(new java.io.File("TryScanner.java"));
} catch(java.io.FileNotFoundException e) {
  e.printStackTrace();
  System.exit(1);
}
```

This fragment will create a `Scanner` object that you can use to scan the file `Scanner.java`.

Getting Input from a Scanner

By default, a `Scanner` object reads tokens assuming they are delimited by whitespace, which corresponds to any character for which the `isWhitespace()` method in the `Character` class returns `true`. Reading a token therefore involves skipping over any delimiter characters until a non-delimiter character is found, then attempting to interpret the sequence of non-delimiter characters in the way you have requested. You can read tokens of primitive types from the scanner source using the following methods:

`nextByte()`	Reads and returns the next token as type `byte`
`nextShort()`	Reads and returns the next token as type `short`
`nextInt()`	Reads and returns the next token as type `int`
`nextLong()`	Reads and returns the next token as type `long`
`nextFloat()`	Reads and returns the next token as type `float`
`nextDouble()`	Reads and returns the next token as type `double`
`nextBoolean()`	Reads and returns the next token as type `boolean`

The first four methods above for type `byte` and the integer types each have an overloaded version that accepts an argument of type `int` specifying the radix to be used in the interpretation of the value. All of these methods will throw an exception of type `java.util.InputMismatchException` if the input does not match the regular expression for the input type being read or of type `java.util.NoSuch ElementException` if the input is exhausted. Note that type `NoSuchElementException` is a superclass of type `InputMismatchException`, so you must put a `catch` clause for the latter first if you intend to catch both types of exceptions separately. The methods can also throw an exception of type `IllegalStateException` if the scanner is closed.

If the input read does not match the token you are trying to read, the invalid input will be left in the input buffer, so you have an opportunity to try an alternative way of matching it. Of course, if it is simply erroneous input, you will want to skip over it before continuing. In this case you can call the `next()` method for the `Scanner` object, which will read the next token up to the next delimiter in the input and return it as a `String` object.

The `Scanner` class also defines `nextBigInteger()` and `nextBigDecimal()` methods that read the next token as a `java.math.BigInteger` object or a `java.math.BigDecimal` object, respectively. The

`BigInteger` class defines objects that encapsulate integers with an arbitrary number of digits and provides the methods you need to work with such values. The `BigDecimal` class does the same thing for non-integral values.

You have enough knowledge to try out a scanner, so let's do it.

Try It Out   Using a Scanner

Here's a simple example that just reads a variety of input from the standard input stream and displays what was read:

```java
import java.util.Scanner;
import java.util.InputMismatchException;

public class TryScanner {
  public static void main(String[] args) {
    Scanner kbScan = new Scanner(System.in);      // Create the scanner
    int selectRead = 1;                           // Selects the read operation
    final int MAXTRIES = 3;                        // Maximum attempts at input
    int tries = 0;                                // Number of input attempts

    while(tries<MAXTRIES) {
      try {
        switch(selectRead) {
          case 1:
          System.out.print("Enter an integer: ");
          System.out.println("You entered: "+ kbScan.nextLong());
          ++selectRead;                            // Select next read operation
          tries = 0;                               // Reset count of tries

          case 2:
          System.out.print("Enter a floating-point value: ");
          System.out.println("You entered: "+ kbScan.nextDouble());
          ++selectRead;                            // Select next read operation
          tries = 0;                               // Reset count of tries

          case 3:
          System.out.print("Enter a boolean value(true or false): ");
          System.out.println("You entered: "+ kbScan.nextBoolean());
        }
        break;
      } catch(InputMismatchException e) {
          String input = kbScan.next();
          System.out.println("\""+ input +"\" is not valid input.");
          if(tries<MAXTRIES) {
            System.out.println("Try again.");
          } else {
            System.out.println(" Terminating program.");
            System.exit(1);
        }
      }
    }
  }
}
```

With my limited typing skills, I got the following output:

```
Enter an integer: 1$
"1$" is not valid input.
Try again.
Enter an integer: 14
You entered: 14
Enter a floating-point value: 2e1
You entered: 20.0
Enter a boolean value(true or false): tree
"tree" is not valid input.
Try again.
Enter a boolean value(true or false): true
You entered: true
```

How It Works

In this example you use a scanner to read values of three different types from the standard input stream. The read operations take place in a loop to allow multiple attempts at correct input. Within the loop you have a rare example of a `switch` statement that doesn't require a `break` statement after each case. In this case you want each case to fall through to the next. The `selectRead` variable that selects a switch case provides the means by which you manage subsequent attempts at correct input, because it records the case label currently in effect.

If an invalid input value is entered, an exception of type `InputMismatchException` will be thrown by the `Scanner` method that is attempting to read a token of a particular type. In the `catch` block, you call the `next()` method for the `Scanner` object to retrieve and thus skip over the input that was not recognized. You then continue with the next `while` loop iteration to allow a further attempt at reading the token.

Testing for Tokens

The `hasNext()` method for a `Scanner` object will return `true` if another token is available from the input source. You can use this in combination with the `next()` method to read a sequence of tokens of any type from a source, delimited by whitespace. For example:

```
java.util.Scanner fileScan = null;
try {
  fileScan = new java.util.Scanner(new java.io.File("TryScanner.java"));
} catch(java.io.IOException e) {
  e.printStackTrace();
  System.exit(1);
}
String token = null;
while(fileScan.hasNext() {
  token = fileScan.next();
  // Do something with the token read...
}
```

Here you are just reading an arbitrary number of tokens at strings. In general, the `next()` method can throw an exception of type `NoSuchElementException`, but this cannot happen here because you use the `hasNext()` method to establish that there is another token to be read before you call the `next()` method.

The `Scanner` object can do better than this. In addition to the `hasNext()` method that checks whether a token of any kind is available, you have methods such as `hasNextInt()` and `hasNextDouble()` for testing for the availability of any of the types that you can read with methods such as `nextInt()` and `nextDouble()`. This enables you to code so that you can process tokens of various types, even when you don't know ahead of time the sequence in which they will be received. For example:

```
while(fileScan.hasNext() {
  if(fileScan.hasNextInt()) {
  // Process integer input...

  } else if(fileScan.hasNextDouble()) {
  // Process floating-point input...

  } else if(fileScan.hasNextBoolean()) {
  // Process boolean input...

  }
}
```

The `while` loop will continue as long as there are tokens of any kind available from the `fileScan` scanner. The `if` statements within the loop decide how the next token is to be processed, assuming it is one of the ones that you are interested in. If you want to skip tokens that you don't want to process within the loop, you can just call the `next()` method for `fileScan`.

Defining Your Own Patterns for Tokens

The `Scanner` class provides a way for you to specify how a token should be recognized. You use one of two overloaded versions of the `next()` method to do this. One version accepts an argument of type `Pattern` that you produce by compiling a regular expression using the static `compile()` method for the `Pattern` class in the way you saw earlier in this chapter. The other accepts an argument of type `String` that specifies a regular expression that will identify the token. In both cases the token is returned as type `String`.

There are also overloaded versions of the `hasNext()` method that accept an argument of type `Pattern` or a reference to a `String` object containing a regular expression that identifies a token. You use these to test for tokens of your own specification. You could see these in action in an example that scans a string for a token specified by a simple pattern.

Try It Out   **Scanning a String**

This example scans a string looking for occurrences of `"had"`:

```
import java.util.Scanner;
import java.util.regex.Pattern;

public class ScanString {
  public static void main(String[] args) {
    String str = "Smith , where Jones had had 'had', had had 'had had'.";
    String regex = "had";
    System.out.println("String is:\n"+str+"\nToken sought is: "+regex);
```

```
        Pattern had = Pattern.compile(regex);
        Scanner strScan = new Scanner(str);
        int hadCount = 0;
        while(strScan.hasNext()) {
          if(strScan.hasNext(had)) {
            ++hadCount;
            System.out.println("Token found!: " + strScan.next(had));
          } else {
            System.out.println("Token is    : " + strScan.next());
          }
        }
        System.out.println(hadCount + " instances of \"" + regex +  "\" were found.");
      }
    }
```

This program will produce the following output:

```
String is:
Smith , where Jones had had 'had', had had 'had had'.
Token sought is: had
Token is    : Smith
Token is    : ,
Token is    : where
Token is    : Jones
Token found!: had
Token found!: had
Token is    : 'had',
Token found!: had
Token found!: had
Token is    : 'had
Token is    : had'.
4 instances of "had" were found.
```

How It Works

After defining the string to be scanned and the regular expression that defines the form of a token, you compile the regular expression into a `Pattern` object. Passing a `Pattern` object to the `hasNext()` method (or the `next()` method) will be much more efficient than passing the original regular expression when you expect to be calling the method more than once. When you pass a `String` object containing a regular expression to the `hasNext()` method, the method will need to compile it to a pattern before it can use it. Thus if you compile the regular expression first and pass the `Pattern` object as the argument, the compile operation will occur only once.

You scan the string, `str`, in the `while` loop. The loop continues as long as there is another token available from the string. Within the loop, you check for the presence of a token defined by `regex` by calling the `hasNext()` method with the `had` pattern as the argument:

```
        if(strScan.hasNext(had)) {
          ++hadCount;
        System.out.println("Token found!: " + strScan.next(had));
        } else {
          System.out.println("Token is    : " + strScan.next());
        }
```

If the `hasNext()` method returns `true`, you increment `hadCount` and output the token returned by `next()` with the argument as `had`. Of course, you could just as well have used the `next()` method with no argument here. If the next token does not correspond to `had`, you read it anyway with the `next()` method. Finally, you output the count of the number of times your token was found.

From the output you can see that only four instances of `"had"` were found. This is because the scanner assumes the delimiter is one or more whitespace characters. If you don't like this you can specify another regular expression that the scanner should use for the delimiter:

```
strScan.useDelimiter("\\s'|\\s*'?[.|,]\\s*|\\s");
```

The `useDelimiter()` method expects an argument of type `String` that specifies a regular expression for recognizing delimiters. In this case the expression implies a delimiter is a whitespace character followed by a single quote, or zero or one whitespace characters followed by a comma or a period followed by zero or more whitespace characters, or just a whitespace character. If you add this statement following the creation of the `Scanner` object the program should find all the `"had"` tokens.

> *I once again want to stress that regular expressions are a very powerful capability that I only touched on in this chapter. You now have a foundation of understanding regular expressions that you can follow into a more in-depth exploration of them. If you want to explore regular expression in more depth, you could try Java Regular Expressions: Taming the java.util.regex Engine by Merhan Habibi (Apress 2004).*

Summary

The important elements that you've covered in this chapter are:

❑ The `java.util.Arrays` class provides static methods for sorting, searching, filling, and comparing arrays.

❑ Objects of type `Random` can generate pseudo-random numbers of type `int`, `long`, `float`, and `double`. The integers are uniformly distributed across the range of the type `int` or `long`. The floating-point numbers are between 0.0 and 1.0. You can also generate numbers of type `double` with a Gaussian distribution with a mean of 0.0 and a standard deviation of 1.0 and random `boolean` values.

❑ Classes derived from the `Observable` class can signal changes to classes that implement the `Observer` interface. You define the `Observer` objects that are to be associated with an `Observable` class object by calling the `addObserver()` method. This is primarily intended to be used to implement the document/view architecture for applications in a GUI environment.

❑ You can create `Date` objects to represent a date and time that you specify in milliseconds since January 1, 1970, 00:00:00 GMT or as the current date and time from your computer clock.

❑ You can use a `DateFormat` object to format the date and time for a `Date` object as a string. The format will be determined by the style and the locale that you specify.

❑ A `GregorianCalendar` object represents a calendar set to an instant in time on a given date.

❑ A regular expression defines a pattern that is used for searching text.

❑ In Java, a regular expression is compiled into a `Pattern` object that you can then use to obtain a `Matcher` object that will scan a given string looking for the pattern.

❑ The `appendReplacement()` method for a `Matcher` object enables you to make substitutions for patterns found in the input text.

❑ A capturing group in a regular expression records the text that matches a subpattern.

❑ By using capturing groups you can rearrange the sequence of substrings in a string matching a pattern.

❑ A `Scanner` object uses a regular expression to segment data from a variety of sources into tokens.

Exercises

You can download the source code for the examples in the book and the solutions to the following exercises from `http://www.wrox.com`.

1. Define a static method to fill an array of type `char[]` with a given value passed as an argument to the method.

2. For the adventurous gambler — use a stack and a `Random` object in a program to simulate a game of Blackjack for one player using two decks of cards.

3. Write a program to display the sign of the Zodiac corresponding to a birth date entered through the keyboard.

4. Write a program using regular expressions to remove spaces from the beginning and end of each line in a file.

5. Write a program using a regular expression to reproduce a file with a sequential line number starting at "0001" inserted at the beginning of each line in the original file. You can use a copy of your Java source file as the input to test this.

6. Write a program using a regular expression to eliminate any line numbers that appear at the beginning of lines in a file. You can use the output from the previous exercise as a test for your program.

Threads

In this chapter you'll investigate the facilities Java has that enable you to overlap the execution of segments of a single program. As well as ensuring your programs run more efficiently, this capability is particularly useful when your program must, of necessity, do a number of things at the same time: for example, a server program on a network that needs to communicate with multiple clients. As you'll see in Chapter 18, threads are also fundamental to any Java application that uses a graphical user interface (GUI), so it's essential that you understand how threads work.

In this chapter you'll learn:

- ❏   What a thread is and how to create threads in your programs

- ❏   How to control interactions between threads

- ❏   What synchronization means and how to apply it in your code

- ❏   What deadlocks are and how to avoid them

- ❏   How to set thread priorities

- ❏   How to get information about the threads in your programs

Understanding Threads

Most programs of a reasonably large size will contain some code segments that are more or less independent of one another and that may execute more efficiently if the code segments could be overlapped in time. Threads provide a way to do this. If you have a machine with two or more processors, then as many computations as you have processors can be executing concurrently. Of course, if your computer has only one processor, you can't execute more than one computation at any instant, but you can still overlap input/output operations with processing.

Another reason for using threads is to allow processes in a program that need to run continuously, such as a continuously running animation, to be overlapped with other activities in the same program. Java applets in a web page are executed under the control of a single program — your browser — and threads make it possible for multiple applets to be executing concurrently. In this case the threads serve to segment the activities running under the control of the browser so that they appear to run concurrently. If you have only one processor, this is an illusion created by your operating system, since only one thread can actually be executing instructions at any given instant, but it's a very effective illusion. To produce animation, you typically put some code that draws a succession of still pictures in a loop that runs indefinitely. The code to draw the picture generally runs under the control of a timer so that it executes at a fixed rate — for example, 20 times per second. Of course, nothing else can happen in the same thread while the loop is running. If you want to have another animation running, it must be in a separate thread. Then the multitasking capability of your operating system can allow the two threads to share the available processor time, thus allowing both animations to run.

Let's get an idea of the principles behind how threads operate. Consider a very simple program that consists of three activities:

❑ Reading a number of blocks of data from a file

❑ Performing some calculation on each block of data

❑ Writing the results of the calculation to another file

You could organize the program as a single sequence of activities. In this case the activities — read file, process, write file — run in sequence, and the sequence is repeated for each block to be read and processed. You could also organize the program so that reading a block from the file is one activity, performing the calculation is a second activity, and writing the results is a third activity. Both of these situations are illustrated in Figure 16-1.

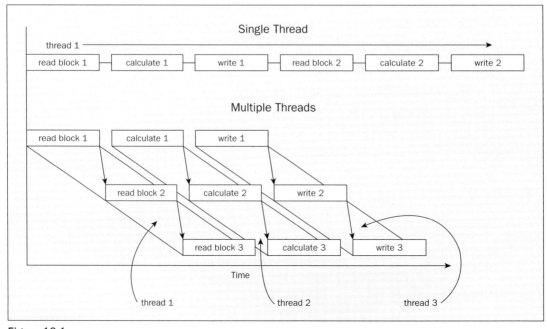

Figure 16-1

Once a block of data has been read, the computation process can start, and as soon as the computation has been completed, the results can be written out. With the program executing each step in sequence (that is, as a single thread), as shown in the top half of Figure 16-1, the total time for execution is the sum of the times for each of the individual activities. However, suppose you were able to execute each of the activities independently, as illustrated in the lower half of Figure 16-1. In this case, reading the second block of data can start as soon as the first block has been read, and in theory you can have all three activities executing concurrently. This is possible even though you have only one processor because the input and output operations are likely to require relatively little processor time while they are executing, so the processor can be doing other things while they are in progress. This can reduce the total execution time for the program.

These three processes that run more or less independently of one another — one to read the file, another to process the data, and a third to write the results — are called **threads**. Of course, the first example at the top of Figure 16-1 has just one thread that does everything in sequence. Every Java program has at least one thread. However, the three threads in the lower example in Figure 16-1 aren't completely independent of one another. After all, if they were, you might as well make them independent programs. You have practical limitations, too — the potential for overlapping these threads is dependent on the capabilities of your computer, and of your operating system. However, if you can get some overlap in the execution of the threads, the program is going to run faster. You'll find no magic in using threads, though. Your computer has only a finite capacity for executing instructions, and if you have many threads running, you may in fact increase the overall execution time because of the overhead implicit in managing the switching of control between threads.

An important consideration when you have a single program running as multiple threads is that the threads are unlikely to have identical execution times, and if one thread is dependent on another you can't afford to have one overtaking the other — otherwise, you'll have chaos. Before you can start calculating in the example in the diagram, you need to be sure that the block of data that the calculation uses has been read, and before you can write the output, you need to know that the calculation is complete. This necessitates having some means for the threads to communicate with one another.

The way I have shown the threads executing in Figure 16-1 isn't the only way of organizing the program. You could have three threads, each of which reads the file, calculates the results, and writes the output, as shown in Figure 16-2.

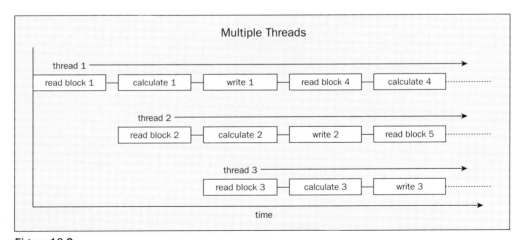

Figure 16-2

Now there's a different sort of contention between the threads. They are all competing to read the file and write the results, so there needs to be some way of preventing one thread from getting at the input file while another thread is already reading from it. The same goes for the output file. There's another aspect of this arrangement that is different from the previous version. For example, if one thread, *thread 1*, reads a block, *block 4*, that needs a lot of time to compute the results, another thread, *thread 2*, could conceivably read a following block, *block 5*, and calculate and write the results for *block 5* before *thread 1* has written the results for *block 4*. If you don't want the results appearing in a different sequence from the input, you should do something about this. However, before I delve into the intricacies of making sure that the threads don't get knotted, let's first look at how you create a thread.

Creating Threads

Your program always has at least one thread: the one created when the program begins execution. In a normal Java application program, this thread starts at the beginning of main(). With an applet, the browser is the main thread. That means that when your program creates a thread, it is in addition to the main thread of execution that created it. As you might have guessed, creating an additional thread involves using an object of a class, and the class you use is java.lang.Thread. Each additional thread that your program creates is represented by an object of the class Thread, or of a subclass of Thread. If your program is to have three additional threads, you will need to create three such objects.

To start the execution of a thread, you call the start() method for the Thread object. The code that executes in a new thread is always a method called run(), which is public, accepts no arguments, and doesn't return a value. Threads other than the main thread in a program always start in the run() method for the object that represents the thread. A program that creates three threads is illustrated diagrammatically in Figure 16-3.

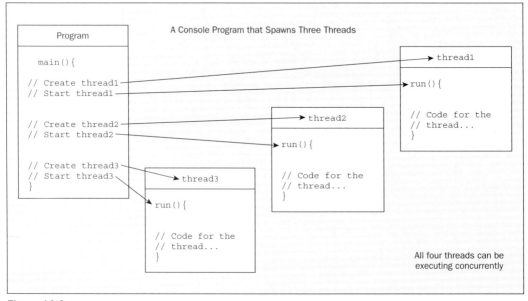

Figure 16-3

For a class representing a thread in your program to do anything, you must implement the run() method, as the version defined in the Thread class does nothing. Your implementation of run() can call any other methods you want. Figure 16-3 shows the main() method creating all three threads, but that doesn't have to be the case. Any thread can create more threads.

Now here comes the bite: You don't call the run() method to start a thread, you call the start() method for the object representing the thread, and that causes the run() method to be called. When you want to stop the execution of a thread that is running, you signal to the Thread object that it should stop itself, by setting a field that the thread checks at regular intervals, for example.

The reason for starting a thread in the way I have described is somewhat complex but basically it boils down to this: threads are always owned and managed by the operating system, and a new thread can be created and started only by the operating system. If you were to call the run() method yourself, it would simply operate like any other method, running in the same thread as the program that calls it.

When you call the start() method for a Thread object, you are calling a native code method that causes the operating system to initiate another thread from which the run() method for the Thread object executes.

In any case, it is not important to understand exactly how this works. Just remember: Always start your thread by calling the start() method. If you try to call the run() method directly yourself, then you will not have created a new thread and your program will not work as you intended.

You can define a class that is to represent a thread in two ways.

❑   One way is to define your class as a subclass of Thread and provide a definition of the method run(), which overrides the inherited method.

❑   The other possibility is to define your class as implementing the interface Runnable, which declares the run() method, and then create a Thread object in your class when you need it.

You'll look at and explore the advantages of each approach in a little more detail.

Try It Out   Deriving a Subclass of Thread

You can see how deriving a subclass of Thread works by using an example. You'll define a single class, TryThread, which you'll derive from Thread. As always, execution of the application starts in the main() method. Here's the code:

```
import java.io.IOException;

public class TryThread extends Thread {
  public TryThread(String firstName, String secondName, long delay) {
    this.firstName = firstName;      // Store the first name
    this.secondName = secondName;    // Store the second name
    aWhile = delay;                  // Store the delay
    setDaemon(true);                 // Thread is daemon
  }

  public static void main(String[] args) {
    // Create three threads
```

```
        Thread first = new TryThread("Hopalong ", "Cassidy ", 200L);
        Thread second = new TryThread("Marilyn ", "Monroe ", 300L);
        Thread third = new TryThread("Slim ", "Pickens ", 500L);

        System.out.println("Press Enter when you have had enough...\n");
        first.start();                      // Start the first thread
        second.start();                     // Start the second thread
        third.start();                      // Start the third thread

        try {
          System.in.read();                 // Wait until Enter key pressed
          System.out.println("Enter pressed...\n");

        } catch (IOException e) {           // Handle IO exception
          System.out.println(e);            // Output the exception
        }
        System.out.println("Ending main()");
        return;
      }

      // Method where thread execution will start
      public void run() {
        try {
          while(true) {                     // Loop indefinitely...
            System.out.print(firstName);    // Output first name
            sleep(aWhile);                  // Wait aWhile msec.
            System.out.print(secondName + "\n"); // Output second name
          }
        } catch(InterruptedException e) {         // Handle thread interruption
          System.out.println(firstName + secondName + e);      // Output the exception
        }
      }

      private String firstName;             // Store for first name
      private String secondName;            // Store for second name
      private long aWhile;                  // Delay in milliseconds
    }
```

If you compile and run the code, you'll see something like this:

```
Press Enter when you have had enough...

Hopalong Marilyn Slim Cassidy
Hopalong Monroe
Marilyn Cassidy
Hopalong Pickens
Slim Monroe
Marilyn Cassidy
Hopalong Cassidy
Hopalong Monroe
Marilyn Pickens
Slim Cassidy
Hopalong Monroe
Marilyn Cassidy
Hopalong Cassidy
Hopalong Monroe
```

```
Marilyn Pickens
Slim Cassidy
Hopalong Cassidy
Hopalong Monroe
Marilyn
Enter pressed...

Ending main()
```

How It Works

You have three instance variables in the `TryThread` class, and these are initialized in the constructor. The two `String` variables hold first and second names, and the variable `aWhile` stores a time period in milliseconds. The constructor for the class, `TryThread()`, will automatically call the default constructor, `Thread()`, for the base class.

The class containing the `main()` method is derived from `Thread` and implements `run()`, so objects of this class represent threads. The fact that each object of your class will have access to the method `main()` is irrelevant — the objects are perfectly good threads. The method `main()` creates three such objects: `first`, `second`, and `third`.

Daemon and User Threads

The call to `setDaemon()`, with the argument `true` in the `TryThread` constructor, makes the thread that is created a **daemon thread**. A daemon thread is simply a background thread that is subordinate to the thread that creates it, so when the thread that created the daemon thread ends, the daemon thread dies with it. In this case, the method `main()` creates the daemon threads so that when `main()` returns, all the threads it has created will also end. If you run the example a few times pressing Enter at random, you should see that the daemon threads die after the `main()` method returns, because, from time to time, you will get some output from one or other thread after the last output from `main()`.

A thread that isn't a daemon thread is called a user thread. The diagram in Figure 16-4 shows two daemon threads and a user thread that are created by the main thread of a program.

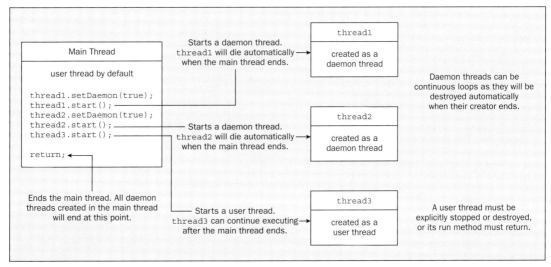

Figure 16-4

A user thread has a life of its own that is not dependent on the thread that creates it. It can continue execution after the thread that created it has ended. The default thread that contains main() is a user thread, as shown in the diagram, but thread3 shown in the diagram could continue to execute after main() has returned. Threads that run for a finite time are typically user threads, but there's no reason why a daemon thread can't be finite. Threads that run indefinitely should usually be defined as daemon threads simply because you need a means of stopping them. A hypothetical example might help you to understand this, so let's consider how a network server handling transactions of some kind might work in principle.

A network server might be managed overall by a user thread that starts one or more daemon threads to listen for requests. When the server starts up, the operator starts the management thread, and this thread creates daemon threads to listen for requests. Each request that is recognized by one of these daemon threads might be handled by another thread that is created by the listening thread, so that each request will be handled independently. Where processing a transaction takes a finite time, and where it is important that the requests are completed before the system shuts down, the thread to handle the request might be created as a user thread to ensure that it runs to completion, even if the listening thread that created it stops. Generally you would not want a program to be able to create an unlimited number of threads because the more threads there are running, the greater the operating system overhead there will be in managing the threads. For this reason, a program will often make use of a **thread pool** of a specified number of threads. When a new thread is required for a particular task, such as servicing a request, one of the threads in the thread pool is allocated to the task. If all the threads in the pool have been allocated, then a new thread cannot be started until one of the threads that is currently running terminates. The class libraries provide help in the creation and management of thread pools through the java.util.concurrent.ThreadPoolExecutor class. When the time comes to shut the system down, the operator doesn't have to worry about how many listening threads are running. When the main thread is shut down, all the listening threads will also shut down because they are daemon threads. Any outstanding threads dealing with specific transactions will then run to completion.

Note that you can call setDaemon() for a thread only before it starts; if you try to do so afterwards, the method will throw an IllegalThreadStateException exception. Also, a thread that is itself created by a daemon thread will be a daemon by default.

Creating Thread Objects

In the main() method you create three Thread variables that store three different objects of type TryThread. As you can see, each object has an individual name pair as the first two arguments to its constructor, and a different delay value passed as the third argument. All objects of the class TryThread are daemon threads because you call setDaemon() with the argument true in the constructor. Since the output can continue indefinitely, you display a message to explain how to stop it.

Once you've created a thread, it doesn't start executing by itself. You need to set it going. As I said earlier, you don't call the run() method for the Thread object to do this, you call its start() method. Thus, you start the execution of each of the threads represented by the objects first, second, and third by calling the start() method that is inherited from Thread for each object. The start() method starts the object's run() method executing and then returns to the calling thread. Eventually, all three threads are executing in parallel with the original application thread, main().

Implementing the run() Method

The run() method contains the code for thread execution. The code in this case is a single, infinite while loop that you have put in a try block because the sleep() method that is called in the loop can throw the InterruptedException exception that is caught by the catch block. The code in the loop outputs the first name, calls the method sleep() inherited from Thread, and then outputs the second name. The sleep() method suspends execution of the thread for the number of milliseconds that you specify in the argument. This gives any other threads that have previously been started a chance to execute. This allows the output from the three threads to become a little jumbled.

Each time a thread calls the method sleep(), one of the other waiting threads jumps in. You can see the sequence in which the threads execute from the output. From the names in the output you can deduce that they execute in the sequence first, second, third, first, first, second, second, first, first, third, and so on. The actual sequence depends on your operating system scheduler, so this is likely to vary from machine to machine. The execution of the read() method that is called in main() is blocked until you press Enter, but all the while the other threads continue executing. The output stops when you press Enter because this allows the main thread to continue and execute the return. Executing return ends the thread for main(), and since the other threads are daemon threads, they also die when the thread that created them dies, although as you may have seen, they can run on a little after the last output from main().

Stopping a Thread

If you did not create the threads in the last example as daemon threads, they would continue executing independently of main(). If you are prepared to terminate the program yourself (use Ctrl+C in a Windows command-line session running Java), you can demonstrate this by commenting out the call to setDaemon() in the constructor. Pressing Enter will end main(), but the other threads will continue indefinitely.

A thread can signal another thread that it should stop executing by calling the interrupt() method for that Thread object. This in itself doesn't stop the thread; it just sets a flag in the thread that indicates an interruption has been requested. This flag must be checked in the run() method to have any effect. As it happens, the sleep() method checks whether the thread has been interrupted, and throws an InterruptedException if it has been. You can see that in action by altering the previous example a little.

Try It Out   Interrupting a Thread

Make sure the call to the setDaemon() method is still commented out in the constructor and modify the main() method as follows:

```
public static void main(String[] args) {
  // Create three threads
  Thread first = new TryThread("Hopalong ", "Cassidy ", 200L);
  Thread second = new TryThread("Marilyn ", "Monroe ", 300L);
  Thread third = new TryThread("Slim ", "Pickens ", 500L);

  System.out.println("Press Enter when you have had enough...\n");
  first.start();                          // Start the first thread
  second.start();                         // Start the second thread
```

```
      third.start();                        // Start the third thread
      try {
        System.in.read();                   // Wait until Enter key pressed
        System.out.println("Enter pressed...\n");

        // Interrupt the threads
        first.interrupt();
        second.interrupt();
        third.interrupt();

      } catch (IOException e) {              // Handle IO exception
        System.out.println(e);              // Output the exception
      }
      System.out.println("Ending main()");
      return;
    }
```

Now the program will produce output that is something like the following:

```
Press Enter when you have had enough...

Slim Hopalong Marilyn Cassidy
Hopalong Monroe
Marilyn Cassidy
Hopalong Pickens
Slim Cassidy
Hopalong Monroe
Marilyn
Enter pressed...

Ending main()
Marilyn Monroe java.lang.InterruptedException: sleep interrupted
Slim Pickens java.lang.InterruptedException: sleep interrupted
Hopalong Cassidy java.lang.InterruptedException: sleep interrupted
```

How It Works

Since the method main() calls the interrupt() method for each of the threads after you press the Enter key, the sleep() method that is called in each thread registers the fact that the thread has been interrupted and throws an InterruptedException. This is caught by the catch block in the run() method and produces the new output that you see. Because the catch block is outside the while loop, the run() method for each thread returns and each thread terminates.

You can check whether a thread has been interrupted by calling the isInterrupted() method for the thread. This returns true if interrupt() has been called for the thread in question. Since this is an instance method, you can use this in one thread to determine whether another thread has been interrupted. For example, in main() you could write:

```
if(first.isInterrupted()) {
  System.out.println("First thread has been interrupted.");
}
```

Note that this determines only whether the interrupted flag has been set by a call to `interrupt()` for the thread — it does not determine whether the thread is still running. A thread could have its interrupt flag set and continue executing — it is not obliged to terminate because `interrupt()` is called. To test whether a thread is still operating you can call its `isAlive()` method. This returns `true` if the thread has not terminated.

The instance method `isInterrupted()` has no effect on the interrupt flag in the thread — if it was set, it remains set. However, the static method `interrupted()` in the `Thread` class is different. It tests whether the currently executing thread has been interrupted, and if it has, it clears the interrupted flag in the current `Thread` object and returns `true`.

When an `InterruptedException` is thrown, the flag that registers the interrupt in the thread is cleared, so a subsequent call to `isInterrupted()` or `interrupted()` will return `false`.

Connecting Threads

If in one thread you need to wait until another thread dies, you can call the `join()` method for the thread that you expect isn't long for this world. Calling the `join()` method with no arguments will halt the current thread for as long as it takes the specified thread to die:

```
thread1.join();              // Suspend the current thread until thread1 dies
```

You can also pass a `long` value to the `join()` method to specify the number of milliseconds you're prepared to wait for the death of a thread:

```
thread1.join(1000);          // Wait up to 1 second for thread1 to die
```

If this is not precise enough, you have a version of `join()` with two parameters. The first is a time in milliseconds and the second is a time in nanoseconds. The current thread will wait for the duration specified by the sum of the arguments. Of course, whether or not you get nanosecond resolution will depend on the capability of your hardware.

The `join()` method can throw an `InterruptedException` if the current thread is interrupted by another thread, so you should put a call to `join()` in a `try` block and catch the exception.

Thread Scheduling

The scheduling of threads depends to some extent on your operating system, but each thread will certainly get a chance to execute while the others are "asleep," that is, when they've called their `sleep()` methods. If your operating system uses preemptive multitasking, the program will work without the call to `sleep()` in the `run()` method (you should also remove the `try` and `catch` blocks if you remove the `sleep()` call). However, if your operating system doesn't schedule in this way, without the `sleep()` call in `run()`, the `first` thread will hog the processor and continue indefinitely.

Figure 16-5 illustrates how four threads might share the processor over time by calling the `sleep()` method to relinquish control.

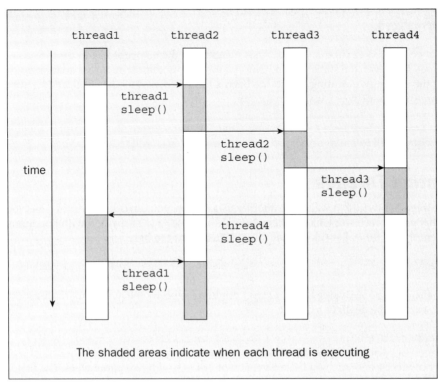

Figure 16-5

Note that there's another method, `yield()`, defined in the `Thread` class, that gives other threads a chance to execute. You would use this when you just want to allow other threads a look-in if they are waiting, but you don't want to suspend execution of the current thread for a specific period of time. When you call the `sleep()` method for a thread, the thread will not continue for at least the time you have specified as an argument, even if no other threads are waiting. Calling `yield()`, on the other hand, causes the current thread to resume immediately if no threads are waiting.

Implementing the Runnable Interface

As an alternative to defining a new subclass of `Thread`, you can implement the `Runnable` interface in a class. You'll find that this is generally much more convenient than deriving a class from `Thread` because you can derive your class from a class other than `Thread` and it can still represent a thread. Because Java allows only a single base class, if you derive your class from `Thread`, it can't inherit functionality from any other class. The `Runnable` interface declares only one method, `run()`, and this is the method that will be executed when the thread is started.

Try It Out   Using the Runnable Interface

To see how this works in practice, you can write another version of the previous example. I've called this version of the program `JumbleNames`:

```
import java.io.IOException;

public class JumbleNames implements Runnable {
  // Constructor
  public JumbleNames(String firstName, String secondName, long delay) {
    this.firstName = firstName;                      // Store the first name
    this.secondName = secondName;                    // Store the second name
    aWhile = delay;                                  // Store the delay
  }

  // Method where thread execution will start
  public void run() {
    try {
      while(true) {                                  // Loop indefinitely...
        System.out.print(firstName);                 // Output first name
        Thread.sleep(aWhile);                        // Wait aWhile msec.
        System.out.print(secondName+"\n");           // Output second name
      }
    } catch(InterruptedException e) {                // Handle thread interruption
      System.out.println(firstName + secondName + e);    // Output the exception
    }
  }

  public static void main(String[] args) {
    // Create three threads
    Thread first = new Thread(new JumbleNames("Hopalong ", "Cassidy ", 200L));
    Thread second = new Thread(new JumbleNames("Marilyn ", "Monroe ", 300L));
    Thread third = new Thread(new JumbleNames("Slim ", "Pickens ", 500L));

    // Set threads as daemon
    first.setDaemon(true);
    second.setDaemon(true);
    third.setDaemon(true);
    System.out.println("Press Enter when you have had enough...\n");
    first.start();                                   // Start the first thread
    second.start();                                  // Start the second thread
    third.start();                                   // Start the third thread
    try {
      System.in.read();                              // Wait until Enter key pressed
      System.out.println("Enter pressed...\n");

    } catch (IOException e) {                         // Handle IO exception
      System.out.println(e);                         // Output the exception
    }
    System.out.println("Ending main()");
    return;
  }

  private String firstName;                          // Store for first name
  private String secondName;                         // Store for second name
  private long aWhile;                               // Delay in milliseconds
}
```

How It Works

You have the same data members in this class as you had in the previous example. The constructor is almost the same as previously, too. You can't call `setDaemon()` in this class constructor because the class isn't derived from `Thread`. Instead, you need to do that in `main()` after you've created the objects that represent the threads. The `run()` method implementation is also very similar. The class doesn't have `sleep()` as a member, but because it's a `public static` member of the `Thread` class, you can call it in the `run()` method by using the class name as the qualifier.

In the `main()` method you still create a `Thread` object for each thread of execution, but this time you use a constructor that accepts an object of type `Runnable` as an argument. You pass an object of our class `JumbleNames` to it. This is possible because the `JumbleNames` class implements `Runnable`.

Thread Names

Threads have a name, which in the case of the `Thread` constructor you're using in the example will be a default name composed of the string `"Thread*"` with a sequence number appended. If you want to choose your own name for a thread, you can use a `Thread` constructor that accepts a `String` object specifying the name you want to assign to the thread. For example, you could have created the `Thread` object `first` with the following statement:

```
Thread first = new Thread(new JumbleNames("Hopalong ", "Cassidy ", 200L),
                          "firstThread");
```

This assigns the name `"firstThread"` to the thread. Note that this name is used only when displaying information about the thread. It has no relation to the identifier for the `Thread` object, and there's nothing, apart from common sense, to prevent several threads being given the same name.

You can obtain the name assigned to a thread by calling the `getName()` method for the `Thread` object. The name of the thread is returned as a `String` object. You can also change the name of a thread by calling the `setName()` method defined in the class `Thread` and passing a `String` object to it.

Once you've created the three `Thread` objects in the example, you call the `setDaemon()` method for each of them. The rest of `main()` is the same as in the original version of the previous example, and you should get similar output when you run this version of the program.

Managing Threads

In all the examples you've seen so far in this chapter, the threads are launched and then left to compete for computer resources. Because all three threads compete in an uncontrolled way for the processor, the output from the threads gets muddled. This isn't normally a desirable feature in a program. In most instances where you use threads, you will need to manage the way in which they execute so that they don't interfere with each other.

Of course, in our examples, the programs are deliberately constructed to release control of the processor partway through outputting a name. While this is very artificial, similar situations can arise in practice, particularly where threads are involved in a repetitive operation. It is important to appreciate that a thread can be interrupted while a source statement is executing. For example, imagine that a bank teller is crediting a check to an account and at the same time the customer with that account is withdrawing some cash through an ATM. This might happen in the following way:

- ❑ The bank teller checks the balance of the customer's account, which is $500.

- ❑ The ATM asks for the account balance.

- ❑ The teller adds the value of the check, $100, to the account balance to give a figure of $600.

- ❑ The ATM takes $50 off the balance of $500, which gives a figure of $450, and spits out 5 $10 bills.

- ❑ The teller assigns the value of $600 to the account balance.

- ❑ The ATM assigns the value $450 to the account balance.

Here you can see the problem very well. Asking the account for its balance and assigning a new balance to the account are two different operations. As long as this is the case, you can never guarantee that this type of problem will not occur.

Where two or more threads share a common resource, such as a file or a block of memory, you'll need to take steps to ensure that one thread doesn't modify a resource while that resource is still being used by another thread. Having one thread update a record in a file while another thread is partway through retrieving the same record is a recipe for disaster. One way of managing this sort of situation is to use **synchronization** for the threads involved. I'll be discussing the basic synchronization capabilities provided by the Java language in this chapter but note that the concurrency library provided as the `java.util.concurrent`, `java.util.concurrent.atomic`, and `java.util.concurrent.locks` packages contains classes that implement specialized thread management facilities.

Synchronization

The objective of synchronization is to ensure that when several threads want access to a single resource, only one thread can access it at any given time. You can use synchronization to manage your threads of execution in two ways:

- ❑ **You can manage code at the method level** — This involves synchronizing methods.

- ❑ **You can manage code at the block level** — This uses synchronizing blocks.

Let's look at how you can use synchronized methods first.

Synchronized Methods

You can make a subset (or indeed all) of the methods for any class object mutually exclusive, so that only one of the methods can execute at any given time. You make methods mutually exclusive by declaring them in the class using the keyword `synchronized`. For example:

```
class MyClass {
  synchronized public void method1() {
    // Code for the method...
  }

  synchronized public void method2() {
    // Code for the method...
```

```
    }

  public void method3() {
    // Code for the method...
  }
}
```

Now, only one of the synchronized methods in a class object can execute at any one time. Only when the currently executing synchronized method for an object has ended can another synchronized method start for the same object. The idea here is that each synchronized method has guaranteed exclusive access to the object while it is executing, at least so far as the other synchronized methods for the class object are concerned.

The synchronization process makes use of an internal **lock** that every object has associated with it. The lock is a kind of flag that is set by a process, referred to as **locking** or a lock action, when a synchronized method starts execution. Each synchronized method for an object checks to see whether the lock has been set by another method. If it has, it will not start execution until the lock has been reset by an **unlock action**. Thus, only one synchronized method can be executing at one time, because that method will have set the lock that prevents any other synchronized method from starting.

> Note that there's no constraint here on simultaneously executing synchronized methods for two *different* objects of the same class. It's only concurrent access to any one object that is controlled.

Of the three methods in `myClass`, two are declared as `synchronized`, so for any object of the class, only one of these methods can execute at one time. The method that isn't declared as synchronized, `method3()`, can always be executed by a thread, regardless of whether a synchronized method is executing in some other thread.

It's important to keep clear in your mind the distinction between an object that has instance methods that you declared as `synchronized` in the class definition and the threads of execution that might use them. A hypothetical relationship between three threads and two objects of the class `myClass` is illustrated in Figure 16-6.

The numbers on the arrows in the figure indicate the sequence of events. **No!** indicates that the thread waits until the method is unlocked so it can execute it. While `method1()` in `obj2` is executing, `method2()` for the same object can't be executed. The synchronization of these two instance methods in an object provides a degree of protection for the object, in that only one synchronized method can mess with the data in the object at any given time.

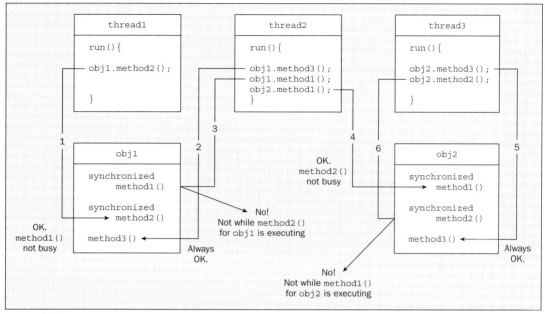

Figure 16-6

However, each object is independent of any other object when it comes to synchronized instance methods. When a thread executes a synchronized method for an object, it is assured exclusive access to the object insofar as the synchronized methods in that object are concerned. Another thread, though, can still call the same method for a different object. While method1() is being executed for obj1, this doesn't prevent method1() for obj2 being executed by some other thread. Also, if there's a method in an object that has not been declared as synchronized—method3() in obj1, for example—any thread can call that at any time, regardless of the state of any synchronized methods in the object.

If you apply synchronization to static methods in a class, only one of those static methods in the class can be executing at any point in time; this is per-class synchronization, and the class lock is independent of any locks for objects of the class.

An important principle that you need to understand is that the only method that is necessarily part of a thread in a class object that represents a thread is the run() method. Other methods for the same class object are only part of the thread if they are called directly or indirectly by the run() method. All the methods that are called directly or indirectly from the run() method for an object are all part of the same thread, but they clearly don't have to be methods for the same Thread object. Indeed, they can be methods that belong to any other objects, including other Thread objects that have their own run() methods.

Chapter 16

Using Synchronized Methods

To see how synchronization can be applied in practice, you'll construct a program that provides a simple model of a bank. This particular bank is a very young business with only one customer account initially, but you'll have two clerks, each working flat out to process transactions for the account, one handling debits and the other handling credits. The objects in our program are illustrated in Figure 16-7.

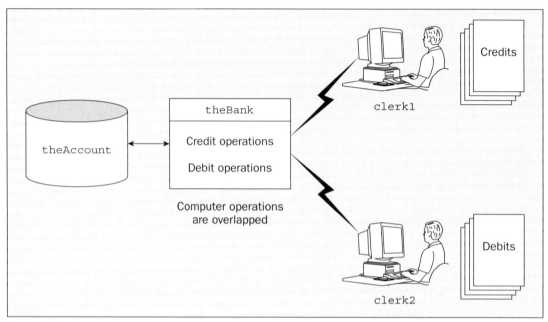

Figure 16-7

The bank in the model is actually a computer that performs operations on the account, and the account is stored separately. Each clerk can communicate directly with the bank. You'll be defining four classes that you will use in the program to model banking operations:

- ❑ A `Bank` class to represent the bank computer
- ❑ An `Account` class to represent the account at the bank
- ❑ A `Transaction` class to represent a transaction on the account — a debit or a credit, for example
- ❑ A `Clerk` class to represent a bank clerk

You'll also define a class containing the method `main()` that will start the process off and determine how it all works.

> **As you develop the code, you won't necessarily get it right the first time, but you will improve as you find out more about how to program using threads. This will expose some of the sorts of errors and complications that can arise when you're programming using threads.**

Try It Out   Defining a Bank Class

The bank computer is the agent that will perform the operations on an account so you'll start with that. You can define the Bank class that will represent the bank computer as follows:

```
// Define the bank
class Bank {
  // Perform a transaction
  public void doTransaction(Transaction transaction) {
    int balance = transaction.getAccount().getBalance();    // Get current balance

    switch(transaction.getTransactionType()) {
      case Transaction.CREDIT:
        // Credits require a lot of checks...
        try {
          Thread.sleep(100);

        } catch(InterruptedException e) {
          System.out.println(e);
        }
        balance += transaction.getAmount();               // Increment the balance
        break;

      case Transaction.DEBIT:
        // Debits require even more checks...
        try {
          Thread.sleep(150);

        } catch(InterruptedException e) {
          System.out.println(e);
        }
        balance -= transaction.getAmount();               // Decrement the balance
        break;

      default:                                            // We should never get here
        System.out.println("Invalid transaction");
        System.exit(1);
    }
    transaction.getAccount().setBalance(balance);    // Restore the account balance
  }
}
```

How It Works

The Bank class is very simple. It keeps no records of anything locally as the accounts will be identified separately, and it has only one method that carries out a transaction. The Transaction object provides all the information about what the transaction is and to which account it applies. You have provided only for debit and credit operations on an account, but the switch could easily be extended to accommodate other types of transactions. Both of the transactions supported involve some delay while the standard nameless checks and verifications that all banks have are carried out. The delay is simulated by calling the sleep() method belonging to the Thread class.

Of course, during this time, other things in other threads may be going on. There are no instance variables to initialize in a `Bank` object, so you don't need a constructor. Since the `Bank` object works using a `Transaction` object, let's define the class for that next.

Try It Out   Defining a Transaction on an Account

The `Transaction` class could represent any transaction on an account, but we are limiting ourselves to debits and credits. You can define the class as follows:

```
class Transaction {
  // Transaction types
  public static final int DEBIT = 0;
  public static final int CREDIT = 1;
  public static String[] types = {"Debit","Credit"};

  // Constructor
  public Transaction(Account account, int transactionType, int amount) {
    this.account = account;
    this.transactionType = transactionType;
    this.amount = amount;
  }

  public Account getAccount() {
    return account;
  }

  public int getTransactionType() {
    return transactionType;
  }

  public int getAmount() {
    return amount;
  }

  public String toString() {
    return types[transactionType] + " A//C: " + ": $" + amount;
  }

  private Account account;
  private int amount;
  private int transactionType;
}
```

How It Works

The type of transaction is specified by the `transactionType` field, which must be one of the values defined for transaction types. You should build in checks in the constructor to ensure that only valid transactions are created, but we'll forego this to keep the code volume down, and you certainly know how to do that sort of thing by now. A transaction records the amount for the transaction and a reference to the account to which it applies, so a `Transaction` object specifies a complete transaction. The methods are very straightforward, just accessor methods for the data members that are used by the `Bank` object, plus the `toString()` method in case you need it.

Defining a Bank Account

You can define an account as follows:

```
// Defines a customer account
public class Account {
  // Constructor
  public Account(int accountNumber, int balance) {
    this.accountNumber = accountNumber;          // Set the account number
    this.balance = balance;                      // Set the initial balance
  }

  // Return the current balance
  public int getBalance() {
    return balance;
  }

  // Set the current balance
  public void setBalance(int balance) {
    this.balance = balance;
  }

  public int getAccountNumber() {
    return accountNumber;
  }

  public String toString() {
    return "A//C No. "+accountNumber+" : $"+balance;
  }

  private int balance;                           // The current account balance
  private int accountNumber;                     // Identifies this account
}
```

How It Works

The Account class is also very simple. It just maintains a record of the amount in the account as a balance and provides methods for retrieving and setting the current balance. Operations on the account are performed externally by the Bank object. You have a bit more than you need in the Account class at the moment, but the methods you don't use in the current example may be useful later.

Defining a Bank Clerk

A clerk is a slightly more complicated animal. He or she retains information about the bank and details of the current transaction, and is responsible for initiating debits and credits on an account by communication with the central bank. Each clerk will work independently of the others so they will each be a separate thread:

```
public class Clerk implements Runnable {
  // Constructor
  public Clerk(Bank theBank) {
    this.theBank = theBank;          // Who the clerk works for
    inTray = null;                   // No transaction initially
  }
```

```
// Receive a transaction
public void doTransaction(Transaction transaction) {
  inTray = transaction;
}

// The working clerk...
public void run() {
  while(true) {
    while(inTray == null) {              // No transaction waiting?
      try {
        Thread.sleep(150);               // Then take a break...

      } catch(InterruptedException e) {
        System.out.println(e);
      }
    }

    theBank.doTransaction(inTray);
    inTray = null;                       // In-tray is empty
  }
}

// Busy check
public boolean isBusy() {
  return inTray != null;                 // A full in-tray means busy!
}

private Bank theBank;                     // The employer - an electronic marvel
private Transaction inTray;               // The in-tray holding a transaction
}
```

How It Works

A Clerk object is a thread since it implements the Runnable interface. Each clerk has an in-tray, capable of holding one transaction, and while the in-tray is not null, the clerk is clearly busy. A clerk needs to be aware of the Bank object that is employing him or her, so a reference is stored in theBank when a Clerk object is created. A transaction is placed in the in-tray for a clerk by calling his or her doTransaction() method. You can check whether a clerk is busy by calling the isBusy() member, which will return true if a transaction is still in progress.

The real work is actually done in the run() method. If the in-tray is empty, indicated by a null value in inTray, then there's nothing to do, so after sleeping a while, the loop goes around again for another look at the in-tray. When a transaction has been recorded, the method in theBank object is called to carry it out, and the inTray is reset to null.

All you need now is the class to drive our model world, which you can call BankOperation. This class requires only the method main(), but there are quite a lot of things to do in this method so you'll put it together piece by piece.

Try It Out   Defining the Operation of the Bank

Apart from setting everything up, the `main()` method has to originate transactions on the accounts and pass them on to the clerks to be expedited. You'll start with just one account and a couple of clerks. Here's the basic structure:

```
import java.util.Random;

public class BankOperation {
  public static void main(String[] args) {
    int initialBalance = 500;      // The initial account balance
    int totalCredits = 0;          // Total credits on the account
    int totalDebits =0;            // Total debits on the account
    int transactionCount = 20;     // Number of debits and credits

    // Create the account, the bank, and the clerks...

    // Create the threads for the clerks as daemon, and start them off

    // Generate the transactions of each type and pass to the clerks

    // Wait until both clerks are done

    // Now output the results
  }
}
```

The `import` for the `Random` class is there because you'll need it for code you'll add a little later. To create the `Bank` object, the clerks, and the account, you need to add the following code:

```
// Create the account, the bank, and the clerks...
Bank theBank = new Bank();                          // Create a bank
Clerk clerk1 = new Clerk(theBank);                  // Create the first clerk
Clerk clerk2 = new Clerk(theBank);                  // Create the second clerk
Account account = new Account(1, initialBalance);   // Create an account
```

The next step is to add the code to create the threads for the clerks and start them going:

```
// Create the threads for the clerks as daemon, and start them off
Thread clerk1Thread = new Thread(clerk1);
Thread clerk2Thread = new Thread(clerk2);
clerk1Thread.setDaemon(true);                       // Set first as daemon
clerk2Thread.setDaemon(true);                       // Set second as daemon
clerk1Thread.start();                               // Start the first
clerk2Thread.start();                               // Start the second
```

The code to generate the transactions looks like a lot but is quite repetitive:

```
// Generate transactions of each type and pass to the clerks
Random rand = new Random();              // Random number generator
Transaction transaction;                 // Stores a transaction
int amount = 0;                          // stores an amount of money
for(int i = 1; i <= transactionCount; i++) {
```

```
        amount = 50 + rand.nextInt(26);           // Generate amount of $50 to $75
        transaction = new Transaction(account,     // Account
                            Transaction.CREDIT,// Credit transaction
                            amount);               //   of amount
        totalCredits += amount;                    // Keep total credit tally

        // Wait until the first clerk is free
        while(clerk1.isBusy()) {
          try {
            Thread.sleep(25);                      // Busy so try later

          } catch(InterruptedException e) {
            System.out.println(e);
          }
        }
        clerk1.doTransaction(transaction);         // Now do the credit

        amount = 30 + rand.nextInt(31);            // Generate amount of $30 to $60
        transaction = new Transaction(account,     // Account
                            Transaction.DEBIT,  // Debit transaction
                            amount);               //   of amount
        totalDebits += amount;                     // Keep total debit tally
        // Wait until the second clerk is free
        while(clerk2.isBusy()) {
          try {
            Thread.sleep(25);                      // Busy so try later

          } catch(InterruptedException e) {
            System.out.println(e);
          }
        }
        clerk2.doTransaction(transaction);         // Now do the debit
      }
```

Once all the transactions have been processed, you can output the results. However, the clerks could still be busy after you exit from the loop, so you need to wait for both of them to be free before outputting the results. You can do this with a `while` loop:

```
      // Wait until both clerks are done
      while(clerk1.isBusy() || clerk2.isBusy()) {
        try {
          Thread.sleep(25);

        } catch(InterruptedException e) {
          System.out.println(e);
        }
      }
```

Lastly, you output the results:

```
      // Now output the results
      System.out.println(
              "Original balance : $" + initialBalance+"\n" +
              "Total credits    : $" + totalCredits+"\n" +
```

```
"Total debits      : $" + totalDebits+"\n" +
"Final balance     : $" + account.getBalance() + "\n" +
"Should be         : $" + (initialBalance + totalCredits - totalDebits));
```

How It Works

The variables in the `main()` method track the total debits and credits, and record the initial account balance. They are there to help you figure out what has happened after the transactions have been processed. The number of times you debit and then credit the account is stored in `transactionCount`, so the total number of transactions will be twice this value. You have added five further blocks of code to perform the functions indicated by the comments, so let's now go through each of them in turn.

The `Account` object is created with the account number as 1 and with the initial balance stored in `initialBalance`. You pass the bank object, `theBank`, to the constructor for each of the `Clerk` objects, so that they can record it.

The `Thread` constructor requires an object of type `Runnable`, so you can just pass the `Clerk` objects in the argument. There's no problem in doing this because the `Clerk` class implements the `Runnable` interface. You can always implicitly cast an object to a type that is any superclass of the object or any interface type that the object class implements.

All the transactions are generated in the `for` loop. The handling of debits is essentially the same as the handling of credits, so I'll go through the code only for the latter in detail. A random amount between $50 and $75 is generated for a credit transaction by using the `nextInt()` method for the `rand` object of type `Random` that you create. You'll recall that `nextInt()` returns an `int` value in the range 0 to one less than the value of the argument, so by passing 26 to the method, you get a value between 0 and 25 returned. You add 50 to this and, presto, you have a value between 50 and 75. You then use this amount to create a `Transaction` object that represents a credit for the account. To keep a check on the work done by the clerks, you add this credit to the total of all the credits generated, which is stored in the variable `totalCredits`. This will allow you to verify whether or not the account has been updated properly.

Before you pass the transaction to `clerk1`, you must make sure that he or she isn't busy. Otherwise, you would overwrite the clerk's in-tray. The `while` loop does this. As long as the `isBusy()` method returns `true`, you continue to call the `sleep()` method for a 25 millisecond delay, before you go round and check again. When `isBusy()` returns `false`, you call the `doTransaction()` method for the clerk, with the reference to the `transaction` object as the argument. The `for` loop will run for 20 iterations, so you'll generate 20 random transactions of each type.

The third `while` loop works in the same way as the previous check for a busy clerk—the loop continues if either of the clerks is busy.

Lastly, you output the original account balance, the totals of credits and debits, and the final balance, plus what it should be for comparison. That's all you need in the method `main()`, so you're ready to give it a whirl. Remember that all four classes need to be in the same directory.

Running the Example

Now, if you run the example, the final balance will be wrong. You should get results something like the following:

```
Original balance   : $500
Total credits      : $1252
```

```
Total debits      : $921
Final balance     : $89
Should be         : $831
```

Of course, your results won't be the same as this, but they should be just as wrong. The customer will not be happy. His account balance is seriously off — in the bank's favor, of course, as always. So how has this come about?

The problem is that both clerks are operating on the same account at the same time. Both clerks call the doTransaction() method for the Bank object, so this method is executed by both clerk threads. Separate calls on the same method are overlapping.

Try It Out   **Synchronizing Methods**

One way you can fix this is by simply declaring the method that operates on an account as synchronized. This will prevent one clerk getting at the method for an account while it is still in progress with the other clerk. To implement this you should amend the Bank class definition as follows:

```
// Define the bank
class Bank {
  // Perform a transaction
  synchronized public void doTransaction(Transaction transaction) {
    // Code exactly as before...
  }
}
```

How It Works

Declaring this method as synchronized will prevent a call to it from being executed while another is still in operation. If you run the example again with this change, the result will be something like:

```
Original balance   : $500
Total credits      : $1201
Total debits       : $931
Final balance      : $770
Should be          : $770
```

The amounts may be different because the transaction amounts are random, but your final balance should be the same as adding the credits to the original balance and subtracting the debits.

As you saw earlier, when you declare methods in a class as synchronized, it prevents concurrent execution of those methods within a single object, *including concurrent execution of the same method*. It is important not to let the fact that there is only one copy of a particular method confuse you. A given method can be potentially executing in any number of threads — as many threads as there are in the program in fact. If it were not synchronized, the doTransaction() method could be executed concurrently by any number of clerks.

Although this fixes the problem you had in that the account balance is now correct, the bank is still amazingly inefficient. Each clerk is kicking his or her heels while another clerk is carrying out a transaction. At any given time a maximum of one clerk is working. On this basis the bank could fire them all bar one and get the same throughput. You can do better, as you'll see.

Synchronizing Statement Blocks

In addition to being able to synchronize methods on a class object, you can also specify a statement or a block of code in your program as `synchronized`. This is more powerful, since you specify which particular object is to benefit from the synchronization of the statement or code block, not just the object that contains the code as in the case of a synchronized method. Here you can set a lock on any object for a given statement block. When the block that is synchronized on the given object is executing, no other code block or method that is synchronized on the same object can execute. To synchronize a statement, you just write:

```
synchronized(theObject)
   statement;              // Synchronized with respect to theObject
```

No other statements or statement blocks in the program that are synchronized on the object *theObject* can execute while this statement is executing. Naturally, this applies even when the statement is a call to a method, which may in turn call other methods. The statement here could equally well be a block of code between braces. This is powerful stuff. Now you can lock a particular object while the code block that is working is running.

To see precisely how you can use this in practice, let's create a modification of the last example. Let's up the sophistication of our banking operation to support multiple accounts. To extend our example to handle more than one account, you just need to make some changes to `main()`. You'll add one extra account to keep the output modest, but you'll modify the code to handle any number of accounts.

Try It Out   Handling Multiple Accounts

You can modify the code in `main()` that creates the account and sets the initial balance to create multiple accounts as follows:

```java
public class BankOperation {
  public static void main(String[] args) {
    int[] initialBalance = {500, 800};            // The initial account balances
    int[] totalCredits = new int[initialBalance.length]; // Two different cr totals
    int[] totalDebits = new int[initialBalance.length];  // Two different db totals
    int transactionCount = 20;                    // Number of debits and of credits

    // Create the bank and the clerks...
    Bank theBank = new Bank();                     // Create a bank
    Clerk clerk1 = new Clerk(theBank );            // Create the first clerk
    Clerk clerk2 = new Clerk(theBank );            // Create the second clerk

    // Create the accounts, and initialize total credits and debits
    Account[] accounts = new Account[initialBalance.length];
    for(int i = 0; i < initialBalance.length; i++) {
      accounts[i] = new Account(i+1, initialBalance[i]); // Create accounts
      totalCredits[i] = totalDebits[i] = 0;
    }

    // Create the threads for the clerks as daemon, and start them off

    // Create transactions randomly distributed between the accounts...
```

```
   // Wait until both clerks are done

      // Now output the results...
   }
}
```

You now create an array of accounts in a loop, the number of accounts being determined by the number of initial balances in the `initialBalance` array. Account numbers are assigned successively starting from 1. The code for creating the bank and the clerks and for creating the threads and starting them is exactly the same as before. The shaded comments that follow the code indicate the other segments of code in `main()` that you need to modify.

The next piece you need to change is the creation and processing of the transactions:

```
// Create transactions randomly distributed between the accounts
Random rand = new Random();
Transaction transaction;                        // Stores a transaction
int amount = 0;                                 // Stores an amount of money
int select = 0;                                 // Selects an account
for(int i = 1; i <= transactionCount; i++) {
  // Choose an account at random for credit operation
  select = rand.nextInt(accounts.length);
  amount = 50 + rand.nextInt(26);               // Generate amount of $50 to $75
  transaction = new Transaction(accounts[select],       // Account
                      Transaction.CREDIT, // Credit transaction
                      amount);            //   of amount
  totalCredits[select] += amount;               // Keep total credit tally

  // Wait until the first clerk is free
  while(clerk1.isBusy()) {
    try {
      Thread.sleep(25);                         // Busy so try later
    } catch(InterruptedException e) {
      System.out.println(e);
    }
  }
  clerk1.doTransaction(transaction);            // Now do the credit

  // choose an account at random for debit operation
  select = rand.nextInt(accounts.length);
  amount = 30 + rand.nextInt(31);               // Generate amount of $30 to $60
  transaction = new Transaction(accounts[select],   // Account
                      Transaction.DEBIT, // Debit transaction
                      amount);            //   of amount
  totalDebits[select] += amount;                // Keep total debit tally

  // Wait until the second clerk is free
  while(clerk2.isBusy()) {
    try {
      Thread.sleep(25);                         // Busy so try later
    } catch(InterruptedException e) {
      System.out.println(e);
    }
  }
  clerk2.doTransaction(transaction);            // Now do the debit
}
```

The last modification you must make to the method `main()` is for outputting the results. You now do this in a loop, as you have to process more than one account:

```
// Now output the results
for(int i = 0; i < accounts.length; i++) {
  System.out.println("Account Number:"+accounts[i].getAccountNumber()+"\n"+
      "Original balance     : $" + initialBalance[i] + "\n" +
      "Total credits        : $" + totalCredits[i] + "\n" +
      "Total debits         : $" + totalDebits[i] + "\n" +
      "Final balance        : $" + accounts[i].getBalance() + "\n" +
      "Should be            : $" + (initialBalance[i]
                                  + totalCredits[i]
                                  - totalDebits[i]) + "\n");
}
```

This is much the same as before except that you now extract values from the arrays you have created. If you run this version it will, of course, work perfectly. A typical set of results is:

```
Account Number:1
Original balance    : $500
Total credits       : $659
Total debits        : $614
Final balance       : $545
Should be           : $545

Account Number:2
Original balance    : $800
Total credits       : $607
Total debits        : $306
Final balance       : $1101
Should be           : $1101
```

How It Works

You now allocate arrays for the initial account balances, the totals of credits and debits for each account, and the totals for the accounts themselves. The number of initializing values in the `initialBalance[]` array will determine the number of elements in each of the arrays. In the `for` loop, you create each of the accounts with the appropriate initial balance and initialize the `totalCredits[]` and `totalDebits[]` arrays to zero.

In the modified transactions loop, you select the account from the array for both the debit and the credit transactions by generating a random index value that you store in the variable `select`. The index `select` is also used to keep a tally of the total of the transactions of each type.

This is all well and good, but by declaring the methods in the class `Bank` as `synchronized`, you're limiting the program quite significantly. No operation of any kind can be carried out while any other operation is in progress. This is unnecessarily restrictive since there's no reason to prevent a transaction on one account while a transaction for a different account is in progress. What you really want to do is constrain the program to prevent overlapping of operations on the same account, and this is where declaring blocks of code to be synchronized on a particular object can help.

Let's consider the methods in the class `Bank` once more. What you really want is the code in the `doTransaction()` method to be synchronized so that simultaneous processing of the same account is prevented, not so that processing of different accounts is inhibited. What you need to do is synchronize the processing code for a transaction on the `Account` object that is involved.

Try It Out   Applying Synchronized Statement Blocks

You can do this with the following changes:

```
class Bank {
  // Perform a transaction
  public void doTransaction(Transaction transaction) {
    switch(transaction.getTransactionType()) {
      case Transaction.CREDIT:
        synchronized(transaction.getAccount()) {
          // Get current balance
          int balance = transaction.getAccount().getBalance();

          // Credits require require a lot of checks...
          try {
            Thread.sleep(100);

          } catch(InterruptedException e) {
            System.out.println(e);
          }
          balance += transaction.getAmount();            // Increment the balance
          transaction.getAccount().setBalance(balance); // Restore account balance
          break;
        }

      case Transaction.DEBIT:
        synchronized(transaction.getAccount()) {
          // Get current balance
          int balance = transaction.getAccount().getBalance();

          // Debits require even more checks...
          try {
            Thread.sleep(150);

          } catch(InterruptedException e) {
            System.out.println(e);
          }
          balance -= transaction.getAmount();           // Increment the balance...
          transaction.getAccount().setBalance(balance);// Restore account balance
          break;
        }

      default:                                          // We should never get here
        System.out.println("Invalid transaction");
        System.exit(1);
    }
  }
}
```

How It Works

The expression in parentheses following the keyword `synchronized` specifies the object for which the synchronization applies. Once one synchronized code block is entered with a given account object, no other code block or method can be entered that has been synchronized on the same object. For example, if the block performing credits is executing with a reference to the object `accounts[1]` returned by the `getAccount()` method for the transaction, the execution of the block carrying out debits cannot be executed for the same object, but it could be executed for a different account.

The object in a synchronized code block acts rather like a baton in a relay race that serves to synchronize the runners in the team. Only the runner with the baton is allowed to run. The next runner in the team can run only once they get hold of the baton. Of course, in any race you have several different batons so you can have several sets of runners. In the same way, you can specify several different sets of `synchronized` code blocks in a class, each controlled by a different object. It is important to realize that code blocks that are synchronized with respect to a particular object don't have to be in the same class. They can be anywhere in your program where the appropriate object can be specified.

Note how you had to move the code to access and restore the account balance inside both synchronized blocks. If you hadn't done this, accessing or restoring the account balance could occur while a synchronized block was executing. This could obviously cause confusion since a balance could be restored by a debit transaction after the balance had been retrieved for a credit transaction. This would cause the effect of the debit to be wiped out.

If you want to verify that we really are overlapping these operations in this example, you can add output statements to the beginning and end of each method in the class `Bank`. Outputting the type of operation, the amount, and whether it is the start or end of the transaction will be sufficient to identify them. For example, you could modify the `doTransaction()` method in the `Bank` class to:

```
// Perform a transaction
public void doTransaction(Transaction transaction) {
  switch(transaction.getTransactionType()) {
    case Transaction.CREDIT:
      synchronized(transaction.getAccount()) {
        System.out.println("Start credit of " +
                transaction.getAccount() + " amount: " +
                transaction.getAmount());

        // code to process credit...

        System.out.println("  End credit of " +
                transaction.getAccount() + " amount: " +
                transaction.getAmount());
      break;
    }

    case Transaction.DEBIT:
      synchronized(transaction.getAccount()) {
        System.out.println("Start debit of " +
                transaction.getAccount() + " amount: " +
                transaction.getAmount());
        // code to process debit...
```

```
            System.out.println("  End debit of " +
                  transaction.getAccount() + " amount: " +
                  transaction.getAmount());
          break;
        }

      default:                                    // We should never get here
        System.out.println("Invalid transaction");
        System.exit(1);
    }
  }
```

This will produce quite a lot of output, but you can always comment it out when you don't need it. You should be able to see how a transaction for an account that is currently being worked on is always delayed until the previous operation on the account is completed. You will also see from the output that operations on different accounts do overlap. Here's a sample of what I got:

```
Start credit of A//C No. 2 : $800 amount: 74
  End credit of A//C No. 2 : $874 amount: 74
Start debit of A//C No. 2 : $874 amount: 52
Start credit of A//C No. 1 : $500 amount: 51
  End debit of A//C No. 2 : $822 amount: 52
  End credit of A//C No. 1 : $551 amount: 51
Start debit of A//C No. 2 : $822 amount: 38
  End debit of A//C No. 2 : $784 amount: 38
Start credit of A//C No. 2 : $784 amount: 74
  End credit of A//C No. 2 : $858 amount: 74
Start debit of A//C No. 1 : $551 amount: 58
Start credit of A//C No. 2 : $858 amount: 53
  End debit of A//C No. 1 : $493 amount: 58
...
```

You can see from the third and fourth lines here that a credit for account 1 starts before the preceding debit for account 2 is complete, so the operations are overlapped. If you want to force overlapping debits and credits on the same account, you can comment out the calculation of the value for `select` for the debit operation in the `for` loop in `main()`. This modification is shown shaded:

```
// Generate a random account index for debit operation
// select = rand.nextInt(accounts.length);
totalDebits[select] += amount;                    // Keep total debit tally
```

This will make the debit transaction apply to the same account as the previous credit, so the transactions will always be contending for the same account.

Of course, this is not the only way of getting the operations to overlap. Another approach would be to equip accounts with methods to handle their own credit and debit transactions and declare these as synchronized methods.

While testing that you have synchronization right is relatively easy in our example, in general it is extremely difficult to be sure you have adequately tested a program that uses threads. Getting the design right first is essential, and you really have no substitute for careful design in programs that have multiple threads (or indeed any real-time program that has interrupt handlers). You can never be sure that a real-world program is 100 percent correct, only that it works correctly most of the time!

Deadlocks

Since you can synchronize code blocks for a particular object virtually anywhere in your program, there's potential for a particularly nasty kind of bug called a **deadlock**. This involves a mutual interdependence between two threads. One way this arises is when one thread executes some code synchronized on a given object, theObject, say, and then needs to execute another method that contains code synchronized on another object, theOtherObject, say. Before this occurs, though, a second thread executes some code synchronized to theOtherObject and needs to execute a method containing code synchronized to the first object, theObject. This situation is illustrated in Figure 16-8.

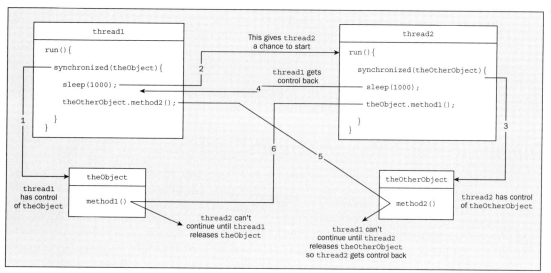

Figure 16-8

The sequence of events is as follows:

❑ thread1 starts first and synchronizes on theObject. This prevents any methods for theObject being called by any other thread.

❑ thread1 then calls sleep() so thread2 can start.

❑ thread2 starts and synchronizes on theOtherObject. This prevents any methods for theOtherObject being called by any other thread.

❑ thread2 then calls sleep(), allowing thread1 another go.

❑ thread1 wakes up and tries to call method2() for theOtherObject, but it can't until the code block in thread2 that is synchronized on theOtherObject completes execution.

❑ thread2 gets another go because thread1 can't proceed and tries to call method1() for theObject. This can't proceed until the code block in thread1 that is synchronized on theObject completes execution.

Neither thread has any possibility of continuing — they are deadlocked. Finding and fixing this sort of problem can be very difficult, particularly if your program is complicated and has other threads that will continue to execute.

You can create a trivial deadlock in the last example by making the `for` loop in `main()` synchronized on one of the accounts. For example:

```
synchronized(accounts[1]) {
  for(int i = 1; i <= transactionCount; i++) {
    // code for generating transactions etc...
  }
}
```

A deadlock occurs as soon as a transaction for `accounts[1]` arises because the `doTransaction()` method in the `theBank` object that is called by a `Clerk` object to handle the transaction will be synchronized to the same object and can't execute until the loop ends. Of course, the loop can't continue until the method in the `theBank` object terminates, so the program hangs.

In general, ensuring that your program has no potential deadlocks is extremely difficult. If you intend to do a significant amount of programming using threads, you will need to study the subject in much more depth than we can deal with here. A good book on the subject is *Concurrent Programming in Java: Design Principles and Patterns* by Doug Lea (Addison-Wesley, 1996).

Communicating between Threads

You've seen how you can lock methods or code blocks using synchronization to avoid the problems that uncontrolled thread execution can cause. While this gives you a degree of control, you're still introducing inefficiencies into the program. In the last example, on several occasions you used a loop to wait for a clerk thread to complete an operation before the current thread could sensibly continue. For example, you couldn't pass a transaction to a `Clerk` object while that object was still busy with the previous transaction. The solution to this was to use a `while` loop to test the busy status of the `Clerk` object from time to time and call the `sleep()` method in between. But there's a much better way.

The `Object` class defines the methods `wait()`, `notify()`, and `notifyAll()`, which you can use to provide a more efficient way of dealing with this kind of situation. Since all classes are derived from `Object`, all classes inherit these methods. You can call these methods only from within a `synchronized` method, or from within a synchronized code block; an exception of type `IllegalMonitorStateException` will be thrown if you call them from somewhere else. The functions that these methods perform are:

Method	Description
`wait()`	There are three overloaded versions of this method.
	This version suspends the current thread until the `notify()` or `notifyAll()` method is called for the object to which the `wait()` method belongs. Note that when any version of `wait()` is called, the thread releases the synchronization lock it has on the object, so any other method or code block synchronized on the same object can execute. As well as enabling `notify()` or `notifyAll()` to be called by another thread, this also allows another thread to call `wait()` for the same object.

Method	Description
	Since all versions of the wait() method can throw an Interrupted Exception, you must call it in a try block with a catch block for this exception, or at least indicate that the method calling it throws this exception.
wait(long timeout)	This version suspends the current thread until the number of milliseconds specified by the argument has expired, or until the notify() or notifyAll() method for the object to which the wait() method belongs is called, if that occurs sooner.
wait(long timeout, int nanos)	This version works in the same way as the previous version, except the time interval is specified by two arguments, the first in milliseconds and the second in nanoseconds.
notify()	This restarts a thread that has called the wait() method for the object to which the notify() method belongs. If several threads have called wait() for the object, you have no control over which thread is notified, in which case it is better to use notifyAll(). If no threads are waiting, the method does nothing.
notifyAll()	This restarts all threads that have called wait() for the object to which the notifyAll() method belongs.

The basic idea of the wait() and notify() methods is that they provide a way for methods or code blocks that are synchronized on a particular object to communicate. One block can call wait() to suspend its operation until some other method or code block synchronized on the same object changes it in some way, and calls notify() to signal that the change is complete. A thread will typically call wait() because some particular property of the object it is synchronized on is not set, or some condition is not fulfilled, and this is dependent on action by another thread. Perhaps the simplest situation is where a resource is busy because it is being modified by another thread, but you are by no means limited to that.

The major difference between calling sleep() and calling wait() is that wait() releases any objects on which the current thread has a lock, whereas sleep() does not. It is essential that wait() should work this way; otherwise, there would be no way for another thread to change things so that the condition required by the current thread is met.

Thus, the typical use of wait() is as follows:

```
synchronized(anObject) {
  while(condition-not-met)
    anObject.wait();
  // Condition is met so continue...
}
```

Here the thread will suspend operation when the wait() method is called until some other thread synchronized on the same object calls notify() (or more typically notifyAll()). This allows the while loop to continue and check the condition again. Of course, it may still not be met, in which case the wait() method will be called again so another thread can operate on anObject. You can see from this that wait() is not just for getting access to an object. It is intended to allow other threads access until some condition has been met. You could even arrange that a thread would not continue until a given number of other threads had called `notify()` on the object to ensure that a minimum number of operations had been carried out.

It is generally better to use `notifyAll()` rather than `notify()` when you have more than two threads synchronized on an object. If you call `notify()` when two or more other threads are suspended having called `wait()`, only one of the threads will be started, but you have no control over which it is. This creates the possibility that the thread that is started calls `wait()` again because the condition it requires is not fulfilled. This will leave all the threads waiting for each other, with no possibility of continuing.

Although the action of each of these methods is quite simple, applying them can become very complex. You have the potential for multiple threads to be interacting through several objects with `synchronized` methods and code blocks. You'll just explore the basics by seeing how you can use `wait()` and `notifyAll()` to get rid of a couple of the `while` loops you had in the last example.

Using wait() and notifyAll() in the Bank Program

In the `for` loop in `main()` that generates the transactions and passes them to the `Clerk` objects, you have two `while` loops that call the `isBusy()` method for a `Clerk` object. These were needed so that you didn't pass a transaction to a clerk while the clerk was still busy. By altering the `Clerk` class so that it can use `wait()` and `notifyAll()`, you can eliminate the need for these.

Try It Out　　**Slimming Down the Transactions Loop**

You want to make the `doTransaction()` method in the `Clerk` class conscious of the state of the `inTray` for the current object. If it is not `null`, you want the method to wait until it becomes so. To use `wait()` you must synchronize the block or method on an object — in this case the `Clerk` object since `inTray` is what you are interested in. You can do this by making the method synchronized:

```
public class Clerk implements Runnable {
  // Constructor
  public Clerk(Bank theBank) {
    this.theBank = theBank;          // Who the clerk works for
    inTray = null;                   // No transaction initially
  }

  // Receive a transaction
  synchronized public void doTransaction(Transaction transaction) {
    while(inTray != null) {
      try {
        wait();

      } catch(InterruptedException e) {
        System.out.println(e);
      }
    }
    inTray = transaction;
    notifyAll();
  }

  // Rest of the methods in the class as before...

  private Bank theBank;                // The employer - an electronic marvel
  private Transaction inTray;          // The in-tray holding a transaction
}
```

When `inTray` is `null`, the transaction is stored, and the `notifyAll()` method is called to notify other threads waiting on a change to this `Clerk` object. If `inTray` is not `null`, this method waits until some other thread calls `notifyAll()` to signal a change to the `Clerk` object. You now need to consider where the `inTray` field is going to be modified elsewhere. The answer is in the `run()` method for the `Clerk` class, of course, so you need to change that, too:

```
public class Clerk implements Runnable {

    synchronized public void run() {
        while(true) {
            while(inTray == null)            // No transaction waiting?
                try {
                    wait();                   // Then take a break until there is
                } catch(InterruptedException e) {
                    System.out.println(e);
                }

            theBank.doTransaction(inTray);
            inTray = null;                    // In-tray is empty
            notifyAll();                      // Notify other threads locked on this clerk
        }
    }

    // Rest of the class as before...
}
```

Just to make it clear which methods are in what threads, the situation in the program is illustrated in Figure 16-9.

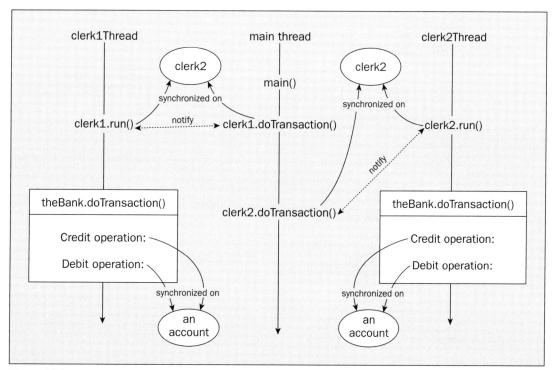

Figure 16-9

Here the `run()` method is synchronized on the `Clerk` object that contains it, and the method waits if `inTray` is `null`. Eventually the `doTransaction()` method for the current object should store a transaction in `inTray` and then notify the thread that is waiting that it should continue.

It may seem odd having two methods in the same object synchronized on one and the same object that owns them, but remember that the `run()` and `doTransaction()` methods for a particular `Clerk` object are in separate threads.

The transaction processing method for the bank can be in both of the clerk threads, whereas the methods that hand over a transaction to a clerk are in the main thread. Figure 16-9 also shows which code is synchronized on what objects.

You can now modify the code in the `for` loop in `main()` to pass the transactions directly to the clerks. Except for deleting the two `while` loops that wait until the clerks are free, the code is exactly as before:

```
// Create transactions randomly distributed between the accounts
for(int i = 1; i <= transactionCount; i++) {
  // Generate a random account index for credit operation

  select = rand.nextInt(accounts.length);
  amount = 50 + rand.nextInt(26);             // Generate amount of $50 to $75
  transaction = new Transaction(accounts[select],    // Account
                          Transaction.CREDIT, // Credit transaction
                          amount);            //  of amount
  totalCredits[select] += amount;             // Keep total credit tally

  clerk1.doTransaction(transaction);          // Now do the credit

  // Generate a random account index for debit operation
  select = rand.nextInt(accounts.length);
  amount = 30 + rand.nextInt(31);             // Generate amount of $30 to $60
  transaction = new Transaction(accounts[select],    // Account
                          Transaction.DEBIT,  // Debit transaction
                          amount);            //  of amount
  totalDebits[select] += amount;              // Keep total debit tally

  clerk2.doTransaction(transaction);          // Now do the debit
}
```

Only the loop blocks that were waiting until a clerk became free have been deleted. This makes the code a lot shorter.

With a small change to the `isBusy()` method in the `Clerk` class, you can also eliminate the need for the `while` loop before we output the results in `main()`:

```
synchronized public void isBusy() {
  while(inTray != null) {                 // Is this object busy?
    try {
      wait();                             // Yes, so wait for notify call
    } catch(InterruptedException e) {
      System.out.println(e);
    }
```

```
        return;                          // It is free now
    }
}
```

Now the isBusy() method will return only when the clerk object has no transaction waiting or in progress, so no return value is necessary. The while loop in main() before the final output statements can be replaced by the following:

```
// Wait until both clerks are done
clerk1.isBusy();
clerk2.isBusy();
```

How It Works

The doTransaction() method for a Clerk object calls the wait() method if the inTray field contains a reference to a transaction object, as this means the Clerk object is still processing a credit or a debit. This will result in the current thread (which is the main thread) being suspended until the notifyAll() method is called by this object's run() method to indicate a change to the clerk.

Because the run() method is also synchronized on the Clerk object, it can also call wait() in this case, if the inTray contains null, since this indicates that there is no transaction waiting for the clerk to expedite. A call to the doTransaction() method for the Clerk object will result in a transaction being stored in inTray, and the notifyAll() call will wake up the run() method to continue execution.

Because you've declared the isBusy() method as synchronized, you can call the wait() method to suspend the current thread if transactions are still being processed. Since the method doesn't return until the outstanding transaction is complete, there's no need for a boolean return value.

Thread Priorities

All threads have a priority that determines which thread is executed when several threads are waiting for their turn. This makes it possible to give one thread more access to processor resources than another. Let's consider an elementary example of how this could be used. Suppose you have one thread in a program that requires all the processor resources — some solid long-running calculation — and some other threads that require relatively few resources. By making the thread that requires all the resources a low-priority thread, you ensure that the other threads are executed promptly, while the processor bound thread can make use of the processor cycles that are left over after the others have had their turn.

The possible values for thread priority are defined in static data members of the class Thread. These members are of type int and are declared as final. The maximum thread priority is defined by the member MAX_PRIORITY, which has the value 10. The minimum priority is MIN_PRIORITY, defined as 1. The value of the default priority that is assigned to the main thread in a program is NORM_PRIORITY, which is set to 5. When you create a thread, its priority will be the same as that of the thread that created it.

You can modify the priority of a thread by calling the setPriority() method for the Thread object. This method accepts an argument of type int that defines the new priority for the thread. An IllegalArgumentException will be thrown if you specify a priority that is less than MIN_PRIORITY or greater than MAX_PRIORITY.

If you're going to be messing about with the priorities of the threads in your program, you need to be able to find out the current priority for a thread. You can do this by calling the getPriority() method for the Thread object. This will return the current priority for the thread as a value of type int.

You need to keep in mind that the actual execution priority of a thread that you set by calling setPriority() depends on the mapping between Java thread priorities and the native operating system priorities. The thread scheduling algorithm that your operating system uses also affects how your Java threads execute and what proportion of the processor time they are allocated.

Using Thread Priorities

In the last example, you could set priorities for the threads by adding statements to main():

```
clerk1Thread.setPriority(Thread.MIN_PRIORITY);    // Credits are a low priority
clerk2Thread.setPriority(Thread.MAX_PRIORITY);    // Debits are a high priority
```

You can put these statements following the call to the start() method for each of the Thread objects for the clerks. However, this can't have much effect in our program as it stands because one clerk can't get ahead of the other. This is because each clerk queues only one transaction, and they are allocated alternately to each clerk.

In the interests of learning more about how thread priorities affect the execution of your program, let's change the example once more to enable a Clerk object to queue transactions. You can do this quite easily using a LinkedList<Transaction> object, which I discussed in Chapter 14. There are a couple of points to be aware of, though.

The first point is that out of the collection classes I discussed in Chapter 14, only the Vector<> class is thread-safe — that is, safe for modification by more than one thread. For the others you must either access them only by methods and code blocks that are synchronized on the collection object or wrap the collection class in a thread-safe wrapper. Let's change the example to incorporate the latter.

The second point is that whether thread priorities have any effect depends on your operating system. If it doesn't support thread priorities, then setting thread priorities in your Java code will have no effect. Let's run it anyway to see how it works.

Try It Out   Setting Thread Priorities

You can extend the Clerk class to handle a number of Transaction objects by giving the in-tray the capacity to store several transactions in a list, but not too many — you don't want to overwork the clerks.

The java.util.Collections class provides methods for creating synchronized sets, lists, and maps from unsynchronized objects. The static synchronizedList() method is a parameterized method in the Collections class that accepts an argument of type List<T> and returns a reference of type List<T> to a collection class object that is synchronized. The Collections class defines other static methods that do the same for maps and sets. You can therefore define the inTray object as a linked list and then use the synchronizedList() to make a synchronized list for storing transactions:

```
import java.util.List;
import java.util.Collections;
import java.util.LinkedList;

public class Clerk implements Runnable {

  // Constructor
  public Clerk(Bank theBank) {
    this.theBank = theBank;          // Who the clerk works for
    //inTray       = null;           // Commented out: don't need this now
  }
  // Plus the rest of the methods in the class...

  private Bank theBank;
  private List<Transaction> inTray =      // The in-tray holding transactions
            Collections.synchronizedList(new LinkedList<Transaction>());
  private int maxTransactions = 8;        // Maximum transactions in the in-tray
}
```

Note that the statement that originally set inTray to null has been deleted from the constructor. Now that you are working with a list, you must change the doTransaction() method in the Clerk class to store the transaction in the list as long as the tray is not full. This means that because you allow a maximum of maxTransactions to be queued, a transaction can be added to the in-tray only when there are less than maxTransactions in the list. Here's the revised code to do this:

```
synchronized public void doTransaction(Transaction transaction) {
  while(inTray.size() >= maxTransactions) {
    try {
      wait();

    } catch(InterruptedException e) {
      System.out.println(e);
    }
    inTray.add(transaction);          // Add transaction to the list
    notifyAll();
  }
}
```

The size() method for the list returns the number of objects it contains so checking this is trivial. You use the add() method to add a new Transaction object to the end of the list.

The run() method for a clerk retrieves objects from the in-tray, so you must update that to deal with a list:

```
synchronized public void run() {
  while(true) {
    while(inTray.size() == 0) {       // No transaction waiting?
      try {
        wait();                       // Then take a break until there is

      } catch(InterruptedException e) {
        System.out.println(e);
```

```
            }
        }
            theBank.doTransaction(inTray.remove(0));
            notifyAll();                    // Notify other threads locked on this clerk
        }
    }
```

The `remove()` method in the `List<>` interface that you are using here removes the object at the index position in the list specified by the argument and returns a reference to it. Because you use 0 as the index, you retrieve the first object in the list to pass to the `doTransaction()` method for the `Bank` object.

As you now use a list to store transactions, the `isBusy()` method for a `Clerk` object also needs to be changed:

```
synchronized public void isBusy() {
    while(inTray.size() != 0) {            // Is this object busy?
        try {
            wait();                        // Yes, so wait for notify call

        } catch(InterruptedException e) {
            System.out.println(e);
        }
    }
    return;                                // It is free now
}
```

Now the clerk is not busy if there are no transactions in the `inTray` list. Hence, you test the value returned by `size()`.

That's all you need to buffer transactions in the in-tray of each clerk. If you reactivate the output statements that you added to the method in the `Bank` class, you'll be able to see how the processing of transactions proceeds.

With the priorities set by the calls to `setPriority()` you saw earlier, the processing of credits should run ahead of the processing of debits, although the fact that the time to process a debit is longer than the time for a credit will also have a significant effect. To make the thread priority the determining factor, set the times in the calls to the `sleep()` method in the `Bank` class to the same value. You could then try changing the values for priorities around to see what happens to the sequence in which transactions are processed. Of course, if your operating system does not support priority scheduling, then it won't have any effect anyway.

How It Works

You've made the `inTray` object a synchronized `List<Transaction>` object, by passing a `LinkedList<Transaction>` object to the static `synchronizedList()` method in the `Collections` class. This method returns a thread-safe `List<>` based on the original `LinkedList<>` object. You use the thread-safe `List<Transaction>` object to store up to `maxTransactions` transactions — eight in this case. The `doTransaction()` method for a `Clerk` object ensures that a transaction is added to the list only if fewer than eight transactions are queued.

The doTransaction() method for the Bank object always obtains the first object in the list, so the transactions will be processed in the sequence in which they were added to the list.

If your operating system supports priority scheduling, altering the thread priority values will change the pattern of servicing of the transactions.

Summary

In this chapter you've learned about threads and the basics of how you can create and manage them. You'll be using threads from time to time in examples later in this book, so be sure you don't move on from here without being comfortable with the basic ideas of how you create and start a thread.

The essential points that I have covered in this chapter are:

❑ Threads are subtasks in a program that can be in execution concurrently.

❑ A thread is represented by an object of the class Thread. Execution of a thread begins with the execution of the run() method defined in the class Thread.

❑ You define the code to be executed in a thread by implementing the run() method in a class derived from Thread, or in a class that implements the interface Runnable.

❑ A thread specified as daemon will cease execution when the thread that created it ends.

❑ A thread that isn't a daemon thread is called a user thread. A user thread will not be terminated automatically when the thread that created it ends.

❑ You start execution of a thread by calling the start() method for its Thread object. If you need to halt a thread before normal completion, you can stop execution of a thread by calling the interrupt() method for its Thread object.

❑ Methods can be declared as synchronized. Only one synchronized instance method for an object can execute at any given time. Only one synchronized static method for a class can execute at one time.

❑ A code block can be declared as synchronized on an object. Only one synchronized code block for an object can execute at any given time.

❑ In a synchronized method or code block, you can call the wait() method inherited from the class Object to halt execution of a thread. Execution of the waiting thread will continue when the notify() or notifyAll() method inherited from Object is called by a thread synchronized on the same object.

❑ The notify() or notifyAll() method can be called only from a method or code block that is synchronized to the same object as the method or block that contains the wait() method that halted the thread.

❑ A deadlock is a situation in which two threads are both waiting for the other to complete some action. Deadlocks can occur in subtle ways in multi-threaded applications, which makes such applications difficult to debug.

❑ You can modify the relative priority of a thread by calling its setPriority() method. This has an effect on execution only in environments that support priority scheduling.

Exercises

You can download the source code for the examples in the book and the solutions to the following exercises from http://www.wrox.com.

1. Modify the last example in the chapter so that each transaction is a debit or a credit at random.

2. Modify the result of the previous exercise to incorporate an array of clerks, each running in their own thread and each able to handle both debits and credits.

3. Extend the result of the previous exercise to incorporate two supervisors for two teams of clerks, where the supervisors each run in their own thread. The supervisor threads should originate transactions and pass them to the clerks they supervise.

Creating Windows

Until now, the programs you have been creating have perhaps not been what you may instinctively think of as a useful program. You can't expect a user to be prepared to enter all the input and get all the output on the command line. A more practical program would be window-based, with one or more windows that provide the interface between the user and the application. These windows, and the environment that the user interacts with, are known as the **graphical user interface (GUI)**.

In this chapter you'll investigate how to create a window for a Java application, and you'll take a first look at some of the components you can assemble to create a graphical user interface in Java.

You will learn:

❑   How you create and display a resizable window

❑   What components and containers are

❑   How you can add components to a window

❑   How you can control the layout of components

❑   How you create a menu bar and menus for a window

❑   What a menu shortcut is and how you can add a shortcut for a menu item

❑   What the restrictions on the capabilities of an applet are

❑   How to convert an application into an applet

Graphical User Interfaces in Java

There is a vast amount of functionality in the Java class libraries devoted to supporting graphical user interface (GUI) creation and management, far more than it is feasible to cover in a single book — even if it is big. Just the JFrame class, which you'll begin to explore in a moment, contains more than 200 methods when you include those inherited from superclasses! I will therefore have to be selective in what I go into detail, in terms of both the specific classes I discuss and their methods. However, I will cover the basic operations that you need to understand to create your own applications and applets. With a good grasp of the basics, you should be able to explore other areas of the Java class library beyond those discussed without too much difficulty.

The fundamental elements that you need to create a GUI reside in two packages, `java.awt` and `javax.swing`. The `java.awt` package was the primary repository for classes you would use to create a GUI way back in Java 1.1 — awt being an abbreviation for **A**bstract **W**indowing **T**oolkit — but many of the classes this package defines have been superseded in Java 2 by `javax.swing`. Note that I said many of the classes, not all. Most of the classes in the `javax.swing` package define GUI elements, referred to as **Swing components**, that provide much-improved alternatives to components defined by classes in `java.awt`. You'll be looking into the `JButton` class in the Swing set that defines a button, rather than the `Button` class in `java.awt`. However, the Swing component classes are generally derived from, and depend on, fundamental classes that are defined within the `java.awt` package, so you can't afford to ignore these.

The Swing classes are part of a more general set of GUI programming capabilities that are collectively referred to as the **Java Foundation Classes**, or **JFC** for short. JFC covers not only the Swing component classes, such as those defining buttons and menus, but also classes for 2D drawing from the `java.awt.geom` package and classes that support drag-and-drop capability in the `java.awt.dnd` package. The JFC also includes an application program interface (API) defined in the `javax.accessibility` package that allows applications to be implemented that provide for users with disabilities.

The Swing component classes are more flexible than the component classes defined in the `java.awt` package because they are implemented entirely in Java. The `java.awt` components depend on native code to a great extent and are, therefore, restricted to a "lowest common denominator" set of interface capabilities. Because Swing components are pure Java, they are not restricted by the characteristics of the platform on which they run. Apart from the added functionality and flexibility of the Swing components, they also provide a feature called **pluggable look-and-feel** that makes it possible to change the appearance of a component. You can programmatically select the look-and-feel of a component from those implemented as standard, or you can create your own look-and-feel for components if you wish. The pluggable look-and-feel of the Swing components has been facilitated by designing the classes in a particular way, called the **Model-View-Controller architecture**.

Model-View-Controller (MVC) Architecture

The design of the Swing component classes is loosely based on something called the **Model-View-Controller architecture**, or **MVC**. This is not of particular consequence in the context of applying the Swing classes, but it's important to be aware of it if you want to modify the pluggable look-and-feel of a component. MVC is not new and did not originate with Java. In fact, the idea of MVC emerged some time ago within the context of the SmallTalk programming language. MVC is an idealized way of modeling a component as three separate parts:

- ❑ The **model** that stores the data that defines the component
- ❑ The **view** that creates the visual representation of the component from the data in the model
- ❑ The **controller** that deals with user interaction with the component and modifies the model and/or the view in response to a user action as necessary

Figure 17-1 illustrates the relationships between the model, the view, and the controller.

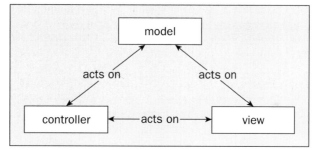

Figure 17-1

In object-oriented terms, each of the three logical parts for a component — the model, the view, and the controller — is ideally represented by a different class type. In practice this turns out to be difficult because of the dependencies between the view and the controller. Since the user interacts with the physical representation of the component, the controller operation is highly dependent on the implementation of the view. For this reason, the view and controller are typically represented by a single composite object that corresponds to a view with an integrated controller. In this case the MVC concept degenerates into the document/view architecture that I introduced when I discussed the `Observable` class and `Observer` interface. Sun calls it the **Separable Model architecture,** and this is illustrated in Figure 17-2.

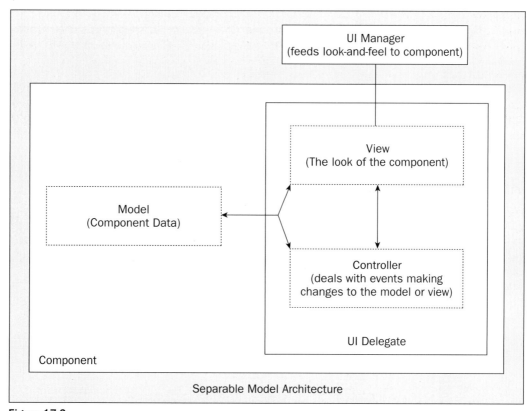

Figure 17-2

The Swing components provide for a pluggable look-and-feel by making the visual appearance of a component and the interface to the user the responsibility of an independent object called the **UI delegate**. This is the view+controller part of the MVC model. Thus, a different UI delegate can provide a component with a new look-and-feel.

The details of how you modify the look-and-feel of a component is beyond the scope of this book, but I'll introduce how you can set one of the standard look-and-feels that are distributed with the Java Development Kit (JDK). It is as well to be aware of the MVC architecture on which the Swing components are based since it appears quite often in the literature around Java, and you may want to change the look-and-feel of a component at some time.

Creating a Window

A basic window in Java is represented by an object of the Window class, which is defined in the java.awt package. Objects of the Window class are hardly ever used directly since borders and a title bar are fairly basic prerequisites for a typical application window, and this class provides neither. The library class JFrame that is defined in the javax.swing package is a much more useful class for creating a window since, in addition to a title bar and a border, it provides a wealth of other facilities. Its superclasses are shown in Figure 17-3.

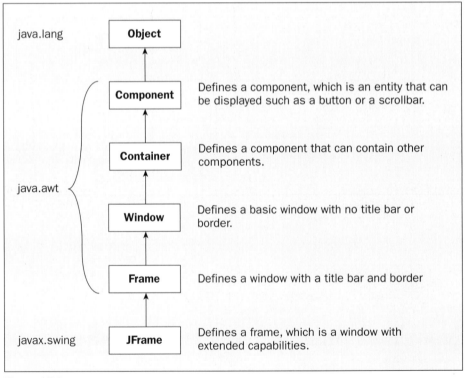

Figure 17-3

The `Component` class is the grandmother of all component classes — it defines the basic properties and methods shared by all components. You'll see later that all the Swing components have the `Component` class as a base. The `Container` class adds the capability for a `Component` object to contain other components, which is a frequent requirement. Since `JFrame` has `Container` as a superclass, a `JFrame` object can contain other components. Beyond the obvious need for a window to be able to contain the components that represent the GUI, a menu bar should contain menus, for example, which in turn will contain menu items; a toolbar will obviously contain toolbar buttons; and there are many other examples. For this reason the `Container` class is also a base for all the classes that define Swing components.

The `Window` class adds methods to the `Container` class that are specific to a window, such as the capability to handle events arising from user interaction with the window. The `Frame` class is the original class in `java.awt` that provided a proper window, with a title bar and a border, with which everyone is familiar. The `JFrame` class adds functionality to the `Frame` class to support much more sophisticated facilities for drawing and displaying other components. You can deduce from the hierarchy in the diagram how a `JFrame` object can easily end up with its 200+ methods, as it has five superclasses from which it inherits members. You aren't going to trawl through all these classes and methods. You'll just look into the ones you need in context as you go along, and then see how they are applied in some examples. This will teach you the most important methods in this class.

You can display an application window simply by creating an object of type `JFrame`, calling a method for the object to set the size of the window, and then calling a method to display the window. Let's try that right away.

Try It Out   Framing a Window

Here's the code:

```java
import javax.swing.JFrame;

public class TryWindow {
  // The window object
  static JFrame aWindow = new JFrame("This is the Window Title");

  public static void main(String[] args) {
    int windowWidth = 400;                          // Window width in pixels
    int windowHeight = 150;                         // Window height in pixels
    aWindow.setBounds(50, 100,                      // Set position
                      windowWidth, windowHeight);   // and size
    aWindow.setDefaultCloseOperation(JFrame.EXIT_ON_CLOSE);
    aWindow.setVisible(true);                       // Display the window
  }
}
```

Under Microsoft Windows, the program will display the window shown in Figure 17-4.

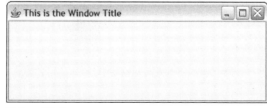

Figure 17-4

This is the default look-and-feel on my system, and it may well be the same on yours. It corresponds to the Java cross-platform look-and-feel that is distributed with the JDK. Each look-and-feel is defined by a class, and on my system the following look-and-feel classes are installed:

```
javax.swing.plaf.metal.MetalLookAndFeel
com.sun.java.swing.plaf.motif.MotifLookAndFeel
com.sun.java.swing.plaf.windows.WindowsLookAndFeel
com.sun.java.swing.plaf.windows.WindowsClassicLookAndFeel
```

The first class corresponds to the Java look-and-feel, which used to be known as the Metal look-and-feel. It is intended to provide a uniform cross-platform look-and-feel, and you can use it on any platform that supports the JFC. The second class defines the Motif look-and-feel that is for use on Unix systems. The last two classes can be used only with Microsoft Windows.

The UIManager class that is defined in the javax.swing package deals with setting the look-and-feel of a Java application. You could list the names of the look-and-feel classes that are installed with the JDK on your system on the command line by adding the following code to main() in the example:

```
UIManager.LookAndFeelInfo[] looks = UIManager.getInstalledLookAndFeels();
  for(UIManager.LookAndFeelInfo look : looks) {
    System.out.println(look.getClassName());
}
```

For this to work, you need the following import statement in the source file:

```
import javax.swing.UIManager;
```

You can set a look-and-feel by passing the fully qualified name of one of your look-and-feel classes to the static setLookAndFeel() method that is defined in the UIManager class. This method can throw an exception of ClassNotFoundException if the look-and-feel class cannot be found, plus other exceptions, so you should put the method call in a try block and arrange to catch the exception. For example:

```
try {
   UIManager.setLookAndFeel("com.sun.java.swing.plaf.motif.MotifLookAndFeel");
   javax.swing.SwingUtilities.updateComponentTreeUI(aWindow);
} catch(Exception e) {
  System.err.println("Look and feel not set.");
}
```

The class name for the cross-platform look-and-feel is returned by the static getCrossPlatformLookAnd FeelClassName() method in the UIManager class, so you can set this explicitly using the following code:

```
try {
   UIManager.setLookAndFeel(UIManager.getCrossPlatformLookAndFeel());
   javax.swing.SwingUtilities.updateComponentTreeUI(aWindow);
} catch(Exception e) {
  System.err.println("Look and feel not set.");
}
```

Calling the static updateComponentTreeUI() method in the SwingUtilities class causes the frame window to be updated with the look-and-feel that is currently set.

Alternatively, you can make your application adopt the look-and-feel for the platform on which it is running by calling the static `getSystemLookAndFeel()` method in the `UIManager` class and passing the class name that it returns to the `setLookAndFeel()` method.

The window for the example is fully operational. You could try resizing the window for the example by dragging a border or a corner with the mouse. You can also try minimizing the window by clicking on the icons to the right of the title bar. Everything should work okay so you are getting quite a lot for so few lines of code. You can close the application by clicking on the X icon.

> **This example will terminate okay if you have entered the code correctly; however, errors could prevent this. If an application doesn't terminate properly for any reason, you will have to get the operating system to end the task. Under MS Windows XP, pressing Ctrl+Alt+Del will bring up the Task Manager window from which you can terminate the application.**

How It Works

The `import` statement adds `JFrame` in the package `javax.swing` to the program. From now on most of your programs will be using the components defined in this package. The object of type `JFrame` is created and stored as the initial value for the `static` data member of the class `TryWindow`, so it will be created automatically when the `TryWindow` class is loaded. The argument to the constructor defines the title to be displayed in the application window.

The `main()` method calls three methods for the `aWindow` object. The method `setBounds()` defines the size and position of the window; the first pair of arguments correspond to the x and y coordinates of the top-left corner of the application window relative to the top-left corner of the display screen, and the second pair of arguments specify the width and height of the window in pixels. The screen coordinate system has the origin point, (0, 0), at the top-left corner of the screen, with the positive x-axis running left to right and the positive y-axis from top to bottom. The positive y-axis in screen coordinates is therefore in the opposite direction to that of the usual Cartesian coordinate system. The coordinate system for screen coordinates is illustrated in Figure 17-5.

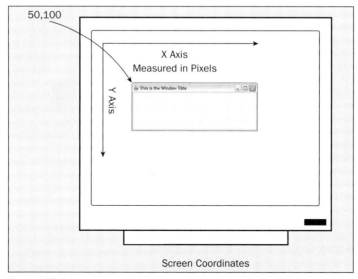

Figure 17-5

773

You have specified the top-left corner of the application window at position (50, 100) on the screen, which will be 50 pixels to the right and 100 pixels down. Since the window will be 400 pixels wide and 150 pixels high, the bottom-right corner will be at position (450, 250). The actual physical width and height of the window, as well as its position relative to the edge of the screen, will depend on the size of your screen and the display resolution. For a given screen size, the higher the display resolution, the smaller the window will be and the closer it will be to the top left-hand corner, simply because the pixels on the screen will be closer together. You'll see how you can get around this potential problem later in this chapter.

The `setDefaultCloseOperation()` method for the `JFrame` object determines what happens when you close the window by either clicking on the X icon or selecting Close from the menu that is displayed when you click on the Java icon in the top-left corner of the window. There are four possible argument values you can use here. The constant you have used at the argument to the method is `EXIT_ON_CLOSE`, which is defined in the `JFrame` class. The effect of this is to close the window, dispose of the window resources and those of any components it contains, and finally to terminate the application. There are three other argument values you could use with the `setDefaultCloseOperation()` method that are defined in the `WindowConstants` interface. These values are:

Argument	Description
DISPOSE_ON_CLOSE	This causes the frame and any components it contains to be destroyed but doesn't terminate the application.
DO_NOTHING_ON_CLOSE	This makes the close operation for the frame window ineffective.
HIDE_ON_CLOSE	This just hides the window by calling its `setVisible()` method with an argument of `false`. This is the default action if you don't call the `setDefaultCloseOperation()` method with a different argument value. When a window is hidden, you can always display the window again later by calling `setVisible()` with an argument of `true`.

Of course, you may want to take some action beyond the options I have discussed here when the user chooses to close the window. If the program involves entering a lot of data for instance, you may want to ensure that the user is prompted to save the data before the program ends. This involves handling an event associated with the Close menu item or the Close button, and you will be investigating this in the next chapter.

The `setVisible()` method with the argument set to `true` displays the application window on top of any other windows that are currently visible on the screen. If you wanted to hide a window at some point during the execution of an application, you would call `setVisible()` with the argument set to `false`.

It's a very *nice* window, but not overly useful. All you can do with it is move, resize, and reshape it. You can drag the borders and maximize and minimize it. The Close icon works because you elected to dispose of the window and exit the program when the `close` operation is selected by setting the appropriate option through the `setDefaultCloseOperation()` method. If you omitted this method call, you would get the default action whereby the window would close, but the program would not terminate.

The setBounds() and setVisible() methods are members of the JFrame class inherited from the Component class, so these are available for any component. However, you don't normally set the size and position of other components, as you'll see. The setDefaultCloseOperation() method is defined in the JFrame class so this method only applies to JFrame window objects.

Before you expand the JFrame example, you need to look a little deeper into the makeup of the component classes.

Components and Containers

A component represents a graphical entity of one kind or another that can be displayed on the screen. A component is any object of a class that is a subclass of Component. As you have seen, a JFrame window is a component, but there are many others. Before getting into specifics, let's first get a feel for the general relationship between the groups of classes that represent components. Part of the class hierarchy with Component as a base is shown in Figure 17-6. The arrows in the diagram point toward the superclass.

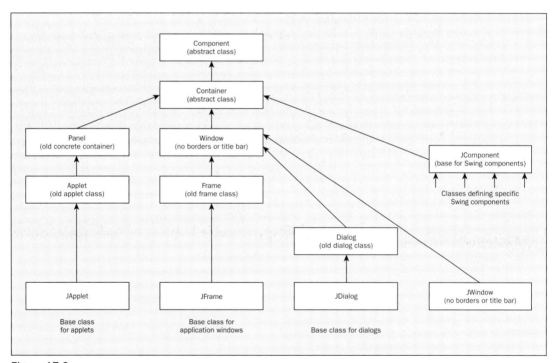

Figure 17-6

This shows some of the subclasses of Component — the ones that are important to you at the moment. I discussed the chain through to JFrame earlier, but the other branches are new. The classes that you'll be using directly are all the most commonly derived classes.

Let's summarize how you would typically use the key classes in this hierarchy:

Class	Use
JFrame	This is used as the basic Java application window. An object of this class has a title bar and provision for adding a menu. You can also add other components to it. You will usually subclass this class to create a window class specific to your application. You'll then be able to add GUI components or draw in this window if required, as you'll see.
JWindow	An object of this class type is a window with no title bar or window management icons. One typical use for a JWindow object is for a subsidiary application window that is displayed on a secondary display where two or more displays are attached to a system.
JDialog	You use this class to define a dialog window that is used for entering data into a program in various ways. You usually code the creation of a dialog in response to some menu item or button being selected.
JApplet	This is the base class for a Java 2 applet—which is a program designed to run embedded in a web page. All your Java 2 applets will have this class as a base. You can draw in a JApplet and also add menus and other components.
JComponent	The subclasses of JComponent define a range of standard components such as menus, buttons, checkboxes, and so on. You'll use these classes to create the GUI for your application or applet.

All the classes derived from Container can contain other objects of any of the classes derived from Component and are referred to generically as **containers**. Since the Container class is a subclass of the Component class, every container object is a Component, too, so a container can contain other containers. The exception is the Window class and its subclasses, as objects of type Window (or of a subclass type) can't be contained in another container. If you try to do this, an exception will be thrown. The JComponent class is the base for all the Swing components used in a window as part of the GUI, and because this class is derived from Container, all of the Swing components are also containers.

As you can see, the JApplet class, which is a base class for all Swing applets, is derived from Component via the Container class. An applet will, therefore, also inherit the methods from the Container and Component classes. It also inherits methods from the old Applet class, which it extends and improves upon. Note that the JApplet, JFrame, and JDialog classes and the JComponent class and its subclasses are all in the package javax.swing. The Applet class is in java.applet, and all the others are in java.awt. The package java.applet is tiny—it contains only the one class plus three related interfaces, but you won't need to use it directly. You will always be using the JApplet class to define an applet, as it's significantly better than Applet.

Window and Frame Components

The basic difference between a JFrame object and a Window object is that a JFrame object represents the main window for an application, whereas a Window object does not—you always need a JFrame object before you can create a Window object.

Since the JDialog class is derived directly from the Window class, you can create a JDialog object in an application only in the context of a JFrame object. Apart from the default constructor, the constructors for the JDialog class generally require a JFrame object to be passed as an argument. This JFrame object is referred to as the **parent** of the JDialog object. A JFrame object has a border, is resizable, and has the ability to hold a built-in menu bar. Since a JFrame object is the top-level window in an application, its size and location are defined relative to the screen. A JDialog object with a JFrame object as a parent will be located relative to its parent.

As I said, the JApplet, JFrame, and JDialog classes are all containers because they have Container as a base class and therefore, in principle, can contain any kind of component. They are also all components themselves since they are derived ultimately from the Component class. However, things are not quite as simple as that. You don't add the components for your application or applet GUI *directly* to the JFrame or JApplet object for your program. Let's look at how it actually works in practice.

Window Panes

When you want to add GUI components or draw in a window displayed from a JFrame object, you add the components to, or draw on, a **window pane** that is managed by the JFrame object. The same goes for an applet. Broadly speaking, window panes are container objects that represent an area of a window, and they come in several different types.

You'll use a window pane called the **content pane** most of the time, but there are others. The relationship between the contentPane object, other window panes, and the application window itself is shown in Figure 17-7.

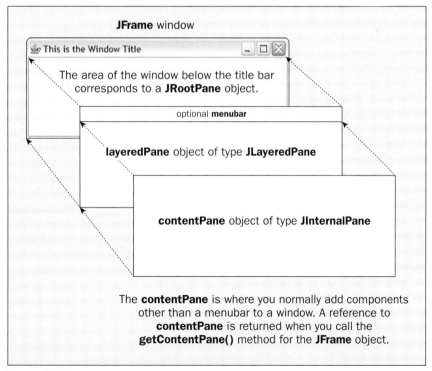

Figure 17-7

As you see, the area below the title bar in a `JFrame` window corresponds to a `JRootPane` object. This contains another pane, the `layeredPane` object in the illustration, which is of type `JLayeredPane`. This pane corresponds to the whole of the area occupied by the `JRootPane` object in the window and manages the menu bar if the window has one. The area in the `layeredPane` below the menu bar corresponds to the `contentPane` object, and it's here that you typically add GUI components. You also display text or do any drawing in the area covered by the content pane.

The `layeredPane` object has special properties for advanced applications that permit groups of components to be managed in separate layers that overlay one another within the pane. With this capability you can control how components are displayed relative to one another, because the layers are displayed in a particular order from back to front. The components in a layer at the front will appear on the screen in front of those in a layer that is towards the back.

There is also an additional pane not shown in Figure 17-7. This is the `glassPane` object, which also corresponds to the complete `JRootPane` area. The contents of the `glassPane` object displays on top of all the other panes, so this is used to display components that you always want to display on top of anything else displayed in the window — such as drop-down menus. You can also use the `glassPane` object to display graphics that need to be updated relatively frequently — such as when you create an animation. When part of what is displayed is to be animated, a static background can be displayed independently via the `contentPane`. Since this doesn't need to be reprocessed each time the animated objects need to be redrawn, the whole process can be much more efficient.

The `JFrame` class defines methods to provide you with a reference to any of the panes:

Method	Description
getRootPane()	Returns the root pane as type `JRootPane`.
getLayeredPane()	Returns the layered pane as type `JLayeredPane`.
getContentPane()	Returns the content pane as type `Container`. This is the method you will use most frequently, since you normally add components to the content pane.
getGlassPane()	Returns the glass pane as type `Component`.

All the classes discussed here that represent panes are themselves Swing components, defined in the `javax.swing` package. A `JApplet` object has the same arrangement of panes as a `JFrame` object, so adding components to an applet, or drawing on it, works in exactly the same way. An applet defined as a `JApplet` object can also have a menu bar just like an application window.

All the panes, as well as the menu bar, are components, so before I start delving into how to add a menu bar or other components to a window, let's unearth a little more about the makeup of components in general.

Basics of Components

You need to understand several basic concepts common to all components before you can apply them properly. They also have applications in many different contexts. While this may seem like something of a catalog of classes and methods, without much in the way of practical application, please stay with it. You'll be using most of these capabilities in a practical context later. To understand the fundamental things you can do with Swing components, you'll be examining what functionality the Swing components inherit from the `Component` and `Container` classes.

When a component is contained within another component, the outer object is referred to as the **parent**. You can obtain a reference to the parent object of any given component by calling its `getParent()` method. This method is inherited from the `Component` class, and it returns the parent as type `Container`, since only a subclass of `Container` can hold other components. If there is no parent, as is the case with a `JFrame` component, this method will return `null`.

Component Attributes

The `Component` class defines attributes, which record the following information about an object:

❑ The **position** is stored as (*x*, *y*) coordinates. This fixes where the object is in relation to its container in the coordinate system of the container object.

❑ The **name** of the component is stored as a `String` object.

❑ The **size** is recorded as values for the width and the height of the object.

❑ The **foreground color** and **background color** that apply to the object. These color values are used when the object is displayed.

❑ The **font** used by the object when text is displayed.

❑ The **cursor** for the object — this defines the appearance of the cursor when it is over the object.

❑ Whether the object is **enabled** or not — when a component is enabled, its enabled state is `true`, and it has a normal appearance. When a component is disabled it is grayed out. Note that a disabled component can still originate events.

❑ Whether the object is **visible** on the screen or not — if an object is not marked as visible, it is not drawn on the screen.

❑ Whether the object is **valid** or not — if an object is not valid, the layout of the entities that make up the object has not been determined. This is the case before an object is made visible. You can make a `Container` object invalid by changing its contents. It will then need to be validated before it is displayed correctly.

You can only modify the characteristics of a `Component` object by calling its methods or affecting it indirectly in some way since none of the data members that store its characteristics are directly accessible — they are all `private`. For example, you can change the name of a `Component` object `myWindow` with the statement:

```
myWindow.setName("The Name");
```

If you subsequently want to retrieve the name of an object, you can use the `getName()` method, which returns the name as a `String` object. For example:

```
String theName = myWindow.getName();
```

The `isVisible()`, `isEnabled()`, and `isValid()` methods return `true` if the object is visible, enabled, and valid, respectively. You can set an object as visible or enabled by passing the value `true` as an argument to the methods `setVisible()` and `setEnabled()`, respectively.

A common misconception with Swing components is that calling `setEnabled(false)` will inhibit events such as mouse clicks from a component. This is not the case. All it does is to set the internal enabled status for the component to `false`, causing the component to be grayed out. To prevent events from a disabled component having an effect, you must call `isEnabled()` for the component in your event handling code to determine whether the component is enabled or not. You can then choose to do nothing when the `isEnabled()` method returns `false`.

Let's see how you can change the size and position of a `Component` object.

The Size and Position of a Component

Position is defined by *x* and *y* coordinates of type `int`, or by an object of type `java.awt.Point`. A `Point` object has two public data members, `x` and `y`, corresponding to the *x* and *y* coordinate values. Size is defined by `width` and `height`, also values of type `int`, or by an object of type `java.awt.Dimension`. The `Dimension` class has two public members of type `int`, namely `width` and `height`. The size and position of a component are often specified together by an object of type `java.awt.Rectangle`. A `Rectangle` object has public data members, `x` and `y`, defining the top-left corner of the rectangle, with `width` and `height` members defining its size. All these data members are of type `int`.

Components have a "preferred" size defined by a `java.awt.Dimension` object encapsulating values for the width and the height. The preferred size will vary depending on the particular object. For example, the preferred size of a `JButton` object that defines a button is the size that accommodates the label for the button. Note that the size of a component is managed automatically when it has a parent component. I'll explain how this works later in this chapter. A component also has a minimum size and a maximum size. The size of the component will lie within the range from the minimum to the maximum, and if the space available to it is less than the minimum size, the component will not be displayed. You can set the preferred size for a component as well as the minimum and maximum size. This provides a way for you to influence the size of a component when it is displayed.

The methods defined in the `Component` class that retrieve the size and position are:

Method	Description
`Rectangle getBounds()`	Returns the position and size of the object as an object of type `Rectangle`.
`Rectangle getBounds(Rectangle rect)`	Stores the position and size in the `Rectangle` object that you pass as the argument and returns a reference to `rect`. This version of the method enables you to reuse an existing `Rectangle` object to store the bounds. If `rect` is `null`, a new `Rectangle` object will be created by the method.

Method	Description
`Dimension getSize()`	Returns the current size of the `Component` object as a `Dimension` object.
`Dimension getSize(Dimension dim)`	Stores the current size in `dim` and returns a reference to `dim`. This enables you to reuse an existing `Dimension` object.
`Point getLocation()`	Returns the position of the `Component` object as an object of type `Point`.
`Point getLocation(Point p)`	Stores the coordinates of the current position of the component in the argument, `p`, and returns a reference to `p`. This enables you to reuse an existing `Point` object to store the position.

You can also change the size and/or position of a component by using the following methods:

Method	Description
`void setBounds(int x, int y, int width, int height)`	Sets the position of the `Component` object to the coordinates (x, y) and the width and height of the object to the values defined by the third and fourth arguments
`void setBounds(Rectangle rect)`	Sets the position and size of the `Component` object to be that of the `Rectangle` argument `rect`
`void setSize(Dimension d)`	Sets the width and height of the `Component` object to the values stored in the members of the object `d`
`setLocation(int x, int y)`	Sets the position of the component to the point defined by (x, y)
`setLocation(Point p)`	Sets the position of the component to the point `p`

You can also set the parameters that determine the range of variation in size that is possible for a component with the following methods:

Method	Description
`void setMinimumSize(Dimension d)`	Sets the minimum size of the `Component` object to the dimensions specified by the argument `d`. A `null` argument will restore the default minimum size for the component.

Table continued on following page

781

Method	Description
`void setMaximumSize(Dimension d)`	Sets the maximum size of the `Component` object to the dimensions specified by the argument d. A `null` argument will restore the default maximum size for the component.
`void setPreferredSize(Dimension d)`	Sets the preferred size of the `Component` object to the dimensions specified by the argument d. A `null` argument will restore the default preferred size for the component.

Another important method defined in the `Component` class is `getToolkit()`. This returns an object of type `Toolkit` that contains information about the environment in which your application is running, including the screen size in pixels. You can use the `getToolkit()` method to help set the size and position of a window on the screen. You can modify the previous example to demonstrate this.

Try It Out   Sizing Windows with Toolkit

You'll use the `Toolkit` object to display the window in the center of the screen, with the width and height set as half of the screen width and height:

```
import javax.swing.JFrame;
import java.awt.Toolkit;
import java.awt.Dimension;

public class TryWindow2 {
  // The window object
  static JFrame aWindow = new JFrame("This is the Window Title");

  public static void main(String[] args) {
    Toolkit theKit = aWindow.getToolkit();       // Get the window toolkit
    Dimension wndSize = theKit.getScreenSize();  // Get screen size

    // Set the position to screen center & size to half screen size
    aWindow.setBounds(wndSize.width/4, wndSize.height/4,    // Position
                      wndSize.width/2, wndSize.height/2);   // Size
    aWindow.setDefaultCloseOperation(JFrame.EXIT_ON_CLOSE);
    aWindow.setVisible(true);                    // Display the window
  }
}
```

If you try this example, you should see the application window centered on your display with a width and height of half that of the screen.

How It Works

You obtain the `Toolkit` object, `theKit`, by calling the `getToolkit()` method for the `JFrame` object, `aWindow`. This object represents the environment on your computer so it encapsulates all the properties and capabilities of that environment as far as Java is concerned, including the screen resolution and size.

> Note that you can't create a `Toolkit` object directly since `Toolkit` is an abstract class. There is only one `Toolkit` object in an application—the one that you get a reference for when you call `getToolKit()` for a component.

The `getScreenSize()` method that is a member of the `Toolkit` object returns an object of type `Dimension` containing data members `width` and `height`. These hold the number of pixels for the width and height of your display. You use these values to set the coordinates for the position of the window and the width and height of the window through the `setBounds()` method.

This is not the only way of centering a window. A `java.awt.GraphicsEnvironment` object contains information about the graphics devices attached to a system, including the display—or displays in systems with more than one. You can obtain a reference to a `GraphicsEnvironment` object that encapsulates information about the graphics devices on the local machine by calling the static `getLocalGraphicsEnvironment()` method in the `GraphicsEnvironment` class, like this:

```
GraphicsEnvironment localGE = GraphicsEnvironment.getLocalGraphicsEnvironment();
```

You can now call this object's `getCenterPoint()` method to obtain a `Point` object containing the coordinates of the center of the screen:

```
Point center = localGE.getCenterPoint();
```

You could try this with a variation on the original version of the example.

Try It Out   **Centering a Window**

Here's the code:

```java
import javax.swing.JFrame;
import java.awt.Point;
import java.awt.GraphicsEnvironment;

public class TryWindow3 {
  // The window object
  static JFrame aWindow = new JFrame("This is the Window Title");

  public static void main(String[] args) {
    Point center =
            GraphicsEnvironment.getLocalGraphicsEnvironment().getCenterPoint();
    int windowWidth = 400;
    int windowHeight = 150;
    // set position and size
    aWindow.setBounds(center.x-windowWidth/2, center.y-windowHeight/2,
                  windowWidth, windowHeight);
    aWindow.setDefaultCloseOperation(JFrame.EXIT_ON_CLOSE);
    aWindow.setVisible(true);                    // Display the window
  }
}
```

When you execute this, you should see the window displayed centered on your screen.

How It Works

This uses the coordinates of the point returned by the `getCenterPoint()` method to position the window. You calculate the position for the top-left corner of the application window by subtracting half the window width and half the height from the *x* and *y* coordinates of the screen center point, respectively. This causes the window to be centered on the screen.

Points and Rectangles

Before continuing with the `Component` class methods, let's digress briefly into more detail concerning the `Point` and `Rectangle` classes, as they are going to come up quite often. As you've seen, both these classes are defined in `java.awt`. You will find many of the methods provided by the `Point` and `Rectangle` classes very useful when drawing in a window. Entities displayed in a window will typically have `Rectangle` objects associated with them that define the areas within the window that they occupy. `Point` objects are used in the definition of other geometric entities such as lines and circles, and to specify their position in a window.

Note that neither `Point` nor `Rectangle` objects have any built-in representation on the screen. They aren't components; they are abstract geometric entities. If you want to display a rectangle you have to draw it. You'll see how to do this in Chapter 19 when you'll meet other classes that define geometric shapes that can be displayed.

Point Objects

As I said, the `Point` class defines a point by two `public` data members of type `int`, x and y. Let's look at the methods that the class provides.

Try It Out   **Playing with Point Objects**

Try the following code:

```java
import java.awt.Point;

public class PlayingPoints {
  public static void main(String[] args) {
    Point aPoint = new Point();                  // Initialize to 0,0
    Point bPoint = new Point(50,25);
    Point cPoint = new Point(bPoint);
    System.out.println("aPoint is located at: " + aPoint);
    aPoint.move(100,50);                         // Change to position 100,50

    bPoint.x = 110;
    bPoint.y = 70;

    aPoint.translate(10,20);                     // Move by 10 in x and 20 in y
    System.out.println("aPoint is now at: " + aPoint);

    if(aPoint.equals(bPoint))
      System.out.println("aPoint and bPoint are at the same location.");
  }
}
```

If you run the program, you should see the following output produced:

```
aPoint is located at: java.awt.Point[x=0,y=0]
aPoint is now at: java.awt.Point[x=110,y=70]
aPoint and bPoint are at the same location.
```

How It Works

You apply the three constructors that the `Point` class provides in the first few lines. You then manipulate the `Point` objects you've instantiated.

You change a `Point` object to a new position with the `move()` method. Alternatively, you can use the `setLocation()` method to set the values of the `x` and `y` members. The `setLocation()` method behaves exactly the same as the `move()` method. It's included in the `Point` class for compatibility with the `setLocation()` method for a component. For the same reason, there's also a `getLocation()` method in the `Point` class that returns a copy of the current `Point` object. As the example shows, you can translate a `Point` object by specified distances in the *x* and *y* directions using the `translate()` method.

Lastly, you compare two `Point` objects using the `equals()` method. This compares the *x* and *y* coordinates of the two `Point` objects and returns `true` if both are equal. The final output statement is executed because the `Point` objects are equal.

Note that this is not the only class that represents points. You will see other classes that define points in Chapter 19 when I discuss how you draw in a window.

Rectangle Objects

As I mentioned earlier, the `Rectangle` class defines four `public` data members, all of type `int`. The position of a `Rectangle` object is defined by the members x and y, and its size is defined by the members `width` and `height`. As they are all `public` class members, you can retrieve or modify any of these directly, but your code will be a little more readable if you use the methods provided.

There are no less than seven constructors that you can use:

Constructor	Description
`Rectangle()`	Creates a rectangle at (0, 0) with zero width and height
`Rectangle(int x, int y, int width, int height)`	Creates a rectangle at (x, y) with the specified width and height
`Rectangle(int width, int height)`	Creates a rectangle at (0, 0) with the specified width and height
`Rectangle(Point p, Dimension d)`	Creates a rectangle at point p with the width and height specified by d
`Rectangle(Point p)`	Creates a rectangle at point p with zero width and height

Table continued on following page

Constructor	Description
Rectangle(Dimension d)	Creates a rectangle at (0, 0) with the width and height specified by d
Rectangle(Rectangle r)	Creates a rectangle with the same position and dimensions as r

You can retrieve or modify the position of a Rectangle object using the method getLocation(), which returns a Point object, and setLocation(), which comes in two versions, one of which requires *x* and *y* coordinates of the new position as arguments and the other of which requires a Point object. You can also apply the translate() method to a Rectangle object, in the same way as the Point object.

To retrieve or modify the size of a Rectangle object, you use the methods getSize(), which returns a Dimension object, and setSize(), which requires either a Dimension object specifying the new size as an argument or two arguments corresponding to the new width and height values as type int.

You can also use several methods to combine Rectangle objects, and to extend a Rectangle object to enclose a point. The effects of each of these methods are shown in Figure 17-8.

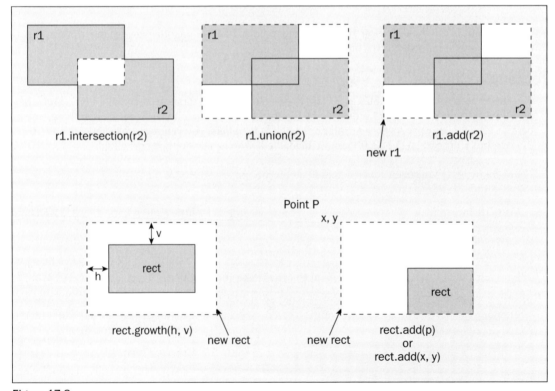

Figure 17-8

The rectangle that results from each operation is shown with dashed line boundaries. The details of the operations provided by the methods illustrated in Figure 17-8 are as follows:

Method	Description
`Rectangle intersection(Rectangle r)`	Returns a `Rectangle` object that is the intersection of the current object and the argument. If the two rectangles do not intersect, the `Rectangle` object returned is at position (0, 0), and the `width` and `height` members are zero, so the rectangle is empty.
`Rectangle union(Rectangle r)`	Returns the smallest `Rectangle` object enclosing both the current `Rectangle` object and the `Rectangle` object r, passed as an argument.
`void add(Rectangle r)`	Expands the current `Rectangle` object to enclose the argument `Rectangle`.
`void add(Point p)`	Expands the current `Rectangle` object to enclose the `Point` object p. The result will be the smallest rectangle that encloses the original rectangle and the point.
`void add(int x, int y)`	Expands the current `Rectangle` object to enclose the point at (x, y).
`void grow(int h, int v)`	Enlarges the current `Rectangle` object by moving the boundary out from the center by h horizontally and v vertically.

You can also test and compare `Rectangle` objects in various ways with the following methods:

Method	Description
`boolean isEmpty()`	Returns `true` if the `width` and `height` members of the current `Rectangle` object are zero, and `false` otherwise.
`boolean equals(Object rect)`	Returns `true` if the `Rectangle` object passed as an argument is equal to the current `Rectangle` object, and `false` otherwise.
	The two rectangles will be equal if they are at the same position and have the same width and height. If the argument is not a `Rectangle` object, `false` is returned.
`boolean intersects(Rectangle rect)`	Returns `true` if the current `Rectangle` object intersects the `Rectangle` object passed as an argument, and `false` otherwise.

Table continued on following page

Method	Description
`boolean contains(Point p)`	Returns `true` if the current `Rectangle` object encloses the `Point` argument p, and `false` otherwise.
`boolean contains(int x, int y)`	Returns `true` if the current `Rectangle` object encloses the point (x, y), and `false` otherwise.

All of these methods will be useful when you are dealing with the contents of a Java window. You will then be dealing with points and rectangles describing the contents drawn in the window. For example, you might want to enable the user of your program to select some geometric shape from among those displayed on the screen, to work with it. You could use the `contains()` method to check whether the point corresponding to the current mouse cursor position is within any of the `Rectangle` objects that enclose each of the circles, lines, or whatever is displayed in the window. This would enable you to decide which of the objects displayed on the screen the user wants to choose.

You'll meet some other classes defining rectangles when you start drawing in a window in Chapter 19.

Visual Characteristics of a Component

Two things determine the visual appearance of a component: the representation of the component created by the Java code in the component class that is executed when the component is displayed and whatever you draw on the component. You can draw on a `Component` object by implementing its `paint()` method. You used this method in Chapter 1 to output the text for our applet. The `paint()` method is called automatically when the component needs to be drawn.

The need to draw a component can arise quite often for a variety of reasons—for example, your program may request that the area that the component occupies should be redrawn, or the user may resize the window containing the component. Your implementation of this method must include code to generate whatever you want drawn within the `Component` object. Note that the component itself—the `JButton` or `JFrame` or whatever—will be drawn for you. You only need to override the `paint()` method for anything additional that you want to draw on it. You'll be overriding the `paint()` method in Chapter 19 to draw in a window, so I'll leave further discussion of it until then.

You can alter some aspects of the appearance of the basic component by calling methods for the object. The following methods have an effect on the appearance of a `Component` object:

Method	Description
`void setBackground(Color aColor)`	Sets the background color to aColor. The background color is the color used for the basic component.
`Color getBackground()`	Retrieves the current background color.
`void setForeground(Color bColor)`	Sets the foreground color to bColor. The foreground color is the color used for anything appearing on the basic component, such as the label on a button, for example.

Method	Description
Color getForeground()	Retrieves the current foreground color
void setCursor(Cursor aCursor)	Sets the cursor for the component to aCursor. This sets the appearance of the cursor within the area occupied by the Component object.
void setFont(Font aFont)	Sets the font for the Component object.
Font getFont()	Returns the Font object used by the component.

To be able to make use of these properly, you need to understand what Color objects are, and you need to know how to create Cursor and Font objects.

Defining Color

A screen color is represented by an object of class Color. You define a color value as a combination of the three primary colors: red, green, and blue. They are usually expressed in that sequence, and are often referred to as **RGB values**. There are other ways of specifying colors in Java, but I'll discuss only RGB. You can specify the intensity of each primary color to be a value between 0 and 255. If the intensities of all three are 0, you have the color black, and if all three are set to 255 you have white. If only one intensity value is positive and the others are zero, you will have a pure primary color; for example, (0, 200, 0) will be a shade of green. You could define variables corresponding to these colors with the following statements:

```
Color myBlack = new Color(0,0,0);          // Color black
Color myWhite = new Color(255,255,255);    // Color white
Color myGreen = new Color(0,200,0);        // A shade of green
```

The three arguments to the constructor correspond to the intensities of the red, green, and blue components of the color, respectively. The Color class defines a number of standard color constants as public final static variables, whose RGB values are given in parentheses:

WHITE	(255, 255, 255)	RED	(255, 0, 0)
PINK	(255, 175, 175)	LIGHT_GRAY	(192, 192, 192)
ORANGE	(255, 200, 0)	MAGENTA	(255, 0, 255)
GRAY	(128, 128, 128)	YELLOW	(255, 255, 0)
CYAN	(0, 255, 255)	DARK_GRAY	(64, 64, 64)
GREEN	(0, 255, 0)	BLUE	(0, 0, 255)
BLACK	(0, 0, 0,)		

So if you want the window in the previous example to have a pink background, you could add the statement:

```
aWindow.setBackground(Color.PINK);
```

When you have created a `Color` object, you can brighten or darken the color it represents by calling its `brighter()` or `darker()` methods, which increase or decrease the intensity of the color components by a predefined factor:

```
thisColor.brighter();            // Brighten the color
thatColor.darker();              // Darken the color
```

The intensities of the component colors will always remain between 0 and 255. When you call `brighter` and a color component is already at 255, it will remain at that value. The other component intensities will be increased if they are less than 255. In a similar way, the `darker()` method will not change a component intensity if it is zero. The factor used for darkening a color component is 0.7. To brighten a color component, the intensity is increased by 1/0.7.

A fundamental point to remember here is that you can obtain only the colors available within the computer and the operating system environment on which your Java program is running. If you have a limited range of colors, the `brighter()` and `darker()` methods may appear to have no effect. Although you can create `Color` objects that are supposed to represent all kinds of colors, if your computer supports only 16 colors you will always end up with one of your 16. If your machine supports 24-bit color and this is supported in your system environment, then everything should be fine and dandy.

You can obtain any of the component intensities by calling `getRed()`, `getGreen()`, or `getBlue()` for a `Color` object. A color can also be obtained as a value of type `int` that is a composite of the red, green, and blue components of the color represented by a `Color` object using the `getRGB()` method. You can also create a `Color` object from a single RGB value of type `int`.

To compare two `Color` objects you can use the `equals()` method. For example, to compare two color objects `colorA` and `colorB`, you could write:

```
if(colorA.equals(colorB)) {
   // Do something...
}
```

The `equals()` method will return `true` if all three components of the two `Color` objects are equal. Don't use the `==` operator to compare `Color` objects. If you do, you are just determining whether the two `Color` object references refer to the same object. Applying the `==` operator to two different `Color` objects that represent the same color will result in `false`.

You could also use the `getRGB()` method for a `Color` object when you are comparing colors:

```
if(colorA.getRGB() == colorB.getRGB()) {
   // Do something....
}
```

This compares the two integer RGB values for equality, so here the `==` operator produces the correct result.

Note that the `Color` class also supports transparency of colors by storing an alpha compositing value in the range 0.0 to 1.0, where 0.0 is completely transparent and 1.0 is completely opaque.

System Colors

The `java.awt` package defines the class `SystemColor` as a subclass of the `Color` class. The `SystemColor` class encapsulates the standard colors that the native operating system uses for displaying various components. The class contains definitions for 24 `public final static` variables of type `SystemColor` that specify the standard system colors used by the operating system for a range of GUI components. For example, the system colors for a window are referenced by:

`window`	Defines the background color for a window
`window_text`	Defines the text color for a window
`window_border`	Defines the border color for a window

You can find the others covering colors used for menus, captions, controls, and so on, if you need them, by looking at the documentation for the `SystemColor` class.

If you want to compare a `SystemColor` value with a `Color` object you have created, then you must use the `getRGB()` method in the comparison. This is because the `SystemColor` class stores the colors internally in a way that makes use of the fields it inherits from the `Color` class differently from a normal `Color` object. For example, to see whether `colorA` corresponds to the system background color for a window, you could write:

```
if(colorA.getRGB() == SystemColor.window.getRGB()) {
    // colorA is the window background color...
}
```

Of course, because `SystemColor` is a subclass of the `Color` class, it inherits all the members of that class, including all the color constants that you saw in the previous section.

Creating Cursors

An object of the `java.awt.Cursor` class encapsulates a bitmap representation of the mouse cursor. The `Cursor` class contains a range of `final static` constants that specify standard cursor types. You use these to select or create a particular cursor. The standard cursor types are:

`DEFAULT_CURSOR`	`N_RESIZE_CURSOR`	`NE_RESIZE_CURSOR`
`CROSSHAIR_CURSOR`	`S_RESIZE_CURSOR`	`NW_RESIZE_CURSOR`
`WAIT_CURSOR`	`E_RESIZE_CURSOR`	`SE_RESIZE_CURSOR`
`TEXT_CURSOR`	`W_RESIZE_CURSOR`	`SW_RESIZE_CURSOR`
`HAND_CURSOR`	`MOVE_CURSOR`	

The resize cursors are the ones you see when resizing a window by dragging its boundaries. Note that these are not like the `Color` constants, which are `Color` objects — these constants are of type `int`, not type `Cursor`, and are intended to be used as arguments to a constructor.

To create a `Cursor` object representing a text cursor you could write:

```
Cursor myCursor = new Cursor(Cursor.TEXT_CURSOR);
```

Alternatively, you can retrieve a cursor of the predefined type using a static class method:

```
Cursor myCursor = Cursor.getPredefinedCursor(Cursor.TEXT_CURSOR);
```

This method is particularly useful when you don't want to store the Cursor object, but just want to pass it to a method, such as setCursor() for a Component object.

If you want to see what the standard cursors look like, you could add a cursor to the previous example, along with the pink background:

Try It Out   Color and Cursors

You can change the background color of the content pane for the application window and try out a different cursor. Make the following changes to TryWindow2.java, which is the example you created earlier that utilizes the toolkit:

```
import javax.swing.JFrame;
import java.awt.Toolkit;
import java.awt.Dimension;
import java.awt.Color;
import java.awt.Cursor;

public class TryWindow4 {
  // The window object
  static JFrame aWindow = new JFrame("This is the Window Title");

  public static void main(String[] args)
  {
    Toolkit theKit = aWindow.getToolkit();        // Get the window toolkit
    Dimension wndSize = theKit.getScreenSize();   // Get screen size

    // Set the position to screen center & size to half screen size
    aWindow.setBounds(wndSize.width/4, wndSize.height/4,    // Position
                      wndSize.width/2, wndSize.height/2);   // Size
    aWindow.setDefaultCloseOperation(JFrame.EXIT_ON_CLOSE);
    aWindow.setCursor(Cursor.getPredefinedCursor(Cursor.CROSSHAIR_CURSOR));
    aWindow.getContentPane().setBackground(Color.PINK);
    aWindow.setVisible(true);                      // Display the window
  }
}
```

You can try all the cursors by plugging in each of the standard cursor names in turn. You could also try out a few variations on the background color.

Selecting Fonts

An object of type Font represents a font. The Font class is actually quite complicated, so I'll only scratch the surface of the class enough for your needs here. The Font class differentiates between a **character**— the letter uppercase Q, say — and a **glyph**, which is the shape defining its appearance when it is displayed or printed. In general, a given character in one font will have a different glyph in a different font. For fonts corresponding to many languages — German, French, or Finnish, for example — a character may involve more than one glyph to display it. This is typically the case for characters that involve

diacritic marks, which are additional graphics attached to a character. The letter *ä*, for example, combines the normal letter *a* with an umlaut, the two dots over it, so it may be represented by two glyphs, one for the appearance of the letter and the other for the appearance of the umlaut. A Font object contains a table that maps the Unicode value for each character to the glyph code or codes that create the visual representation of the character.

To create a Font object you must supply the font name, the style of the font, and the point size. For example, consider the following statement:

```
Font myFont = new Font("Serif", Font.ITALIC, 12);
```

This defines a 12-point Times Roman italic font. The other options you could use for the style are PLAIN and BOLD. The name you have given to the font here, "Serif", is a **logical font name**. Other logical font names you could have used are "Dialog", "DialogInput", "Monospaced", or "SansSerif". Instead of a logical font name, you can supply a physical font face name — the name of a particular font, such as "Times New Roman" or "Palatino". Swing components work with either logical fonts or physical fonts, whereas AWT components can use only logical fonts. Logical fonts have the advantage that they will work on any platform, so you can use a logical font without needing to verify its availability. However, the appearance of a logical font may vary from one platform to another. Using physical fonts provides a lot more flexibility, but the font you are using must be available on the platform on which your code is executing.

It is important to keep in mind that fonts are for presenting characters visually, on the screen or on a printer, for example. Although Java has a built-in capability to represent characters by Unicode codes, it doesn't have any fonts because it doesn't display or print characters itself. The responsibility for this rests entirely with your operating system. Although your Java programs can store strings of Japanese or Tibetan characters, if your operating system doesn't have fonts for these characters you can't display or print them. Therefore, to display or print text in the way that you want, you need to know what font face names are available in the system on which your code is running. I will come back to this in a moment.

You can specify combined font styles by ORing or adding them together because each style is a single-bit integer. If you want myFont to be BOLD and ITALIC you would have written the statement as follows:

```
Font myFont = new Font("Serif", Font.ITALIC + Font.BOLD, 12);
```

You retrieve the style and size of an existing Font object by calling its methods getStyle() and getSize(), both of which return a value of type int. You can also check the individual font style for a Font object with the methods isPlain(), isBold(), and isItalic(). Each of these methods returns a boolean value indicating whether the Font object has that style.

Before you create a font using a particular font face name, you need to know whether the font is available on the system where your code is executing. For this you need to use a method, getAllFonts(), in the GraphicsEnvironment class defined in the java.awt package. You met this class earlier when you were centering a window. You could obtain an array of the fonts available as follows:

```
GraphicsEnvironment e = GraphicsEnvironment.getLocalGraphicsEnvironment();
Font[] fonts = e.getAllFonts();              // Get the fonts
```

You get a reference to the GraphicsEnvironment object for the current machine by calling the static method getLocalGraphicsEnvironment(). You then use the reference that is returned to call its getAllFonts() method. The getAllFonts() method returns an array of Font objects consisting of those available on the current system. You can then check this list for the font you want to use. Each of the Font instances in the array will be of a 1-point size, and since 1 point is approximately 1/72 of an inch, or 0.353 mm, you will typically want to change this unless your screen and eyesight are really exceptional. To change the size and/or style of a font, you call its deriveFont() method. This method comes in three versions, each of which returns a new Font object with the specified size and/or style:

deriveFont() Method	Description
deriveFont(int Style)	Creates a new Font object with the style specified — one of PLAIN, BOLD, ITALIC, or BOLD+ITALIC
deriveFont(float size)	Creates a new Font object with the size specified
deriveFont(int Style, float size)	Creates a new Font object with the style and size specified

To use the last font from the array of Font objects to create an equivalent 12-point font you could write:

```
Font newFont = fonts[fonts.length-1].deriveFont(12.0f);
```

If you look in the documentation for the Font class, you will see that there is a fourth version of deriveFont() that involves an object of type java.awt.geom.AffineTransform, but I'll defer discussion of AffineTransform objects until Chapter 20.

Getting a Font object for every font in the system can be a time-consuming process if you have many fonts installed. A much faster alternative is to get the font names and then use one of these to create the Font object that you require. You can get the face names for all the fonts in a system like this:

```
GraphicsEnvironment e = GraphicsEnvironment.getLocalGraphicsEnvironment();
String[] fontnames = e.getAvailableFontFamilyNames();
```

The array fontnames will contain the names of all the font faces available, and you can use one or more of these to create the Font objects you need.

Try It Out Getting the List of Fonts

This program will output your screen's size and resolution, as well as the list of font family names installed on your machine:

```
import java.awt.Toolkit;
import java.awt.GraphicsEnvironment;
import java.awt.Font;
import java.awt.Dimension;

public class FontInfo {
  public static void main(String[] args) {
    Toolkit theKit = Toolkit.getDefaultToolkit();

    System.out.println("\nScreen Resolution: "
                     + theKit.getScreenResolution() + " dots per inch");
```

```
            Dimension screenDim = theKit.getScreenSize();
            System.out.println("Screen Size: "
                              + screenDim.width + " by "
                              + screenDim.height + " pixels");

            GraphicsEnvironment e = GraphicsEnvironment.getLocalGraphicsEnvironment();
            String[] fontnames = e.getAvailableFontFamilyNames();
            System.out.println("\nFonts available on this platform: ");
            int count = 0;
            for (String fontname : fontnames) {
              System.out.printf("%-30s", fontname);
              if(++count % 3 == 0) {
                System.out.println();
              }
            }
        return;
        }
    }
```

On my system I get the following output:

```
Screen Resolution: 96 dots per inch
Screen Size: 1024 by 768 pixels

18thCentury              Alien Encounters        Almonte Snow
Arial                    Arial Black             Arial Narrow
Arial Unicode MS         Asimov                  Baby Kruffy
Balloonist               Batang                  BN Jinx
BN Machine               Bobcat                  Book Antiqua
Bookman Old Style        Candles                 Century
Century Gothic           Chinyen                 Comic Sans MS
Courier New              Cracked Johnnie         Creepygirl
Dialog                   DialogInput             Digifit
```

. . . plus many more font names.

How It Works

You first get a `Toolkit` object by calling the `static` method `getDefaultToolkit()` — this is the key to the other information. The `getScreenResolution()` method returns the number of pixels per inch as a value of type `int`. The `getScreenSize()` method returns a `Dimension` object that specifies the width and height of the screen in pixels.

You use the `getAvailableFontFamilyNames()` method discussed previously to get a `String` array containing the names of the fonts, which you output to the command line.

Font Metrics

Every component has a `getFontMetrics()` method that you can use to retrieve **font metrics** — the wealth of dimensional data about a font. You pass a `Font` object as an argument to the method, and it returns an object of type `FontMetrics` that you can use to obtain data relating to the particular font. For example, if `aWindow` is a `Frame` object and `myFont` is a `Font` object, you could obtain a `FontMetrics` object corresponding to the font with the following statement:

```
FontMetrics metrics = aWindow.getFontMetrics(myFont);
```

You could use the `getFont()` method for a component to explore the characteristics of the font that the component contains. For example:

```
FontMetrics metrics = aWindow.getFontMetrics(aWindow.getFont());
```

You can now call any of the following `FontMetrics` methods for the object to get at the basic dimensions of the font:

Method	Description
int getAscent()	Returns the **ascent** of the font, which is the distance from the baseline to the top of the majority of the characters in the font. The **baseline** is the line on which the characters rest. Depending on the font, some characters can extend beyond the ascent.
int getMaxAscent()	Returns the maximum ascent for the font. No character will exceed this ascent.
int getDescent()	Returns the **descent** of the font, which is the distance from the baseline to the bottom of most of the font characters that extend below the baseline. Depending on the font, some characters may extend beyond the descent for the font.
int getMaxDescent()	Returns the maximum descent of the characters in the font. No character will exceed this descent.
int getLeading()	Returns the **leading** for the font, which is the line spacing for the font — that is the spacing between the bottom of one line of text and the top of the next. The term originated when type was actually made of lead, and there was a strip of lead between one line of type and the next when a page was typeset.
int getHeight()	Returns the height of the font, which is defined as the sum of the ascent, the descent, and the leading.

Figure 17-9 shows how the dimensions relate to the font.

The **advance width** for a character is the distance from the reference point of the character to the reference point of the next character. The **reference point** for a character is on the baseline at the left edge of the character. Each character will have its own advance width, which you can obtain by calling a `FontMetrics` method `charWidth()`. For example, to obtain the advance width for the character `'X'`, the following statement could be used:

```
int widthX = metrics.charWidth('X');
```

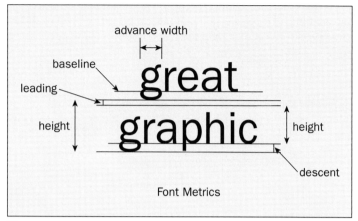

Figure 17-9

You can also obtain the advance widths for all the characters in the font as an array of type `int` with the method `getWidths()`:

```
int[] widths = metrics.getWidths();
```

The numerical value for the character is used to index the array, so you can get the advance width for the character `'X'` with the expression `widths['X']`. If you just want the maximum advance width for the characters in the font, you can call the method `getMaxAdvance()`. Lastly, you can get the total advance width for a `String` object by passing the object to the method `stringWidth()`. The advance width is returned as a value of type `int`. It's important to appreciate that the advance width for a string is not necessarily the sum of the widths of the characters that it contains.

Although you now know a great deal about how to create and manipulate fonts, you haven't actually created and used one. You'll remedy this after you have a feel for what Swing components can do and have learned a little about using containers.

Swing Components

Swing components all have the `JComponent` class as a base, which itself extends the `Component` class to add the following capability:

❑ Supports pluggable look-and-feel for components, allowing you to change the look-and-feel programmatically, or implement your own look-and-feel for all components displayed.

❑ Support for tooltips — a **tooltip** being a message describing the purpose of a component when the mouse cursor lingers over it. Tooltips are defined by the `JTooltip` class.

❑ Support for automatic scrolling in a list, a table, or a tree when a component is dragged with the mouse.

❑ Special debugging support for graphics, providing component rendering in slow motion so you can see what is happening.

❑ Component classes can be easily extended to create your own custom components.

All the Swing component classes are defined in the `javax.swing` package and have class names that begin with `J`. There are quite a few Swing components, so I'll give you an overview of what's available and how the classes relate to one another and then go into the detail of particular components when you use them in examples.

Buttons

The Swing button classes in the `javax.swing` package define various kinds of buttons operated by clicking with a mouse. The button classes have the `AbstractButton` class as a base, as shown in Figure 17-10.

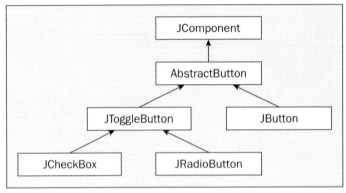

Figure 17-10

The `JButton` class defines a regular pushbutton that you would use as a dialog button—OK and Cancel buttons, for example—or in a toolbar, where the buttons might provide alternatives to using menu items.

Figure 17-11

Figure 17-11 is an example of a JButton object as it might be used in a dialog. This component is not the default appearance of a button but has a border of type BevelBorder added to it.

The `JToolBar` class is used in conjunction with the `JButton` class to create a toolbar containing buttons. A toolbar is dockable without any additional programming effort on your part, as you'll see.

The JToggleButton class defines a two-state button, pressed or not, and two more specialized versions are defined by JCheckBox and JRadioButton. Radio buttons defined as JRadioButton objects generally operate in a group so that only one button can be in the pressed state at any one time. This grouping is established by adding the JRadioButton object to a ButtonGroup object that takes care of the state of the buttons in the group.

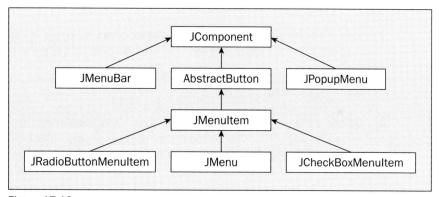

Figure 17-12

A JCheckBox object is a button with a square checkbox to the left (see Figure 17-12). Clicking on the checkbox changes its state from checked to unchecked or vice versa.

All the buttons can be displayed with a text label, an icon, or both.

Menus

The Swing components include support for pop-up or context menus as well as menu bars. The classes defining elements of a menu are shown in Figure 17-13.

Figure 17-13

The JMenuBar class defines a **menu bar** usually found at the top of an application window. A JMenu object represents a top-level menu item on a menu bar that drops down a list of menu items when it is clicked. The items in a menu are defined by the JMenuItem class. The JPopupMenu class defines a context menu that is typically implemented to appear at the current cursor position when the right mouse button is clicked. A JCheckBoxMenuItem component is a menu item with a checkbox that is ticked when the item is selected. The JRadioButtonMenuItem class defines a menu item that is part of a group where only one item can be selected at any time. The group is created by adding JRadioButtonMenuItem objects to a ButtonGroup object. You'll be implementing a menu in an application and an applet later in this chapter.

Text Components

The capability of the Swing text components is very wide indeed. The classes in the javax.swing packages that represent text components are shown in Figure 17-14. Like all Swing components, they have the JComponent class as a base.

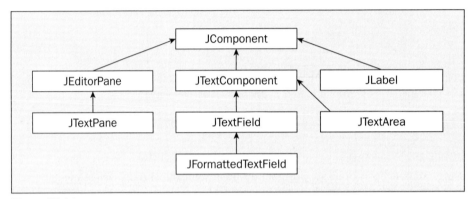

Figure 17-14

Figure 17-15
The most elementary text component is a JLabel object, as shown in Figure 17-15. A JLabel component is passive and does not react to input events so you can't edit it.

A JTextField component looks similar to a label in that it displays a single line of text, but in this case it is editable. An example is shown in Figure 17-16.

10-Apr-2004
Figure 17-16
A JFormattedTextField component is a JTextField component that can control and format the data that is displayed or entered. It can supply automatic formatting in many instances. In Figure 17-16, it has automatically displayed a Date object as a date.

Tis a dog's delight to bark and bite
And little birds to sing,
And if you sit on a red hot brick,
Tis a sign of an early spring!

The JTextArea class defines a component that allows editing of multiline text, as shown in Figure 17-17. A JTextArea component does not support scrolling directly, but it's easy to add scrollbars by placing the JTextArea component in a JScrollPane container.

Figure 17-17

The JEditorPane and JTextPane components are a different order of complexity from the others and enable you to implement sophisticated editing facilities relatively easily. The JEditorPane supports editing of plaintext, text in HTML, and RTF (Rich Text Format). The JTextPane class extends JEditorPane and enables you to embed images or other components within the text managed by the component.

Other Swing Components

Other Swing components you will use regularly include the JPanel component. The JPanel class defines something like a physical panel that you can use as a container to group a set of components. For example, you might use two `JPanel` objects to support two separate groups of `JButton` components in the content pane of an application window.

Shadrach
Meshak
Abednego

Figure 17-18

The `JList` and JTable components are also very useful. A `JList` component that implements a list of items is shown in Figure 17-18 with a line border around it.

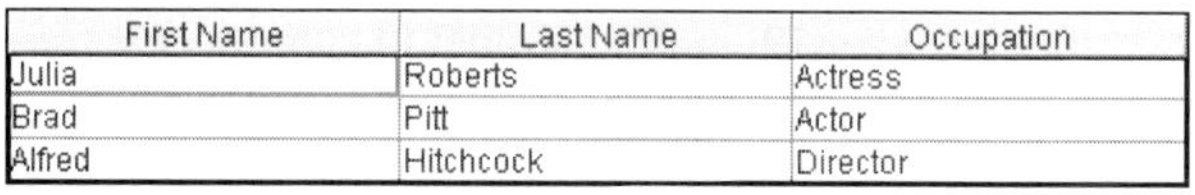

First Name	Last Name	Occupation
Julia	Roberts	Actress
Brad	Pitt	Actor
Alfred	Hitchcock	Director

Figure 17-19

Figure 17-19 shows a `JTable` component that implements a table of items from which you can select a row, a column, or a single element.

A `JTable` component automatically takes care of reordering the columns when a column is dragged to a new position using the mouse.

In principle, any component can have a border added, and the `javax.swing.borders` package contains eight classes that represent different kinds of borders you can use for a component. However, you can also place a component to which you want to add a border in a `JPanel` container, and add the border to the `JPanel` object. You'll be using `JPanel` containers quite a lot throughout the rest of the book.

I have not introduced all the Swing component classes by any means, and you'll be meeting a few more as you progress through the rest of the chapters.

Using Containers

A container is any component of a type that has the `Container` class as a base; so all the Swing components are containers. The `Container` class is the direct base class for the `Window` class, and it provides the capability for a window to contain other components. Since the `Container` class is an `abstract` class, you cannot create instances of `Container`. Instead, it's objects of the subclasses such as `Window`, `JFrame`, or `JDialog` that inherit the capability to contain other components.

> Note that a container cannot contain an object of the class `Window`, or an object of any of the classes derived from `Window`. An object of any other class that is derived from `Component` can be added to a container.

The components within a container are displayed within the area occupied by the container on the display screen. A dialog box, for example, might contain a `JList` object offering some options; `JCheckbox` objects offering other options and `JButton` objects representing buttons enabling the user to end the dialog or enter the selections — all these components would appear within the boundaries of the dialog box. Of course, for the contained components to be visible, the container must itself be displayed, as the container effectively "owns" its components. The container also controls how its embedded components are laid out by means of an object called a **layout manager**.

Before I introduce you to what a layout manager is and how the layout of the components in a container is determined, let's consider the basic methods that the `Container` class defines that are available to all containers.

You can find out about the components in a `Container` object by using the following methods that are defined in the `Container` class:

Method	Description
`int getComponentCount()`	Returns a count of the number of components contained by the current component.
`Component getComponent(int index)`	Returns the component identified by the `index` value. The `index` value is an array index so it must be between 0 and one less than the number of components contained; otherwise, an `ArrayIndex OutOfBoundsException` will be thrown.
`Component[] getComponents()`	Returns an array of all the components in the current container.

You can also obtain a reference to a component that contains a given point within the area occupied by the container by calling the `getComponentAt()` method, with the *x* and *y* coordinates of the point as arguments. If more than one component contains the point, a reference to the component closest to index 0 in the container will be returned.

If you have a `Container` object, `content`, perhaps the content pane of a `JFrame` window, you could iterate through the components in the `Container` with the following statements:

```
Component component = null;                             // Stores a Component
int numComponents = content.getComponentCount();        // Get the count

for(int i = 0; i < numComponents; i++) {
   component = content.getComponent(i);                 // Get each component
   // Do something with component...
}
```

This retrieves the components in `content` one at a time in the `for` loop. Alternatively, you could retrieve them from the container all at once:

```
Component[] theComponents = content.getComponents();   // Get all components

for(Component component : theComponents) {
   // Do something with component...
}
```

Adding Components to a Container

The components that you add to a container are recorded in an array within the `Container` object. The array is increased in size when necessary to accommodate as many components as are present. To add a component to a container, you use the add() method. The Container class defines the following four overloaded versions of the add() method:

add() Method	Description
Component add(Component c)	Adds the component c to the end of the list of components stored in the container. The return value is c.
Component add(Component c, int index)	Adds the component c to the list of components in the container at the position specified by index. If index is -1, the component is added to the end of the list. If the value of index is not -1, it must be less than the number of components in the container and greater than or equal to 0. The return value is c.
void add(Component c, Object constraints)	Adds the component c to the end of the list of components stored in the container. The position of the component relative to the container is subject to the constraints defined by the second parameter. You'll learn about constraints in the next section.
void add(Component c, Object constraints, int index)	Adds the component c to the list of components in the container at the position specified by index and the position subject to constraints. If index is -1, the component is added to the end of the list. If the value of index is not -1, it must be less than the number of components in the container and greater than or equal to 0.

Note that adding a component does not displace any components already in the container. When you add a component at a given position, other components are moved in the sequence to make room for the new one. However, a component can be in only one container at a time. Adding a component to a container that is already in another container will remove it from the original container.

Before you can try adding components to a container, you need to understand the constraints that appear in some of the add() methods and look at how the layout of components in a container is controlled.

Container Layout Managers

As I said earlier, an object called a **layout manager** determines the way that components are arranged in a container. All containers will have a default layout manager, but you can choose a different layout manager when necessary. Many layout manager classes are provided in the java.awt and javax.swing packages, so I'll introduce those that you are most likely to need. It is also possible to create your own layout manager classes, but creating layout managers is beyond the scope of this book. The layout manager for a container determines the position and size of all the components in the container, so you should not generally change the size and position of such components yourself; just let the layout manager take care of it.

Since the classes that define layout managers all implement the LayoutManager interface, you can use a variable of type LayoutManager to store any of them if necessary. I'll introduce six layout manager classes in a little more detail. The names of these classes and the basic arrangements that they provide are as follows:

Layout Manager	Description
FlowLayout	Places components in successive rows in a container, fitting as many on each row as possible and starting on the next row as soon as a row is full. This works in much the same way as your text processor places words on a line. Its primary use is for arranging buttons, although you can use it with other components. It is the default layout manager for JPanel objects.
BorderLayout	Places components against any of the four borders of the container and in the center. The component in the center fills the available space. This layout manager is the default for the contentPane in a JFrame, JDialog, or JApplet object.
CardLayout	Places components in a container one on top of the other — like a deck of cards. Only the "top" component is visible at any one time.
GridLayout	Places components in the container in a rectangular grid with the number of rows and columns that you specify.
GridBagLayout	This also places the components into an arrangement of rows and columns, but the rows and columns can vary in length. This is a complicated layout manager with a lot of flexibility in how you control where components are placed in a container.
BoxLayout	This arranges components either in a row or in a column. In either case the components are clipped to fit if necessary, rather than wrapping to the next row or column. The BoxLayout manager is the default for the Box container class.
SpringLayout	Allows components to have their position defined by "springs" or "struts" fixed to an edge of the container or another component in the container.

The BoxLayout, SpringLayout, and Box classes are defined in the javax.swing package. The other layout manager classes in the list above are defined in java.awt.

One question you might ask is why do you need layout managers at all? Why can't you just place components at some given position in a container? The basic reason is to ensure that the GUI elements for your Java program are displayed properly in every possible Java environment. Layout managers automatically adjust the size and positions of components to fit within the space available. If you fix the size and position of each of the components, they could run into one another and overlap if the screen area available to your program is reduced.

To set the layout manager for a `Container` object, you can call its `setLayout()` method. For example, you could change the layout manager for the `Container` object `aWindow` of type `JFrame` from its default `BorderLayout` layout manager to flow layout with the following statements:

```
FlowLayout flow = new FlowLayout();
aWindow.getContentPane().setLayout(flow);
```

Remember that components that you want to display in the client area of a `JFrame` object should be added to its content pane. The same goes for `JDialog` and `JApplet` objects. In fact, if you use the `add()` method for a `JFrame`, `JDialog`, or `JApplet` object to add a component, it will be redirected to the content pane, so everything will be as it should be. This convenience facility is there for consistency with similar AWT components. However, for some other operations — setting the background color, for example — you *must* call the method belonging to the content pane object for things to turn out as you expect. For this reason I think it's better to explicitly perform all operations on the content pane rather than rely on redirection by the parent frame object. That way you won't forget that it's the content pane you are working with.

With some containers you can set the layout manager in the constructor for that container, as you'll see in later examples. Let's look at how the layout managers work, and some examples of how you might use them in practice.

The Flow Layout Manager

The flow layout manager places components in a row, and when the row is full, it automatically spills components onto the next row. The default positioning of the row of components is centered in the container, and the default orientation is from left to right. You have five possible row-positioning options that you specify by constants of type `int` that are defined in the `FlowLayout` class. These are `LEFT`, `RIGHT`, `CENTER`, `LEADING`, and `TRAILING`. `LEADING` and `TRAILING` specify the edge of the component to which the row should be justified. The effects of the first three on the alignment of a row of components are what you would expect. The `CENTER` option is the default. By default, components in a row are separated by a five-unit gap and successive rows are separated by the same distance.

The flow layout manager is very easy to use, so let's jump straight in and see it working in an example.

Try It Out   Using a Flow Layout Manager

As I said earlier, this layout manager is used primarily to arrange a few components whose relative position is unimportant. Let's implement a `TryFlowLayout` program based on the `TryWindow` example:

```
import javax.swing.JFrame;
import javax.swing.JButton;

import java.awt.Toolkit;
import java.awt.Dimension;
import java.awt.Container;
import java.awt.FlowLayout;

public class TryFlowLayout {
  // The window object
  static JFrame aWindow = new JFrame("This is a Flow Layout");
```

```
   public static void main(String[] args) {
      Toolkit theKit = aWindow.getToolkit();          // Get the window toolkit
      Dimension wndSize = theKit.getScreenSize();     // Get screen size
      // Set the position to screen center & size to half screen size
      aWindow.setBounds(wndSize.width/4, wndSize.height/4,      // Position
                        wndSize.width/2, wndSize.height/2);    // Size
      aWindow.setDefaultCloseOperation(JFrame.EXIT_ON_CLOSE);

      FlowLayout flow = new FlowLayout();              // Create a layout manager
      Container content = aWindow.getContentPane();    // Get the content pane
      content.setLayout(flow);                         // Set the container layout mgr

      // Now add six button components
      for(int i = 1; i <= 6; i++)
         content.add(new JButton("Press " + i));       // Add a Button to content pane

      aWindow.setVisible(true);                        // Display the window
   }
}
```

The new or modified code compared to the `TryWindow` example is highlighted.

How It Works

The new code is quite simple. You create a `FlowLayout` object and make this the layout manager for `aWindow` by calling `setLayout()`. You then add six `JButton` components of a default size to `aWindow` in the loop.

If you compile and run the program, you should get a window similar to the one shown in Figure 17-20:

Figure 17-20

The `Button` objects are positioned by the layout manager flow. As you can see, they have been added to the first row in the window, and the row is centered. You can confirm that the row is centered and see how the layout manger automatically spills the components onto the next row once a row is full by reducing the size of the window by dragging the window boundaries. The result on my computer is shown in Figure 17-21.

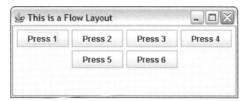

Figure 17-21

Here the second row is clearly centered. Each button component has been set to its preferred size, which comfortably accommodates the text for the label. The centering is determined by the alignment constraint for the layout manager, which defaults to CENTER.

It can also be set to RIGHT or LEFT by using a different constructor. For example, you could have created the layout manager with the statement:

```
FlowLayout flow = new FlowLayout(FlowLayout.LEFT);
```

The flow layout manager then left aligns each row of components in the container. If you run the program with this definition and resize the window, you should be able to make it will look like Figure 17-22.

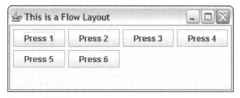

Figure 17-22

Now the buttons are clearly left aligned. I have reduced the width of the window so two of the buttons have spilled from the first row to the second because there is insufficient space across the width of the window to accommodate them all.

Changing the Gap

The flow layout manager in the previous examples applies a default gap of 5 pixels between components in a row, and between one row and the next. You can choose values for the horizontal and vertical gaps by using yet another `FlowLayout` constructor. You can set the horizontal gap to 20 pixels and the vertical gap to 30 pixels in the last example with the statement:

```
FlowLayout flow = new FlowLayout(FlowLayout.LEFT, 20, 30);
```

If you rerun the program with this definition of the layout manager, you should see a window with the buttons arranged as in Figure 17-23.

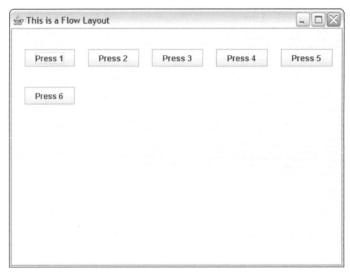

Figure 17-23

You can also set the gaps between components and rows explicitly by calling the setHgap() or the setVgap() method. To set the horizontal gap to 35 pixels, you would write:

```
flow.setHgap(35);                         // Set the horizontal gap
```

Don't be misled by this. You can't get differential spacing between components by setting the gap before adding each component to a container. The last values for the gaps between components that you set for a layout manager will apply to all the components in a container. This is because the layout is recalculated dynamically each time the container is displayed. Of course, many different events may necessitate a container being redisplayed while an application is running. The methods getHgap() and getVgap() will return the current setting for the horizontal or vertical gap as a value of type int.

The initial size at which the application window is displayed is determined by the values you pass to the setBounds() method for the JFrame object. If you want the window to assume a size that just accommodates the components it contains, you can call the pack() method for the JFrame object. Add the following line immediately before the call to setVisible():

```
aWindow.pack();
```

If you recompile and run the example again, the application window should fit the components and appear as shown in Figure 17-24.

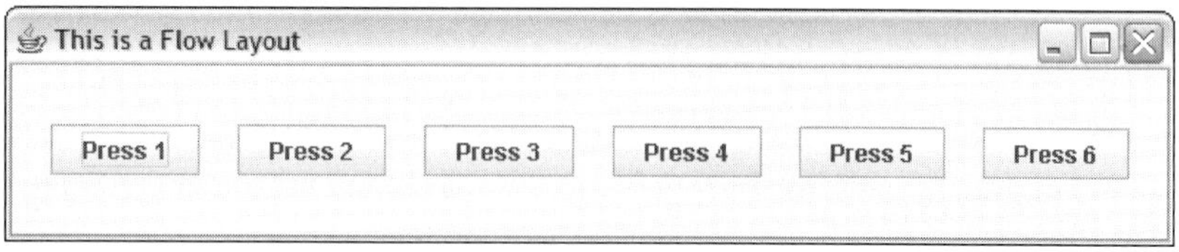

Figure 17-24

As I've said, you add components to an applet created as a `JApplet` object in the same way as for a `JFrame` application window. You can verify this by adding some buttons to an example of an applet. You can try out a `Font` object and add a border to the buttons to brighten them up a bit at the same time.

Try It Out   Adding Buttons to an Applet

You can define the class for an applet displaying buttons as follows:

```java
import javax.swing.JButton;
import javax.swing.JApplet;

import java.awt.Font;
import java.awt.Container;
import java.awt.FlowLayout;

import javax.swing.border.BevelBorder;

public class TryApplet extends JApplet {
  public void init() {
    Container content = getContentPane();                    // Get content pane
    content.setLayout(new FlowLayout(FlowLayout.RIGHT)); // Set layout

    JButton button;                                          // Stores a button
    Font[] fonts = { new Font("Serif", Font.ITALIC, 10), // Two fonts
                     new Font("Dialog", Font.PLAIN, 14)
                   };

    BevelBorder edge = new BevelBorder(BevelBorder.RAISED); // Bevelled border

    // Add the buttons using alternate fonts
    for(int i = 1; i <= 6; i++) {
      content.add(button = new JButton("Press " + i));  // Add the button
      button.setFont(fonts[i%2]);                       // One of our own fonts
      button.setBorder(edge);                           // Set the button border
    }
  }
}
```

Of course, to run the applet you will need an `.html` file containing the following:

```html
<APPLET CODE="TryApplet.class" WIDTH=300 HEIGHT=200>
</APPLET>
```

This specifies the width and height of the applet — you can use your own values here if you wish. You can save the file as `TryApplet.htm`.

Once you have compiled the applet source code using `javac`, you can execute it with the `appletviewer` program by entering the following command from the folder containing the .htm file and the `.class` file:

```
appletviewer TryApplet.htm
```

You should see the Applet Viewer window displaying the applet as in Figure 17-25.

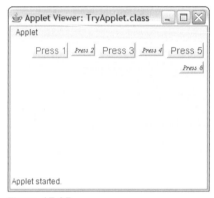

Figure 17-25

The arrangement of the buttons is now right-justified in the flow layout. You have the button labels alternating between the two fonts that you created. The buttons also look more like buttons with a beveled edge.

How It Works

As you saw in Chapter 1, an applet is executed rather differently from a Java program, and it is not really an independent program at all. The browser (or `appletviewer` in this case) initiates and controls the execution of the applet. An applet does not require a `main()` method. To execute the applet, the browser first creates an instance of our applet class, `TryApplet`, and then calls the `init()` method for it. This method is inherited from the `Applet` class (the base for `JApplet`) and you typically override this method to provide your own initialization.

Before creating the buttons, you create a `BevelBorder` object that you'll use to specify the border for each button. In the loop that adds the buttons to the content pane for the applet, you select one or other of the `Font` objects you have created, depending on whether the loop index is even or odd and then set `edge` as the border by calling the `setBorder()` member. This would be the same for any component. Note how the size of each button is automatically adjusted to accommodate the button label. Of course, the fonts in the example are both logical fonts, so they'll be available on every system. If you want to try physical fonts, choose two from those that you have installed on your system.

The buttons look much better with raised edges. If you wanted them to appear sunken, you would specify `BevelBorder.LOWERED` as the constructor argument. You might like to try out a `SoftBevelBorder`, too. All you need to do is use the class name, `SoftBevelBorder`, when creating the border. Don't forget the import statement for the class name; the border classes are defined in the `javax.swing.border` package.

Using a Border Layout Manager

The border layout manager is intended to place up to five components in a container. With this layout manager you can place components on any of the four borders of the container and in the center. Only one component can be at each position. If you add a component at a position that is already occupied, the previous component will be displaced. A border is selected by specifying a constraint that can be NORTH, SOUTH, EAST, WEST, or CENTER. These are all `final static` constants defined in the `BorderLayout` class.

You can't specify the constraints in the `BorderLayout` constructor since a different constraint has to be applied to each component. You specify the position of each component in a container when you add it using the `add()` method. You can modify the earlier application example to add five buttons to the content pane of the application window in a border layout:

Try It Out   **Testing the BorderLayout Manager**

Make the following changes to `TryFlowLayout.java` to try out the border layout manager and exercise another border class:

```java
import javax.swing.JFrame;
import javax.swing.JButton;

import java.awt.Toolkit;
import java.awt.Dimension;
import java.awt.Container;
import java.awt.BorderLayout;

import javax.swing.border.EtchedBorder;

public class TryBorderLayout {
  // The window object
  static JFrame aWindow = new JFrame("This is a Border Layout");

  public static void main(String[] args) {
    Toolkit theKit = aWindow.getToolkit();        // Get the window toolkit
    Dimension wndSize = theKit.getScreenSize();  // Get screen size

    // Set the position to screen center & size to half screen size
    aWindow.setBounds(wndSize.width/4, wndSize.height/4,   // Position
                      wndSize.width/2, wndSize.height/2);  // Size
    aWindow.setDefaultCloseOperation(JFrame.EXIT_ON_CLOSE);

    BorderLayout border = new BorderLayout();           // Create a layout manager
    Container content = aWindow.getContentPane();      // Get the content pane
    content.setLayout(border);                          // Set the container layout mgr
    EtchedBorder edge = new EtchedBorder(EtchedBorder.RAISED);  // Button border
    // Now add five JButton components and set their borders
    JButton button;
```

```
        content.add(button = new JButton("EAST"), BorderLayout.EAST);
        button.setBorder(edge);
        content.add(button = new JButton("WEST"), BorderLayout.WEST);
        button.setBorder(edge);
        content.add(button = new JButton("NORTH"), BorderLayout.NORTH);
        button.setBorder(edge);
        content.add(button = new JButton("SOUTH"), BorderLayout.SOUTH);
        button.setBorder(edge);
        content.add(button = new JButton("CENTER"), BorderLayout.CENTER);
        button.setBorder(edge);

      aWindow.setVisible(true);                           // Display the window
    }
  }
```

If you compile and execute the example, you'll see the window shown in Figure 17-26.

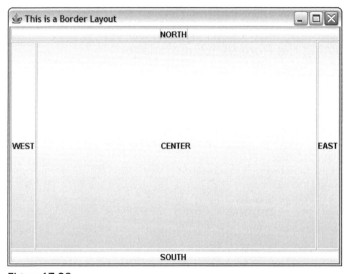

Figure 17-26

You can see here how a raised `EtchedBorder` edge to the buttons looks.

How It Works

Components laid out with a border layout manager are extended to fill the space available in the container. The "NORTH" and "SOUTH" buttons are the full width of the window and the "EAST" and "WEST" buttons occupy the height remaining unoccupied once the "NORTH" and "SOUTH" buttons are in place. It always works like this, regardless of the sequence in which you add the buttons — the "NORTH" and "SOUTH" components occupy the full width of the container and the "CENTER" component takes up the remaining space. If there are no "NORTH" and "SOUTH" components, the "EAST" and "WEST" components will extend to the full height of the container.

The width of the `"EAST"` and `"WEST"` buttons is determined by the space required to display the button labels. Similarly, the `"NORTH"` and `"SOUTH"` buttons are determined by the height of the characters in the labels.

You can alter the spacing between components by passing arguments to the `BorderLayout` constructor — the default gaps are zero. For example, you could set the horizontal gap to 20 pixels and the vertical gap to 30 pixels with the following statement:

```
content.setLayout(new BorderLayout(20, 30));
```

Like the flow layout manager, you can also set the gaps individually by calling the methods `setHgap()` and `setVgap()` for the `BorderLayout` object. For example:

```
BorderLayout border = new BorderLayout();    // Construct the object
content.setLayout(border);                   // Set the layout
border.setHgap(20);                          // Set horizontal gap
```

This sets the horizontal gap between the components to 20 pixels and leaves the vertical gap at the default value of zero. You can also retrieve the current values for the gaps with the `getHgap()` and `getVgap()` methods.

Using a Card Layout Manager

The card layout manager generates a stack of components, one on top of the other. The first component that you add to the container will be at the top of the stack, and therefore visible, and the last one will be at the bottom. You can create a `CardLayout` object with the default constructor, `CardLayout()`, or you can specify horizontal and vertical gaps as arguments to the constructor. The gaps in this case are between the edge of the component and the boundary of the container. You can see how this works in an applet:

Try It Out   Dealing Components

Because of the way a card layout works, you need a way to interact with the applet to switch from one component to the next. You'll implement this by enabling mouse events to be processed, but I won't explain the code that does this in detail here. I'll leave that to the next chapter.

Try the following code:

```
import javax.swing.JApplet;
import javax.swing.JButton;

import java.awt.Container;
import java.awt.CardLayout;

import java.awt.event.ActionEvent;                     // Classes to handle events
import java.awt.event.ActionListener;

public class TryCardLayout extends JApplet implements ActionListener {
  CardLayout card = new CardLayout(50,50);              // Create layout

  public void init() {
    Container content = getContentPane();
    content.setLayout(card);                            // Set card as the layout mgr
```

```
      JButton button;                              // Stores a button
      for(int i = 1; i <= 6; i++) {
        content.add(button = new JButton(" Press " + i), "Card" + i); // Add a button
        button.addActionListener(this);            // Add listener for button
      }
    }

    // Handle button events
    public void actionPerformed(ActionEvent e) {
      card.next(getContentPane());                 // Switch to the next card
    }
  }
```

You'll need an HTML file to execute the applet containing the following:

```
<APPLET CODE="TryCardLayout.class" WIDTH=300 HEIGHT=200>
</APPLET>
```

If you run the program using `appletviewer`, the applet should be as shown in Figure 17-27. Click on the button — and the next button will be displayed.

Figure 17-27

How It Works

You create the `CardLayout` object, `card`, with horizontal and vertical gaps of 50 pixels. In the `init()` method for the applet, you set `card` as the layout manager and add six buttons to the content pane. Note that you have two arguments to the `add()` method, the first being the reference to the component you are adding to the container. Using card layout requires that you identify each component by an object of some class type and you supply this via the second argument to the `add()` method — the method parameter is of type `Object`. In this example, you pass a `String` object as the second argument to the `add()` method because you are using an arbitrary string to identify each component consisting of the string `"Card"` with the sequence number of the button appended to it.

Within the loop you call the addActionListener() method for each button to identify the applet object as the object that will handle events generated for the button (such as clicking on it with the mouse). When you click on a button, the actionPerformed() method for the applet object will be called. This just calls the next() method for the layout object to move the next component in sequence to the top. You'll be looking at event handling in more detail in the next chapter.

The argument to the next() method identifies the container as the TryCardLayout object that is created when the applet starts. The CardLayout class has other methods that you can use for selecting from the stack of components:

Method	Description
void previous(Container parent)	Selects the previous component in the container parent.
void first(Container parent)	Selects the first component in the container parent.
void last(Container parent)	Selects the last component in the container parent.
void show(Container parent, String name)	Selects the component in the container parent associated with the String object name. This must be one of the String objects specified when you called the add() method to add components.

Using the next() or previous() methods, you can cycle through the components repeatedly, since the next component after the last is the first, and the component before the first is the last.

The String object that you supplied when adding a button to the container identifies the button and can be used to switch to any of them. For example, you could switch to the button associated with "Card4" before the applet is displayed by adding the following statement after the loop that adds the buttons:

```
card.show(content, "Card4");    // Switch to button "Card4"
```

This calls the show() method for the layout manager. The first argument is the container and the second argument is the object identifying the component to be at the top, and therefore the one that is visible when the window is displayed.

Using a Grid Layout Manager

A grid layout manager arranges components in a rectangular grid within the container. You have three constructors for creating GridLayout objects:

Constructor	Description
`GridLayout()`	Creates a grid layout manager that will arrange components in a single row (that is, a single column per component) with no gaps between components
`GridLayout(int rows,` `          int cols)`	Creates a grid layout manager that arranges components in a grid with `rows` number of rows and `cols` number of columns, and with no gaps between components

`GridLayout(int rows,`
`          int cols,`
`          int hgap,`
`          int vgap)`
	Creates a grid layout manager that arranges components in a grid with `rows` number of rows and `cols` number of columns, and with horizontal and vertical gaps between components of `hgap` and `vgap` pixels, respectively

In the second and third constructors shown in the preceding table, you can specify the number of rows or the number of columns as zero (but not both). If you specify the number of rows as zero, the layout manager will provide as many rows in the grid as are necessary to accommodate the number of components you add to the container. Similarly, setting the number of columns as zero indicates an arbitrary number of columns. If you fix both the rows and the columns, and add more components to the container than the grid will accommodate, the number of columns will be increased appropriately.

You can try out a grid layout manager in a variation of a previous example.

Try It Out   Gridlocking Buttons

Here's the code to demonstrate a `GridLayout` layout manager in action:

```
import javax.swing.JFrame;
import javax.swing.JButton;
import javax.swing.border.EtchedBorder;

import java.awt.Toolkit;
import java.awt.Dimension;
import java.awt.GridLayout;
import java.awt.Container;

public class TryGridLayout {
  // The window object
  static JFrame aWindow = new JFrame("This is a Grid Layout");

  public static void main(String[] args) {
    Toolkit theKit = aWindow.getToolkit();          // Get the window toolkit
    Dimension wndSize = theKit.getScreenSize();      // Get screen size

    // Set the position to screen center & size to half screen size
    aWindow.setBounds(wndSize.width/4, wndSize.height/4,      // Position
                wndSize.width/2, wndSize.height/2);      // Size
    aWindow.setDefaultCloseOperation(JFrame.EXIT_ON_CLOSE);
```

```
    GridLayout grid = new GridLayout(3,4,30,20);    // Create a layout manager
    Container content = aWindow.getContentPane();   // Get the content pane
    content.setLayout(grid);                        // Set the container layout mgr

    EtchedBorder edge = new EtchedBorder(EtchedBorder.RAISED);   // Button border

    // Now add ten Button components
    JButton button = null;                                      // Stores a button
    for(int i = 1; i <= 10; i++) {
      content.add(button = new JButton(" Press " + i));   // Add a Button
      button.setBorder(edge);                             // Set the border
    }
    aWindow.pack();                                     // Size for components
    aWindow.setVisible(true);                           // Display the window
  }
}
```

When you run this example, the application window will appear as shown in Figure 17-28.

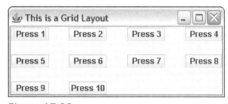

Figure 17-28

How It Works

You create a grid layout manager, `grid`, for three rows and four columns, and with horizontal and verti-cal gaps between components of 30 and 20 pixels, respectively. You set `grid` as the layout manager for the content pane of the application window. You add ten buttons, each with a raised etched border, in the `for` loop. The layout manager causes the buttons to be arranged in a rectangular grid arrangement, with gaps of 30 units between buttons in a row and a gap of 20 units between rows.

Using a BoxLayout Manager

The `javax.swing.BoxLayout` class defines a layout manager that arranges components in either a sin-gle row or a single column. You specify whether you want a row-wise or a columnar arrangement when creating the `BoxLayout` object. The `BoxLayout` constructor requires two arguments. The first is a refer-ence to the container to which the layout manager applies, and the second is a constant value that can be either `BoxLayout.X_AXIS` for a row-wise arrangement or `BoxLayout.Y_AXIS` for a column-wise arrangement.

Components are added from left to right in a row, or from top to bottom in a column. Components in a given row or column do not spill onto the next row or column when the row is full. When more com-ponets have been added to a row or column than can be accommodated within the space available, the layout manager will reduce the size of the components or even clip them if necessary and keep them all in a single row or column. With a row of components, the box layout manager will try to make all the components the same height and try to set a column of components to the same width.

The `javax.swing.Box` container class is particularly convenient when you need to use a box layout since it has a `BoxLayout` manager built in. It also has some additional facilities that provide more flexibility in the arrangement of components than is provided by other containers, such as `JPanel` objects. The `Box` constructor accepts a single argument that specifies the orientation as either `BoxLayout.X_AXIS` or `BoxLayout.Y_AXIS`. The class also has two static methods, `createHorizontalBox()` and `createVerticalBox()`, that each return a reference to a `Box` container with the orientation implied.

As I said earlier, a container can contain another container, so you can easily place one `Box` container inside another to get any arrangement of rows and columns that you want. Let's try that out.

Try It Out   Boxes Containing Boxes

In this example you'll create an application that has a window containing a column of radio buttons on the left, a column of checkboxes on the right, and a row of buttons across the bottom. Here's the code:

```
import java.awt.Toolkit;
import java.awt.Dimension;
import java.awt.Container;
import java.awt.BorderLayout;

import javax.swing.JFrame;
import javax.swing.JButton;
import javax.swing.BoxLayout;
import javax.swing.Box;
import javax.swing.ButtonGroup;
import javax.swing.JRadioButton;
import javax.swing.JCheckBox;
import javax.swing.JPanel;
import javax.swing.BorderFactory;
import javax.swing.border.Border;

public class TryBoxLayout {
  // The window object
  static JFrame aWindow = new JFrame("This is a Box Layout");

  public static void main(String[] args) {
    Toolkit theKit = aWindow.getToolkit();        // Get the window toolkit
    Dimension wndSize = theKit.getScreenSize();   // Get screen size

    // Set the position to screen center & size to half screen size
    aWindow.setBounds(wndSize.width/4, wndSize.height/4,    // Position
                      wndSize.width/2, wndSize.height/2);   // Size
    aWindow.setDefaultCloseOperation(JFrame.EXIT_ON_CLOSE);
    // Create left column of radio buttons
    Box left = Box.createVerticalBox();
    ButtonGroup radioGroup = new ButtonGroup();               // Create button group
    JRadioButton rbutton;                                     // Stores a button
    radioGroup.add(rbutton = new JRadioButton("Red"));        // Add to group
    left.add(rbutton);                                        // Add to Box
    radioGroup.add(rbutton = new JRadioButton("Green"));
    left.add(rbutton);
    radioGroup.add(rbutton = new JRadioButton("Blue"));
```

```
            left.add(rbutton);
            radioGroup.add(rbutton = new JRadioButton("Yellow"));
            left.add(rbutton);

            // Create right columns of checkboxes
            Box right = Box.createVerticalBox();
            right.add(new JCheckBox("Dashed"));
            right.add(new JCheckBox("Thick"));
            right.add(new JCheckBox("Rounded"));

            // Create top row to hold left and right
            Box top = Box.createHorizontalBox();
            top.add(left);
            top.add(right);
            // Create bottom row of buttons
            JPanel bottomPanel = new JPanel();
            Border edge = BorderFactory.createRaisedBevelBorder();   // Button border
            JButton button;
            Dimension size = new Dimension(80,20);
            bottomPanel.add(button = new JButton("Defaults"));
            button.setBorder(edge);
            button.setPreferredSize(size);
            bottomPanel.add(button = new JButton("OK"));
            button.setBorder(edge);
            button.setPreferredSize(size);
            bottomPanel.add(button = new JButton("Cancel"));
            button.setBorder(edge);
            button.setPreferredSize(size);

            // Add top and bottom panel to content pane
            Container content = aWindow.getContentPane();    // Get content pane
            content.setLayout(new BorderLayout());           // Set border layout manager
            content.add(top, BorderLayout.CENTER);
            content.add(bottomPanel, BorderLayout.SOUTH);
            aWindow.pack();
            aWindow.setVisible(true);                        // Display the window
        }
    }
```

When you run this example and try out the radio buttons and checkboxes, it should produce a window something like the one shown in Figure 17-29.

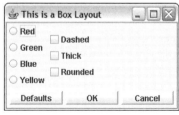

Figure 17-29

It's not an ideal arrangement, but you'll improve on it.

How It Works

The shaded code is of interest — the rest you have seen before. The first block in `main()` creates the left column of radio buttons providing a color choice. You use a `Box` object with a vertical orientation to contain the radio buttons. If you tried the radio buttons, you will have found that only one of them can ever be selected. This is the effect of the `ButtonGroup` object that is used — to ensure that radio buttons operate properly, you must add them to a `ButtonGroup` object.

The `ButtonGroup` object ensures that only one of the radio buttons it contains can be selected at any one time. Each time you click on a radio button to select it, any other button that is selected will be deselected. Note that a `ButtonGroup` object is not a component — it's just a logical grouping of radio buttons — so you can't add it to a container. You must add the buttons independently of the `Box` container that manages their physical arrangement. The `Box` object for the right-hand group of `JCheckBox` objects works in the same way as that for the radio buttons.

Both the `Box` objects holding the columns are added to another `Box` object that implements a horizontal arrangement to position them side-by-side. Note how the vertical `Box` objects adjust their width to match that of the largest component in the column. That's why the two columns are bunched toward the left side. You'll see how to improve on this in a moment.

You use a `JPanel` object to hold the buttons. This has a flow layout manager by default, which is what you want here. Calling the `setPreferredSize()` method for each button sets the preferred width and height to that specified by the `Dimension` object `size`. This ensures that, space permitting, each button will be 80 pixels wide and 20 pixels high.

I have introduced another way of obtaining a border for a component here. The `javax.swing.BorderFactory` class contains static methods that return standard borders of various kinds. The `createBevelBorder()` method returns a reference to a `BevelBorder` object as type `Border` — `Border` being an interface that all border objects implement. You use this border for each of the buttons. You'll try some more of the methods in the `BorderFactory` class later.

To improve the layout of the application window, you can make use of some additional facilities provided by a `Box` container.

Struts and Glue

The `Box` class contains static methods to create an invisible component called a **strut**. A vertical strut has a given height in pixels and zero width. A horizontal strut has a given width in pixels and zero height. The purpose of these struts is to enable you to insert space between your components, either vertically or horizontally. By placing a horizontal strut between two components in a horizontally arranged `Box` container, you fix the distance between the components. By adding a horizontal strut to a vertically arranged `Box` container, you can force a minimum width on the container. You can use a vertical strut in a horizontal box to force a minimum height. The way in which you might use struts to fix the vertical spacing between radio buttons is illustrated in Figure 17-30.

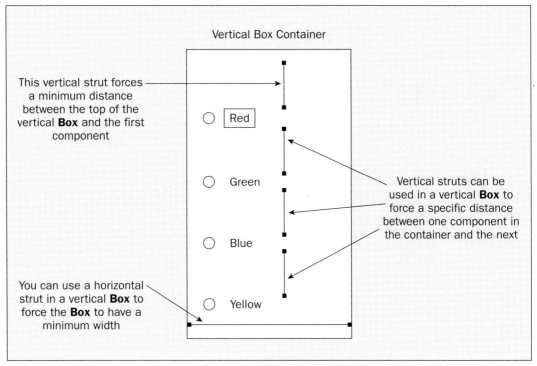

Figure 17-30

Note that although vertical struts have zero width, they have no maximum width so they can expand horizontally to have a width that takes up any excess space. Similarly, the height of a horizontal strut will expand when excess vertical space is available.

A vertical strut is returned as an object of type Component by the static createVerticalStrut() method in the Box class. The argument to the method specifies the height of the strut in pixels. To create a horizontal strut, you use the createHorizontalStrut() method.

You can space out your radio buttons in the previous example by inserting struts between them:

```
// Create left column of radio buttons
Box left = Box.createVerticalBox();
left.add(Box.createVerticalStrut(30));                    // Starting space
ButtonGroup radioGroup = new ButtonGroup();               // Create button group
JRadioButton rbutton;                                     // Stores a button
radioGroup.add(rbutton = new JRadioButton("Red"));        // Add to group
left.add(rbutton);                                        // Add to Box
left.add(Box.createVerticalStrut(30));                    // Space between
radioGroup.add(rbutton = new JRadioButton("Green"));
left.add(rbutton);
left.add(Box.createVerticalStrut(30));                    // Space between
radioGroup.add(rbutton = new JRadioButton("Blue"));
left.add(rbutton);
```

```
        left.add(Box.createVerticalStrut(30));                    // Space between
        radioGroup.add(rbutton = new JRadioButton("Yellow"));
        left.add(rbutton);
```

The extra statements add a 30-pixel vertical strut at the start of the columns, and a further strut of the same size between each radio button and the next. You can do the same for the checkboxes:

```
        // Create right columns of checkboxes
        Box right = Box.createVerticalBox();
        right.add(Box.createVerticalStrut(30));                   // Starting space
        right.add(new JCheckBox("Dashed"));
        right.add(Box.createVerticalStrut(30));                   // Space between
        right.add(new JCheckBox("Thick"));
        right.add(Box.createVerticalStrut(30));                   // Space between
        right.add(new JCheckBox("Rounded"));
```

If you run the example with these changes, the window will look like the one shown in Figure 17-31.

Figure 17-31

It's better, but far from perfect. The columns are now equally spaced in the window because the vertical struts have assumed a width to take up the excess horizontal space that is available. The distribution of surplus space vertically is different in the two columns because the number of components is different. You can control where surplus space goes in a Box object with **glue**. Glue is an invisible component that has the sole function of taking up surplus space in a Box container.

While the name *glue* gives the impression that it binds components together, in fact glue provides an elastic connector between two components that can expand or contract as necessary, so it acts more like a spring. Glue components can be placed between the actual components in the Box and at either or both ends. Any surplus space that arises after the actual components have been accommodated is distributed between the glue components added. If you wanted all the surplus space to be at the beginning of a Box container, for example, you should first add a single glue component in the container.

You create a component that represents glue by calling the createGlue() method for a Box object. You then add the glue component to the Box container in the same way as any other component wherever you want surplus space to be taken up. You can add glue at several positions in a row or column, and spare space will be distributed between the glue components. You can add glue after the last component in each column to make all the spare space appear at the end of each column of buttons. For the radio buttons you can add the following statement:

```
// Statements adding radio buttons to left Box object...
left.add(Box.createGlue());                          // Glue at the end
```

You can do the same for the right box:

```
// Statements adding check boxes to right Box object...
right.add(Box.createGlue());                         // Glue at the end
```

The glue component at the end of each column of buttons will take up all the surplus space in each vertical Box container. This will make the buttons line up at the top. Running the program with added glue will result in the application window shown in Figure 17-32.

Figure 17-32

It's better now, but let's put together a final version of the example with some additional embroidery.

Try It Out   Embroidering Boxes

You'll use some JPanel objects with a new kind of border to contain the vertical Box containers:

```
import java.awt.Toolkit;
import java.awt.Dimension;
import java.awt.Container;
import java.awt.BorderLayout;
import java.awt.Color;

import javax.swing.JFrame;
import javax.swing.JButton;
import javax.swing.BoxLayout;
import javax.swing.Box;
import javax.swing.ButtonGroup;
```

```java
import javax.swing.JRadioButton;
import javax.swing.JCheckBox;
import javax.swing.JPanel;
import javax.swing.BorderFactory;
import javax.swing.border.Border;
import javax.swing.border.TitledBorder;
import javax.swing.border.EtchedBorder;
import javax.swing.border.CompoundBorder;
import javax.swing.border.BevelBorder;

public class TryBoxLayout4 {
  // The window object
  static JFrame aWindow = new JFrame("This is a Box Layout");

  public static void main(String[] args) {
    // Set up the window as before...

    // Create left column of radio buttons with struts and glue as above...
    // Create a panel with a titled border to hold the left Box container
    JPanel leftPanel = new JPanel(new BorderLayout());
    leftPanel.setBorder(new TitledBorder(
                               new EtchedBorder(),     // Border to use
                               "Line Color"));         // Border title
    leftPanel.add(left, BorderLayout.CENTER);

    // Create right columns of checkboxes with struts and glue as above...
    // Create a panel with a titled border to hold the right Box container
    JPanel rightPanel = new JPanel(new BorderLayout());
    rightPanel.setBorder(new TitledBorder(
                               new EtchedBorder(),     // Border to use
                               "Line Properties"));    // Border title
    rightPanel.add(right, BorderLayout.CENTER);

    // Create top row to hold left and right
    Box top = Box.createHorizontalBox();
    top.add(leftPanel);
    top.add(Box.createHorizontalStrut(5));             // Space between vertical boxes
    top.add(rightPanel);

    // Create bottom row of buttons
    JPanel bottomPanel = new JPanel();
    bottomPanel.setBorder(new CompoundBorder(
          BorderFactory.createLineBorder(Color.black, 1),        // Outer border
          BorderFactory.createBevelBorder(BevelBorder.RAISED))); // Inner border

    // Create and add the buttons as before...
    Container content = aWindow.getContentPane();  // Set the container layout mgr
    BoxLayout box = new BoxLayout(content, BoxLayout.Y_AXIS);
                                               // Vertical for content pane
    content.setLayout(box);                    // Set box layout manager
    content.add(top);
    content.add(bottomPanel);
    aWindow.pack();
    aWindow.setVisible(true);                  // Display the window
  }
}
```

The example will now display the window shown in Figure 17-33.

Figure 17-33

How It Works

Both vertical boxes are now contained within a JPanel container. Because JPanel objects are Swing components, you can add a border to them, and this time you add a TitledBorder border that you create directly using the constructor. A TitledBorder is a combination of the border that you specify by the first argument to the TitledBorder constructor and a title that is a String object you specify as the second argument to the constructor. You use a border of type EtchedBorder here, but you can use any type of border.

You introduce space between the two vertically aligned Box containers by adding a horizontal strut to the Box container that contains them. If you wanted space at each side of the window, you could add struts to the container before and after the components.

The last improvement is to the panel holding the buttons along the bottom of the window. You now have a border that is composed of two types, one inside the other: a LineBorder and a BevelBorder. A CompoundBorder object defines a border that is a composite of two border objects, the first argument to the constructor being the outer border and the second being the inner border. The LineBorder class defines a border consisting of a single line of the color specified by its first constructor argument and a thickness in pixels specified by the second. There is a static method defined for the class, createBlackLineBorder(), that creates a black line border that is 1 pixel wide, so you could have used that here.

Using a GridBagLayout Manager

The java.awt.GridBagLayout manager is much more flexible than the other layout managers you have seen and, consequently, rather more complicated to use. The basic mechanism arranges components in an arbitrary rectangular grid, but the rows and columns of the grid are not necessarily the same height or width. A component is placed at a given cell position in the grid specified by the coordinates of the cell, where the cell at the top-left corner is at position (0, 0). You can spread a component over several cells in a row and/or column in the grid, but a component always occupies a rectangular group of cells.

825

Each component in a GridBagLayout has its own set of constraints. These are defined by an object of type GridBagConstraints that you associate with each component before adding the component to the container. The location of each component, its relative size, and the area it occupies in the grid are all determined by its associated GridBagConstraints object.

A GridBagConstraints object has no less than 11 public instance variables that may be set to define the constraints for a component. Since they also interact with each other, there's more entertainment here than with a Rubik's cube. Let's first get a rough idea of what these instance variables in a GridBagConstraints object do:

Instance Variable	Description
gridx and gridy	Determines the position of the component in the container as coordinate positions of cells in the grid, where (0, 0) is the top-left position in the grid
gridwidth and gridheight	Determines the size of the area occupied by the component in the container
weightx and weighty	Determines how free space is distributed between components in the container
anchor	Determines where a component is positioned within the area allocated to it in the container
ipadx and ipady	Determines by how much the component size is to be increased above its minimum size
fill	Determines how the component is to be enlarged to fill the space allocated to it
insets	Specifies the free space that is to be provided around the component within the space allocated to it in the container

All that should seem straightforward enough. You can now explore the possible values you can set for these and then try them out.

GridBagConstraints Instance Variables

A component will occupy at least one grid position, or **cell**, in a container that uses a GridBagLayout object, but it can occupy any rectangular array of cells. The total number of rows and columns, and thus the cell size, in the grid for a container is variable and determined by the constraints for all of the components in the container. Each component will have a specified position in the grid plus the area it is allocated within the grid defined by a number of horizontal and vertical grid positions. This is illustrated in Figure 17-34.

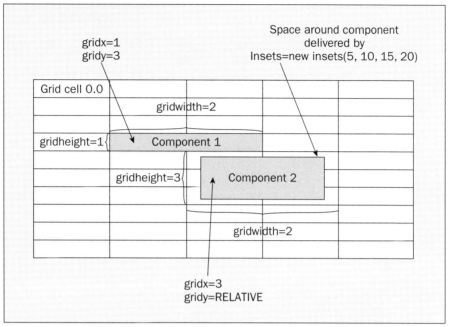

Figure 17-34

The top-left cell in a layout is at position (0, 0). You specify the position of a component by defining where the top-left cell that it occupies is, either relative to the grid origin or relative to the last component that was added to the container. You specify the position of the top-left cell that a component occupies in the grid by setting the gridx and gridy members of the GridBagConstraints object to appropriate values of type int. The default value for gridx is GridBagConstraints.RELATIVE—a constant that places the top-left grid position for the component in the column immediately to the right of the previous component. The same value is the default for gridy, which places the next component immediately below the previous one.

You specify the number of cells to be occupied by a component horizontally and vertically by setting values for the gridwidth and gridheight instance variables for the GridBagConstraints object. The default value for both of these is 1. You can use two constants as values for these variables. With a value of GridBagConstraints.REMAINDER, the component will be the last one in the row or column and occupy the remaining cells. If you specify the value as GridBagConstraints.RELATIVE, the component will be the penultimate one in the row or column.

If the preferred size of the component is less than the display area, you can control how the size of the component is adjusted to fit the display area by setting the fill and insets instance variables for the GridBagConstraints object.

Variable	Description
fill	The value for this variable is of type int, and it determines how the size of the component is adjusted in relation to the array of cells it occupies. The default value of GridBagConstraints.NONE means that the component is not resized. A value of GridBagConstraints.HORIZONTAL adjusts the width of the component to fill the display area. A value of GridBagConstraints.VERTICAL adjusts the height of the component to fill the display area. A value of GridBagConstraints.BOTH adjusts the height and the width to completely fill the display area.
insets	This variable stores a reference to an object of type Insets. An Insets object defines the space allowed between the edges of the components and boundaries of the display area it occupies. Four parameter values to the class constructor define the top, left-side, bottom, and right-side padding from the edges of the component. The default value is Insets(0, 0, 0, 0).

If you don't intend to expand a component to fill its display area, you may still want to enlarge the component from its minimum size. You can adjust the dimensions of the component by setting the following GridBagConstraints instance variables:

Variable	Description
ipadx	An int value that defines the number of pixels by which the top and bottom edges of the component are to be expanded. The default value is 0.
ipady	An int value that defines the number of pixels by which the left and right edges of the component are to be expanded. The default value is 0.

If the component is still smaller than its display area in the container, you can specify where it should be placed in relation to its display area by setting a value for the anchor instance variable of the GridBagConstraints object. Possible values are NORTH, NORTHEAST, EAST, SOUTHEAST, SOUTH, SOUTH-WEST, WEST, NORTHWEST, and CENTER, all of which are defined in the GridBagConstraints class.

The last GridBagConstraints instance variables to consider are weightx and weighty, which are of type double. These determine how space in the container is distributed between components in the horizontal and vertical directions. You should always set a value for these; otherwise, the default of 0 will cause the components to be bunched together adjacent to one another in the center of the container. The absolute values for weightx and weighty are not important. It is the relative values that matter. If you set all the values the same (but not zero), the space for each component will be distributed uniformly. Space is distributed between components in the proportions defined by the values of weightx and weighty you have set.

For example, if three components in a row have weightx values of 1.0, 2.0, and 3.0, the first will get 1/6 of the total in the x direction, the second will get 2/6, which is 1/3, and the third will get 3/6, which is half. The proportion of the available space that a component gets in the x direction is the weightx value for the component divided by the sum of the weightx values in the row. This also applies to the weighty values for allocating space in the y direction.

I'll start with a simple example of placing two buttons in a window and introduce another way of obtaining a standard border for a component.

Try It Out   Applying the GridBagConstraints Object

You can compile and execute the following program to try out the `GridBagLayout` manager:

```java
import java.awt.Toolkit;
import java.awt.Dimension;
import java.awt.GridBagLayout;
import java.awt.GridBagConstraints;
import javax.swing.JFrame;
import javax.swing.JButton;
import javax.swing.BorderFactory;
import javax.swing.border.Border;

public class TryGridBagLayout {
  // The window object
  static JFrame aWindow = new JFrame("This is a Gridbag Layout");

  public static void main(String[] args) {
    Toolkit theKit = aWindow.getToolkit();            // Get the window toolkit
    Dimension wndSize = theKit.getScreenSize();       // Get screen size

    // Set the position to screen center & size to half screen size
    aWindow.setBounds(wndSize.width/4, wndSize.height/4,     // Position
                      wndSize.width/2, wndSize.height/2);    // Size
    aWindow.setDefaultCloseOperation(JFrame.EXIT_ON_CLOSE);

    GridBagLayout gridbag = new GridBagLayout();      // Create a layout manager
    GridBagConstraints constraints = new GridBagConstraints();
    aWindow.getContentPane().setLayout(gridbag);      // Set the container layout mgr

    // Set constraints and add first button
    constraints.weightx = constraints.weighty = 10.0;
    constraints.fill = constraints.BOTH;              // Fill the space
    addButton(" Press ", constraints, gridbag);       // Add the button

    // Set constraints and add second button
    constraints.gridwidth = constraints.REMAINDER;    // Rest of the row
    addButton("GO", constraints, gridbag);            // Create and add button

    aWindow.setVisible(true);                         // Display the window
  }

  static void addButton(String label,
                        GridBagConstraints constraints,
                        GridBagLayout layout) {
    // Create a Border object using a BorderFactory method
    Border edge = BorderFactory.createRaisedBevelBorder();

    JButton button = new JButton(label);              // Create a button
    button.setBorder(edge);                           // Add its border
```

```
        layout.setConstraints(button, constraints);     // Set the constraints
        aWindow.getContentPane().add(button);           // Add button to content pane
    }
}
```

The program window will look like that shown in Figure 17-35.

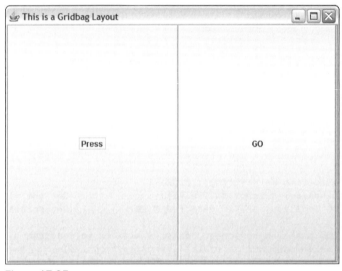

Figure 17-35

As you see, the left button is slightly wider than the right button. This is because the length of the button label affects the size of the button.

How It Works

Because the process will be the same for every button added, you have implemented a helper method, addButton(). This method creates a Button object, associates the GridBagConstraints object with it in the GridBagLayout object, and then adds it to the content pane of the frame window.

After creating the layout manager and GridBagConstraints objects, you set the values for weightx and weighty to 10.0. A value of 1.0 or 100.0 would have the same effect because it is the relative values that these variables have for the constraints on components in a column or row, not their absolute values. You set the fill constraint to BOTH to make the component fill the space it occupies. Note that when the setConstraints() method is called to associate the GridBagConstraints object with the button object, it creates a copy of the constraints object that you pass as the argument, and a reference to the copy is stored in the layout — not a reference to the object that you created. This allows you to change the constraints object that you created and use it for the second button without affecting the constraints for the first.

The buttons are more or less equal in size in the *x* direction (they would be exactly the same size if the labels were the same length) because the weightx and weighty values are the same for both. Both buttons fill the space available to them because the fill constraint is set to BOTH. If fill was set to

HORIZONTAL, for example, the buttons would be the full width of the grid positions they occupy, but just high enough to accommodate the label, since they would have no preferred size in the *y* direction.

If you alter the constraints for the second button to

```
// Set constraints and add second button
constraints.weightx = 5.0;                            // Weight half of first
constraints.insets = new java.awt.Insets(10, 30, 10, 20);  // Left 30 & right 20
constraints.gridwidth = constraints.RELATIVE;        // Rest of the row
addButton("GO", constraints, gridbag);               // Add button to content pane
```

the application window will be as shown in Figure 17-36.

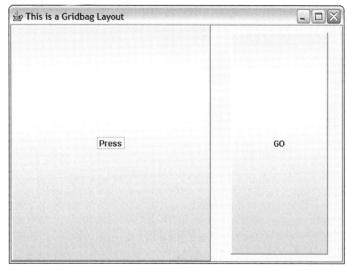

Figure 17-36

Now the second button occupies one third of the space in the *x* direction—that corresponds to 5/(5+10) of the total space in *x* that is available—and the first button occupies two-thirds. Note that the buttons still occupy one grid cell each—the default values for `gridwidth` and `gridheight` of 1 apply—but the `weightx` constraint values have altered the relative sizes of the cells for the two buttons in the *x* direction.

The second button is also within the space allocated—10 pixels at the top and bottom, 30 pixels on the left, and 20 on the right (set by the `insets` constraint). You can see that for a given window size here, the size of a grid position depends on the number of objects. The more components there are, the less space each will be allocated.

Suppose you wanted to add a third button, the same width as the Press button, and immediately below it. You could do that by adding the following code immediately after that for the second button:

```
// Set constraints and add third button
constraints.insets = new java.awt.Insets(0,0,0,0);   // No insets
constraints.gridx = 0;                               // Begin new row
constraints.gridwidth = 1;                            // Width as "Press"
addButton("Push", constraints, gridbag);             // Add button to content pane
```

You reset the `gridx` constraint to zero to put the button at the start of the next row. It has a default `gridwidth` of 1 cell, like the others. The window would now look like the one shown in Figure 17-37.

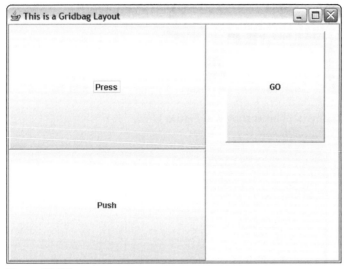

Figure 17-37

Having seen how it looks now, clearly it would be better if the GO button were the height of Press and Push combined. To arrange them like this, you need to make the height of the GO button twice that of the other two buttons. The height of the Press button is 1 by default, so by making the height of the GO button 2, and resetting the `gridheight` constraint of the Push button to 1, you should get the desired result. Modify the code for the second and third buttons to:

```
// Set constraints and add second button
constraints.weightx = 5.0;                          // Weight half of first
constraints.gridwidth = constraints.RELATIVE;       // Rest of the
rowconstraints.insets = new java.awt.Insets(10, 30, 10, 20); // Left 30 & right 20
constraints.gridheight = 2;                          // Height 2x "Press"
addButton("GO", constraints, gridbag);              // Add button to content pane

// Set constraints and add third button
constraints.insets = new java.awt.Insets(0, 0, 0, 0);    // No insets
constraints.gridx = 0;                              // Begin new row
constraints.gridwidth = 1;                          // Width as "Press"
constraints.gridheight = 1;                         // Height as "Press"
addButton("Push", constraints, gridbag);            // Add button to content pane
```

With these code changes, the window will be as shown in Figure 17-38.

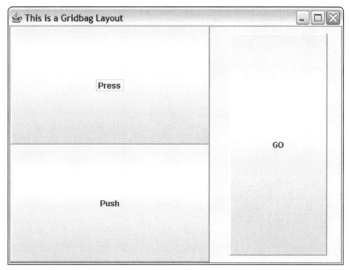

Figure 17-38

You could also see the effect of padding the components out from their preferred size by altering the button constraints a little:

```
// Create constraints and add first button
constraints.weightx = constraints.weighty = 10.0;
constraints.fill = constraints.NONE;
constraints.ipadx = 30;                         // Pad 30 in x
constraints.ipady = 10;                         // Pad 10 in y
addButton("Press", constraints, gridbag);       // Add button to content pane

// Set constraints and add second button
constraints.weightx = 5.0;                      // Weight half of first
constraints.fill = constraints.BOTH;            // Expand to fill space
constraints.ipadx = constraints.ipady = 0;      // No padding
constraints.gridwidth = constraints.REMAINDER;  // Rest of the row
constraints.gridheight = 2;                     // Height 2x "Press"
constraints.insets = new Insets(10, 30, 10, 20); // Left 30 & right 20
addButton("GO", constraints, gridbag);          // Add button to content pane

// Set constraints and add third button
constraints.gridx = 0;                          // Begin new row
constraints.fill = constraints.NONE;
constraints.ipadx = 30;                         // Pad component in x
constraints.ipady = 10;                         // Pad component in y
constraints.gridwidth = 1;                      // Width as "Press"
constraints.gridheight = 1;                     // Height as "Press"
constraints.insets = new Insets(0, 0, 0, 0);    // No insets
addButton("Push", constraints, gridbag);        // Add button to content pane
```

With the constraints for the buttons as before, the window will look as shown in Figure 17-39.

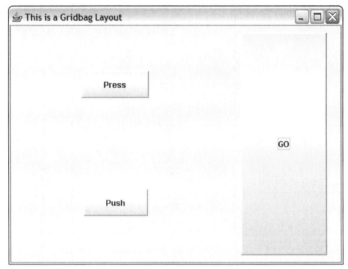

Figure 17-39

Both the Push and the Press button occupy the same space in the container, but because `fill` is set to NONE they are not expanded to fill the space in either direction. The `ipadx` and `ipady` constraints specify by how much the buttons are to be expanded from their preferred size — by 30 pixels on the left and right and 10 pixels on the top and bottom. The overall arrangement remains the same.

You need to experiment with using `GridBagLayout` and `GridBagConstraints` to get a good feel for how the layout manager works because it's only with experience that you'll appreciate what you can do with it.

Using a SpringLayout Manager

You can set the layout manager for the content pane of a `JFrame` object, aWindow, to be a `javax.swing.SpringLayout` manager like this:

```
SpringLayout layout = new SpringLayout();          // Create a layout manager
Container content = aWindow.getContentPane();      // Get the content pane
content.setLayout(layout);
```

The layout manager defined by the `SpringLayout` class determines the position and size of each component in the container according to a set of constraints that are defined by `javax.swing.Spring` objects. Every component within a container using a `SpringLayout` manager has an object associated with it of type `SpringLayout.Constraints` that defines constraints on the position of each of the four edges of the component. Before you can access the `SpringLayout.constraints` object for a component object, you must first add the component to the container. For example:

```
JButton button = new JButton("Press Me");
content.add(button);
```

Now you can call the `getConstraint()` method for the `SpringLayout` object to obtain the object encapsulating the constraints:

```
SpringLayout.Constraints constraints = layout.getConstraints(button);
```

The argument to the `getConstraints()` method identifies the component in the container for which you want to access the `constraints` object. To constrain the location and size of the `button` object, you'll call methods for the `constraints` object to set individual constraints.

Understanding Constraints

The top, bottom, left, and right edges of a component are referred to by their compass points, north, south, west, and east. When you need to refer to a particular edge in your code — for setting a constraint, for example — you use constants that are defined in the `SpringLayout` class, NORTH, SOUTH, WEST, and EAST, respectively. This is shown in Figure 17-40.

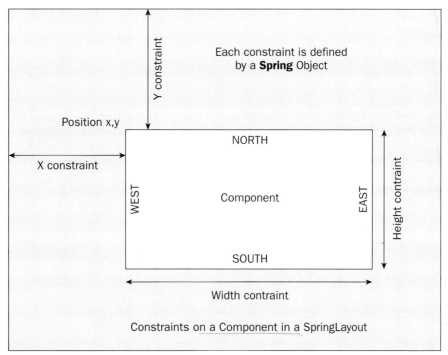

Figure 17-40

As Figure 17-40 shows, the position of a component is determined by a horizontal constraint on the *x* coordinate of the component and a vertical constraint on the *y* coordinate. These obviously also determine the location of the WEST and NORTH edges of the component, since the position determines where the top-left corner is located. The width and height are determined by horizontal constraints that relate the position of the EAST and SOUTH edges to the positions of the WEST and NORTH edges, respectively. Thus, the constraints on the positions of the EAST and SOUTH edges are determined by constraints that are derived from the others, as follows:

```
EAST_constraint = X_constraint + width_constraint
SOUTH_constraint = Y_constraint + height_constraint
```

You can set the X, Y, width, and height constraints independently, as you'll see in a moment, and you can set a constraint explicitly for any edge. Obviously, it is possible to set constraints such that the preceding relationships between the constraints may be violated. In this case, the layout manager will adjust one or other of the constraints so that the preceding relationships still apply. The constraint that is adjusted depends on which constraint you set to potentially cause the violation, as shown in the table:

If you set a constraint for a component on:	The layout manager will make the adjustment:
X or the WEST edge	width value set to EAST-X
The width	EAST edge is set to X+width
EAST edge	X is set to EAST-width
Y or the NORTH edge	height is set to SOUTH-Y
The height	SOUTH edge is set to Y+height
The SOUTH edge	Y is set to SOUTH-height

The SpringLayout manager automatically adds Spring constraints that will control the width and height of a component based on the component's minimum, maximum, and preferred sizes. The width or height will be set to a value between the maximum and minimum for the component. These sizes are obtained dynamically by calling the getMinimumSize(), getMaximumSize(), and getPreferredSize() methods for the component. Normally these constraints on the width and height will expand or contract the component as the size of the container changes, but when the getPreferredSize() and getMaximumSize() methods return the same value, the layout manager will not alter the width and height of the component as the container size is changed.

Defining Constraints

The Spring class in the javax.swing package defines an object that represents a constraint. A Spring object is defined by three integer values that relate to the notional length of the spring: the minimum length, the preferred length, and the maximum length. A Spring object will also have an actual length value that lies between the minimum and the maximum, and that will determine the location of the edge to which it applies. You can create a Spring object like this:

```
Spring spring = Spring.constant(10, 30, 50);    // min=10, pref=30, max=50
```

The static constant() method in the Spring class creates a Spring object from the three arguments that are the minimum, preferred, and maximum values for the Spring object. If all three values are

equal, the object is called a strut because its value is fixed at the common value you set for all three. There's an overloaded version of the `constant()` method for creating struts that has just one parameter:

```
Spring strut = Spring.constant(40); // min, pref, and max all set to 40
```

The `Spring` class also defines static methods that operate on `Spring` objects:

`sum(Spring spr1, Spring spr2)`	Returns a reference to a new `Spring` object that has minimum, preferred, and maximum values that are the sum of the corresponding values of the arguments
`minus(Spring spr)`	Returns a reference to a new `Spring` object with minimum, preferred, and maximum values that are the same magnitude as those of the argument but with opposite signs
`max(Spring spr1, Spring spr2)`	Returns a reference to a new `Spring` object that has minimum, preferred, and maximum values that are the maximum of the corresponding values of the arguments

Setting Constraints for a Component

The `setX()` and `setY()` methods for a `SpringLayout.Constraints` object set the constraints for the WEST and NORTH edges of the component, respectively. For example:

```
SpringLayout.Constraints constraints = layout.getConstraints(button);
Spring xSpring = Spring.constant(5,10,20);      // Spring we'll use for X
Spring ySpring = Spring.constant(3,5,8);        // Spring we'll use for Y
constraints.setX(xSpring);                      // Set the WEST edge constraint
constraints.setY(xSpring);                      // Set the NORTH edge constraint
```

The `layout` variable references a `SpringLayout` object that has been set as the layout manager for the container that contains the `button` component. The `setX()` method defines a constraint between the WEST edge of the container and the WEST edge of the `button` component. Similarly, the `setY()` method defines a constraint between the NORTH edge of the container and the NORTH edge of the `button` component. This fixes the location of the component in relation to the origin of the container, as illustrated in Figure 17-41.

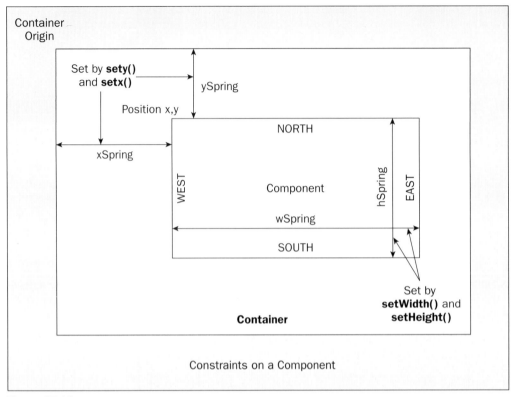

Constraints on a Component

Figure 17-41

To set the width and height of the component, you call the setWidth() and setHeight() methods for its SpringLayout.Constraints object and supply a Spring object that you want to control the dimension. Here's how you could specify specific Spring objects of your choosing:

```
Spring wSpring = Spring.constant(30,50,70);   // Spring we'll use for width
Spring hSpring = Spring.constant(15);         // Strut we'll use for height
constraints.setWidth(wSpring);                // Set component width constraint
constraints.setHeight(hSpring);               // Set component height constraint
```

The width constraint is applied between the WEST and EAST edges and the height constraint applies between the component's NORTH and SOUTH edges. Since you have specified a strut for the height, there is no leeway on this constraint; its value is fixed at 15.

The Spring class defines the static methods width() and height() that return a Spring object based on the minimum, maximum, and preferred sizes of the component that you pass as the argument to the method. These are the constraints that the layout manager will apply to the width and height by default, but there may be circumstances where you wish to reapply them. You could use these methods to create Spring objects to control the width and height of the button object like this:

```
constraints.setWidth(Spring.width(button));   // Set component width constraint
constraints.setHeight(Spring.width(button));  // Set component height constraint
```

The springs you have set here will adjust the width and height based of the values for the minimum, maximum, and preferred sizes for the component.

If you want to explicitly set an edge constraint for a component, you call the `setConstraint()` method for the component's `SpringLayout.Constraints` object:

```
layout.getConstraints(newButton)
      .setConstraint(StringLayout.EAST, Spring.sum(xSpring, wSpring));
```

This statement ties the EAST edge of the `newButton` component to the WEST edge of the container by a `Spring` object that is the sum of `xSpring` and `wSpring`.

You can also set constraints between pairs of vertical or horizontal edges, where one edge can belong to a different component from the other. For example, you could add another button to the container like this:

```
JButton newButton = new JButton("Push");
content.add(newButton);
```

You can now constrain its WEST and NORTH edges by tying the edges to the EAST and SOUTH edges of the `button` component that you added to the container previously. You use the `putConstraint()` method for the `SpringLayout` object to do this:

```
SpringLayout.Constraints newButtonConstr = layout.getConstraints(newButton);
layout.putConstraint(SpringLayout.WEST,
                     newButton,
                     xSpring,
                     SpringLayout.EAST,
                     button);
```

The first two arguments to the `putConstraint()` method for the layout object are the edge specification and a reference to the dependent component, respectively. The third argument is a `Spring` object defining the constraint. The fourth and fifth arguments specify the edge and a reference to the component to which the dependent component is anchored. Obviously, since constraints can only be horizontal or vertical, both edges should have the same orientation. There is an overloaded version of the `putConstraint()` method for which the third argument is a value of type `int` that defines a fixed distance between the edges.

Let's look at a simple example using a `SpringLayout` object as the layout manager.

Try It Out   Using a SpringLayout Manager

Here's the code for an example that displays six buttons in a window:

```
import javax.swing.JButton;
import javax.swing.JFrame;
import javax.swing.SpringLayout;
import javax.swing.Spring;

import java.awt.Container;
import java.awt.Dimension;
import java.awt.Toolkit;
```

```
public class TrySpringLayout {
  // The window object
  static JFrame aWindow = new JFrame("This is a Spring Layout");

  public static void main(String[] args) {
    Toolkit theKit = aWindow.getToolkit();            // Get the window toolkit
    Dimension wndSize = theKit.getScreenSize();       // Get screen size

    // Set the position to screen center & size to two-thirds screen size
    aWindow.setBounds(wndSize.width/6, wndSize.height/6,       // Position
                      2*wndSize.width/3, 2*wndSize.height/3);  // Size
    aWindow.setDefaultCloseOperation(JFrame.EXIT_ON_CLOSE);

    SpringLayout layout = new SpringLayout();         // Create a layout manager
    Container content = aWindow.getContentPane();     // Get the content pane
    content.setLayout(layout);                        // Set the container layout mgr

    JButton[] buttons = new JButton[6];               // Array to store buttons
    SpringLayout.Constraints constr = null;
    for(int i = 0; i < buttons.length; i++) {
      buttons[i] = new JButton("Press " + (i+1));
      content.add(buttons[i]);                        // Add a Button to content pane
    }

    Spring xSpring = Spring.constant(5,15,25);     // x constraint for first button
    Spring ySpring = Spring.constant(10,30, 50);   // y constraint for first button

    // Connect x,y for first button to left and top of container by springs
    constr = layout.getConstraints(buttons[0]);
    constr.setX(xSpring);
    constr.setY(ySpring);

    // Hook buttons together with springs
    for(int i = 1 ; i< buttons.length ; i++) {
      constr = layout.getConstraints(buttons[i]);
      layout.putConstraint(SpringLayout.WEST, buttons[i],
                           xSpring,SpringLayout.EAST, buttons[i-1]);
      layout.putConstraint(SpringLayout.NORTH, buttons[i],
                           ySpring,SpringLayout.SOUTH, buttons[i-1]);
    }
    aWindow.setVisible(true);                         // Display the window
  }
}
```

When you compile and run this you should get a window with the buttons laid out as shown in Figure 17-42.

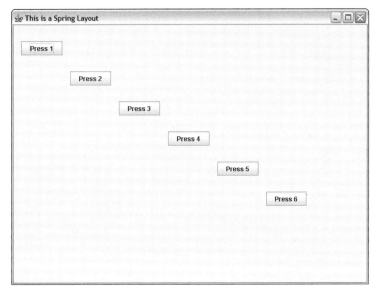

Figure 17-42

How It Works

You first create a variable that will store a reference to a `SpringLayout.Constraints` object and array to hold references to `JButton` objects:

```
JButton[] buttons = new JButton[6];              // Array to store buttons
SpringLayout.Constraints constr = null;
```

You create and add six buttons to the content pane of the window in a loop:

```
for(int i = 0; i < buttons.length; i++) {
   buttons[i] = new JButton("Press " + (i+1));
   content.add(buttons[i]);                       // Add a Button to content pane
}
```

As each button is added to the container, the layout manager will apply the contraints to the height and width of the container that I discussed earlier. Unless these are overridden because the component is overconstrained, these constraints will adjust the size of the button based on the minimum, maximum, and preferred sizes for the component.

After adding six buttons to the content pane of the window, you define two `Spring` objects that you'll use to position the first button relative to the container:

```
Spring xSpring = Spring.constant(5,15,25);     // x constraint for first button
Spring ySpring = Spring.constant(10,30, 50);   // y constraint for first button
```

You then set the location of the first button relative to the container:

```
constr = layout.getConstraints(buttons[0]);
constr.setX(xSpring);
constr.setY(ySpring);
```

This fixes the top-left corner of the first button. You can define the positions of each of the remaining buttons relative to its predecessor. You do this by adding constraints between the NORTH and WEST edges of each button and the SOUTH and EAST edges of its predecessor. This is done in the for loop:

```
for(int i = 1 ; i< buttons.length ; i++) {
    constr = layout.getConstraints(buttons[i]);
    layout.putConstraint(SpringLayout.WEST, buttons[i],
                    xSpring,SpringLayout.EAST, buttons[i-1]);
    layout.putConstraint(SpringLayout.NORTH, buttons[i],
                    ySpring,SpringLayout.SOUTH, buttons[i-1]);
}
```

This places each component after the first relative to the bottom-right corner of its predecessor, so the buttons are laid out in a cascade fashion.

Relating the Container Size to the Components

Of course, the size of the application window in our example is independent of the components within it. If you resize the window the springs have no effect. If you call pack() for the aWindow object before calling its setVisible() method, the window will shrink to a width and height just accommodating the title bar so you won't see any of the components. This is because SpringLayout does not adjust the size of the container by default so the effect of pack() is as though the content pane were empty.

You can do much better than this. You can set constraints on the edges of the container using springs that will control its size. You can therefore place constraints on the height and width of the container in terms of the springs that you used to determine the size and locations of the components. This will have the effect of relating all the springs that determine the size and position of the buttons to the size of the application window. Try adding the following code to the example, immediately preceding the call to setVisible() for the window object:

```
SpringLayout.Constraints constraint = layout.getConstraints(content);
constraint.setConstraint(SpringLayout.EAST,
                Spring.sum(constr.getConstraint(SpringLayout.EAST),
                        Spring.constant(15)));
constraint.setConstraint(SpringLayout.SOUTH,
                Spring.sum(constr.getConstraint(SpringLayout.SOUTH),
                        Spring.constant(10)));
aWindow.pack();
```

This sets the constraint on the EAST edge of a container that is the Spring constraining the EAST edge of the last button plus a strut 15 units long. This positions the right edge of the container 15 units to the right of the right edge of the last button. The bottom edge of the container is similarly connected by a fixed link, 10 units long, to the bottom edge of the last button. If you recompile with these additions and run the example again, you should find that not only is the initial size of the window set to accommodate all the buttons, but when you resize the window the size and positions of the buttons adapt accordingly. Isn't that nice?

Note how the width and height of each button is maintained as you resize the window, even when the content pane is too small to accommodate all the buttons. This is because a `JButton` object returns a maximum size that is the same as the preferred size, so the layout manager will not alter the width or the height.

The `SpringLayout` manager is extremely flexible and can do much of what the other layout mangers can do if you choose the constraints on the components appropriately. It's well worth experimenting to see the effect of various configurations of springs on your application.

Adding a Menu to a Window

As I've already mentioned, a `JMenuBar` object represents the menu bar that is placed at the top of a window. You can add `JMenu` or `JMenuItem` objects to a `JMenuBar` object, and these will be displayed on the menu bar. A `JMenu` object is a menu with a label that can display a list of menu items when clicked. A `JMenuItem` object represents a menu item in a menu, with a label that results in some program action when clicked — such as opening a dialog. A `JMenuItem` object can have an icon in addition to, or instead of, a `String` label. Each item on the menu encapsulated in a `JMenu` object can be an object of either type `JMenu`, `JMenuItem`, `JCheckBoxMenuItem`, or `JRadioButtonMenuItem`. If an item in a menu is a `JMenu` object, then it represents a second level of menu containing further menu items.

A `JCheckBoxMenuItem` is a simple menu item with a checkbox associated with it. The checkbox can be checked and unchecked and typically indicates that that menu item was selected last time the drop-down menu was displayed. You can also add separators in a drop-down menu. These are simply bars to separate one group of menu items from another. A `JRadioButtonMenuItem` is a menu item much like a radio button in that it is intended to be one of a group of like menu items added to a `ButtonGroup` object. Both `JCheckBoxMenuItem` and `JRadioButtonMenuItem` objects can have icons.

Creating JMenu and JMenuItem

To create a menu you call a `JMenu` class constructor and pass a `String` object to it that contains the label for the menu. For example, to create a File menu you could write:

```
JMenu fileMenu = new JMenu("File");
```

The string that is passed as the argument is the text that will appear.

Creating a menu item is much the same as creating a menu:

```
JMenuItem openMenu = new JMenuItem("Open");
```

The argument is the text that will appear on the menu item.

If you create a `JCheckboxMenuItem` object by passing just a `String` argument to the constructor, the object will represent a checkbox menu item that is initially unchecked. For example, you could create an unchecked item with the following statement:

```
JCheckboxMenuItem circleItem = new JCheckboxMenuItem("Circle");
```

Another constructor for this class allows you to set the check mark by specifying a second argument of type `boolean`. For example:

```
JCheckboxMenuItem lineItem = new JCheckboxMenuItem("Line", true);
```

This creates an item with the label, `Line`, which will be checked initially. You can, of course, also use this constructor to explicitly specify that you want an item to be unchecked by setting the second argument to `false`.

A `JRadioButtonMenuItem` object is created in essentially the same way:

```
JRadioButtonMenuItem item = new JRadioButtonMenuItem("Curve", true);
```

This creates a radio button menu item that is selected.

If you want to use a menu bar in your application window, you must create your window as a `JFrame` object, since the `JFrame` class incorporates the capability to manage a menu bar. You can also add a menu bar to `JDialog` and `JApplet` objects. Let's explore how you create a menu on a menu bar.

Creating a Menu

To create a window with a menu bar, you'll define your own window class as a subclass of `JFrame`. This will provide a much more convenient way to manage all the details of the window compared to using a `JFrame` object directly as you have been doing up to now. By extending the `JFrame` class, you can add your own members that will customize a `JFrame` window to your particular needs. You can also override the methods defined in the `JFrame` class to modify their behavior, if necessary.

You'll be adding functionality to this example over several chapters, so create a directory for it with the name Sketcher. You'll be developing this program into a window-based sketching program that will enable you to create sketches using lines, circles, curves, and rectangles, and to annotate them with text. By building an example in this way, you'll gradually create a much larger Java program than the examples seen so far, and you will also gain experience in combining many of the capabilities of `javax.swing` and other standard packages in a practical situation.

Try It Out   **Building a Menu**

To start with, you'll have two class files in the Sketcher program. The file `Sketcher.java` will contain the `main()` method where execution of the application will start, and the `SketchFrame.java` file will contain the class defining the application window.

You can define a preliminary version of the window class as follows:

```
// Frame for the Sketcher application
import javax.swing.JFrame;
import javax.swing.JMenuBar;
```

```java
import javax.swing.JMenu;

public class SketchFrame extends JFrame {
  // Constructor
  public SketchFrame(String title) {
    setTitle(title);                          // Set the window title
    setDefaultCloseOperation(EXIT_ON_CLOSE);

    setJMenuBar(menuBar);                     // Add the menu bar to the window

    JMenu fileMenu = new JMenu("File");       // Create File menu
    JMenu elementMenu = new JMenu("Elements"); // Create Elements menu

    menuBar.add(fileMenu);                    // Add the file menu
    menuBar.add(elementMenu);                 // Add the element menu
  }

  private JMenuBar menuBar = new JMenuBar();  // Window menu bar
}
```

Save this code as `SketchFrame.java` in the `Sketcher` directory.

Next, you can enter the code for the `Sketcher` class in a separate file:

```java
// Sketching application
import java.awt.Toolkit;
import java.awt.Dimension;

public class Sketcher {
  public static void main(String[] args) {
    window = new SketchFrame("Sketcher");     // Create the app window
    Toolkit theKit = window.getToolkit();     // Get the window toolkit
    Dimension wndSize = theKit.getScreenSize(); // Get screen size

    // Set the position to screen center & size to half screen size
    window.setBounds(wndSize.width/4, wndSize.height/4,      // Position
                    wndSize.width/2, wndSize.height/2);      // Size

    window.setVisible(true);
  }

  private static SketchFrame window;          // The application window
}
```

Save this file as `Sketcher.java` in the `Sketcher` directory. If you compile and run `Sketcher`, you should see the window shown in Figure 17-43.

Figure 17-43

How It Works

The `Sketcher` class has a `SketchFrame` variable, `window`, as a data member that you'll use to store the application window object. You must declare this variable as `static` as there will be no instances of the `Sketcher` class around. The `window` variable is initialized in the method `main()` that is called when program execution begins. Once the `window` object exists, you set the size of the window based on the screen size in pixels, which you obtain using the `Toolkit` object. This is exactly the same process that you saw earlier in this chapter. Finally, in the `main()` method you call the `setVisible()` method for the window object with the argument `true` to display the application window.

In the constructor for the `SketchFrame` class, you could pass the title for the window to the superclass constructor to create the window with the title bar directly. However, later when you have developed the application a bit more, you will want to add to the title, so you call the `setTitle()` member to set the window title here. Next you call the `setJMenuBar()` method that is inherited from the `JFrame` class to specify `menuBar` as the menu bar for the window. To define the two menus that are to appear on the menu bar, you create one `JMenu` object with the label `"File"` and another with the label `"Elements"` — these labels will be displayed on the menu bar. You add the `fileMenu` and `elementMenu` objects to the menu bar by calling the `add()` method for the `menuBar` object.

The field that you have defined in the `SketchFrame` class represents the menu bar. Both items on the menu bar are of type `JMenu` and are therefore menus, so you'll be adding menu items to each of them. The File menu will provide the file input, file output, and print options, and you'll eventually use the Elements menu to choose the kind of geometric figure you want to draw. Developing the menu further, you can now add the menu items.

Adding Menu Items to a Menu

Both menus on the menu bar need menu items to be added — they can't do anything by themselves because they are of type JMenu. You use a version of the add() method that is defined in the JMenu class to add items to a menu.

The simplest version of the add() method creates a menu item with the label that you pass as an argument. For example:

```
JMenuItem newMenu = fileMenu.add("New");                    // Add the menu item "New"
```

This will create a menu item as a JMenuItem object with the label "New", add it to the menu represented by the fileMenu object, and return a reference to the menu item. You'll need the reference to the menu item to enable the program to react to the user clicking the item.

You can also create the JMenuItem object explicitly and use another version of the add() method for the JMenu object to add it:

```
JMenuItem newMenu = new JMenuItem("New");          // Create the item
fileMenu.add(newMenu);                             // and add it to the menu
```

You can operate on menu items by using the following methods defined in the JMenuItem class:

Method	Description
void setEnabled(boolean b)	If b has the value true, the menu item is enabled. If b has the value false, the menu item is disabled. The default state is enabled.
void setText(String label)	Sets the menu item label to the string stored in the label.
String getText()	Returns the current menu item label.

Since the JMenu class is a subclass of JMenuItem, these methods also apply to JMenu objects.

To add a separator to a menu you call the addSeparator() method for the JMenu object. The separator will appear following the last menu item that you added to the menu.

Let's now create the drop-down menus for the File and Element menus on the menu bar in the Sketcher application and try out some of the menu items.

Try It Out   Adding Drop-Down Menus

You can change the definition of our SketchFrame class to do this:

```
// Frame for the Sketcher application
import javax.swing.JFrame;
import javax.swing.JMenuBar;
import javax.swing.JMenu;
```

```java
import javax.swing.JMenuItem;
import javax.swing.JRadioButtonMenuItem;
import javax.swing.JCheckBoxMenuItem;
import javax.swing.ButtonGroup;

public class SketchFrame extends JFrame {
  // Constructor
  public SketchFrame(String title) {
    setTitle(title);                                    // Set the window title
    setDefaultCloseOperation(EXIT_ON_CLOSE);

    setJMenuBar(menuBar);                               // Add the menu bar to the window

    JMenu fileMenu = new JMenu("File");                // Create File menu
    JMenu elementMenu = new JMenu("Elements");         // Create Elements menu

    // Construct the file drop-down menu
    newItem = fileMenu.add("New");                     // Add New item
    openItem = fileMenu.add("Open");                   // Add Open item
    closeItem = fileMenu.add("Close");                 // Add Close item
    fileMenu.addSeparator();                           // Add separator
    saveItem = fileMenu.add("Save");                   // Add Save item
    saveAsItem = fileMenu.add("Save As...");           // Add Save As item
    fileMenu.addSeparator();                           // Add separator
    printItem = fileMenu.add("Print");                 // Add Print item

    // Construct the Element drop-down menu
    elementMenu.add(lineItem = new JRadioButtonMenuItem("Line", true));
    elementMenu.add(rectangleItem = new JRadioButtonMenuItem("Rectangle", false));
    elementMenu.add(circleItem = new JRadioButtonMenuItem("Circle", false));
    elementMenu.add(curveItem = new JRadioButtonMenuItem("Curve", false));
    ButtonGroup types = new ButtonGroup();
    types.add(lineItem);
    types.add(rectangleItem);
    types.add(circleItem);
    types.add(curveItem);

    elementMenu.addSeparator();

    elementMenu.add(redItem = new JCheckBoxMenuItem("Red", false));
    elementMenu.add(yellowItem = new JCheckBoxMenuItem("Yellow", false));
    elementMenu.add(greenItem = new JCheckBoxMenuItem("Green", false));
    elementMenu.add(blueItem = new JCheckBoxMenuItem("Blue", true));
```

```
      menuBar.add(fileMenu);                            // Add the file menu
      menuBar.add(elementMenu);                         // Add the element menu
  }

  private JMenuBar menuBar = new JMenuBar();            // Window menu bar

  // File menu items
  private JMenuItem newItem,  openItem,   closeItem,
                  saveItem, saveAsItem, printItem;

  // Element menu items
  private JRadioButtonMenuItem lineItem,   rectangleItem, circleItem,  // Types
                              curveItem, textItem;
  private JCheckBoxMenuItem    redItem,    yellowItem,                  // Colors
                              greenItem, blueItem ;
}
```

If you recompile Sketcher once more, you can run the application again to try out the menus. If you extend the File menu by clicking on it, you'll see that it has the menu items that you have added. The window is shown in Figure 17-44.

Figure 17-44

Now if you extend the Elements menu it should appear as shown with the Line and Blue items checked, as shown in Figure 17-45.

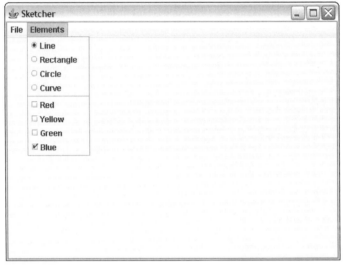

Figure 17-45

How It Works

You have defined the fields that store references to the menu items for the drop-down menus as private members of the class. For the File menu, the menu items are of type JMenuItem. In the Element menu the items select a type of shape to be drawn, and because these are clearly mutually exclusive, you use objects of type JRadioButtonMenuItem for them. You could use objects of the same type for the element color menu items, but to try it out you are using the JCheckBoxMenuItem type.

To create the items in the File menu, you pass the String object for the label for each menu item to the add() method and leave it to the JMenu object to create the JMenuItem object. The add() method returns a reference to the object that it creates and you store the reference in one of the fields you have defined for that purpose. You'll need access to the menu item objects later when you add code to service events that arise from the user clicking a menu item.

The first group of Elements menu items are JRadioButtonMenuItem objects, and you create each of these in the argument to the add() method. To ensure only one is checked at a time, you also add them to a ButtonGroup object. The color menu items are of type JCheckBoxMenuItem, so the current selection is indicated by a check mark on the menu. You'll make Line the default element type and Blue the default color, so you set both of these as checked by specifying true as the second argument to the constructor.

The other items will be unchecked initially because you have specified the second argument as false. You could have omitted the second argument to leave these items unchecked by default. It then means that you need to remember the default to determine what is happening, so it is much better to set the checks explicitly.

You can see the effect of the `addSeparator()` method from the `JMenu` class. It produces the horizontal bar separating the items for element type from those for color. If you select any of the unchecked element type items on the Elements drop-down menu, they will be checked automatically, and only one can appear checked. More than one of the color items can be checked at the moment, but you'll add some code in the next chapter to make sure only one of these items is checked at any given time.

You could try putting the color selection item in an additional drop-down menu. You can do this by changing the code that follows the statement adding the separator in the Elements menu as follows:

```
elementMenu.addSeparator();

JMenu colorMenu = new JMenu("Color");                 // Color submenu
elementMenu.add(colorMenu);                           // Add the submenu
colorMenu.add(redItem = new JCheckBoxMenuItem("Red", false));
colorMenu.add(yellowItem = new JCheckBoxMenuItem("Yellow", false));
colorMenu.add(greenItem = new JCheckBoxMenuItem("Green", false));
colorMenu.add(blueItem = new JCheckBoxMenuItem("Blue", true));
```

Now you add a `JMenu` object, `colorMenu`, to the drop-down menu for Elements. This has its own drop-down menu consisting of the color menu items. The Color item will be displayed on the Elements menu with an arrow to show that a further drop-down menu is associated with it. If you run the application again and extend the drop-down menus, the window should be as shown in Figure 17-46.

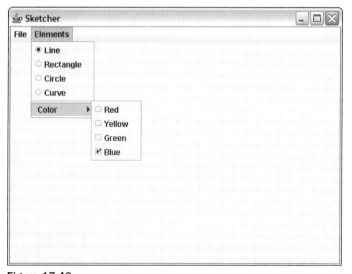

Figure 17-46

Whether you choose this menu structure or the previous one is a matter of taste. It might even be better to have a separate item on the menu bar, but let's leave it at that for now. You'll see in the next chapter that the programming necessary to deal with menu selections by the user is the same in either case.

Adding a Shortcut for a Menu Item

A **shortcut** is a unique key combination used to select a menu on the menu bar directly from the keyboard to display the drop-down menu. A typical shortcut under MS Windows would be the Alt key plus a letter from the menu item label, so the shortcut for the File menu item might be Alt+F. When you enter this key combination the menu is displayed. You can add shortcuts for the File and Elements menu items by adding the following statements after you add the menu items to the menu bar:

```
fileMenu.setMnemonic('F');               // Create shortcut
elementMenu.setMnemonic('E');            // Create shortcut
```

The setMnemonic() method is inherited from the AbstractButton class, so all subclasses of this class inherit this method. The argument is a character in the String that is the label for the item that is to be the shortcut character — under Windows, the File menu would then pop up if you key Alt+F. The effect of setMnemonic() is to implement the shortcut and underline the shortcut character letter in the menu label. Naturally, the shortcut for each menu on the menu bar must be a unique key combination.

An **accelerator** is a key combination that you can enter to select an item from a drop-down menu without having to go through the process of displaying the menu. Under Windows, the Ctrl key is frequently used in combination with a letter as an accelerator for a menu item, so Ctrl+L might be the combination for the Line item in the Elements menu. To define the accelerator for a menu item, you call the setAccelerator() method for the object that encapsulates the menu item. For example, for the Line menu item you could write:

```
lineItem.setAccelerator(KeyStroke.getKeyStroke('L', InputEvent.CTRL_DOWN_MASK ));
```

The javax.swing.KeyStroke class defines a keystroke combination. The static method getKeyStroke() in the KeyStroke class returns the KeyStroke object corresponding to the arguments. The first argument is a character in the keystroke combination and the second argument specifies one or more modifier keys. The modifier keys are specified as a combination of single-bit constants that are defined in the InputEvent class that appears in the java.awt.event package. The InputEvent class defines constants that identify control keys on the keyboard and mouse buttons. In this context, the constants you are interested are SHIFT_DOWN_MASK, ALT_DOWN_MASK, META_DOWN_MASK, and what you used in the preceding statement, CTRL_DOWN_MASK. If you want to express a combination of the Alt and Ctrl keys for example, you can add them as shown in the following expression:

```
InputEvent.ALT_DOWN_MASK + InputEvent.CTRL_DOWN_MASK
```

Of course, when you add accelerators for menu items, if the accelerators are to work properly, you must make sure that each accelerator key combination is unique. Let's see how this works in practice.

Try It Out   Adding Menu Shortcuts

You can add some shortcuts to Sketcher by amending the statements that add the items to the File menu in the SketchFrame class constructor:

```
// Frame for the Sketcher application
import javax.swing.JFrame;
import javax.swing.JMenuBar;
import javax.swing.JMenu;
```

```
import javax.swing.JMenuItem;
import javax.swing.JRadioButtonMenuItem;
import javax.swing.JCheckBoxMenuItem;
import javax.swing.ButtonGroup;
import javax.swing.KeyStroke;
import static java.awt.event.InputEvent.*;          // For modifier constants

public class SketchFrame extends JFrame {
  // Constructor
  public SketchFrame(String title) {
    setTitle(title);                                 // Call the base constructor
    setDefaultCloseOperation(EXIT_ON_CLOSE);
    setJMenuBar(menuBar);                            // Add the menu bar to the window

    JMenu fileMenu = new JMenu("File");              // Create File menu
    JMenu elementMenu = new JMenu("Elements");       // Create Elements menu
    fileMenu.setMnemonic('F');                       // Create shortcut
    elementMenu.setMnemonic('E');                    // Create shortcut

    // Construct the file drop-down menu as before...

    // Add File menu accelerators
    newItem.setAccelerator(KeyStroke.getKeyStroke('N',CTRL_DOWN_MASK ));
    openItem.setAccelerator(KeyStroke.getKeyStroke('O', CTRL_DOWN_MASK));
    saveItem.setAccelerator(KeyStroke.getKeyStroke('S', CTRL_DOWN_MASK));
    printItem.setAccelerator(KeyStroke.getKeyStroke('P', CTRL_DOWN_MASK));

    // Construct the Element drop-down menu as before...

    // Add element type accelerators
    lineItem.setAccelerator(KeyStroke.getKeyStroke('L', CTRL_DOWN_MASK));
    rectangleItem.setAccelerator(KeyStroke.getKeyStroke('E', CTRL_DOWN_MASK));
    circleItem.setAccelerator(KeyStroke.getKeyStroke('I', CTRL_DOWN_MASK));
    curveItem.setAccelerator(KeyStroke.getKeyStroke('V', CTRL_DOWN_MASK));

    elementMenu.addSeparator();

    // Create the color submenu as before...

    // Add element color accelerators
    redItem.setAccelerator(KeyStroke.getKeyStroke('R', CTRL_DOWN_MASK));
    yellowItem.setAccelerator(KeyStroke.getKeyStroke('Y', CTRL_DOWN_MASK));
    greenItem.setAccelerator(KeyStroke.getKeyStroke('G', CTRL_DOWN_MASK));
    blueItem.setAccelerator(KeyStroke.getKeyStroke('B', CTRL_DOWN_MASK));

    menuBar.add(fileMenu);                           // Add the file menu
    menuBar.add(elementMenu);                        // Add the element menu
  }

  // File menu items and the rest of the class as before...
}
```

If you save SketchFrame.java after you have made the changes, you can recompile Sketcher and run it again. The file menu will now appear as shown in Figure 17-47.

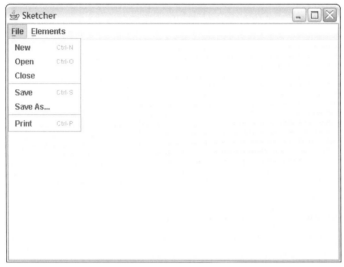

Figure 17-47

How It Works

You have added an import statement for the KeyStroke class, and a static import statement for the constants in the InputEvent class. The names of the constants are already wordy and importing the names saves having to add qualifiers to them.

You use the setMnemonic() method to set the shortcuts for the menu bar items, and the setAccelerator() method to add accelerators to the submenu items. You must make sure that you do not use duplicate key combinations, and the more menu items you have accelerators for, the trickier this gets. The File menu here defines the standard Windows accelerators. You can see that the setAccelerator() method adds the shortcut key combination to the item label.

The menus don't actually work at the moment but at least they look good! You'll start adding the code to implement menu operations in the next chapter.

More on Applets

Applets are a peculiar kind of program, as they are executed in the context of a web browser. This places some rather severe restrictions on what you can do in an applet to protect the environment in which it executes. Without these restrictions an applet would be a very direct means for someone to interfere with your system — in short, a virus delivery vehicle.

System security in Java programs is managed by a **security manager**. This is simply an object that provides methods for setting and checking security controls that determine what is and what is not allowed for a Java program. What an applet can and cannot do is determined by both the security manager that the browser running the applet has installed and the security policy that is in effect for the system.

Unless permitted explicitly by the security policy in effect, the main default limitations on an applet are:

❑ An applet cannot have any access to files on the local computer.

❑ An applet cannot invoke any other program on the local computer.

❑ An applet cannot communicate with any computer other than the computer from which the HTML page containing the applet was downloaded.

Obviously there will be circumstances where these restrictions are too stringent. In this case you can set up a security policy that allows certain operations for specific trusted programs, applets, or sites by authorizing them explicitly in a **policy file**. A policy file is an ASCII text file that defines what is permitted for a particular code source. I won't be going into details on this, but if you need to set up a policy file for your system, it is easiest to use the `policytool` program supplied with the JDK.

Because they are normally shipped over the Internet as part of an HTML page, applets should be compact. This doesn't mean that they are inevitably simple or unsophisticated. Because they can access the host computer from which they originated, they can provide a powerful means of enabling access to files on that host, but they are usually relatively small to enable them to be easily downloaded.

The `JApplet` class includes the following methods, which are all called automatically by the browser or applet viewer controlling the applet:

Method	Description
`void init()`	You implement this method to do any initialization that is necessary for the applet. This method is called once by the browser when the applet starts execution.
`void start()`	You implement this method to start the processing for the applet. For example, if your applet displays an animated image, you would start a thread for the animation in this method.
	This method is called by the browser immediately after `init()`. It is also called if the user returns to the current `.html` page after leaving it.
`void stop()`	This method is called by the browser when the user moves off the page containing the applet. You implement this to stop any operations that you started in the `start()` method.
`void destroy()`	This method is called after the `stop()` method when the browser is shut down. In this method you can release any resources your applet uses that are managed by the local operating system. This includes such things as resources used to display a window.

These are the basic methods you need to implement in the typical applet. You really need some graphics knowledge to go further with implementing an applet, so you'll return to the practical application of these methods in Chapter 18.

Converting an Application to an Applet

Subject to the restrictions described in the previous section, you can convert an application to an applet relatively easily. You just need to be clear about how each part of program executes. You know that an application is normally started in the method `main()`. The `main()` method is not called for an applet but the method `init()` is, so one thing you should do is add an `init()` method to the application class. The other obvious difference is that an applet always extends the `JApplet` class.

I can demonstrate how you can convert an application so that it also works as an applet by changing the definition of the `Sketcher` class and making a slight modification to the `SketchFrame` class. Sketcher doesn't make a very sensible applet, but you'll be able to see the principles at work. I suggest you copy the current `Sketcher.java` and `SketchFrame.java` class files for use with this example as you'll be discarding the applet version of Sketcher after you've tried it out.

Try It Out   Running Sketcher as an Applet

Having the applet code exit when you close the window is not really consistent with the notion of how an applet works, so you'll need to remove or comment out the following statement in the `SketchFrame` class constructor:

```
setDefaultCloseOperation(EXIT_ON_CLOSE);
```

You need to modify the contents of `Sketcher.java` so that it contains the following:

```java
// Sketching application
import java.awt.Dimension;
import java.awt.Toolkit;
import javax.swing.JApplet;

public class Sketcher extends JApplet {
  public static void main(String[] args) {
    theApp = new Sketcher();              // Create the application object
    theApp.init();                        // ...and initialize it
  }

  public void init() {
    window = new SketchFrame("Sketcher");           // Create the app window
    Toolkit theKit = window.getToolkit();           // Get the window toolkit
    Dimension wndSize = theKit.getScreenSize();     // Get screen size

    // Set the position to screen center & size to half screen size
    window.setBounds(wndSize.width/4, wndSize.height/4,          // Position
                     wndSize.width/2, wndSize.height/2);         // Size

    // The field theApp will be null when Sketcher is an applet
    if(theApp != null) {
      window.setDefaultCloseOperation(window.EXIT_ON_CLOSE);
    }

    window.setVisible(true);
  }
```

```
    private static SketchFrame window;              // The application window
    private static Sketcher theApp;                 // The application object
}
```

To run Sketcher as an applet, you should add an .htm file to the Sketcher directory with the contents:

```
<APPLET CODE="Sketcher.class" WIDTH=300 HEIGHT=200>
</APPLET>
```

If you recompile the revised version of the Sketcher class, you can run it as before, or using appletviewer, or even within your browser.

How It Works

The class now extends the class JApplet, and an import statement has been added for the javax.swing.JApplet class name.

The init() method now does most of what the method main() did before. The method main() now creates an instance of the Sketcher class and stores it in the static data member theApp. The method main() then calls the init() method for the new Sketcher object.

When Sketcher runs as an application, execution starts with the main() method, which creates an instance of the Sketcher class and stores it in the theApp field. The main() method then calls the init() method for the object referenced by theApp, and this will create the application window. When Sketcher executes as an applet, a Sketcher object will be instantiated by the environment executed by the applet, but the field, theApp, will not be initialized, so it will be null by default. This enables you to test theApp in the init() method to decide whether or not to call the setDefaultCloseOperation() for the window object. If you were to call this method in an applet, the security manager would not allow the applet to execute.

Even if Sketcher is running as an applet, the application window appears as a detached window from the Applet Viewer window, and it is still positioned relative to the screen.

Of course, when you implement the File menu, it will no longer be legal to derive the Sketcher class from the JApplet class since it will contravene the rule that an applet must not access the files on the local machine. It is also not recommended to create frame windows from within an untrusted applet, so you may get a warning from the appletviewer about this. As I previously mentioned, Sketcher doesn't make a very sensible applet, so you'll continue in the next chapter developing Sketcher from the previous version, when it was simply an application.

Summary

In this chapter you have learned how to create an application window, and how to use containers in the creation of the GUI for a program. I discussed the following important points:

❑   The package javax.swing provides classes for creating a graphical user interface (GUI).

❑   A component is an object that is used to form part of the GUI for a program. All components have the class Component as a superclass.

❏ A container is a component that can contain other components. A container object is created with a class that is a subclass of Container. The classes JPanel, JApplet, JWindow, JFrame, and JDialog are containers.

❏ The class JApplet is the base class for an applet. The JFrame class is a base class for an application window with a title bar, borders, and a menu.

❏ The arrangement of components in a container is controlled by a layout manager.

❏ The default layout manager for the content pane of JFrame, JApplet, and JDialog objects is BorderLayout.

❏ The GridBagLayout provides the most flexible control of the positioning of components in a container. The position of a component in a GridBagLayout is controlled by a GridBagConstraints object.

❏ A Box container can be used to arrange components or containers in rows and columns. You can use multiple nested Box containers in combination to easily create complex arrangements that otherwise might require GridBagLayout to be used.

❏ A layout manager of type SpringLayout arranges components by applying constraints in the form of Spring objects to their edges.

❏ A menu bar is represented by a JMenuBar object. Menu items can be objects of type JMenu, JMenuItem, JCheckBoxMenuItem, or JRadioButtonMenuItem.

❏ You associate a drop-down menu with an item of type JMenu.

❏ You can create a shortcut for a menu by calling its setMnemonic() method, and you can create an accelerator key combination for a menu item by calling its setAccelerator() method.

In the next chapter you'll move on to look at events — that is, how you associate program actions with menu items and components within a window.

Exercises

You can download the source code for the examples in the book and the solutions to the following exercises from http://www.wrox.com.

1. Create an application with a square window in the center of the screen that is half the height of the screen by deriving your own window class from JFrame.

2. Add six buttons to the application in the previous example in a vertical column on the left side of the application window.

3. Add a menu bar containing the items File, Edit, Window, and Help.

4. Add a drop-down menu for Edit containing two groups of items of your own choice with a separator between them.

5. Add another item to the Edit drop-down menu, which itself has a drop-down menu, and provide accelerators for the items in the menu.

6. Here's an exercise to tickle the brain cells — use a `SpringLayout` to obtain the button arrangement shown in Figure 17-48 in an application window.

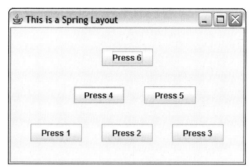

Figure 17-48

Handling Events

In this chapter you'll learn how a window-based Java application is structured and how to respond to user actions in an application or an applet. This is the fundamental mechanism you'll be using in virtually all of your graphical Java programs. Once you understand how user actions are handled in Java, you'll be equipped to implement the application-specific code that is necessary to make your program do what you want.

You will learn:

- ❑ What an event is
- ❑ What an event-driven program is and how it is structured
- ❑ How events are handled in Java
- ❑ How events are categorized in Java
- ❑ How components handle events
- ❑ What an event listener is and how you create one
- ❑ What an adapter class is and how you can use it to make programming the handling of events easier
- ❑ What actions are and how you use them
- ❑ How to create a toolbar

Window-Based Java Programs

Before you get into the programming specifics of window-based programs, you need to understand a little of how such programs are structured, and how they work. There are fundamental differences between the console programs that you have been producing up to now and a window-based Java program. With a console program, you start the program, and the program code determines the sequences of events. Generally everything is predetermined. You enter data when required, and the program will output data when it wants. At any given time, the specific program code that will execute next is generally known.

A window-based application, or an applet for that matter, is quite different. The operation of the program is driven by what you do with the graphical user interface (GUI). Selecting menu items or buttons using the mouse, or through the keyboard, causes particular actions within the program. At any given moment you have a whole range of possible interactions available to you, each of which will result in a different program action. Until you do something, the specific program code that is to be executed next is not known.

Event-Driven Programs

Your actions when you're using the GUI for a window-based program or an applet — clicking a menu item or a button, moving the mouse, and so on — are first recognized by the operating system. For each action, the operating system determines which of the programs currently running on your computer should know about it and passes the action on to that program. When you click a mouse button, it's the operating system that registers this and notes the position of the mouse cursor on the screen. It then decides which application controls the window where the cursor was when you pressed the button, and communicates the mouse button-press to that program. The signals that a program receives from the operating system as a result of your actions are called **events**. The basic idea of how actions and events are communicated to your program code is illustrated in Figure 18-1.

A program is not obliged to respond to any particular event. If you just move the mouse, for example, the program need not invoke any code to react to that. If it doesn't, the event is quietly disposed of. Each event that the program does recognize is associated with one or more methods, and when the event occurs — when you click a menu item, for example — the appropriate methods will be called automatically. A window-based program is called an **event-driven program** because the sequence of events created as a result of your interaction with the GUI drives and determines what happens in the program.

> **Events are not limited to window-based applications — they are a quite general concept. Most programs that control or monitor things in the real world are event-driven. Any occurrence external to a program, such as a switch closing or a preset temperature being reached, can be registered as an event. In Java you can even create events within your program to signal some other part of the code that something noteworthy has happened. However, I'm going to concentrate on the kinds of events that occur when you interact as a user with a program.**

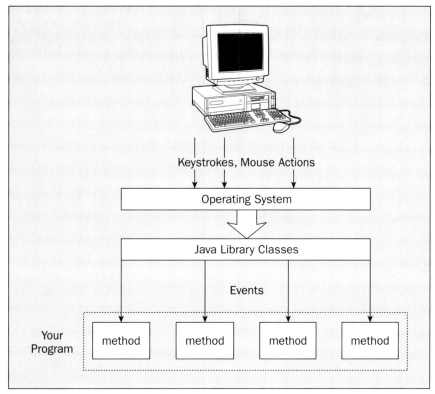

Figure 18-1

The Event-Handling Process

To manage the user's interaction with the components that make up the GUI for a program, you must understand how events are handled in Java. To get an idea of how this works, let's consider a specific example. Don't worry too much about the class names and other details here. Just try to get a feel for how things connect.

Suppose the user clicks a button in the GUI for your program. The button is the source of this event. The event that is generated as a result of the mouse click is associated with the JButton object in your program that represents the button on the screen. An event always has a source object — in this case the JButton object. When the button is clicked, it creates a new object that represents and identifies this event — in this case an object of type `ActionEvent`. This object contains information about the event and its source. Any event that is passed to a Java program will be represented by a particular event object — and this object will be passed as an argument to the method that is to handle the event. Figure 18-2 illustrates this mechanism.

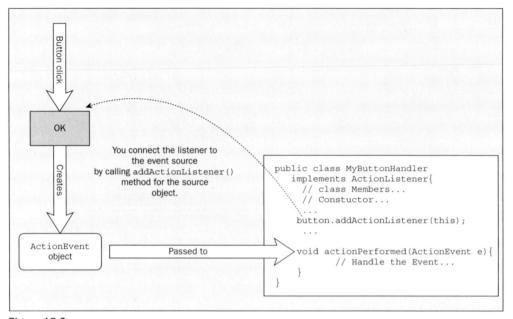

Figure 18-2

The event object corresponding to the button click will be passed to any **listener object** that has previously registered an interest in this kind of event — a listener object being simply an object that listens for particular events. A listener is also called a target for an event. Here, "passing the event to the listener" just means the event source calls a particular method in the listener object and passes the event object to it as an argument. A listener object can listen for events for a particular object — just a single button, for example — or it can listen for events for several different objects — a group of menu items, for example. Which approach you take when you define a class representing listeners depends on the context and which is most convenient from a programming point of view. Your programs will often involve both.

So how do you define a class that represents a listener? You can make the objects of any class listener objects by making the class implement a **listener interface**. You will find quite a variety of listener interfaces, to cater to different kinds of events. In the case of our button click, the `ActionListener` interface needs to be implemented to receive the event from the button. The code that is to receive this event object and respond to the event is implemented in a method declared in the listener interface. In this example, the `actionPerformed()` method in the `ActionListener` interface is called when the event occurs, and the event object is passed as an argument. Each kind of listener interface defines particular methods for receiving the events that that listener has been designed to deal with.

Simply implementing a listener interface isn't sufficient to link the listener object to an event source. You still have to connect the listener to the source, or sources, of the events that you want it to deal with. You register a listener object with a source by calling a particular method in the source object. To register a listener to listen for button-click events, you call the `addActionListener()` method for the `JButton` object and pass the listener object as the argument to the method.

This mechanism for handling events using listeners is very flexible and very efficient, particularly for GUI events. Any number of listeners can receive a particular event. However, a particular event is passed only to the listeners that have registered to receive it, so only interested parties are involved in responding to each event. Since being a listener just requires a suitable interface to be implemented, you can receive and handle events virtually anywhere you like. The way in which events are handled in Java, using listener objects, is referred to as the **delegation event model**. This is because the responsibility for responding to events that originate with a component, such as a button or a menu item, is not handled by the objects that originated the events themselves — but is delegated to separate listener objects.

> *Not all event handling necessarily requires a separate listener. A component can handle its own events, as you'll see a little later in this chapter.*

A very important point to keep in mind when writing code to handle events is that all such code executes in the same thread, the event-dispatching thread, which is separate from the thread in which `main()` executes. This implies that while your event-handling code is executing, no other events can be processed. The code to handle the next event will start executing only when the current event-handler finishes. Thus, the responsiveness of your program to the user is dependent on how long your event-handling code takes to execute. For snappy performance, your event handlers must take as little time as possible to execute. Also, because events are processed in a separate thread from the main thread, you must not modify or query the GUI for an application from the main thread once the GUI has been displayed or is ready to be displayed. Otherwise, a deadlock may result.

Avoiding Deadlocks in GUI Code

Preparing the application window and any components it contains and displaying it is described as **realizing** the window. Calling `setVisible()` for an application window object realizes the window. As I said in the previous section, once an application GUI has been realized, modifying or querying it on the main thread can cause deadlock because user interactions with the GUI, such as clicking a menu item, are handled in the event-dispatching thread. There is also the rare possibility with some types of Swing components that deadlocks can occur even when it is not apparent that you are modifying the GUI after it has been realized. You can avoid any possibility of deadlock in your application arising from your GUI creation code by arranging to execute all the code that creates the GUI on the event-dispatching thread.

The `javax.swing.SwingUtilities` class provides the static `invokeLater()` method, which makes creating the GUI on the event-dispatching thread very easy. The `invokeLater()` method expects an argument of type `Runnable`, which is a reference to an object of a type that implements the `Runnable` interface. A simple way of defining a `Runnable` object that will create the GUI for an application is to use an anonymous class. Let's see how that works.

Try It Out   **Creating the GUI on the Event-Dispatching Thread**

You can modify the last version of the Sketcher application in Chapter 17 to use the `invokeLater()` method from the `SwingUtilities` class. Copy the `Sketcher.java` and `SketchFrame.java` files to a new directory and modify the `Sketcher` class definition as follows:

```java
import java.awt.Toolkit;
import java.awt.Dimension;
import javax.swing.SwingUtilities;

public class Sketcher {
  public static void main(String[] args) {
    SwingUtilities.invokeLater(
      new Runnable() {                      // Anonymous Runnable class object
          public void run() {               // Run method executed in thread
            creatGUI();                     // Call static GUI creator
          }
      } );
  }

  static void creatGUI() {
    window = new SketchFrame("Sketcher");       // Create the app window
    Toolkit theKit = window.getToolkit();       // Get the window toolkit
    Dimension wndSize = theKit.getScreenSize(); // Get screen size

    // Set the position to screen center & size to half screen size
    window.setBounds(wndSize.width/4, wndSize.height/4,       // Position
                     wndSize.width/2, wndSize.height/2);      // Size

    window.setVisible(true);
  }

  private static SketchFrame window;                // The application window
}
```

If you look in the directory after you have recompiled Sketcher, you'll see there are three `.class` files, the two corresponding to the `Sketcher` and `SketchFrame` classes and the third corresponding to the anonymous class. This version of Sketcher will display the application window with the File and Elements menus exactly as the last example in the previous chapter.

How It Works

All the GUI creation code that was in `main()` is now in a separate static method `createGUI()`. The `main()` method now calls the static `invokeLater()` method that is defined in the `SwingUtilities` class. The `invokeLater()` method executes the `run()` method for the object that is passed as the argument on the event-dispatching thread after all pending events have been processed. It is sometimes useful to call this method from within event-handling code that is already executing in the event-dispatching thread because it provides a way for you to defer execution of the `run()` method in your `Runnable` object until after outstanding events have been processed when this is desirable.

You pass an object of an anonymous class that implements the `Runnable` interface to the `invokeLater()` method. You have defined the anonymous class as:

```
new Runnable() {                  // Anonymous Runnable class object
    public void run() {           // Run method executed in thread
        createGUI();              // Call static GUI creator
    }
}
```

You'll recall from Chapter 16 that the `Runnable` interface defines just the `run()` method that is called when the object is executed in a new thread, so the anonymous class needs to define only that method. The `run()` method just calls the static method in the `Sketcher` class that creates the window and its components, so it is this code that will now execute on the event-dispatching thread.

Let's now get down to looking at the specifics of what kinds of events you can expect and the range of listener interfaces that processes them.

Event Classes

Your program may need to respond to many different kinds of events — from menus, from buttons, from the mouse, from the keyboard, and from a number of other components. To have a structured approach to handling events, the events are broken down into subsets. At the topmost level, there are two broad categories of events in Java:

❑ **Low-Level Events** — These are system-level events that arise from the keyboard or from the mouse, or events associated with operations on a window, such as reducing it to an icon or closing it. The meaning of a low-level event is something like "the mouse was moved," "this window has been closed," or "this key was pressed."

❑ **Semantic Events** — These are specific component-related events such as pressing a button by clicking it to cause some program action or adjusting a scrollbar. They originate, and you interpret them, in the context of the GUI you have created for your program. The meaning of a semantic event is typically along the lines of "the OK button was pressed," or "the Save menu item was selected." Each kind of component, a button or a menu item, for example, can generate a particular kind of semantic event.

These two categories can seem to be a bit confusing as they overlap in a way. If you click a button, you create a semantic event as well as a low level event. The click produces a low-level event object in the form of 'the mouse was clicked' as well as a semantic event 'the button was pushed'. In fact it produces more than one mouse event, as you'll see. Whether your program handles the low-level events or the semantic events, or possibly both kinds of events, depends on what you want to do.

Most of the events relating to the GUI for a program are represented by classes that are defined in the `java.awt.event` package. This package also defines the listener interfaces for the various kinds of events that it defines. The package `javax.swing.event` defines classes for events that are specific to Swing components.

Low-Level Event Classes

You can elect to handle four kinds of low-level events in your programs. They are represented by the following classes in the `java.awt.event` package:

Event	Description
FocusEvent	Objects of this class represent events that originate when a component gains or loses the keyboard focus. Only the component that has the focus can receive input from the keyboard, so it will usually be highlighted or have the cursor displayed.
MouseEvent	Objects of this class represent events that result from user actions with the mouse, such as moving the mouse or pressing a mouse button.
KeyEvent	Objects of this class represent events that arise from pressing keys on the keyboard.
WindowEvent	Objects of this class represent events that relate to a window, such as activating or deactivating a window, reducing a window to its icon, or closing a window. These events relate to objects of the `Window` class or any subclass of `Window`.

The `MouseEvent` class has two subclasses that identify more specialized mouse events. One is the `MenuDragMouseEvent` class that defines event objects signaling when the mouse has been dragged over a menu item. The other is the `MouseWheelEvent` class that defines event objects indicating when the mouse wheel is rotated.

> **Just so that you know, this isn't an exhaustive list of all of the low-level event classes. It's a list of the ones you need to know about. For example, there's also the `PaintEvent` class that is concerned with the internals of how components are painted on the screen. There's also another low-level event class, `ContainerEvent`, that defines events relating to a container, such as adding or removing components. You can ignore these classes, as these events are handled automatically.**

Each of these event classes defines methods that enable you to analyze the event. For a `MouseEvent` object, for example, you can get the coordinates of the cursor when the event occurred. These low-level event classes also inherit methods from their superclasses and are related in the manner shown in Figure 18-3.

The `AWTEvent` class is itself a subclass of `java.util.EventObject`. The `EventObject` class implements the `Serializable` interface, so all objects of the event classes in the diagram are serializable. It also defines a method, `getSource()`, that returns the object that is the source of an event as type `Object`. All the event classes shown inherit this method.

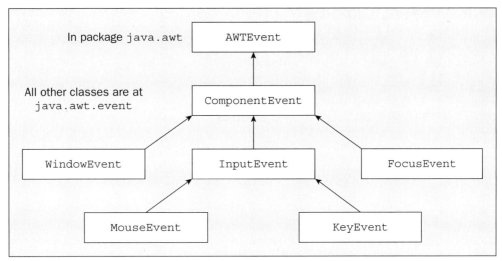

In package `java.awt`

AWTEvent

All other classes are at
`java.awt.event`

ComponentEvent

WindowEvent

InputEvent

FocusEvent

MouseEvent

KeyEvent

Figure 18-3

The `AWTEvent` class defines constants that are public final values identifying the various kinds of events. These constants are named for the sake of consistency as the event name in capital letters, followed by _MASK. The constants identifying the low-level events that you are most likely to be interested in are:

MOUSE_EVENT_MASK	MOUSE_MOTION_EVENT_MASK
MOUSE_WHEEL_EVENT_MASK	KEY_EVENT_MASK
ADJUSTMENT_EVENT_MASK	WINDOW_EVENT_MASK
WINDOW_FOCUS_EVENT_MASK	WINDOW_STATUS_EVENT_MASK
TEXT_EVENT_MASK	ITEM_EVENT_MASK
FOCUS_EVENT_MASK	

Each of these constants is a value of type `long` with a single bit set to 1 and all the remaining set to 0. Because they are defined this way you can combine them using a bitwise OR operator and you can separate a particular constant out from a combination by using a bitwise AND.

> **The list of event masks above is not exhaustive. There are masks for component events represented by objects of the class `ComponentEvent` and for container events. These events occur when a component is moved or resized, or a component is added to a container, for example. There is also a mask for events associated with components that receive text input. You won't normally need to get involved in these events so I won't be discussing them further.**

You use the identifiers for event masks to enable a particular group of events in a component object. You call the `enableEvents()` method for the component, and pass the variable for the events you want enabled as an argument. However, you do this only when you aren't using a listener. Registering a listener automatically enables the events that the listener wants to hear, so you don't need to call the `enableEvents()` method. The circumstance when you might do this is when you want an object to handle some of its own events, although you can achieve the same result using a listener.

Making a Window Handle Its Own Events

Using listeners is the preferred way of handling events since it is easier than enabling events directly for an object, and the code is clearer. Nonetheless, you should take a look at how events are dealt with after calling `enableEvents()` in case you come across it elsewhere. An example of where you might want to call `enableEvents()` exists in the `SketchFrame` class in the Sketcher program.

As you may recall from the previous chapter, you used the `setDefaultCloseOperation()` method to determine what happens when you close the window by clicking the X icon. Although the `EXIT_ON_CLOSE` argument value that you used disposed of the frame and closed the application, it didn't provide any opportunity to do any checking or cleanup before causing the program to exit. You can respond to the close icon being clicked in the program yourself, rather than letting the `JFrame` facilities handle the associated event within the window object itself. This will eventually enable you to prompt the user to save any data that has been created before shutting down the application when a close event occurs, so let's give it a try.

Try It Out   Closing a Window

You need to modify the `SketchFrame` class definition from the previous example as follows:

```
// Frame for the Sketcher application
import javax.swing.JFrame;
import javax.swing.JMenuBar;
import javax.swing.JMenu;
import javax.swing.JMenuItem;
import javax.swing.JRadioButtonMenuItem;
import javax.swing.JCheckBoxMenuItem;
import javax.swing.ButtonGroup;
import javax.swing.KeyStroke;
import java.awt.Event;
import static java.awt.event.InputEvent.*;
import static java.awt.AWTEvent.*;
import java.awt.event.WindowEvent;

public class SketchFrame extends JFrame {
  // Constructor
  public SketchFrame(String title) {
    setTitle(title);                            // Set the window title
    //   setDefaultCloseOperation(EXIT_ON_CLOSE);

    // rest of code as before...

    menuBar.add(fileMenu);                       // Add the file menu
    menuBar.add(elementMenu);                    // Add the element menu
    enableEvents(WINDOW_EVENT_MASK);             // Enable window events
  }
```

```
      // Handle window events
      protected void processWindowEvent(WindowEvent e) {
        if (e.getID() == WindowEvent.WINDOW_CLOSING) {
          dispose();                     // Release resources
          System.exit(0);                // Exit the program
        }
        super.processWindowEvent(e);     // Pass on the event
      }

      private JMenuBar menuBar = new JMenuBar();        // Window menu bar

      // File menu items
      private JMenuItem newItem,    openItem,    closeItem,
                    saveItem, saveAsItem, printItem;

      // Element menu items
      private JRadioButtonMenuItem lineItem,   rectangleItem, circleItem,   // Types
                                   curveItem, textItem;
      private JCheckBoxMenuItem    redItem,    yellowItem,                   // Colors
                                   greenItem, blueItem ;
    }
```

You add the call to enableEvents() as the last in the constructor. Note that the statement that sets EXIT_ON_CLOSE as the close option for the window is commented out. You could delete the statement if you want. When you compile SketchFrame and run Sketcher again, you'll be able to close the window as before, and the program will shut down gracefully. However, this time it's your method that's doing it.

How It Works

The additional import statements make the constants defined in the AWTEvent class and the WindowEvent class name available to your source file without the need to qualify them with the package names. You call enableEvents() in the constructor with WINDOW_EVENT_MASK as the argument to enable window events. This enables all the window events represented by the WindowEvent class. An object of this class can represent one of a number of different window events that are each identified by an event ID, which is a constant defined within the WindowEvent class. The event IDs for the WindowEvent class are:

Event ID	Description
WINDOW_OPENED	The event that occurs the first time a window is made visible.
WINDOW_CLOSING	The event that occurs as a result of the close icon being selected or Close being selected from the window's system menu.
WINDOW_CLOSED	The event that occurs when the window has been closed.
WINDOW_ACTIVATED	The event that occurs when the window is activated — obtains the focus, in other words. When another GUI component has the focus, you could make the window obtain the focus by clicking on it, for example.

Table continued on following page

Event ID	Description
WINDOW_DEACTIVATED	The event that occurs when the window is deactivated — loses the focus, in other words. Clicking on another window would cause this event, for example.
WINDOW_GAINED_FOCUS	The event that occurs when the window gains the focus. This implies that the window or one of its components will receive keyboard events.
WINDOW_LOST_FOCUS	The event that occurs when the window loses the focus. This implies that keyboard events will not be delivered to the window or any of its components.
WINDOW_ICONIFIED	The event that occurs when the window is minimized and reduced to an icon.
WINDOW_DEICONIFIED	The event that occurs when the window is restored from an icon.
WINDOW_STATE_CHANGED	The event that occurs when the window state changes — when it is maximized or minimized, for instance.

If any of these events occur, the processWindowEvent() method that you have added to the SketchFrame class will be called. Your version of the method overrides the base class method that is inherited from java.awt.Window, and is responsible for passing the event to any listeners that have been registered. The argument of type WindowEvent that is passed to the method will contain the event ID that identifies the particular event that occurred. To obtain the ID of the event, you call the getID() method for the event object, and compare that with the ID identifying the WINDOW_CLOSING event. If the event is WINDOW_CLOSING, you call the dispose() method for the window to close the window and release the system resources it is using. You then close the application by calling the exit() method defined in the System class.

The getID() method is defined in the AWTEvent class, which is a superclass of all the low-level event classes I have discussed, so all event objects that encapsulate low-level events have this method.

In the SketchFrame class, the dispose() method is inherited originally from the Window class via the base class JFrame. This method releases all the resources for the window object, including those for all components owned by the object. Calling the dispose() method doesn't affect the window object itself in the program. It just tells the operating system that the resources used to display the window and the components it contains on the screen are no longer required. The window object is still around together with its components, so you could call its methods or even open it again.

> Note that you call the processWindowEvent() method in the superclass if it is not the closing event. It is very important that you do this as it allows the event to be passed on to any listeners that have been registered for these events. If you don't call processWindowEvent() for the superclass, any events that you do not handle in your processWindowEvent() method will be lost, because the base class method is normally responsible for passing the event to the listeners that have been registered to receive it.

If you had not commented out the call to the `setDefaultCloseOperation()` method, your `processWindowEvent()` method would still have been called when the close icon was clicked. In this case you would not need to call `dispose()` and `exit()` in the method. This would all have been taken care of automatically after your `processWindowEvent()` method had finished executing. This would be preferable as it means there would be less code in your program, and the code to handle the default close action is there in the `JFrame` class anyway.

Enabling Other Low-level Events

The `enableEvents()` method is inherited from the `Component` class. This means that any component can elect to handle its own events. You just call the `enableEvents()` method for the component and pass an argument defining the events you want the component to handle. If you want to enable more than one type of event for a component, you just combine the event masks from `AWTEvent` that you saw earlier by linking them with a bitwise OR. To make the window object handle mouse events as well as window events, you could write:

```
enableEvents(WINDOW_EVENT_MASK | MOUSE_EVENT_MASK);
```

Of course, you must now also implement the `processMouseEvent()` method for the `SketchFrame` class. Like the `processWindowEvent()` method, this method is protected and has `void` as the return type. It receives the event as an argument of type `MouseEvent`. There are two other methods specific to the `Window` class that handle events:

Event-Handling Methods	Description
`processWindowFocusEvent(WindowEvent e)`	This method is called for any window focus events that arise as long as such events are enabled for the window.
`processWindowStateEvent(WindowEvent e)`	This method is called for events arising as a result of the window changing state.

These methods and the `processWindowEvent()` method are available only for objects of type Window or of a type that is a subclass of Window, so don't try to enable window events on other components.

The other event-handling methods that you can override to handle component events are:

Event-Handling Methods	Description
`processEvent(AWTEvent e)`	This method is called first for any events that are enabled for the component. If you implement this method and fail to call the base class method, none of the methods for specific groups of events will be called.
`processFocusEvent(FocusEvent e)`	This method will be called for focus events, if they are enabled for the component.

Table continued on following page

Event-Handling Methods	Description
`processKeyEvent(KeyEvent e)`	This method will be called for key events, if they are enabled for the component.
`processMouseEvent(MouseEvent e)`	This method will be called for mouse button events, if they are enabled for the component.
`processMouseMotionEvent(MouseEvent e)`	This method will be called for mouse move and drag events, if they are enabled for the component.
`processMouseWheelEvent(MouseWheelEvent e)`	This method will be called for mouse wheel rotation events, if they are enabled for the component.

All the event-handling methods for a component are protected methods that have a return type of `void`. The default behavior implemented by these methods is to dispatch the events to any listeners registered for the component. If you don't call the base class method when you override these methods after your code has executed, this behavior will be lost.

> **Although it seemed to be convenient to handle the window-closing event in the `SketchFrame` class by implementing `processWindowEvent()`, as a general rule you should use listeners to handle events. Using listeners is the recommended approach to handling events in the majority of circumstances, since separating the event handling from the object that originated the event results in a simpler code structure that is easier to understand and is less error prone. You will change the handling of the window-closing event in the Sketcher code to use a listener a little later in this chapter.**

Low-Level Event Listeners

To create a class that defines an event listener, your class must implement a listener interface. All event listener interfaces extend the interface `java.util.EventListener`. This interface doesn't declare any methods, though — it's just used to identify an interface as being an event listener interface. It also allows a variable of type `EventListener` to be used for storing a reference to any kind of event listener object.

There is a very large number of event listener interfaces. You'll consider just eight at this point that are concerned with low-level events. The following sections describe these interfaces and the methods they declare.

The WindowListener Interface

This interface defines methods to respond to events reflecting changes in the state of a window.

Defined Methods	Description
windowOpened(WindowEvent e)	Called the first time the window is opened
windowClosing(WindowEvent e)	Called when the system menu Close item or the window close icon is selected
windowClosed(WindowEvent e)	Called when the window has been closed
windowActivated(WindowEvent e)	Called when the window is activated — by clicking on it, for example
windowDeactivated(WindowEvent e)	Called when a window is deactivated — by clicking on another window, for example
windowIconified(WindowEvent e)	Called when a window is minimized and reduced to an icon
windowDeiconified(WindowEvent e)	Called when a window is restored from an icon

The WindowFocusListener Interface

This interface defines methods to respond to a window gaining or losing the focus. When a window has the focus, one of its child components can receive input from the keyboard. When it loses the focus, keyboard input via a child component of the window is not possible.

Defined Methods	Description
windowGainedFocus(WindowEvent e)	Called when the window gains the focus such that the window or one of its components will receive keyboard events.
windowLostFocus(WindowEvent e)	Called when the window loses the focus. After this event, neither the window nor any of its components will receive keyboard events.

The WindowStateListener Interface

This interface defines a method to respond to any change in the state of a window.

Defined Method	Description
windowStateChanged(WindowEvent e)	Called when the window state changes — when it is maximized or iconified, for example

The MouseListener Interface

This interface defines methods to respond to events arising when the mouse cursor is moved into or out of the area occupied by a component, or one of the mouse buttons is pressed, released, or clicked.

Defined Methods	Description
mouseClicked(MouseEvent e)	Called when a mouse button is clicked on a component — that is, when the button is pressed and released
mousePressed(MouseEvent e)	Called when a mouse button is pressed on a component
mouseReleased(MouseEvent e)	Called when a mouse button is released on a component
mouseEntered(MouseEvent e)	Called when the mouse enters the area occupied by a component
mouseExited(MouseEvent e)	Called when the mouse exits the area occupied by a component

The MouseMotionListener Interface

This interface defines methods that are called when the mouse is moved or dragged with a button pressed.

Defined Methods	Description
mouseMoved(MouseEvent e)	Called when the mouse is moved within a component
mouseDragged(MouseEvent e)	Called when the mouse is moved within a component while a mouse button is held down

The MouseWheelListener Interface

This interface defines a method to respond to the mouse wheel being rotated. This is frequently used to scroll information that is displayed, but you can use it in any way that you want.

Defined Method	Description
mouseWheelMoved(MouseWheelEvent e)	Called when the mouse wheel is rotated

The KeyListener Interface

This interface defines methods to respond to events arising when a key on the keyboard is pressed or released.

Defined Methods	Description
keyTyped(KeyEvent e)	Called when a key on the keyboard is pressed and then released
keyPressed(KeyEvent e)	Called when a key on the keyboard is pressed
keyReleased(KeyEvent e)	Called when a key on the keyboard is released

The FocusListener Interface

This interface defines methods to respond to a component gaining or losing the focus. You might implement these methods to change the appearance of the component to reflect whether or not it has the focus.

Defined Methods	Description
focusGained(FocusEvent e)	Called when a component gains the keyboard focus
focusLost(FocusEvent e)	Called when a component loses the keyboard focus

There is a further listener interface, MouseInputListener, that is defined in the javax.swing.event package. This listener implements both the MouseListener and MouseMotionListener interfaces so it declares methods for all possible mouse events in a single interface.

The WindowListener, WindowFocusListener, and WindowStateListener interfaces define methods corresponding to each of the event IDs defined in the WindowEvent class that you saw earlier. If you deduced from this that the methods in the other listener interfaces correspond to event IDs for the other event classes, well, you're right. All the IDs for mouse events are defined in the MouseEvent class. These are:

MOUSE_CLICKED	MOUSE_PRESSED	MOUSE_DRAGGED
MOUSE_ENTERED	MOUSE_EXITED	MOUSE_RELEASED
MOUSE_MOVED	MOUSE_WHEEL	

The MOUSE_MOVED event corresponds to just moving the mouse. The MOUSE_DRAGGED event arises when you move the mouse while keeping a button pressed.

The event IDs that the KeyEvent class defines are:

KEY_TYPED	KEY_PRESSED	KEY_RELEASED

Those defined in the FocusEvent class are:

FOCUS_GAINED	FOCUS_LOST

To implement a listener for a particular event type, you just need to implement the methods declared in the corresponding interface. You could handle some of the window events for the SketchFrame class by making the application class the listener for window events.

Try It Out   Implementing a Low-Level Event Listener

First, delete the call to the enableEvents() method in the SketchFrame() constructor. Then delete the definition of the processWindowEvent() method from the class definition.

Now you can modify the previous version of the Sketcher class so that it is a listener for window events:

```
// Sketching application
import java.awt.Dimension;
import java.awt.Toolkit;
import java.awt.event.WindowListener;
import java.awt.event.WindowEvent;

public class Sketcher implements WindowListener {
  public static void main(String[] args) {
    theApp = new Sketcher();             // Create the application object
    SwingUtilities.invokeLater(
      new Runnable() {                   // Anonymous Runnable class object
                    public void run() {  // Run method executed in thread
                      theApp.creatGUI(); // Call static GUI creator
                    }
                 }     );
  }

  // Method to create the application GUI
  private void creatGUI() {
    window = new SketchFrame("Sketcher");        // Create the app window
    Toolkit theKit = window.getToolkit();        // Get the window toolkit
    Dimension wndSize = theKit.getScreenSize();  // Get screen size

    // Set the position to screen center & size to half screen size
    window.setBounds(wndSize.width/4, wndSize.height/4,        // Position
                wndSize.width/2, wndSize.height/2);       // Size

    window.addWindowListener(this);               // theApp as window listener
    window.setVisible(true);
  }

  // Handler for window closing event
  public void windowClosing(WindowEvent e) {
    window.dispose();                      // Release the window resources
    System.exit(0);                        // End the application
  }

  // Listener interface functions you must implement - but don't need
  public void windowOpened(WindowEvent e) {}
  public void windowClosed(WindowEvent e) {}
```

```
      public void windowIconified(WindowEvent e) {}
      public void windowDeiconified(WindowEvent e) {}
      public void windowActivated(WindowEvent e) {}
      public void windowDeactivated(WindowEvent e) {}

   private SketchFrame window;                    // The application window
   private static Sketcher theApp;                // The application object
}
```

If you run the Sketcher program again, you will see it works just as before, but now the Sketcher class object is handling the close operation.

How It Works

You have added import statements for the WindowEvent and WindowListener class names. The Sketcher class now implements the WindowListener interface, so an object of type Sketcher can handle window events. The main() method now creates a Sketcher object and stores the reference in the static class member theApp.

The createGUI() method is now an instance method, and this executes on the event-dispatching thread as shown in the previous example. The createGUI() method creates the application window object as before, but now the reference is stored in a field belonging to theApp. After setting up the window components, the createGUI() method calls the addWindowListener() method for the window object. The argument to the addWindowListener() method is a reference to the listener object that is to receive window events. Here it is the variable this, which refers to the application object, theApp. If you had other listener objects that you wanted to register to receive this event, you would just need to add more calls to the addWindowListener() method — one call for each listener.

When you implement the WindowListener interface in the Sketcher class, you must implement all seven methods that are declared in the interface. If you failed to do this, the class would be abstract and you could not create an object of type Sketcher. Only the windowClosing() method contains code here — the bodies of all the other methods are empty because you don't need to use them. The windowClosing() method does the same as the processWindowEvent() method that you implemented for the previous version of the SketchFrame class, but here you don't need to check the object passed to it because the windowClosing() method is called only for a WINDOW_CLOSING event. You don't need to pass the event on either; this is necessary only when you handle events in the manner I discussed earlier. Here, if there were other listeners around for the window events, they would automatically receive the event.

You have included the code that calls dispose() and exit() here, but if you set the default close operation in SketchFrame to EXIT_ON_CLOSE, you could omit these, too. You really need to put your application cleanup code only in the windowClosing() method, and this will typically display a dialog to just prompt the user to save any application data. You will get to that eventually.

Having to implement six methods that you don't need is rather tedious. But you have a way to get around this — by using what is called an adapter class, to define a listener.

Using Adapter Classes

An adapter class is a term for a class that implements a listener interface with methods that have no content, so they do nothing. The idea of this is to enable you to derive your own listener class from any of the adapter classes that are provided, and then implement just the methods that you are interested in. The other empty methods will be inherited from the adapter class so you don't have to worry about them.

There's an adapter class defined in the `javax.swing.event` package that defines the methods for the `MouseInputListener` interface. There are five further adapter classes defined in the `java.awt.event` package that cover the methods in the other low-level listener interfaces you have seen:

FocusAdapter	WindowAdapter	KeyAdapter
MouseAdapter	MouseMotionAdapter	MouseInputAdapter

The `WindowAdapter` class implements all of the methods defined in the `WindowListener`, `WindowFocusListener`, and `WindowStateListener` interfaces. The other five each implement the methods in the corresponding listener interface.

To handle the window closing event for the `Sketcher` application, you could derive your own class from the `WindowAdapter` class and just implement the `windowClosing()` method. If you also make it an inner class for the `Sketcher` class, it will automatically have access to the members of the `Sketcher` object, regardless of their access specifiers. Let's change the structure of the `Sketcher` class once more to make use of an adapter class.

Try It Out   Implementing an Adapter Class

The version of the `Sketcher` class to implement this will be as follows, with changes to the previous version highlighted:

```
// Sketching application
import java.awt.Toolkit;
import java.awt.Dimension;
import javax.swing.SwingUtilities;
import java.awt.event.WindowEvent;
import java.awt.event.WindowAdapter;

public class Sketcher {
  public static void main(String[] args) {
    theApp = new Sketcher();               // Create the application object
    SwingUtilities.invokeLater(
      new Runnable() {                      // Anonymous Runnable class object
                    public void run() {     // Run method executed in thread
                      theApp.createGUI();   // Call static GUI creator
                    }
                  }       );
  }

  // Method to create the application GUI
  private void creatGUI() {
    window = new SketchFrame("Sketcher");       // Create the app window
    Toolkit theKit = window.getToolkit();       // Get the window toolkit
    Dimension wndSize = theKit.getScreenSize(); // Get screen size
```

```
    // Set the position to screen center & size to half screen size
    window.setBounds(wndSize.width/4, wndSize.height/4,      // Position
                 wndSize.width/2, wndSize.height/2);    // Size
    window.addWindowListener(new WindowHandler()); // Add window listener
    window.setVisible(true);                       // Display the window
  }

  // Handler class for window events
  class WindowHandler extends WindowAdapter {
    // Handler for window closing event
    public void windowClosing(WindowEvent e) {
      window.dispose();                            // Release the window resources
      System.exit(0);                              // End the application
    }
  }

  private SketchFrame window;                       // The application window
  private static Sketcher theApp;                   // The application object
}
```

This example will display the same application window as the previous example.

How It Works

As the Sketcher class is no longer the listener for window, it doesn't need to implement the WindowListener interface. The WindowHandler class is the listener class for window events. Because the WindowHandler class is an inner class to the Sketcher class, it has access to all the members of the class, so calling the dispose() method for the window object is still quite straightforward — you just access the window field of the top-level class.

The WindowAdapter object that is the listener for the window object is created in the argument to the addWindowListener() method for window. You don't need an explicit variable to contain it because it will be stored in a data member of the Window class object. This data member is inherited from the Window superclass of the SketchFrame class.

> An easy mistake to make when you're using adapter classes is to misspell the name of the method that you are using to implement the event — typically by using the wrong case for a letter. In this case, you won't be overriding the adapter class method at all; you'll be adding a new method. Your code will compile perfectly well but your program will not handle any events. They will all be passed to the method in the adapter class with the name your method should have had — which does nothing, of course. This can be a bit mystifying until you realize where the problem is.

You haven't finished with low-level events yet by any means, and you'll return to handling more low-level events in the next chapter when you begin to add drawing code to the Sketcher program. In the meantime, let's start looking at how you can manage semantic events.

Semantic Events

As you saw earlier, semantic events relate to operations on the components in the GUI for your program. If you select a menu item or click a button, for example, a semantic event is generated. Three classes represent the basic semantic events you'll be dealing with most of the time, and they are derived from the AWTEvent class, as shown in Figure 18-4.

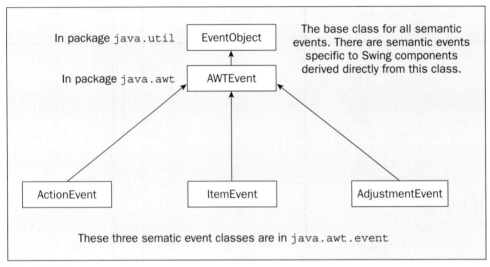

Figure 18-4

An ActionEvent is generated when you perform an action on a component such as clicking on a menu item or a button. An ItemEvent occurs when a component is selected or deselected, and an AdjustmentEvent is produced when an adjustable object, such as a scrollbar, is adjusted.

Different kinds of components can produce different kinds of semantic events. The components that can originate these events are:

Event Type	Produced by Objects of Type
ActionEvent	Buttons: JButton, JToggleButton, JcheckBox Menus: JMenuItem, JMenu, JCheckBoxMenuItem, JradioButtonMenuItem Text: JTextField

Event Type	Produced by Objects of Type
ItemEvent	Buttons: JButton, JToggleButton, JcheckBox Menus: JMenuItem, JMenu, JCheckBoxMenuItem, JRadioButtonMenuItem
AdjustmentEvent	JScrollbar

These three types of event are also generated by the old AWT components, but I won't go into these here as you are concentrating on the Swing components. Of course, any class you derive from these component classes to define your own customized components can be the source of the event that the base class generates. If you define your own class for buttons — MyFancyButton, say — your class will have JButton as a base class and inherit all of the methods from the JButton class, and objects of your class will originate events of type ActionEvent and ItemEvent.

Quite a large number of semantic events are specific to Swing components. Classes that have AbstractButton as a base, which includes menu items and buttons, can generate events of type ChangeEvent that signal some change in the state of a component. Components corresponding to the JMenuItem class and classes derived from JMenuItem can generate events of type MenuDragMouseEvent and of type MenuKeyEvent. An AncestorEvent is an event that is communicated to a child component from a parent component. You'll look at the details of some of these additional events when you need to handle them for the components in question.

As with low-level events, the most convenient way to handle semantic events is to use listeners, so I'll delve into the listener interfaces for semantic events next.

Semantic Event Listeners

You have a listener interface defined for each of the three semantic event types that I have introduced so far, and they each declare a single method:

Listener Interface	Method
ActionListener	void actionPerformed(ActionEvent e)
ItemListener	void itemStateChanged(ItemEvent e)
AdjustmentListener	void adjustmentValueChanged(AdjustmentEvent e)

Since each of these semantic event listener interfaces declares only one method, there's no need for corresponding adapter classes. The adapter classes for the low-level events were there only because of the number of methods involved in each listener interface. To define your semantic event listener objects, you just define a class that implements the appropriate listener interface. You can try that out by implementing a simple applet now, and then see how you can deal with semantic events in a more complicated context by adding to the Sketcher program later.

Semantic Event Handling in Applets

Event handling in an applet is exactly the same as in an application, but you ought to see it for yourself. Let's see how you might handle events for buttons in an applet. You can create an applet that uses some buttons that have listeners. To make this example a bit more gripping, I'll throw in the possibility of monetary gain. That's interesting to almost everybody.

Let's suppose you want to implement an applet that will create a set of random numbers for a lottery entry. The requirement is to generate six different random numbers between 1 and 49. It would also be nice to be able to change a single number if you don't like it, so you'll add that capability as well. Since the local lottery may not be like this, you'll implement the applet to make it easily adaptable to fit local requirements.

By displaying the six selected numbers on buttons, you can provide for changing one of the choices by processing the action event for that button. Thus, clicking a button will provide another number. You'll also add a couple of control buttons, one to make a new selection for a complete set of lottery numbers, and another just for fun to change the button color. Figure 18-5 shows how the applet will look when running under `appletviewer`:

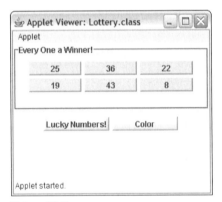

Figure 18-5

Try It Out   A Lottery Applet

You can outline the broad structure of the applet's code as follows:

```
// Applet to generate lottery entries
import javax.swing.JButton;
import javax.swing.JApplet;
import javax.swing.JPanel;
import javax.swing.BorderFactory;
import javax.swing.SwingUtilities;

import java.awt.GridLayout;
import java.awt.FlowLayout;
import java.awt.Dimension;
import java.awt.Container;
import java.awt.Color;
```

```
import java.util.Random;                    // For random number generator
import java.awt.event.ActionListener;
import java.awt.event.ActionEvent;

public class Lottery extends JApplet {
  // Initialize the applet
  public void init() {
    // Create interface components on event dispatch thread...
  }

  // Create User Interface for applet
  public void createGUI() {
    // Set up the lucky numbers buttons...

    // Set up the control buttons...
  }

  // Class defining custom buttons showing lottery selection
  // Each button listens for its own events
  class Selection extends JButton implements ActionListener {
    // Constructor
    public Selection(int value) {
      // Create the button showing the value...
    }

    // Handle selection button event
    public void actionPerformed(ActionEvent e) {
      // Change the current selection value to a new selection value
    }
    // Details of the rest of the selection class definition...
  }

  // Class defining a handler for a control button
  class HandleControlButton implements ActionListener {
    // Constructor...

    // Handle button click
    public void actionPerformed(ActionEvent e) {
      // Handle button click for a particular button...
    }

    // Rest of the inner class definition...
  }

  final static int numberCount = 6;                 // Number of lucky numbers
  final static int minValue = 1;                    // Minimum in range
  final static int maxValue = 49;                   // Maximum in range
  static int[] values = new int[maxValue-minValue+1]; // Array of possible values
  static {                                          // Initialize array
    for(int i = 0 ; i<values.length ; i++)
      values[i] = i + minValue;
  }
```

```
        // An array of custom buttons for the selected numbers
        private Selection[] luckyNumbers = new Selection[numberCount];

        private static Random choice = new Random();          // Random number generator
    }
```

How It Works

The applet class is called Lottery, and it contains two inner classes, Selection and
HandleControlButton. The Selection class provides a custom button that will show a number
as its label, the number being passed to the constructor as an argument. You can make an object of
the Selection class listen for its own action events. As I said at the outset, an event for a selection
button will change the label of the button to a different value, so of course, you'll need to make sure
this doesn't duplicate any of the values for the other buttons.

The two control buttons will use separate listeners to handle their action events, and the response to an
event will be quite different for each of them. One control button will create a new set of lucky numbers
while the other control button will just change the color of the buttons.

The numberCount member of the Lottery class sets the number of values that is created. The minValue
and maxValue members specify the range of possible values that lottery numbers can have. The possible
values for selections are stored in the values array, and this is set up in the static initialization block. The
Lottery class has an array of Selection objects as a data member — you can have arrays of components
just like arrays of any other kind of object. Since the Selection buttons will all be the same, it's very convenient to create them as an array, and having an array of components enables you to set them up in a
loop. You also have a Random object as a class member that you'll use to generate random integers.

You can now set about filling in the sections of the program that you have roughed out.

Filling in the Details

The generation of maxCount random values from the elements in the values array is quite independent
of everything else here, so you can define a static method in the Lottery class to do this:

```
public class Lottery extends JApplet {
    // Generate numberCount random selections from the values array
    static int[] getNumbers() {
        int[] numbers = new int[numberCount];     // Store for the numbers to be returned
        int candidate = 0;                        // Stores a candidate selection
        for(int i = 0; i < numberCount; i++) {    // Loop to find the selections

            search:
            // Loop to find a new selection different from any found so far
            for(;;) {
                candidate = values[choice.nextInt(values.length)];
                for(int j = 0 ; j<i ; j++) {           // Check against existing selections
                    if(candidate==numbers[j]) {        // If it is the same
                        continue search;               // get another random selection
                    }
                }
```

```
        numbers[i] = candidate;          // Store the selection in numbers array
        break;                           // and go to find the next
      }
    }
    return numbers;                      // Return the selections
  }

  // Plus the rest of the class definition...
}
```

The `getNumbers()` method returns a reference to an array of values of type `int` that represent the selections — which must all be different, of course. You start the process by creating an array to hold the selections, and a variable, `candidate`, to hold a potential selection for the `values` array. You generate a new selection for each iteration of the outer `for` loop. The process for finding an acceptable selection is quite simple. In the indefinite `for` loop with the label `search`, you choose a random value from the `values` array using the random number generator and then check its value against any selections already stored in the `numbers` array. If it is the same as any of them, the labeled `continue` statement will go to the next iteration of the indefinite `for` loop. This will continue until a selection is found that is different from the others. In this way you ensure that you end up with a set of selections that are all different.

Let's implement the `init()` method and the `creatGUI()` method for the `Lottery` class next, as these set up the `Selection` buttons and the rest of the applet.

Try It Out   Setting Up the Lucky Number Buttons

The `init()` method has to execute only the `createGUI()` method on the event-dispatching thread:

```java
// Initialize the applet
public void init() {
  SwingUtilities.invokeLater(           // Create interface components
    new Runnable() {                    // on the event dispatching thread
      public void run() {
        createGUI();
      }
    } );
}
```

In the class outline, you identified two tasks for the `createGUI()` method. The first was setting up the lucky number buttons to be contained in the `luckyNumbers` array.

Here's the code to do that:

```java
// Create User Interface for applet
public void creatGUI() {
  // Set up the selection buttons
  Container content = getContentPane();
  content.setLayout(new GridLayout(0,1)); // Set the layout for the applet

  // Set up the panel to hold the lucky number buttons
  JPanel buttonPane = new JPanel();       // Add the pane containing numbers
```

```
        // Let's have a fancy panel border
        buttonPane.setBorder(BorderFactory.createTitledBorder(
                        BorderFactory.createEtchedBorder(Color.cyan,
                                                         Color.blue),
                                                 "Every One a Winner!"));

        int[] choices = getNumbers();          // Get initial set of numbers
        for(int i = 0; i<numberCount; i++) {
         luckyNumbers[i] = new Selection(choices[i]);
         buttonPane.add(luckyNumbers[i]);
        }
        content.add(buttonPane);

        // Set up the control buttons...
    }
```

How It Works

The init() method uses the invokeLater() method from the SwingUtilities class to execute the createGUI() method on the event-dispatching thread. This guarantees that there is no possibility of a deadlock arising in the GUI construction process. This is the same technique that you used in the previous example.

The first step in the createGUI() method is to define the layout manager for the applet. To make the layout easier, you'll use one panel to hold the selection buttons and another to hold the control buttons. You position these panels one above the other by specifying the layout manager for the content pane of the applet as a grid layout with one column. The top panel will contain the lucky number buttons and the bottom panel will contain the control buttons.

The buttonPane panel that holds the lucky number buttons is of type JPanel, so it has a FlowLayout object as its layout manager by default. A flow layout manager allows components to assume their "natural" or "preferred size," so you'll set the preferred size for the buttons in the Selection class constructor. You decorate the panel with a border by calling its setBorder() method. The argument is the reference that is returned by the static createTitledBorder() method from the BorderFactory class. The first argument passed to createTitledBorder() is the border to be used, and the second argument is the title.

You use an etched border that is returned by another static method in the BorderFactory class. The two arguments to this method are the highlight and shadow colors to be used for the border. A big advantage of using the BorderFactory methods rather than creating border objects from the border class constructors directly is that border objects will be shared where possible, so you can use a particular border in various places in your code and only one object will be created.

The buttons to display the chosen numbers will be of type Selection, and you'll get to the detail of this inner class in a moment. You call the static getNumbers() method to obtain the first set of random values for the buttons. You then create and store each button in the luckyNumbers array and add it to the panel in the for loop. Since these buttons are going to listen for their own events, you don't need to worry about setting separate action listeners for them. The last step here is to add the buttonPane panel to the content pane for the applet.

You can now add the code for the control buttons to the createGUI() method.

Try It Out   **Setting Up the Control Buttons**

The listeners for each of the control buttons will be of the same class type, so the listener object will need some way to determine which button originated a particular event. One way to do this is to use constants as IDs to identify the control buttons and pass the appropriate ID to the class constructor for the listener object.

You can define the constants `PICK_LUCKY_NUMBERS` and `COLOR` as fields in the `Lottery` class for this purpose. The `COLOR` control button will also reference a couple of variables of type `Color`, `startColor`, and `flipColor`. You can add the following statements to the `Lottery` class after the definition of the `luckyNumbers` array:

```
// An array of custom buttons for the selected numbers
private Selection[] luckyNumbers = new Selection[numberCount];

final public static int PICK_LUCKY_NUMBERS = 1;       // Select button ID
final public static int COLOR = 2;                    // Color button ID

// swap colors
Color flipColor = new Color(Color.YELLOW.getRGB()^Color.RED.getRGB());

Color startColor = Color.YELLOW;                      // start color
```

The `startColor` field is initialized with the `YELLOW` color from the `Color` class. The `flipColor` field is set to the color that results from ORing the colors `YELLOW` and `RED`. Of course, to get a sensible color as a result you must OR the RGB values that you obtain from the `Color` objects, not the references to the `Color` objects! You'll be using the `flipColor` field to change the color of the buttons.

The code to add the other panel and the control buttons is as follows:

```
// Create User Interface for applet
public void createGUI() {
    // Setting up the selections buttons as previously...

    // Add the pane containing control buttons
    JPanel controlPane = new JPanel(new FlowLayout(FlowLayout.CENTER, 5, 10));

    // Add the two control buttons
    JButton button;                                  // A button variable
    Dimension buttonSize = new Dimension(100,20);    // Button size

    controlPane.add(button = new JButton("Lucky Numbers!"));
    button.setBorder(BorderFactory.createRaisedBevelBorder());
    button.addActionListener(new HandleControlButton(PICK_LUCKY_NUMBERS));
    button.setPreferredSize(buttonSize);

    controlPane.add(button = new JButton("Color"));
    button.setBorder(BorderFactory.createRaisedBevelBorder());
    button.addActionListener(new HandleControlButton(COLOR));
    button.setPreferredSize(buttonSize);

    content.add(controlPane);
}
```

How It Works

You create another JPanel object to hold the control buttons and just to show that you can, you pass a layout manager object to the constructor. It's a FlowLayout manager again, but this time you explicitly specify that the components are to be centered and the horizontal and vertical gaps are to be 5 and 10 pixels, respectively.

You declare the button variable to use as a temporary store for the reference to each button while you set it up. You also define a Dimension object that you'll use to set a common preferred size for the buttons. The buttons in this case are JButton components, not custom components, so you must set each of them up here with a listener and a border. You add a raised bevel border to each button to make them look like buttons — again using a BorderFactory method.

The listener for each button is an object of the inner class HandleControlButton, and you pass the appropriate button ID to the constructor for reasons that will be apparent when you define that class. To set the preferred size for each button object, you call its setPreferredSize() method. The argument is a Dimension object that specifies the width and height. Finally, after adding the two buttons to controlPane, you add that to the content pane for the applet.

The inner class HandleControlButton defines the listener object for each control button, so let's implement that next.

Try It Out   Defining the Control Button Handler Class

You have already determined that the HandleControlButton class constructor will accept an argument that identifies the particular button for which it is listening. This is to enable the actionPerformed() method in the listener class to choose the course of action appropriate to the button. Here's the inner class definition to do that:

```
class HandleControlButton implements ActionListener {
  // Constructor
  public HandleControlButton(int buttonID) {
    this.buttonID = buttonID;                        // Store the button ID
  }

  // Handle button click
  public void actionPerformed(ActionEvent e) {
    switch(buttonID) {
      case PICK_LUCKY_NUMBERS:
        int[] numbers = getNumbers();                // Get maxCount random numbers
        for(int i = 0; i < numberCount; i++) {
          luckyNumbers[i].setValue(numbers[i]);      // Set the button values
        }
        break;
      case COLOR:
        Color color = new Color(
            flipColor.getRGB()^luckyNumbers[0].getBackground().getRGB());
        for(int i = 0; i < numberCount; i++)
          luckyNumbers[i].setBackground(color);   // Set the button colors
        break;
    }
  }
}
```

```
        private int buttonID;
    }
```

How It Works

The constructor stores its argument value in the `buttonID` field so each listener object will have the ID for the button available. The `actionPerformed()` method uses the button ID to select the appropriate code to execute for a particular button. Each case in the `switch` statement corresponds to a different button. You could extend this to enable the class to handle as many different buttons as you want by adding case statements. Because of the way you have implemented the method, each button must have a unique ID associated with it. Of course, this isn't the only way to do this, as you'll see in a moment.

For the `PICK_LUCKY_NUMBERS` button event, you just call the `getNumbers()` method to produce a set of numbers, and then call the `setValue()` method for each selection button and pass a number to it. You'll implement the `setValue()` method when you define the `Selection` class in detail, in a moment.

For the `COLOR` button event, you create a new color by exclusive ORing (that is, XOR) the RGB value of `flipColor` with the current button color. You'll recall from the discussion of the ^ operator (in Chapter 2) that you can use it to exchange two values, and that is what you are doing here. You defined `flipColor` as the result of exclusive ORing the two colors, `Color.YELLOW` and `Color.RED`, together. Exclusive ORing `flipColor` with either color will produce the other color, so you flip from one color to the other automatically for each button by exclusive ORing the background and `flipColor`. As I said earlier, you must get the RGB value for each color and operate on those — you can't apply the ^ operator to the object references. You then turn the resulting RGB value back into a `Color` object.

Let's now add the inner class, `Selection`, which defines the lucky number buttons.

Try It Out   Defining the Selection Buttons

Each button will need to store the value shown on the label, so the class will need a data member for this purpose. The class will also need a constructor, a `setValue()` method to set the value for the button to a new value, and a method to compare the current value for a button to a given value. You need to be able to set the value for a button for two reasons — you'll need the capability when you set up all six selections in the listener for the control button, and you'll want to reset the value for a button to change it individually.

The method to compare the value set for a button to a given integer will enable you to exclude a number that was already assigned to a button when you are generating a new set of button values. You'll also need to implement the `actionPerformed()` method to handle the action events for the button, as the buttons are going to handle their own events. Here's the basic code for the class definition:

```
class Selection extends JButton implements ActionListener {
  // Constructor
  public Selection(int value) {
    super(Integer.toString(value));     // Call base constructor and set the label
    this.value = value;                 // Save the value
    setBackground(startColor);
    setBorder(BorderFactory.createRaisedBevelBorder());    // Add button border
    setPreferredSize(new Dimension(80,20));
    addActionListener(this);            // Button listens for itself
  }
```

```
    // Handle selection button event
    public void actionPerformed(ActionEvent e) {
      // Change this selection to a new selection
      int candidate = 0;
      for(;;) {                                   // Loop to find a different selection
        candidate = values[choice.nextInt(values.length)];
        if(isCurrentSelection(candidate)) {   // If it is not different
          continue;                            // find another
        }
        setValue(candidate);                   // We have one so set the button value
        return;
      }
    }
    // Set the value for the selection
    public void setValue(int value) {
      setText(Integer.toString(value));        // Set value as the button label
      this.value = value;                      // Save the value
    }

    // Check the value for the selection
    boolean hasValue(int possible) {
      return value==possible;                  // Return true if equals current value
    }

    // Check the current choices
    boolean isCurrentSelection(int possible) {
      for(int i = 0; i < numberCount; i++) {       // For each button
        if(luckyNumbers[i].hasValue(possible)) {   // check against possible
          return true;                             // Return true for any =
        }
      }
      return false;                            // Otherwise return false
    }

    private int value;                         // Value for the selection button
  }
```

How It Works

The constructor calls the base class constructor to set the initial label for the button. It also stores the value of type int that is passed as an argument. The setValue() method just updates the value for a selection button with the value passed as an argument and changes the button label by calling the setText() method, which is inherited from the base class, JButton. The hasValue() method returns true if the argument value passed to it is equal to the current value stored in the data member value, and false otherwise.

The actionPerformed() method has a little more meat to it, but the technique is similar to that in the getNumbers() method. To change the selection, you must create a new random value for the button from the numbers values array, but excluding all the numbers currently assigned to the six buttons. To do this you just check each candidate against the six existing selections by calling the isCurrentSelection() method and continue choosing a new candidate until you find one that's different.

In the `isCurrentSelection()` method, you just work through the array of `Selection` objects, `luckyNumbers`, comparing each value with the `possible` argument using the `hasValue()` method. If any button has the same value as `possible`, the method returns `true`; otherwise, it returns `false`.

You're ready to start generating lottery entries. If you compile the `Lottery.java` file, you can run the applet using `appletviewer`. You will need an HTML file, of course. The following contents for the file will do the job:

```
<APPLET CODE="Lottery.class" WIDTH=300 HEIGHT=200>
</APPLET>
```

You can adjust the width and height values to suit your monitor resolution if necessary.

The applet should produce a selection each time you click the left control button. Clicking any of the selection buttons will generate an action event that causes a new value to be created for the button. This enables you to replace any selection that you know to be unlucky with an alternative.

Undoubtedly, anyone who profits from using this applet will have immense feelings of gratitude and indebtedness towards the author, who will not be offended in the slightest by any offers of a portion of that success, however large!

Alternative Event-Handling Approaches

As I indicated in the discussion, there are various approaches to implementing listeners. Let's look at a couple of other ways in which you could have dealt with the control button events.

Instead of passing a constant to the listener class constructor to identify which button was selected, you could have exploited the fact that the event object has a method, `getSource()`, that returns a reference to the object that is the source of the event. To make use of this, a reference to both button objects would need to be available to the `actionPerformed()` method. You could easily arrange for this to be the case by adding a couple of fields to the `Lottery` class:

```
JButton pickButton = new JButton("Lucky Numbers!");
JButton colorButton = new JButton("Color");
```

The inner class could then be defined as follows:

```
class HandleControlButton implements ActionListener {
  // Handle button click
  public void actionPerformed(ActionEvent e) {
    Object source = e.getSource();                    // Get source object reference

    if(source == pickButton) {                        // Is it the pick button?
        int[] numbers = getNumbers();                 // Get maxCount random numbers
        for(int i = 0; i < numberCount; i++) {
          luckyNumbers[i].setValue(numbers[i]);       // Set the button values
        }
    } else if(source == colorButton) {                // Is it the color button?
      Color color = new Color(
                  flipColor.getRGB()^luckyNumbers[0].getBackground().getRGB());
```

```
        for(int i = 0; i < numberCount; i++) {
          luckyNumbers[i].setBackground(color);     // Set the button colors
        }
      }
    }
  }
```

You no longer need to define a constructor, as the default will do. The actionPerformed() method now decides what to do by comparing the reference returned by the getSource() method for the event object with the two button references in the JButton fields of the Lottery class. With the previous version of the listener class, you stored the ID as a data member, so a separate listener object was needed for each button. In this case there are no data members in the listener class, so you can use one listener object for both buttons.

The code to add these buttons in the createGUI() method would then be:

```
// Add the two control buttons
Dimension buttonSize = new Dimension(100,20);
pickButton.setPreferredSize(buttonSize);
pickButton.setBorder(BorderFactory.createRaisedBevelBorder());

colorButton.setPreferredSize(buttonSize);
colorButton.setBorder(BorderFactory.createRaisedBevelBorder());

HandleControlButton controlHandler = new HandleControlButton();
pickButton.addActionListener(controlHandler);
colorButton.addActionListener(controlHandler);

controlPane.add(pickButton);
controlPane.add(colorButton);
content.add(controlPane);
```

The only fundamental difference here is that you use one listener object for both buttons.

There is another possible way to implement listeners for these buttons. You could define a separate class for each listener — this would not be unreasonable, as the actions to be performed in response to the semantic events for each button are quite different. You could use anonymous classes in this case — as I discussed back in Chapter 6. You could do this by adding the listeners for the button objects in the createGUI() method like this:

```
// Add the two control buttons
Dimension buttonSize = new Dimension(100,20);
pickButton.setPreferredSize(buttonSize);
pickButton.setBorder(BorderFactory.createRaisedBevelBorder());

colorButton.setPreferredSize(buttonSize);
colorButton.setBorder(BorderFactory.createRaisedBevelBorder());

pickButton.addActionListener(
    new ActionListener() {
      public void actionPerformed(ActionEvent e) {
        int[] numbers = getNumbers();
```

```
                for(int i = 0; i < numberCount; i++) {
                   luckyNumbers[i].setValue(numbers[i]);
                }
             }
          });

       colorButton.addActionListener(
          new ActionListener() {
             public void actionPerformed(ActionEvent e) {
                Color color = new Color(flipColor.getRGB()^luckyNumbers[0]
                                               .getBackground().getRGB());
                for(int i = 0; i < numberCount; i++) {
                   luckyNumbers[i].setBackground(color);
                }
             }
          });

       controlPane.add(pickButton);
       controlPane.add(colorButton);
       content.add(controlPane);
```

Now the two listeners are defined by anonymous classes, and the implementation of the
`actionPerformed()` method in each just takes care of the particular button for which it is listening.
This is a very common technique when the action to be performed in response to an event is simple.

Handling Low-Level and Semantic Events

I said earlier in this chapter that a component generates both low-level and semantic events, and you
could handle both if you want. I can demonstrate this quite easily with a small extension to the Lottery
applet. Suppose you want to change the cursor to a hand cursor when it is over one of the selection buttons. This would be a good cue that you can select these buttons individually. You can do this by adding
a mouse listener for each button.

Try It Out   **A Mouse Listener for the Selection Buttons**

There are many ways in which you could define the listener class. Here you'll define it as a separate
class called MouseHandler:

```
// Mouse event handler for a selection button
import java.awt.Cursor;
import java.awt.event.MouseEvent;
import java.awt.event.MouseAdapter;

class MouseHandler extends MouseAdapter {
   Cursor handCursor = new Cursor(Cursor.HAND_CURSOR);
   Cursor defaultCursor = new Cursor(Cursor.DEFAULT_CURSOR);

   // Handle mouse entering the selection button
   public void mouseEntered(MouseEvent e) {
      e.getComponent().setCursor(handCursor);     // Switch to hand cursor
   }
```

```
       // Handle mouse exiting the selection button
     public void mouseExited(MouseEvent e) {
       e.getComponent().setCursor(defaultCursor); // Change to default cursor
     }
   }
 }
```

All you need to do to expedite this is to add a mouse listener for each of the six selection buttons. You need only one listener object and after creating this you need to change the loop only in the `createGUI()` method for the applet to add the listener:

```
    int[] choices = getNumbers();                    // Get initial set of numbers
    MouseHandler mouseHandler = new MouseHandler();   // Create the listener
    for(int i = 0 ; i<numberCount ; i++) {
      luckyNumbers[i] = new Selection(choices[i]);
      luckyNumbers[i].addMouseListener(mouseHandler);
      buttonPane.add(luckyNumbers[i]);
    }
```

How It Works

The `mouseEntered()` method will be called when the mouse enters the area of the component with which the listener is registered, and the method then changes the cursor for the component to a hand cursor. When the cursor is moved out of the area occupied by the component, the `mouseExited()` method is called, which restores the default cursor.

Just two extra statements in `createGUI()` create the listener object and then add it for each selection button within the loop. If you recompile the applet and run it again, a hand cursor should appear whenever the mouse is over the selection buttons. Of course, you are not limited to just changing the cursor in the event handler. You could highlight the button by changing its color for instance. You could apply the same technique for any kind of component where the mouse is the source of actions for it.

Semantic Event Listeners in an Application

The Sketcher program is an obvious candidate for implementing semantic event listeners to support the operation of the menu bar in the `SketchFrame` class. When you click on an item in one of the pull-down menus, a semantic event will be generated that you can listen for and then use to determine the appropriate program action.

Listening to Menu Items

Let's start with the `Elements` menu. This is concerned with identifying the type of graphic element to be drawn next, and the color in which it will be drawn. You won't be drawing them for a while, but you can put in the infrastructure to set the type and color for an element without worrying about how it will actually be created and drawn.

To identify the type of element, you can define constants that will act as IDs for the four types of element you have provided for in the menu so far. This will help with the operation of the listeners for the menu item as well as provide a way to identify a particular type of element. Since you'll accumulate quite a number of application-wide constants, it will be convenient to define them as static fields in a class from which they can be imported statically. To be able to import the static fields, the class must be in a named package, so let's set that up. To put the class in a package with the name `Constants`, you need to set up a directory with this name at a suitable location on your disk, and then use the `-classpath` option when you compile the class in the `Constants` package to identify the path to the `Constants` directory. Here's the initial definition, including constants to define line, rectangle, circle, and curve elements:

```
// Defines application wide constants
package Constants;

public class SketcherConstants {
  // Element type definitions
  public final static int LINE      = 101;
  public final static int RECTANGLE = 102;
  public final static int CIRCLE    = 103;
  public final static int CURVE     = 104;

  // Initial conditions
  public final static int DEFAULT_ELEMENT_TYPE = LINE;
}
```

Save this as `SketcherConstants.java` in the `Constants` directory you have created. Each element type ID in the class is an integer constant with a unique value, and you can obviously extend the variety of element types if necessary. Of course, you could also have defined the element IDs as enumeration constants, but then you would have more than one class involved in the definition of constants for Sketcher.

You have defined the `DEFAULT_ELEMENT_TYPE` constant to specify the initial element type to apply when the Sketcher application starts. You could do the same thing for the `Color` submenu and supply a constant that specifies the default initial element color:

```
// Defines application wide constants
package Constants;
import java.awt.Color;

public class SketcherConstants {
  // Element type definitions
  public final static int LINE      = 101;
  public final static int RECTANGLE = 102;
  public final static int CIRCLE    = 103;
  public final static int CURVE     = 104;

  // Initial conditions
  public final static int DEFAULT_ELEMENT_TYPE = LINE;
  public final static Color DEFAULT_ELEMENT_COLOR = Color.BLUE;
}
```

You have defined the `DEFAULT_ELEMENT_COLOR` field as type `Color`, so you have added an `import` statement for the `Color` class name. When you want to change the default startup color or element type, you just need to change the values of the constants in the `SketcherConstants` class. This will automatically take care of setting things up — as long as you implement the program code appropriately.

You can add fields to the `SketchFrame` class to store the current element type and color, since these are application-wide values, and are not specific to a view:

```
    private Color elementColor = DEFAULT_ELEMENT_COLOR;    // Current element color
    private int elementType = DEFAULT_ELEMENT_TYPE;        // Current element type
```

You can now use these to ensure that the menu items are checked appropriately when the application starts. Of course, for the class to compile, you also want the names of the constants from the SketcherConstants class imported into the SketchFrame class, so make the following changes to the SketchFrame class definition:

```
import javax.swing.JFrame;
import javax.swing.JMenuBar;
import javax.swing.JMenu;
import javax.swing.JMenuItem;
import javax.swing.JRadioButtonMenuItem;
import javax.swing.JCheckBoxMenuItem;
import javax.swing.ButtonGroup;
import javax.swing.KeyStroke;
import static java.awt.event.InputEvent.*;
import static java.awt.AWTEvent.*;
import java.awt.event.WindowEvent;
import java.awt.Color;
import static java.awt.Color.*;
import static Constants.SketcherConstants.*;

public class SketchFrame extends JFrame {
  // Constructor
  public SketchFrame(String title) {
    setTitle(title);                          // Set the window title
    setJMenuBar(menuBar);                     // Add the menu bar to the window
    setDefaultCloseOperation(EXIT_ON_CLOSE);

    // Code to create the File menu...

    // Construct the Element drop-down menu...
    elementMenu.add(lineItem = new JRadioButtonMenuItem(
                                   "Line", elementType==LINE));
    elementMenu.add(rectangleItem = new JRadioButtonMenuItem(
                                   "Rectangle", elementType==RECTANGLE));
    elementMenu.add(circleItem = new JRadioButtonMenuItem(
                                   "Circle", elementType==CIRCLE));
    elementMenu.add(curveItem = new JRadioButtonMenuItem(
                                   "Curve", elementType==CURVE));
    ButtonGroup types = new ButtonGroup();

    // ...plus the rest of the code for the element types as before...

    elementMenu.addSeparator();

    elementMenu.add(colorMenu);                    // Add the sub-menu
    colorMenu.add(redItem = new JCheckBoxMenuItem(
                          "Red", elementColor.equals(RED)));
    colorMenu.add(yellowItem = new JCheckBoxMenuItem(
                         "Yellow", elementColor.equals(YELLOW)));
    colorMenu.add(greenItem = new JCheckBoxMenuItem(
                         "Green", elementColor.equals(GREEN)));
```

```
        colorMenu.add(blueItem = new JCheckBoxMenuItem(
                          "Blue", elementColor.equals(BLUE)));

    // Add element color accelerators...
    // ... plus the rest of the constructor as before...
  }

    // ...plus the rest of the class and include the two new data members...
    private Color elementColor = DEFAULT_ELEMENT_COLOR;    // Current element color
    private int elementType = DEFAULT_ELEMENT_TYPE;        // Current element type
  }
```

You have imported static constants from the `Color` class, so you can use the names of the standard color objects that the class defines without qualifying them. When you construct the element objects, you use the `elementType` and `elementColor` members to set the state of each menu item. Only the element type menu item corresponding to the default type set in `elementType` will be checked because that's the only comparison that will produce a true result as an argument to the `JRadioButtonMenuItem` constructor. The mechanism is the same for the color menu items, but note that you use the `equals()` method defined in the `Color` class for a valid comparison of `Color` objects. You might just get away with using == because you are using only constant `Color` values that are defined in the class, but as soon as you use a color that is not one of these, this would no longer work. Of course, you have to use == for the element type items because the IDs are of type `int`.

At this point it would be a good idea to recompile Sketcher to make sure everything is as it should be. Because you now have your own package containing the `SketcherConstants` class definition, you must use the `-classpath` option to tell the compiler where to find it. Assuming the `Constants` directory is a sub-directory of the `C:/Packages` directory, and the current directory is the one containing `Sketcher.java` and `SketchFrame.java`, you will need to use the following command to compile Sketcher:

```
javac -classpath ".;C:/Packages" Sketcher.java
```

The `-classpath` option defines two paths: the current directory, specified by the period, and `C:/Packages`, which is the path to the `Constants` directory that contains the `SketcherConstants.java` source file. This command should compile everything, including your package.

Having got that sorted out, you can have a go at implementing the listeners for the `Elements` menu, starting with the type menu items.

Try It Out   Handling Events for the Element Type Menu

You'll add an inner class to `SketchFrame` that will define listeners for the menu items specifying the element type. This class will implement the `ActionListener` interface because you want to respond to actions on these menu items. Add the following definition as an inner class to `SketchFrame`:

```
    // Handles element type menu items
    class TypeListener implements ActionListener {
      // Constructor
      TypeListener(int type) {
        this.type = type;
      }
```

```
  // Sets the element type
  public void actionPerformed(ActionEvent e) {
    elementType = type;
  }

  private int type;                          // Store the type for the menu
}
```

Now you can use objects of this class as listeners for the menu items. Add the following code to the SketchFrame constructor, after the code that sets up the type menu items for the Elements menu just before the last two lines of the constructor:

```
  // Add type menu item listeners
  lineItem.addActionListener(new TypeListener(LINE));
  rectangleItem.addActionListener(new TypeListener(RECTANGLE));
  circleItem.addActionListener(new TypeListener(CIRCLE));
  curveItem.addActionListener(new TypeListener(CURVE));

  menuBar.add(fileMenu);                      // Add the file menu
  menuBar.add(elementMenu);                   // Add the element menu
}
```

It will also be necessary to add the following two import statements to the source file for the SketchFrame class:

```
import java.awt.event.ActionListener;
import java.awt.event.ActionEvent;
```

Recompile Sketcher and see how it looks. Don't forget the -classpath option when you compile the application. You'll also need to specify the same -classpath option when you execute it; otherwise, the SketcherConstants .class file won't be found.

How It Works

The application window won't look any different, as the listeners just set the current element type in the SketchFrame object. The listener class is remarkably simple. Each listener object stores the type corresponding to the menu item that is passed as the constructor argument. When an event occurs, the actionPerformed() method just stores the type in the listener object in the elementType member of the SketchFrame object.

Now you can do the same for the color menu items.

Try It Out   Implementing Color Menu Item Listeners

You'll define another inner class to SketchFrame that defines listeners for the Color menu items:

```
  // Handles color menu items
  class ColorListener implements ActionListener {
    public ColorListener(Color color) {
      this.color = color;
    }
```

```
    public void actionPerformed(ActionEvent e) {
      elementColor = color;
    }

    private Color color;
}
```

You just need to create listener objects and add them to the color menu items. Add the following code at the end of the SketchFrame constructor after the code that sets up the Color submenu:

```
// Add color menu item listeners
redItem.addActionListener(new ColorListener(RED));
yellowItem.addActionListener(new ColorListener(YELLOW));
greenItem.addActionListener(new ColorListener(GREEN));
blueItem.addActionListener(new ColorListener(BLUE));

menuBar.add(fileMenu);                          // Add the file menu
menuBar.add(elementMenu);                       // Add the element menu
}
```

This adds a listener object for each menu item in the Color menu.

How It Works

The ColorListener class works in the same way as the TypeListener class. Each class object stores an identifier for the menu item for which it is listening — in this case a Color object corresponding to the color the menu item sets up. The actionPerformed() method just stores the Color object from the listener object in the elementColor member of the SketchFrame object.

Of course, the menu doesn't quite work as it should. The Color menu item check marks are not being set correctly, as you can see in Figure 18-6. You want an exclusive check, as with the radio buttons; having more than one color checked at one time doesn't make sense.

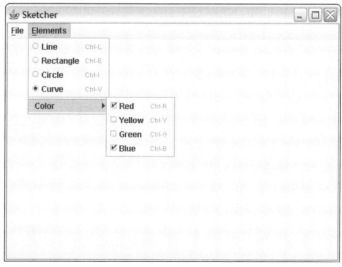

Figure 18-6

Fixing the Color Menu Check Marks

One way to deal with the problem is to make the listener object for a color menu item set the check marks for all the menu items. You could code this in the `ColorListener` class as follows:

```
class ColorListener implements ActionListener {
  public void actionPerformed(ActionEvent e) {
    elementColor = color;
    // Set the checks for all menu items
    redItem.setState(color.equals(RED));
    greenItem.setState(color.equals(GREEN));
    blueItem.setState(color.equals(BLUE));
    yellowItem.setState(color.equals(YELLOW));
  }
  // Rest of the class as before...
}
```

This calls the `setState()` method for each menu item. If the argument to the method is `true` the check mark is set, and if it is `false`, it isn't. Clearly this will set the check mark only for the item that corresponds to the color referenced by `color`. This is quite straightforward, but there is a better way.

A `ButtonGroup` object works with `JCheckBoxMenuItem` objects because they have `AbstractButton` as a base class. Therefore, you could add these menu items to their own button group in the `SketchFrame` constructor, and it will all be taken care of for you. The `ButtonGroup` object tracks the state of all of the buttons in the group. When any button is turned on, all the others are turned off, so only one button in the group can be on at one time. So add the following code — it could go anywhere after the items have been created but place it following the code that adds the items to the `Color` menu for consistency with the element type code:

```
ButtonGroup colors = new ButtonGroup();       // Color menu items button group
colors.add(redItem);
colors.add(yellowItem);
colors.add(greenItem);
colors.add(blueItem);
```

Now the `Color` menu check marks are set automatically, so you can forget about them.

Using Actions

One difficulty with the code that you have added to support the menus is that it is very menu specific. What I mean by this is that if you are going to do a proper job on the Sketcher application, you will undoubtedly want it to have a toolbar. The toolbar will surely have a whole bunch of buttons that perform exactly the same actions as the menu items you have just implemented, so you'll be in the business of doing the same thing all over again in the toolbar context. Of course, the only reason I brought it up, as I'm sure you've anticipated, is that there is another way of working with menus, and that is to use an `Action` object.

An `Action` object is a bit of a strange beast. It can be quite hard to understand at first, so I'll take it slowly. First of all let's look at what is meant by an "action" here, as it is a precise term in this context. An action is an object of any class that implements the `javax.swing.Action` interface. This interface declares methods that operate on an action object — for example, storing properties relating to the action, enabling it and disabling it. The Action interface happens to extend the ActionListener interface, so an action object is a listener as well as an action. Now that you know an Action object can get and set properties and is also a listener, how does that help us in implementing the Sketcher GUI?

The answer is in the last capability of an Action object. Some Swing components, such as those of type JMenu and JToolBar, have an add() method that accepts an argument of type Action. When you add an Action object to these using the add() method, the method creates a component from the Action object that is automatically of the right type. If you add an Action object to a JMenu object, a JMenuItem will be created and returned by the add() method. On the other hand, when you add exactly the same Action object to a JToolBar object, an object of type JButton will be created and returned. This means that you can add the very same Action object to both a menu and a toolbar, and since the Action object is its own listener, you automatically get both the menu item and the toolbar button supported by the same action. Clever, eh?

First, you should look at the Action interface.

The Action Interface

In general, **properties** are items of information that relate to a particular object and are stored as part of the object. Properties are often stored in a map, where a key identifies a particular property, and the value corresponding to that property can be stored in association with the key. The Properties class that is defined in the java.util package does exactly that. The Action interface has provision for storing seven basic standard properties that relate to an Action object:

❑ **A name** — A String object that is used as the label for a menu item or a toolbar button.

❑ **A small icon** — A javax.swing.Icon object to be displayed on a toolbar button.

❑ **A short description of the action** — A String object to be used as a tooltip.

❑ **An accelerator key for the action** — Defined by a javax.swing.KeyStroke object.

❑ **A long description of the action** — A String object that is intended to be used as context-sensitive help.

❑ **A mnemonic key for the action** — This is a key code of type int.

❑ **An action command key** — Defined by an entry in a javax.swing.ActionMap object associated with a component. The ActionMap object for a component defines mappings between objects that are keys and actions.

Just so you are aware of them I have included the complete set here, but you will concentrate on just using the first three. You haven't met Icon objects before, but you'll get to them a little later in this chapter.

You are not obliged to provide for all of these properties in your action classes, but the Action interface provides the framework for it. These properties are stored internally in a map collection in your action class, so the Action interface defines constants that you use as keys for each of the standard properties. These constants are all of type String, and the ones you are interested in are NAME, SMALL_ICON, and SHORT_DESCRIPTION. The others are ACCELERATOR_KEY, LONG_DESCRIPTION, MNEMONIC_KEY, and ACTION_COMMAND_KEY. There is another constant of type String defined in the interface with the name DEFAULT, but this is not used currently. The Action interface also declares the following methods:

Method	Description
`void putValue(String key, Object value)`	Stores the value with the key `key` in the map supported by the action class. To store the name of an action within a class method, you might write: `putValue(NAME, theName);` This uses the standard key `NAME` to store the object `theName`.

`Object getValue(String key)`	This retrieves the object from the map corresponding to the key `key`. To retrieve a small icon within an action class method, you might write:
	
	`Icon lineIcon = (Icon)getValue`
	`(SMALL_ICON);`

`boolean isEnabled()`	This returns `true` if the action object is enabled and `false` otherwise.
`void setEnabled(boolean state)`	This sets the `Action` object as enabled if the argument state is `true` and disabled if it is `false`. This operates on both the toolbar button and the menu item if they have been created using the same object.
`void addPropertyChangeListener(` `        PropertyChangeListener listener)`	This adds the listener passed as an argument, which listens for changes to properties such as the enabled state of the object. This is used by a container for an `Action` object to track property changes.
`void removePropertyChangeListener(` `        PropertyChangeListener listener)`	This removes the listener passed as an argument. This is also for use by a `Container` object.

Of course, since the `Action` interface extends the `ActionListener` interface, it also incorporates the `ActionPerformed()` method that you are already familiar with. So far, all you seem to have gained with this interface is a license to do a lot of work in implementing it, but it's not as bad as that. The `javax.swing` package defines the `AbstractAction` class that already implements the `Action` interface. If you extend this class to create your own action class, you get a basic infrastructure for free. Let's try it out in the context of Sketcher.

Using Actions as Menu Items

This will involve major surgery on the `SketchFrame` class. Although you'll be throwing away all those fancy varieties of menu items you spent so much time putting together, at least you know how they work now, and you'll end up with much less code after re-engineering the class, as you'll see. As the saying goes, you've got to crack a few eggs to make a soufflé.

You'll go back nearly to square one and reconstruct the class definition. First you'll delete a lot of code from the existing class definition. Comments will show where you'll add code to re-implement the menus using actions. Get your definition of the `SketchFrame` class to the following state:

```java
// Frame for the Sketcher application
import javax.swing.JMenu;
import javax.swing.JMenuItem;
import javax.swing.JRadioButtonMenuItem;
import javax.swing.JCheckBoxMenuItem;
import javax.swing.ButtonGroup;
import javax.swing.KeyStroke;
import javax.swing.Action;
import javax.swing.AbstractAction;

import java.awt.event.WindowEvent;
import java.awt.event.ActionListener;
import java.awt.event.ActionEvent;

import java.awt.Color;

import static java.awt.event.InputEvent.*;
import static java.awt.AWTEvent.*;
import static java.awt.Color.*;
import static Constants.SketcherConstants.*;

public class SketchFrame extends JFrame {
  // Constructor
  public SketchFrame(String title) {
    setTitle(title);                             // Set the window title
    setJMenuBar(menuBar);                        // Add the menu bar to the window
    setDefaultCloseOperation(EXIT_ON_CLOSE);     // Default is exit the application

    JMenu fileMenu = new JMenu("File");          // Create File menu
    JMenu elementMenu = new JMenu("Elements");   // Create Elements menu
    fileMenu.setMnemonic('F');                   // Create shortcut
    elementMenu.setMnemonic('E');                // Create shortcut

    // You will construct the file drop-down menu here using actions...
    // you will add the types menu items here using actions...

    elementMenu.addSeparator();

    JMenu colorMenu = new JMenu("Color");        // Color sub-menu
    elementMenu.add(colorMenu);                  // Add the sub-menu
```

```
      // You will add the color menu items here using actions...

      menuBar.add(fileMenu);                        // Add the file menu
      menuBar.add(elementMenu);                     // Add the element menu
    }

    // You will add inner classes defining action objects here...

    // You will add action objects as members here...

    private JMenuBar menuBar = new JMenuBar();           // Window menu bar
    private Color elementColor = DEFAULT_ELEMENT_COLOR;  // Current element color
    private int elementType = DEFAULT_ELEMENT_TYPE;      // Current element type
  }
```

Note that you have restored the statement to set the default close operation as EXIT_ON_CLOSE, so you won't need to call dispose() and exit() in the window event handler. Now would be a good time to delete the statements from the windowClosing() method in the inner WindowHandler class to the Sketcher class. The old inner classes in SketchFrame have been deleted, as well as the fields storing references to menu items. All the code to create the menu items has been wiped as well, along with the code that added the listeners. You are ready to begin reconstruction. You can rebuild it stronger, faster, better!

Defining Action Classes

You'll need three inner classes defining actions, one for the File menu items, another for the element type menu items, and the third for element colors. You'll derive each of these classes from the javax.swing.AbstractAction class that already implements the Action interface. The AbstractAction class has three constructors:

Method	Description
AbstractAction()	Defines an object with a default name and icon
AbstractAction(String name)	Defines an object with the name specified by the argument and a default icon
AbstractAction(String name, Icon icon)	Defines an object with the name and icon specified by the arguments

The AbstractAction class definition already provides the mechanism for storing action properties. For the last two constructors, the argument values that you pass will be stored using the standard keys that I described earlier in the context of the Action interface. For the moment, you'll take advantage only of the second constructor and leave icons till a little later.

You can define the FileAction inner class as follows:

```
    // Inner class defining Action objects for File menu items
    class FileAction extends AbstractAction {
      // Constructor
      FileAction(String name) {
```

```
      super(name);
    }

    // Constructor
    FileAction(String name, KeyStroke keystroke) {
      this(name);
      if(keystroke != null) {
        putValue(ACCELERATOR_KEY, keystroke);
      }
    }

    // Event handler
    public void actionPerformed(ActionEvent e) {
      // You will add action code here eventually...
    }
  }
```

You have two constructors. The first just stores the name for the action by calling the base class constructor. The second stores the name by calling the first constructor and then stores the accelerator keystroke using the appropriate key if the argument is not `null`. Calling the other constructor rather than the base class constructor is better here, in case you add code to the other constructor later on (as you certainly will!).

Because the class is an action listener, you have implemented the `actionPerformed()` method in it. You don't yet know what you are going to do with the File menu item actions, so you can leave it open for now and let the `actionPerformed()` method do nothing. Add the `FileAction` class as an inner class to `SketchFrame` where the comment indicated.

The `SketchFrame` class will need a data member of type `FileAction` for each menu item you intend to add, so add the following statement to the `SketchFrame` class definition where the comment indicated:

```
    // File actions
    private FileAction newAction, openAction, closeAction,
                       saveAction, saveAsAction, printAction;
```

You can define an inner class for the element type menus next:

```
    // Inner class defining Action objects for Element type menu items
    class TypeAction extends AbstractAction {
      TypeAction(String name, int typeID) {
        super(name);
        this.typeID = typeID;
      }

      public void actionPerformed(ActionEvent e) {
        elementType = typeID;
      }

      private int typeID;
    }
```

Add this definition to the `SketchFrame` class following the previous inner class. The only extra code here compared to the previous action class is that you retain the `typeID` concept to identify the element type. This makes the listener operation simple and fast. Because each object corresponds to a particular element type, there is no need for any testing of the event — you just store the current `typeID` as the new element type in the `SketchFrame` class object. You won't be adding accelerator key combinations for type menu items, so you don't need to provide for them in the class.

Add the following statement to the `SketchFrame` class for the members that will store references to the `TypeAction` objects, following the statement defining the fields that store `FileAction` references:

```
// Element type actions
private TypeAction lineAction, rectangleAction, circleAction, curveAction;
```

The third inner class to `SketchFrame` is just as simple:

```
// Handles color menu items
class ColorAction  extends AbstractAction {
  public ColorAction(String name, Color color) {
    super(name);
    this.color = color;
  }

  public void actionPerformed(ActionEvent e) {
    elementColor = color;

    // This is temporary - just to show it works...
    getContentPane().setBackground(color);
  }

  private Color color;
}
```

You also use the same idea that you used in the listener class for the `Color` menu items in the previous implementation of `SketchFrame`. Here you have a statement in the `actionPerformed()` method that sets the background color of the content pane to the element color. When you click on a color menu item, the background color of the content pane will change so you will be able to see that it works. You'll remove this code later.

Add the following statement to the `SketchFrame` class for the color action members following the `TypeAction` fields:

```
// Element color actions
  private ColorAction redAction, yellowAction,
                    greenAction, blueAction;
```

You can try these action classes out now.

Try It Out   Actions in Action

Fundamentally, all you need to do to create the menu items is use the `JMenuItem` constructor, which accepts an `Action` argument, and then use the `add()` method for the `JMenu` object to add the menu item to a menu. This all happens in the `SketchFrame` constructor — with the aid of a helper method that will economize on the number of lines of code you need:

```
public SketchFrame(String title) {
  setTitle(title);                              // Set the window title
  setJMenuBar(menuBar);                         // Add the menu bar to the window
  setDefaultCloseOperation(EXIT_ON_CLOSE);      // Default is exit the application

  JMenu fileMenu = new JMenu("File");           // Create File menu
  JMenu elementMenu = new JMenu("Elements");    // Create Elements menu
  fileMenu.setMnemonic('F');                    // Create shortcut
  elementMenu.setMnemonic('E');                 // Create shortcut

  // Create the action items for the file menu
  newAction = new FileAction("New", KeyStroke.getKeyStroke('N', CTRL_DOWN_MASK));
  openAction = new FileAction("Open",
                              KeyStroke.getKeyStroke('O', CTRL_DOWN_MASK));
  closeAction = new FileAction("Close");
  saveAction = new FileAction("Save",
                              KeyStroke.getKeyStroke('S', CTRL_DOWN_MASK));
  saveAsAction = new FileAction("Save As...");
  printAction = new FileAction("Print",
                               KeyStroke.getKeyStroke('P', CTRL_DOWN_MASK));

  // Construct the file drop-down menu
  fileMenu.add(new JMenuItem(newAction));
  fileMenu.add(new JMenuItem(openAction));
  fileMenu.add(new JMenuItem(closeAction));
  fileMenu.addSeparator();                      // Add separator
  fileMenu.add(new JMenuItem(saveAction));
  fileMenu.add(new JMenuItem(saveAsAction));
  fileMenu.addSeparator();                      // Add separator
  fileMenu.add(new JMenuItem(printAction));

  // Construct the Element drop-down menu
  elementMenu.add(new JMenuItem(lineAction = new TypeAction("Line", LINE)));
  elementMenu.add(new JMenuItem(rectangleAction =
                            new TypeAction("Rectangle", RECTANGLE)));
  elementMenu.add(new JMenuItem(circleAction =
                                new TypeAction("Circle", CIRCLE)));
  elementMenu.add(new JMenuItem(curveAction = new TypeAction("Curve", CURVE)));

  elementMenu.addSeparator();

  JMenu colorMenu = new JMenu("Color");         // Color sub-menu
  elementMenu.add(colorMenu);                   // Add the sub-menu
  colorMenu.add(new JMenuItem(redAction = new ColorAction("Red", RED)));
  colorMenu.add(new JMenuItem(yellowAction = new ColorAction("Yellow", YELLOW)));
  colorMenu.add(new JMenuItem(greenAction = new ColorAction("Green", GREEN)));
  colorMenu.add(new JMenuItem(blueAction = new ColorAction("Blue", BLUE)));

  menuBar.add(fileMenu);                         // Add the file menu
  menuBar.add(elementMenu);                      // Add the element menu
}
```

You have added four blocks of code. The first two are for the File menu, one block creating the action objects and the other creating the menu items. The other two blocks of code are for the element type and color menus. You create the action items for these menus in the arguments to the JMenuItem constructor calls. It's convenient to do this here as the constructor calls are relatively simple. You could adopt the same approach with the File menu items, but the statements will begin to look rather complicated.

When you create a JMenuItem object from an Action object, the accelerator key combination is automatically set for the menu item when the Action object defines one.

If you recompile and run Sketcher, you will get a window that looks like the one shown in Figure 18-7.

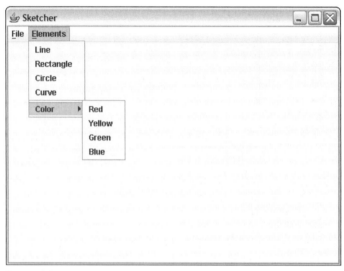

Figure 18-7

How It Works

You create an Action object for each item in the File menu. You then create the menu items corresponding to the Action objects and add them to the File menu. The JMenuItem constructor automatically adds an accelerator key for a menu item if it exists in the Action object.

The items for the other menus are created in essentially the same way except that you create and store the Action objects in the expressions that produce the arguments to the JMenuItem constructor calls. These objects are then passed to the add() method for the menu object. It's reasonable to create the Action objects in the expressions for the arguments to the constructor, as they are relatively simple expressions. Because you store the references to the Action objects, they will be available later when you want to create toolbar buttons corresponding to the menu items. The accelerators for the Elements menu items have been omitted here on the grounds that they were not exactly standard or convenient.

If you try out the color menus you should see the background color change. If it doesn't, there's something wrong somewhere. Now that you have the menus set up using Action objects, you are ready to tackle adding a toolbar to the Sketcher application.

Adding a Toolbar

A toolbar is a bar, usually positioned below the menu bar, which contains a row of buttons that typically provides a more direct route to menu options. You could add a toolbar to the Sketcher program for the menu items that are likely to be most popular. Just so that you know where you are heading, the kind of toolbar you will end up with ultimately is shown in Figure 18-8.

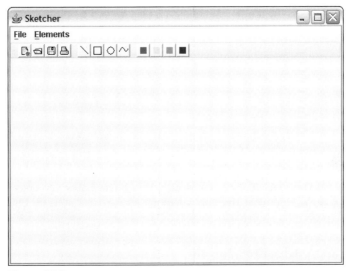

Figure 18-8

The four buttons in the first group are for the most frequently used functions in the File menu. The other two groups of four buttons select the element type and element color, respectively. So how are you going to put this toolbar together?

Adding the toolbar itself couldn't be easier. A toolbar is a Swing component defined by the `javax.swing.JToolBar` class. You can add a member to the `SketchFrame` class for a toolbar by adding the following field to the class definition:

```
private JToolBar toolBar = new JToolBar();          // Window toolbar
```

You can position this following the declaration of the `menuBar` member. It simply creates a `JToolBar` object as a member of the class. Of course, you'll need to add an `import` statement to the `SketchFrame` class for `javax.swing.JToolbar`.

To add the toolbar to the application window, you need to add the following statement after the existing code in the `SketchFrame` constructor:

```
getContentPane().add(toolBar, BorderLayout.NORTH);
```

This adds the (currently empty) toolbar to the top of the content pane for the frame window. The content pane has the `BorderLayout` manager as the default, which is very convenient. A `JToolBar` object should be added to a `Container` using the `BorderLayout` manager since it is normally positioned at one of the four sides of a component. The other three sides of the content pane would be identified by the `SOUTH`, `EAST`, and `WEST` constants in the `BorderLayout` class. An empty toolbar is not much use so let's see how you add buttons to it.

Adding Buttons to a Toolbar

The `JToolBar` class inherits the `add()` methods from the `Container` class, so you can create `JButton` objects and add them to the toolbar using this method. The `JButton` class defines a constructor that accepts an argument of type Action, and creates a button based on the `Action` object that is passed to it. You can use this to create buttons for any of the `Action` objects that you created for the menus, and have the toolbar button events taken care of without any further work.

For example, you could add a button for the `openAction` object corresponding to the `Open` menu item in the File menu with the following statements:

```
JButton button = new JButton(openAction);    // Create button from Action
toolBar.add(button);                         // Add a toolbar button
```

That's all you need basically. The `JButton` constructor will create a `JButton` object based on the `Action` object that you pass as the argument. The `add()` method for `toolBar` adds the `JButton` object to the toolbar. You could still modify the button later—by adding a border, for example. Let's see how that looks.

Try It Out   Adding a Toolbar Button

Assuming you have added the declaration for the `toolBar` object to the `SketchFrame` class, you just need to add a couple of statements preceding the last statement in the constructor to add the toolbar to the content pane:

```
public SketchFrame(String title) {
  // Constructor code as before...
  JButton button = new JButton(openAction);                    // Create button
  button.setBorder(BorderFactory.createRaisedBevelBorder());// Add button border
  toolBar.add(button);
  getContentPane().add(toolBar, BorderLayout.NORTH);
}
```

You'll also need to add `import` statements for `javax.swing.JButton`, `javax.swing.BorderFactory`, and `java.awt.BorderLayout` to the `SketchFrame` class.

If you recompile Sketcher and run it, the window should look like that shown in Figure 18-9.

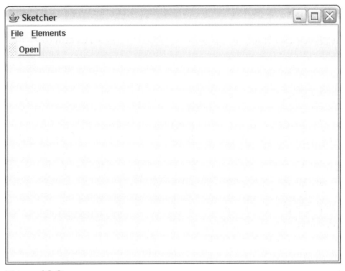

Figure 18-9

How It Works

There's not much to say about this. The add() method for the toolBar object creates a button based on the openAction object that you passed as the argument. You store the reference returned in the button so that you can add a border to the button.

A feature that comes for free with a JToolBar object is that it is automatically dockable and can float as an independent window. You can drag the toolbar using the mouse by holding mouse button 1 down with the cursor in the gray area to the left of the button and then dragging it to a new position. The toolbar will turn into a free-floating window, as Figure 18-10 shows.

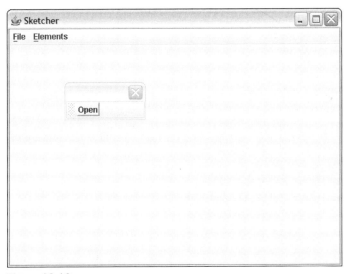

Figure 18-10

You can also drag the toolbar to its original docked position again at the top of the content pane. You must drag with the cursor in the gray area of the toolbar to redock it. Dragging with the cursor in the toolbar title area just moves the window. It's not always convenient to have the toolbar floating. You can inhibit the capability to drag the toolbar around by calling the setFloatable() method for the JToolBar object with the argument specified as false. Let's do this for Sketcher, so add the following statement to the SketchFrame constructor before the statement that adds the toolbar to the content pane:

```
    toolBar.setFloatable(false);                    // Inhibit toolbar floating
    getContentPane().add(toolBar, BorderLayout.NORTH);
}
```

A true argument to the setFloatable() method will allow the toolbar to float, so you can switch this on and off in an application as you wish. You can also test whether the toolbar can float by calling the isFloatable() method for the JToolBar object. This will return true if the toolbar is floatable and false otherwise. If you recompile SketchFrame and run Sketcher again you will see that the gray bit at the left-hand end of the toolbar is no longer there, and you cannot drag the toolbar around.

The toolbar would probably look a little better with a border to differentiate it from the menu bar. You can add an etched border by inserting the following statement in the SketchFrame constructor immediately before you add the toolbar to the content pane:

```
    toolBar.setBorder(BorderFactory.createEtchedBorder(WHITE, LIGHT_GRAY));
```

The button that has been created in the toolbar uses the name from the Action object as its label by default. You really want toolbar buttons with icons instead of text, so that's the next step.

Adding Icons

A reference to an icon is generally stored in a variable of type javax.swing.Icon. Icon is an interface that declares methods that return the height and width of an icon in pixels — these are the getHeight() and getWidth() methods, respectively. The Icon interface also declares a method to paint the icon image on a component — the paint() method. One class that implements the Icon interface is javax.swing.ImageIcon, and it is this class that you use to create an icon object in your program from a file that contains the data defining the icon image.

The ImageIcon class provides several constructors, and the one you'll be using accepts a String argument that specifies the file in which the icon image is found. The String object that you pass as the argument can be just a file name, in which case the file should be in the current directory, which is the one that contains the .class files for the application or applet. You can also supply a string that specifies the path and file name where the file containing the image is to be found. The ImageIcon constructors accept icon files in PNG format (Portable Network Graphics format, which have .png extensions), GIF format (Graphics Interchange Format, or .gif files), or JPEG format (Joint Photographic Experts Group format, or .jpg files) formats, but I'll assume GIF files in the Sketcher code. If you want to use files in one of the other formats, just modify the code accordingly.

You'll put the files containing the icons for the Sketcher application in a subdirectory of the Sketcher directory called Images, so create a subdirectory to your Sketcher application directory with this name. To create an icon for the openAction object from an image in a file open.gif in the Images directory, you could write:

```
openAction.putValue(Action.SMALL_ICON, new ImageIcon ("Images/open.gif"));
```

This stores the ImageIcon object in the Action object associated with the SMALL_ICON key. The add() method for the toolbar object will then look for the icon for the toolbar button that it creates using this key. Let's see if it works.

You will need to obtain, or create for yourself, the GIF files containing the icons for the toolbar buttons. You can use any graphics editor that can save files in the GIF format to create them — Paint Shop Pro, Microsoft Paint, or GIMP, for example. If you are creating your own icons, make sure the background pixels have a transparent color. You won't get the rollover action if they aren't. If you are using your own icons, make sure the file for the openAction object is called open.gif and stored in the Images subdirectory. You'll need GIF files for other buttons, too, and they will each have a file name that is the same as the label on the corresponding menu item. If you want to put all the icon files together for the toolbar buttons, for the File menu you'll need save.gif, new.gif, and print.gif; for the element types you'll need line.gif, rectangle.gif, circle.gif, and curve.gif; and for the colors you'll need red.gif, yellow.gif, green.gif, and blue.gif.

GIF files for all the icons that the Sketcher application uses are included with the Sketcher source code that you can download from the Wrox Press web site: http://www.wrox.com.

You can also download icons for a variety of applications from the Java look-and-feel graphics repository at http://java.sun.com/developer/techDocs/hi/repository. These icons have been designed specifically to go with the Java look-and-feel. The icons are available as 16x16 pixels and 24x24 pixels. The first four icons on the toolbar shown at the beginning of this section are 16x16 icons from this set — the others I created for myself.

Try It Out   A Button with an Icon

You can add the statement to create the icon for the Action object just before you create the toolbar button:

```
public SketchFrame(String title) {
  // Constructor code as before...

    openAction.putValue(Action.SMALL_ICON, new ImageIcon ("Images/open.gif"));
    JButton button = new JButton(openAction);                 // Create button
    button.setBorder(BorderFactory.createRaisedBevelBorder());// Add button border
    toolBar.add(button);
    toolBar.setFloatable(false);                              // Inhibit toolbar floating
    toolBar.setBorder(BorderFactory.createEtchedBorder(WHITE, LIGHT_GRAY));
    getContentPane().add(toolBar, BorderLayout.NORTH);
  }
```

In fact, you could put the statement anywhere after the openAction object has been created, but here will be convenient. You'll need an import statement in SketchFrame.java for the javax.swing.ImageIcon class name. If you recompile Sketcher and run it again, you should see the window shown in Figure 18-11.

Figure 18-11

How It Works

The ImageIcon object that you store in the openAction object is automatically used by the add() method for the toolBar object to add the icon to the button. Unfortunately, you get the label on the toolbar button as well as the icon so you'll want to get rid of the label. If you look at the corresponding menu item though, you get both the label and the icon here, too, and you may want to inhibit the icon in this context. I'll return to modifying the menu items a little later in this chapter, after you've finished with the toolbar. Removing the label from the toolbar button is simple — you just call the setText() method for the button with the argument as null.

It would be better if you altered the inner classes that define the Action objects to add icons automatically when a suitable .gif file is available. You can take care of the labels as well. Let's try that now.

Try It Out   Adding All the Toolbar Buttons

You can modify the constructor for each inner class to add the corresponding icon. Here's how you can implement this in the FileAction class:

```
FileAction(String name) {
  super(name);
  String iconFileName = "Images/" + name + ".gif";
  if(new File(iconFileName).exists()) {
    putValue(SMALL_ICON, new ImageIcon(iconFileName));
  }
}
```

This takes care of both class constructors because the other constructor calls this constructor. Because you refer to the `File` class here, you need to add an `import` statement for `java.io.File` to the beginning of the `SketchFrame.java` source file. This code assumes all icon files follow the convention that their name is the same as the `String` associated with the `NAME` key. If you want to have any file name, you could pass the `String` defining the file name to the constructor. If the icon file is not available then nothing happens, so the code will work whether or not an icon is defined.

The code that you need to add to the constructors for the `TypeAction` and `ColorAction` inner classes is exactly the same as you have added to the `FileAction` class, so go ahead and copy it across to the constructor in each of these classes.

You can reduce the amount of code in the `SketchFrame` constructor a little by defining a helper method in the `SketchFrame` class to create toolbar buttons as follows:

```
// Method to add a button to the toolbar
private JButton addToolBarButton(Action action) {
   JButton button = new JButton(action);
   button.setBorder(BorderFactory.createRaisedBevelBorder());// Add button border
   button.setText(null);
   toolBar.add(button);
   return button;
}
```

The argument is the `Action` object for the toolbar button that is to be added, and the code is similar to the specific code you had in the `SketchFrame` constructor to create the button for the `openAction` object. The `setText()` method call for the button will remove the label so the toolbar buttons will just have icons. You can remove the statement from the `SketchFrame` constructor that created the toolbar button for the `openAction` action and replace it by the following code to create all the toolbar buttons that you need:

```
public SketchFrame(String title) {
   // Constructor code as before...

   // Add file buttons
   toolBar.addSeparator();                          // Space at the start
   addToolBarButton(newAction);
   addToolBarButton(openAction);
   addToolBarButton(saveAction);
   addToolBarButton(printAction);

   // Add element type buttons
   toolBar.addSeparator();
   addToolBarButton(lineAction);
   addToolBarButton(rectangleAction);
   addToolBarButton(circleAction);
   addToolBarButton(curveAction);

   // Add element color buttons
   toolBar.addSeparator();
   addToolBarButton(redAction);
   addToolBarButton(yellowAction);
   addToolBarButton(greenAction);
   addToolBarButton(blueAction);
   toolBar.addSeparator();                          // Space at the end
```

```
        toolBar.setFloatable(false);                        // Inhibit toolbar floating
        toolBar.setBorder(BorderFactory.createEtchedBorder(WHITE, LIGHT_GRAY));
        getContentPane().add(toolBar, BorderLayout.NORTH); // Add the toolbar
    }
```

Now you should get the window shown in Figure 18-8, with a nice neat toolbar. You can see the color buttons in action since they will change the background color. Note how the buttons automatically show when the mouse cursor is over the button. There is also visual feedback when you click a button. You'll lose this functionality if the background color for your icons is not transparent.

How It Works

The extra code in the inner class constructors stores an icon in each object if there is a GIF file with the appropriate name in the `Images` subdirectory. You create each of the toolbar buttons by calling our `addToolBarButton()` helper method with an `Action` item corresponding to a menu item. The helper method passes the `Action` object to the `add()` method for the `JToolBar` object to create a `JButton` object. It also adds a border to the button. The `addToolBarButton()` method returns a reference to the button object in case you need it.

Fixing the Menus

Things are perhaps still not quite as you would have them. If you take a look at the menus in Figure 18-12 you'll see what I mean.

Figure 18-12

All of the menu items now have icons too. While this is a helpful cue to what the toolbar icons are, maybe you would rather not have them as they look a little cluttered. You could get rid of the icons very easily by modifying the menu items created in the expression that is the argument to the `add()` method for the `JMenu` objects. The `JMenuItem` class has a `setIcon()` method that accepts a reference of type `Icon` to set an icon for a menu item. If you want to remove the icon for a menu item, you just call its `setIcon()` method with the argument as `null`.

Try It Out   **Removing Menu Item Icons**

You just need to modify the statements that add the menu items in the `SketchFrame` constructor to remove the icons for all the menu items, like this:

```
public SketchFrame(String title) {
  // Code as before...

  // Construct the file drop-down menu
  fileMenu.add(new JMenuItem(newAction)).setIcon(null);
  fileMenu.add(new JMenuItem(openAction)).setIcon(null);
  fileMenu.add(new JMenuItem(closeAction)).setIcon(null);
  fileMenu.addSeparator();                     // Add separator
  fileMenu.add(new JMenuItem(saveAction)).setIcon(null);
  fileMenu.add(new JMenuItem(saveAsAction)).setIcon(null);
  fileMenu.addSeparator();                     // Add separator
  fileMenu.add(new JMenuItem(printAction))  .setIcon(null);

  // Construct the Element drop-down menu
  elementMenu.add(new JMenuItem(lineAction =
                   new TypeAction("Line", LINE))).setIcon(null);
  elementMenu.add(new JMenuItem(rectangleAction =
                   new TypeAction("Rectangle", RECTANGLE))).setIcon(null);
  elementMenu.add(new JMenuItem(circleAction =
                   new TypeAction("Circle", CIRCLE))).setIcon(null);
  elementMenu.add(new JMenuItem(curveAction =
                   new TypeAction("Curve", CURVE))).setIcon(null);
  elementMenu.addSeparator();

  JMenu colorMenu = new JMenu("Color");         // Color sub-menu
  elementMenu.add(colorMenu);                   // Add the sub-menu

  colorMenu.add(new JMenuItem(redAction =
                   new ColorAction("Red", RED))).setIcon(null);
  colorMenu.add(new JMenuItem(yellowAction =
                   new ColorAction("Yellow", YELLOW))).setIcon(null);
  colorMenu.add(new JMenuItem(greenAction =
                   new ColorAction("Green", GREEN))).setIcon(null);
  colorMenu.add(new JMenuItem(blueAction =
                   new ColorAction("Blue", BLUE))).setIcon(null);
  // Rest of the code as before...
}
```

When you run Sketcher with this modification to `SketchFrame`, you should see the menu items without icons.

How It Works

When you construct each of the menu items using our helper method, `addMenuItem()`, you remove the icon from the `JMenuItem` that is created by passing `null` to its `setIcon()` method. Thus none of the menu item objects has an icon associated with it. Of course, the toolbar buttons are unaffected and retain the icons defined by the `Action` objects they are created from. I rather like the icons on the menu items, so I'm going to leave them in. Further versions of Sketcher will include the icons in the menus.

Adding Tooltips

I'm sure you have seen tooltips in operation. These are the little text prompts that appear automatically when you let the mouse cursor linger over certain GUI elements on the screen for a second or two. They disappear automatically when you move the cursor. I think you will be surprised at how easy it is to implement support for tooltips in Java.

The secret is in the `Action` objects that you are using. `Action` objects have a built-in capability to store tooltip text because it is already provided for with the `SHORT_DESCRIPTION` key that is defined in the interface. All you have to do is store the tooltip text in the inner classes that are derived from `AbstractAction`. The tooltip will then be automatically available on the toolbar buttons that you create. Let's work through the `Action` classes and provide for tooltip text.

Try It Out   Implementing Tooltips

You can provide for tooltip text in each of the inner classes by adding constructors with an extra parameter for the text that is to be the tooltip. You need two additional constructors in the `FileAction` class, one for when the `Action` item has an accelerator key and the other for when it doesn't. The definition of the first new `FileAction` class constructor will be:

```
// Constructor to implement an accelerator and a tooltip
FileAction(String name, KeyStroke keystroke, String tooltip) {
  this(name, keystroke);                      // Call the other constructor
  if(tooltip != null) {                       // If there is tooltip text
    putValue(SHORT_DESCRIPTION, tooltip);     // ...squirrel it away
  }
}
```

This just calls the constructor that accepts arguments defining the name and the keystroke. It then stores the tooltip string using the `SHORT_DESCRIPTION` key, as long as it isn't null. Although you wouldn't expect a null to be passed for the tooltip text reference, it's best not to assume it as this could crash the program. If the string for the tooltip text is null, you do nothing.

The other constructor will take care of a tooltip for an `Action` item without an accelerator keystroke:

```
// Constructor to implement a tooltip
FileAction(String name, String tooltip) {
  this(name);                                 // Call the other constructor
  if(tooltip != null) {                       // If there is tooltip text
    putValue(SHORT_DESCRIPTION, tooltip);     // ...squirrel it away
  }
}
```

Of course, you must now change the code in the `SketchFrame` constructor that creates `FileAction` items so that you incorporate the tooltip argument:

```
// Create the action items for the file menu
newAction = new FileAction("New", KeyStroke.getKeyStroke('N',
                              CTRL_DOWN_MASK), "Create new sketch");
openAction = new FileAction("Open", KeyStroke.getKeyStroke('O',
                              CTRL_DOWN_MASK), "Open existing sketch");
closeAction = new FileAction("Close", "Close sketch");
```

```
                saveAction = new FileAction("Save", KeyStroke.getKeyStroke('S',
                                   CTRL_DOWN_MASK), "Save sketch");
                saveAsAction = new FileAction("Save As...", "Save as new file");
                printAction = new FileAction("Print", KeyStroke.getKeyStroke('P',
                                   CTRL_DOWN_MASK), "Print sketch");
```

You can do exactly the same with the `TypeAction` class—just add the following constructor to the class definition:

```
       // Constructor to implement a tooltip
       TypeAction(String name, int typeID, String tooltip) {
         this(name, typeID);
         if(tooltip != null) {                      // If there is a tooltip
           putValue(SHORT_DESCRIPTION, tooltip);    // ...squirrel it away
         }
       }
```

You can now modify the code in the `SketchFrame` constructor to pass a tooltip string when you create a `TypeAction` object:

```
       // Construct the Element drop-down menu
       elementMenu.add(new JMenuItem(lineAction =
                        new TypeAction("Line", LINE, "Draw lines")));
       elementMenu.add(new JMenuItem(rectangleAction =
                        new TypeAction("Rectangle", RECTANGLE, "Draw rectangles")));
       elementMenu.add(new JMenuItem(circleAction =
                        new TypeAction("Circle", CIRCLE, "Draw circles")));
       elementMenu.add(new JMenuItem(curveAction =
                        new TypeAction("Curve", CURVE, "Draw curves")));
```

And you need to add a constructor that does exactly the same as in the other action classes to the `ColorAction` class:

```
       // Constructor to implement a tooltip
       public ColorAction(String name, Color color, String tooltip) {
         this(name, color);
         if(tooltip != null) {                      // If there is a tooltip
           putValue(SHORT_DESCRIPTION, tooltip);    // ...squirrel it away
         }
       }
```

The corresponding changes required in the `SketchFrame` constructor are:

```
       JMenu colorMenu = new JMenu("Color");                  // Color sub-menu
       elementMenu.add(colorMenu);                            // Add the sub-menu
       colorMenu.add(new JMenuItem(redAction =
                        new ColorAction("Red", RED, "Draw in red")));
       colorMenu.add(new JMenuItem(yellowAction =
                        new ColorAction("Yellow", YELLOW, "Draw in yellow")));
       colorMenu.add(new JMenuItem(greenAction =
                        new ColorAction("Green", GREEN, "Draw in green")));
       colorMenu.add(new JMenuItem(blueAction =
                        new ColorAction("Blue", BLUE, "Draw in blue")));
```

Of course, if you want to use your own tooltip text for any of these, you can. You should keep it short since it is displayed on the fly. You can try the tooltips out now that you have the last piece in place. Just recompile the SketchFrame class and run Sketcher again. You should be able to see the tooltip when you let the cursor linger over a button, as Figure 18-13 illustrates.

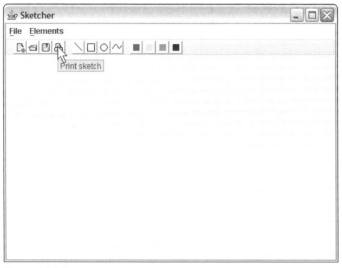

Figure 18-13

How It Works

Action objects act as a repository for the tooltip text for components that implement the actions, so this works for the toolbar buttons in Sketcher. If an Action object contains a tooltip property, a toolbar button that you create from it will automatically have the tooltip operational. Try lingering the cursor over a menu item. Since the menu items are also created from Action items, tooltips are available for them, too.

Disabling Actions

You won't want to have all of the menu items and toolbar buttons enabled all of the time. For example, while there is no sketch active, the Save and Print menu items should not be operational, and neither should the corresponding buttons. The Action objects provide a single point of control for enabling or disabling menu items and the corresponding toolbar buttons. To disable an action, you call the setEnabled() method for the Action object with an argument of false. You can restore the enabled state by calling the method with a true argument. The isEnabled() method for an Action object returns true if the action is enabled, and false otherwise.

Let's see toolbar button inaction in action in Sketcher.

Try It Out   **Disabling Actions**

You'll disable the actions corresponding to the `Save`, `Close`, and `Print` actions. Add the following statements to the end of the `SketchFrame` constructor:

```
// Disable actions
saveAction.setEnabled(false);
closeAction.setEnabled(false);
printAction.setEnabled(false);
```

That's all that's necessary. If you run the modified version of Sketcher, menu items and toolbar buttons corresponding to the `Action` objects you have disabled will be grayed out and non-operational. Figure 18-14 shows the application window with the disabled toolbar buttons grayed out.

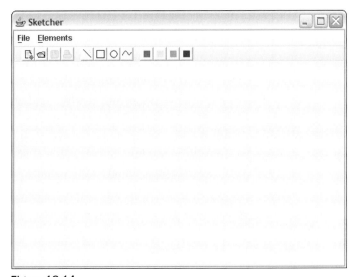

Figure 18-14

If you extend the File menu, you will see that the corresponding menu items are grayed out, too.

How It Works

The state of both the `JMenuItem` and `JButton` objects created from an `Action` object is determined by the state of the `Action` object. Disabling the `Action` object disables any menus or toolbar buttons created from it. If you want a demonstration that they really are disabled, try disabling a couple of the color actions.

Summary

In this chapter you have learned how to handle events in your applications and in your applets. Events are fundamental to all window-based applications, as well as most applets, so you'll be applying the techniques you have seen this chapter throughout the rest of the book.

The most important points I have discussed in this chapter are:

❏ A user interaction generates an event in the context of a component.

❏ Two categories of events are associated with a component: low-level events from the mouse or keyboard, or window system events such as opening or closing a window; and semantic events that represent component actions such as pressing a button or selecting a menu item.

❏ Both low-level and semantic events can arise simultaneously.

❏ An event for a component can be handled by the component object itself, or by a separate object that implements a listener interface corresponding to the event type.

❏ A component that is to handle its own events does so by calling its `enableEvents()` method and implementing the class method to process the kind of event that has been enabled.

❏ A listener object that is registered with a component will receive notification of the events originating with the component that correspond to the type(s) of events the listener can handle.

❏ A listener interface for low-level events requires several event-handling methods to be implemented.

❏ A listener interface for semantic events declares a single event-handling method.

❏ An adapter class defines a set of empty methods for one or more low-level event interfaces. You can create your own class defining a low-level event listener by deriving your class from an adapter class and then implementing the event-handling methods in which you are interested.

❏ Events in applications and in applets are handled in exactly the same way.

❏ An `Action` object is an object of a class that implements the `Action` interface. `Action` objects can be used to create menu items and associated toolbar buttons.

❏ An `Action` object is automatically the listener for the menu item and toolbar button that are created from it.

Exercises

You can download the source code for the examples in the book and the solutions to the following exercises from `http://www.wrox.com`.

1. Modify Sketcher to add an `Exit` action for the File menu and the toolbar.

2. Modify the `Lottery` applet to present the six numbers selected in ascending sequence.

3. Replace the action listener for the selection buttons in the `Lottery` applet with a mouse listener and use the `mousePressed()` method to update the selection with a new value.

4. Modify the `Lottery` applet to implement the mouse listener for a selection button as an inner class to the `Lottery` class.

5. Modify the `Lottery` applet to implement the control buttons on a toolbar based on `Action` objects.

6. Change the `Lottery` applet to handle the `MOUSE_ENTERED` and `MOUSE_EXITED` events within the toolbar buttons you added in the previous exercise and display a hand cursor.

7. Add tooltips to the lucky number buttons and the toolbar buttons in the `Lottery` applet. (You can make the tooltip the same for each of the lucky number buttons.)

Drawing in a Window

In this chapter you'll look at how you can draw using the Java 2D facilities that are part of the Java Foundation Classes (JFC). You'll explore how you draw in an applet and in an application. You'll investigate how you can combine the event-handling capability that you learned about in the previous chapter with the drawing facilities you'll explore in this chapter to implement an interactive graphical user interface for creating a sketch.

By the end of this chapter you will have learned:

- ❑   What components are available for creating a GUI
- ❑   How coordinates are defined for drawing on a component
- ❑   How you implement drawing on a component
- ❑   How to structure the components in a window for drawing
- ❑   What kinds of shapes you can draw on a component
- ❑   How you implement mouse listener methods to enable interactive drawing operations

Using the Model/View Architecture

You need to develop an idea of how you're going to manage the data for a sketch in the Sketcher program before you start drawing a sketch, because this will affect where and how you handle events. You already have a class that defines an application window, SketchFrame, but this class would not be a very sensible place to store the underlying data that defines a sketch. For one thing, you'll want to save a sketch in a file, and serialization is the easiest way to do that. If you're going to use serialization to store a sketch, you won't want all the stuff in the implementation of the SketchFrame class muddled up with the data relating to the sketch you have created.

For another thing, it will make the program easier to implement if you separate out the basic data defining a sketch from the definition of the GUI. This will be along the lines of the **Model-View-Controller** (MVC) architecture that I first mentioned in Chapter 17, a variant of which is used in the definition of Swing components. Ideally, you should manage the sketch data in a class designed specifically for that purpose—this class will be the model for a sketch.

A class representing a view of the data in the model class will display the sketch and handle user interactions — so this class will combine viewing functions and a sketch controller. The general GUI creation and operations not specific to a view will be dealt with in the SketchFrame class. This is not the only way of implementing the things you want in the Sketcher program, but it's quite a good way.

The model object will contain a mixture of text and graphics that will make up a sketch. You can call the model class SketchModel, and the class that will represent a view of the model can have the name SketchView, although you won't be adding the view to the program until the next chapter. Figure 19-1 illustrates the relationships between the classes you'll have in Sketcher.

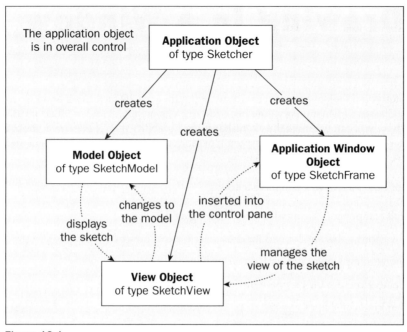

Figure 19-1

The application object will have overall responsibility for managing links between the other objects involved in the program. Any object that has access to the application object will be able to communicate with any other object as long as the application class has methods to make each of the objects available. Thus, the application object will act as the communication channel between objects.

Note that SketchFrame is not the view class — it just defines the application window and the GUI components associated with that. When you create a SketchView object in the next chapter, you'll arrange to insert the SketchView object into the content pane of the SketchFrame object and manage it using the layout manager for the content pane. By defining the view class separately from the application class, you separate the view of a sketch from the menus and other components that you use to interact with the program. One benefit of this is that the area in which you display a sketch has its own coordinate system, independent of that of the application window.

To implement the foundations for the model/view design in Sketcher, you need to define classes for the model and the view, at least in outline. You can define in skeleton form the class to contain the data defining a sketch:

```
import java.util.Observable;

class SketchModel extends Observable {
  // Detail of the rest of class to be filled in later...
}
```

You obviously have a bit more work to do on this class to make it effective! You'll add to this as you go along. Since the SketchModel class extends the Observable class, you'll be able to register the view class with it as an observer and automatically notify the view of any changes to the model. This facility will come into its own when you have multiple views. You can define the view class as a component by deriving it from the JComponent class. This will build in all the methods for operating as a component and you can override any of these as necessary. The view class also needs to implement the Observer interface so that you can register it with the model to receive notification when the model changes. Here's the outline:

```
import javax.swing.JComponent;
import java.util.Observer;
import java.util.Observable;

class SketchView extends JComponent implements Observer {
  public SketchView(Sketcher theApp) {
    this.theApp = theApp;
  }

  // Method called by Observable object when it changes
  public void update(Observable o, Object rectangle) {
    // Code to respond to changes in the model...
  }

  private Sketcher theApp;              // The application object
}
```

The view is definitely going to need access to the model to display it, but rather than store a reference to the model, the constructor has a parameter to enable the application object to be passed to it. By storing the application object in the view, rather than a reference to the model and adding a method to the application object to return a reference to the model, you make the view object independent of the model object. If a completely different object represents the model because, for example, a new file is loaded, you don't need to change the view object. As long as the view object is registered as an observer for the new model, the view will automatically redraw the new sketch when it is notified by the model that it has changed.

To integrate a model and its view into the Sketcher application, you just need to add some code to the Sketcher class:

```
import java.awt.Toolkit;
import java.awt.Dimension;
import java.awt.BorderLayout;
import javax.swing.SwingUtilities;
```

```
import java.awt.event.WindowEvent;
import java.awt.event.WindowAdapter;

public class Sketcher {
  public static void main(String[] args) {
    theApp = new Sketcher();
    SwingUtilities.invokeLater(
       new Runnable() {                          // Anonymous Runnable class object
                      public void run() {         // Run method executed in thread
                        theApp.createGUI();       // Call static GUI creator
                      }
                    }     );
  }

  public void createGUI() {
    window = new SketchFrame("Sketcher", this);  // Create the app window
    Toolkit theKit = window.getToolkit();        // Get the window toolkit
    Dimension wndSize = theKit.getScreenSize();  // Get screen size

    // Set the position to screen center & size to 2/3 screen size
    window.setBounds(wndSize.width/6, wndSize.height/6,        // Position
                2*wndSize.width/3, 2*wndSize.height/3);    // Size
    window.addWindowListener(new WindowHandler()); // Add window listener

    sketch = new SketchModel();                  // Create the model
    view = new SketchView(this);                 // Create the view
    sketch.addObserver(view);                    // Register view with the model
    window.getContentPane().add(view, BorderLayout.CENTER);
    window.setVisible(true);
  }

  // Return a reference to the application window
  public SketchFrame getWindow() {
    return window;
  }

  // Return a reference to the model
  public SketchModel getModel() {
    return sketch;
  }

  // Return a reference to the view
  public SketchView getView() {
    return view;
  }

  // Handler class for window events
  class WindowHandler extends WindowAdapter {
    // Handler for window closing event
    public void windowClosing(WindowEvent e) {
      // Code to be added here later...
    }
  }
}
```

```
private SketchModel sketch;              // The data model for the sketch
private SketchView view;                 // The view of the sketch
private static SketchFrame window;       // The application window
private static Sketcher theApp;          // The application object
}
```

There is no code in the `windowClosing()` method at present, so this assumes you have restored `EXIT_ON_CLOSE` as the default closing action in the `SketchFrame` class as I suggested in the previous chapter. You'll be adding code to the `windowClosing()` method in the `WindowHandler` inner class when you save sketches on disk.

The `SketchFrame` constructor needs to be modified as follows:

```
public SketchFrame(String title, Sketcher theApp) {
    setTitle(title);                              // Set the window title
    this.theApp = theApp;                         // Save app. object reference
    setJMenuBar(menuBar);                         // Add the menu bar to the window
    setDefaultCloseOperation(EXIT_ON_CLOSE);      // Default is exit the application

    // Rest of the constructor as before...
}
```

You can add a field to the `SketchFrame` class that will store the reference to the application object:

```
private Sketcher theApp;                          // The application object
```

There are new methods in the `Sketcher` class that return a reference to the application window, the model, and the view, so all of these are now accessible from anywhere in the Sketcher application code where you have a reference to the application object available.

After creating the model and view objects in the `createGUI()` method in the `Sketcher` class, you register the view as an observer for the model to enable the model to notify the view when any changes occur. You then add the view to the content pane of the window object, which is the main application window. Since you add the view in the center using the `BorderLayout` manager for the content pane, it will occupy all the remaining space in the pane.

Now that you know roughly the direction in which you are heading, let's move on down the road.

Coordinate Systems in Components

In Chapter 17, you saw how your computer screen has a coordinate system that is used to define the position and size of a window. You also saw how you can add components to a container with their position established by a layout manager. The coordinate system used by a container to position components within it is analogous to the screen coordinate system. The origin is at the top-left corner of the container, with the positive *x*-axis running horizontally from left to right, and the positive *y*-axis running from top to bottom. The positions of buttons in a `JWindow` or a `JFrame` object are specified as a pair of (*x*, *y*) pixel coordinates, relative to the origin at the top-left corner of the container object on the screen. In Figure 19-2 you can see the coordinate system for the `Sketcher` application window.

Positive Y-Axis

Window origin at 0,0

Positive X-Axis

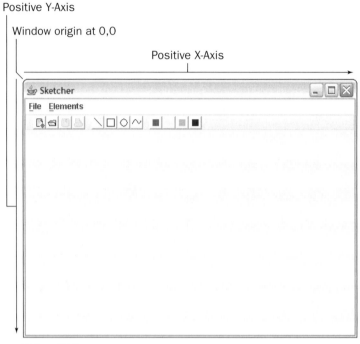

Figure 19-2

Of course, the layered pane for the window object will have its own coordinate system, with the origin in the top-left corner of the pane, and this is used to position the menu and the content pane. The content pane will have its own coordinate system, too, which will be used to position the components that it contains.

It's not just containers and windows that have their own coordinate system: Each JButton object also has its own system, as do JToolBar objects. In fact, every component has its own coordinate system, and some examples are illustrated in Figure 19-3.

Origin for the toolbar

Origin for the line button

Origin for the color button

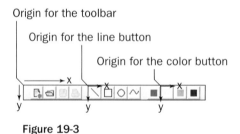

Figure 19-3

It's clear that a container needs a coordinate system for specifying the positions of the components it contains. You also need a coordinate system to draw on a component — to draw a line, for example, you need to be able to specify where it begins and ends in relation to the component — and while the coordinate system you use for drawing on a component is similar to that used for positioning components in a container, it's not exactly the same. It's more complicated when you are drawing — but for very good reasons. Let's see how the coordinate system for drawing works.

Drawing on a Component

Before I get into the specifics of how you draw on a component, let's understand the principle ideas behind it. When you draw on a component using the Java 2D capabilities, two coordinate systems are involved. When you draw something — a line or a curve, for example — you specify the line or the curve in a device-independent logical coordinate system called the **user coordinate system** for the component, or **user space**. By default, this coordinate system has the same orientation as the system that I discussed for positioning components in containers. The origin is at the top-left corner; the positive *x*-axis runs from left to right, and the positive *y*-axis from top to bottom. Coordinates are usually specified as floating-point values, although you can also use integers.

A particular graphical output device will have its own device coordinate system, or device space, as illustrated in Figure 19-4. This coordinate system has the same orientation as the default user coordinate system, but the coordinate units depend on the characteristics of the device. Your display, for example, will have a different device coordinate system for each configuration of the screen resolution, so the coordinate system when your display is set to a resolution 1024x768 pixels will be different from the coordinate system for 800x600 pixels.

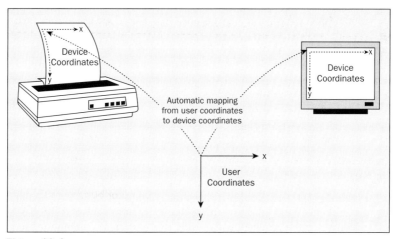

Figure 19-4

*Incidentally, the drawing process is often referred to as **rendering**, because graphical output devices are generally raster devices and the drawing elements such as lines, rectangles, text, and so on need to be rendered into a rasterized representation before they can be output to the device.*

Having a device-independent coordinate system for drawing means that you can use essentially the same code for writing graphical information to a variety of different devices — to your display screen, for example, or to your printer, even though these devices themselves have quite different coordinate systems with different resolutions. The fact that your screen might have 90 pixels per inch while your printer may have 600 dots per inch is automatically taken care of. Java 2D will deal with converting your user coordinates to the device coordinate system that is specific to the output device you are using.

With the default mapping from user coordinates to device coordinates, the units for user coordinates are assumed to be 1/72 of an inch. Since for most screen devices the pixels are approximately 1/72 inch apart, the conversion amounts to an identity transformation. If you want to use user coordinates that are in some other units, you have to provide for this yourself. You'll look into the mechanism that you would use to do this when I discuss transformations in the next chapter.

Graphics Contexts

The user coordinate system for drawing on a component using Java 2D is encapsulated in an object of type Graphics2D, which is usually referred to as a **graphics context**. It provides all the tools you need to draw whatever you want on the surface of the component. A graphics context enables you to draw lines, curves, shapes, filled shapes, as well as images, and gives you a great deal of control over the drawing process.

The Graphics2D class is derived from the Graphics class that defined device contexts in earlier versions of Java, so if you feel the need to use the old drawing methods, they are all inherited in the Graphics2D class. I'll be concentrating on the more powerful and flexible facilities provided by Graphics2D, but as you'll see, references to graphics contexts are usually passed around as type Graphics, so you need to be aware of it. Note that both the Graphics and Graphics2D classes are abstract classes, so you can't create objects of either type directly. An object representing a graphics context is entirely dependent on the component to which it relates, so a graphics context is always obtained for use with a particular component.

The Graphics2D object for a component takes care of mapping user coordinates to device coordinates, so it contains information about the device that is the destination for output as well as the user coordinates for the component. The information required for converting user coordinates to device coordinates is encapsulated in three different kinds of objects:

❑ A GraphicsEnvironment object encapsulates all the graphics devices (as GraphicsDevice objects) and fonts (as Font objects) that are available on your computer.

❑ A GraphicsDevice object encapsulates information about a particular device, such as a screen or a printer, and stores it in one or more GraphicsConfiguration objects.

❑ A GraphicsConfiguration object defines the characteristics of a particular device, such as a screen or a printer. Your display screen will typically have several GraphicsConfiguration objects associated with it, each corresponding to a particular combination of screen resolution and number of displayable colors.

The graphics context also maintains other information necessary for drawing operations, such as the drawing color, the line style, and the specification of the fill color and pattern for filled shapes. You'll see how to work with these attributes in examples later in this chapter.

Because a graphics context defines the drawing context for a specific component, you must have a reference to the graphics context object for a component before you can draw on the component. For the most part, you'll draw on a component by implementing the paint() method that is called whenever the component needs to be reconstructed. An object representing the graphics context for the component is passed as an argument to the paint() method, and you use this object to do the drawing. The graphics context includes all the methods that you use to draw on a component, and you'll be looking into many of these in this chapter.

The paint() method is not the only way of drawing on a component. You can obtain a graphics context for a component at any time just by calling its getGraphics() method and then using methods for the Graphics object to specify the drawing operations.

There are occasions when you want to get a component redrawn while avoiding a direct call of the paint() method. In such cases you should call repaint() for the component. Five versions of this method are available; you'll look at four:

repaint() Method	Description
repaint()	Causes the entire component to be repainted by calling its paint() method after all of the currently outstanding events have been processed.
repaint(long msec)	Requests that the entire component be repainted within msec milliseconds.

repaint(int msec,
        int x, int y,
        int width, int height)
	Adds the region specified by the arguments to the dirty region list if the component is visible. The dirty region list is simply a list of areas of the component that need to be repainted. The component will be repainted by calling its paint() method when all currently outstanding events have been processed, or within msec milliseconds. The region is the rectangle at position (x, y), with the width and height as specified by the last two arguments.

repaint(Rectangle rect)	Adds the rectangle specified by rect to the dirty region list if the component is visible.

You will find that the first and the last methods are the ones you use most of the time.

That's enough theory for now. It's time to get a bit of practice. Let's get an idea of how you can draw on a component by drawing on the SketchView object that you added to Sketcher. All you need to do is implement the paint() method in the SketchView class.

Try It Out   Drawing in a View

Add the following implementation of the paint() method to the SketchView class:

```
import javax.swing.JComponent;
import java.util.Observer;
import java.util.Observable;
```

```
import java.awt.Graphics;
import java.awt.Graphics2D;
import java.awt.Color;

class SketchView extends JComponent implements Observer {
  public void paint(Graphics g) {
    // Temporary code
    Graphics2D g2D = (Graphics2D)g;                       // Get a Java 2D device context

    g2D.setPaint(Color.RED);                              // Draw in red
    g2D.draw3DRect(50, 50, 150, 100, true);              // Draw a raised 3D rectangle
    g2D.drawString("A nice 3D rectangle", 60, 100); // Draw some text
  }

  // Rest of the class as before...
}
```

If you recompile the file SketchFrame.java and run Sketcher once again, you can see what the paint() method produces. You should see the window shown in Figure 19-5.

Figure 19-5

Okay, it's not your traditional meaning of 3D. In this case, the edges of the rectangle are highlighted so that they appear to be beveled and lift from the top left-hand corner (or the coordinate origin).

How It Works

The graphics context is passed as the argument to the paint() method as type Graphics (the base class for Graphics2D), so to use the methods defined in the Graphics2D class you must first cast it to that type. The paint() method still has a parameter type of Graphics for compatibility with applications written using older versions of Java.

Once you have cast the graphics context, you then set the color in which you will draw by calling the setPaint() method for the Graphics2D object and passing the drawing color as the argument. All subsequent drawing operations will now be in the color Color.RED. You can change this with another call to setPaint() whenever you want to draw in a different color.

Next, you call the draw3DRect() method for the Graphics2D object, and this draws the 3D rectangle. The first two arguments are integers specifying the x and y coordinates of the top-left corner of the rectangle to be drawn, relative to the user space origin of the component, which in this case is the top-left corner of the view object in the content pane. The third and fourth arguments are the width and height of the rectangle, respectively, also in units determined by the user coordinate system.

The drawString() method draws the string specified as the first argument at the position determined by the second and third arguments — these are the x and y coordinates in user coordinates of the bottom-left corner of the first letter of the string. The string will be drawn by obtaining the glyphs for the current Font object in the device context corresponding to the characters in the string. As I said when I discussed Font objects, the glyphs for a font define the physical appearance of the characters.

However, there's more to drawing than is apparent from this example. The graphics context has information about the line style to be drawn, as well as the color, the font to be used for text, and more besides. Let's dig a little deeper into what is going on.

The Drawing Process

A Graphics2D object maintains a whole heap of information that determines how things are drawn. Most of this information is contained in six attributes within a Graphics2D object:

❑ The **paint** attribute determines the drawing color for lines. It also defines the color and pattern to be used for filling shapes. The paint attribute is set by calling the setPaint(Paint paint) method for the graphics context. java.awt.Paint is an interface that is implemented by the Color class that defines a color. It is also implemented by the java.awt.GradientPaint and java.awt.TexturePaint classes, which represent a color pattern and a texture, respectively. You can therefore pass references of any of these types to the setPaint() method. The default paint attribute is the color of the component.

❑ The **stroke** attribute defines a pen that determines the line style, such as solid, dashed, or dotted lines, and the line thickness. It also determines the shape of the ends of lines. The stroke attribute is set by calling the setStroke(Stroke s) method for a graphics context. The default stroke attribute defines a square pen that draws a solid line with a thickness of 1 user coordinate unit. The ends of the line are square, and joins are mitered. The java.awt.Stroke interface is implemented by the java.awt.BasicStroke class, which defines a basic set of attributes for rendering lines.

❑ The **font** attribute determines the font to be used when drawing text. The font attribute is set by calling the setFont(Font font) method for the graphics context. The default font is the font set for the component.

❑ The **transform** attribute defines the transformations to be applied during the rendering process. What you draw can be translated, rotated, and scaled as determined by the transforms currently in effect. There are several methods for applying transforms to what is drawn, as you'll see. The default transform is the identity transform, which leaves things unchanged.

❑ The **clip** attribute defines the boundary of an area on a component. Rendering operations are restricted so that drawing takes place only within the area enclosed by the clip boundary. The clip attribute is set by calling one of the two `setClip()` methods for a graphics context. With one version of `setClip()` you define the boundary of the area to be rendered as a rectangle that you specify by the coordinates of its top-left corner and the height and width of the rectangle. The other `setClip()` method expects the argument to be a reference of type `java.awt.Shape`. The `Shape` interface is implemented by a variety of classes in the `java.awt.geom` package that define geometric shapes of various kinds, such as lines, circles, polygons, and curves. The default clip attribute is the whole component area.

❑ The **composite** attribute determines how overlapping shapes are drawn on a component. You can alter the transparency of the fill color of a shape so an underlying shape shows through. You set the composite attribute by calling the `setComposite(Composite comp)` method for the graphics context. The default composite attribute causes a new shape to be drawn over whatever is already there, taking account of the transparency of any of the colors used.

All of the objects that represent attributes are stored as references within a `Graphics2D` object. Therefore, you must always call a `setXXX()` method to alter an attribute in a graphics context, not try to modify an external object directly. If you externally alter an object that has been used to set an attribute, the results are unpredictable.

*You can also affect how the rendering process deals with "jaggies" when drawing lines. The process to eliminate jaggies on sloping lines is called **antialiasing**, and you can change the antialiasing that is applied by calling one of the two `setRenderingHints()` methods for a graphics context. I won't be going into this aspect of drawing further, though.*

There's a huge amount of detail on attributes under the covers. Rather than going into all that here, you'll be exploring how to apply new attributes to a graphics context piecemeal where it is relevant to the various examples you'll create.

Rendering Operations

You have the following basic methods available with a `Graphics2D` object for rendering various kinds of graphic entities:

Method	Description
`draw(Shape shape)`	Renders a shape using the current attributes for the graphics context. I'll be discussing what a shape is next.
`fill(Shape shape)`	Fills a shape using the current attributes for the graphics context. You'll see how to do this later in this chapter.
`drawString(String text)`	Renders a text string using the current attributes for the graphics context. You'll be applying this further in the next chapter.
`drawImage()`	Renders an image using the current attributes for the graphics context. This is quite a complicated operation so you won't be getting very far into this.

Let's see what shapes are available. They'll help make Sketcher a lot more useful.

Shapes

Classes that define geometric shapes are contained in the `java.awt.geom` package, but the `Shape` interface that these classes implement is defined in `java.awt`. Objects that represent shapes are often passed around as references of type `Shape`, so you'll usually need to import class names from both packages into your source file. Any class that implements the `Shape` interface defines a shape, and visually a shape will be some composite of straight lines and curves. Straight lines, rectangles, ellipses, and curves are all shapes.

A graphics context knows how to draw objects of a type that implements the `Shape` interface. To draw a shape on a component, you just need to pass the object defining the shape to the `draw()` method for the `Graphics2D` object for the component. To explore this in detail, I'll split the shapes into three groups: straight lines and rectangles, arcs and ellipses, and freeform curves. First, though, you must take a look at how points are defined.

Classes Defining Points

Two classes in the `java.awt.geom` package define points, `Point2D.Float` and `Point2D.Double`. From the class names you can see that these are both inner classes to the `Point2D` class, which also happens to be an abstract base class for both classes too. The `Point2D.Float` class defines a point from a pair of (*x*, *y*) coordinates of type `float`, whereas the `Point2D.Double` class defines a point as a coordinate pair of type `double`. The `Point` class in the `java.awt` package also defines a point, but in terms of a coordinate pair of type `int`. The `Point` class also has `Point2D` as a base, and the hierarchy of classes that represents points is shown in Figure 19-6.

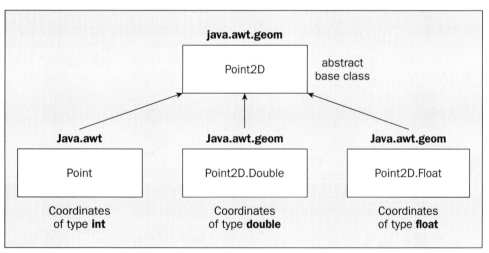

Figure 19-6

The `Point` class actually predates the `Point2D` class, but the `Point` class was redefined to make it a subclass of `Point2D` when `Point2D` was introduced, hence the somewhat unusual class hierarchy with only two of the subclasses as inner classes. The merit of this arrangement is that all of the subclasses inherit the methods defined in the `Point2D` class, so operations on each of the three kinds of point are the same. Objects of all three concrete types that represent points can be passed around as references of type `Point2D`.

The three subclasses of `Point2D` define a default constructor that defines the point (0,0) and a constructor that accepts a pair of coordinates of the type appropriate to the class type.

The operations that each of the three concrete point classes inherits are:

1. **Accessing coordinate values** — The `getX()` and `getY()` methods return the x and y coordinates of a point as type `double`, regardless of how the coordinates are stored. These are abstract methods in the `Point2D` class, so they are defined in each of the subclasses. Although you get coordinates as values of type `double` from all three concrete classes via these methods, you can always access the coordinates with their original type directly since the coordinates are stored in public fields with the same names, `x` and `y`, in each case.

2. **Calculating the distance between two points** — You have no less than three overloaded versions of the `distance()` method for calculating the distance between two points, and returning it as type `double`:

`distance(`
    `double x1, double y1,`
    `double x2, double y2)`
	This is a static version of the method that calculates the distance between the points $(x1, y1)$ and $(x2, y2)$.

`distance(` `double xNext, double yNext)`	This calculates the distance from the current point (the object for which the method is called) and the point $(xNext, yNext)$.
`distance(Point2D nextPoint)`	This calculates the distance from the current point to the point `nextPoint`. The argument can be any of the subclass types, `Point`, `Point2D.Float`, or `Point2D.Double`.

Here's how you might calculate the distance between two points:

```
Point2D.Double p1 = new Point2D.Double(2.5, 3.5);
Point p2 = new Point(20, 30);
double lineLength = p1.distance(p2);
```

You can also calculate this distance without creating the points by using the static method:

```
double lineLength = Point2D.distance(2.5, 3.5, 20, 30);
```

Corresponding to each of the three `distance()` methods is a convenience method, `distanceSq()`, with the same parameter list that returns the square of the distance between two points as a value of type `double`.

3. **Comparing points** — The `equals()` method compares the current point with the point object referenced by the argument and returns `true` if they are equal and `false` otherwise.

4. **Setting a new location for a point** — The inherited `setLocation()` method comes in two versions. One accepts an argument that is a reference of type `Point2D` and sets the coordinate values of the current point to those of the point passed as an argument. The other accepts two arguments of type `double` that are the *x* and *y* coordinates of the new location. The `Point` class also defines a version of `setLocation()` that accepts two arguments of type `int` to define the new coordinates.

Lines and Rectangles

The `java.awt.geom` package contains the following classes for shapes that are straight lines and rectangles:

Class	Description
Line2D	This is an abstract base class defining a line between two points. Two concrete subclasses — `Line2D.Float` and `Line2D.Double` — define lines in terms of user coordinates of type `float` and `double`, respectively. You can see from their names that the subclasses are nested classes to the abstract base class `Line2D`.
Rectangle2D	This is the abstract base class for the `Rectangle2D.Double` and `Rectangle2D.Float` classes that define rectangles. A rectangle is defined by the coordinates of the position of its top-left corner plus its width and height. The `Rectangle2D` class is also the abstract base class for the `Rectangle` class in the `java.awt` package, which stores the position coordinates and the height and width as values of type `int`.
RoundRectangle2D	This is the abstract base class for the `RoundRectangle2D.Double` and `RoundRectangle2D.Float` classes, which define rectangles with rounded corners. The rounded corners are specified by a width and height.

Like the `java.awt.Point` class, the `Rectangle` class that is defined in the `java.awt` package predates the `Rectangle2D` class, but the definition of the `Rectangle` class was changed to make `Rectangle2D` a base for compatibility reasons. Note that there is no equivalent to the `Rectangle` class for lines defined by integer coordinates. If you are browsing the documentation, you may notice there is a `Line` interface, but this declares operations for an audio channel and has nothing to do with geometry.

Figure 19-7 illustrates how, lines, rectangles, and round rectangles are defined.

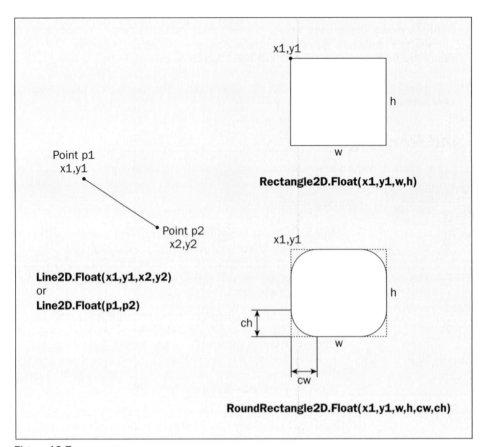

Figure 19-7

You can define a line by supplying two `Point2D` objects to a constructor, or two pairs of (x, y) coordinates. For example, here's how you define a line by two coordinate pairs:

```
Line2D.float line = new Line2D.Float(5.0f, 100.0f, 50.0f, 150.0f);
```

This draws a line from the point (5.0, 100.0) to the point (50.0, 150.0). You could also create the same line using `Point2D.Float` objects, like this:

```
Point2D.Float p1 = new Point2D.Float(5.0f, 100.0f);
Point2D.Float p2 = new Point2D.Float(50.0f, 150.0f);
Line2D.float line = new Line2D.Float(p1, p2);
```

You draw a line using the `draw()` method for a `Graphics2D` object. For example:

```
g2D.draw(line);                              // Draw the line
```

To create a rectangle, you specify the coordinates of its top-left corner, and the width and height of the rectangle:

```
float width = 120.0f;
float height = 90.0f;
Rectangle2D.Float rectangle = new Rectangle2D.Float(50.0f, 150.0f, width, height);
```

The default constructor creates a rectangle at the origin with a zero width and height. You can set the position, width, and height of a rectangle by calling its setRect() method. There are three versions of this method. One of them accepts arguments for the coordinates of the top-left corner and the width and height as values of type float, exactly as in the constructor. Another accepts arguments with the same meaning but of type double. The third setRect() method accepts an argument of type Rectangle2D so you can pass any type of rectangle object to it.

A Rectangle2D object has getX() and getY() methods for retrieving the coordinates of the top-left corner, and getWidth() and getHeight() methods that return the width and height of the rectangle, respectively.

A round rectangle is a rectangle with rounded corners. The corners are defined by a width and a height and are essentially a quarter segment of an ellipse (I'll get to the details of ellipses later). Of course, if the corner width and height are equal, then the corner will be a quarter of a circle.

You can define a round rectangle using coordinates of type double with the following statements:

```
Point2D.Double position = new Point2D.Double(10, 10);
double width = 200.0;
double height = 100;
double cornerWidth = 15.0;
double cornerHeight = 10.0;
RoundRectangle2D.Double roundRect = new RoundRectangle2D.Double(
                       position.x, position.y,      // Position of top-left
                       width, height,               // Rectangle width & height
                       cornerWidth, cornerHeight);   // Corner width & height
```

The only difference between this and defining an ordinary rectangle is the addition of the width and height to be applied for the corner rounding.

Combining Rectangles

You can combine two rectangles to produce a new rectangle that is either the union of the two original rectangles or the intersection. Let's take a couple of specifics to see how this works. You can create two rectangles with the statements:

```
float width = 120.0f;
float height = 90.0f;
Rectangle2D.Float rect1 = new Rectangle2D.Float(50.0f, 150.0f, width, height);
Rectangle2D.Float rect2 = new Rectangle2D.Float(80.0f, 180.0f, width, height);
```

You can obtain the intersection of the two rectangles with the statement:

```
Rectangle2D.Float rect3 = rect1.createIntersection(rect2);
```

The effect is illustrated in Figure 19-8 by the shaded rectangle. Of course, the result is the same if you call the method for `rect2` with `rect1` as the argument. If the rectangles don't overlap, the rectangle that is returned will be the rectangle from the bottom right of one rectangle to the top right of the other that does not overlap either of the original rectangles.

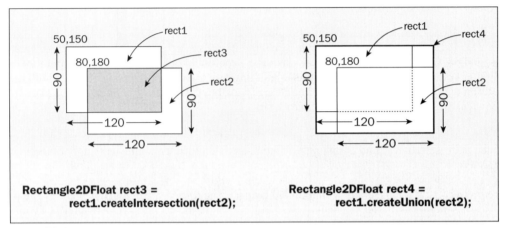

Figure 19-8

The following statement produces the union of the two rectangles:

```
Rectangle2D.Float rect3 = rect1.createUnion(rect2);
```

The result is shown in Figure 19-8 by the rectangle with the heavy boundary that encloses the other two.

Testing Rectangles

Perhaps the simplest test you can apply to a `Rectangle2D` object is for an empty rectangle. The `isEmpty()` method that is implemented in all the rectangle classes returns `true` if the `Rectangle2D` object is empty — which is when either the width or the height (or both) are zero.

You can also test whether a point lies inside any type of rectangle object by calling its `contains()` method. There are `contains()` methods for all the rectangle classes that accept either a `Point2D` argument, or a pair of (*x*, *y*) coordinates of a type matching that of the rectangle class: They return `true` if the point lies within the rectangle and `false` otherwise. Every shape class defines a `getBounds2D()` method that returns a `Rectangle2D` object that encloses the shape.

The `getBounds2D()` method is frequently used in association with the `contains()` method to provide an efficient test of whether the cursor lies within a particular shape. Testing whether the cursor is within the enclosing rectangle will be a lot faster in general than testing whether it is within the precise boundary of the shape and is good enough for many purposes — for example, when you are selecting a particular shape on the screen to manipulate it in some way.

You also have versions of the `contains()` method to test whether a given rectangle lies within the area occupied by a rectangle object — this obviously enables you to test whether a shape lies within another shape. You can pass the given rectangle to the `contains()` method as the coordinates of its top-left corner, and its height and width as type `double`, or as a `Rectangle2D` reference. The method returns `true` if the rectangle object completely contains the given rectangle.

Let's try drawing a few simple lines and rectangles by inserting some code in the `paint()` method for the view in Sketcher.

Try It Out   Drawing Lines and Rectangles

Begin by adding `import` statements to `SketchView.java` for the class names from the `java.awt.geom` package that you'll be using:

```
import java.awt.geom.Rectangle2D;
import java.awt.geom.Point2D;
import java.awt.geom.Line2D;
```

Now you can replace the previous code in the `paint()` method in the `SketchView` class with the following:

```
public void paint(Graphics g) {
   // Temporary code - to be deleted later...
   Graphics2D g2D = (Graphics2D)g;                      // Get a Java 2D device context

   g2D.setPaint(Color.RED);                             // Draw in red

   // Position width and height of first rectangle
   Point2D.Float p1 = new Point2D.Float(50.0f, 10.0f);
   float width1 = 60;
   float height1 = 80;

   // Create and draw the first rectangle
   Rectangle2D.Float rect = new Rectangle2D.Float(p1.x, p1.y, width1, height1);
   g2D.draw(rect);

   // Position width and height of second rectangle
   Point2D.Float p2 = new Point2D.Float(150.0f, 100.0f);
   float width2 = width1 + 30;
   float height2 = height1 + 40;

   // Create and draw the second rectangle
   g2D.draw(new Rectangle2D.Float(
                    (float)(p2.getX()), (float)(p2.getY()), width2, height2));
   g2D.setPaint(Color.BLUE);                            // Draw in blue

   // Draw lines to join corresponding corners of the rectangles
   Line2D.Float line = new Line2D.Float(p1,p2);
   g2D.draw(line);
```

```
    p1.setLocation(p1.x + width1, p1.y);
    p2.setLocation(p2.x + width2, p2.y);
    g2D.draw(new Line2D.Float(p1,p2));

    p1.setLocation(p1.x, p1.y + height1);
    p2.setLocation(p2.x, p2.y + height2);
    g2D.draw(new Line2D.Float(p1,p2));

    p1.setLocation(p1.x - width1, p1.y);
    p2.setLocation(p2.x - width2, p2.y);
    g2D.draw(new Line2D.Float(p1, p2));

    p1.setLocation(p1.x, p1.y - height1);
    p2.setLocation(p2.x, p2.y - height2);
    g2D.draw(new Line2D.Float(p1, p2));

    g2D.drawString("Lines and rectangles", 60, 250); // Draw some text
  }
```

If you type this in correctly and recompile the SketchView class, the Sketcher window will look like the one shown in Figure 19-9.

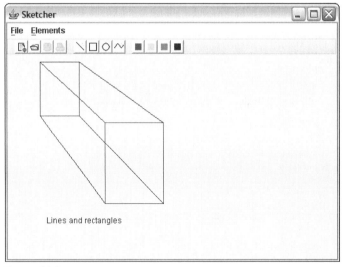

Figure 19-9

How It Works

After casting the graphics context object that is passed to the paint() method to type Graphics2D, you set the drawing color to red. All subsequent drawing that you do will be in red until you change the color with another call to setPaint(). You define a Point2D.Float object to represent the position of the first rectangle, and you define variables to hold the width and height of the rectangle. You use these to create the rectangle by passing them as arguments to the constructor that you saw earlier in this chapter and display the rectangle by passing the `rect` object to the `draw()` method for the graphics context, `g2D`. The second rectangle is defined by essentially the same process, except that this time you create the `Rectangle2D.Float` object in the argument expression for the `draw()` method.

Note that you have to cast the values returned by the `getX()` and `getY()` members of the `Point2D` object, as they are returned as type `double`. It is generally more convenient to reference the x and y fields directly as you do in the rest of the code.

You change the drawing color to blue so that you can see quite clearly the lines you are drawing. You use the `setLocation()` method for the point objects to move the point on each rectangle to successive corners and draw a line at each position. The caption also appears in blue since that is the color in effect when you call the `drawString()` method to output the text string.

Arcs and Ellipses

There are shape classes defining both arcs and ellipses. The abstract class representing a generic ellipse is:

Class	Description
Ellipse2D	This is the abstract base class for the `Ellipse2D.Double` and `Ellipse2D.Float` classes that define ellipses. An ellipse is defined by the top-left corner, width, and height of the rectangle that encloses it.

The class representing an elliptic arc is:

Class	Description
Arc2D	This is the abstract base class for the `Arc2D.Double` and `Arc2D.Float` classes that define arcs as a portion of an ellipse. The full ellipse is defined by the position of the top-left corner and the width and height of the rectangle that encloses it. The arc length is defined by a start angle measured in degrees anticlockwise relative to the horizontal axis of the full ellipse, plus an angular extent measured anticlockwise from the start angle in degrees. You can specify an arc as OPEN, which means the ends are not connected; as CHORD, which means the ends are connected by a straight line; or as PIE, which means the ends are connected by straight lines to the center of the whole ellipse. These constants are defined as static members of the `Arc2D` class.

Arcs and ellipses are closely related since an arc is just a segment of an ellipse. Constructors for the `Ellipse2D.Float` and `Arc2d.Float` classes are shown in Figure 19-10. To define an ellipse you supply the data necessary to define the enclosing rectangle—the coordinates of the top-left corner, the width, and the height. To define an arc you supply the data to define the ellipse, plus additional data that defines the segment of the ellipse that you want. The seventh argument to the arc constructor determines the type, whether OPEN, CHORD, or PIE.

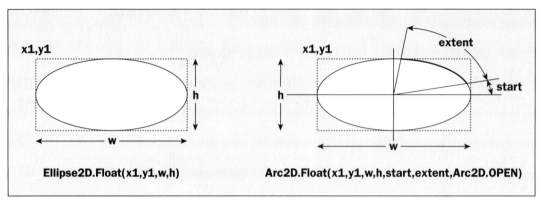

Figure 19-10

You could define an ellipse with the following statements:

```
Point2D.Double position = new Point2D.Double(10,10);
double width = 200.0;
double height = 100;
Ellipse2D.Double ellipse = new Ellipse2D.Double(
                    position.x, position.y,  // Top-left corner
                    width, height);          // width & height of rectangle
```

You could define an arc that is a segment of the previous ellipse with this statement:

```
Arc2D.Double arc = new Arc2D.Double(
                    position.x, position.y,  // Top-left corner
                    width, height,           // width & height of rectangle
                    0.0, 90.0,               // Start and extent angles
                    Arc2D.OPEN);             // Arc is open
```

This defines the upper-right quarter segment of the whole ellipse as an open arc. The angles are measured counterclockwise from the horizontal in degrees. As shown in Figure 19-10, the first angular argument is where the arc starts, and the second is the angular extent of the arc.

Of course, a circle is just an ellipse for which the width and height are the same, so the following statement defines a circle with a diameter of 150:

```
double diameter = 150.0;
Ellipse2D.Double circle = new Ellipse2D.Double(
                    position.x, position.y,  // Top-left corner
                    diameter, diameter);     // width & height of rectangle
```

This presumes the point `position` is defined somewhere. You will often want to define a circle by its center and radius—adjusting the arguments to the constructor a little does this easily:

```
Point2D.Double center = new Point2D.Double(200, 200);
double radius = 150;
Ellipse2D.Double newCircle = new Ellipse2D.Double(
            center.x-radius, center.y-radius,  // Top-left corner
            2*radius, 2*radius);               // width & height of rectangle
```

The fields that store the coordinates of the top-left corner of the enclosing rectangle and the width and height are public members of `Ellipse2D` and `Arc2D` objects. They are `x`, `y`, `width`, and `height`, respectively. An `Arc2D` object also has public members, `start` and `extent`, that store the angles.

Try It Out   **Drawing Arcs and Ellipses**

Let's modify the `paint()` method in `SketchView.java` once again to draw some arcs and ellipses. First modify the `import` statements for `Rectangle2D` and `Line2D`:

```
import java.awt.geom.Ellipse2D;
import java.awt.geom.Arc2D;
import java.awt.geom.Point2D;
```

Now you can replace the code in the body of the `paint()` method:

```
public void paint(Graphics g) {
  // Temporary code - to be deleted later...
  Graphics2D g2D = (Graphics2D)g;                    // Get a Java 2D device context
  Point2D.Double position = new Point2D.Double(50,10);  // Initial position
  double width = 150;                                // Width of ellipse
  double height = 100;                               // Height of ellipse
  double start = 30;                                 // Start angle for arc
  double extent = 120;                               // Extent of arc
  double diameter = 40;                              // Diameter of circle

  // Define open arc as an upper segment of an ellipse
  Arc2D.Double top = new Arc2D.Double(position.x, position.y,
                         width, height,
                         start, extent,
                         Arc2D.OPEN);

  // Define open arc as lower segment of ellipse shifted up relative to 1st
  Arc2D.Double bottom = new Arc2D.Double(
                         position.x, position.y - height + diameter,
                         width, height,
                         start + 180, extent,
                         Arc2D.OPEN);

  // Create a circle centered between the two arcs
  Ellipse2D.Double circle1 = new Ellipse2D.Double(
                         position.x + width/2 - diameter/2,position.y,
                         diameter, diameter);

  // Create a second circle concentric with the first and half the diameter
  Ellipse2D.Double circle2 = new Ellipse2D.Double(
                 position.x + width/2 - diameter/4, position.y + diameter/4,
                 diameter/2, diameter/2);

  // Draw all the shapes
  g2D.setPaint(Color.BLACK);                         // Draw in black
  g2D.draw(top);
  g2D.draw(bottom);
```

```
        g2D.setPaint(Color.BLUE);                    // Draw in blue
        g2D.draw(circle1);
        g2D.draw(circle2);
        g2D.drawString("Arcs and ellipses", 80, 100);    // Draw some text
    }
```

Running Sketcher with this version of the paint() method in SketchView will produce the window shown in Figure 19-11.

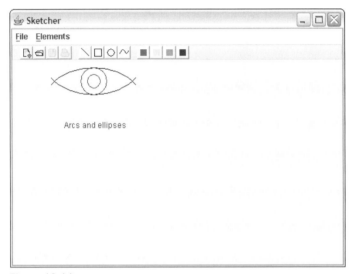

Figure 19-11

How It Works

This time you create all the shapes first and then draw them. The two arcs are segments of ellipses of the same height and width. The lower arc segment is shifted up with respect to the first arc segment so that they intersect, and the distance between the top of the rectangle for the first arc and the bottom of the rectangle for the second arc is diameter, which is the diameter of the first circle you create.

Both circles are created centered between the two arcs and are concentric. Finally, you draw all the shapes — the arcs in black and the circles in blue.

Next time you change the code in Sketcher, you'll be building the application as it should be, so you can now remove the temporary code from the paint() method and the code that sets the background color in the ColorAction inner class to the SketchFrame class.

Curves

There are two classes that define arbitrary curves, one defining a quadratic or second-order curve, and the other defining a cubic curve. The cubic curve just happens to be a Bézier curve (so called because it was developed by a Frenchman, Monsieur Pierre Bézier, and first applied in the context of defining contours for programming numerically controlled machine tools for manufacturing car body forms). The classes defining these curves are:

Class	Description
QuadCurve2D	This is the abstract base class for the QuadCurve2D.Double and Quad Curve2D.Float classes that define a quadratic curve segment. The curve is defined by its end points plus a control point that defines the tangent at each end. The tangents are the lines from the end points to the control point.
CubicCurve2D	This is the abstract base class for the CubicCurve2D.Double and Cubic Curve2D.Float classes that define a cubic curve segment. The curve is defined by its end points plus two control points that define the tangent at each end. The tangents are the lines from the end points to the corresponding control point.

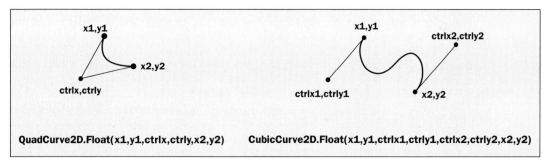

QuadCurve2D.Float(x1,y1,ctrlx,ctrly,x2,y2)   **CubicCurve2D.Float(x1,y1,ctrlx1,ctrly1,ctrlx2,ctrly2,x2,y2)**

Figure 19-12

In general, there are many other methods for modeling arbitrary curves, but the two defined in Java have the merit that they are both easy to understand and the effect on the curve segment when you move a control point is quite intuitive.

An object of each curve type defines a curve segment between two points. The control points — one for a QuadCurve2D curve and two for a CubicCurve2D curve — control the direction and magnitude of the tangents at the end points. A QuadCurve2D curve constructor has six parameters corresponding to the x and y coordinates of the starting point for the segment, the x and y coordinates of the control point, and the x and y coordinates of the end point. You can define a QuadCurve2D curve from a point start to a point end, plus a control point, control, with the following statements:

```
Point2D.Double startQ = new Point2D.Double(50, 150);
Point2D.Double endQ = new Point2D.Double(150, 150);
Point2D.Double control = new Point2D.Double(80,100);

QuadCurve2D.Double quadCurve
        = new QuadCurve2D.Double(startQ.x, startQ.y,     // Segment start point
                                 control.x, control.y,    // Control point
                                 endQ.x, endQ.y);         // Segment end point
```

The `QuadCurve2D` subclasses have public members storing the end points and the control point so you can access them directly. The coordinates of the start and end points are stored in the fields x1, y1, x2, and y2. The coordinates of the control point are stored in ctrlx and ctrly.

Defining a cubic curve segment is very similar — you just have two control points, one for each end of the segment. The arguments are the (x, y) coordinates of the start point, the control point for the start of the segment, the control point for the end of the segment, and finally the end point. You could define a cubic curve with the following statements:

```
Point2D.Double startC = new Point2D.Double(50, 300);
Point2D.Double endC = new Point2D.Double(150, 300);
Point2D.Double controlStart = new Point2D.Double(80, 250);
Point2D.Double controlEnd = new Point2D.Double(160, 250);

CubicCurve2D.Double cubicCurve = new CubicCurve2D.Double(
                    startC.x, startC.y,              // Segment start point
                    controlStart.x, controlStart.y,  // Control point for start
                    controlEnd.x, controlEnd.y,      // Control point for end
                    endC.x, endC.y);                 // Segment end point
```

The cubic curve classes also have public members for all the points: x1, y1, x2, and y2 for the end points and ctrlx1, ctrly1, ctrlx2, and ctrly2 for the corresponding control points. You could therefore use the default constructor to create a curve object with all the fields set to 0 and set them yourself. The following statements create the same curve as the previous fragment:

```
CubicCurve2D.Double cubicCurve = new CubicCurve2D.Double();
cubicCurve.x1 = 50;
cubicCurve.y1 = 300;
cubicCurve.x2 = 150;
cubicCurve.y2 = 300;
cubicCurve.ctrlx1 = 80;
cubicCurve.ctrly1 = 250;
cubicCurve.ctrlx2 = 160;
cubicCurve.ctrly2 = 250;
```

Of course, you could use the same approach to create a quadratic curve.

You will understand these curve classes better if you try them out. This time let's do it with an applet.

Try It Out   Drawing Curves

You can define an applet to display the curves I used as examples in the previous section:

```
import javax.swing.JApplet;
import javax.swing.JComponent;

import java.awt.Color;
import java.awt.Graphics2D;
import java.awt.Container;
import java.awt.Graphics;
```

```
import java.awt.geom.Point2D;
import java.awt.geom.CubicCurve2D;
import java.awt.geom.QuadCurve2D;

public class CurveApplet extends JApplet {
  // Initialize the applet
  public void init() {
    pane = new CurvePane();                    // Create pane containing curves
    Container content = getContentPane();      // Get the content pane

    // Add the pane displaying the curves to the content pane for the applet
    content.add(pane);                         // BorderLayout.CENTER is default position
  }

  // Class defining a pane on which to draw
  class CurvePane extends JComponent {
    // Constructor
    public CurvePane() {
      quadCurve = new QuadCurve2D.Double(            // Create quadratic curve
                     startQ.x, startQ.y,             // Segment start point
                     control.x, control.y,           // Control point
                     endQ.x, endQ.y);                // Segment end point

      cubicCurve = new CubicCurve2D.Double(          // Create cubic curve
                     startC.x, startC.y,             // Segment start point
                     controlStart.x, controlStart.y, // Control point for start
                     controlEnd.x, controlEnd.y,     // Control point for end
                        endC.x, endC.y);             // Segment end point
    }

    public void paint(Graphics g) {
      Graphics2D g2D = (Graphics2D)g;                // Get a 2D device context

      // Draw the curves
      g2D.setPaint(Color.BLUE);
      g2D.draw(quadCurve);
      g2D.draw(cubicCurve);
    }
  }
  // Points for quadratic curve
  Point2D.Double startQ = new Point2D.Double(50, 75);      // Start point
  Point2D.Double endQ = new Point2D.Double(150, 75);       // End point
  Point2D.Double control = new Point2D.Double(80, 25);     // Control point

  // Points for cubic curve
  Point2D.Double startC = new Point2D.Double(50, 150);     // Start point
  Point2D.Double endC = new Point2D.Double(150, 150);      // End point
  Point2D.Double controlStart = new Point2D.Double(80, 100);  // 1st control point
  Point2D.Double controlEnd = new Point2D.Double(160, 100);   // 2nd control point
  QuadCurve2D.Double quadCurve;                            // Quadratic curve
  CubicCurve2D.Double cubicCurve;                          // Cubic curve
  CurvePane pane = new CurvePane();                        // Pane to contain curves
}
```

You will need an HTML file to run the applet. The contents can be something like:

```
<applet code="CurveApplet.class" width=300 height=300></applet>
```

If you run the applet using `appletviewer`, you will get a window that looks like the one shown in Figure 19-13.

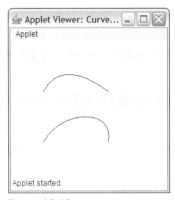

Figure 19-13

How It Works

To display the curves, you need an object of your own class type so that you can implement the `paint()` method for it. You define the inner class, `CurvePane`, for this purpose with `JComponent` as the base class so it is a Swing component. You create an object of this class (which is a member of the `CurveApplet` class) and add it to the content pane for the applet using its inherited `add()` method. The layout manager for the content pane is `BorderLayout`, and the default positioning is `BorderLayout.CENTER` so the `CurvePane` object fills the content pane.

The points defining the quadratic and cubic curves are defined as fields in the `CurveApplet` class and the fields that store references to the curve objects are used in the `paint()` method for the `CurvePane` class to display curves. The fields that store points are used in the `CurvePane` class constructor to create the objects encapsulating curves. You draw the curves in the `paint()` method by calling the `draw()` method for the `Graphics2D` object and passing a reference to a curve object as the argument. The classes that define curves implement the `Shape` interface so any curve object can be passed to the `draw()` method that has a parameter of type `Shape`.

It's hard to see how the control points affect the shape of the curve, so let's add some code to draw the control points.

Displaying the Control Points

You can mark the position of each control point by drawing a small circle around it. You can define a marker using an inner class of `CurveApplet` that you can define as follows:

```
// Inner class defining a control point marker
class Marker {
  public Marker(Point2D.Double control)  {
    center = control;                        // Save control point as circle center

    // Create circle around control point
    circle = new Ellipse2D.Double(control.x-radius, control.y-radius,
                                  2.0*radius, 2.0*radius);
  }

    // Draw the marker
    public void draw(Graphics2D g2D) {
      g2D.draw(circle);
    }

   // Get center of marker - the control point position
    Point2D.Double getCenter() {
      return center;
  }

  Ellipse2D.Double circle;                // Circle around control point
  Point2D.Double center;                  // Circle center - the control point
  static final double radius = 3;         // Radius of circle
}
```

The argument to the constructor is the control point that is to be marked. The constructor stores this control point in the member `center` and creates an `Ellipse2D.Double` object that is the circle to mark the control point. The class also has a method, `draw()`, to draw the marker using the `Graphics2D` object reference that is passed to it, so `Marker` objects can draw themselves, given a graphics context. The `getCenter()` method returns the center of the marker as a `Point2D.Double` reference. You'll use the `getCenter()` method when you draw tangent lines from the end points of a curve to the corresponding control points.

You can now add fields to the `CurveApplet` class to define the `Marker` objects for the control points. These definitions should follow the members that define the points:

```
// Markers for control points
Marker ctrlQuad = new Marker(control);
Marker ctrlCubic1 = new Marker(controlStart);
Marker ctrlCubic2 = new Marker(controlEnd);
```

You can now add code to the `paint()` method for the `CurvePane` class to draw the markers and the tangents from the end points of the curve segments:

```
public void paint(Graphics g) {
  // Code to draw curves as before...

  // Create and draw the markers showing the control points
  g2D.setPaint(Color.red);                        // Set the color
  ctrlQuad.draw(g2D);
  ctrlCubic1.draw(g2D);
  ctrlCubic2.draw(g2D);
  // Draw tangents from the curve end points to the control marker centers
  Line2D.Double tangent = new Line2D.Double(startQ, ctrlQuad.getCenter());
  g2D.draw(tangent);
  tangent = new Line2D.Double(endQ, ctrlQuad.getCenter());
  g2D.draw(tangent);

  tangent = new Line2D.Double(startC, ctrlCubic1.getCenter());
  g2D.draw(tangent);
  tangent = new Line2D.Double(endC, ctrlCubic2.getCenter());
  g2D.draw(tangent);
}
```

If you recompile the applet with these changes, when you execute it again you should see the window shown in Figure 19-14.

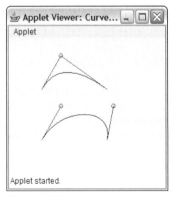

Figure 19-14

How It Works

In the `Marker` class constructor, the top-left corner of the rectangle enclosing the circle for a control point is obtained by subtracting the radius from the x and y coordinates of the control point. You then create an `Ellipse2D.Double` object with the width and height as twice the value of `radius` — which is the diameter of the circle.

In the `paint()` method, you call the `draw()` method for each of the `Marker` objects to draw a red circle around each control point. The tangents to the curves are just lines from the end points of each curve segment to the centers of the corresponding `Marker` objects.

It would be good to see what happens to a curve segment when you move the control points around. Then you could really see how the control points affect the shape of the curve. That's not as difficult to implement as it might sound, so let's give it a try.

Try It Out   Moving the Control Points

You'll arrange to allow a control point to be moved by positioning the cursor on it, pressing a mouse button, and dragging it around. Releasing the mouse button will stop the process for that control point, so the user will then be free to manipulate another control point. To implement this functionality in the applet you will add another inner class to `CurveApplet` that will handle mouse events:

```
class MouseHandler extends MouseInputAdapter {
  public void mousePressed(MouseEvent e) {
    // Check if the cursor is inside any marker
    if(ctrlQuad.contains(e.getX(), e.getY()))
      selected = ctrlQuad;
    else if(ctrlCubic1.contains(e.getX(), e.getY()))
      selected = ctrlCubic1;
    else if(ctrlCubic2.contains(e.getX(), e.getY()))
      selected = ctrlCubic2;
  }

  public void mouseReleased(MouseEvent e) {
    selected = null;                          // Deselect any selected marker
  }

  public void mouseDragged(MouseEvent e) {
    if(selected != null) {                    // If a marker is selected
      // Set the marker to current cursor position
      selected.setLocation(e.getX(), e.getY());
      pane.repaint();                         // Redraw pane contents
    }
  }

  Marker selected = null;                 // Stores reference to selected marker
}
```

You need to add two `import` statements to the beginning of the source file, one because you reference the `MouseInputAdapter` class and the other because you refer to the `MouseEvent` class:

```
import javax.swing.event.MouseInputAdapter;
import java.awt.event.MouseEvent;
```

The `mousePressed()` method calls a `contains()` method for a `Marker` that should test whether the point defined by the arguments is inside the marker. You can implement this in the `Marker` class like this:

```
    // Test if a point x,y is inside the marker
    public boolean contains(double x, double y) {
      return circle.contains(x,y);
    }
```

This just calls the `contains()` method for the circle object that is the marker. This will return `true` if the point (x, y) is inside the circle, and `false` if it isn't.

The `mouseDragged()` method calls a `setLocation()` method for the selected `Marker` object that is supposed to move the marker to a new position, so you need to implement this in the `Marker` class, too:

```
    // Sets a new control point location
    public void setLocation(double x, double y) {
       center.x = x;                           // Update control point
       center.y = y;                           // coordinates
       circle.x = x-radius;                    // Change circle position
       circle.y = y-radius;                    // correspondingly
    }
```

After updating the coordinates of the point `center`, you also update the position of the circle by setting its data member directly. You can do this because `x` and `y` are public members of the `Ellipse2D.Double` class and store the coordinates of the center of the ellipse.

You can create a `MouseHandler` object in the `init()` method for the applet and set it as the listener for mouse events for the `pane` object:

```
  public void init() {
    pane = new CurvePane();                  // Create pane containing curves
    Container content = getContentPane();    // Get the content pane

    // Add the pane displaying the curves to the content pane for the applet
    content.add(pane);                       // BorderLayout.CENTER is default position

    MouseHandler handler = new MouseHandler();   // Create the listener
    pane.addMouseListener(handler);              // Monitor mouse button presses
    pane.addMouseMotionListener(handler);        // as well as movement
  }
```

Of course, to make the effect of moving the control points apparent, you must update the curve objects before you draw them. You can add the following code to the `paint()` method to do this:

```
    public void paint(Graphics g) {
      Graphics2D g2D = (Graphics2D)g;                       // Get a 2D device context

      // Update the curves with the current control point positions
      quadCurve.ctrlx = ctrlQuad.getCenter().x;
      quadCurve.ctrly = ctrlQuad.getCenter().y;
      cubicCurve.ctrlx1 = ctrlCubic1.getCenter().x;
      cubicCurve.ctrly1 = ctrlCubic1.getCenter().y;
      cubicCurve.ctrlx2 = ctrlCubic2.getCenter().x;
      cubicCurve.ctrly2 = ctrlCubic2.getCenter().y;

      // Rest of the method as before...
```

You can update the data members that store the control point coordinates for the curves directly because they are public members of each curve class. You get the coordinates of the new positions for the control points from their markers by calling the getCenter() method for each Marker object and then using the appropriate data member of the Point2D.Double object that is returned to update the fields for the curve objects.

If you recompile the applet with these changes and run it again you should get something like the window shown in Figure 19-15.

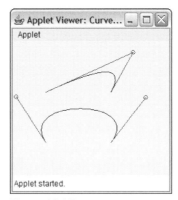

Figure 19-15

You should be able to drag the control points around with the mouse and see the curves change shape. If you find it's a bit difficult to select the control points, just make the value of radius a bit larger. Note how the angle of the tangent as well as its length affects the shape of the curve.

How It Works

The mousePressed() method in the MouseHandler class will be called when you press a mouse button. In this method you check whether the current cursor position is within any of the markers enclosing the control points. You do this by calling the contains() method for each Marker object and passing the coordinates of the cursor position to it. The getX() and getY() methods for the MouseEvent object supply the coordinates of the current cursor position. If one of the markers does enclose the cursor, you store a reference to the Marker object in the selected member of the MouseHandler class for use by the mouseDragged() method.

In the mouseDragged() method, you set the location for the Marker object referenced by selected to the current cursor position, and call repaint() for the pane object. The repaint() method causes the paint() method to be called for the component, so everything will be redrawn, taking account of the modified control point position.

Releasing the mouse button will cause the mouseReleased() method to be called. In here you just set the selected field back to null so no Marker object is selected. Remarkably easy, wasn't it?

Complex Paths

You can define a more complex geometric shape as an object of type GeneralPath. A GeneralPath object can be a composite of lines, Quad2D curves, and Cubic2D curves, or even other GeneralPath objects.

In general, closed shapes such as rectangles and ellipses can be filled with a color or pattern quite easily because they consist of a closed path enclosing a region. In this case, whether a given point is inside or outside a shape can be determined quite simply. With more complex shapes such as those defined by a GeneralPath object, it can be more difficult. Such paths may be defined by an exterior bounding path that encloses interior "holes," and the "holes" may also enclose further interior paths. Therefore, it is not necessarily obvious whether a given point is inside or outside a complex shape. In these situations, the determination of whether a point is inside or outside a shape is made by applying a **winding rule**. When you crate a GeneralPath object, you have the option of defining one of two winding rules that will then be used to determine whether a given point is inside or outside the shape. The winding rules that you can specify are defined by static constants defined in the GeneralPath class:

Winding Rule	Description
WIND_EVEN_ODD	In this case, a point is interior to a GeneralPath object if the boundary is crossed an odd number of times by a line from a point exterior to the GeneralPath to the point in question. When you use this winding rule for shapes with holes, a point is determined to be interior to the shape if it is enclosed by an odd number of boundaries.
WIND_NON_ZERO	In this case, whether a point is inside or outside a path is determined by considering how the path boundaries cross a line drawn from the point in question to infinity, taking account of the direction in which the path boundaries are drawn.

Looking along the line from the point, the point is interior to the GeneralPath object if the difference between the number of times the line is crossed by a boundary from left to right, and the number of times the line is crossed from right to left, is non-zero. When you use this rule for shapes bounded by more than one contiguous path — with holes, in other words — the result will vary depending on the direction in which each path is drawn. If an interior path is drawn in the opposite direction to the outer path, the interior of the inner path will be determined as not being interior to the shape.

The way these winding rules affect the filling of a complex shape is illustrated in Figure 19-16.

The region of the shape that is determined as being inside the shape is shown shaded in Figure 19-16. The directions in which the boundaries are drawn are indicated by the arrows on the boundaries. As you can see, the region where P3 lies is determined as being outside the shape by the WIND_EVEN_ODD rule, and as being inside the shape by the WIND_NON_ZERO rule.

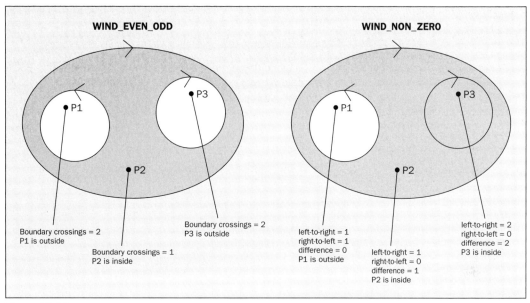

Figure 19-16

You have four constructors available for creating `GeneralPath` objects:

Constructor	Description
`GeneralPath()`	Defines a general path with a default winding rule of `WIND_NON_ZERO`
`GeneralPath(int rule)`	Creates an object with the winding rule specified by the argument. You can specify the argument as `WIND_NON_ZERO` or `WIND_EVEN_ODD`.
`GeneralPath(int rule, int capacity)`	Creates an object with the winding rule specified by the first argument and the number of path segments specified by the second argument. In any event, the capacity is increased when necessary.
`GeneralPath(Shape shape)`	Creates an object from the object passed as an argument.

You can create a `GeneralPath` object with the following statement:

```
GeneralPath p = new GeneralPath(GeneralPath.WIND_EVEN_ODD);
```

A `GeneralPath` object embodies the notion of a **current point** of type `Point2D` from which the next path segment will be drawn. You set the initial current point by passing a pair of (x, y) coordinates as values of type `float` to the `moveTo()` method for the `GeneralPath` object. For example, for the object generated by the previous statement, you could set the current point with the following statement:

```
p.moveTo(10.0f,10.0f);            // Set the current point to 10,10
```

When you add a segment to a general path, the segment is added starting at the current point, and the end of the segment becomes the new current point that will be used as the starting point for the next segment. Of course, if you want disconnected segments in a path, you can call `moveTo()` to move the current point to wherever you want before you add a new segment. If you need to get the current position at any time, you can call the `getCurrentPoint()` method for a `GeneralPath` object, and the current point will be returned as a reference of type `Point2D`.

You can use the following methods to add segments to a `GeneralPath` object:

Methods to Add Segments	Description
`lineTo(float x, float y)`	Draws a line from the current point to the point (x, y)

`quadTo(float ctrlx,`
`        float ctrly,`
`        float x2, float y2)`
	Draws a quadratic curve segment from the current point to the point $(x2, y2)$ with (`ctrlx`, `ctrly`) as the control point

`curveTo(float ctrlx1,`
`         float ctrly1,`
`         float ctrlx2, float ctrly2,`
`         float x2, float y2)`
	Draws a Bezier curve segment from the current point with control point (`ctrlx1`, `ctrly1`) to (`x2`, `y2`) with (`ctrlx2`, `ctrly2`) as the control point

Each of these methods updates the current point to be the end of the segment that is added. A path can consist of several subpaths since a new subpath is started by a `moveTo()` call. The `closePath()` method closes the current subpath by connecting the current point at the end of the last segment to the point defined by the previous `moveTo()` call.

Let's illustrate how this works with a simple example. You could create a triangle with the following statements:

```
GeneralPath p = new GeneralPath(GeneralPath.WIND_EVEN_ODD);
p.moveTo(50.0f, 50.0f);                  // Start point for path
p.lineTo(150.0f, 50.0f);                 // Line from 50,50 to 150,50
p.lineTo(150.0f, 250.0f);                // Line from 150,50 to 150,250
p.closePath();                           // Line from 150,250 back to start
```

The first line segment starts at the current position set by the moveTo() call. Each subsequent segment begins at the end point of the previous segment. The closePath() call joins the latest end point to the point set by the previous moveTo() call — which in this case is the beginning of the path. The process is much the same using quadTo() or curveTo() method calls, and of course you can intermix them in any sequence you like.

Once you have created a path for a GeneralPath object by calling its methods to add segments to the path, you can remove them all by calling its reset() method. This empties the path.

The GeneralPath class implements the Shape interface, so a Graphics2D object knows how to draw a path. You just pass a reference to a GeneralPath object as the argument to the draw() method for the graphics context. To draw the path, p, that was defined in the preceding example in the graphics context g2D, you would write:

```
    g2D.draw(p);                                    // Draw path p
```

Let's try an example.

Try It Out   Reaching for the Stars

You won't usually want to construct a GeneralPath object as I did in the preceding example. You will probably want to create a particular shape — a triangle or a star, say — and then draw it at various points on a component. You might think you can do this by subclassing GeneralPath, but the GeneralPath class is declared as final so subclassing is not allowed. However, you can always add a GeneralPath object as a member of your class. You can try drawing some stars using your own Star class. You'll use a GeneralPath object to create the star shown in Figure 19-17.

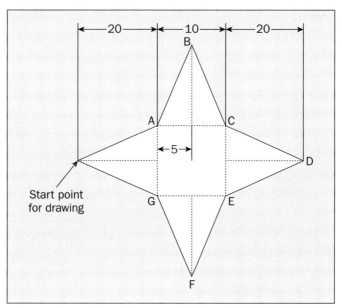

Figure 19-17

Here's the code for a class defining the star:

```java
import java.awt.geom.Point2D;
import java.awt.geom.GeneralPath;
import java.awt.Shape;

public class Star {
  public Star(float x, float y) {
    start = new Point2D.Float(x, y);              // store start point
    createStar();
  }

  // Create the path from start
  private void createStar() {
    Point2D.Float point = start;
    p = new GeneralPath(GeneralPath.WIND_NON_ZERO);
    p.moveTo(point.x, point.y);
    p.lineTo(point.x + 20.0f, point.y - 5.0f);    // Line from start to A
    point = (Point2D.Float)p.getCurrentPoint();
    p.lineTo(point.x + 5.0f, point.y - 20.0f);    // Line from A to B
    point = (Point2D.Float)p.getCurrentPoint();
    p.lineTo(point.x + 5.0f, point.y + 20.0f);    // Line from B to C
    point = (Point2D.Float)p.getCurrentPoint();
    p.lineTo(point.x + 20.0f, point.y + 5.0f);    // Line from C to D
    point = (Point2D.Float)p.getCurrentPoint();
    p.lineTo(point.x - 20.0f, point.y + 5.0f);    // Line from D to E
    point = (Point2D.Float)p.getCurrentPoint();
    p.lineTo(point.x - 5.0f, point.y + 20.0f);    // Line from E to F
    point = (Point2D.Float)p.getCurrentPoint();
    p.lineTo(point.x - 5.0f, point.y - 20.0f);    // Line from F to g
    p.closePath();                                // Line from G to start
  }

  // Modify the location of this star
  public Shape atLocation(float x, float y) {
    start.setLocation(x, y);                      // Store new start
    p.reset();                                    // Erase current path
    createStar();                                 // create new path
    return p;                                     // Return the path
  }

  // Make the path available
  public Shape getShape() {
    return p;
  }

  private Point2D.Float start;                    // Start point for star
  private GeneralPath p;                          // Star path
}
```

You can now define an applet that will draw stars:

```java
import javax.swing.JApplet;
import javax.swing.JComponent;
import java.awt.Graphics;
```

```
import java.awt.Graphics2D;

public class StarApplet extends JApplet {
  // Initialize the applet
  public void init() {
    StarPane pane = new StarPane();      // Pane containing stars
    getContentPane().add(pane);          // BorderLayout.CENTER is default position
  }

  // Class defining a pane on which to draw
  class StarPane extends JComponent {
    public void paint(Graphics g) {
      Graphics2D g2D = (Graphics2D)g;
      Star star = new Star(0,0);                    // Create a star
      float delta = 60f;                            // Increment between stars
      float starty = 0f;                            // Starting y position

      // Draw 3 rows of 4 stars
      for(int yCount = 0; yCount < 3; yCount++) {
        starty += delta;                            // Increment row position
        float startx = 0f;                          // Start x position in a row

        // Draw a row of 4 stars
        for(int xCount = 0; xCount<4; xCount++) {
          g2D.draw(star.atLocation(startx += delta, starty));
        }
      }
    }
  }
}
```

The HTML file for this applet could contain:

```
<applet code="StarApplet.class" width=360 height=240></applet>
```

This is large enough to accommodate our stars. If you compile and run the applet, you should see the Applet Viewer window shown in Figure 19-18.

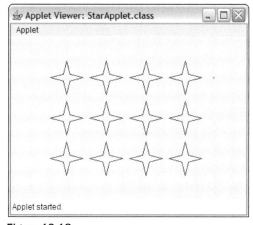

Figure 19-18

How It Works

The Star class has a GeneralPath object, p, as a member that will reference the path for a star. The constructor sets the coordinates of the start point from the arguments and calls the createStar() method, which creates the path for the star. The first line is drawn relative to the start point that is set by the call to moveTo() for p. For each subsequent line, you retrieve the current position by calling getCurrentPoint() for p and drawing the line relative to that. The last line to complete the star is drawn by calling closePath().

You always need a Shape reference to draw a Star object, so you have included in the class a getShape() method that simply returns a reference to the current GeneralPath object as type Shape. The atLocation() method recreates the path for the star starting at the new position specified by the arguments and returns a reference to it.

The StarApplet class draws stars on a component defined by the inner class StarPane. You draw the stars using the paint() method for the StarPane object, which is a member of the StarApplet class. Each star is drawn in the nested loop with the position specified by (x, y). The y coordinate defines the vertical position of a row, so this is incremented by delta on each iteration of the outer loop. The coordinate x is the position of a star within a row so this is incremented by delta on each iteration of the inner loop.

Note that you could have defined the Star class so that it implemented the Shape interface. This would allow references of type Star to be used directly as the argument for the draw() method for a Graphics2D object. Implementing the Shape interface would have been quite easy, if a little tedious. It would just have involved defining the 10 methods from the Shape interface in the Star class, which you could do by making each method call the corresponding method for the field p in the Star class.

Filling Shapes

Once you know how to create and draw a shape, filling it is easy. You just call the fill() method for the Graphics2D object and pass a reference of type Shape to it. This works for any shape but for sensible results the boundary should be closed. The way the enclosed region will be filled is determined by the window rule in effect for the shape.

Let's try it out by modifying the applet example that displayed stars.

Try It Out   Filling Stars

To fill the stars you just need to call the fill() method for each star in the paint() method of the StarPane object. Modify the paint() method as follows:

```
public void paint(Graphics g) {
  Graphics2D g2D = (Graphics2D)g;
  Star star = new Star(0,0);              // Create a star
  float delta = 60;                       // Increment between stars
  float starty = 0;                       // Starting y position

  // Draw 3 rows of 4 stars
  for(int yCount = 0 ; yCount<3; yCount++) {
```

```
        starty += delta;                                 // Increment row position
        float startx = 0;                                // Start x position in a row

      // Draw a row of 4 stars
      for(int xCount = 0 ; xCount<4; xCount++) {
        g2D.setPaint(Color.BLUE);                        // Drawing color blue
        g2D.draw(star.atLocation(startx += delta, starty));
        g2D.setPaint(Color.GREEN);                       // Color for fill is green
        g2D.fill(star.getShape());                       // Fill the star
      }
    }
  }
}
```

You also need an `import` statement for the `Color` class name in the `StarApplet.java` source file:

```
import java.awt.Color;
```

Now the applet window will look something like that shown in Figure 19-19, but in color, of course.

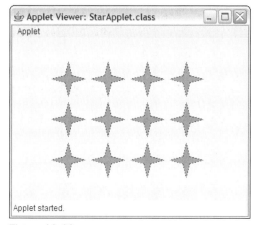

Figure 19-19

How It Works

You set the color for drawing and filling the stars separately, simply to show that you can get both. The stars are displayed in green with a blue boundary. You can fill a shape without drawing a boundary for it — just call the `fill()` method. You could amend the example to do this by modifying the inner loop to:

```
      for(int xCount = 0 ; xCount<4; xCount++) {
        g2D.setPaint(Color.GREEN);                          // Color for fill is green
        g2D.fill(star.atLocation(startx += delta, starty)); // Fill the star
      }
```

Now all you will get is the green fill for each shape — no outline.

967

Gradient Fill

You are not limited to filling a shape with a uniform color. You can create a `GradientPaint` object that represents a graduation in shade from one color to another and pass that to the `setPaint()` method for the graphics context. There are four `GradientPaint` class constructors:

Constructor	Description

`GradientPaint(`
    `Point2D p1, Color c1,`
    `Point2D p2, Color c2)`
	Defines a gradient from point p1 with the color c1 to the point p2 with the color c2. The color varies linearly from color c1 at point p1 to color c2 at point p2.
	
	By default the gradient is acyclic, which means the color variation applies only between the two points. Beyond either end of the line the color is the same as the nearest end point.

`GradientPaint(`
    `float x1, float y1, Color c1,`
    `float x2, float y2, Color c2)`
	This does same as the previous constructor but with the points specified by their coordinates.

`GradientPaint(`
    `Point2D p1, Color c1,`
    `Point2D p2, Color c2,`
    `boolean cyclic)`
	With the last argument specified as `false`, this is identical to the first constructor. If you specify `cyclic` as `true`, the color gradation repeats cyclically off either end of the line — that is, you get repetitions of the color gradient in both directions.

`GradientPaint(`
    `float x1, float y1,`
    `Color c1, float x2, float y2,`
    `Color c2, boolean cyclic)`
	This is the same as the previous constructor except for the explicit point coordinates.

Points that are off the line defining the color gradient will have the same color as the normal (that is, right-angle) projection of the point onto the line. This stuff is easier to demonstrate than to describe, so Figure 19-20 shows the output from the example you're going to try out next.

You can see that points along lines at right angles to the line defined by p1 and p2 have the same color as the point on the line. The window shows both cyclic and acyclic gradient fill.

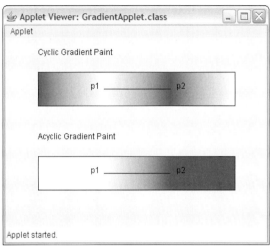

Figure 19-20

Try It Out   Color Gradients

You'll create an example similar to the star applet, except that the applet will draw rectangles with
`GradientPaint` fills. Here's the complete code:

```
import javax.swing.JComponent;
import javax.swing.JApplet;

import java.awt.Color;
import java.awt.GradientPaint;
import java.awt.Graphics2D;
import java.awt.Graphics;

import java.awt.geom.Rectangle2D;
import java.awt.geom.Point2D;
import java.awt.geom.Line2D;

public class GradientApplet extends JApplet {
  // Initialize the applet
  public void init() {
    GradientPane pane = new GradientPane();  // Pane containing filled rectangles
    getContentPane().add(pane);              // BorderLayout.CENTER is default position
  }

  // Class defining a pane on which to draw
  class GradientPane extends JComponent {
    public void paint(Graphics g) {
      Graphics2D g2D = (Graphics2D)g;
```

```
      Point2D.Float p1 = new Point2D.Float(150.f, 75.f);    // Gradient line start
      Point2D.Float p2 = new Point2D.Float(250.f, 75.f);    // Gradient line end
      float width = 300;
      float height = 50;
      GradientPaint g1 = new GradientPaint(p1, Color.WHITE,
                                   p2, Color.DARK_GRAY,
                                   true);                    // Cyclic gradient
      Rectangle2D.Float rect1 = new Rectangle2D.Float(
                           p1.x-100, p1.y-25, width,height);
      g2D.setPaint(g1);                                      // Gradient color fill
      g2D.fill(rect1);                                       // Fill the rectangle
      g2D.setPaint(Color.BLACK);                             // Outline in black
      g2D.draw(rect1);                                       // Fill the rectangle
      g2D.draw(new Line2D.Float(p1, p2));
      g2D.drawString("Cyclic Gradient Paint", p1.x-100, p1.y-50);
      g2D.drawString("p1", p1.x-20, p1.y);
      g2D.drawString("p2", p2.x+10, p2.y);

      p1.setLocation(150, 200);
      p2.setLocation(250, 200);
      GradientPaint g2 = new GradientPaint(p1, Color.WHITE,
                                   p2, Color.DARK_GRAY,
                                   false);                   // Acyclic gradient
      rect1.setRect(p1.x-100, p1.y-25, width, height);
      g2D.setPaint(g2);                                      // Gradient color fill
      g2D.fill(rect1);                                       // Fill the rectangle
      g2D.setPaint(Color.BLACK);                             // Outline in black
      g2D.draw(rect1);                                       // Fill the rectangle
      g2D.draw(new Line2D.Float(p1, p2));
      g2D.drawString("Acyclic Gradient Paint", p1.x-100, p1.y-50);
      g2D.drawString("p1", p1.x-20, p1.y);
      g2D.drawString("p2", p2.x+10, p2.y);
    }
  }
}
```

If you run this applet with the following HTML, you should get the window previously shown in Figure 19-20:

```
<applet code="GradientApplet.class" width=400 height=280></applet>
```

Note that to get a nice smooth color gradation, your monitor needs to be set up for at least 16-bit colors (65536 colors), and preferably 24-bit colors (16.7 million colors).

How It Works

The applet displays two rectangles, and they are annotated to indicate which is which. The applet also displays the gradient lines, which lie in the middle of the rectangles. You can see the cyclic and acyclic gradients quite clearly. You can also see how points off the gradient line have the same color as the normal projection onto the line.

The first block of shaded code in the `paint()` method creates the upper rectangle where the `GradientPaint` object that is used is `g1`. This is created as a cyclic gradient between the points p1 and p2, and varying from white to dark gray. I chose these shades because the book is printed in black and white, but you can try the example with any color combination you like. To set the color gradient for the fill, you call `setPaint()` for the `Graphics2D` object and pass `g1` to it. Any shapes that are drawn and/or filled subsequent to this call will use the gradient color, but here you just fill the rectangle, `rect1`.

To make the outline and the annotation clearer, you set the current color back to black before calling the `draw()` method to draw the outline of the rectangle and the `drawString()` method to annotate it.

The code for the lower rectangle is essentially the same as that for the first. The only important difference is that you specify the last argument to the constructor as `false` to get an acyclic gradient fill pattern. This causes the colors of the ends of the gradient line to be the same as the end points. You could have omitted the `boolean` parameter here, getting an acyclic gradient by default.

The applet shows how points off the gradient line have the same color as the normal projection onto the line. This is always the case, regardless of the orientation of the gradient line. You could try changing the definition of `g1` for the upper rectangle to:

```
GradientPaint g1 = new GradientPaint(p1.x, p1.y - 20, Color.WHITE,
                                     p2.x, p2.y + 20, Color.DARK_GRAY,
                                     true);                // Cyclic gradient
```

You'll also need to draw the gradient line in its new orientation:

```
g2D.draw(rect1);                                          // Fill the rectangle

//g2D.draw(new Line2D.Float(p1, p2));
g2D.draw(new Line2D.Float(p1.x, p1.y - 20, p2.x, p2.y + 20));
```

The annotation for the end points will also have to be moved:

```
g2D.drawString("p1",p1.x - 20,p1.y - 20);
g2D.drawString("p2",p2.x + 10,p2.y + 20);
```

If you run the applet with these changes, you can see in Figure 19-21 how the gradient is tilted and how the color of a point off the gradient line matches that of the point that is the orthogonal projection onto it.

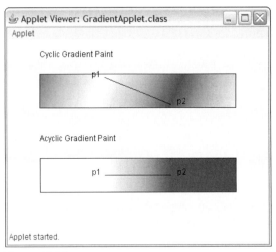

Figure 19-21

Managing Shapes

When you create shapes in Sketcher, you'll have no idea of the sequence of shape types that will occur. This is determined totally by the person using the program to produce a sketch. You'll therefore need to be able to draw shapes and perform other operations on them without knowing what they are — and of course polymorphism can help here.

You don't want to use the shape classes defined in java.awt.geom directly as you'll want to add your own attributes such as color or line style for the shapes that can be drawn in Sketcher and store them as part of the object. You could consider using the shape classes as base classes for your shapes, but you couldn't use the GeneralPath class in this scheme of things because, as I said earlier, the class has been defined as final and therefore cannot be subclassed. You could consider defining an interface that all your shape classes would implement. However, some methods have a common implementation in all your shape classes, which would mean that you would need to repeat this code in every class.

Taking all of this into account, the easiest approach might be to define a common base class for the Sketcher shape classes and include a member in each class to store a shape object of one kind or another. You'll then be able to include a polymorphic method to return a reference to a shape as type Shape for use with the draw() method of a Graphics2D object.

You can start by defining a base class, Element, from which you'll derive the classes defining specific types of shapes for Sketcher. The Element class will have data members that are common to all types of shapes, and you can put the methods that you want to be able to execute polymorphically in this class too. All you need to do is make sure that each shape class that is derived from the Element class has its own implementation of these methods.

Figure 19-22 shows the initial members that you'll define in the `Element` base class. The only field for now is the `color` member to store the color of a shape. The `getShape()` and `getBounds()` methods will be abstract here since the `Element` class is not intended to define a shape, but you'll be able to implement the `getColor()` method in this class. The other methods will be implemented by the subclasses of `Element`.

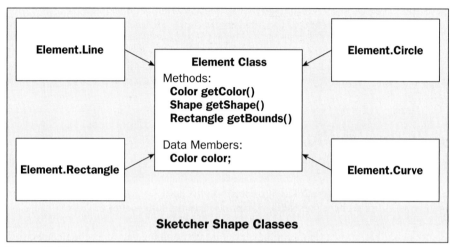

Figure 19-22

Initially, you'll define the five classes shown Figure 19-22 that represent shapes, with the `Element` class as a base. They provide objects that represent straight lines, rectangles, circles, freehand curves, and blocks of text. These classes will all inherit the fields that you define for the `Element` class. As you can see from the names of the Sketcher shape classes, they are all inner classes to the `Element` class. The `Element` class will serve as the base class, as well as house the shape classes. This will avoid any possible confusion with other classes that might have names such as `Line` or `Circle`, for example. Since there will be no `Element` objects around, you'll declare the shape classes as static members of the `Element` class.

You can now define the base class, `Element`. Note that this won't be the final version, as you'll be adding more functionality in later chapters. Here's the code that needs to go in `Element.java` in the same directory as `Sketcher.java`:

```java
import java.awt.Color;
import java.awt.Shape;

public abstract class Element {
  public Element(Color color) {
    this.color = color;
  }

  public Color getColor() {
    return color;
  }
```

973

```
    public abstract Shape getShape();
    public abstract java.awt.Rectangle getBounds();

    protected Color color;                              // Color of a shape
}
```

You have defined a constructor to initialize the `color` data member and the `getColor()` method to provide access to the current shape color. The other methods are abstract, so they must be implemented by the subclasses.

Note that the return type for the abstract `getBounds()` method is fully qualified using the package name. This is to prevent confusion with your own `Rectangle` class that you'll be adding later on in this chapter.

Storing Shapes in the Model

Even though you haven't defined the classes for the shapes that Sketcher will create, you can implement the mechanism for storing them in the `SketchModel` class. You'll be storing all of them as objects of type `Element`, so you can use a `LinkedList<Element>` collection class object to hold an arbitrary number of `Element` objects. A linked list also has the advantage that deleting a shape is fast.

You can add a member to the `SketchModel` class that you defined earlier in the Sketcher program to store elements:

```
import java.util.Observable;
import java.util.LinkedList;

class SketchModel extends Observable {
    protected LinkedList<Element> elements = new LinkedList<Element>();
}
```

You'll definitely want methods to add and delete `Element` objects from the linked list. It will also be very useful if the `SketchModel` class implements the `Iterable<Element>` interface because that will allow a collection-based `for` loop to be used to iterate over the `Element` objects stored in the model. Here's how the class looks to accommodate that:

```
import java.util.Observable;
import java.util.LinkedList;
import java.util.Iterator;

class SketchModel extends Observable implements Iterable<Element> {
    public boolean remove(Element element) {
        boolean removed = elements.remove(element);
        if(removed) {
            setChanged();
            notifyObservers(element.getBounds());
        }

        return removed;
    }
```

```
      public void add(Element element) {
        elements.add(element);
        setChanged();
        notifyObservers(element.getBounds());
      }

      public Iterator<Element> iterator() {
        return elements.iterator();
      }

    protected LinkedList<Element> elements = new LinkedList<Element>();
  }
```

All three methods make use of methods that are defined for the LinkedList<Element> object elements, so they are very simple. When you add or remove an element, the model is changed; therefore, you call the setChanged() method inherited from Observable to record the change and the notifyObservers() method to communicate this to any observers that have been registered with the model. You pass the Rectangle object that is returned by getBounds() for the shape to notifyObservers(). Each of the shape classes defined in the java.awt.geom package implements the getBounds() method to return the rectangle that bounds the shape. You'll be able to use this in the view to specify the area that needs to be redrawn.

In the remove() method, it is possible that the element was not removed — because it was not there, for example — so you test the boolean value that is returned by the remove() method for the LinkedList<Element> object. You also return this value from the remove() method in the SketchModel class, as the caller may want to know if an element was removed or not.

Next, even though you haven't defined any of the specific shape classes that Sketcher will support, you can still make provision for displaying them in the view class.

Drawing Shapes

You'll draw the shapes in the paint() method for the SketchView class, so if you haven't already done so, remove the old code from the paint() method now. You can replace it with code for drawing Sketcher shapes like this:

```
import javax.swing.JComponent;
import javax.swing.JComponent;
import java.util.Observer;
import java.util.Observable;
import java.awt.Graphics;
import java.awt.Graphics2D;

class SketchView extends JComponent implements Observer {
  public SketchView(Sketcher theApp) {
    this.theApp = theApp;
  }

  // Method called by Observable object when it changes
  public void update(Observable o, Object rectangle) {
    // Code to respond to changes in the model...
  }
```

```
public void paint(Graphics g) {
  Graphics2D g2D = (Graphics2D)g;                // Get a 2D device context
  for(Element element : theApp.getModel()) {     // Go through the list
    element = (Element)elements.next();           // Get the next element
    g2D.setPaint(element.getColor());             // Set the element color
    g2D.draw(element.getShape());                 // Draw its shape
  }
}

// Method called by Observable object when it changes
public void update(Observable o, Object rectangle) {
  // Code to respond to changes in the model...
}

private Sketcher theApp;               // The application object
}
```

The getModel() method that you implemented in the Sketcher class returns a reference to the SketchModel object, and because SketchModel implements the Iterable<> interface, you can use a collection-based for loop to iterate over the Element objects it contains. For each element, you obtain its color and pass that to the setPaint() method for the graphics context. You then pass the Shape reference that the getShape() method returns to the draw() method for g2D. This will draw the shape in the color you passed previously to the setPaint() method. In this way you draw all the elements that are stored in the model.

It's time you put in place the mechanism for creating Sketcher shapes.

Drawing Using the Mouse

You've drawn shapes so far just using data internal to the program. In the Sketcher program you want to be able to draw a shape using the mouse in the view and then store the finished shape in the model. Ideally, the process should be as natural as possible, so you'll implement a mechanism that allows you to draw by pressing the left mouse button (more accurately, button 1) and dragging the cursor to draw the selected type of shape. So for a line, the point where you depress the mouse button will be the start point for the line, and the point where you release the button will be the end point. This process is illustrated in Figure 19-23.

As the user drags the mouse with the button down, Sketcher will display the line as it looks at that point. Thus, the line will be displayed dynamically all the time the mouse cursor is being dragged and the left button remains pressed. This process is called **rubber-banding**.

You can use essentially the same process of pressing the mouse button and dragging the cursor for all four of the shapes you saw when I discussed the Element class. Thus, two points will define each shape — the cursor position where the mouse button is pressed and the cursor position where the mouse button is released (plus the color for the shape, of course). This implies that the shape constructors will all have three parameters, corresponding to the two points and the color. Let's look at how you handle mouse events to make this work.

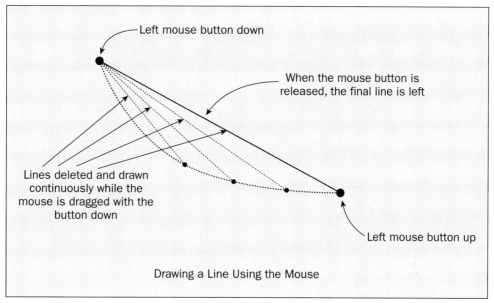

Drawing a Line Using the Mouse

Figure 19-23

Handling Mouse Events

Because all the drawing operations for a sketch will be accomplished using the mouse, you must implement the process for creating elements within the methods that handle the mouse events. The mouse events you're interested in will originate in the SketchView object because the mouse events that relate to drawing shapes will originate in the content pane for the application window, which is the view object. You'll make the view responsible for handling all its own events, which includes events that occur in the drawing process as well as interactions with existing shapes.

Drawing a shape, such as a line, interactively will involve you in handling three different kinds of mouse event. Let's summarize what they are, and what you need to do when they occur:

Event	Action
Left Button (Button 1) pressed	Save the cursor position somewhere as the starting point for the line. You'll store this in a data member of the inner class to SketchView that you'll create to define listeners for mouse events.
Mouse dragged	Save the current cursor position somewhere as the end point for the line. Erase any previously drawn temporary line, and create a new temporary line from the starting point that was saved initially. Draw the new temporary line.
Left Button (Button 1) released	If there's a reference to a temporary line stored, add it to the sketch model and redraw it.

977

You'll remember from the previous chapter that there are two mouse listener interfaces: `MouseListener`, which has methods for handling events that occur when the mouse buttons are pressed or released, and `MouseMotionListener`, which has methods for handling events that arise when the mouse is moved. You'll also recall that the `MouseInputAdapter` class implements both, and since you need to implement methods from both interfaces, you'll add an inner class to the `SketchView` class that extends the `MouseInputAdapter` class.

Since there's quite a lot of code involved in this, you'll first define the bare bones of the class to handle mouse events and then continue to add the detail incrementally until it does what you want.

Try It Out   Implementing a Mouse Listener

Add the following class outline as an inner class to `SketchView`:

```
import javax.swing.JComponent;
import java.util.Observer;
import java.util.Observable;
import java.awt.Graphics;
import java.awt.Graphics2D;
import java.awt.Point;
import java.awt.event.MouseEvent;
import javax.swing.event.MouseInputAdapter;

class SketchView extends JComponent implements Observer {
  // Rest of the class as before...

  class MouseHandler extends MouseInputAdapter {
    public void mousePressed(MouseEvent e)  {
      // Code to handle mouse button press...
    }

    public void mouseDragged(MouseEvent e) {
      // Code to handle the mouse being dragged...
    }

    public void mouseReleased(MouseEvent e) {
      // Code to handle the mouse button being release...
    }

    private Point start;             // Stores cursor position on press
    private Point last;              // Stores cursor position on drag
    private Element tempElement;     // Stores a temporary element
  }
}
```

You have implemented the three methods that you'll need to create an element. The `mousePressed()` method will store the position of the cursor in the `start` member of the `MouseHandler` class, so this point will be available to the `mouseDragged()` method that will be called repeatedly when you drag the mouse cursor with the button pressed. The `mouseDragged()` method will create an element using the current cursor position and the position saved in `start` and store a reference to it in the `tempElement` member of the class. The `last` member of the `MouseHandler` class will be used to store the cursor position when `mouseDragged()` is called. Both `start` and `last` are of type `Point` since this is the type that you'll get for the cursor position, but remember that `Point` is a subclass of `Point2D`, so you can always cast a `Point` reference to `Point2D` when necessary. The process ends when you release the mouse button, causing the `mouseReleased()` method to be called.

An object of type `MouseHandler` will be the listener for mouse events for the view object, so you should put this in place in the `SketchView` constructor. Add the following code at the end of the existing code:

```
public SketchView(Sketcher theApp) {
  this.theApp = theApp;
  MouseHandler handler = new MouseHandler();      // create the mouse listener
  addMouseListener(handler);                       // Listen for button events
  addMouseMotionListener(handler);                 // Listen for motion events
}
```

You call the `addMouseListener()` and `addMotionListener()` methods and pass the same listener object as the argument to both because the listener class deals with both types of event. Both these methods are inherited in the `SketchView` class from the `Component` class, which also defines an `addMouseWheelListener()` method for when you want to handle mouse wheel events.

Let's go for the detail of the `MouseHandler` class now, starting with the `mousePressed()` method.

Handling Mouse Button Press Events

The first thing you'll need to do is find out which button is pressed. It is generally a good idea to make mouse button operations specific to a particular button. That way you avoid potential confusion when you extend the code to support more functionality. This is very easy to do. The `getButton()` method for the `MouseEvent` object that is passed to a handler method returns a value of type `int` that indicates which of the three supported buttons changed state. It can return one of four constant values that are defined in the `MouseEvent` class, BUTTON1, BUTTON2, BUTTON3, or NOBUTTON, the last constant being the return value when no button has changed state in the current mouse event. On a two-button mouse or a wheel mouse, BUTTON1 for a right-handed user corresponds to the left button and BUTTON2 corresponds to the right button. Of course, the buttons associated with these constants are reversed if you have a left-handed mouse setup. BUTTON3 corresponds to the middle button when there is one. You can detect when button 1 is pressed by using the following code in the `mousePressed()` method:

```
public void mousePressed(MouseEvent e) {
  if(e.getButton() == MouseEvent.BUTTON1)
    // Code to handle button 1 press...
}
```

The `MouseEvent` object that is passed as the argument to the `mousePressed()` method records the current cursor position, and you can get a `Point` reference to it by calling the `getPoint()` method for the object. For example:

```
public void mousePressed(MouseEvent e) {
  start = e.getPoint();                           // Save the cursor position in start
  if(e.getButton() == MouseEvent.BUTTON1) {
    // Rest of the code to handle button 1 press...
  }
}
```

This saves the current cursor position in the start field of the MouseHandler object. You save it before the if statement because you are likely to want the current cursor position available whichever button was pressed.

As well as saving the cursor position, your implementation of the mousePressed() method must set things up to enable the mouseDragged() method to create an element and display it. One thing the mouseDragged() method needs to know is whether button 1 is down or not, because you only want to draw a shape while button 1 is down. After all, you may want to use dragging with button 2 down for some other function. The getButton() method won't tell you which button is pressed in this case because it records which button changed state in the event, not which button is down, and the button state won't change as a consequence of a mouse dragged event. You can store the state of button 1 when the mousePressed() method is called, though. Then it will be available to the mouseDragged() method. First, you need to add a suitable field to the MouseHandler class:

```
private boolean button1Down = false;     // Flag for button 1 state
```

Now you can store the state of button 1 when the mousePressed() method executes:

```
public void mousePressed(MouseEvent e) {
  start = e.getPoint();                   // Save the cursor position in start
  if(button1Down = (e.getButton() == MouseEvent.BUTTON1)) {
    // Rest of the code to handle button 1 press...
  }
}
```

The mouseDragged() method is going to be called very frequently, and to implement rubber-banding of the element each time, the redrawing of the element needs to be very fast. You don't want to have the whole view redrawn each time, as this will carry a lot of overhead. You need a different approach.

Using XOR Mode

One way to do this is to draw in **XOR mode**. You set XOR mode by calling the setXORMode() method for a graphics context and passing a color to it—usually the background color. In this mode the pixels are not written directly to the screen. The color in which you are drawing is combined with the color of the pixel currently displayed together with a third color that you specify, by exclusive ORing them together, and the resultant pixel color is written to the screen. The third color is usually set to be the background color, so the color of the pixel that is written is the result of the following operation:

```
resultant_Color = foreground_color^background_color^current_color
```

If you remember the discussion of the exclusive OR operation, back in Chapter 2, you'll realize that the effect of this is to flip between the drawing color and the background color. The first time you draw a shape, the result will be in the color you are drawing with, except for overlaps with other shapes, since they won't be in the background color. When you draw the same shape a second time, the result will be the background color so the shape will disappear. Drawing a third time will make it reappear.

Based on the way XOR mode works, you can now implement the `mousePressed()` method for the `MouseHander` class like this:

```
public void mousePressed(MouseEvent e) {
  start = e.getPoint();                          // Save the cursor position in start
  if(button1Down = (e.getButton() == MouseEvent.BUTTON1)) {
    g2D = (Graphics2D)getGraphics();                      // Get graphics context
    g2D.setXORMode(getBackground());                      // Set XOR mode
    g2D.setPaint(theApp.getWindow().getElementColor()); // Set color
  }
}
```

Note that the `getGraphics()` method being called in this method is for the view object; the `MouseHandler` class has no such method because the method is defined in the `Component` class, which is not a base class for the `MouseHandler` class. If button 1 was pressed, you obtain a graphics context for the view and store it in `g2D`, so you must add `g2D` as a field in the `MouseHandler` class:

```
private Graphics2D g2D = null;                       // Temporary graphics context
```

You use the `g2D` object to set XOR mode, because you'll use this mode in the `mouseDragged()` method to erase a previously drawn shape without reconstructing the whole sketch. The last thing that is done here is to retrieve the current drawing color, which is recorded in the `SketchFrame` object. You'll remember that this is set when you select a menu item or a toolbar button. You use `theApp` object stored in the view to get the `SketchFrame` object, and then call its `getElementColor()` member to retrieve the color in which an element should be drawn. This method doesn't exist in `SketchFrame` yet, but it's not difficult to implement. Add the following method to the `SketchFrame` class definition:

```
public Color getElementColor() {
  return elementColor;
}
```

With the button press code in place, you can have a go at implementing `mouseDragged()`.

Handling Mouse Dragging Events

You obtain the cursor position in the `mouseDragged()` method in the same way as you did in the `mousePressed()` method, which is by calling `getPoint()` for the event object that is passed as the argument, so you could write:

```
last = e.getPoint();                         // Get cursor position
```

But you want to handle drag events only for button 1, so you'll make this conditional upon the `button1Down` field having the value `true`. When `mouseDragged()` is called for the first time, you won't have created an element, so you can just create one from the points stored in `start` and `last` and then draw it using the graphics context saved by the `mousePressed()` method. The `mouseDragged()` method will be called lots of times while you drag the mouse though, and for every occasion other than the first, you must take care to redraw the old element before creating the new one so that you effectively erase it. Because the graphics context is in XOR mode, drawing the element a second time will draw it in the background color, so it will disappear. Here's how you can do all that:

```
        public void mouseDragged(MouseEvent e) {
          last = e.getPoint();                              // Save cursor position

          if(button1Down) {
            if(tempElement == null) {                       // Is there an element?
              tempElement = createElement(start, last);     // No, so create one
            } else {
              g2D.draw(tempElement.getShape());             // Yes - draw to erase it
              tempElement.modify(start, last);              // Now modify it
            }
            g2D.draw(tempElement.getShape());               // and draw it
          }
        }
```

If button 1 is pressed, `button1Down` will be `true` so you are interested. You first check for an existing element by comparing the reference in `tempElement` with `null`. If there isn't one, you create an element of the current type by calling a method, `createElement()`, that you'll add to the `SketchView` class in a moment. You save a reference to the element that is created in the `tempElement` member of the listener object.

If `tempElement` is not `null` then an element already exists, so you modify the existing element to incorporate the latest cursor position by calling the method `modify()` for the element object. You will need to add an implementation of this method for each element type. Finally, you draw the latest version of the element that is referenced by `tempElement`. Since you expect to call the `modify()` method for an element polymorphically, you should add it to the base class, `Element`. It will be abstract in the `Element` class, so add the following declaration to the `Element` class definition:

```
        public abstract void modify(Point start, Point last);
```

Since you reference the `Point` class here, you should add an `import` statement for it in the `Element.java` file:

```
        import java.awt.Point;
```

You can implement the `createElement()` method as a private member of the `MouseHandler` class because it's not needed anywhere else. The parameters for the method are just the two points that will be used to define each element. Here's the code:

```
        private Element createElement(Point start, Point end) {
          switch(theApp.getWindow().getElementType()) {
            case LINE:
              return new Element.Line(start, end,
                                      theApp.getWindow().getElementColor());
            case RECTANGLE:
              return new Element.Rectangle(start, end,
                                      theApp.getWindow().getElementColor());

            case CIRCLE:
              return new Element.Circle(start, end,
                                      theApp.getWindow().getElementColor());
            case CURVE:
              return new Element.Curve(start, end,
```

```
                                           theApp.getWindow().getElementColor());
          default:
            assert false;                        // We should never get to here
        }
      return null;
    }
```

Since you refer to the constants identifying element types here, you must import the static members of the `SketcherConstants` class that you defined in the `Constants` package into the `SketchView.java` source file. Add the following `import` statement:

```
import static Constants.SketcherConstants.*;
```

The `createElement()` method returns a reference to a shape as type `Element`. You determine the type of shape to create by retrieving the element type ID stored in the `SketchFrame` class by the menu item listeners that you put together in the previous chapter. The `getElementType()` method isn't there in the `SketchFrame` class yet, but you can add it now as follows:

```
public int getElementType() {
  return elementType;
}
```

The `switch` statement in the `createElement()` method selects the constructor to be called, and as you see, they are all essentially of the same form. If the code falls through the switch with an ID that you haven't provided for, you return `null`. Of course, none of these shape class constructors exists in the Sketcher program yet, so if you want to try compiling the code you have so far, you will need to comment out each of the return statements. The form of the constructor calls implies that all the shape classes are inner classes to the `Element` class, which is what was decided earlier. You'll be implementing these very soon, but first let's add the next piece of mouse event handling that's required — handling button release events.

Handling Button Release Events

When the mouse button is released, you will have created an element. In this case all you need to do is to add the element that is referenced by the `tempElement` member of the `MouseHandler` class to the `SketchModel` object that represents the sketch. One thing you need to consider though — someone might click the mouse button without dragging it. In this case there won't be an element to store, so you'll just clean up the data members of the `MouseHandler` object:

```
public void mouseReleased(MouseEvent e) {
  if(button1Down = (e.getButton()==MouseEvent.BUTTON1)) {
    button1Down = false;                   // Reset the button 1 flag

    if(tempElement != null) {              // If there is an element...
      theApp.getModel().add(tempElement);  // ...add it to the model...
      tempElement = null;                  // ...and reset the field
    }
    if(g2D != null) {                      // If there's a graphics context
      g2D.dispose();                       // ...release the resource...
      g2D = null;                          // ...and reset field to null
    }
```

```
        start = last = null;                        // Remove the points
      }
    }
```

When button 1 for the mouse is released it will change state, so you can use the `getButton()` method here to verify that this occurred. Of course, once button 1 is released, you should reset the flag `button1Down`. If there is a reference stored in `tempElement`, you add it to the model by calling the `add()` method that you defined for the `SketchModel` class and set `tempElement` back to `null`. It is most important that you set `tempElement` back to `null` here. Failing to do that would result in the old element reference being added to the model when you click the mouse button.

When you add the new element to the model, the view will be notified as an observer, so the `update()` method for the view object will be called. You can implement the `update()` method in the `SketchView` class like this:

```
public void update(Observable o, Object rectangle) {
   if(rectangle != null & rectangle instanceof Rectangle) {
     repaint((Rectangle)rectangle);
   } else {
     repaint();
   }
}
```

If the reference passed to `update()` is not `null`, then you should have a reference to a `Rectangle` object that was provided by the `notifyObservers()` method call in the `add()` method for the `SketchModel` object. To make doubly sure, you also verify that the argument is indeed of type `Rectangle` before you attempt to cast it to that type. This rectangle is the area occupied by the new element, so when you pass this to the `repaint()` method for the view object, just this area will be added to the area to be redrawn on the next call of the `paint()` method. If `rectangle` is `null` or not of type `Rectangle`, you call the version of `repaint()` that has no parameter to redraw the whole view. Of course, you'll need to import the `Rectangle` class name into the source file for the `SketchView` class:

```
import java.awt.Rectangle;
```

Another important operation that the `mouseReleased()` method carries out is to call the `dispose()` method for the `g2D` object. Every graphics context makes use of finite system resources. If you use a lot of graphics context objects and you don't release the resources they use, your program will consume more and more resources. Under some versions of MS Windows, for example, the amount of such resources that you can have is limited, so you may eventually run out, your computer will stop working, and you'll have to reboot. When you call `dispose()` for a graphics context object, it can no longer be used, so you set `g2D` back to `null` to be on the safe side.

> A reminder about a potential error in using adapter classes: Be sure to spell the method names correctly. If you don't, your method won't get called, but the base class member will. The base class method does nothing so your code won't work as you expect. There will be no warning or error messages about this because your code will be perfectly legal — though quite wrong. You will simply have added an additional and quite useless method to those defined in the adapter class.

You have implemented all three methods that you need to draw shapes. You could try it out if only you had a shape to draw, but before I get into that I'll digress briefly to introduce you to another class that you can use to get information about where the mouse cursor is.

Locating the Mouse Cursor Using MouseInfo Class Methods

The `java.awt.MouseInfo` class provides a way for you to get information about the mouse at any time. The `MouseInfo` class defines a static method, `getPointerInfo()`, that returns a reference to an object of type `java.awt.PointerInfo`, which encapsulates information about where the mouse cursor was when the method was called. To find the location of the mouse cursor from a `PointerInfo` object you call its `getLocation()` method. This method returns a reference to a `Point` object that identifies the mouse cursor location. Thus you can find out where the mouse cursor is at any time like this:

```
Point position = MouseInfo.getPointerInfo().getLocation();
```

After executing this code fragment, the `position` object will contain the coordinates of the mouse cursor at the time you call the `getPointerInfo()` method. Note that the `PointerInfo` object that this method returns does not get updated when the mouse cursor is moved, so there's no point in saving each. You must always call the `getPointerInfo()` method each time you want to find out where the cursor is.

Where you have multiple display devices attached, you can find out which display the mouse cursor is on by calling the `getDevice()` method for the `PointerInfo` object. This returns a reference to a `java.awt.GraphicsDevice` object that encapsulates the display that shows the cursor.

The `MouseInfo` class also defines a static method `getNumberOfButtons()`, which returns a value of type `int` specifying the number of buttons on the mouse. This is useful when you want to make your code adapt automatically to the number of buttons on the mouse when the code executes. You can make your program take advantage of the second or third buttons on the mouse and also adapt to use alternative GUI mechanisms when they are not available — by using a mouse button combined with keyboard key presses, for example.

Most of the time you will want to find the cursor location from within a mouse event-handling method. In these cases you'll find it is easiest to obtain the mouse cursor location from the `MouseEvent` object that is passed to the method handling the event. However, when you don't have a `MouseEvent` object available, you still have the `MouseInfo` class methods to fall back on.

Now, I'll return to the subject of how you can define shapes.

Defining Your Own Shape Classes

All the classes that define shapes in Sketcher will be static nested classes of the `Element` class. As I said earlier, as well as being a convenient way to keep the shape class definitions together, this will also avoid possible conflicts with the names of standard classes such as the `Rectangle` class in the `java.awt` package.

You can start with the simplest type of Sketcher shape — a class representing a line.

Defining Lines

A line will be defined by two points and its color. You can define the Line class as a nested class in the base class Element as follows:

```java
import java.awt.Color;
import java.awt.Shape;
import java.awt.Point;
import java.awt.geom.Line;

public abstract class Element {
  // Code defining the base class...
  // Nested class defining a line
  public static class Line extends Element {
    public Line(Point start, Point end, Color color) {
      super(color);
      line = new Line2D.Double(start, end);
    }

    // Method to return the line as a Shape reference
    public Shape getShape() {
      return line;
    }

    // Obtain the rectangle bounding the line
    public java.awt.Rectangle getBounds() {
      return line.getBounds();
    }

    // Change the end point for the line
    public void modify(Point start, Point last) {
      line.x2 = last.x;
      line.y2 = last.y;
    }

    private Line2D.Double line;
  }
}
```

You have to specify the Line class as static to avoid a dependency on an Element object being available. The Element class is abstract, so there's no possibility of creating objects of this type. The Line constructor has three parameters, the two end points of the line as type Point and the color. You could specify the Point parameters to the constructor as type Point2D because Point2D is a superclass of Point, but since all the points you'll be working with originate from mouse events as type Point, you might as well stick to that type for the parameters. After passing the color to the base class constructor, you create the line as a Line2D.Double object. Because this class implements the Shape interface, you can return it as type Shape from the getShape() method.

The getBounds() method couldn't be simpler. You just return the Rectangle object produced by the getBounds() method for the line object. However, note how the return type is fully qualified. This is because you'll be adding a Rectangle class as a nested class to the Element class. When you do, the compiler will interpret the type Rectangle within the code for the Element class as your rectangle class, and not the one defined in the java.awt package. You can always use a fully qualified class name when conflicts like this arise.

Try It Out   Drawing Lines

If you have saved the Element class definition as Element.java in the same directory as the rest of the Sketcher classes, all you need to do is make sure all the constructor calls other than Element.Line are commented out in the createElement() member of the MouseHandler class that is an inner class to SketchView. The code for the method should look like this:

```
private Element createElement(Point start, Point end) {
    switch(theApp.getWindow().getElementType()) {
        case LINE:
            return new Element.Line(start, end,
                              theApp.getWindow().getElementColor());
        case RECTANGLE:
//          return new Element.Rectangle(start, end,
//                                  theApp.getWindow().getElementColor());

        case CIRCLE:
//          return new Element.Circle(start, end,
//                                  theApp.getWindow().getElementColor());

        case CURVE:
//          return new Element.Curve(start, end,
//                                  theApp.getWindow().getElementColor());
        default:
            assert false;                         // We should never get to here
    }
    return null;
}
```

If you compile and run Sketcher, you should be able to draw a figure like that shown in Figure 19-24.

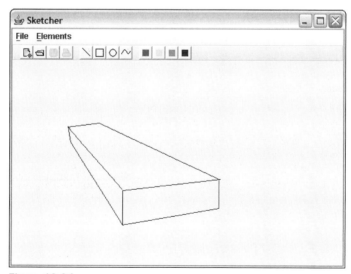

Figure 19-24

You can only draw lines at this point though. Trying to draw anything else will result in an assertion because the code will fall through the cases in the `switch` in the `createElement()` method until you hit the default case.

How It Works

As you drag the mouse, `Element.Line` objects are being repeatedly created and drawn to produce the rubber-banding effect. Each line is from the point where you pressed the mouse button to the current cursor position. Try drawing lines in different colors. It should all work. If it doesn't, maybe you forgot to remove the `getContentPane().setBackground(color)` call that you put temporarily in the `actionPerformed()` method in the `ColorAction` inner class to `SketchFrame`.

If you are typing in the code as you go (and I hope that you are!), you may have made a few mistakes, as there's been such a lot of code added to Sketcher. In this case don't look back at the code in the book first to find out why. Before you do that, try using the Java debugger that comes with the JDK, or even just implementing the methods that might be the problem with `println()` calls of your own so you can trace what's going on. It's good practice for when you are writing your own code.

Defining Rectangles

The interactive mechanism for drawing a rectangle is similar to that for a line. When you are drawing a rectangle, the point where the mouse is pressed will define one corner of the rectangle, and as you drag the mouse, the cursor position will define an opposite corner, as illustrated in Figure 19-25.

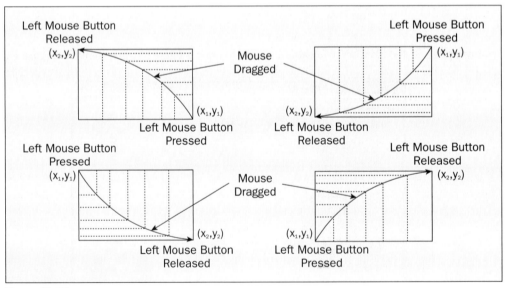

Figure 19-25

Releasing the mouse button will establish the final rectangle shape to be stored in the model. As you can see, the cursor position when you press the mouse button can be any corner of the rectangle. This is fine from a usability standpoint, but our code needs to take account of the fact that a `Rectangle2D` object is always defined by the top-left corner, plus a width and a height.

Figure 19-25 shows the four possible orientations of the mouse path as it is dragged in relation to the rectangle drawn. The top-left corner will have coordinates that are the minimum x and the minimum y from the points at the ends of the diagonal. The width will be the absolute value of the difference between the x coordinates for the two ends, and the height will be the absolute value of the difference between the y coordinates. From that you can define the Rectangle class for Sketcher.

Try It Out   The Element.Rectangle Class

Here's the definition of the class for a rectangle object:

```
import java.awt.Color;
import java.awt.Shape;
import java.awt.Point;
import java.awt.geom.Line2D;
import java.awt.geom.Rectangle2D;

class Element {
  // Code for the base class definition...

  // Nested class defining a line...

  // Nested class defining a rectangle
  public static class Rectangle extends Element {
    public Rectangle(Point start, Point end, Color color) {
      super(color);
      rectangle = new Rectangle2D.Double(
        Math.min(start.x, end.x), Math.min(start.y, end.y),     // Top-left corner
        Math.abs(start.x - end.x), Math.abs(start.y - end.y)); // Width & height
    }

    // Method to return the rectangle as a Shape reference
    public Shape getShape() {
      return rectangle;
    }

    // Method to return the rectangle enclosing this rectangle
    public java.awt.Rectangle getBounds() {
      return rectangle.getBounds();
    }

    // Method to redefine the rectangle
    public void modify(Point start, Point last) {
      rectangle.x = Math.min(start.x, last.x);
      rectangle.y = Math.min(start.y, last.y);
      rectangle.width = Math.abs(start.x - last.x);
      rectangle.height = Math.abs(start.y - last.y);
    }

    private Rectangle2D.Double rectangle;
  }
}
```

If you uncomment the line in the `createElement()` method that creates rectangles and recompile the Sketcher program, you will be ready to draw rectangles as well as lines. You need to recompile only `Element.java` and `SketchView.java`. The rest of Sketcher is still the same. If you run it again, you should be able to draw rectangles and lines—in various colors, too. A typical high-quality artistic sketch that you are now able to create is shown in Figure 19-26.

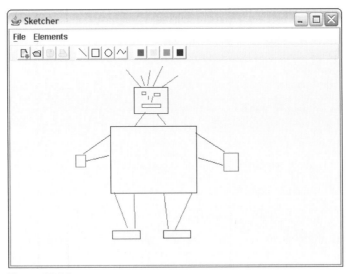

Figure 19-26

How It Works

The code that enables rectangles to be drawn works in essentially the same way as for lines. You can drag the mouse in any direction to create a rectangle. The constructor sorts out the correct coordinates for the top-left corner. This is because the rectangle is being defined from its diagonal, so the rectangle is always defined from the point where the mouse button was pressed to the current cursor position. Because its top-left corner always defines the position of a `Rectangle2D` object, you can no longer tell from this object which diagonal was used to define it.

Defining Circles

The most natural mechanism for drawing a circle is to make the point where the mouse button is pressed the center, and the point where the mouse button is released the end of the radius—that is, on the circumference. You'll need to do a little calculation to make it work this way.

Figure 19-27 illustrates the drawing mechanism for a circle. Circles will be drawn dynamically as the mouse is dragged, with the cursor position being on the circumference of the circle. You'll have the center of the circle and a point on the circumference available in the methods that handle the mouse events, but the `Ellipse2D` class that you'll use to define a circle will expect it to be defined by the coordinates of the point on the top-right corner of the rectangle that encloses the circle plus its height and width. This means you have to calculate the position, height, and width of the rectangle from the center and radius of the circle.

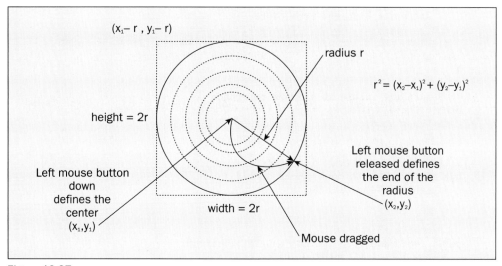

Figure 19-27

Pythagoras' theorem provides the formula that you might use to calculate the radius of the circle from the point at the center and the point on the circumference, and this is shown in Figure 19-27. The formula may look a little complicated but Java makes this easy. Remember the `distance()` method defined in `Point2D` class? That does exactly what is shown here, so you'll be able to use that to obtain the radius directly from two points. When you have the radius, you can then calculate the coordinates of the top-left point by subtracting the radius value from the coordinates of the center. The height and width of the enclosing rectangle for the circle will be just twice the radius.

Try It Out   Adding Circles

Here's how this is applied in the definition of the `Element.Circle` class:

```
import java.awt.Color;
import java.awt.Shape;
import java.awt.Point;
import java.awt.geom.Line2D;
import java.awt.geom.Rectangle2D;
import java.awt.geom.Ellipse2D;

class Element {
  // Code defining the base class...

  // Nested class defining a line...

  // Nested class defining a rectangle...

  // Nested class defining a circle
  public static class Circle extends Element {
    public Circle(Point center, Point circum, Color color) {
      super(color);
```

```
       // Radius is distance from center to circumference
       double radius = center.distance(circum);
       circle = new Ellipse2D.Double(center.x - radius, center.y - radius,
                                     2.*radius, 2.*radius);
     }

     // Return the circle as a Shape reference
     public Shape getShape() {
       return circle;
     }

     // Return the rectangle bounding this circle
     public java.awt.Rectangle getBounds() {
       return circle.getBounds();
     }

     // Recreate this circle
     public void modify(Point center, Point circum) {
       double radius = center.distance(circum);
       circle.x = center.x - (int)radius;
       circle.y = center.y - (int)radius;
       circle.width = circle.height = 2*radius;
     }

     private Ellipse2D.Double circle;
   }
 }
```

If you amend the `createElement()` method in the `MouseHandler` class by uncommenting the line that creates `Element.Circle` objects and recompile the Sketcher program, you'll be ready to draw circles. You are now equipped to produce artwork of the astonishing sophistication shown in Figure 19-28.

Figure 19-28

How It Works

The circle is generated with the button down point as the center and the cursor position while dragging as a point on the circumference. The distance() method defined in the Point2D class calculates the radius, and then this value is used to calculate the coordinates of the top-left corner of the enclosing rectangle. The width and height of the rectangle enclosing the circle are just twice the radius value, so the circle is stored as an Ellipse2D.Double object with a width and height as twice the radius.

Drawing Curves

Curves are a bit trickier to deal with than the other shapes. You want to be able to create a freehand curve by dragging the mouse, so that as the cursor moves the curve extends. This needs to be reflected in how you define the Element.Curve class. Let's first consider how the process of drawing a curve is going to work and define the Element.Curve class based on that.

The QuadCurve2D and CubicCurve2D classes are not very convenient or easy to use here. A curve is going to be entered freehand, and the data that you get will be a series of points that are relatively close together, but you don't know ahead of time how many there are going to be; as long as the mouse is being dragged you'll collect more points. This gives us a hint as to the approach you could adopt for creating a curve to keep it as simple as possible. Figure 19-29 illustrates one approach you could take.

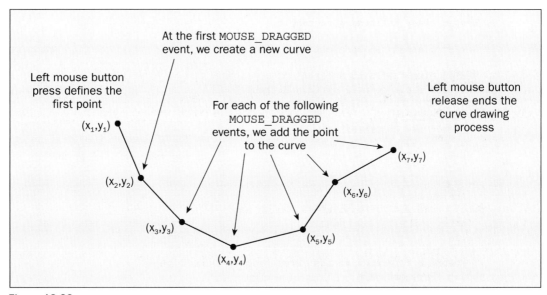

Figure 19-29

Since successive points that define the freehand curve will be quite close together, you could create a visual representation of the curve by joining the points to forms a series of connected line segments. Since the lengths of the line segments will be short, it should look like a reasonable curve.

This looks like a job for a `GeneralPath` object. A `GeneralPath` object can handle any number of segments, and you can add to it. If you construct an initial path as soon as you have two points — which will be when you process the first `MOUSE_DRAGGED` event — you can extend the curve by calling the `modify()` method to add another segment using the point that you get for each of the subsequent `MOUSE_DRAGGED` events.

Try It Out   The Element.Curve Class

The approach described in the previous section means that the outline of the `Curve` class is going to be:

```java
import java.awt.Color;
import java.awt.Shape;
import java.awt.Point;
import java.awt.geom.Line2D;
import java.awt.geom.Rectangle2D;
import java.awt.geom.Ellipse2D;
import java.awt.geom.GeneralPath;

class Element {
  // Code defining the base class...

  // Nested class defining a line...

  // Nested class defining a rectangle...

  // Nested class defining a circle...

  // Nested class defining a curve
  public static class Curve extends Element {
    public Curve(Point start, Point next, Color color) {
      super(color);
      curve = new GeneralPath();
      curve.moveTo(start.x, start.y);           // Set current position as start
      curve.lineTo(next.x, next.y);             // Add segment line to next
    }

    // Add another segment
    public void modify(Point start, Point next) {
      curve.lineTo(next.x, next.y);             // Add segment to next point
    }

    // Return a reference to the curve path as type Shape
    public Shape getShape()  {
      return curve;
    }

    // Return the rectangle bounding the path
    public java.awt.Rectangle getBounds() {
      return curve.getBounds();
    }

    private GeneralPath curve;
  }
}
```

The `Curve` class constructor creates a `GeneralPath` object and adds a single line segment to it by moving the current point for the path to `start` by calling `moveTo()` and then calling the `lineTo()` method for the `GeneralPath` object with `next` as the argument. Additional segments are added by the `modify()` method. This calls `lineTo()` for the `GeneralPath` member of the class with the new point, `next`, as the argument. This will add a line from the end of the last segment that was added to the new point.

Try It Out   Drawing Curves

Of course, you'll need to uncomment the line creating an `Element.Curve` object in the `createElement()` method in the `MouseHandler` inner class to `SketchFrame`. Then you're ready to roll again. If you recompile Sketcher you'll be able to give freehand curves a whirl, and produce elegant sketches such as that in Figure 19-30.

Figure 19-30

How It Works

Drawing curves works in essentially the same way as drawing the other elements. The use of XOR mode is superfluous with drawing a curve since you only extend it, but it would be quite a bit of work to treat it as a special case. This would be justified only if drawing curves were too slow and produced excessive flicker.

You may be wondering if you can change from XOR mode back to the normal mode of drawing in a graphics context. Certainly you can: just call the `setPaintMode()` method for the graphics context object to get back to the normal drawing mode.

There's some fabricated text in the last screenshot — if you can recognize it as such. In the next chapter you'll add a rather more sophisticated facility for adding text to a sketch. Don't draw too many masterpieces yet. You won't be able to preserve them for the nation and posterity by saving them in a file until Chapter 21.

Summary

In this chapter you have learned how to draw on components and how you can use mouse listeners to implement a drawing interface. The important points I have covered in this chapter are:

- ❑ A Graphics2D component represents the drawing surface of the component.

- ❑ You draw on a component by calling methods for its Graphics2D object.

- ❑ The user coordinate system for drawing on a component has the origin in the top-left corner of the component by default, with the positive x-axis from left to right, and the positive y-axis from top to bottom. This is automatically mapped to the device coordinate system, which is in the same orientation.

- ❑ You normally draw on a component by implementing its paint() method. The paint() method is passed a Graphics2D object that is the graphics context for the component but as type Graphics. You must cast the Graphics object to type Graphics2D to be able to access the Graphics2D class methods. The paint() method is called whenever the component needs to be redrawn.

- ❑ You can't create a Graphics2D object. If you want to draw on a component outside of the paint() method, you can obtain a Graphics2D object for the component by calling its getGraphics() method.

- ❑ There is more than one drawing mode that you can use. The default mode is paint mode, where drawing overwrites the background pixels with pixels of the current color. Another mode is XOR mode, where the current color is combined with the background color. This is typically used to alternate between the current color and a color passed to the setXORMode() method.

- ❑ The Graphics2D class defines methods for drawing outline shapes as well as filled shapes.

- ❑ The java.awt.geom package defines classes that represent 2D shapes.

Exercises

You can download the source code for the examples in the book and the solutions to the following exercises from http://www.wrox.com.

1. Add code to the Sketcher program to support drawing an ellipse.

2. Modify the Sketcher program to include a button for switching fill mode on and off.

3. Extend the classes defining rectangles, circles, and ellipses to support filled shapes.

4. Extend the curve class to support filled shapes.

5. (Harder — for curve enthusiasts!) Implement an applet to display a curve as multiple CubicCurve2D objects from points on the curve entered by clicking the mouse. The applet should have two buttons — one to clear the window and allow points on the curve to be entered and the other to display the curve. Devise your own scheme for default control points.

6. (Also harder!) Modify the previous example to ensure that the curve is continuous — this implies that the control points on either side of an interior point, and the interior point itself, should be on a straight line. Allow control points to be dragged with the mouse, but still maintaining the continuity of the curve.

Extending the GUI

In this chapter you'll investigate how you can improve the graphical user interface (GUI) for Sketcher. After adding a status bar, you'll be creating dialogs and exploring how you can use them to communicate with the user and manage input. Another GUI capability you'll be looking at is context menus, which are pop-up menus that vary depending on the context in which they are displayed. You'll be using context menus to enhance the functionality of the Sketcher application. All of this will give you a lot more practice in implementing event listeners, and much more besides.

In this chapter you'll learn:

- ❏ How to create a status bar
- ❏ How to create a dialog
- ❏ What a modal dialog is and how it differs from a non-modal dialog
- ❏ How to create a message box dialog
- ❏ How you can use components in a dialog to receive input
- ❏ What a pop-up menu is
- ❏ How you can apply and use transformations to the user coordinate system when drawing on a component
- ❏ What context menus are and how you can implement them

Creating a Status Bar

One limitation of the Sketcher program as it stands is that you have no direct feedback on what current element type and color have been selected. As a gentle start to this chapter, let's fix that now. A window status bar at the bottom of an application window is a common and very convenient way of displaying the status of various application parameters, each in its own pane.

You can make up your own class, StatusBar, for example, that will define a status bar. Ideally you would design a class for a generic status bar and customize it for Sketcher, but as space is limited you'll take the simple approach of designing a class that is specific to Sketcher. The JPanel class would be a good base for the StatusBar class since it represents a panel, and you can add objects representing status bar panes to it. You can use the JLabel class as a base for defining status bar panes and add sunken borders to them for a distinct appearance.

Let's start with a status bar at the bottom of the Sketcher application that contains two panes to show the current element type and color. Then the user will know exactly what they are about to draw. You can start by defining the StatusBar class that will represent the status bar in the application window, and you'll define the StatusPane class that defines a region within the status bar as an inner class to StatusBar.

Try It Out   Defining a Status Bar Class

Here's an initial stab at the definition for the StatusBar class:

```java
// Class defining a status bar
import javax.swing.JPanel;
import javax.swing.JLabel;
import javax.swing.BorderFactory;
import javax.swing.border.BevelBorder;
import java.awt.Color;
import java.awt.Font;
import java.awt.FlowLayout;
import java.awt.Dimension;
import static Constants.SketcherConstants.*;

class StatusBar extends JPanel {
  // Constructor
  public StatusBar() {
    setLayout(new FlowLayout(FlowLayout.LEFT, 10, 3));
    setBackground(Color.LIGHT_GRAY);
    setBorder(BorderFactory.createLineBorder(Color.DARK_GRAY));
    setColorPane(DEFAULT_ELEMENT_COLOR);
    setTypePane(DEFAULT_ELEMENT_TYPE);
    add(colorPane);                              // Add color pane to status bar
    add(typePane);                               // Add type pane to status bar
  }

  // Set color pane label
  public void setColorPane(Color color) {
  // Code to set the color pane text...
  }

  // Set type pane label
  public void setTypePane (int elementType) {
  // Code to set the type pane text....
  }

  // Panes in the status bar
  private StatusPane colorPane = new StatusPane("BLUE");
  private StatusPane typePane = new StatusPane("LINE");

  // Class defining a status bar pane
```

```
class StatusPane extends JLabel {
  public StatusPane(String text) {
    setBackground(Color.LIGHT_GRAY);      // Set background color
    setForeground(Color.BLACK);
    setFont(paneFont);                     // Set the fixed font
    setHorizontalAlignment(CENTER);        // Center the pane text
    setBorder(BorderFactory.createBevelBorder(BevelBorder.LOWERED));
    setPreferredSize(new Dimension(100,20));
    setText(text);                         // Set the text in the pane
  }

  // Font for pane text
  private Font paneFont = new Font("Serif", Font.PLAIN, 10);
}
}
```

How It Works

Since the StatusBar class imports the names of static members of the SketcherConstants class that you defined in the Constants package, all the constants that represent possible element types and colors are available. This outline version of StatusBar has two fields of type StatusPane, which will be the panes showing the current color and element type. The initial information to be displayed by a StatusPane object is passed to the constructor as a String object.

The StatusBar constructor updates the information to be displayed in each pane by calling the setColorPane() and setTypePane() methods. These ensure that initially the StatusPane objects display the default color and type that you've defined for the application. One or other of these methods will be called whenever it is necessary to update the status bar. You'll complete the definitions for setColorPane() and setTypePane() when you've been through the detail of the StatusPane class.

The StatusBar panel has a FlowLayout manager that is set in the constructor. The panes in the status bar need display only a small amount of text, so you've derived the StatusPane class from the JLabel class — so a pane for the status bar will be a specialized kind of JLabel. This means that you can call the setText() method that is inherited from JLabel to set the text for the StatusPane objects. The StatusPane objects will be left-justified when they are added to the status bar, as a result of the first argument to the setLayout() method call in the StatusBar constructor. The layout manager will leave a 10-pixel horizontal gap between successive panes in the status bar, and a 3-pixel vertical gap between rows of components. The border for the status bar is a single dark gray line that you add using the BorderFactory method.

The only field in the StatusPane class is the Font object font. You've defined the font to be used for pane text as a standard 10-point Serif font. The StatusPane constructor sets the background color to light gray, the foreground color to dark gray, and sets the standard font for the pane. The constructor also sets the alignment of the text as centered by calling the inherited method setHorizontalAlignment(), and passing the value CENTER to it — this value is defined in the base class JLabel.

If you can maintain a fixed width for each pane, it will prevent the size of the pane from jumping around when you change the text. So you've set the setPreferredSize() at the minimum necessary for accommodating the longest text field that needs to be displayed. Lastly, the StatusPane constructor sets the initial text to be displayed in the pane by calling the inherited setText() method.

 Updating the Panes

You can code the `setColorPane()` method as follows:

```
// Set color pane label
public void setColorPane(Color color) {
  String text = null;                          // Text for the color pane
  if(color.equals(Color.RED)) {
    text = "RED";
  } else if(color.equals(Color.YELLOW)) {
    text = "YELLOW";
  } else if(color.equals(Color.GREEN)) {
    text = "GREEN";
  } else if(color.equals(Color.BLUE)) {
    text = "BLUE";
  } else {
    text = "CUSTOM COLOR";
  }
  colorPane.setForeground(color);
  colorPane.setText(text);                     // Set the pane text
}
```

In the code for the `setTypePane()` method, you can use a `switch` statement rather than `if` statements to test the parameter value because it is of type `int`:

```
// Set type pane label
public void setTypePane(int elementType) {
  String text = null;                          // Text for the type pane
  switch(elementType) {
    case LINE:
      text = "LINE";
      break;
    case RECTANGLE:
      text = "RECTANGLE";
      break;
    case CIRCLE:
      text = "CIRCLE";
      break;
    case CURVE:
      text = "CURVE";
      break;
    default:
      assert false;
  }
  typePane.setText(text);                       // Set the pane text
}
```

How It Works

This code is quite simple. The text to be displayed in the color pane is selected in the series of `if-else` statements. They each compare the color that is passed as the argument with the standard colors you use in Sketcher and set the `text` variable accordingly. The last `else` should never be reached at the moment, but it will be obvious if it is. This provides the possibility of adding more flexibility in the drawing color later on. Note that you also set the foreground color to the currently selected element color, so the text will be drawn in the color to which it refers.

The type pane uses a `switch` as it is more convenient, but the basic process is the same as for the color pane. If something goes wrong somewhere that results in an invalid element type, the program will assert through the default case.

All you need now is to implement the status bar in the `SketchFrame` class. For this you must add a field to the `SketchFrame` class that stores a reference to the status bar, modify the `SketchFrame` class constructor to add the status bar to the content pane of the window, and extend the `actionPerformed()` methods in the `TypeAction` and `ColorAction` classes to update the status bar when the element type or color is altered.

Try It Out   The Status Bar in Action

You can add the following statement to the `SketchFrame` class to define the status bar as a data member, following the members that define the menu bar and toolbar:

```
private StatusBar statusBar = new StatusBar();        // Window status bar
```

You create `statusBar` as a data member so that it can be accessed throughout the class definition, including from within the `Action` classes. You need to add one statement to the end of the `SketchFrame` class constructor:

```
public SketchFrame(String title, Sketcher theApp) {
  // Constructor code as before...
  getContentPane().add(statusBar, BorderLayout.SOUTH);    // Add the statusbar
}
```

This adds the status bar to the bottom of the application window. To update the status bar when the element type changes, you can add one statement to the `actionPerformed()` method in the inner class `TypeAction`:

```
public void actionPerformed(ActionEvent e) {
  elementType = typeID;
  statusBar.setTypePane(typeID);
}
```

The type pane is updated by calling the `setTypePane()` method for the status bar and passing the current element type to it as an argument. You can add a similar statement to the `actionPerformed()` method to update the color pane:

```
public void actionPerformed(ActionEvent e) {
  elementColor = color;
  statusBar.setColorPane(color);
}
```

If you now recompile and run Sketcher again, you'll see the status bar in the application, as shown in Figure 20-1.

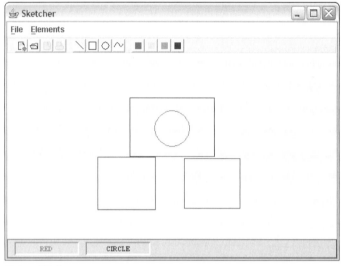

Figure 20-1

As you change the element type and color through the menus or toolbar buttons, the status bar will be updated automatically.

Using Dialogs

A dialog is a window that is displayed within the context of another window — its parent. You use dialogs to manage input that can't be handled conveniently through interaction with the view — selecting from a range of options, for example, or enabling data to be entered from the keyboard. You can also use dialogs for information messages or warnings. The JDialog class in the javax.swing package defines dialogs, and a JDialog object is a specialized sort of Window. A JDialog object will typically contain one or more components for displaying information or allowing data to be entered, plus buttons for selection of dialog options (including closing the dialog), so there's quite a bit of work involved in putting one together. However, for many of the typical dialogs that you will want to use, the JOptionPane class provides an easy shortcut to creating dialogs. Figure 20-2 shows a dialog that you'll create later in this chapter using just one statement.

Figure 20-2

You'll use this dialog to provide a response to clicking on a Help/About menu item that you'll add to Sketcher in a moment. First, though, you need to understand a little more about how dialogs work.

Modal and Non-Modal Dialogs

There are two different kinds of dialog that you can create, and they have distinct operating characteristics. You have a choice of creating either a **modal dialog** or a **non-modal dialog**.

When you display a modal dialog — typically by selecting a menu item or clicking a button — it inhibits the operation of any other windows in the application until you close the dialog. The dialog in Figure 20-2 that displays a message is a modal dialog. The dialog window retains the focus as long as it is displayed, and operation of the application cannot continue until you click the OK button. Modal dialogs that manage input will normally have at least two buttons, an OK button that you use to accept whatever input has been entered and then close the dialog, and a Cancel button to just close the dialog and abort the entry of the data. Dialogs that manage input are almost always modal dialogs, simply because you won't generally want to allow other interactions to be triggered until your user's input is complete.

A non-modal dialog can be left on the screen for as long as you want, since it doesn't block interaction with other windows in the application. You can also switch the focus back and forth between using a non-modal dialog and using any other application windows that are on the screen.

Whether you create a modal or a non-modal dialog is determined either by an argument to a dialog class constructor, or by which constructor you choose, because some of them create non-modal dialogs by default. The default, no-argument `JDialog` constructor creates a non-modal dialog with an empty title bar. Since you have no provision for specifying a parent window for the dialog with the no-argument constructor, a shared hidden frame will be used as the parent in this case. You have a choice of five constructors for creating a `JDialog` object where the parent can be a window of type `Frame` or `JFrame`:

Constructor	Description		
	Title Bar	**Parent Window**	**Mode**
`JDialog(Frame parent)`	(empty)	parent	non-modal
`JDialog(Frame parent, String title)`	title	parent	non-modal
`JDialog(Frame parent, boolean modal)`	(empty)	parent	modal (when `modal` is true) non-modal (when `modal` is false)

Table continued on following page

Constructor	Description		
	Title Bar	Parent Window	Mode
JDialog(Frame parent, String title, boolean modal)	title	parent	modal (when modal is true) non-modal (when modal is false)
JDialog(Frame parent, String title, boolean modal, GraphicsConfiguration gc)	title	parent	modal (when modal is true) non-modal (when modal is false)

Because the first parameter to each of these constructors is of type Frame, you can supply a reference of type Frame or of type JFrame. There are a further five constructors for creating JDialog objects with a Dialog or JDialog object as the parent. The only difference between these and the ones in the table is that the type of the first parameter is Dialog rather than Frame. Any of these constructors can throw an exception of type HeadlessException if the system on which the code is executing does not have a display attached.

After you've created a JDialog object using any of the constructors, you can change the kind of dialog window it will produce from modal to non-modal, or vice versa, by calling the setModal() method for the object. If you specify the argument to the method as true, the dialog will be modal, and a false argument will make it non-modal. You can also check whether a JDialog object is modal or not. The isModal() method for the object will return true if it represents a modal dialog and false otherwise.

All JDialog objects are initially invisible, so to display them you must call the setVisible() method for the JDialog object with the argument true. This method is inherited from the Component class via the Container and Window classes. If you call setVisible() with the argument false, the dialog window is removed from the screen. Once you've displayed a modal dialog window, the user can't interact with any of the other application windows until you call setVisible() for the dialog object with the argument false, so you typically do this in the event handler that is called to close the dialog. Note that the setVisible() method affects only the visibility of the dialog. You still have a perfectly good JDialog object so when you want to display the dialog again, you just call its setVisible() method with an argument set to true. Of course, if you call dispose() for the JDialog object, or set the default close operation to DISPOSE_ON_CLOSE, then you won't be able to use the JDialog object again.

To set or change the title bar for a dialog, you just pass a String object to the setTitle() method for the JDialog object. If you want to know what the current title for a dialog is, you can call the getTitle() method, which will return a reference to a String object that contains the title bar string.

Dialog windows are resizable by default, so you can normally change the size of a dialog window by dragging its boundaries. If you don't want to allow a dialog window to be resized, you can inhibit this by calling the `setResizable()` method for the `JDialog` object with the argument as `false`. An argument value of `true` re-enables the resizing capability.

A Simple Modal Dialog

The simplest kind of dialog is one that just displays some information. You could see how this works by adding a Help menu with an About menu item, and then displaying an About dialog to provide information about the application.

You'll derive your own dialog class from `JDialog` so you can create an About dialog. `AboutDialog` seems like a good name for the new class.

Try It Out   Defining the AboutDialog Class

The constructor for the `AboutDialog` class will need to accept three arguments — the parent `Frame` object, which will be the application window in Sketcher; a `String` object defining what should appear on the title bar; and a `String` object for the message that you want to display. You'll need only one button in the dialog window, an OK button to close the dialog. You can make the whole thing self-contained by making the `AboutDialog` class the action listener for the button, and because it's relevant only in the context of the `SketchFrame` class, you can define it as an inner class to `SketchFrame`:

```java
// Import statements as before...
import javax.swing.JDialog;
import javax.swing.JPanel;
import javax.swing.JLabel;
import java.awt.Dimension;
import java.awt.Point;

public class SketchFrame extends JFrame {
  // SketchFrame class as before...

  // Class defining a general purpose message box
  class AboutDialog extends JDialog implements ActionListener   {
    public AboutDialog(JFrame parent, String title, String message)  {
      super(parent, title, true);
      // If there was a parent, set dialog position inside
      if(parent != null) {
        Dimension parentSize = parent.getSize(); // Parent size
        Point p = parent.getLocation();          // Parent position
        setLocation(p.x+parentSize.width/4,p.y+parentSize.height/4);
      }

      // Create the message pane
      JPanel messagePane = new JPanel();
      messagePane.add(new JLabel(message));
      getContentPane().add(messagePane);

      // Create the button pane
      JPanel buttonPane = new JPanel();
      JButton button = new JButton("OK");        // Create OK button
      buttonPane.add(button);                     // add to content pane
```

```
          button.addActionListener(this);
          getContentPane().add(buttonPane, BorderLayout.SOUTH);
          setDefaultCloseOperation(DISPOSE_ON_CLOSE);
          pack();                                    // Size window for components
          setVisible(true);
        }

        // OK button action
        public void actionPerformed(ActionEvent e)  {
          setVisible(false);                         // Set dialog invisible
          dispose();                                 // Release the dialog resources
        }
      }
    }
```

How It Works

The constructor first calls the base `JDialog` class constructor to create a modal dialog with the title bar given by the `title` argument. It then defines the position of the dialog relative to the position of the frame.

> When you create an instance of the `AboutDialog` class in the Sketcher program a little later in this chapter, you'll specify the `SketchFrame` object as the parent for the dialog. The parent relationship between the application window and the dialog implies a lifetime dependency. When the `SketchFrame` object is destroyed, the `AboutDialog` object will be, too, because it is a child of the `SketchFrame` object. This doesn't just apply to `JDialog` objects — any `Window` object can have another `Window` object as a parent.

By default the `AboutDialog` window will be positioned relative to the top-left corner of the screen. To position the dialog in a more sensible position relative to the application window, you set the coordinates of the top-left corner of the dialog as one quarter of the distance across the width of the application window, and one quarter of the distance down from the top-left corner of the application window.

You add the components you want to display in a dialog to the content pane for the `JDialog` object. The content pane has a `BorderLayout` manager by default, just like the content pane for the application window, and this is quite convenient for the `AboutDialog` layout. The dialog contains two `JPanel` objects that are created in the constructor, one to hold a `JLabel` object for the message that is passed as an argument to the constructor and the other to hold the OK button that will close the dialog. The `messagePane` object is added so that it fills the center of the dialog window. The `buttonPane` position is specified as `BorderLayout.SOUTH`, so it will be at the bottom of the dialog window. Both `JPanel` objects have a `FlowLayout` manager by default.

You want the `AboutDialog` object to be the listener for the OK button so you pass the `this` variable as the argument to the `addActionListener()` method call for the button.

The `pack()` method is inherited from the `Window` class. This method packs the components in the window, setting the window to an optimal size for the components it contains before laying out the components. Note that if you don't call `pack()` here, the size for your dialog will not be set and you won't be able to see it.

The `actionPerformed()` method will be called when the OK button is selected. This just disposes of the dialog by calling the `dispose()` method for the `AboutDialog` object so the dialog window will disappear from the screen and the resources it was using will be released.

To add a Help menu with an About item to the Sketcher application, you need to insert some code into the `SketchFrame` class constructor.

Try It Out   Creating an About Menu Item

You shouldn't have any trouble with this. You can make the `SketchFrame` object the listener for the About menu item, so add `ActionListener` as the interface implemented by `SketchFrame`:

```
public class SketchFrame extends JFrame implements ActionListener {
```

The changes to the constructor to add the Help menu will be:

```
public SketchFrame(String title , Sketcher theApp) {
  setTitle(title);                              // Set the window title
  this.theApp = theApp;                         // Save application object reference
  setJMenuBar(menuBar);                         // Add the menu bar to the window
  setDefaultCloseOperation(EXIT_ON_CLOSE);      // Default is exit the application

  JMenu fileMenu = new JMenu("File");           // Create File menu
  JMenu elementMenu = new JMenu("Elements");    // Create Elements menu
  JMenu helpMenu = new JMenu("Help");           // Create Help menu
  fileMenu.setMnemonic('F');                    // Create shortcut
  elementMenu.setMnemonic('E');                 // Create shortcut
  helpMenu.setMnemonic('H');                    // Create shortcut

  // All the stuff for the previous menus and the toolbar, as before...

  // Add the About item to the Help menu
  aboutItem = new JMenuItem("About");           // Create the item
  aboutItem.addActionListener(this);            // Listener is the frame
  helpMenu.add(aboutItem);                      // Add item to menu
  menuBar.add(helpMenu);                        // Add the Help menu
}
```

Add `aboutMenu` as a private member of the `SketchFrame` class:

```
// Sundry menu items
private JMenuItem aboutItem;
```

Lastly, you need to implement the method in the `SketchFrame` class to handle the About menu item's events:

```
// Handle About menu action events
public void actionPerformed(ActionEvent e)  {
  if(e.getSource() == aboutItem) {
    // Create about dialog with the app window as parent
    AboutDialog aboutDlg = new AboutDialog(this, "About Sketcher",
                                 "Sketcher Copyright Ivor Horton 2004");
  }
}
```

You can now recompile `SketchFrame.java` to try out your smart new dialog, which you can see in Figure 20-3.

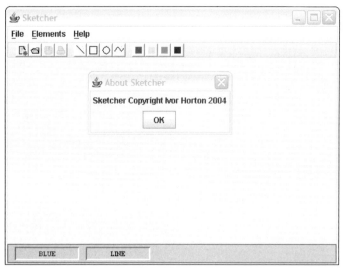

Figure 20-3

The dialog pops up when you select the About item in the Help menu. Until you select the OK button in the About Sketcher dialog, you can't interact with the application window at all because you created this as a modal dialog. By changing the last argument in the call to the superclass constructor in the `AboutDialog` constructor, you can make it non-modal and see how that works. This kind of dialog is usually modal though.

If you resize the application window before you display the About dialog, you'll see that the position of the dialog relative to the application window is adjusted accordingly.

How It Works

This is stuff that should be very familiar to you by now. You create a `JMenu` object for the Help item on the menu bar, and add a shortcut for it by calling its `setMnemonic()` member. You create a `JMenuItem` object, which is the About menu item, and call its `addActionListener()` method to make the `SketchFrame` object the listener for the item. After adding the menu item to the Help menu, you add the `helpMenu` object to the `menubar` object.

You create an `AboutDialog` object in the `actionPerformed()` method for the `SketchFrame` object, as this method will be called when the About menu item is clicked. Before you display the dialog, you verify that the source of the event is the menu item, `aboutItem`. This is not important now, but you'll add other menu items later, and you'll want to handle their events using the same `actionPerformed()` method. The dialog object is self-contained and disposes of itself when the OK button is clicked. The dialog that you want to display here will always display the same message, so there's no real point in creating and destroying it each time you want to display it. You could arrange for the dialog box object to be created once, and the reference stored as a member of the `SketchFrame` class. Then you could make it visible in the `actionPerformed()` method for the menu item and make it invisible in the `actionPerformed()` method responding to the dialog OK button event.

This is all very well, but it was a lot of work just to get a dialog with a message displayed. Deriving a class from `JDialog` gives you complete flexibility as to how the dialog works, but you didn't really need it in this case. Didn't I say there was an easier way?

Instant Dialogs

The `JOptionPane` class in the `javax.swing` package defines a number of static methods that will create and display standard modal dialogs for you. The simplest dialog you can create this way is a message dialog rather like the About message dialog in the previous example. The following static methods in the `JOptionPane` class produce message dialogs:

Dial-a-Dialog Methods	Description

`showMessageDialog(`
　　　`Component parent,`
　　　`Object message)`
	This method displays a modal dialog with the default title `"Message"`. The first argument is the parent for the dialog. The `Frame` object containing the component will be used to position the dialog. If the first argument is `null`, a default `Frame` object will be created and that will be used to position the dialog centrally on the screen.
	
	The second argument specifies what is to be displayed in addition to the default OK button. This can be a `String` object specifying the message or an `Icon` object defining an icon to be displayed. It can also be a `Component`, in which case the component will be displayed. If some other type of object is passed as the second argument, its `toString()` method will be called, and the `String` object that is returned will be displayed. You will usually get a default icon for an information message along with your message.
	
	You can pass multiple items to be displayed by passing an array of type `Object[]` for the second argument. Each array element will be processed as above according to its type and they will be arranged in a vertical stack. Clever, eh?

Table continued on following page

Dial-a-Dialog Methods	Description

showMessageDialog(
    Component parent,
    Object message,
    String title,
    int messageType)
	This displays a dialog just as the preceding method, but with the title specified by the third argument. The fourth argument, messageType, can be:
	
	ERROR_MESSAGE
	INFORMATION_MESSAGE
	WARNING_MESSAGE
	QUESTION_MESSAGE
	PLAIN_MESSAGE
	
	These determine the style of the message constrained by the current look-and-feel. This will usually include a default icon, such as a question mark for QUESTION_MESSAGE.

showMessageDialog(
    Component parent,
    Object message,
    String title,
    int messageType,
    Icon icon)
	This displays a dialog just as the preceding method except that the icon will be what you pass as the fifth argument. Specifying a null argument for the icon will produce a dialog just as the previous version of the method.

You could have used one of these for the About dialog instead of all that messing about with inner classes. Let's see how.

Try It Out   An Easy About Dialog

Delete the inner class AboutDialog from SketchFrame — you won't need that any longer. Change the implementation of the actionPerformed() method in the SketchFrame class to the following:

```
public void actionPerformed(ActionEvent e) {
  if(e.getSource() == aboutItem) {
    // Create about dialog with the menu item as parent
    JOptionPane.showMessageDialog(this,                        // Parent
                      "Sketcher Copyright Ivor Horton 2004",   // Message
                      "About Sketcher",                        // Title
                      JOptionPane.INFORMATION_MESSAGE);        // Message type
  }
}
```

Add an `import` statement for `JOptionPane` to `SketchFrame.java` and then recompile `SketchFrame` and run Sketcher once more. When you click on the Help/About menu item, you should get something like the window shown in Figure 20-4.

Figure 20-4

The pretty little icon comes for free.

How It Works

All the work is done by the static `showMessageDialog()` method in the `JOptionPane` class. What you get is controlled by the arguments that you supply, and the Swing look-and-feel that is in effect. By default this will correspond to the cross-platform look-and-feel, and this is what Figure 20-4 shows. You get the icon you see because you specified the message type as `INFORMATION_MESSAGE`. You can try plugging in the other message types to see what you get.

Input Dialogs

`JOptionPane` also has four static methods that you can use to create standard modal input dialogs:

```
showInputDialog(Object message)
```

This method displays a default modal input dialog with a text field for input. The message you pass as the argument is set as the caption for the input field and the default also supplies an OK button, a Cancel button, and Input as a title. For example, if you pass the message "Enter Input:" as the argument, as in the following statement,

```
String input = JOptionPane.showInputDialog("Enter Input:");
```

the dialog shown in Figure 20-5 will be displayed.

Figure 20-5

When you click the OK button, whatever you entered in the text field will be returned by the showInputDialog() method and stored in input; this will be "This is the input..." in this case. If you click the Cancel button, null will be returned. Note that this is not the same as *no* input. If you click OK without entering anything in the text field, a reference to an empty String object will be returned.

You could also use the overloaded version of the method that has the following form:

```
String showInputDialog(Component parent, Object message)
```

This version produces the same dialog as the previous method, but with the component you specify as the first argument as the parent of the dialog.

Another possibility is to use the method with the following form:

```
String showInputDialog(Component parent, Object message,
                       String title, int messageType)
```

In this case the title of the dialog is supplied by the third argument, and the style of the message is determined by the fourth argument. The values for the fourth argument can be any of those I discussed earlier in the context of message dialogs. For example, you could display the dialog shown in Figure 20-6 with the following statement:

```
String input = JOptionPane.showInputDialog(null, "Enter Input:",
                       "Dialog for Input", JOptionPane.WARNING_MESSAGE);
```

Figure 20-6

The data that you enter in the text field is returned by the `showInputDialog()` method when the OK button is pressed as before.

You also have a version that accepts seven arguments:

```
String showInputDialog(Component parent, Object message,
                       String title, int messageType,
                       Icon icon, Object[] selections,
                       object initialSelection)
```

This version of the method displays a dialog with a list of choices in a drop-down list box. You pass the items that are the set of choices as the sixth argument to the method in the form of an array, and it can be an array of elements of any class type. The initial selection to be shown when the dialog is first displayed is specified by the seventh argument. Whatever is chosen when the OK button is clicked will be returned as type `Object`, and if the Cancel button is clicked, `null` will be returned. You can specify your own icon to replace the default icon by passing a reference of type `Icon` as the fifth argument. The following statements display the dialog shown in Figure 20-7:

```
String[] choices = {"Money", "Health", "Happiness", "This", "That", "The Other"};
String input = (String)JOptionPane.showInputDialog(null, "Choose now...",
                      "The Choice of a Lifetime",
                      JOptionPane.QUESTION_MESSAGE,
                      null,              // Use default icon
                      choices,           // Array of choices
                      choices[1]);       // Initial choice
```

Figure 20-7

Note that you have to cast the reference returned by this version of the `showInputDialog()` method to the type of choice value you have used. Here you are using type `String`, but the selections could be type `Icon`, or whatever you want.

Using a Dialog to Create Text Elements

It would be good if our Sketcher program also provided a means of adding text to a picture—after all, you might want to put your name to a sketch. A dialog is the obvious way to provide the mechanism for entering the text when you create text elements. You can use one of the `showInputDialog()` methods for this, but first you need to add a `Text` menu item to the `Elements` menu, and you'll have to define a class to represent text elements, which will be the `Element.Text` class, of course, with `Element` as a base class. Let's start with the `Element.Text` class.

Text is a little tricky. For one thing, you can't treat it just like another element. There is no object that implements the `Shape` interface that represents a text string, so unless you want to define one, you can't use the `draw()` method for a graphics context to display text. You have to use the `drawString()` method. You'll also have to figure out the bounding rectangle for the text on screen for yourself. With `Shape` objects, you can rely on the `getBounds()` method supplied by the 2D shape classes in `java.awt.geom`, but with text you're on your own.

Ideally you want to avoid treating text elements as a special case. Having many tests for types while you're drawing a sketch in the `paint()` method for the view generates considerable processing overhead that you would be better off without. One way around this is to make every element draw itself. You could implement a polymorphic method in each element class — `draw()`, say — and pass a `Graphics2D` object to it. Each shape or text element could then figure out how to draw itself. The `paint()` method in the view class would not need to worry about what type of element was being drawn at all.

Try It Out   Defining the Element.Text Class

Let's see how that works out. You can start by adding an abstract `draw()` method to the `Element` class definition:

```
public abstract class Element {
  public Element(Color color) {
    this.color = color;
  }

  public   Color getColor() {
    return color;
  }

  public abstract java.awt.Rectangle getBounds();
  public abstract void modify(Point start, Point last);
  public abstract void draw(Graphics2D g2D);

  protected Color color;                   // Color of a shape

  // Plus definitions for our shape classes...
}
```

Note that the `getShape()` method declaration has been deleted from the `Element` class as you won't be needing it further. You can remove the definitions of the `getShape()` method from all the nested classes of the `Element` class. You also need to make the `Graphics2D` class name accessible so add an `import` statement for it to `Element.java`:

```
import java.awt.Graphics2D;
```

The `draw()` method now needs to be implemented in each of the nested classes to the `Element` class, but because each of the current inner classes has a `Shape` member, it will be essentially the same in each. The version for the `Element.Line` class will be:

```
public void draw(Graphics2D g2D) {
  g2D.setPaint(color);                      // Set the line color
  g2D.draw(line);                           // Draw the line
}
```

This just sets the color and passes the Shape object that is a member of the class to the draw() method for the Graphics2D object. To implement the draw() method for the other element classes, just replace the argument to the g2D.draw() method call, with the name of the Shape member of the class, and update the comments.

You can now change the implementation of the paint() method in the SketchView class to:

```
public void paint(Graphics g) {
  Graphics2D g2D = (Graphics2D)g;                    // Get a 2D device context
  for(Element element : theApp.getModel()) {         // Go through the list
    element.draw(g2D);                               // Element draws itself
  }
}
```

The paint() method is now quite a lot shorter, as the element sets its own color in the graphics context before it draws itself.

You must not forget to update the mouseDragged() method in the MouseHandler class in SketchView to use the new mechanism for drawing elements:

```
public void mouseDragged(MouseEvent e) {
  last = e.getPoint();                               // Save cursor position

  if(button1Down) {
    if(tempElement == null) {                        // Is there an element?
      tempElement = createElement(start, last);      // No, so create one
    } else {
      tempElement.draw(g2D);                         // Yes - draw to erase it
      tempElement.modify(start, last);               // Now modify it
    }
    tempElement.draw(g2D);                           // and draw it
  }
}
```

The mousePressed() method doesn't need to set the color in the graphics context, as the draw() methods for the shapes do that now. You can delete the following statement from the definition of mousePressed() in the Sketcher view class:

```
    g2D.setPaint(theApp.getWindow().getElementColor()); // Set color
```

You are now ready to get back to the Element.Text class. You can define the Element.Text class quite easily. The constructor will need five arguments, though — the font to be used for the string, the string to be displayed, the position where it is to be displayed, its color, and its bounding rectangle. To get the bounding rectangle for a string, you need access to a graphics context, so it will be easier to create the bounding rectangle before you create a text element, and then pass it to the constructor.

Here's the class definition for objects that define text elements:

```
import java.awt.Color;
import java.awt.Shape;
import java.awt.Point;
import java.awt.Font;
```

```
import java.awt.Graphics2D;
import java.awt.geom.Line2D;
import java.awt.geom.Rectangle2D;
import java.awt.geom.Ellipse2D;
import java.awt.geom.GeneralPath;

class Element {
  // Code that defines the base class...
  // Definitions for the other shape classes...

  // Nested class defining text elements
  public static class Text extends Element  {
    public Text(Font font, String text, Point position, Color color,
                                      java.awt.Rectangle bounds) {
      super(color);
      this.font = font;
      this.position = position;
      this.text = text;
      this.bounds = bounds;
      this.bounds.setLocation(position.x, position.y - (int)bounds.getHeight());
    }

    public java.awt.Rectangle getBounds() {
      return bounds;
    }

    public void draw(Graphics2D g2D)   {
      g2D.setPaint(color);
      Font oldFont = g2D.getFont();              // Save the old font
      g2D.setFont(font);                         // Set the new font
      g2D.drawString(text, position.x, position.y);
      g2D.setFont(oldFont);                      // Restore the old font
    }

    public void modify(Point start, Point last) {
      // No code is required here, but you must supply a definition
    }

    private Font font;                    // The font to be used
    private String text;                  // Text to be displayed
    private Point position;               // Position of the text
    private java.awt.Rectangle bounds;    // The bounding rectangle
  }
}
```

How It Works

The Element.Text class constructor passes the color to the superclass constructor and stores the other argument values in data members of the Element.Text class. When you create the bounding rectangle to pass to the constructor, the default reference point for the top-left corner of the rectangle will be (0, 0). This is not what you want for the text object so you have to modify it, as shown in Figure 20-8.

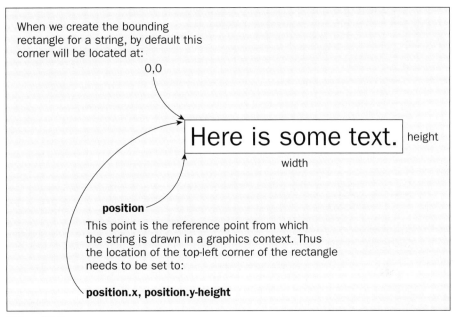

When we create the bounding rectangle for a string, by default this corner will be located at:

0,0

Here is some text. height

width

position

This point is the reference point from which the string is drawn in a graphics context. Thus the location of the top-left corner of the rectangle needs to be set to:

position.x, position.y-height

Figure 20-8

In the constructor, you adjust the coordinates of the top-left corner of the bounding rectangle relative to the point, `position`, where the string will be drawn. Remember that the point coordinates that you pass to the `drawString()` method must correspond to the bottom-left corner of the first character in the string.

The code to draw text is not difficult—it's just different from drawing shapes. It amounts to calling `setPaint()` to set the text color, setting the font in the graphics context by calling its `setFont()` method, and finally calling `drawString()` to display the text. You don't know whether some other method may be relying on the font that's already set for the graphics context, so you save the old font before changing it and then restore it when you are done.

You could do with a menu item and a toolbar button to work with text that will set the element type to `TEXT`, so let's deal with that next.

Try It Out   Adding the Text Menu Item

First, you can add a `textAction` member to the `SketchFrame` class, so amend the declaration for the `TypeAction` members to:

```
private TypeAction lineAction, rectangleAction, circleAction,
                curveAction, textAction;
```

You'll need an icon in the `Images` directory that is a subdirectory to the `Sketcher` directory if you want to create a toolbar button for text. I just created an icon with `'T'` on it, but you can create something fancier if you have a mind to. The file containing the icon should have the name `Text.gif`, because that's what the `TypeAction` object will assume.

You can add a statement to the `SketchFrame` constructor that will add the menu item, following the statements that create the other items in the element menu:

```java
public class SketchFrame extends JFrame implements ActionListener {
  // Constructor
  public SketchFrame(String title, Sketcher theApp) {
    // Code as before...

    // Code to add the other Element menu items as before...
    addMenuItem(elementMenu, textAction = new TypeAction("Text", TEXT,
                                                   "Draw text"));

    // Code as before...
  }
  // Rest of the code for the SketchFrame class...
}
```

The new statement assumes you have defined the value of `TEXT` in the `SketcherConstants` class, so now add that to the class as well as a default font for use with text elements:

```java
package Constants;
import java.awt.Color;
import java.awt.Font;

public class SketcherConstants {
  // Element type definitions
  public final static int LINE      = 101;
  public final static int RECTANGLE = 102;
  public final static int CIRCLE    = 103;
  public final static int CURVE     = 104;
  public final static int TEXT      = 105;
  // Initial conditions
  public final static int DEFAULT_ELEMENT_TYPE = LINE;
  public final static Color DEFAULT_ELEMENT_COLOR = Color.BLUE;
  public final static Font DEFAULT_FONT = new Font("SansSerif",Font.PLAIN, 12);
}
```

If you don't like the SansSerif font, choose another font that you have on your machine. You'll need a data member in the application window object to hold a reference to the current font. It will start out as the default font, but you'll be adding the means to alter this later. Add the following data member after the others in `SketchFrame`:

```java
private Color elementColor = DEFAULT_ELEMENT_COLOR;   // Current element color
private int elementType = DEFAULT_ELEMENT_TYPE;       // Current element type
private Font font = DEFAULT_FONT;                      // Current font
```

Of course, you also need a method in the `SketchFrame` class to retrieve the current font from the application window object:

```java
public Font getCurrentFont() {
  return font;
}
```

Don't forget to add an `import` statement for `java.awt.Font` to the `SketchFrame` source file. Now the view will be able to get the current font when necessary, via the application object.

If you want the toolbar button as well, you will need to add one statement to the `SketchFrame` constructor, following the others, that adds element type selection buttons:

```
// Add element type buttons
toolBar.addSeparator();
addToolBarButton(lineAction);
addToolBarButton(rectangleAction);
addToolBarButton(circleAction);
addToolBarButton(curveAction);
addToolBarButton(textAction);
```

The action events for the menu item and toolbar button for text are taken care of and the final piece is dealing with mouse events when you create a text element.

Text elements are going to be different from shapes in how they are created and displayed. More information is required for a text element. To create a text element you need to know what the text is, its color, its font, and where it is to be placed. You'll also have to construct its bounding rectangle. This sounds as though it might not be much harder than creating geometric elements, but there are complications.

Try It Out   Creating Text Elements

You start the process of creating geometric elements in `SketchView`'s `MouseHandler` class, but you can't simply start with the `mousePressed()` method, as would at first seem logical. The problem is the sequence of events. You want to display a dialog to manage the text entry, but if you display a dialog in the `mousePressed()` method, the `mouseReleased()` event will get lost, unless you're happy to hold down the mouse button while typing into the text field with the other hand!

A simple solution is to separate the creation of text elements altogether and create them in the `mouseClicked()` method. This method is called after the mouse button is released, so all the other events will have occurred and been dealt with.

You can implement the `mouseClicked()` method in the inner class, `MouseHandler`, so that it will create a text element. The code for the method will be along the following lines:

```
public void mouseClicked(MouseEvent e) {
   if((e.getButton()== MouseEvent.BUTTON1) &&
      (theApp.getWindow().getElementType() == TEXT)) {

    start = e.getPoint();                  // Save cursor position - start of text
    String text = JOptionPane.showInputDialog(
                 (Component)e.getSource(),    // Used to get the frame
                 "Enter Text:",               // The message
                 "Dialog for Text Element",   // Dialog title
                 JOptionPane.PLAIN_MESSAGE);  // No icon

    if(text != null && text.length()!= 0)  { // If we have text
                                             // create the element
       // Code to create the Element.Text element
       // and add it to the sketch model...
    }
   }
}
```

You'll need to import `JOptionPane` from the `javax.swing` package into `SketchView.java` as well as the `Component` and `Font` class names from the `java.awt` package, so add the following `import` statements to the source file:

```
import java.awt.Component;
import java.awt.Font;
import javax.swing.JOptionPane;
```

You want to do something in the `mouseClicked()` method only if it was mouse button 1 that was clicked *and* the current element type is `TEXT`, so the `if` statement tests for that. When the `if` condition is `true`, you save the cursor position and pop a dialog to permit the text string to be entered. If a string that is not an empty was entered, you go ahead and create a text element and add it to the sketch model.

You still have to add the code for creating a text element. The tricky part is figuring out what the size of the rectangle that bounds the text is. The `Font` class defines a `getStringBounds()` method that returns a rectangle indicating the logical bounds for a string in a given context in which the string is drawn. Unfortunately, as the documentation for this method says, it does not always return a rectangle enclosing all of the text. If you were to use this, parts of the text could get chopped off when displayed. To get a rectangle that completely encloses the text in every case, you must create a `TextLayout` object for the text and use its `getBounds()` method to obtain a rectangle.

This `TextLayout` class is defined in the `java.awt.font` package, so you'll need an `import` statement for that in the `SketchView.java` file:

```
import java.awt.font.TextLayout;
```

A `TextLayout` object encapsulates the graphical representation of a given text string on a particular graphics device, so, as well as the text and the font, a `TextLayout` class constructor needs information on the dimensions of the font in the context of the graphical device. The `FontRenderContext` class in the `java.awt.font` package defines an object that encapsulates the information necessary to display text in a given graphics context. You obtain a `FontRenderContext` object from a `Graphics2D` object, `g2D`, like this:

```
FontRenderContext frc = g2D.getFontRenderContext();
```

All you need now is a `Graphics2D` object. You can get that by calling the `getGraphics()` method that the `SketchView` object inherits from the `JComponent` class:

```
Graphics2D g2D = (Graphics2D)getGraphics();
```

You have all the pieces you need to create the bounding rectangle for the text, and hence the `Element.Text` object. Here's the code that goes in the `if` statement in the `mouseClicked()` method that will create the text element and add it to the model:

```
if(text != null) {                              // If we have text
                                                // create the element
    g2D = (Graphics2D)getGraphics();
    Font font = theApp.getWindow().getCurrentFont();
    tempElement = new Element.Text(
      font,                                     // The font
      text,                                     // The text
      start,                                    // Position of the  text
```

```
              theApp.getWindow().getElementColor(),   // The text color
              new java.awt.font.TextLayout(text, font, // The bounding rectangle
              g2D.getFontRenderContext()).getBounds().getBounds()
                                     );

    if(tempElement != null) {                      // If we created one
      theApp.getModel().add(tempElement);          // add it to the model
      tempElement = null;                          // and reset the field
    }
    g2D.dispose();                                 // Release context resources
    g2D = null;
    start = null;
  }
```

The bounding rectangle for the text is produced by the rather fearsome looking expression for the last argument to the `Element.Text` constructor. It's much easier than it looks so let's take it apart.

The `TextLayout` constructor you are using expects three arguments: the text string, the font, and a `FontRenderContext` object for the context in which the text is to be displayed. You call the `getBounds()` method for the `TextLayout` object, which returns a reference to a rectangle of type `Rectangle2D`. Since you want a rectangle of type `Rectangle` to pass to the `Element.Text` constructor, you call the `getBounds()` method for the `Rectangle2D` object, hence the repetition in the code.

Once the element has been created, you just add it to the model, and clean up the variables that you were using.

You must now make sure that the other mouse event handlers do nothing when the current element is TEXT. You don't want the XOR mode set when you are just creating text elements, for example. A simple additional condition that tests the current element type will take care of it in the `mousePressed()` method:

```
public void mousePressed(MouseEvent e) {
  // Code to handle mouse button press...
  start = e.getPoint();                     // Save the cursor position in start
  if((button1Down = (e.getButton()==MouseEvent.BUTTON1)) &&
     (theApp.getWindow().getElementType() != TEXT)) {
    g2D = (Graphics2D)getGraphics();                     // Get graphics context
    g2D.setXORMode(getBackground());                     // Set XOR mode
  }
}
```

The `if` expression will be `true` only if button 1 was pressed and the current element type is not TEXT. You can update the `mouseDragged()` method in a similar way:

```
public void mouseDragged(MouseEvent e) {
  last = e.getPoint();                                   // Save cursor position

  if(button1Down && (theApp.getWindow().getElementType() != TEXT)) {
    if(tempElement == null) {                  // Is there an element?
      tempElement = createElement(start, last);  // No, so create one
    } else {
      tempElement.draw(g2D);                     // Yes - draw to erase it
      tempElement.modify(start, last);           // Now modify it
```

```
        }
        g2D.draw(tempElement.getShape());              // and draw it
      }
    }
```

The change to the `mouseReleased()` method is exactly the same as for `mousePressed()`, so go ahead and modify the `if` condition in that method, too. The only other change you need is to make the status bar respond to the TEXT element type being set. To do this you can make a small addition to the definition of the `setTypePane()` method in the `StatusBar` class:

```
    public void setTypePane(int elementType) {
      String text;           // Text for the type pane
      switch(elementType) {
        // case labels as before...

        case TEXT:
          text = "TEXT";
          break;
        default:
          assert false;
      }
      typePane.setText(text);                           // Set the pane text
    }
```

How It Works

The `mouseClicked()` handler responds to mouse button 1 being clicked when the element type is TEXT. This method will be called after the `mouseReleased()` method has been called. Within the `if` statement that determines that the current element is of type TEXT, you create a dialog to receive the text input by calling the static `showInputDialog()` in the `JOptionPane` class. If the Cancel button is clicked in the dialog, `text` will be `null`, so in this case you do nothing. If text is not `null`, you create an `Element.Text` object at the current cursor position containing the text string that was entered in the dialog. You then add this to the model, as long as it's not `null`. It's important to reset the `start` and `tempElement` members back to `null`; otherwise, subsequent event-handling operations will be confused.

Incidentally, although there isn't a method to detect double-clicks on the mouse button, it's easy to implement. The `getClickCount()` method for the `MouseEvent` object that is passed to `mouseClicked()` returns the click count. To respond to a double-click, you could write the following statements:

```
    if(e.getClickCount() == 2) {
      //Response to double-click...
    }
```

The other event-handling methods behave as before so far as the geometric elements are concerned, and do nothing if the element type is TEXT. You can try it out.

All you need to do now is recompile Sketcher and run it again. To open the text dialog, select the new toolbar button or the menu item and click in the view where you want the text to appear.

You just type the text that you want and click the OK button. The text will be displayed starting at the point in the view where you clicked the mouse button. You can draw text in any of the colors — just like the geometric elements. The application window may look something like that in Figure 20-9 when the text dialog is displayed.

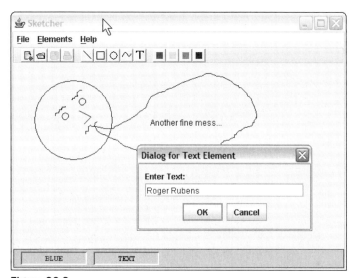

Figure 20-9

A Font Selection Dialog

You don't really want to be stuck with a 12-point SansSerif font. You need to be able to release your creativity so your sketches will astound and delight! A font dialog that pops up in response to a click on a suitable menu item should enable you to change the font for text elements to any of those available on the system. It will also give you a chance to see how you can get at and process the fonts that are available. You'll also learn more about how to add components to a dialog window. The first step is to establish what the font dialog will do.

You want to be able to choose the font name from those available on the system on which the application is executing. You'll also want to select the style of the font, whether plain, bold, or italic, as well as the point size. It would also be nice to see what a font looks like before you decide to use it. The dialog will therefore need to obtain a list of the fonts available and display them in a component. It will also need a component to allow the point size to be selected and some means for choosing the style for the font.

This is not going to be a wimpy pathetic excuse for a dialog like those you have seen so far. This is going to be a real chunky Java programmer's dialog. You'll drag in a diversity of components here, just for the experience, and you'll be building it step-by-step, as it involves quite a lot of code. Just so that you know where you're headed, the finished dialog is shown in Figure 20-10.

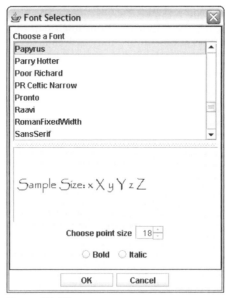

Figure 20-10

The component that provides the choice of font in the dialog is a Swing component of type `javax.swing.JList` that can display a list of any type of component. Below that is a panel holding a `JLabel` object, which displays a sample of the current font. The list of font names and the panel below are displayed in a split pane defined by the `JSplitPane` class. Here the pane is split vertically, but a `JSplitPane` object can also hold two panels side by side. The point size is displayed in another Swing component called a spinner, which is an object of type `javax.swing.JSpinner`. The choice for the font style options is provided by two radio buttons, and either, neither, or both may be selected. Finally, you have two buttons to close the dialog.

You can set the foundations by defining the `FontDialog` class with its data members and its constructor, and then build on that.

Try It Out   A FontDialog Class

The major work will be in the dialog class constructor. That will set up all the GUI elements as well as the necessary listeners to respond to operations with the dialog. The dialog object will need to know that the `SketchFrame` object that represents the Sketcher application window is the parent, so you'll pass a `SketchFrame` reference to the constructor.

Here's the code for the outline of the `FontDialog` class:

```
// Class to define a dialog to choose a font
import java.awt.Font;
import javax.swing.JDialog;

class FontDialog extends JDialog {
  // Constructor
  public FontDialog(SketchFrame window) {
    // Code to initialize the data members...

    // Code to create buttons and the button panel...

    // Code to create the data input panel...

    // Code to create the font choice and add it to the input panel...

    // Code to create the font size choice and add it to the input panel...

    // Code to create the font style checkboxes and add them to the input panel...

    // ...and then some!
  }
  private Font font;                          // Currently selected font
  private int fontStyle;                      // Font style - Plain,Bold,Italic
  private int fontSize;                       // Font point size
}
```

You'll be adding a few more data members shortly, but at least you know you'll need the three that are shown here. The code to initialize the data members within the `FontDialog` constructor is easy. You can initialize the `font` member and the associated `fontStyle` and `fontSize` members from the current font that is stored in the application window:

```
public FontDialog(SketchFrame window) {
  // Call the base constructor to create a modal dialog
  super(window, "Font Selection", true);

  font = window.getCurrentFont();           // Get the current font
  fontStyle = font.getStyle();              // ...style
  fontSize = font.getSize();                // ...and size

  // Plus the code for the rest of the constructor...
}
```

You call the base class constructor and pass the `window` object to it as the parent. The second argument is the title for the dialog, and the third argument determines that the dialog is modal. The `getCurrentFont()` method returns the font stored in the `window` object, and you use this to initialize the `fontStyle` and `fontSize` members; therefore, the first time you open the dialog this will be the default setting.

Creating the Font Dialog Buttons

Next you can add the code to the constructor that will create the button panel with the OK and Cancel buttons. You can place the button panel at the bottom of the content pane for the dialog using the default `BorderLayout` manager:

```
public FontDialog(SketchFrame window) {
  // Initialization as before...

  // Create the dialog button panel
  JPanel buttonPane = new JPanel();                  // Create a panel to hold buttons

  // Create and add the buttons to the buttonPane
  buttonPane.add(ok = createButton("OK"));           // Add the OK button
  buttonPane.add(cancel = createButton("Cancel"));   // Add the Cancel button
  getContentPane().add(buttonPane, BorderLayout.SOUTH);// Add pane to content pane

  // Plus the code for the rest of the constructor...
}
```

The `buttonPane` object will have a `FlowLayout` manager by default, so this will take care of positioning the buttons. You add the button pane to the dialog content pane using the `BorderLayout.SOUTH` specification to place it at the bottom of the window. Because creating each button involves several steps that are the same for both buttons, you are using a helper method, `createButton()`, that requires only the button label as an argument. You can see that you store each button reference in a class field, so you must add these as members of the `FontDialog` class:

```
private JButton ok;        // OK button
private JButton cancel;    // Cancel button
```

You'll use these fields in the listener for the button events, as you'll see in a moment.

You can code the `createButton()` method as a member of the `FontDialog` class as follows:

```
JButton createButton(String label) {
  JButton button = new JButton(label);             // Create the button
  button.setPreferredSize(new Dimension(80,20));   // Set the size
  button.addActionListener(this);                  // Listener is the dialog
  return button;                                   // Return the button
}
```

You set the preferred size of the button here to ensure that the buttons are all of the same size. Without this call, each button would be sized to fit its label, so the dialog would look a bit untidy. The listener is the `FontDialog` class object, so the `FontDialog` class must implement the `ActionListener` interface, which implies that an `actionPerformed()` method must be defined in the class:

```
import java.awt.Font;
import java.awt.BorderLayout;
import java.awt.Dimension;
import java.awt.event.ActionListener;
import java.awt.event.ActionEvent;
import javax.swing.JDialog;
```

```
import javax.swing.JButton;
import javax.swing.JPanel;
class FontDialog extends JDialog implements ActionListener {
  // Constructor definition...

  // createButton() definition...

  public void actionPerformed(ActionEvent e) {
    if(e.getSource()== ok)  {                        // Is it the OK button?
      ((SketchFrame)getOwner()).setCurrentFont(font); // Set the selected font
    }
    // Now hide the dialog - for ok or cancel
    setVisible(false);
  }
  // Plus the rest of the class definition...
}
```

The getSource() member of the ActionEvent object e returns a reference to the object that originated the event, so you can use this to determine the button for which the method is being called. You just compare the source object (which is holding the reference to the object to which the event applies) to the OK button object to determine whether it was clicked. If it is the OK button, you call the setCurrentFont() method in the SketchFrame object that is the parent for this dialog to set the font. You then just hide the dialog so Sketcher can continue. This will be the sole action when the Cancel button is selected for the dialog.

Of course, you must add the definition of setCurrentFont() to the SketchFrame class:

```
// Method to set the current font
public void setCurrentFont(Font font) {
  this.font = font;
}
```

Let's now get back to the FontDialog constructor.

Adding the Data Pane

You can now add a panel to contain the components that will receive input. You'll be using a JList object for the font names, a JSpinner object for the point size of the font, and two JRadioButton objects for selecting the font style. You can add the code to create the panel first:

```
public FontDialog(SketchFrame window) {
  // Initialization as before...
  // Button panel code as before...

  // Code to create the data input panel
  JPanel dataPane = new JPanel();                    // Create the data entry panel
  dataPane.setBorder(BorderFactory.createCompoundBorder(   // Create pane border
              BorderFactory.createLineBorder(Color.BLACK),
              BorderFactory.createEmptyBorder(5, 5, 5, 5)));
  GridBagLayout gbLayout = new GridBagLayout();       // Create the layout
  dataPane.setLayout(gbLayout);                       // Set the pane layout
  GridBagConstraints constraints = new GridBagConstraints();

  // Plus the code for the rest of the constructor...
}
```

Here you use a `GridBagLayout` manager so you can set constraints for each component that you add to the `dataPane` container. You also set a black line border for `dataPane` with an inset empty border 5 pixels wide. This uses the `BorderFactory` static methods that you have seen before. You have many other possible layout managers that you could use here. `BoxLayout` managers are very easy to use to lay out components in vertical columns and horizontal rows.

The first component that you'll add to `dataPane` will be a label that prompts for the font selection:

```
public FontDialog(SketchFrame window) {
    // Initialization as before...
    // Button panel code as before...
    // Set up the data input panel to hold all input components as before...

    // Code to create the font choice and add it to the input panel
    JLabel label = new JLabel("Choose a Font");
    constraints.fill = GridBagConstraints.HORIZONTAL;
    constraints.gridwidth = GridBagConstraints.REMAINDER;
    gbLayout.setConstraints(label, constraints);
    dataPane.add(label);

    // Plus the code for the rest of the constructor...
}
```

With the `fill` constraint set as `HORIZONTAL`, the components in a row will fill the width of the `dataPane` container, but without affecting the height. With the width constraint set to `REMAINDER`, the `label` component will fill the width of the row.

You need a few more `import` statements in the `FontDialog` source file, so add the following statements:

```
import java.awt.Color;
import java.awt.GridBagLayout;
import java.awt.GridBagConstraints;
import javax.swing.JLabel;
import javax.swing.BorderFactory;
```

Implementing the Font List

You'll add the `JList` object that displays the list of fonts next, but you won't add this directly to the `dataPane` panel because the list is likely to be long enough to need scrolling capability. The list of fonts will have to be obtained using the `GraphicsEnvironment` object that encapsulates information about the system in which the application is running. You'll recall that you call a `static` method in the `GraphicsEnvironment` class to get the `GraphicsEnvironment` object. Here's the code to create the list of font names:

```
public FontDialog(SketchFrame window) {
    // Initialization as before...

    // Button panel code as before...
    // Set up the data input panel to hold all input components as before...
    // Add the font choice prompt label as before...
```

```
        // Code to set up font list choice component
        GraphicsEnvironment e = GraphicsEnvironment.getLocalGraphicsEnvironment();
        String[] fontNames = e.getAvailableFontFamilyNames();  // Get the font names

        fontList = new JList(fontNames);                       // Create list of font names
        fontList.setValueIsAdjusting(true);                    // single event selection
        fontList.setSelectionMode(ListSelectionModel.SINGLE_SELECTION);// Choose 1 font
        fontList.setSelectedValue(font.getFamily(),true);
        fontList.addListSelectionListener(this);
        JScrollPane chooseFont = new JScrollPane(fontList);    // Scrollable list
        chooseFont.setMinimumSize(new Dimension(300,100));
        chooseFont.setWheelScrollingEnabled(true);             // Enable mouse wheel scroll

    // Plus the code for the rest of the constructor...
    }
```

You obtain the list of font family names for the system on which Sketcher is running by calling the `getAvailableFontFamilyNames()` method for the `GraphicsEnvironment` object. The `fontList` variable will need to be accessible in the method-handling events for the list, so this will be another data member of the class:

```
    private JList fontList;                                 // Font list
```

The `fontNames` array holds `String` objects, but you can create a `JList` object for any kind of object — images, for example. You can also create a `JList` object by passing a `Vector<>` object that contains the objects you want in the list to the constructor. It is possible to allow multiple entries from a list to be selected, in which case the selection process may cause multiple events — when you drag the cursor over several list items, for example. You can make certain that there is only one event for a selection, even though multiple items are selected, by calling the `setValueIsAdjusting()` method with the argument `true`. Calling `setSelectionMode()` with the argument `SINGLE_SELECTION` ensures that only one font name can be selected.

You have two possible multiple selections that you can enable for a `JList` object. Passing the value `SINGLE_INTERVAL_SELECTION` to the `setSelectionMode()` method allows a series of consecutive items to be selected. Passing `MULTIPLE_SELECTION_INTERVAL` provides you with total flexibility and allows any number of items anywhere to be selected. The initial selection in the list is set by the `setSelectedValue()` call. You pass the family name for the current font as the argument specifying the initial selection. There is a complementary method, `getSelectedValue()`, that you'll be using in the event handler.

There's a special kind of listener for `JList` selection events that is an object of a class type that implements the `ListSelectionListener` interface. Since you set the `FontDialog` object as the listener for the list in the call to the `addListSelectionListener()` method, you had better make sure the `FontDialog` class implements the interface:

```
    class FontDialog extends JDialog
                     implements ActionListener,              // For buttons etc.
                                ListSelectionListener {       // For list box
```

There's only one method in the `ListSelectionListener` interface, and you can implement it in the `FontDialog` class like this:

```
// List selection listener method
public void valueChanged(ListSelectionEvent e) {
  if(!e.getValueIsAdjusting()) {
    font = new Font((String)fontList.getSelectedValue(), fontStyle, fontSize);
    fontDisplay.setFont(font);
    fontDisplay.repaint();
  }
}
```

This method will be called when you select an item in the list. You have only one list, so you don't need to check which object was the source of the event. If you were handling events from several lists, you could call the `getSource()` method for the event object that is passed to `valueChanged()`, and compare it with the references to the `JList` objects being used.

The `ListSelectionEvent` object that is passed to the `valueChanged()` method contains records of the index positions of the list items that changed. You can obtain these as a range by calling the `getFirstIndex()` method for the event object to get the first in the range, and the `getLastIndex()` method will return the last in the range. You don't need to worry about any of this in the `FontDialog` class because you have disallowed multiple selections and you just want the newly selected item in the list.

You have to be careful though. Since you start out with an item already selected, selecting another font name from the list will cause two events — one for deselecting the original font name and the other for selecting the new name. You make sure that you deal only with the last event by calling the `getValueIsAdjusting()` method for the event object in the `if` expression. This returns `false` for the event when all changes due to a selection are complete, and `true` if things are still changing when the event occurred. Thus your implementation of the `valueChanged()` method will do nothing when the `getValueIsAdjusting()` method returns `true`.

Once you are sure nothing further is changing, which will be when `getValueIsAdjusting()` returns `false`, you retrieve the selected font name from the list by calling its `getSelectedValue()` method. The item is returned as type `Object` so you have to cast it to type `String` before using it. You create a new `Font` object using the selected family name and the current values for `fontStyle` and `fontSize`. You store the new font in the data member `font` and also call the `setFont()` member of a data member, `fontDisplay`, that you haven't added to the `FontDialog` class yet. This will be a `JLabel` object displaying a sample of the current font. After you've set the new font, you call `repaint()` for the label `fontDisplay` to get it redrawn.

> *If you allow multiple selections on the list with the* `SINGLE_SELECTION_INTERVAL` *method, you can use the* `getFirstIndex()` *and* `getLastIndex()` *methods to get the range of index values for the item that may have changed. If on the other hand you employ the* `MULTIPLE_SELECTION_INTERVAL` *option, you would need to figure out which items in the range were actually selected. You could do this by calling the* `getSelectedIndices()` *method or the* `getSelectedValues()` *method for the list object. The first of these returns an array of index values of type* int *for the selected items, and the second returns an array of elements of type* Object *that reference the selected items.*

A `JList` object doesn't support scrolling directly, but it is scrolling "aware." To get a scrollable list, one with scrollbars, you just need to pass the `JList` object to the `JScrollPane` constructor, as you have in the `FontDialog` constructor. A `JScrollPane` object creates a pane with scrollbars — either vertical, horizontal, or both — as necessary for whatever it contains. You set a minimum size for the `JScrollPane` object to limit how small it can be made in the split pane into which you'll insert it in a moment. Note how easy it is to get the mouse wheel supported for scrolling here. You just call the `setWheelScrollingEnabled()` method for the scroll pane with the argument as `true`, and it's done.

The new code that you've added requires a few more `import` statements:

```
import java.awt.GraphicsEnvironment;
import javax.swing.JList;
import javax.swing.ListSelectionModel;
import javax.swing.JScrollPane;
import javax.swing.event.ListSelectionListener;
import javax.swing.event.ListSelectionEvent;
```

Displaying the Selected Font

You'll display the selected font in a `JLabel` object that you'll place in another `JPanel` pane. Adding the following code to the constructor will do this:

```
public FontDialog(SketchFrame window) {
  // Initialization as before...
  // Button panel code as before...
  // Set up the data input panel to hold all input components as before...
  // Add the font choice prompt label as before...
  // Set up font list choice component as before...

    // Panel to display font sample
    JPanel display = new JPanel();
    fontDisplay = new JLabel("Sample Size: x X y Y z Z");
    fontDisplay.setPreferredSize(new Dimension(300,100));
    display.add(fontDisplay);

    // Plus the code for the rest of the constructor...
  }
```

You create the `JPanel` object `display` and add the `JLabel` object `fontDisplay` to it. Remember, you update this object in the `valueChanged()` handler for selections from the list of font names. You'll also be updating it when the font size or style is changed. The `fontDisplay` object just represents some sample text. You can choose something different if you like.

It's not strictly necessary here but just for the experience you'll use a split pane to hold the scroll pane containing the list, `chooseFont`, and the `display` panel.

Using a Split Pane

A `JSplitPane` object represents a pane with a movable horizontal or vertical split, so that it can hold two components. The split pane divider can be adjusted by dragging it with the mouse. Here's the code to do that:

```
public FontDialog(SketchFrame window) {
  // Initialization as before...
```

```
// Button panel code as before...
// Set up the data input panel to hold all input components as before...
// Add the font choice prompt label as before...
// Set up font list choice component as before...
// Panel to display font sample as before...

//Create a split pane with font choice at the top
// and font display at the bottom
JSplitPane splitPane = new JSplitPane(JSplitPane.VERTICAL_SPLIT,
                                      true,
                                      chooseFont,
                                      display);
gbLayout.setConstraints(splitPane, constraints);    // Split pane constraints
dataPane.add(splitPane);                             // Add to the data pane

// Plus the code for the rest of the constructor...
}
```

You'll need an `import` statement for `javax.swing.JSplitPane` in `FontDialog.java`.

The constructor does it all. The first argument specifies that the pane supports two components, one above the other. You can probably guess that for side-by-side components you would specify `JSplitPane.HORIZONTAL_SPLIT`. If the second constructor argument is `true`, the components are redrawn continuously as the divider is dragged. If it is `false` the components are not redrawn until you stop dragging the divider.

The third argument is the component to go at the top, or to the left for `HORIZONTAL_SPLIT`, and the fourth argument is the component to go at the bottom, or to the right, as the case may be.

You don't need to do it here, but you can change the components in a split pane. You have four methods to do this: `setLeftComponent()` *and* `setRightComponent()` *for a horizontal arrangement of the panes and* `setTopComponent()` *and* `setBottomComponent()` *for a vertical arrangement of the panes. You just pass a reference to the component you want to set to whichever method you want to use. There are also corresponding get methods to retrieve the components in a split pane. You can even change the orientation by calling the* `setOrientation()` *method and passing either* `JSplitPane.HORIZONTAL_SPLIT` *or* `JSplitPane.VERTICAL_SPLIT` *to it.*

There is a facility to provide a widget on the divider to collapse and restore either pane. You don't need it, but if you want to try this here, you can add the following statement after the `JSplitPane` constructor call:

```
splitPane.setOneTouchExpandable(true);
```

Calling this method with the argument as `false` will remove the widget.

Once you have created the `splitPane` object, you add it to the `dataPane` panel with constraints that make it fill the full width of the container.

Next you can add the font size selection mechanism.

Using a Spinner

You could use another list for this, but to broaden your horizons you'll use another Swing component, a `javax.swing.JSpinner` object. A `JSpinner` object displays a sequence of numbers or objects and the user can select any one from the set. The spinner displays up and down arrows at the side of the spinner for stepping through the list. You can also use the keyboard up and down arrow keys for this.

The sequence of choices in a spinner is managed by a `javax.swing.SpinnerModel` object. There are three concrete spinner model classes defined in the `javax.swing` package. The one you use depends on what sort of items you are choosing from:

Class	Description
SpinnerNumberModel	A model for a sequence of numbers. Numbers are stored internally and returned as type `Number`, which is the superclass of the classes encapsulating the primitive numerical types — `Integer`, `Long`, `Double`, etc. `Number` is also the superclass of other classes such as `BigDecimal`, but only the classes corresponding to the primitive types are supported.
SpinnerListModel	A model for a sequence defined by an array of objects of any type, or by a `java.util.List<>` object. You could use this to use a sequence of strings as the choices in the spinner.
SpinnerDateModel	A model for a sequence of dates specified as `java.util.Date` objects.

I won't be able to go through all the detail on these, so let's just take a `JSpinner` object using a `SpinnerNumberModel` class to contain the sequence, as that fits with selecting a font size.

You'll be using a fixed range of point sizes to choose from, so let's add some constants to the `SketcherConstants` class to define this:

```
public final static int pointSizeMin = 8;      // Minimum font point size
public final static int pointSizeMax = 24;     // Maximum font point size
public final static int pointSizeStep = 2;     // Point size step
```

Thus the smallest point size that can be chosen is 8, the largest is 24, and the step from 8 onwards is 2.

You create a `JSpinner` object by passing a `SpinnerModel` reference to it. For example:

```
JSpinner spinner = new JSpinner(spinnerModel);
```

In the font dialog, the spinner model will be of type `SpinnerNumberModel`, and the constructor you'll use to create the object expects four arguments: a current value that will be the one displayed initially, a minimum value, a maximum value, and the step size. Here's how you can create that for the font dialog:

```
public FontDialog(SketchFrame window) {
  // Initialization as before...
  // Button panel code as before...
```

```
// Set up the data input panel to hold all input components as before...
// Add the font choice prompt label as before...
// Set up font list choice component as before...
// Panel to display font sample as before...
// Create a split pane with font choice at the top as before...

// Set up the size choice using a spinner
JPanel sizePane = new JPanel();                  // Pane for size choices
label = new JLabel("Choose point size");         // Prompt for point size
sizePane.add(label);                             // Add the prompt

chooseSize = new JSpinner(new SpinnerNumberModel(fontSize,
                           pointSizeMin, pointSizeMax, pointSizeStep));
chooseSize.addChangeListener(this);  sizePane.add(chooseSize);

 // Add spinner to pane
gbLayout.setConstraints(sizePane, constraints);   // Set pane constraints
dataPane.add(sizePane);                           // Add the pane

// Plus the code for the rest of the constructor...
}
```

Add `import` statements for the two new class names you are referencing here and a static `import` statement for the constants in the `SketcherConstants` class:

```
import javax.swing.JSpinner;
import javax.swing.SpinnerNumberModel;
import static Constants.SketcherConstants.*;
```

You again create a panel to contain the spinner and its associated prompt, as it makes the layout easier. The default `FlowLayout` in the panel is fine for what you want. You had better add a couple more members to the `FontDialog` class to store the references to the `chooseSize` and `fontDisplay` objects:

```
private JSpinner chooseSize;              // Font size options
private JLabel fontDisplay;               // Font sample
```

A spinner generates an event of type `ChangeEvent` when an item is selected that will be sent to listeners of type `ChangeListener`. The listener for our spinner is the `FontDialog` object so you need to specify that it implements the `ChangeListener` interface:

```
class FontDialog extends JDialog
            implements ActionListener,           // For buttons etc.
                       ListSelectionListener,     // For list box
                       ChangeListener {           // For the spinner
```

The `ChangeListener` interface defines one method, `stateChanged()`, which has a parameter of type `ChangeEvent`. You obtain a reference to the source of the event by calling `getSource()` for the event object. You then need to cast the reference to the type of the source — in this case, `JSpinner`. For example, you could code it like this:

```
public void stateChanged(ChangeEvent e) {
  JSpinner source = (JSpinner)e.getSource();
  // ...plus code to deal with the spinner event for source...
}
```

Of course, you want the value that is now selected in the spinner, and the getValue() method will return a reference to this as type Object. Since you are using a SpinnerNumberModel object as the spinner model, the object encapsulating the value will actually be of type Number, so you can cast the reference returned by getValue() to this type. You can get a little closer to what you want by amending our stateChanged() method to:

```
public void stateChanged(ChangeEvent e) {
    Number value = (Number)((JSpinner)e.getSource()).getValue();
}
```

You're not really interested in a Number object though. What you want is the integer value it contains, so you can store it in the fontSize member of the dialog and then derive a new font. The intValue() method for the Number object will produce that. You can therefore arrive at the final version of setChanged() that does what you want:

```
public void stateChanged(ChangeEvent e) {
    fontSize = ((Number)(((JSpinner)e.getSource()).getValue())).intValue();
    font = font.deriveFont((float)fontSize);
    fontDisplay.setFont(font);
    fontDisplay.repaint();
}
```

That first statement looks quite daunting but since you put it together one step at a time, you should see that it isn't really difficult — there are just a lot of parentheses to keep in sync. You now need to add import statements for the ChangeListener interface and the ChangeEvent class:

```
import javax.swing.event.ChangeListener;
import javax.swing.event.ChangeEvent;
```

Using Radio Buttons to Select the Font Style

Two JRadioButton objects will provide the means for selecting the font style. One will select bold or not, and the other will select italic or not. A plain font is simply one that is neither bold nor italic. You could use JCheckBox objects here if you prefer — they would work just as well. Here's the code:

```
public FontDialog(SketchFrame window) {
    // Initialization as before...
    // Button panel code as before...
    // Set up the data input panel to hold all input components as before...
    // Add the font choice prompt label as before...
    // Set up font list choice component as before...
    // Panel to display font sample as before...
    // Create a split pane with font choice at the top as before...
    // Set up the size choice using a spinner as before...

    // Set up style options using radio buttons
    JRadioButton bold = new JRadioButton("Bold", (fontStyle & Font.BOLD) > 0);
    JRadioButton italic = new JRadioButton("Italic",
                                           (fontStyle & Font.ITALIC) > 0);
    bold.addItemListener(new StyleListener(Font.BOLD));    // Add button listeners
    italic.addItemListener(new StyleListener(Font.ITALIC));
    JPanel stylePane = new JPanel();                       // Create style pane
    stylePane.add(bold);                                   // Add buttons
    stylePane.add(italic);                                 // to style pane...
```

```
        gbLayout.setConstraints(stylePane, constraints);     // Set pane constraints
        dataPane.add(stylePane);                              // Add the pane

        getContentPane().add(dataPane, BorderLayout.CENTER);
        pack();
        setVisible(false);
    }
```

You can add another `import` statement, too:

```
    import javax.swing.JRadioButton;
```

It looks like a lot of code, but it's repetitive as you have two radio buttons. The second argument to the `JRadioButton` constructor sets the state of the button. If the existing style of the current font is BOLD and/or *ITALIC*, the initial states of the buttons will be set accordingly. You add a listener of type `StyleListener` for each button, and you'll add a definition for this type as an inner class to `FontDialog` in a moment. Note that you pass the style constant that corresponds to the set state of the button to the constructor for the listener.

The `stylePane` object presents the buttons using the default `FlowLayout` manager, and this pane is added as the last row to `dataPane`. The final step is to add the `dataPane` object as the central pane in the content pane for the dialog. The call to `pack()` lays out the dialog components with their preferred sizes if possible, and the `setVisible()` call with the argument `false` means that the dialog is initially hidden. Since this is a complex dialog, you won't want to create a new object each time you want to display the font dialog. You'll just call the `setVisible()` method for the dialog object with the argument `true` when you want to display it.

Listening for Radio Buttons

The inner class, `StyleListener`, in the `FontDialog` class will work on principles that you have seen before. A radio button (or a checkbox) generates events of type `java.awt.ItemEvent`, and the listener class must implement the `java.awt.ItemListener` interface:

```
    class StyleListener implements ItemListener {
      public StyleListener(int style) {
        this.style = style;
      }

      public void itemStateChanged(ItemEvent e) {
        if(e.getStateChange()==ItemEvent.SELECTED) { // If style was selected
          fontStyle |= style;                         // turn it on in the font style
        } else {
          fontStyle &= ~style;                        // otherwise turn it off
        }
        font = font.deriveFont(fontStyle);            // Get a new font
        fontDisplay.setFont(font);                    // Change the label font
        fontDisplay.repaint();                        // repaint
      }

      private int style;                              // Style for this listener
    }
```

The constructor accepts an argument that is the style for the button, so the value of the member, `style`, will be the value you want to set in the `fontStyle` member that you use to create a new `Font` object, either `Font.BOLD` or `Font.ITALIC`. Since the listener for a particular button already contains the corresponding style, the `itemStateChanged()` method that is called when an item event occurs just switches the value of `style` in the `fontStyle` member of `FontDialog` either on or off, depending on whether the radio button was selected or deselected. It then derives a font with the new style, sets it in the `fontDisplay` label, and repaints it.

This code calls for two more `import` statements in the `FontDialog` source file:

```
import java.awt.event.ItemListener;
import java.awt.event.ItemEvent;
```

You have now completed the `FontDialog` class. If you have been creating the code yourself, now would be a good time to try compiling the class to see what missing — `import` statements usually. All you need now is some code in the `SketchFrame` class to make use of it.

Try It Out   Using the Font Dialog

To get the font dialog operational in Sketcher, you'll add a new menu, Options, to the menu bar with a Choose font... menu item and install a listener for the menu item. To keeps things vaguely shipshape it would be best to add the fragments of code in the `SketchFrame` constructor in the places where you do similar things.

Create the Options menu with the following code in the `SketchFrame` constructor:

```
JMenu fileMenu = new JMenu("File");          // Create File menu
JMenu elementMenu = new JMenu("Elements");   // Create Elements menu
JMenu optionsMenu = new JMenu("Options");    // Create options menu
JMenu helpMenu = new JMenu("Help");          // Create Help menu

fileMenu.setMnemonic('F');                   // Create shortcut
elementMenu.setMnemonic('E');                // Create shortcut
optionsMenu.setMnemonic('O');                // Create shortcut
helpMenu.setMnemonic('H');                   // Create shortcut
```

You can add the menu item like this somewhere in the constructor:

```
// Add the font choice item to the options menu
fontItem = new JMenuItem("Choose font...");
fontItem.addActionListener(this);
optionsMenu.add(fontItem);
```

You can add a declaration for the `fontItem` member of the `SketchFrame` class by adding it to the existing declaration for the `aboutItem`, which is probably somewhere near the end in your file. It may take some hunting to find it with the amount of code you now have in this class:

```
private JMenuItem aboutItem, fontItem;
```

You need to add the Options menu to the menu bar before the Help menu to be consistent with convention:

```
menuBar.add(fileMenu);                      // Add the file menu
menuBar.add(elementMenu);                   // Add the element menu
menuBar.add(optionsMenu);                   // Add the options menu
```

You can create a `FontDialog` object by adding a statement to the end of the `SketchFrame` constructor:

```
fontDlg = new FontDialog(this);             // Create the font dialog
```

You can reuse the `FontDialog` object as often as you want. When you need to display it, you simply call its `setVisible()` method. Of course, you'll declare `fontDlg` as a member of the `SketchFrame` class:

```
private FontDialog fontDlg;                 // The font dialog
```

You can modify the `actionPerformed()` method in the `SketchFrame` class to handle the events for the new menu item:

```
public void actionPerformed(ActionEvent e) {
  if(e.getSource() == aboutItem) {

    // Create about dialog with the menu item as parent
    JOptionPane.showMessageDialog(this,                        // Parent
                     "Sketcher Copyright Ivor Horton 2000",// Message
                     "About Sketcher",                         // Title
                     JOptionPane.INFORMATION_MESSAGE);    // Message type
  } else if(e.getSource() == fontItem) {       // Set the dialog window position
    Rectangle bounds = getBounds();
    fontDlg.setLocation(bounds.x + bounds.width/3, bounds.y + bounds.height/3);
    fontDlg.setVisible(true);                  // Show the dialog
  }
}
```

The new `else if` block makes the dialog visible after setting its location in relation to the application window. You'll need an `import` statement for the `Rectangle` class name in the source file for `SketchFrame`:

```
import java.awt.Rectangle;
```

If you recompile Sketcher, you will be able to play with fonts to your heart's content. Figure 20-11 shows what I mean.

How It Works

This last piece is relatively trivial. The additional menu is added to the menu bar just like the other menus. The menu item is a `JMenuItem` object rather than an `Action` object and the `actionPerformed()` method is called when the Choose font... menu item is clicked. This sets the top-left corner of the dialog window one-third of the way in from the top and left sides of the application window. It then calls `setVisible()` for the dialog object to display it.

Figure 20-11

Pop-Up Menus

The `javax.swing` package defines the `JPopupMenu` class, which represents a menu that you can pop up at any position within a component, but conventionally you display it at the current mouse cursor position when a particular mouse button is pressed, usually button 2. There are two constructors in the `PopupMenu` class: one to which you pass a `String` object that defines a name for the menu, and a default constructor that defines a menu without a name. If you specify a name for a pop-up menu with a statement such as

```
generalPopup = new PopupMenu("General");
```

the name you supply is primarily for identification purposes and is not always displayed when the menu is popped up: it depends on your environment. Under MS Windows, for example, it doesn't appear. This is different from a menu on a menu bar where the string you pass to the constructor is what appears on the menu bar. Don't forget to add an `import` statement for `javax.swing.JPopupMenu`.

Let's add a pop-up menu to the `SketchFrame` class by adding a data member of type `JPopupMenu`:

```
private JPopupMenu popup = new JPopupMenu("General");        // Window pop-up
```

To populate a pop-up menu with menu items, you add JMenuItem objects by passing each of them to the add() method for the JPopupMenu object. If you're using Action objects because you also want to implement toolbar buttons, you can create the JMenuItem object using a constructor that accepts a reference of type Action and then pass it to the add() method for the pop-up menu object. You can also pass a String object to add(), which will create a JMenuItem object and add it to the pop-up. A reference to the menu item object is always returned by the various overloaded add() methods. Handling the events for the menu items is an identical process to that for regular menu items, and Action objects handle their own events, as you have seen.

You'll now add menu items to the pop-up that you have created as a member of a SketchFrame object by adding the following code to the SketchFrame class constructor:

```
// Create pop-up menu
popup.add(new JMenuItem(lineAction));
popup.add(new JMenuItem(rectangleAction));
popup.add(new JMenuItem(circleAction));
popup.add(new JMenuItem(curveAction));
popup.add(new JMenuItem(textAction));
popup.addSeparator();
popup.add(new JMenuItem(redAction));
popup.add(new JMenuItem(yellowAction));
popup.add(new JMenuItem(greenAction));
popup.add(new JMenuItem(blueAction));
```

This adds the element menu items to the pop-up. You might want to add the font choice menu item to the pop-up, but you must not try to add the same JMenuItem object to two different menus. You could either create an Action object that would pop up the font dialog and create two menu item objects from that, or you could create an independent menu item that did the same thing as the original when it was clicked and add that to the pop-up. The former approach would be better because a single Action object would handle events from either menu item.

Displaying a Pop-Up Menu

You can display a pop-up within the coordinate system of any component, by calling the show() method for the JPopupMenu object. The method requires three arguments to be specified: a reference to the parent component that is the context for the pop-up, and the x and y coordinates where the menu is to be displayed, relative to the origin of the parent. For example:

```
generalPopup.show(view, xCoord, yCoord);
```

This displays the pop-up at position (xCoord, yCoord) in the coordinate system for the component, view.

A pop-up menu is usually implemented as a **context menu**. The principal idea of a context menu is that it's not just a single menu: It displays a different set of menu items depending on the context — that is, what is under the mouse cursor when the button is clicked. The mouse button that you press to display a context menu is sometimes called a **pop-up trigger**, simply because pressing it triggers the display of the pop-up. On systems that support the notion of a pop-up trigger, the pop-up trigger is fixed, but it can be different between systems. It is usually the right mouse button on a two- or three-button mouse for right-handed users. On systems with a one-button mouse, you typically have to hold down a modifier key while pressing the mouse button to fire the pop-up trigger.

The `MouseEvent` class has a special method, `isPopupTrigger()`, that returns `true` when the event should display a pop-up menu. This method will return `true` only in the `mousePressed()` or `mouseReleased()` methods. It will always return `false` in methods corresponding to other mouse events. This method helps solve the problem of different mouse buttons being used on different systems to display a pop-up. If you use this method to decide when to display a pop-up, you've got them covered — well, almost. You would typically use this with the following code to display a pop-up:

```
public void mouseReleased(MouseEvent e) {
    if(e.isPopupTrigger()) {
        // Code to display the pop-up menu...
    }
}
```

I have shown conceptual code for the `mouseReleased()` method here. This would be fine for Windows, but unfortunately it may not work on some other systems — Solaris, for example. This is because in some operating system environments, the `isPopupTrigger()` returns `true` only when the button is pressed, not when it is released. The pop-up trigger is not just a particular button — it is a either a mouse-pressed event or a mouse-released event associated with a particular button. This implies that if you want your code to work on a variety of systems using the "standard" mouse button to trigger the pop-up in every case, you must implement the code to call `isPopupTrigger()` and pop the menu in both the `mousePressed()` and `mouseReleased()` methods. The method will return `true` only in one or the other. Of course, you could always circumvent this by ignoring convention and pop the menu for a specific button press with code like this:

```
if((e.getButton() == e.BUTTON3) {
    // Code to display the pop-up menu...
}
```

Now the pop-up would operate only with button 3, regardless of the convention for the underlying operating system, but the user may not be particularly happy about having to use a different pop-up trigger for your Java program compared to other applications on the same system.

Try It Out   Displaying a Pop-Up Menu

In Sketcher, the pop-up menu would sensibly operate in the area where the sketch is displayed — in other words, triggering the pop-up menu has to happen in the view. Assuming you have already added the code to `SketchFrame` that will create the pop-up menu as I discussed earlier, you just need to add a method to `SketchFrame` to make the pop-up available to the view:

```
// Retrieve the pop-up menu
public JPopupMenu getPopup() {
    return popup;
}
```

Now a `SketchView` object can get a reference to the pop-up in the `SketchFrame` object by using the application object to get to this method.

To maintain proper cross-platform operation for Sketcher, you'll implement the pop-up triggering in both the mousePressed() and the mouseReleased() methods. To make it easier, you can implement the processing of the pop-up trigger event in a separate method in the MouseHandler inner class to SketchView:

```
// Process pop-up trigger event
public void processPopupTrigger(MouseEvent e) {
  start = e.getPoint();                  // Save the cursor position in start
  theApp.getWindow().getPopup().show((Component)e.getSource(),
                                            start.x, start.y);

  start = null;
}
```

The response to the event is to display the pop-up menu at the position defined by start. You obtain a reference to the JPopupMenu object from the application window object, which you access via the application object reference that is stored in the view. You then call the show() method for the pop-up menu object, passing a reference to the source of the event as the parent. Note that the method retrieves the cursor position from the MouseEvent object. You could use the position stored in start by the mousePressed() method, but if the event is associated with the mouse released event and the user drags the cursor before releasing the button, the menu will appear at a different position from where the button is released.

Here's how mousePressed() should be implemented in the MouseHandler inner class to SketchView:

```
public void mousePressed(MouseEvent e)  {
  if(e.isPopupTrigger()) {
    processPopupTrigger(e);
  } else if((button1Down = (e.getButton() == MouseEvent.BUTTON1)) &&
                   (theApp.getWindow().getElementType() != TEXT)) {
    start = e.getPoint();                  // Save the cursor position in start
    g2D = (Graphics2D)getGraphics();               // Get graphics context
    g2D.setXORMode(getBackground());               // Set XOR mode
  }
}
```

The method checks for a pop-up trigger event. If that's what it is, the method calls the processPopupTrigger() method to handle the event. If it's not the pop-up trigger event, things process exactly as before. The cursor position is now retrieved from the event object inside the body of the second if statement.

Implementing the mouseReleased() method is just as easy:

```
public void mouseReleased(MouseEvent e) {
  if(e.isPopupTrigger()) {
    processPopupTrigger(e);
  } else if(button1Down = (e.getButton()==MouseEvent.BUTTON1) &&
                   (theApp.getWindow().getElementType() != TEXT)) {
    button1Down = false;                  // Reset the button 1 flag

    if(tempElement != null) {             // If there is an element...
      theApp.getModel().add(tempElement);  // ...add it to the model...
      tempElement = null;                  // ...and reset the field
```

```
        }
        if(g2D != null) {                    // If there's a graphics context
          g2D.dispose();                     // ...release the resource...
          g2D = null;                        // ...and reset field to null
        }
        start = last = null;                 // Remove the points
      }
    }
```

If you recompile Sketcher and run it again, the pop-up menu should appear in response to a right-button click, or whatever button triggers a context menu on your system. The way it looks on my system is shown in Figure 20-12.

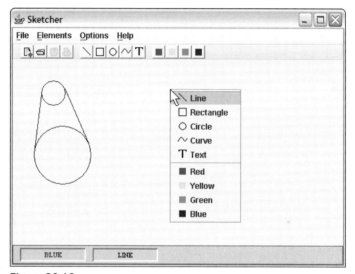

Figure 20-12

Note how you get the icons and the label for each of the menu items. This is because both are defined in the Action objects that were used to generate the menu, and they have not been set to null by calling the setIcon() method for the menu items.

How It Works

The isPopupTrigger() method for the MouseEvent object returns true when the button corresponding to a context menu is pressed or released. In this case you call the processPopupTrigger() method that you implemented to display the pop-up menu. When you click on a menu item in the pop-up, or click elsewhere, the pop-up menu is automatically hidden. Now any element type or color is a couple of clicks away.

This is just a pop-up menu, not a context menu. A context menu should be different depending on what's under the cursor. You'll now look more closely at how you could implement a proper context menu capability in Sketcher.

Implementing a Context Menu

As a context menu displays a different menu depending on the context, it follows that the program needs to know what is under the cursor at the time the pop-up trigger button is pressed. Let's take the specific instance of the view in Sketcher where you are listening for mouse events. You could define two contexts for the cursor in the view — one when an already drawn element is under the cursor and another when there is no element under the cursor. In the first context, you could display a special pop-up menu that provides operations that apply specifically to the element under the cursor — with menu items to delete or move the element, for example. In the second context, when there is no element under the cursor, you could display the pop-up menu that you created in the previous example. The context menu that will be displayed when an element is under the cursor is going to look like that shown in Figure 20-13.

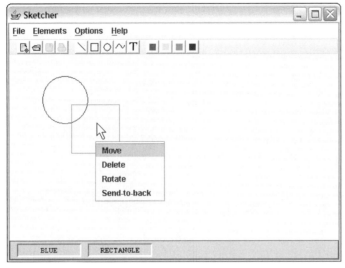

Figure 20-13

That's where you're headed, but there are a few bridges to be crossed on the way. For starters, if the context menu is to be really useful, users will need to know which element is under the cursor before they pop up the context menu, otherwise they can't be sure to which element the pop-up menu operations will apply, particularly when elements overlap on the screen. Deleting the wrong element could be irritating to say the least.

What you need is some visual feedback to show when an element is under the cursor — highlighting the element under the cursor by changing its color, for example.

Try It Out   Highlighting an Element

You could draw an element in magenta rather than its normal color to highlight that it's the one under the mouse cursor. Every element will need a `boolean` field to indicate whether it is highlighted or not so the object will know which color to use in the `draw()` method when drawing the element You can add this variable as a field in the `Element` class:

```
protected boolean highlighted = false;          // Highlight flag
```

You can add this line immediately following the statement for the other data members in the `Element` class definition. The `highlighted` field will be inherited by all of the subclasses of `Element`.

You'll need a method to set the `highlighted` flag in the `Element` class:

```
// Set or reset highlight color
public void setHighlighted(boolean highlighted) {
    this.highlighted = highlighted;
}
```

This method will also be inherited by all of the subclasses of `Element`.

To implement the basis for getting highlighting to work, you need to change one line in the `draw()` method for each of the subclasses of `Element` — that is, `Element.Line`, `Element.Circle`, `Element.Curve`, `Element.Rectangle`, and `Element.Text`. The line to change is the one that sets the drawing color — it's the first line in each of the `draw()` methods. You should change it to:

```
g2D.setPaint(highlighted ? Color.MAGENTA : color);
```

Now each element can potentially be highlighted.

How It Works

The `setHighlighted()` method accepts a `boolean` value as an argument and stores it in the data member `highlighted`. When you want an element to be highlighted, you just call this method with the argument as `true`. To switch highlighting off for an element, you call this method with the argument `false`.

Previously, the `setPaint()` statement just set the color stored in the data member `color` as the drawing color. Now, if `highlighted` is `true`, the color will be set to magenta, and if `highlighted` is `false`, the color stored in the data member `color` will be used.

To make use of highlighting to provide the visual feedback necessary for a user-friendly implementation of the context menu, you need to determine at all times what is under the cursor. This means you must track and analyze all mouse moves *all the time*!

Tracking Mouse Moves

Whenever the mouse is moved, the `mouseMoved()` method in the `MouseMotionListener` interface is called. You can therefore track mouse moves by implementing this method in the `MouseHandler` class, which is an inner class to the `SketchView` class. Before I get into that, I need to define what I mean by an element being under the cursor, and more crucially, how you are going to find out to which element, if any, this applies.

It's not going to be too difficult. You can arbitrarily decide that an element is under the cursor when the cursor position is inside the bounding rectangle for an element. This is not too precise a method, but it has the great attraction that it is extremely simple. Precise hit-testing on an element would carry considerably more processing overhead. Electing to add any greater complexity will not help you to understand the principles here, so you'll stick with the simple approach.

So what is going to be the methodology for finding the element under the cursor? Brute force basically: Whenever the mouse is moved, you can just search through the bounding rectangles for each of the elements in the model until you find one that encloses the current cursor position. You'll then arrange for the first element that you find to be highlighted. If you check all the elements in the model without finding a bounding rectangle that encloses the cursor, then there isn't an element under the cursor. The mechanism for the various geometric elements is illustrated in Figure 20-14.

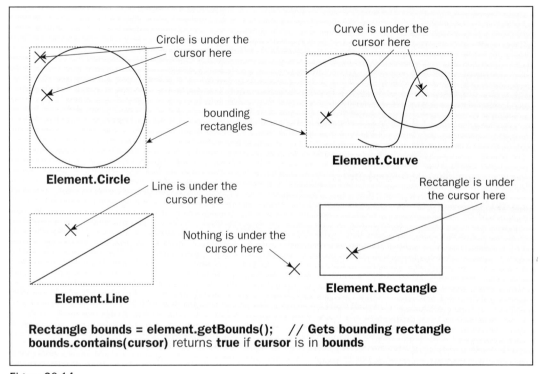

Circle is under the cursor here

Curve is under the cursor here

bounding rectangles

Element.Curve

Element.Circle

Line is under the cursor here

Rectangle is under the cursor here

Nothing is under the cursor here

Element.Line

Element.Rectangle

Rectangle bounds = element.getBounds();   // Gets bounding rectangle
bounds.contains(cursor) returns **true** if **cursor** is in **bounds**

Figure 20-14

To record a reference to the element that is under the cursor, you'll add a data member of type `Element` to the `SketchView` class. If there isn't an element under the cursor, you'll make sure that this data member is `null`.

Try It Out   Referring to Elements

Add the following statement after the statement that declares the `theApp` data member in the `SketchView` class definition:

```
    private Element highlightElement;                        // Highlighted element
```

The `mouseMoved()` method is going to be called very frequently, so you must make sure it executes as quickly as possible. This means that for any given set of conditions, you execute the minimum amount of code. Here's the implementation of the `mouseMoved()` method in the `MouseHandler` class in `SketchView`:

```
// Handle mouse moves
public void mouseMoved(MouseEvent e) {
  Point currentCursor = e.getPoint();   // Get current cursor position

  for(Element element : theApp.getModel())  {  // Go through the list
    if(element.getBounds().contains(currentCursor)) { // Under the cursor?
      if(element==highlightElement) {          // If it's already highlighted
        return;                                // we are done
      }
      // The element under the cursor is not highlighted
      g2D = (Graphics2D)getGraphics();         // Get graphics context

      // Un-highlight any old highlighted element
      if(highlightElement!=null)   {           // If an element is highlighted
        highlightElement.setHighlighted(false);// un-highlight it and
        highlightElement.draw(g2D);            // draw it normal color
      }

      element.setHighlighted(true);            // Set highlight for new element
      highlightElement = element;              // Store new highlighted element
      element.draw(g2D);                       // Draw it highlighted
      g2D.dispose();                           // Release graphic context resources
      g2D = null;
      return;
    }
  }

  // Here there is no element under the cursor so...
  if(highlightElement!=null)   {           // If an element is highlighted
    g2D = (Graphics2D)getGraphics();       // Get graphics context
    highlightElement.setHighlighted(false);// ...turn off highlighting
    highlightElement.draw(g2D);            // Redraw the element
    highlightElement = null;               // No element highlighted
    g2D.dispose();                         // Release graphic context resources
    g2D = null;
  }
}
```

To check that highlighting works, recompile Sketcher and run it again. If you draw a few elements, you should see them change color as the cursor moves over them.

How It Works

This method is a fair amount of code so let's work through it step by step. The first statement saves the current cursor position in the local variable `currentCursor`. You use a collection-based `for` loop to iterate over all the elements in the model. In the loop, you obtain the bounding rectangle for each element by calling its `getBounds()` method, and then call the `contains()` method for the rectangle that is returned with the current cursor position as the argument. This will return `true` if the rectangle encloses the point, and `false` if it doesn't. When you find an element under the cursor, it is quite possible that the element is already highlighted because the element was found the last time the `mouseMoved()` method was called. This will occur when you move the cursor within the rectangle bounding an element. In this case you don't need to do anything, so you return from the method.

If the element found is not the same as last time, you obtain a graphics context object for the view because you definitely need it to draw the new element you have found under the cursor in the highlight color. You then check that the variable highlightElement is not null — it will be null if the cursor newly entered the rectangle for an element and previously none were highlighted. If highlightElement is not null, you must restore the normal color to the old element before you highlight the new one. To do this you call its setHighlighted() method with the argument false, and then call its draw() method. You don't need to involve the paint() method for the view here since you are not adding or removing elements — you are simply redrawing an element that is already displayed. To highlight the new element, you call its setHighlighted() method with the argument true, and then store a reference to the element in highlightElement and call its draw() method to get it drawn in the highlight color. Finally, you release the graphics context resources by calling the dispose() method for g2D, set the variable back to null, and return.

The next block of code in the method executes if you exit the for loop because no element is under the cursor. In this case you must check if there was an element highlighted last time around. If there was, you un-highlight it, redraw it in its normal color, and reset highlightElement to null.

Defining the Other Context Menu

You already have the menu defined in SketchFrame for when the cursor is not over an element. It's sensible to keep it there because the menu items are a subset of those from the application windows menus. The context menu when the cursor is over an element will have a new set of menu items, specific to operating on individual elements, so it can be defined in the view. All you need is the code to define the new context menu — plus the code to decide which menu to display when isPopupTrigger() returns true for a mouse event.

You already know that you will have four menu items in the element context menu:

❑ **Move** — This moves the element under the cursor to a new position. This operation works by dragging it with the left mouse button down (button 1).

❑ **Delete** — This operation will delete the element under the cursor.

❑ **Rotate** — This operation will allow you to rotate the element under the cursor about the top-left corner of its bounding rectangle by dragging it while holding button 1 (normally the left mouse button) down.

❑ **Send-to-back** — This operation overcomes the problem of an element not being accessible, never highlighted that is, because it is masked by the bounding rectangle of another element.

Since you highlight an element by searching the list from the beginning, an element towards the end may never be highlighted if the rectangle for an earlier element completely encloses it. Moving the earlier element that is hogging the highlighting to the end of the list will allow the formerly masked element to be highlighted, so this is what the Send-to-back operation will do.

Try It Out   Creating Context Menus

First, add the data members to the SketchView class that will store the element pop-up reference and the JMenuItem objects that will be the pop-up menu items:

```
private JPopupMenu elementPopup = new JPopupMenu("Element");
private JMenuItem moveItem, deleteItem, rotateItem, sendToBackItem;
```

You must also add `import` statements for `JPopupMenu` and `JMenuItem`:

```
import javax.swing.JPopupMenu;
import javax.swing.JMenuItem;
```

You can create the `elementPopup` context menu in the `SketchView` constructor:

```
public SketchView(Sketcher theApp) {
    this.theApp = theApp;
    MouseHandler handler = new MouseHandler();       // create the mouse listener
    addMouseListener(handler);                       // Listen for button events
    addMouseMotionListener(handler);                 // Listen for motion events

    // Add the pop-up menu items
    moveItem = elementPopup.add(new JMenuItem("Move"));
    deleteItem = elementPopup.add(new JMenuItem("Delete"));
    rotateItem = elementPopup.add(new JMenuItem("Rotate"));
    sendToBackItem = elementPopup.add(new JMenuItem("Send-to-back"));

    // Add the menu item listeners
    moveItem.addActionListener(this);
    deleteItem.addActionListener(this);
    rotateItem.addActionListener(this);
    sendToBackItem.addActionListener(this);
}
```

You add the menu items using the `add()` method that accepts a `JMenuItem` argument, and returns a reference to the `JMenuItem` object that it creates. You create each `JMenuItem` object in the expression that is the argument to the `add()` method. You then use the references to the `JMenuItem` objects to add the view object as the listener for all the menu items in the pop-up.

You must make the `SketchView` class implement the `ActionListener` interface:

```
class SketchView extends JComponent
                 implements Observer, ActionListener {
```

You can add to `SketchView` the `actionPerformed()` method, which will handle action events from the menu items:

> **As with the new data members above, be careful to add this to the `SketchView` class and not inside the inner `MouseHandler` class by mistake!**

```
// Handle context menu events
public void actionPerformed(ActionEvent e ) {
  Object source = e.getSource();
  if(source == moveItem) {
    // Process a move...

  } else if(source == deleteItem) {
    // Process a delete...

  } else if(source == rotateItem) {
```

```
          // Process a rotate

      } else if(source == sendToBackItem) {
        // Process a send-to-back...
      }
   }
```

Of course, you'll need two more `import` statements in the `SketchView.java` file:

```
import java.awt.event.ActionEvent;
import java.awt.event.ActionListener;
```

To pop the menu you need to modify the code in the `processPopupTrigger()` method of the `MouseHandler` inner class a little:

```
public void processPopupTrigger(MouseEvent e) {
    start = e.getPoint();                      // Save the cursor position in start
    if(highlightElement == null) {
      theApp.getWindow().getPopup().show((Component)e.getSource(),
                                                      start.x, start.y);
    } else {
      elementPopup.show((Component)e.getSource(), start.x, start.y);
    }
    start = null;
}
```

This just adds an `if-else` to display the element dialog when an element is highlighted. If you recompile Sketcher you should get a different context menu depending on whether an element is under the cursor or not.

How It Works

The `processPopupTrigger()` method in the `MouseHandler` inner class now pops one or other of the two pop-ups you have, depending on whether the reference in `highlightElement` is `null` or not. The `processPopupTrigger()` method will be called either by the `mousePressed()` method or the `mouseReleased()` method, depending on how the pop-up trigger is defined in your environment. You can select items from the general pop-up to set the color or the element type, but the element pop-up menu does nothing at present. It just needs a few lines of code somewhere to do moves and rotations and stuff. Don't worry—it'll be like falling off a log—but not so painful.

Deleting Elements

Let's take the easiest one first—deleting an element. All that's involved here is calling `remove()` for the model object from the `actionPerformed()` method in `SketchView`. Let's give it a try.

Try It Out   Deleting Elements

The code you need to add to `actionPerformed()` in the `SketchView` class looks like this:

```
public void actionPerformed(ActionEvent e) {
    Object source = e.getSource();
```

```
    if(source == moveItem) {
      // Process a move...

    } else if(source == deleteItem) {
      if(highlightElement != null) {            // If there's an element
        theApp.getModel().remove(highlightElement);   // then remove it
        highlightElement = null;                // Remove the reference
      }
    } else if(source == rotateItem) {
      // Process a rotate
    } else if(source == sendToBackItem) {
      // Process a send-to-back...
    }
  }
}
```

This is a cheap operation requiring only six lines. Recompile, create a few elements, and then watch them disappear before your very eyes with a right button click.

How It Works

After verifying in the `actionPerformed()` method that `highlightElement` is not `null`, you call the `remove()` method that you added in the `SketchModel` class way back. This will delete the element from the list, so when the view is repainted, it will no longer be displayed. The repaint occurs automatically because the `update()` method for the view — the method that you implemented for the `Observer` interface — will be called because the model has changed. Of course, you must remember to set `highlightElement` to `null` too; otherwise, it could get drawn by a mouse handler even though it is no longer in the model.

Let's do another easy one — send-to-back.

Implementing the Send-to-Back Operation

The send-to-back operation is really an extension of the delete operation. You can move an element from wherever it is in the list by deleting it and then adding it again at the end of the list.

Try It Out   **The Send-to-Back Operation**

The `actionPerformed()` method in the `SketchView` class has the job of removing the highlighted element from wherever it is in the model and then adding it back at the end:

```
public void actionPerformed(ActionEvent e) {
  Object source = e.getSource();
  if(source == moveItem) {
    // (Process a move...)

  } else if(source == deleteItem) {
    // Code as inserted here earlier...

  } else if(source == rotateItem) {
    // (Process a rotate)

  } else if(source == sendToBackItem) {
```

```
        if(highlightElement != null) {
          theApp.getModel().remove(highlightElement);
          theApp.getModel().add(highlightElement);
          highlightElement.setHighlighted(false);
          highlightElement = null;
          repaint();
        }
      }
    }
```

A little harder this time — eight lines of code. You can try this by drawing a few concentric circles, with the outermost drawn first. An outer circle will prevent an inner circle from being highlighted, but applying send-to-back to the outer circle will make the inner circle accessible.

How It Works

This uses the `remove()` method in `SketchModel` to remove the highlighted element, and then calls the `add()` method to put it back — it will automatically be added to the end of the elements in the list. You switch off the highlighting of the element to indicate that it's gone to the back of the queue, and reset `highlightElement` back to `null`. You call `repaint()` for the view object to get the highlighted element that you have reset drawn in its normal color.

You have run out of easy operations. You must now deal with a not quite so easy one — the move operation. To handle this you must look into a new topic — transforming the user coordinate system. If you are not of a mathematical bent, some of what I'll discuss here can sound complicated. But even if your math is very rusty, you should not have too many problems. Like a lot of things, it's the unfamiliarity of the jargon that makes it seem more difficult than it is.

Transforming the User Coordinate System

I said when you started learning how to draw on a component that the drawing operations are specified in a user coordinate system, and the user coordinates are converted to a device coordinate system. The conversion of coordinates from the user system to the device system is taken care of by the methods in the graphics context object that you use to do the drawing, and they do this by applying a **transformation** to the user coordinates. The term *transformation* refers to the computational operations that perform the conversion.

By default, the origin, the (0, 0) point in the user coordinate system, corresponds to the (0, 0) point in the device coordinate system. The axes are also coincident, too, with positive *x* heading from left to right, and positive *y* from top to bottom. However, you can move the origin of the user coordinate system relative to its default position. Such a move is called a **translation**, and this is illustrated in Figure 20-15.

A fixed value, `deltaX`, say, is added to each *x* coordinate, and another value, `deltaY`, say, is added to every *y* coordinate, and the effect of this is to move the origin of the user coordinate system relative to the device coordinate system: Everything will be shifted to the right and down compared to where it would have been without the translation. Of course, the `deltaX` and `deltaY` values can be negative, in which case it would shift things to the left and up.

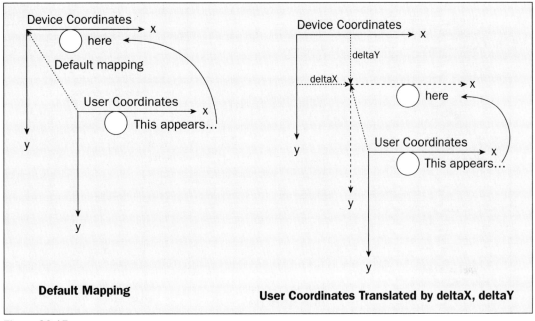

Figure 20-15

A translation is one kind of **affine transformation**. (*Affine* is a funny word. Some say it goes back to Laurel and Hardy where Ollie says, "This is affine mess you've got us into," but I don't subscribe to that.) An affine transformation is actually a linear transformation that leaves straight lines still straight and parallel lines still parallel. As well as translations, there are other kinds of affine transformation that you can define:

❑ **Rotation** — The user coordinates system is rotated through a given angle about its origin.

❑ **Scale** — The *x* and *y* coordinates are each multiplied by a scaling factor, and the multipliers for *x* and *y* can be different. This enables you to enlarge or reduce something in size. If the scale factor for one coordinate axis is negative, then objects will be reflected in the other axis. Setting the scale factor for *x* coordinates to –1, for example, will make all positive coordinates negative and vice versa, so everything is reflected in the *y* axis.

❑ **Shear** — This is perhaps a less familiar operation. It adds to each *x* coordinate a value that depends on the *y* coordinate, and adds to each *y* coordinate a value that depends on the *x* coordinate. You supply two values to specify a shear, sX and sY, say, and they change the coordinates in the following way:

Each *x* coordinate becomes (x + sX * y)

Each *y* coordinate becomes (y + sY * x)

The effect of this can be visualized most easily if you first imagine a rectangle that is drawn normally. A shearing transform can squash it by tilting the sides—rather like when you flatten a carton—but keep opposite sides straight and parallel. Figure 20-16 illustrates the three affine transformations that I've just described.

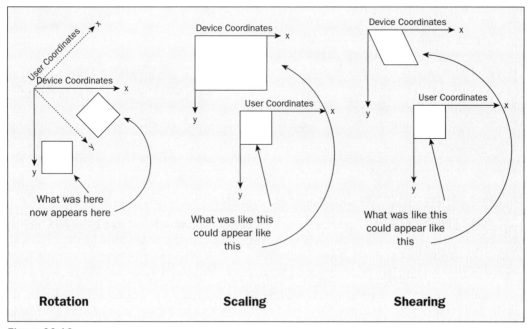

Figure 20-16

Figure 20-16 shows:

❑ A rotation of -π/4 radians, which is the same as a rotation of –45 degrees. Rotation angles are expressed in radians, and a positive angle rotates everything from the positive x-axis toward the positive y-axis—therefore clockwise. The rotation in the illustration is negative and therefore counterclockwise.

❑ A scaling transformation corresponding to an x scale of 2.5 and a y scale of 1.5

❑ A shearing operation where only the x coordinates have a shear factor. The factor for the y coordinates is 0 so they are unaffected, and the transformed shape is the same height as the original.

The AffineTransform Class

In Java, the AffineTransform class in the java.awt.geom package represents an affine transformation. Every Graphics2D graphics context has one. The default AffineTransform object in a graphics context is the **identity transform**, which leaves user coordinates unchanged. It is applied to the user coordinate system anyway for everything you draw, but all the coordinates for an entity that is displayed are unaltered by default. You can retrieve a copy of the current transform for a graphics context object by calling its getTransform() method. For example:

```
AffineTransform at = g2D.getTransform();     // Get current transform
```

While this retrieves a copy of the current transform for a graphics context, you can also replace it by another transform object:

```
g2D.setTransform(at);
```

You can retrieve the transform currently in effect with `getTransform()`, set it to some other operation before you draw some shapes, and then restore the original transform later with `setTransform()` when you're finished. The fact that `getTransform()` returns a reference to a copy, rather than a reference to the original transform object, is important. It means you can alter the existing transform and then restore the copy later.

Although the default transform object for a graphics context leaves everything unchanged, you could set it to do something by calling one of its member functions. All of these have a return type of `void`, so none of them return anything:

Transform Default	Description

setToTranslation(
    double deltaX,
    double deltaY)
	This method makes the transform a translation of `deltaX` in x and `deltaY` in y. This replaces whatever the previous transform was for the graphics context. You could apply this to the transform for a graphics context with the statements:
	
	`// Save current transform and set a new one`
	
	`AffineTransform at = g2D.getTransform();`
	
	`at.setToTranslation(5.0, 10.0);`
	
	The effect of the new transform will be to shift everything that is drawn in the graphics context g2D 5.0 to the right and down by 10.0. This will apply to everything that is drawn in g2D subsequent to the statement that sets the new transform.

setToRotation(double angle)	You call this method for a transform object to make it a rotation of `angle` radians about the origin. This replaces the previous transform. To rotate the axes 30 degrees clockwise, you could write: `g2D.getTransform().setToRotation(30*Math.PI/180);` This statement gets the current transform object for g2D and sets it to be the rotation specified by the expression `30*Math.PI/180`. Since (radians is 180 degrees, this expression produces the equivalent of 30 degrees measured in radians.

Table continued on following page

Transform Default	Description

setToRotation(
      double angle,
      double deltaX,
      double deltaY)
	This method defines a rotation of `angle` radians about the point `deltaX, deltaY`. It is equivalent to three successive transform operations — a translation by `deltaX, deltaY`, then a rotation through angle radians about the new position of the origin, and then a translation back by `-deltaX, -deltaY` to restore the previous origin point.
	
	 You could use this to draw a shape rotated about the shape's reference point. For example, if the reference point for a shape were at `shapeX, shapeY`, you could draw the shape rotated through (/3 radians with the following:
	
	 `g2D.getTransform().setToRotation(Math.PI/3,`
	
	 `shapeX, shapeY);`
	
	 `// Draw the shape...`
	
	 The coordinate system has been rotated about the point `shapeX, shapeY` and will remain so until you change the transformation in effect. You would probably want to restore the original transform after drawing the shape rotated.

setToScale(
      double scaleX,
      double scaleY)
	This method sets the transform object to scale the *x* coordinates by `scaleX`, and the *y* coordinates by `scaleY`. To draw everything half scale you could set the transformation with the following statement:
	
	 `g2D.getTransform().setToScale(0.5, 0.5);`

setToShear(
      double shearX,
      double shearY)
	The *x* coordinates are converted to x+shearX*y, and the *y* coordinates are converted to y+shearY*x.

All of the methods that I've discussed here replace the transform in an `AffineTransform` object. You can modify the existing transform object in a graphics context, too.

Modifying the Transformation for a Graphics Context

Modifying the current transform for a `Graphics2D` object involves calling a method for the `Graphics2D` object. The effect in each case is to *add* whatever transform you are applying to whatever the transform did before. You can add each of the four kinds of transforms that I discussed before by using the following methods that are defined in the `Graphics2D` class:

```
translate(double deltaX, double deltaY)
translate(int deltaX, int deltaY)
rotate(double angle)
rotate(double angle, double deltaX, double deltaY)
```

```
scale(double scaleX, double scaleY)
shear(double shearX, double shearY)
```

Each of these adds or **concatenates** the transform specified to the existing transform object for a `Graphics2D` object. Therefore, you can cause a translation of the coordinate system followed by a rotation about the new origin position with the following statements:

```
g2D.translate(5, 10);              // Translate the origin
g2D.rotate(Math.PI/3);             // Clockwise rotation 60 degrees
g2D.draw(line);                    // Draw in translate and rotated space
```

Of course, you can apply more than two transforms to the user coordinate system — as many as you like. However, it is important to note that the order in which you apply the transforms matters. To see why, look at the example shown in Figure 20-17.

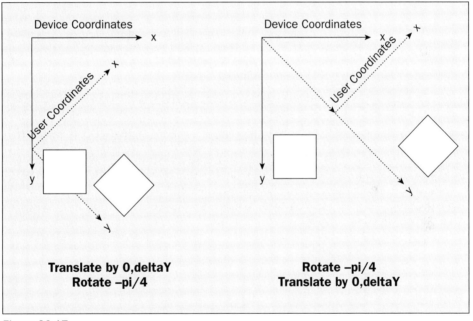

Figure 20-17

This shows just two transforms in effect, but it should be clear that the sequence in which they are applied makes a big difference. This is because the second transform is always applied relative to the new position of the coordinate system after the first transform has been applied. If you need more convincing that the order in which you apply transforms matters, you can apply some transforms to yourself. Stand with your back to any wall in the room. Now apply a translation — take three steps forward. Next apply a rotation — turn through 45 degrees clockwise. Make a mental note of where you are. If you now go back and stand with your back to the wall in the original position and first turn through 45 degrees before you take the three steps forward, you will clearly be in quite a different place in the room from the first time around.

Next on your affine tour — how you can create completely new `AffineTransform` objects.

Creating AffineTransform Objects

Of course, there are constructors for `AffineTransform` objects: the default "identity" constructor and a number of other constructors, but I don't have space to go into them here. The easiest way to create transform objects is to call a `static` member of the `AffineTransform` class. There are four static methods corresponding to the four kinds of transforms that I discussed earlier:

```
getTranslateInstance(double deltaX, double deltaY)
getRotateInstance(double angle)
getScaleInstance(double scaleX, double scaleY)
getShearInstance(double shearX, double shearY)
```

Each of these returns an `AffineTransform` object containing the transform that you specify by the arguments. To create a transform to rotate the user space by 90 degrees, you could write:

```
AffineTransform at = AffineTransform.getRotateInstance(Math.PI/2);
```

Once you have an `AffineTransform` object, you can apply it to a graphics context by passing it as an argument to the `setTransform()` method. It has another use, too: You can use it to transform a Shape object. The `createTransformedShape()` method for the `AffineTransform` object does this. Suppose you define a `Rectangle` object with the following statement:

```
Rectangle rect = new Rectangle(10, 10, 100, 50);
```

You now have a rectangle that is 100 wide by 50 high, at position (10, 10). You can create a transform object with the statement:

```
AffineTransform at = getTranslateInstance(25, 30);
```

This is a translation in *x* of 25, and a translation in *y* of 30. You can create a new `Shape` object from the original rectangle with the statement:

```
Shape transRect = at.createTransformedShape(rect);
```

The new `transRect` object will look the same as the original rectangle but translated by 25 in *x* and 30 in *y*, so its top-left corner will now be at (35, 40). Figure 20-18 illustrates this operation.

However, although it will still look like a rectangle, it will not be a `Rectangle` object. The `createTransformedShape()` method always returns a `GeneralPath` object since it has to work with any transform. This is because some transformations will deform a shape—applying a shear to a rectangle, for example, results in a shape that is no longer a rectangle. The method also has to be able to apply any transform to any `Shape` object, and returning a `GeneralPath` shape makes this possible.

Let's try some of this out. A good place to do this is with the Sketcher shape classes. At the moment you draw each shape or text element in the place where the cursor happens to be. Let's use a translation to change how this works. You can redefine each nested class to `Element` so that it translates the user coordinate system to where the shape should be and then draws the shape that it represent at the origin, (0, 0). You could try to implement this yourself as an exercise before reading on. You just need to apply some of the transform methods I have been discussing.

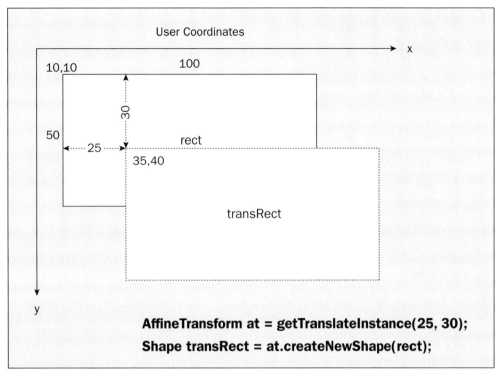

Figure 20-18

Try It Out   Translation

To make this work you'll need to save the position for each element that is passed to the element constructor — this is the start point recorded in the `mousePressed()` method — and use this to create a translation transform in the `draw()` method for the element. Since you are going to store the position of every class object that has `Element` as a base, you might as well store the location in a data member of the base class. You can modify the `Element` class to do this:

```
// import statements as before...
public abstract class Element {
  public Element(Color color) {
    this.color = color;
  }

  public Color getColor(){
    return color;
  }

  // Set or reset highlight color
  public void setHighlighted(boolean highlighted) {
    this.highlighted = highlighted;
  }
```

```
    // Get the current position of the element
    public Point getPosition() {
      return position;
    }

    public abstract java.awt.Rectangle getBounds();
    public abstract void modify(Point start, Point last);
    public abstract void draw(Graphics2D g2D);

    protected Color color;                          // Color of a shape
    protected boolean highlighted = false;          // Highlight flag
    final static Point origin = new Point();         // Point 0,0
    protected Point position;                        // Element position

    // Definitions for the shape classes...
  }
```

You might consider passing the start point to the `Element` constructor, but this wouldn't always work. This is because you need to figure out what the reference point is in some cases — for rectangles, for example. The position of a rectangle will always be the top-left corner, but this is not necessarily the start point. A method to retrieve the position of an element has been added, as I'm sure you are going to need it. You also have added another member, `origin`, which is the point $(0, 0)$. This will be useful in all the derived classes, as you'll now draw every element at that point. Since you only need one, it is `static`, and since you won't want to change it, it is `final`.

Let's start with the nested class, `Line`.

Translating Lines

You need to update the constructor first of all:

```
    public Line(Point start, Point end, Color color) {
      super(color);
      position = start;
      line = new Line2D.Double(origin, new Point(end.x - position.x,
                                                 end.y - position.y));
    }
```

You've saved the point start in `position` and created the `Line2D.Double` shape as the origin. Of course, you have to adjust the coordinates of the end point so that it is relative to $(0, 0)$.

You can now implement the `draw()` method to use a transform to move the coordinate system to where the line should be drawn. You can economize on the code in the element classes a little by thinking about this because a lot of the code is essentially the same. Here's how you would implement the method for the `Element.Line` class directly:

```
    public void draw(Graphics2D g2D) {
      g2D.setPaint(highlighted ? Color.MAGENTA : color);   // Set the line color
      AffineTransform old = g2D.getTransform();        // Save the current transform
      g2D.translate(position.x, position.y);           // Translate to position
      g2D.draw(line);                                  // Draw the line
      g2D.setTransform(old);                           // Restore original transform
    }
```

Before you expedite this, let's cover what it does. To draw the line in the right place, you have to apply a translation to the coordinate system before the draw() operation. Saving a copy of the old transform is most important, as that enables you to restore the original scheme after you've drawn the line. If you don't do this, subsequent draw operations in the same graphics context will have more and more translations applied cumulatively, so objects get further and further away from where they should be. Only one line of code here involves the element itself, however, and that is the following statement:

```
g2D.draw(line);                                    // Draw the line
```

All the rest will be common to most of the types of shapes — text being the sole exception. You could add an overloaded draw() method to the base class Element that you can define like this:

```
protected void draw(Graphics2D g2D, Shape element) {
   g2D.setPaint(highlighted ? Color.MAGENTA : color);  // Set the element color
   AffineTransform old = g2D.getTransform();       // Save the current transform
   g2D.translate(position.x, position.y);          // Translate to position
   g2D.draw(element);                              // Draw the element
   g2D.setTransform(old);                          // Restore original transform
}
```

You'll need to add an import for java.awt.geom.AffineTransform. This draw() method will draw any Shape object after applying a translation to the point position. You can now call this method from the draw() method in the Element.Line class:

```
public void draw(Graphics2D g2D) {
   draw(g2D, line);                                // Call base draw method
}
```

You can now go ahead and implement the draw() method in exactly the same way for all the nested classes to Element, with the exception of the Element.Text class. Just pass the underlying Shape reference for each class as the second argument to the overloaded draw() method. You can't use the base class helper method in the Element.Text class because text is not a Shape object. You'll have to treat the class defining text as a special case, but let's complete the process for drawing the geometric shapes first.

You must think about the bounding rectangle for a line now. You don't want the bounding rectangle for a line to be at (0, 0). You want it to be defined in terms of the coordinate system before it is translated. This is because no transforms are in effect when you use it for highlighting. For highlighting of elements to work, the bounding rectangle must be in the same reference frame.

This means that for a line, for example, you must apply the translation to the bounding rectangle that corresponds to the Line2D.Double shape. A base class helper method will come in handy here, too:

```
protected java.awt.Rectangle getBounds(java.awt.Rectangle bounds) {
   AffineTransform at = AffineTransform.getTranslateInstance(position.x,
                                                             position.y);
   return at.createTransformedShape(bounds).getBounds();
}
```

Add the definition of this method to the code for the Element class.

You first create an AffineTransform object that applies a translation to the point position. Then you apply the createTransformedShape() method to the rectangle that is passed as the argument — which will be the bounding rectangle for a shape at (0, 0); this produces a corresponding shape translated to its proper position. Even though you get a GeneralPath object back from the createTransformedShape() method, you can get a rectangle from that quite easily by calling its getBounds() method. Thus our helper method accepts a reference to an object of type java.awt.Rectangle and returns a reference to the rectangle that results from translating this to the point position. This is precisely what you want to do with the bounding rectangles you get with the shapes defined at the origin. You can now use this to implement the getBounds() method for the Element.Line class:

```java
public java.awt.Rectangle getBounds() {
  return getBounds(line.getBounds());
}
```

You just pass the reference to the line member of the class as the argument to the base class version of getBounds() and return the rectangle that is returned by that method. The getBounds() methods for the nested classes Rectangle, Circle, and Curve will be essentially the same — just change the argument to the base class getBounds() call to the Shape reference corresponding to each class. Implementing the getBounds() method for the Text class is slightly different, but still easy; you can just pass the bounds member of that class as the argument to the base class getBounds() method.

You must also update the modify() method, and this is going to be specific to each class. To adjust the end point of a line so that it is relative to the start point at the origin, you must change the method in the Element.Line class as follows:

```java
public void modify(Point start, Point last) {
  line.x2 = last.x - position.x;
  line.y2 = last.y - position.y;
}
```

That's the Element.Line class complete. You can apply essentially the same thing to all the other classes in the Element class.

Translating Rectangles

Here are the changes to the Element.Rectangle constructor:

```java
public Rectangle(Point start, Point end, Color color) {
  super(color);
  position = new Point(Math.min(start.x, end.x),
                       Math.min(start.y, end.y));
  rectangle = new Rectangle2D.Double(origin.x,
                                     origin.y,
                                     Math.abs(start.x - end.x),      // Width
                                     Math.abs(start.y - end.y));     // & height
}
```

The expressions for the coordinates of the point position ensure that you set it as the location of the top-left corner. The rectangle object is defined with its top-left corner at the origin, and its width and height as before.

You have to adjust the `modify()` method so that it adjusts the location stored in `position` and leaves the rectangle defined at the origin:

```
public void modify(Point start, Point last) {
   position.x = Math.min(start.x, last.x);
   position.y = Math.min(start.y, last.y);
   rectangle.width = Math.abs(start.x - last.x);
   rectangle.height = Math.abs(start.y - last.y);
}
```

You should already have added the revised version of the `draw()` and `getBounds()` methods for an `Element.Rectangle` object essentially the same as that for lines.

Translating Circles

The `Element.Circle` class constructor is also very easy:

```
public Circle(Point center, Point circum, Color color) {
   super(color);

   // Radius is distance from center to circumference
   double radius = center.distance(circum);
   position = new Point(center.x - (int)radius,
                        center.y - (int)radius);

   circle = new Ellipse2D.Double(origin.x, origin.y,      // Position - top-left
                                 2.*radius, 2.*radius );   // Width & height
}
```

The radius is calculated as before, and you make the top-left corner of the `Ellipse2D.Double` object the origin point. Thus `position` is calculated as for the top-left corner in the previous version of the constructor.

You can adjust the `modify()` method for the `Element.Circle` class to record the new coordinates of `position`:

```
public void modify(Point center, Point circum) {
   double radius = center.distance(circum);
   position.x = center.x - (int)radius;
   position.y = center.y - (int)radius;
   circle.width = circle.height = 2*radius;
}
```

The `draw()` and `getBounds()` methods are already done, so it's curves next.

Translating Curves

The `Element.Curve` class is just as simple:

```
public Curve(Point start, Point next, Color color) {
   super(color);
   curve = new GeneralPath();
```

```
        position = start;
        curve.moveTo(origin.x, origin.y);
        curve.lineTo(next.x - position.x,
                     next.y - position.y);
    }
```

You store the start point in `position`, and create the curve starting at (0, 0). The end point has to be adjusted so that it is defined relative to (0, 0).

Adding a new segment in the `modify()` method also has to be changed to take into account the new origin for the curve relative to the start point:

```
    public void modify(Point start, Point next) {
        curve.lineTo(next.x - start.x,
                     next.y - start.y);
    }
```

You just subtract the coordinates of the original start point that you saved in `position` from the coordinates of the point `next`. The methods for drawing the curve and getting the bounding rectangle have already been updated, so the last piece is the `Element.Text` class.

Translating Text

The first step is to remove the declaration for the member `position` from this class, as you'll now be using the member of the same name that is inherited from the base class.

The only changes you need to make to the constructor are as follows:

```
    public Text(Font font, String text, Point position,
                Color color, java.awt.Rectangle bounds) {
        super(color);
        this.font = font;
        this.position = position;
        this.position.y -= (int)bounds.getHeight();
        this.text = text;
        this.bounds = new java.awt.Rectangle(origin.x, origin.y,
                                             bounds.width, bounds.height);
    }
```

The bounding rectangle for the text object now has its top-left corner at the origin. The point `position` that defines where the text is to be drawn is set to correspond to the top-left corner of the rectangle bounding the text, to be consistent with the way it is defined for the other elements. You'll need to take account of this in the implementation of the `draw()` method because the `drawString()` method expects the position for the text to be the bottom-left corner:

```
    public void draw(Graphics2D g2D) {
        g2D.setPaint(highlighted ? Color.MAGENTA : color);
        Font oldFont = g2D.getFont();                       // Save the old font
        g2D.setFont(font);                                  // Set the new font
```

```
        AffineTransform old = g2D.getTransform();     // Save the current transform
        g2D.translate(position.x, position.y);        // Translate to position
        g2D.drawString(text, origin.x, origin.y+(int)bounds.getHeight());
        g2D.setTransform(old);                         // Restore original transform

        g2D.setFont(oldFont);                          // Restore the old font
    }
```

The transformation that you apply in the draw() method here is essentially the same as for the other classes. You now add the height of the bounding rectangle to the *y* coordinate of position in the argument to drawString(). This specifies the bottom-left corner of the first text character.

You can now recompile Sketcher for another trial. If you have done everything right it should still work as before.

How It Works

All the classes defining elements now create the elements at the origin and store their location in a member, position, that is inherited from the base class, Element. The draw methods all apply a transform to move the coordinate system to the point stored in position before drawing the element. The draw() methods then restore the original transform to leave the graphics context unchanged. Each of the getBounds() methods returns a bounding rectangle in the original untransformed coordinate system, because that is the context in which it will be used. You are now ready to try moving elements around.

Moving an Element

Now you can implement the move operation that you provided for in the context menu. Taking the trouble to define all the elements relative to the origin and using a transform to position them correctly really pays off when you want to apply other transformations to the elements. You can add a move() method to the base class Element that will move any element, and the body of the method is just two lines of code:

```
    // Move an element
    public void move(int deltax, int deltay) {
       position.x += deltax;
       position.y += deltay;
    }
```

Let's review the process that you be implementing to move an element. From a user's point of view, to move an element you just click on the Move menu item in the context menu and then drag the highlighted element to where you want it to be with button 1 held down.

In programming terms, moving an element will be initiated in the actionPerformed() method in SketchView that responds to a menu selection. When the Move menu item is clicked, you'll set the operating mode to what you'll define as MOVE mode, so that you can detect this in the mouse handler methods that will expedite a move. The Rotate menu will work in exactly the same way by setting a ROTATE mode. To accommodate this you'll add a new member, mode, of type int to the SketchView class that will store the current operating mode. By default, it will be NORMAL.

Add the following member declaration to SketchView:

```
    private int mode = NORMAL;
```

1065

You'll add the definitions of the constants that identify these operating modes to the SketcherConstants class in the Constants package by adding the following statements:

```
// Operating modes
public final static int NORMAL = 0;
public final static int MOVE   = 1;
public final static int ROTATE = 2;
```

When you set the operating mode to other than NORMAL, the methods that deal with mouse events will need to know to which element the mode applies, so you'll add another member to SketchView to record this:

```
private Element selectedElement;
```

Now you can change the actionPerformed() method in the SketchView class as follows:

```
public void actionPerformed(ActionEvent e) {
  Object source = e.getSource();
  if(source == moveItem) {
    mode = MOVE;
    selectedElement = highlightElement;
  } else if(source == deleteItem) {
    if(highlightElement != null)   {                    // If there's an element
      theApp.getModel().remove(highlightElement);       // then remove it
      highlightElement = null;                          // Remove the reference
    }
  } else if(source == rotateItem) {
    mode = ROTATE;
    selectedElement = highlightElement;
  } else if(source == sendToBackItem) {
    if(highlightElement != null) {
      theApp.getModel().remove(highlightElement);
      theApp.getModel().add(highlightElement);
      highlightElement.setHighlighted(false);
      highlightElement = null;
      repaint();
    }
  }
}
```

All moving of the highlighted element will be managed in the mouseDragged() method in the MouseHandler inner class to SketchView. Figure 20-19 illustrates how it will work.

Each move will be from the previous cursor position stored in start to the current cursor position when the MOUSE_DRAGGED event occurred. The current cursor position will be obtained by calling the getPoint() method for the event object passed to the mouseDragged() method. Once each mouse move has been processed, the current cursor position will then be stored in the variable start, ready for the next event. For each MOUSE_DRAGGED event, you'll move the element the distance between successive cursor positions.

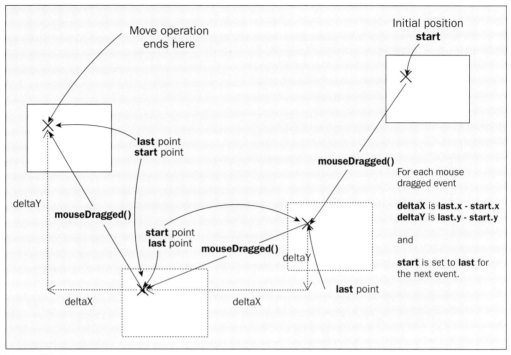

Figure 20-19

Try It Out   Moving Elements

Since the element classes are equipped to move, and you have kitted out SketchView to handle the menu item action, you just need to add the code to the methods in MouseHandler. The mousePressed() method records the start point for a move, and it also sets up the XOR mode for drawing. That's precisely what you'll need to move or rotate elements; geometric elements are okay. However, you also want to move or rotate text, and for this to work the mousePressed() method will have to set XOR mode for a TEXT element, too. This is simple to fix:

```
public void mousePressed(MouseEvent e)  {
  if(e.isPopupTrigger()) {
    processPopupTrigger(e);
  } else if((button1Down = (e.getButton() == MouseEvent.BUTTON1))) {
    start = e.getPoint();                  // Save the cursor position in start
    g2D = (Graphics2D)getGraphics();                // Get graphics context
    g2D.setXORMode(getBackground());                // Set XOR mode
  }
}
```

All that was necessary was to remove the test for TEXT mode in the else if condition. Now XOR mode is set whenever button 1 is pressed.

You have to test for the setting of mode in the mouseDragged() method, and in principle, execute differ-ent code depending on what it is. You have three possibilities: NORMAL, where you do as you did before; MOVE, where you'll execute a move operation; and ROTATE, where you'll execute a rotate operation, which I'll come to later. Here's the new version of mouseDragged() to accommodate moving elements:

```java
public void mouseDragged(MouseEvent e) {
  last = e.getPoint();                              // Save cursor position

  if(button1Down && (theApp.getWindow().getElementType() != TEXT)
                  && (mode == NORMAL)) {
    if(tempElement == null) {                       // Is there an element?
      tempElement = createElement(start, last);     // No, so create one
    } else {
      tempElement.draw(g2D);                        // Yes - draw to erase it
      tempElement.modify(start, last);              // Modify it
    }
    tempElement.draw(g2D);                          // and draw it

  } else if(button1Down && mode == MOVE && selectedElement != null) {
    selectedElement.draw(g2D);                      // Draw to erase the element
    selectedElement.move(last.x-start.x, last.y-start.y);  // Move it
    selectedElement.draw(g2D);                      // Draw in its new position
    start = last;                                   // Make start current point
  }
}
```

Now the method only executes the previous code in NORMAL mode. For MOVE mode, if button 1 is down and there is an element selected to move, you move it by erasing it at the current position, moving the element by calling its move() method, and drawing it at the new position. The current last will be start for the next MOUSE_DRAGGED event.

The final alterations to the code occur in the mouseReleased() method:

```java
public void mouseReleased(MouseEvent e) {
  if(e.isPopupTrigger()) {
    processPopupTrigger(e);
  } else if((e.getButton()==MouseEvent.BUTTON1) &&
           (theApp.getWindow().getElementType() != TEXT) && mode == NORMAL) {
    button1Down = false;                            // Reset the button 1 flag
    if(tempElement != null) {
      theApp.getModel().add(tempElement);           // Add element to the model
      tempElement = null;                           // No temporary element now stored
    }
  } else if((e.getButton()==MouseEvent.BUTTON1) &&
           (mode == MOVE || mode == ROTATE)) {
    button1Down = false;                            // Reset the button 1 flag
    if(selectedElement != null) {
      repaint();
    }
    mode = NORMAL;
  }

  if(g2D != null) {
```

```
        g2D.dispose();                        // Release graphic context resource
        g2D = null;                           // Set it to null
      }
    start = last = null;                      // Remove the points
    selectedElement = tempElement = null;     // Reset elements
  }
```

The last block of code is not entirely new — some of it has been relocated from earlier in the code for the previous version. You have an extra condition in the original `if` expression to check for NORMAL mode. The next `if` tests for MOVE mode or ROTATE mode because in either case you will have changed an element by dragging it around, so the view will need to be redrawn. This is the one place where you must do this explicitly because the model is not aware of these changes. If `selectedElement` is not `null`, you call `repaint()` for the view to get it redrawn, and you restore NORMAL mode. Outside of all the `if`s you reset everything back to `null`.

If you recompile Sketcher and rerun it, you can now produce sketches like the one shown of Figure 20-20.

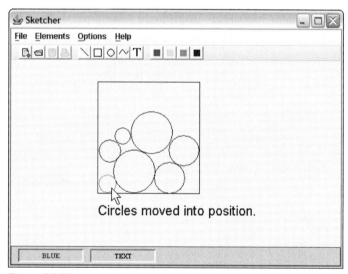

Figure 20-20

How It Works

Using a transform to position each element means that expediting a move operation consists of just altering the `position` member of an element. The move operation depends on setting a MOVE mode for the mouse event-handling methods to respond to. A move for each element is the same: drawing the element in XOR mode in its original position to erase it, moving it, and then drawing it again in the new position. You may see pixels left behind as you move elements, particularly text.

This is due to rounding in the floating-point operations mapping user coordinates to device coordinates. They all disappear when the move is complete and the whole picture is redrawn.

Now that you have made Move work, Rotate will be a piece of cake.

Rotating Elements

Clearly you are going to make use of another transform to implement this. You know how to create a rotation transform, so all you need to figure out is the mechanics of how the user accomplishes the rotation of an element.

The first step is already in place—the `actionPerformed()` method in `SketchView` already sets `ROTATE` mode in response to the Rotate menu action. The user will then drag the element to the angle required with the mouse, while holding button 1 down. You need to work out the rotation angle for each `MOUSE_DRAGGED` event. Figure 20-21 shows what happens when the mouse is dragged for a rotation.

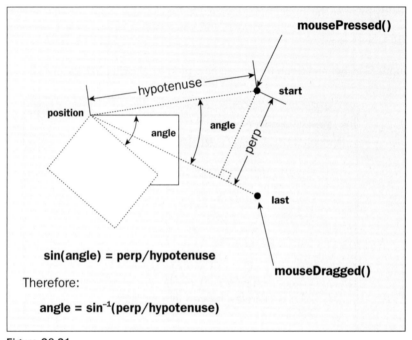

Figure 20-21

The angle in Figure 20-21 is exaggerated so you can see what is going on. The `mousePressed()` method is called when the button is first pressed at some arbitrary position, and the cursor position is recorded in `start`. When the `mouseDragged()` method is called, you record the cursor position in `last`, and you now need to calculate `angle`. You must apply a little high school math to get this, which you can ignore if your recall of trigonometry is nonexistent.

You can get the length of the perpendicular from the point `start` in Figure 20-21 to the line extending from `position` to `last` by using a static method in the `Line2D` class:

```
double perp = Line2D.ptLineDist(position.x, position.y,
                                last.x, last.y,
                                start.x, start.y);
```

The `ptLineDist()` method calculates the perpendicular distance of the point specified by the last two arguments to the line specified by the first four arguments — the first pair of arguments being the coordinates of the beginning of the line, and the second pair being the coordinates of the end point.

You know how to get the distance from `position` to `start`. You just apply the `distance()` method that is defined in the `Point` class:

```
double hypotenuse = position.distance(start);
```

From Figure 20-21 you can see that you can calculate `angle` as:

```
sin-1(perp/hypotenuse)
```

This comes from the definition of what the sine of an angle is. The `Math` class provides a method to calculate `sin-1` values (also called arcsine values), so you can calculate `angle` as:

```
double angle = Math.asin(perp/hypotenuse);
```

The `asin()` method returns an angle in radians between -(/2 and (/2, which is fine for the situation you are dealing withh. You are unlikely to create an angle outside this range for a `mouseDragged()` event unless there is something seriously awry with your PC.

Of course, you need to know which way the rotation is going, clockwise or counterclockwise. Another static method in the `Line2D` class can help out here. The `relativeCCW()` method determines where a point lies with respect to a line. If you have to rotate the line clockwise to reach the point, the method returns −1, and if you have to rotate the line counterclockwise, it returns +1. You can use this method to test whether the point `last` is clockwise or counterclockwise with respect to the line from `position` to `start`. Since angles rotating the coordinate system clockwise are positive, you can calculate a suitably signed value for `angle` with the following statement:

```
double angle = -Line2D.relativeCCW(position.x, position.y,
                                   start.x, start.y,
                                   last.x, last.y)*Math.asin(perp/hypotenuse);
```

The minus sign is necessary because the method returns −1 when `last` is clockwise with respect to the line from `position` to `start`. That's all the math you need. Let's do it.

Try It Out   Rotating Elements

To deal with `ROTATE` mode in the `mouseDragged()` method, you can add an extra `else if` clause after the one you added for `MOVE`:

```
        } else if(button1Down && mode == ROTATE && selectedElement != null) {
          selectedElement.draw(g2D);                    // Draw to erase the element
          selectedElement.rotate(getAngle(selectedElement.getPosition(),
                                                            start, last));
          selectedElement.draw(g2D);                    // Draw in its new position
          start = last;                                 // Make start current point
        }
```

After drawing the element to erase it, you call its `rotate()` method to rotate it and then redraw it in the new position. You'll add the definition for the `rotate()` method to the `Element` class in a moment.

The argument to the `rotate()` method is the angle in radians through which the element is to be rotated, and that is returned by a helper method, `getAngle()`. You can add that to the `MouseHandler` class as:

```
// Helper method for calculating the rotation angle
double getAngle(Point position, Point start, Point last) {
  // Get perpendicular distance from last to the line from position to start
  double perp = Line2D.ptLineDist(position.x, position.y,
                                  last.x, last.y, start.x, start.y);
  // Get the distance from position to start
  double hypotenuse = position.distance(start);
  if(hypotenuse == 0.0) {                        // Make sure it's
    hypotenuse = 1.0;                            // non-zero
  }

  // Angle is the arc sine of perp/hypotenuse. Clockwise is positive angle
  return -Line2D.relativeCCW(position.x, position.y,
                 start.x, start.y,
                 last.x, last.y)*Math.asin(perp/hypotenuse);
}
```

This is basically just an assembly of the code fragments calculating the angle in the last section. You'll need an `import` statement for `Line2D` in the source file for `SketchView`:

```
import java.awt.geom.Line2D;
```

You completed the `mouseReleased()` method when you dealt with MOVE mode, so there's nothing further to add there.

Now you must empower the `Element` objects to rotate themselves. You'll add a data member to the base class to store the rotation angle and a method to rotate the element:

```
public abstract class Element {
  public Element(Color color) {
  this.color = color; }

  public   Color getColor()   {
  return color;   }

  // Set or reset highlight color
  public void setHighlighted(boolean highlighted) {
    this.highlighted = highlighted;
  }

  public Point getPosition() {
    return position;
  }

  protected void draw(Graphics2D g2D, Shape element) {
    g2D.setPaint(highlighted ? Color.MAGENTA : color);  // Set the element color
    AffineTransform old = g2D.getTransform();         // Save the current transform
    g2D.translate(position.x, position.y);            // Translate to position
```

```
    g2D.rotate(angle);                          // Rotate about position
    g2D.draw(element);                          // Draw the element
    g2D.setTransform(old);                      // Restore original transform
  }

  protected java.awt.Rectangle getBounds(java.awt.Rectangle bounds) {
    AffineTransform at = AffineTransform.getTranslateInstance(
                                              position.x, position.y);
    at.rotate(angle);
    return  at.createTransformedShape(bounds).getBounds();
  }

  public void move(int deltax, int deltay) {
    position.x += deltax;
    position.y += deltay;
  }

  // Increment the element rotation angle
  public void rotate(double angle) {
    this.angle += angle;
  }

  public abstract Rectangle getBounds();
  public abstract void draw(Graphics2D g2D);
  public abstract void modify(Point start, Point last);

  protected Color color;                     // Color of a shape
  protected boolean highlighted = false;     // Highlight flag
  final static Point origin = new Point();   // Point 0,0
  protected Point position;                  // Element position
  protected double angle = 0.0;              // Rotation angle

  // inner shape classes defined here...
}
```

All the `rotate()` method does is add the angle that is passed to it as the argument to the current value of `angle`. The value of `angle` is assumed to be in radians. Naturally, when you create an element the value of `angle` will be zero. You have modified the `draw()` method in the base class to apply a rotation through `angle` radians about the point `position`. It is important that you apply the rotation *after* the translation; otherwise, the translation would be applied in the rotated coordinate system, which would give quite a different result from what you require. Since you now have the possibility of rotated shapes, the `getBounds()` method also has to take account of this, so you apply a rotation here, too. You must also remember that the `draw()` method in the `Element.Text` class is a special case. You need to add a line to this method to apply the rotation:

```
public void draw(Graphics2D g2D) {
    g2D.setPaint(highlighted ? Color.MAGENTA : color);
    Font oldFont = g2D.getFont();                     // Save the old font
    g2D.setFont(font);                                // Set the new font

    AffineTransform old = g2D.getTransform();         // Save the current transform
    g2D.translate(position.x, position.y);            // Translate to position
```

```
        g2D.rotate(angle);                                  // Rotate about position
        g2D.drawString(text, origin.x, origin.y+(int)bounds.getHeight());
        g2D.setTransform(old);                              // Restore original transform
        g2D.setFont(oldFont);                               // Restore the old font
    }
```

Recompile all the stuff you have changed and try out the new context menus. Having a rotate capability adds flexibility, and with the move operation giving you much more precision in positioning elements relative to one another, this should enable a massive leap forward in the quality of your artwork. Figure 20-22 shows the sort of standard you might be able to achieve.

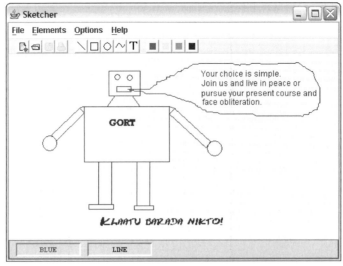

Figure 20-22

How It Works

Rotating elements just involves adding an extra transform before each element is drawn. Because you draw each element at the origin, rotating an element becomes relatively simple.

Choosing Custom Colors

You made provision in the status bar for showing a custom color. It would be a shame not to make use of this, so let's add a dialog to enable any color to be chosen. This is going to be a lot easier than you imagine.

To keep it simple, you'll implement this as a facility on the general pop-up menu, although in practice you would probably want it accessible from the main menu and the toolbar. You can add a member to the SketchFrame class for the menu item:

```
private JMenuItem customColorItem;
```

You should add this to the pop-up and add an action listener for it. This requires two statements in the SketchFrame constructor:

```
customColorItem = popup.add(new JMenuItem("Custom Color...")); // Add the item
customColorItem.addActionListener(this);                       // and add its listener
```

You can add these statements following the others that set up the pop-up menu. Selecting this menu item will now cause the actionPerformed() method in the SketchFrame class to be called so you will implement the custom color choice in there. Let's put that together and try it out.

Try It Out   Choosing a Custom Color

You'll use the facilities provided by the javax.swing.JColorChooser class that does precisely what you want. Here's how you can use it in the actionPerformed() method:

```
// Handle About menu action events
public void actionPerformed(ActionEvent e)  {
  if(e.getSource() == aboutItem) {
    // Create about dialog with the menu item as parent
    JOptionPane.showMessageDialog(this,                        // Parent
                          "Sketcher Copyright Ivor Horton 2004", // Message
                          "About Sketcher",                     // Title
                          JOptionPane.INFORMATION_MESSAGE);     // Message type

  } else if(e.getSource() == fontItem) {      // Set the dialog window position
    Rectangle bounds = getBounds();
    fontDlg.setLocation(bounds.x + bounds.width/3, bounds.y + bounds.height/3);
    fontDlg.setVisible(true);                 // Show the dialog

  } else if(e.getSource() == customColorItem) {
    Color color = JColorChooser.showDialog(this, "Select Custom Color",
                                            elementColor);

    if(color != null) {
      elementColor = color;
      statusBar.setColorPane(color);
    }
  }
}
```

With the `JColorChooser` class imported, recompile and rerun Sketcher and select the Custom Color... menu item from the general pop-up. You will see the dialog shown in Figure 20-23.

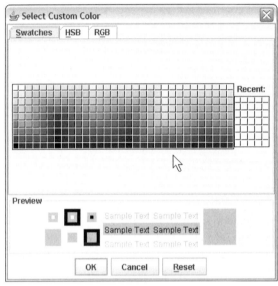

Figure 20-23

How It Works

The `JColorChooser` class defines a complete color choosing facility that you can use in your own dialog, or you can create a complete modal dialog by calling the `static` method `showDialog()` as you have done here. The arguments to `showDialog()` are a reference to the parent component for the dialog, the title for the dialog, and the initial color selection. You can choose a color using any of the three tabs, which provide different mechanisms for defining the color that you want. When you click OK, the color that you chose is returned as type `Color`. If you exit the dialog by any means other than selecting the OK button, the dialog returns `null`. You just store the color that is returned in `elementColor` and set it in the status bar pane. Subsequent sketching operations will be in the custom color.

Summary

In this chapter you've learned how to use dialogs to manage data input. You have also learned how to implement context menus, which can bring a professional feel to the GUI in your applications. You have applied scrollbars to varying data values as well as scrolled a window, so you should be in a position to use them in whatever context you need.

The important points I have covered in this chapter are:

❑ A modal dialog blocks input from other windows in the same application as long as it is displayed.

❑   A non-modal dialog does not block input to other windows. You can switch the focus between a non-modal dialog and other windows in the application whenever necessary.

❑   The `JOptionPane` class provides `static` methods for creating simple dialogs.

❑   A pop-up menu is a menu that can be displayed at any point within the coordinate system of a component.

❑   A context menu is a pop-up menu that is specific to what lies at the point where the menu is displayed — so the contents of the menu depend on the context.

❑   A context menu is displayed as a result of a pop-up trigger, which is usually a right mouse-button click for a right-handed mouse setup.

❑   The `AffineTransform` class defines an affine transformation that can be applied to a graphics context and to a `Shape` object.

❑   A `Graphic2D` object always contains an `AffineTransform` object, and the default transform leaves coordinates unchanged.

❑   The transform for a graphics context is applied immediately before user coordinates for a shape are converted to device coordinates.

❑   You can create four kinds of transforms: translations, rotations, scaling, and shearing.

❑   You can combine any number of transformations in a single `AffineTransform` object.

Exercises

You can download the source code for the examples in the book and the solutions to the following exercises from `http://www.wrox.com`.

1.   Implement a dialog initiated from a toolbar button to select the current element color.

2.   Add a menu item to the `Element` context menu that will display information about the element at the cursor in a dialog — what it is and its basic defining data.

3.   Display a special context menu when the cursor is over a `TEXT` object that provides a menu option to edit the text through a dialog.

4.   Change the implementations of the element classes to make use of the combined translate and rotate operation.

5.   Add a toolbar button to switch highlighting on and off. The same button should turn it on when it is off and vice versa, so you need to change the button label appropriately.

6.   Add a Scale menu item to the element context menu that will allow a geometric element to be scaled by dragging the mouse cursor.

7.   Implement a main menu item and a toolbar button for choosing a custom color.

Filing and Printing Documents

In this chapter you'll explore serializing and printing documents in an application and adding these as the finishing touches to the Sketcher program. These capabilities are not available to an untrusted applet for security reasons, so everything I'll cover here applies only to applications and trusted applets. Although you have already covered serialization in Chapter 12, you'll find that there is quite a difference between understanding how the basic methods for object input and output work and applying them in a practical context.

In this chapter you'll learn:

- ❏ How to use the `JFileChooser` class
- ❏ How to save a sketch in a file as objects
- ❏ How to implement the Save As menu mechanism
- ❏ How to open a sketch stored in a file and integrate it into the application
- ❏ How to create a new sketch and integrate it into the application
- ❏ How to ensure that the current sketch is saved before the application is closed or a new sketch is loaded
- ❏ How printing in Java works
- ❏ How to print in landscape orientation rather than portrait orientation
- ❏ How to implement multipage printing
- ❏ How to output components to your printer

Serializing the Sketch

The Sketcher program can be considered to be a practical application only if you can save sketches in a file and retrieve them later — in other words, you need to implement serialization for a SketchModel object and use that to make the File menu work. Ideally, you want to be able to write the model for a sketch to a file and be able to read it back at a later date and reconstruct exactly the same model object. One obvious way to do this is to use serialization because the primary purpose of serialization is the accurate storage and retrieval of objects, so that's what you'll implement in this chapter. In Chapter 23 you'll explore another possibility — saving sketches in Extensible Markup Language (XML).

You've seen how to serialize objects back in Chapter 12. All you have to do to serialize a sketch document in our Sketcher program is to apply what you learned there. Of course, quite a few classes are involved in a sketch document but it will be remarkably easy considering the potential complexity of a sketch — I promise!

Putting in place the graphical user interface (GUI) functionality for saving a sketch on disk and reading it back from a file will be significantly more work than implementing serialization for the model. The logic of opening and saving files so as not to lose anything accidentally can get rather convoluted. Before you get into that, there is a more fundamental point I should address — a sketch doesn't have a name. You should at least make provision for assigning a file name to a sketch, and maybe displaying the name of the current sketch in the title bar of the application window.

Try It Out   Assigning a Document Name

Since the sketch is going to have a name because you intend to store it somewhere, let's define a default directory to hold sketches. Add the following lines to the end of the SketcherConstants class (SketcherConstants.java) that you defined in the Constants package:

```
public final static File DEFAULT_DIRECTORY = new File("C:/Sketches");
public final static String DEFAULT_FILENAME = "Sketch.ske";
```

If you want to store your sketches in a different directory you can set the definition of DEFAULT_DIRECTORY to suit your needs. The file extension .ske to identify sketches is also arbitrary. You can change this if you would prefer to use a different extension. Since you reference the File class here, you must add an import statement to the SketcherConstants source file to get at it:

```
import java.io.File;
```

You'll want to store information related to saving a sketch, and the application window object is a suitable repository for it so add the following data members to the SketchFrame class definition:

```
private String frameTitle;                        // Frame title
private String filename = DEFAULT_FILENAME; // Current model file name
private File modelFile;                           // File for the current sketch
```

The frameTitle member specifies the basic title for the Sketcher application window. You'll append the file name for the sketch to it and display the result in the title bar. The modelFile member will hold a reference to the File object identifying the file containing the current sketch, once the sketch has been saved.

You can arrange for the frameTitle field to be initialized and the default file name to be appended to the basic window title in the SketchFrame constructor. You can also make sure that DEFAULT_DIRECTORY exists and is valid. The following code will do this:

```
public SketchFrame(String title, Sketcher theApp) {
  frameTitle = title + ": ";
  setTitle(frameTitle + filename);

  if(!DEFAULT_DIRECTORY.exists()) {
    if(!DEFAULT_DIRECTORY.mkdirs()) {
      JOptionPane.showMessageDialog(this,
                                    "Error creating default directory",
                                    "Directory Creation Error",
                                    JOptionPane.ERROR_MESSAGE);
      System.exit(1);
    }
  }
  this.theApp = theApp;                          // Save application object

  // Rest of the code in the constructor as before...
}
```

If the default directory is found not to exist, you try to create it by calling the mkdirs() method for the DEFAULT_DIRECTORY object. If that fails, something is seriously wrong, so you pop a dialog with an error message and terminate the program.

Since you'll be implementing the event handling for the File menu, you can remove or comment out the statements from the constructor that disable the actions for this:

```
// Disable actions
//saveAction.setEnabled(false);
//closeAction.setEnabled(false);
//printAction.setEnabled(false);
```

If you recompile Sketcher and run it, you should now see the default file name for a sketch displayed in the title bar, as Figure 21-1 shows. All the toolbars buttons are enabled, too.

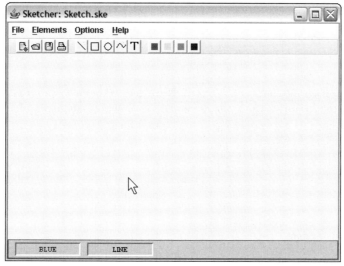

Figure 21-1

You now have a name assigned to the document, but there's another point to consider if you're preparing to store a sketch. When you close the application, there should be a means of checking whether the sketch needs to be saved. Otherwise, it will be all too easy to close Sketcher and lose the brilliant sketch that you have just spent 3 hours crafting. Checking whether the sketch needs to be saved isn't difficult. You just need to record the fact that the model has changed.

Try It Out   Recording Changes to a Sketch

To provide the means of recording whether or not a sketch has been changed you can add a `boolean` field to the `SketchFrame` class that you'll set to `true` when the `SketchModel` object changes, and `false` when it is in a new and original condition — as is the case when it has just been loaded or saved in a file. Add the following data member definition to the `SketchFrame` class:

```
private boolean sketchChanged = false;          // Model changed flag
```

This sort of variable is sometimes referred to as a "dirty" flag for the model because it records when something has been done to sully the pristine state of the model data. The flag is `false` by default because the sketch is empty and therefore unchanged by definition. Any change that the user makes to the model should result in the flag being set to `true`, and whenever the model is written to a file, the flag should be reset to `false`. By checking the state of this flag you'll be able to avoid unnecessary save operations while the sketch in memory remains unchanged.

You already have in place the means to signal changes to a sketch, since the `SketchModel` class has `Observable` as a base class. As you know, an `Observable` object can automatically notify any registered `Observer` objects when a change takes place. All you need to do is to make the `SketchFrame` class implement the `Observer` interface and register the application window as an observer of the sketch object:

```
public class SketchFrame extends JFrame implements ActionListener, Observer {

  // Method called by SketchModel object when it changes
  public void update(Observable o, Object obj) {
    sketchChanged = true;
  }

  // Rest of the class as before...
}
```

The `Observer` interface and the `Observable` class are defined in the `java.util` package, so you must import them into the `SketchFrame.java` file with the following statements:

```
import java.util.Observer;
import java.util.Observable;
```

You can register the application window as an observer for the `SketchModel` object by adding one statement to the `createGUI()` method in the `Sketcher` class:

```
private void creatGUI() {
// Code as before...
  sketch = new SketchModel();              // Create the model
  view = new SketchView(this);             // Create the view
```

```
            sketch.addObserver(view);                    // Register view with the model
            sketch.addObserver(window);                  // Register window with the model
            window.getContentPane().add(view, BorderLayout.CENTER);
            window.setVisible(true);
        }
```

The window field in the Sketcher object stores a reference to the application window. Whenever an element is added to the sketch, or deleted from it, the application window object will be notified. You can now press ahead with serializing the model for a sketch.

Implementing the Serializable Interface

As I hope you still remember, the fundamental step in making objects serializable is to implement the Serializable interface in every class that defines objects you want written to a file. You need a methodical approach here, so how about top-down—starting with the SketchModel class.

Try It Out   **Serializing SketchModel Objects**

This is where you get a great deal from astonishingly little effort. To implement serialization for the SketchModel class you must first modify the class definition header to:

```
class SketchModel extends Observable implements Iterable<Element>, Serializable {
```

The Serializable interface is defined in the java.io package, so you need to add the following import statement to the beginning of the SketchModel.java file:

```
import java.io.Serializable;
```

The Serializable interface declares no methods—so that's it so far as the SketchModel class is concerned!

Is that enough to serialize a sketch? Not quite. For a class to be serializable, all its data members must be serializable or declared as transient. If this is not the case, then an exception of type NotSerializableException will be thrown when you try to serialize an object. To avoid this you must trawl through the data elements of the SketchModel class, and if any of these are your own classes, you must make sure they either implement the Serializable interface or are declared as transient.

You also cannot assume that objects of a standard class type are serializable because some most definitely are not. It's a fairly quick fishing trip though, because the SketchModel class has only one data member—the linked list of elements that make up the sketch. If the SketchModel object is to be serializable you simply need to make sure the elements field is serializable.

Serializing the List of Elements

If you look through the Java Development Kit (JDK) documentation, you'll see that the LinkedList<> generic class implements the Serializable interface, so all you need to worry about are the list elements themselves. You can make the base class for the shapes in a sketch serializable by declaring that the Element class implements the Serializable interface:

```
public abstract class Element implements Serializable {
```

Don't forget that you now need an `import` statement for the `Serializable` interface in `Element.java`:

```
import java.io.Serializable;
```

The data members of the `Element` class that are object references are of type `java.awt.Color` or of type `java.awt.Point`, and since both of these classes are serializable, as you can verify from the JDK documentation, the `Element` class is serializable. Now you need to look at the subclasses of `Element`.

Subclasses of `Element` will inherit the implementation of the `Serializable` interface, so they are all declared to be serializable by default; however, there is a tiny snag. At the time of writing, none of the classes in the `java.awt.geom` package that implement the `java.awt.Shape` interface are serializable, and you've been using them all over the place.

You're not completely scuppered, though. Remember that you can always implement the `readObject()` and `writeObject()` methods in a class and then implement your own serialization. You can take the data that you need to re-create the required `Shape` object and serialize that in your implementation of the `writeObject()` method. You'll then be able to reconstruct the object from the data you get back from a file in the `readObject()` method. Let's start with the `Element.Line` class.

Serializing Lines

Just to remind you of one of the things I discussed way back in the I/O chapters, the `writeObject()` method that serializes objects must have the following form:

```
private void writeObject(ObjectOutputStream out) throws IOException {
  // Code to serialize the object...
}
```

Our `Element.Line` objects are always drawn from (0, 0) so there's no sense in saving the start point in a line — it's always the same. You just need to serialize the end point, so add the following implementation of the `writeObject()` method to the `Element.Line` class:

```
// Method to serialize a line
private void writeObject(ObjectOutputStream out) throws IOException {
  out.writeDouble(line.x2);
  out.writeDouble(line.y2);
}
```

You don't need to worry about exceptions that might be thrown by the `writeDouble()` method at this point. These will be passed on to the method that calls `writeObject()`. You'll need `import` statements for the `IOException` and `ObjectOutputStream` class name in `Element.java`:

```
import java.io.IOException;
import java.io.ObjectOutputStream;
```

The coordinates that you pass to the `writeDouble()` method are public members of the `Line2D.Double` object so you can reference them directly to write them to the stream. The rest of the data relating to a line is stored in the base class, `Element`, and as I said earlier, they are all taken care of. The base class members will be serialized automatically when an `Element.Line` object is written to a file. You just need the means to read it back.

To recap what you already know, the `readObject()` method to deserialize an object is also of a standard form:

```
private void readObject(ObjectInputStream in)
                          throws IOException,  ClassNotFoundException {
  // Code to deserialize an object...
}
```

For the `Element.Line` class, the `readObject()` implementation will read the coordinates of the end point of the line and reconstitute `line` — the `Line2D.Double` member of the class. Adding the following method to the `Element.Line` class will do that:

```
// Method to deserialize a line
private void readObject(ObjectInputStream in)
                          throws IOException, ClassNotFoundException {
  double x2 = in.readDouble();
  double y2 = in.readDouble();
  line = new Line2D.Double(0,0,x2,y2);
}
```

This calls for another `import` statement in `Element.java`:

```
import java.io.ObjectInputStream;
```

That's lines serialized. It looks as though it's going to be easy. You can do rectangles next.

Serializing Rectangles

A rectangle is always drawn with its top-left corner at the origin, so you need to write only the width and height to the file:

```
// Method to serialize a rectangle
private void writeObject(ObjectOutputStream out) throws IOException {
  out.writeDouble(rectangle.width);
  out.writeDouble(rectangle.height);
}
```

The width and height members of the `Rectangle2D.Double` object are public, so you can access them directly to write them to the stream.

Deserializing an `Element.Rectangle` object is almost identical to the way you deserialized a line:

```
// Method to deserialize a rectangle
private void readObject(ObjectInputStream in)
            throws IOException, ClassNotFoundException {
  double width = in.readDouble();
  double height = in.readDouble();
  rectangle = new Rectangle2D.Double(0,0,width,height);
}
```

Don't forget that the base class fields such as the color and position of an object are all taken care of automatically. You only have to worry about the fields that belong specifically to the subclasses of `Element`.

You may be surprised and delighted to hear that serializing an `Element.Circle` object is actually going to be easier.

Serializing Circles

A circle is drawn as an ellipse with the top-left corner of the bounding rectangle at the origin. Therefore, the only item of data that you need to reconstruct a circle is the diameter:

```
// Method to serialze a circle
private void writeObject(ObjectOutputStream out) throws IOException {
  out.writeDouble(circle.width);
}
```

The diameter is recorded in the `width` member (and also in the `height` member) of the `Ellipse2D.Double` object. You just write it to the file.

You can read a circle back from a file with the following code:

```
// Method to deserialize a circle
private void readObject(ObjectInputStream in)
                        throws IOException, ClassNotFoundException {
  double width = in.readDouble();
  circle = new Ellipse2D.Double(0,0,width,width);
}
```

This reconstitutes the circle using the diameter that was written to the file.

Serializing Curves

Curves are a little trickier. One complication is that you create a curve as a `GeneralPath` object, and you have no idea how many segments make up the curve. You can obtain a special iterator object of type `PathIterator` for a `GeneralPath` object that will make available all the information you need to create the `GeneralPath` object. `PathIterator` is an interface that declares methods for retrieving details of the segments that make up a `GeneralPath` object, so a reference to an object of type `PathIterator` encapsulates all the data defining that path.

The `getPathIterator()` method for a `GeneralPath` object returns a reference of type `PathIterator`. The argument to `getPathIterator()` is an `AffineTransform` object that is applied to the path. This is based on the assumption that a single `GeneralPath` object may be used to create a number of different appearances on the screen simply by applying different transformations to the same object. You might have a `GeneralPath` object that defines a complicated object, a boat, for example. You could draw several boats on the screen simply by applying a transform before you draw each boat to set its position and orientation and use the same `GeneralPath` object for all. This avoids the overhead of creating multiple instances of what are essentially identical objects. That's why the `getPathIterator()` method enables you to obtain an iterator for a particular transformed instance of a `GeneralPath` object. However, in Sketcher you want an iterator for the unmodified path to get the basic data that you need, so you pass a default `AffineTransform` object, which does nothing.

The `PathIterator` interface declares four methods:

Method	Description
`currentSegment(double[] coords)` `currentSegment(float[] coords)`	Returns the current segment. See the text following this table for a detailed description.
`getWindingRule()`	Returns a value of type `int` that identifies the winding rule in effect. The value can be `WIND_EVEN_ODD` or `WIND_NON_ZERO`.
`next()`	Moves the iterator to the next segment as long as there is another segment.
`isDone()`	Returns `true` if the iteration is complete, and `false` otherwise.

The array argument `coords` that you pass to either version of the `currentSegment()` method is used to store data relating to the current segment and should have six elements to record the coordinates of one, two, or three points, depending on the current segment type.

The `currentSegment()` method returns a value of type `int` that indicates the type of the segment, and can be one of the following values:

Segment Type	Description
`SEG_MOVETO`	The segment corresponds to a `moveTo()` operation. The coordinates of the point moved to are returned as the first two elements of the array `coords`.
`SEG_LINETO`	The segment corresponds to a `lineTo()` operation. The coordinates of the end point of the line are returned as the first two elements of the array `coords`.
`SEG_QUADTO`	The segment corresponds to a `quadTo()` operation. The coordinates of the control point for the quadratic segment are returned as the first two elements of the array `coords`, and the end point is returned as the third and fourth elements.
`SEG_CUBICTO`	The segment corresponds to a `curveTo()` operation. The array `coords` will contain coordinates of the first control point, the second control point, and the end point of the cubic curve segment.
`SEG_CLOSE`	The segment corresponds to a `closePath()` operation. The segment closes the path by connecting the current point to the first point in the path. No values are returned in the coords array.

You have all the tools you need to get the data on every segment in the path. You just need to get a `PathIterator` reference and use the `next()` method to go through the segments in the path. The case for an `Element.Curve` object is simple: You have only a single `moveTo()` segment that is always (0, 0), and this is followed by one or more `lineTo()` segments. You'll still test the return type though, to show how it's done, and in case there are errors. You're going to end up with an array of coordinates with an unpredictable number of elements: It sounds like a case for a `Vector<>` container, particularly since `Vector<>` objects are serializable.

The coordinates you'll get for each segment in a general path will be of type `float`, so you can use a container of type `Vector<Float>` to store them, and the automatic boxing and unboxing of the values will take care of conversions to and from type `Float`. The first segment is a special case. It is always a move to (0, 0), whereas all the others will be lines. Thus the procedure will be to get the first segment and discard it after verifying it is a move and then get the remaining segments in a loop. Here's the code:

```
// Method to serialize a curve
private void writeObject(ObjectOutputStream out) throws IOException {
   PathIterator iterator = curve.getPathIterator(new AffineTransform());
   Vector<Float> coords = new Vector<Float>();
   int maxCoordCount = 6;
   float[] temp = new float[maxCoordCount];     // Stores segment data

   int result = iterator.currentSegment(temp);  // Get first segment
   assert(result == iterator.SEG_MOVETO);
   iterator.next();                             // Next segment
   while(!iterator.isDone()) {                  // While there are segments
      result = iterator.currentSegment(temp);   // Get the segment data
      assert(result == iterator.SEG_LINETO);

      coords.add(temp[0]);                      // Add x coordinate to Vector
      coords.add(temp[1]);                      // Add y coordinate
      iterator.next();                          // Go to next segment
   }

   out.writeObject(coords);                     // Save the Vector
}
```

You'll also need to add two more `import` statements to `Element.java`:

```
import java.awt.geom.PathIterator;
import java.util.Vector;
```

You obtain a `PathIterator` object for the `Element.Curve` object that you use to extract the segment data for the curve. You create a `Vector<Float>` object in which you will store the coordinate data, and you'll serialize this vector in the serialization of the curve. You also create an array of type `float[]` to hold the numerical coordinate values for a segment. All six elements are used when the segment is a cubic Bézier curve. In our case fewer are used but you must still supply an array with six elements as an argument to the `currentSegment()` method because that's what the method expects to receive.

After verifying that the first segment is a move-to segment, you use the path iterator to extract the segment data that defines the curve. You store the coordinates in the `Vector<>` object `coords`. The assertion is there to make sure that the curve consists only of line segments after the initial move-to.

It's worth considering how you might handle a GeneralPath object that consisted of a variety of different segments in arbitrary sequence. For the case where the path consisted of a set of line, quad, or cubic segments, you could use a vector of type Vector<float[]>. Don't forget, arrays are objects too, so there's nothing to prevent you from using a type argument that is an array type. If you arrange to store the coordinate values in an array of a suitable length for the segment type, you could deduce the type of segment from the number of coordinates you have stored in each array for a segment, since line, cubic, and quad segments each require a difference number of points. In the general case you would need to define classes to represent the segments of various types, plus moves, of course. If these had a common base class, Segment, say, then you could store all the objects for a path in a vector of type Vector<Segment>. Of course, you would need to make sure your segment classes were serializable, too.

To deserialize a curve, you just have to read the Vector<Float> object from the file and recreate the GeneralPath object for the Element.Curve class:

```
// Method to deserialize a curve
private void readObject(ObjectInputStream in)
                    throws IOException, ClassNotFoundException {
  Vector<Float> coords = (Vector<Float>)in.readObject();  // Read vector
  curve = new GeneralPath();                              // Create a path
  curve.moveTo(0,0);                                      // Move to the origin

  for(int i = 0 ; i<coords.size() ; i += 2 ) {    // For each pair of elements
    curve.lineTo(coords.get(i), coords.get(i+1));  // Create a line segment
  }
}
```

This should be very easy to follow. You read the data that you wrote to the stream — the vector of Float objects. The readObject() method returns the vector object as type Object, so you must cast it to the appropriate type, which is Vector<Float>. Because this cast is unchecked, you'll get a warning message from the compiler.

The first segment is always a move to the origin, so you insert that into the GeneralPath object you have created. All the succeeding segments are lines specified by pairs of elements from the Vector<>. Automatic unboxing takes care of converting the Float objects that you retrieve from the vector to the parameter type float for the lineTo() method.

Serializing Text

Element.Text is the last element type you have to deal with. Fortunately, Font, String, and java.awt.Rectangle objects are all serializable already, which means that Element.Text is serializable by default, and you have nothing further to do. You can now start implementing the listener operations for the File menu.

Supporting the File Menu

To support the menu items in the File menu, you must add some code to the actionPerformed() method in the FileAction class. You can try to put a skeleton together but a problem presents itself immediately: The ultimate source of an event will be either a toolbar button (a JButton object) or a menu item (a JMenuItem object) that was created from a FileAction object. How do you figure out what action originated the event? You only have one definition of the actionPerformed() method shared amongst all FileAction class objects so you need a way to determine which particular FileAction object originated the event. That way you can decide what you should do in response to the event.

Each FileAction object stores a String object that was passed to the constructor as the name argument, and this string was then passed on to the base class constructor. If only you had thought of saving it, you could compare the name for the current object with the name for each of the FileAction objects in the SketchFrame class. Then you could determine for which object the actionPerformed() method was called.

All is not lost though. You can call the getValue() method for the ActionEvent object to retrieve the name for the action object that caused the event. You'll be able to compare that with the name for each of the FileAction objects that you store as members of the SketchFrame class. You can therefore implement the actionPerformed() member of the FileAction inner class like this:

```java
public void actionPerformed(ActionEvent e) {
    String name = (String)getValue(NAME);
    if(name.equals(saveAction.getValue(NAME))) {
        // Code to handle file Save operation...
    } else if(name.equals(saveAsAction.getValue(NAME))) {
        // Code to handle file Save As operation...
    } else if(name.equals(openAction.getValue(NAME))) {
        // Code to handle file Open operation...
    } else if(name.equals(newAction.getValue(NAME))) {
        // Code to handle file New operation...
    } if(name.equals(printAction.getValue(NAME))) {
        // Code to handle Print operation..
    }
}
```

Calling getValue() with the argument as the NAME key that is defined in the Action interface returns the String object that was stored for the FileAction object when it was created. If the name for the current object matches that of a particular FileAction object, then that must be the action to which the event applies, so you know what to do. You have one if or else-if block for each action, and you'll develop the code for these one by one.

Many of these operations will involve dialogs. You'll want to get at the file system and display the list of directories and files to choose from, for an Open operation for instance. It sounds like a lot of work, and it certainly would be, if it weren't for a neat facility provided by the javax.swing.JFileChooser class.

Using a File Chooser

The JFileChooser class in the javax.swing package provides an easy-to-use mechanism for creating file dialogs for opening and saving files. You can use a single object of this class to create all the file dialogs you need, so add a member to the SketchFrame class to store a reference to a JFileChooser object that you'll create in the constructor:

```java
private JFileChooser files;                    // File chooser dialog
```

While you're about it, you can add an `import` for the `JFileChooser` class name, too. There are several `JFileChooser` constructors, but I'll discuss only a couple of them here. The default constructor creates an object with the current directory as the default directory, but that won't quite do for our purposes. What you want is for the default directory to be the `DEFAULT_DIRECTORY`, which you defined in the `SketcherConstants` class, so you'll use the constructor that accepts an argument of type `File` that specifies the directory containing the files that the dialog will display initially. Add the following statement to the `SketchFrame` constructor, following the statements that you added earlier that verified `DEFAULT_DIRECTORY` actually existed on the hard drive:

```
files = new JFileChooser(DEFAULT_DIRECTORY);
```

The dialog that the `files` object encapsulates will display the contents of the directory specified by `DEFAULT_DIRECTORY`. You can now use the `files` object to implement the event handling for the `File` menu. There are a considerable number of methods in the `JFileChooser` class, so rather than trying to summarize them all, which would take many pages of text and be incredibly boring, let's try out the ones that you can apply to Sketcher to support the `File` menu.

File Save Operations

In most cases you'll want to display a modal file save dialog when the Save menu item or toolbar button is selected. As luck would have it, the `JFileChooser` class has a `showSaveDialog()` method that does precisely what you want. All you have to do is call the method with a reference to the `Component` object that will be the parent for the dialog to be displayed as the argument. The method returns a value indicating how the dialog was closed. You could display a save dialog in a method for a `FileAction` object with the following statement:

```
int result = files.showSaveDialog(SketchFrame.this);
```

This will automatically create a file save dialog with the `SketchFrame` object as parent, and with Save and Cancel buttons. The `SketchFrame.this` notation is used to refer to the `this` member for the `SketchFrame` object from within a method of an inner class object of type `FileAction`. To reference the `this` variable for an outer class object from a non-static inner class object, you just qualify `this` with the outer class name. The file chooser dialog will be displayed centered in the parent component, which is the `SketchFrame` object here. If you specify the parent component as `null`, the dialog will be centered on the screen. This also applies to all the other methods I'll discuss that display file chooser dialogs.

When you need a file open dialog, you can call the `showOpenDialog()` member of a `JFileChooser` object. Don't be fooled here though. A save dialog and an open dialog are essentially the same. They differ only in minor details — the title bar and one of the button labels. The sole purpose of both dialogs is simply to select a file — for whatever purpose. If you wanted to be perverse, you could pop up a save dialog to open a file and vice versa!

You can also display a customized dialog from a `JFileChooser` object. Although it's not strictly necessary for the Sketcher application — the standard file dialogs are quite adequate — you'll adopt a custom approach as it will give you some experience of using a few more `JFileChooser` methods.

You can display a custom dialog by calling the `showDialog()` method for the `JFileChooser` object supplying two arguments. The first argument is the parent component for the dialog window, and the second is the approve button text — the approve button being the button that you click on to expedite the operation rather than cancel it. You could display a dialog with a Save button with the following statement:

```
int result = files.showDialog(SketchFrame.this, "Save");
```

If you pass `null` as the second argument here, the button text will be whatever was set previously—possibly the default.

Before you display a custom dialog, though, you would normally do a bit more customizing of what is to be displayed. You'll be using the following `JFileChooser` methods to customize the dialogs for Sketcher:

Method	Description
setDialogTitle(String text)	The `String` object that you pass as the argument is set as the dialog's title bar text.
setApproveButtonText(String text)	The `String` object that you pass as the argument is set as the approve button label.
setApproveButtonToolTipText(String text)	The `String` object that you pass as the argument is set as the approve button tooltip.

A file chooser can be set to select files, directories, or both. You can determine what can be selected in a dialog by calling the `setFileSelectionMode()` method. The argument must be one of the constants `FILES_ONLY`, `DIRECTORIES_ONLY`, and `FILES_AND_DIRECTORIES` that are defined as static members of the `JFileChooser` class; `FILES_ONLY` is the default. You also have the `getFileSelectionMode()` method with which you can determine what selection mode is set. To allow multiple selections to be made from the list in the file dialog, you call the `setMultiSelectionEnabled()` method for your `JFileChooser` object with the argument `true`.

If you want the dialog to have a particular file selected when it opens, you can pass a `File` object specifying that file to the `setSelectedFile()` method for the `JFileChooser` object. This will pre-select the file in the file list for the dialog if the file already exists, and insert the name in the file name field if it doesn't. The file list is created when the `JFileChooser` object is created, but naturally files may be added or deleted over time, and when this occurs you will need to reconstruct the file list. Calling the `rescanCurrentDirectory()` method before you display the dialog will do this for you. You can change the current directory at any time by passing a `File` object specifying the directory you want to make current to the `setCurrentDirectory()` method.

That's enough detail for now. Let's put the customizing code together.

Try It Out   Creating a Customized File Dialog

You'll first add a method to the `SketchFrame` class to create the customized file dialog and return the `File` object encapsulating the file that has been selected, or `null` if a file was not selected:

```
        // Display a custom file save dialog
      private File showDialog(String dialogTitle,
                              String approveButtonText,
                              String approveButtonTooltip,
                              File file) {              // Current file - if any

      files.setDialogTitle(dialogTitle);
      files.setApproveButtonText(approveButtonText);
      files.setApproveButtonToolTipText(approveButtonTooltip);
      files.setFileSelectionMode(files.FILES_ONLY);
      files.rescanCurrentDirectory();
      files.setSelectedFile(file);
      int result = files.showDialog(SketchFrame.this, null);   // Show the dialog
      return (result == files.APPROVE_OPTION) ? files.getSelectedFile() : null;
    }
```

This method accepts four arguments that are used to customize the dialog — the dialog title, the button label, the button tooltip, and the `File` object representing the file for the current sketch. Each of the options is set using one of the methods for the `JFileChooser` object that I discussed earlier. The last argument is used to select a file in the file list initially. If it is `null`, no file will be selected from the file list.

Note that you reconstruct the file list for the dialog by calling the `rescanCurrentDirectory()` method. This is to ensure that you always display an up-to-date list of files. If you didn't do this, the dialog would always display the list of files that were in the directory when you created the `JFileChooser` object. Any changes to the contents of the directory since then would not be taken into account.

The value that is returned by the `showDialog()` member of the `JFileChooser` object indicates whether the approve button was selected or not. If it was, you return the `File` object from the file chooser that represents the selected file; otherwise, you return `null`. A method that calls your `showDialog()` method to display the dialog can determine whether or not a file was chosen by testing the return value for `null`.

You can now use this method when you implement handling of a Save menu item action event. A save operation is a little more complicated than you might imagine at first sight, so let's consider it in a little more detail.

Implementing the Save Operation

First of all, what happens in a save operation depends on whether the current file has been saved before. If it has, the user won't want to see a dialog every time. Once it has been saved the first time, the user will want it written away without displaying the dialog. You can use the `modelFile` member of the `SketchFrame` class to determine whether you need to display a dialog or not. You added this earlier to hold a reference to the `File` object for the sketch. Before a sketch has been saved, this will be `null`, so if it is not `null` you can conclude that the sketch has been saved previously and you don't want to show the dialog. When the sketch has been saved, you'll store a reference to the `File` object in `modelFile`, so this file will generally hold a reference to the file that holds the last version of the sketch that was saved.

Secondly, if the sketch is unchanged — which will be indicated by the `sketchChanged` member being false — either because it is new and therefore empty or because it hasn't been altered since it was last saved, you really don't need to save it at all.

You can package up these checks for when you need to save and for when you should display the dialog in another method in the SketchFrame class. You can call it saveOperation() and make it a private member of the SketchFrame class:

```
// Save the sketch if it is necessary
private void saveOperation() {
  if(!sketchChanged) {
    return;
  }

  File file = modelFile;
  if(file == null) {
    file = showDialog("Save Sketch",
                      "Save",
                      "Save the sketch",
                      new File(files.getCurrentDirectory(), filename));
    if(file == null ||   (file.exists() &&      // Check for existence
        JOptionPane.NO_OPTION ==                // Overwrite warning
          JOptionPane.showConfirmDialog(SketchFrame.this,
                                        file.getName()+" exists. Overwrite?",
                                        "Confirm Save As",
                                        JOptionPane.YES_NO_OPTION,
                                        JOptionPane.WARNING_MESSAGE)))
          return;                               // No selected file
  }
  saveSketch(file);
}
```

You first check the sketchChanged flag. If the flag is false, either the sketch is empty or it hasn't been changed since the last save. Either way, there's no point in writing it to disk, so you return immediately from the method. If the flag is true you initialize the local variable file with the reference stored in modelFile. If modelFile was not null, then you skip the entire if that displays the dialog and just call the saveSketch() method to write the sketch to the file specified by modelFile — I'll get to the detail of the saveSketch() method in a moment.

The condition tested in the nested if looks rather complicated, but this is primarily due to the plethora of arguments in the showConfirmDialog() call. You can break the condition down into its component parts quite easily. The condition comprises two logical expressions separated by the || operator, so if either expression is true, then you execute a return. The first expression just checks for file being null, so if this is the case, you return immediately. If the first expression is false, file is not null, and the second expression will be evaluated.

The second expression will be true if file references a file that already exists *and* the value returned from the showConfirmDialog() method is JOptionPane.NO_OPTION. The confirm dialog just warns of the overwrite potential, so if JOptionPane.NO_OPTION is returned, then the user has elected not to overwrite the file. Remember that with the || operator, if the left operand is true, then the right operand will not be evaluated. Similarly, with the && operator, if the left operand is false, then the right operand will not be evaluated. This means that the showConfirmDialog() method will be executed only if file is not null, which implies the left operand for the || operation is false, and file references a file that does already exist, so the left operand for the && operation is true. If you don't execute the return statement, then you fall through the if to call the helper method saveSketch() with file as the argument.

Writing a Sketch to a File

Writing a sketch to a file just involves making use of what you learned about writing objects to a file. You have already made sure that a `SketchModel` object is serializable, so you can write the sketch to an `ObjectOutputStream` with the following method in the `SketchFrame` class:

```
// Write a sketch to outFile
private void saveSketch(File outFile) {
  try {
    ObjectOutputStream out =  new ObjectOutputStream(
                              new BufferedOutputStream(
                              new FileOutputStream(outFile)));
    out.writeObject(theApp.getModel());        // Write the sketch to the stream
    out.close();                               // Flush & close it
  } catch(IOException e) {
    System.err.println(e);
    JOptionPane.showMessageDialog(SketchFrame.this,
                        "Error writing a sketch file.",
                        "File Output Error",
                        JOptionPane.ERROR_MESSAGE);
    return;                                     // Serious error - return
  }
  if(outFile != modelFile) {                    // If we are saving to a new file
                                                // we must update the window
    modelFile = outFile;                        // Save file reference
    filename = modelFile.getName();             // Update the file name
    setTitle(frameTitle + modelFile.getPath()); // Change the window title
  }
  sketchChanged = false;                        // Set as unchanged
}
```

You'll need some more `import` statements in `SketchFrame.java`:

```
import java.io.ObjectOutputStream;
import java.io.BufferedOutputStream;
import java.io.FileOutputStream;
import java.io.IOException;
```

The `saveSketch()` method writes the current `SketchModel` object to the object output stream that you create from the `File` object that is passed to it. If an error occurs, an exception of type `IOException` will be thrown, in which case you write the exception to the standard error output stream and pop up a dialog indicating that an error has occurred. You assume that the user might want to retry the operation, so you just return from the method rather than terminating the application.

If the write operation succeeds, then you need to consider whether the data members in the `window` object that relate to the file need to be updated. This will be the case when the `File` object reference that was passed to the `saveSketch()` method is not the same as the reference stored in `modelFile`. If this is so, you update the `modelFile` and file name members of the `window` object, and set the window title to reflect the new file name and path. In any event, the `sketchChanged` flag is reset to `false`, as the sketch is now safely stored away in the file.

You can now put together the code that will handle the Save menu item event.

Try It Out   Saving a Sketch

The code to handle the Save menu item event will go in the `actionPerformed()` method of the inner class `FileAction`. You have done all the real work, so it amounts to just one statement:

```
public void actionPerformed(ActionEvent e) {
    String name = (String)getValue(NAME);
    if(name.equals(saveAction.getValue(NAME))) {
        saveOperation();
} else if(name.equals(saveAsAction.getValue(NAME))) {
    // Code to handle file Save As operation...
} else if(name.equals(openAction.getValue(NAME))) {
    // Code to handle file Open operation...
} else if(name.equals(newAction.getValue(NAME))) {
    // Code to handle file New operation...
} if(name.equals(printAction.getValue(NAME))) {
    // Code to handle Print operation..
}
    }
```

You can recompile Sketcher and run it again. The Save menu item and toolbar button should now be working. When you select either of them, you should get the dialog displayed in Figure 21-2.

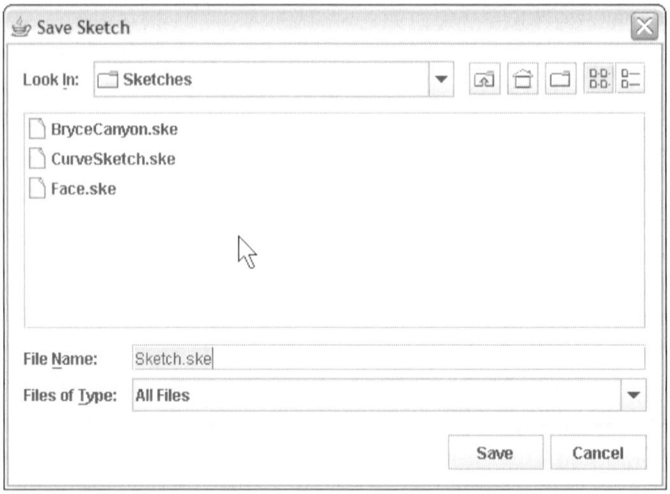

Figure 21-2

All the buttons in the dialog are fully operational. Go ahead and try them out and then save the sketch using the default name. Next time you save the sketch, the dialog won't appear. Be sure to check out the button tooltips.

Once you have created a few sketch files, you should get the warning shown in Figure 21-3 if you attempt to overwrite an existing sketch file with a new one.

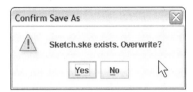

Figure 21-3

You can now save any sketch in a file — regardless of its complexity — with protection against accidentally overwriting existing files. I hope you agree that the save operation was remarkably easy to implement.

How It Works

This just calls the `saveOperation()` method for the `SketchFrame` object that is the parent of the `FileAction` object containing the `actionPerformed()` method. This carries out the save operation that writes the `SketchModel` object to a file.

Creating a File Filter

One customizing option you haven't used but might like to try is to supply a file filter for the sketch files. The default file filter in a `JFileChooser` object accepts any file or directory, but you can add filters of your own that are of a type that has the `javax.swing.filechooser.FileFilter` class as a superclass. Two abstract methods are declared in the `FileFilter` class that your filter class will have to implement:

Method	Description
`accept(File file)`	Returns `true` if the file represented by the object `file` is accepted by the file filter, and `false` otherwise
`getDescription()`	Returns a `String` object describing the filter — for example, "Sketch files"

Note that there is also a `FileFilter` interface defined in the `java.io` package that declares just one method, `accept()`, which has essentially the same function as the method in the `FileFilter` class. Objects of classes that implement the `FileFilter` interface are for use with the `listFiles()` method that is defined in the `File` class, not for `JFileChooser` objects, so make sure you don't confuse the `FileFilter` class with the `FileFilter` interface.

You can define your own file filter class for use with the Sketcher program as follows:

```
import javax.swing.filechooser.FileFilter;
import java.io.File;

public class ExtensionFilter extends FileFilter {
  public ExtensionFilter(String ext, String descr) {
    extension = ext.toLowerCase();            // Store the extension as lower case
    description = descr;                       // Store the description
  }
```

```
    public boolean accept(File file) {
      return(file.isDirectory()||file.getName().toLowerCase().endsWith(extension));
    }

    public String getDescription() {
      return description;
    }

    private String description;                // Filter description
    private String extension;                  // File extension
  }
```

To create a filter for files with the extension .ske you could write:

```
    ExtensionFilter sketchFilter = new ExtensionFilter(".ske", "Sketch files (*.ske)");
```

If you add the ExtensionFilter.java source file to the Sketcher program directory, you could try this out by adding a little code to the showDialog() method in the SketchFrame class.

Try It Out   Using a File Filter

You need to add only three lines of code:

```
    private File showDialog(String dialogTitle,
                            String approveButtonText,
                            String approveButtonTooltip,
                            File file) {            // Current file - if any

      files.setDialogTitle(dialogTitle);
      files.setApproveButtonText(approveButtonText);
      files.setApproveButtonToolTipText(approveButtonTooltip);
      files.setFileSelectionMode(files.FILES_ONLY);
      ExtensionFilter sketchFilter = new ExtensionFilter(".ske",
                                            "Sketch files (*.ske)");
      files.addChoosableFileFilter(sketchFilter);        // Add the filter
      files.setFileFilter(sketchFilter);                 // and select it
      files.rescanCurrentDirectory();
      files.setSelectedFile(file);
      int result = files.showDialog(SketchFrame.this, null);
      return(result == files.APPROVE_OPTION) ? files.getSelectedFile() : null;
    }
```

Now when you display a file save dialog, it will use the Sketcher file filter by default, and will display only directories or files with the extension .ske. The user can override this by selecting the All Files option in the dialog, whereupon all files in the current directory will be displayed.

How It Works

The file filter `sketchFilter` that you create is added to the list of available filters in the `JFileChooser` object by passing a reference to the `addChoosableFileFilter()` method. You then set this filter as the one in effect by calling the `setFileFilter()` method. The `JFileChooser` object will check each file in the file list by passing each `File` object to the `accept()` method for the file filter object that is in effect. The new file filter you have created will return `true` only for directories or files with the extension `.ske`, so only those files will be displayed in the dialog. The description of the filter is obtained by the `JFileChooser` object calling the `getDescription()` method for the Sketcher `FileFilter` object and this description is displayed in the dialog.

Of course, the available list of file filters will include the "accept all" filter that is there by default. You might want to suppress this in some situations, and there is a method defined in the `JFileChooser` class to do this:

```
files.setAcceptAllFileFilter(false);          // Remove 'all files' filter
```

Of course, passing an argument of `true` to this method will restore the filter to the list. You can also discover whether the all-files filter is used by calling the `isAcceptAllFileFilterUsed()` method, which will return `true` if it is or `false` if it isn't.

You can also remove specific `FileFilter` objects from the list maintained by the `JFileChooser` object. This allows you to adapt a `JFileChooser` object to suit circumstances at different points in a program. To remove a filter just pass a `FileFilter` reference to the `removeChoosableFileFilter()` method for your file chooser object. For example:

```
files.removeChoosableFileFilter(sketchFilter);    // Removes our filter
```

This would remove the filter you have defined for Sketcher files.

File Save As Operations

For Save As... operations, you'll always want to display a save dialog, regardless of whether the file has been saved before and ignoring the state of the dirty flag. Apart from that and some cosmetic differences in the dialog itself, the operation is identical to the Save menu item event handling. With the `showDialog()` method that you have added to the `SketchFrame` class, the implementation becomes almost trivial.

Try It Out   File Save As Operations

The code in the `else if` block in the `actionPerformed()` method in the `FileAction` class for this operation will be:

```
else if(name.equals(saveAsAction.getValue(NAME))) {
    File file = showDialog("Save Sketch As",
                           "Save",
                           "Save the sketch",
    modelFile == null ? new File(files.getCurrentDirectory(),filename): modelFile);

    if(file != null) {
```

```
            if(file.exists() && !file.equals(modelFile))
              if(JOptionPane.NO_OPTION ==                    // Overwrite warning
                 JOptionPane.showConfirmDialog(SketchFrame.this,
                                     file.getName()+" exists. Overwrite?",
                                     "Confirm Save As",
                                     JOptionPane.YES_NO_OPTION,
                                     JOptionPane.WARNING_MESSAGE))
                return;                                      // No file selected
            saveSketch(file);
          }
          return;
        }
```

Recompile Sketcher with these additions and you will have a working Save As... option on the File menu, with a file filter in action, too!

How It Works

Most of this is the same as the code for the `saveOperation()` method that implements the Save menu. You have a fancy expression as the last argument to the `showDialog()` method. This is because the Save As... operation could be used with a sketch that has been saved previously or with a sketch that has never been saved. The expression passes `modelFile` as the argument if it is not `null` and creates a new `File` object as the argument from the current directory and file name if `modelFile` is `null`. If you get a non-null `File` object back from the `showDialog()` method, then you check for a potential overwrite of an existing file. This will be the case if the selected file exists and is also different from `modelFile`. In this instance you display a YES/NO dialog warning of this, just to verify that overwriting the existing file really is intended. If the user closes the dialog by selecting the No button, you just return from the method; otherwise, you save the current sketch in the file.

Since you have sketches written to disk, let's now look at how you can implement the operation for the Open menu item so you can try reading them back.

File Open Operations

Supporting the file/open operation is in some ways a little more complicated than save. You have to consider the currently displayed sketch first of all. Opening a new sketch will replace it, so does it need to be saved before the file open operation? If it does, you must deal with that before you can read a new sketch from the file. Fortunately, most of this is already done by the `saveOperation()` method that you implemented in the `SketchFrame` class. You just need to add a prompt for the save operation when necessary. You could put this in a `checkForSave()` method that you can implement in the `SketchFrame` class as:

```
        // Prompt for save operation when necessary
        public void checkForSave() {
          if(sketchChanged && JOptionPane.YES_OPTION ==
                 JOptionPane.showConfirmDialog(SketchFrame.this,
                             "Current file has changed. Save current file?",
                             "Confirm Save Current File",
                             JOptionPane.YES_NO_OPTION,
                             JOptionPane.WARNING_MESSAGE)) {
            saveOperation();
          }
        }
```

This method will be useful outside the `SketchFrame` class a little later on, so you have declared it as a `public` member of the class. If the `sketchChanged` flag is `true`, the expression that is the right operand for the `&&` operator will be evaluated. This will pop up a confirm dialog to verify that the sketch needs to be saved. If it does, you call the `saveOperation()` method to do just that. Of course, if `sketchChanged` has the value `false`, the right operand to the `&&` operator will not be evaluated and so the dialog won't be displayed.

When you get to the point of reading a sketch from the file, some further slight complications arise. You must replace the existing `SketchModel` object and its view in the application with a new `SketchModel` object and its view.

With those few thoughts, you are now ready to make it happen.

Try It Out   Implementing the Open Menu Item Operation

The file open process is similar to a save operation, but instead of writing the file, it will read it. You'll add another helper method, `openSketch()`, to the `SketchFrame` class that will do the reading, given a `File` object identifying the source of the data. Using this method, the code to handle the `Open` menu item event in the `actionPerformed()` method for the `FileAction` class will be:

```
} else if(name.equals(openAction.getValue(NAME))) {
  checkForSave();

  // Now open a sketch file
  File file = showDialog(
                    "Open Sketch File",          // Dialog window title
                    "Open",                      // Button lable
                    "Read a sketch from file",   // Button tooltip text
                    null);                       // No file selected
  if(file != null) {                            // If a file was selected
    openSketch(file);                           // then read it
  }
}
```

You can implement the `openSketch()` method in the `SketchFrame` class as follows:

```
// Method for opening file
public void openSketch(File inFile) {
  try {
    ObjectInputStream in = new ObjectInputStream(new BufferedInputStream(
                                new FileInputStream(inFile)));
    theApp.insertModel((SketchModel)in.readObject());
    in.close();
    modelFile = inFile;
    filename = modelFile.getName();              // Update the file name
    setTitle(frameTitle+modelFile.getPath());    // Change the window title
    sketchChanged = false;                       // Status is unchanged
  } catch(Exception e) {
    System.out.println(e);
    JOptionPane.showMessageDialog(SketchFrame.this,
                    "Error reading a sketch file.",
                    "File Input Error",
                    JOptionPane.ERROR_MESSAGE);
```

```
      }
   }
```

Of course, you need three more `import` statements in `SketchFrame.java`:

```
import java.io.ObjectInputStream;
import java.io.BufferedInputStream;
import java.io.FileInputStream;
```

The `SketchModel` object that is read from the file is passed to a new method in the Sketcher class, `insertModel()`. This method has to replace the current sketch with the new one that is passed as the argument. You can implement the method like this:

```
// Insert a new sketch model
public void insertModel(SketchModel newSketch) {
   sketch = newSketch;                    // Store the new sketch
   sketch.addObserver(view);              // Add the view as observer
   sketch.addObserver(window);            // Add the app window as observer
   view.repaint();                        // Repaint the view
}
```

After you have loaded the new model, you update the window title bar and record the status as unchanged in the `SketchFrame` object. If you compile Sketcher once more, you can give the file open operation a workout. The Open dialog should be as shown in Figure 21-4.

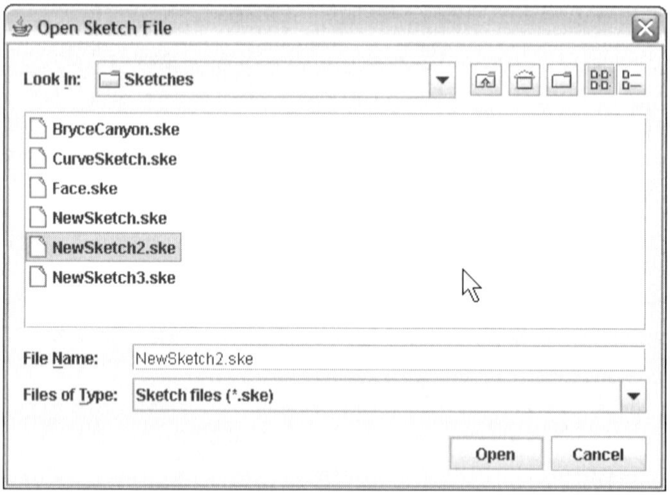

Figure 21-4

Don't forget to try out the tooltip for the Open button.

How It Works

After dealing with saving the current sketch in the `actionPerformed()` member of the `FileAction` class, you use the `showDialog()` method that you defined in the `SketchFrame` class to display a file open dialog. The `showDialog()` method is all-purpose — you can put any kind of label on the button or title in the title bar so you can use it to display any of the dialogs you need for file operations.

If a `File` object was selected in the dialog, you pass this to the `openSketch()` member of the `SketchFrame` object to read a new sketch from the file. The `openSketch()` method creates an `ObjectInputStream` object from the File object that was passed as an argument and reads a `SketchModel` object from the stream by calling the `readObject()` method. The object returned by the `readObject()` method has to be cast to the appropriate type — `SketchModel` in this case. You pass this `SketchModel` object to the `insertModel()` method for the application object. This replaces the current sketch reference in the `sketch` member of the application object with a reference to the new sketch and then sets the view and the application window as observers. Calling `repaint()` for the view object displays the new sketch, since the `paint()` method for the view object obtains a reference to the current model by calling the `getModel()` member of the application object, which will return the reference to the new model.

Starting a New Sketch

The File ⇨ New menu item simply starts a new sketch. This is quite similar to the open operation except that you must create an empty sketch rather than read a new one from disk. The processes of checking for the need to save the current sketch and inserting the new `SketchModel` object into the application will be the same.

Try It Out   Implementing the New Operation

You need to place the code to create a new empty sketch in the `else-if` block corresponding to the `newAction` object event. This is in the `actionPerformed()` method in the `FileAction` inner class:

```
else if(name.equals(newAction.getValue(NAME))) {
  checkForSave();
  theApp.insertModel(new SketchModel());       // Insert new empty sketch
  modelFile = null;                            // No file for it
  filename = DEFAULT_FILENAME;                 // Default name
  setTitle(frameTitle + files.getCurrentDirectory() + "\\" + filename);
  sketchChanged = false;                       // Not changed yet
}
```

Now you can create a new sketch.

How It Works

All the saving of the existing sketch is dealt with by the `checkForSave()` method that you added to the `SketchFrame` class. The new part is the last five lines of the highlighted code above. You call the `SketchModel` constructor to create a new empty sketch, and pass it to the `insertModel()` method for the application object. This will insert the new sketch into the application and get the view object to display it. You then update the data members of the window that record information about the file for the current sketch and its status. You also set the `sketchChanged` flag to `false`, as it's an empty sketch.

Preventing Data Loss on Close

At the moment you're still not calling `checkForSave()` when you close the application with the window icon. This means you could lose hours of work in an instant. But the solution is very simple. You just need to get the event handler for the window closing event to call the `checkForSave()` method for the window object.

To implement this you can use the `WindowListener` object for the application window that you have already added in the `Sketcher` class. This listener receives notification of events associated with opening and closing the window as well as minimizing and maximizing it. You just need to add some code to the body of the `windowClosing()` method for the listener. You require one extra line in the Sketcher class definition:

```
// Handler class for window events
class WindowHandler extends WindowAdapter {
  // Handler for window closing event
  public void windowClosing(WindowEvent e) {
    window.checkForSave();
  }
}
```

The `WindowHandler` class is a subclass of the `WindowAdapter` class. In the subclass you just define the methods you are interested in to override the empty versions in the adapter class. The `WindowListener` interface declares the following seven methods corresponding to various window events:

Method	Description
`windowActivated(WindowEvent e)`	Called when the window receives the focus and becomes the currently active window
`windowDeactivated(WindowEvent e)`	Called when the window ceases to be the currently active window
`windowIconified(WindowEvent e)`	Called when the window is minimized
`windowDeiconified(WindowEvent e)`	Called when the window returns to its normal state from a minimized state
`windowOpened(WindowEvent e)`	Called the first time a window is made visible
`windowClosed(WindowEvent e)`	Called when a window has been closed by calling its `dispose()` method
`windowClosing(WindowEvent e)`	Called when the user selects the close icon or the Close item from the system menu for the window

Clearly, using the `WindowAdapter` class as a base saves a lot of time and effort. Without it you would have to define all seven of the methods declared in the interface in our class. Because the `WindowHandler` class is an inner class its methods can access the fields of the `Sketcher` class, so the windowClosing() method you have defined can call the checkForSave() method for the window member of the Sketcher class object.

Now if you close the application window without having saved your sketch, you will be prompted to save it.

Defining the WindowHandler inner class with just one method is not necessary. You could choose to use an anonymous class, as the method is so simple. First, delete the WindowHandler inner class to the Sketcher class. Next, replace the statement that adds the window listener for the window object with the following statement:

```
window.addWindowListener(new WindowAdapter() {// Add window listener
                        public void windowClosing(WindowEvent e) {
                          window.checkForSave();
                        }
                     } );
```

You define an anonymous class derived from the WindowHandler class in the expression that is the argument to the addWindowListener() method. The syntax is exactly the same as if you were defining an anonymous class that implements an interface. The class defines just one method, the windowClosing() method that you defined previously in the WindowHandler class.

If you recompile the Sketcher program, you should find that it works just as well as before.

How It Works

This makes use of the code that you implemented for the save operation, packaged in the checkForSave() method. This does everything necessary to enable the sketch to be saved before the application window is closed. Defining methods judiciously makes for economical coding.

This still leaves you with the now redundant File | Close button to tidy up. As it's not really any different from the File | New function, let's change it to an application Exit button and reposition it at the bottom of the File menu. First, delete the statements that create the closeAction object and add it to the File menu. Next you can insert statements for an else if block corresponding to the closeAction object event in the actionPerformed() method for the FileAction inner class to SketchFrame that will provide the close action functionality — checking to see whether the file should be saved before exiting the program:

```
      } if(name.equals(printAction.getValue(NAME))) {
        // Code to handle Print operation..
      } else if(name.equals(closeAction.getValue(NAME))) {
        checkForSave();
        System.exit(0);
      }
```

Then you can redo the menu layout in the File menu constructor and add the mnemonic key Ctrl-X for the Exit menu item:

```
      // Create the action items for the file menu
      newAction = new FileAction("New",
              KeyStroke.getKeyStroke('N', CTRL_DOWN_MASK), "Create new sketch");
```

```
openAction = new FileAction("Open",
            KeyStroke.getKeyStroke('O', CTRL_DOWN_MASK),"Open existing sketch");
saveAction = new FileAction("Save",
            KeyStroke.getKeyStroke('S', CTRL_DOWN_MASK), "Save sketch");
saveAsAction = new FileAction("Save As...");
printAction = new FileAction("Print",
            KeyStroke.getKeyStroke('P', CTRL_DOWN_MASK), "Print sketch");
closeAction = new FileAction("Exit",
            KeyStroke.getKeyStroke('X', CTRL_DOWN_MASK ), "Exit Sketcher");

// Construct the file drop-down menu
fileMenu.add(new JMenuItem(newAction));
fileMenu.add(new JMenuItem(openAction));
fileMenu.addSeparator();                        // Add separator
fileMenu.add(new JMenuItem(saveAction));
fileMenu.add(new JMenuItem(saveAsAction));
fileMenu.addSeparator();                        // Add separator
fileMenu.add(new JMenuItem(printAction));
fileMenu.addSeparator();                        // Add separator
fileMenu.add(new JMenuItem(closeAction));
```

All but one of the file actions are now operable. To complete the set you just need to get printing up and running.

Printing in Java

Printing is always a messy business — inevitably so, because you have to worry about tedious details such as the size of a page, the margin sizes, and how many pages you're going to need for your output. As you might expect, the process for printing an image is different from printing text, and you may also have the added complication of several printers with different capabilities being available, so with certain types of documents you need to select an appropriate printer. The way through this is to take it one step at a time. Let's understand the general principles first.

There are five packages dedicated to supporting printing capabilities in Java:

Package	Description
javax.print	Defines classes and interfaces that enable you to determine what printers are available and what their capabilities are. It also enables you to identify types of documents to be printed.
javax.print.attribute	Defines classes and interfaces supporting the definition of sets of printing attributes. For example, you can define a set of attributes required by a particular document when it is printed, such as color output and two-sided printing.

Package	Description
`javax.print.attribute.standard`	Defines classes that identify a set of standard printing attributes.
`javax.print.event`	Defines classes that identify events that can occur while printing and interfaces that identify listeners for printing events.
`java.awt.print`	Defines classes and attributes for expediting the printing of 2D graphics and text.

The first four of these packages make up what is called the Print Service API. This allows printing on all Java platforms and has facilities for discovering and using multiple printers with varying capabilities. Since in all probability you have just a single printer available, you'll concentrate in the first instance on understanding the classes and interfaces defined in the `java.awt.print` package that carry out print operations on a given printer, and stray into classes and interfaces from the other packages when necessary.

Four classes are defined in the `java.awt.print` package, and you'll be using all of them eventually:

`PrinterJob`	An object of this class type controls printing to a particular print service (such as a printer or fax capability).
`PageFormat`	An object of this class type defines the size and orientation of a page that is to be printed.
`Paper`	An object of this class type defines the size and printable area of a sheet of paper.
`Book`	An object of this class type defines a multipage document where pages may have different formats and require different rendering processes.

The `PrinterJob` class drives the printing process. Don't confuse this with the `PrintJob` class in the `java.awt` package — this is involved in the old printing process that was introduced in Java 1.1, and the `PrinterJob` class now supersedes this. A `PrinterJob` class object provides the interface to a printer in your environment, and you use `PrinterJob` class methods to set up and initiate the printing process for a particular document. You start printing off one or more pages in a document by calling the `print()` method for the `PrinterJob` object.

A `PageFormat` object encapsulates information about a page, such as its dimensions, margin sizes, and orientation. An object of type `Paper` describes the characteristics of a physical sheet of paper that will be part of a `PageFormat` object. A `Book` object encapsulates a document consisting of a collection of pages that are typically processed in an individual way. You'll be getting into the details of how you work with these a little later in this chapter.

There are three interfaces in the `java.awt.print` package:

`Printable`	Implemented by a class to print a single page
`Pageable`	Implemented by a class to print a multipage document, where each page may be printed by a different `Printable` object
`PrinterGraphics`	Declares a method for obtaining a reference to the `PrinterJob` object for use in a method that is printing a page

When you print a page, an object of a class that implements the `Printable` interface determines what is actually printed. Such an object is referred to as a **page painter**. Figure 21-5 illustrates the basics of how the printing process works.

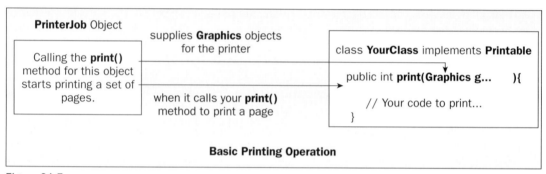

Figure 21-5

The `Printable` interface defines only one method, `print()`, which is called by a `PrinterJob` object when a page should be printed. Therefore, the `print()` method from the `Printable` interface does the printing of a page. Note that I have mentioned two `print()` methods, one defined in the `PrinterJob` class that you call to starting the printing process and another declared in the `Printable` interface that you implement in your class that is to do the printing legwork for a single page.

The printing operation that you must code when you implement the `print()` method declared in the `Printable` interface works through a graphics context object that provides the means for writing data to your printer. The first argument passed to your `print()` method when it is called by a `PrinterJob` object is a reference of type `Graphics` that represents the graphics context for the printer. The object that it references is actually of type `Graphics2D`, which parallels the process you are already familiar with for drawing on a component that is displayed on the screen. Just as with writing to the screen, you use the methods defined in the `Graphics` and `Graphics2D` classes to print what you want, and the basic mechanism for printing 2D graphics or text on a page is identical to drawing on a component. The `Graphics` object for a printer also happens to implement the `PrinterGraphics` interface (not to be confused with the `PrintGraphics` interface in the `java.awt` package!) that declares just one method, `getPrinterJob()`. You call this method to obtain a reference to the object that is managing the print process. You would do this if you need to call `PrinterJob` methods to extract information about the print job, such as the job name or the user name.

A class that implements the `Pageable` interface defines an object that represents a set of pages to be printed rather than a single page. You would implement this interface for more complicated printing situations in which a different page painter may print each page using an individual `PageFormat` object. It's the job of the `Pageable` object to supply information to the `PrinterJob` object about which page painter and `PageFormat` object should be used to print each page. The `Pageable` interface declares three methods:

`getNumberOfPages()`	Returns the number of pages to be printed as type `int`, or the constant value `UNKNOWN_NUMBER_OF_PAGES` if the number of pages is not known. This constant is defined as a value of type `int` in the `Pageable` interface.
`getPageFormat(int pageIndex)`	Returns a `PageFormat` object describing the size and orientation of the page specified by the argument. An exception of type `IndexOutOfBoundsException` will be thrown if the page does not exist.
`getPrintable(int pageIndex)`	Returns a reference to the `Printable` object responsible for printing the page specified by the argument. An exception of type `IndexOutOfBoundsException` will be thrown if the page does not exist.

A `Book` object also encapsulates a document that consists of a number of pages, each of which may be processed individually for printing. The difference between this and an object of a class that implements the `Pageable` interface is that you can add individual pages to a `Book` object programmatically, whereas a class that implements `Pageable` encapsulates all the pages. You'll look at how both of these options work later in this chapter.

Creating and Using PrinterJob Objects

Because the `PrinterJob` class encapsulates and manages the printing process for a given physical printer that is external to the Java Virtual Machine (JVM), you can't create an object of type `PrinterJob` directly using a constructor. You obtain a reference to a `PrinterJob` object for the default printer on a system by calling the static method `getPrinterJob()` that is defined in the `PrinterJob` class:

```
PrinterJob printJob = PrinterJob.getPrinterJob(); // For the default printer
```

The `printJob` object provides the interface to the default printer and controls each print job that you send to it.

A printer is encapsulated by a `javax.print.PrintService` object, and you can obtain a reference of type `PrintService` to an object encapsulating the printer that will be used by a `PrinterJob` object by calling its `getPrintService()` method:

```
PrintService printer = printJob().getPrintService();
```

You can query the object that is returned for information about the capabilities of the printer and the kinds of documents it can print, but I won't divert down that track for the moment. One point you should keep in mind is that sometimes a printer may not be available on the machine on which your code is running. In this case the getPrintService() method will return null, so it's a good idea to call the method and test the reference that is returned, even if you don't want to obtain details of the printer.

If multiple print services are available, such as several printers or perhaps a fax capability, you can obtain an array of PrintService references for them by calling the static lookupPrintServices() method that is defined in the PrinterJob class. For example:

```
PrintService[] printers = PrinterJob.lookupPrintServices();
```

The printers array will have one element for each print service that is available. If no print services are available, the array will have zero length. If you want to select a specific printer for the PrinterJob object to work with, you just pass the array element corresponding to the print service of your choice to the setPrintService() method for the PrinterJob object. For example:

```
if(printers.length>0) {
  printJob.setPrintService(printers[0]);
}
```

The if statement checks that there are some print services before attempting to set the print service. Without this you could get an IndexOutOfBoundsException exception if the printers array has no elements. Of course, more realistically you would use methods defined in the PrintService interface to query the printers, and use the results to decide which printer to use.

Displaying a Print Dialog

When you want to provide the user with control over the printing process, you can display a print dialog by calling the printDialog() method for a PrinterJob object. This method displays the modal dialog that applies to your particular print facility. There are two versions of the printDialog() method for a PrinterJob object. The version without arguments will display the native dialog if the PrinterJob object is printing on a native printer, so I'll introduce that first and return to the other version later.

If the dialog is closed using the button that indicates printing should proceed, the printDialog() method will return true; otherwise, it will return false. The method will throw an exception of type java.awt.HeadlessException if there is no display attached to the system. Thus, to initiate printing, you can call the printDialog() method to put the decision to proceed in the hands of the user, and if the method returns true, call the print() method for the PrinterJob object to start printing. Note that the print() method will throw an exception of type java.awt.print.PrinterException if an error in the printing system causes the operation to be aborted.

Of course, the PrinterJob object has no prior knowledge of what you want to print, so you have to call a method to tell the PrinterJob object where the printed pages are coming from before you initiate printing. The simplest way to do this is to call the setPrintable() method and pass a reference to an object of a class that implements the Printable interface as the argument.

In Sketcher, the obvious candidate to print a sketch is the SketchView object (a reference to which is stored in the view member of the application object). Thus, you could provide for the possibility of sketches being printed by making the SketchView class implement the Printable interface. That done, you could then set the source of the printed output just by passing a reference to the view to the setPrintable() method for a PrinterJob object. You might consider the SketchModel object to be a candidate to do the printing, but printing is not really related to a sketch, any more than plotting or displaying a sketch on the screen is. The model is the input to the printing process, not the owner of it. It is generally better to keep the model dedicated to encapsulating the data that represents the sketch.

Starting the Printing Process

Let's use what you now know about printing to add some code to the `actionPerformed()` method in the `FileAction` class. This will handle the event for the `printAction` object in the `SketchFrame` class:

```
if(name.equals(printAction.getValue(NAME))) {
  // Get a printing object
  PrinterJob printJob = PrinterJob.getPrinterJob();
  PrintService printer = printJob.getPrintService();
  if(printer == null) {                    // See if there is a printer
    JOptionPane.showMessageDialog(SketchFrame.this,
                          "No default printer available.",
                          "Printer Error",
                          JOptionPane.ERROR_MESSAGE);
    return;
  }
  // The view is the page source
  printJob.setPrintable(theApp.getView());

  if(printJob.printDialog()) {             // Display print dialog

    try {                                  // and if true is returned...
      printJob.print();                    // ...then print
    } catch(PrinterException pe) {
      System.out.println(pe);
      JOptionPane.showMessageDialog(SketchFrame.this,
                          "Error printing a sketch.",
                          "Printer Error",
                          JOptionPane.ERROR_MESSAGE);
    }
  }
} else if(name.equals(closeAction.getValue(NAME))) {
  checkForSave();
  System.exit(0);
}
```

The code here obtains a `PrinterJob` object, and after verifying that there is a printer to print on, sets the view as the printable source. You don't need access to the `PrinterService` object to print, but it's one way of verifying that a printer is available. The expression for the second `if` will display a print dialog, and if the return value from the `printDialog()` method call is `true`, you call the `print()` method for the `printJob` object to start the printing process. This is one of two overloaded `print()` methods that the `PrinterJob` class defines. You'll look into the other one when you try out the alternative `printDialog()` method a little later in this chapter.

Three more `import` statements are needed in the `SketchFrame.java` file:

```
import javax.print.PrintService;
import java.awt.print.PrinterJob;
import java.awt.print.PrinterException;
```

1111

The SketchFrame class still won't compile at the moment, as you haven't made the SketchView class implement the Printable interface yet.

Printing Pages

The class object that you pass to the setPrintable() method is responsible for all the details of the printing process. This class must implement the Printable interface, which implies defining the print() method in the class. You can make the SketchView class implement the Printable interface like this:

```
import javax.swing.*;                    // For various Swing components
// Import statements as before...
import java.awt.print.Printable;
import java.awt.print.PageFormat;
import java.awt.print.PrinterException;

class SketchView extends JComponent
                  implements Observer, ActionListener, Printable {
  // Method to print the sketch
  public int print(Graphics g,              // Graphics context for printing
                   PageFormat pageFormat,    // The page format
                   int pageIndex)            // Index number of current page
              throws PrinterException {
    // Code to do the printing...
  }

  // Rest of the class definition as before...
}
```

The code that you added to the actionPerformed() method in the FileAction inner class to SketchFrame identified the SketchView object to the PrinterJob object as responsible for executing the printing of a page. The PrinterJob object will therefore call the print() method that you have defined here for each page to be printed. This process starts when you call the print() method for the PrinterJob object that has overall control of the printing process; this occurs in the actionPerformed() method in the FileAction class. You can see that the print() method in SketchView can throw an exception of type PrinterException. If you identify a problem within your print() method code, the way to signal the problem to the PrinterJob object is to throw an exception of this type.

Keep in mind that you should not assume that the PrinterJob object will call the print() method for your Printable object just once per page. In general, the print() method is likely to be called several times for each page, as the output destined for the printer is buffered within the Java printing system, and the buffer will not necessarily be large enough to hold a complete page. You don't need to worry about this unduly. Just don't build any assumptions into your code about how often print() is called for a given page.

Of course, the PrinterJob object in the actionPerformed() method code has no way of knowing how many pages need to be printed. When you call the PrinterJob object's print() method, it will continue calling the SketchView object's print() method until the value returned indicates there are no more pages to be printed. You can return one of two values from the print() method in the Printable interface—either PAGE_EXISTS, to indicate you have rendered a page, or NO_SUCH_PAGE if there are no more pages to be printed. Both of these constants are defined in the `Printable` interface. The `PrinterJob` object will continue calling the `print()` method for the `Printable` object until the method returns the value `NO_SUCH_PAGE`. If you don't make sure the `print()` method returns this value at some point, you'll have an indefinite loop in the program.

You can see that three arguments are passed to the `print()` method in the `Printable` interface. The first is the graphics context that you must use to write to the printer. The reference passed to the method is actually of type `Graphics2D`, so you will typically cast it to this type before using it—just as you did within the `paint()` method for a component to draw on the screen. In the `print()` method in our view class, you could draw the sketch on the printer with the following statements:

```
public int print(Graphics g,              // Graphics context for printing
                 PageFormat pageFormat,    // The page format
                 int pageIndex)            // Index number of current page
               throws PrinterException {
  Graphics2D g2D = (Graphics2D) g;
  paint(g2D);
  return PAGE_EXISTS;
}
```

This will work after a fashion, but you have more work to do before you can try this out. At the moment, it will print the same page over and over, indefinitely, so let's take care of that as a matter of urgency!

It's the third argument that carries an index value for the page. The first page in a print job will have index value 0, the second will have index value 1, and so on for as long as there are more pages to be printed. If you intend to print our sketch on a single page, you can stop the printing process by checking the page index:

```
public int print(Graphics g,              // Graphics context for printing
                 PageFormat pageFormat,    // The page format
                 int pageIndex)            // Index number of current page
                 throws PrinterException {
  if(pageIndex>0) {
    return NO_SUCH_PAGE;
  }
  Graphics2D g2D = (Graphics2D) g;
  paint(g2D);                              // Draw the sketch
  return PAGE_EXISTS;
}
```

You want to print only one page, so if the value passed as the third parameter is greater than 0, you return `NO_SUCH_PAGE` to stop the printing process.

While at least you won't now print endlessly, you still won't get an output formatted the way you want it. You must look into how you can use the information provided by the second argument that is passed to the `print()` method, the `PageFormat` object, to position the output properly on the paper.

The PageFormat Class

The `PageFormat` reference that is passed as the second argument to the `print()` method for a page provides details of the page size, the position and size of the printable area on the page, and the orientation — portrait or landscape.

Perhaps the most important pieces of information you can get are where the top-left corner of the printable area (or **imageable** area to use the terminology of the method names) is on the page, and its width and height, since this is the area you have available for printing your output. The printable area on a page is simply the area within the current margins that are defined for your printer. The position of the printable area is returned by the methods `getImageableX()` and `getImageableY()` for the `PageFormat` object. These return the *x* and *y* coordinates of the top-left corner of the printable area in user coordinates for the printing context as values of type `double`, which happen to be in units of 1/72 of an inch, which, as luck would have it, corresponds to a **point** — as in *point* size for a font. The width and height of the printable area on the page are returned in the same units by the `getImageableWidth()` and `getImageableHeight()` methods for the `PageFormat` object.

The origin of the page coordinate system, the point (0,0), corresponds initially to the top-left corner of the paper. If you want the output to be placed in the printable area on the page, the first step will be to move the origin of the graphics context that you will use for writing to the printer to the position of the top-left corner of the printable area. Figure 21-6 illustrates the way you do this.

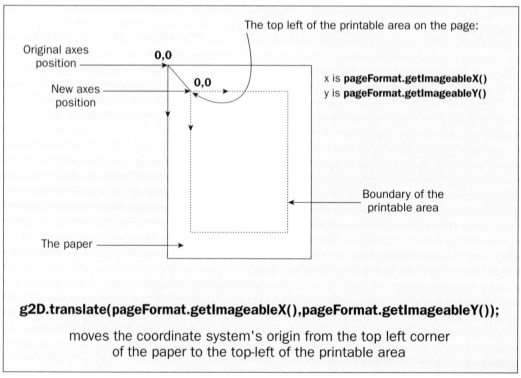

Figure 21-6

You know how to do this; it's exactly what you have been doing in the draw() method for each of our element classes. You call the translate() method for the graphics context to move the origin for the user coordinate system. Here's how this would work for the print() method in the SketchView class:

```
public int print(Graphics g,                  // Graphics context for printing
                  PageFormat pageFormat,       // The page format
                  int pageIndex)               // Index number of current page
                  throws PrinterException {
  if(pageIndex>0) {
    return NO_SUCH_PAGE;
  }
  Graphics2D g2D = (Graphics2D) g;

  // Move origin to page printing area corner
  g2D.translate(pageFormat.getImageableX(), pageFormat.getImageableY());

  paint(g2D);                                  // Draw the sketch
  return PAGE_EXISTS;
}
```

Calling the translate() method for the Graphics2D object moves the user coordinate system so that the (0,0) point is positioned at the top-left corner of the printable area on the page.

Let's see if that works in practice.

Try It Out   Printing a Sketch

You should have added the code you saw earlier to the actionPerformed() method to handle the Print menu item event and the code to SketchView to implement the Printable interface that you have evolved. Don't forget the import statements for the classes in the java.awt.print package. If you compile and run Sketcher, you should be able to print a sketch.

On my system, when I select the toolbar button to print, I get the dialog shown in Figure 21-7.

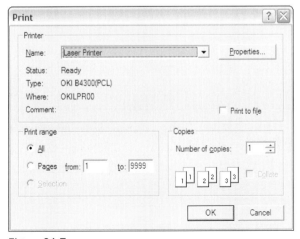

Figure 21-7

This is the standard dialog for my printer under Windows XP. In your environment you will get a dialog for your default printer. The reason why the dialog indicates that there are 9999 pages to be printed is that you haven't specified how many, so the maximum is assumed.

How It Works

The code in the `actionPerformed()` method in the `FileAction` class executes when you click the toolbar button or menu item to print a sketch. This first displays the print dialog by calling the `printDialog()` method for the `PrinterJob` object that you obtain. Clicking the OK button causes the dialog to close and the `print()` method for the `PrinterJob` object to be called. This in turn causes the `print()` method in the `SketchView` class to be called one or more times for each page that is to be printed, and one more time to end the process. The number of pages that are printed is determined by the `print()` method in the `SketchView` class. Only when this method returns the value `NO_SUCH_PAGE` will the `PrinterJob` object cease calling the method.

In the `print()` method in `SketchView`, you adjust the origin of the user coordinate system for the graphics context so that its position is at the top-left corner of the printable area on the page. Only one page is printed because you return `NO_SUCH_PAGE` when the page index value that is passed to the `print()` method is greater than 0. Incidentally, if you want to see how many times the `print()` method is called for a page, just add a statement at the beginning of the method to output some trace information to the console.

I used the print facility to print the sketch shown in Figure 21-8, and frankly, I was disappointed.

Figure 21-8

The picture that I get printed on the paper is incomplete. There are only two flowers in view, and that interesting cross between a rabbit and a cat has lost its tail.

The boulder on the left appears only in part. I know it's not all on the screen, but it's all in the model, so I was hoping to see the picture in its full glory. If you think about it, though, it's very optimistic to believe that you could automatically get the whole sketch printed. First of all, neither the `PrinterJob` object nor the view object has any idea how big the sketch is. That's a fairly fundamental piece of data if you want a complete sketch printed. Another consideration is that the left extremity of the boulder on the left of the sketch is to the left of the y axis, but I'd rather like to see it in the picture. It would be nice if you could take account of that too. Let's see how you might do it.

> *Note that material change to the `Element` subclasses will cause problems in retrieving old sketches. Sketches that were serialized before the changes will not deserialize afterwards because the class definition you use to read the data is different from the class definition when you wrote it.*

Printing the Whole Sketch

A starting point is to figure out the extent of the sketch. Ideally you need a rectangle that encloses all the elements in the sketch. It's really surprisingly easy to get that. Every element has a `getBounds()` method that returns a `java.awt.Rectangle` object enclosing the element. As you saw in Chapter 17, the `Rectangle` class also defines an `add()` method that combines the `Rectangle` object that you pass as the argument with the `Rectangle` object for which you called the method, and returns the smallest `Rectangle` object that encloses both; this is referred to as the union of the two rectangles. With these two bits of information and by accessing the elements in the list in the `SketchModel` object, you can get a rectangle that encloses the entire sketch by implementing the following method in the `SketchModel` class:

```
// Get the rectangle enclosing an entire sketch
Rectangle getModelExtent() {
  Rectangle rect = new Rectangle();           // An empty rectangle
  for(Element element : elements) {           // Go through the list
    rect.add(element.getBounds());            // Expand union
  }
  if(rect.width == 0) {                       // Make sure width
    rect.width = 1;                           // is non-zero
  }
  if(rect.height == 0) {                      // and the height
    rect.height = 1;
  }
  return rect;
}
```

Don't forget to add an `import` statement for the `Rectangle` class name to the `SketchModel` source file:

```
import java.awt.Rectangle;
```

Using the collection-based `for` loop to iterate over the elements in the list, you generate the union of the bounding rectangles for all the elements, so you end up with a rectangle that bounds everything in the sketch. A zero width or height for the rectangle is unlikely, but you want to be sure it can't happen because you'll use these values as divisors later.

You can see from Figure 21-9 how the rectangle returned by the `getModelExtent()` method is simply the rectangle that encloses all the bounding rectangles for the individual elements. If you visualize the origin of the user coordinate system being placed at the top-left corner of the printable area on the page, you can appreciate that a section of the sketch in the illustration will be hanging out to the left outside the printable area. This can arise quite easily in Sketcher—when you are drawing a circle with the center close to either of the axes, for example, or if you move a shape so this is the case. You can avoid missing part of the sketch from the printed output by first translating the origin of the coordinate system to the top-left corner of rect and then translating the origin of the graphics context at this position to the top-left corner of the printable area on the page.

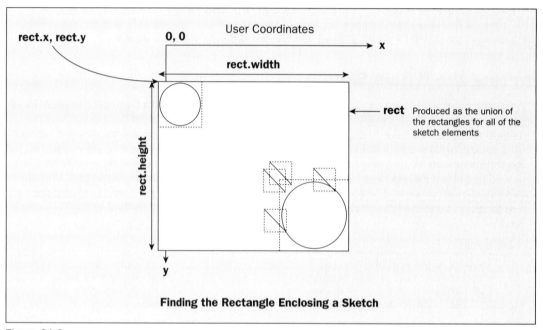

Finding the Rectangle Enclosing a Sketch

Figure 21-9

The following code in the print() method in the SketchView class will do this:

```
public int print(Graphics g,                  // Graphics context for printing
                 PageFormat pageFormat,       // The page format
                 int pageIndex)               // Index number of current page
             throws PrinterException {
  if(pageIndex>0) {
    return NO_SUCH_PAGE;
  }
  Graphics2D g2D = (Graphics2D) g;

  // Get sketch bounds
  Rectangle rect = theApp.getModel().getModelExtent();

  // Move origin to page printing area corner
  g2D.translate(pageFormat.getImageableX(), pageFormat.getImageableY());

  // Move origin to rect top left
  g2D.translate(-rect.x, -rect.y);
```

```
    paint(g2D);                                  // Draw the sketch
    return PAGE_EXISTS;
}
```

You get the rectangle bounding the sketch by calling the `getModelExtent()` method that you put together just now. You move the origin for the graphics context so that it corresponds to the top-left corner of the printable area on the page. You then use `rect` in the second statement that calls `translate()` for the `Graphics2D` object to position the top-left corner of `rect` at the origin. You could have combined these two translations into one, but it's better in this instance to keep them separate, first to make it easier to see what is going on, and second because you'll later be adding some other transformations in between these translations. There is a potentially puzzling aspect to the second translation — why are the arguments to the `translate()` method negative?

To understand this, it is important to be clear about what you are doing. It's easy to get confused by this, so I'll take it step by step. First of all, remember that the paper is a physical entity with given dimensions, and its coordinate system just defines where each point will end up on the paper when you print something. Of course, you can move the coordinate system about in relation to the paper, and you can scale or even rotate it to get something printed where you want.

Now consider our sketch. The point (`rect.x`, `rect.y`) is the top-left corner of the rectangle bounding our sketch, the area you want to transfer to the page, and this point is fixed — you can't change it to make it the origin, for instance. With the current paper coordinates at the top-left corner of the printable area, it might print something like that shown in Figure 21-10.

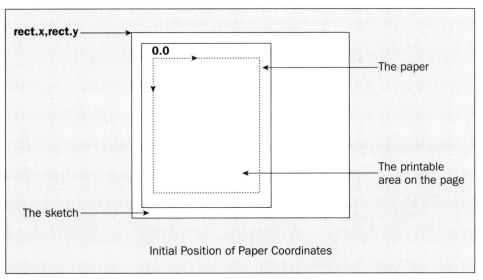

Figure 21-10

When you print a sketch you really want the point (rect.x, rect.y) to end up at the top-left corner of the printable area on the page. In other words, you have to move the origin of the coordinate system for the paper so that the point (rect.x, rect.y) in the new coordinate system is the top-left corner of the printable area. To do this you must move the origin to the new position shown in Figure 21-11.

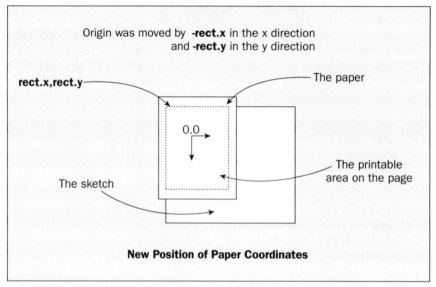

Figure 21-11

Thus a translation of the origin to the point (-rect.x, -rect.y) does the trick.

You have the sketch in the right place on the page, but it won't necessarily fit into the space available on the paper. You must scale the sketch so that it doesn't hang out beyond the right side or below the bottom of the printable page area.

Scaling the Sketch to Fit

You saw earlier that you can get the width and height of the printable area on a page by calling the getImageableWidth() and getImageableHeight() methods for the PageFormat object that is passed to the print() method. You also have the width and height of the rectangle that encloses the entire sketch. This provides the information that you need to scale the sketch to fit on the page. There are a couple of tricky aspects that you need to think about, though. Figure 21-12 shows what happens when you scale up by a factor of 2, for example.

First, note that when you scale a coordinate system, a unit of length along each of the axes changes in size, so things move relative to the origin as well as relative to one another. When you scale up with a factor greater than 1, everything moves away from the origin. You can see in Figure 21-12 how scaling up by a factor of 2 causes the dimensions of the rectangle to double, but the distances of the new rectangle from each of the axes are also doubled.

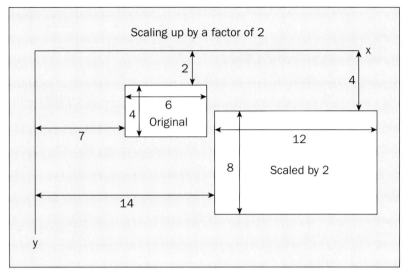

Figure 21-12

The reverse happens with scale factors less than 1. You want to make sure that you scale the sketch to fit the page while keeping its top-left corner at the top left of the printable area. This means that you can't just apply the scaling factor necessary to make the sketch fit the page in the new coordinate system I showed in the previous illustration. If you were to scale with this coordinate system, the sketch would move in relation to the origin, away from it if you are scaling up as is the case in Figure 21-12, or towards it if you are scaling down. As a consequence, the top-left corner of the sketch would no longer be at the top left of the printable area. Thus you must apply the scaling operation to make the sketch fit on the page *after* you have translated the paper origin to the top-left corner of the printable area, but *before* you translate this origin point to make the top-left corner of the sketch appear at the top-left corner of the printable area. This ensures that the sketch is scaled to fit the page and the top-left corner of the sketch stays at the top-left corner of the printable area on the page and doesn't move to some other point.

Secondly, you want to make sure that you scale *x* and *y* by the same factor. If you apply different scales to the *x* and *y* axes in the user coordinate system, the relative proportions of a sketch will not be maintained and circles will become ellipses and squares will become rectangles.

You can calculate the scale factors you need to apply to get the sketch to fit within the printable area of the page with the following statements:

```
// Calculate the x and y scales to fit the sketch to the page
double scaleX = pageFormat.getImageableWidth()/rect.width ;
double scaleY = pageFormat.getImageableHeight()/rect.height;
```

You are using variables of type `double` for the scale factors here because the `getImageableWidth()` and `getImageableHeight()` methods return values of type `double`. The scale factor for the *x*-axis needs to be such that when you multiply the width of the sketch, `rect.width`, by the scale factor, the result is the width of the printable area on the page returned by `getImageableWidth()`, and similarly for scaling the *y*-axis. Since you want to apply the same scale to both axes, you should calculate the minimum of the scale factors scaleX and scaleY. If you then apply this minimum to both axes, the sketch will fit within the width and height of the page and still be in proportion.

Try It Out   Printing the Whole Sketch

You just need to add some code to the print() method in SketchView to calculate the required scale factor and then use the scale() method for the Graphics2D object to apply the scaling transformation:

```
public int print(Graphics g,              // Graphics context for printing
                 PageFormat pageFormat,    // The page format
                 int pageIndex)            // Index number of current page
                 throws PrinterException {
  if(pageIndex>0) {
    return NO_SUCH_PAGE;
  }
  Graphics2D g2D = (Graphics2D) g;
  // Get sketch bounds
  Rectangle rect = theApp.getModel().getModelExtent();

  // Calculate the scale to fit sketch to page
  double scaleX = pageFormat.getImageableWidth()/rect.width;
  double scaleY = pageFormat.getImageableHeight()/rect.height;

  // Get minimum scale factor
  double scale = Math.min(scaleX, scaleY);

  // Move origin to page printing area corner
  g2D.translate(pageFormat.getImageableX(), pageFormat.getImageableY());

  g2D.scale(scale, scale);                 // Apply scale factor

  g2D.translate(-rect.x, -rect.y);         // Move origin to rect top left

  paint(g2D);                              // Draw the sketch
  return PAGE_EXISTS;
}
```

If you compile and run Sketcher with these changes, you should now be able to print each sketch within a page. Note that you need to create a new sketch. Any sketches that you created before these changes will not be readable because of the changes you have made to the SketchModel class definition.

How It Works

You calculate the scaling factors for each axis as the ratio of the dimension of the printable area on the page to the corresponding dimension of the rectangle enclosing the sketch. You then take the minimum of these two scale factors as the scale to be applied to both axes. As long as the scale transformation is applied after the translation of the coordinate system to the top-left corner of the printable page area, one or other dimension of the sketch will fit exactly within the printable area of the page.

The output is now fine, but if the width of the sketch is greater than the height, you waste a lot of space on the page. Ideally in this situation you would want to print with a landscape orientation rather than the default portrait orientation. Let's see what possibilities you have for doing that.

Printing in Landscape Orientation

You can easily determine when a landscape orientation would be preferable by comparing the width of a sketch with its height. If the width is larger than the height, a landscape orientation will make better use of the space on the paper and you will get a larger-scale picture.

You can set the orientation of the output in relation to the page by calling the setOrientation() method for the PageFormat object. You can pass one of three possible argument values to this method, which are defined within the PageFormat class:

Argument Value	Description
PORTRAIT	The origin is at the top-left corner of the page, with the positive x-axis running from left to right and the positive y-axis running from top to bottom. This is the MS Windows and Postscript portrait definition.
LANDSCAPE	The origin is at the bottom-left corner of the page, with the positive x-axis running from bottom to top and the positive y-axis running from left to right.
REVERSE_LANDSCAPE	The origin is at the top-right corner of the page, with the positive x-axis running from top to bottom and the positive y-axis running from right to left. This is the Apple Macintosh landscape definition.

In each case the long side of the paper is in the same orientation as the y-axis, but note that a Macintosh landscape specification has the origin at the top-right corner of the page rather than the top-left or bottom-left.

You might think that you can incorporate LANDSCAPE orientation into the print() method in SketchView by changing the PageFormat object:

```
public int print(Graphics g,              // Graphics context for printing
                 PageFormat pageFormat,    // The page format
                 int pageIndex)            // Index number of current page
```

```
              throws PrinterException {
  if(pageIndex>0) {
    return NO_SUCH_PAGE;
  }
  Graphics2D g2D = (Graphics2D) g;

  // Get sketch bounds
  Rectangle rect = theApp.getModel().getModelExtent();

  // If the width is more than the height, set landscape
  if(rect.width>rect.height) {
    pageFormat.setOrientation(pageFormat.LANDSCAPE);
  }

  // Rest of the code as before...
}
```

Having set the orientation for the `PageFormat` object, the methods returning the coordinates for the position of the printable area and the width and height all return values consistent with the orientation. Thus the width of the printable area will be greater than the height if the orientation has been set to `LANDSCAPE`. Everything looks fine until you try it out. It just doesn't work. The `PageFormat` object that is passed to the `print()` method here is a carrier of information — the information that the `PrinterJob` method used when it created the graphics context object. The coordinate system in the graphics context has already been set up with whatever paper orientation was set in the `PageFormat` object, and changing it here is too late. The solution is to make sure the `PrinterJob` object that controls the printing process works with a `PageFormat` object that has the orientation set the way that you want.

If you had known ahead of time back in the `actionPerformed()` method in the `FileAction` inner class to `SketchFrame`, you could have set up the `PageFormat` object for the print job before the `print()` method for the view object ever gets called. This can be done by modifying the code that initiates printing in the `actionPerformed()` method like this:

```
// Get a printing object
PrinterJob printJob = PrinterJob.getPrinterJob();
PrintService printer = printJob.getPrintService();
if(printer == null) {
  JOptionPane.showMessageDialog(SketchFrame.this,
                          "No default printer available.",
                          "Printer Error",
                          JOptionPane.ERROR_MESSAGE);
  return;
}
PageFormat pageFormat = printJob.defaultPage();
Rectangle rect = theApp.getModel().getModelExtent(); // Get sketch bounds

// If the sketch width is greater than the height, print landscape
if(rect.width>rect.height) {
  pageFormat.setOrientation(pageFormat.LANDSCAPE);
}
printJob.setPrintable(theView, pageFormat);
```

Calling the `defaultPage()` method for a `PrinterJob` object returns a reference to the default page for the current printer. You can then change that to suit the conditions that you want to apply in the printing operation and pass the reference to an overloaded version of the `setPrintable()` method. The call to `setPrintable()` here makes the `printJob` object use the `view` object as the `Printable` object, and supply the `PageFormat` object specified by the second argument when it calls the `print()` method for the view. With this code you don't need to worry about the orientation in the `print()` method for the `Printable` object. It is taken care of before `print()` ever gets called. You'll need an `import` statement for the `PageFormat` class name in the `SketchFrame.java` file for this to compile.

If you recompile and try printing a sketch that is wider than it is long, it should come out perfectly in landscape orientation. While everything works, the way printing has been implemented could be better. The `PrinterJob` and `PrintService` objects are recreated every time the event handler executes. This has a detrimental effect on the performance of the printing event handler in the `FileAction` class, and what's more, it's not necessary. You'll fix this in the next section.

Improving the Printing Facilities

Of course, there are many situations where choosing the best orientation from a paper usage point of view may not be what the user wants. Instead of automatically setting landscape or portrait orientation based on the dimensions of a sketch, you could leave it to the user with a dialog to select the page setup parameters in the print dialog that you display. The mechanism for the user to set the job parameters is already in place in Sketcher. Clicking the Properties button on the dialog usually displays an additional dialog in which you can set the parameters for the print job, including whether the output is portrait or landscape. Whatever is set in the print dialog will override the orientation that you determine programmatically in the `actionPerformed()` method in the `FileAction` class.

However, the printing facilities in Sketcher are not implemented in the way that is usual for an application. For one thing, the toolbar button and the File | Print menu item do exactly the same thing, but typically it's the menu item that pops a print dialog, and the toolbar button just initiates printing of the current document. For another, there's often a separate menu item that allows the page to be set up for printing, independent of the process of printing a document. You can fix that without too much difficulty though.

In the `actionPerformed()` method in the `FileAction` class, you'll need to be able to determine whether it was the toolbar button or the menu item that initiated the event. You can get a reference to the object that originated the event by calling the `getSource()` method for the `ActionEvent` object that is passed to the `actionPerformed()` method. All you need then is a reference to the toolbar button or the menu item for print operations — either will do.

First, add a field to the `SketchFrame` class to store a reference to the toolbar button for printing:

```
    private JButton printButton;                    // Toolbar button for printing
```

The `addToolbarButton()` method in the `SketchFrame` class returns a reference to the button that it creates. You can use this to initialize the `printButton` field in the `SketchFrame` constructor:

```
    // Add file buttons
    toolBar.addSeparator();                         // Space at the start
    addToolBarButton(newAction);
```

```
addToolBarButton(openAction);
addToolBarButton(saveAction);
printButton = addToolBarButton(printAction);
```

Now you can compare the reference returned by the `getSource()` method for the `ActionEvent` object with `printButton`, and if they are one and the same, it was the button the originated the event. Otherwise it was the menu item. You can now update the code in the `actionPerformed()` method in the `FileAction` inner class so you get the print dialog displayed only when the menu item is selected:

```
// The view is the page source
printJob.setPrintable(theApp.getView(), pageFormat);
boolean printIt = true;
if(e.getSource() != printButton) {        // If it's not the toolbar button
    printIt = printJob.printDialog();      // ...display the print dialog
}
if(printIt) {                              // If printIt is true...
    try {
        printJob.print();                  // ...then print
    } catch(PrinterException pe) {
        System.out.println(pe);
        JOptionPane.showMessageDialog(SketchFrame.this,
                        "Error printing a sketch.",
                        "Printer Error",
                        JOptionPane.ERROR_MESSAGE);
    }
}
```

The value of the `printIt` flag you have defined is `true` by default. It can get reset to `false` by the value returned by the `printDialog()` method. This method only gets called when the menu item caused the event for printing, not for the toolbar button, so you only get the print dialog displayed for the menu item.

If you've completed all the changes I've described, recompile Sketcher and run it again. You should now get different behavior depending on whether you use the toolbar button or the menu item for printing.

Implementing Page Setup

You can add a menu item to the File menu to provide for setting up the printer page. First, add a field to store a reference to the menu item:

```
private JMenuItem printSetupItem;
```

Since you are not going to add a toolbar button for this, you don't need to use an `Action` object. `Action` objects carry more overhead that a simple component, so it's best not to use them unless you need the capability they provide.

Add the shaded code to the `SketchFrame` constructor to create the `JMenuItem` object for the new menu item and add the menu item to the File menu:

```
printSetupItem = new JMenuItem("Print Setup...");
printSetupItem.addActionListener(this);

// Construct the file drop-down menu
fileMenu.add(new JMenuItem(newAction));
fileMenu.add(new JMenuItem(openAction));
fileMenu.addSeparator();                        // Add separator
fileMenu.add(new JMenuItem(saveAction));
fileMenu.add(new JMenuItem(saveAsAction));
fileMenu.addSeparator();                        // Add separator
fileMenu.add(new JMenuItem(printAction));
fileMenu.add(printSetupItem);
fileMenu.addSeparator();                        // Add separator
fileMenu.add(new JMenuItem(closeAction));
```

There's no provision for an accelerator for the print setup menu item, but you could add one by calling the setAccelerator() method for the JMenuItem object and passing a reference to an appropriate KeyStroke object as the argument. The listener for the new menu item is the SketchFrame object, so you must put the code that will handle events for this menu item in the actionPerformed() method in the SketchFrame class. The only thing you need to decide is what this code is going to do.

A PrinterJob object will help because it provides a pageDialog() method that displays a dialog specifically for printing page setup. Data from the PageFormat object you supply as the argument is used to set the values in controls in the dialog. The method stores the user selections from the dialog in a new PageFormat object that it creates and returns a reference to it, so you must save it. A reference to the PageFormat object that you pass to the method will be returned only if the user does not change any page parameters. Of course, you'll need to arrange to preserve the PageFormat object that the pageDialog() method returns so that it can be used when you call the print() method for a PrinterJob object to initiate a print operation. It would therefore be a good idea to create fields in the SketchFrame class that will store the PrinterJob object for the printer you'll use and a PageFormat object to go with it. Then you just need to update the PageFormat object in the event handlers when necessary.

Add the following fields to the SketchFrame class:

```
PrinterJob printJob;                            // The current printer job
PageFormat pageFormat;                          // The printing page format
PrintService printer;                           // The printer to be used
```

You can initialize the first two fields in the SketchFrame constructor. Add the following statements at the end of the existing code in the constructor:

```
PrinterJob printJob = PrinterJob.getPrinterJob(); // Get a printing object
PageFormat pageFormat = printJob.defaultPage();   // Get the page format
printer = printJob.getPrintService();             // Get the default printer
```

Of course, the fields concerned with printing are accessible through the SketchFrame class code, including the inner classes such as the FileAction class.

You'll need to change the code in the `actionPerformed()` method in the `FileAction` class to make use of the fields you have just added to the `SketchFrame` class and to initialize the `PrintService` field:

```
      } if(name.equals(printAction.getValue(NAME))) {
        // Verify there is a default printer
        if(printer == null) {
          JOptionPane.showMessageDialog(SketchFrame.this,
                                   "No default printer available.",
                                   "Printer Error",
                                   JOptionPane.ERROR_MESSAGE);
          return;
        }

        // The view is the page source
        printJob.setPrintable(theApp.getView(), pageFormat);
        boolean printIt = true;
        if(e.getSource() != printButton) {      // If it's not the toolbar button
          printIt = printJob.printDialog();     // ...display the print dialog
        }
        if(printIt) {                           // If printIt is true...
          try {
            printJob.print();                   // ...then print
          } catch(PrinterException pe) {
            System.out.println(pe);
            JOptionPane.showMessageDialog(SketchFrame.this,
                                   "Error printing a sketch.",
                                   "Printer Error",
                                   JOptionPane.ERROR_MESSAGE);
          }
        }
      } else if(name.equals(closeAction.getValue(NAME))) {
        checkForSave();
        System.exit(0);
      }
```

You no longer need to set up the `PrinterJob` object or the `PrinterService` object here as it's already done in the `SketchFrame` class constructor. You only need to check that the printer field in the `SketchFrame` class is not `null` before you print. If it is, you pop up a message dialog and return immediately. I've removed the code that sets the page orientation based on the extent of the sketch, because it overrides the effect of the page setup dialog that you'll add in a moment.

You can now update the `actionPerformed()` method in the `SketchFrame` class to respond to events for the Print Setup... menu item:

```
  public void actionPerformed(ActionEvent e)  {
    Object source = e.getSource();
    if(source == aboutItem) {
      // Create about dialog with the menu item as parent
      JOptionPane.showMessageDialog(this,                          // Parent
                         "Sketcher Copyright Ivor Horton 2004",    // Message
                         "About Sketcher",                         // Title
                         JOptionPane.INFORMATION_MESSAGE);         // Message type
```

```
    } else if(e.getSource() == fontItem) {         // Set the dialog window position
        Rectangle bounds = getBounds();
        fontDlg.setLocation(bounds.x + bounds.width/3, bounds.y + bounds.height/3);
        fontDlg.setVisible(true);                   // Show the dialog
    } else if(source == customColorItem) {
        Color color = JColorChooser.showDialog(this, "Select Custom Color",
                                                      elementColor);

        if(color != null) {
            elementColor = color;
            statusBar.setColorPane(color);
        }
    } else if(source == printSetupItem) {
        pageFormat = printJob.pageDialog(pageFormat);      // update the page format
    }
}
```

As you now are handling events from three different sources in the method, you now obtain the reference to the source of the event and store it in a local variable. Servicing the event for the printSetupItem object just involves calling the pageDialog() method for the printJob object that is stored as a field in the SketchFrame object. You pass a reference to pageFormat that holds the current page settings as the argument to the method. You store the PageFormat reference that the method returns in the pageFormat field. This will either be a reference to the original object you passed as the argument or a new object containing updated data relating to the page.

On my system, the pageDialog() method displays the dialog shown in Figure 21-13.

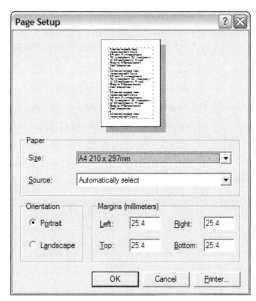

Figure 21-13

As you can see, with my printer I can select the paper size and the source tray. I can also set the margin sizes as well as select portrait or landscape orientation. The bottom-right button has provision for selecting an alternative printer, but this information will not be recorded in the `PageFormat` object. When the dialog is closed normally with the OK button, the method returns a new `PageFormat` object that incorporates the values set by the user in the dialog. If the Cancel button is used to close the dialog, the original reference that was passed as an argument is returned. The printing operations that are initiated in the `actionPerformed()` method in the `FileAction` class will use the updated `PageFormat` object. You achieve this by passing `pageFormat` as the second argument to the overloaded `setPrintable()` method with two parameters. The first argument is the object that implements the `Printable` interface and thus carries out the printing.

Using the Java Print Dialog

The overloaded version of the `printDialog()` method that I sidestepped earlier generates a Java-based print dialog rather than using the native dialog. This method requires a single argument of type `PrintRequestAttributeSet`. This interface type is defined in the `javax.print.attribute` package and declares methods for adding attributes relating to a print request to a set of such attributes. These attributes specify things such as the number of copies to be printed, the orientation of the image on the paper, or the media or media tray to be selected for the print job. The `HashPrintRequestAttributeSet` class that is defined in the same package implements this interface and encapsulates a set of print request attributes stored as a hash map. It will be useful if you can define a set of attributes that have some persistence in Sketcher so they can be carried forward from one print request to the next. You can add an initially empty set of print request attributes to the `SketchFrame` class like this:

```
private HashPrintRequestAttributeSet printAttr =
                          new  HashPrintRequestAttributeSet();
```

There are other `HashPrintRequestAttributeSet` class constructors that will create non-empty attribute sets, but this will suffice for Sketcher. You'll need an `import` statement for the class in the `SketchFrame.java` file:

```
import javax.print.attribute.HashPrintRequestAttributeSet;
```

Now you have a print request attribute set object; you can modify the `actionPerformed()` method in the `FileAction` inner class to use the Java print dialog:

```
// Verify there is a default printer
if(printer == null) {
    JOptionPane.showMessageDialog(SketchFrame.this,
                                  "No default printer available.",
                                  "Printer Error",
                                  JOptionPane.ERROR_MESSAGE);
```

```
      return;
    }

    // The view is the page source
    printJob.setPrintable(theApp.getView(), pageFormat);
    boolean printIt = true;
    if(e.getSource() != printButton) {          // If it's not the toolbar button
      printIt = printJob.printDialog(printAttr); // ...display the print dialog
    }
    if(printIt) {                                // If printIt is true...
      try {
        printJob.print(printAttr);               // ...then print
      } catch(PrinterException pe) {
        System.out.println(pe);
        JOptionPane.showMessageDialog(SketchFrame.this,
                             "Error printing a sketch.",
                             "Printer Error",
                             JOptionPane.ERROR_MESSAGE);
      }
    }
```

Note that you also use an overloaded version of the print() method for the PrinterJob object to which you pass the print request attribute set. Thus the print operation will use whatever attributes were set or modified in the print dialog displayed by the printDialog() method.

As you are using print attributes when printing, you should make the page dialog that is displayed in response to the Print Setup... menu item use them, too. There's a slight complication in that the behavior of the pageDialog() method that has a parameter of type PrintRequestAttributeSet is different from that of the method with a parameter of type PageFormat when the Cancel button in the dialog is clicked. The former version returns null, whereas the latter version returns a reference to the PageFormat object that was passed as the argument. If you don't take account of this, canceling the page setup dialog will cause printing to fail because the pageFormat field in SketchFrame will be set to null. You therefore must modify the code in the actionPerformed() method in the SketchFrame class like this:

```
    } else if(source == printSetupItem) {
      PageFormat pf = printJob.pageDialog(printAttr);
      if(pf != null) {
        pageFormat = pf;     // update the page format
      }
    }
```

Now you update pageFormat only if the return value from the pageDialog() method is not null.

If you run Sketcher with these changes you should see a dialog with three tabs, similar to that shown in Figure 21-14, when you print a sketch:

Figure 21-14

Now you have the ability to set attributes on any of the tabs in the dialog and the attributes will be stored in the `PrintAttr` member of the `SketchFrame` class that you passed to the `printDialog()` method. Since you also pass this reference to the `print()` method for the `PrinterJob` object, the print request will be executed using these attributes. This is accomplished by passing a `PageFormat` object to the `Printable` object, which prints a page that has its size, orientation, and other attributes set from the print request attributes defined by `PrintAttr`. You can see that the page count has been set to 1 by default in this dialog. You can set attributes related to a print job and store them in the `PrintRequestAttributeSet` object that you pass to the `printDialog()` method. Let's explore that a little further.

Setting Print Request Attributes Programmatically

Print request attributes are specifications of the kinds of options displayed in the dialog you just saw. They specify things like the number of copies, whether printing is in color or monochrome, the page margin sizes, and so on. Each print request attribute is identified by a class that implements the `PrintRequestAttribute` interface, and the `javax.print.attributes.standard` package defines a series of classes for standard print request attributes, as well as classes for other types of print attributes. There is a large number of standard classes for print request attributes, and I don't have the space to go into the details of them all here. So I will just pick one to show how you can query and set them.

All the classes that implement the `PrintRequestAttribute` interface are identified in the interface documentation. You can use the `Copies` class in the `javax.print.attributes.standard` package that specifies the number of printed copies to be produced.

You'll be adding an instance of the `Copies` class to our `PrintAttr` object to specify the number of copies to be printed, and this will be displayed by the print dialog. You can create an object specifying the number of copies to be produced by extending the code relating to printer setup in the `SketchFrame` constructor, like this:

```
// Set up the printer and page format objects
printJob = PrinterJob.getPrinterJob(); // Get a printing object
pageFormat = printJob.defaultPage();    // Get the page format
printer = printJob.getPrintService();   // Get the default printer
Copies twoCopies = new Copies(2);
if (printer.isAttributeCategorySupported(twoCopies.getCategory())) {
  printAttr.add(twoCopies);
}
```

The argument to the `Copies` class constructor specifies the number of copies to be produced. Our object specifies just two copies but you can go for more if you have the paper, the time, and the inclination.

Before you add this object to the print request attribute set though, you verify that the printer does actually support the production of multiple copies. Obviously, it only makes sense to set an attribute for a printer that has the appropriate capability — you won't be able to print in color on a monochrome printer, for instance. You can call the `isAttributeCategorySupported()` method for the `PrintService` object that you obtained from the `PrinterJob` object to do this.

The `isAttributeCategorySupported()` method requires an argument of type `Class` to identify the attribute category that you are querying, and you obtain this by calling the `getCategory()` method for the `Copies` object. If the attribute is supported, you add the `twoCopies` object to the set encapsulated by `printAttr` by calling its `add()` method.

You should add an `import` statement for the `Copies` class to `SketchFrame.java`:

```
import javax.print.attribute.standard.Copies;
```

If you recompile and run Sketcher once more, the print dialog should come up with two copies set initially.

Of course, setting things like margin sizes and page orientation once and for all for every page in a document may not be satisfactory in many cases. It is easy to envisage situations where you may want to print some pages in a document in portrait orientation while others, perhaps containing illustrations, are printed in landscape orientation. You'll look next at how you can handle that in Java, but before going any further, delete the following code from the `SketchFrame` constructor:

```
Copies twoCopies = new Copies(2);
if (printer.isAttributeCategorySupported(twoCopies.getCategory())) {
  printAttr.add(twoCopies);
}
```

You can remove the `import` statement for the `Copies` class name, too.

Multipage Document Printing

If you need to print a document that contains multiple pages in a print job, you can include code for accommodating this possibility in the implementation of the `print()` method declared in the `Printable` interface. The `PrinterJob` object will continue to call this method until the value `NO_SUCH_PAGE` is returned. However, this won't be convenient in every case. In a more complicated application than Sketcher, as well as having different page orientations, you may want to have different class objects printing different kinds of pages — rendering the same data as graphical or textual output, for instance. You can't do this conveniently with just one class implementing the `Printable` interface. You also need something more flexible than just passing a class object that does printing to the `PrinterJob` object by calling its `setPrintable()` method.

The solution is to implement the `Pageable` interface in a class, and call the `setPageable()` method for the `PrinterJob` object instead of `setPrintable()`. The essential difference between the `Printable` and `Pageable` interfaces is that a `Printable` object is intended to encapsulate a single page to be printed, whereas a `Pageable` object encapsulates multiple pages. Each of the pages to be printed by a `Pageable` object is encapsulated by a `Printable` object though.

Implementing the Pageable Interface

A class that implements the `Pageable` interface defines a set of pages to be printed. A `Pageable` object must be able to supply the `PrinterJob` object with a count of the number of pages for a job, a reference of type `Printable` for the object that is to print each page, plus a `PageFormat` object defining the format of each page. The `PrinterJob` object acquires this information by calling the three methods declared in the `Pageable` interface:

Method	Description
`getNumberOfPages()`	Must return a value of type `int` that specifies the number of pages to be printed. If the number of pages cannot be determined then the value `UNKNOWN_NUMBER_OF_PAGES` can be returned. This value is defined in the `Pageable` interface.
`getPageFormat(int pageIndex)`	This method must return a `PageFormat` object for the page specified by the page index that is passed to it.
`getPrintable(int pageIndex)`	This method must return a reference of type `Printable` to the object responsible for printing the page specified by the page index that is passed to it.

At the start of a print job that was initiated by a call to the `setPageable()` method for a `PrinterJob` object, the `PrinterJob` object will call the `getNumberOfPages()` method for the `Pageable` object to determine how many pages are to be printed. If you return the value `UNKNOWN_NUMBER_OF_PAGES`, then the process relies on a `Printable` object returning `NO_SUCH_PAGE` at some point to stop printing. It is therefore a good idea to supply the number of pages when it can be determined.

The `PrinterJob` object assumes each page in a print job is associated with a page index value, with the first page being index 0, the second being index 1, and so on. For each page index, the `PrinterJob` object will call the `getPageFormat()` method to obtain the `PageFormat` object to be used to print the page, and it will then call the `getPrintable()` method for the `Pageable` object to obtain a reference to the `Printable` object that will do the printing. Of course, just because you *can* supply a different `Printable` object for each page doesn't mean that you *must*. You could use as many or as few as you need for your application and control how different pages are printed by making the `getPageFormat()` method for the `Pageable` object return different `PageFormat` objects. Remember, though, that the `print()` method for a `Printable` object may be called more than once by the `PrinterJob` object to print a particular page, and the same page should be rendered each time the same page index is passed as an argument to the `print()` method, so you must not code the method in a way that presumes otherwise.

Creating PageFormat Objects

As you saw earlier, you can get the default `PageFormat` object for the print service you are using by calling the `defaultPage()` method for the `PrinterJob` object. The default `PageFormat` class constructor can also be used to create an object that is portrait-oriented, but in this case you have no guarantee that it is compatible with the current print service. A `PageFormat` object encapsulates information about the size of the paper and the margins in effect, so the object produced by the default constructor may not correspond with your printer setup. If you want to go this route, you can pass a reference to a `PageFormat` object to the `validatePage()` method for a `PrinterJob` object. For example:

```
// Object for current printer
PrinterJob printJob = PrinterJob.getPrinterJob();

// Validated page
PageFormat pageFormat = printJob.validatePage(new PageFormat());
```

Note that the `validatePage()` method does not return the same reference that you pass as the argument. The method clones the object that was passed to it and returns a reference to the clone, which will have been modified where necessary to suit the current printer. Since it does not modify the object in place, you always need to store the reference that is returned. This is obviously well suited to multipage printing because you can create a series of distinct `PageFormat` objects from the same argument.

Fundamentally, a `PageFormat` object encapsulates all the information needed to print on a page, as Figure 21-15 illustrates.

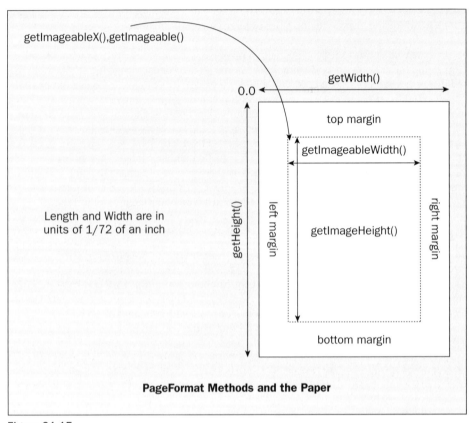

Figure 21-15

Once you have a `PageFormat` object, you can modify the orientation of the page by calling its `setOrientation()` method as you know, the possible values for the argument being `LANDSCAPE`, `PORTRAIT`, or `REVERSE_LANDSCAPE`. The `PageFormat` class defines several methods to retrieve information about the paper — you have seen that you can get the position and size of the printable area on the page, for instance, by calling the `getImageableX()`, `getImageableY()`, `getImageableWidth()`, and `getImageableHeight()` methods. You also have `getWidth()` and `getHeight()` methods in the `PageFormat` class that return the overall width and height of the page, respectively. These are all properties of the paper itself, which is represented by an object of the `java.awt.print.Paper` class that is associated with a `PageFormat` object. You can also work with the `Paper` object for a `PageFormat` object directly.

Dealing with Paper

The `Paper` class encapsulates the size of the paper and the size and position of the printable area on the page. The default constructor for the `Paper` class creates an American letter-sized sheet with one-inch margins—the printable area being the area inside the margins. You can change the size of the paper by calling the setSize() method for the Paper object, as you'll see in a moment.

Rather than creating an independent Paper object, you would normally retrieve a reference to the Paper object for a PageFormat object by calling its getPaper() method. If you then want to change the size of the paper, or the printable area—the page margins, in other words—you can call the setSize() or the setImageableArea() method for the Paper object. You can restore the paper details by passing an object of type Paper back to the PageFormat object by calling its setPaper() method with a reference to the Paper object as the argument.

The setSize() method for a Paper object has two parameters of type double that specify the width and height of the paper in units of 1/72 of an inch. If you use A4 paper, you could specify the size of the paper for a PageFormat object with the following statements:

```
Paper paper = pageFormat.getPaper();
final double MM_TO_PAPER_UNITS = 72.0/25.4;       // 25.4 mm to an inch
double widthA4 = 210*MM_TO_PAPER_UNITS;
double heightA4 = 297*MM_TO_PAPER_UNITS;
paper.setSize(widthA4, heightA4);
```

If you use letter size paper that is 8.5 by 11 inches, it's somewhat simpler:

```
Paper paper = pageFormat.getPaper();
double widthLetterSize = 72.0*8.5;
double heightLetterSize = 72.0*11.0;
paper.setSize(widthLetterSize, heightLetterSize);
```

The setImageableArea() method expects you to supply four arguments of type double. The first two are the coordinates of the top-left corner of the printable area and the next two are the width and the height. All these values are in units of 1/72 of an inch. To set 20 mm margins on your A4 sheet you could write:

```
double marginSize = 20.0* MM_TO_PAPER_UNITS;       // 20 mm wide
paper.setImageableArea(marginSize, marginSize,     // Top left
                  widthA4-2.0*marginSize,          // Width
                  heightA4-2.0*marginSize);        // Height
```

If you are printing on letter-size paper, a one-inch margin might be more appropriate, so you would write:

```
double marginSize = 72.0;                              // 1 inch wide
paper.setImageableArea(marginSize, marginSize,         // Top left
                  widthLetterSize-2.0*marginSize,      // Width
                  heightLetterSize-2.0*marginSize);    // Height
```

Of course, there's no reason why a class that implements the Pageable interface cannot also implement Printable, so you could do this in Sketcher, just to get a feel for the Pageable interface in action.

Try It Out   Using the Pageable Interface

You'll just print two pages in a print job in Sketcher, a cover page with a title for the sketch plus the sketch itself, which may be portrait or landscape, of course. You could produce both pages in `SketchView`, but to make it more interesting, let's define a separate class to represent a `Printable` object for the cover page:

```
import java.awt.Graphics;
import java.awt.Graphics2D;
import java.awt.Color;
import java.awt.Font;
import java.awt.geom.GeneralPath;
import java.awt.geom.Rectangle2D;import java.awt.print.Printable;
import java.awt.print.PageFormat;
import java.awt.print.PrinterException;

class SketchCoverPage implements Printable {
  public SketchCoverPage(Sketcher theApp) {
    this.theApp = theApp;
  }

  // Print the cover page
  public int print(Graphics g,
               PageFormat pageFormat,
               int pageIndex)
               throws PrinterException {
    // If it's page 0 print the cover page...
  }

  private Sketcher theApp;
}
```

The sole reason for having the `Sketcher` field in the class is so you can get at the name of the sketch to print on the cover page. Since the need has come up, you should add a `getSketchName()` method to the `SketchFrame` class that will supply a reference to the `String` object containing the file name:

```
// Method to return the name of the current sketch
public String getSketchName() {
  return filename;
}
```

You can use this method in the implementation of the `print()` method in the `SketchCoverPage` class. The `print()` method needs to recognize when it is being called to print the first page — that is, when the page index is zero — and then print the cover page. You could do whatever you like here to produce a fancy cover page, but I'll just put the code to draw a line border inset from the page and put the sketch file name in the middle in a box. Here's how you could do that:

```
public int print(Graphics g,
             PageFormat pageFormat,
             int pageIndex)
          throws PrinterException {
```

```
        if(pageIndex>0) {
          return NO_SUCH_PAGE;
        }
        Graphics2D g2D = (Graphics2D) g;
        float x = (float)pageFormat.getImageableX();
        float y = (float)pageFormat.getImageableY();

        GeneralPath path = new GeneralPath();
        path.moveTo(x+1, y+1);
        path.lineTo(x+(float)pageFormat.getImageableWidth()-1, y+1);
        path.lineTo(x+(float)pageFormat.getImageableWidth()-1,
                    y+(float)pageFormat.getImageableHeight()-1);
        path.lineTo(x+1, y+(float)pageFormat.getImageableHeight()-1);
        path.closePath();

        g2D.setPaint(Color.red);
        g2D.draw(path);

        // Get a 12 pt bold version of the default font
        Font font = g2D.getFont().deriveFont(12.f).deriveFont(Font.BOLD);

        g2D.setFont(font);                      // Set the new font
        String sketchName = theApp.getWindow().getSketchName();
        Rectangle2D textRect = new java.awt.font.TextLayout(sketchName, font,
                              g2D.getFontRenderContext()).getBounds();
        double centerX = pageFormat.getWidth()/2;
        double centerY = pageFormat.getHeight()/2;
        Rectangle2D.Double surround = new Rectangle2D.Double(
                                      centerX-textRect.getWidth(),
                                      centerY-textRect.getHeight(),
                                      2*textRect.getWidth(),
                                      2*textRect.getHeight());
        g2D.draw(surround);

        // Draw text in the middle of the printable area
        g2D.setPaint(Color.blue);
        g2D.drawString(sketchName, (float)(centerX-textRect.getWidth()/2),
                          (float)(centerY+textRect.getHeight()/2));
        return PAGE_EXISTS;
      }
```

To center the file name on the page you need to know the width and height of the text string when it is printed. The `getStringBounds()` method in the `Font` class returns the rectangle bounding the string. The second argument is a reference to an object of type `FontRenderContext` that is returned by the `getFontRenderContext()` method you have called here for `g2D`. A `FontRenderContext` object contains all the information the `getStringBounds()` method needs to figure out the rectangle bounding the text when it is printed. This includes information about the size of the font as well as the resolution of the output device — the printer, in our case.

You can now implement the `Pageable` interface in the `SketchView` class. You must add three methods to the class: `getNumberOfPages()`, which returns the number of pages to be printed, `getPrintable()`, which returns a reference to a `Printable` object that will print a page with a given index, and getPageFormat(), which returns a reference to a PageFormat object corresponding to a particular page:

```
// Import statements as before...
import java.awt.print.Pageable;
import java.awt.print.Paper;

class SketchView extends     JComponent
                  implements Observer, ActionListener, Printable, Pageable {

  // Method to return page count - always two pages
  public int getNumberOfPages() {
    return 2;
  }

  // Method to return the Printable object that will render the page
  public Printable getPrintable(int pageIndex) {
    if(pageIndex == 0)                         // For the first page
      return new SketchCoverPage(theApp);      // return the cover page
    else
      return this;
  }

  public PageFormat getPageFormat(int pageIndex) {
    // Code to define the PageFormat object for the page...
  }
  // Method to print the sketch
  public int print(Graphics g,                 // Graphics context for printing
                   PageFormat pageFormat,       // The page format
                   int pageIndex)               // Index number of current page
             throws PrinterException {
    // Code to test pageIndex removed...
    Graphics2D g2D = (Graphics2D) g;
    // Get sketch bounds
    Rectangle rect = theApp.getModel().getModelExtent();
    // Rest of the code as before...
  }

  // Plus the rest of the class as before...
}
```

The first two methods are already fully defined here. You will always print two pages, the first page being printed by a SketchCoverPage object and the second page by the view object. The print() method should now print the page when called without testing the pageIndex value for zero. The page with index 0 will be printed by the SketchCoverPage object.

Let's see how you can produce the PageFormat object for a page. You'll want to use the PageFormat object that's stored as a field in the application window, so add a method to the SketchFrame class to make it accessible:

```
// Method to return a reference to the current PageFormat object
public PageFormat getPageFormat() {
  return pageFormat;
}
```

To make use of some of the methods in the `Paper` class that I've discussed, you'll arbitrarily double the size of the margins for the cover page but leave the margins for the other page at their default sizes. You also set the cover page to landscape orientation, but leave the second page as whatever is set in the `pageFormat` field of the application object. Here's the code to do that:

```
public PageFormat getPageFormat(int pageIndex) {
    if(pageIndex==0) {                       // If it's the cover page...
                                             // ...make the margins twice the size
        // Create a duplicate of the current page format
        PageFormat pageFormat = (PageFormat)
                                (theApp.getWindow().getPageFormat().clone());
        Paper paper = pageFormat.getPaper();

        // Get top and left margins - x & y coordinates of top-left corner
        // of imageable area are the left & top margins
        double leftMargin = paper.getImageableX();
        double topMargin = paper.getImageableY();

        // Get right and bottom margins
        double rightMargin = paper.getWidth()-paper.getImageableWidth()-leftMargin;
        double bottomMargin = paper.getHeight()-paper.getImageableHeight()-topMargin;

        // Double the margin sizes
        leftMargin *= 2.0;
        rightMargin *= 2.0;
        topMargin *= 2.0;
        bottomMargin *= 2.0;

        // Set new printable area for the paper
        paper.setImageableArea(leftMargin, topMargin,
                        paper.getWidth()-leftMargin-rightMargin,
                        paper.getHeight()-topMargin-bottomMargin);

        pageFormat.setPaper(paper);                  // Restore the paper
        pageFormat.setOrientation(PageFormat.LANDSCAPE);
        return pageFormat;                           // Return the page format
    }
    // For pages after the first, use the object from the app window
    return theApp.getWindow().getPageFormat();
}
```

You don't want to mess up the `PageFormat` object from the application window for use when you are printing the cover page, so you duplicate it by calling its `clone()` method. The `PageFormat` class specifically overrides the `clone()` method that it inherits from the `Object` class with a `public` member to allow the `PageFormat` object to be cloned. The `clone()` method always returns a reference of type `Object`, so you must cast it to the correct type. The left and top margins correspond to the x and y coordinates of the top-left corner of the imageable area for the page, so you call the methods for the `Paper` object to retrieve these values. You calculate the size of the right margin by subtracting the width of the imageable area and the value for the left margin from the overall width of the page. You produce the value for the size of the bottom margin in a similar way. After doubling the margin sizes, you redefine the position and size of the imageable area for the `Paper` objects from these, and then restore the modified Paper object in the `PageFormat` object.

If it's not the cover page, you just return a reference to the `PageFormat` object that is stored in the application window object.

The last thing you need to do is alter the code in the `actionPerformed()` method for the inner class `FileAction` in `SketchFrame`. You must replace the `setPrintable()` method call with a `setPageable()` call:

```
      } if(name.equals(printAction.getValue(NAME))) {
         // Verify there is a default printer
         if(printer == null) {
            JOptionPane.showMessageDialog(SketchFrame.this,
                                 "No default printer available.",
                                 "Printer Error",
                                 JOptionPane.ERROR_MESSAGE);
            return;
         }

         // The view is the page source
         printJob.setPageable(theApp.getView());
         boolean printIt = true;
         if(e.getSource() != printButton) {       // If it's not the toolbar button
           printIt = printJob.printDialog();       // ...display the print dialog
         }
         if(printIt) {                             // If printIt is true...
           try {
             printJob.print(printAttr);            // ...then print
           } catch(PrinterException pe) {
             System.out.println(pe);
             JOptionPane.showMessageDialog(SketchFrame.this,
                                 "Error printing a sketch.",
                                 "Printer Error",
                                 JOptionPane.ERROR_MESSAGE);
           }
         }
      } else if(name.equals(closeAction.getValue(NAME))) {
         checkForSave();
         System.exit(0);
      }
```

This code is the earlier version that uses the `printDialog()` method without an argument to show the effect in this context. If you comment out the most recent code, you can try both versions by juggling the commented out code. On my system, the print dialog now shows that pages numbered from 1 to 2 should be printed, courtesy of the `Pageable` interface implementation that you added to Sketcher. You can see my print dialog in Figure 21-16.

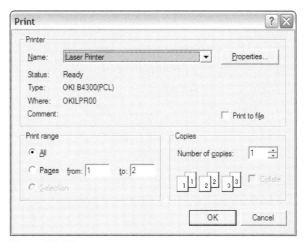

Figure 21-16

How It Works

The PrinterJob object now calls methods in the Pageable interface that you have implemented in the SketchView class that defines the view object. The number of pages in the document is now determined by the getNumberOfPages() method, and the PageFormat and Printable objects are now obtained individually for each page.

If you switch the code back to using the printDialog() and print() methods with an argument of type PrintRequestAttributeSet, the print operation will run in the same way. The print attributes passed to the print() method will not override those specified in the PageFormat object returned by the getPageFormat() method for the Pageable object. If the attribute set passed to the print method includes attributes not determined by the Pageable object — such as a Copies attribute object — these will have an effect on the printing process. Similarly, if you set the page orientation to landscape using the dialog displayed by the Print Setup... menu item, the second page that contains the sketch will print in landscape orientation.

Printing Using a Book

A Book object is a repository for a collection of pages where the pages may be printed using different formats. The page painter for a page in a book is represented by a Printable object and each Printable object within a book can print one or possibly several pages with a given format. Figure 21-17 shows an example of a Book object that uses three Printable objects to print a total of seven pages.

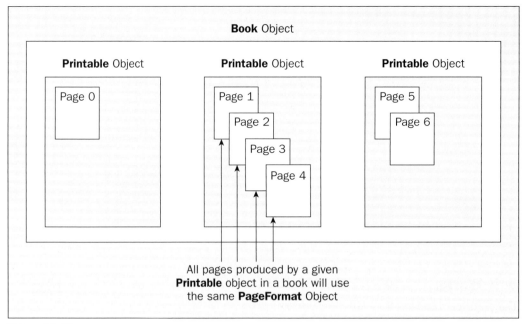

Figure 21-17

Because the Book class implements the Pageable interface, you print a book in the same way as you print a Pageable object. Once you have assembled all the pages you want in a Book object, you just pass a reference to it to the setPageable() method for your PrinterJob object. Let's take it from the top.

The Book class has only a default constructor, and that creates an empty book. Thus, you create a book like this:

```
Book sketchBook = new Book();
```

You add a page to a book by calling the append() method for the Book object. There are two overloaded versions of append(): one to add a Printable object that represents a single page, and the other to add a Printable object that represents several pages. In the latter case, all the pages are printed using the same PageFormat object.

The first version of append() accepts two arguments: a reference to the Printable object and a reference to an associated PageFormat object. Suppose you wanted to create a Book object for Sketcher, and the object would be created in the SketchFrame object somewhere. You could add the cover page of a sketch just as in the previous example to the sketchBook object like this:

```
PageFormat pageFormat = pageFormat.clone();
Paper paper = pageFormat.getPaper();

double leftMargin = paper.getImageableX();    // Top left corner is indented
double topMargin = paper.getImageableY();        // by the left and top margins
double rightMargin = paper.getWidth()-paper.getImageableWidth()-leftMargin;
double bottomMargin = paper.getHeight()-paper.getImageableHeight()-topMargin;
```

```
    leftMargin *= 2.0;                      // Double the left margin...
    rightMargin *= 2.0;                     // ...and the right...
    topMargin *= 2.0;                       // ...and the top...
    bottomMargin *= 2.0;                    // ...and the bottom

    paper.setImageableArea(leftMargin, topMargin,   // Set new printable area
                      paper.getWidth()-leftMargin-rightMargin,
                      paper.getHeight()-topMargin-bottomMargin);
    pageFormat.setPaper(paper);                     // Restore the paper
    sketchBook.append(new SketchCoverPage(theApp), pageFormat);
```

Apart from the first statement and the last statement that appends the `Printable` object that represents the page painter, all this code is essentially the same as the code in the previous example for creating the `PageFormat` object for the cover page.

To add the second page of the sketch to the `Book` object, you could write:

```
    sketchBook.append(theApp.getView(), pageFormat);
```

The arguments to the `append()` method specify that the view object will print the page, and that the `PageFormat` object that should be used is the one stored in the `pageFormat` field in the `SketchFrame` class.

Now that you have assembled the book containing the two pages for the print job, you can tell the `PrinterJob` object that you want to print the book:

```
    printJob.setPageable(sketchBook);               // The book is the source of pages
```

Now all you need to do is call the `print()` method for the `PrinterJob` object to start printing. To expedite printing, the `PrinterJob` object will communicate with the `Book` object to get the number of pages to be printed and to get the page painter and page format appropriate to print each page. The total number of pages is returned by the `getNumberOfPages()` method for the `Book` object. In this case it would always return 2. A reference to the `Printable` object for a given page index is returned by the `getPrintable()` method for the `Book` object, and the `PageFormat` object for a given page index is returned by the `getPageFormat()` method. Obviously, in the case of Sketcher, using a `Book` object doesn't offer much advantage over the `Pageable` object that you used in the previous example. In situations where you have more complex documents with a lot of pages with diverse formats it can make things much easier.

You use the other version of `append()` for a `Book` object to add a given number of pages to a book that will be produced by a single `Printable` object, and where all the pages have the same format. Here's an example:

```
    Book book = new Book();
    book.append(painter, pageFormat, pageCount);
```

Here the `painter` argument is a reference of type `Printable` that will print `pageCount` pages all with the same format, `pageFormat`. A typical instance where you might use this might be a long text document. The document could consist of many pages, but they all are printed with the same page format. The view object for the document would typically provide a method to figure out the number of pages that are necessary to output the document.

Printing Swing Components

Printing components is easier than you might think. Swing components are particularly easy to print because they already know how to draw themselves. You should not call a Swing component's paint() method when you want to print it though. Rendering of Swing components is buffered by default to improve the efficiency of displaying them but printing one by calling its paint() method adds a lot of unnecessary overhead to the printing operation. Instead you should call the print() method that is defined in the JComponent class. This will render the component directly to the graphics context that is passed as an argument, so there is no buffering of the output. The method automatically prints any child components that the component contains, so you need to call print() directly only for a top-level component.

The print() method for a Swing component that has JComponent as a base calls three protected methods to actually carry out the printing:

printComponent(Graphics g)	Prints the component
printBorder(Graphics g)	Prints the component border
printChildren(Graphics g)	Prints components that are children of the component

If you want to customize how a Swing component is printed, you can subclass the component and override any or all of these. This doesn't apply to a JFrame component though. The JFrame class is a subclass of Frame and does not have JComponent as a superclass. However, you can still call the print() method for a JFrame component to print it. In this case it's inherited from the Container class.

Let's implement a capability to print the Sketcher application window to see how this can be done.

Try It Out   Printing the Sketcher Window

First you can add a field in the SketchFrame class to store a reference to a new menu item that you'll add to the File menu in Sketcher to print the window:

```
private JMenuItem printWindowItem;
```

Next you can add a statement to the SketchFrame contructor that will create the menu item and add the application window as the event listener:

```
printSetupItem = new JMenuItem("Print Setup...");
printSetupItem.addActionListener(this);
printWindowItem = new JMenuItem("Print Window");
printWindowItem.addActionListener(this);
```

To install the menu item in the File menu you need to add another statement in the constructor:

```
// Construct the file drop-down menu
fileMenu.add(new JMenuItem(newAction));
fileMenu.add(new JMenuItem(openAction));
fileMenu.addSeparator();                    // Add separator
fileMenu.add(new JMenuItem(saveAction));
```

```
fileMenu.add(new JMenuItem(saveAsAction));
fileMenu.addSeparator();                        // Add separator
fileMenu.add(new JMenuItem(printAction));
fileMenu.add(printSetupItem);
fileMenu.add(printWindowItem);
fileMenu.addSeparator();                        // Add separator
fileMenu.add(new JMenuItem(closeAction));
```

You can add the code to handle events for the new menu item to the `actionPerformed()` method in the `SketchFrame` class:

```
  } else if(source == printSetupItem) {
    PageFormat pf = printJob.pageDialog(printAttr);
    if(pf != null) {
      pageFormat = pf;       // update the page format
    }
  } else if(source == printWindowItem) {
    if(printer == null) {
      JOptionPane.showMessageDialog(this,
                          "No default printer available.",
                          "Printer Error",
                          JOptionPane.ERROR_MESSAGE);
      return;
    }
    // The app window is the page source
    printJob.setPrintable(this, pageFormat);
    try {
      printJob.print();                      // ...then print
    } catch(PrinterException pe) {
      System.out.println(pe);
      JOptionPane.showMessageDialog(SketchFrame.this,
                          "Error printing the application window.",
                          "Printer Error",
                          JOptionPane.ERROR_MESSAGE);
    }
  }
}
```

The application window, which is the `SketchFrame` object `window`, is responsible for printing the window because it is obviously best placed to do this, so you must make the `SketchFrame` class implement the `Printable` interface. Change the first line of the class definition to:

```
public class SketchFrame extends      JFrame
                       implements ActionListener, Observer, Printable {
```

Now you can add the definition of the `print()` method to the `SketchFrame` class:

```
  // Print the window
  public int print(Graphics g,
                 PageFormat pageFormat,
                 int pageIndex)
           throws PrinterException {

    if(pageIndex>0)    // Only one page page 0 to be printed
```

```
        return NO_SUCH_PAGE;

      // Scale the component to fit
      Graphics2D g2D = (Graphics2D) g;

      // Calculate the scale factor to fit the window to the page
      double scaleX = pageFormat.getImageableWidth()/getWidth();
      double scaleY = pageFormat.getImageableHeight()/getHeight();

      double scale = Math.min(scaleX,scaleY);  // Get minimum scale factor

      // Move paper origin to page printing area corner
      g2D.translate(pageFormat.getImageableX(), pageFormat.getImageableY());
      g2D.scale(scale,scale);                   // Apply the scale factor

      print(g2D);                               // Draw the component
      return PAGE_EXISTS;
    }
```

The getWidth() and getHeight() methods you are calling here are inherited in the SketchFrame class from the Component class and they return the width and height of the window, respectively.

Make sure you have the necessary additional imports:

```
    import java.awt.print.Printable;
    import java.awt.Graphics;
    import java.awt.Graphics2D;
```

If you recompile and run Sketcher once more, the File | Print window menu item should be operational.

How It Works

The menu operation and the printing mechanism function as I have already discussed. The SketchFrame object is the page painter for the window so the print() method is where it all happens. After checking the page index value and casting the Graphics reference passed to the method to Graphics2D, you calculate the scaling factor to fit the window to the page. The getWidth() and getHeight() methods inherited in our SketchFrame class return the width and height of the window, respectively. You then apply the scale just as you did for printing a sketch. The coordinates of the top-left corner of the window are at (0, 0) so you can just print it once you have applied the scaling factor. Calling the inherited print() method with g2D as the argument does this.

I'm sure you will have noticed that the output has deficiencies. The title bar and window boundary are missing. Of course, a JFrame object is a top-level window, and since it is derived from the Frame class, it is a heavyweight component with its appearance determined by its native peer, which is outside the Java code. The print() method for the JFrame object that you call to print the window does not include the peer-created elements of the window. The printAll() method that the JFrame class inherits from the Component class does though. Modify the code in the print() method to call printAll() rather than print(), like this:

```
        printAll(g2D);                          // Draw the component
        return PAGE_EXISTS;
```

Now you should get the whole application window printed.

Summary

In this chapter you have added full support for the File menu to the Sketcher application for both sketch storage and retrieval and for printing. You should find that the techniques that you have used here are readily applicable in other Java applications. The approach to saving and restoring a model object is not usually dependent on the kind of data it contains. Of course, if your application is a word processor, you will have a little more work to do taking care that the number of lines printed on each page is a whole number of lines. In other words, you will have to make sure you avoid having the top half of a line of text on one page and the bottom half on the next. There are other Java classes to help with that, however, and I don't really have the space to discuss them here — but look them up — the `javax.swing.text` package is a veritable gold mine for text handling!

If you have been following all the way with Sketcher, you now have an application that consists of well over 1500 lines of code, so you should be pretty pleased with yourself. And you're not finished with Sketcher yet — you'll add the capability to export and import sketches in XML over the next two chapters.

The important points I've covered in this chapter are:

❑ You can implement writing your model object to a file and reading it back by making it serializable.

❑ The `JFileChooser` class provides a generalized way for displaying a dialog to enable a file to be chosen.

❑ A printing operation is initiated by creating a `PrinterJob` object. This object encapsulates the interface to your printer and is used to manage the printing process.

❑ A `PrintService` object encapsulates a printer.

❑ A `PageFormat` object defines the format for a page, and methods for this object can provide information on the paper size and orientation and the printable area on the page.

❑ An object of type `Paper` defines a page.

❑ You can display a print dialog by calling the `printDialog()` method for a `PrinterJob` object. The no-argument version of `printDialog()` will display the native print dialog, whereas the version accepting a single argument of type `PrintRequestAttributeSet` displays a Java print dialog.

❑ Printing a page is always done by an object of a class that implements the `Printable` interface.

❑ You print a page by calling methods for the `Graphics` object passed to the `print()` method in the `Printable` interface by the `PrinterJob` object.

❑ You can manage multipage print jobs by implementing the `Pageable` interface in a class. This will enable different types of class objects to be used to print different pages.

❑ A `Book` object can encapsulate a series of pages to be printed. Each `Printable` object that is appended to a book prints one or more pages in a given format.

Exercises

You can download the source code for the examples in the book and the solutions to the following exercises from `http://www.wrox.com`.

1. Modify the Sketcher program to print the title at the top of the page on which the sketch is printed.

2. Modify the printing of a sketch so that a solid black boundary line is drawn around the sketch on the page.

3. Modify Sketcher to print a single sketch laid out on four pages. The sketch should be enlarged to provide the best fit on the four pages without distorting circles — that is, the same scale should be applied to the x and y axes.

4. Use a `Book` object to print a cover page plus the sketch spread over four pages as in the previous exercise.

Java and XML

The Java Development Kit (JDK) includes capabilities within the standard set of class libraries for processing **Extensible Markup Language** (**XML**) documents. The classes that support XML processing are collectively referred to as JAXP, the **J**ava **A**PI for **X**ML **P**rocessing (JAXP). In this chapter and the next you'll be exploring not only how you can read XML documents, but also how you can create and modify them. This chapter provides a brief outline of XML and some related topics, plus a practical introduction to reading XML documents from within your Java programs using one of the two available mechanisms for this. In the next chapter I'll discuss the second approach to reading XML documents, as well as how you modify them and how you create new XML documents programmatically. Inevitably, I can only skim the surface in a lot of areas because XML itself is a huge topic. However, you should find enough in this chapter and the next to give you a good feel for what XML is about and how you can handle XML documents in Java.

In this chapter you'll learn:

- ❑   What a well-formed XML document is
- ❑   What constitutes a valid XML document
- ❑   What the components in an XML document are and how they are used
- ❑   What a DTD is and how it is defined
- ❑   What namespaces are and why you use them
- ❑   What the SAX and DOM APIs are and how they differ
- ❑   How you read documents using SAX

XML

XML, or the Extensible Markup Language to give it its full title, is a system- and hardware-independent language for defining data and its structure within an XML document. An **XML document** is a Unicode text file that contains data together with **markup** that defines the structure of the data. Because an XML document is a text file, you can create XML using any plaintext editor, although an editor designed for creating and editing XML will obviously make things easier. The precise definition of XML is in the hands of the World Wide Web Consortium (W3C), and if you want to consult the current XML specifications, you can find them at `http://www.w3.org/XML`.

The term *markup* derives from a time when the paper draft of a document to be printed was *marked up* by hand to indicate to the typesetter how the printed form of the document should look. Indeed the ancestry of XML can be traced back to a system that was originally developed by IBM in the 1960s to automate and standardize markup for system reference manuals for IBM hardware and software products. XML markup looks similar to HTML in that it consists of tags and attributes added to the text in a file. However, the superficial appearance is where the similarity between XML and HTML ends. XML and HTML are profoundly different in purpose and capability.

Firstly, although an XML document can be created, read, and understood by a person, XML is primarily for communicating data from one computer to another. XML documents will therefore more typically be generated and processed by computer programs. An XML document defines the structure of the data it contains so a program that receives it can properly interpret it. Thus XML is a tool for transferring information and its organization between computer programs. The purpose of HTML, on the other hand, is solely the description of how data should look when it is displayed or printed. The only structuring information that generally appears in an HTML document relates to the appearance of the data as a visible image. The purpose of HTML is data presentation.

Secondly, HTML provides you with a set of tags that is essentially fixed and geared to the presentation of data. XML is a language in which you can define new sets of tags and attributes to suit different kinds of data — indeed to suit any kind of data including *your* particular data. Because XML is extensible, it is often described as a **meta-language** — a language for defining new languages, in other words. The first step in using XML to exchange data is to define the language that you intend to use for that purpose in XML.

Of course, if I invent a set of XML markup to describe data of a particular kind, you will need to know the rules for creating XML documents of this type if you want to create, receive, or modify them. As you'll see, the definition of the markup that has been used within an XML document can be included as part of the document. It also can be provided as a separate entity, in a file identified by a URI, for example, that can be referenced within any document of that type. The use of XML has already been standardized for very diverse types of data. XML languages exist for describing the structures of chemical compounds and musical scores, as well as plain old text such as in this book.

The Java **API** for **XML** **P**rocessing (**JAXP**) provides you with the means for reading, creating, and modifying XML documents from within your Java programs. To understand and use this application program interface (API) you need to be reasonably familiar with two basic topics:

❑　What an XML document is for and what it consists of

❑　What a DTD is and how it relates to an XML document

You also need to be aware of what an XML namespace is, if only because JAXP has methods relating to handling these. You can find more information on JAXP at `http://java.sun.com/xml/jaxp/index.jsp`.

Just in case you are new to XML, I'll introduce the basic characteristics of XML and DTDs before explaining how you apply the classes and methods provided by JAXP to process XML documents. I'll also briefly explore what XML namespaces are for. If you are already comfortable with these topics you can skip most of this chapter and pick up where I start talking about SAX. Let's start by looking into the general organization of an XML document.

XML Document Structure

An XML document basically consists of two parts, a **prolog** and a **document body**:

❏ The **prolog** provides information necessary for the interpretation of the contents of the document body. It contains two optional components, and since you can omit both, the prolog itself is optional. The two components of the prolog, in the sequence in which they must appear, are as follows:

  ❏ An **XML declaration** that defines the version of XML that applies to the document and may also specify the particular Unicode character encoding used in the document and whether the document is standalone or not. Either the character encoding or the standalone specification can be omitted from the XML declaration, but if they do appear, they must be in the given sequence.

  ❏ A **document type declaration** specifying an external **Document Type Definition (DTD)** that identifies markup declarations for the elements used in the body of the document, or explicit markup declarations, or both.

❏ The **document body** contains the data. It comprises one or more **elements** where each element is defined by a begin tag and an end tag. The elements in the document body define the structure of the data. There is always a single **root element** that contains all the other elements. All of the data within the document is contained within the elements in the document body.

Processing instructions (PI) for the document may also appear at the end of the prolog and at the end of the document body. Processing instructions are instructions intended for an application that will process the document in some way. You can include comments that provide explanations or other information for human readers of the XML document as part of the prolog and as part of the document body.

When an XML document is said to be **well-formed**, it just means that it conforms to the rules for writing XML as defined by the XML specification. Essentially, an XML document is well-formed if its prolog and body are consistent with the rules for creating these. In a well-formed document there must be only one root element, and all elements must be properly nested. I will summarize more specifically what is required to make a document well-formed a little later in this chapter, after you have looked into the rules for writing XML.

An **XML processor** is a software module that is used by an application to read an XML document and gain access to the data and its structure. An XML processor also determines whether an XML document is well-formed or not. Processing instructions are passed through to an application without any checking or analysis by the XML processor. The XML specification describes how an XML processor should behave when reading XML documents, including what information should be made available to an application for various types of document content.

Here's an example of a well-formed XML document:

```
<proverb>Too many cooks spoil the broth.</proverb>
```

The document just consists of a root element that defines a proverb. There is no prolog, and formally, you don't have to supply one, but it would be much better if the document did include at least the XML version that is applicable, like this:

```
<?xml version="1.0"?>
<proverb>Too many cooks spoil the broth.</proverb>
```

The first line is the prolog, and it consists of just an XML declaration, which specifies that the document is consistent with XML version 1.0. The XML declaration must start with `<?xml` with no spaces within this five character sequence. You could also include an encoding declaration following the version specification in the prolog that specifies the Unicode encoding used in the document. For example:

```
<?xml version="1.0" encoding="UTF-8"?>
<proverb>Too many cooks spoil the broth.</proverb>
```

The first line states that as well as being XML version 1.0, the document uses the `"UTF-8"` Unicode encoding. If you omit the encoding specification, `"UTF-8"` or `"UTF-16"` will be assumed, and because "UTF-8" includes ASCII as a subset, you don't need to specify an encoding if all you are using is ASCII text. The version and the character encoding specifications must appear in the order shown. If you reverse them you have broken the rules, so the document would no longer be well-formed.

If you want to specify that the document is not dependent on any external definitions of markup, you can add a `standalone` specification to the prolog like this:

```
<?xml version="1.0" encoding="UTF-8" standalone="yes"?>
<proverb>Too many cooks spoil the broth.</proverb>
```

Specifying the value for `standalone` as `"yes"` indicates to an XML processor that the document is self-contained. A value of `"no"` would indicate that the document is dependent on an external definition of the markup used.

Valid XML Documents

A **valid** XML document is a well-formed document that has an associated **D**ocument **T**ype **D**efinition, or **DTD** (you will learn more about DTDs later in this chapter). In a valid document the DTD must be consistent with the rules for creating a DTD and the document body must be consistent with the DTD. A DTD essentially defines a markup language for a given type of document and is identified in the DOC-TYPE declaration in the document prolog. It specifies how all the elements that may be used in the document can be structured, and the elements in the body of the document must be consistent with it.

The previous example is well-formed, but not valid, because it does not have an associated DTD that defines the `<proverb>` element. Note that there is nothing *wrong* with an XML document that is not valid. It may not be ideal, but it is a perfectly legal XML document. *Valid* in this context is a technical term that means only that a document has a DTD.

An XML processor may be **validating** or **non-validating**. A validating XML processor will check that an XML document has a DTD and that its contents are correctly specified. It will also verify that the document is consistent with the rules expressed in the DTD and report any errors that it finds. A non-validating XML processor will not check that the document body is consistent with the DTD. As you'll see, you can usually choose whether the XML processor that you use to read a document is validating or non-validating simply by switching the validating feature on or off.

Here's a variation on the example from the previous section with a document type declaration added:

```
<?xml version="1.0" encoding="UTF-8" standalone="no"?>
<!DOCTYPE proverb SYSTEM "proverb.dtd">
<proverb>Too many cooks spoil the broth.</proverb>
```

A document type declaration always starts with `<!DOCTYPE` so it is easily recognized. The name that appears in the `DOCTYPE` declaration, in this case `proverb`, must always match that of the root element for the document. I have specified the value for `standalone` as `"no"`, but it would still be correct if I left it out because the default value for `standalone` is "no" if there are external markup declarations in the document. The `DOCTYPE` declaration indicates that the markup used in this document can be found in the DTD at the URI `proverb.dtd`. You'll see a lot more about the `DOCTYPE` declaration later in this chapter.

Having an external DTD for documents of a given type does not eliminate all the problems that may arise when exchanging data. Obviously confusion may arise when several people independently create DTDs for the same type of document. My DTD for documents containing sketches created by Sketcher is unlikely to be the same as yours. Other people with sketching applications may be inventing their versions of a DTD for representing a sketch, so the potential for conflicting definitions for markup is considerable. To obviate the difficulties that this sort of thing would cause, standard markup languages are being developed in XML that can be used universally for documents of common types. For example, the Mathematical Markup Language (MathML) is a language defined in XML for mathematical documents, and the Synchronized Multimedia Integration Language (SMIL) is a language for creating documents that contain multimedia presentations. There is also the Scalable Vector Graphics (SVG) language for representing 2D graphics such as design drawings or even sketches created by Sketcher.

Let's understand a bit more about what XML markup consists of.

Elements in an XML Document

XML markup divides the contents of a document into **elements** by enclosing segments of the data between tags. As I said, there will always be one root element that contains all the other elements in a document. In the example above, the following is an element:

```
<proverb> Too many cooks spoil the broth.</proverb>
```

In this case, this is the only element and is therefore the root element. A **start tag**, `<proverb>`, indicates the beginning of an element, and an **end tag**, `</proverb>`, marks its end. The name of the element, `proverb` in this case, always appears in both the start and end tags. The text between the start and end tags for an element is referred to as **element content** and in general may consist of just data, which is referred to as **character data**; other elements, which is described as **markup**; or a combination of character data and markup; or it may be empty. An element that contains no data and no markup is referred to as an **empty element**.

When an element contains plain text, the content is described as **parsed character data** (PCDATA). This means that the XML processor will parse it — it will analyze it, in other words — looking to see if it can be broken down further. In fact, PCDATA allows for a mixture of ordinary data and other elements, referred to as **mixed content**, so a parser will be looking for the characters that delimit the start and end of markup tags. Consequently, ordinary text must not contain characters that might cause it to be recognized as a tag. Thus you can't include < or & characters explicitly as part of the text within an element, for example. Since it could be a little inconvenient to completely prohibit such characters within ordinary text, you can include them by using **predefined** entities when you need to. XML recognizes the following predefined entities that represent characters that would otherwise be recognized as part of markup:

Character	Predefined Entity
&	&
'	'
"	"
<	<
>	>

Here's an element that makes use of a predefined entity:

```
<text> This is parsed character data within a &lt;text&gt; element.</text>
```

The content of this element is the following string:

```
This is parsed character data within a <text> element.
```

Here's an example of an XML document containing several elements:

```
<?xml version="1.0"?>
<address>
  <buildingnumber>29</buildingnumber>
  <street> South Lasalle Street</street>
  <city>Chicago</city>
  <state>Illinois</state>
  <zip>60603</zip>
</address>
```

This document evidently defines an address. Each tag pair identifies and categorizes the information between the tags. The data between <address> and </address> is an address, which is a composite of five further elements that each contain character data that forms part of the address. You can easily identify what each of the components of the address is from the tags that enclose each sub-unit of the data.

Rules for Tags

The tags that delimit an element have a precise form. Each element start tag must begin with < and end with >, and each element end tag must start with </ and end with >. The tag name — also known as the element type name — identifies the element and differentiates it from other elements. Note that the element name must immediately follow the opening < in the case of a start tag and the </ in the case of an end tag. If you insert a space here it is incorrect and will be flagged as an error by an XML processor.

Since the `<address>` element contains all of the other elements that appear in the document, this is the root element. When one element encloses another, it must always do so completely if the document is to be well-formed. Unlike HTML, where a somewhat cavalier use of the language is usually tolerated, XML elements must *never* overlap. For example, you can't have:

```
<address><zip>60603</address></zip>
```

An element that is enclosed by another element is referred to as the **child** of the enclosing element, and the enclosing element is referred to as the **parent** of the child element. In the earlier example of a document that defined an address, the `<address>` element is the parent of the other four because it directly encloses each of them, and the enclosed elements are child elements of the `<address>` element. In a well-formed document, each start tag must always be matched by a corresponding end tag, and vice versa. If this isn't the case, the document is not well-formed.

Don't forget that there must be only one root element that encloses all the other elements in a document. This implies that you cannot have an element of the same type as the root element as a child of any element in the document.

Empty Elements

You already know that an element can contains nothing at all, so just a start tag immediately followed by an end tag is an **empty element**. For example:

```
<commercial></commercial>
```

You have an alternative way to represent empty elements. Instead of writing a start and end tag with nothing between them, you can write an empty element as a single tag with a forward slash immediately following the tag name:

```
<commercial/>
```

This is equivalent to a start tag followed by an end tag. There must be no spaces between the opening < and the element name, or between the / and the > marking the end of the tag.

You may be thinking at this point that an empty element is of rather limited use, whichever way you write it. Although by definition an empty element has no content, it can and often does contain additional information that is provided within **attributes** that appear within the tag. You'll see how you add attributes to an element a little later in this chapter. Additionally, an empty element can be used as a marker or flag to indicate something about the data within its parent. For example, you might use an empty element as part of the content for an `<address>` element to indicate that the address corresponds to a commercial property. Absence of the `<commercial/>` element would indicate a private residence.

Document Comments

When you create an XML document using an editor, it is often useful to add explanatory text to the document. You can include comments in an XML document like this:

```
<!-- Prepared on 14th January 2004 -->
```

Comments can go just about anywhere in the prolog or the document body, but not inside a start tag or an end tag, or within an empty element tag. You can spread a comment over several lines if you wish, like this:

```
<!--
   Eeyore, who is a friend of mine,
    has lost his tail.
-->
```

For compatibility with SGML from which XML is derived, the text within a comment should not contain a sequence of two or more hyphens and it must not end with a hyphen. A comment that ends with `--->` is not well-formed and will be rejected by an XML processor. While an XML processor of necessity scans comments to distinguish them from markup and document data, they are not part of the character data within a document. XML processors need not make comments available to an application, although some may do so.

Element Names

If you're going to be creating elements, then you're going to have to give them names, and XML is very generous in the names you're allowed to use. For example, there aren't any reserved words to avoid in XML, as there are in most programming languages, so you do have a lot of flexibility in this regard. However, there are certain rules that you must follow. The names you choose for elements must begin with either a letter or an underscore and can include digits, periods, and hyphens. Here are some examples of valid element names:

```
net_price   Gross-Weight   _sample   clause_3.2   pastParticiple
```

In theory you can use colons within a name but because colons have a special purpose in the context of names, as you'll see later, you should not do so. Since XML documents use the Unicode character set, any national language alphabets defined within that set may be used for names. HTML users need to remember that tag names in XML are case-sensitive, so `<Address>` is not the same as `<address>`.

Note also that names starting with uppercase or lowercase x followed by m followed by l are reserved, so you must not define names that begin `xml` or `XmL` or any of the other six possible sequences.

Defining General Entities

There is a frequent requirement to repeat a given block of parsed character data in the body of a document. An obvious example of this is some kind of copyright notice that you may want to insert in various places. You can define a named block of parsed text like this:

```
<!ENTITY copyright "(c) 2004 Ivor Horton">
```

This is an example of declaration of a **general entity**. You can put declarations of general entities within a `DOCTYPE` declaration in the document prolog or within an external DTD. We will describe how a little later in this chapter. The block of text that appears between the double quotes in the entity declaration is identified by the name `copyright`. You could equally well use single quotes as delimiters for the string. Wherever you want to insert this text in the document, you just need to insert the name delimited by an `&` at the beginning and `;` at the end, thus:

```
&copyright;
```

This is called an **entity reference**. This is exactly the same notation as the predefined entities representing markup characters that you saw earlier. It will cause the equivalent text to be inserted at this point when the document is parsed. Of course, since a general entity is parsed text, you need to take care that the document is still well-formed and valid after the substitution has been made.

An entity declaration can include entity references. For example, we could declare the copyright entity like this:

```
<!ENTITY copyright "(c) 2004 Ivor Horton &documentDate;">
```

The text contains a reference to a documentDate entity. Entity references may appear in a document only after their corresponding entity declarations, so the declaration for the documentDate entity must precede the declaration for the copyright entity:

```
<!ENTITY documentDate "24th January 2004">
<!ENTITY copyright "(c) 2004 Ivor Horton &documentDate;">
```

Entity declarations can contain nested entity references to any depth, so the declaration for the documentDate entity could contain other entity references. Substitutions for entity references will be made recursively by the XML processor until all references have been resolved. An entity declaration must not directly or indirectly contain a reference to itself though.

You can also use general entities that are defined externally. You use the SYSTEM keyword followed by the URL for where the text is stored in place of the text in the ENTITY declaration. For example:

```
<!ENTITY usefulstuff SYSTEM "http://www.some-server.com/inserts/stuff.txt">
```

The reference &usefulstuff; represents the contents of the file stuff.txt.

CDATA Sections

It is possible to embed **unparsed character data** (**CDATA**) anywhere in a document where character data can occur. You do this by placing the unparsed character data in a CDATA section, which begins with <![CDATA[and ends with]]>. The data is described as unparsed because the XML processor will not analyze it in any way, but will make it available to an application. The data within a CDATA section can be anything at all—it can even be binary data. You can use a CDATA section to include markup in a document that you don't want to have parsed. For example:

```
<explanation> A typical circle element is written as:
<![CDATA[
  <circle radius="15">
    <position x="30" y="50"/>
  </circle>
]]>
</explanation>
```

The lines shown shaded are within a CDATA section, and although they look suspiciously like markup, an XML processor looking for markup will not scan them. I have used some of the reserved characters in here without escaping them, but since the data in a CDATA section is not parsed, they will not be identified as markup.

Element Attributes

You can put additional information within an element in the form of one or more **attributes**. An attribute is identified by an attribute name, and the value is specified as a string between single or double quotes. For example:

```
<elementname attributename="Attribute value"> ... </elementname>
```

As I said earlier, empty elements frequently have attributes. Here's an example of an empty element with three attributes:

```
<color red="255" green="128" blue="64"></color>
```

This would normally be written in the shorthand form, like this:

```
<color red="255" green="128" blue="64" />
```

You can also use single quotes to delimit an attribute value if you wish.

The names of the three attributes here are `red`, `green`, and `blue`, which identify the primary components of the color, and the values between 0 and 255 represent the contribution of each primary color to the result. Attribute names are defined using the same rule as element names. The attributes in an element follow the element name in the start tag (or the only tag in the case of an empty element) and are separated from it by at least one space. If a tag has multiple attributes, they must be separated by spaces. You can also put spaces on either side of the = sign, but it is clearer without, especially where there are several attributes. HTML fans should note that a comma separator between attributes is not allowed in XML and will be reported as an error.

A string that is an attribute value must not contain a delimiting character explicitly within the string, but you can put a double quote as part of the value string if you use single quotes as delimiters, and vice versa. For example, you could write the following:

```
<textstuff answer="it's mine" explanation='He said"It is mine"'/>
```

The value for the `answer` attribute uses double quotes as delimiters, so it can contain a single quote explicitly; thus the value is `it's mine`. Similarly, the value for the second attribute uses single quotes so the string can contain a double quote, so its value is `He said "It is mine"`. Of course, someone is bound to want both a single quote and a double quote as part of the value string. Easy, just use an escape sequence within the value for the one that is a delimiter. For example, you could rewrite the previous example as:

```
<textstuff answer='it&apos;s mine' explanation="He said&quot;It's mine&quot;"/>
```

In general, it's easiest to stick to a particular choice of delimiter for strings and always escape occurrences of the delimiter within a string.

In the Sketcher program, you can create circles that are specified by a radius and a position. You can easily define a circle in XML — in fact, there are many ways in which you could do this. Here's one example:

```
<circle radius="15">
  <position x="30" y="50"/>
</circle>
```

The `radius` attribute for the `<circle>` tag specifies the radius, and its position is specified by an empty `<position/>` tag, with the *x* and *y* coordinates of the circle's position specified by attributes x and y. A reasonable question to ask is whether this is the best way of representing a circle. I should therefore explore the options in this context a little further.

Attributes versus Elements

Obviously you could define a circle without using attributes, maybe like this:

```
<circle>
  <radius>15</radius>
  <position>
    <x-coordinate>30</x-coordinate>
    <y-coordinate>50</y-coordinate>
  </position>
</circle>
```

This is the opposite extreme. There are no attributes here, only elements. Where the content of an element is one or more other elements — as in the case of the `<circle>` and `<position>` elements here — it is described as **element content**. A document design in which all the data is part of element content and no attributes are involved is described as **element-normal**.

Of course, it is also possible to represent the data defining a circle just using attributes within a single element:

```
<circle positionx="30" positiony="50" radius="15"/>
```

Now you have just one element defining a circle with all the data defined by attribute values. Where all the data in a document is defined as attribute values, it is described as **attribute-normal**.

An element can also contain a mixture of text and markup — so-called **mixed content** — so you have a further way in which you could define a circle in XML, like this:

```
<circle>
  <position>
    <x-coordinate>30</x-coordinate>
    <y-coordinate>50</y-coordinate>
  </position>
  15
</circle>
```

Now the value for the radius just appears as text as part of the content of the `<circle>` element along with the position element. The disadvantage of this arrangement is that it's not obvious what the text is, so some information about the structure has been lost compared to the previous example.

So which is the better approach, to go for attributes or elements? Well, it can be either, or both, if you see what I mean. It depends on what the structure of the data is, how the XML is generated, and how it will be used. One overriding consideration is that an attribute is a single value. It has no inner structure, so anything that does have substructure must be expressed using elements. Where data is essentially hierarchical, representing family trees in XML, for example, you will want to use nested elements to reflect the structure of the data. Where the data is serial or tabular, temperature and rainfall or other weather data over time, for example, you may well use attributes within a series of elements within the root element.

If you are generating an XML document interactively using an editor, then readability is an important consideration since poor readability will encourage errors. You'll lean towards whatever makes the editing easier — and for the most part elements are easier to find and edit than attributes. Attribute values should be short for readability, so this limits the sort of data that you can express as an attribute. You probably would not want to see the soliloquy from Shakespeare's *Hamlet* appearing as an attribute value, for example. That said, if the XML is computer-generated and is not primarily intended for human viewing, the choice is narrowed down to the most efficient way to handle the data in the computer. Attributes and their values are readily identified in a program, so documents are likely to make use of attributes wherever the structure of the data does not require otherwise. You'll see how this works out in practice when you get to use the Java API for processing XML.

Whitespace and Readability

The indentation shown in the examples so far have been included just to provide you with visual cues to the structure of the data. It is not required, and an XML processor will ignore the whitespace between elements. When you are creating XML in an editor, you can use whitespace generally between elements to present the XML document visually so that it is easier for a human reader to understand. Whitespace can consist of spaces, tabs, carriage returns, and linefeed characters. You can see that a circle expressed without whitespace, as shown below, would be significantly less readable:

```
<circle><position><x-coordinate>30</x-coordinate><y-coordinate>50</
y-coordinate></position>15</circle>
```

Having said that, you don't have complete freedom in deciding where you put whitespace within a tag, as you have already seen. The tag name must immediately follow the opening < or </ in a tag, and there can be no space within an opening </ delimiter, or a closing /> delimiter in the case of an empty element. You must also separate an attribute from the tag name or from another attribute with at least one space. Beyond that you can put additional spaces within a tag wherever you like.

Data Structure in XML

The ability to nest elements is fundamental to defining the structure of the data in a document. We can easily represent the structure of the data in our XML fragment defining an address, as shown in Figure 22-1.

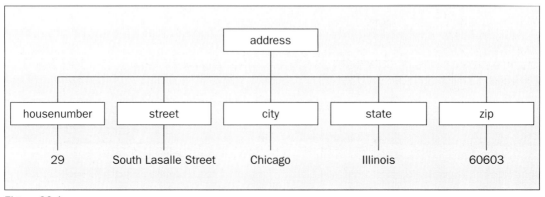

Figure 22-1

The structure follows directly from the nesting of the elements. The `<address>` element contains all of the others directly, so the nested elements are drawn as subsidiary or child elements of the `<address>` element. The items that appear within the tree structure — the elements and the data items — are referred to as **nodes**.

Figure 22-2 shows the structure of the first circle definition in XML that you saw in the previous section. Even though there's an extra level of elements in this diagram, there are strong similarities to the structure shown in Figure 22-1.

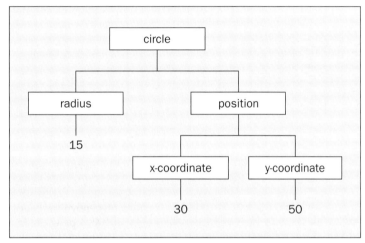

Figure 22-2

You can see that both structures have a single root element, `<address>` in the first example and `<circle>` in the second. You can also see that each element contains either other elements or some data that is a segment of the document content. In both diagrams all the document content lies at the bottom. Nodes at the extremities of a tree are referred to as **leaf nodes**.

In fact an XML document *always* has a structure similar to this. Each element in a document can contain other elements, or text, or elements and text, or it can be empty.

Document Type Definitions

You have seen several small examples of XML and in each case it was fairly obvious what the content was meant to represent, but where are the rules that ensure such data is represented consistently and correctly in different documents? Do the `<radius>` and `<position>` elements have to be in that sequence in a `<circle>` element and could you omit either of them?

Clearly there has to be a way to determine what is correct and what is incorrect for any particular element in a document. As I mentioned earlier, a **Document Type Definition (DTD)** defines how valid elements are constructed for a particular type of document, so the XML for purchase order documents in a company could be defined by one DTD, and sales invoice documents by another. The Document Type

Definition for a document is specified in a **document type declaration** — commonly known as a DOC-TYPE declaration — that appears in the document prolog following any XML declaration. A DTD essentially defines a **vocabulary** for describing data of a particular kind — the set of elements that you use to identify the data, in other words. It also defines the possible relationships between these elements — how they can be nested. The contents of a document of the type identified by a particular DTD must be defined and structured according to rules that make up the DTD. Any document of a given type can be checked for validity against its DTD.

A DTD can be an integral part of a document, but it is usually, and more usefully, defined separately. Including a DTD in an XML document makes the document self-contained, but it does increase its bulk. It also means that the DTD has to appear within every document of the same type. A separate DTD that is external to a document avoids this and provides a single reference point for all documents of a particular type. An external DTD also makes maintenance of the DTD for a document type easier as it only needs to be changed in one place for all documents that make use of it. Let's look at how you identify the DTD for a document and then investigate some of the ways in which elements and their attributes can be defined in a DTD.

Declaring a DTD

You use a document type declaration (a DOCTYPE declaration) in the prolog of an XML document to specify the DTD for the document. An XML 1.0 document can have only one DOCTYPE declaration. You can include the markup declarations for elements used in the document explicitly within the DOCTYPE statement, in which case the declarations are referred to as the **internal subset**. You can also specify a URI that identifies the DTD for the document, usually in the form of a URL. In this case the set of declarations is referred to as the **external subset**. If you include explicit declarations as well as a URI referencing an external DTD, the document has both an internal and an external subset. Here is an example of an XML document that has an external subset:

```
<?xml version="1.0"?>
<!DOCTYPE address SYSTEM "http://docserver/dtds/AddressDoc.dtd">
<address>
  <buildingnumber> 29 </buildingnumber>
  <street> South Lasalle Street</street>
  <city>Chicago</city>
  <state>Illinois</state>
  <zip>60603</zip>
</address>
```

The name following the DOCTYPE keyword must always match the root element name in the document, so the DOCTYPE declaration here indicates that the root element in the document has the name address. The declaration also indicates that the DTD in which this and the other elements in the document are declared is an external DTD located at the URI following the SYSTEM keyword. This URI, which is invariably a URL, is called the **system ID** for the DTD.

In principle you can also specify an external DTD by a **public ID** using the keyword PUBLIC in place of SYSTEM. A public ID is just a unique public name that identifies the DTD — a Uniform Resource Name (URN), in other words. As you probably know, the idea behind URNs is to get over the problem of changes to URLs. Public IDs are intended for DTDs that are available as public standards for documents of particular types, such as SVG. However, there is a slight snag. Since there is no mechanism defined for resolving public IDs to find the corresponding URL, if you specify a public ID, you still have to supply a system ID with a URL so the XML processor can find it, so you won't see public IDs in use much.

If the file containing the DTD is stored on the local machine, you can specify its location relative to the directory containing the XML document. For example, the following DOCTYPE declaration implies that the DTD is in the same directory as the document itself:

```
<!DOCTYPE address SYSTEM "AddressDoc.dtd">
```

The AddressDoc.dtd file includes definitions for the elements that may be included in a document containing an address. In general, a relative URL is assumed to be relative to the location of the document containing the reference.

Defining a DTD

In looking at the details of how we put a DTD together I'll use examples in which the DTD is an internal subset, but the declarations in an external DTD are exactly the same. Here's an example of a document with an integral DTD:

```
<?xml version="1.0"?>
<!DOCTYPE proverb [ <!ELEMENT proverb (#PCDATA)> ]>
<proverb>A little knowledge is a dangerous thing.</proverb>
```

All the internal definitions for elements used within the document appear between the square brackets in the DOCTYPE declaration. In this case just one element is declared, the root element, and the element content is PCDATA — parsed character data.

You could define an external DTD in a file with the name proverbDoc.dtd in the same directory as the document. The file would contain just a single line:

```
<!ELEMENT proverb (#PCDATA)>
```

The XML document would then be:

```
<?xml version="1.0"?>
<!DOCTYPE proverb SYSTEM "proverbDoc.dtd">
<proverb>A little knowledge is a dangerous thing.</proverb>
```

The DTD is referenced by a relative URI that is relative to the directory containing the document.

When you want both an internal and external subset, you just put both in the DOCTYPE declaration, with the external DTD reference appearing first. Entities from both are available for use in the document, but where there is any conflict between them, the entities defined in the internal subset take precedence over those declared in the external subset.

The syntax for defining elements and their attributes is rather different from the syntax for XML markup. It also can get quite complex, so I won't be able to go into it comprehensively here. However, you do need to have a fair idea of how a DTD is put together in order to understand the operation of the Java API for XML, so let's look at some of the ways in which you can define elements in a DTD.

Defining Elements in DTDs

The DTD will define each type of element that can appear in the document using an ELEMENT type declaration. For example, the <address> element could be defined like this:

```
<!ELEMENT address (buildingnumber, street, city, state, zip)>
```

This defines the element with the name address. The information between the parentheses specifies what can appear within an <address> element. The definition states that an <address> element contains exactly one each of the elements <buildingnumber>, <street>, <city>, <state>, and <zip>, in that sequence. This is an example of **element content** since only elements are allowed within an <address> element. Note the space that appears between the element name and the parentheses enclosing the content definition. This is required, and a parser will flag the absence of at least one space here as an error. The ELEMENT identifier must be in capital letters and must immediately follow the opening "<!".

The preceding definition of the <address> element makes no provision for anything other than the five elements shown, and in that sequence. Thus, any whitespace that you put between these elements in a document is not part of the content and will be ignored by a parser; therefore, it is known as **ignorable whitespace**. That said, you can still find out if there is whitespace there when the document is parsed, as you'll see.

You can define the <buildingnumber> element like this:

```
<!ELEMENT buildingnumber (#PCDATA)>
```

This states that the element can contain only parsed character data, specified by #PCDATA. This is just ordinary text, and since it will be parsed, it cannot contain markup. The # character preceding the word PCDATA is necessary just to ensure it cannot be confused with an element or attribute name — it has no other significance. Since element and attribute names must start with a letter or an underscore, the # prefix to PCDATA ensures that it cannot be interpreted as such.

The PCDATA specification does provide for markup — child elements — to be mixed in with ordinary text. In this case you must specify the names of the elements that can occur mixed in with the text. If you wanted to allow a <suite> element specifying a suite number to appear alongside the text within a <buildingnumber> element, you could express it like this:

```
<!ELEMENT buildingnumber (#PCDATA|suite)*>
```

This indicates that the content for a <buildingnumber> element is parsed character data, and the text can be combined with <suite> elements. The | operator here has the same meaning as the | operator you met in the context of regular expressions in Chapter 15. It means one or other of the two operands but not both. The * following the parentheses is required here and has the same meaning as the * operator that you also met in the context of regular expressions. It means that the operand to the left can appear zero or more times.

If you want to allow several element types to be optionally mixed in with the text, you separate them by |. Note that it is not possible to control the sequence in which mixed content appears.

The other elements used to define an address are similar, so you could define the whole document with its DTD like this:

```
<?xml version="1.0"?>
<!DOCTYPE address
[
    <!ELEMENT address (buildingnumber, street, city, state, zip)>
    <!ELEMENT buildingnumber (#PCDATA)>
    <!ELEMENT street (#PCDATA)>
    <!ELEMENT city (#PCDATA)>
    <!ELEMENT state (#PCDATA)>
    <!ELEMENT zip (#PCDATA)>
]>
<address>
  <buildingnumber> 29 </buildingnumber>
  <street> South Lasalle Street</street>
  <city>Chicago</city>
  <state>Illinois</state>
  <zip>60603</zip>
</address>
```

Note that you have no way to constrain the text in an element definition. It would be nice to be able to specify that the building number had to be numeric, for example, but the DTD grammar and syntax provide no way to do this. This is a serious limitation of DTDs and one of the driving forces behind the development of XML Schema, which is an XML-based description language that supports data types and offers an alternative to DTDs. I'll introduce XML Schemas a little later in this chapter.

If you were to create the DTD for an address document as a separate file, the file contents would just consist of the element definitions:

```
<!ELEMENT address (buildingnumber, street, city, state, zip)>
<!ELEMENT buildingnumber (#PCDATA)>
<!ELEMENT street (#PCDATA)>
<!ELEMENT city (#PCDATA)>
<!ELEMENT state (#PCDATA)>
<!ELEMENT zip (#PCDATA)>
```

The DOCTYPE declaration identifies the DTD for a particular document, so it is not part of the DTD. If the preceding DTD were stored in the AddressDoc.dtd file in the same directory as the document, the DOCTYPE declaration in the document would be:

```
<?xml version="1.0"?>
<!DOCTYPE address SYSTEM "AddressDoc.dtd">
<address>
  <buildingnumber> 29 </buildingnumber>
  <street> South Lasalle Street</street>
  <city>Chicago</city>
  <state>Illinois</state>
  <zip>60603</zip>
</address>
```

Of course, the DTD file would also include definitions for element attributes, if there were any. These will be useful later, so save the DTD as AddressDoc.dtd, and the preceding XML file (as Address.xml perhaps) in your Beg Java Stuff directory.

One further possibility you need to consider is that in many situations it is desirable to allow some child elements to be omitted. For example, `<buildingnumber>` may not be included in some cases. The `<zip>` element, while highly desirable, might also be left out in practice. We can indicate that an element is optional by using the **cardinality operator**, ?. This operator expresses the same idea as the equivalent regular expression operator, and it indicates that a child element may or may not appear. The DTD would then look like this:

```
<!DOCTYPE address
[
    <!ELEMENT address (buildingnumber?, street, city, state, zip?)>
    <!ELEMENT buildingnumber (#PCDATA)>
    <!ELEMENT street (#PCDATA)>
    <!ELEMENT city (#PCDATA)>
    <!ELEMENT state (#PCDATA)>
    <!ELEMENT zip (#PCDATA)>
]>
```

The ? operator following an element indicates that the element may be omitted or may appear just once. This is just one of three **cardinality** operators that you use to specify how many times a particular child element can appear as part of the content for the parent. The cardinality of an element is simply the number of possible occurrences for the element. The other two cardinality operators are *, which you have already seen, and +. In each case the operator follows the operand to which it applies. You now have four operators that you can use in element declarations in a DTD, and they are each similar in action to their equivalent in the regular expression context:

+	This operator indicates that there can be one or more occurrences of its operand. In other words, there *must* be at least one occurrence, but there may be more.
*	This operator indicates that there can be zero or more occurrences of its operand. In other words, there can be none or any number of occurrences of the operand to which it applies.
?	This indicates that its operand may appear once or not at all.
|	This operator indicates that there can be an occurrence of either its left operand or its right operand, but not both.

You might want to allow a building number or a building name in an address, in which case the DTD could be written:

```
<!ELEMENT address ((buildingnumber | buildingname), street, city, state, zip?)>
<!ELEMENT buildingnumber (#PCDATA)>
<!ELEMENT buildingname (#PCDATA)>
<!ELEMENT street (#PCDATA)>
<!ELEMENT city (#PCDATA)>
<!ELEMENT state (#PCDATA)>
<!ELEMENT zip (#PCDATA)>
```

The DTD now states that either `<buildingnumber>` or `<buildingname>` must appear as the first element in `<address>`. But you might want to allow neither, in which case you would write the third line as:

```
<!ELEMENT address ((buildingnumber | buildingname)?, street, city, state, zip?)>
```

The ? operator applies to the parenthesized expression (buildingnumber | buildingname), so it now states that either <buildingnumber> or <buildingname> may or may not appear, so you allow one, or the other, or none.

Of course, you can use the | operator repeatedly to express a choice between any number of elements, or indeed, sub-expressions between parentheses. For example, given that you have defined elements Linux, Solaris, and Windows, you might define the element operatingsystem as:

```
<!ELEMENT operatingsystem (Linux | Solaris | Windows)>
```

If you wanted to allow an arbitrary operating system to be identified as a further alternative, you could write:

```
<!ELEMENT operatingsystem (AnyOS | Linux | Solaris | Windows)>
<!ELEMENT AnyOS (#PCDATA)>
```

You can combine the operators you've seen to produce definitions for content of almost unlimited complexity. For example:

```
<!ELEMENT breakfast ((tea|coffee), orangejuice?,
                     ((egg+, (bacon|sausage)) | cereal) , toast)>
```

This states that <breakfast> content is either a <tea> or <coffee> element, followed by an optional <orangejuice> element, followed by either one or more <egg> elements and a <bacon> or <sausage> element, or a <cereal> element, with a mandatory <toast> element bringing up the rear. However, while you can produce mind-boggling productions for defining elements, it is wise to keep things as simple as possible.

After all this complexity, you mustn't forget that an element may also be empty, in which case it can be defined like this:

```
<!ELEMENT position EMPTY>
```

This states that the <position> element has no content. Elements can also have attributes so let's take a quick look at how they can be defined in a DTD.

Defining Element Attributes

You use an ATTLIST declaration in a DTD to define the attributes for a particular element. As you know, attributes are name-value pairs associated with a particular element, and values are typically, but not exclusively, text. Where the value for an attribute is text, it is enclosed between quotation marks, so it is always unparsed character data. Attribute values that consist of text are therefore specified just as CDATA. No preceding # character is necessary in this context since there is no possibility of confusion.

You could declare the elements for a document containing circles as follows:

```
<?xml version="1.0"?>

<!DOCTYPE circle
[
    <!ELEMENT circle (position)>
    <!ATTLIST circle
```

```
                radius CDATA #REQUIRED
    >

    <!ELEMENT position EMPTY>
    <!ATTLIST position
                x CDATA #REQUIRED
                y CDATA #REQUIRED
    >
]>

<circle radius="15">
  <position x="30" y="50"/>
</circle>
```

Three items define each attribute — the attribute name, the type of value (CDATA), and whether or not the attribute is mandatory. This third item may also define a default value for the attribute, in which case this value will be assumed if the attribute is omitted. The #REQUIRED specification against an attribute name indicates that it must appear in the corresponding element. You specify the attribute as #IMPLIED if it need not be included. In this case the XML processor will not supply a default value for the attribute. An application is expected to have a default value of its own for the attribute value that is implied by the attribute's omission.

Save this XML in your /Beg Java Stuff directory with a suitable name such as "circle with DTD.xml"; it will come in handy later.

You specify a default value for an attribute between double quotes. For example:

```
    <!ATTLIST circle
            radius CDATA "1"
    >
```

This indicates that the value of radius will be 1 if the attribute is not specified for a <circle> element.

You can also insist that a value for an attribute must be one of a fixed set. For example, suppose you had a color attribute for your circle that could be only red, blue, or green. You could define it like this:

```
    <!ATTLIST circle
            color (red|blue|green) #IMPLIED
    >
```

The value for the color attribute in a <circle> element must be one of the options between the parentheses. In this case the attribute can be omitted because it is specified as #IMPLIED, and an application processing it will supply a default value. To make the inclusion of the attribute mandatory, we would define it as:

```
    <!ATTLIST circle
            color (red|blue|green) #REQUIRED
    >
```

An important aspect of defining possible attribute values by an enumeration like this is that an XML editor can help the author of a document by prompting with the list of possible attribute values from the DTD when the element is being created.

An attribute that you declare as #FIXED must always have the default value. For example:

```
<!ATTLIST circle
        color (red|blue|green) #REQUIRED
        line_thickness medium  #FIXED
  >
```

Here the XML processor will supply an application only with the value medium for the thickness attribute. If you were to specify this attribute for the <circle> element in the body of the document you can use only the default value; otherwise, it is an error.

Defining Parameter Entities

You will often need to repeat a block of information in different places in a DTD. A **parameter entity** identifies a block of parsed text by a name that you can use to insert the text at various places within a DTD. Note that parameter entities are for use only within a DTD. You cannot use parameter entity references in the body of a document. You declare general entities in the DTD when you want to repeat text within the document body.

The form for a parameter entity is very similar to what you saw for general entities except that a % character appears between ENTITY and the entity name, separated from both by a space. For example, it is quite likely that you would want to repeat the x and y attributes that you defined in the <position> element in the previous section in other elements. You could define a parameter entity for these attributes and then use that wherever these attributes should appear in an element declaration. Here's the parameter entity declaration:

```
<!ENTITY % coordinates "x CDATA #REQUIRED y CDATA #REQUIRED">
```

Now you can use the entity name to insert the x and y attribute definitions in an attribute declaration:

```
<!ATTLIST position %coordinates; >
```

A parameter entity declaration must precede its use in a DTD.

The substitution string in a parameter entity declaration is parsed and can include parameter and general entity references. As with general entities, a parameter entity can also be defined by a reference to a URI containing the substitution string.

Other Types of Attribute Value

There are a further eight possibilities for specifying the type of the attribute value. I won't go into detail on these, but so you can recognize them, they are as follows:

ENTITY	An entity defined in the DTD. An entity here is a name identifying an unparsed entity defined elsewhere in the DTD by an `ENTITY` tag. The entity may or may not contain text. An entity could represent something very simple such as `&lt;`, which refers to a single character, or it could represent something more substantial such as an image.
ENTITIES	A list of entities defined in the DTD, separated by spaces.
ID	An ID is a unique name identifying an element in a document. This is to enable internal references to a particular element from elsewhere in the document.
IDREF	A reference to an element elsewhere in a document via its ID.
IDREFS	A list of references to IDs, separated by spaces.
NMTOKEN	A name conforming to the XML definition of a name. This just says that the value of the attribute will be consistent with the XML rules for a name.
NMTOKENS	A list of name tokens, separated by spaces.
NOTATION	A name identifying a notation — which is typically a format specification for an entity such as a JPEG or PostScript file. The notation will be identified elsewhere in the DTD using a `NOTATION` tag that may also identify an application capable of processing an entity in the given format.

A DTD for Sketcher

With what you know of XML and DTDs, you can have a stab at putting together a DTD for storing Sketcher files as XML. As I said before, an XML language has already been defined for representing and communicating two-dimensional graphics. This is called Scalable Vector Graphics, and you can find it at `http://www.w3.org/TR/SVG/`. While this would be the choice for transferring 2D graphics as XML documents in a real-world context, the objective here is to exercise your knowledge of XML and DTDs, so you'll reinvent your own version of this wheel, even though it will have fewer spokes and may wobble a bit.

First, let's consider what the general approach is going to be. Since the objective is to define a DTD that will enable you to exercise the Java API for XML with Sketcher, you'll define the language to make it an easy fit to Sketcher, rather than worry about the niceties of the best way to represent each geometric element. Since Sketcher itself was a vehicle for trying out various capabilities of the Java class libraries, it evolved in a somewhat topsy-like fashion with the result that the classes defining geometric entities are not necessarily ideal. However, you'll just map these directly in XML to avoid the mathematical jiggery-pokery that would be necessary if you adopted a more formal representation of geometry in XML.

A sketch is a very simple document. It's basically a sequence of lines, circles, rectangles, curves, and text. You can therefore define the root element `<sketch>` in the DTD as:

```
<!ELEMENT sketch (line|circle|rectangle|curve|text)*>
```

This just says that a sketch consists of zero or more of any of the elements between the parentheses. You now need to define each of these elements.

A line is easy. It is defined by its location, which is its start point and an end point. It also has an orientation — its rotation angle — and a color. You could define a `<line>` element like this:

```
<!ELEMENT line (color, position, endpoint)>
  <!ATTLIST line
        angle CDATA                    #REQUIRED
  >
```

A line is fully defined by two points, but the `Line` class includes a rotation field, so you have included that, too. Of course, a position is also a point, so it would be possible to use a `<point>` element for this, but differentiating the position for a geometric element will make it a bit easier for a human reader to read an XML document containing a sketch.

You could define color by a `color` attribute to the `<line>` element with a set of alternative values, but to allow the flexibility for lines of any color, it would be better to define a `<color>` element with three attributes for RGB values. In this case you can define the `<color>` element as:

```
<!ELEMENT color EMPTY>
  <!ATTLIST color
        R CDATA                    #REQUIRED
        G CDATA                    #REQUIRED
        B CDATA                    #REQUIRED
  >
```

You must now define the `<position>` and `<endpoint>` elements. These are both points defined by an (x, y) coordinate pair, so you would sensibly define them consistently. Empty elements with attributes are the most economical way here, and you can use a parameter entity for the attributes:

```
<!ENTITY % coordinates "x CDATA #REQUIRED y CDATA #REQUIRED">
<!ELEMENT position EMPTY>
  <!ATTLIST position %coordinates;>
<!ELEMENT endpoint EMPTY>
  <!ATTLIST endpoint %coordinates;>
```

A rectangle will be defined very similarly to a line since it is defined by its position, which corresponds to the top-left corner, plus the coordinates of the bottom-right corner. It also has a color and a rotation angle. Here's how this will look in the DTD:

```
<!ELEMENT rectangle (color, position, bottomright)>
  <!ATTLIST rectangle
        angle CDATA                    #REQUIRED
  >
<!ELEMENT bottomright EMPTY>
  <!ATTLIST bottomright %coordinates;>
```

You don't need to define the `<color>` and `<position>` elements because you have already defined these earlier for the `<line>` element.

The `<circle>` element is no more difficult. Its position is the center, and it has a radius and a color. It also has a rotation angle. You can define it like this:

```
<!ELEMENT circle (color, position)>
  <!ATTLIST circle
              radius CDATA                   #REQUIRED
              angle CDATA                    #REQUIRED
  >
```

The `<curve>` element is a little more complicated because it's defined by an arbitrary number of points, but it's still quite easy:

```
<!ELEMENT curve (color, position, point+)>
  <!ATTLIST curve  angle CDATA   #REQUIRED>
<!ELEMENT point EMPTY>
  <!ATTLIST point %coordinates;>
```

The start point of the curve is defined by the `<position>` element, and it includes at least one `<point>` element, which is specified by the + operator.

Lastly, you have the element that defines a text element in Sketcher terms. You need to allow for the font name and its style and point size, a rotation angle for the text, and a color — plus the text itself, of course, and its position. A `Text` element is also a little different from the other elements, as its bounding rectangle is required to construct it, so you must also include that. You have some options as to how you define this element. You could use mixed element content in a `<text>` element, combining the text string with `<font>` and `<position>` elements, for example.

The disadvantage of this is that you cannot limit the number of occurrences of the child elements and how they are intermixed with the text. You can make the definition more precisely controlled by enclosing the text in its own element. Then you can define the `<text>` element as having element content — like this:

```
<!ELEMENT text (color, position, font, string)>
  <!ATTLIST text  angle CDATA   #REQUIRED>

<!ELEMENT font EMPTY>
  <!ATTLIST font
              fontname   CDATA                #REQUIRED
              fontstyle (plain|bold|italic)  #REQUIRED
              pointsize  CDATA                #REQUIRED
  >
<!ELEMENT string (#PCDATA|bounds)*>

<!ELEMENT bounds EMPTY>
  <!ATTLIST point
              width CDATA    #REQUIRED
              height CDATA   #REQUIRED
  >
```

The `<string>` element content will be a `<bounds>` element defining the height and width of the bounding rectangle plus the text to be displayed. The `<font>` element provides the name, style, and size of the font as attribute values, and since nothing is required, beyond that it is an empty element. Children of the `<text>` element that you have already defined specify the color and position of the text.

That's all you need. The complete DTD for Sketcher documents will be:

```
<?xml version="1.0" encoding="UTF-8"?>
<!ELEMENT sketch (line|circle|rectangle|curve|text)*>

<!ELEMENT color EMPTY>
   <!ATTLIST color
             R CDATA                    #REQUIRED
             G CDATA                    #REQUIRED
             B CDATA                    #REQUIRED
   >

<!ENTITY % coordinates "x CDATA #REQUIRED y CDATA #REQUIRED">

<!ELEMENT position EMPTY>
   <!ATTLIST position %coordinates;>

<!ELEMENT endpoint EMPTY>
   <!ATTLIST endpoint %coordinates;>

<!ELEMENT line (color, position, endpoint)>
   <!ATTLIST line
             angle CDATA                #REQUIRED
   >

<!ELEMENT rectangle (color, position, bottomright)>
   <!ATTLIST rectangle
             angle CDATA                #REQUIRED
   >

<!ELEMENT bottomright EMPTY>
   <!ATTLIST bottomright %coordinates;>

<!ELEMENT circle (color, position)>
   <!ATTLIST circle
             radius CDATA               #REQUIRED
             angle CDATA                #REQUIRED
   >

<!ELEMENT curve (color, position, point+)>
   <!ATTLIST curve  angle CDATA  #REQUIRED>

<!ELEMENT point EMPTY>
   <!ATTLIST point %coordinates;>

<!ELEMENT text (color, position, font, string)>
   <!ATTLIST text  angle CDATA  #REQUIRED>

<!ELEMENT font EMPTY>
   <!ATTLIST font
             fontname  CDATA                        #REQUIRED
             fontstyle (plain|bold|italic|bold-italic) #REQUIRED
             pointsize CDATA                        #REQUIRED
   >
```

```
<!ELEMENT string (#PCDATA|bounds)*>

<!ELEMENT bounds EMPTY>
   <!ATTLIST bounds
            width     CDATA                #REQUIRED
            height    CDATA                #REQUIRED
   >
```

You can use this DTD to represent any sketch in XML. Stash it away in your `Beg Java Stuff` directory as `sketcher.dtd`. You'll try it out later.

Rules for a Well-Formed Document

Now that you know a bit more about XML elements and what goes into a DTD, I can formulate what you must do to ensure your XML document is well-formed. The rules for a document to be well-formed are quite simple:

1. If the XML declaration appears in the prolog, it must include the XML version. Other specifications in the XML document must be in the prescribed sequence — character encoding followed by `standalone` specification.

2. If the document type declaration appears in the prolog, the DOCTYPE name must match that of the root element, and the markup declarations in the DTD must be according to the rules for writing markup declarations.

3. The body of the document must contain at least one element, the root element, which contains all the other elements, and an instance of the root element must not appear in the content of another element. All elements must be properly nested.

4. Elements in the body of the document must be consistent with the markup declarations identified by the DOCTYPE declaration.

The rules for writing an XML document are absolutely strict. Break one rule and your document is not well-formed and will not be processed. This strict application of the rules is essential because you are communicating data and its structure. If any laxity were permitted, it would open the door to uncertainty about how the data should be interpreted. HTML used to be quite different from XML in this respect. Until recently, the rules for writing HTML were only loosely applied by HTML readers such as web browsers.

For example, even though a paragraph in HTML should be defined using a start tag, `<p>`, and an end tag, `</p>`, you can usually get away with omitting the end tag, and you can use both capital and lowercase *p*, and indeed close a capital *P* paragraph with a lowercase *p*, and vice versa. You can often have overlapping tags in HTML and get away with that, too. While it is not to be recommended, a loose application of the rules for HTML is not so harmful since HTML is concerned only with data presentation. The worst that can happen is that the data does not display quite as you intended.

In 2000, the W3C released the XHTML 1.0 standard that makes HTML an XML language, so you can expect more and more HTML documents to conform to this. The enduring problem is, of course, that the Internet has accumulated a great deal of material over many years that is still very useful but that will never be well-formed XML, so browsers may never be fully XML-compliant.

XML Namespaces

Even though they are very simple, XML namespaces can be very confusing. The confusion arises because it is so easy to make assumptions about what they imply when you first meet them. Let's look briefly at why you have XML namespaces in the first place, and then see what an XML namespace actually is.

You saw earlier that an XML document can have only one DOCTYPE declaration. This can identify an external DTD by a URI or include explicit markup declarations, or it may do both. What happens if you want to combine two or more XML documents that each has its own DTD into a single document? The short answer is that you can't—not easily anyway. Since the DTD for each document will have been defined without regard for the other, element name collisions are a real possibility. It may be impossible to differentiate between different elements that share a common name, and in this case major revisions of the documents' contents as well as a new DTD will be necessary to deal with this. It won't be easy.

XML namespaces are intended to help deal with this problem. They enable names used in markup to be qualified so that you can make duplicate names that are used in different markup unique by putting them in separate namespaces. An XML namespace is just a collection of element and attribute names that is identified by a URI. Each name in an XML namespace is qualified by the URI that identifies the namespace. Thus, different XML namespaces may contain common names without causing confusion since each name is notionally qualified by the unique URI for the namespace that contains it.

I say "notionally qualified" because you don't usually qualify names using the URI directly, although you could. Normally, in the interests of not making the markup overly verbose, you use another name called a **namespace prefix** whose value is the URI for the namespace. For example, I could have a namespace that is identified by the URI http://www.wrox.com/Toys and a namespace prefix toys that contains a declaration for the name rubber_duck. I could have a second namespace with the URI http://www.wrox.com/BathAccessories and the namespace prefix bathAccessories that also defines the name rubber_duck. The rubber_duck name from the first namespace is referred to as toys:rubber_duck and that from the second namespace is bathAccessories:rubber_duck, so there is no possibility of confusing them. The colon is used in the qualified name to separate the namespace prefix from the local name, which is why I said earlier in the chapter that you should avoid the use of colons in ordinary XML names.

Let's come back to the confusing aspects of namespaces for a moment. There is a temptation to imagine that the URI that identifies an XML namespace also identifies a document somewhere that specifies the names in the namespace. This is not required by the namespace specification. The URI is just a unique identifier for the namespace and a unique qualifier for a set of names. It does not necessarily have any other purpose, or even have to refer to a real document; it only needs to be unique. The definition of how names within a given namespace relate to one another and the rules for markup that uses them is an entirely separate question. This may be provided by a DTD or some other mechanism such as an XML Schema.

Namespace Declarations

A namespace is associated with a particular element in a document, which of course can be, but does not have to be, the root element. A typical namespace declaration in an XML document looks like this:

```
<sketcher:sketch xmlns:sketcher="http://www.wrox.com/dtds/sketches">
```

A namespace declaration uses a special reserved attribute name, `xmlns`, within an element, and in this instance the namespace applies to the `<sketch>` element. The name `sketcher` that is separated from `xmlns` by a colon is the namespace prefix, and it has the value `http://www.wrox.com/dtds/sketches`. You can use the namespace prefix to qualify names within the namespace, and since this maps to the URI, the URI is effectively the qualifier for the name. The URL that I've given here is hypothetical — it doesn't actually exist, but it could. The sole purpose of the URI identifying the namespace is to ensure that names within the namespace are unique, so it doesn't matter whether it exists or not. You can add as many namespace declarations within an element as you want, and each namespace declared in an element is available within that element and its content.

With the namespace declared with the `sketcher` prefix, you can use the `<circle>` element that is defined in the `sketcher` namespace like this:

```
<sketcher:sketch xmlns:sketcher="http://www.wrox.com/dtds/sketches">
    <sketcher:circle radius="15" angle="0">
      <sketcher:color R="150" G="250" B="100"/>
      <sketcher:position x="30" y="50"/>
    </sketcher:circle>
</sketcher:sketch>
```

Each reference to the element name is qualified by the namespace prefix `sketcher`. A reference in the same document to a `<circle>` element that is defined within another namespace can be qualified by the prefix specified in the declaration for that namespace. By qualifying each element name by its namespace prefix, you avoid any possibility of ambiguity.

A namespace has **scope** — a region of an XML document over which the namespace declaration is visible. The scope of a namespace is the content of the element within which it is declared, plus all direct or indirect child elements. The preceding namespace declaration applies to the `<sketch>` element and all the elements within it. If you declare a namespace in the root element for a document, its scope is the entire document.

You can declare a namespace without specifying a prefix. This namespace then becomes the default namespace in effect for this element, and its content and unqualified element names are assumed to belong to this namespace. Here's an example:

```
<sketch xmlns="http://www.wrox.com/dtds/sketches">
```

There is no namespace prefix specified so the colon following `xmlns` is omitted. This namespace becomes the default, so you can use element and attribute names from this namespace without qualification and they are all implicitly within the default namespace. For example:

```
<sketch xmlns="http://www.wrox.com/dtds/sketches">
  <circle radius="15" angle="0">
    <color R="150" G="250" B="100"/>
    <position x="30" y="50"/>
  </circle>
</sketch>
```

This markup is a lot less cluttered than the earlier version that used qualified names, which makes it much easier to read. It is therefore advantageous to declare the namespace that you use most extensively in a document as the default.

You can declare several namespaces within a single element. Here's an example of a default namespace in use with another namespace:

```
<sketch xmlns="http://www.wrox.com/dtds/sketches"
        xmlns:print="http://www.wrox.com/dtds/printed">
  <circle radius="15" angle="0">
    <color R="150" G="250" B="100"/>
    <position x="30" y="50"/>
  </circle>
  <print:circle print:lineweight="3" print:linestyle="dashed"/>
</sketch>
```

Here the namespace with the prefix `print` contains names for elements relating to hardcopy presentation of sketch elements. The `<circle>` element in the `print` namespace is qualified by the namespace prefix so it is distinguished from the element with the same name in the default namespace.

XML Namespaces and DTDs

For a document to be valid, you must still have a DTD, and the document must be consistent with it. The way in which a DTD is defined has no specific provision for namespaces. The DTD for a document that uses namespaces must therefore define the elements and attributes using qualified names and must also make provision for the `xmlns` attribute with or without its prefix in the markup declaration for any element in which it can appear. Because the markup declarations in a DTD have no specific provision for accommodating namespaces, a DTD is a less than ideal vehicle for defining the rules for markup when namespaces are used. The XML Schema specification provides a much better solution, and overcomes a number of other problems associated with DTDs.

XML Schemas

Because of the limitations of DTDs that I mentioned earlier, the W3C has developed the XML Schema language for defining the content and structure of sets of XML documents, and this language is now a W3C standard. You use the XML Schema Definition language to create descriptions of particular kinds of XML documents in a similar manner to the way you use DTDs, and such descriptions are themselves referred to as XML Schemas and fulfill the same role as DTDs. The XML Schema language is itself defined in XML and is therefore implicitly extensible to support new capabilities when necessary. Because the XML Schema language enables you to specify the type and format of data within an XML document, it provides a way for you to define and create XML documents that are inherently more precise, and therefore safer than documents described by a DTD.

It's easy to get confused when you are working with XML Schemas. One primary source of confusion is the various levels of language definition you are involved with. At the top level, you have XML — everything you are working with in this context is defined in XML. At the next level you have the XML Schema Definition language — defined in XML of course — and you use this language to define an XML Schema, which is a specification for a set of XML documents. At the lowest level you define an XML document — such as a document describing a Sketcher sketch — and this document is defined according to the rules you have defined in your XML Schema for Sketcher documents. Figure 22-3 shows the relationships between these various XML documents.

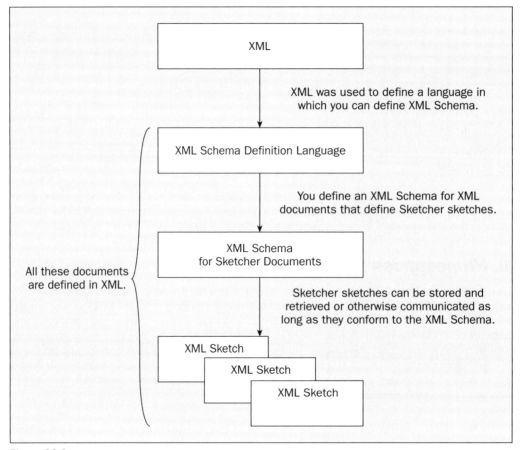

Figure 22-3

The XML Schema language is sometimes referred to as **XSD**, from **XML S**chema **D**efinition language. The XML Schema namespace is usually associated with the prefix name xsd, and files containing a definition for a class of XML documents often have the extension .xsd. You'll also often see the prefix xs used for the XML Schema namespace, but in fact you can use anything you like. A detailed discussion of the XML Schema language is a substantial topic that really requires a whole book to do it justice, so I'll just give you enough of a flavor of how you define your own XML documents schemas so that you're able to how it differs from a DTD.

Defining a Schema

The elements in a schema that defines the structure and content of a class of XML documents are organized in a similar way to the elements in a DTD. A schema has a single root element that is unique, and all other elements must be contained within the root element and must be properly nested. Every schema consists of a `schema` root element with a number of nested sub-elements. Let's look at a simple example.

Here's a possible schema for XML documents that contain an address:

```
<?xml version="1.0" ?>
<xsd:schema xmlns:xsd="http://www.w3.org/2001/XMLSchema">

<xsd:annotation>
    <xsd:documentation>
        This schema defines documents that contain an address.
    </xsd:documentation>
</xsd:annotation>

<!--This declares document content. -->
<xsd:element name="address" type="AddressType"/>

<!--This defines an element type that is used in the declaration of content. -->
<xsd:complexType name="AddressType">
  <xsd:sequence>
   <xsd:element name="buildingnumber" type="xsd:positiveInteger"/>
   <xsd:element name="street" type="xsd:string"/>
   <xsd:element name="city"   type="xsd:string"/>
   <xsd:element name="state"  type="xsd:string"/>
   <xsd:element name="zip"    type="xsd:decimal"/>
  </xsd:sequence>
 </xsd:complexType>
</xsd:schema>
```

You might like to contrast this schema with the DTD you saw earlier that defined XML documents with similar content. This schema defines documents that consist of an `<address/>` root element that contains a sequence of child elements with the names, `buildingnumber`, `street`, `city`, `state`, and `zip`.

The root element in the schema definition is the `xsd:schema` element, and that has an attribute with the name `xmlns` that identifies an XML namespace. The value you specify for the `xmlns` attribute is a URI that is the namespace name for the content document, and since the current document is a schema, the namespace is the one corresponding to elements in the XML Schema Definition language. The `xsd` that follows the colon is the prefix that will be used to identify element names from the `"http://www.w3.org/2001/XMLSchema"` namespace, so `xsd` is shorthand for the full namespace name. Thus `schema`, `complexType`, `sequence`, and `element` are all names of elements in a namespace defined for the XML Schema Definition language. The root element for every XML Schema will be a `schema` element. Don't lose sight of what a schema is; it's a definition of the form of XML documents of a particular type, so it declares the elements that can be used in such a document and how they may be structured. A document that conforms to a particular schema does not have to identify the schema, but it can. I'll come back to how you reference a schema when you are defining an XML document a little later in this chapter.

The example uses an `<annotation/>` element to include some simple documentation in the schema definition. The text that is the documentation appears within a child `<documentation/>` element. You can also use an `<appInfo/>` child element within a `<annotation/>` element to reference information located at a given URI. Of course, you can also use XML comments, `<!--comment-->`, within a schema, as the example shows.

In an XML Schema, a **declaration** specifies an element that is content for a document, whereas a **definition** defines an element type. The `xsd:element` element is a declaration that the content of a document consists of an `<address/>` element. Contrast this with the `xsd:complexType` element, which is a definition of the `AddressType` type for an element and does not declare document content. The `xsd:element` element in the schema declares that the `address` element is document content and happens to be of type `AddressType`, which is the type defined by the `xsd:complexType` element.

Now let's take a look at some of the elements that you use to define a document schema in a little more detail.

Defining Elements

As I said, the `xsd:complexType` element in the sample schema defines a type of element, not an element in the document. A complex element is simply an element that contains other elements, or that has attributes, or both. Any elements that are complex elements will need a `xsd:complexType` definition in the schema to define a type for the element. You place the definitions for child elements for a complex element between the `complexType` start and end tags. You also place the definitions for any attributes for a complex element between the `complexType` start and end tags. You can define a simple type using an `xsd:simpleType` definition in the schema. You would use a simple type definition to constrain attribute values or element content in some way. You'll see examples of this a little later in this chapter.

In the example you specify that any element of type `AddressType` contains a sequence of **simple elements** — a `buildingnumber` element, a `street` element, a `city` element, a `state` element, and a `zip` element. A simple element is an element that does not have child elements or attributes; it can contain only data, which can be of a variety of standard types or of a type that you define. The definition of each simple element that appears within an element of type `AddressType` uses an `xsd:element` element in which the `name` attribute specifies the name of the element being defined and the `type` attribute defines the type of data that can appear within the element. You can also control the number of occurrences of an element by specifying values for two further attributes within the `xsd:element` tag, as follows:

Attribute	Description
minOccurs	The value defines the minimum number of occurrences of the element and must be a positive integer (which can be 0). If this attribute is not defined, then the minimum number of occurrences of the element is 1.
maxOccurs	The value defines the maximum number of occurrences of the element and can be a positive integer or the value unbounded. If this attribute is not defined, then the maximum number of occurrences of the element is 1.

Thus, if both of these attributes are omitted, as is the case with the child element definitions in the sample schema for elements of type `AddressType`, the minimum and maximum numbers of occurrences are both one, so the element must appear exactly once. If you specify `minOccurs` as 0, then the element is optional. Note that you must not specify a value for `minOccurs` that is greater than `maxOccurs`, and the value for `maxOccurs` must not be less than `minOccurs`. You should keep in mind that both attributes have default values of 1 when you specify a value for just one attribute.

Specifying Data Types

In the example, each of the definitions for the five simple elements within an address element has a type specified for the data that it'll contain, and you specify the data type by a value for the `type` attribute. The data in a `buildingnumber` element is specified to be of type `positiveInteger`, and the others are all of type `string`. These two types are relatively self-explanatory, corresponding to positive integers greater than or equal to 0, and strings of characters. The XML Schema Definition language allows you to specify many different values for the `type` attribute in an `element` definition. Here are a few other examples:

Data Type	Examples of Data
integer	25, -998, 12345, 0, -1
negativeInteger	-1, -2, -3, -12345, and so on
nonNegativeInteger	0, 1, 2, 3, and so on
hexBinary	0DE7, ADD7
long	25, 123456789, -9999999
float	2.71828, 5E5, 500.0, 0, -3E2, -300.0, NaN, INF, -INF
double	3.1415265, 1E30, -2.5, NaN, -INF, INF
boolean	true, false, 1, 0
date	2004-12-31
language	en-US, en, de

The `float` and `double` types correspond to values within the ranges for 32-bit and 64-bit floating-point values, respectively. There are many more standard types of data within the XML Schema Definition language, and because this is extensible, you can also define data types of your own.

You can also define a default value for a simple element by using the `default` attribute within the definition of the element. For example, within an XML representation of a sketch you will undoubtedly need to have an element defining a color. You might define this as a simple element like this:

```
<xsd:element name="color" type="xsd:string" default="blue"/>
```

This defines a color element containing data that is a string and a default value for the string of `"blue"`. In a similar way, you can define the content for a simple element to be a fixed value by specifying the content as the value for the `fixed` attribute within the `xsd:element` tag.

Defining Attributes for Complex Elements

You use the xsd:attribute tag to define an attribute for a complex element. Let's take an example to see how you do this. Suppose you decided that you would define a circle in an XML document for a sketch using a <circle/> element, where the coordinates of the center, the radius, and the color are specified by attributes. Within the document schema, you might define the type for an element representing a circle like this:

```
<xsd:complexType name="CircleType">
 <xsd:attribute name="x" type="xsd:double"/>
 <xsd:attribute name="y" type="xsd:double"/>
 <xsd:attribute name="radius" type="xsd:double"/>
 <xsd:attribute name="color" type="xsd:string"/>
</xsd:complexType>
```

The elements that define the attributes for the <circle/> element type appear within the complexType element, just like child element definitions. You specify the attribute name and the data type for the value in exactly the same way as for an element. The type specification is not mandatory. If you leave it out, it just means that anything goes as a value for the attribute.

You can also specify in the definition for an attribute whether it is optional or not by specifying a value for the use attribute within the xsd:attribute element. The value for the use attribute can be either "optional" or "required". For a circle element, none of the attributes are optional, so you might modify the complex type definition to the following:

```
<xsd:complexType name="CircleType">
 <xsd:attribute name="x" type="xsd:double" use="required"/>
 <xsd:attribute name="y" type="xsd:double" use="required"/>
 <xsd:attribute name="radius" type="xsd:double" use="required"/>
 <xsd:attribute name="color" type="xsd:string" use="required"/>
</xsd:complexType>
```

You might also want to restrict the values that can be assigned to an attribute. For example, the radius certainly cannot be zero or negative, and the color may be restricted to standard colors. You could do this by adding a simple type definition that defines restrictions on these values. For example:

```
<xsd:complexType name="circle">
 <xsd:attribute name="x" type="xsd:double" use="required"/>
 <xsd:attribute name="y" type="xsd:double" use="required"/>
 <xsd:attribute name="radius" use="required">
  <xsd:simpleType>
   <xsd:restriction base="xsd:double">
    <xsd:minExclusive value="0"/>
   </xsd:restriction
  </xsd:simpleType>
 </xsd:attribute>
 <xsd:attribute name="color" use="required">
  <xsd:simpleType>
   <xsd:restriction base="xsd:string">
    <xsd:enumeration value="red"/>
    <xsd:enumeration value="blue"/>
    <xsd:enumeration value="green"/>
```

```
            <xsd:enumeration value="yellow"/>
        </xsd:restriction>
      </xsd:simpleType>
    </xsd:attribute>
  </xsd:complexType>
```

The `radius` and `color` attributes have restrictions on the values that can be assigned to them. The `simpleType` element that appears within the `xsd:attribute` elements specifies the constraints on the values for each attribute. You can also use the `simpleType` element with an `xsd:element` element definition to constrain the content for an element in a similar way. The `xsd:restriction` element defines the constraints, and you have a considerable range of options for specifying them, many more than I can possibly explain here. The `base` attribute in the `xsd:restriction` element defines the type for the value that is being restricted, and this attribute specification is required.

I've used an `xsd:minExclusive` specification to define an exclusive lower limit for values of the `radius` attribute, and this specifies that the value must be greater than `"0"`. Alternatively, you might prefer to use `xsd:minExclusive` with a value of `"1"` to set a sensible minimum value for the radius. You also have the option of specifying an upper limit on the values by specifying either `maxInclusive` or `maxExclusive` values. For the `color` attribute definition, I've introduced a restriction that the value must be one of a fixed set of values. Each value that is allowed is specified in an `xsd:enumeration` element, and there can be any number of these. Obviously, this doesn't just apply to strings; you can restrict the values for numeric types to be one of an enumerated set of values. For the color attribute the value must be one of the four string values specified.

Defining Groups of Attributes

Sometimes several different elements have the same set of attributes. To avoid having to repeat the definitions for the elements in such a set for each element that requires them, you can define an attribute group. Here's an example of a definition for an attribute group:

```
<xsd:attributeGroup name="coords">
    <xsd:attribute name="x" type="xsd:double" use="required"/>
    <xsd:attribute name="y" type="xsd:double" use="required"/>
</xsd:attributeGroup>
```

This defines a group of two attributes with names x and y that specify x and y coordinates for a point. The name of this attribute group is `coords`. In general, an attribute group can contain other attribute groups. You could use the `coords` attribute group within a complex type definition like this:

```
<xsd:complexType name="PointType">
    <xsd:attributeGroup ref="coords"/>
</xsd:complexType>
```

This defines the element type `PointType` as having the attributes that are defined in the `coords` attribute group. The `ref` attribute in the `xsd:attributeGroup` element specifies that this is a reference to a named attribute group. You can now use the `PointType` element type to define elements. For example:

```
<xsd:element name="position" type="PointType"/>
```

This declares a `<point/>` element to be of type `PointType`, and thus have the required attributes x and y.

Specifying a Group of Element Choices

The xsd:choice element in the Schema Definition language enables you to specify that one out of a given set of elements included in the choice definition must be present. This will be useful in specifying a schema for Sketcher documents because the content is essentially variable — it can be any sequence of any of the basic types of elements. Suppose that you have already defined types for the geometric and text elements that can occur in a sketch. You could use an xsd:choice element in the definition of a complex type for a <sketch/> element like this:

```
<xsd:complexType name="SketchType">
    <xsd:choice minOccurs="0" maxOccurs="unbounded">
        <xsd:element name="line" type="LineType"/>
        <xsd:element name="rectangle" type="RectangleType"/>
        <xsd:element name="circle" type="CircleType"/>
        <xsd:element name="curve" type="CurveType"/>
        <xsd:element name="text" type="TextType"/>
    </xsd:choice>
</xsd:complexType>
```

This defines that an element of type SketchType contains zero or more elements that are each one of the five types identified in the xsd:choice element. Thus, each element can be any of the types LineType, RectangleType, CircleType, CurveType, or TextType, which are types for the primitive elements in a sketch that will be defined elsewhere in the schema. Given this definition for SketchType, you can declare the content for a sketch to be:

```
<xsd:element name="sketch" type="SketchType"/>
```

This declares the contents of an XML document for a sketch to be a <sketch/> element that has zero or more elements of any of the types that appeared in the preceding xsd:choice element. This is exactly what is required to accommodate any sketch, so this single declaration defines the entire contents of all possible sketches. All you need is to fill in a few details for the element types. I think you know enough about XML Schema to put together a schema for Sketcher documents.

A Schema for Sketcher

As I noted when I discussed a DTD for Sketcher, an XML document that defines a sketch can have a very simple structure. Essentially, it can consist of a <sketch/> element that contains a sequence of zero or more elements that define lines, rectangles, circles, curves, or text. These child elements may be in any sequence, and there can be any number of them. To accommodate the fact that any given child element must be one of five types of elements, you could use some of the XML fragments from earlier sections to make an initial stab at an outline of a Sketcher schema like this:

```
<?xml version="1.0" encoding="UTF-8"?>
<xsd:schema xmlns:xsd="http://www.w3.org/2001/XMLSchema">

    <!--The entire document content -->
    <xsd:element name="sketch" type="SketchType"/>

    <!--Type for a sketch root element -->
    <xsd:complexType name="SketchType">
        <xsd:choice minOccurs="0" maxOccurs="unbounded">
```

```
            <xsd:element name="line" type="LineType"/>
            <xsd:element name="rectangle" type="RectangleType"/>
            <xsd:element name="circle" type="CircleType"/>
            <xsd:element name="curve" type="CurveType"/>
            <xsd:element name="text" type="TextType"/>
        </xsd:choice>
    </xsd:complexType>

    <!--Other definitions that are needed...  -->
</xsd:schema>
```

This document references the XML Schema language namespace, so it's evidently a definition of a schema. The documents that this schema defines have no namespace specified, so elements on documents conforming to this schema do not need to be qualified. The entire content of a Sketcher document is declared to be an element with the name sketch that is of type SketchType. The <sketch/> element is the root element, and because it can have child elements, it must be defined as a complex type. The child elements within a <sketch/> element are the elements specified by the xsd:choice element, which represents a selection of one of the five complex elements that can occur in a sketch. The minOccurs and maxOccurs attribute values for the xsd:choice element determines that there may be any number of such elements, including zero. Thus, this definition accommodates XML documents describing any Sketcher sketch. All you now need to do is fill in the definitions for the possible varieties of child elements.

Defining Line Elements

Let's define the same XML elements in the schema for Sketcher as the DTD for Sketcher defines. On that basis, a line element will have three child elements specifying the color, position, and end point for a line, plus an attribute that specifies the rotation angle. You could define the type for a <line/> element in the schema like this:

```
<xsd:complexType name="LineType">
    <xsd:sequence>
        <xsd:element name="color" type="ColorType"/>
        <xsd:element name="position" type="PointType"/>
        <xsd:element name="endpoint" type="PointType"/>
    </xsd:sequence>
    <xsd:attribute name="angle" type="xsd:double" use="required"/>
</xsd:complexType>
```

This defines the type for a <line/> element in a sketch. An element of type LineType contains three elements, <color/>, <position/>, and <endpoint/>. These are enclosed within a <sequence/> schema definition element, so they must all be present and must appear in a sketch document in the sequence in which they are specified here. The element type definition also specifies an attribute with the name angle that must be included in any element of type LineType.

Of course, you now must define the types that you've used in the definition of the complex type, LineType: the ColorType and PointType element types.

Defining a Type for Color Elements

As I discussed in the context of the DTD for Sketcher, the data for a `<color/>` element will be supplied by three attributes that specify the RGB values for the color. You can therefore define the element type like this:

```
<xsd:complexType name="ColorType">
    <xsd:attribute name="R" type="xsd:nonNegativeInteger" use="required"/>
    <xsd:attribute name="G" type="xsd:nonNegativeInteger" use="required"/>
    <xsd:attribute name="B" type="xsd:nonNegativeInteger" use="required"/>
</xsd:complexType>
```

This is a relatively simple complex type definition. There are just the three attributes — R, G, and B — that all have integer values that can be 0 or greater, and are all mandatory.

Defining a Type for Point Elements

You saw a definition for the `PointType` element type earlier:

```
<xsd:complexType name="PointType">
    <xsd:attributeGroup ref="coords"/>
</xsd:complexType>
```

This references the attribute group with the name `coords`, so this must be defined elsewhere in the schema. You've also seen this attribute group definition before:

```
<xsd:attributeGroup name="coords">
  <xsd:attribute name="x" type="xsd:double" use="required"/>
  <xsd:attribute name="y" type="xsd:double" use="required"/>
</xsd:attributeGroup>
```

You'll be able to use this attribute group in the definitions for other element types in the schema. The definition of this attribute group must appear at the top level in the schema, within the root element; otherwise, it will not be possible to refer to it from within an element declaration.

Defining a Rectangle Element Type

The definition of the type for a `<rectangle/>` element is almost identical to the `LineType` definition:

```
<xsd:complexType name="RectangleType">
    <xsd:sequence>
        <xsd:element name="color" type="ColorType"/>
        <xsd:element name="position" type="PointType"/>
        <xsd:element name="bottomright" type="PointType"/>
    </xsd:sequence>
    <xsd:attribute name="angle" type="xsd:double" use="required"/>
</xsd:complexType>
```

This references the element types `ColorType` and `PointType`, and both of these have already been defined. Note how you can declare two different elements, `position` and `bottomright`, to be of the same element type.

Defining a Circle Element Type

There's nothing new in the definition of `CircleType`:

```xsd
<xsd:complexType name="CircleType">
    <xsd:sequence>
        <xsd:element name="color" type="ColorType"/>
        <xsd:element name="position" type="PointType"/>
    </xsd:sequence>
    <xsd:attribute name="radius" type="xsd:double" use="required"/>
    <xsd:attribute name="angle" type="xsd:double" use="required"/>
</xsd:complexType>
```

The child elements appear within a sequence element, so their sequence is fixed. You have the radius and angle for a circle specified by attributes that both have values of type `double`, and are both mandatory.

Defining a Curve Element Type

A type for the curve element does introduce something new because the number of child elements is variable. A curve is defined by the origin plus one or more points, so the type definition must allow for an unlimited number of child elements defining points. Here's how you can accommodate that:

```xsd
<xsd:complexType name="CurveType">
    <xsd:sequence>
        <xsd:element name="color" type="ColorType"/>
        <xsd:element name="position" type="PointType"/>
        <xsd:element name="point" type="PointType" minOccurs="1"
                                                 maxOccurs="unbounded"/>
    </xsd:sequence>
    <xsd:attribute name="angle" type="xsd:double" use="required"/>
</xsd:complexType>
```

The flexibility in the number of `<point/>` elements is specified through the `minOccurs` and `maxOccurs` attribute values. The value of 1 for `minOccurs` ensures that there will always be at least one, and the unbounded value for `maxOccurs` allows an unlimited number of `<point/>` elements to be present.

Defining a Text Element Type

The type for `<text/>` elements is the odd one out, but it's not difficult. It involves four child elements for the color, the position, the font, and the text itself, plus an attribute to specify the angle. The type definition will be as follows:

```xsd
<xsd:complexType name="TextType">
    <xsd:sequence>
        <xsd:element name="color" type="ColorType"/>
        <xsd:element name="position" type="PointType"/>
        <xsd:element name="font" type="FontType"/>
        <xsd:element name="string" type="xsd:string"/>
    </xsd:sequence>
    <xsd:attribute name="angle" type="xsd:double" use="required"/>
</xsd:complexType>
```

The text string itself is a simple `<string/>` element, but the font is a complex element that requires a type definition:

```
<xsd:complexType name="FontType">
    <xsd:attribute name="fontname" type="xsd:string" use="required"/>
    <xsd:attribute name="fontstyle" use="required">
        <xsd:simpleType>
            <xsd:restriction base="xsd:string">
                <xsd:enumeration value="plain"/>
                <xsd:enumeration value="bold"/>
                <xsd:enumeration value="italic"/>
                <xsd:enumeration value="bold-italic"/>
            </xsd:restriction>
        </xsd:simpleType>
    </xsd:attribute>
</xsd:complexType>
```

The style attribute for the `<font/>` element can be only one of four fixed values. You impose this constraint by defining an enumeration of the four possible string values within a `simpleType` definition for the attribute value. The `xsd:simpleType` definition is implicitly associated with the `style` attribute value because the type definition is a child of the `xsd:attribute` element.

The Complete Sketcher Schema

If you assemble all the fragments into a single file, you'll have the following definition for the Sketcher schema that defines XML documents containing a sketch:

```
<?xml version="1.0" encoding="UTF-8"?>
<xsd:schema xmlns:xsd="http://www.w3.org/2001/XMLSchema">
    <xsd:element name="sketch" type="SketchType"/>

    <!--Type for a sketch root element -->
    <xsd:complexType name="SketchType">
        <xsd:choice minOccurs="0" maxOccurs="unbounded">
            <xsd:element name="line" type="LineType"/>
            <xsd:element name="rectangle" type="RectangleType"/>
            <xsd:element name="circle" type="CircleType"/>
            <xsd:element name="curve" type="CurveType"/>
            <xsd:element name="text" type="TextType"/>
        </xsd:choice>
    </xsd:complexType>

    <!--Type for a line element -->
    <xsd:complexType name="LineType">
        <xsd:sequence>
            <xsd:element name="color" type="ColorType"/>
            <xsd:element name="position" type="PointType"/>
            <xsd:element name="endpoint" type="PointType"/>
        </xsd:sequence>
        <xsd:attribute name="angle" type="xsd:double"/>
    </xsd:complexType>

    <!--Type for a rectangle element -->
    <xsd:complexType name="RectangleType">
        <xsd:sequence>
```

```xml
            <xsd:element name="color" type="ColorType"/>
            <xsd:element name="position" type="PointType"/>
            <xsd:element name="bottomright" type="PointType"/>
        </xsd:sequence>
        <xsd:attribute name="angle" type="xsd:double"/>
    </xsd:complexType>

    <!--Type for a circle element -->
    <xsd:complexType name="CircleType">
        <xsd:sequence>
            <xsd:element name="color" type="ColorType"/>
            <xsd:element name="position" type="PointType"/>
        </xsd:sequence>
        <xsd:attribute name="radius" type="xsd:double"/>
        <xsd:attribute name="angle" type="xsd:double"/>
    </xsd:complexType>

    <!--Type for a curve element -->
    <xsd:complexType name="CurveType">
        <xsd:sequence>
            <xsd:element name="color" type="ColorType"/>
            <xsd:element name="position" type="PointType"/>
            <xsd:element name="point" type="PointType" minOccurs="1"
                                                      maxOccurs="unbounded"/>
        </xsd:sequence>
        <xsd:attribute name="angle" type="xsd:double"/>
    </xsd:complexType>

    <!--Type for a text element -->
    <xsd:complexType name="TextType">
        <xsd:sequence>
            <xsd:element name="color" type="ColorType"/>
            <xsd:element name="position" type="PointType"/>
            <xsd:element name="font" type="FontType"/>
            <xsd:element name="string" type="xsd:string"/>
        </xsd:sequence>
        <xsd:attribute name="angle" type="xsd:double"/>
    </xsd:complexType>

    <!--Type for a font element -->
    <xsd:complexType name="FontType">
        <xsd:attribute name="fontname" type="xsd:string" use="required"/>
        <xsd:attribute name="fontstyle" use="required">
            <xsd:simpleType>
                <xsd:restriction base="xsd:string">
                    <xsd:enumeration value="plain"/>
                    <xsd:enumeration value="bold"/>
                    <xsd:enumeration value="italic"/>
                    <xsd:enumeration value="bold-italic"/>
                </xsd:restriction>
            </xsd:simpleType>
        </xsd:attribute>
    </xsd:complexType>

    <!--Type for elements representing points -->
    <xsd:complexType name="PointType">
```

```
            <xsd:attributeGroup ref="coords"/>
      </xsd:complexType>

      <!--Type for a color element -->
      <xsd:complexType name="ColorType">
          <xsd:attribute name="R" type="xsd:nonNegativeInteger" use="required"/>
          <xsd:attribute name="G" type="xsd:nonNegativeInteger" use="required"/>
          <xsd:attribute name="B" type="xsd:nonNegativeInteger" use="required"/>
      </xsd:complexType>

      <!-- Attribute group specifying point coordinates -->
      <xsd:attributeGroup name="coords">
          <xsd:attribute name="x" type="xsd:double" use="required"/>
          <xsd:attribute name="y" type="xsd:double" use="required"/>
      </xsd:attributeGroup>
   </xsd:schema>
```

This is somewhat longer than the DTD for Sketcher, but it does provide several advantages. All the data in the document now has types specified so the document is more precisely defined. This schema is XML, so the documents and the schema are defined in fundamentally the same way and are equally communicable. There is no problem combining one schema with another because namespaces are supported, and every schema can be easily extended. You can save this as a file Sketcher.xsd.

A Document That Uses a Schema

A document that has been defined in accordance with a particular schema is called an **instance document** for that schema. An instance document has to identify the schema to which it conforms, and this is done using attribute values within the root element of the document. Here's an XML document for a sketch that identifies the location of the schema:

```
<sketch
   xmlns:xsi="http://www.w3.org/2001/XMLSchema-instance"
   xsi:noNamespaceSchemaLocation="file:/C:/Beg%20Java%20Stuff/Sketcher.xsd">
   <!-- Elements defined for the sketch... -->
</sketch>
```

The value for the xmlns attribute identifies the namespace name http://www.w3.org/2001/XMLSchema-instance and specifies xsi as the prefix used to represent this namespace name. In an instance document, the value for the noNamespaceSchemaLocation attribute in the xsi namespace is a hint about the location where the schema for the document can be found. Here the value for noNamespaceSchemaLocation is a URI for a file on the local machine, and the spaces are escaped because this is required within a URI. The value you specify for the xsi:noNamespaceSchema Location attribute is always regarded as a hint, so in principle an application or parser processing this document is not obliged to take account of this. In practice though, this usually will be taken account of when the document is processed, unless there is good reason to ignore it.

You define a value for the `noNamespaceSchemaLocation` attribute because a sketch document has no namespace; if it had a namespace, you would define a value for the `schemaLocation` attribute that includes two URIs separated by whitespace within the value specification— the URI for the namespace and a URI that is a hint for the location of the namespace. Obviously, since one or more spaces separate the two URIs, the URIs cannot contain unescaped spaces.

Programming with XML Documents

Right at the beginning of this chapter I introduced the notion of an XML processor as a module that is used by an application to read XML documents. An XML processor parses the contents of a document and makes the elements, together with their attributes and content, available to the application, so it is also referred to as an **XML parser**. In case you haven't met the term before, a **parser** is just a program module that breaks down text in a given language into its component parts. A natural language processor would have a parser that identifies the grammatical segments in each sentence. A compiler has a parser that identifies variables, constants, operators, and so on in a program statement. An application accesses the content of a document through an API provided by an XML parser and the parser does the job of figuring out what the document consists of.

Java supports two complementary APIs for processing an XML document:

❏   **SAX**, which is the **S**imple **A**PI for **X**ML parsing

❏   **DOM**, which is the **D**ocument **O**bject **M**odel for XML

The support in JDK 5.0 is for DOM level 3 and for SAX version 2.0.2. JDK 5.0 also supports **XSLT** version 1.0, where **XSL** is the **E**xtensible **S**tylesheet **L**anguage and **T** is **T**ransformations—a language for transforming one XML document into another, or into some other textual representation such as HTML. However, I'll concentrate on the basic application of DOM and SAX. XSLT is such an extensive topic that there are several books devoted entirely to it.

Before I get into detail on these APIs, let's look at the broad differences between SAX and DOM, and get an idea of the circumstances in which you might choose to use one rather than the other.

SAX Processing

SAX uses an **event-based** process for reading an XML document that is implemented through a callback mechanism. This is very similar to the way in which you handle GUI events in Java. As the parser reads a document, each parsing event, such as recognizing the start or end of an element, results in a call to a particular method associated with that event. Such a method is often referred to as a **handler**. It is up to you to implement these methods to respond appropriately to the event. Each of your methods then has the opportunity to react to the event, which will result in it being called in any way that you wish. In Figure 22-4 you can see the events that would arise from the XML document example that you saw earlier.

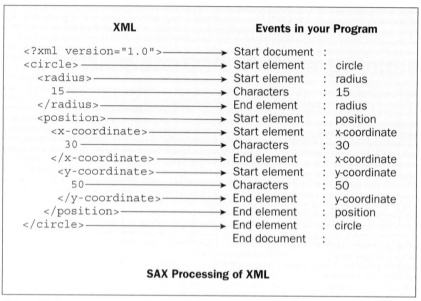

Figure 22-4

Each type of event results in a different method in your program being called. There are, for example, different events for registering the beginning and end of a document. You can also see that the start and end of each element results in two further kinds of events, and another type of event occurs for each segment of document data. Thus, this particular document will involve five different methods in your program being called — some of them more than once, of course, so there is one method for each type of event.

Because of the way SAX works, your application inevitably receives the document a piece at a time, with no representation of the whole document. This means that if you need to have the whole document available to your program with its elements and content properly structured, you have to assemble it yourself from the information supplied piecemeal to your callback methods.

Of course, it also means that you don't have to keep the entire document in memory if you don't need it, so if you are just looking for particular information from a document, all <phonenumber> elements, for example, you can just save those as you receive them through the callback mechanism, and discard the rest. As a consequence, SAX is a particularly fast and memory efficient way of selectively processing the contents of an XML document.

First of all, SAX itself is not an XML document parser; it is a public domain definition of an interface to an XML parser, where the parser is an external program. The public domain part of the SAX API is in three packages that are shipped as part of the JDK:

❑   `org.xml.sax` — This defines the Java interfaces specifying the SAX API and the `InputSource` class that encapsulates a source of an XML document to be parsed.

❑   `org.xml.sax.helpers` — This defines a number of helper classes for interfacing to a SAX parser.

❑   `org.xml.sax.ext` — This defines interfaces representing optional extensions to SAX2 to obtain information about a DTD, or to obtain information about comments and CDATA sections in a document.

In addition to these, the `javax.xml.parsers` package provides factory classes that you use to gain access to a parser, and the `javax.xml.transform` package defines interfaces and classes for XSLT 1.0 processing of an XML document.

In Java terms there are several interfaces involved. The `XMLReader` interface defined in the `org.xml.sax` package specifies the methods that the SAX parser will call, as it recognizes elements, attributes, and other components of an XML document. You must provide a class that implements these methods and responds to the method calls in the way that you want.

DOM Processing

DOM works quite differently than SAX. When an XML document is parsed, the whole document tree is assembled in memory and returned to your application as an object of type `Document` that encapsulates it, as Figure 22-5 illustrates.

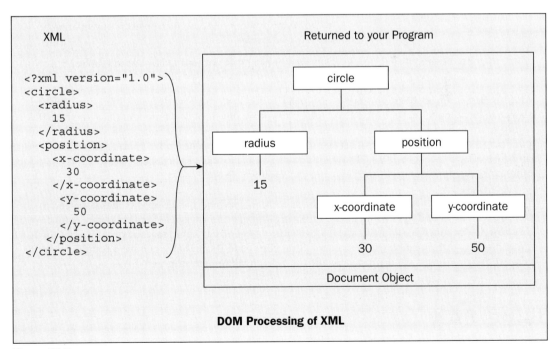

DOM Processing of XML

Figure 22-5

Once you have the `Document` object available, you can call the `Document` object's methods to navigate through the elements in the document tree starting with the root element. With DOM, the entire document is available for you to process as often and in as many ways as you want. This is a major advantage over SAX processing. The downside to this is the amount of memory occupied by the document — there is no choice, you get it all, no matter how big it is. With some documents the amount of memory required may be prohibitively large.

DOM has one other unique advantage over SAX. It allows you to modify existing documents or create new ones. If you want to create an XML document programmatically and then transfer it to an external destination such as a file or another computer, DOM is the API for this since SAX has no direct provision for creating or modifying XML documents. I will go into detail on how you can use a DOM parser in the next chapter.

Accessing Parsers

The `javax.xml.parsers` package defines four classes supporting the processing of XML documents:

`SAXParserFactory`	Enables you to create a configurable factory object that you can use to create a `SAXParser` object encapsulating a SAX-based parser
`SAXParser`	Defines an object that wraps a SAX-based parser
`DocumentBuilderFactory`	Enables you to create a configurable factory object that you can use to create a `DocumentBuilder` object encapsulating a DOM-based parser
`DocumentBuilder`	Defines an object that wraps a DOM-based parser

All four classes are abstract. This is because JAXP is designed to allow different parsers and their factory classes to be plugged in. Both DOM and SAX parsers are developed independently of the Java JDK so it is important to be able to integrate new parsers as they come along. The Xerces parser that is currently distributed with the JDK is controlled and developed by the Apache Project, and it provides a very comprehensive range of capabilities. However, you may want to take advantage of the features provided by other parsers from other organizations, and JAXP allows for that.

These abstract classes act as wrappers for the specific factory and parser objects that you need to use for a particular parser and insulate your code from a particular parser implementation. An instance of a factory object that can create an instance of a parser is created at run time, so your program can use a different parser without changing or even recompiling your code. Now that you have a rough idea of the general principles, let's get down to specifics and practicalities, starting with SAX.

Using SAX

To process an XML document with SAX, you first have to establish contact with the parser that you want to use. The first step toward this is to create a `SAXParserFactory` object like this:

```
SAXParserFactory spf = SAXParserFactory.newInstance();
```

The `SAXParserFactory` class is defined in the `javax.xml.parsers` package along with the `SAXParser` class that encapsulates a parser. The `SAXParserFactory` class is abstract but the static `newInstance()` method will return a reference to an object of a class type that is a concrete implementation of `SAXParserFactory`. This will be the factory object for creating an object encapsulating a SAX parser.

Before you create a parser object, you can condition the capabilities of the parser object that the `SAXParserFactory` object will create. For example, the `SAXParserFactory` object has methods for determining whether the parser that it will attempt to create will be namespace aware or will validate the XML as it is parsed:

`isNamespaceAware()`	Returns `true` if the parser to be created is namespace aware, and `false` otherwise
`isValidating()`	Returns `true` if the parser to be created will validate the XML during parsing, and `false` otherwise

You can set the factory object to produce namespace aware parsers by calling its `setNamespaceAware()` method with an argument value of `true`. An argument value of `false` sets the factory object to produce parsers that are not namespace aware. A parser that is namespace aware can recognize the structure of names in a namespace — with a colon separating the namespace prefix from the name. A namespace aware parser can report the URI and local name separately for each element and attribute. A parser that is not namespace aware will report only an element or attribute name as a single name even when it contains a colon. In other words, a parser that is not namespace aware will treat a colon as just another character that is part of a name.

Similarly, calling the `setValidating()` method with an argument value of `true` will cause the factory object to produce parsers that can validate the XML as a document is parsed. A validating parser can verify that the document body has a DTD or a schema, and that the document content is consistent with the DTD or schema identified within the document.

You can now use the `SAXParserFactory` object to create a `SAXParser` object as follows:

```
SAXParser parser = null;
try {
  parser = spf.newSAXParser();
}catch(SAXException e){
    e.printStackTrace(System.err);
    System.exit(1);
} catch(ParserConfigurationException e) {
    e.printStackTrace(System.err);
    System.exit(1);
}
```

The `SAXParser` object that you create here will encapsulate the parser supplied with the JDK. The `newSAXParser()` method for the factory object can throw the two exceptions you are catching here. A `ParserConfigurationException` will be thrown if a parser cannot be created consistent with the configuration determined by the `SAXParserFactory` object, and a `SAXException` will be thrown if any other error occurs. For example, if you call the `setValidating()` option and the parser does not have the capability for validating documents, this exception would be thrown. This should not arise with the parser supplied with the JDK though, because it supports both of these features.

1197

The `ParserConfigurationException` class is defined in the `javax.xml.parsers` package and the `SAXException` class is in the `org.xml.sax` package. Now let's see what the default parser is by putting the code fragments you have looked at so far together in a working example.

Try It Out   Accessing a SAX Parser

Here's the code to create a `SAXParser` object and output some details about it to the command line:

```
import javax.xml.parsers.SAXParserFactory;
import javax.xml.parsers.SAXParser;
import javax.xml.parsers.ParserConfigurationException;
import org.xml.sax.SAXException;
public class TrySAX {
  public static void main(String args[]) {
    // Create factory object
    SAXParserFactory spf = SAXParserFactory.newInstance();
    System.out.println("Parser will "+(spf.isNamespaceAware()?"":"not ") +
                    "be namespace aware");
    System.out.println("Parser will "+(spf.isValidating()?"":"not ") +
                    "validate XML");

    SAXParser parser = null;              // Stores parser reference
    try {
     parser = spf.newSAXParser();         // Create parser object
    }catch(ParserConfigurationException e){// Thrown if a parser cannot be created
                                           // that is consistent with the
      e.printStackTrace(System.err);       // configuration in spf
      System.exit(1);
    } catch(SAXException e) {              // Thrown for any other error
      e.printStackTrace(System.err);
      System.exit(1);
    }

    System.out.println("Parser object is: "+ parser);
  }
}
```

When I ran this I got the following output:

```
Parser will not be namespace aware
Parser will not validate XML
Parser object is: com.sun.org.apache.xerces.internal.jaxp.SAXParserImpl@118f375
```

How It Works

The output shows that the default configuration for the SAX parser produced by the `SAXParserFactory` object `spf` will be neither namespace aware nor validating. The parser supplied with the JDK is the Xerces parser from the XML Apache Project. This parser implements the W3C standard for XML, the de facto SAX2 standard, and the W3C DOM standard. It also provides support for the W3C standard for XML Schema. You can find detailed information on the advantages of this particular parser on the `http://xml.apache.org` web site.

The code to create the parser works as I have already discussed. Once you have an instance of the factory method, you use that to create an object encapsulating the parser. Although the reference is returned as type SAXParser, the object is of type SAXParserImpl, which is a concrete implementation of the abstract SAXParser class for a particular parser.

The Xerces parser is capable of validating XML and can be namespace aware. All you need to do is specify which of these options you require by calling the appropriate method for the factory object. You can set the parser configuration for the factory object spf so that you get a validating and namespace aware parser by adding two lines to the program:

```
// Create factory object
SAXParserFactory spf = SAXParserFactory.newInstance();
spf.setNamespaceAware(true);
spf.setValidating(true);
```

If you compile and run the code again, you should get output something like:

```
Parser will be namespace aware
Parser will validate XML
Parser object is: com.sun.org.apache.xerces.internal.jaxp.SAXParserImpl@867e89
```

You arrive at a SAXParser instance without tripping any exceptions, and you clearly now have a namespace aware and validating parser. By default the Xerces parser will validate an XML document with a DTD. To get it to validate a document with an XML Schema, you need to set another option for the parser, as I'll discuss in the next section.

Using a Different Parser

You might like to try a different parser at some point. The simplest way to try out an alternative parser is to include the path to the .jar file that contains the parser implementation in the -classpath option on the command line. For example, suppose you have downloaded a newer version of the Xerces 2 parser from the Apache web site that you want to try. Once you have extracted the zip files and stored them on your C:\ drive, say, you could run the example with the new Xerces parser with a command similar to this:

```
java -classpath .;C:\xerces-2_6_2\xercesImpl.jar -enableassertions TrySAX
```

Don't forget the period in the classpath definition that specifies the current directory. Without it the TrySAX.class file will not be found. If you omit the -classpath option, the program will revert to using the default parser. Of course, you can use this technique to select a particular parser when you have several installed on your PC. Just add the path to the directory that contains the JAR for the parser to the classpath.

Parser Features and Properties

Specific parsers, such as the Xerces parser that you get with the JDK, define their own features and properties that control and report on the processing of XML documents. A **feature** is an option in processing XML that is either on or off, so a feature is set as a boolean value, either true or false. A **property** is a parameter that you set to a particular object value, usually of type String. There are standard SAX2 features and properties that may be common to several parsers, and non-standard features and properties that are parser-specific. Note that although a feature or property may be standard for SAX2, this does not mean that a SAX2 parser will necessarily support it.

Querying and Setting Parser Features

Namespace awareness and validating capability are both features of a parser, and you already know how you tell the parser factory object that you want a parser with these features turned on. In general, each parser feature is identified by a name that is a fully qualified URI, and the standard features for SAX2 parsing have names within the namespace `http://xml.org/sax/features/`. For example, the feature specifying namespace awareness has the name `http://xml.org/sax/features/namespaces`. Here are a few of the standard features that are defined for SAX2 parsers:

Feature	Description
namespaces	When `true`, the parser replaces prefixes to element and attribute names with the corresponding namespace URIs. If you set this feature to `true`, the document must have a schema that supports the use of namespaces. All SAX parsers must support this feature.
namespace-prefixes	When `true`, the parser reports the original prefixed names and attributes used for namespace declarations. The default value for this feature is `false`. All SAX parsers must support this feature.
validation	When `true`, the parser will validate the document and report any errors. The default value for the validation feature is `false`.
external-general-entities	When `true`, the parser will include general entities.
string-interning	When `true`, all element and attribute names, namespace URIs, and local names use Java string interning so each of these corresponds to a unique object. This feature is always `true` for the Xerces parser.
external-parameter-entities	When `true`, the parser will include external parameter entities and the external DTD subset.
lexical-handler/parameter-entities	When `true`, the beginning and end of parameter entities will be reported.

There are other non-standard features for the Xerces parser. Consult the documentation for the parser on the Apache web site for more details. Apart from the `namespaces` and `namespaces-prefixes` features that all SAX2 parsers are required to implement, there is no set collection of features for a SAX2 parser, so a parser may implement any number of arbitrary features that may or may not be in the list of standard features.

You have two ways to query and set features for a parser. You can call the `getFeature()` and `setFeature()` methods for the `SAXParserFactory` object to do this before you create the `SAXParser` object. The parser that is created will then have the features switched on. Alternatively, you can create a `SAXParser` object using the factory object and then obtain an `org.sax.XMLReader` object reference from it by calling the `getXMLReader()` method. You can then call the `getFeature()` and `setFeature()` methods for the `XMLReader` object. `XMLReader` is the interface that a concrete SAX2 parser implements to allow features and properties to be set and queried. The principle difference in use between calling the factory object methods and calling the `XMLReader` object methods is that the methods for a `SAXParserFactory` object can throw an exception of type `javax.xml.parsers.ParserConfigurationException` if a parser cannot be created with the feature specified.

Once you have created an `XMLParser` object, you can obtain an `XMLReader` object reference from the parser like this:

```
XMLReader reader = null;
try{
   reader = parser.getXMLReader();
} catch(org.xml.sax.SAXException e) {
   System.err.println(e.getMessage());
}
```

The `getFeature()` method that the `XMLReader` interface declares for querying a feature expects an argument of type `String` that identifies the feature you are querying. The method returns a `boolean` value that indicates the state of the feature. The `setFeature()` method expects two arguments; the first argument is of type `String` and identifies the feature you are setting, and the second is of type `boolean` and specifies the state to be set. The `setFeature()` method can throw exceptions of type `org.xml.SAXNotRecognizedException` if the feature is not found, or of type `org.xml.sax.SAXNotSupportedException` if the feature name was recognized but cannot be set to the `boolean` value you specify. Both exception types have `SAXException` as a base, so you can use this type to catch either of them. Here's how you might set the features for the Xerces parser so that it will support namespace prefixes:

```
String nsPrefixesFeature = "http://xml.org/sax/features/namespace-prefixes";
XMLReader reader = null;
try{
   reader = parser.getXMLReader();
   reader.setFeature(nsPrefixesFeature, true);
} catch(org.xml.sax.SAXException e) {
   System.err.println(e.getMessage());
}
```

This sets the feature to make the parser report the original prefixed element and attribute names.

If you want to use the `SAXParserFactory` object to set the features before you create the parser object, you could do it like this:

```
String nsPrefixesFeature = "http://xml.org/sax/features/namespace-prefixes";
SAXParserFactory spf = SAXParserFactory.newInstance();
SAXParser parser = null;
try {
  spf.setFeature(nsPrefixesFeature, true);
```

```
      parser = spf.newSAXParser();
      System.out.println("Parser object is: "+ parser);
    }
  catch(SAXException e) {
    e.printStackTrace(System.err);
    System.exit(1);
  }
  catch(ParserConfigurationException e) {
    e.printStackTrace(System.err);
    System.exit(1);
  }
```

You must call the `setFeature()` method for the `SAXParserFactory` object in a `try` block because of the exceptions it may throw. The `catch` block for exceptions of type `SAXException` will catch the `SAXNotRecognizedException` and `SAXNotSupportedException` exceptions if they are thrown.

Setting Parser Properties

As I said at the outset, a **property** is a parser parameter with a value that is an object, usually a `String` object. Some properties have values that you set to influence the parser's operation, while the values for other properties are set by the parser for you to retrieve to provide information about the parsing process.

You can set the properties for a parser by calling the `setProperty()` method for the `SAXParser` object after you have created it. The first argument to the method is the name of the property as type `String`, and the second argument is the value for the property. A property value can be of any class type, as the parameter type is `Object`, but it is usually of type `String`. The `setProperty()` method will throw a `SAXNotRecognizedException` if the property name is not recognized or a `SAXNotSupported Exception` if the property name is recognized but not supported. Both of these exception classes are defined in the `org.xml.sax` package. Alternatively, you can get and set properties using the `XMLReader` object reference that you used to set features. The `XMLReader` interface declares the `getProperty()` and `setProperty()` methods with the same signatures as those for the `SAXParser` object.

You can also retrieve the values for some properties during parsing to obtain additional information about the most recent parsing event. You use the parser's `getProperty()` method in this case. The argument to the method is the name of the property, and the method returns a reference to the property's value.

As with features, there is no defined set of parser properties, so you need to consult the parser documentation for information on these. There are four standard properties for a SAX parser, none of which are required to be supported by a SAX parser. Since these properties involve the more advanced features of SAX parser operation, they are beyond the scope of this book, but if you are interested, they are documented in the description for the `org.xml.sax` package that you'll find in the JDK documentation.

Parsing Documents with SAX

To parse a document using the `SAXParser` object you simply call its `parse()` method. You have to supply two arguments to the `parse()` method. The first identifies the XML document, and the second is a reference of type `DefaultHandler` to a handler object that you will have created to process the contents of the document. The `DefaultHandler` object must contain a specific set of public methods that the `SAXParser` object expects to be able to call for each event, where each type of event corresponds to a particular syntactic element it finds in the document.

The `DefaultHandler` class that is defined in the `org.xml.sax.helpers` package already contains do-nothing definitions of all the callback methods that the `SAXParser` object expects to be able to call. Thus, all you have to do is to define a class that extends the `DefaultHandler` class and then override the methods in the `DefaultHandler` class for the events that you are interested in. But let's not gallop too far ahead. You need to look into the versions of the `parse()` method that you have available before you get into handling parsing events.

The `SAXParser` class defines ten overloaded versions of the `parse()` method, but you'll be interested in only five of them. The other five use a deprecated handler type `HandlerBase` that was applicable to SAX1, so you can ignore those and just look at the versions that relate to SAX2. All versions of the method have a return type of `void`, and the five varieties of the `parse()` method that you'll consider are as follows:

`parse(File aFile,` `        DefaultHandler handler)`	Parses the document in the file specified by `aFile` using `handler` as the object containing the callback methods called by the parser. This will throw an exception of type `IOException` if an I/O error occurs, and of type `IllegalArgumentException` if `aFile` is null.
`parse(String uri,` `        DefaultHandler handler)`	Parses the document specified by `uri` using `handler` as the object defining the callback methods. This will throw an exception of type `SAXException` if `uri` is null, and an exception of type `IOException` if an I/O error occurs.
`parse(InputStream input,` `        DefaultHandler handler)`	Parses `input` as the source of the XML with `handler` as the event handler. This will throw an exception of type `IOException` if an I/O error occurs, and of type `IllegalArgumentException` if `input` is null.

`parse(InputStream input,`
`        DefaultHandler handler,`
`        String systemID)`
	Parses `input` as the previous method, but uses `systemID` to resolve any relative URIs.

`parse(InputSource source,` `        DefaultHandler handler)`	Parses the document specified by `source` using `handler` as the object providing the callback methods to be called by the parser.

The `InputSource` class is defined in the `org.xml.sax` package. It defines an object that wraps a variety of sources for an XML document that you can use to pass a document reference to a parser. You can create an `InputSource` object from a `java.io.InputStream` object, a `java.io.Reader` object encapsulating a character stream, or a `String` specifying a URI — either a public name or a URL. If you specify the document source as a URL, it must be fully qualified.

Implementing a SAX Handler

As I said, the `DefaultHandler` class in the `org.xml.sax.helpers` package provides a default do-nothing implementation of each of the callback methods a SAX parser may call when parsing a

document. These methods are declared in four interfaces that are all implemented by the
DefaultHandler class:

❑ The ContentHandler interface declares methods that will be called to identify the content of a
document to an application. You will usually want to implement all the methods defined in this
interface in your subclass of DefaultHandler.

❑ The EntityResolver interface declares one method, resolveEntity(), that is called by a
parser to pass a public and/or system ID to your application to allow external entities in the
document to be resolved.

❑ The DTDHandler interface declares two methods that will be called to notify your application of
DTD-related events.

❑ The ErrorHandler interface defines three methods that will be called when the parser has
identified an error of some kind in the document.

All four interfaces are defined in the org.xml.sax package. Of course, the parse() method for the
SAXParser object expects you to supply a reference of type DefaultHandler as an argument, so you
have no choice but to extend the DefaultHandler class in which you are defining your handler class.
This accommodates just about anything you want to do since you decide which base class methods you
want to override.

The methods that you must implement to deal with parsing events that relate to document content are
those declared by the ContentHandler interface so let's concentrate on those first. All the methods have
a void return type, and they are as follows:

startDocument()	Called when the start of a document is recognized.
endDocument()	Called when the end of a document is recognized.

startElement(String uri,
      String localName,
      String qName,
      Attributes attr)
	Called when the start of an element is recognized. Up to three names may be provided for the element:
	
	uri is the namespace URI for the element name. This will be an empty string if there is no URI or if namespace processing is not being done.
	
	localName is the unqualified local name for the element. This will be an empty string if namespace processing is not being done. In this case the element name is reported via the qName parameter.
	
	qName is the qualified name for the element. This will be just the name if the parser is not namespace aware. (A colon, if it appears, is then just an ordinary character.)

	The `attr` reference encapsulates the attributes for the element that have explicit values.

`endElement(String uri,`
`         String localName,`
`         String qName)`
	Called when the end of an element is recognized. The references passed to the method are as described for the `startElement()` method.

`characters(char[] ch,`
`           int start,`
`           int length)`
	Called for each segment of character data that is recognized. Note that a contiguous segment of text within an element can be returned as several chunks by the parser via several calls to this method. The characters that are available are from `ch[start]` to `ch[start+length-1]`, and you must not try to access the array outside these limits.

`ignorableWhitespace(char[] ch,`
`                    int start,`
`                    int length)`
	Called for each segment of ignorable whitespace that is recognized within the content of an element. Note that a contiguous segment of ignorable whitespace within an element can be returned as several chunks by the parser via several calls to this method. The whitespace characters are that available are from `ch[start]` to `ch[start+length-1]`, and you must not try to access the array outside these limits.

`startPrefixMapping(String prefix,` `                   String uri)`	Called when the start of a prefix URI namespace mapping is identified. Most of the time you can disregard this method, as a parser will automatically replace prefixes for elements and attribute names by default.
`endPrefixMapping(String prefix)`	Called when the end of a prefix URI namespace mapping is identified. Most of the time you can disregard this method for the reason noted in the preceding method.
`processingInstruction(String target,` `                      String data)`	Called for each processing instruction recognized.
`skippedEntity(String name)`	Called for each entity that the parser skips.
`setDocumentLocator(Locator locator)`	Called by the parser to pass a `Locator` object to your code that you can use to determine the location in the document of any SAX document event. The `Locator` object can provide the public identifier, the system ID, the line number, and the column number in the document for any event. Just implement this method if you want to receive this information for each event.

Your implementations of these methods can throw an exception of type SAXException if an error occurs.

When the startElement() method is called, it receives a reference to an object of type org.xml.sax.Attributes as the last argument. This object encapsulates information about all the attributes for the element. The Attributes interface declares methods you can call for the object to obtain details of each attribute name, its type, and its value. There are methods for obtaining this information about an attribute using either an index value to select a particular attribute, or using an attribute name — either a prefix qualified name or a name qualified by a namespace name. I'll just describe the methods relating to using an index because that's what the code examples will use. Index values start from 0. The methods that the Attributes interface declares for accessing attribute information using an index are as follows:

getLength()	Returns a count of the number of attributes encapsulated in the object
getLocalName(int index)	Returns a reference to a String object containing the local name of the attribute for the index value passed as the argument
getQName(int index)	Returns a reference to a String object containing the XML 1.0 qualified name of the attribute for the index value passed as the argument
getType(int index)	Returns a reference to a String object containing the type of the attribute for the index value passed as the argument. The type is returned as one of the following: "CDATA", "ID", "IDREF", "IDREFS", "NMTOKEN", "NMTOKENS", "ENTITY", "ENTITIES", "NOTATION"
getValue(int index)	Returns a reference to a String object containing the value of the attribute for the index value passed as the argument
getURI(int index)	Returns a reference to a String object containing the attribute's namespace URI, or the empty string if no URI is available

If the index value that you supply to any of the getXXX() methods here is out of range, then the method returns null.

Given a reference, attr, of type Attributes, you can retrieve information about all the attributes with the following code:

```
int attrCount = attr.getLength();
if(attrCount>0) {
  System.out.println("Attributes:");
  for(int i = 0 ; i<attrCount ; i++) {
    System.out.println("  Name : " + attr.getQName(i));
    System.out.println("  Type : " + attr.getType(i));
    System.out.println("  Value: " + attr.getValue(i));
  }
}
```

This is very straightforward. You look for data on attributes only if the value returned by the `getLength()` method is greater than zero. You then retrieve information about each attribute in the `for` loop.

The `DefaultHandler` class is just like the adapter classes you have used for defining GUI event handlers. All you have to do to implement your own handler is extend the `DefaultHandler` class and define your own implementations for the methods you are interested in. The same caveat applies here that applied with adapter classes—you must take care that the signatures of your methods are correct. Otherwise, you are simply adding a new method rather than overriding one of the inherited methods. In this case, your program will then do nothing for the given event since the original do-nothing version of the method will execute, rather than your version. Let's try implementing a handler class.

Try It Out   Handling Parsing Events

Let's first define a handler class to deal with document parsing events. You'll just implement a few of the methods from the `ContentHandler` interface in this—only those that apply to a very simple document—and you won't worry about errors for the moment. Here's the code:

```
import org.xml.sax.helpers.DefaultHandler;
import org.xml.sax.Attributes;

public class MySAXHandler extends DefaultHandler {
  public void startDocument() {
    System.out.println("Start document: ");
  }
  public void endDocument()   {
    System.out.println("End document: ");
  }

  public void startElement(String uri, String localName, String qname,
                                            Attributes attr) {
    System.out.println("Start element: local name: " + localName + " qname: "
                                + qname + " uri: "+uri);

    int attrCount = attr.getLength();
    if(attrCount>0) {
      System.out.println("Attributes:");
      for(int i = 0 ; i<attrCount ; i++) {
        System.out.println("  Name : " + attr.getQName(i));
        System.out.println("  Type : " + attr.getType(i));
        System.out.println("  Value: " + attr.getValue(i));
      }
    }
  }

  public void endElement(String uri, String localName, String qname) {
    System.out.println("End element: local name: " + localName + " qname: "
                                + qname + " uri: "+uri);
  }

  public void characters(char[] ch, int start, int length) {
    System.out.println("Characters: " + new String(ch, start, length));
```

```
    }

    public void ignorableWhitespace(char[] ch, int start, int length) {
      System.out.println("Ignorable whitespace: " + new String(ch, start, length));
    }
  }
```

Each handler method just outputs information about the event to the command line.

Now you can define a program to use a handler of this class type to parse an XML document. You can make the example read the name of the XML file to be processed from the command line. Here's the code:

```
import javax.xml.parsers.SAXParserFactory;
import javax.xml.parsers.SAXParser;
import javax.xml.parsers.ParserConfigurationException;
import org.xml.sax.SAXException;
import java.io.File;
import java.io.IOException;

public class TrySAXHandler {
  public static void main(String args[]) {
    if(args.length == 0) {
      System.out.println("No file to process. Usage is:"
                                        +"\njava TrySax \"filename\" ");
      return;
    }
    File xmlFile = new File(args[0]);
    process(xmlFile);
  }

  private static void process(File file) {
    SAXParserFactory spf = SAXParserFactory.newInstance();
    SAXParser parser = null;
    spf.setNamespaceAware(true);
    spf.setValidating(true);
    System.out.println("Parser will "+(spf.isNamespaceAware()?"":"not ")
                                      + "be namespace aware");
    System.out.println("Parser will "+(spf.isValidating()?"":"not ")
                                      + "validate XML");
    try {
     parser = spf.newSAXParser();
     System.out.println("Parser object is: "+ parser);

    } catch(SAXException e) {
      e.printStackTrace(System.err);
      System.exit(1);

    } catch(ParserConfigurationException e) {
      e.printStackTrace(System.err);
      System.exit(1);
    }

    System.out.println("\nStarting parsing of "+file+"\n");
```

```
        MySAXHandler handler = new MySAXHandler();
        try {
            parser.parse(file, handler);
        } catch(IOException e) {
          e.printStackTrace(System.err);

        } catch(SAXException e) {
          e.printStackTrace(System.err);
        }
      }
    }
```

I created the `circle.xml` file with the following content:

```
<?xml version="1.0"?>
<circle radius="20" angle="0">
  <color R="255" G="0" B="0"/>
  <position x="10" y="15"/>
</circle>
```

I saved this in my `C:\Beg Java Stuff` directory, but you can put it wherever you want and adjust the command-line argument accordingly. If you put it in the same directory as the source file, you can just use the file name as the command-line argument. The command to execute `TrySAXHandler` with this file in the `C:/Beg Java Stuff` directory is:

```
java TrySAXHandler "C:/Beg Java Stuff/circle.xml"
```

On my computer the program produced the following output:

```
Parser will be namespace aware
Parser will validate XML
Parser object is: com.sun.org.apache.xerces.internal.jaxp.SAXParserImpl@1d8957f

Starting parsing of circle.xml

Start document:
Start element: local name: circle qname: circle uri:
Attributes:
  Name : radius
  Type : CDATA
  Value: 20
  Name : angle
  Type : CDATA
  Value: 0
Characters:

Start element: local name: color qname: color uri:
Attributes:
  Name : R
  Type : CDATA
  Value: 255
  Name : G
  Type : CDATA
```

```
      Value: 0
      Name : B
      Type : CDATA
      Value: 0
End element: local name: color qname: color uri:
Characters:

Start element: local name: position qname: position uri:
Attributes:
      Name : x
      Type : CDATA
      Value: 10
      Name : y
      Type : CDATA
      Value: 15
End element: local name: position qname: position uri:
Characters:

End element: local name: circle qname: circle uri:
End document:
```

How It Works

Much of the code in the `TrySAXHandler` class is the same as in the previous example. The `main()` method first checks for a command-line argument. If there isn't one, you output a message and end the program. You might want to add some code following the command-line argument check to make sure the file does exist. You saw how to do this way back in the chapters on file I/O.

Next you call the static `process()` method with a reference to the `File` object for the XML document as the argument. This method creates the `XMLParser` object in the way you've seen previously and then creates a handler object of type `MySAXHandler` for use by the parser. The parsing process is started by calling the `parse()` method for the parser object, `parser`, with the `file` reference as the first argument and the `handler` reference as the second argument. This identifies the object whose methods will be called for parsing events.

You have overridden six of the do-nothing methods that are inherited from `DefaultHandler` in the `MySAXHandler` class and the output indicates which ones are called. Your method implementations just output a message along with the information that is passed as arguments. You can see from the output that there is no URI for a namespace in the document so the value for qname is identical to `localname`.

Note how you form a `String` object in the `characters()` method from the specified sequence of elements in the ch array. You must access only the `length` elements from this array that start with the element ch(start).

The output also shows that the `characters()` method is sometimes called with just whitespace passed to the method in the ch array. This whitespace is ignorable whitespace that appears between the elements, but the parser is not recognizing it as such. This is because there is no DTD to define how elements are to be constructed in this document so the parser has no way to know what can be ignored.

You can see that the output shows string values for both a `local name` and a qname. This is because you have the namespace awareness feature switched on. If you comment out the statement that calls setNamespaceAware() and recompile and re-execute the example, you'll see that only a qname is reported. Both the local name and URI outputs will be empty.

You get all the information about the attributes, too, so the processing of attributes works without a DTD or a schema.

Processing a Document with a DTD

You can run the example again with the Address.xml file that you saved earlier in the C:/Beg Java Stuff directory to see how using a DTD affects processing. This should have the following contents:

```
<?xml version="1.0"?>
<!DOCTYPE address SYSTEM "AddressDoc.dtd">
<address>
   <buildingnumber> 29 </buildingnumber>
   <street> South Lasalle Street</street>
   <city>Chicago</city>
   <state>Illinois</state>
   <zip>60603</zip>
</address>
```

The AddressDoc.dtd file in the same directory as Address.xml should contain:

```
<!ELEMENT address (buildingnumber, street, city, state, zip)>
    <!ELEMENT buildingnumber (#PCDATA)>
    <!ELEMENT street (#PCDATA)>
    <!ELEMENT city (#PCDATA)>
    <!ELEMENT state (#PCDATA)>
    <!ELEMENT zip (#PCDATA)>
```

If the path to the file contains spaces, you'll need to specify the path between double quotes in the command-line argument. I got the following output:

```
Parser will be namespace aware
Parser will validate XML
Parser object is: com.sun.org.apache.xerces.internal.jaxp.SAXParserImpl@1d8957f

Starting parsing of Address.xml

Start document:
Start element: local name: address qname: address uri:
Ignorable whitespace:

Start element: local name: buildingnumber qname: buildingnumber uri:
Characters:   29
End element: local name: buildingnumber qname: buildingnumber uri:
Ignorable whitespace:

Start element: local name: street qname: street uri:
Characters:   South Lasalle Street
End element: local name: street qname: street uri:
Ignorable whitespace:
```

```
Start element: local name: city qname: city uri:
Characters: Chicago
End element: local name: city qname: city uri:
Ignorable whitespace:

Start element: local name: state qname: state uri:
Characters: Illinois
End element: local name: state qname: state uri:
Ignorable whitespace:

Start element: local name: zip qname: zip uri:
Characters: 60603
End element: local name: zip qname: zip uri:
Ignorable whitespace:

End element: local name: address qname: address uri:
End document:
```

You can see that with a DTD, the ignorable whitespace is recognized as such, and is passed to your `ignorableWhitespace()` method. A validating parser must call this method to report whitespace in element content. Although the parser is validating the XML, you still can't be sure that the document is valid based on the output you are getting. If any errors are found, the default do-nothing error-handling methods that are inherited from the `DefaultHandler` class will be called so there's no indication of when errors are found. You can fix this quite easily by modifying the `MySAXHandler` class, but let's first look at processing some other XML document flavors.

Processing a Document with Namespaces

You can convert the `Address.xml` file to use a namespace by modifying the root element like this:

```
<address xmlns="http://www.wrox.com/AddressNamespace">
```

With this change to the XML file, the URI for the default namespace is `http://www.wrox.com/AddressNamespace`. This doesn't really exist, but it doesn't need to. It's just a unique qualifier for the names within the namespace.

You'll also need to use a different DTD that takes account of the use of a namespace, so you must modify the `DOCTYPE` declaration in the document:

```
<!DOCTYPE address SYSTEM "AddressNamespaceDoc.dtd">
```

You can now save the revised XML document with the name `AddressNamespace.xml`.

You must also create the new DTD. This is the same as the previous one with the addition of a declaration for the `xmlns` attribute for the `<address>` element:

```
<!ATTLIST address xmlns CDATA #IMPLIED>
```

If you run the previous example with this version of the XML document, you should see the URI in the output. Since the namespace is the default, there is no prefix name, so the values for the `localname` and `qname` parameters to the `startElement()` and `endElement()` methods are the same.

Using Qualified Names

You can change the document to make explicit use of the namespace prefix like this:

```
<?xml version="1.0"?>
<!DOCTYPE addresses:address SYSTEM "AddressNamespaceDoc.dtd">
<addresses:address  xmlns:addresses=" http://www.wrox.com/AddressNamespace">
  <addresses:buildingnumber> 29 </addresses:buildingnumber>
  <addresses:street> South Lasalle Street</addresses:street>
  <addresses:city>Chicago</addresses:city>
  <addresses:state>Illinois</addresses:state>
  <addresses:zip>60603</addresses:zip>
</addresses:address>
```

Unfortunately, you also have to update the DTD. Otherwise, if the qualified names are not declared in the DTD, they will be regarded as errors. You need to change the DTD to the following:

```
<!ELEMENT addresses:address (addresses:buildingnumber, addresses:street,
                             addresses:city, addresses:state, addresses:zip)>
<!ATTLIST addresses:address xmlns:addresses CDATA #IMPLIED>
<!ELEMENT addresses:buildingnumber (#PCDATA)>
<!ELEMENT addresses:street (#PCDATA)>
<!ELEMENT addresses:city (#PCDATA)>
<!ELEMENT addresses:state (#PCDATA)>
<!ELEMENT addresses:zip (#PCDATA)>
```

The namespace prefix is `addresses`, and each element name is qualified by the namespace prefix. You can usefully add implementations for two further callback methods in the `MySAXHandler` class:

```
public void startPrefixMapping(String prefix, String uri) {
   System.out.println("Start \"" + prefix + "\" namespace scope. URI: " + uri);
}
```

```
public void endPrefixMapping(String prefix) {
   System.out.println("End \"" + prefix + "\" namespace scope.");
}
```

The parser won't call these methods by default. You have to switch the `http://xml.org/sax/features/namespace-prefixes` feature on to get this to happen. You can add a call to the `setFeature()` method for the parser factory object to do this in the `process()` method that you defined in the `TrySAXHandler` class, immediately before you create the parser object in the `try` block:

```
spf.setFeature("http://xml.org/sax/features/namespace-prefixes",true);
parser = spf.newSAXParser();
```

You place the statement here rather than after the call to the `setValidating()` method because the `setFeature()` method can throw an exception of type `ParserConfigurationException` and it needs to be in a `try` block. Now the parser will call the `startPrefixMapping()` method at the beginning of each namespace scope, and the `endPrefixMapping()` method at the end. If you parse this document, you will see that each of the `qname` values is the local name qualified by the namespace prefix. You should also see that the start and end of the namespace scope are recorded in the output.

Handling Other Parsing Events

I have considered only events arising from the recognition of document content, those declared in the
`ContentHandler` interface. In fact, the `DefaultHandler` class defines do-nothing methods declared in
the other three interfaces that you saw earlier. For example, when a parsing error occurs, the parser calls
a method to report the error. Three methods for error reporting are declared in the `ErrorHandler` interface and are implemented by the `DefaultHandler` class:

`warning(SAXParseException spe)`	Called to notify you of conditions that are not errors or fatal errors. The exception object, `spe`, that is passed to the method contains information to enable you to locate the error in the original document.
`error(SAXParseException spe)`	Called to notify you that an error has been identi-fied. An error is anything in a document that vio-lates the XML specification but is recoverable and allows the parser to continue processing the document normally.
`fatalError(SAXParseException spe)`	A fatal error is a non-recoverable error. After a fatal error the parser will not continue normal processing of the document.

Each of these methods is declared to throw an exception of type `SAXException`, but you don't have to
implement them so that they do this. With the `warning()` and `error()` methods you'll probably want
to output an error message and return to the parser so it can continue processing. Of course, if your
`fatalError()` method is called, processing of the document will not continue anyway, so it would be
appropriate to throw an exception in this case.

Obviously your implementation of any of these methods will want to make use of the information from
the `SAXParseException` object that is passed to the method. This object has four methods that you can
call to obtain additional information that will help you locate the error:

`getLineNumber()`	Returns the line number of the end of the docu-ment text where the error occurred as type `int`. If this information is not available, –1 is returned.
`getColumnNumber()`	Returns the line number within the document that contains the end of the text where the error occurred as type `int`. If this information is not available, –1 is returned. The first column in a line is column 1.
`getPublicID()`	Returns the public identifier of the entity where the error occurred as type `String`, or `null` if no public identifier is available.
`getSystemID()`	Returns the system identifier of the entity where the error occurred as type `String`, or `null` if no system identifier is available.

A simple implementation of the `warning()` method could be like this:

```
public void warning(SAXParseException spe) {
    System.out.println("Warning at line "+spe.getLineNumber());
    System.out.println(spe.getMessage());
}
```

This outputs a message indicating the document line number where the error occurred. It also outputs the string returned by the `getMessage()` method inherited from the base class, `SAXException`. This will usually indicate the nature of the error that was detected.

You could implement the `error()` callback method similarly, but you might want to implement `fatalError()` so that it throws an exception. For example:

```
public void fatalError(SAXParseException spe) throws SAXException {
    System.out.println("Fatal error at line "+spe.getLineNumber());
    System.out.println(spe.getMessage());
    throw spe;
}
```

Here you just rethrow the `SAXParseException` after outputting an error message indicating the line number that caused the error. The `SAXParseException` class is a subclass of `SAXException` so you can rethrow `spe` as the superclass type. Don't forget the `import` statements in the `MySAXHandler` source file for the `SAXException` and `SAXParseException` class names from the `org.xml.sax` package.

You could try these out with the previous example by adding these methods to the `MySAXHandler` class. You could introduce a few errors into the XML file to get these methods called. Try deleting the `DOCTYPE` declaration or deleting the forward slash on an element end tag or even just deleting one character in an element name.

Parsing a Schema Instance Document

You can create a simple instance of a document the uses the `Sketcher.xsd` schema that you developed earlier. Here's the definition of the document contents:

```
<?xml version="1.0" encoding="UTF-8"?>
<sketch xmlns:xsi="http://www.w3.org/2001/XMLSchema-instance"
        xsi:noNamespaceSchemaLocation="file:/C:/Beg%20Java%20Stuff/Sketcher.xsd">
    <circle radius="15" angle="0">
        <color R="255" G="0" B="0"/>
        <position x="10" y="10"/>
    </circle>
    <line angle="0">
        <color R="0" G="0" B="255"/>
        <position x="10" y="10"/>
        <endpoint x="30" y="40"/>
    </line>
    <rectangle angle="0">
        <color R="255" G="0" B="0"/>
        <position x="30" y="40"/>
        <bottomright x="50" y="70"/>
    </rectangle>
</sketch>
```

This defines a sketch that consists of three elements: a circle, a line, and a rectangle. The location of the schema is specified by the value for the noNamespaceSchemaLocation attribute, which here corresponds to the Sketcher.xsd file in the C:/Beg Java Stuff directory.

An XML document may have the applicable schema identified by the value for the noNamespaceSchemaLocation attribute, or the schema may not be identified explicitly in the document. You have the means for dealing with both of these situations in Java.

A javax.xml.validation.Schema object encapsulates a schema. You create a Schema object by calling methods for a javax.xml.validation.SchemaFactory object that you generate by calling the static newInstance() method for the SchemaFactory class. It works like this:

```
SchemaFactory sf = SchemaFactory.newInstance("http://www.w3.org/2001/XMLSchema");
```

A SchemaFactory object compiles a schema from an external source in a given Schema Definition Language into a Schema object that can subsequently be used by a parser. The argument to the static newInstance() method in the SchemaFactory class identifies the schema language that the schema factory will be able to process. The only possibility for this argument apart from that used in the example to specify the XML Schema language is "http://relaxng.org/ns/structure/1.0", which is another schema language for XML. At the time of writing, Schema objects encapsulating DTDs are not supported.

The javax.xml.XMLConstants class defines String constants for basic values required when you are processing XML. The class defines a constant with the name W3C_XML_NS_URI that corresponds to the URI for the Schema Definition Language, so you could use this as the argument to the newInstance() method in the SchemaFactory class, like this:

```
SchemaFactory sf = SchemaFactory.newInstance(W3C_XML_NS_URI);
```

This statement assumes you have statically imported the names from the XMLConstants class.

Once you have identified the Schema Definition Language that will be used, you can create a Schema object from a schema definition. Here's an example of how you might do this:

```
File schemaFile = new File("C:/Beg Java Stuff/sketcher.xsd");
try {
   Schema schema = sf.newSchema(schemaFile);
}catch(SAXException e) {
 e.printStyackTrace(System.err);
   System.exit(1);
}
```

The newSchema() method for the SchemaFactory object creates and returns a Schema object from the file specified by the File object you pass as the argument. There are versions of the newSchema() method with parameters of type java.net.URL and java.xml.transform.Source. An object that implements the Source interface represents an XML source. There's also a version of newSchema() that accepts an argument that is an array of Source object references and generates a Schema object from the input from all of the array elements.

Now that you have a `Schema` object, you can pass it to the `SAXParserFactory` object before you create your `SAXParser` object to process XML documents:

```
SAXParserFactory spf = SAXParserFactory.newInstance();
spf.setSchema(schema);
```

The parser you create by calling the `newSAXParser()` method for the `SAXParserFactory` object will validate documents using the schema you have specified. XML documents will be validated in this instance, even when the `isValidating()` method returns `false`, so it's not essential that you configure the parser to validate documents.

In many situations the document itself will identify the schema to be used. In this case you call the `newSchema()` method for the `SchemaFactory` object with no argument specified:

```
try {
   Schema schema = sf.newSchema();
}catch(SAXException e) {
  e.printStyackTrace(System.err);
   System.exit(1);
}
```

A special `Schema` object is created by the `newSchema()` method that assumes the schema for the document is identified by hints within the document. Note that you still need to call `newSchema()` within a `try` block here because the method will throw an exception of type `SAXException` if the operation fails for some reason. If the operation is not supported, an exception of type `UnsupportedOperationException` will be thrown, but because this is a subclass of `RuntimeException`, you are not obliged to catch it.

Try It Out   Parsing a Schema Instance Document

Here's a variation on the `TrySAXHandler` class that will parse a schema instance document:

```
import javax.xml.parsers.SAXParserFactory;
import javax.xml.parsers.SAXParser;
import javax.xml.parsers.ParserConfigurationException;
import javax.xml.validation.SchemaFactory;
import org.xml.sax.SAXException;
import java.io.File;
import java.io.IOException;

import static javax.xml.XMLConstants.*;

public class TryParsingSchemaInstance {
   public static void main(String args[]) {
      if(args.length == 0) {
        System.out.println("No file to process. Usage is:"
                +"\n   java TrySax \"xmlFilename\" "
                +"\nor:\n   java TrySaxHandler \"xmlFilename\" \"schemaFileName\" ");
        return;
      }
      File xmlFile = new File(args[0]);
      File schemaFile = args.length>1 ? new File(args[1]) : null;
```

```
      process(xmlFile, schemaFile);
  }

  private static void process(File file, File schemaFile) {
    SAXParserFactory spf = SAXParserFactory.newInstance();
    SAXParser parser = null;
    spf.setNamespaceAware(true);
    try {
      SchemaFactory sf =
                    SchemaFactory.newInstance(W3C_XML_SCHEMA_NS_URI);
      spf.setSchema(schemaFile == null ? sf.newSchema() : sf.newSchema(schemaFile));
      parser = spf.newSAXParser();
    } catch(SAXException e) {
      e.printStackTrace(System.err);
      System.exit(1);
    } catch(ParserConfigurationException e) {
      e.printStackTrace(System.err);
      System.exit(1);
    }

    System.out.println("\nStarting parsing of "+file+"\n");
    MySAXHandler handler = new MySAXHandler();
    try {
      parser.parse(file, handler);
    }  catch(IOException e) {
      e.printStackTrace(System.err);
    }
    catch(SAXException e) {
      e.printStackTrace(System.err);
    }
  }
}
```

You need to copy the MySAXHandler.java source file from the previous example to the folder you are using for this example. You have the option of supplying an additional command-line argument when you run the program. The first argument is the name of the XML file to be parsed, as in the TrySAXHandler example; the second argument is the path to the schema that is to be used to parse the file. When the second argument is present, the program will process the XML file using the specified schema. If the second argument is absent, the XML file will be processed using the schema specified by hints in the document.

I processed the sketch.xml file that I defined in the previous section with the following command:

```
java -ea TryParsingSchemaInstance sketch.xml
```

This resulted in the following output:

```
Starting parsing of sketch.xml

Start document:
Start element: local name: sketch qname: sketch uri:
Attributes:
  Name : xsi:noNamespaceSchemaLocation
```

```
  Type : CDATA
  Value: file:/C:/Beg%20Java%20Stuff/Sketcher.xsd
Ignorable whitespace: 5 Characters.
Start element: local name: circle qname: circle uri:
Attributes:
  Name : radius
  Type : CDATA
  Value: 15
  Name : angle
  Type : CDATA
  Value: 0
Ignorable whitespace: 9 Characters.
```

followed by a lot more output that ends . . .

```
Start element: local name: rectangle qname: rectangle uri:
Attributes:
  Name : angle
  Type : CDATA
  Value: 0
Ignorable whitespace: 9 Characters.
Start element: local name: color qname: color uri:
Attributes:
  Name : R
  Type : CDATA
  Value: 255
  Name : G
  Type : CDATA
  Value: 0
  Name : B
  Type : CDATA
  Value: 0
End element: local name: color qname: color uri:
Ignorable whitespace: 9 Characters.
Start element: local name: position qname: position uri:
Attributes:
  Name : x
  Type : CDATA
  Value: 30
  Name : y
  Type : CDATA
  Value: 40
End element: local name: position qname: position uri:
Ignorable whitespace: 9 Characters.
Start element: local name: bottomright qname: bottomright uri:
Attributes:
  Name : x
  Type : CDATA
  Value: 50
  Name : y
  Type : CDATA
  Value: 70
End element: local name: bottomright qname: bottomright uri:
Ignorable whitespace: 5 Characters.
```

```
End element: local name: rectangle qname: rectangle uri:
Ignorable whitespace: 1 Characters.
End element: local name: sketch qname: sketch uri:
End document:
```

Of course, you can also try the example specifying the schema location by the second argument on the command line.

How It Works

The only significant difference from what you had in the previous example is the creation of the `Schema` object to identify the schema to be used. When you supply a second command-line argument, a `File` object encapsulating the schema file path is created and a reference to this is passed as the second argument to the `process()` method. The `process()` method uses the second argument that you pass to it to determine how to create the `Schema` object that is passed to the `setSchema()` method for the `SAXParserFactory` object:

```
SchemaFactory sf = SchemaFactory.newInstance(W3C_XML_SCHEMA_NS_URI);
spf.setSchema(schemaFile == null ? sf.newSchema() : sf.newSchema(schemaFile));
```

The argument to the `newInstance()` method is the constant from the `XMLConstants` class that defines the URI for the Schema Definition Language. There's a static `import` statement for the static names in this class, so we don't need to qualify the name of the constant. The `Schema` object is created either by passing the non-null `File` reference `schemaFile` to the `newSchema()` method or by calling the `newSchema()` method with no argument. In both cases the `Schema` object that is created is passed to the `setSchema()` method for the parser factory object. The parser that is subsequently created by the `SAXParserFactory` object will use the schema encapsulated by the `Schema` object to validate documents. In this way the program is able to process documents for which the schema is specified by hints in the document as well as documents for which the schema is specified independently through the second command-line argument.

Summary

In this chapter I have discussed the fundamental characteristics of XML and how Java supports the analysis and synthesis of XML documents. The key points I've covered include the following:

❑ XML is a language for describing data that is to be communicated from one computer to another. Data is described in the form of text that contains the data plus markup that defines the structure of the data.

❑ XML is also a meta-language because you can use XML to create new languages for defining and structuring data.

❑ Markup consists of XML elements that may also include attributes, where an attribute is a name-value pair.

❑ The structure and meaning of a particular type of document can be defined within a Document Type Definition (DTD).

❏   A DTD can be defined in an external file or it can be part of a document.

❏   A DTD is identified by a DOCTYPE declaration in a document.

❏   The Schema Definition language provides a more flexible alternative to DTDs.

❏   An XML namespace defines a set of names qualified by a prefix that corresponds to a URI.

❏   The SAX API defines a simple event-driven mechanism for analyzing XML documents.

❏   A SAX parser is a program that parses an XML document and identifies each element in a document by calling a particular method in your program. The methods that are called are those defined by the SAX API.

Exercises

You can download the source code for the examples in the book and the solutions to the following exercises from http://www.wrox.com.

1.   Write a program using SAX that will count the number of occurrences of each element type in an XML document and display them. The document file to be processed should be identified by the first command-line argument.

2.   Modify the program resulting from the previous exercise so that it will accept optional additional command-line arguments that are the names of elements. When there are two or more command-line arguments, the program should count and report only on the elements identified by the second and subsequent command-line arguments.

Creating and Modifying XML Documents

In this chapter you'll be exploring what you can do with the Document Object Model (DOM) application program interface (API). As I outlined in the previous chapter, DOM uses a mechanism that is completely different to Simple API for XML (SAX). As well as providing an alternative mechanism for parsing XML documents, DOM also adds the capability for you to modify them and create new ones.

In this chapter you'll learn:

- ❏ What a Document Object Model is
- ❏ How you create a DOM parser
- ❏ How you access the contents of a document using DOM
- ❏ How you create and update a new XML document
- ❏ How to modify Sketcher to read and write sketches as XML documents

The Document Object Model (DOM)

As you saw in the previous chapter, a DOM parser presents you with an object encapsulating the entire XML structure. You can then call methods belonging to this object to navigate through the document tree and process the elements and attributes in the document in whatever way you want. This is quite different to SAX as I've already noted, but nonetheless there is quite a close relationship between DOM and SAX.

The mechanism for getting access to a DOM parser is very similar to what you used to obtain a SAX parser. You start with a factory object that you obtain like this:

```
DocumentBuilderFactory builderFactory = DocumentBuilderFactory.newInstance();
```

The `newInstance()` method is a `static` method in the `javax.xml.parsers.DocumentBuilderFactory` class for creating factory objects. As with SAX, this approach of dynamically creating a factory object that you then use to create a parser allows you to change the parser you are using without modifying or recompiling your code. You use the factory object to create a `javax.xml.parsers.DocumentBuilder` object that encapsulates a DOM parser:

```
DocumentBuilder builder = null;
try {
  builder = builderFactory.newDocumentBuilder();
} catch(ParserConfigurationException e) {
  e.printStackTrace();
}
```

As you'll see, when a DOM parser reads an XML document, it makes it available in its entirety as an object of type `Document`. The name of the class that encapsulates a DOM parser has obviously been chosen to indicate that it can also build new `Document` objects. A DOM parser can throw exceptions of type `SAXException`, and parsing errors in DOM are handled in essentially the same way as in SAX2. The `DocumentBuilderFactory`, `DocumentBuilder`, and `ParserConfigurationException` classes are all defined in the `javax.xml.parsers` package. Let's jump straight in and try this out for real.

Try It Out   Creating an XML Document Builder

Here's the code to create a document builder object:

```
import javax.xml.parsers.DocumentBuilderFactory;
import javax.xml.parsers.DocumentBuilder;
import javax.xml.parsers.ParserConfigurationException;
import org.xml.sax.SAXException;

public class TryDOM {
  public static void main(String args[]) {
    DocumentBuilderFactory builderFactory = DocumentBuilderFactory.newInstance();
    DocumentBuilder builder = null;
    try {
      builder = builderFactory.newDocumentBuilder();
    }
    catch(ParserConfigurationException e) {
      e.printStackTrace();
      System.exit(1);
    }
    System.out.println("Builder Factory = " + builderFactory +"\nBuilder = "
                                            + builder);
  }
}
```

I got the following output:

```
Builder Factory =
com.sun.org.apache.xerces.internal.jaxp.DocumentBuilderFactoryImpl@18a47e0
Builder = com.sun.org.apache.xerces.internal.jaxp.DocumentBuilderImpl@174cc1f
```

How It Works

The static `newInstance()` method in the `DocumentBuilderFactory` class returns a reference to a factory object. You call the `newDocumentBuilder()` method for the factory object to obtain a reference to a `DocumentBuilder` object that encapsulates a DOM parser. This will be the default parser. If you want the parser to validate the XML or provide other capabilities, you can set the parser features before you create the `DocumentBuilder` object by calling methods for the `DocumentBuilderFactory` object.

You can see that you get a version of the Xerces parser as a DOM parser. Many DOM parsers are built on top of SAX parsers, and this is the case with the Xerces parser.

Setting DOM Parser Features

The idea of a feature for a DOM parser is the same as with SAX — a parser option that can be either on or off. The `DocumentBuilderFactory` object has the following methods for setting DOM parser features:

`setNamespaceAware(boolean aware)`	Calling this method with a `true` argument sets the parser to be namespace aware. The default setting is `false`.
`setValidating(boolean validating)`	Calling this method with a `true` argument sets the parser to validate the XML in a document as it is parsed. The default setting is `false`.
`setIgnoringElementContentWhitespace(boolean ignore)`	Calling this method with a `true` argument sets the parser to remove ignorable whitespace in element content so the `Document` object produced by a parser will not contain ignorable whitespace. The default setting is `false`.
`setIgnoringComments(boolean ignore)`	Calling this method with a `true` argument sets the parser to remove comments as the document is parsed. The default setting is `false`.
`setExpandEntityReferences(boolean expand)`	Calling this method with a `true` argument sets the parser to expand entity references. The default setting is `true`.
`setCoalescing(boolean coalesce)`	Calling this method with a `true` argument sets the parser to convert CDATA sections to text and append it to any adjacent text. The default setting is `false`.

There is a possibility that XML documents being processed by a parser could be a security risk. There is a `setSecureProcessing()` method defined for `DocumentBuilderFactory` objects that you use to enable secure processing of documents by the parser. You pass an object of type `javax.xml.SecureProcessing` to the method that sets limits on processing actions such as the maximum entity expansion that can occur, and the maximum number of occurrences for an element in `Schema` declarations. You can also inhibit the execution of arbitrary functions in transformations.

As you see from the previous table, by default the parser that is produced is neither namespace aware nor validating. You should at least set these two features before creating the parser. This is quite simple:

```
DocumentBuilderFactory builderFactory = DocumentBuilderFactory.newInstance();
builderFactory.setNamespaceAware(true);
builderFactory.setValidating(true);
```

If you add the shaded statements to the example, the newDocumentBuilder() method for the factory object should now return a validating and namespace aware parser. With a validating parser, you should define an ErrorHandler object that will deal with parsing errors. You identify the ErrorHandler object to the parser by calling the setErrorHandler() method for the DocumentBuilder object:

```
builder.setErrorHandler(handler);
```

Here handler refers to an object that implements the three methods declared in the org.xml.sax.ErrorHandler interface. I discussed these in the previous chapter in the context of SAX parser error handling, and the same applies here. If you do create a validating parser, you should always implement and register an ErrorHandler object. Otherwise, the parser may not work properly.

The factory object has methods corresponding to each of the setXXX() methods in the preceding table to check the status of parser features. The checking methods all have corresponding names of the form isXXX(), so to check whether a parser will be namespace aware, you call the isNamespaceAware() method. Each method returns true if the parser to be created will have the feature set, and false otherwise.

You can identify a schema to be used by a DOM parser when validating documents. You pass a reference to a Schema object as an argument to the setSchema() method for the DocumentBuilderFactory object. The parser that you create will then use the specified schema when validating a document.

Parsing a Document

Once you have created a DocumentBuilder object, you just call its parse() method with a document source as an argument to parse a document. The parse() method will return a reference of type Document to an object that encapsulates the entire XML document. The Document interface is defined in the org.w3c.dom package.

There are five overloaded versions of the parse() method that provide various options for you to identify the source of the XML document. They all return a reference to a Document object:

parse(File file)	Parses the document in the file identified by file.
parse(String uri)	Parses the document at the URI uri.
parse(InputSource source)	Parses the document from source.
parse(InputStream stream)	Parses the document read from the input stream stream.
parse(InputStream stream, String systemID)	Parses the document read from the input stream stream. The second argument, systemID, is used to resolve relative URIs.

All five versions of the `parse()` method can throw three types of exception. An exception of type `IllegalArgumentException` will be thrown if you pass `null` to the method for the parameter that identifies the document source. The method will throw an exception of type `IOException` if any I/O error occurs, and of type `SAXException` in the event of a parsing error. Both these last exceptions must be caught. Note that it is a `SAXException` that can be thrown here. Exceptions of type `DOMException` arise only when you are navigating the element tree for a `Document` object.

You could `parse()` a document using the `DocumentBuilder` object `builder` like this:

```
File xmlFile = new File("D:/Beg Java Stuff/circlewithDTD.xml");
Document xmlDoc = null;
  try {
    xmlDoc = builder.parse(xmlFile);
  }
    catch(SAXException e) {
    e.printStackTrace();
    System.exit(1);
  }
    catch(IOException e) {
    e.printStackTrace();
    System.exit(1);
  }
```

This code fragment requires `imports` for the `File` and `IOException` classes in the `java.io` package as well as the `org.w3c.dom.Document` class name. Once this code executes, you can call methods for the `xmlDoc` object to navigate through the elements in the document tree structure. Let's look at what the possibilities are.

Navigating a Document Object Tree

The `Node` interface that is defined in the `org.w3c.dom` package is fundamental to all objects that encapsulate components of an XML document, and this includes the `Document` object itself. It represents a type that encapsulates a node in the document tree. `Node` is also a super-interface of a number of other interfaces that declare methods relating to access document components of various kinds. The sub-interfaces of `Node` that identify components of a document are:

`Element`	Represents an XML element.
`Attr`	Represents an attribute for an element.
`Text`	Represents text that is part of element content. This interface is a sub-interface of `CharacterData`, which in turn is a sub-interface of `Node`. References of type `Text` will therefore have methods from all three interfaces.
`CDATASection`	Represents a CDATA section — unparsed character data.
`Comment`	Represents a document comment. This interface also extends the `CharacterData` interface.
`DocumentType`	Represents the type of a document.

Table continued on following page

`Document`	Represents the entire XML document.
`DocumentFragment`	Represents a lightweight document object that is used to encapsulate a sub-tree of a document.
`Entity`	Represents an entity that may be parsed or unparsed.
`EntityReference`	Represents a reference to an entity.
`Notation`	Represents a notation declared in the DTD for a document. A notation is a definition of an unparsed entity type.
`ProcessingInstruction`	Represents a processing instruction for an application.

Each of these interfaces declares its own set of methods and inherits the method declared in the `Node` interface. Every XML document will be modeled as a hierarchy of nodes that are accessible as one or other of the interface types in the table above. At the top of the node hierarchy for a document will be the `Document` node that is returned by the `parse()` method. Each type of node may or may not have child nodes in the document hierarchy, and those that do can have only certain types of child nodes. The types of nodes in a document that can have children are as follows:

Node Type	Possible Children
`Document`	`Element` (only 1), `DocumentType` (only 1), `Comment`, `ProcessingInstruction`
`Element`	`Element`, `Text`, `Comment`, `CDATASection`, `EntityReference`, `ProcessingInstruction`
`Attr`	`Text`, `EntityReference`
`Entity`	`Element`, `Text`, `Comment`, `CDATASection`, `EntityReference`, `ProcessingInstruction`
`EntityReference`	`Element`, `Text`, `Comment`, `CDATASection`, `EntityReference`, `ProcessingInstruction`

Of course, what each node may have as children follows from the XML specification, not just the DOM specification. There is one other type of node that extends the `Node` interface — `DocumentFragment`. This is not formally part of a document in the sense that a node of this type is a programming convenience. It is used to house a fragment of a document — a sub-tree of elements — for use when moving fragments of a document around, for example, so it provides a similar function to a `Document` node but with less overhead. A `DocumentFragment` node can have the same range of child nodes as an `Element` node.

The starting point for exploring the entire document tree is the root element for the document. You can obtain a reference to an object that encapsulates the root element by calling the `getDocumentElement()` method for the `Document` object:

```
Element root = xmlDoc.getDocumentElement();
```

This method returns the root element for the document as type `Element`. You can also get the node corresponding to the `DOCTYPE` declaration as type `DocumentType` like this:

```
DocumentType doctype = xmlDoc.getDoctype();
```

If there is no DOCTYPE declaration or the parser cannot find the DTD for the document, the getDocType() method will return null. If the value returned is not null, you can obtain the contents of the DTD as a string by calling the getDocumentElement() method for the DocumentType object:

```
System.out.println("Document type:\n" + doctype.getInternalSubset());
```

This statement will output the contents of the DTD for the document.

Once you have an object encapsulating the root element for a document, the next step is to obtain its child nodes. You can use the getChildNodes() method that is defined in the Node interface for this. This method returns a NodeList reference that encapsulates all the child elements for that element. You can call this method for any node that has children, including the Document node if you wish. You can therefore obtain the child elements for the root element with the following statement:

```
NodeList children = root.getChildNodes();
```

A NodeList reference encapsulates an ordered collection of Node references, each of which may be one or other of the possible node types for the current node. So with an Element node, any of the Node references in the list that is returned can be of type Element, Text, Comment, CDATASection, EntityReference, or ProcessingInstruction. Note that if there are no child nodes, the getChildNodes() method will return a NodeList reference that is empty, not null. You call the getChildNodes() method to obtain a list of child nodes for any node type that can have them.

The NodeList interface declares just two methods:

getLength()	Returns the number of nodes in the list as type int
item(int index)	Returns a reference of type Node to the object at position index in the list

You can use these methods to iterate through the child elements of the root element, perhaps like this:

```
Node[] nodes = new Node[children.getLength()];
for(int i = 0 ; i<nodes.getLength() ; i++) {
  nodes[i] = children.item(i);
}
```

You allocate sufficient elements in the nodes array to accommodate the number of child nodes and then populate the array in the for loop.

Node Types

Of course, you will normally be interested in the specific types of nodes that are returned so you will want to extract them as specific types or at least determine what they are before processing them. This is not difficult. One possibility is to test the type of any node using the instanceof operator. Here's one way you could extract just the child nodes that are of type Element:

```
java.util.Vector<Element> elements = new java.util.Vector<Element>();
Node node = null;
for(int i = 0 ; i<nodes.getLength() ; i++) {
  node = children.item(i);
  if(node instanceof Element) {
    elements.add(node);
  }
}
```

Another possibility is provided by the getNodeType() method that is declared in the Node interface. This method returns a value of type short that will be one of the following constants defined in the Node interface:

DOCUMENT_NODE	DOCUMENT_TYPE_NODE
DOCUMENT_POSITION_FOLLOWING	DOCUMENT_POSITION_PRECEDING
DOCUMENT_POSITION_IMPLEMENTATION_SPECIFIC	DOCUMENT_FRAGMENT_NODE
DOCUMENT_POSITION_CONTAINED_BY	DOCUMENT_POSITION_CONTAINS
PROCESSING_INSTRUCTION_NODE	DOCUMENT_POSITION_DISCONNECTED
COMMENT_NODE	CDATA_SECTION_NODE
NOTATION_NODE	TEXT_NODE
ENTITY_NODE	ENTITY_REFERENCE_NODE
ELEMENT_NODE	ATTRIBUTE_NODE

The advantage of using the getNodeType() method is that you can test for the node type using a switch statement with the constants in the preceding table as case values. This makes it easy to farm out processing for nodes of various types to separate methods.

A simple loop like the one in the previous code fragment is not a very practical approach to navigating a document. In general, you will have no idea of the level to which elements are nested in a document, and this loop examines only one level. You need an approach that will allow any level of nesting. This is a job for recursion. Let's put together a working example to illustrate how you can do this.

Try It Out   Listing a Document

You can extend the previous example to list the nodes in a document. You'll add a static method to the TryDOM class to list child elements recursively. You'll also add a helper method that will identify what each node is. The program will output details of each node followed by its children. Here's the code:

```
import javax.xml.parsers.DocumentBuilderFactory;
import javax.xml.parsers.DocumentBuilder;
```

```
import javax.xml.parsers.ParserConfigurationException;
import org.xml.sax.SAXException;
import org.xml.sax.SAXParseException;
import org.xml.sax.ErrorHandler;
import org.w3c.dom.Node;
import org.w3c.dom.Document;
import org.w3c.dom.DocumentType;
import org.w3c.dom.NodeList;
import java.io.File;
import java.io.IOException;
import static org.w3c.dom.Node.*;                   // For node type constants

public class TryDOM implements ErrorHandler {
  public static void main(String args[]) {
    if(args.length == 0) {
      System.out.println("No file to process."+
                         "Usage is:\njava TryDOM \"filename\"");

      System.exit(1);
    }
    File xmlFile = new File(args[0]);
    DocumentBuilderFactory builderFactory = DocumentBuilderFactory.newInstance();
    builderFactory.setNamespaceAware(true);         // Set namespace aware
    builderFactory.setValidating(true);             // and validating parser feaures

    DocumentBuilder builder = null;
    try {
      builder = builderFactory.newDocumentBuilder();  // Create the parser
      builder.setErrorHandler(new TryDOM()); //Error handler is instance of TryDOM
    } catch(ParserConfigurationException e) {
      e.printStackTrace();
      System.exit(1);
    }
    Document xmlDoc = null;

    try {
      xmlDoc = builder.parse(xmlFile);

    } catch(SAXException e) {
      e.printStackTrace();

    } catch(IOException e) {
      e.printStackTrace();
    }
    DocumentType doctype = xmlDoc.getDoctype();      // Get the DOCTYPE node
    if(doctype == null) {                            // If it's not null...
      System.out.println("DOCTYPE is null");
    } else {                                         // ...output it
      System.out.println("DOCTYPE node:\n" + doctype.getInternalSubset());
    }

    System.out.println("\nDocument body contents are:");
    listNodes(xmlDoc.getDocumentElement(),"");       // Root element & children
  }
```

```
// output a node and all its child nodes
static void listNodes(Node node, String indent) {
  // List the current node
  String nodeName = node.getNodeName();
  System.out.println(indent+" Node: " + nodeName);
  System.out.println(indent+" Node Type: " + nodeType(node.getNodeType()));
  NodeList list = node.getChildNodes();          // Get the list of child nodes
  if(list.getLength() > 0) {                      // As long as there are some...
    System.out.println(indent+" Child Nodes of "+nodeName+" are:");
    for(int i = 0 ; i<list.getLength() ; i++) {//...list them & their children...
      listNodes(list.item(i),indent+"  ");     // by calling listNodes() for each
    }
  }
}

// Method to identify the node type
static String nodeType(short type) {
  switch(type) {
    case ELEMENT_NODE:                   return "Element";
    case DOCUMENT_TYPE_NODE:             return "Document type";
    case ENTITY_NODE:                    return "Entity";
    case ENTITY_REFERENCE_NODE:          return "Entity reference";
    case NOTATION_NODE:                  return "Notation";
    case TEXT_NODE:                      return "Text";
    case COMMENT_NODE:                   return "Comment";
    case CDATA_SECTION_NODE:             return "CDATA Section";
    case ATTRIBUTE_NODE:                 return "Attribute";
    case PROCESSING_INSTRUCTION_NODE:    return "Attribute";
  }
  return "Unidentified";
}

public void fatalError(SAXParseException spe) throws SAXException {
  System.out.println("Fatal error at line "+spe.getLineNumber());
  System.out.println(spe.getMessage());
  throw spe;
}

public void warning(SAXParseException spe) {
  System.out.println("Warning at line "+spe.getLineNumber());
  System.out.println(spe.getMessage());
}

public void error(SAXParseException spe) {
  System.out.println("Error at line "+spe.getLineNumber());
  System.out.println(spe.getMessage());
}
}
```

I have removed the statement that outputs details of the parser to reduce the output a little. Run this with a document file `AddressWithDTD.xml` that has the following contents:

```
<?xml version="1.0"?>
<!DOCTYPE address
[
```

```
    <!ELEMENT address (buildingnumber, street, city, state, zip)>
    <!ATTLIST address xmlns CDATA #IMPLIED>
    <!ELEMENT buildingnumber (#PCDATA)>
    <!ELEMENT street (#PCDATA)>
    <!ELEMENT city (#PCDATA)>
    <!ELEMENT state (#PCDATA)>
    <!ELEMENT zip (#PCDATA)>
]>

<address>
  <buildingnumber> 29 </buildingnumber>
  <street> South Lasalle Street</street>
  <city>Chicago</city>
  <state>Illinois</state>
  <zip>60603</zip>
</address>
```

This is the `Address.xml` document from the previous chapter with the DTD now included in the document. If you store this file in the same directory as the source file, you can just put the file name as the command-line argument, like this:

```
java TryDOM AddressWithDTD.xml
```

The program produces quite a lot of output starting with:

```
DOCTYPE node:
<!ELEMENT address (buildingnumber,street,city,state,zip)>
<!ATTLIST address xmlns CDATA #IMPLIED>
<!ELEMENT buildingnumber (#PCDATA)>
<!ELEMENT street (#PCDATA)>
<!ELEMENT city (#PCDATA)>
<!ELEMENT state (#PCDATA)>
<!ELEMENT zip (#PCDATA)>


Document body contents are:
Node: address
 Node Type: Element
 Child Nodes of address are:
   Node: #text
   Node Type: Text
   Node: buildingnumber
   Node Type: Element
   Child Nodes of buildingnumber are:
     Node: #text
     Node Type: Text
```

and so on down to the last few lines:

```
   Node: zip
   Node Type: Element
   Child Nodes of zip are:
     Node: #text
     Node Type: Text
   Node: #text
   Node Type: Text
```

How It Works

Since you have set the parser configuration in the factory object to include validating the XML, you have to provide an `org.xml.sax.ErrorHandler` object for the parser. The `TryDOM` class implements the `warning()`, `error()`, and `fatalError()` methods declared by the `ErrorHandler` interface, so an instance of this class takes care of it.

You call the `getDoctype()` method for the `Document` object to obtain the node corresponding to the DOCTYPE declaration:

```
DocumentType doctype = xmlDoc.getDoctype();          // Get the DOCTYPE node
if(doctype == null) {                                // If it's not null...
  System.out.println("DOCTYPE is null");
} else {                                             // ...output it
  System.out.println("DOCTYPE node:\n" + doctype.getInternalSubset());
}
```

You can see from the output that you get the complete text of the DTD from the document.

After outputting a header line showing where the document body starts, you output the contents, starting with the root element. The `listNodes()` method does all the work. You pass a reference to the root element that you obtain from the `Document` object with the following statement:

```
listNodes(xmlDoc.getDocumentElement(),"");          // Root element & children
```

The first argument to `listNodes()` is the node to be listed, and the second argument is the current indent for output. On each recursive call of the method, you append a couple of spaces. This results in each nested level of nodes being indented in the output by two spaces relative to the parent node output.

The first step in the `listNodes()` method is to get the name of the current node by calling its `getNodeName()` method:

```
String nodeName = node.getNodeName();       // Get name of this node
```

The next statement outputs the node itself:

```
System.out.println(indent+" " + nodeName);
```

You then output the type of the current node with the following statement:

```
System.out.println(indent+" Node Type: " + nodeType(node.getNodeType()));
```

The `indent` parameter defines the indentation for the current node. Calling `getNodeType()` for the node object returns a value of type `short` that identifies the node type. You then pass this value to the `nodeType()` helper method that you've added to the `TryDOM` class. The code for the helper method is just a `switch` statement with the constants from the `Node` interface that identify the types of nodes as case values. I just included a representative set in the code, but you can add case labels for all 18 constants if you wish.

The remainder of the `listNodes()` code iterates through the child nodes of the current node if it has any:

```
NodeList list = node.getChildNodes();              // Get the list of child nodes
if(list.getLength() > 0) {                          // As long as there are some...
   System.out.println(indent+"Child Nodes of "+nodeName+" are:");
      for(int i = 0 ; i<list.getLength() ; i++) {   //...list them & their children...
         listNodes(list.item(i),indent+"  ");       // by calling listNodes() for each
      }
```

The `for` loop simply iterates through the list of child nodes obtained by calling the `getChildNodes()` method. Each child is passed as an argument to the `listNodes()` method, which will list the node and iterate through its children. In this way the method will work through all the nodes in the document. You can see that you append an extra couple of spaces to `indent` in the second argument to the `listNodes()` call for a child node. The `indent` parameter in the next level down will reference a string that is two spaces longer. This ensures that the output for the next level of nodes will be indented relative to the current node.

Ignorable Whitespace and Element Content

Some of the elements have multiple `#text` elements recorded in the output. The `#text` elements arise from two things: text that represents element content and ignorable whitespace that is there to present the markup in a readable fashion. If you don't want to see the ignorable whitespace, you can get rid of it quite easily. You just need to set another parser feature in the factory object:

```
builderFactory.setNamespaceAware(true);          // Set namespace aware
builderFactory.setValidating(true);              // and validating parser features
builderFactory.setIgnoringElementContentWhitespace(true);
```

Calling this method will result in a parser that will not report ignorable whitespace as a node, so you won't see it in the `Document` object. If you run the example again with this change, the `#text` nodes arising from ignorable whitespace will no longer be there.

That still leaves some other `#text` elements that represent element content, and you really do want to access that and display it. In this case you can use the `getWholeText()` method for a node of type `Text` to obtain all of the content as a single string. You could modify the code in the `listNodes()` method in the example to do this:

```
static void listNodes(Node node, String indent) {
   // List the current node
   String nodeName = node.getNodeName();
   System.out.println(indent+" Node: "+nodeName);
   short type =node.getNodeType();
   System.out.println(indent+" Node Type: " + nodeType(type));
   if(type == TEXT_NODE){
     System.out.println(indent+" Content is: "+((Text)node).getWholeText());
   }

   // Now list the child nodes
   NodeList list = node.getChildNodes();        // Get the list of child nodes
   if(list.getLength() > 0) {                    // As long as there are some...
     System.out.println(indent+" Child Nodes of "+nodeName+" are:");
      for(int i = 0 ; i<list.getLength() ; i++) {//...list them & their children...
        listNodes(list.item(i),indent+"  ");     // by calling listNodes() for each
```

```
                }
            }
        }
```

Here you store the integer identifying the node type in a variable, type, that you test subsequently to see if it is a text node. If it is, you get the contents by calling the getWholeText() method for the node. You have to cast the node reference from type Node to type Text; otherwise, you would not be able to call the getWholeText() method because it is declared in the Text interface, which is a sub-interface of Node. If you run the example again with this further addition, you'll get the contents of the nodes displayed, too. You'll need to add an import statement for the org.w3c.dom.Text interface name.

Even though you have set the parser feature to ignore ignorable whitespace, you could still get #text elements that contained just whitespace. The Text interface declares the isElementContentWhitespace() method that you can use to check for this — when you don't want to display an empty line, for example.

Accessing Attributes

You'll usually want to access the attributes for an element, but only if it has some. You can test whether an element has attributes by calling its hasAttributes() method. This will return true if the element has attributes and false otherwise, so you might use it like this:

```
short type =node.getNodeType();
if(type == ELEMENT_NODE && node.hasAttributes()) {
    // Process the element with its attributes

} else {
    // Process the element without attributes
}
```

The getAttributes() method for an element returns a NamedNodeMap reference that contains the attributes, the NamedNodeMap interface being defined in the org.w3c.dom package. In general, a NamedNodeMap object is a collection of Node references that can be accessed by name, or serially by iterating through the collection. Since the nodes are attributes in this instance, the nodes will actually be of type Attr. In fact, you can call the getAttributes() method for any node type, and it will return null if an element has no attributes. Thus, you could omit the test for the element type in the if condition, and the code will work just as well.

The NamedNodeMap interface declares the following methods for retrieving nodes from the collection:

item(int index)	Returns the Node reference at index position index
getLength()	Returns the number of Node references in the collection as type int
getNamedItem(String name)	Returns the Node reference with the node name name
getNamedItemNS(String uri, String localName)	Returns the Node reference with the name localName in the namespace at uri

Obviously the last two methods apply when you know what attributes to expect. You can apply the first two methods to iterate through the collection of attributes in a NamedNodeMap:

```
if(node.hasAttributes()) {
   NamedNodeMap attrs = node.getAttributes();
   for(int i = 0 ; i<attrs.getLength() ; i++) {
     Attr attribute = (Attr)attrs.item(i);
     // Process the attribute...
   }
}
```

You now are in a position to obtain each of the attributes for an element as a reference of type Attr. To get at the attribute name and value you call the getName() and getValue() methods declared in the Attr interface, respectively, both of which return a value of type String. You can put that into practice in another example.

Try It Out   Listing Elements with Attributes

You can modify the listNodes() method in the previous example to include attributes with the elements. Here's the revised version:

```
static void listNodes(Node node) {
    System.out.println(indent+" Node: "+nodeName);
    short type =node.getNodeType();
    System.out.println(indent+" Node Type: " + nodeType(type));
    if(type == TEXT_NODE){
      System.out.println(indent+" Content is: "+((Text)node).getWholeText());
    } else if(node.hasAttributes()) {
      System.out.println(indent+" Element Attributes are:");
      NamedNodeMap attrs = node.getAttributes();        //...get the attributes
      for(int i = 0 ; i<attrs.getLength() ; i++) {
        Attr attribute = (Attr)attrs.item(i);           // Get an attribute
        System.out.println(indent+ " " + attribute.getName()
                                     + " = "+attribute.getValue());
      }
    }

    NodeList list = node.getChildNodes();        // Get the list of child nodes
    if(list.getLength() > 0) {                    // As long as there are some...
      System.out.println(indent+"Child Nodes of "+nodeName+" are:");
      for(int i = 0 ; i<list.getLength() ; i++){ //...list them & their children
        listNodes(list.item(i),indent+" ");      // by calling listNodes()
    }
  }
}
```

Don't forget to update the import statements in the example. The complete set will now be:

```
import javax.xml.parsers.DocumentBuilderFactory;
import javax.xml.parsers.DocumentBuilder;
import javax.xml.parsers.ParserConfigurationException;
import org.xml.sax.SAXException;
import org.xml.sax.SAXParseException;
import org.xml.sax.ErrorHandler;
```

```
import org.w3c.dom.Node;
import org.w3c.dom.Text;
import org.w3c.dom.Document;
import org.w3c.dom.DocumentType;
import org.w3c.dom.NodeList;
import org.w3c.dom.Attr;
import org.w3c.dom.NamedNodeMap;
import java.io.File;
import java.io.IOException;
import static org.w3c.dom.Node.*;
```

You can recompile the code with these changes and run the example with the `circlewithDTD.xml` file that you created back when I was discussing DTDs. The content of this file is:

```
<?xml version="1.0"?>
<!DOCTYPE circle
[
    <!ELEMENT circle (position)>
    <!ATTLIST circle
                radius CDATA #REQUIRED
    >

    <!ELEMENT position EMPTY>
    <!ATTLIST position
                x CDATA #REQUIRED
                y CDATA #REQUIRED
    >
]>

<circle radius="15">
  <position x="30" y="50"/>
</circle>
```

The output from the example processing this file should be:

```
DOCTYPE node:
<!ELEMENT circle (position)>
<!ATTLIST circle radius CDATA #REQUIRED>
<!ELEMENT position EMPTY>
<!ATTLIST position x CDATA #REQUIRED>
<!ATTLIST position y CDATA #REQUIRED>


Document body contents are:
 Node: circle
 Node Type: Element
 Element Attributes are:
 radius = 15
 Child Nodes of circle are:
   Node: position
```

```
Node Type: Element
Element Attributes are:
x = 30
y = 50
```

How It Works

All the new code to handle attributes is in the `listNodes()` method. After verifying that the current node does have attributes, you get the collection of attributes as a `NamedNodeMap` object. You then iterate through the collection extracting each node in turn. Nodes are indexed from zero, and you obtain the number of nodes in the collection by calling its `getLength()` method. Since an attribute node is returned by the `item()` method as type `Node`, you have to cast the return value to type `Attr` to call the methods in this interface. You output the attribute and its value, making use of the `getName()` and `getValue()` methods for the `Attr` object in the process of assembling the output string.

It isn't used in the example, but the `Attr` interface also declares a `getSpecified()` method that returns `true` if the attribute value was explicitly set in the document rather than being a default value from the DTD. The `Attr` interface also declares a `getOwnerElement()` method that returns an `Element` reference to the element to which this attribute applies.

I'll bet analyzing XML documents was a whole lot easier than you expected. You'll now put DOM into reverse and look into how you can synthesize XML documents.

Creating XML Documents

You can create an XML document in a file programmatically by a two-step process. You can first create a `Document` object that encapsulates what you want in your XML document. Then you can use the `Document` object to create the hierarchy of elements that has to be written to the file. You'll first look at how you create a suitable `Document` object.

The simplest way to create a `Document` object programmatically is to call the `newDocument()` method for a `DocumentBuilder` object, and it will return a reference to a new empty `Document` object:

```
Document newDoc = builder.newDocument();
```

This is rather limited, especially since there's no way to modify the `DocumentType` node to reflect a suitable `DOCTYPE` declaration because the `DocumentType` interface does not declare any.

There's an alternative approach that provides a bit more flexibility, but it is not quite so direct. You first call the `getDOMImplementation()` method for the `DocumentBuilder` object:

```
DOMImplementation domImpl = builder.getDOMImplementation();
```

This returns a reference of type `DOMImplementation` to an object that encapsulates the underlying DOM implementation. This interface type is defined in the `org.w3c.dom` package.

There are three methods you can call for a `DOMImplementation` object:

`createDocument(String namespaceURI,`
`            String qualifiedName,`
`            DocumentType doctype)`
	Creates a `Document` object with the root element having the name `qualifiedName` that is defined in the namespace specified by `namespaceURI`. The third argument specifies the `DOCTYPE` node to be added to the document. If you don't want to declare a `DOCTYPE`, then `doctype` can be specified as `null`.
	
	This method will throw an exception of type `DOMException` if the second argument is incorrect in some way.

`createDocumentType(String qualifiedName,`
`                String publicID,`
`                String systemID)`
	Creates a node of type `DocumentType` that represents a `DOCTYPE` declaration. The first argument is the qualified name of the root element, the second argument is the public ID of the external subset of the DTD, and the third argument is its system ID. This method will also throw an exception of type `DOMException` if the first argument contains an illegal character or is not of the correct form.

`hasFeature(String feature,` `          String version)`	Returns `true` if the DOM implementation has the feature with the name `feature`. The second argument specifies the DOM version number of the feature and can be either `"1.0"` or `"2.0"` with DOM Level 2.

You can see from the first two methods here that there is a big advantage to using a `DOMImplementation` object to create a document. First of all, you can create a `DocumentType` object by calling the `createDocumentType()` method:

```
DocumentType doctype = null;
try {
   doctype = domImpl.createDocumentType("sketch", null, "sketcher.dtd");

} catch(DOMException e) {
   // Handle the exception
}
```

This code fragment creates a `DocumentType` node for an external `DOCTYPE` declaration with the name sketch, and with the system ID `sketcher.dtd`. There is no public ID in this case since you specified the second argument as `null`. You can now use the `DocumentType` object in the creation of a document:

```
Document newDoc = null;
try {
   doctype = domImpl.createDocumentType("sketch", null, "sketcher.dtd");
   newDoc = domImpl.createDocument(null, "sketch", doctype);
}
catch(DOMException e) {
   // Handle the exception
}
```

If you were creating a document without a DTD, you would just specify the third argument to the `createDocument()` method as null.

The `DOMException` object that may be thrown by either the `createDocumentType()` or the `createDocument()` method has a public field of type `int` that has the name `code`. This field stores an error code identifying the type of error that caused the exception, so you can check the value of `code` to determine the cause of the error. This exception can be thrown by a number of different methods that you use to create nodes in a document, so the values that `code` can have are not limited to the two methods you have just used. There are 17 possible values for `code` that are defined in the `DOMException` class, but obviously you would check only for those that apply to the code in the `try` block where the exception may arise.

The possible values for `code` in a `DOMException` object are:

`INVALID_CHARACTER_ERR`	The second argument specifying the root element name contains an invalid character.
`DOMSTRING_SIZE_ERR`	The specified range of text does not fit into a `DOMString` value. A `DOMString` value is defined in the DOM Level 3 specification and is equivalent to a Java `String` type.
`HIERARCHY_REQUEST_ERR`	You tried to insert a node where it doesn't belong.
`WRONG_DOCUMENT_ERR`	You tried to use a node in a different document from the one that created it.
`NO_DATA_ALLOWED_ERR`	You specified data for a node that does not support data.

1241

NO_MODIFICATION_ALLOWED_ERR	You attempted to modify an object where modifications are prohibited.
NOT_FOUND_ERR	You tried to reference a node that does not exist.
NOT_SUPPORTED_ERR	The object type or operation that you requested is not supported.
INUSE_ATTRIBUTE_ERR	You tried to add an attribute that is in use elsewhere.
INVALID_STATE_ERR	You tried to use an object that is not usable.
SYNTAX_ERR	You specified an invalid or illegal string.
INVALID_MODIFICATION_ERR	You tried to modify the type of the underlying object.
NAMESPACE_ERR	You tried to create or modify an object such that it would be inconsistent with namespaces in the document.
INVALID_ACCESS_ERR	A parameter or operation is not supported by the underlying object.
VALIDATION_ERR	An operation to remove or insert a node relative to an existing node would make the node invalid.
TYPE_MISMATCH_ERR	The type of an object is not compatible with the expected type of the parameter associated with the object.
WRONG_DOCUMENT_ERR	The document does not support the DocumentType node specified.

The createDocument() method can throw an exception of type DOMException with code set to INVALID_CHARACTER_ERR, NAMESPACE_ERR, NOT_SUPPORTED_ERR, or WRONG_DOCUMENT_ERR. The createDocumentType() method can also throw an exception of type DOMException with code set to any of the first three values for createDocument().

You therefore might code the catch block in the previous fragment like this:

```
catch(DOMException e) {
  switch(e.code) {
    case DOMException.INVALID_CHARACTER_ERR:
      System.err.println("Qualified name contains an invalid character.");
      break;
    case DOMException.NAMESPACE_ERR:
      System.err.println("Qualified name is malformed or invalid.");
      break;
    case DOMException.WRONG_DOCUMENT_ERR:
      System.err.println("Document does not support this doctype");
      break;
    case DOMException.NOT_SUPPORTED_ERR:
      System.err.println("Implementation does not support XML.");
      break;
  }
  System.err.println(e.getMessage());
}
```

Of course, you can also output the stack trace, return from the method, or even end the program here if you want.

Adding to a Document

The `org.w3c.Document` interface declares methods for adding nodes to a `Document` object. You can create nodes encapsulating elements, attributes, text, entity references, comments, CDATA sections, and processing instructions, so you can assemble a `Document` object representing a complete XML document. The methods declared by the `Document` interface are:

`createElement(String name)`	Returns a reference to an `Element` object encapsulating an element with `name` as the tag name. The method will throw an exception of type `DOMException` with `INVALID_CHARACTER_ERR` set if `name` contains an invalid character.
`createElementNS(String nsURI,` `              String qualifiedName)`	Returns a reference to an `Element` object encapsulating an element with `qualifiedName` as the tag name in the namespace `nsURI`. The method will throw an exception of type `DOMException` with `INVALID_CHARACTER_ERR` set if `qualifiedName` contains an invalid character, or `NAMESPACE_ERR` if it has a prefix `"xml"` and `nsURI` is not `http://www.w3.org/XML/1998/namespace`.
`createAttribute(String name)`	Returns a reference to an `Attr` object encapsulating an attribute with `name` as the attribute name and its value as `""`. The method will throw an exception of type `DOMException` with `INVALID_CHARACTER_ERR` set if `name` contains an invalid character.

Table continued on following page

1243

`createAttribute(String nsURI,` `            String qualifiedName)`	Returns a reference to an `Attr` object encapsulating an attribute with `qualifiedName` as the attribute name in the namespace `nsURI` and its value as `""`. The method will throw an exception of type `DOMException` with `INVALID_CHARACTER_ERR` set if the name contains an invalid character, or `NAMESPACE_ERR` if the name conflicts with the namespace.
`createTextNode(String text)`	Returns a reference to a `Text` node containing the string `text`.
`createComment(String comment)`	Returns a reference to a `Comment` node containing the string `comment`.
`createCDATASection(String data)`	Returns a reference to a `CDATASection` node with the value `data`. Throws a `DOMException` if you try to create this node if the `Document` object encapsulates an HTML document.
`createEntityReference(String name)`	Returns a reference to an `EntityReference` node with the name specified. Throws a `DOMException` with the code `INVALID_CHARACTER_ERR` if `name` contains invalid characters, and `NOT_SUPPORTED_ERR` if the `Document` object is an HTML document.

`createProcessingInstruction(String target,` `                            String name)`	Returns a reference to a `ProcessingInstruction` node with the specified name and target. Throws a `DOMException` with the code `INVALID_CHARACTER_ERR` if `target` contains illegal characters, and `NOT_SUPPORTED_ERR` if the `Document` object is an HTML document.
`createDocumentFragment()`	Creates an empty `DocumentFragment` object. You can insert a `DocumentFragment` object into a `Document` object using methods that the `Document` interface (and the `DocumentFragment` interface) inherits from the `Node` interface. You can use the same methods to insert nodes into a `DocumentFragment` object.

The references to HTML in the preceding table arise because a `Document` object can be used to encapsulate an HTML document. Our interest is purely XML, so I won't be discussing this aspect further.

Of course, having a collection of nodes within a document does not define any structure. To establish the structure of a document you have to associate each attribute node that you have created with the appropriate element, and you must also make sure that each element other than the root is a child of some element. Along with all the other types of node, the `Element` interface inherits two methods from the `Node` interface that enable you to make one node a child of another:

`appendChild(Node child)`	Appends the node `child` to the end of the list of existing child nodes. This method throws a `DOMException` with the code `HIERARCHY_REQUEST_ERR` if the current node does not allow children, the code `WRONG_DOCUMENT_ERR` if `child` belongs to another document, or the code `NO_MODIFICATION_ALLOWED_ERR` if the current node is read-only.
`insertBefore(Node child,` `            Node existing)`	Insert `child` as a child node immediately before `existing` in the current list of child nodes. This method can throw `DOMException` with the same error codes as above, plus `NOT_FOUND_ERR` if `existing` is not a child of the current node.

The `Element` interface also declares four methods for adding attributes:

`setAttributeNode(Attr attr)`	Adds the node `attr` to the element. If an attribute node with the same name already exists, it will be replaced by `attr`. The method returns either a reference to an existing `Attr` node that has been replaced or `null`. The method can throw a `DOMException` with the following codes: `WRONG_DOCUMENT_ERR` if `attr` belongs to another document `NO_MODIFICATION_ALLOWED_ERR` if the element is read-only `INUSE_ATTRIBUTE_ERR` if `attr` already belongs to another element
`setAttributeNodeNS(Attr attr)`	As previous but applies to an element defined within a namespace.

`setAttribute(String name,` `            String value)`	Adds a new attribute node with the specified name and value. If the attribute has already been added, its value is changed to `value`. The method can throw DOMException with the following codes: INVALID_CHARACTER_ERR if name contains an illegal character NO_MODIFICATION_ALLOWED_ERR if the element is read-only

`setAttributeNS(String nsURI,`
`               String qualifiedName,`
`               String value)`
	As previous but with the attribute within the namespace nsURI. In addition, this method can throw a DOMException with the code NAMESPACE_ERR if qualifiedName is invalid or not within the namespace.

Since you know enough about constructing a `Document` object to have a stab at putting together an object encapsulating a real XML document, let's have a stab at it.

Storing a Sketch as XML

You have already defined a DTD in the previous chapter that is suitable for defining a sketch. You can see how you can put together the code to store a sketch as an XML document instead of as a serialized object. Obviously you'll use the DTD you already have, and you can create a `Document` object with a `DocumentType` node via a `DOMImplementation` object from a `DocumentBuilder` object. You can do this with two statements in a `try` block:

```
Document doc = null;
try {
  DOMImplementation domImpl = DocumentBuilderFactory.newInstance()
                                      .newDocumentBuilder()
                                      .getDOMImplementation();

  doc = domImpl.createDocument(null, "sketch",
                  domImpl.createDocumentType("sketch", null, "sketcher.dtd"));

} catch(ParserConfigurationException e) {
  e.printStackTrace(System.err);
  // Display the error and terminate the current activity...

} catch(DOMException e) {
  e.printStackTrace(System.err);
  // Determine the kind of error from the error code,
  // display the error, and terminate the current activity...
}
```

They are rather long statements since they accomplish in a single statement what you previously did in several steps. However, they are quite simple. The first statement creates a `DocumentBuilderFactory` object from which a `DocumentBuilder` object is created from which a reference `DOMImplementation` object is obtained and stored in domImpl. This is used in the next statement to create the Document object for a sketch and its DocumentType object defining the DOCTYPE declaration for sketcher.dtd. Eventually you will add this code to the SketchModel class, but let's leave that to one side for the moment while you look at how you can fill out the detail of the Document object from the objects representing elements in a sketch.

A sketch in XML is a simple two-level structure. The root node in an XML representation of a sketch will be a <sketch> element, so to define the structure you need only to add an Element node to the content for the root node for each element in the sketch. A good way to implement this would be to add a method to each of the sketch Element classes that adds its own org.w3c.dom.Element node to the Document object. This will make each object representing a sketch element able to create its own XML representation.

The Sketcher classes you have to modify are the inner classes to the Element class, plus the Element class itself. The inner classes are Element.Line, Element.Rectangle, Element.Circle, Element.Curve, and Element.Text. The nodes that have to be added for each kind of geometric element derive directly from the declaration in the DTD, so it will help if you have this in hand while you go through these classes. If you typed it in when I discussed it in the last chapter, maybe you can print a copy.

Adding Element Nodes

Polymorphism is going to be a big help in this, so let's first define an abstract method in the Element base class to add an element node to a document. You can add the declaration immediately after the declaration for the abstract draw() method, like this:

```
public abstract void draw(Graphics2D g2D);
public abstract void addElementNode(Document document);
```

Each of the inner classes will need to implement this method since they are derived from the Element class.

You will need a couple of import statements at the beginning of the Element.java file in Sketcher:

```
import org.w3c.dom.Document;
import org.w3c.dom.Attr;
```

Note that you definitely *don't* want to use the * notation to import all of the names from this package. If you do, you will get the Sketcher Element class confused with the Element interface in the org.w3c.dom package. You are going to have to use qualified names wherever there is a potential clash.

The XML elements that you'll create for geometric elements in a sketch will all need <position> and <color> elements as children. If you define methods in the base class Element to create these, they will be inherited in each of the subclasses of Element. Here's how you can define a method in the Element class to create a <color> element:

```
protected org.w3c.dom.Element createColorElement(Document doc) {
  org.w3c.dom.Element colorElement = doc.createElement("color");

  Attr attr = doc.createAttribute("R");
  attr.setValue(String.valueOf(color.getRed()));
```

```
        colorElement.setAttributeNode(attr);

        attr = doc.createAttribute("G");
        attr.setValue(String.valueOf(color.getGreen()));
        colorElement.setAttributeNode(attr);

        attr = doc.createAttribute("B");
        attr.setValue(String.valueOf(color.getBlue()));
        colorElement.setAttributeNode(attr);
        return colorElement;
    }
```

The method for creating the node for a `<position>` element will use essentially the same process, but you have several nodes that represent points that are the same apart from their names. You can share the code by putting it into a method that you call with the appropriate type name:

```
    protected org.w3c.dom.Element createPointTypeElement(Document doc,
                                                 String name,
                                                 String xValue,
                                                 String yValue) {
        org.w3c.dom.Element element = doc.createElement(name);

        Attr attr = doc.createAttribute("x");        // Create attribute x
        attr.setValue(xValue);                       // and set its value
        element.setAttributeNode(attr);              // Insert the x attribute

        attr = doc.createAttribute("y");             // Create attribute y
        attr.setValue(yValue);                       // and set its value
        element.setAttributeNode(attr);              // Insert the y attribute
        return element;
    }
```

This will create an element with the name specified by the second argument, so you can use this in another method in the `Element` class to create a node for a `<position>` element:

```
    protected org.w3c.dom.Element createPositionElement(Document doc) {
        return createPointTypeElement(doc, "position",
                                  String.valueOf(position.getX()),
                                  String.valueOf(position.getY()));
    }
```

You'll be able to create `<endpoint>`, `<bottomright>`, or `<point>` nodes in the same way in methods in the subclasses of `Element`.

Adding a Line Node

The method to add a `<line>` node to the `Document` object will create a `<line>` element with an `angle` attribute and then add three child elements: `<color>`, `<position>`, and `<endpoint>`. You can add the following implementation of the `addElementNode()` method to the `Element.Line` class:

```
    public void addElementNode(Document doc) {
        org.w3c.dom.Element lineElement = doc.createElement("line");

        // Create the angle attribute and attach it to the <line> node
```

```
         Attr attr = doc.createAttribute("angle");
         attr.setValue(String.valueOf(angle));
         lineElement.setAttributeNode(attr);

         // Append the <color>, <position>, and <endpoint> nodes as children
         lineElement.appendChild(createColorElement(doc));
         lineElement.appendChild(createPositionElement(doc));
         lineElement.appendChild(createEndpointElement(doc));

         // Append the <line> node to the document root node
         doc.getDocumentElement().appendChild(lineElement);
      }
```

When you have a <Line> element in a sketch, calling this method with a reference to a Document object as an argument will add a child node corresponding to the <line> element. To complete this you must add the createEndpointElement() method to the Element.Line class:

```
      private org.w3c.dom.Element createEndpointElement(Document doc) {
         return createPointTypeElement(doc, "endpoint",
                              String.valueOf(line.x2+position.x),
                              String.valueOf(line.y2+position.y));
      }
```

This calls the createPointTypeElement() method that is inherited from the base class. Since the position of a line is recorded in the base class and the end point of the line is relative to that point, you must add the coordinates of position in the base class to the coordinates of the end point of the line in order to get the original end point coordinates back.

Adding a Rectangle Node

The code to add a <rectangle> node to the Document object is almost the same as adding a <line> node:

```
      public void addElementNode(Document doc) {
         org.w3c.dom.Element rectElement = doc.createElement("rectangle");

         // Create the angle attribute and attach it to the <rectangle> node
         Attr attr = doc.createAttribute("angle");
         attr.setValue(String.valueOf(angle));
         rectElement.setAttributeNode(attr);

         // Append the <color>, <position>, and <bottomright> nodes as children
         rectElement.appendChild(createColorElement(doc));
         rectElement.appendChild(createPositionElement(doc));
         rectElement.appendChild(createBottomrightElement(doc));

         doc.getDocumentElement().appendChild(rectElement);
      }
```

You also must define the `createBottomrightElement()` method in the `Element.Rectangle` class:

```
private org.w3c.dom.Element createBottomrightElement(Document doc) {
  return createPointTypeElement(doc, "bottomright",
                          String.valueOf(rectangle.width+position.x),
                          String.valueOf(rectangle.height+position.y));
}
```

A rectangle is defined relative to the origin, so you have to adjust the coordinates of the bottom right corner by adding the corresponding `position` coordinates.

Adding a Circle Node

Creating the node for a `<circle>` element is not very different:

```
public void addElementNode(Document doc) {
  org.w3c.dom.Element circleElement = doc.createElement("circle");

  // Create the radius attribute and attach it to the <circle> node
  Attr attr = doc.createAttribute("radius");
  attr.setValue(String.valueOf(circle.width/2.0));
  circleElement.setAttributeNode(attr);

  // Create the angle attribute and attach it to the <circle> node
  attr = doc.createAttribute("angle");
  attr.setValue(String.valueOf(angle));
  circleElement.setAttributeNode(attr);

  // Append the <color> and <position> nodes as children
  circleElement.appendChild(createColorElement(doc));
  circleElement.appendChild(createPositionElement(doc));

  doc.getDocumentElement().appendChild(circleElement);
}
```

There's nothing new here. You can use either the `width` or the `height` member of the `Ellipse2D.Double` class object to get the diameter of the circle. You divide the `width` field for the `circle` object by `2.0` to get the radius.

Adding a Curve Node

Creating a `<curve>` node is a bit more long-winded, as a `GeneralPath` object represents a curve, and you have to extract the arbitrary number of defining points from it. The code that does this is more or less what you used in the `writeObject()` method for a curve, so it is nothing new:

```
public void addElementNode(Document doc) {
  org.w3c.dom.Element curveElement = doc.createElement("curve");

  // Create the angle attribute and attach it to the <curve> node
  Attr attr = doc.createAttribute("angle");
  attr.setValue(String.valueOf(angle));
  curveElement.setAttributeNode(attr);

  // Append the <color> and <position> nodes as children
```

```
        curveElement.appendChild(createColorElement(doc));
        curveElement.appendChild(createPositionElement(doc));

        // Get the defining points via a path iterator
        PathIterator iterator = curve.getPathIterator(new AffineTransform());
        int maxCoordCount = 6;                          // Maximum coordinates for a segment
        float[] temp = new float[maxCoordCount];        // Stores segment data

        int result = iterator.currentSegment(temp);     // Get first segment
        assert result == iterator.SEG_MOVETO;           // ... should be move to

        iterator.next();                                // Next segment
        while(!iterator.isDone())    {                  // While you have segments
          result = iterator.currentSegment(temp);       // Get the segment data
          assert result == iterator.SEG_LINETO;         // Should all be lines

          // Create a <point> node and add it to the list of children
          curveElement.appendChild(createPointTypeElement(doc, "point",
                                 String.valueOf(temp[0]+position.x),
                                 String.valueOf(temp[1]+position.y)));
          iterator.next();                              // Go to next segment
        }

        doc.getDocumentElement().appendChild(curveElement);
      }
```

You add one <point> node as a child of the Element node for a curve for each defining point after the first. Since the defining points for the GeneralPath object were created relative to the origin, you have to add the corresponding coordinates of position to the coordinates of each defining point.

Adding a Text Node

A text node is a little different and involves quite a lot of code. As well as the usual <color> and <position> child nodes, you also have to append a <font> node to define the font and a <string> node. The <font> node has three attributes that define the font name, the font style, and the point size. The <string> node has the text as well as a <bounds> element that has two attributes defining the width and height of the text. Here's the code:

```
    public void addElementNode(Document doc) {
      org.w3c.dom.Element textElement = doc.createElement("text");

      // Create the angle attribute and attach it to the <text> node
      Attr attr = doc.createAttribute("angle");
      attr.setValue(String.valueOf(angle));
      textElement.setAttributeNode(attr);

      // Append the <color> and <position> nodes as children
      textElement.appendChild(createColorElement(doc));
      textElement.appendChild(createPositionElement(doc));

      // Create and apppend the <font> node
      org.w3c.dom.Element fontElement = doc.createElement("font");
```

```
    attr = doc.createAttribute("fontname");
    attr.setValue(font.getName());
    fontElement.setAttributeNode(attr);

    attr = doc.createAttribute("fontstyle");
    String style = null;
    int styleCode = font.getStyle();
    if(styleCode == Font.PLAIN) {
      style = "plain";
    } else if(styleCode == Font.BOLD) {
      style = "bold";
    } else if(styleCode == Font.ITALIC) {
      style = "italic";
    } else if(styleCode == Font.ITALIC+Font.BOLD) {
        style = "bold-italic";
    }
    assert style != null;
    attr.setValue(style);
    fontElement.setAttributeNode(attr);

    attr = doc.createAttribute("pointsize");
    attr.setValue(String.valueOf(font.getSize()));
    fontElement.setAttributeNode(attr);
    textElement.appendChild(fontElement);

    // Create the <string> node
    org.w3c.dom.Element string = doc.createElement("string");

    // Create the <bounds> node and its attributes
    org.w3c.dom.Element bounds = doc.createElement("bounds");
    attr = doc.createAttribute("width");
    attr.setValue(String.valueOf(this.bounds.width));
    bounds.setAttributeNode(attr);
    attr = doc.createAttribute("height");
    attr.setValue(String.valueOf(this.bounds.height));
    bounds.setAttributeNode(attr);
    string.appendChild(bounds);       // Set <bounds> element as <string> content

    string.appendChild(doc.createTextNode(text));
    textElement.appendChild(string);// Set <text> as <string> content
    doc.getDocumentElement().appendChild(textElement);
  }
```

Since the font style can be "plain", "bold", "bold-italic", or just "italic", you have a series of if statements to determine the value for the attribute. The style is stored in a Font object as an integer with different values for plain, bold, and italic. The values corresponding to bold and italic can be combined, in which case the style is "bold-italic".

All the element objects in a sketch can now add their own node to a Document object. You should now be able to make a SketchModel object use this capability to create a document that encapsulates the entire sketch.

Creating a Document Object for a Complete Sketch

You can add a `createDocument()` method to the `SketchModel` class to create a `Document` object and populate it with the nodes for the elements in the current sketch model. Creating the `Document` object will use the code fragment you saw earlier. You need to add some `import` statements at the beginning of the `SketchModel.java` source file for the new interfaces and classes you will be using:

```
import javax.swing.JOptionPane;
import javax.xml.parsers.DocumentBuilderFactory;
import javax.xml.parsers.ParserConfigurationException;
import org.w3c.dom.Document;
import org.w3c.dom.DOMImplementation;
import org.w3c.dom.DOMException;
```

Here's the method definition you can add to the class:

```
// Creates a DOM Document object encapsulating the current sketch
public Document createDocument() {
  Document doc = null;
  try {
    DOMImplementation domImpl = DocumentBuilderFactory.newInstance()
                                                      .newDocumentBuilder()
                                                      .getDOMImplementation();
    doc = domImpl.createDocument(null, "sketch",
              domImpl.createDocumentType("sketcher", null, "sketcher.dtd"));

  } catch(ParserConfigurationException e) {
    JOptionPane.showInternalMessageDialog(null,
                "Parser configuration error while creating document",
                "DOM Parser Error",
                JOptionPane.ERROR_MESSAGE);
    System.err.println(e.getMessage());
    e.printStackTrace(System.err);
    return null;

  } catch(DOMException e) {
    JOptionPane.showInternalMessageDialog(null,
                "DOM exception thrown while creating document",
                "DOM Error",
                JOptionPane.ERROR_MESSAGE);
    System.err.println(e.getMessage());
    e.printStackTrace(System.err);
    return null;
  }

  // Each element in the sketch can create its own node in the document
  for(Element element : elements) {             // For each element...
    element.addElementNode(doc);                // ...add its node.
  }
  return doc;
}
```

Now notice that this requires that the DTD file for Sketcher should be in the same folder as a saved sketch, so copy `Sketcher.dtd` from wherever you put it to the current directory for this version of Sketcher.

You now pop up a dialog and return `null` if something goes wrong when you are creating the `Document` object. In case of an exception of type `DOMException` being thrown, you could add a `switch` statement to analyze the value in the `code` member of the exception and provide a more specific message in the dialog.

The `SketchModel` object can now create a DOM `Document` object encapsulating the entire sketch. All you now need is some code to use this to write an XML file.

Saving a Sketch as XML

Of course, you could modify Sketcher so that it could optionally save sketches either as objects or as XML, but to keep things simple you'll add menu items to the File menu to export or import a sketch as XML. In broad terms, here's what you have to do to the `SketchFrame` class to save a sketch as an XML file:

❑ Add Import XML and Export XML menu items.

❑ Add XML `ImportAction` and `XMLExportAction` inner classes to `SketchFrame` defining the `Action` types for the new menu items, either to save the current sketch as an XML file or to replace the current sketch by a new sketch created from an XML file.

❑ Implement the process of creating an XML document as text from the `Document` object created by the `createDocument()` method that you added to the `SketchModel` class.

❑ Implement writing the text for the XML document to a file.

By adding new `Action` classes for the two new menu items, you avoid cluttering up the existing `FileAction` class any further. Clearly, a lot of the work will be in the implementation of the new `Action` classes, so let's start with the easy bit—adding the new menu items to the File menu. First, you can add two new fields for the menu items by changing the existing definition in the `SketchFrame` class:

```
private FileAction newAction,  openAction,   closeAction,
                  saveAction, saveAsAction, printAction;
private XMLExportAction exportAction;      // Action for XML export menu item
private XMLImportAction importAction;      // Action for XML import menu item
```

These store the references to the `Action` objects for the new menu items.

You can create the Action objects for the two new menu items in the `SketchFrame` constructor, following the creation of the `Action` item for the Save As menu item:

```
saveAsAction = new FileAction("Save As...");
exportAction = new XMLExportAction("Export XML",
                                    "Export sketch as an XML file");
importAction = new XMLImportAction("Import XML",
                                    "Import sketch from an XML file");
printAction = new FileAction("Print",
              KeyStroke.getKeyStroke('P', CTRL_DOWN_MASK), "Print sketch");
```

You can also add the menu items in the `SketchFrame` constructor, immediately following the menu separator definition that comes after the `saveAsAction` menu item:

```
addMenuItem(fileMenu, saveAction);
addMenuItem(fileMenu, saveAsAction);
fileMenu.addSeparator();                            // Add separator
fileMenu.add(new JMenuItem(exportAction));
fileMenu.add(new JMenuItem(importAction));
fileMenu.addSeparator();                            // Add separator
```

Now you can add code in the `SketchFrame` class for the two inner classes. You can define the `ExportAction` class within the `SketchFrame` class like this:

```
class XMLExportAction extends AbstractAction {
  public XMLExportAction(String name, String tooltip) {
    super(name);
    if(tooltip != null) {                           // If there is tooltip text
      putValue(SHORT_DESCRIPTION, tooltip);         // ...squirrel it away
    }
  }

  public void actionPerformed(ActionEvent e) {
    JFileChooser chooser = new JFileChooser(DEFAULT_DIRECTORY);
    chooser.setDialogType(chooser.SAVE_DIALOG);
    chooser.setDialogTitle("Export Sketch as XML");
    chooser.setApproveButtonText("Export");
    ExtensionFilter xmlFiles = new ExtensionFilter(".xml",
                                        "XML Sketch files (*.xml)");
    chooser.addChoosableFileFilter(xmlFiles);       // Add the filter
    chooser.setFileFilter(xmlFiles);                // and select it
    File file = null;
    if(chooser.showDialog(SketchFrame.this, null) == chooser.APPROVE_OPTION){
      file = chooser.getSelectedFile();
      if(file.exists()) {                           // Check file exists
        if(JOptionPane.NO_OPTION ==                 // Overwrite warning
          JOptionPane.showConfirmDialog(SketchFrame.this,
                      file.getName()+" exists. Overwrite?",
                      "Confirm Save As",
                      JOptionPane.YES_NO_OPTION,
                      JOptionPane.WARNING_MESSAGE))
          return;                                   // No overwrite
      }
      saveXMLSketch(file);
    }
  }
}
```

This is very similar to the code that appears in the `FileAction` class. The constructor provides only for what you use — a menu item name plus a tooltip. If you want to have the option for an icon for use on a toolbar button, you can add that in the same way as for the `FileAction` constructors. The `actionPerformed()` method pops up a `CFFileChooser` dialog to enable the destination file for the XML to be selected. The chosen file is passed to a new method that you will put together, `saveXMLSketch()`, which will handle writing the XML document to the file.

You can define the `XMLImportAction` inner class like this:

```
class XMLImportAction extends AbstractAction {
    public XMLImportAction(String name, String tooltip) {
        super(name);
        if(tooltip != null) {                      // If there is tooltip text
            putValue(SHORT_DESCRIPTION, tooltip);  // ...squirrel it away
        }
    }

    public void actionPerformed(ActionEvent e) {
        JFileChooser chooser = new JFileChooser(DEFAULT_DIRECTORY);
        chooser.setDialogTitle("Import Sketch from XML");
        chooser.setApproveButtonText("Import");
        ExtensionFilter xmlFiles = new ExtensionFilter(".xml",
                                         "XML Sketch files (*.xml)");
        chooser.addChoosableFileFilter(xmlFiles);        // Add the filter
        chooser.setFileFilter(xmlFiles);                 // and select it
        if(chooser.showDialog(SketchFrame.this, null) == chooser.APPROVE_OPTION)
            openXMLSketch(chooser.getSelectedFile());
    }
}
```

This is more of the same but in the opposite direction, as Stanley might have said. Once the name of the file to be imported has been identified in the `JFileChooser` dialog, you call `openXMLSketch()` to read the XML from the file and create the corresponding sketch.

Now you can go on to the slightly more difficult bits. Since you can't test the process for reading a sketch as XML until you have written some, you'll start by looking at how you can write an XML document to a file.

Writing the XML File

Before you start on the code, you can add a few constants that you'll need to the `SketcherConstants` class that you defined in the `Constants` package:

```
public final static String QUOTE_ENTITY = "&quot;";
public final static char QUOTE = '\"';
public final static char NEWLINE = '\n';
public final static char TAG_START = '<';
public final static char TAG_END = '>';
public final static String EMPTY_TAG_END = "/>";
public final static String END_TAG_START = "</";
```

It would be a good idea to standardize on using a double quote as a string delimiter in the XML that Sketcher will generate. You'll therefore substitute the `QUOTE_ENTITY` constant for any double quotes that appear in the text for a Sketcher `Text` element. The other constants will be useful when you are assembling XML markup for a sketch.

You can make the `saveXMLSketch()` method a member of the `SketchFrame` class. This method will obtain a `FileChannel` object for the `File` object that is passed as an argument. The `FileChannel` object can then be used to write the XML to the file. Here's how you can define this method:

```
    private void saveXMLSketch(File outFile) {
      FileOutputStream outputFile = null;       // Stores an output stream reference
      try {
        outputFile = new FileOutputStream(outFile);    // Output stream for the file
        FileChannel outChannel = outputFile.getChannel(); // Channel for file stream
        writeXMLFile(theApp.getModel().createDocument(), outChannel);

      } catch(FileNotFoundException e) {
        e.printStackTrace(System.err);
        JOptionPane.showMessageDialog(SketchFrame.this,
                      "Sketch file " + outFile.getAbsolutePath() + " not found.",
                      "File Output Error",
                      JOptionPane.ERROR_MESSAGE);
        return;                                   // Serious error - return
      }
    }
```

This calls another method that you have yet to write. The `writeXMLFile()` method will assemble the XML from the `Document` object passed as the first argument and write that to the `FileChannel` referenced by the second argument.

You don't really expect to end up in the `catch` block. If you do, something is seriously wrong somewhere. Don't forget to import the `FileChannel` class name. The `import` statement you must add to `SketchFrame` is:

```
    import java.nio.channels.FileChannel;
```

The `writeXMLFile()` method that you'll put together next will have to navigate the `Document` object and its nodes to create all the well-formed and valid XML that has to be written to the file to form a complete XML document.

Creating the XML document for a sketch won't be difficult. You already know how to navigate a `Document` object and write the nodes to the command line. You did that in an example a few pages back. You'll need to make sure the code you use here writes everything that is necessary to produce well-formed XML, but it will be essentially the same as what you have seen. The only difference here is that you are writing to a file channel rather than the command line, but that should not be any trouble since you know how to do that, too. If you take a little care in the appearance of the XML, you should be able to end up with an XML file defining a sketch that is reasonably readable.

Since you want to be able to look at the XML file for a sketch in an editor, you'll write it as the 8-bit Unicode subset `UTF-8`. By applying all the knowledge and experience you have accumulated up to now, you can implement `writeXMLFile()` in the `SketchFrame` class like this:

```
    private void writeXMLFile(org.w3c.dom.Document doc, FileChannel channel) {
      StringBuffer xmlDoc = new StringBuffer(
                          "<?xml version=\"1.0\" encoding=\"UTF-8\"?>");
      xmlDoc.append(NEWLINE).append(getDoctypeString(doc.getDoctype()));
      xmlDoc.append(getDocumentNode(doc.getDocumentElement(), ""));

      try {
        channel.write(ByteBuffer.wrap(xmlDoc.toString().getBytes("UTF-8")));
```

```
        } catch(UnsupportedEncodingException e) {
          System.out.println(e.getMessage());

        } catch(IOException e) {
          JOptionPane.showMessageDialog(SketchFrame.this,
                                 "Error writing XML to channel.",
                                 "File Output Error",
                                 JOptionPane.ERROR_MESSAGE);
          e.printStackTrace(System.err);
          return;
        }
    }
```

Initially you create a `StringBuffer` object that will eventually contain the entire XML document. It starts out initialized with the XML declaration, and you append the text corresponding to the DOCTYPE declaration. You use the `getDoctypeString()` method to generate this, and this method will be virtually identical to the method of the same name from the example earlier in this chapter, as you'll see in a moment. This method accepts an argument of type `DocumentType`, assembles a complete DOCTYPE declaration from that, and returns it as type `String`. This is appended to `xmlDoc` following a newline character that will start the declaration on a new line.

You introduce another new method in the code for the `writeXMLFile()` method in the statement:

```
        xmlDoc.append(getDocumentNode(doc.getDocumentElement(), ""));
```

This is for good reason. You'll need a recursive method to navigate the nodes in the `Document` object that represent the body of the document and create the XML for that. The string that is returned will be the entire document body, so once you have appended this to `xmlDoc`, you have the complete document. You'll implement the `getDocumentNode()` method shortly.

The other statement deserving some explanation is the one in the `try` block that writes the complete document to the file:

```
        channel.write(ByteBuffer.wrap(xmlDoc.toString().getBytes("UTF-8")));
```

Starting from the inside and working outwards: Calling the `toString()` method for `xmlDoc` returns the contents as type `String`. You then call the `getBytes()` method for the `String` object to obtain an array of type `byte[]` containing the contents of the `String` object encoded as UTF-8. You then call the static `wrap()` method in the `ByteBuffer` class (that will need importing) to create a `ByteBuffer` object that wraps the array. The buffer that is returned has its limit and position set ready for the buffer contents to be written to a file. You can therefore pass this `ByteBuffer` object directly to the `write()` method for the `FileChannel` object to write the contents of the buffer, which will be the entire XML document, to the file. How's that for a powerful statement.

The code for the `getDoctypeString()` method will be:

```
    private String getDoctypeString(org.w3c.dom.DocumentType doctype) {
        // Create the opening string for the DOCTYPE declaration with its name
        String str = doctype.getName();
        StringBuffer doctypeStr = new StringBuffer("<!DOCTYPE ").append(str);

        // Check for a system ID
```

```
      if((str = doctype.getSystemId()) != null) {
        doctypeStr.append(" SYSTEM ").append(QUOTE).append(str).append(QUOTE);
      }

      // Check for a public ID
      if((str = doctype.getPublicId()) != null) {
        doctypeStr.append(" PUBLIC ").append(QUOTE).append(str).append(QUOTE);
      }

      // Check for an internal subset
      if((str = doctype.getInternalSubset()) != null) {
        doctypeStr.append('[').append(str).append(']');
      }

      return doctypeStr.append(TAG_END).toString();  // Append '>' & return string
    }
```

This assembles a DOCTYPE declaration from the information stored in the DocumentType object that is
passed as the argument to the method, and returns it as a string.

Creating XML for the Document Body

The recursive getDocumentNode() method to assemble the XML for the document body is a little more
work than the others, but it will work much like the method you wrote earlier to list nodes in a document. The method will find out the specific type of the current node and then append the appropriate
XML string to a StringBuffer object. If the current node has child nodes, the method will call itself to
deal with each of these nodes. You can implement the writeDocumentNode() method like this:

```
    private String getDocumentNode(Node node, String indent) {
      StringBuffer nodeStr = new StringBuffer().append(NEWLINE).append(indent);
      String nodeName = node.getNodeName();        // Get name of this node

      switch(node.getNodeType()) {
        case Node.ELEMENT_NODE:
        nodeStr.append(TAG_START);
        nodeStr.append(nodeName);
        if(node.hasAttributes()) {                 // If the element has attributes...
          org.w3c.dom.NamedNodeMap attrs = node.getAttributes();   // ...get them
          for(int i = 0 ; i<attrs.getLength() ; i++) {
            org.w3c.dom.Attr attribute = (org.w3c.dom.Attr)attrs.item(i);
            // Append " name="value" to the element string
            nodeStr.append(' ').append(attribute.getName()).append('=')
                      .append(QUOTE).append(attribute.getValue()).append(QUOTE);
          }
        }
        if(!node.hasChildNodes()) {           // Check for no children for this element
          nodeStr.append(EMPTY_TAG_END);      // There are none-close as empty element
          return nodeStr.toString();          // and return the completed element

        } else {                                   // It has children
          nodeStr.append(TAG_END);                 // so close start-tag
          NodeList list = node.getChildNodes();    // Get the list of child nodes
          assert list.getLength()>0;               // There must be at least one
```

```
          // Append child nodes and their children...
            for(int i = 0 ; i<list.getLength() ; i++) {
              nodeStr.append(getDocumentNode(list.item(i), indent+" "));
            }
          }
          nodeStr.append(NEWLINE).append(indent).append(END_TAG_START)
                                          .append(nodeName).append(TAG_END);
          break;

          case Node.TEXT_NODE:
          nodeStr.append(replaceQuotes(((org.w3c.dom.Text)node).getData()));
          break;

          default:
          assert false;
        }
        return nodeStr.toString();
    }
```

You start out by creating the `StringBuffer` object and appending a newline and the indent to it to make each element start on a new line. This should result in a document you can read comfortably in a text editor.

After saving the name of the current node in `nodeName`, you determine what kind of node you are dealing with in the `switch` statement. You could have used the `instanceof` operator and `if` statements to do this, but here there's a chance to try out the alternative approach that I discussed earlier. You identify only two cases in the switch, corresponding to the constants `Node.ELEMENT_NODE` and `Node.TEXT_NODE`. This is because our DTD for Sketcher doesn't provide for any others, so you don't expect to find them.

For a node that is an element, you begin appending the start tag for the element, including the element name. You then check for the presence of attributes for this element. If there are some, you get them as a `NamedNodeMap` object in the same manner as our earlier example. You then just iterate through the collection of attributes and build the text that corresponds to each, appending the text to the `StringBuffer` object `nodeStr`.

Once you have finished with the attributes for the current node, you determine whether it has child nodes. If it has no child nodes, it has no content, so you can complete the tag for the current node making it an empty element. Since the element is now complete, you can return it as a `String`. If the current element has child nodes, you obtain those in a `NodeList` object. You then iterate through the nodes in the `NodeList` and call `getDocumentNode()` for each with an extra space appended to `indent`. The `String` that is returned for each call is appended to `nodeStr`. When all the child nodes have been processed, you are done, so you can exit the switch and return the contents of `nodeStr` as a `String`.

The other possibility is that the current node is text. This will arise from an `Element.Text` object in the sketch. It is also possible that this text may contain double quotes — the delimiter that you are using for strings in our XML. You therefore call `replaceQuotes()` to replace all occurrence of `QUOTE` in the text with the `QUOTE_ENTITY` constant that you defined in our `Constants` interface, before appending the string to `nodeStr`.

You can implement the `replaceQuotes()` method in `SketchFrame` as follows:

```
public String replaceQuotes(String str) {
  StringBuffer buf = new StringBuffer();
  for(int i = 0 ; i<str.length() ; i++) {
    if(str.charAt(i)==QUOTE) {
      buf.append(QUOTE_ENTITY);
    } else {
      buf.append(str.charAt(i));
    }
  }
  return buf.toString();
}
```

This just tests each character in the original string. If it's a delimiter for an attribute value, it's replaced by the entity reference `&quot;` in the output string `buf`.

Well, you're done—almost. You must not forget the extra `import` statements you need in the `SketchFrame.java` file:

```
import java.io.FileNotFoundException;
import java.io.UnsupportedEncodingException;
import java.nio.ByteBuffer;
import java.nio.channels.FileChannel;
import org.w3c.dom.Node;
import org.w3c.dom.NodeList;
```

These cover the new classes that you used in our new code for I/O and for DOM without using fully qualified names.

Try It Out   Writing a Sketch as XML

You call one method that you have yet to define—the `openXMLSketch()` method that is called in the `XMLImportAction` class. You can add an empty definition for this method to `SketchFrame` to make the code compilable:

```
private void openXMLSketch(File xmlFile) {
}
```

Recompile sketcher with the new code. Once you have fixed any errors, you can run Sketcher and export your sketch as XML. You can then inspect the file in your editor. You can also process the file with the `TryDOM` and `TrySAX` programs to check that the XML is valid.

How It Works

You've been through the detailed mechanics of this. The `SketchModel` object creates a `Document` object that is populated by nodes encapsulating the sketch elements. Each node is created by the corresponding sketch element. You then navigate through the nodes in the document to create the XML for each node.

You can now have a go at importing an XML sketch.

Reading an XML Representation of a Sketch

The Import XML operation will also be implemented in the `SketchFrame` class. You have already added the menu item and the `XMLImportAction` class that is used to create it. You just need to implement the `openXMLSketch()` method that is called by the `actionPerformed()` method in the `XMLImportAction` class.

Assuming the XML representation of a sketch that you have created is well-formed and valid, creating a `Document` object encapsulating a sketch will be a piece of cake. You will just get a DOM parser to do it — and it will verify that the document is well-formed and valid along the way. You will need an `ErrorHandler` object to deal with parsing errors, so first add an inner class to our `SketchFrame` class for that:

```
class DOMErrorHandler implements org.xml.sax.ErrorHandler {
  public void fatalError(org.xml.sax.SAXParseException spe)
     throws org.xml.sax.SAXException {
    JOptionPane.showMessageDialog(SketchFrame.this,
                                  "Fatal error at line "+spe.getLineNumber()
                         + "\n"+spe.getMessage(),
                                  "DOM Parser Error",
                                  JOptionPane.ERROR_MESSAGE);
    throw spe;
  }

  public void warning(org.xml.sax.SAXParseException spe) {
    JOptionPane.showMessageDialog(SketchFrame.this,
                                  "Warning at line "+spe.getLineNumber()
                         + "\n"+spe.getMessage(),
                                  "DOM Parser Error",
                                  JOptionPane.ERROR_MESSAGE);
  }

  public void error(org.xml.sax.SAXParseException spe) {
    JOptionPane.showMessageDialog(SketchFrame.this,
                                  "Error at line "+spe.getLineNumber()
                         + "\n"+spe.getMessage(),
                                  "DOM Parser Error",
                                  JOptionPane.ERROR_MESSAGE);
  }
}
```

This implements the three methods declared in the `ErrorHandler` interface. In contrast to the previous example using a DOM error handler, rather than writing error information to the command line, here you display it in a suitable dialog.

Here's how you can implement the `openXMLSketch()` method in the `SketchFrame` class:

```
private void openXMLSketch(File xmlFile) {
    DocumentBuilderFactory builderFactory = DocumentBuilderFactory.newInstance();
    builderFactory.setValidating(true);              // Add validating parser feature
    builderFactory.setIgnoringElementContentWhitespace(true);
```

```
        try {
          DocumentBuilder builder = builderFactory.newDocumentBuilder();
          builder.setErrorHandler(new DOMErrorHandler());
          checkForSave();
          theApp.insertModel(createSketchModel(builder.parse(xmlFile)));
          filename = xmlFile.getName();            // Update the file name
          setTitle(frameTitle+xmlFile.getPath());  // Change the window title
          sketchChanged = false;                   // Status is unchanged

        } catch(ParserConfigurationException e) {
          JOptionPane.showMessageDialog(SketchFrame.this,
                                        e.getMessage(),
                                        "DOM Parser Factory Error",
                                        JOptionPane.ERROR_MESSAGE);
          e.printStackTrace(System.err);
        } catch(org.xml.sax.SAXException e) {
          JOptionPane.showMessageDialog(SketchFrame.this,
                                        e.getMessage(),
                                        "DOM Parser Error",
                                        JOptionPane.ERROR_MESSAGE);
          e.printStackTrace(System.err);
        } catch(IOException e) {
          JOptionPane.showMessageDialog(SketchFrame.this,
                                        e.getMessage(),
                                        "I/O Error",
                                        JOptionPane.ERROR_MESSAGE);
          e.printStackTrace();
        }
      }
```

Most of the code here is devoted to catching exceptions that you hope will not get thrown. You set up the parser factory object to produce a validating parser that will ignore surplus whitespace. The latter feature will avoid extraneous nodes in the Document object that will be created by the parser from the XML file.

After storing a reference to the DOM parser that is created in builder, you create a DOMErrorHandler object and set that as the handler for any parsing errors that arise. If the parser finds any errors, you'll see a dialog displayed indicating what the error is. You use the builder object to parse the XML file that is identified by the File object xmlFile and pass the Document object that is returned by the parse() method to the createSketchModel() method that you'll be adding to the SketchFrame class next. This method has the job of creating a new SketchModel object from the Document object.

Let's see how you can create a new SketchModel object encapsulating a new sketch by analyzing the Document object.

Creating the Model

You know that a sketch in XML is a two-level structure. There is a root element <sketch> that contains one XML element for each of the elements in the original sketch. Therefore, to recreate the sketch, you just need to extract the children of the root node in the Document object and then figure out what kind of sketch element each child represents. Whatever it is, you want to create a sketch element object of that type and add it to a model. The simplest way to create sketch element objects from a given document node is to add a constructor to each of the classes that define sketch elements. You'll add these constructors after you have defined the `createSketchModel()` method in the `SketchFrame` class. Here's the code for that:

```
    private SketchModel createSketchModel(org.w3c.dom.Document doc) {
        SketchModel model = new SketchModel();        // The new model object

        // Get the first child of the root node
        org.w3c.dom.Node node = doc.getDocumentElement().getFirstChild();

        // Starting with the first child, check out each child in turn
        while (node != null) {
          assert node instanceof org.w3c.dom.Element; // Should all be Elements

          String name = ((org.w3c.dom.Element)node).getTagName(); // Get the name

          if(name.equals("line")) {                          // Check for a line
            model.add(new Element.Line((org.w3c.dom.Element)node));

          } else if(name.equals("rectangle")) {       // Check for a rectangle
            model.add(new Element.Rectangle((org.w3c.dom.Element)node));

          } else if(name.equals("circle")) {          // Check for a circle
        model.add(new Element.Circle((org.w3c.dom.Element)node));

          } else if(name.equals("curve")) {           // Check for a curve
        model.add(new Element.Curve((org.w3c.dom.Element)node));

          } else if(name.equals("text")) {            // Check for a text
            model.add(new Element.Text((org.w3c.dom.Element)node));
          }
          node = node.getNextSibling();               // Next child node
        }
      return model;
    }
```

You'll need three more `import` statements in `SketchFrame` for the new names you use here:

```
  import javax.xml.parsers.DocumentBuilder;
  import javax.xml.parsers.DocumentBuilderFactory;
  import javax.xml.parsers.ParserConfigurationException;
```

This method works in a straightforward fashion. You get the first child node of the root node by calling `getDocumentElement()` for the document object to obtain a reference to the `org.w3c.dom.Element` object that encapsulates the root node, and then call its `getFirstChild()` method to obtain a reference of type `Node` to its first child. All the children of the root element should be `Element` nodes, and the assertion verifies this.

You determine what kind of element each child node is by checking its name. You call a sketch `Element` constructor corresponding to the node name to create the sketch element to be added to the model. Each of these constructors creates an object from the `org.w3c.dom.Element` object reference that is passed as the argument. You just have to implement these constructors in the subclasses of `Element`, and you're done.

Creating Sketch Elements from XML Elements

Every element has to have the `color` field in the base class set to a color determined from a `<color>` element in the document. You can therefore usefully add a base class method to take care of this. Add the following to the `Element` class definition:

```
protected void setElementColor(org.w3c.dom.Element colorElement) {
    color = new Color(Integer.parseInt(colorElement.getAttribute("R")),
                      Integer.parseInt(colorElement.getAttribute("G")),
                      Integer.parseInt(colorElement.getAttribute("B")));
}
```

The method expects to receive a reference to an `org.w3c.dom.Element` object as an argument that contains the RGB values for the color. You extract the value of each of the attributes in the `colorElement` object by calling its `getAttribute()` method with the attribute name as the argument. You pass each of the values obtained to the `Color` constructor, and you store the reference to this object in `color`. Because the attribute values are strings, you have to convert them to numerical values using the static `parseInt()` method that is defined in the `Integer` class.

The same applies to the position field in the `Element` class, so you should define a method in the `Element` class to initialize it from an `org.w3c.dom.Element` object:

```
protected void setElementPosition(org.w3c.dom.Element posElement) {
    position = new Point();
    position.setLocation(Double.parseDouble(posElement.getAttribute("x")),
                         Double.parseDouble(posElement.getAttribute("y")));
}
```

This uses essentially the same mechanism as the previous method. Here the attribute strings represent `double` values, so you use the static `parseDouble()` method from the `Double` class to convert them to the numeric equivalent.

Every Sketcher element has a color, a position, and an angle, which are stored in base class fields, so you can create a base class constructor to initialize these from the document node for the element:

```
protected Element(org.w3c.dom.Element xmlElement) {
    // Get the <color> element
    org.w3c.dom.NodeList list = xmlElement.getElementsByTagName("color");
    setElementColor((org.w3c.dom.Element)list.item(0));        // Set the color

    list = xmlElement.getElementsByTagName("position");        // Get <position>
    setElementPosition((org.w3c.dom.Element)list.item(0));     // Set the position

    angle = Double.parseDouble(xmlElement.getAttribute("angle")); // Set the angle
}
```

You have declared this constructor as `protected` to prevent the possibility of it being called externally.

Every one of the new constructors in the inner classes to `Element` will call this constructor first. An important point to remember is that if a constructor for a derived class object does not call a base class constructor as the first statement in the body of the constructor, the compiler will insert a call to the no-arg constructor for the base class. This means that a base class always has to have a no-arg constructor if the derived class constructors do not call a base class constructor with arguments.

You first extract the child element for the current element with the name `"color"` by calling the `getElementsByTagName()` method for `xmlElement`. This method is declared in the `org.w3c.dom.Element` interface and returns a `NodeList` object containing all the child nodes with the given name. If you pass the string `"*"` as the argument to this method, it will return all child `org.w3c.dom.Element` objects in the node list. There's another method, `getElementsByTagNameNS()`, that is declared in the `Element` interface that does the same for documents using namespaces. The first argument in this case is the namespace URI, and the second argument is the element name. The strings to either or both arguments can be `"*"`, in which case all namespaces and/or names will be matched.

You pass the reference to the element with the name `"color"` to the `setElementColor()` method that is inherited from the base class. This sets the value of the `color` field in the base class.

Next you initialize the `position` field in the `Element` class by calling the `setElementPosition()` method. The process is much the same as for the `color` field. Lastly, you set the `angle` field by converting the string that is the value for the angle attribute for the current node to type `double`.

Now you're ready to add the new constructors to the subclasses to create sketch elements from XML elements.

Creating a Line Element

You can construct an `Element.Line` object by first calling the base class constructor you have just defined to set the `color`, `position`, and `angle` fields and then setting the `line` field in the derived class. Here's the code for the constructor:

```
// Content is <color>, <position>, <endpoint> elements. Attribute is angle.
public Line(org.w3c.dom.Element xmlElement) {
   super(xmlElement);

   org.w3c.dom.NodeList list = xmlElement.getElementsByTagName("endpoint");
   org.w3c.dom.Element endpoint = (org.w3c.dom.Element)list.item(0);
   line = new Line2D.Double(origin.x, origin.y,
             Double.parseDouble(endpoint.getAttribute("x"))-position.getX(),
             Double.parseDouble(endpoint.getAttribute("y"))-position.getY());
}
```

To save you having to refer back to the DTD, the comment preceding the constructor definition outlines the XML corresponding to the element. You first call the base class constructor and then extract the child element that is the `<endpoint>` element. You will doubtless recall that all our sketch elements are defined at the origin. This makes moving an element very easy and allows all elements to be moved in the same way — by modifying the `position` field. You therefore create the `Line2D.Double` object as a line starting at the origin. The coordinates of its end point are the values stored in the `<endpoint>` child element minus the corresponding coordinates of `position` that were set in the base class constructor.

Creating a Rectangle Element

This constructor will be almost identical to the previous constructor for a line:

```
   // Rectangle has angle attribute. Content is <color>,<position>,<bottomright>
   public Rectangle(org.w3c.dom.Element xmlElement) {
     super(xmlElement);

     org.w3c.dom.NodeList list = xmlElement.getElementsByTagName("bottomright");
     org.w3c.dom.Element bottomright = (org.w3c.dom.Element)list.item(0);
     rectangle = new Rectangle2D.Double(origin.x, origin.y,
           Double.parseDouble(bottomright.getAttribute("x"))-position.getX(),
           Double.parseDouble(bottomright.getAttribute("y"))-position.getY());
   }
```

Spot the differences! This code is so similar to that of the `Line` constructor that I don't think it requires further explanation.

Creating a Circle Element

Here's the code for the `Circle` constructor:

```
   // Circle has radius, angle attributes. Content is <color>, <position>
   public Circle(org.w3c.dom.Element xmlElement) {
     super(xmlElement);

     double radius = Double.parseDouble(xmlElement.getAttribute("radius"));
     circle = new Ellipse2D.Double(origin.x, origin.y,       // Position - top-left
                             2.*radius, 2.*radius);   // Width & height
   }
```

If this code is compared to the previous two constructors, the only change you will find is the last bit where you use the `radius` attribute value to define the `Ellipse2D.Double` object representing the circle.

Creating a Curve Element

Before you nod off, this one's a little more challenging because there can be an arbitrary number of child nodes:

```
   // Curve has angle attribute. Content is <color>, <position>, <point>+
   public Curve(org.w3c.dom.Element xmlElement) {
     super(xmlElement);

     curve = new GeneralPath();
     curve.moveTo(origin.x, origin.y);
     org.w3c.dom.NodeList nodes = xmlElement.getElementsByTagName("point");
     for(int i = 0 ; i<nodes.getLength() ; i++) {
       curve.lineTo(
                   (float)(Double.parseDouble(
           ((org.w3c.dom.Element)nodes.item(i)).getAttribute("x")) - position.x),
                   (float)(Double.parseDouble(
           ((org.w3c.dom.Element)nodes.item(i)).getAttribute("y")) - position.y));
     }
   }
```

Having said that, the first part calls the base class constructor the same as ever. It's more interesting when you get the list of Element nodes with the name "point" by calling getElementsByTagName() for the xmlElement object. These are the nodes holding the coordinates of the points that define the curve. It is important to us here that the method returns the nodes in the NodeList object in the sequence in which they were originally added to the XML document. If it didn't, you would have no way to reconstruct the curve. With the data encapsulated in the nodes from the NodeList object that is returned, you can reconstruct the GeneralPath object that describes the curve. The first point on the curve is always the origin, so the first definition in the path is defined by calling its moveTo() method to move to the origin.

Each of the <point> nodes contains a point on the path in absolute coordinates. Since you want the curve to be defined relative to the origin, you subtract the coordinates of the start point position from the corresponding coordinates stored in each node. You use the resulting coordinates to define the end on each line segment by passing them to the lineTo() method for the path object.

Creating a Text Element

Recreating an Element.Text object from a <text> element is the messiest of all. It certainly involves the most code. It's not difficult though. There are just a lot of bits and pieces to take care of:

```
// Text has angle attribute. Content is <color>, <position>, <font>, <string>
// <font> has attributes fontname, fontstyle, pointsize
// fontstyle is "plain", "bold", "italic", or "bold-italic"
// <string> content is text plus <bounds>
public Text(org.w3c.dom.Element xmlElement) {
  super(xmlElement);

  // Get the font details
  org.w3c.dom.NodeList list = xmlElement.getElementsByTagName("font");
  org.w3c.dom.Element fontElement = (org.w3c.dom.Element)list.item(0);
  String styleStr = fontElement.getAttribute("fontstyle");
  int style = 0;
  if(styleStr.equals("plain")) {
    style = Font.PLAIN;
  } else if(styleStr.equals("bold")) {
    style = Font.BOLD;
  } else if(styleStr.equals("italic")) {
    style = Font.ITALIC;
  } else if(styleStr.equals("bold-italic")) {
    style = Font.BOLD + Font.ITALIC;
  } else {
    assert false;
  }
  font = new Font(fontElement.getAttribute("fontname"), style,
                  Integer.parseInt(fontElement.getAttribute("pointsize")));

  // Get string bounds
  list = xmlElement.getElementsByTagName("bounds");
  org.w3c.dom.Element boundsElement = (org.w3c.dom.Element)list.item(0);

  this.bounds = new java.awt.Rectangle(origin.x, origin.y,
                  Integer.parseInt(boundsElement.getAttribute("width")),
                  Integer.parseInt(boundsElement.getAttribute("height")));
```

```
        // Get the string
        list = xmlElement.getElementsByTagName("string");
        org.w3c.dom.Element string = (org.w3c.dom.Element)list.item(0);
        list = string.getChildNodes();

        StringBuffer textStr = new StringBuffer();
        for(int i = 0 ; i<list.getLength() ; i++) {
            if(list.item(i).getNodeType()==org.w3c.dom.Node.TEXT_NODE) {
                textStr.append(((org.w3c.dom.Text)list.item(i)).getData());
            }
        }
        text = textStr.toString().trim();
    }
```

The attributes of the `<string>` element define the font. Only the `fontstyle` attribute needs some analysis since you have to represent the style by an integer constant. This means testing for the possible values for the string and setting the appropriate integer value in `style`. Of course, you could have stored the style as a numeric value, but that would have been meaningless to a human reader. Making the attribute value a descriptor string makes it completely clear. After obtaining the style code, you have an assertion to make sure it actually happened. Because the XML was created by Sketcher, the only reasons why this would assert are if there is an error in the code somewhere if the XML was written by a different version of Sketcher, or if the XML was generated by hand. Of course, errors in the XML due to inconsistencies with the DTD would be caught by the parser and signaled by one or other of the `ErrorHandler` methods.

Text content for an element can appear distributed among several child `<Text>` nodes. You accommodate this possibility by concatenating the data from all the child `<Text>` nodes that you find, and then trimming any leading and trailing whitespace from the string before storing it in `text`.

That's all the code you need. If everything compiles, you are ready to try exporting and importing sketches. If it doesn't compile, chances are good there's an `import` statement missing.

Try It Out   Sketches in XML

You can try various combinations of elements to see how they look in XML. Be sure to copy the `sketcher.dtd` file to the directory in which you are storing exported sketches. If you don't, you won't be able to import them since the DTD will not be found. Don't forget you can look at the XML using any text editor and in most browsers. I created the sketch shown in Figure 23-1.

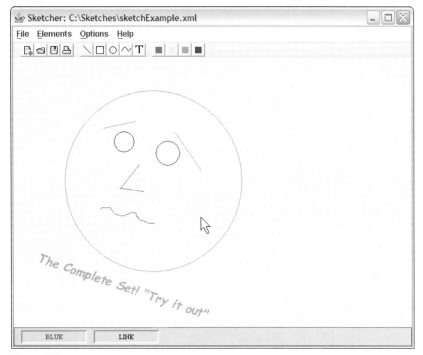

Figure 23-1

When I exported this sketch I got an XML file with the following contents:

```xml
<?xml version="1.0" encoding="UTF-8"?>
<!DOCTYPE sketch SYSTEM "sketcher.dtd">
<sketch>
 <circle radius="15.0" angle="0.0">
  <color B="255" G="0" R="0"/>
  <position x="153.0" y="109.0"/>
 </circle>
 <circle radius="18.027756377319946" angle="0.0">
  <color B="255" G="0" R="0"/>
  <position x="217.0" y="123.0"/>
 </circle>
 <circle radius="134.61797799699713" angle="0.0">
  <color B="255" G="0" R="0"/>
  <position x="78.0" y="48.0"/>
 </circle>
 <line angle="0.0">
  <color B="0" G="0" R="255"/>
  <position x="191.0" y="158.0"/>
  <endpoint x="162.0" y="194.0"/>
 </line>
 <line angle="0.0">
  <color B="0" G="0" R="255"/>
  <position x="162.0" y="193.0"/>
```

```
 <endpoint x="197.0" y="198.0"/>
 </line>
 <line angle="0.0">
  <color B="0" G="255" R="0"/>
  <position x="185.0" y="94.0"/>
  <endpoint x="137.0" y="104.0"/>
 </line>
 <line angle="0.0">
  <color B="0" G="255" R="0"/>
  <position x="246.0" y="110.0"/>
  <endpoint x="285.0" y="166.0"/>
 </line>
 <curve angle="0.0">
  <color B="0" G="0" R="255"/>
  <position x="132.0" y="224.0"/>
  <point x="132.0" y="223.0"/>
  <point x="133.0" y="222.0"/>
  <point x="134.0" y="222.0"/>
  <point x="137.0" y="222.0"/>
  <!-- points cut here for the sake of brevity -->
  <point x="211.0" y="245.0"/>
  <point x="212.0" y="245.0"/>
  <point x="213.0" y="245.0"/>
  <point x="214.0" y="245.0"/>
 </curve>
 <text angle="0.3183694064160789">
  <color B="0" G="255" R="0"/>
  <position x="42.0" y="283.0"/>
  <font fontname="Comic Sans MS" fontstyle="bold-italic" pointsize="18"/>
  <string>
   <bounds width="271" height="21"/>
   The Complete Set! &quot;Try it out&quot;
  </string>
 </text>
 </sketch>
```

This file is also available as sketchexample.xml in the code download for this book from the Wrox Press web site, http://www.wrox.com. You could try importing it into Sketcher and see if you get the same sketch.

Summary

In this chapter I've discussed how you can use a DOM parser to analyze XML and how JAXP supports the synthesis and modification of XML documents using DOM. The key points I have covered include the following:

❑ An object of type DocumentBuilder encapsulates a DOM parser.

❑ You create an object encapsulating a DOM parser by using a DocumentBuilderFactory object that you obtain by calling the static newInstance() method that is defined in the DocumentFactoryBuilder class.

❏ You can parse an XML document by passing the document as an argument to the `parse()` method for a `DocumentBuilder` object.

❏ A DOM parser creates a `Document` object that encapsulates an entire XML document as a tree of `Node` objects.

❏ The DOM API defines the methods of a `Document` object that enable you to analyze an XML document by navigating through the nodes in the `Document` object.

❏ The DOM API also defines methods for creating a new XML document encapsulated by a `Document` object.

❏ When you want to create a new XML document that includes a DTD, you should use the `createDocument()` method for a `DOMImplementation` object, rather than the `newDocument()` method for a `DocumentBuilder` object.

Exercises

You can download the source code for the examples in the book and the solutions to the following exercises from `http://www.wrox.com`.

1. Write a program using DOM that will count the number of occurrences of each element type in an XML document and display them. The document file should be identified by the first command-line argument. The program should also accept optional, additional command-line arguments that are the names of elements. When there are two or more command-line arguments, the program should count and report only on the elements identified by the second and subsequent command-line arguments.

2. Implement the XML Import capability in Sketcher using SAX, rather than DOM.

Talking to Databases

In the next two chapters, you're going to look at how Java programs can interface with relational databases or any database that can be accessed using Structured Query Language (SQL). You'll be executing SQL statements by using classes that come with the Java Development Kit (JDK).

First I'll introduce the basic ideas behind databases and how they store data. This leads naturally into a discussion of SQL, the language that is used with many relational databases to both define and query data and which is a prerequisite for database access in Java. Then you'll look into the Java Database Connectivity (JDBC) class library, which provides a standard way for establishing and maintaining a Java program's connection to a database. Once you have a connection to a database, you can use SQL to access and process the contents.

In this first chapter, you'll take a brief tour of database concepts, SQL and JDBC. In the next chapter you'll go into more depth on the capabilities provided by JDBC and develop a database browsing application. In this chapter you will learn:

❑   What databases are

❑   What the basic SQL statements are and how you apply them

❑   What the rationale behind JDBC is

❑   How to write a simple JDBC program

❑   What the key elements of the JDBC API are

JDBC Concepts and Terminology

To make sure we have a common understanding of the jargon, I'll first take a look at database terminology. First, in general, **data access** is the process of retrieving or manipulating data that is taken from a remote or local **data source**. Data sources don't have to be relational — they can come in a variety of different forms. Some common examples of data sources that you might access are:

❑ A remote relational database on a server — for example, SQL Server

❑ A local relational database on your computer — for example, Personal Oracle or Microsoft Access

❑ A text file on your computer

❑ A spreadsheet

❑ A remote mainframe/midrange host providing data access

❑ An online information service (such as a stock market ticker, for example)

JDBC is, by definition, an interface to **relational** data sources. While it is conceivable that non-relational sources may be accessible through JDBC, you'll be concentrating on relational databases throughout this chapter and the next. If you haven't met relational databases before, you should still be able to follow the discussion. The structure of a relational database is logical and fairly easy to learn, and while I can't provide a comprehensive tutorial on it here, I'll cover enough of the basics to make what you are doing understandable, even if you've never worked with databases before.

The Java Database Connectivity (JDBC) library provides the means for you to execute SQL statements within a Java program to access and operate on a relational database. JDBC was designed as an object-oriented, Java-based application program interface (API) for database access and is intended to be a standard to which Java developers and database vendors can adhere.

> *JDBC is based on other standard program-database interfaces — largely the X/Open SQL CLI (Call Level Interface) specification, but knowledge of these standards isn't necessary to use JDBC. However, if you've programmed database access before, you should be able to draw on that experience when using JDBC.*

The library is implemented in the `java.sql` package. It is a set of classes and interfaces that provides a uniform API for access to a broad range of databases.

Figure 24-1 shows the basic contents of the `technical_library` database (available as part of the code download for this book from the Wrox web site — `www.wrox.com`) that I'll be using both to illustrate some key concepts and as a base for the examples.

This shows the tables that make up the sample database. In case you are unfamiliar with relational databases, I'll be going into what tables are in a moment.

The operations that you want to carry out on a relational database are expressed in a language that was designed specifically for this purpose, the **Structured Query Language** — more commonly referred to as SQL. SQL is not like a conventional programming language, such as Java. SQL is a **declarative** language, which means that SQL statements tell the database server *what* you want to do, but not *how* it should be done — the *how* is up to the server. Each SQL command is analyzed by the database server, and the operation it describes is carried out by a separate piece of software that is usually referred to as the **database engine**. A database engine will be associated with a particular implementation of a relational database, although not necessarily uniquely. Different commercial database implementations may use a common database engine.

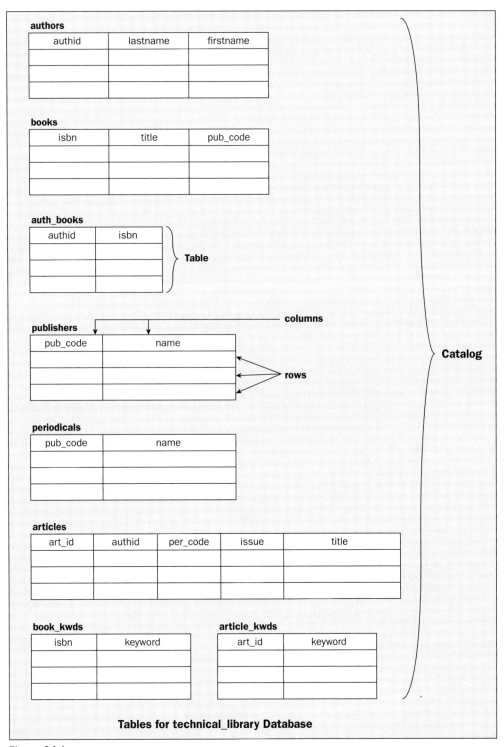

Tables for technical_library Database

Figure 24-1

Tables

A relational database consists of a number of tables. A **table**, such as the `authors` table in the example in Figure 24-1, is the primary database construct that you'll be dealing with. Any time that you define, create, update, or delete data, you'll do so within the context of a table.

When you create a table within a database, you are creating a "template" for a rectangular grid that will contain the data. In relational parlance, a table is a collection of rows conforming to the specifications of the corresponding columns, and the table is called a **relation**. Each row implies that the set of data items that it contains are related in some way — it expresses a relationship between the data items, and a table can contain as many rows as you want.

The technical term for a row in a table is a **tuple**. The columns define the constituent parts of a row and are referred to as **fields**, and these column-defined items of data in a row are called **attributes**. Thus, the number of columns for a given table is fixed. Figure 24-2 shows the `authors` table from the `technical_library` database.

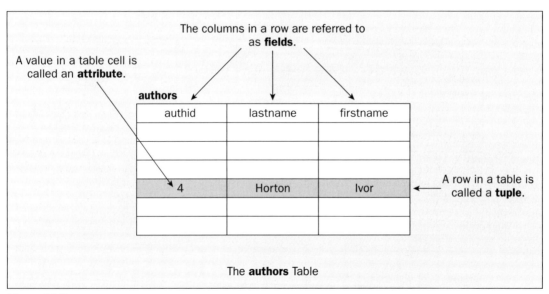

Figure 24-2

Although a table is logically a set of rows with a fixed number of columns, the physical organization doesn't have to be like that. The physical organization can be anything at all as long as the logical organization — the way it appears when you access it — is as I have described.

Table Columns

As I said, a table behaves as if it is a rectangular grid of cells. The grid has a given number of columns and an arbitrary number of rows. Each column of cells in the grid stores data of a particular kind. Not only is the data of a particular data type, but it is also a specific category of information specified by the field name. For example, in Figure 24-2, the field with the name `lastname` is one of three fields defined for the `authors` table. It stores the last name of the authors that appear in the table, and the type of the data will be a text string. SQL has data types that correspond to the basic Java data types — I'll list them later.

It's fundamental to a relational database that the data items in each column in a table have consistent data types *and* semantics. For example, in the `authors` table, the `lastname` column, which is defined as a text field, will be used to store text only — not numbers, so the data type is preserved. The column's semantics must also be preserved, and since the column represents the last name of an author, you would not use this column to store an author's hobbies or favorite movie, even though such data items may be of the same type. If you wanted to record that information, you would need to create new columns in the table.

Table Rows

Each **row** in a table is the collection of data elements that make up an entity referred to as a **tuple**. Some data sources refer to a row as a **record**, and you will often see the term *record* used in a general-purpose programming context when accessing a relational database. The term **recordset** is used to describe a collection of rows that is produced by executing an SQL command.

A row from the `authors` table in the database shown in Figure 24-2 would look like the following:

4	Horton	Ivor

This row contains data items for the `authid`, `lastname`, and `firstname` columns. Although in this case there is a data item corresponding to each column, this does not have to be the case. A data item can be empty, but it still appears in the row. Note that empty is not the same as zero, and `NULL` is used in SQL to denote the absence of a value. A rough analogy might be a variable in Java of type `Integer` that could contain a reference to an object that represents zero (or some other integer value, of course) or could contain `null`. I'll come back to the notion of `NULL` when I introduce SQL data types.

Database Catalog

In general, the **catalog** refers to the database **system tables**. System tables are similar to the tables used by your application, except that they are used to store information about the databases, the tables, and the composition of those tables, rather than storing application data. The catalog can be queried to find out what tables are available from a data source, what columns are defined for a given table, and so forth. The data describing the contents of a database is also referred to as **metadata** — data about data — or collectively as the **data dictionary**.

In Figure 24-1, "Catalog" refers to the entire `technical_library` database.

Depending on the particular database to which you're connected, the catalog may contain other information related to accessing the database, such as security details, foreign keys, and stored procedures.

The column values that together uniquely identify a particular row in a table make up what is referred to as the primary key. Such columns are also called primary key fields or primary key values. Rows may also contain values that refer to key values in different tables. For example, the auth_books table contains a column authid whose value is the primary key for a row in the authors table. When a table contains columns that are key columns for another table, values in those columns are referred to as foreign keys. Figure 24-3 shows key fields and foreign keys.

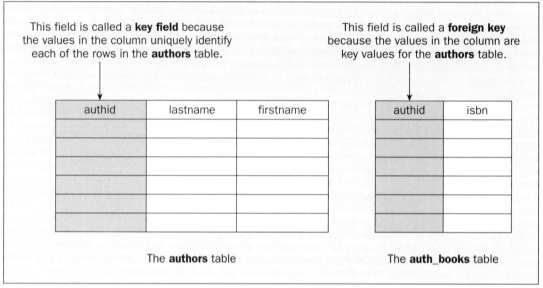

Figure 24-3

Many database servers are capable of executing pre-built scripts, as well as SQL statements. These server-based scripts are called by the application, and are executed by the database server. They are frequently referred to as **stored procedures**, or just **procedures.** They are used to package up commonly used operations on the database, particularly those that enforce specific business rules.

Introducing SQL

Structured Query Language (SQL) is accepted internationally as the official standard for relational database access. A major reason for the acceptance of SQL as *the* relational query language was the move toward client/server architectures that began in the late 1980s.

> Not all versions and dialects of SQL are created equal, however. As vendors have incorporated SQL into their products, extensions to the grammar have often been added. That was convenient for the database vendors but tough for anyone else trying to work with more than one database vendor. To ensure SQL's place as a standard for database access, organizations like the ISO and ANSI have worked with the industry to develop standards for SQL. The current ISO operating standard is SQL-92, to which JDBC adheres. Conformance to the standard does not guarantee that your SQL will work in every case though. A database system that is in conformance with the standard for SQL is not obliged to implement all the capabilities that the standard defines. Indeed, most database systems do not do so.

SQL is different from other programming languages that you may be familiar with in that it is declarative, not procedural. In other words, you don't use SQL to define complex processes; you use SQL to issue commands that define and manipulate data.

The first thing that strikes you about SQL is that it is very readable. The way that each query is structured reads like a sentence in English. The syntax is easy to learn, and the constructs and concepts are very easy to grasp. Secondly, with SQL you always issue commands. You send the command to the database and the database either returns the required data or performs the required action.

Let's look at the example of a database that you saw earlier in Figure 24-1 — the `technical_library` database. How would you go about defining the tables you need to implement this database?

Try It Out   Designing Database Tables

The first step in designing the tables you need in your database is to decide what information you want to capture. Then you can design the tables around that information.

With the `technical_library` database, you want to keep track of the following kinds of things:

❑   Books

❑   Articles

❑   Authors

❑   Publishers

For each of these information categories, called **entities** in database jargon, you will want to record a specific set of data items, as follows:

Entity	Attribute
Books	ISBN
	Book title
	Author(s)
	Publisher

Table continued on following page

Entity	Attribute
Articles	Author(s)
	Title
	Periodical it was published in
	Issue of publication
Authors	Last name
	First name
	Books published
	Articles published
Publishers	Publisher code
	Name

Let's start out with a table to keep track of the authors. You'll call this table `authors` and describe the columns that you want for this table:

Column Heading	Description
`authid`	Unique identifier for an author — you need this because several authors could have the same name
`lastname`	Family name
`firstname`	First name
`address1`	Address line one
`address2`	Address line two
`city`	City
`state_prov`	State or province
`postcode`	Zip or postal code
`country`	Country
`phone`	Contact phone number
`fax`	Fax number
`email`	E-mail address

You need to assign a data type to each column heading that prescribes the form of the data in the column as it is stored in the table. Of course, these need to be data types meaningful to SQL, not necessarily Java data types. The data types for data in a relational database are those recognized by the SQL implementation supported by the database engine, and these types will have to be mapped to Java data types. Let's look at some examples of SQL data types:

SQL Data Type	Description
CHAR	Fixed-length string of characters
VARCHAR	Variable-length string of characters
BOOLEAN	Logical value — true or false
SMALLINT	Small integer value, from -127 to +127
INTEGER	Larger integer value, from -32767 to +32767
NUMERIC	A numeric value with a given **precision** — which is the number of decimal digits in the number — and a given **scale** — which is the number of digits after the decimal point. For example, the value 234567.89 has a precision of 8 and a scale of 2.
FLOAT	Floating-point value
CURRENCY	Stores monetary values
DOUBLE	Higher precision floating-point value
DATE	Date
TIME	Time
DATETIME	Date and time
RAW	Raw binary data (can be used to store objects in a streamed binary format)

As I said earlier, NULL represents the absence of a value for any SQL type of data, but it is not the same as the null we have been using in Java. For one thing, in SQL you can't compare one NULL with another NULL, you can only determine whether a particular attribute is or is not NULL. One effect of this is to introduce four potential values of type BOOLEAN — TRUE and FALSE, which you would expect; NULL meaning the absence of a BOOLEAN value; and UNKNOWN, which arises when the result cannot be determined — when you compare two NULL values, for example. Note that not all database systems allow BOOLEAN values to be NULL however.

Based on the types of information in the authors table listed earlier, you can assign a data type for each column in the table that is appropriate for the kind of information in the column:

Column Name	Data Type
authid	INTEGER
lastname	VARCHAR
firstname	VARCHAR
address1	VARCHAR
address2	VARCHAR
city	VARCHAR

Table continued on following page

Column Name	Data Type
state_prov	VARCHAR
pzipcode	VARCHAR
country	VARCHAR
phone	VARCHAR
fax	VARCHAR
email	VARCHAR

How It Works

The column names tell us something about the information that will be stored in that field, but they don't tell the computer what type of information has been stored or how to store it. While you are interested in the information stored in the columns, all the database engine wants to know is the *type* of information, and that's where the data type comes in.

You probably noticed that a column labeled authid has been placed at the top of the list of columns in the authors table. This is to give each record a unique identifier so that an individual record can easily be retrieved. Think of the nightmare you'd have if you were managing books and journals for a large library and you had several authors named John Smith. You wouldn't have any way of distinguishing one John Smith from another. It's essential to give each row, or record, a unique identifier, and the author's ID serves this purpose here. Of course, it is not always necessary to introduce a column or columns specifically for this purpose. If your table already contains a column or combination of columns that will uniquely identify each row, then you can just use that.

Most of the data in the authors table is string information, so the VARCHAR data type was chosen as most convenient, since it allows as much or as little text information to be stored in that field as necessary. However, in practice it is likely to be more efficient to choose fixed-length character fields.

> Not all databases support VARCHAR. In such cases, you will have to define these fields as CHAR type anyway and estimate the maximum number of characters these fields will require. You'll be doing this a little later when you get to a final definition of the database tables to allow the same table definitions to work with Microsoft Access and other databases.

The next requirement is to be able to store information about books. One possibility is to store the data in the authors table using extra columns. If you wanted to store books in the authors table, you might consider adding two columns — title and publisher. However, this would seriously restrict the amount of information about books written by a particular author — to just one book in fact. Since each record in the authors table has a unique author ID, each author can have only one record in the table, and thus only one book could be recorded for each author. In practice, authors will frequently write more than one book or article, so you must have a way to cope with this. A much more realistic approach is to store books in a separate table.

Try It Out   Defining the Books Table

You can easily store information about individual books by creating a table that will store the following information:

Column Heading	Description
isbn	ISBN is a globally unique identifier for a book
title	Title of the book
pub_code	Code identifying the publisher of the book

You also need an SQL data type assignment for each column in our books table.

Column Heading	Data Type
isbn	VARCHAR
title	VARCHAR
pub_code	CHAR(8)

Here the publisher's code is a fixed-length character field. The other two fields vary in length so you have assigned VARCHAR as the most convenient type. Where this is not supported, you would have to use the CHAR type with a length sufficient to accommodate whatever data might turn up — something that is not always easy to decide.

How It Works

The books table allows you to record the ISBN for each book, which uniquely identifies the book, its title, and the publisher of the book. Notice, however, that I haven't included any information about the author. This isn't an oversight. Since more than one author can be involved in the writing of a book and an author can be involved in the writing of more than one book, you need to add some more information linking an author with a book that will be independent of the books table. Let's see how you might do that.

Designing an Intersection Table

It is not difficult to see that you could create the link between an author and a book by using the isbn (the book identifier) and the authid. If you create a table with these two pieces of information, you can make a record of each combination of authors and the books they authored or co-authored. This table is simple enough — it merely contains a column for the author identifier and the ISBN. The data types must match the corresponding columns in the authors and books tables:

Column Heading	Data Type
authid	INTEGER
isbn	VARCHAR

This table effectively provides links between the `authors` table and the `books` table. A table like this that links two or more tables is called an **intersection table** and is illustrated in Figure 24-4.

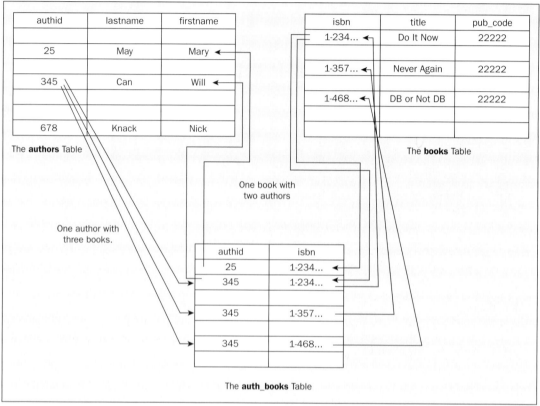

Figure 24-4

Now that you've decided on the design of the tables, let's see how you use SQL to create and add information to them. Rather than use the VARCHAR type for text fields, which is less widely supported, you'll use fixed-length CHAR types so that the database can be created in more environments. It may also be a bit more efficient.

SQL Statements

Most SQL statements, and certainly the ones you'll be using, fall neatly into two groups:

- ❑ **Data Definition Language (DDL)** statements that are used to describe the tables and the data they contain.

- ❑ **Data Manipulation Language (DML)** statements that are used to operate on data in the database. DML can be further divided into two groups:

  - ❑ **SELECT statements** — Statements that return a set of results
  - ❑ **Everything else** — Statements that don't return a set of results

To create the tables in the example, you would use DDL, which defines a syntax for commands such as CREATE TABLE and ALTER TABLE. You would use DDL statements to define the structure of the database. To carry out operations on the database — adding rows to a table or searching the data, for example — you would use DML statements.

Here's an example of a typical DDL statement:

```
CREATE TABLE authors (
   authid INT NOT NULL PRIMARY KEY,
   lastname CHAR(25) NOT NULL,
   firstname CHAR(15),
   address1 CHAR(25),
   address2 CHAR(25),
   city CHAR(25),
   state_prov CHAR(25),
   zipcode CHAR(10),
   country CHAR(15),
   phone CHAR(20),
   fax CHAR(20),
   email CHAR(25));
```

This is not dissimilar to the data type assignments that I described earlier, but as you can see, in this SQL statement I've used fixed-length CHAR fields rather than VARCHAR types. The values between parentheses are the number of characters in the field. Note that while it is not mandatory, by convention keywords in SQL are written in uppercase.

The clause NOT NULL PRIMARY KEY for the authid column tells the database two things. First, it indicates that no row of the table is allowed to contain a NULL value in this column. Every row in this column must always contain a valid value. Second, because this column is a primary key field, the database should create a unique index in the authid column. This ensures that there will be no more than one row with any given author ID. This greatly assists the database operations when searching through and ordering records. Think how difficult it would be to search for an entry in an encyclopedia without an index of unique values in one of the volumes.

This is the same principle on which database indexes work. Just to make sure you have some concrete information identifying an author, the lastname field is also not allowed to be NULL. Of course, all the tables in a database have to have unique names; otherwise, it would not be possible to determine to which table you were referring. The names for the columns within a table must all be different for the same reason, and it is also helpful if you give all the non-key columns in all the tables in the database unique names, but this is not mandatory.

Now that you have a table created, you need to put data into the table. The SQL INSERT statement does exactly that.

INSERT Statements

There are three basic parts to an **INSERT statement**:

- ❏   Defining the target table for inserting data
- ❏   Defining the columns that will have values assigned
- ❏   Defining the values for those columns

An INSERT statement begins with the keywords INSERT INTO, followed by the name of the target table:

```
INSERT INTO authors
```

You then supply a list of the names of the columns that will receive values, enclosed between parentheses:

```
(authid, lastname, firstname, email)
```

Lastly, you put the keyword VALUES followed by the values between parentheses for the columns you have identified:

```
VALUES (99, 'Phillips', 'Ron', 'ronp@happykitty.com')
```

Thus, the complete INSERT statement is:

```
INSERT INTO authors (authid, lastname, firstname, email)
        VALUES (99, 'Phillips', 'Ron', 'ronp@happykitty.com')
```

The result of executing this statement is a new row inserted into the authors table. This statement does not fill in values for every column in the table, however. The SQL database will supply a NULL value where no values were supplied by the INSERT statement. If you had attempted to insert a row without a value for authid, the database would have reported an error, since the table was created with the authid column specified as NOT NULL.

You can use a variation on the INSERT statement when all column values are being filled; when no columns are specified in an INSERT statement, SQL assumes that the values following the VALUES keyword correspond to each column in the order that they were specified when the table was created. For example, you could add a row to the books table with the following statement:

```
INSERT INTO books (isbn, title, pub_code)
    VALUES ('186100088X', 'Beginning Visual C++ 6', 'WROX')
```

Since the books table contains only the three columns, the following statement has exactly the same results:

```
INSERT INTO books
    VALUES ('186100088X', 'Beginning Visual C++ 6', 'WROX')
```

Note how I have been spreading the SQL statements over two lines, just for readability. Whitespace is ignored generally in SQL, except in the middle of a string, of course, so you can add whitespace wherever it helps to make your SQL code more readable.

Now, let's look at a basic SELECT statement, as this will provide a starting point for getting some data back from the database that you prepared earlier.

SELECT Statements

You use the SELECT statement to retrieve information from a database. There are four parts to an SQL SELECT statement:

- ❏ Defining what you want to retrieve

- ❏ Defining where you want to get it from

- ❏ Defining the conditions for retrieval — joining tables and record filtering

- ❏ Defining the order in which you want to see the data

So, how do you define what you want to retrieve? The first keyword in the SELECT statement, unsurprisingly, is SELECT. This tells the database that you intend to get some data back in the form of a **resultset**, sometimes referred to as a **recordset**. A **resultset** is just a table of data — with fixed numbers of columns and rows — that corresponds to some subset of data from a database table generated as a result of the SELECT statement.

The next identifier enables you to define what you want to see — it allows you to specify which columns you want to retrieve and to have as the resultset table headers. You specify each column name as part of a comma-separated list.

So the sample SELECT statement so far looks like this:

```
SELECT firstname, lastname, authid
```

You now have to specify which table you want to retrieve the data from. When creating a table, there is nothing to stop the developer giving similar column names to each table, so you must ensure that there are no ambiguities when selecting similar column names from two or more tables.

You specify the table or tables that you wish to retrieve data from in a **FROM clause**. This clause immediately follows the SELECT clause. A FROM clause consists of the keyword FROM, followed by a comma-separated list of tables that you wish to access:

```
FROM authors
```

Giving:

```
SELECT firstname, lastname, authid FROM authors
```

This is a complete statement that will retrieve the name, surname, and author ID from each row in the authors table.

When you retrieve a resultset from the database, each resultset column has a label that, by default, is derived from the column names in the SELECT statement. It is also possible to provide **aliases** for the table column names that are to be used for the resultset column names. Aliases are also referred to as **correlation names** and are often used so that column names can be abbreviated. Column aliases appear after the column names in the SELECT statement following the keyword AS. For example:

```
SELECT firstname, lastname, authid AS author_identifier
    FROM authors
```

would alias the authid as author_identifier. If you require an alias for a column name that includes whitespace, just put the alias between double quotes in the SELECT statement.

If you want to select all columns from a table in a SELECT statement, there is a wildcard notation you can use. You just specify the columns as * to indicate that you want to select all the columns in a table. For example, to select all the columns from the authors table you would write:

```
SELECT * FROM authors
```

Suppose you wanted to limit the rows returned by a SELECT operation to include only authors that reside within the UK. To accomplish that, you would add a WHERE clause. WHERE clauses are used to filter the set of rows produced as the result of a SELECT operation. For example, to get a list of authors in the UK:

```
SELECT lastname, firstname FROM authors
   WHERE country = 'UK'
```

You can also specify multiple criteria for row selection in a WHERE clause. For example, you might want to get a list of authors in the UK for whom an e-mail address is also on record:

```
SELECT lastname, firstname, phone FROM authors
   WHERE country = 'UK'
      AND email IS NOT NULL
```

Note the construction of the WHERE clause—there are two conditions that a row is required to satisfy before it will be returned. Firstly, the country field must contain a value that is equal to the string value UK, and the email field must not be NULL. If you wanted to find rows in which the field is NULL, you would omit the NOT.

Let's look at one final example of a SELECT statement—a **table join**. Suppose you want to see a list of all authors and the books they have written. You can write a statement that will return this information like this:

```
SELECT a.lastname, a.firstname, b.title
   FROM authors a, books b, auth_books ab
   WHERE a.authid = ab.authid
      AND b.isbn = ab.isbn
```

The table join appears in the first line of the WHERE clause; for each row, you specify the condition that the authid columns of the authors table and the auth_books table must be equal. You also specify that the isbn column of books and auth_books must be equal.

Notice also one small addition to the statement. As you saw earlier, you can alias table names by specifying an alternative name after each table identifier, or expression using the AS keyword. In this statement you are aliasing the table names in the FROM clause by simply putting the alias following the table name. The authors table is aliased as a, the books table is aliased as b, and the auth_books table is aliased as ab. Back in the first part of the SELECT statement, the column names are "qualified" by the aliases for each table. This is how column name ambiguities are removed. Since the authid column name appears in more than one table, if you did not have a qualifier in front of each usage of the authid column name, the database engine would have no way of knowing from which table the column was required. Note that if you specify an alias in the FROM clause, column names in the WHERE clause must be qualified with the appropriate table alias.

UPDATE Statements

UPDATE statements provide a way of modifying existing data in a table. Update statements are constructed in a similar way to SELECT statements. You first start with the UPDATE keyword, followed by the name of the table you wish to modify:

```
UPDATE authors
```

You then specify the SET keyword and the data members you wish to modify with their new values:

```
SET lastname = 'Burk'
```

Finally, the WHERE clause is used to filter the records that you wish to update. An UPDATE statement cannot be performed across a table join, so the WHERE clause is not used to specify a join of this type.

```
WHERE authid = 27
```

The full statement:

```
UPDATE authors SET lastname = 'Burk' WHERE authid = 27
```

will update the author record to reflect a change in last name for the author with the ID of 27.

UPDATE statements do not return a resultset, they merely modify data in the database.

Delete Statements

DELETE statements provide a way of deleting particular rows from tables in a database. DELETE statements consist of the DELETE keyword, a FROM clause, and a WHERE clause. For example:

```
DELETE FROM books WHERE isbn = '0131259075'
```

deletes the record in the books table with the ISBN value '0131259075'. In the case of the books table, there can only be one row with this value, since its primary key is the ISBN. If a similar DELETE statement were executed against the auth_books table, however, it would delete all rows with the matching ISBN value.

By now you should have a reasonably clear idea of:

- ❑ The way SQL is constructed
- ❑ How to read SQL statements
- ❑ How to construct basic SQL statements

> You can expect SQL statements to work with relational databases that adhere to ANSI standards, although each database typically implements a subset of the full standard. For this reason, you always need to understand the functionality of the SQL that is used by the underlying database you are using, as this will affect the way you use JDBC to write your Java applications.

The JDBC Package

The JDBC library was designed as an interface for executing SQL statements, and not as a high-level abstraction layer for data access. So, although it wasn't designed to automatically map Java classes to rows in a database, it allows large-scale applications to be written to the JDBC interface without worrying too much about which database will be deployed with the application. A JDBC application is well insulated from the particular characteristics of the database system being used and therefore doesn't have to be re-engineered for specific databases. From the user's point of view, a Java application working with a database looks conceptually as shown in Figure 24-5.

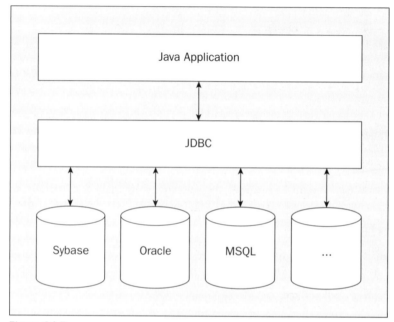

Figure 24-5

JDBC manages to operate with a variety of different relational database systems by having an implementation of the JDBC interface for each specific database—a driver. This handles the mapping of Java method calls in the JDBC classes to the database API. You'll learn more about this later on.

Relating JDBC to ODBC

One of the fundamental principles of JDBC's design was to make it practical to build JDBC drivers based on other database APIs. There is a very close mapping between the JDBC architecture and API and the **O**pen **D**ata**B**ase **C**onnectivity (ODBC) counterparts, fundamentally because they are all based on the same standard, the SQL X/Open CLI; but JDBC is a lot easier to use. Because of their common ancestry, they share some important conceptual components:

Driver Manager	Loads database drivers and manages the connections between the application and the driver
Driver	Translates API calls into operations for a specific data source
Connection	A session between an application and a database
Statement	A SQL statement to perform a query or update operation
Metadata	Information about returned data, the database, and the driver
Resultset	Logical set of columns and rows of data returned by executing a statement

JDBC Basics

Assuming you have followed the instructions given at the start of the chapter, and have the requisite sample database and database driver installed on your machine, you are ready to look at a basic JDBC program that involves the following steps:

1. Import the necessary classes.
2. Load the JDBC driver.
3. Identify the data source.
4. Allocate a `Connection` object.
5. Allocate a `Statement` object.
6. Execute a query using the `Statement` object.
7. Retrieve data from the returned `ResultSet` object.
8. Close the `ResultSet`.
9. Close the `Statement` object.
10. Close the `Connection` object.

Throughout this chapter you will work toward accumulating a sufficient understanding of JDBC to implement the essential elements of such a program.

The JDBC architecture is based on a collection of Java interfaces and classes that together enable you to connect to data sources, to create and execute SQL statements, and to retrieve and modify data in a database. These operations are illustrated in Figure 24-6.

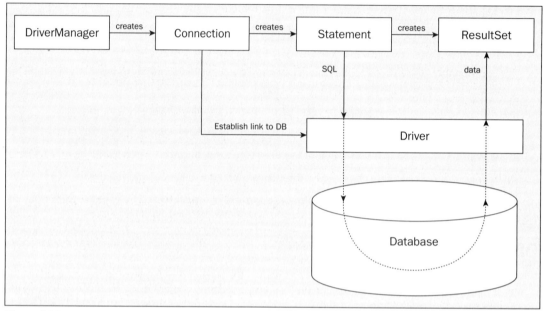

Figure 24-6

Each of the boxes in Figure 24-6 represents a JDBC class or interface that has a fundamental role in accessing a relational database. All your work with JDBC will begin with the java.sql.DriverManager class, but before you look at that, let's set up the technical_library database so that you will be ready to use it as you progress.

Setting Up a Database

Before you get started on learning about the DriverManager class, it's worthwhile setting up a sample database and a suitable JDBC driver for our code to use. The database is called technical_library, and it stores information on technical books that you might have in your library. This is implemented as a Microsoft Access 2000 database, and you can download it together with the sample code from the book from the Wrox web site.

In Microsoft Windows, to use this database with the application that you are going to construct in this chapter, you can set up an Access database driver for the database in the ODBC Data Source Administrator dialog box, which can be found by selecting Start| Settings | Control Panel and then double-clicking the ODBC Data Sources icon. Select the System DSN tab at the top of the dialog box, and click the Add... button at the right. In the list box that comes up, select Microsoft Access Driver (*.mdb) and then click Finish. A further dialog box will then come up with the title ODBC Microsoft Access Setup. In the Data Source Name text box at the top of the dialog, type in technical_library. Type in a suitable description in the Description text field if you wish. In the Database section of the dialog, click the

Select button, and in the file browsing dialog box that comes up, find and select your saved version of technical_library.mdb; then click OK. Now click OK in the ODBC Microsoft Access Setup dialog. The System DSN section of the initial ODBC Data Source Administrator dialog should now have technical_library in the list of system data sources available. Click the OK button at the bottom of the dialog to exit. Barring unforeseen problems, you should now be able to use this database with the programs in this chapter.

If you're working with a database program other than Access, you will need to obtain an appropriate driver for it if you do not already have one. An up-to-date list of suitable drivers for various databases can be found at http://servlet.java.sun.com/products/jdbc/drivers. If you have a database other than Access and the correct driver is already set up, you can use a small Java class, build_tables, that is also included with the book's code, to create the sample database's tables.

If you are using something other than Access, you may need to edit the first few lines of the source file to use the appropriate database driver, and possibly edit the data defining the String array of SQL statements to accommodate the data types used by your database system. It is quite common for database systems not to support all of the SQL capabilities defined by the ANSI standard. If you have no luck getting the sample database up and running first time around, try reading on in this chapter and then re-reading your driver and database documentation before having another go. Once you have a suitable database and JDBC driver installed, you can try running the InteractiveSQL program that you'll be using in this chapter to show how to send commands to a database. You'll build the application at the end of this chapter, by which time its workings should be plain to you.

> **In all the examples you will write in this chapter, you'll be using the JDBC-ODBC Bridge driver** — sun.jdbc.odbc.JdbcOdbcDriver — **to access the MS Access 2000 database** technical_library.mdb **that I've assumed has been set up with a Microsoft Access ODBC driver as described in the section earlier.**

DriverManager

JDBC database drivers are defined by classes that implement the Driver interface. The DriverManager class is responsible for establishing connections to the data sources that you want to access through the JDBC drivers. If any JDBC driver has been identified in the "jdbc.drivers" system property (see later in this section) on your computer, then the DriverManager class will attempt to load that when it is loaded.

The system properties are actually stored in a Properties object. The java.util.Properties class associates values with keys in a map, and the contents of the map defines a set of system properties. In general, each key is supplied as a String and the value corresponding to a key can be any valid object. Thus, you can use a Properties object to supply as much information as is required by your driver — or anything else that interacts with the system properties for that matter. You just set the key/value pairs for the Properties object that are needed.

You can set the "jdbc.drivers" system property by calling the setProperty() method for the System class, for example:

```
System.setProperty("jdbc.drivers","sun.jdbc.odbc.JdbcOdbcDriver");
```

The first argument is the key for the property to be set and the second argument is the value. This statement identifies the JDBC-ODBC Bridge driver in the system property. This driver supports connections to any ODBC-supported database. If you want to specify multiple drivers in the system property value, you should separate the driver names within the string by colons.

If the security manager permits it, you can obtain a reference to the `Properties` object for your system by calling the static `getProperties()` method for the `System` class. If there is no `Properties` object defined containing the system properties, one will be created with a default set of properties. The `Properties` class defines a `list()` method that you can use to list all your system properties as follows:

```
System.getProperties().list(System.out);    // List all properties
```

You could try this out in a simple program of your own if you want to see what your system properties are. The `Properties` class also defines a `setProperty()` method, so once you have a `Properties` object, you can set properties directly by calling this method for the object.

If a security manager is in effect and a security policy has been set up on your system, it may be that you will not be allowed to set the system property, in which case the `setProperty()` call will throw an exception of type `SecurityException`. In this situation, to include the driver that you want to use, you can load the driver explicitly by calling the static `forName()` method in the `Class` class and passing a `String` object as an argument containing the driver class name. For example:

```
Class.forName("sun.jdbc.odbc.JdbcOdbcDriver");    // Load the ODBC driver
```

The `forName()` method can throw an exception of type `ClassNotFoundException` if the driver class cannot be found, and this must be caught; so a call to the function has to appear in a `try` block with an appropriate `catch` block.

Each driver class will typically create an instance of itself when it is loaded, and register that instance by calling the `DriverManager` class method automatically. You don't need to—indeed you can't—create `DriverManager` objects, and all the methods in the `DriverManager` class are `static`. There are `DriverManager` class methods that can be used to determine which drivers have been loaded, as well as methods that register or unregister drivers "on the fly." However, for the most part you will need to call only the method that establishes a connection to a data source.

When you need a connection to a JDBC driver, you don't create a new object encapsulating the connection yourself—you ask the `DriverManager` to do it for you. The `DriverManager` class provides several `static` methods for creating objects that implement the `Connection` interface and encapsulate a connection to a database. These are all overloaded versions of the `getConnection()` method.

Creating a Connection to a Data Source

A connection to a specific data source is represented by an object of a class that implements the `java.sql.Connection` interface. Before you can execute any SQL statements, you must first have a `Connection` object. A `Connection` object represents an established connection to a particular data source, and you use it to create a `java.sql.Statement` object that enables you to define and execute specific SQL statements. A `Connection` object can also be used to query the data source for information about the data in the database (the metadata), including the names of the available tables, information about the columns for a particular table, and so on.

There are three overloaded `getConnection()` methods in the `DriverManager` class that return a `Connection` object. In the simplest case you can obtain a `Connection` object that represents a session for your database with the following statement:

```
Connection databaseConnection = DriverManager.getConnection(source);
```

The argument, `source`, is a `String` object defining the URL that identifies where the database is located. Note that this is a `String` object specifying the URL, not an object of the `URL` class that you have seen earlier.

URLs and JDBC

A URL references an electronic resource, such as a World Wide Web page or a file on an FTP server, in a manner that uniquely identifies that resource. URLs play a central role in networked application development in Java. JDBC uses URLs to identify the locations of both drivers and data sources. JDBC URLs have the following format:

```
jdbc:subprotocol:data_source_identifier
```

The scheme `jdbc` indicates that the URL refers to a JDBC data source. The sub-protocol identifies which JDBC driver to use. For example, the JDBC-ODBC Bridge uses the driver identifier `odbc`.

The JDBC driver dictates the format of the data source identifier. In the previous example, the JDBC-ODBC Bridge simply uses the ODBC data source name. To use the ODBC driver with the `technical_library` ODBC data source, you would create a URL with the following format:

```
jdbc:odbc:technical_library
```

The next step to getting data to or from a database is to create a `Connection` object. The `Connection` object essentially establishes a context in which you can create and execute SQL commands. Since the data source that you will use in this chapter's examples doesn't require a user name or password, the simplest form of the `getConnection()` method can be used.

You could exercise the `getConnection()` method in a working example.

Try It Out   Making a Connection

The following source code is a minimal JDBC program that creates a `Connection` object. In this instance the connection will be established using only the URL for the data source. In the next section you'll look at how you can also supply a user ID and a password when this is necessary.

```java
import java.sql.Connection;
import java.sql.DriverManager;
import java.sql.SQLException;

public class MakingTheConnection {
  public static void main(String[] args) {
    // Load the driver
    try {
      // Load the driver class
      Class.forName("sun.jdbc.odbc.JdbcOdbcDriver");

      // Define the data source for the driver
```

```
        String sourceURL = "jdbc:odbc:technical_library";

        // Create a connection through the DriverManager
        Connection databaseConnection = DriverManager.getConnection(sourceURL);
        System.out.println("Connection is: "+databaseConnection);
      } catch(ClassNotFoundException cnfe) {
        System.err.println(cnfe);
      } catch(SQLException sqle) {
        System.err.println(sqle);
      }
   }
}
```

This should output a line something like the following:

```
Connection is: sun.jdbc.odbc.JdbcOdbcConnection@4a5ab2
```

How It Works

As usual, you import the class and interface names that you use in the program—in this case they are all from the `java.sql` package. The `forName()` method call at the beginning of `main()` ensures that the JDBC driver class required by our program is loaded. This guarantees that any initialization that the JDBC driver must do will be completed before your code actually uses the driver. As I said earlier, the `forName()` method will throw a `ClassNotFoundException` if the driver class cannot be found, and this exception must be caught.

The `forName()` method call causes the Java interpreter's class loader to load the class for the driver specified by the argument. When the driver class is loaded, the class loader will determine if the driver class has any `static` initialization code. If it does, it will execute the `static` initialization code immediately after the class has been loaded. That is how the driver class is able to instantiate itself and register the instance that is created with the `DriverManager` object. It can also execute other initialization code that may be required, such as loading a dynamic link library if the driver uses native methods, for example, and since this all happens when the class is loaded, it is guaranteed to happen before any other driver methods are called.

Most JDBC methods handle errors by throwing an exception of type `SQLException`, and the `getConnection()` method of the `DriverManager` class does exactly that, so you also have a `catch` block that handles the `SQLException` exception. In this example, a simple message will be displayed in the event of a problem loading the JDBC driver or creating a `Connection` to the data source. In the next chapter, you will learn more sophisticated error-handling techniques.

More Complex Connections

If the database requires a user name and password to gain access to it, you can use the second form of the `getConnection()` method:

```
databaseConnection = DriverManager.getConnection(sourceURL,
                                       myUserName,
                                       myPassword);
```

All three arguments here are of type `String`. In some cases, however, the user name and password may not be enough to establish a connection. To accommodate those situations, the `DriverManager` class provides another `getConnection()` method that accepts a `Properties` object as an argument.

To supply the properties required by your JDBC driver, you can create a `Properties` object using the default class constructor and then set the properties that you need by calling its `setProperty()` method. In general, at least the user name and password need to be set.

The code fragment below illustrates creation of a connection for the JBDC driver for ODBC:

```
import java.util.Properties;

// ...

    String driverName = "sun.jdbc.odbc.JdbcOdbcDriver";
    String sourceURL = "jdbc.odbc:technical_library";

    try {
      Class.forName (driverName);
      Properties prop = new Properties();
      prop.setProperty("user", "ItIsMe");
      prop.setProperty("password", "abracadabra");
      Connection databaseConnection = DriverManager.getConnection(sourceURL, prop);
    } catch(ClassNotFoundException cnfe) {
      System.err.println("Error loading " + driverName);
    } catch(SQLException sqle) {
      System.err.println(sqle);
    }
```

Of course, you'll also need to import the `Properties` class name from the `java.util` package.

While this pretty much covers everything that most developers will ever do to establish a connection to a data source, the `DriverManager` class defines other static methods that may be useful. You'll take a look at these next.

Logging JDBC Driver Operations

The `DriverManager` class provides a pair of access methods for the `PrintWriter` object that is used by the `DriverManager` class and all JDBC drivers to record logging and trace information. These allow you to set, or reroute, the `java.io.PrintWriter` that the driver uses to log information. The two access methods are:

```
public static void setLogWriter(PrintWriter out)
public static PrintWriter getLogWriter()
```

You can disable logging by passing a `null` argument to the `setLogWriter()` method.

Examining the log can be pretty interesting. If you want to find out what's going on behind the scenes, take a look at the information generated by the JDBC-ODBC driver. You'll get a very good idea of how that driver works.

Your application can write to the `PrintWriter` stream using the static `println()` method that is defined in the `DriverManager` class. Just pass a `String` object as an argument containing the message you want to record in the log. This method is typically used by JDBC drivers, but it may prove useful for debugging or logging database-related errors or events.

Setting the Login Timeout

The `DriverManager` class provides a pair of access methods for the login timeout period. These allow you to specify a timeout period (in seconds) that limits the time that a driver is prepared to wait for logging in to the database. The two access methods are:

`setLoginTimeout(int secs)`	Sets the maximum time the driver will wait to connect to a database to `secs` seconds
`getLoginTimeout()`	Returns the number of seconds that the driver is prepared to wait to establish a connection to a database as a value of type `int`

Specifying a non-default timeout period can be useful for troubleshooting applications that are having difficulty connecting to a remote database server. For example, if your application is trying to connect to a very busy server, the application might appear to have hung. You can tell the `DriverManager` to fail the connection attempt by specifying a timeout period. The code fragment below tells the `DriverManager` to fail the login attempt after 60 seconds:

```
String driverName = "sun.jdbc.odbc.JdbcOdbcDriver";
String sourceURL =  "jdbc:odbc:technical_library";
try {
  Class.forName(driverName);

  DriverManager.setLoginTimeout(60);              // fail after 60 seconds
  Connection databaseConnection = DriverManager.getConnection(sourceURL);
} catch(ClassNotFoundException cnfe) {
  System.err.println("Error loading " + driverName);
} catch(SQLException sqle) {
  System.err.println(sqle);
}
```

More on Drivers

When the `DriverManager` class has been loaded, it is then possible to connect to a data source using a particular driver. A driver is represented by an object of type `java.sql.Driver`. Driver implementations come in four flavors:

- ❏   JDBC-ODBC Bridge driver
- ❏   Native API/partly Java

❑ Net protocol all-Java client

❑ Native protocol all-Java

Understanding a little of how drivers are built, and their limitations, will help you to decide which driver is most appropriate for your application.

JDBC-ODBC Bridge Driver

The JDBC-ODBC Bridge— `"sun.jdbc.odbc.JdbcOdbcDriver"` —is included with the JDK, and it enables Java applications to access data through drivers written to the ODBC standard. The driver bridge is very useful for accessing data in data sources for which no pure JDBC drivers exist.

The bridge works by translating the JDBC methods into ODBC function calls. It has the advantage of working with a huge number of ODBC drivers, but it works only under the Microsoft Windows and Sun Solaris operating systems.

Native API/Partly Java Driver

This class of driver is quite similar to the bridge driver. It consists of Java code that accesses data through native methods — typically, calls to a particular vendor library. Like the bridge driver, this class of driver is convenient when a C data access library already exists, but it isn't usually very portable across platforms.

Net Protocol All-Java Client

This class of driver is implemented as "middleware," with the client driver completely implemented in Java. This client driver communicates with a separate middleware component (usually through TCP/IP), which translates JDBC requests into database access calls. This form of driver is an extension of the previous class, with the Java and native API separated into separate client and proxy processes.

Native Protocol All-Java

This class of driver communicates directly to the database server using the server's native protocol. Unlike the previous driver type, there is no translation step that converts the Java-initiated request into some other form. The client talks directly to the server. If this class of driver is available for your database, then this is the one you should use.

> **A large number of JDBC drivers are available. As I mentioned earlier, the best source of up-to-date information about JDBC drivers is from the JavaSoft JDBC drivers page on Java's web site:** `http://servlet.java.sun.com/products/jdbc/drivers`.

The only time that you are likely to come into contact with the `Driver` object is when you install it. Your applications need not ever interact directly with the `Driver` object itself since the `DriverManager` class takes care of all such communications. When you call the `getConnection()` method of the

DriverManager class, it iterates through the drivers that are registered with the DriverManager and asks each one in turn if it can handle the URL that you have passed to it. The first driver that can satisfy the connection defined by the URL creates a Connection object, which is passed back to the application by way of the DriverManager (see Figure 24-7).

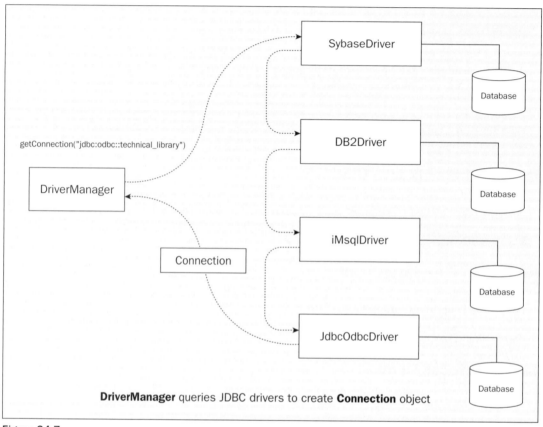

Figure 24-7

There are occasions, however, when you may want to query a specific driver for information, such as its version number. For example, you may know that a particular feature that your program makes use of wasn't incorporated into a driver until version 2.1. You can query the driver to get the version number so your program can handle an earlier version intelligently.

To get the Driver object, you call the static getDriver() method that is defined in the DriverManager class, passing the URL of the data source to it as the argument. If the DriverManager finds a driver that can accommodate the data source, the method returns a reference to a Driver object encapsulating it. The code fragment below illustrates testing the version of a JDBC driver, looking for versions that are 1.1 or greater:

```
// Load the driver class
Class.forName("sun.jdbc.odbc.JdbcOdbcDriver");

// Define the data source for the driver
String sourceURL = "jdbc:odbc:technical_library";

// Test for driver version
int verMajor = 0;                              // Major version number
float verComplete = 0.0f;                      // Complete version number
float verPreferred = 1.1f;                     // The minimum preferred version


Driver theDriver = DriverManager.getDriver(sourceURL); // Set the driver

// Get the version number to the left of the decimal point, e.g. 1 out of 1.0
verMajor = theDriver.getMajorVersion();

// Make the complete version number type float by adding the minor number
// to verMajor (to the right of the decimal point, e.g. 1108 out of 1.1108)
verComplete = Float.parseFloat(verMajor + "." + theDriver.getMinorVersion());

// Test to see if we have a suitable version of the driver
if(verComplete >= verPreferred) {
    System.out.println("Version " + verComplete + " found");
    //Make the connection...
} else {
    System.out.println("Required version of driver (" +
            verPreferred + ") not found");
    // Otherwise drop out...
}
```

In practice, you could do a lot more that just output messages, depending on the version of the driver that is available. Your program might choose to operate differently to account for the limitations of an earlier version, for example.

Statement Objects

A `java.sql.Statement` object is an object of a class that implements the `Statement` interface. When a `Statement` object is created, it provides a workspace for you to create an SQL query, execute it, and retrieve any results that are returned. You can also assemble multiple SQL statements into a batch, and submit them for processing as a batch to the database.

`Statement` objects are created by calling the `createStatement()` method of a valid `Connection` object. Once you have created a `Statement` object, you can use it to execute an SQL query by calling the `executeQuery()` method for your `Statement` object. You pass a `String` object containing the text of your SQL query as the argument to the method.

The resultset from the query is returned as an object of type `java.sql.ResultSet`. For example, if you have a `Statement` object, `statement`, you could write:

```
ResultSet results = statement.executeQuery(
                        "SELECT lastname, firstname FROM authors");
```

This will execute the SELECT statement that appears as the argument.

When you want to batch several SQL statements, you call the addBatch() method in the Statement object for each of them, passing a String object containing an SQL statement as the argument. When you finally want to execute the batch of SQL that you have created, you call the executeBatch() method for the statement object. To clear the batch of statements in readiness for a new set, you call the clearBatch() method for the Statement object. Because a batch of SQL statements can generate multiple resultsets, accessing them is a little complicated. It involves calling the getResultSet() method for the Statement object to retrieve the first resultset and then using getXXX() methods for the object reference that is returned to access the contents. To move to the next resultset, you call getMoreResults() for the Statement object. This returns true if the next result is another resultset and false if the next result is not a resultset or there are no more results. You can then call getResultSet() again to obtain a reference to the next resultset if there is one. This is a relatively rare requirement, so I won't go into further detail on this.

JDBC provides two other kinds of objects that you can use to execute SQL statements. These objects implement interfaces that are subinterfaces of the Statement interface—the java.sql.Prepared Statement interface, which extends the Statement interface, and the java.sql.CallableStatement interface, which extends the PreparedStatement interface.

You obtain a reference to a PreparedStatement object by calling the prepareStatement() method for a Connection object. In the simplest case, you just pass a String object specifying the text of an SQL statement as the argument to the prepareStatement() method, but there is a more complex version of the method that provides you with more control over the resultset that is produced. PreparedStatement objects differ from Statement objects in that the SQL statement is pre-compiled and can have placeholders for runtime parameter values. PreparedStatement objects are particularly useful when a statement will be executed many times (for example, when you are adding a large number of new rows to a table), since substantial performance gains can be achieved in many cases.

This is due to the fact that a prepared statement is parsed once and reused, whereas the SQL for a Statement object has to be parsed by the server each time it is executed. PreparedStatement objects are also helpful when it is not convenient to create a single string containing the entire SQL statement. You'll see an example later in this chapter that will show the same SQL statement executed via both Statement and PreparedStatement objects.

A CallableStatement reference is returned by the prepareCall() method for a Connection object. There are two overloaded versions of this method, one requiring a single String JDBC-ODBC Bridge argument that defines the SQL for the stored procedure, and the other with additional parameters providing more control over the resultset that is produced. You use a CallableStatement object for calling procedures on the database. As I said earlier, many database engines have the ability to execute procedures on the database. This allows business logic and rules to be defined at the server level, rather than relying on applications to replicate and enforce those rules.

Whichever type of Statement reference you are using, the results of an SQL query are always returned in the same way, so let's look at that.

ResultSet Objects

The results of executing an SQL query are returned in the form of an object that implements the ResultSet interface and contains the table produced by the SQL query. The ResultSet object contains something called a **cursor** that you can manipulate to refer to any particular row in the resultset. This initially points to a position immediately preceding the first row. Calling the `next()` method for the `ResultSet` object will move the cursor to the next position. You can reset the cursor to the first or last row at any time by calling the `first()` or `last()` method for the `ResultSet` object. You also have methods `beforeFirst()` and `afterLast()` to set the cursor position before the first row or after the last. The `previous()` method for the `ResultSet` object moves the cursor from its current position to the previous row. This ability to scroll backwards through a resultset is dependent on your database and whether your driver supports this capability.

Usually you will want to process rows from a resultset in a loop, and you have a couple of ways to do this. Both the `next()` and `previous()` methods return `true` if the move is to a valid row and `false` if you fall off the end, so you can use this to control a `while` loop. You could process all the rows in a resultset with the following loop:

```
while(resultset.next()) {
    // Process the row...
}
```

This code fragment assumes that `resultset` is the object returned as a result of executing a query and the `resultset` object starts out in its default state with the cursor set to 1 before the first row. You can also use the `isLast()` or `isFirst()` methods to test whether you have reached the end or the beginning of the resultset.

Now you know how to get at the rows in a resultset; let's look into how you access the fields in a row.

Accessing Data in a Resultset

Using the `ResultSet` reference, you can retrieve the value of any column for the current row (as specified by the cursor) by name or by position. You can also determine information about the columns, such as the number of columns returned or the data types of columns. The `ResultSet` interface declares the following basic methods for retrieving column data for the current row as Java types:

getAsciiStream()	getTimestamp()	getTime()
getBoolean()	getBinaryStream()	getString()
getDate()	getBytes()	getByte()
getInt()	getFloat()	getDouble()
getShort()	getObject()	getLong()

Note that this is not a comprehensive list, but it is not likely you will need to know about the others. For a full list of the methods available take a look at the documentation for the `ResultSet` interface. There are overloaded versions of each of the methods shown in the preceding table that provide two ways of identifying the column containing the data. The column can be selected by passing the SQL column name as a `String` argument or by passing an index value for the column of type `int`, where the first column has the index value 1. Note that column names are not case-sensitive so `"FirstName"` is the same as `"firstname"`.

The `getDate()`, `getTime()`, and `getTimestamp()` methods return objects of type `java.sql.Date`, `java.sql.Time`, and `java.sql.TimeStamp`, respectively. The `getAsciiStream()` method returns an object of type `java.io.InputStream` that you can use to read the data as a stream of ASCII characters. This is primarily for use with values of the SQL type LONGVARCHAR, which can be very long strings that you would probably want to read piecemeal. Most of the basic data access methods are very flexible in converting from SQL data types to Java data types. For example, if you use `getInt()` on a field of type CHAR, the method will attempt to parse the characters assuming they specify an integer. Equally, you can read numeric SQL types using the `getString()` method.

With all these methods, an absence of a value, which is an SQL NULL, is returned either as the equivalent of zero, or as `null` if an object reference is returned. Thus a NULL boolean field will return `false`, and a NULL numeric field will return 0. If a database access error occurs when executing a `getXXX()` method for a resultset, an exception of type `SQLException` will be thrown.

The JDBC API provides access to metadata not only for the `Connection` object, but also for the `ResultSet` object. The JDBC API provides a `ResultSetMetaData` object that lets you peek into the data behind the `ResultSet` object. If you plan on providing interactive browsing facilities in your JDBC applications, you'll find this particularly useful and you'll see how to do this later.

Together, these classes and interfaces make up the bulk of the JDBC components that you will be working with. Let's now put them into action with a simple example.

Try It Out   Using a Connection

You'll do something useful with the `Connection` object created by changing our `MakingTheConnection` class into a new class for accessing the `technical_library` database. The code for this example is shown below:

```java
import java.sql.Connection;
import java.sql.DriverManager;
import java.sql.SQLException;
import java.sql.Statement;
import java.sql.ResultSet;

public class MakingAStatement {
  public static void main(String[] args) {
    // Load the driver
    try {
      // Load the driver class
      Class.forName("sun.jdbc.odbc.JdbcOdbcDriver");

      // This defines the data source for the driver
      String sourceURL = new String("jdbc:odbc:technical_library");

      // Create connection through the DriverManager
      Connection databaseConnection =
                          DriverManager.getConnection(sourceURL);

      Statement statement = databaseConnection.createStatement();
      ResultSet authorNames = statement.executeQuery(
                          "SELECT lastname, firstname FROM authors");

      // Output the resultset data
      while(authorNames.next()) {
```

```
                System.out.println(authorNames.getString("lastname")+" "+
                                        authorNames.getString("firstname"));
        }
    } catch(ClassNotFoundException cnfe) {
        System.err.println(cnfe);
    } catch(SQLException sqle) {
        System.err.println(sqle);
    }
  }
}
```

You can save this as `MakingAStatement.java`. This program will list all the author names, one author to a line, with the last name first on each line.

How It Works

Once the connection has been established by the `getConnection()` method call, the next step is to create a `Statement` object that enables you to execute an SQL statement and retrieve the results. To create a `Statement` object you simply call the `createStatement()` method for the `Connection` object.

Once you have created the `statement` object, you execute an SQL query against the connected database by passing a `String` object as the argument to the `executeQuery()` method for the `statement` object. The `executeQuery()` method returns an object that implements the `ResultSet` interface. As the name implies, the `ResultSet` interface enables you to get at information that was retrieved by the query. You can think of the `ResultSet` interface as providing row-at-a-time access to a virtual table of results. The `ResultSet` object provides an internal **cursor** or logical pointer to keep track of its current row. When the `ResultSet` is first returned, the cursor is positioned just before the first row of data. This mechanism is illustrated in Figure 24-8.

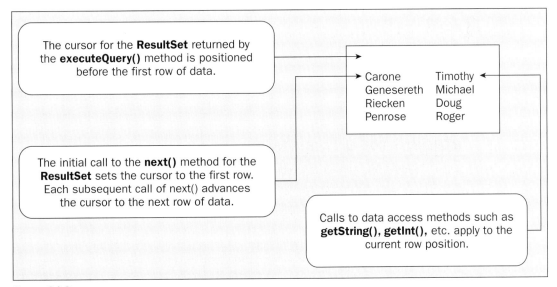

Figure 24-8

After executing the query, the row position needs to be advanced by calling the next() method before any column data can be accessed, and you do this in the while loop condition. The next() method advances the row position and returns a boolean value indicating whether the ResultSet is positioned at a valid row (true) or there are no more rows (false). Thus, the while loop continues until you have output the data from all the rows in the authorNames resultset.

Within the while loop, you access the data in the columns using the getString() method for the ResultSet object. In both cases you use the column names to reference the column. Accessing the columns by name has the advantage that you don't need to know the order of the columns. On the other hand, you do need to know the column names. If you wanted to process the columns by their index position, you would just use the index values 1 and 2 to refer to data in the first and second columns, respectively. Using the column position is slightly faster than using the column name since there is no additional overhead in matching a column name to determine a particular column position. It can also be more convenient to refer to columns using their position when you want to identify the column by means of an expression.

Note that the rows in the resultset are not ordered. If you want to output the rows in lastname order, you need to change the SQL statement to sort the rows, as follows:

```
ResultSet authorNames = statement.executeQuery(
                "SELECT lastname, firstname FROM authors ORDER BY lastname");
```

The rows in the resultset will be sorted in lastname order — in ascending sequence by default. To sort in descending sequence you should add the keyword DESC to the end of the SQL statement. You can sort on multiple columns by separating the column names by commas. The sorting applies to the columns successively from left to right, so if you specify the sort columns as lastname, firstname in the SELECT statement, then the rows in the resultset will be ordered by lastname, and where two last names are the same, by first name. For example, if you want the rows in the resultset authorNames to be sorted in descending sequence, you could write:

```
ResultSet authorNames = statement.executeQuery(
            "SELECT lastname, firstname FROM authors
                ORDER BY lastname DESC, firstname DESC");
```

Note that you must supply the DESC keyword for each column name to which you want to apply it. If you omit it for a column, the default ascending sequence will apply.

Getting Metadata for a Resultset

The getMetaData() method for a ResultSet object returns a reference to an object of type java.sql.ResultSetMetaData that encapsulates the metadata for the resultset. The ResultSetMetaData interface declares methods that enable you to get items of metadata for the resultset.

The getColumnCount() method returns the number of columns in the resultset as a value of type int. For each column, you can get the column name and column type by calling the getColumnName() and getColumnType() methods, respectively. In both cases you specify the column by its index value. The column name is returned as a String object, and the column type is returned as a value of type int that identifies the SQL type. The Types class in the java.sql package defines public fields of type int that identify the SQL types, and the names of these class data members are the same as the SQL types they represent — such as CHAR, VARCHAR, DOUBLE, INT, TIME, and so on. Thus, you could list the names of the columns in a resultset that were of type CHAR with the following code:

```
ResultSetMetaData metadata = results.getMetaData();
int columns = metadata.getColumnCount();              // Get number of columns

for(int i = 1 ; i<= columns ; i++) {                  // For each column
  if(metadata.getColumnType(i) == Types.CHAR) {       // if it is CHAR
     System.out.println(metadata.getColumnName(i));   // display the name
  }
}
```

You could output the data value of each row of a ResultSet object results that was of SQL type CHAR with the following code:

```
ResultSetMetaData metadata = results.getMetaData();
int columns = metadata.getColumnCount();              // Get number of columns

int row = 0;                                          // Row number
while(results.next()) {                               // For each row
  System.out.print("\nRow "+(++row)+":");             // increment row count
  for(int i = 1 ; i<= columns ; i++)                  // For each column
    if(metadata.getColumnType(i) == Types.CHAR) {     // if it is CHAR display it
       System.out.print(" "+results.getString(i));
    }
}
```

You can also get the type name for a column as a String by calling the getColumnTypeName() method with the column number as the argument. Another very useful method is getColumnDisplaySize(), which returns the normal maximum number of characters required to display the data stored in the column. You pass the index number of the column that you are interested in as the argument. The return value is type int. You can use this to help format the output of column data.

A whole range of other methods supplies other metadata for a resultset, and you will find those methods in the documentation for the ResultSetMetaData interface. Here's a list of a few more that you may find useful — they all require an argument that is the column number as type int:

getTableName()	Returns the table name for the column as type String
getColumnLabel()	Returns a String object that is the suggested label for a column for use in printouts
getPrecision()	Returns the number of decimal digits for a column as type int
getScale()	Returns the number of decimal digits to the right of the decimal point for a column as type int
isSigned()	Returns true if the column contains signed numbers
isCurrency()	Returns true if the column contains currency values

Table continued on following page

isNullable()	Returns an int value that can be:
	columnNoNulls indicating NULL is not allowed
	columnNullable indicating NULL is allowed
	columnNullableUnknown indicating it is not known if NULL is allowed
isWritable()	Returns true if a write on the column is likely to succeed

The Essential JDBC Program

You now have all the pieces to make up the essential JDBC program, one that will initialize the environment, create Connection and Statement objects, and retrieve data by both position and column name.

Try It Out   Putting It All Together

This application will execute two queries, one that selects specific columns by name and another that selects all columns. First you'll define the application class in outline, with the data members and the main() function and the other methods in the class:

```
import java.sql.Connection;
import java.sql.Statement;
import java.sql.DriverManager;
import java.sql.ResultSet;
import java.sql.ResultSetMetaData;
import java.sql.SQLException;

public class EssentialJDBC {

  public static void main (String[] args) {
    EssentialJDBC SQLExample = new EssentialJDBC();    // Create application object

    SQLExample.getResultsByColumnName();
    SQLExample.getResultsByColumnPosition();
    SQLExample.getAllColumns();
    SQLExample.closeConnection();
  }

  public EssentialJDBC() {
    // Constructor to establish the connection and create a Statement object...
  }

  void getResultsByColumnName() {
    // Execute wildcard query and output selected columns...
  }

  void getResultsByColumnPosition() {
    // Execute ID and name query and output results...
```

```
   }

   void getAllColumns() {
     // Execute wildcard query and output all columns...
   }
   // Close the connection
   void closeConnection() {
     if(connection != null) {
       try {
         connection.close();
         connection = null;
       } catch (SQLException ex) {
         System.out.println("\nSQLException------------------\n");
         System.out.println("SQLState: " + ex.getSQLState());
         System.out.println("Message : " + ex.getMessage());
       }
     }
   }


   Connection connection;
   Statement statement;
   String sourceURL = "jdbc:odbc:technical_library";
   String queryIDAndName = "SELECT authid, lastname, firstname FROM authors";
   String queryWildcard = "SELECT * FROM authors";          // Select all columns
}
```

The data source is identified by a URL in the form jdbc:driver_name:datasource. The data source identifier format is defined by the driver. In the case of the JDBC-ODBC Bridge, the data source is the ODBC source name. You have defined a closeConnection() method here that closes the connection when you are done. Notice that this method tests the value of the connection to ensure that you don't try to close a null connection.

Next you can fill in the details of the constructor for the class. This will establish a connection with the database and create a Statement object that will be used for executing queries:

```
   public EssentialJDBC() {
     try {
       Class.forName("sun.jdbc.odbc.JdbcOdbcDriver");
       connection = DriverManager.getConnection(sourceURL);
       statement = connection.createStatement();
     } catch(SQLException sqle) {
       System.err.println("Error creating connection");
     } catch(ClassNotFoundException cnfe) {
       System.err.println(cnfe.toString());
     }
   }
```

Next you can code the getResultsByColumnName() method. You will be using the statement object created from the connection object in the constructor to execute the SQL query to get a resultset back. A while loop with a call to next() as the condition will iterate through all the rows starting at the first:

```
void getResultsByColumnName() {
  try {
    ResultSet authorResults = statement.executeQuery(queryWildcard);
    int row = 0;

    while(authorResults.next()) {
      System.out.println("Row " + (++row) + ") "+
                          authorResults.getString("authid")+ " " +
                          authorResults.getString("lastname")+ " , "+
                          authorResults.getString("firstname"));
    }
    authorResults.close();
  } catch (SQLException sqle) {
    System.err.println ("\nSQLException-------------------\n");
    System.err.println ("SQLState: " + sqle.getSQLState());
    System.err.println ("Message : " + sqle.getMessage());
  }
}
```

The SQLException handling code here doesn't provide very elegant error handling for this program, but you are obliged to catch this exception.

You can now define the getResultsByColumnPosition() method. This will use the query for the ID and names columns, where the order of the columns is determined by the order of the column names in the query:

```
void getResultsByColumnPosition() {
  try {
    ResultSet authorResults = statement.executeQuery(queryIDAndName);

    int row = 0;
    while (authorResults.next()) {
      System.out.print("\nRow " + (++row) + ") ");
      for(int i = 1 ; i<=3 ; i++) {
        System.out.print((i>1?", ":" ")+authorResults.getString(i));
      }
    }
    authorResults.close();                              // Close the resultset
  } catch (SQLException ex) {
    System.err.println("\nSQLException-------------------\n");
    System.err.println("SQLState: " + ex.getSQLState());
    System.err.println("Message : " + ex.getMessage());
  }
}
```

Next you can define the getAllColumns() method. This uses the wildcard form of the SELECT statement where the * for the columns to be selected will retrieve all columns in the authors table. In general you won't necessarily know how many columns are returned in the resultset, but you can implement the method so that it will deal with any number of columns as well as any number of rows:

```
void getAllColumns() {
  try {
    ResultSet authorResults = statement.executeQuery(queryWildcard);
```

```
        ResultSetMetaData metadata = authorResults.getMetaData();
        int columns = metadata.getColumnCount();            // Column count
        int row = 0;
        while (authorResults.next()) {
          System.out.print("\nRow " + (++row) + ") ");
          for(int i = 1 ; i<=columns ; i++) {
            System.out.print((i>1?", ":" ")+authorResults.getString(i));
          }
        }
        authorResults.close();                              // Close the resultset
      } catch (SQLException ex) {
        System.err.println("\nSQLException-------------------\n");
        System.err.println("SQLState: " + ex.getSQLState());
        System.err.println("Message : " + ex.getMessage());
      }
    }
  }
```

Running the `EssentialJDBC` program produces three sets of results. The first two sets are the same and consist of the ID and the name columns from the `authors` table. The third set lists all columns. Although the additional columns are `null`, you can see that you get them all in this case.

How It Works

The `EssentialJDBC` class provides a `main()` method to declare and allocate an `EssentialJDBC` object by calling the class constructor. It then calls the `getResultsByColumnName()`, `getResultsByColumnPosition()`, and `getAllColumns()` methods of the new object.

The constructor initializes member variables and loads the `JdbcOdbc` driver class. It then creates a `Connection` object by calling the static `getConnection()` method of the `DriverManager` class. It then uses the `Connection` object to create a `Statement` object.

The bulk of the work is done in the three `getXXX()` methods. All three use the same `Statement` object to execute an SQL query. The difference between the three methods is how they retrieve the returned data.

The `getResultsByColumnName()` method executes the wildcard form of an SQL `SELECT` statement where the column names are specified by an `*`, and the column ordering of the returned results is determined by the database engine. This query is executed by calling the `executeQuery()` method of the `Statement` object, and this method returns the data in a `ResultSet` object. Since the column ordering is unknown ahead of time, you retrieve data by explicitly specifying the column names. The column data is retrieved as strings and written to the standard output stream. Finally, the `ResultSet` is closed. Note that the garbage collection of Java will handle this automatically anyway, but calling `close()` explicitly ensures that the resources, used by the `ResultSet` object, will be cleaned up sooner.

The `getResultsByColumnPosition()` method executes a `SELECT` statement that explicitly specifies the columns required by name, so the column ordering in the resultset is the same as the sequence of column names in the `SELECT` statement. You can therefore use the column position index values to retrieve the data from the `ResultSet`. Like the previous method, the column data is retrieved as strings and printed to the console for each row returned. Finally, the `ResultSet` object is closed as before.

The `getAllColumns()` method uses the wildcard form of the `SELECT` statement to retrieve a resultset containing all columns from the `authors` table — the entire table, in other words. The method gets the count of the number of columns by means of the `ResultSetMetaData` object for the `ResultSet` object created as a result of the query. This is used to output however many columns there are in the resultset.

Using a PreparedStatement Object

Let's put a prepared statement into action now to go through the mechanics in a practical context. This won't really show the capabilities of this—I'll get to that in the next chapter. You will code an example that executes the same SQL SELECT statement using both Statement and PreparedStatement objects. For each of these, the results will be displayed along with the metadata.

Try It Out   Statements and Metadata

First you'll define an outline of the StatementTest class and its member data. The main() method will instantiate a StatementTest object and then call the methods doStatement() and doPreparedStatement() for that object:

```
import java.sql.Connection;
import java.sql.Statement;
import java.sql.PreparedStatement;
import java.sql.DriverManager;
import java.sql.ResultSet;
import java.sql.ResultSetMetaData;
import java.sql.SQLException;

public class StatementTest {
  public static void main(String[] args) {
    try {
      StatementTest SQLExample = new StatementTest();
      SQLExample.doStatement();
      SQLExample.doPreparedStatement();
    } catch(SQLException sqle) {
      System.err.println("SQL Exception: " + sqle);
    } catch(ClassNotFoundException cnfe) {
      System.err.println(cnfe.toString());
    }
  }

  Connection databaseConnection;          // Connection to the database
  String driverName;                      // Database driver name
  String sourceURL;                       // Database location
}
```

Next you can define the StatementTest class constructor. This constructor will assign the driver name and the source URL that defines where the data will come from. It will then load the driver and call the static getConnection() method of the DriverManager class to establish the database connection:

```
public StatementTest() throws SQLException, ClassNotFoundException {
  driverName = "sun.jdbc.odbc.JdbcOdbcDriver";
  sourceURL = "jdbc:odbc:technical_library";

  Class.forName (driverName);
  databaseConnection = DriverManager.getConnection(sourceURL);
}
```

Next you can define the `doStatement()` method that is called in `main()`. This method shows once again how you create a `Statement` object and use it to execute a query. The `ResultSet` object that is returned by the `executeQuery()` method of the `Statement` object is passed to the `showResults()` method of the `StatementTest` class to display the results:

```
public void doStatement() throws SQLException {
   Statement myStatement = databaseConnection.createStatement();
   ResultSet myResults = myStatement.executeQuery(
            "SELECT authid, lastname, firstname FROM authors ORDER BY authid");

   showResults(myResults);
}
```

Next you can add a definition for the `doPreparedStatement()` method. This method will demonstrate how a `PreparedStatement` is created and executed. For the time being you will define it so that it operates in the same fashion as the `doStatement()` method:

```
public void doPreparedStatement() throws SQLException {
   PreparedStatement myStatement = databaseConnection.prepareStatement(
            "SELECT authid, lastname, firstname FROM authors ORDER BY authid");
   ResultSet myResults = myStatement.executeQuery();
   showResults(myResults);
}
```

This method calls the `showResults()` method, which you can define next. You pass a `ResultSet` object to the `showResults()` method from which it will extract both data and metadata:

```
public void showResults(ResultSet myResults) throws SQLException {
   // Retrieve ResultSetMetaData object from ResultSet
   ResultSetMetaData myResultMetadata = myResults.getMetaData();

   // How many columns were returned?
   int numColumns = myResultMetadata.getColumnCount();

   System.out.println(
            " --------------------Query Results------------------------");
   // Loop through the ResultSet and get data
   while(myResults.next()) {
      System.out.printf("%-5d", myResults.getInt(1));     // 1st Column only
      for(int column = 2; column <= numColumns; column++) {
        System.out.print(myResults.getString(column)+"   ");
      }
      System.out.print("\n");
   }
   System.out.println("\n\n----------Query Metadata---------------");
   System.out.println("ResultSet contains " + numColumns + " columns");
   for (int column = 1; column <= numColumns; column++) {
      System.out.println("\nColumn " + column);
      // Print the column name
      System.out.println("   column          : " +
                              myResultMetadata.getColumnName(column));

      // Print the label name
      System.out.println("   label           : " +
                              myResultMetadata.getColumnLabel(column));
      // Print the column's display size
```

```
                System.out.println("   display width : " +
                                     myResultMetadata.getColumnDisplaySize(column) +
                                     " characters");
            // Print the column's type
            System.out.println("   data type    : " +
                                     myResultMetadata.getColumnTypeName(column));
        }
    }
```

Notice that the first thing this method does is retrieve the `ResultSetMetaData` object, from which it determines the number of columns returned. It then loops through and retrieves each column value as a string and prints it out. After the data is displayed, the method extracts information about each column and displays that, too.

When you run the `StatementTest` program, you should get the following results twice:

```
--------------------Query Results------------------------
1     Gamma                                   Erich
2     Helm                                    Richard
3     Johnson                                 Ralph
      . . .
13    Riecken                                 Doug
14    Genesereth                              Michael
15    Carone                                  Timothy

-----------Query Metadata----------------
ResultSet contains 3 columns

Column 1
    column         : authid
    label          : authid
    display width : 11 characters
    data type      : INTEGER

Column 2
    column         : lastname
    label          : lastname
    display width : 48 characters
    data type      : CHAR

Column 3
    column         : firstname
    label          : firstname
    display width : 48 characters
    data type      : CHAR
```

How It Works

All you've done in this example is to take the concepts that you've seen in this chapter and put them all together into a working program.

The program creates and executes both a `Statement` and a `PreparedStatement` object, which should produce identical results. In this case, there were no parameters for the `PreparedStatement` (not to worry — you'll have more than enough `PreparedStatement` objects in the next chapter!). Since the results were identical, the `ResultSetMetaData` is identical for the two executed SQL statements as well.

Notice that all of the exception handling for this example is handled within `main()`. Each of the other methods that might generate exceptions declares those exceptions in its `throws` clause. If an exception is thrown within any of those methods, the method will simply pass that exception back to the calling routine — `main()`.

Creating an Interactive SQL Tool

So far the examples with database operations have all been console applications. In practice you will want to implement your database programs as interactive windowed applications, so let's apply what you know to creating an example. You will build an interactive SQL tool that will execute SQL statements to retrieve a resultset.

The interactive SQL tool will be a simple front end to the JDBC API. It will provide a means of entering and executing SQL statements, and have a display area for viewing results. This tool will be pretty basic in terms of functionality, but may come in handy for experimenting with SQL statements. You can always add extensions to this utility as you become more familiar with JDBC.

You'll set the requirements for the `InteractiveSQL` tool class to be fairly simple:

❑   Enable the user to enter and execute an SQL command

❑   Display the resultset from an SQL query

❑   Display error information where appropriate

You will implement this as an application with a window based on the Swing class `JFrame`. You will also use a Swing component that is particularly useful for database applications — a table defined by the `JTable` class. The `JTable` class is defined in the `javax.swing.table` package along with some other classes and interfaces that support tables of data. The resultset that is generated when you execute an SQL `SELECT` statement is a rectangular table of data values, so a `JTable` component is ideal for displaying resultsets. Let's first explore the basics of the `JTable` component so you can apply it to the `InteractiveSQL` program.

Using Tables

You use a `JTable` component to display a rectangular array of data on the screen. The items of data in the table do not have to be of all the same type; in fact, each column of data in the table can be of a different type, either a basic type or class type. This is precisely the situation you have with a resultset. There are several ways to create a `JTable` component, but I'll just consider the most convenient in the database context, which is to use an object that encapsulates the data that is to be displayed in the table and implements the `javax.swing.table.TableModel` interface. You can create a `JTable` object directly from such an object by passing a reference of type `TableModel` to a `JTable` constructor. For example:

```
JTable table = new JTable(model);
```

Here, `model` is a variable of type `TableModel` that stores a reference to an object that encapsulates the data to be displayed — the resultset, in other words. All you need is a class to define this object, so the obvious next step is to investigate how you implement the `TableModel` interface.

Understanding the TableModel Interface

The `TableModel` interface declares methods that are used by a `JTable` object to access the data item to be displayed at each position in the table. This interface is defined in the `javax.swing.table` package, along with the `JTable` class. Our class encapsulating a resultset will need to implement this interface and therefore define all the methods that the interface declares. The bad news is that there are nine of them. The good news is that there is an abstract class, `AbstractTableModel`, that implements six of them, so if you extend this class you have a minimum of three methods to define. The full set of methods declared in the `TableModel` interface is as follows:

`getColumnCount()`	Returns the number of columns in the table model as type `int`.
`getRowCount()`	Returns the number of rows in the table model as type `int`.
`getValueAt(int row, int column)`	Returns the value of the data item in the table model at the position specified by the argument as type `Object`.
`getColumnClass(int column)`	Returns the class type of the data in the columns specified by the argument as type `Class`.
`getColumnName(int column)`	Returns the name of the columns specified by the argument as type `String`.
`setValueAt(Object value, int row, int column)`	Sets the value `value` for the data item in the table model at the position specified by the last two arguments. There is no return value.
`isCellEditable(int row, int column)`	Returns `true` if the data item at the position specified by the arguments is editable, and `false` otherwise.
`addTableModelListener(TableModelListener tml)`	Adds a listener that is notified each time the table model is altered.
`removeTableModelListener(TableModelListener tml)`	Removes a listener that was listening for table model changes.

Remember that all these methods are called by the `JTable` object, so these provide the means whereby the `JTable` object accesses and manipulates data in the table model. The `AbstractTableModel` class provides default implementations for the last six methods in the list above, so the minimum you have to supply when you extend this class are the first three.

Defining a Table Model

You want to define a class that encapsulates a `ResultSet` object, and it will be convenient to make the object of this class type have the capability to replace the existing `ResultSet` object by a new one at any time. This will enable a single `JTable` object to display a series of different resultsets, just by setting a new resultset in the underlying `TableModel` object. You can do this by providing a method that will accept a `ResultSet` object as an argument and making the contents available through the `TableModel` interface. With this in mind, the basic outline of the class will be:

```
import java.sql.ResultSet;
import java.sql.ResultSetMetaData;
import java.sql.SQLException;
import javax.swing.table.AbstractTableModel;
import java.util.Vector;

class ResultsModel extends AbstractTableModel {
   public void setResultSet(ResultSet results) {
      // Make the data in the resultset available through the TableModel interface...
   }

   public int getColumnCount() {
      // Return number of columns...
   }

   public int getRowCount() {
      // Return number of rows...
   }

   public String getValueAt(int row, int column) {
      // Return the value at position row,column...
   }

   public String getColumnName(int column) {
      // Return the name for the column...
   }
}
```

You could access the data to be returned by the `TableModel` interface methods by going back to the original `ResultSet` object as necessary. This may involve going back to the database each time, and it will be generally more convenient and probably more efficient to cache the data from the resultset in the `ResultsModel` object. This means that the `setResultSet()` method will need to set this up. You will need to store two sets of information in a `ResultsModel` object — the column names, which are `String` objects, and the data in the table, which could be any of the types matching the SQL data types. To keep things simple, you'll access the data using the `getString()` method for the `ResultSet` object. Any of the SQL data types you will be using can be extracted as type `String`, and with this approach you'll have to deal only with strings at this point.

You can store the column names in a `String` array, so you can add a data member to the `ResultsModel` class to provide for this:

```
private String[] columnNames = new String[0];   // Empty array of names
```

Defining `columnNames` as an array with zero elements ensures that you start out with a non-null array, even though there is no resultset initially. You won't know in advance how many rows or columns of data there are, so you won't want to use an array. A `Vector<>` object will provide sufficient flexibility to accommodate whatever you need. You can store the contents of a row as an array of `String` objects that you can then store as an element in the `Vector<>`. You can define the data member that stores the rows of data values as:

```
private Vector<String[]> dataRows = new Vector<String[]>(); // Vector of rows
```

Of course, you have set the type for all the data items in a row to `String` here, but if you wanted to accommodate different types within a row, you could use an array of type `Object[]` object to store each row. You mustn't forget the `import` statement for the `Vector` class name — it's defined in `java.util`.

You can now implement the `setResultSet()` method in the `ResultsModel` class as:

```
public void setResultSet(ResultSet results) {
  try {
    ResultSetMetaData metadata = results.getMetaData();

    int columns = metadata.getColumnCount();     // Get number of columns
    columnNames = new String[columns];           // Array to hold names

    // Get the column names
    for(int i = 0; i < columns; i++) {
      columnNames[i] = metadata.getColumnLabel(i+1);
    }

    // Get all rows
    dataRows.clear();                            // Empty vector to store the data
    String[] rowData;                           // Stores one row
    while(results.next()) {                     // For each row...
      rowData = new String[columns];            // create array to hold the data
      for(int i = 0; i < columns; i++) {        // For each column
        rowData[i] = results.getString(i+1);    // retrieve the data item
      }
      dataRows.addElement(rowData);             // Store the row in the vector
    }
    fireTableChanged(null);         // Signal the table there is new model data
  }
  catch (SQLException sqle) {
    System.err.println(sqle);
  }
}
```

To get the column names and the number of columns, you need access to the `ResultSetMetaData` object corresponding to the `ResultSet` object. The `getColumnLabel()` method for the `metadata` object returns the label to be used to name the column. This will either be the name of the column as known to the database, or the alias if you specify one in the `SELECT` statement used to create the resultset. The column names are stored in the array `columnNames`.

You call the `clear()` method for the `Vector<String[]>` object to remove any existing references from the vector. Each element in the vector will be a reference to an array of `String` objects, `rowData`, that you create in the `while` loop, and you set the values of its elements in the nested `for` loop. Once you have created the array, you store a reference to it in `dataRows`. After all the rows from the resultset have been stored, you call the `fireTableChanged()` method that the `ResultsModel` class inherits from the base class. This method notifies all listeners for the `JTable` object for this model that the model has changed, so the `JTable` object should redraw itself from scratch. The argument to the `fireTableChanged()` method is a reference to an object of type `TableModelEvent` that you can use to record the parts of the model that have changed, and this is passed to the listeners. You pass a `null` here, as you want to invalidate the whole table.

The method to return the number of columns is now very easy to implement:

```
public int getColumnCount() {
    return columnNames.length;
}
```

The column count is the number of elements in the `columnNames` array.

Supplying the row count is just as easy:

```
public int getRowCount() {
    return dataRows == null ? 0 : dataRows.size();
}
```

The number of rows corresponds to the size of the `Vector<>` object, `dataRows`. You check to verify that the value of the `dataRows` vector is not `null` to ensure that the initialization of the `InteractiveSQL` GUI can take place even when the vector has not been initialized.

The next method you need to define provides access to the data values. You can implement this as follows:

```
public String getValueAt(int row, int column) {
    return dataRows.elementAt(row)[column];
}
```

The `elementAt()` method returns the element in the `Vector<>` object at the position specified by the argument. This will be a reference to an array of type `String[]` so you just index this with the value of the `column` parameter to select the element to be returned.

The last method you must add to the class is `getColumnName()`, which will return the column name given a column index. You can implement this as:

```
public String getColumnName(int column) {
    return columnNames[column] == null ? "No Name" : columnNames[column];
}
```

You take the precaution here of dealing with a `null` column name by supplying a default column name in this case.

The Application GUI

Figure 24-9 shows the user interface for the `InteractiveSQL` tool. The text field at the top provides an entry area for typing in the SQL statement and will be implemented using a `JTextField` component. The results display provides a scrollable area for the results of the executed SQL command. This will be implemented using a `JScrollPane` component. A status line, implemented as a `JTextArea` component, provides the user with the number of rows returned from the query, or the text of any `SQLException` object generated by the query.

Figure 24-9

Figure 24-9 also shows the menu items in the File menu and the tooltip prompt for the SQL input area. The Clear query menu item will just clear the input area where you enter an SQL query.

Try It Out   Defining the GUI

You will derive the `InteractiveSQL` class from the `JFrame` class and make this the foundation for the application. Its constructor will be responsible for loading the JDBC driver class, creating a connection to the database, and creating the user interface. The code is as follows:

```
import java.awt.BorderLayout;
import java.awt.event.WindowAdapter;
import java.awt.event.WindowEvent;
import javax.swing.JFrame;
import javax.swing.JTextField;
```

```java
import javax.swing.JTextArea;
import javax.swing.JMenu;
import javax.swing.JMenuBar;
import javax.swing.JMenuItem;
import javax.swing.JScrollPane;
import javax.swing.JTable;
import java.sql.DriverManager;
import java.sql.Connection;
import java.sql.Statement;
import java.sql.SQLException;

public class InteractiveSQL extends JFrame {
  public static void main(String[] args) {
    // Create the application object
    InteractiveSQL theApp = new InteractiveSQL("sun.jdbc.odbc.JdbcOdbcDriver",
                                               "jdbc:odbc:technical_library",
                                               "guest",
                                               "guest");

  }

  public InteractiveSQL(String driver, String url,
                        String user , String password) {
    super("InteractiveSQL");                      // Call base constructor
    setBounds(0, 0, 400, 300);                    // Set window bounds
    setDefaultCloseOperation(DISPOSE_ON_CLOSE);   // Close window operation
    addWindowListener(new WindowAdapter() {       // Listener for window close
            // Handler for window closing event
            public void windowClosing(WindowEvent e) {
              dispose();                          // Release the window resources
              System.exit(0);                     // End the application
            }
          } );

    // Add the input for SQL statements at the top
    command.setToolTipText("Key SQL commmand and press Enter");
    getContentPane().add(command, BorderLayout.NORTH);

    // Add the status reporting area at the bottom
    status.setLineWrap(true);
    status.setWrapStyleWord(true);
    getContentPane().add(status, BorderLayout.SOUTH);

    // Create the menubar from the menu items
    JMenu fileMenu = new JMenu("File");           // Create File menu
    fileMenu.setMnemonic('F');                    // Create shortcut
    fileMenu.add(clearQueryItem);                 // Add clear query item
    fileMenu.add(exitItem);                       // Add exit item
    menuBar.add(fileMenu);                        // Add menu to the menubar
    setJMenuBar(menuBar);                         // Add menubar to the window
    // Establish a database connection and set up the table
    try {
      Class.forName(driver);                      // Load the driver
      connection = DriverManager.getConnection(url, user, password);
      statement = connection.createStatement();
```

```
          model = new ResultsModel();              // Create a table model
          JTable table = new JTable(model);         // Create a table from the model
          table.setAutoResizeMode(JTable.AUTO_RESIZE_OFF);   // Use scrollbars
          resultsPane = new JScrollPane(table);     // Create scrollpane for table
          getContentPane().add(resultsPane, BorderLayout.CENTER);
        } catch(ClassNotFoundException cnfe) {
          System.err.println(cnfe);                 // Driver not found
        } catch(SQLException sqle) {
          System.err.println(sqle);                 // error connection to database
        }
      pack();
      setVisible(true);
    }

    JTextField command = new JTextField();          // Input area for SQL
    JTextArea status = new JTextArea(3,1);          // Output area for status and errors
    JScrollPane resultsPane;

    JMenuBar menuBar = new JMenuBar();                        // The menu bar
    JMenuItem clearQueryItem = new JMenuItem("Clear query");  // Clear SQL item
    JMenuItem exitItem = new JMenuItem("Exit");               // Exit item

    Connection connection;                          // Connection to the database
    Statement statement;                            // Statement object for queries
    ResultsModel model;                             // Table model for resultset
  }
```

You can try running the application as it is, and you should see the basic application interface displayed in the window with a working close operation.

How It Works

The constructor is passed the arguments required to load the appropriate driver and create a `Connection` to a database. The first executable statement in this constructor calls the constructor for the `JFrame` class, passing a default window title to it. The constructor then creates and arranges the user interface components. Most of this should be familiar to you, but let's pick out a few things that are new, or are worthy of a second look.

You can see how you add a tooltip for the `JTextField` component `command` — the input area for an SQL statement. Don't forget that you can add a tooltip for any Swing component in the same way.

You define the `JTextArea` object, `status`, so that it can display three lines of text. The first argument to the `JTextArea` constructor is the number of lines of text, and the second argument is the number of columns. Some of the error messages can be quite long, so you call both the `setLineWrap()` method to make lines wrap automatically, and the `setWrapStyleWord()` method to wrap a line at the end of a word — that is, on whitespace — rather than in the middle of a word. In both cases the `true` argument switches the facility on.

You create the `JTable` object using the default `ResultsModel` object, which will contain no data initially. Since the number of columns in a resultset will vary depending on the SQL query that is executed, you wrap the `JTable` object in a `JScrollPane` object to provide automatic scrolling as necessary. The scrollbars will appear whenever the size of the `JTable` object is larger than the size of the scroll pane. By default, a `JTable` object will resize the width of its columns to fit within the width of the `JTable` component. To inhibit this and allow the scroll pane scrollbars to be used, you call the `setAutoResizeMode()` method with the argument as `JTable.AUTO_RESIZE_OFF`.

This not only inhibits the default resizing action when the table is displayed, but also allows you to change the size of a column when the table is displayed without affecting the size of the other columns. You change the size of a column by dragging the side of the column name using the mouse. There are other values defined in the `JTable` class that you can pass to the `setAutoResizeMode()` method to determine how resizing is handled:

`AUTO_RESIZE_ALL_COLUMNS`	Adjusts the sizes of all columns to take up the change in width of the column being resized. This maintains the overall width of the table.
`AUTO_RESIZE_NEXT_COLUMN`	Adjusts the size of the next column to provide for the change in the column being altered in order to maintain the total width of the table.
`AUTO_RESIZE_LAST_COLUMN`	Adjusts the size of the last column to provide for the change in the column being altered in order to maintain the total width of the table.
`AUTO_RESIZE_SUBSEQUENT_COLUMNS`	Adjusts the size of the columns to the right to provide for the change in the column being altered in order to maintain the total width of the table.

Handling Events

Of course, the program doesn't do anything because there's no code in the program to respond to SQL commands that you enter in the text field or to menu item selection. The first step is to make the `InteractiveSQL` class implement the `ActionListener` interface. Change the first line of the class definition to:

```
public class InteractiveSQL extends JFrame implements ActionListener {
```

You can define the `actionPerformed()` method in the `InteractiveSQL` class like this:

```
public void actionPerformed(ActionEvent e) {
  Object source = e.getSource();
  if(source == command) {                    // Enter key for text field input
    executeSQL();
  } else if(source == clearQueryItem) {      // Clear query menu item
    command.setText("");                     // Clear SQL entry
  } else if(source == exitItem) {            // Exit menu item
    dispose();                               // Release the window resources
    System.exit(0);                          // End the application
  }
}
```

This method is handling events from the text field and the menu items, so the action to be carried out depends on the object that originated the event. You determine which object originated the event by comparing the reference returned by the getSource() method for the event object with the three fields in the InteractiveSQL object. If it's the text field, you call the executeSQL() method that you'll add next; this will execute the SQL command that was entered. If it's the clearQueryItem menu item, you call the setText() method for the JTextField object to reset the contents to an empty string. If it's the exitItem menu item, you just exit the program after releasing the window resources.

You can define the method that will enter the SQL command that was entered like this:

```
public void executeSQL() {
   String query = command.getText();              // Get the SQL statement
   if(query == null ||query.length() == 0) {      // If there's nothing we are done
     return;
   }
   try {
     model.setResultSet(statement.executeQuery(query));
     status.setText("Resultset has " + model.getRowCount() + " rows.");
   } catch (SQLException sqle) {
     status.setText(sqle.getMessage());           // Display error message
   }
 }
```

Calling the getText() method for the JTextField object returns a reference to the string that was entered. If it's null or an empty string, there's nothing to be done, so the method returns immediately. If it's not null, you pass the query string to the executeQuery() method for the Statement object. This will return a reference to a ResultSet object containing the results of the query, and you pass this to the setResultSet() method for the ResultsModel object. This sets the new resultset in the model and causes the JTable object to redisplay itself with the new data from the table model. Finally, you display the number of rows returned by the query in the text area below the table.

Of course, you still have to identify the InteractiveSQL object as the listener for the text field and the two menu items, so add the following code to the constructor after the code that sets up the menu:

```
menuBar.add(fileMenu);              // Add menu to the menubar
setJMenuBar(menuBar);               // Add menubar to the window

// Add listeners for text field and menu items
command.addActionListener(this);
clearQueryItem.addActionListener(this);
exitItem.addActionListener(this);
```

You need to add two more import statements to the source file for InteractiveSQL:

```
import java.awt.event.ActionEvent;
import java.awt.event.ActionListener;
```

If you recompile the program and rerun it, you should now be able to enter SQL commands and see the results displayed in the application window.

The program works only with the database and driver that you have hard-coded in the program. You can make it a lot more flexible by allowing command-line arguments to be supplied that specify the database and driver, as well as the user ID and password.

Handling Command-Line Arguments

All you need to do is to alter the `main()` method to accept up to four command-line arguments; these will be the values for the user name, password, database URL, and JDBC driver.

Try It Out   **Using Command-Line Parameters**

You need to modify the code in `main()` to:

```java
public static void main(String[] args) {
    // Set default values for the command line args
    String user     = "guest";
    String password = "guest";
    String url      = "jdbc:odbc:technical_library";
    String driver   = "sun.jdbc.odbc.JdbcOdbcDriver";

    // Up to 4 arguments in the sequence database url,driver url, user ID, password
    switch(args.length) {
      case 4:                                   // Start here for four arguments
        password = args[3];
        // Fall through to the next case
      case 3:                                   // Start here for three arguments
        user = args[2];
        // Fall through to the next case
      case 2:                                   // Start here for two arguments
        driver = args[1];
        // Fall through to the next case
      case 1:                                   // Start here for one argument
        url = args[0];
    }
    InteractiveSQL theApp = new InteractiveSQL(driver, url, user, password);
}
```

How It Works

Now the program enables you to optionally specify the JDBC URL, the JDBC driver, the user name, and the password on the command line. If you don't supply any command-line arguments, the program works as before, accessing the `technical_library` database.

The mechanism that handles the optional parameters is pretty simple. The `switch` statement tests the number of parameters that were specified on the command line. If one parameter was passed, it is interpreted as the JDBC URL. If two parameters were passed, the second parameter is assumed to be the driver URL, and so on. There are no `break` statements, so control always drops through from the starting case to include each of the following cases.

Summary

In this chapter you've been introduced to JDBC programming and seen it in action. The important points covered in this chapter include the following:

❑ The fundamental classes in JDBC are as follows:

    ❑ `DriverManager` manages the loading of JDBC drivers and connections to client applications.

    ❑ `Connection` provides a connection to a specific data source.

    ❑ `Statement` provides a context for executing SQL statements.

    ❑ `ResultSet` provides a means for accessing data returned from an executed `Statement`.

❑ The essential JDBC program has the following basic sequence when writing:

    ❑ Import the necessary classes.

    ❑ Load the JDBC driver.

    ❑ Identify the data source.

    ❑ Allocate a `Connection` object.

    ❑ Allocate a `Statement` object.

    ❑ Execute a query using the `Statement` object.

    ❑ Retrieve data from the returned `ResultSet` object.

    ❑ Close the `ResultSet`.

    ❑ Close the `Statement` object.

    ❑ Close the `Connection` object.

❑ The `JTable` component provides an easy and convenient way to display the results of database queries.

❑ A table model can provide the data to be displayed by a `JTable` component. A table model is an object of a class that implements the `TableModel` interface.

Exercises

You can download the source code for the examples in the book and the solutions to the following exercises from `http://www.wrox.com`.

1. Write a program that outputs all authors in the `technical_library` database with last names starting with the letters A through H.

2. Write a program that lists all books and the authors for those books. (Hint: You will need an SQL join and the `auth_books` table.)

3. Modify the `InteractiveSQL` program to allow the user to specify which database to use.

4. Modify the `InteractiveSQL` program to provide separate input areas for each part of a SELECT statement — one for the table columns, one for the table, one for a possible WHERE clause, and so on.

The JDBC in Action

In this chapter I'll expand on the topics that I introduced in the previous chapter, and go into more detail on the Java Database Connectivity (JDBC) application program interface (API). In this chapter you're going to learn more about:

❑ How you map relational data onto Java objects

❑ The mapping between SQL and Java data types

❑ How you limit the data created in a resultset

❑ How you constrain the time spent executing a query

❑ How you use a PreparedStatement object to create a parameterized SQL statement

❑ How you can execute database update and delete operations in your Java programs

❑ How you can get more information from SQLException objects

❑ What an SQLWarning object is and what you can do with it

Data Types and JDBC

In all of the examples so far, all of the data extracted from a resultset was retrieved as a String. You'll certainly need to get other types of data, and as you saw in the previous chapter, the ResultSet provides a number of methods for retrieving different data types. To use these effectively, you need to look at the SQL data types and understand how they map to the Java data types in your program.

Mapping between Java and SQL Data Types

The SQL-92 standard defines a set of data types that don't map one-for-one with those in Java. As you write applications that move data from SQL to Java and back, you'll have to take account of how JDBC performs that mapping. That is, you need to know the Java data type you need to represent a given SQL data type, and vice versa.

The `Types` class in the `java.sql` package defines constants of type `int` that represent each of the supported SQL types. The name given to the data member storing each constant is the same as that of the corresponding SQL type. For example, when you retrieve the SQL type of a table column by calling the `getColumnType()` method for a `ResultSetMetaData` object, the SQL type is returned as one of the constants defined in the `Types` class.

When you're retrieving data from a JDBC data source, the `ResultSet` implementation will map the SQL data onto Java data types. The following table shows the SQL-to-Java mappings:

SQL Data Type	Java Data Type
CHAR	String
VARCHAR	String
LONGVARCHAR	String
NUMERIC	java.math.BigDecimal
DECIMAL	java.math.BigDecimal
BIT	boolean
TINYINT	byte
SMALLINT	short
INTEGER	int
BIGINT	long
REAL	float
FLOAT	double
DOUBLE	double
BINARY	byte[]
VARBINARY	byte[]
LONGVARBINARY	byte[]
DATE	java.sql.Date
TIME	java.sql.Time
TIMESTAMP	java.sql.Timestamp

Note that the last three are Java class types defined in the `java.sql` package. The `Date`, `Time`, and `Timestamp` classes here that accommodate the requirements of the SQL types are derived from the `Date` class defined in the `java.util` package.

Conversely, when you are relating Java-to-SQL data types, the following mappings apply:

Java Data Type	SQL Data Type
String	VARCHAR, LONGVARCHAR
java.math.BigDecimal	NUMERIC
boolean	BIT
byte	TINYINT
short	SMALLINT
int	INTEGER
long	BIGINT
float	REAL
double	DOUBLE
byte[]	VARBINARY, LONGVARBINARY
java.sql.Date	DATE
java.sql.Time	TIME
java.sql.Timestamp	TIMESTAMP

> Note that some databases implement INTEGER data types as NUMERIC. When accessing INTEGER elements through the JDBC, it is important to associate the JDBC data type with the internal data type that is actually stored in the database.

Most likely you'll know ahead of time what the SQL type is for the data you are accessing in a database. When this is not the case, you can easily determine the SQL type for each column in a resultset by calling the getColumnType() method for the ResultSetMetaData object. You can then compare the return value with the constants defined in the Types class to select the getXXX() method for the ResultSet object that is appropriate for retrieving the data.

Mapping Relational Data onto Java Objects

In the previous chapter, you saw how you could get the basic attribute data from a JDBC ResultSet object. Since Java is object-oriented, in many cases you won't want to deal with individual data items such as the authors' names and IDs — you'll want to work with Author objects that represent the authors. That's what I'll focus on now, and in the process, you'll get some more experience with the Statement and ResultSet interfaces.

The way that information is handled at the object level is usually different from the way that data is stored in a relational database. In the world of objects, the underlying principle is to make those objects exhibit the same characteristics (information and behavior) as their real-world counterparts — in other words, objects function at the level of the conceptual model. Relational databases, on the other hand, work at the data model level. As you saw in the previous chapter, relational databases store information using normalized forms, where conceptual objects like invoices and customers can be decomposed into a number of tables. So how do you deal with the problem of mapping objects to relational data models?

Sometimes there is a straightforward relationship between the columns in a table and the member variables in an object. In that case, the mapping task consists simply of matching the data types of the database with those of Java. Figure 25-1 shows this simple application-level SQL-to-object mapping.

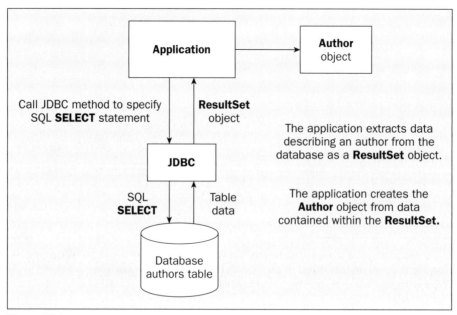

Figure 25-1

Try It Out   A Simple Mapping from SQL Rows to Java Objects

The authors table in the sample database is a good example of a simple mapping. To recap, this table has the following definition:

Column	Data Type	Description
authid	int	Unique identifier for each author
lastname	char(48)	Last name of author
firstname	char(48)	First name of author
address1	char(80)	First line of address
address2	char(80)	Second line of address
city	char(25)	City
state_prov	char(25)	State or province

Column	Data Type	Description
postcode	char(10)	Postal code
country	char(15)	Country
phone	char(20)	Daytime phone number
fax	char(20)	Fax number
email	char(25)	E-mail address

Let's define a Java class to encapsulate an author. Take a look back at the table that shows you how to map SQL to Java data types. Based on those mappings, you can define the member variables for an `Author` class, and add a constructor, member access methods, and a `toString()` method:

```java
public class Author {
   public Author(int authid, String lastname, String firstname,
                 String address[], String city, String state,
                 String postcode, String country,
                 String phone, String fax, String email)
   {
     this.authid = authid;
     this.lastname = lastname;
     this.firstname = firstname;
     this.address = address;
     this.city = city;
     this.state = state;
     this.postcode = postcode;
     this.country = country;
     this.phone = phone;
     this.fax = fax;
     this.email = email;
   }

   public int getId() {
     return authid;
   }

   public String getLastName() {
     return lastname;
   }

   public String getFirstName() {
     return firstname;
   }

   public String[] getAddress() {
     return address;
   }

   public String getCity() {
     return city;
   }
```

```
    public String getState() {
       return state;
    }

    public String getCountry() {
       return country;
    }

    public String getPostCode() {
       return postcode;
    }

    public String getPhone() {
       return phone;
    }

    public String getFax() {
       return fax;
    }

    public String getEmail() {
       return email;
    }

    public String toString() {
       return new String
              ("author ID: " + Integer.toString(authid) +
               "\nname     : " + lastname + "," + firstname +
               "\naddress  : " + address[0] +
               "\n         : " + address[1] +
               "\n         : " + city + " " + state +
               "\n         : " + postcode + " " + country +
               "\nphone    : " + phone +
               "\nfax      : " + fax +
               "\nemail    : " + email);
    }

    int authid;
    String lastname;
    String firstname;
    String address[];
    String city;
    String state;
    String postcode;
    String country;
    String phone;
    String fax;
    String email;
}
```

Next, you need to get the data from the database into the Author object. Your initial strategy for doing this is going to be pretty basic — the application class will create the Connection, Statement, and ResultSet objects and read the data from the database. The Author class constructor will be called using each row of data read. For this example, you'll use an SQL statement that is a literal string in the code, rather than creating a PreparedStatement:

```
import java.sql.DriverManager;
import java.sql.Connection;
import java.sql.Statement;
import java.sql.ResultSet;
import java.sql.SQLException;

public class TrySimpleMapping {
  public static void main (String[] args) {
    TrySimpleMapping SQLtoJavaExample;
    try {
      SQLtoJavaExample = new TrySimpleMapping();
      SQLtoJavaExample.listAuthors();
    } catch(SQLException sqle) {
      System.err.println(sqle);
    } catch(ClassNotFoundException cnfe) {
      System.err.println(cnfe);
    }
  }

  public TrySimpleMapping() throws SQLException, ClassNotFoundException {
    Class.forName (driverName);
    connection = DriverManager.getConnection(sourceURL, user, password);
  }

  public void listAuthors() throws SQLException {
    Author author = null;

    String query = "SELECT authid, lastname, firstname, address1,"+
                   "address2, city, state_prov, postcode, country,"+
                   "phone, fax, email FROM authors";

    Statement statement = connection.createStatement();
    ResultSet authors = statement.executeQuery(query);

    while(authors.next()) {
      int id             = authors.getInt(1);
      String lastname    = authors.getString(2);
      String firstname   = authors.getString(3);

      String[] address   = { authors.getString(4), authors.getString(5)};
      String city        = authors.getString(6);
      String state       = authors.getString(7);
      String postcode    = authors.getString(8);
      String country     = authors.getString(9);
      String phone       = authors.getString(10);
      String fax         = authors.getString(11);
      String email       = authors.getString(12);

      author = new Author(id, lastname, firstname,
                          address, city, state, postcode,
                          country, phone, fax, email);

      System.out.println("\n" + author);
    }
    authors.close();
    connection.close();
```

1335

```
        }

        Connection connection;
        String driverName = "sun.jdbc.odbc.JdbcOdbcDriver";
        String sourceURL = "jdbc:odbc:technical_library";
        String user = "guest";
        String password = "guest";
    }
```

You should get the following output when you execute the preceding example:

```
author ID: 15
name      : Carone                                    , Timothy
address   : null
          : null
          : null null
          : null null
phone     : null
fax       : null
email     : null

author ID: 14
name      : Genesereth                                , Michael
address   : null
          : null
          : null null
          : null null
phone     : null
fax       : null
email     : null

and so on...
```

How It Works

Everything in this example should look pretty familiar, but there are just a couple of new things I need to cover.

Note first that there's an extra step after the data is read that creates the Author object by calling its constructor with that data. Also, in the while loop, as each row is read from the ResultSet, the application uses the appropriate getXXX() method of the ResultSet object to perform the mapping from SQL to Java data types. In each of these method calls, the argument is the index value to select the column. Since the query selects the columns by name, the columns in the resultset will be in the same sequence as the column names in the SQL query. To display the data for each Author object, you simply call System.out.println() and pass the Author object reference to it. This will automatically invoke the toString() method for the object. Notice that in the output, the literal null appears where there are null values in the database.

> This example uses the JDBC-ODBC Bridge driver with a data source that does not require a user name or password. If you need a user name and password to access that data source, simply modify the code in the TrySimpleMapping constructor to use the appropriate driver, URL, and getConnection() method of the DriverManager.

A Better Mapping Strategy

As you saw, the simple strategy described in the previous section does in fact transfer the data between the relational database and the Java objects successfully (and this approach can be used in reverse to get data back to the database, as you'll see shortly). It does, however, leave quite a lot to be desired because the movement of data between the database and the Java object is left completely to the application code.

A better, more object-oriented strategy would be to make the Author class handle its own data extraction from a ResultSet object. To do this, you could add to the Author class a static factory method (a method that manufactures Author objects) that will synthesize Author objects from data in the database. The code calling the factory method must still do the work of creating the Connection and Statement objects and use the Statement object to execute the query that retrieves the data. It will also need to ensure that the ResultSet contains the columns required for populating the Author object.

You need to establish an implied "contract" between this factory method and any code that calls it:

❑   The current row of the ResultSet object that is passed to the factory method must be positioned at a valid row.

❑   The ResultSet must contain all the columns from the authors table.

You can implement the factory method in the Author class as:

```
public static Author fromResults(ResultSet authors) throws SQLException {
    String[]address = {
                authors.getString("address1"),
                authors.getString("address2")
            };

    return new Author(
                authors.getInt("authid"),
                authors.getString("lastname"),
                authors.getString("firstname"),
                address,
                authors.getString("city"),
                authors.getString("state_prov"),
                authors.getString("postcode"),
                authors.getString("country"),
                authors.getString("phone"),
                authors.getString("fax"),
                authors.getString("email"));
}
```

Here you access the columns by name, so there is no dependency on the order in which they are retrieved in the query. This gives a little added flexibility to the application — to use the wildcard notation, for example. The only requirement is that all the columns should be present in the ResultSet object. If any are not, an exception of type SQLException will be thrown, and this will need to be caught by the calling method. Of course, the Author.java file must now have import statements added for the ResultSet and SQLException names from the java.sql package.

You can see this in action with another example.

Try It Out   Encapsulated Mapping of SQL Rows to Java Objects

You just need to create the application class. This class is nearly identical to `TrySimpleMapping`, except that there's less code in the `listAuthors()` method:

```java
import java.sql.DriverManager;
import java.sql.Connection;
import java.sql.Statement;
import java.sql.ResultSet;
import java.sql.SQLException;

public class TryEncapsulatedMapping {
  public static void main (String[] args) {
    TryEncapsulatedMapping SQLtoJavaExample;
    try {
      SQLtoJavaExample = new TryEncapsulatedMapping();
      SQLtoJavaExample.listAuthors();
    } catch(SQLException sqle) {
      System.err.println(sqle);
    } catch(ClassNotFoundException cnfe) {
      System.err.println(cnfe);
    }
  }

  public TryEncapsulatedMapping() throws SQLException,
                                    ClassNotFoundException {
    Class.forName (driverName);
    connection = DriverManager.getConnection(sourceURL, user, password);
  }

  public void listAuthors() throws SQLException {
    Author author;
    String query = "SELECT authid, lastname, firstname, address1,"+
                   "address2, city, state_prov, postcode, country,"+
                   "phone, fax, email FROM authors";

    Statement statement = connection.createStatement();
    ResultSet authors = statement.executeQuery(query);

    while(authors.next())
      System.out.println("\n" + Author.fromResults(authors));
    authors.close();
    connection.close();
  }

  Connection connection;
  String driverName = "sun.jdbc.odbc.JdbcOdbcDriver";
  String sourceURL = "jdbc:odbc:technical_library";
  String user = "guest";
  String password = "guest";
}
```

When you run the example, you should get results that are exactly the same as those from the previous example.

How It Works

All you've really done in this example is push the work of extracting Java types from the ResultSet to the class that is using the data. Instead of reading from the ResultSet and instantiating a new Author object for each row in the listAuthors() method, you just call the static fromResults() method of the Author class, which will create a new Author object from the data in the current row of the ResultSet.

This approach is better than the previous example because the class itself is responsible for ensuring that the correct mapping is performed between the database and the Java object. That way, applications don't have to duplicate that logic and don't have the opportunity to attempt bad mappings (such as converting an SQL REAL type to an int). The mapping is also independent of the sequence of columns in the resultset. Encapsulation of the mapping from the database data to the class object is important for ensuring that classes can be reused easily within and between applications; therefore, although it's a little more work than the simple mapping method, it's well worth it.

The Statement and PreparedStatement Interfaces

In this section you're going to look in more detail at the Statement and PreparedStatement interfaces.

You'll start with the Statement interface, where you'll learn about the methods that allow you to constrain the query and how to handle data definition and data manipulation. Next, you'll look at the PreparedStatement, explore the differences between static and dynamic statements, and work with the PreparedStatement interface.

The Statement Interface

You were introduced to the Statement interface in the previous chapter. The Statement interface defines a set of methods that are implemented by an object returned to your program when you call the createStatement() method for the Connection object:

```
try {
  Statement queryStatement = connection.createStatement();
  // ...
} catch(SQLException sqle) {
  System.err.println(sqle);
}
```

Like pretty much every other method defined by JDBC, this code must be within a try block and include a catch block for SQLException.

Once the Statement interface has been created, defining the query is as simple as building a String containing a valid SQL statement and passing that statement as the argument to the executeQuery() method of the Statement object. The SQL query can be a literal, or it can be a String value that you build at run time, as was the case in the InteractiveSQL application in the previous chapter, where the application obtains the SQL string from the text field just before the statement is executed.

Constraining the Resultset

In general, you won't normally know how much data will be returned from executing a query. In the technical_library example, there isn't any possibility of getting into difficulties because of the volume of data, but with production databases you may need some controls. Getting a million rows back from a SELECT operation could be an embarrassment, not only because a substantial amount of time will be involved, but also because a large amount of memory will be needed to store the data. The Statement interface allows you to set constraints on the consequences of executing a query. You can limit the number of rows in the resultset that are returned, as well as specify the maximum field size. You can also limit the amount of time that is allowed for a query to execute.

Maximum Number of Rows

The JDBC driver may impose a limitation on how many rows may be returned by a query, and you may wish to impose your limit on how many rows are returned in a resultset. The Statement interface defines the getMaxRows() and setMaxRows() methods that allow you to query and set the maximum number of rows returned in the ResultSet object. An argument value 0 is defined as no limit.

A particular JDBC driver may default to a practical limit on the number of rows in a resultset or may even have implementation restrictions that limit the number of rows that are returned. To determine the row limit in effect, you can call the getMaxRows() method for your Statement object:

```
Statement statement = connection.createStatement();
int maxRows = statement.getMaxRows();
```

When you wish to limit the number of rows returned from a query in an application, to prevent an extremely lengthy query process, for example, you call setMaxRows() to limit the number of rows returned:

```
SQLStatement.setMaxRows(30);
```

> **It's important to realize that when the maximum row count is set to a non-zero value (zero being unlimited), you won't get any indication when the data that would have been returned has been truncated. If the total number of rows exceeds the maximum value, the maximum number of rows are returned in the resultset, and any remaining rows that meet the query criteria will be silently left behind.**

Maximum Field Size

The Statement interface also enables you to query and set the maximum field size that applies to all column values returned in a ResultSet. Querying this value will tell you if the JDBC driver imposes a practical or absolute limit on the size of the columns returned. The value 0 is defined as no limit.

To determine the maximum field size for statement results, simply call the getMaxFieldSize() method of the Statement:

```
Statement statement = connection.createStatement();
int maxFieldSize = statement.getMaxFieldSize();
```

The value returned is the maximum number of bytes permitted for any field returned in a resultset. Like the maximum row method pair, there is a corresponding `setMaxFieldSize()` method to set the maximum field size:

```
SQLStatement.setMaxFieldSize(4096);
```

Note that the `setMaxFieldSize()` method applies only to columns with the following SQL data types:

BINARY	VARBINARY	LONGVARBINARY
CHAR	VARCHAR	LONGVARCHAR

Any bytes in a field in excess of the maximum you have set will be silently discarded.

Query Time-Out

Depending on your JDBC driver and the database to which it is attached, there may be an execution timeout period after which a query will fail and the `executeQuery()` method will throw an exception. You can check the value for the time-out period with the `getQueryTimeout()` method for a `Statement` object; you can also set the time-out period (for example, if you want a query to fail after a fixed time period) using the `setQueryTimeout()` method. The time-out period is defined in seconds, and a time-out value of 0 indicates that there is no limit on the time that a query can take.

Here's a simple program that will test the default query constraints for your JDBC driver. You can substitute an appropriate URL and driver name if you have other JDBC drivers available.

Try It Out   Query Constraints

Since this program is tiny, you'll incorporate everything into the `main()` method:

```java
import java.sql.DriverManager;
import java.sql.Connection;
import java.sql.Statement;
import java.sql.SQLException;

public class TestQueryTimeOut {
  public static void main(String[] args) {
    Statement statement = null;
    try {
       String url = "jdbc:odbc:technical_library";
       String driver = "sun.jdbc.odbc.JdbcOdbcDriver";
       String username = "guest";
       String password = "guest";
       Class.forName(driver);
       Connection connection = DriverManager.getConnection(url, username, password);
       statement = connection.createStatement();
       System.out.println("Driver          :  " + driver);
    } catch (ClassNotFoundException cnfe) {
       System.out.println(cnfe);
    } catch (SQLException sqle) {
       System.out.println(sqle);
    }
```

```
   // Put each method call in a separate try block to execute them all
   try {
      System.out.print("\nMaximum rows    :");
      int maxRows = statement.getMaxRows();
      System.out.print(maxRows == 0 ? " No limit" : " " + maxRows);
   } catch (SQLException sqle) {
      System.err.print(sqle);
   }
   try {
      System.out.print("\nMax field size   :");
      int maxFieldSize = statement.getMaxFieldSize();
      System.out.print(maxFieldSize == 0 ? " No limit" : " " + maxFieldSize);
   } catch (SQLException sqle) {
      System.err.print(sqle);
   }
   try {
      System.out.print("\nTimeout          :" );
      int queryTimeout = statement.getQueryTimeout();
      System.out.print(queryTimeout == 0 ? " No limit" : " " + queryTimeout);
   } catch (SQLException sqle) {
      System.err.print(sqle);
   }
 }
}
```

Running this with Access, I got the following output:

```
Driver          :  sun.jdbc.odbc.JdbcOdbcDriver

Maximum rows    : No limit
Max field size  :java.sql.SQLException: [Microsoft][ODBC Microsoft Access
Driver]Optional feature not implemented
Timeout          :java.sql.SQLException: [Microsoft][ODBC Microsoft Access
Driver]Optional feature not implemented
```

You can see that the underlying ODBC driver doesn't support time-out or field size constraints — more sophisticated drivers are likely to support these methods.

How It Works

This code is pretty simple. It creates a `Connection` using a URL defining an Access database called `technical_library`. Once the connection is established, a `Statement` object is created, and using that the values for the query time-out period, the maximum column size, and the maximum number of rows can be executed. All three methods providing this information will throw an exception of type `SQLException` if the information is not available — as is the case with the Microsoft Access driver. To make sure that you do call all three methods, even when an exception is thrown, each method call is in a separate `try` block.

Executing DDL and DML

As you know, the `executeQuery()` method is used to execute an SQL query statement — a statement that is expected to return some results in a resultset. As I indicated in the previous chapter, there are other types of SQL statements that do not return results. These statements fall into two primary categories: Data Definition Language (DDL) statements and Data Manipulation Language (DML) statements.

❏ DDL statements are those that change the structure of a database, such as CREATE TABLE and DROP TABLE.

❏ DML statements are those that change the contents of the database, such as INSERT, UPDATE, and DELETE statements.

So far, all of the examples you have seen, including the InteractiveSQL application, have used the executeQuery() method. If you tried to execute an SQL statement that didn't produce a resultset with the InteractiveSQL program, such as any DDL or DML, you would see an exception message reported on the status line. This is shown in Figure 25-2.

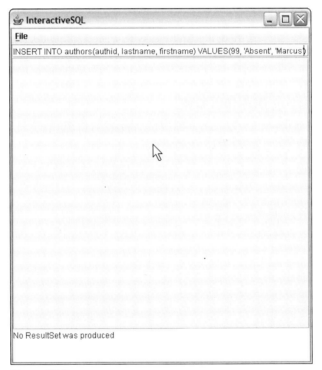

Figure 25-2

The exception containing the message "No ResultSet was produced" is thrown because the executeQuery() method expects only an SQL statement that generates results (note that even though an exception was thrown in this case, the SQL statement was still executed).

The Statement interface provides the executeUpdate() method to execute statements that change the contents of the database rather than return results. Like executeQuery(), the executeUpdate() method accepts a single argument of type String specifying the SQL statement that is to be executed. You can use the executeUpdate() method to execute UPDATE, INSERT, or DELETE SQL statements. You can also use it to execute DDL statements. The method returns a value of type `int` that indicates the number of rows affected by the operation when the database contents are changed, or 0 for statements that do not alter the database.

The code fragment below illustrates use of the `executeUpdate()` method to add a row to the `authors` table:

```
int rowsAdded = 0;

Statement statement = connection.createStatement();
rowsAdded = statement.executeUpdate(
            "INSERT INTO authors (authid, lastname, firstname)" +
            "VALUES(65,'Einstein','Albert')");
```

I split the SQL command into two strings simply because it will not fit on a single line in the book.

Using the `executeUpdate()` method, it is pretty easy to write a utility to create and populate a table. The next example does exactly that. In fact, this example is similar to the `build_tables` utility included with the book's source code, except that the latter reads an SQL statement from an external file.

Try It Out   Executing DDL and DML

Again, this is a small example, so the code will all be contained in the `main()` method. The URL and the driver are identified by the `url` and `driver` strings:

```
import java.sql.DriverManager;
import java.sql.Connection;
import java.sql.Statement;
import java.sql.SQLException;

public class BuildTables {
  public static void main(String[] args) {
    try {
      String username = "guest";
      String password = "guest";
      String url = "jdbc:odbc:technical_library";
      String driver = "sun.jdbc.odbc.JdbcOdbcDriver";

      String[] SQLStatements = {
      "CREATE TABLE online_resources (pub_id int, name char(48), url char(80))",
      "INSERT INTO online_resources VALUES(1, 'Wrox Home Page'," +
                                          " 'http://www.wrox.com')",
      "INSERT INTO online_resources VALUES(2, 'JavaSoft Home Page'," +
                                          " 'http://www.javasoft.com')",
      "INSERT INTO online_resources VALUES(3, 'Apress Home Page'," +
                                          " 'http://www.apress.com')",
      "INSERT INTO online_resources VALUES(4, 'Addison Wesley Home Page'," +
                                          " 'http://www.awprofessional.com')",
      "INSERT INTO online_resources VALUES(5, 'Java Developer Connection'," +
                                          " 'http://java.sun.com')"
      };
      Class.forName(driver);
```

```
        Connection connection = DriverManager.getConnection(url, username, password);
        Statement statement = connection.createStatement();

        for (String SQLStatement : SQLStatements) {
          statement.executeUpdate(SQLStatement);
          System.out.println(SQLStatement);
        }
      } catch (ClassNotFoundException cnfe) {
        System.err.println(cnfe);
      } catch (SQLException sqle) {
        System.err.println(sqle);
      }
    }
  }
}
```

The `SQLStatements` `String` array contains the DDL and DML that will be executed by this program. The `for` loop simply iterates through each statement in the array and executes it using the `executeUpdate()` method of the `Statement`.

You can check the results by running the `InteractiveSQL` application on the table you created and observing that the rows were inserted. To do this, start that application and execute the SQL statement:

```
SELECT * FROM online_resources
```

After you're satisfied with your results, feel free to delete the table. Using a new instance of the `InteractiveSQL` application, execute the statement:

```
DROP TABLE online_resources
```

`InteractiveSQL` will complain that no `ResultSet` is produced, but will dispose of the table nevertheless.

How It Works

The `BuildTables` program is very simple. The `String` array `SQLStatements` contains all of the SQL statements that you want to execute with `executeUpdate()` — one statement in each element of the array. Note that you concatenate two `String` literals for three of the array element values just to make the presentation clearer on the page here. The `for` loop iterates through that array and executes and prints each statement in turn. As usual, the code is inside a `try` block to catch any exceptions that might be thrown.

The only differences between this example and the other examples you've seen are that the SQL statements are executed with the `executeUpdate()` method instead of the `executeQuery()` method, and instead of a `ResultSet` being returned, the method returns the number of rows affected by the operation.

The PreparedStatement Interface

Earlier in this chapter, you saw that you can build SQL strings on the fly and execute them with the `executeQuery()` method of a `Statement`. That is one way to introduce parameters into an SQL statement, but it is not the only way, nor is it necessarily the most convenient. The `PreparedStatement` interface provides an alternative mechanism that enables you to define an SQL statement with **placeholders** for arguments. Placeholders are tokens that appear in the SQL statement that are replaced by actual values before the SQL statement is executed. This is usually much easier than building an SQL statement with specific values by concatenating strings.

Like a `Statement` object, you create a `PreparedStatement` object by calling a method for a `Connection` object. Instead of calling the `createStatement()` method of the `Connection` object, you call the `prepareStatement()` method when you want to create a `PreparedStatement` object. While you can use a `Statement` object to execute any number of different SQL statements, a `PreparedStatement` object executes only one predefined SQL statement that has placeholders for the variable parts of the statement. You specify the SQL statement that a `PreparedStatement` object represents by an argument of type `String` to the `prepareStatement()` method. The argument specifies the SQL statement with each placeholder for a value represented by a `?` character. For example:

```
String newLastName = "UPDATE authors SET lastname = ? WHERE authid = ?";
PreparedStatement updateLastName = connection.prepareStatement(newLastName);
```

The first statement defines a `String` object specifying an `UPDATE` statement with placeholders for the last name and the author ID values. This string is passed as the argument to the `prepareStatement()` method call that creates the `PreparedStatement` object, `updateLastName`. This will allow any value for `lastname` to be set for any `authid`.

Setting Query Parameters

You must set values for all the placeholders that appear in the statement encapsulated by the `updateLastName` reference before the statement can be executed. You supply the value for each placeholder by calling one of the `setXXX()` methods of the `PreparedStatement` interface:

setAsciiStream()	setBigDecimal()	setBinaryStream()
setBoolean()	setByte()	setBytes()
setDate()	setDouble()	setFloat()
setInt()	setLong()	setNull()
setObject()	setShort()	setString()
setTime()	setTimestamp()	setUnicodeStream()

These methods accept, minimally, a position argument that identifies which placeholder you are referring to and a value argument that is the value to be substituted for the placeholder. Placeholders are indexed in sequence from left to right starting at 1, so you reference the leftmost placeholder with a position index of 1, and any placeholders that follow with index values of 2, 3, and so on.

The method that you call for a particular placeholder for an input value depends of the SQL type of the destination column. You must select the method that corresponds to the field type, so you would use `setInt()` for type `INTEGER`, for example. After calling the appropriate `setXXX()` method for each placeholder in the `PreparedStatement` object, you can execute the SQL statement that the `PreparedStatement` object represents either by calling its `executeQuery()` method if the statement generates a resultset or by calling its `executeUpdate()` method to update or otherwise alter the database. Neither method requires an argument since the `PreparedStatement` object already has its SQL statement defined.

Once all the placeholders have values set and you have executed the statement, you can update any or all of the placeholders (or even none) before re-executing the statement. The following code fragment shows the `PreparedStatement` placeholder value replacement in action:

```
// Create a PreparedStatement to update the lastname field for an author
String changeLastName = "UPDATE authors SET lastname = ? WHERE authid = ?";
PreparedStatement updateLastName = connection.prepareStatement(changeLastName);
updateLastName.setString(1,"Martin");          // Set lastname placeholder value
updateLastName.setInt(2,4);                     // Set author ID placeholder value
int rowsUpdated = updateLastName.executeUpdate();   // execute the update
```

Note that placeholders for string arguments are not quoted — they are just a ? character, and the `PreparedStatement` automatically sets up the empty placeholder. Also, it's perfectly okay to set parameters in whatever order you choose — you don't have to set the first placeholder first, the second one next, and so forth, just so long as they are all set before the statement is executed.

Let's try the code fragment above in an example that will change the last name of the author whose `authid` is 4.

Try It Out   Using a PreparedStatement Object

Try out the following code — only the bits that are of particular interest are shaded here:

```
import java.sql.DriverManager;
import java.sql.Connection;
import java.sql.PreparedStatement;
import java.sql.SQLException;

public class TryPlaceHolders {
  public static void main(String[] args) {
    try {
      String url = "jdbc:odbc:technical_library";
      String driver = "sun.jdbc.odbc.JdbcOdbcDriver";
      String user = "guest";
      String password = "guest";
      Class.forName(driver);
      Connection connection = DriverManager.getConnection(url);
      String changeLastName = "UPDATE authors SET lastname = ? WHERE authid = ?";
      PreparedStatement updateLastName =
                          connection.prepareStatement(changeLastName);

      updateLastName.setString(1," Martin");    // Set lastname placeholder value
      updateLastName.setInt(2,4);               // Set author ID placeholder value

      int rowsUpdated = updateLastName.executeUpdate();      // execute the update
      System.out.println("Rows affected: " + rowsUpdated);
      connection.close();
    } catch (ClassNotFoundException cnfe) {
      System.err.println(cnfe);
    } catch (SQLException sqle) {
      System.err.println(sqle);
    }
  }
}
```

This should produce the following output:

```
Rows affected: 1
```

How It Works

The `PreparedStatement` object is created from the `Connection` object by calling the `prepareStatement()` method. The statement is also defined with the placeholders marked as question marks. Those placeholders, for the last name and author ID columns, respectively, are then filled with values at run time by calling the `setString()` and `setInt()` methods of the `PreparedStatement` interface.

The statement is executed by calling the `executeUpdate()` method, which returns the number of rows affected by the update operation. No arguments are passed to the method since the SQL statement was defined when the `PreparedStatement` object was created.

Note that if no change was made to the database, which would occur for example if the primary key value, `authid`, did not exist in the `authors` table, the 0 would be returned as the number of rows affected. If you want to verify that the change was made, you can use the `InteractiveSQL` program to inspect the list of authors.

Statement versus PreparedStatement

There will be times where the choice between using a `Statement` object or a `PreparedStatement` object may not be entirely clear. `PreparedStatement` objects are great when:

- ❑ You need to execute the same statement several times and need to change only specific values.
- ❑ You are working with large chunks of data that make concatenation unwieldy.
- ❑ You are working with a large number of parameters in the SQL statement that make string concatenation unwieldy.

Conversely, `Statement` objects work well when you have simple statements; and of course, you have no option if your JDBC driver doesn't support the `PreparedStatement` interface.

Working with Input Streams

One of the most intriguing features of the `PreparedStatement` interface is the ability to use a stream as the source of data to be inserted in a statement in place of a placeholder. It's very often more convenient to deal with streams when you're working with data types like LONGVARCHAR and LONGVARBINARY. For example, an application storing binary images can very efficiently populate a LONGVARBINARY column by creating a `FileInputStream` object representing the source file.

The `PreparedStatement` interface provides three methods for extracting data from input streams:

Method	Description
setAsciiStream()	Use for columns with the SQL type LONGVARCHAR
setUnicodeStream()	Use for columns with the SQL type LONGVARCHAR
setBinaryStream()	Use for columns with the SQL type LONGVARBINARY

Each of these methods requires three argument values that indicate the placeholder position, the InputStream object that is the source of the data, and the number of bytes to be read from the stream. If an end of file is encountered before the designated number of bytes have been read, the methods throw an exception of type SQLException.

The next example is a simple illustration of using the setAsciiStream() method of the PreparedStatement to store Java source code in a database. It opens a Java source code file as an InputStream object and uses that InputStream object to populate a column in the database. Access does not support the LONGVARCHAR SQL type, and you have to use LONGTEXT as the type for the field that will store the source code in the CREATE TABLE command.

Try It Out   PreparedStatement and Input Streams

The program starts out with the usual code for establishing a connection to the database. Then a FileInputStream object is created from the source code file for this program. The number of bytes contained by the file is obtained by calling the available() method:

```
import java.sql.DriverManager;
import java.sql.Connection;
import java.sql.Statement;
import java.sql.PreparedStatement;
import java.sql.SQLException;
import java.io.FileInputStream;

public class TryInputStream {
  public static void main(String[] args) {
    try {
      String url = "jdbc:odbc:technical_library";
      String driver = "sun.jdbc.odbc.JdbcOdbcDriver";
      String user = "guest";
      String password = "guest";
      FileInputStream fis = new FileInputStream("TryInputStream.java");
      Class.forName(driver);
      Connection connection = DriverManager.getConnection(url, user, password);
      Statement createTable = connection.createStatement();

      // Execute the SQL to create the table
      createTable.executeUpdate(
              "CREATE TABLE source_code (name CHAR(20), source LONGTEXT)");

      // Create a PreparedStatement to INSERT a row in the table
```

```
      String ins = "INSERT INTO source_code VALUES(?,?)";
      PreparedStatement statement = connection.prepareStatement(ins);

      // Set values for the placeholders
      statement.setString(1, "TryInputStream");            // Set first field
      statement.setAsciiStream(2, fis, fis.available());   // Stream is source

      int rowsUpdated = statement.executeUpdate();
      System.out.println("Rows affected: " + rowsUpdated);
      connection.close();
    } catch (Exception e) {
      System.err.println(e);
    }
  }
}
```

The code can throw exceptions of types `IOException`, `ClassNotFoundException`, and `SQLException`, and they all need to be caught. The `FileInputStream` constructor and the `setAsciiStream()` method of the `PreparedStatement` interface can throw `IOException` exceptions. Since all you'll do in each case is output the exception to the error stream, you can economize on the code by catching them all in the same `catch` block that uses `Exception` as the type. This works because all exception objects have the `Exception` class as a base.

You might want to check your results by running the `InteractiveSQL` application to verify that the table was created and the rows were inserted. Start that application and execute the SQL statement:

```
SELECT * FROM source_code
```

After you're satisfied with your results, feel free to delete the table. Having restarted the `InteractiveSQL` application, execute the statement:

```
DROP TABLE source_code
```

Note that once the table exists, executing the `CREATE TABLE` command will fail, so if you want to run the example more than once be sure to delete the table each time.

How It Works

This program is very similar to the previous example. A `FileInputStream` object is created from the file `TryInputStream.java`. Since the `setXXXStream()` methods need to know how many bytes to read from the stream, you have to get the file size of the `TryInputStream.java` file by calling the `available()` method of the `FileInputStream` object.

You first create the table by executing the CREATE TABLE SQL command using the Statement object createTable. Then the PreparedStatement object statement is created, and the placeholder value for the first column is set by calling the setString() method for the statement object. The real magic happens in the setAsciiStream() method — all you have to do is supply the method with the placeholder position, the InputStream, and the number of bytes to be read — returned by the available() method for the FileInputStream object. When the SQL INSERT statement is executed, the bytes are read from the stream and stored in the second column of the row inserted in the database table source_code.

When your JDBC applications will be dealing with large chunks of data, the Stream methods of the PreparedStatement interface are a real help.

The ResultSet

Now that you have a good understanding of the capabilities of the Statement and PreparedStatement interfaces, it's time to dig a little deeper into the details of getting the data back from the query. In this section, you'll add to what you learned about the ResultSet object in the last chapter. You'll explore the getXXX() methods in more depth and look at some of the special SQL data types and how they are handled. You'll also look at how to use streams with a ResultSet object.

Retrieving Column Data for Specified Data Types

So far you've retrieved data from a resultset as type String because data of any SQL type can be retrieved in this way. As you saw briefly in the previous chapter, like the Statement and PreparedStatement interfaces, the ResultSet interface provides methods for working with a variety of data types and retrieving data as a Java type that is more consistent with the original SQL type.

Most of these methods work in a similar way and come in two overloaded forms. One form specifies the column by the column name:

```
xxxType resultSet.getXXX(String columnName)
```

The other specifies the column name by its index position, the first position index being 1:

```
xxxType resultSet.getXXX(int columnPosition)
```

The mechanics of calling these methods is quite straightforward, but to use these methods effectively, you need to understand the possible mappings between Java data types and SQL data types in both directions.

The table in Figure 25-3 illustrates the mappings between SQL data types and the appropriate `ResultSet getXXX()` methods. To decide which `getXXX()` method you should use, look in the table for the method that maps the column data type to the Java type you'll use. The "preferred" method for a type is indicated with the Y character. That means that it is the closest mapping to the SQL type. Other methods that may also work are indicated by the ± *symbol*.

	TINYINT	SMALLINT	INTEGER	BIGINT	REAL	FLOAT	DOUBLE	DECIMAL	NUMERIC	BIT	CHAR	VARCHAR	LONGVARCHAR	BINARY	VARBINARY	LONGVARBINARY	DATE	TIME	TIMESTAMP
getByte()	Y	±	±	±	±	±	±	±	±	±	±	±	±						
getShort()	±	Y	±	±	±	±	±	±	±	±	±	±	±						
getInt()	±	±	Y	±	±	±	±	±	±	±	±	±	±						
getLong()	±	±	±	Y	±	±	±	±	±	±	±	±	±						
getFloat()	±	±	±	±	Y	±	±	±	±	±	±	±	±						
getDouble()	±	±	±	±	±	Y	Y	±	±	±	±	±	±						
getBigDecimal()	±	±	±	±	±	±	±	Y	Y	±	±	±	±						
getBoolean()	±	±	±	±	±	±	±	±	±	Y	±	±	±						
getString()	±	±	±	±	±	±	±	±	±	±	Y	Y	±	±	±	±	±	±	±
getBytes()														Y	Y	±			
getDate()											±	±	±				Y		
getTime()											±	±	±					Y	±
getTimeStamp()											±	±	±					±	Y
getAsciiStream()											±	±	Y	±	±	±			
getUnicodeStream()											±	±	Y	±	±	±			
getBinaryStream()														±	Y	Y			
getObject()	±	±	±	±	±	±	±	±	±	±	±	±	±	±	±	±	±	±	±

ResultSet Method to SQL Data Type Mapping

Figure 25-3

Working with Null Values

As I've said, NULL is a special value in the world of SQL. NULL is not the same thing as an empty string for text columns, nor is it the same thing as zero for a numeric field. NULL means that no data is defined for a column value within a relation. For example, recall the authors table, which has several values that may or may not have values assigned, including the email column. To determine which authors do not have an e-mail address recorded, you could use the following query:

```
SELECT authid FROM authors WHERE email = NULL
```

This query will return the ID for each author without an e-mail address.

The ResultSet interface provides a method for testing a column value within a resultset to determine if it is null. The wasNull() method returns a boolean value that is true if the last column read from the ResultSet object was a null, and false if it was some other value.

You'll need to use the capability to detect a null value for a field in your code unless you created your tables with every column defined as NOT NULL, which tells the database system that it must never allow a null value in any column. However, that's not always a practical or desirable way to design tables.

Let's consider a simple example that selects and displays the author ID, last name, first name, and e-mail address for each row in the authors table. If any of these values are not assigned a value, the code could throw a NullPointerException when the program attempts to display the value. To avoid that sort of bad program behavior, this example will use the wasNull() method of the ResultSet to check for empty fields. Notice that the wasNull() method is called after the value is retrieved from the ResultSet.

Try It Out   Testing for Null Values in the ResultSet

Here's the code for the example:

```java
import java.sql.Connection;
import java.sql.DriverManager;
import java.sql.Statement;
import java.sql.ResultSet;

public class TestNullValues {
   public static void main(String[] args) {
      String url = "jdbc:odbc:technical_library";
      String driver = "sun.jdbc.odbc.JdbcOdbcDriver";
      String theStatement = "SELECT authid, lastname, firstname, email FROM authors";

      try {
        Class.forName(driver);
        Connection connection = DriverManager.getConnection(url, "guest", "guest");
        Statement queryAuthors = connection.createStatement();
        ResultSet results = queryAuthors.executeQuery(theStatement);

        String lastname, firstname, email;
        int id;
        while(results.next()) {
           id = results.getInt(1);
           lastname = results.getString(2);
           firstname = results.getString(3);
           email = results.getString(4);
```

```
                    if(results.wasNull()) {
                       email = "no email";
                    }
                    System.out.println(Integer.toString(id) + ", " +
                                        lastname.trim() + ", " +
                                        firstname.trim() +", " +
                                        email.trim());
                 }
              queryAuthors.close();
           } catch (Exception e) {
              System.err.println(e);
           }
        }
     }
```

Running this code produces the following results:

```
1, Gamma, Erich, no email
2, Helm, Richard, no email
3, Johnson, Ralph, no email
4, Horton, Ivor, no email
...
```

How It Works

In `TestNullValues`, the SQL statement is executed, and the values for the author ID, last name, first name, and e-mail address are extracted into local variables. The rows in the resultset are ordered by `authid` because of the ORDER BY clause in the SQL query. Because the value for `email` can be `null` in the table, you call the `wasNull()` method immediately after retrieving that column from `results` to test if the value read was a `null` value. If so, you replace the literal string referenced by `email`, so outputting the report will work without throwing an exception. Since the `authid`, `lastname`, and `firstname` columns are required, there's no need to test those column values for `null` values.

Working with Special Data Types

The JDBC `java.sql` package defines some special data types to accommodate the characteristics of particular SQL types that don't readily map to a standard Java data type. A `ResultSet` class object has methods for accessing data of these special types. The `ResultSet` class also defines methods that access values of SQL types that map to Java data types defined in the `java.math` package that are designed to handle numbers with a large number of digits of precision. These types are as follows:

Date

The `java.sql.Date` class defines the object that is returned by the `ResultSet.getDate()` method. This class subclasses the `Date` class defined in the `java.util` package, so all of the methods for `java.util.Date` objects can be applied to objects of type `java.sql.Date`. The `java.sql.Date` class defines three nondeprecated methods:

❑   A `toString()` method that formats the value of the date as a string in the form *yyyy-mm-dd*

❑   A static `valueOf()` method that converts a string representation (*yyyy-mm-dd* form) of a date into a `java.sql.Date` object

❏ A setTime() method that accepts an argument of type long that is a millisecond value relative to 1st January 1970, 00:00:00 GMT, and sets the date value encapsulated by the current java.sql.Date object to this value

Time

Like java.sql.Date, the java.sql.Time class wraps the java.util.Date class as a subclass. The class defines a static valueOf() method that returns a Time object from a string representation (*hh:mm:ss* form) of time into a Time object and a toString() method that returns a string representation of the time encapsulated by the object in the form *hh:mm:ss*.

Timestamp

The java.sql.Timestamp class also subclasses java.util.Date, but provides additional support for SQL timestamps with support for nanoseconds (java.util.Date supports time only to the nearest millisecond). The static valueOf() method creates a Timestamp object from a string representation (*yyyy-mm-dd hh:mm:ss.fffffffff* form). It also overloads accessor methods and comparison methods — before() and after() — to support nanoseconds.

Big Numbers

The SQL NUMERIC and DECIMAL types are mapped to the Java BigDecimal class type. This class is defined in the java.math package along with the BigInteger class that defines objects that encapsulate integers of arbitrary precision, with negative values in 2's complement form. A BigDecimal object defines a decimal value of arbitrary precision that can be positive or negative. A BigDecimal object is implemented as an arbitrary precision signed integer — a BigInteger object, plus a scale value that specifies the number of digits to the right of the decimal point. Thus, the value of a BigDecimal object is the integer value divided by 10^{scale}. To read a column value of either NUMERIC or DECIMAL SQL type as a Java BigDecimal object, you use the getBigDecimal() method for the ResultSet object.

The BigInteger and BigDecimal classes are very useful for applications that require a large number of digits of precision, such as security keys, very large monetary values, and so forth. The BigInteger and BigDecimal classes provide mathematical methods for addition, subtraction, multiplication, and division, as well as comparison methods and methods for returning their value as standard Java types. Additionally, BigInteger objects support bitwise and shift operations. The BigDecimal class provides methods for tailoring the rounding behavior in arithmetic operations.

Like Java String objects, the value of a BigInteger or BigDecimal object is immutable. That is, once an object has been created, you can't change its value. When you apply arithmetic operations to BigInteger and BigDecimal objects using their methods, such as multiply() and divide(), you always get a new object as a result, in much the same way as you get a new String object when you use the concat() or substring() methods of String.

You can get an idea of the usefulness of these classes if you consider the difficulties you would have if you had to use type double for computations where which you needed to maintain a great deal of accuracy. Suppose you had to calculate the product of the following two floating-point numbers:

```
98765423462576235623562346234623462.35632456234567890
```

and

```
98982345232356246643764376346743734346547.34586558
```

If you were to calculate the product of two variables of type double that you have initialized with these values, you would probably be very disappointed when your code produced the result:

```
9.776033242192577E74
```

Considering the number of digits of precision you entered originally for the factors, you could not claim that accuracy has been maintained. Of course, the problem is that the precision for values of type double is fixed and limited to the number of digits that you see in the preceding result. Enter the BigDecimal class. Let's see how it would work with that.

Try It Out   The BigDecimal Class

You can do the calculation and produce the sort of result that you want using BigDecimal objects as follows:

```java
import java.math.BigDecimal;

public class TestBigDecimal {
  public static void main(String[] args) {
    BigDecimal bn1 = new BigDecimal(
        "9876542346257623562356234623462346234623462.35632456234567890");
    BigDecimal bn2 = new BigDecimal(
        "98982345232356246643764376347634674373436547.34586558");
    BigDecimal bn3 = bn1.multiply(bn2);
    System.out.println(bn3);
  }
}
```

When you run the code, the program displays the result of the multiplication:

```
97760332421925786372389351223148078503101925277904720859519667576821933 9448.7733135
102106926932422620
```

How It Works

The BigDecimal class has remarkable capabilities. It can support numbers of virtually limitless precision. The precision and scale are both 32-bit signed integer values, so they can be as large as 2,147,483,647 digits — and that's a huge number of decimal digits! In the example, you create two BigDecimal objects, bn1 and bn2, representing the original values that you want to multiply. You multiply them using the multiply() method for bn1 and store the reference to the BigDecimal object that is returned containing the result in bn3. You can use this in a println() method call since the BigDecimal class implements the toString() method.

The BigDecimal class defines methods that implement all of the usual arithmetic operators, add(), subtract(), multiply(), divide(), and remainder(), as well as a range of methods supporting other operations, including max(), min(), pow(), and compareTo(). Just about anything that you can do with a primitive numeric type you can also do with BigDecimal objects.

The BigInteger class is just as impressive — it provides the same arbitrary precision characteristics for integer values. Of course, there is a price to pay for that precision. Computations using the BigInteger and BigDecimal classes are notably slower than their counterparts using native Java types.

The BigInteger and BigDecimal classes manage digits as objects in a vector, so to get the flexibility of unlimited precision, you have to trade off computing time for operations on the numbers. Nonetheless, this class is invaluable for many applications.

Working with Streams

Earlier, you looked at using streams to populate LONGVARCHAR and LONGVARBINARY columns because it's frequently much easier to use streams when you're working with large objects.

The ResultSet interface provides three methods for retrieving data from a database as a stream. These methods are:

Method	Description
getAsciiStream()	Use for LONGVARCHAR columns
getCharacterStream()	Use for LONGVARCHAR columns
getBinaryStream()	Use for LONGVARBINARY columns

Each of these methods requires an argument to be supplied that indicates the column either by name or by index position. The getCharacterStream() method returns a reference to a Reader object, whereas the other two methods return a reference to an InputStream object from which you can read the data for the column.

The next example shows a simple example of using the getAsciiStream() method of the ResultSet. This example extends the TryInputStream.java program that you saw in the previous chapter.

Try It Out   ResultSet Columns as Streams

Here's a version of the TryInputStream.java program that uses a stream:

```
import java.sql.Connection;
import java.sql.DriverManager;
import java.sql.Statement;
import java.sql.PreparedStatement;
import java.sql.ResultSet;
import java.io.FileInputStream;
import java.io.BufferedReader;
import java.io.InputStreamReader;

public class TryInputStream2 {
  public static void main(String[] args) {
    try {
      String url = "jdbc:odbc:technical_library";
      String driver = "sun.jdbc.odbc.JdbcOdbcDriver";
      String user = "guest";
      String password = "guest";

      FileInputStream fis = new FileInputStream("TryInputStream2.java");

      Class.forName(driver);
```

```
Connection connection = DriverManager.getConnection(url, user, password);
Statement createTable = connection.createStatement();
createTable.executeUpdate(
"CREATE TABLE source_code (name char(20), source LONGTEXT)");
String ins = "INSERT INTO source_code VALUES(?,?)";
PreparedStatement statement = connection.prepareStatement(ins);

statement.setString(1, "TryInputStream2");
statement.setAsciiStream(2, fis, fis.available());

int rowsUpdated = statement.executeUpdate();
System.out.println("Rows affected: " + rowsUpdated);
// Create a statement object and execute a SELECT
Statement getCode = connection.createStatement();
ResultSet theCode = getCode.executeQuery(
                     "SELECT name,source FROM source_code");
BufferedReader reader = null;              // Reader for a column
String input = null;                       // Stores an input line

while(theCode.next()) {                     // For each row
  // Create a buffered reader from the stream for a column
  reader = new BufferedReader(
                   new InputStreamReader(theCode.getAsciiStream(2)));

  // Read the column data from the buffered reader
  while((input = reader.readLine()) != null) { // While there is a line
    System.out.println(input);                 // display it
  }
}
connection.close();
} catch (Exception e) {
System.err.println(e);
}
}
}
}
```

Make sure that the source_code table doesn't exist before you run the program. If it does, you can delete it using the InteractiveSQL program, as you've seen before. You should see the text of this source code printed out. After you're satisfied with your results, you can delete the table using the InteractiveSQL application.

How It Works

Most of this code sets up and populates the source_code table with the data from the program source file, TryInputStream2.java. Once that is done you get a Statement object from the connection that you'll use to retrieve the data from the table. The while loop iterates through all the rows in the resultset that contains the result of the SQL query in the way that you are now very familiar with.

Using the ResultSet object that is returned from executeQuery(), you get an InputStream object corresponding to the second column in the current row by calling its getAsciiStream() method with the position index argument as 2. The InputStream object that is returned is used to create an InputStreamReader object, which in turn is used to create a BufferedReader object that provides buffered stream input for the column data. The readLine() method for the BufferedReader object returns a `String` object containing a line of input. When the end of the stream is reached, the `readLine()` method returns `null` so the inner `while` loop will then terminate.

Calling Procedures

Many database systems support **stored procedures**, which are predefined sequences of SQL commands that you can call when you want to execute the function that the stored procedure defines. This is a very powerful facility with a lot of ramifications, so I'll only touch on the basics of how to use this here, just so that you are aware of it. JDBC provides support for this sort of capability through the `java.sql.CallableStatement` interface, which is derived from the `PreparedStatement` interface. You can obtain a `CallableStatement` reference corresponding to a stored procedure call by calling the `prepareCall()` method for a `Connection` object.

The argument to the `prepareCall()` method is a `String` object that defines a string in a format described as **SQL escape syntax**. The purpose of SQL escape syntax is to enable the driver to determine that this is not an ordinary SQL statement and needs to be transformed into a form that will be understood by the database system. This enables the idiosyncrasies of how stored procedures are called in different database systems to be accommodated, since it is up to the driver to recognize that the string is SQL escape syntax and transform it to the format required by the underlying database. Let's first consider the simplest possible form for a string to call a stored procedure:

```
"{call procedureName}"
```

The braces are always present. The procedure to be called has the name `procedureName`. Given that you have a `Connection` object `connection`, you could call the procedure with the following code:

```
CallableStatement call = connection.prepareCall("{call procedureName}");
ResultSet result = call.executeQuery();          // Execute the procedure call
```

Now you can obtain the data from the `ResultSet` object that is returned by the procedure using `getXXX()` methods in the usual way. This code assumes that the stored procedure produces a single resultset. Of course, it is possible that a procedure may produce multiple resultsets, in which case you would use the `execute()` method to execute the procedure and `getResultSet()` to retrieve the resultset. If the procedure updated the database, you would call the `executeUpdate()` method to execute it.

Stored procedures can have arguments that specify input values (called `IN` parameters) to the operation. In this case you specify the parameter list between parentheses following the procedure name. Each parameter is denoted by `?`, as for a `PreparedStatement` command, and you set the values for the parameters using the `setXXX()` methods in the way you have seen for `PreparedStatement` objects. For example:

```
CallableStatement call = connection..prepareCall("{call getMonthData(?, ?)}");
call.setInt(1, 6);                              // Set first argument value
call.setInt(2,1999);                            // Set second argument value
ResultSet result = call.executeQuery();         // Execute the procedure call
```

As you have seen, each parameter is identified by an index value, the first parameter having the index value 1.

Procedures can also have parameters for returning a result—referred to as OUT parameters—and you can set these, too. The placeholder for an OUT parameter is ?—no different from an IN parameter—but obviously the process for setting the parameter is significantly different. For each OUT parameter, you must identify the type of the output value as one of the types defined in the java.sql.Types class by calling the registerOutParameter() method for the CallableStatement object. The first argument is the index position of the OUT parameter, and the second argument is the type. For example:

```
call.registerOutParameter(2, Types.INTEGER);   // Second parameter OUT and INTEGER
```

Of course, if you don't want to qualify the type constants from the Types class in the code, you can always use a static import statement to import the names into your source file.

Once the OUT parameters have been registered, you then execute the procedure call in the way you have seen. If a resultset is returned, you can access the data from that in the usual way. To get the value for each OUT parameter, you must call the getXXX() method for the CallableStatement object that corresponds to the parameter type, so for the preceding example you would write:

```
int value = call.getInt(2);                      // Read second parameter value
```

Procedures can also have parameters that serve as both input and output, so-called INOUT parameters. In this case you just combine what I've discussed for IN and OUT parameters, using setXXX() for the input value, registerOutParameter() to set the type for the output, and getXXX() to retrieve the output value.

Finally, a stored procedure may return a value—not as part of the parameter list but as a return value as for a method. In this case you specify it as follows:

```
CallableStatement call = connection.prepareCall("{? = call getData(?, ?)}");
```

This has two parameters plus a return value specified by the first ?—preceding the = in the string. This placeholder is at index position 1, and the two other parameters will be at index position 2 and 3. You now need to register the type of the value that is returned by the procedure before you execute the procedure call. You do this in the same way as for any other OUT parameter:

```
call.registerOutParameter(1,Types.DECIMAL);
```

When the procedure has been executed, you can retrieve the return value using the getDouble() method for the call object.

Handling Errors

In all of the examples that you've used so far in this chapter, I've glossed over the issue of errors, warnings, and exceptions. The examples up until this point have all been predicated on the hope that everything will work okay.

Unfortunately, life is a bit less predictable than that, and you need to take some extra steps in your JDBC applications to handle conditions that generate warnings or errors. In this section, you'll see how to build mechanisms to trap errors, how to use the extra facilities built into JDBC to get detailed warning and error information from the data source, and how to gracefully recover from JDBC exceptions. The first place where you get some extra help is from the SQLException class.

SQLException

Most of the examples that you've seen so far have just output the basic exception that is thrown when an error occurred:

```
try {
    //do JDBC stuff
} catch(SQLException sqle) {
    System.err.println(sqle);
}
```

This invokes the toString() method for the exception object and displays the result. Every method of every JDBC class and interface can throw an exception of type SQLException. Using the SQLException exception in this way is a pretty broad-brush approach to handling errors in JDBC, and it is certainly possible to do a little better.

To do useful things with the SQLException, you need to know that three important pieces of information are available from the exception object that is thrown. How you use these pieces of information depends on what is possible in the context of your application.

The Exception Message

The boilerplate information that you get with just about any exception is a string that describes the exception, and as you've seen, it's returned by the getMessage() method of the exception object. For the examples that I've presented so far, this is the most useful piece of information. However, this string varies depending on the JDBC driver that you're using, so while this information is useful for humans as an indication of why things are not working out as they should, it's difficult for programs to make decisions based on this information. For that you need to use something a little different.

SQL State

There is another piece of information that is available when an error occurs — the SQL state — which you can use within a program to make decisions about how best to proceed. The SQL state is a string that contains a state as defined by the X/Open SQL standard. You obtain the SQL state value from the SQLException object by calling its getSQLState() method.

The X/Open standard defines the SQL state as a five-character string that consists of two parts. The first two characters of the string define the **class** of the state — for example, the characters 01 represent the SQL state "success with warning". Class here is merely a classification — it has nothing to do with class types.

The next three characters define the subclass of the state. The X/Open standard defines specific subclasses and also provides the value 000 as a general subclass. Specific database implementations may define state subclasses of their own using the values 900 through ZZZ where the standard does not provide a specific subclass.

The following table shows the SQL state strings defined in the X/Open standard. When these state codes are set, they may not be directly attributable to your JDBC code, but may reflect an error occurring in the underlying driver. For example, if you're using the JDBC-ODBC Bridge, a SQL state can reflect an error occurring at the ODBC driver level.

Class	Subclass	Description
01		Success with warning
	002	Disconnect error
	004	String data, right truncation
	006	Privilege not revoked
02	000	No data
07		Dynamic SQL error
	001	Using-clause does not match dynamic parameters
	006	Restricted data type attribute violation
	008	Invalid descriptor count
08		Connection exception
	001	Server rejected the connection
	002	Connection name in use
	003	Connection does not exist
	004	Client unable to establish connection
	007	Transaction state unknown
	S01	Communication failure
21		Cardinality violation
	S01	Insert value list does not match column list
	S02	Degree of derived table does not match column list
22		Data exception
	001	String data, right truncation
	003	Numeric value out of range
	005	Error in assignment
	012	Divide by zero
23	000	Integrity constraint violation
24	000	Invalid cursor state
25	000	Invalid transaction state
	S02	Transaction still active
	S03	Transaction is rolled back

Class	Subclass	Description
2D	000	Invalid transaction termination
34	000	Invalid cursor name
37	000	Syntax error or access violation
40	000	Transaction rollback
	001	Statement completion unknown
42	000	Syntax error or access violation
HZ	000-ZZZ	RDA (Remote Data Access) errors
S0		Invalid name
	001	Base table or view already exists
	002	Base table not found
	011	Index already exists
	012	Index not found
	021	Column already exists
S1		Call Level Interface specific
	001	Memory allocation error
	002	Invalid column number
	003	Program type out of range
	004	SQL data type out of range
	008	Operation canceled
	009	Invalid argument value
	010	Function sequence error
	012	Invalid transaction operation code
	013	Memory management error
	015	No cursor name available
	900-ZZZ	Implementation defined

The SQL state string is a very useful piece of information if you want to handle exceptions programmatically. As you can see from the table, the subclasses indicate specific problems that in many cases may be recoverable. Using the SQL state value, you can make decisions in your program as to whether it is possible to recover from an exception or not.

For example, if your application creates tables, an exception indicating SQL state S0001 means that the table already exists. Depending on your application, this may not represent a fatal error, and your program can continue. This was the case in the example that generated to the source_code table, for example, and then output the source code from the table to the screen. As written, the example terminated when the exception was thrown, but it would obviously be possible to code the example to use the SQL state information and allow the program to continue with the output operation if the table was already there.

Vendor Error Code

The third piece of information that you can get from the SQLException object is a vendor-specific error code. This value is returned as an integer, and its meaning is completely defined by the driver vendor. You can obtain this value by calling the getErrorCode() method for the SQLException object.

Let's use an example to take a look at the additional information you can get when an exception is thrown.

Try It Out   Extracting Information from SQLException

In this example, you'll intentionally create errors in the executed SQL statements to generate exceptions, and then extract the message, vendor code, and SQL state from the exception. To generate the exception, I've misspelled the name of the table in the variable theStatement.

```java
import java.sql.Connection;
import java.sql.DriverManager;
import java.sql.Statement;
import java.sql.ResultSet;
import java.sql.SQLException;

public class ExtractSQLExceptionInfo {
  public static void main(String[] args) {
    String url = "jdbc:odbc:technical_library";
    String driver = "sun.jdbc.odbc.JdbcOdbcDriver";
    String user = "guest";
    String password = "guest";

    // Following statement contains a deliberate mistake
    String theStatement = "SELECT lastname, firstname FROM autors";

    try {
      Class.forName(driver);
      Connection connection = DriverManager.getConnection(url, user, password);
      Statement queryAuthors = connection.createStatement();
      ResultSet theResults =  queryAuthors.executeQuery(theStatement);

      queryAuthors.close();
    } catch (ClassNotFoundException cnfe) {
      System.err.println(cnfe);
    } catch (SQLException sqle) {
      String sqlMessage = sqle.getMessage();
      String sqlState  = sqle.getSQLState();
      int vendorCode = sqle.getErrorCode();
      System.err.println("Exception occurred:");
      System.err.println("Message: " + sqlMessage);
      System.err.println("SQL state: " + sqlState);
      System.err.println("Vendor code: " + vendorCode +
```

```
                                      "\n----------------");
        }
      }
    }
```

When I ran this example, it produced the following output:

```
Exception occurred:
Message: [Microsoft][ODBC Microsoft Access Driver] The Microsoft Jet database
engine cannot find the input table or query 'autors'.  Make sure it exists and that
its name is spelled correctly.
SQL state: S0002
Vendor code: -1305
```

How It Works

In the `SQLException` exception handler, you extract the message, the SQL state, and the vendor-specific error code. In this elementary example, this information is simply formatted and displayed. In a more sophisticated application, you might want to decide how the program proceeds based on the information, and log this information to a file to help you troubleshoot your application.

The message that is returned is quite self-explanatory. The text will vary, of course, from driver to driver — hence, the importance of the SQL state value. If you look back to the previous table, you'll see that the SQL state reported in this exception corresponds to the SQL state "Base table not found," which correctly identifies the problem. Lastly, the vendor code that was returned indicates the driver vendor's numeric code for the exception.

Chaining SQLExceptions

When an SQL exception is thrown, more than one exception object associated with the error that caused the exception may be thrown. To handle this situation, the `SQLException` may be linked to another in a chain of exceptions. This situation is shown in Figure 25-4.

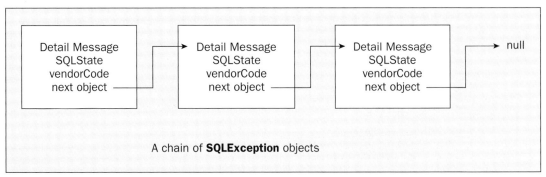

A chain of **SQLException** objects

Figure 25-4

An `SQLException` object is essentially a node in a linked list. The `SQLException` class defines the `setNextException()` method for JDBC drivers and applications — the code throwing the exception, in other words — to link a new exception to the chain. When a `catch` block in your program catches an exception of type SQLException, it is always the first node in a chain of one or more exception objects. You can call the getNextException() method for the SQLException object that is passed to a catch block to obtain the next exception object in the chain if one exists. This method returns either a reference to the next SQLException object in the chain, or null if there are no more exceptions.

Thus, when your program catches an SQLException, you should always use the getNextException() method in a loop to get all of the exceptions. The code fragment below illustrates a simple technique for looping:

```
try {
    // call a method that can throw SQLException
    theProgram.doSQLQuery();
} catch(SQLException sqle) {
    do {                                  // loop through each exception
        // do something with each exception
        System.err.println("Exception occurred:\nMessage: " + sqle.getMessage());
        System.err.println("SQL state: " + sqle.getSQLState());
        System.err.println("Vendor code: " + sqle.getErrorCode());
    } while((sqle = sqle.getNextException()) != null);
}
```

In the do-while loop, you output information from the exception object sqle, which is passed to the catch block on the first iteration. The loop condition stores the references returned by the getNextException() for the sqle object back in sqle, and if it is not null, the loop continues. In this way you iterate through all the exceptions in the chain, outputting the information from each.

The next example shows the mechanics of how an application can add a new exception to a chain of SQLException objects in its exception handling. This technique is useful if you are defining a class that wraps one of the JDBC classes and you want to provide additional information when an exception is thrown.

Try It Out   Chaining SQLExceptions

You'll contrive to add an SQLException object to a chain of exceptions by executing the database operations in a method, doQuery(). This method will catch the SQLException when it is thrown, add a new exception object to the chain, and then rethrow the exception so that it can be caught in main(). Here's the code:

```
import java.sql.Connection;
import java.sql.DriverManager;
import java.sql.Statement;
import java.sql.ResultSet;
import java.sql.SQLException;

public class ChainSQLExceptions {
    public static void main(String[] args) {
        ChainSQLExceptions theApp = new ChainSQLExceptions();
        try {
            theApp.doQuery();                  // Call the method that deals with the DB
        } catch(SQLException sqle) {            // Catch the exception thrown by the method
            do {                               // loop through each exception
                // do something with each exception
                System.err.println("Exception occurred:\nMessage: " + sqle.getMessage());
```

```
            System.err.println("SQL state: " + sqle.getSQLState());
            System.err.println("Vendor code: " + sqle.getErrorCode() +
                              "\n----------------");
        } while((sqle = sqle.getNextException()) != null);
    }
}

// Method to add an exception to a chain of SQLExceptions
public void doQuery() throws SQLException {
    String url = "jdbc:odbc:technical_library";
    String driver = "sun.jdbc.odbc.JdbcOdbcDriver";
    String user = "guest";
    String password = "guest";
    String theStatement = "SELECT lastname, firstname FROM autors";

    try {
        Class.forName(driver);
        Connection connection = DriverManager.getConnection(url, user, password);
        Statement queryAuthors = connection.createStatement();
        ResultSet theResults = queryAuthors.executeQuery(theStatement);

        queryAuthors.close();
    } catch(ClassNotFoundException cnfe) {
        System.out.println(cnfe);
    } catch(SQLException sqle) {
        SQLException generatedException = new SQLException(        // New exception
                                   "SQL operation cancelled", // Message
                                   "S1008",                   // SQL state
                                   0);                        // Vendor code
        generatedException.setNextException(sqle);      // Append the old exception
        throw generatedException;      }               // and throw the chain
    }
}
```

When I ran the program with the JDBC-ODBC driver I got the following:

```
Exception occurred:
Message: SQL operation cancelled
SQL state: S1008
Vendor code: 0
----------------
Exception occurred:
Message: [Microsoft][ODBC Microsoft Access Driver] The Microsoft Jet database
engine cannot find the input table or query 'autors'.  Make sure it exists and that
its name is spelled correctly.
SQL state: S0002
Vendor code: -1305
----------------
```

How It Works

This example demonstrates the code that you saw earlier for handling chains of SQLException objects and how you can add exceptions to the chain.

The `main()` method calls the `doQuery()` method, which can throw a `SQLException`. The exception handler in `main()` starts with the exception object that is passed to the exception handler and follows the chain of exceptions, outputting the information for each one. For each exception, the message, `SQLState`, and vendor code are displayed.

The `doQuery()` method contains an exception handler that appends a new `SQLException` to the chain when an exception is thrown because of an error in the database access code. You just append the old exception to your `generatedException` and throw it again.

SQLWarnings

JDBC provides a means of obtaining warning information from JDBC objects. Sometimes conditions may arise that may not be serious enough to throw an exception, but do merit the program being signaled that all is not completely well. Warnings are represented by objects of type `java.sql.SQLWarning`, and an `SQLWarning` object is silently appended to a JDBC object when an operation using the object causes something odd to occur.

The `SQLWarning` class is derived from `SQLException`; therefore, it inherits the ability of the `SQLException` objects to define a message, an `SQLState` code, and a vendor code. An `SQLWarning` object can also be chained to one or more other `SQLWarning` objects. The techniques described in the previous section for traversing `SQLException` object chains apply just as well to `SQLWarning` object chains. In most respects, the `SQLWarning` looks a lot like `SQLException`, except for one very important distinction: You have to ask for an `SQLWarning` object explicitly. If you don't ask, you won't get it.

The `ResultSet`, `Connection`, and `Statement` interfaces all declare the `getWarnings()` method, which returns an `SQLWarning` object if warnings are present, and `null` otherwise.

To better understand how `SQLWarning` objects arise, consider one special class of warnings — data truncation. There is nothing preventing an application from retrieving data from a column as a Java type that is not particularly suitable for the SQL type — for example, accessing a floating-point column as an integer type. Of course, this can and probably will result in data loss. This sort of thing will cause an `SQLWarning` object to be chained to the `ResultSet` object that requested the inappropriate data conversion. To detect this the application can call the `getWarnings()` method of the `ResultSet` object.

Since data truncation is a particularly common type of warning, JDBC provides a `DataTruncation` class that is itself derived from `SQLWarning`. Let's give it a go.

Try It Out   **Using SQLWarning**

This example is basically the same code as the previous example, except that here you intentionally retrieve floating-point values from the PRODUCTS table integers to force a warning. Any warnings arising from data access operations are detected by the `checkForWarning()` method that you've added to the class. Here's the code:

```
import java.sql.Connection;
import java.sql.DriverManager;
import java.sql.Statement;
```

```java
import java.sql.ResultSet;
import java.sql.SQLException;
import java.sql.SQLWarning;

public class TestSQLWarning {
  public static void main(String[] args) {
    TestSQLWarning theApp = new TestSQLWarning();
    try {
      theApp.doQuery();                 // Call the method that deals with the DB
    } catch(SQLException sqle) {         // Catch the exception thrown by the method
      do {                              // loop through each exception
        // do something with each exception
        System.err.println("Exception occurred:\nMessage: " + sqle.getMessage());
        System.err.println("SQL state: " + sqle.getSQLState());
        System.err.println("Vendor code: " + sqle.getErrorCode() +
                           "\n----------------");
      } while((sqle = sqle.getNextException()) != null);
    }
  }

  public void doQuery() throws SQLException {
    String url = "jdbc:odbc:technical_library";
    String driver = "sun.jdbc.odbc.JdbcOdbcDriver";
    String user = "guest";
    String password = "guest";
    String theStatement =
            "SELECT title, price FROM books WHERE price <> NULL";
    try {
      Class.forName(driver);
      Connection connection = DriverManager.getConnection(url, user, password);
      Statement queryBooks = connection.createStatement();
      ResultSet results = queryBooks.executeQuery(theStatement);
      int price;
      String title;
      while(results.next()) {
        title = results.getString("title");
        checkForWarning(results.getWarnings());

        price = results.getInt("price");
        checkForWarning(results.getWarnings());

        System.out.println(title + " " + price);
      }
      queryBooks.close();
    } catch (ClassNotFoundException cnfe) {
      System.out.println(cnfe);
    } catch (SQLException sqle) {
      SQLException generatedException =
              new SQLException("SQL operation canceled","S1008", 0);
      SQLException lastException = sqle;
      while(lastException.getNextException() != null)
        lastException = lastException.getNextException();
```

```
            lastException.setNextException(generatedException);
            throw sqle;
        }
    }

    boolean checkForWarning(SQLWarning w) {
        if(w == null) {
            return false;
        }
        do {
            System.err.println("Warning:\nMessage: " + w.getMessage());
            System.err.println("SQL state: " + w.getSQLState());
            System.err.println("Vendor code: " + w.getErrorCode() +
                                "\n----------------");
        } while((w = w.getNextWarning())!=null);
        return true;
    }
}
```

When you run the program you should see the following output:

```
Warning:
Message: Data truncation
SQL state: 01004
Vendor code: 0
----------------
Beginning Visual C++ 6                                          49
Warning:
Message: Data truncation
SQL state: 01004
Vendor code: 0
----------------
Beginning C. Third Edition                                     44
Warning:
Message: Data truncation
SQL state: 01004
Vendor code: 0
----------------
Beginning ANSI C++: The Complete Language, Third Edition       59

Warning:
Message: Data truncation
SQL state: 01004
Vendor code: 0
----------------
```

```
Beginning Java 2 JDK 5 Edition                                    49
Warning:
Message: Data truncation
SQL state: 01004
Vendor code: 0
----------------
and so on...
```

How It Works

Since SQLWarning objects are just attached to the ResultSet object when unusual conditions arise, the code needs to check the ResultSet object after extracting each value to find out if any warnings were produced. The ResultSet.getWarnings() method returns an SQLWarning object if any warnings were generated, and null otherwise. The value returned by the method call is passed to your checkForWarning() method, which checks for a non-null value and iterates through the chain of SQLWarning objects in the way you have seen applied to a chain of SQLException objects. For each warning the method outputs the message, the SQL state, and the vendor code. The method also returns a boolean value that is true if there was a warning, just in case the calling method needs to know about it. As you can see, you don't make use of this in the code here.

The results displayed by running the program reflect the fact that the books don't generally have prices that are an integral number of dollars, so in most cases retrieving the price as an integer results in data truncation.

Browsing a Database

It's time you put together another "proper" application with a decent GUI. As a final example on JDBC operations, you'll put together an application that will enable you to browse any relational database for which you have a JDBC driver available—plus the necessary authority to get at the data, of course. Along the way, you'll learn a bit more about how you can get hold of metadata for a database—you'll need that to start the browsing process off. You'll also explore some new components that will be useful in this context, as well as discover a few wrinkles about some that you are already familiar with.

Let's start by deciding the basic appearance of the application window. You'll need to provide for an input area where the database URL, user ID, and password can be entered. These will basically be single-line text input fields, so JTextField objects will do nicely. You can use JLabel objects to annotate the entry areas. The password entry ought to have some protection from prying eyes though, and you can provide this by using the JPasswordField class, which happens to be a subclass of JTextField. The main feature of a JPasswordField object is that the input data is displayed as asterisks, so you can't read what was typed.

You need a regular application window so you can derive the application class from JFrame. It will be convenient to locate all the input at the top of the window, and you can arrange the fields and their labels quite easily using Box containers, as shown in Figure 25-5.

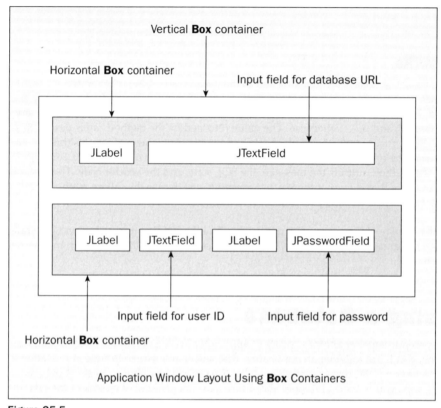

Figure 25-5

You'll recall that the Box container uses the BoxLayout layout manager, and this arranges everything in a single row or column, depending on the orientation of the Box object. Here you have a vertical Box container with two horizontal Box containers inside it. The horizontal Box containers are used to align the input fields and their labels. You could start your application off by putting the code for this together, along with a JTextArea component at the bottom of the window to display messages to the user.

Try It Out   Building the Basic GUI

You'll call the application class DatabaseBrowse, so the initial code will be as follows:

```
import javax.swing.JFrame;
import javax.swing.JTextField;
import javax.swing.JPasswordField;
import javax.swing.JTextArea;
import javax.swing.JLabel;
import javax.swing.Box;
```

```
import javax.swing.BorderFactory;
import javax.swing.SwingUtilities;
import java.awt.BorderLayout;
import javax.swing.border.BevelBorder;

class DatabaseBrowse extends JFrame {
  public static void main(String[] args) {
        SwingUtilities.invokeLater(new Runnable() {
            public void run() {
                createGUI();
            }
        });
  }

  private static void createGUI() {
   DatabaseBrowse theApp = new DatabaseBrowse();       // Create application object
  }

  // Constructor
  public DatabaseBrowse() {
    super("Database Browser");

    setBounds(0, 0, 400, 300);
    setDefaultCloseOperation(DISPOSE_ON_CLOSE);

    // Create labels for input fields
    JLabel dbURLLabel  = new JLabel( "Database URL: ");
    JLabel userIDLabel = new JLabel( "User ID:", JLabel.RIGHT);
    userIDLabel.setPreferredSize(dbURLLabel.getPreferredSize()); // Set same size
    JLabel passwordLabel = new JLabel("Password: ");
    // Box for database URL input
    Box dbPane = Box.createHorizontalBox();
    dbPane.add(dbURLLabel);
    dbPane.add(database);

    // Box for user ID and password input fields
    Box loginPane = Box.createHorizontalBox();
    loginPane.add(userIDLabel);
    loginPane.add(userIDInput);
    loginPane.add(passwordLabel);
    loginPane.add(passwordInput);

    Box inputPane = Box.createVerticalBox();
    inputPane.add(dbPane);
    inputPane.add(loginPane);
    getContentPane().add(inputPane, BorderLayout.NORTH);

    // Add message area
    status.setText("Enter a database URL and/or press Enter");
    status.setEditable(false);                  // No user input
    status.setLineWrap(true);                   // Lines wrap
    status.setWrapStyleWord(true);              // on word boundaries
    status.setBorder(BorderFactory.createBevelBorder(BevelBorder.LOWERED));
    getContentPane().add(status, BorderLayout.SOUTH);
```

```
        setVisible(true);                      // Set window visible
        database.requestFocus();               // Focus to the url input field
    }

    private String userID = "guest";
    private String password = "guest";
    private String url = "jdbc:odbc:technical_library";

    private JTextField database = new JTextField(url);
    private JTextField userIDInput = new JTextField(userID);
    private JPasswordField passwordInput = new JPasswordField(password);
    private JTextArea status = new JTextArea(3,30);
}
```

You can compile and run this as it is. You should see the window shown in Figure 25-6 when it executes.

Figure 25-6

The cursor is on the database URL input field and the default password value appears as asterisks, just as it should.

How It Works

You should have no trouble seeing how this works as it's all standard stuff. The first bit sets up the window with the default window closing operation being DISPOSE_ON_CLOSE. The window is created in a separate thread from the main thread to avoid any possibility of deadlocks.

The JTextField and JPasswordField objects and the String objects they display are all members of the DatabaseBrowse class because you'll need to refer to these objects elsewhere in the code. You set the preferred size of the label for the user ID field to be the same as that for the database URL label just to get them to line up nicely.

Note how you specify the userIDLabel text as right-justified; the second argument to the JLabel constructor can have values of RIGHT, LEFT, or CENTER. These values are actually defined in the javax.swing.SwingConstants interface that is implemented by the JLabel class. To arrange the input fields and their labels, you just add them all to their respective horizontal Box containers in the appropriate sequence, and then add these horizontal Box containers to the vertical Box container. This last Box container serves to arrange the other two one above the other. You then add the vertical Box container to the top of the content pane for the application window.

The message display area at the bottom of the screen is a JTextArea object that displays three lines. You don't want anyone entering data here, and since input is allowed by default, you set it as not editable by calling its setEditable() method with the argument false. You also ensure you get line wrapping on word boundaries by calling the setLineWrap() and setWrapStyleWord() methods, both with the argument true.

Once the components are set up, you set the window as visible by calling its setVisible() method. You finally call requestFocus() for the URL input field so that it will have the focus initially. Note that calling this method works only when the component is visible on the screen.

Displaying Database Data

You have two kinds of information to display; you have the metadata for a database, which in our case will be the table names and the column names for each table, and you have the contents of a particular table, as selected by the user. This suggests that you'll need two display areas to accommodate these, and a javax.swing.JSplitPane component provides just what you need.

The JSplitPane class defines a pane with either a horizontal or vertical divider that can be moved by dragging with the mouse. Each half of the split pane can display a separate component. For example, you can create a pane with a vertical divider with the following statement:

```
JSplitPane splitpane = new JSplitPane(JSplitPane.HORIZONTAL_SPLIT,
                            true,                // Continuous relayout
                            leftComponent,       // Left pane content
                            rightComponent);     // Right pane content
```

For a pane divided by a horizontal divider, you would specify the first argument as the constant, VERTICAL_SPLIT. The second argument defines what happens when the divider is dragged with the mouse. With a true argument the two panes are redrawn continuously as the divider is dragged. On a slow machine or with very complicated content for the two halves, you might want to set this to false, which will update the two halves only when the divider drag operation ends. The last two arguments specify the components to appear in the left or right panes — or the top and bottom panes in the case of a horizontal divider. Any component can appear in either half of a split pane, including another JSplitPane component. In this way you can create a pane that is split into however many panes you need.

In this case you'll use a `JSplitPane` object that is split into two panes side by side. You'll display the metadata in the left pane, and the contents of a table in the right pane. When it is complete, the application window will look as shown in Figure 25-7.

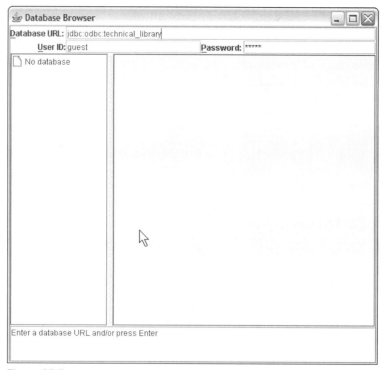

Figure 25-7

To display the table data in the right pane, you'll use the same mechanism that you used in the `InteractiveSQL` example from the previous chapter — a `JTable` object with an underlying `ResultsModel` object displayed in a `JScrollPane` to allow scrolling of the data. For the metadata you'll use something new — a `JTree` component — also within a scroll pane. Let's look at the basics of using a `JTree` component.

Using a JTree Component

The `JTree` class defines a component that displays data organized in a tree-like structure. There's a bit of jargon used with trees that you need to understand. Each element in a tree is referred to as a **node**, and the base node of the tree is referred to as the **root node**. A **parent node** is a node that has other nodes attached to it, and nodes that have a parent node, which will be all nodes other than the root node, are called **child nodes**. Nodes that have no children are called **leaf nodes**. An example of nodes in a simple tree is shown in Figure 25-8.

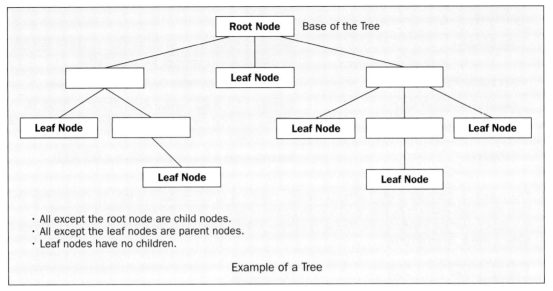

- All except the root node are child nodes.
- All except the leaf nodes are parent nodes.
- Leaf nodes have no children.

Example of a Tree

Figure 25-8

You can visualize the data in a relational database as a very simple tree that has a fixed number of levels—always three. The root node at the top level is the database itself, and that has child nodes on the next level that are tables. Each table node has child nodes on the next level that are the columns in the table, and since the columns are the lowest level, these will be leaf nodes.

The JTree class has vastly more capability than you'll be using to display database metadata, both in terms of the complexity of the structures it can handle and in terms of the nature of the nodes in the structure. You can use a JTree component to display virtually any tree structure where the nodes in the tree can be any kind of object—and they can all be different if you want. You could use it to display people in the management structure of a company, for example, complete with photos of everyone, and different visual cues denoting the level of each person in the hierarchy. I won't be going into this level of detail, but now that you have an idea of the potential, you may want to explore it further for yourself.

Defining Tree Nodes

A node in a tree can be any object of a class that implements the TreeNode interface. The methods declared by the TreeNode interface provide the means of navigating a tree:

Method	Description
getParent()	Returns the parent node as a TreeNode reference and null if there isn't one—that is, it's a root node.
getChildCount()	Returns the number of child nodes as type int.
getChildAt(int index)	Returns the child node at position index—child nodes being indexed from 0.

Table continued on following page

Method	Description
children()	Returns a reference to an Enumeration object that can be used to iterate through the child nodes.
getIndex(TreeNode node)	Returns the index value for the child node node.
getAllowsChildren()	Returns true if the current node allows children. By default children are allowed, but classes that implement this interface can inhibit children for a node.
isLeaf()	Returns true if the current node is a leaf node.

The TreeNode interface doesn't provide enough capability to link nodes in a tree. To create a tree structure, each node needs to be able to refer to its parent node and any child nodes that it has. The MutableTreeNode interface extends the TreeNode interface and adds declarations for the methods that allow a tree to be constructed:

Method	Description
insert(MutableTreeNode child, int index)	Inserts the node child as a child of the current node at position index.
remove(int index)	Removes the child node at position index for the current node.
remove(MutableTreeNode node)	Removes node from the set of children of the current node.
removeFromParent()	Removes the current node from the list of children for its parent node.
setParent(MutableTreeNode parent)	Sets parent as the parent of the current node.
setUserObject(Object o)	Sets the object o as the object to be displayed for the node in a tree. This is where you set your node information — the table name for a node representing a database table, for example.

While you can create your own class to define nodes if you want, the DefaultMutableTreeNode class in the javax.swing.tree package is adequate for most purposes. This class implements the MutableTreeNode interface and adds a few more methods of its own. The default constructor creates an object with no parent and no children. You can also construct a DefaultMutableTreeNode object containing an object of your own, again with no parent and no children, by using the constructor that accepts a single argument of type Object — any class type, in other words. For example:

```
DefaultMutableTreeNode tableNode = new DefaultMutableTreeNode("authors");
```

A third DefaultMutableTreeNode constructor accepts a second argument of type boolean, and a value of false prevents the node from having children — forcing it to be a leaf node, in other words. You won't need to go into the methods that the `DefaultMutableTreeNode` class has beyond those I have already discussed, but you do need to know more about how the `JTree` class works before you can use it.

Tree Models

Like the `JTable` component, the `JTree` component works with an underlying model object that supplies the data that is to be displayed in the tree. A class that defines a model for a tree implements the `TreeModel` interface, which appears in the `javax.swing.tree` package. This is quite an extensive interface, with eight methods declared in it, so to save you the work of creating a class from scratch, the `javax.swing.tree` package includes a `DefaultTreeModel` class that implements `TreeModel` and that you can use "as is" in many situations. You create a `DefaultTreeModel` object using a single node that is the root node for your tree. For example:

```
DefaultMutableTreeNode dbNode = new DefaultMutableTreeNode("No Database");
DefaultTreeModel dbTreeModel = new DefaultTreeModel(dbNode);
```

Here, you first construct a node object with the `String` argument as the object it stores. You then use this as the root node to create a tree model object model. Now that you have a `DefaultTreeModel` object, you can create a `JTree` object from it using the `JTree` class constructor that accepts a `TreeModel` reference as the argument:

```
Tree dbTree = new JTree(dbTreeModel);
```

The `dbTree` object doesn't do very much. When you want to actually store a database in the tree, you can call the `setRoot()` method for the `DefaultTreeModel` object to set a new root node that you can then add table nodes to using the methods from the `MutableTreeNode` interface. Before I get to that, you need to put the component together in the GUI that will display the metadata. Let's try adding the code for that to our example.

Try It Out	Creating and Displaying a Tree

You'll first add the data members to the `DatabaseBrowse` class that you'll need to access in various class methods:

```
private DefaultMutableTreeNode dbNode;      // Root node for the database tree
private DefaultTreeModel dbTreeModel;       // Model for the database metadata
private JTree dbTree;                        // Tree to display the metadata
private JScrollPane treePane;                // Scroll pane holding the tree
```

You'll also need to add `import` statements to the `DatabaseBrowse.java` file for names from the package supporting trees:

```
import javax.swing.tree.DefaultMutableTreeNode;
import javax.swing.tree.DefaultTreeModel;
import javax.swing.tree.TreePath;
```

You'll also need `import` statements for the `Color`, `JTree`, and `JScrollPane` class names:

```
import javax.swing.JTree;
import javax.swing.JScrollPane;
import java.awt.Color;
```

Now you can add code to the `DatabaseBrowse` class constructor to create the tree and place it in a scroll pane:

```
// Create tree to go in left split pane
dbNode = new DefaultMutableTreeNode("No database");
dbTreeModel = new DefaultTreeModel(dbNode);
dbTree = new JTree(dbTreeModel);
treePane = new JScrollPane(dbTree);
treePane.setBorder(BorderFactory.createLineBorder(Color.darkGray));
```

This code will go just before the call to `setVisible()` in the constructor. As you can see, you are just applying the code you saw earlier to first create a root node and then to create a model from the root node. Then a tree object is created from the model, and finally you place the tree in a scroll pane.

You'll want to put the scroll pane containing the tree in the left half of a split pane, but first you need to put together the component that goes in the other half that will eventually display the table data. As I discussed earlier, this will be another `JScrollPane` object containing a `JTable` object — just as you had in the `InteractiveSQL` example. You'll use the `ResultsModel` class here, too, so copy the source file for the class from the directory containing the `InteractiveSQL` files to the directory for our current example. You'll need `import` statements for the `JTable` and `JSplitPane` class names in the `DatabaseBrowse` source file:

```
import javax.swing.JSplitPane;
import javax.swing.JTable;
```

You'll need three data members in the `DatabaseBrowse` class to store the model, the table, and the scroll pane object that will contain the table:

```
private ResultsModel tableModel;        // Model for table
private JTable table;                    // Table holding table data
private JScrollPane tablePane;           // Scroll pane holding the table
```

The code to add the table can go immediately following the previous block of code that you added to create the tree:

```
// Create table to go in right split pane
tableModel = new ResultsModel();
JTable table = new JTable(tableModel);
table.setAutoResizeMode(JTable.AUTO_RESIZE_OFF);
tablePane = new JScrollPane(table);
tablePane.setBorder(BorderFactory.createLineBorder(Color.darkGray));
```

You have no idea at this point how many rows and columns there will be in a table. This will vary depending on the table currently selected. By putting the table in a scroll pane you can deal with a table with any number of rows. If there are too many to fit within the available space, the scroll pane will automatically insert a scrollbar to manage the rows. You call `setAutoResizeMode()` with the argument `JTable.AUTO_RESIZE_OFF` to prevent the columns being squashed up to fit within the available space for the table. This way you'll get a horizontal scrollbar if the column headings exceed the width of the scroll pane. You'll also be able to change the width of a column by dragging the right boundary of the column header.

Now you can create the split pane containing the tree and the table and add it to the content pane of the application window. This code can follow the code fragment that you added previously in the constructor:

```
JSplitPane splitpane = new JSplitPane(JSplitPane.HORIZONTAL_SPLIT,
                              true,        // Continuous relayout
                              treePane,    // Left pane content
                              tablePane);  // Right pane content
getContentPane().add(splitpane, BorderLayout.CENTER);
splitpane.setDividerLocation(200);           // Left pane 200 pixels wide
```

You should also call `pack()` for the window to lay out the components at their appropriate sizes:

```
pack();
```

Place this statement immediately before the `setVisible()` method call in the constructor.

If you compile the application again and run it, the window should be similar to the screenshot that you saw earlier.

How It Works

The JTree and the JTable objects have been set up to display data in the left and right panes of the JSplitPane object. They each have their respective model objects that will supply the data that is to be displayed. They each have their own scroll pane that will provide scrolling capability when the data is outside the area that is displayed. Each JScrollPane object has its own line border, and when you have data to display, you'll replace this with a titled border that will show the name of the data that is displayed — the database URL for the left pane, and the table name for the right pane.

Try dragging the split pane divider with the mouse. The JSplitPane object manages this quite automatically and will arrange for the contents of the panes to be redrawn as necessary — when you have some, that is.

Getting Database Metadata

You need to obtain the database metadata that will be displayed by the JTree object in the left scroll pane. You can do this when a connection has been established, for which you need the database URL plus the user ID and password. Before you can establish a connection, you want to be sure the driver is loaded, so add the following data member to the DatabaseBrowse class to store the driver names:

```
private String[] drivers = {
                        "sun.jdbc.odbc.JdbcOdbcDriver",       // ODBC bridge
                        "com.imaginary.sql.msql.MsqlDriver"   // mSQL driver
                      };
```

I have added the driver for mSQL — which is a mini SQL implementation that is available as shareware — just to show how easy it is to have multiple drivers. If the driver is not present on your system the program will record an error message in the lower part of the application window, but you can ignore that. You can add the names of your own drivers between the braces if you wish. You'll put code in the constructor that will try to load all the drivers in the drivers array, and failing to load a driver won't matter, as long as you don't need it, of course. Add the following code to the end of the code for the constructor:

```
// Attempt to load all drivers
for(String driver : drivers) {
   try {
      Class.forName(driver);
   } catch(ClassNotFoundException cnfe) {
      System.err.println(cnfe);
      status.setText("Driver load failed: " + cnfe.getMessage());
   }
}
```

The `try` and `catch` blocks are both within the scope of the `for` loop, so failing to load one driver will not prevent the others from being loaded.

The trigger to open a connection with a database will be pressing the Enter key for any of the input fields. By default, this will create an action event, so you can respond to this by making the `DatabaseBrowse` class implement the `ActionListener` interface. This involves defining the `actionPerformed()` method in the class, and adding the class object as the action listener for all three input fields. The first line of the class definition will be:

```
class DatabaseBrowse extends JFrame implements ActionListener {
```

The `actionPerformed()` method definition will be:

```
public void actionPerformed(ActionEvent e) {
   Object source = e.getSource();             // Get source of the event
   if(source == database    ||                // If its URL input,
      source == userIDInput ||                // or userID input,
      source == passwordInput) {              // or password input...
      // ...try for a connection
      url = database.getText();               // Get database URL
      userID = userIDInput.getText();         // Get user ID

      char[] pw = passwordInput.getPassword(); // Get password
      if(pw != null) {
         password = new String(pw);
      }
      if(url == null || url.length() == 0) {
         status.setText("Please specify a database URL ");
         return;
      }
      openConnection();
      password = null;                        // For security
   }
}
```

Here you get all the input you need and then call a method `openConnection()` that you'll need to add to the `DatabaseBrowse` class before you try compiling the code again. You also need to register the application object as the listener for the events, so add the following code to the constructor preceding the call to `pack()`:

```
                // Add event listeners
                database.addActionListener(this);
                userIDInput.addActionListener(this);
                passwordInput.addActionListener(this);
```

Since the `this` pointer references the current object, the application object will be registered as the action listener for all three input fields.

You must add `import` statements for the `ActionEvent` and `ActionListener` names to `DatabaseBrowse`:

```
    import java.awt.event.ActionEvent;
    import java.awt.event.ActionListener;
```

If you add the `openConnection()` method to the `DatabaseBrowse` class, you could take the application for another run.

Try It Out   Opening a Connection

The `DatabaseBrowse` application class will need data members to store a `Connection` reference and to store a `Statement` reference that you'll use to execute an SQL query when you want to display table data. You can do this by adding the following fields to the class:

```
    private Connection connection;
    private Statement statement;
```

You can add `import` statements for the names you'll be referencing from the `java.sql` package, too, at this point:

```
    import java.sql.Connection;
    import java.sql.DriverManager;
    import java.sql.Statement;
    import java.sql.DatabaseMetaData;
    import java.sql.ResultSet;
    import java.sql.SQLException;
```

Because it will be called each time the user enters a new URL and presses Enter, the `openConnection()` method will need to close any existing connection before opening a new connection. It will also need to reset the contents of the split pane—both the metadata and any table data that is displayed. To facilitate resetting the contents of the `JTable` object displayed in the right split pane, you can amend the `ResultsModel` class method `setResultSet()` to reset the data when a `null` argument is passed to it. You can do this as follows:

```
        public void setResultSet(ResultSet results) {
          if(results == null) {
            columnNames = new String[0];      // Reset the columns names
            dataRows.clear();                 // Remove all entries in the Vector
            fireTableChanged(null);           // Tell the table there is new model data
            return;
          }
          // Rest of the code as before...
        }
```

So by passing `null` to this method, you'll reset the `JTable` object that it supports to display nothing.

You can now implement the first part of the `openConnection()` method in our `DatabaseBrowse` class as follows:

```
public void openConnection() {
  try {
    if(connection != null) {              // If there is a connection
      connection.close();                 // close it

      // Reset the table data
      tableModel.setResultSet(null);
      tablePane.setBorder(BorderFactory.createLineBorder(Color.darkGray));
      // Reset the tree displaying metadata
      dbNode = new DefaultMutableTreeNode("No database");
      dbTreeModel.setRoot(dbNode);
      dbTree.setRootVisible(true);
      treePane.setBorder(BorderFactory.createLineBorder(Color.darkGray));
      dbTreeModel.reload();
    }

    // Code to open the new connection will go here...

  } catch(SQLException sqle) {
    status.setText(sqle.getMessage());       // Display first message
    do {                                     // loop through exceptions
      System.err.println("Exception occurred:\nMessage: " + sqle.getMessage());
      System.err.println("SQL state: " + sqle.getSQLState());
      System.err.println("Vendor code: " + sqle.getErrorCode() +
                         "\n----------------");
    } while((sqle = sqle.getNextException()) != null);
  }
}
```

If connection is not `null`, you call the `close()` method for the connection object to close it and reset any table data that is displayed by calling the `setResultSet()` member of the model object supporting the table. You also have to reset the border for the scroll pane that contains the table, because you'll put a title border in place showing the table name when you display data from a table.

To reset the `JTree` object, you first set a new root node for the underlying `TreeModel` object by calling its `setRoot()` method and passing a new node object as the argument. When you display the metadata for a database, what you want to see are the table names, and optionally the columns in each table, and since the root node takes up unnecessary real estate within the application window, you'll set it as invisible to provide maximum space for what you want to see. However, you restore the visibility of the `"No database"` root node when there are no tables in the tree as you reset the model, and this is done by calling the `setRootVisible()` method for the `JTree` object `dbTree` with the argument `true`. Lastly, you have to reset the border for the scroll pane to a line border, because you'll use a title border to display the database name when the metadata is displayed.

To open the new connection you can add the following code:

```
public void openConnection() {
  try {
```

```
                // Code to close the old connection as before....

                // Now open the new connection
                connection = DriverManager.getConnection(url, userID, password);
                status.setText("Database connection established");
                statement = connection.createStatement();   // Create statement for query
                dbNode = new DefaultMutableTreeNode(url);    // Root node is URL
                dbTreeModel.setRoot(dbNode);                 // Set root in model
                setupTree(connection.getMetaData());         // Set up tree with metadata

                treePane.setBorder(BorderFactory.createTitledBorder(
                          BorderFactory.createLineBorder(Color.darkGray),
                          url,
                          TitledBorder.CENTER,
                          TitledBorder.DEFAULT_POSITION));
                dbTree.setRootVisible(false);                // Now hide the root node
                dbTreeModel.reload();                        // Get the tree redisplayed
            } catch(SQLException sqle) {
                status.setText(sqle.getMessage());           // Display first message
                do {                                         // loop through exceptions
                  System.err.println("Exception occurred:\nMessage: " + sqle.getMessage());
                  System.err.println("SQL state: " + sqle.getSQLState());
                  System.err.println("Vendor code: " + sqle.getErrorCode() +
                                   "\n---------------");
                } while((sqle = sqle.getNextException()) != null);
            }
        }
```

You open the connection and create a `Statement` object in the way you have seen previously. You create a new root node for the tree model and store the `String` object containing the URL as the user object in the node. To populate the tree with the metadata, you call the method `setupTree()` in the application class — you'll come to the implementation of this in a moment. The argument is a `DatabaseMetaData` reference that is returned by the `getMetaData()` method that you call for the `connection` object. To show the database name in the left split pane, you reset the border for the scroll pane containing the tree to a title border showing the database URL. You'll need to add an `import` statement for the `TitledBorder` class name:

```
    import javax.swing.border.TitledBorder;
```

As I discussed previously, you won't want to see the root node while the table names are displayed, so you set the root node as invisible by calling the `setRootVisible()` method for the tree with the argument `false`. Calling the `reload()` method for the `DefaultTreeModel` object causes the data to be reloaded into the tree, so the tree display will be updated.

Any exceptions that are thrown in all this will be caught by the `catch` block. To let the user know directly when an error occurs, you display the message for the exception in the status area at the bottom of the application window. You then iterate through the potential chain of exceptions using the technique that you saw earlier.

If you want to try compiling and running the application again, you can add an empty definition for the `setupTree()` method to the `DatabaseBrowse` class:

```
    private void setupTree(DatabaseMetaData metadata) {
      // Code to be added here...
    }
```

When you press Enter when the application window is initially displayed, the connection will be established and the application window will then look something like that shown in Figure 25-9.

Figure 25-9

How It Works

Pressing the Enter key with the focus in any of the input fields will cause the openConnection()
method to be called if a database URL is available. This opens the connection to the database and displays the URL in the border of the left scroll pane. There are no scrollbars yet because there is no data in
the scroll pane. As you can see, the status is displayed at the bottom of the screen. Try entering an
invalid database URL and see the effect.

Loading the Database Metadata

The setupTree() method will be responsible for retrieving the metadata using the DatabaseMetaData
reference that is passed as the argument. The DatabaseMetaData interface declares well in excess of 100
methods, so I won't be going through all of them — I'll just pick a few that are relevant in the present
context, and you can explore the rest in the JDK documentation. One word of caution — all of these
methods depend on the underlying driver and database engine supporting access to the metadata that is
required, and in many cases this will not be available, in which case the requesting method will throw
an exception. For example, although it would be nice to be able to display the key fields in a table in our

example by using the `getPrimaryKeys()` method in the `DatabaseMetaData` interface, unfortunately this capability is not supported by the ODBC driver for Access.

You can potentially get at several different kinds of metadata. One broad classification is information related to the capability of the database engine in general. You can request the SQL types supported by calling the `getTypesInfo()` method, for example, or the maximum length of an SQL statement by calling the `getMaxStatementLength()` method. A whole series of methods provides data on the limits on table size, row length, and other constraints implicit in the database system. You would use this kind of data to condition your application code to work within the prescribed limits. This provides the possibility of your code being able to adapt itself to accommodate the constraints that are peculiar to the current database and thus avoid exceptions being thrown when attempting operations outside those limits. Of course, if the database and/or driver do not make the data available, it won't be particularly effective, but the architects of JDBC have at least had the foresight to provide for the possibility.

Retrieving Table Names

Most of the time, the metadata that you'll be interested in relates to the particular database that you want to access. You can get information about the tables within the database with the `getTables()` method, which is of the following form:

```
ResultSet getTables(String catalog,
                    String schemaPattern,
                    String tableNamePattern,
                    String[] types)
```

The parameters form the basis for deciding which tables in the database are to be identified, and each parameter provides a separate way of filtering out the tables that you are interested in. The first parameter is a database catalog name, and data will be returned on the tables within the catalog that you specify. If you supply an empty string, `""`, as the argument here, you'll get information on tables without a catalog. If you supply `null` as the argument, you'll get tables with and without a catalog.

The second parameter is a pattern for a schema name. A database schema is a set of declarations for the tables and other entities such as views that make up the database. Only tables for schemas conforming to the pattern will be selected. A pattern is a string of characters where `'%'` means any substring and `'_'` means any character. For example, the pattern `"%data"` specifies any string ending `"data"`, so `"Mydata"` or `"Yourdata"` would be in, and `"Mydata1"` would be out. The pattern `"data_"` would select `"data1"` or `"dataA"`, but not `"Adata"` or `"Mydata"`. If you supply an empty string, `""`, as the argument, you'll get information on tables without a schema. If you supply `null`, you'll get tables with and without a schema.

The third parameter is a pattern for selecting the table names, with the pattern defined as described in the preceding paragraph. Only data on tables with names corresponding to the pattern will be returned. If you specify the argument as `null`, information on all tables consistent with the other arguments will be returned.

The fourth parameter is an array of table type names. Examples of table types are `"TABLE"`, `"SYSTEM TABLE"`, or `"VIEW"` — which is a virtual table constructed from actual tables. A `null` argument selects all table types.

The information on the tables is returned in a `ResultSet` object, with each row supplying information about a particular table. The resultset will have five columns:

Column Name	Column Data
TABLE_CAT	A String object specifying the table catalog, which can be null
TABLE_SCHEM	A String object specifying the table schema, which can be null
TABLE_NAME	A String object specifying the table name
TABLE_TYPE	A String object specifying the table type
REMARKS	A String object describing the table

If an error of any kind occurs when accessing the database, the getTables() method will throw an exception of type SQLException.

Given a DatabaseMetaData reference, metadata, you could retrieve all the tables for a database with the statements:

```
String[] tableTypes = { "TABLE"};
ResultSet tables = metadata.getTables(null,
                                      null,
                                      null,
                                      tableTypes);
```

This will return information on tables that are real data tables in the database, not views or system tables. This is because you have included only type "TABLE" in the tableTypes array. Of course, you would need to take care of handling the exception that could be thrown here.

Retrieving Column Names

To get the column names for particular tables, you can call the getColumns() method for a Database MetaData object. The first three arguments are the catalog, schemaPattern, and tableNamePattern, as described for the getTables() method. The fourth argument is a String object specifying a pattern for selecting column names. This method returns a ResultSet object containing no less than 18 columns, where each row provides information about a particular column. The ones you are most likely to be interested in are:

Column Name	Column Data
TABLE_CAT	A String object specifying the catalog for the table containing the column, which can be null
TABLE_SCHEM	A String object specifying the schema for the table containing the column, which can be null
TABLE_NAME	A String object specifying the name of the table containing the column

Column Name	Column Data
COLUMN_NAME	A String object specifying the name of the column
DATA_TYPE	A String object specifying the SQL type for the data in the column
COLUMN_SIZE	The maximum number of characters in the case of character or date types, or the precision for NUMERIC or DECIMAL types

Of course, using the third argument that specifies the table name pattern, you can get data on the columns for a specific table, just by supplying the table name here. The getColumns() method can also throw an exception of type SQLException if an error occurs.

Now you have enough knowledge to implement the setupTree() method, so let's try it.

Try It Out   **Displaying Metadata**

You just need to apply the DatabaseMetaData methods that I have just discussed. You won't catch the exceptions in the method. You can let the calling method openConnection() catch them instead. Here's the code for the setupTree() method:

```
private void setupTree(DatabaseMetaData metadata) throws SQLException {
   String[] tableTypes = { "TABLE"};              // We want only tables
   ResultSet tables = metadata.getTables(         // Get the tables info
                              null,
                              null,
                              null,
                              tableTypes);

   String tableName;                       // Stores a table name
   DefaultMutableTreeNode tableNode;       // Stores a tree node for a table
   while(tables.next()) {                         // For each table
     tableName = tables.getString("TABLE_NAME");  // get the table name
     tableNode = new DefaultMutableTreeNode(tableName);
     dbNode.add(tableNode);                        // Add the node to the tree

     // Get all the columns for the current table
     ResultSet columnNames = metadata.getColumns(null, null, tableName, null);

     // Add nodes for the columns as children of the table node
     while(columnNames.next()) {
       tableNode.add(new
               DefaultMutableTreeNode(columnNames.getString("COLUMN_NAME")));
     }
   }
}
```

You can try compiling and executing the application again. Pressing Enter should display the tables as shown in Figure 25-10.

Figure 25-10

Single-clicking a table name will select it. Double-clicking it will expand the tree to show the column names. Double-clicking the node for an expanded table will contract it again. All this function comes for free with the JTree component. If you expand the tree so that its extent is outside the pane, the scroll-bars will appear automatically.

Note that holding the Ctrl key down enables you to select several individual nodes one after another. When you have selected one node, you can select a block of nodes from the currently selected node to any other node by holding the Shift key down.

How It Works

You have a simple application of the getTables() and getColumns() methods from the Database MetaData interface. The call to getTables() returns a ResultSet object that provides access to infor-mation on the tables of type "TABLE". You iterate through the rows in the resultset in the outer while loop. For each row, you retrieve and save the table name, and you add a new node as a child to the root node in the tree model dbTreeModel. You use the table name that you have saved in tableName to retrieve information on the columns in that table by calling the getColumns() method for metadata. In the inner while loop, you iterate through all the rows in the resultset relating to the columns, and add a child node to the table node corresponding to each column name. This process will add a table node to the root node in `dbTreeModel` for each table, and add a column node to a table node for every column in the table. Simple really, isn't it?

The last thing you need to figure out is how to display the contents of a table. You could do this in various ways, but you'll display the contents of a table by listening to the tree.

Using Tree Listeners

You can add three different kinds of listeners to a `JTree` object, each of which has an interface defining the methods involved.

❑ The `TreeExpansionListener` interface declares two methods that are called when a node in a tree is expanded or contracted.

    ❑ The `treeExpanded()` method is called when a tree node is expanded.

    ❑ Unsurprisingly, the `treeCollapsed()` method is called when a tree node is collapsed.

  Each method is passed an event object of type `TreeExpansionEvent`.

❑ Knowing that the tree was expanded may be too late in some circumstances. You may need to do things immediately before the expansion or contraction takes place. In this case you can use a `TreeWillExpandListener`. The `TreeWillExpandListener` declares `treeWillExpand()` and `treeWillCollapse()` methods with the obvious applications.

❑ In the `DatabaseBrowse` application, you'll use the third kind of listener for a tree, of type `TreeSelectionListener`. This declares a single method, `valueChanged()`, which is called when a selection within the tree changes — that is, when a node is selected or deselected. When the method is called, it is passed an object of type `TreeSelectionEvent` as the argument. This object provides methods that you can use to discover which nodes changed their selection state. Since you can make individual selections, multiple selections, or select a block of nodes, a single event can signal that several nodes have changed their selection state.

The methods in the `JTree` class that you use to add the listeners I've been talking about are `addTreeExpansionListener()`, `addTreeWillExpandListener()`, and `addTreeSelectionListener()`. Note that the tree event classes and listener interfaces are defined in the `javax.swing.event` package, so you'll need that following `import` statements in the `DatabaseBrowse.java` file:

```
import javax.swing.event.TreeSelectionEvent;
import javax.swing.event.TreeSelectionListener;
```

Tree Paths

A node that has changed state is identified by a `TreePath` object. A `TreePath` object defines a path to a node from the root node; in other words, it contains the sequence of nodes from the root to a particular node. To get a reference to the node identified by a `TreePath` object, you can call its `getLastPathComponent()` method. To provide maximum flexibility, the node is returned as type `Object`, but for a `DefaultTreeNodeModel` the node will actually be of type `TreeNode`.

You have lots of ways to iterate through the nodes in a path. You can use the `getParentPath()` method in conjunction with the `getLastPathComponent()` method. The `getParentPath()` method returns a

TreePath object that is the parent of the current path—in other words, a path that is like the current path, but without the last node in the path. You can also get all the nodes in a path as an array of elements of type Object by calling the getPath() method for a TreePath object. You could use an object treepath of type TreePath like this:

```
MutableTreeNode[] nodes = (MutableTreeNodes[])treepath.getPath();
for(int i = 0 ; i < nodes.length ; i++) {
  System.out.println("Node " + (i+1) + " is " + nodes[i]);
}
```

This just outputs each node on a separate line.

You can also get a count of the number of nodes in a path by calling the getPathCount() method for the TreePath object. You could then use the getPathComponent() method, which accepts a zero-based index to a node as an argument, to select each node and return the node as type Object. For example, you could get the same effect as the previous code fragment like this:

```
for(int i = 0 ; i < treepath.getPathCount() ; i++) {
  System.out.println("Node " + (i+1) + " is " +
                                  ((MutableTreeNode)getPathComponent (i)));
}
```

A TreeSelectionEvent object provides methods to obtain all the paths for nodes that have changed their selection state. The getPath() method will return the first path, and you can test whether the first path was selected or deselected by calling isAddedPath() for the event object. This returns true if the path is for a node that was selected—added in other words—and false otherwise—when the node was deselected. The getPaths() method for the event object will return all paths to nodes that have changed. To tell whether a particular path is to a node that was selected or deselected, you can call an overloaded version of the isAddedPath() method in the TreeSelectionEvent class that expects an argument of type TreeNode.

Dealing with the paths from a TreeSelectionEvent that are a combination of paths to selected and deselected nodes can be quite complicated. If you are interested only in the paths that are selected, you can avoid all this by going directly to the horse's mouth—the JTree object. You can use this to get at just the selected nodes. If you have several JTree objects you are listening for, you can get a reference to the object originating the event by calling the getSource() method for the event object. This method is inherited in the TreeSelectionEvent class from the EventObject class. If you have only one tree, as you do in the example, you can use your JTree reference directly to call the getSelectionPaths() method. This returns an array of TreePath objects that represent paths to nodes selected in the tree. I think you know enough about tree paths to complete the example now, so let's do that.

Try It Out   Displaying Table Data

Make sure you added the import statements for the TreeSelectionEvent and TreeSelectionListener names from the javax.swing.event package. You'll make the application class a tree selection listener, so you should declare that it implements the interface:

```
class DatabaseBrowse2 extends JFrame
                implements ActionListener, TreeSelectionListener {
```

You mustn't forget to add the application object as the tree selection listener. Add the following statement after the other three statements in the class constructor that add listeners:

```
dbTree.addTreeSelectionListener(this);
```

The `valueChanged()` method will display some or all of the columns from a table in the right-hand split pane, depending on what is selected. Because you have allowed complete flexibility to select any number of nodes (you can restrict the possibilities though), you need to give a little thought to the problem of what you do under various selection states that can arise. For example, several table nodes may be selected, possibly with column names selected, too. You can deal with this by defining the following rules:

❑ If any table name is selected, you display the entire table for the first table name that you find.

❑ If only columns are selected, you display the selected columns for the first table that you find with selected columns.

You now can add the definition for the `valueChanged()` method to handle selection events:

```java
public void valueChanged(TreeSelectionEvent e) {
  TreePath[] paths = dbTree.getSelectionPaths();
  if(paths == null) {
    return;
  }

  boolean tableSelected = false;        // Set true if a table is selected
  String column = null;                 // Stores a column name from a path
  String tableName = null;              // Stores a table name from a path
  String columnsParam = null;           // Column names in SQL SELECT
  String tableParam = null;             // Table name in SQL SELECT
  String message = null;                // Message for status area
  for(TreePath path : paths) {
    switch(path.getPathCount()) {
      case 2:                           // We have a table selected
        tableParam = (String)
                (((DefaultMutableTreeNode)
                      (path.getPathComponent(1))).getUserObject());
        columnsParam = "*";             // Select all columns
        tableSelected = true;           // Set flag for a table selected
        message = "Complete " + tableParam + " table displayed";
        break;

      case 3:                           // Column selected
        tableName = (String)
                (((DefaultMutableTreeNode)
                      (path.getPathComponent(1))).getUserObject());
        if(tableParam == null) {
          tableParam = tableName;

        } else if(tableParam != tableName) {
          break;
        }
        column = (String)
                (((DefaultMutableTreeNode)
```

```
                                  (path.getPathComponent(2))).getUserObject());
          if(columnsParam == null) {           // If no previous columns
            columnsParam = column;             // add the column
          } else {                             // otherwise
            columnsParam += "," + column;      // we need a comma too
          }
          message = columnsParam + " displayed from " + tableParam + " table.";
          break;
        }
        if(tableSelected) {                    // If a table was selected
          break;                               // we are done
        }
      }
    }
    try {
      // Display the columns and change the scroll pane border
      tableModel.setResultSet(
          statement.executeQuery("SELECT " + columnsParam+" FROM " + tableParam));
      tablePane.setBorder(BorderFactory.createTitledBorder(
                    BorderFactory.createLineBorder(Color.darkGray),
                    tableParam,
                    TitledBorder.CENTER,
                    TitledBorder.DEFAULT_POSITION));
    } catch(SQLException sqle) {
      message = "Selection event Error\n" + sqle.getMessage();
      System.err.println(message);
    }
    if(message != null) {
      status.setText(message);
    }
  }
}
```

If you recompile the program with these additions, and you have managed to enter all the code without typos, the whole program should now be working, and you can select table data as illustrated in Figure 25-11.

The table data that is displayed is updated as you select or deselect tables or columns. Don't forget you can use the Shift and Ctrl keys when selecting nodes. If you have one, you can also enter a different database URL.

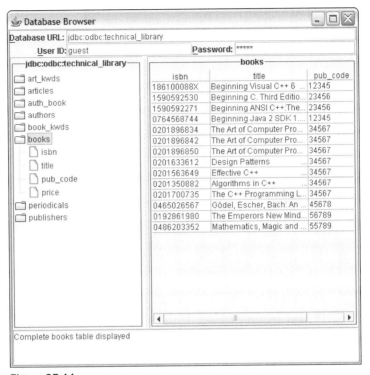

Figure 25-11

How It Works

The valueChanged() method is a little tricky, with some fearsome looking statements, but they are not as tough as they look. The objective of the valueChanged() method is to assemble an SQL SELECT statement for a table and then execute it. The set of columns in the statement will be assembled in the variable columnsParam, and the table name will be stored in the tableParam variable.

First of all, you are interested only in paths to selected nodes here, so you get this information directly from the dbTree object. Since a database tree has a fixed structure with three levels — as I discussed way back — a TreePath will always have either two or three nodes in the path, two when a table is selected, and three when a column is selected. This guides our approach to processing the paths for selected nodes.

You iterate through the paths in the for loop. For each path, there will be either two or three elements in the path, and this is returned by the getPathCount() method for the path. You use this value to select one or other of the cases in the switch. When the value is 2, you have found a table name that is selected, so you retrieve the name with the expression:

```
(String)(((DefaultMutableTreeNode)(path.getPathComponent(1)))).getUserObject())
```

This expression is easy to understand if you take it from the inside out. The expression `path.getPathComponent(1)` returns the second node object from the current path, `path`, as type `Object` — which will be the node storing the table name. You want to call the `getUserObject()` method for the node, but before you can do that, you must cast it to type `DefaultMutableTreeNode`, and you need parentheses around that because of operator precedence. The reference returned by `getUserObject()` is type `Object`, so you have to cast that to type `String` before storing it as the table name in `tableParam`. To select all the columns in the table, you set `columnsParam` to `"*"`, and set the `tableSelected` flag to `true` so you'll exit the loop because of the `if` statement that tests this value at the end, and thus you won't look at any other paths.

If the value returned by `getPathCount()` is 3, you have found a column that is selected. You get the column name using essentially the same expression as you used to get the table name. If `columnsParam` is `null`, then this is the first column name you have found, so you just store the name. If `columnsParam` is not `null`, you have an additional column name, so you append it following a comma to the existing string in `columnsParam`. In this way you accumulate all the names of the selected columns. If a table name turns up, you abandon the column names you have recorded and display the whole table.

The last bit after you exit the `for` loop is easy. You pass a SELECT statement formed from the `columnsParam` and `tableParam` strings to the `executeQuery()` method `for` statement. This produces a `ResultSet` object containing the table data that you pass to the `setResultSet()` method for our `ResultsModel` object that supplies data to the table. Finally, you update the border for the scroll pane containing the table to display the table name.

Summary

In this chapter, you've applied the basic JDBC skills you learned about in the previous chapter in some new ways, extended your detailed knowledge of some of the topics I covered there, and even got into some new ones. The important elements that I introduced in this chapter include:

- ❑ You can create Java objects directly from JDBC data sources by adding a factory method to a class to extract data from a `ResultSet` object and build a class object.

- ❑ The `Statement` interface provides methods that enable you to limit the field size and number of rows that can be generated in a resultset. You can also set a maximum duration for an SQL query.

- ❑ A `PreparedStatement` object encapsulates a parameterized SQL statement and provides methods for you to set values for the parameters. Placeholders for the parameters in the SQL statement are represented by a question mark.

- ❑ JDBC provides a set of preferred mappings between SQL types and Java types. The methods provided for transferring data between your program and a database also support conversions to other than the preferred types.

- ❑ The SQL NUMERIC and DECIMAL data types are mapped to the `BigDecimal` class type that is defined in the `java.math` package. You can use this class and the `BigInteger` class for applications that need numerical precision beyond the capabilities of the primitive numeric types.

❏ When exceptions are thrown by JDBC methods, a chain of SQLException objects can be linked together. You can access successive objects in the chain by calling the getNextException() method for each SQLException object in the chain.

❏ If problems are detected by JDBC that do not warrant throwing an exception, an object of type SQLWarning is attached to the object originating the problem. SQLWarning objects can be attached to Connection, Statement, and ResultSet objects. You can check for a warning by calling the getWarnings() method for the JDBC object you are using to access the database.

❏ You can use a JTree component to display data structured as a tree.

❏ The getMetaData() method for a Connection object returns a DatabaseMetaData object containing methods that make database metadata available. These work only if the driver and database engine support the capability implied by the methods you are using.

Remember, you've only skimmed the facilities offered by many of the classes I've discussed in this chapter. You'll find much more capability under the covers, and time spent browsing the class methods will be very rewarding in most cases.

Exercises

You can download the source code for the examples in the book and the solutions to the following exercises from http://www.wrox.com.

With some additional features, you'll find the InteractiveSQL utility very useful. Add the following features to InteractiveSQL:

1. Keep the last ten queries that were executed and allow the user to select from that list of previously run queries.

2. Provide a menu option that lets the user close the current connection and open a new one. Prompt the user for the URL, driver name, user name, and password.

3. Modify the program to provide full, detailed information about any SQLException exceptions that are thrown. You may want to use a separate window that provides more space and keeps a running list of exceptions until these are cleared by the user.

There are also lots of potential extensions to the DatabaseBrowse application. Try the following:

4. It would be more efficient to separate the execution of the SELECT statement from the selection events from the tree. Add a button to execute a SELECT statement with whatever table or columns are selected in the tree.

5. Extend the application to allow a WHERE condition to be applied. (This is quite hard. You'll need to provide an additional mechanism for specifying the WHERE conditions — which means you'll need to track the columns selected. You could keep a list that you record in the TreeSelectionEvent handler and supply a dialog to allow the condition to be specified.)

6. Extend the application to allow an ORDER BY condition to be applied to the SELECT statement. (If you have done the previous exercise, this will be a piece of cake.)

Keywords

The following keywords are reserved in Java, so you must not use them as names in your programs:

abstract	assert	boolean	break
byte	case	catch	char
class	const	continue	default
do	double	else	enum
extends	final	finally	float
for	goto	if	implements
import	instanceof	int	interface
long	native	new	package
private	protected	public	return
short	static	strictfp	super
switch	synchronized	this	throw
throws	transient	try	void
volatile	while		

You should also not attempt to use the boolean values true and false or null as names in your programs.

Computer Arithmetic

In the chapters of this book, I have deliberately kept discussion of binary arithmetic to a minimum. However, it is important overall, and fundamental to understanding how some operators work, so I've included a summary of the subject in this appendix. If you feel confident about your math knowledge, this will all be old hat to you and you need read no farther. If you find the math parts tough, then this section should show you how easy it really is.

Binary Numbers

First let's consider what you mean when you write a common everyday number such as 321 or 747. Put more precisely you mean

321 is:

3 x 10 x 10 + 2 x 10 + 1

and 747 is:

7 x 10 x 10 + 4 x 10 + 7

Because it is built around powers of ten, you call this the decimal system (derived from the Latin *decimalis* meaning of *tithes*, which was a tax of 10 percent — ah, those were the days . . .).

Representing numbers in this way is very handy for people with ten fingers and ten toes, or creatures with ten of any kind of appendage for that matter. However, your PC is quite unhandy in this context, being built mainly of switches that are either on or off. This is okay for counting up to two, but not spectacular at counting to ten. For this reason your computer represents numbers to base 2 rather than base 10. This is called the **binary** system of counting, analogous to the **bi**cycle (two wheels), but nothing whatever to do with bibacity, which means an inclination to drink a lot. With the decimal system, to base 10, the digits used can be from 0 to 9. In the binary system, to base 2, the digits can only be 0 or 1, ideal when you have only on/off switches to represent them; off is usually 0, and on is 1, simple. Each digit in the binary system is called a **bit**, which is a contraction of **binary digit**. In an exact analogy to the usual base 10 counting, the binary number 1101 is therefore

$1 \times 2 \times 2 \times 2 + 1 \times 2 \times 2 + 0 \times 2 + 1$

which, if you work it out, amounts to 13 in the decimal system. In the following table you can see the decimal equivalents of 8-bit binary numbers illustrated.

Binary	Decimal	Binary	Decimal
0000 0000	0	1000 0000	128
0000 0001	1	1000 0001	129
0000 0010	2	1000 0010	130
...	...	...	...
0001 0000	16	1001 0000	144
0001 0001	17	1001 0001	145
...	...	...	...
0111 1100	124	1111 1100	252
0111 1101	125	1111 1101	253
0111 1110	126	1111 1110	254
0111 1111	127	1111 1111	255

Note that by using just 7 bits you can represent all the decimal numbers from 0 to 127, which is a total of 2^7, or 128 numbers; and using all 8 bits you get 256, which corresponds to 2^8 numbers. In general, if you have n bits available, you can represent 2^n positive integers with values from 0 to 2^n-1.

Hexadecimal Numbers

When you get to work with larger binary numbers — for example, numbers with 24 bits:

1111 0101 1011 1001 1110 0001

the notation starts to be a little cumbersome, particularly when you consider that if you apply the method you saw in the previous section to work out what this is in decimal notation, it's only 16,103,905, a miserable 8 decimal digits. You can sit more angels on a pinhead than that. Well, as it happens, you have an excellent alternative.

Arithmetic to base 16 is a very convenient option. Each digit can have values from 0 to 15 (the digits from 10 to 15 being represented by the letters A to F as shown in the next table, or by a to f if you're averse to capitalization) and values from 0 to 15 correspond quite nicely with the range of values that four binary digits can represent.

Hexadecimal	Decimal	Binary
0	0	0000
1	1	0001
2	2	0010
3	4	0011
4	4	0100
5	5	0101
6	6	0110
7	7	0111
8	8	1000
9	9	1001
A	10	1010
B	11	1011
C	12	1100
D	13	1101
E	14	1110
F	15	1111

Because a hexadecimal digit corresponds exactly to 4 binary bits, you can represent a binary number as a hexadecimal number just by taking successive groups of four binary digits starting from the right, and writing the equivalent base 16 digit for each group. Look as this binary number:

1111 0101 1011 1001 1110 0001

If you replace each group of 4 bits with the equivalent hexadecimal digit, you'll get:

F5B9E1

You have six hexadecimal digits corresponding to the six groups of four binary digits. Just to show it all really works out with no cheating, you can convert this number directly from hexadecimal to decimal, by again using the analogy with the meaning of a decimal number, as follows:

F5B9E1 is:

15 x 16 x 16 x 16 x 16 x 16 + 5 x 16 x 16 x 16 x 16 + 11 x 16 x 16 x 16 + 9 x 16 x 16 + 14 x16 + 1

This in turn turns out to be:

15,728,640 + 327,680+ 45,056 + 2304 + 224 + 1

which fortunately totals to the same number you got when you converted the original binary number to a decimal value.

Negative Binary Numbers

There is another aspect to binary arithmetic that you need to understand — how negative numbers are represented. So far you have assumed everything is positive — the optimist's view, if you will — your glass is still half full. But you can't avoid the negative side of life forever — the pessimist's perspective that your glass is already half empty. How do you indicate a negative number? Well, you have only binary digits at your disposal, so they must contain the solution.

For numbers where you want to allow the possibility of negative values (referred to as **signed** numbers) you must first decide on a fixed length (in other words, fix the number of binary digits in a number) and then designate the leftmost binary digit as a sign bit. You have to fix the length to avoid any confusion about which bit is the sign bit as opposed to other bits that are digits. A single bit is quite capable of representing the sign of a number because a number can be either positive — corresponding to a sign bit being 0, or negative — indicated by the sign bit being 1.

Of course, you can have some numbers with 8 bits, and some with 16 bits, or whatever number of bits you like, as long as you know what the length is in each case. If the sign bit is 0 the number is positive, and if it is 1, the number is negative. This would seem to solve the problem, but not quite. If you add -8 in binary to +12 you would really like to get the answer +4. If you carry out that operation simplistically, just putting the sign bit of the positive value to 1 to make it negative, and then doing the arithmetic with conventional carries from one bit position to the next on the left, it doesn't quite work:

12 in binary is	0000 1100
-8 in binary you suppose is	1000 1000

Since +8 is 0000 1000, the binary representation for -8 is the same, but with the leftmost bit set to 1. If we now add these together we get:

12 + (-8) is	1001 0100

The value 1001 0100 seems to be -20 according to the rules, which is not what you wanted at all. It's definitely not +4, which you know is 0000 0100. Ah, I hear you say, you can't treat a sign just like another digit. But that is just what you do have to do when dealing with computers because, dumb things that they are, they have trouble coping with anything else. So you really need a different representation for negative numbers if the same process for addition is to work regardless of the sign of the operands. Well, as the same process for arithmetic operations should work regardless of the signs of the operands, you could try subtracting +12 from +4 and see what you get. Whatever the result is should be -8:

+4 is	0000 0100
Take away +12	0000 1100
and you get	1111 1000

For each digit from the fourth from the right onwards you had to borrow 1 to do the sum, analogously to our usual decimal method for subtraction. This supposedly is -8, and even though it doesn't look much like it, it really is. Just try adding it to +12 or +15 in binary and you will see that it works. So what is it? It turns out that the answer is what is called the **2's complement** representation of negative binary numbers.

Now here I am going to demand a little faith on your part and avoid getting into explanations of why it works. I'll just show you how the 2's complement form of a negative number can be constructed from a positive value and that it does work so you can prove it to yourself. Let's return to the previous example where you need the 2's complement representation of -8. We start with +8 in binary:

0000 1000

You now flip each digit—if it is one make it zero, and vice versa:

1111 0111

This is called the 1's complement form, and if you now add 1 to this, you'll get the 2's complement form:

	1111 0111
Add one to this	0000 0001
and we get:	1111 1000

Now this looks pretty similar to the representation of -8 you got from subtracting +12 from +4. So just to be sure, let's try the original sum of adding -8 to +12:

+12 is	0000 1100
Our version of -8 is	1111 1000
and you get:	0000 0100

So the answer is 4—magic! It works! The carry propagates through all the leftmost 1's, setting them back to zero. One fell off the end, but you shouldn't worry about that. It's probably the one you borrowed from off the end in the subtraction sum you did earlier to get -8. In fact, what is happening is that you are making the assumption that the sign bit, 1 or 0, repeats forever to the left. If you try a few examples of your own, you'll find it always works quite automatically. The really great thing is, it makes arithmetic very easy (and fast) for your computer.

Floating-Point Numbers

You often have to deal with very large numbers: the number of protons in the universe, for example, which needs around 79 decimal digits. Clearly there are lots of situations where you need more than the 10 decimal digits you get from a 4-byte binary number. Equally, there are lots of very small numbers: the amount of time in minutes, for example, that it takes the typical car salesman to accept your cash offer on his wonderful 1982 Ford LTD (and only driven 380,000 miles . . .). A mechanism for handling both these kinds of numbers is — as you will have guessed from the title of this section — **floating-point** numbers.

A floating-point representation of a number is a decimal point followed by a fixed number of digits multiplied by a power of 10 to get the number you want. It's easier to demonstrate than explain, so let's take some examples. The number 365 in normal decimal notation would be written in floating-point form as:

```
0.365E03
```

Here, the E stands for *exponent* and is the power of ten that the 0.365 (the mantissa) is multiplied by, to get the required value. That is:

```
0.365 x 10 x 10 x 10
```

which is clearly 365.

Now let's look at a smallish number:

```
.365E-04
```

This is evaluated as .365 x 10^{-4}, which is .0000365 — exactly the time in minutes required by the car salesman to accept your money.

The number of digits in the mantissa of a floating-point number depends on the type of the floating-point number that you are using. The Java type float provides the equivalent of approximately 7 decimal digits, and the type double provides around 17 decimal digits. The number of digits is approximate because the mantissa is binary, not decimal, and there's not an exact mapping between binary and decimal digits.

Suppose you have a large number such as 2,134,311,179. How does this look as a floating-point number? Well, as type float it looks like:

```
0.2134311E10
```

It's not quite the same. You have lost three low-order digits, so you have approximated our original value as 2,134,311,000. This is a small price to pay for being able to handle such a vast range of numbers, typically from 10^{-38} to 10^{+38} either positive or negative, as well as having an extended representation that goes from a minute 10^{-308} to a mighty 10^{+308}. As you can see, they are called floating-point numbers for the fairly obvious reason that the decimal point "floats" depending on the exponent value.

Aside from the fixed precision limitation in terms of accuracy, there is another aspect you may need to be conscious of. You need to take great care when adding or subtracting numbers of significantly different magnitudes. A simple example will demonstrate the kind of problem that can arise. You can first consider adding .365E-3 to .365E+7. You can write this as a decimal sum:

```
.000365 + 3,650,000
```

This produces the result:

```
3,650,000.000365
```

which when converted back to floating point with seven-digit accuracy becomes:

```
.3650000E+7
```

So you might as well not have bothered. The problem lies directly with the fact that you carry only seven-digit precision. The seven digits of the larger number are not affected by any of the digits of the smaller number because they are all farther to the right. Oddly enough, you must also take care when the numbers are very nearly equal. If you compute the difference between such numbers you may end up with a result that has only one or two digits precision. It is quite easy in such circumstances to end up computing with numbers that are total garbage.

One final point about using floating-point values — many values that have an exact representation as a decimal value cannot be represented exactly in binary floating-point form. For example, 0.2 as a decimal value cannot be represented exactly as a binary floating-point value. This means that when you are working with such values, you have tiny errors in your values right from the start. One effect of this is that accumulating the sum of 100 values that are all 0.2 will not produce 20 as the result. If you try this out in Java the result will be 20.000004, slightly more than you bargained for.

You can conclude from this that while floating-point numbers are a powerful way of representing a very wide range of values in your programs, you must always keep in mind their limitations. If you are conscious of the range of values that you are likely to be working with, you can usually adopt an approach to performing the calculations that you need that avoids the sorts of problems I have described. In other words, if you keep the pitfalls in mind when working with floating-point values, you have a reasonable chance of stepping around or over them.

Index